Special Edition

USING
Windows NT®
Server 4

Que®

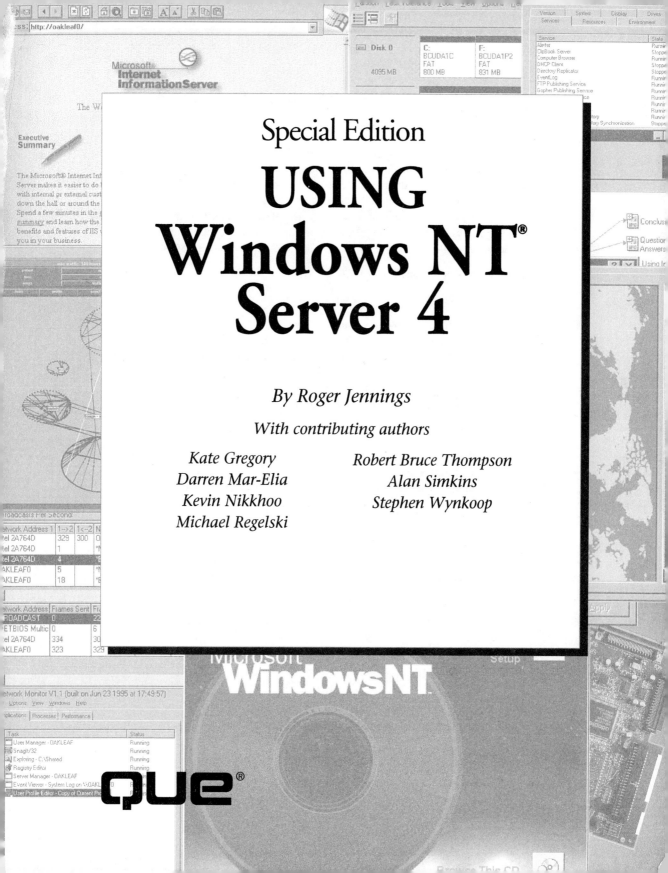

Special Edition

USING
Windows NT®
Server 4

By Roger Jennings

With contributing authors

Kate Gregory
Darren Mar-Elia
Kevin Nikkhoo
Michael Regelski

Robert Bruce Thompson
Alan Simkins
Stephen Wynkoop

que®

Special Edition Using Windows NT Server 4

Library of Congress Catalog No.: 95-73277

ISBN: 0-7897-0251-7

98 97 96   6 5 4 3 2

Interpretation of the printing code: the rightmost double-digit number is the year of the book's printing; the rightmost single-digit number, the number of the book's printing. For example, a printing code of 96-1 shows that the first printing of the book occurred in 1996.

Screen reproductions in this book were created using Collage Plus from Inner Media, Inc., Hollis, NH.

Composed in *Stone Serif* and *MCPdigital* by Que Corporation

Credits

President
Roland Elgey

Publisher
Joseph B. Wikert

Publishing Manager
Fred Slone

Senior Title Manager
Bryan Gambrel

Editorial Services Director
Elizabeth Keaffaber

Managing Editor
Sandy Doell

Director of Marketing
Lynn E. Zingraf

Product Director
Rob Tidrow

Production Editor
Susan Shaw Dunn

Editors
Kelli M. Brooks
Thomas Cirtin
Sherri Fugit
Hetty Gray
Patrick Kanouse

Assistant Product Marketing Manager
Christy M. Miller

Strategic Marketing Manager
Barry Pruett

Technical Editors
Bob Chronister
Christopher Corry
Robert Green
Randall Maxey
Michele Petrovsky
Sundar Rajan

Technical Support Specialist
Nadeem Muhammed

Acquisitions Coordinator
Carmen Krikorian

Software Relations Coordinator
Patty Brooks

Editorial Assistants
Jennifer Condon
Andrea Duvall

Book Designer
Ruth Harvey

Cover Designer
Dan Armstrong

Production Team
Stephen Adams
Debra Bolhuis
Jason Carr
Erin M. Danielson
Maribeth Echard
DiMonique Ford
Trey Frank
Julie Geeting
Jason Hand
Daniel Harris
Tony McDonald
Steph Mineart
Anjy Perry
Casey Price
Laura Robbins
Bobbi Satterfield
Lisa Stumpf

Indexer
Chris Barrick

This book is dedicated to Aaron Weule, who's on his way to becoming a Microsoft Certified Systems Engineer specializing in Microsoft BackOffice integration.

About the Author

Roger Jennings is a principal of OakLeaf Systems, a northern California consulting firm specializing in Windows client/server database and digital video applications. Roger is the author of Que Publishing's *Using Access 2 for Windows*, Special Edition; *Special Edition Using Access 95*; *Unveiling Windows 95*; *Access Hot Tips*; and *Discover Windows 3.1 Multimedia*. He was a contributing author for Que's *Killer Windows Utilities*; *Using Windows 3.11*, Special Edition; *Special Edition Using Windows 95*; and *Excel Professional Techniques*. He has also written two books for Windows database developers, and has contributed to the Microsoft Developer Network CD-ROM and Microsoft Developer Network News.

Roger was a member of the beta test team for Microsoft Windows 3.1 and 95; Windows NT 3.1, 3.5, 3.51, and 4.0 (Workstation and Server); Exchange Server; SQL Server 6.0 and 6.5; Proxy Server (code-named *Catapult*); ActiveMovie; Media Server (code-named *Cougar*) and every release of Access and Visual Basic. Roger's also a contributing editor for Fawcette Technical Publication, Inc.'s *Visual Basic Programmer's Journal*. You can reach him on CompuServe at **70233,2161** or via the Internet at **70233.2161@ compuserve.com**.

Acknowledgements

Kate Gregory (chapters 4, 6, and 9) is a freelance writer, trainer, and programmer, and is a partner in Gregory Consulting, founded in 1986. Based in rural Ontario, Canada, Gregory Consulting provides clients throughout North America, including Microsoft and IBM, with programming, training, and Web development services. Kate programs exclusively in Visual C++ with an emphasis on Internet projects, and has developed and taught courses on UNIX, C++, the Internet, and HTML. She holds a doctorate in chemical engineering from the University of Toronto but finds programming and the Internet a lot more fun than modeling blood coagulation. Kate was lead author on Que's *Using Usenet Newsgroups* and *Building Internet Applications with Visual C++*, and she contributed to Que's *The Official Visual Basic Programmer's Journal Guide to Visual Basic 4*, *Designing Windows 95 Help Systems*, and *Special Edition Using Visual C++ 4*. She is lead author on a complete rewrite of Que's *Special Edition Using Visual C++*, scheduled for release in the fall of 1996. Kate can be reached at **kate@gregcons.com**, and her main Web site is at **http://www.gregcons.com**.

Darren Mar-Elia (chapters 11, 15, and 16) is a Windows NT and Networking specialist for a large financial services firm in San Francisco. He has more than 10 years' experience in systems and network administration, and was a member of a design team that rolled out 7,000 Windows NT workstations and servers nationwide. A graduate in organizational behavior from the University of California at Berkeley, Darren is certified by Novell as a CNE and is currently working on his Microsoft CSE. He was a contributing author of Que's *Upgrading and Repairing Networks*. You can reach him at **dmarelia@earthlink.net**.

Kevin Nikkhoo (Chapter 24) has more than 15 years' experience in the computer industry and has held positions of senior manager, systems administrator, software developer, and network manager for Fortune 500 firms and smaller companies. He earned an MBA from the University of Southern California and a master's in computer engineering from California State University, Los Angeles, as well as a BSCE from McGill University. Kevin is president of Vertex Systems, Inc., a Microsoft Solution Provider and one of the leading computer technology consulting firms in California. He's a frequent speaker at computer industry conferences and serves on Microsoft's Solution Provider Advisory Council. You can e-mail Kevin at **KevinN@VertexSystems.com** or contact Vertex Systems, Inc. at (310) 571-2222 (voice).

Michael Regelski (chapters 12 and 14) is the director of software development at Lenel Systems International in Fairport, New York. Lenel Systems is one of the leading suppliers of industrial security products, including photo ID management and access control. Michael has an MS in software development and management and a BS in computer engineering from Rochester Institute of Technology. He has contributed to several other Que books, including *Special Edition Using Visual Basic 4* and *Building Multimedia Applications with Visual Basic 4.*

Robert Bruce Thompson (chapters 2, 5, 7, 8, 10, 13, and 17) is president of Triad Technology Group, Inc., a network consulting firm in Winston-Salem, North Carolina. He has 24 years' experience in programming, systems analysis, microcomputers, data communications, and network administration. Bob is certified by Novell as a Master CNE, by IBM in Advanced Connectivity, by AT&T in Network Systems Design, and is now working on his Microsoft CSE. He holds an MBA from Wake Forest University. Bob specializes in network systems design, branch office networking, and the application of technology to the needs of small businesses. He's the lead author of Que's *Windows NT Workstation 4.0 Internet and Networking Handbook,* and a contributing author for Que's *Upgrading and Repairing Networks.* You can reach him via Internet mail at **rbt@ttgnet.com**. Triad Technology Group, Inc. may be contacted at (910) 748-9867 (voice) or (910) 748-8714 (fax).

Alan Simkins (Chapter 19) is director of systems at Online System Services, Inc., a Denver-based Internet service and content provider and Microsoft Solutions Provider. He has been involved with personal computers since 1984 and holds a BS and MS in computer systems engineering from the University of Arkansas. Alan is a Microsoft Certified Systems Engineer and has held positions as network administrator, network engineer, client/server systems team leader, and database administrator. His current responsibilities include Web administration, database design, and interactive Web development. You can reach Alan via the Internet at **asimkins@ossinc.net** or by telephone at (303) 296-9200.

Stephen Wynkoop (chapters 20 and 23, and additions to Chapter 19) is an author and lecturer working almost exclusively with Microsoft-based products and technologies, with emphasis on the Internet and client-server systems. Stephen has been developing applications and consulting in the computer industry for more than 14 years. He's the author of Que's *The BackOffice Intranet Kit* and is a co-author of *Special Edition Using Microsoft SQL Server 6.5*, as well as a contributing author for other Que titles on Internet technologies. Stephen is a regular speaker at Microsoft's TechEd conferences and has written books on Microsoft Access and Office 95 integration. Stephen also is a Microsoft Certified Professional (MCP) for both Windows for Workgroups and Windows NT technologies. You can reach Stephen via the Internet at **swynk@pobox.com**.

Thanks to all of the Microsoft product support personnel who manned the Windows NT 4.0 beta forum on CompuServe. Their prompt responses to issues uncovered during the beta test program for Windows NT 4.0 are greatly appreciated.

Fred Slone, publishing manager, made sure that I didn't fall too far behind the manuscript submission schedule. Robert Tidrow, development editor, provided valuable insight and suggestions for this book's content and organization. Susan Dunn, production editor, put in long hours to add last-minute changes from the last beta to the retail release version of Windows NT Server 4.0. The responsibility for any errors or omissions, however, rests solely on my shoulders. Finally, thanks to Que publisher Joe Wikert for granting me the privilege to write this book.

We'd Like to Hear from You!

As part of our continuing effort to produce books of the highest possible quality, Que would like to hear your comments. To stay competitive, we *really* want you, as a computer book reader and user, to let us know what you like or dislike most about this book or other Que products.

You can mail comments, ideas, or suggestions for improving future editions to the address below, or send us a fax at (317) 581-4663. For the online inclined, Macmillan Computer Publishing has a forum on CompuServe (type **GO QUEBOOKS** at any prompt) through which our staff and authors are available for questions and comments. The address of our Internet site is **http://www.mcp.com** (World Wide Web).

In addition to exploring our forum, please feel free to contact me personally to discuss your opinions of this book: I'm **fslone@que.mcp.com** on the Internet.

Thanks in advance—your comments will help us to continue publishing the best books available on computer topics in today's market.

Fred Slone
Publishing Manager
Que Corporation
201 W. 103rd Street
Indianapolis, Indiana 46290
USA

Contents at a Glance

Introduction 1

**Networking with Windows
NT Server 4.0** **17**

1 Placing Windows NT
Server in Perspective 19

2 Planning Your Windows NT
Network Installation 55

3 Understanding the Windows
NT Operating System 85

4 Choosing Network Protocols 107

5 Purchasing Networking
Hardware 129

Networking

**Deploying Windows NT
Server 4.0** **183**

6 Making the Initial Server
Installation 185

7 Setting Up Redundant Arrays
of Inexpensive Disks (RAID) 217

8 Installing File Backup Systems 263

9 Understanding the
Windows NT Registry 303

10 Configuring Windows 95
Clients for Networking 331

11 Connecting Other PC
Clients to the Network 377

Deploying Windows NT

**Administering a Secure
Network** **413**

12 Managing User and Group
Accounts 415

13 Sharing and Securing
Network Resources 457

14 Optimizing Network
Server Performance 501

15 Troubleshooting Network
Problems 527

Administering a Network

**Wide Area Networking
and the Internet** **565**

16 Distributing Network
Services with Domains 567

17 Integrating Windows NT
with Heterogeneous
Networks 597

18 Managing Remote Access
Service 653

19 Setting Up the Internet
Information Server 687

20 Administering Intranet and
World Wide Web Sites 729

WANs and the Internet

**Windows NT Server and
Microsoft BackOffice** **775**

21 Taking Advantage of
BackOffice Server Integration 777

22 Running Microsoft SQL
Server 6.5 797

23 Messaging with Microsoft
Exchange Server 837

24 Adminstering Clients with
System Management Server 881

Glossary 913

Index 937

Microsoft BackOffice

Contents

Introduction   **1**

    Networking with Windows NT Server 4.0 3
    Windows NT Server 4.0, the Internet,
        and Intranets 4
    The Future of Windows NT 4
    Who Should Read This Book? 5
    How This Book Is Organized 6
        Part I: Networking with Windows NT Server 4.0 6
        Part II: Deploying Windows NT Server 4.0 7
        Part III: Administering a Secure Network 8
        Part IV: Wide Area Networking and the Internet 8
        Part V: Windows NT Server and Microsoft BackOffice 9
        Glossary 9
    How This Book Is Designed 9
    Typographic Conventions Used in This Book 10
        Typefaces and Fonts 10
        Key Combinations and Menu Choices 10
    Bibliography 11
        Print and CD-ROM Publications 11
        Online Sources of Windows NT Server Information 14

**I Networking with Windows NT
Server 4.0**   **17**

1 Placing Windows NT Server in Perspective   **19**

    What's New in Windows NT Server 4.0 20
        Server Usability 20
        Client-Side Features 26
        Network Performance and Scalability Features 28
        TCP/IP and NetWare Integration Features 30
        Troubleshooting Tools 31
        Internet, Intranet, and Remote Access Services 36
        Distributed Component Object Model (DCOM) 39
        Telephony API (TAPI) 2.0 40
    Understanding Windows NT Marketing and Pricing
        Strategies 41

Embracing and Extending the Internet 44
    Intranetworking and Internet Information Server 2.0.......46
    Managing Internet Information Server 2.0 48
Forging Alliances for Scalable Windows NT Server Hardware ...50
    Digital Equipment Corporation 51
    Tandem Computers, Inc. 51
    Compaq Computer, Inc. 52
    Amdahl Corporation 52
From Here... 52

2 Planning Your Windows NT Network Installation   55

Developing the Network Implementation Plan 55
    Meeting Business Objectives 56
    Determining User and Workgroup Needs 57
    Establishing Security 59
    Determining Fault-Tolerance Requirements 64
    Incorporating Existing Infrastructure 66
    Connecting to the Outside World 69
    Developing an Implementation Schedule 70
    Considering Network Management Needs 70
    Providing for Future Growth 72
    Working Within a Budget 74
    Training Users 76
Managing the Project..77
    Using Project-Management Software to Manage
       Resources and Schedules 77
    Getting Outside Help 80
Balancing Resources and Requirements 81
    Establishing a Minimum Configuration 82
    Allocating Remaining Funds 82
Dealing with Vendors 83
From Here... 84

3 Understanding the Windows NT Operating System   85

Gaining a Historical View of Windows NT 86
    Windows NT 3.1 87
    Windows NT 3.5 and 3.51...87
    The Shell Update Release and Windows NT 4.0 88
    Cairo and 64-Bit Windows NT 89
Summarizing Windows NT Operating System Features.............91
    The Windows NT Executive 93
    Clients and Protected Subsystem Servers 95
Handling Files with NTFS 97
    Understanding the Master File Table 99
    Implementing Recoverability with Transactions 101
Calling Remote Procedures 102
Networking with Windows NT 105
From Here... 106

4 Choosing Network Protocols   107

Understanding the OSI
    Seven-Layer Model 107
        The Physical Layer 108
        The Data-Link Layer 108
        The Network Layer 109
        The Transport Layer 109
        The Session Layer 110
        The Presentation Layer 110
        The Application Layer 110
        Comparing Windows NT and OSI Network Layers 111
Networking with Windows NT's Protocols 112
        NetBEUI and NetBEUI Frame 112
        TCP/IP 113
        NWLink (IPX/SPX) 117
        DLC 117
        AppleTalk 117
        RAS 118
        Streams 118
Supporting a Variety of PC Clients 119
        Windows NT Workstations 119
        Windows 95 120
        Windows for Workgroups 3.1x 120
        Windows 3.1+ 121
        DOS-Only PCs 121
        OS/2 Clients 122
        Apple Macintosh Computers 122
        UNIX Workstations 122
Supporting Multiple Servers 122
        Other Windows NT Servers 122
        Novell NetWare Servers 123
        UNIX Servers 123
        Local Intranet Servers 123
        The Internet 123
        Mainframes 124
Planning for Network Interoperability 124
Making the Final Protocol Choice 126
From Here… 126

5 Purchasing Networking Hardware   129

Selecting a Media Access Method 129
        ARCnet 130
        Token Ring 130
        Ethernet 132
        High-Speed Ethernet Variants 133
        Other High-Speed Media Access Methods 135
        Media Access Recommendations 137

Designing a Network Cabling System 138
    Network Topologies 139
    Cable Types 141
    Structured Cabling Systems 147
    Cabling System Recommendations 147
    Designing for Expandability and Ease of Maintenance ... 148
Selecting Active Network Components 149
    Network Interface Cards 149
    Repeaters 152
    Simple Hubs 153
    Bridges 155
    Routers 156
    Routing vs. Bridging 157
    Gateways 158
    Enterprise Hubs, Collapsed Backbones, Ethernet
        Switches, and Virtual LANs 158
    Summary Recommendations for Active Network
        Components 162
Specifying Server Hardware 163
    General Types of Servers 164
    Conformance to the Microsoft Windows NT
        Hardware Compatibility List 165
    Warranties, Maintainability, and Local Service 165
    Choosing the Server Components 165
From Here... 182

II Deploying Windows NT Server 4.0   183

6 Making the Initial Server Installation   185

Gathering Information and Making Decisions 185
    Preparing to Upgrade from Another Version
        of Windows 186
    Knowing Your Hardware 187
    Providing Names and Identification 191
    Choosing to Install as a Domain Controller 192
Backing Up Data on an Existing Computer 192
Starting the Basic Installation 193
    Running the Setup Program 194
    Choosing to Install or Repair 197
    Detecting Mass Storage 198
    Choosing to Upgrade or Install from Scratch 198
    Confirming Basic System Information 199
    Setting Up Your Fixed-Disk Drives 199
    Watching the Copying Process 200
    Identifying the User, Company Name, Licensing
        Terms, and Computer Name 201

Choosing the Type of Domain Controller 201
Setting the Administrator Password 202
Dealing with the Pentium Floating-Point
    Division Bug 202
Specifying Creation of an Emergency Repair Disk 202
Fine-Tuning the Installation 202
Joining the Network 203
Finishing Setup 209
Installing Internet Information Server 209
Creating the Emergency Repair Disk 211
Restarting the Server for the Last Time 212
Preparing the Server for Use 212
Repairing the Windows NT Server Operating
    System Installation 213
From Here... 215

7 Setting Up Redundant Arrays of Inexpensive Disks (RAID) 217

Understanding RAID Levels 218
The RAID Advisory Board 219
RAID 0 219
RAID 1 222
RAID 2 226
RAID 3 226
RAID 4 228
RAID 5 228
Proprietary and Non-Standard RAID Levels 231
Stacked RAID 232
Sizing the Array 233
Specifying a RAID Implementation 234
Picking the Best RAID Level for Your Needs 234
Understanding RAID Product Features 236
Implementing RAID in Hardware 238
Understanding Windows NT Server 4.0
    Software RAID 243
Creating Windows NT Server Stripe and Mirror Sets 245
Summarizing RAID Recommendations 259
From Here... 260

8 Installing File Backup Systems 263

Understanding Backup Types 264
The Archive Bit 264
Normal Backups 264
Copy Backups 265
Incremental Backups 265
Differential Backups 267
Daily Copy Backups 268
Choosing Among the Backup Types 268

Developing a Backup Strategy 270
    Organizing Disk Storage 270
    Ensuring Backup Integrity 271
    Backing Up Open Files...................................... 272
    Matching Backup Media Capacity to Disk Size 273
    Organizing Rotation Methods 274
    Using Hierarchical Storage Management (HSM) 279
    Considering Enterprise Backup Solutions 280
    Storing Data Off Site 281
    Developing a Restore Plan 282
Choosing Backup Hardware 283
    Tape Drives and Formats 284
    Writable Optical Drives 287
    WORM Drives 288
Using the Windows NT Server 4.0 Backup Application 288
    Setting Up NTBACKUP for Use with Your Tape Drive 289
    Backing Up Using NTBACKUP 291
    Restoring Using NTBACKUP................................... 297
Looking Beyond NTBACKUP 300
From Here… 300

9 Understanding the Windows NT Registry   303

Tracking Configuration Settings in the Registry 303
    What Types of Information Are Registered? 303
    The Importance of the Windows NT Registry................. 304
    The Danger of Changing Registry Values 305
    How the Windows NT and Windows 95
        Registries Vary 306
Viewing the Registry's Organization 306
    Keys 306
    Subkeys 307
    Value Entries 308
    Hives 309
Understanding Some Important Keys 310
    HKEY_LOCAL_MACHINE 310
    HKEY_CURRENT_CONFIG 315
    HKEY_CLASSES_ROOT 315
    HKEY_CURRENT_USER 316
    HKEY_USERS 316
Using the Windows NT Diagnostics Utility 317
Backing Up the Registry 318
Using the Registry Editor 318
    Working with Keys and Value Entries...................... 318
    Using the Registry Editor Menus 320
Inspecting Another Computer's Registry 323
    Choosing to Edit Remotely 323
    Preparing for Remote Registry Editing 323
    Opening the Remote Registry.............................. 324

Maintaining Registry Security 324
Restricting Access to Registry Keys 325
Viewing an Audit Log 327
Understanding the Interaction of .INI and CONFIG.SYS
Files with the Registry 328
From Here... 330

10 Configuring Windows 95 Clients for Networking 331

Windows 95 Networking Features 331
Installing Network Support 333
Installing Network Interface Cards 334
Changing NIC Settings 336
Installing and Removing Network Clients 338
Completing the Identification Page 341
Completing the Access Control Page 342
Configuring Network Clients 343
Configuring the Client for Microsoft Networks 343
Configuring the Client for NetWare Networks 344
Setting the Primary Network Logon 345
Configuring Network Protocols 347
Configuring NetBEUI 347
Configuring NWLink 348
Configuring TCP/IP 351
Installing File and Printer Sharing 356
File and Printer Sharing for Microsoft Networks 356
File and Printer Sharing for NetWare Networks 357
Managing Windows 95 on the Network 359
Installing Windows 95 from the Network 359
Setting Up User Profiles on the Server 364
Using System Policies 366
Managing Windows 95 Clients Remotely 369
Enabling Remote Management 370
Using Remote Management 371
From Here... 375

11 Connecting Other PC Clients to the Network   377

Connecting Windows 3.1 Clients 378
Creating Client Installation Diskettes 378
Installing the MS-DOS and Windows Client 379
Viewing Changes Made to Windows 3.1
Configuration and Initialization Files 384
Setting Up Windows to Use the Network Drivers 385
Connecting to Windows NT File
and Printer Resources 386
Connecting Windows for Workgroups 3.11 Clients 387
Installing the 32-bit TCP/IP Network Protocol 388
Viewing Changes Made to WfWg 3.1+ Configuration
and Initialization Files 391

Logging On and Connecting to Windows NT
Server 4.0 Resources 392
Connecting Windows NT Workstation 4.0 Clients 395
Installing the Network Software 395
Attaching to Domain Resources 398
Connecting Macintosh Clients 400
Adding Services for Macintosh on Windows NT
Server 400
Setting Up Macintosh Clients 403
Accessing Windows NT Server Resources from the
Macintosh 404
From Here... 412

III Administering a Secure Network   413

12 Managing User and Group Accounts   415

Defining Account and Group Terminology 415
Working with User Manager for Domains 416
Starting the User Manager for Domains 417
Starting Multiple Instances of User Manager 418
Selecting a New Domain with User Manager 420
Using a Low-Speed Connection to Connect
to a Domain 420
Managing User Accounts 421
Managing the Built-In User Accounts 421
Adding New User Accounts 423
Modifying User Accounts 427
Managing User Account Properties 428
Assigning Group Membership to a User Account 428
Defining and Managing User Profiles 429
Managing Logon Hours 433
Restricting Logon Privileges to Assigned Workstations ... 435
Managing Account Information 436
Setting User Dial-In Permissions 437
Using the Add User Account Wizard 437
Administering the Domain Account Policy 442
Setting the Account Policy for Passwords 443
Setting the Account Lockout Policy 444
Managing User Groups 444
Examining the Built-In Groups of Windows NT
Server 4.0 445
Adding Local Groups 446
Adding Global Groups 448
Copying a Group 448
Deleting Groups from the Domain 449

Deciding When to Use Local Groups or
Global Groups 449
Providing Users in Trusted Domains Access to
Resources in Trusting Domains 449
Using the Group Management Wizard 450
Managing User Rights Policy 453
Determining User Rights 453
Assigning New User Rights 454
From Here... 455

13 Sharing and Securing Network Resources   457

Sharing and Securing Folders and Files 457
Windows NT Server File Systems 458
Understanding Folder Shares 458
Using the Managing Folder and File Access Wizard 464
Understanding NTFS Permissions 468
Replicating Folders 477
Creating a Replication User 478
Starting the Replication Service 478
Configuring Folder Replication 480
Sharing and Securing Network Printers 482
Configuring Locally Attached Server Printers as
Shared Resources 483
Configuring Network Printer Servers as Shared
Resources 488
Configuring Printer Properties 491
From Here... 498

14 Optimizing Network Server Performance   501

Using Performance Monitor 501
Using Objects and Counters in Performance Monitor 502
Charting Performance Characteristics 505
Using Performance Monitor to Set Alerts 508
Using Performance Monitor Log Files 511
Optimizing Windows NT 4.0 File and Print Servers 514
Minimizing Disk Bottlenecks 515
Eliminating Unneeded Network Protocols 518
Changing the Binding Order of Multiple Protocols 519
Overcoming Network Media Limitations 519
Reducing File Fragmentation 520
Optimizing Windows NT 4.0 as an Application Server 521
Examining an Application Server's CPU Usage 521
Examining Memory Usage in an Application Server 522
From Here... 526

15 Troubleshooting Network Problems **527**

Relating Network Protocols and Troubleshooting Issues 527
NetBEUI Broadcasting 528
IPX/SPX 529
TCP/IP 529
Using Windows NT's Troubleshooting Tools 533
Using Protocol Analyzers 533
Using Windows NT 4.0's Network Monitor 535
Using Performance Monitor as a Network
Troubleshooting Tool 541
Using Windows NT's Network-Related Commands
and Utilities 545
Taking Advantage of Other Resources 553
Solving Windows NT Server
Network Problems 553
Understanding and Solving Connectivity Problems 553
Browsing 554
Routing 557
Troubleshooting Trusts 557
Understanding WINS and DNS Name Resolution 560
From Here… 563

**IV Wide Area Networking and
the Internet** **565**

16 Distributing Network Services with Domains **567**

Understanding Domain Architecture and Security 567
Understanding Windows NT Security Identifiers 569
Understanding the Roles of Domain Controllers 570
Understanding the Domain Synchronization Process 573
Adding Backup Domain Controllers to a New
Domain 575
Adding Windows NT Clients to the Domain 575
Moving Machines Between Domains and Renaming
Domains 577
Implementing Domains and Trusts Between Domains 580
Distributing Authentication Services 580
Understanding Trust Relationships 584
Understanding Windows NT's Domain Models 588
The Single Domain Model 588
The Single Master Model 589
The Multiple Master Model 589
Complete Trust 590
Hybrid Domain Models 592
Deciding on the Right Design 593

Using the Windows NT Resource Kit's
Domain Planner 594
Implementing Resource Sharing 594
From Here... 595

17 Integrating Windows NT with Heterogeneous Networks 597

Spanning Multiple Network Protocols 597
Integration Feuds 598
Windows NT Network and Transport Protocols 598
Integrating Windows NT Server with Novell NetWare 599
Accessing Novell NetWare Servers Using Microsoft
Clients 601
Accessing Microsoft Windows NT Servers Using
NetWare Clients 614
Other Windows NT Server Integration Tools
for NetWare 622
Integrating Windows NT Server with UNIX 632
Windows NT Server Integration Tools for UNIX 633
Sharing Windows NT Files with UNIX 642
Building Universal Clients for Microsoft Windows NT,
Novell NetWare, and UNIX 645
Configuring Windows 3.11 for Workgroups as a
Universal Client 646
Using Windows 95 as a Universal Client 649
Integrating Windows NT in IBM SNA Environments 649
Migrating from Novell NetWare to Windows NT Server 650
From Here... 652

18 Managing Remote Access Service 653

Touring the New Communications Features of
Windows NT Server 4.0 654
Deciding on a Dial-Up Networking Architecture 655
Understanding TAPI 2.0 658
Setting Up Windows NT Server 4.0
Remote Access Service 659
Installing Internal or External Modems 660
Configuring Dial-Up Networking 665
Granting Client Access with the Remote Access
Admin Application 668
Installing and Testing Dial-Up
Networking on Clients 669
Windows 95 Clients 670
Windows NT Clients 676
Monitoring Connections with Remote Access Admin 683

Using the Point-to-Point Tunneling Protocol 685
From Here... 686

19 Setting Up the Internet Information Server   687

Viewing Microsoft's Internet Product Line 687
Planning Your Site 689
Connecting to the Internet 690
Choosing an Internet Service Provider 691
Understanding Connection Types 692
Name Resolution and the Domain Name System 698
An Overview of IIS and Its Components 700
Understanding World Wide Web Service 700
Understanding the File Transfer Protocol Service 703
Understanding the Gopher Service 705
Understanding How IIS Interacts with
the Windows NT Domain Model 705
Installing the Internet Information Server 706
Preparing to Install the Gopher Service 707
Making an Initial Installation or Upgrading a Prior
Version of IIS 707
Using the Internet Service Manager 710
Testing the Default IIS 2.0 Installation 711
Setting Audit and Logging Options 713
WWW Server Options and Logging Parameters 713
Setting FTP Server Options 723
Setting the Gopher Server Options 725
Understanding URLs 727
From Here... 728

20 Administering Intranet and World Wide
Web Sites   729

Logging to an ODBC Data Source 729
Creating the Logging Database 730
Adding the Logging Table 730
Setting Up ODBC System Data Sources 735
Specifying the ODBC System Data Source for Logging.... 740
Writing Sample Queries for Reviewing Logs 741
Using SQL Server Web Assistant to Distribute Activity
Reports 742
Using Performance Monitor 747
Enhancing Your Site with Dynamic Database Access 750
Using the Internet Database Connector 750
Considering User Rights and Database Security 757
Using Microsoft dbWeb 758

Managing the Content of Your Web Site with Microsoft
FrontPage 764
Installing FrontPage 1.1 and the IIS 2.0 Server
Extension 764
Experimenting with FrontPage Explorer and Editor 770
From Here… 773

V Windows NT Server and Microsoft BackOffice **775**

21 Taking Advantage of BackOffice Server Integration **777**

Aiming at a Moving BackOffice Target 778
Licensing BackOffice Components 779
Per-Seat vs. Per-Server Licensing 780
BackOffice Server and Client Access Licenses 781
Windows NT 4.0 License Packages and Cost 782
SQL Server 6.5 Licensing 782
Exchange Server 4.0 Licensing 783
System Management Server 1.2 Licensing 784
SNA Server 2.11 Licensing 784
Licensing Costs for All BackOffice Components 785
The Annuity Model for BackOffice Upgrades 786
Using Windows NT Server 4.0's License Manager 787
Control Panel's License Tool 787
License Manager 789
From Here… 794

22 Running Microsoft SQL Server 6.5 **797**

Positioning SQL Server in the RDBMS Market 797
Installing SQL Server 6.5 799
Installing Files from the Distribution CD-ROM 800
Starting SQL Server and SQL Executive 806
Using SQL Enterprise Manager 807
Installing SQL Enterprise Manager on a 32-Bit Client 807
Registering Servers 808
Specifying and Testing Backup Tape Devices 812
Creating and Managing Database Devices 814
Creating a New Database Device 814
Importing Table Structures and Data 817
Working with SQL Tables, Indexes, Tasks, and
Triggers 821

Viewing Triggers 825
Viewing Standard Stored Procedures 826
Executing Queries 827
Setting Up Transaction Logging 828
Establishing Database Permissions 830
Using SQL Security Manager to Assign Group
Accounts 831
Viewing Logins and Setting Permissions in SQL
Enterprise Manager 834
From Here... 835

23 Messaging with Microsoft Exchange Server   837

Comparing Microsoft Exchange and Microsoft Mail 837
Microsoft Mail 3.x 838
Microsoft Exchange Server 839
Client/Server Messaging and Remote Procedure Calls 843
Installing Exchange Server 844
Maximizing Exchange Server Performance 846
Planning for Exchange Accounts 847
Running the Exchange Setup Program 847
Using the Exchange Server Optimizer Utility 851
Using the Client Load Simulator Utility 854
Using the Migration Wizard 857
Migrating from Microsoft Mail 3.x 858
Using Migration Files 864
Installing the Exchange Client 865
Installing the Client Software on the Server 866
Installing the Client Software 867
Specifying Client Options 869
Working with User Manager and Exchange Mailboxes 874
Using the Exchange Administrator Utility 877
From Here... 878

**24 Administering Clients with System
Management Server   881**

Introducing System Management Server 881
Remote Control and Troubleshooting 882
Hardware and Software Inventory 883
Software Distribution and Installation 883
Network Protocol Analysis 883
Remote Performance Monitoring 883
Customized Data Analysis, Transfer, and Reporting 884
Differences Between SMS and Network Management
Applications 884
Server Requirements 884

Supported Networks 885
Wide Area Network Options 885
Clients Supported 885
Planning for System Management Server 886
Enterprise Site Topology 886
Component Terminology and Concepts 887
Installing System Management Server 888
Creating a Service Account 888
Setting Up SQL Server 890
Installing System Management Server on the
     Primary Site Server 890
Using SMS Administrator 893
Sites Window 895
Packages Window 897
Jobs Window 899
Queries Window 900
Alerts Window 903
Machine Groups Window 903
Site Groups Window 903
Program Groups Window 903
Events Window 904
Installing and Configuring Client Software 904
Manual Client Software Installation 904
Automatic Installation 905
Client Inventory Management 905
Remote Control 907
Network Monitor 909
Building Sites for Enterprise Networks 910
Communication Between Sites with Senders.................. 911
Coexistence with NetWare Environments 911
From Here... 912

Glossary   **913**

Index   **937**

Introduction

Microsoft Corporation introduced Windows NT 3.1 in July 1993. Windows NT version 3.5, the first major upgrade to the Windows NT operating system, appeared September 21, 1994. During the second half of 1994, the computer press was devoting much of its coverage of operating systems to the yet-to-be-released Microsoft Windows 95 (then code-named Chicago) and, to a lesser degree, IBM OS/2 Warp. Thus, the release of Windows NT 3.5 was eclipsed by stories about products which, at the time, were best categorized as "projectorware."

A point upgrade, Windows NT 3.51, which was intended to provide compatibility with the forthcoming Windows 95 and Object Linking and Embedding (OLE) 2+, appeared with even less fanfare in May 1995. In mid-1996, as this book was being written, Windows NT 3.51 Server and, to a lesser extent, the Workstation edition began to receive the press attention and market acceptance that Windows NT deserves.

> **Note**
>
> This book uses the term *Windows NT* without a type (Server or Workstation) or version number when referring to the basic architecture and attributes of the operating system. The *Workstation* or *Server* identifier is added when discussing features that only are applicable to or are most often used by one version or the other. When comparing features of Windows NT Server 4.0 to features of preceding versions of Windows NT, the version number is included. *Windows NT 3.x* is used when the discussion applies to earlier versions 3.1, 3.5, *and* 3.51. The term *Windows 3.1+* includes Windows 3.1 and 3.11, and *Windows for Workgroups (WfWg) 3.1+* includes versions 3.1 and 3.11.

Windows NT Server is a remarkable network operating system, but it's only now beginning to meet with remarkable commercial success. Windows NT 3.1 didn't live up to Microsoft's initial sales projections primarily because of what was considered at the time to be big-time resource requirements (a minimum of 16M of RAM and about 70M of fixed-disk space, substantially more for the Server version). The lack of 32-bit Windows applications and a reputation for running 16-bit Windows applications somewhat slower than Windows 3.1+ also acted as a throttle on acceptance of the Workstation version. Further, Microsoft's marketing program targeted Windows NT Server to "enterprise computing," a term that, along with "mission-critical," has become a cliché. Large corporations and other sizable institutions rarely adopt a network operating system that doesn't have a proven track record for production use. Relatively few buyers of Windows NT 3.1 Advanced Server installed the product in a production environment, because corporate network and PC administrators considered Windows NT 3.1 to be an "immature" operating system, compared with UNIX and NetWare. Those who took the Windows NT 3.1 plunge, however, quickly found Windows NT 3.1 Advanced Server lived up to most, if not all, of Microsoft's claims for its new network operating system.

Windows NT 4.0 is the fourth iteration of Windows NT and now qualifies as a "mature" operating system, although Windows NT has been on the market only six years. Unlike other Microsoft operating systems, Windows NT is a cross-platform product; identical versions are available for Intel X86, Digital Alpha, Silicon Graphics MIPS, and Apple/IBM/Motorola PowerPC computers. Major hardware manufacturers such as Hewlett-Packard, IBM, Digital, Tandem, Amdahl, and Unisys offer high-end servers designed specifically to run Windows NT. The endorsement of Windows NT by these firms, which market proprietary operating systems and/or their own flavors of UNIX, adds substantial credibility to Windows NT Server in the large-scale networking arena.

The most obvious change between Windows NT 3.5+ and Windows NT 4.0 is the adoption of Windows 95's user interface (UI) and operating system shell. The primary visible change to the shell, aside from the taskbar and desktop, is the substitution of Windows Explorer for File Manager. Microsoft calls Windows NT 4.0 the *Shell Update Release* (SUR), a term that dates from late 1995, when Microsoft planned to provide the Windows 95 UI and shell in the form of a Service Pack update, rather than as a full version upgrade to Windows NT. The Windows 95 facelift to Windows NT 3.5+ primarily benefits users of Windows NT Workstation 4.0, eliminating the need to train users for and support the legacy UI of Windows 3.1+ used by Windows NT 3.5+ and the new UI of Windows 95.

Beneath the cosmetic improvements, Windows NT Server 4.0 provides several new networking features, the most important of which for networking are the Distributed Common Object Model (DCOM, formerly called NetworkOLE) and a substantial improvement in the Domain Name Service (DNS) for TCP/IP networks. Microsoft needs DCOM to implement its plans for distributing ActiveX (formerly OLE) controls and documents via the Internet and to fully implement three-tier client/server computing using Automation (formerly OLE Automation). Microsoft intends to use DNS as the underpinnings of its directory services for the next version of Windows NT, currently code-named Cairo and scheduled for release in late 1997 or early 1998.

Other new networking features of Windows NT Server 4.0 include an improved print spooler, plus Point-to-Point Tunneling Protocol (PPTP) and the Telephony API (TAPI) 1.0 to provide secure communication and ease support of mobile users of Windows NT Server 4.0's Remote Access Service (RAS). Each new feature of Windows NT Server 4.0 receives detailed coverage in this book.

Networking with Windows NT Server 4.0

Networking, the primary subject of this book, is where Microsoft has made the greatest improvement in Windows NT 4.0. Microsoft claims that Windows NT Server 4.0's file services are more than twice as fast as the original version, and printing has been given a speed-up, too. Windows NT 4.0 includes Microsoft's new IPX/SPX stack, which appears to offer equal or better performance than Novell's own NetWare drivers. What's more important, however, is that Microsoft has adopted the Internet's venerable TCP/IP (Transport Control Protocol/Internet Protocol) as the network protocol of choice, making Windows NT Server 4.0 more attractive to Microsoft's target market, Fortune 1000 firms. UNIX servers running TCP/IP over 10BaseT (unshielded twisted-pair) Ethernet cabling currently dominate enterprise-wide corporate local area networks. Although 60 percent or more of today's networked PCs may "speak" NetWare's IPX/SPX, by the end of the 1990s TCP/IP is likely to displace the standard Novell protocol in all but the smallest-scale networks.

Windows NT 4.0 also thrives in heterogeneous networks using a combination of TCP/IP, IPX/SPX, and even NetBEUI protocols. What's more, you don't pay extra for Windows NT Server 4.0's capability to run simultaneous multiple network protocols.

> **Note**
>
> International Data Corp. (IDC), a market research firm in Framingham, Massachusetts, estimates that by the turn of the century, the number of Windows NT Server shipments will surpass those of NetWare. IDC's Server Operating Forecast Updated, issued in mid-May 1996, predicts year 2000 shipments of 1.5 million units of Windows NT, 1.4 million units of NetWare, 928,000 units of UNIX (all flavors), and 498,000 units of OS/2. IDC expects Windows NT Server to achieve an average annual compounded growth rate of 31 percent during the period 1994 through 2000.

Windows NT 3.1 Advanced Server established a new standard for ease of installation of a network operating system, and the Setup program of Windows NT Server 4.0 is even more streamlined. You can install Windows NT Server 4.0 from the CD-ROM in about 30 minutes and upgrade a Windows 95 or Windows for Workgroups 3.1+ peer-to-peer network with 20 to 30 clients in a day or so. On average, it takes about 15 minutes to reconnect each client to a Windows NT Server 4.0 domain, including reconnecting clients to a relocated Microsoft Mail postoffice. You need a few more minutes per client if you use TCP/IP or IPX/SPX, rather than the Windows Network's simpler NetBEUI protocol.

Ease of installation, especially in a workgroup environment that might connect 20 to 100 clients, isn't the only benefit of using Windows NT Server 4.0. Since its inception, Windows NT Server has required substantially fewer administrative and support resources than its NetWare and UNIX competitors. Windows NT 4.0 offers various administrative tools, notably User Manager for Domains and Server Manager, with improved graphical user interfaces that simplify the life of network administrators. In the longer term, it's not the license fee and installation time that determines the economics of a network operating system—it's the annual administrative and support costs that make or break information system budgets.

Windows NT Server 4.0, the Internet, and Intranets

The remarkable growth of the Internet, brought about primarily by the proliferation of Web servers, is one of the principal contributors to increased adoption of Windows NT Server by organizations of all sizes. Today, most Internet servers run UNIX, but Windows NT Server rapidly is gaining ground as the network operating system of choice for delivering Web pages. Windows NT's advantages are lower cost for the hardware and software needed to set up a Windows NT Web site, combined with easier administration and reduced support requirements than for UNIX "boxes."

Microsoft arrived late at the Internet table, having waited until December 7, 1995, to elucidate its "Embrace and Extend" Internet strategy. A flurry of press releases and white papers announced Microsoft's intent to become a major player in the Internet server and browser markets. To gain market presence, Microsoft let you download its Internet Information Server (IIS) and Internet Explorer (IE) browser from **http://www. microsoft.com** for only the cost of connect time. Microsoft's objective in giving away these two products obviously is to increase the size of the market for Windows NT Server and Windows 95, respectively. Whether this strategy succeeds in displacing Netscape Navigator as the undisputed leader of the browser business remains to be seen. It's clear, however, that much of the very rapid increase in sales of Windows NT Server during the first half of 1996 derived from the free IIS offer. You no longer need to download IIS and IE from Microsoft's Web site; IIS 2.0 and IE 2.0 are included on the Windows NT Server 4.0 CD-ROM.

The "real money" on the server side of the Internet business comes from setting up private intranets, not creating Internet sites. Intranets offer the convenience of allowing users to browse for information on a corporate local area network (LAN) or wide area network (WAN) using a conventional Internet browser. Navigating hyperlinks to related HTML-encoded documents with connections to server-resident applications is demonstrably easier for the average PC user than running special-purpose, often complex client-side applications. Conventional database query tools and dedicated database front ends often require a substantial amount of user training. Inexperienced users quickly gain a knack for finding the information they need by clicking text and iconic hyperlinks of Web pages. Thus, organizations setting up intranets minimize training costs and, because simple Web-based applications are relatively easy to code, save programming expense. Microsoft sells a license for Windows NT Server with each free copy of IIS, and gains the opportunity to sell a copy of its forthcoming Proxy Server (currently code-named Catapult) for Internet security and Merchant Services for conducting Internet commerce.

The Future of Windows NT

Windows NT remains a constantly moving target, with new features added by Service Packs and, less frequently, point or full-version releases at various intervals. What Microsoft now calls "the next version of Windows NT" (and everyone else calls Cairo) is expected to provide the NT Directory Service based on the client/server model of Microsoft Exchange Server, instead of the originally planned Object File System (OFS).

Microsoft now intends to incorporate the content-related query features of OFS as an element of the existing NT File System (NTFS). Using the Exchange approach, directory services can use DNS and Internet domain names to provide improved integration with the Internet and intranets. Cairo undoubtedly will include or provide for clustering of Windows NT servers to compete with the scalability now offered by high-end UNIX systems.

Before Cairo arrives in late 1997 or early 1998, you can expect to see at least the following new server-based applications for Windows NT:

- *Windows NT clustering* solutions from third parties, with initial offerings of two-server fail-over software that assures continued operation if one server dies. Product announcements of clustering products for Windows NT Server began to appear as this book was being written.

- *Proxy Server* to create firewalls for managing outbound access to the Internet and securing inbound Internet access to LANs for mobile users.

- *Merchant Services* for creating Internet storefronts and conducting Internet commerce with Secure Transaction Technology (STT).

- *Media Server* (formerly Tiger, now code-named *Cougar*), originally designed for the mythical 500 channels of interactive TV. Microsoft is reported to be "repurposing" Cougar for its "Broadcast PC" initiative that's intended to create links between TV programming and the Web, as well as for high-bandwidth cable modems that can deliver interactive magazines enhanced with full-screen, full-motion video and high-fidelity audio content.

- *Normandy*, the code name for a suite of server-based applications designed for Internet service providers (ISPs). Microsoft derived the Normandy components from the software used to reimplement The Microsoft Network as an Internet service. Much of the code for Normandy comes from Merchant Services and the accounting system developed for the original Tiger project.

Who Should Read This Book?

Special Edition Using Windows NT Server 4 is intended for an eclectic audience, from networking neophytes to network designers and administrators responsible for setting up and maintaining large networks using Windows NT Server 4.0, either alone or with other network operating systems. This book isn't designed as an introduction to Windows NT.

Folks for whom *Special Edition Using Windows NT Server 4* offers the most usefulness fall into the following general categories:

- Network architects designing local area or wide area networks that incorporate Windows NT servers, either in a Microsoft-only or in a heterogeneous networking environment

- Network administrators handling the day-to-day chores necessary to assure network availability, security, and reliability

- Database administrators seeking to provide networked users with expedited access to corporate "information warehouses"

- Information systems (IS) managers responsible for planning and administering downsizing (or upsizing) corporate data distribution systems

- Human resources directors responsible for overseeing remote-access telecommuting services for their firm's employees

- Network support personnel keeping Windows Networking clients online and helping users gain the maximum benefit from the Windows NT 4.0 domain(s) to which they connect

- Microsoft Solution Providers who provide network management and database consulting services

- Value-added resellers (VARs) of complete networking solutions, which include Windows NT servers

- Manufacturers and marketers of hubs, bridges, routers, and other networking paraphernalia who need insight into the networking systems management features of Windows NT and System Management Server

- Educational institutions and training firms needing an advanced-level text on Windows NT networking for their students

- Line management personnel who are members of re-engineering committees charged with integrating information management into the re-engineering process

- Television broadcast/cable executives and technical personnel involved in evaluating and/or deploying Internet and/or intranet connectivity with cable modems or other data-related services, such as InterCast

- Users of various UNIX flavors who find Windows NT encroaching on the sacred ground of their erstwhile "open system"

The preceding list includes only the most obvious classifications of the potential audience for this book. Even if you're just curious about Microsoft's future operating system and client-server strategies, you'll find this book useful.

How This Book Is Organized

Special Edition Using Windows NT Server 4 consists of 28 chapters divided into six parts of progressively increasing technical complexity. The organization of the book follows the process of establishing a new Windows NT network, either as a self-contained entity or connected into a heterogeneous WAN. The following sections describe the content of each part and chapter of this book.

Part I: Networking with Windows NT Server 4.0

Part I contains chapters that describe Microsoft's design strategy for the Windows NT operating system and its networking features, plus planning and budgeting for a network based on Windows NT Server 4.0.

■ Chapter 1, "Placing Windows NT Server in Perspective," supplies a brief history of the development of Windows NT, explains the new features Microsoft added to Windows NT Server 4.0, describes how Windows NT fits into the PC server markets of the late 1990s, and compares the features of Windows NT Server 4.0 with those of its primary competitors, Novell NetWare and UNIX.

■ Chapter 2, "Planning Your Windows NT Network Installation," details the steps required to plan and budget for networks ranging in size from small workgroup LANs to company-wide, multisite WANs.

■ Chapter 3, "Understanding the Windows NT Operating System," introduces you to the technical foundation of Windows NT and the Windows NT File System (NTFS).

■ Chapter 4, "Choosing Network Protocols," explains how to select one or more of the three principal networking protocols supported by Windows NT based on your network configuration.

■ Chapter 5, "Purchasing Networking Hardware," provides guidance in the selection of the adapter cards, cabling, hubs, routers, and related equipment required to complete the physical network installation.

Part II: Deploying Windows NT Server 4.0

Part II covers the basics of installing and starting up Windows NT Server, along with fixed-disk arrays and backup tape drives, and connecting a variety of client PCs to your server.

■ Chapter 6, "Making the Initial Server Installation," guides you through Windows NT Server 4.0's Setup application, with emphasis on preparing you to answer the questions posed in the Setup dialogs.

■ Chapter 7, "Setting Up Redundant Arrays of Inexpensive Disks (RAID)," describes how to choose between software and hardware RAID implementation and how to take best advantage of Windows NT Server 4.0's software RAID capabilities.

■ Chapter 8, "Installing File Backup Systems," explains the tradeoffs between different types and formats of backup systems, and how to manage server backup operations to ensure against lost data in case of a fixed-disk failure.

■ Chapter 9, "Understanding the Windows NT Registry," introduces you to Windows NT Server 4.0's registration database, which is similar but not identical to the Windows 95 Registry.

■ Chapter 10, "Configuring Windows 95 Clients for Networking," shows you how to set up PCs running Windows 95 to take maximum advantage of Windows NT 4.0 networks, including the use of server-based desktop configurations and policies.

■ Chapter 11, "Connecting Other PC Clients to the Network," provides the details on setting up Windows 3.1+, Windows for Workgroups 3.1+, Windows NT Workstation 4.0, and Macintosh clients to communicate with Windows NT 4.0.

Part III: Administering a Secure Network

Part III encompasses the administrative side of network management with chapters covering user and group accounts, sharing file and printer resources, tuning Windows NT server, and solving the inevitable problems that arise in homogeneous and heterogeneous networks.

- Chapter 12, "Managing User and Group Accounts," describes how to use Windows NT Server 4.0's User Manager for Domains, take advantage of the new Add User Accounts and Group Management wizards, and utilize the built-in user groups of Windows NT.

- Chapter 13, "Sharing and Securing Network Resources," explains Windows NT Server's security system for shared file, folder, and printer resources and how to use the new Managing File and Folder Access Wizard and the Add Printer Wizard to simplify sharing Windows NT Server 4.0's resources.

- Chapter 14, "Optimizing Network Server Performance," describes the Windows NT Server 4.0 Performance Monitor and explains tuning methodology to help you maintain optimum network throughput as your network usage grows.

- Chapter 15, "Troubleshooting Network Problems," provides solutions for typical problems encountered when running multiple network protocols, and how to use the command-line tools included with Windows NT 4.0 and the Windows NT Resource Kit to isolate network problems. A brief description of the use of System Management Server's Network Monitor also is included.

Part IV: Wide Area Networking and the Internet

Part IV is devoted to the general topic of WANs, including networks with multiple domains, heterogeneous networks, remote access services, and establishing and managing an Internet or intranet site.

- Chapter 16, "Distributing Network Services with Domains," covers Windows NT Server's trusted domains and other distributed networking features that allow a single-user logon for multiple network servers and server-based applications running on LANs and WANs.

- Chapter 17, "Integrating Windows NT with Heterogeneous Networks," shows you how to set up and administer Windows NT Server within a Novell NetWare or UNIX networking environment.

- Chapter 18, "Managing Remote Access Service," explains how to configure Windows NT Server 4.0's RAS component to support dial-in access to shared network resources by mobile users.

- Chapter 19, "Setting Up the Internet Information Server," provides a step-by-step description of the process of establishing an Internet or intranet server with Microsoft's IIS 2.0, which is included with Windows NT Server 4.0.

- Chapter 20, "Administering Intranet and World Wide Web Sites," describes key elements of maintaining a Web site that reliably distributes the content of

HTML-encoded documents, outlines a Webmaster's duties, and briefly describes the integration of popular HTML authoring tools with an intranet or Internet server.

Part V: Windows NT Server and Microsoft BackOffice

Part V covers the three primary components of BackOffice that run as services under Windows NT Server 4.0: Microsoft SQL Server 6.5, Exchange Server 4.0, and System Management Server 1.2.(SNA Server, used to connect mainframes and IBM AS/400 minicomputers, is beyond the scope of this book.)

- Chapter 21, "Taking Advantage of BackOffice Server Integration," explains Microsoft's approach to developing client/server business solutions by using BackOffice and Office components. This chapter also covers licensing issues and how to use Windows NT 4.0's Licensing service.

- Chapter 22, "Running Microsoft SQL Server 6.5," describes the basic features of Microsoft's most recent update to SQL Server that includes new database replication features and a SQL Web Page Wizard.

- Chapter 23, "Messaging with Microsoft Exchange Server," introduces you to installation and management of Microsoft Mail 4.0, Microsoft's new client/server replacement for file-oriented Microsoft Mail 3+.

- Chapter 24, "Administering Clients with System Management Server," covers the basics of planning, administration, and management for Microsoft SMS 1.2.

Glossary

At the end of this book, the Windows NT Glossary supplies definitions of many of the new buzzwords and technical terms used to describe 32-bit Windows operating systems and applications.

How This Book Is Designed

The following special features are included in this book to assist you as you read:

- This icon appears next to sections that describe features in Windows NT Server 4.0 that weren't implemented in version 3.x or were added to version 3.5 through a Service Pack.

- The Internet icon appears next to sections that describe features in Windows NT Server 4.0 that are of importance in setting up and maintaining an Internet or intranet server.

- *Cross-references* include the names of sections elsewhere in this book that contain information related to the associated text and the page on which you'll find the sections.

◀◀ See "Section That Appears Earlier in the Book," p. xxx.
▶▶ See "Section That Appears Later in the Book," p. xxx.

> **Note**
>
> Notes offer suggestions and comments related to the text that precedes the note. Some notes provide references to Web sites that provide content related to the subject matter of the preceding text.

> **Tip**
>
> Tips describe shortcuts and alternative approaches to gaining an objective. Many of these tips are based on the experience the authors gained during months of testing successive beta versions of Windows NT Server 4.0.

> **Caution**
>
> Cautions appear where an action might lead to an unexpected or unpredictable result, including possible loss of data or other serious consequences. The text provides an explanation of how you can avoid such a result.

Typographic Conventions Used in This Book

This book uses various typesetting styles to distinguish between explanatory and instructional text, text you enter in dialogs, and text you enter in code-editing windows.

Typefaces and Fonts

The following type attributes are applied to the text of this book to make reading easier:

- A special `monospaced` font is used for on-screen prompts, code, and SQL statements.

- The **bold** attribute is used for World Wide Web URLs, other Internet addresses, and FTP sites.

- The text you type at the command prompt or into text boxes is **`bold monospace`**.

- The *italic* attribute is used for definitions (instead of double quotation marks) and to set off initial items in bulleted lists, where appropriate. The *italic* attribute also is used for emphasis.

- When you must substitute a name of your own making for an entry, the **`lowercase monospace bold italic`** attribute is used for the substitutable portion, as in the example **`filename.mdb`**. Here, you substitute the name of your file for **`filename`**, but the .mdb extension is required because it's in a roman (not italic) style.

Key Combinations and Menu Choices

Key combinations that you use to perform Windows operations are indicated with the keys joined by a plus sign; Alt+F4, for example, indicates that you press and hold the Alt key while pressing the function key F4. In the rare cases when you must press and release a control key and *then* enter another key, the keys are separated by a comma: Alt, F4, for example.

> **Note**
>
> Key combinations that perform menu operations requiring more than one keystroke are called *shortcut keys*. An example of such a shortcut is the combination Ctrl+C, which substitutes for the Copy choice of the Edit menu in most Windows applications.

Accelerator keys (Alt+*Key*) for menu choices are indicated by the underscore attribute, as in "Choose Open from the File menu," duplicating the appearance of Windows NT Server 4.0's menu text.

Successive entries in dialogs follow the *tab order* of the dialog—the sequence in which the focus (selection) moves when you press Tab to move from one entry or control option to another. Command buttons, option buttons, and check box choices are treated similarly to menu choices, but their access key letters don't have the underscore attribute.

File names of 32-bit applications and documents created by 32-bit applications appear in mixed case, regardless of the use of long file names (LFNs) or the conventional DOS 8.3 (8-character maximum file name and 3-character extension). This style conforms to the file name display of Windows NT 4.0's Explorer. File names of 16-bit applications and related document files are set in all uppercase.

Bibliography

Publishing limitations preclude a full bibliography for Windows NT and its related BackOffice components. The following sections show you where to obtain additional information in the form of books, CD-ROMs, and online product support for Windows NT Workstation and Server, plus the individual members of the BackOffice suite that were released when this book was written.

Print and CD-ROM Publications

Windows NT has spawned various Microsoft and third-party publications in printed and CD-ROM formats. Most the books available on Windows NT have been directed primarily to developers (programmers) of 32-bit applications for Windows NT and now Windows 95. Following is a list of books from Que Corporation and other publishers, plus specialized CD-ROM titles, that are particularly useful for administrators of Microsoft Windows NT Server networks and the BackOffice server suite:

- *Windows NT Workstation 4.0 Internet and Networking Handbook* by Robert Bruce Thompson (Que, ISBN 0-7897-0817-5) is an indispensable aid for linking Windows NT Workstation 4.0 users with Windows NT Server 4.0 over a wide variety of communications channels, including POTS, ISDN, Switched-56, and frame-relay services. This book is the companion volume to Chapter 18, "Managing Remote Access Service." Thompson, a principal of Triad Technology Group, Inc. in Winston-Salem, North Carolina, is the primary contributing author for *Special Edition Using Windows NT Server 4*, having written chapters 2, 5, 7, 8, 10, 13, and 17.

- *The BackOffice Intranet Kit* by Stephen Wynkoop (Que, ISBN 0-7897-0848-5) describes how to take advantage of the BackOffice components, such as SQL Server 6.5, to develop an effective intranet site that provides Web-page access to databases and mainframes. Wynkoop is the contributing author for this book's Chapter 20, "Administering Intranet and World Wide Web Sites," and Chapter 23, "Messaging with Microsoft Exchange Server."

- *Special Edition Using Windows NT Workstation 4.0* by Paul Sanna, et al. (Que, ISBN 0-7897-0673-3) complements this book by providing coverage of the client-side features of Windows NT 4.0 that are beyond the scope of this book.

- *Special Edition Using the Windows NT 4.0 Registry* by Jerry Honeycutt (Que, ISBN 0-7897-0842-6) provides thorough coverage of Windows NT 4.0's Registry, complementing Chapter 9, "Understanding the Windows NT Registry."

- *Special Edition Using Microsoft Internet Information Server* (Que, ISBN 0-7897-0850-7) supplies detailed instructions for setting up an Internet or intranet Web site using IIS 2.0. This book extends the coverage of Chapter 19, "Setting Up the Internet Information Server," and Chapter 20, "Administering Intranet and World Wide Web Sites."

- *Special Edition Using Microsoft FrontPage* by Neil Randall and Dennis Jones (Que, ISBN 0-7897-0821-3) supplements the meager written documentation accompanying FrontPage 1.1 with detailed instructions for designing and implementing Web pages for intranets.

- *Special Edition Using BackOffice* by G.A. Sullivan (Que, ISBN 0-7897-0688-1) combines coverage of all the components of Microsoft BackOffice 2.0 in a single volume.

- *Special Edition Using Microsoft SQL Server 6.5* by Bob Branchek, Peter Hazelhurst, Stephen Wynkoop, and Scott Warner (Que, ISBN 0-7897-0097-2) is designed to bring system and database administrators, as well as developers, up-to-date on the latest version of Microsoft SQL Server.

- *Special Edition Using Microsoft Exchange Server* by Mark Kapczynski (Que, ISBN 0-7897-0687-3) is a detailed tutorial and reference for Exchange Server 4.0.

- *Special Edition Using Microsoft System Management Server* (Que, ISBN 0-7897-0820-5) shows you how to get the most out of SMS 1.2 when managing Windows 3.1+, Windows 95, and Windows NT 4.0 clients.

- *Platinum Edition Using Windows 95* by Ron Person, et al. (Que, ISBN 0-7897-0797-7) is a 1,300+ page book that covers all aspects of Windows 95 in detail and is especially useful as a reference for Windows 95 client networking and user/policy management.

> **Note**
>
> Additional information on Que's series of books on Microsoft Windows NT, Internet Information Server, and BackOffice and its components is available from the Macmillan Superlibrary at **http://www.mcp.com**.

- *Inside Windows NT* by Helen Custer (Microsoft Press, ISBN 1-55615-481-X) describes the development history and design philosophy of Windows NT, and delves more deeply into details of the operating system than this book.

- *Inside the Windows NT File System* by Helen Custer (Microsoft Press, ISBN 1-55615-660-X) is a monograph that adds a detailed description of Windows NT's NTFS (New Technology File System) to Custer's original book. A brief discussion of the compression system for NTFS files also is included.

- *Windows NT Resource Kit* (Microsoft Press) is an indispensable source of technical information about Windows NT. The Resource Kit for Windows NT 4.0 wasn't published when this book was written. Most of the information in the Windows NT 3.5 Resource Kit with the Version 3.51 Update is applicable to Windows NT 4.0.

- *Showstopper! The Breakneck Race to Create Windows NT and the Next Generation at Microsoft* by G. Pascal Zachary (The Free Press, ISBN 0-02-935671-7) uses a battle-field metaphor to depict the behind-the-scenes strategy and tactics of Microsoft's development program for Windows NT. As John Soat put it in his review of *Showstopper!* in the November 7, 1994, issue of *Information Week*, this book demonstrates that creating new operating system software "ain't for sissies."

- *Windows NT Magazine* is a monthly publication of Duke Communications International, Inc., designed to help power users and network administrators get the most out of Windows NT. For subscription information, check **http://www. winntmag.com**, or call (800) 621-1544 or (970) 663-4700.

- *Microsoft Interactive Developer,* published by Fawcette Technical Publications, Inc., covers Internet- and intranet-related topics, with emphasis on Internet Information Server. You can subscribe from Fawcette's Development Exchange Web site, **http:/ /www.windx.com/**, from **http:/www.microsoft.com/mind** or by calling (800) 848-5523 or (415) 833-7100.

- *Microsoft TechNet* is a CD-ROM subscription service designed to aid persons who are responsible for supporting Microsoft productivity applications and systems, including Windows NT and BackOffice. For further information, check out **http:// www.microsoft.com/technet/**.

- *Microsoft Developers Network* (MSDN) is a tiered CD-ROM subscription service directed primarily to developers of 32-bit Windows applications. The MSDN CD-ROMs also include white papers on Windows NT and application development strategies for 32-bit Windows. MSDN Library Subscription (formerly Level I) is the basic service, with quarterly updates. MSDN Professional Subscription (formerly Level II) adds copies of Microsoft client operating systems and environments.

The Enterprise Subscription (formerly Level III) supplements the preceding versions with developer copies of Windows NT Server and the BackOffice components. A new Universal Subscription adds Microsoft productivity applications to the Enterprise Subscription. For more information on subscribing to MSDN, go to **http://www.microsoft.com/support/**.

Online Sources of Windows NT Server Information

The Internet is rapidly becoming the source of product knowledge and support for all PC-oriented products. Even the traditional online services, such as CompuServe and Prodigy, have announced their transition to the Internet and the World Wide Web. The following sections list the most important Web sites and newsgroups that pertain to Windows NT Server 4.0 and BackOffice. Windows NT-related support forums on CompuServe also are listed.

Internet Web Sites. As Microsoft continues to "embrace and extend" the Internet and the World Wide Web, much of the information about and support for Microsoft products formerly found on commercial online services, such as CompuServe, America Online, and The Microsoft Network, is moving to the Internet. Following are Web sites that are devoted to Windows NT, BackOffice, and Internet Information Server:

- The *Microsoft BackOffice* home page at **http://www.microsoft.com/BackOffice/** leads to sources of information on Windows NT Server 4.0 and the components of BackOffice 2.0+.

- *Information Week* magazine's online Resource Center at **http://techweb.cmp.com/iw/center/nt.html** provides reviews of and other news articles about Windows NT Server, BackOffice, and server hardware and software.

- The *Windows NT Frequently Asked Questions* Web site's FAQ pages (**http://www.iea.com/~daler/nt/faq/toc.html**) are compiled from two newsgroups, **comp.os.ms-windows.nt.misc** and **comp.os.ms-windows.nt.setup**, and the mailing list **windows-nt-request@mailbase.ac.uk**, as well as individual user contributions.

- *Windows NT Magazine*'s Professional Support Forums for Windows NT Server and Workstation are located at **http://www.winntmag.com/Forums/index.html**.

- *Avatar Magazine*, an online service of Fawcette Technical Publications, Inc., complements *Microsoft Interactive Developer* as "an interactive publication for creators of interactive media ... from Web sites to digital video." Check out the Avatar site at **http://www.avatarmag.com/**.

- *DevX*, Fawcette Technical Publications' new Web site for Windows developers at **http://www.windx.com/**, offers a wide range of news, features, and product reviews of interest to Windows NT Server administrators and programmers.

- Microsoft's *AnswerPoint* home page, **http://www.microsoft.com/supportnet/answerpoint/**, provides information about Microsoft's no-fee and low-fee support services for all its products. For other support options, go to **http://www.microsoft.com/Support/**.

Internet Newsgroups. Microsoft established its own Network News Transport Protocol (NNTP) news server, **msnews.microsoft.com**, in the spring of 1996. You must config-ure Internet Explorer 2.0 to read newsgroups by choosing <u>O</u>ptions from the <u>V</u>iew menu to open the Internet Properties sheet and making the appropriate settings on the News page. Alternatively, you can download the Internet Mail and News readers from **http://www.microsoft.com/ie/imn/**. Following are Microsoft-sponsored and Usenet newsgroups with Windows NT Server 4.0 content:

- A list of the Microsoft-sponsored newsgroups for Windows NT appears at **http://www.microsoft.com/support/news/winnt.htm**. These newsgroups don't provide support by Microsoft employees, but instead rely on user-to-user support. The newsgroups carry the prefix **microsoft.public.windowsnt**.

- Lists of similar Microsoft-sponsored newsgroups for Internet Information Server and each BackOffice component, with links to the newsgroups, are available through the Microsoft Newsgroup drop-down list of the **http://www.microsoft.com/support/** home page.

- Windows NT Usenet newsgroups are found at **comp.os.ms-windows.nt**. Subcat-egories are **admin**, **advocacy**, **misc**, **pre-release**, **setup**, and **software**. You can expect to find the greatest initial traffic on Windows NT 4.0 in the **comp.os.ms-windows.nt.pre-release** newsgroup.

The Microsoft Network. Although The Microsoft Network (MSN) is reported to have more than 1 million members, there's little in the way of message traffic in the MS Windows NT Server Member BBS, which features peer-to-peer support from Microsoft-anointed Most Valuable Professionals (MVPs). To see whether activity has increased since this book was written, try the go word msbackoffice_sd to navigate to the Microsoft BackOffice and Microsoft Windows NT Workstation area.

CompuServe Forums. In early 1996, Microsoft abandoned direct support of its products on CompuServe by its Product Support Specialists (PSS) in favor of user-to-user support under the auspices of the Windows User Group Network (WUGNet) and other indepen-dent organizations. (Unlike its newsgroups and MSN offerings, Microsoft doesn't sponsor the CompuServe support forums, with the exception of MSKB and MSL.) Following are the forums on CompuServe that are of primary interest to users of Windows NT:

- The Windows NT Forum (GO WINNT), run by WUGNet, is a source of support for both Windows NT Workstation and Server. You can access the Fixes & Updates library to obtain new Service Packs, drivers, and patches for Windows NT.

- The Windows NT Server (GO NTSERVER) and Windows NT Workstation (GO NTWORK) forums, run by WUGNet, also provide user-to-user support but have less message traffic than WINNT.

- The Microsoft Networks Forum (GO MSNET), run by Stream (a major software reseller), primarily addresses System Management Server (SMS) topics.

■ The SQL Server Forum (GO MSSQL), run by Stream, is devoted to support for Microsoft SQL Server versions 4.21a and higher.

■ The Windows NT SNA Server Forum (GO MSSNA), also run by Stream, provides support for IBM mainframe and AS/400 connectivity using protocols supported by SNA Server.

■ The Microsoft Knowledge Base (GO MSKB) is a Microsoft forum with a searchable database of bug fixes, workarounds, technical papers, and press releases for all Microsoft products. The Microsoft Software Library (GO MSL) provides downloadable updates and patches for Microsoft products.

■ The Windows Connectivity Forum (GO WINCON), run by WUGNet, covers a wide range of networking and other connectivity issues related to Windows 3.1+, Windows 95, and Windows NT.

■ The Windows Users Group Forum (GO WUGNET) offers broad-spectrum coverage of Windows topics from the user's perspective.

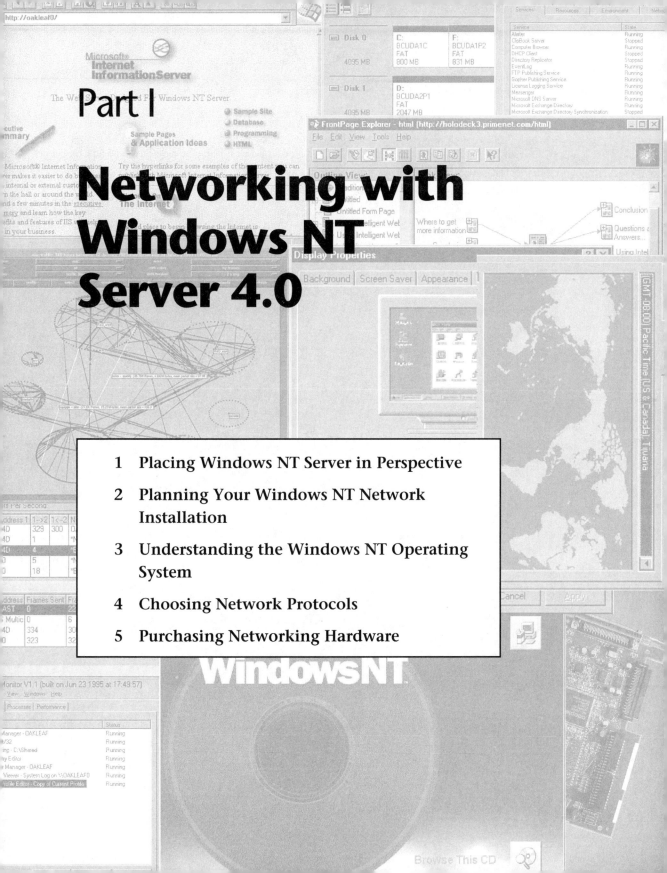

Part I

Networking with Windows NT Server 4.0

1 Placing Windows NT Server in Perspective

2 Planning Your Windows NT Network Installation

3 Understanding the Windows NT Operating System

4 Choosing Network Protocols

5 Purchasing Networking Hardware

Chapter 1

Placing Windows NT Server in Perspective

Windows NT Server is on a roll. According to International Data Corporation, a major market research organization, sales of Windows NT Server increased by more than 370 percent in 1995 and are slated to almost double during 1996. If IDC's 1996 prediction pans out, Windows NT Server sales will be running neck and neck with shipments of Novell NetWare 4.1, and will account for 25 percent of worldwide server operating system sales by the time you read this book. Over a span of less than four years, Windows NT Server has emerged from niche status as an application server to become a major contender in the mainstream PC file- and printer-sharing server market now dominated by NetWare and, to a lesser extent, UNIX servers.

Microsoft's determination to make Windows NT the primary player in the Internet server market is sure to fuel a substantial proportion of the increase in sales of Windows NT Server 4.0 for 1996 and onward. Although the Internet's public World Wide Web garners most of the publicity, private *intranets* represent the market with the greatest growth potential for Windows NT Server 4.0.

Intranets, which run over existing local area networks (LANs) and wide area networks (WANs), deliver documents coded with the Web's HyperText Markup Language (HTML) to clients equipped with low-cost or no-cost Web browsing applications. Just as the Internet Information Server 2.0 is fully integrated with Windows NT Server 4.0, Microsoft's 32-bit Internet Explorer 3.0 is scheduled to become an integrated component of the Windows NT 4.0 and Windows 95 operating systems by the end of 1996.

This chapter provides an introduction to the fourth iteration of Windows NT Server, which Microsoft originally called the Shell Update Release (SUR), but which now is officially Windows NT 4.0.

This chapter introduces the following subjects:

- New features of Windows NT Server 4.0

- Microsoft's marketing and pricing strategies for Windows NT Server

- Windows NT Server 4.0 and the Internet

- Setting up intranets with Internet Information Server 2.0

- Windows NT Server hardware alliances

Each topic is covered in much greater detail in the remaining chapters of this book.

> **Note**
>
> The first official use of "Version 4.0" with Windows NT appeared in the boot window of an alpha test release in late 1995 of the Windows 95 user-interface upgrade to Windows NT 3.51. At that time, Microsoft insisted that the SUR would be distributed as a maintenance release (Service Pack) for Windows NT 3.51—not as a new version.
>
> Microsoft's plan was to reserve the official "4.0" designation for the repeatedly delayed Cairo operating system, then scheduled to begin beta testing in 1996. (Microsoft calls Cairo the "next major version of Windows NT.") Microsoft explained that "4.0" was required to notify Windows 95-compliant applications that the upgraded Windows NT operating system supported Windows 95's shell functions.
>
> As the projected release date for Cairo extended into 1997 (and possibly into early 1998), Microsoft acquiesced to the inevitable and made Windows NT 4.0 an "official" version.

What's New in Windows NT Server 4.0

Special Edition Using Windows NT Server 4 is devoted to a new release of an existing operating system, making a list of newly added features obligatory. The following sections briefly describe the new features of Windows NT Server 4.0, many of which also apply to Windows NT Workstation 4.0.

 Brief descriptions of new features are of greater significance to readers now using or at least familiar with prior versions of Windows NT Server than to those planning to adopt or in the process of adopting Windows NT Server 4.0 as their network operating system. Detailed descriptions of each new Windows NT Server 4.0 feature that appear in the remaining chapters of this book are indicated by the New Feature of Windows NT Server 4.0 margin icon next to this paragraph.

The new features of Windows NT Server 4.0 described in the following sections are grouped in the following categories:

- Server usability
- Client-side features
- Network performance and scalability
- TCP/IP and NetWare integration
- Troubleshooting tools
- Internet, intranet, and remote access services
- Distributed Component Object Model (DCOM)

Server Usability

Microsoft's usability improvements for Windows NT Server 4.0 arise primarily from features inherited from Windows 95, such as the Windows 95 user interface, Explorer, and taskbar, and from the wizards of the Microsoft Office productivity software suite. The following sections describe the most important new features that affect Windows NT Server 4.0's usability from the perspective of a network administrator.

> **Note**
>
> Unfortunately, Windows NT Server 4.0 didn't inherit all of Windows 95's usability improvements. Windows NT 4.0 doesn't support Plug-and-Play installation of adapter cards, printers, monitors, and other Plug-and-Play-compliant devices. Windows NT 4.0 also lacks Windows 95's Device Manager page of the System tool. These features are expected to be included in the Cairo release.

Windows 95 User Interface. Microsoft's initial objective for the SUR was simply to graft the Windows 95 user interface (UI) to Windows NT in order to give the high-end operating system the "modern look and feel" before the release of Cairo. There's little controversy that the Windows 95 UI is a substantial improvement over that of Windows 3.1+. Although Windows 95 didn't achieve Microsoft's sales objectives for corporate desktops, Windows 95 has enjoyed great success in the consumer and small-office/home-office (SOHO) markets.

Unfortunately, Microsoft elected to retain in Windows NT Server 4.0 the consumer-oriented My Computer and Network Neighborhood icons, whose names are believed to have originated with the ill-fated Microsoft Bob shell for Windows 3.1+. Fortunately, you can rename these two icons with more appropriate captions, such as the server name and Network Browser, respectively, as shown in figure 1.1.

Fig. 1.1   Windows NT Server 4.0 desktop with Windows Explorer open.

Windows Explorer. Windows Explorer (refer to fig. 1.1) substitutes for Windows NT 3.x's File Manager, which in turn was derived from the original File Manager tool of Windows 3.0. From Explorer's File menu, members of groups with the required rights can

- Share drives and folders (but not individual files) in the Sharing page of the *Foldername* Properties sheet

- Establish share permissions, audit access, and take ownership of files and folders in the Security page of the *Foldername* Properties sheet (see fig. 1.2)

- Compress and decompress drives and files or folders (optionally including subfolders) of Windows NT File System (NTFS) volumes

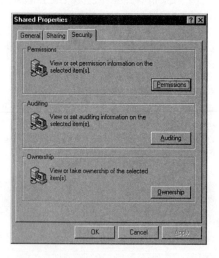

Fig. 1.2   The Security page of the *Foldername* Properties sheet for the Shared folder.

The *Foldername* Properties sheet is identical to that of Windows 95 except for the Security page, which isn't available in Windows 95. Windows NT compression isn't available for volumes formatted for the file allocation table (FAT) system used by DOS, Windows 3.x, and Windows 95. You can establish permissions, auditing, and ownership for a selected file—shared or not—in the *Filename* Properties sheet.

Note

This book uses the term *property sheet* when referring to dialogs used to set property values of a Windows NT object, such as a folder, file, user, or group. Property sheets originated with ActiveX controls (formerly OLE Controls, or OCXs), first introduced with Access 2.0. Most Windows NT property sheets are tabbed dialogs that use the Windows 95 common dialog design. For consistency with ActiveX terminology, the term *property page* describes the view for the tab you click. When Cairo arrives, all components of Windows NT will be objects, and property sheets and pages are destined to become part of Cairo's universal object nomenclature.

Task Manager. The Windows NT 4.0 Task Manager provides a substantial extension to the Task Manager tool of Windows NT 3.x. To open Task Manager, right-click the taskbar and choose Task Manager from the popup menu. The Task Manager window includes the following tabbed pages:

■ *Applications* lists the applications launched and the status of each. (see fig. 1.3) Right-clicking an application entry displays the popup menu that provides such choices as jumping to a process or terminating a task.

Fig. 1.3 The Applications page of Windows NT Server 4.0's improved Task Manager.

■ *Processes* lists all running executable files and allows you to check the percentage of processor time consumed by each process as well as a variety of other information about the process. Choosing Select Columns from the View menu allows you to customize the Processes display (see fig. 1.4).

■ *Performance* provides graphical displays of current and historical memory and CPU usage (see fig. 1.5).

Administrative Wizards. Microsoft wizards, which originated with Access 1.0, provide step-by-step guidance in the execution of administrative operations that involve an ordered sequence of tasks. All the components of Microsoft Office and Windows 95 have adopted wizards to assist users in performing sequential operations or to streamline single-step tasks. Windows NT Server 4.0 provides the following wizards:

■ The *Add User Account Wizard* guides you through the process of adding new user accounts to a Windows NT Server 4.0 network (see fig. 1.6).

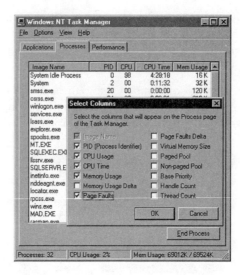

Fig. 1.4 Customizing the display of Task Manager's Processes page.

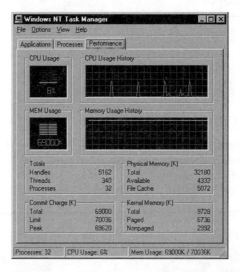

Fig. 1.5 Task Manager's graphical display of server memory and CPU usage.

■ The *Group Management Wizard* allows you to create and manage groups of users in order to minimize the effort needed to assign rights to individual user accounts.

■ The *Managing File and Folder Access Wizard* provides a five-step method for sharing and securing drives or folders with Microsoft Network, Apple Macintosh, and Novell NetWare clients (see fig. 1.7).

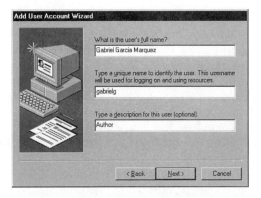

Fig. 1.6 The second step in adding a new user account with the Add User Account Wizard.

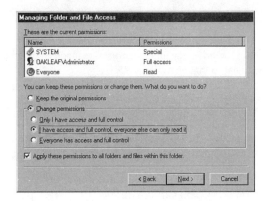

Fig. 1.7 The third step in sharing a server folder with the Managing File and Folder Access Wizard.

- The *Add Printer Wizard* sets up local or network printers for printer sharing. The wizard also installs the necessary printer drivers on the server that are automatically downloaded to Windows NT clients when printing to a shared printer.

- The *Network Client Administrator Wizard* automates the installation and updating of client software on networked PCs.

- The *License Wizard* lets administrators track software licenses for servers and clients to ensure compliance with licensing agreements.

- The *Add/Remove Programs Wizard* provides a shortcut to Control Panel's Add/Remove Programs tool for installing or removing applications and their associated libraries and Registry keys.

- The *Install New Modem Wizard* detects and sets up modems connected to the server.

The first three wizards in this list are especially useful for administrators new to Windows NT Server. The Network Client Administrator Wizard and License Wizard aid new and experienced network administrators. The last two wizards primarily are of interest to users of Windows NT Workstation 4.0.

Client-Side Features

Windows 95 introduced the concept of server-stored *system policies* and *user profiles* for centralized management of Windows 95 clients and to provide each networked user with his own custom desktop when logging on to the network from any location. Windows NT Server 4.0 extends system policies and user profiles to clients running Windows NT Workstation 4.0. The following sections describe Windows NT Server 4.0's new System Policy Editor for establishing system policies and user profiles, and support for diskless Windows 95 clients.

> **Note**
>
> The structure of Windows NT 4.0 system policy and user profile files differs from that of Windows 95. Windows NT Server 4.0's methodology for creating and managing system policies and user profiles, however, is very similar to that of Windows 95.

System Policy Editor. System administrators use system policies to enforce standardization of client desktops, as well as to limit users' capability to modify the client environment. As an example, you might want to restrict users from editing the client's Registry because making an incorrect Registry entry can render the client unbootable.

Windows NT Server 4.0's new System Policy Editor is based on the PolEdit.exe application of Windows 95 (see fig. 1.8). You can create specific system policies for each user group or for individual users. Policy files are stored in the virtual netlogon share (the physical \Winnt\System32\Repl\Import\Scripts folder) and accessed by clients during startup of Windows NT Workstation 4.0. Information stored in the System Policy file modifies the HKEY_CURRENT_USER and HKEY_LOCAL_MACHINE keys of the client's Registry. Chapter 9, "Understanding the Windows NT Registry," describes Windows NT's Registry.

User Profiles. User profiles contain values of the user-definable settings that control the operating environment of client (and server) PCs running Windows NT 4.0. You create and edit Windows NT 4.0 user profiles for user groups and individual user accounts with Upedit.exe (see fig. 1.9).

> **Note**
>
> The Windows NT Server 4.0 Setup program doesn't install the User Profile Editor. You install Upedit.exe and its associated help file from the d:\Clients\SvrTools\WinNT\i386\ folder of the distribution CD-ROM.

Fig. 1.8   Restricting user options for Windows NT 4.0 PCs with the System Policy Editor.

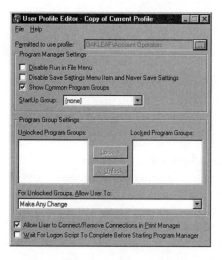

Fig. 1.9   Setting a user group profile for account operators with the User Profile Editor.

Remote Server Administration from Windows 95 Clients. The Windows NT Server 4.0 distribution CD-ROM includes separate sets of remote server administration utilities for networked PCs running Windows 95 and Windows NT Workstation 4.0. The Windows 95 version installs the following tools in the Start menu's Programs, Windows NT Tools group:

■ *Event Viewer* lets you read the System, Security, and Application logs of any Windows NT computer on the network. Figure 1.10 shows the Windows 95 Event Viewer displaying System events from a Windows NT 4.0 server.

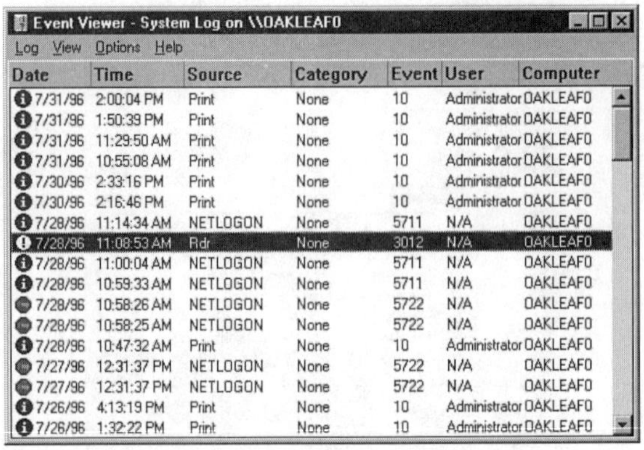

Fig. 1.10 Displaying server system events remotely with the Windows 95 version of Event Viewer.

■ *Server Manager* lets you manage user connections, shared folders, open resources, replications, and alerts on Windows NT servers.

■ *User Manager for Domains* lets you manage groups and users in any domain for which you have Administrator privileges.

Windows 95 Remote Program Load. Windows 95 *Remote Program Load* (RPL) lets diskless Windows 95 clients boot from Windows NT Server 4.0. Diskless Windows 95 clients are very uncommon, perhaps non-existent; running Windows 95 from a server creates very heavy network traffic. It's likely that Microsoft provided RPL in an effort to counter the Network Computer (NC) proposed by Oracle Corp. The acceptance of NCs in the business and consumer markets of 1997 and beyond remains to be proven.

Network Performance and Scalability Features

Ever-increasing network traffic and expansion of LANs and WANs to accommodate a larger number of domains requires commensurate enhancement of server capabilities, and especially the performance of servers used as domain controllers. The following sections discuss the new features of Windows NT Server 4.0 that provide faster access by clients to shared server resources.

Faster File Sharing on High-Speed LANs. The rapidly declining cost of 100mbps adapter cards and switchable hubs is making implementation of Fast Ethernet cost-effective for LANs with heavy traffic, such as that generated by videoconferencing or delivery of full-screen, full-motion video to clients. Microsoft claims up to double the throughput over 100BaseT networks compared with Windows NT Server 3.51, based on tests conducted by National Software Testing Laboratories (NTSL).

Server Scalability. *Scalability* is a measure of the capability of multiprocessing operating systems to provide increased performance by adding additional processors. A perfectly scalable system delivers four times the performance when you install three additional processors to a conventional single-processor system. High-end UNIX operating systems traditionally have offered better scalability than PC-based network operating systems such as Windows NT and NetWare. Microsoft claims that the *symmetrical multiprocessing* (SMP) of Windows NT Server 4.0 delivers better performance scalability with high-end server hardware, especially systems with more than four processors.

> **Note**
>
> Scalability with SMP requires that such services as relational database management systems (RDBMSs) and Web servers be written to take maximum advantage of multithreading. (SMP assigns an application thread for execution by the processor with the lightest workload.) There is overhead in the thread assignment process, so achieving 100 percent (perfect) scalability is impossible. The architecture of the system motherboard and the operating system have a pronounced influence on scalability.

The few SMP servers announced in mid-1996 are based on Intel Corporation's new four-Pentium Pro motherboard, which uses an Intel chipset for memory management and the other operations required to support multiple processors effectively. Eight-processor servers are expected to be available from several vendors in late 1996. When a four-processor server runs out of steam, server clustering technology is likely to be a better choice than adding more processors. Microsoft and third-party approaches to Windows NT Server 4.0 clustering is the primary subject of the "Forging Alliances for Scalable Windows NT Server Hardware" section near the end of this chapter.

Expanded Directory Services. The Windows NT Directory Service accommodates a larger number of entries (objects), depending on the amount of RAM installed in the server. (There's no limit to the number of trusting domains.) Windows NT Server 4.0 expands the recommended number of trusted domains from a maximum of 128 in version 3.51 to 140 for 32M, 250 for 64M, and 500 for 128M of RAM. The administrator can override the recommendations and, for example, increase the size of the non-paged pool (NPP) to accommodate 500 trusted domains with a server having 64M of RAM.

Printing Enhancements. Windows NT 4.0 uses *server-based* rendering of print jobs for printers that don't use the Adobe PostScript page description language. Server-based rendering minimizes the time spent by clients processing complex print jobs generated by desktop publishing, image editing, and similar applications. The file-sharing enhancements of Windows NT Server 4.0 for 100BaseT networks, noted earlier in the section "Faster File Sharing on High-Speed LANs," also speed the processing of print jobs.

Application Server APIs and Fibers for Developers. New APIs for writing server-based applications provide improved performance by updated services, such as SQL Server 6.5. Lightweight threads, which Microsoft calls *fibers*, make it easier for developers to optimize scheduling within multithreaded applications. Microsoft says that Windows NT 4.0 uses "[l]onger quantums to reduce context switches and cache churning" and has "[c]onditional critical section acquire." It's hoped that application programmers will take full advantage of such arcane (but important) new features of Windows NT Server 4.0 when writing 32-bit server applications. (Developer features of Windows NT Server 4.0 are beyond the scope of this book.)

TCP/IP and NetWare Integration Features

Each release of Windows NT Server has improved integration with TCP/IP and NetWare networks. (Built-in support for the TCP/IP protocol was introduced with Windows NT Server 3.5.) The following sections describe the new features of Windows NT Server 4.0 for heterogeneous networks.

Graphical Domain Name Service Tool. Windows NT Server 4.0 now offers a dynamic Domain Name Service (DNS) derived from Microsoft's proprietary Windows Internet Name Service (WINS) protocol. DNS is an Internet-standard service that translates character-based addresses (host names), such as www.msn.com, to numeric IP addresses, such as 204.255.247.121. You also can use DNS compound names, such as \\oakleaf1.oakleaf.com*whatever*, to access a server share.

Combining DNS with WINS simplifies the integration of Windows NT Server 4.0 with TCP/IP networks of all types, not just the Internet. Previously, Windows NT Server's DNS was static and required the network administrator to create a text-based list of host names and their corresponding IP addresses. Windows NT Server 4.0 allows DNS to query WINS for name resolution. The new graphical Domain Name Service Manager tool of Windows NT Server 4.0 speeds the mapping of DNS server names (see fig. 1.11).

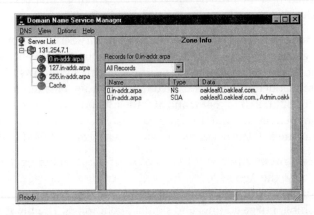

Fig. 1.11   Displaying addresses for a DNS server in the Domain Name Service Manager.

Novell NetWare Interoperability. Windows NT 4.0's Client for NetWare and Gateway Services for NetWare (GSNW) now support NetWare Directory Services (NDS), enabling browsing of NDS resources (using NetWare 3.1x bindery emulation mode), NDS authentication, and NDS printing. (Gateway Services for NetWare allows a Windows NT 4.0 server to process dial-in connections to resources located on NetWare servers.) Figure 1.12 illustrates GSNW's Configure Gateway dialog with a NetWare share added. Windows NT Server 4.0 also supports authentication to multiple NDS trees and can process NetWare logon scripts.

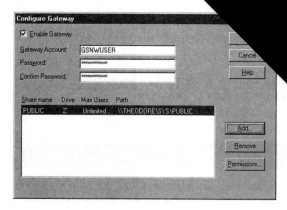

Fig. 1.12 A NetWare share added to a Windows NT 4.0 server with the Gateway Service for NetWare feature.

Note

File and Print Services for NetWare (FPNW) is a utility that allows Windows NT Server 4.0 to emulate a NetWare 3.12-compatible file and print server. The objective is to allow networked PCs with only Novell client software to access file and print services on a Windows NT 4.0 server. Clients also can run the Windows NT versions of applications now installed as NetWare Loadable Modules (NLMs).

FPNW isn't included with Windows NT Server 4.0, and individual server licenses must be purchased from Microsoft. The purpose of FPNW is to simplify the transition from NetWare to Windows NT servers by eliminating the need to substitute Microsoft for Novell network drivers on the clients.

Multi-Protocol Router (MPR). The *Multi-Protocol Router* (MPR) allows Windows NT Server to route packets and dynamically exchange routing data for TCP/IP, Novell IPX, and AppleTalk protocols using the *Routing Internet Protocol* (RIP) with other routers using RIP. You need two network cards in the server PC to take advantage of MPR for LAN-to-LAN routing. MPR consists of RIP for TCP/IP, RIP for NWLink IPX/SPX, and BOOTP (Boot Protocol) for Windows NT Server's Dynamic Host Configuration Protocol (DHCP). MPR first appeared in the Service Pack 2 update to Windows NT 3.51; technically, MPR isn't a new feature of Windows NT Server 4.0.

Troubleshooting Tools

As the complexity of server hardware, software, and networks increases, network administrators require sophisticated diagnostic tools to aid in troubleshooting networking problems. The following sections describe Windows NT Server 4.0's improvement to version 3.51's diagnostics program and the new Network Monitor included with Windows NT Server 4.0.

Improved Diagnostics Tool. Windows NT Server 4.0 includes a new Windows NT Diagnostics tool, which centralizes the display of Windows NT system properties in a single window with nine tabbed pages. The pages display only system property values; you

...ctive

...applications to make changes to these ...tool's pages and the function of each

...list of all applications and tools that run ...t status, such as Running or Stopped, plus ...l's Services tool to change the status of

...HCP Client, or SQL Server—that can be ex-
...ess. Windows NT services are similar in concept
...ons.

Fig. 1.13 The Services page of the Windows NT Diagnostics tool.

- *Resources* selectively shows the interrupts (IRQ), I/O ports, DMA channels, and upper memory blocks used by installed hardware, plus a list of hardware devices in use.

- *Environment* displays the values of environmental variables for the system (the server PC) and the location of the local user's temporary files.

- *Network* provides information about logged-on users, the transports in use, network settings, and networking statistics (see fig. 1.14).

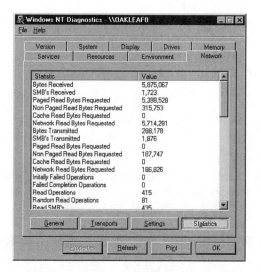

Fig. 1.14 Networking statistics displayed by the Network page of the Windows NT Diagnostics tool.

- *Version* shows the current version of Windows NT Server 4.0 in use and registration information.

- *System* displays the identifier (AT/AT COMPATIBLE for Intel PCs), the Hardware Abstraction Layer (HAL) in use, information on the server's BIOS, and a list of the installed processors.

- *Display* shows information about your graphics adapter card and the Windows NT drivers that support the card.

- *Drives* supplies details about the server's removable, fixed, CD-ROM, and network-connected drives.

- *Memory* provides statistics on the available and consumed RAM, along with the size and usage of the paging file.

Network Monitor. Windows NT Server 4.0's new Network Monitor tool allows you to capture a snapshot of network traffic that you can analyze later in order to uncover network performance bottlenecks or to perform other troubleshooting tasks. Network Monitor—derived from the SMS Network Monitor of Microsoft System Management Server (SMS) 1.2—provides many of the features of dedicated network analysis systems, such as Network General's Sniffers. The built-in Network Monitor tool captures only traffic to and from the server; the SMS Network Monitor captures all network traffic on the network segment.

Figure 1.15 shows the default arrangement of Network Monitor's window. The following list describes the information presented in the window's four panes:

- *Graphs* displays five bar graphs in the upper left pane that show the percentage of network usage, plus the number of frames, bytes, broadcasts, and multicasts per second.

- Below the bar graphs, *Session Stats* displays detailed information on conversations between nodes defined by Network Address 1 and Network Address 2.

- At the bottom of the window, *Station Stats* presents a columnar list of all network nodes visible to the server, together with individual frame and byte counts for each node.

- *Total Stats*, at the upper right of the window, displays Network Statistics, Capture Statistics, Per Second Statistics, Network Card (MAC) Statistics, and Network Card (MAC) Error Statistics in a scrolling list.

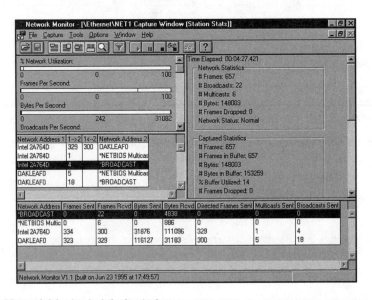

Fig. 1.15   Network Monitor's default window.

After you install the Network Monitor tools and Agent Service from Control Panel's Network tool, you click the toolbar's Start Capture button (with the VCR play symbol) to begin the logging process. Then click the Stop Capture and View button (with the VCR stop symbol and glasses) when you've captured the desired number of frames. During the capture process, the bar graphs display network activity. The Capture Summary pane takes over Network Monitor's window, as shown in figure 1.16.

Double-clicking an entry in the Capture Summary pane displays the two additional panes (see fig. 1.17). The middle Capture Detail pane displays the frame data by OSI component layers. The bottom Capture Hex pane displays a hex and ASCII dump of the content of the selected frame.

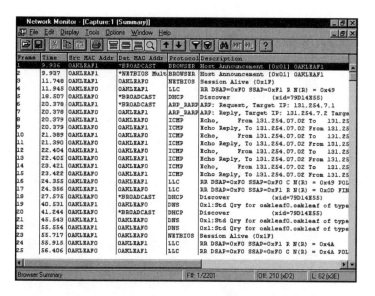

Fig. 1.16   Displaying information for all frames captured in the Capture Summary pane.

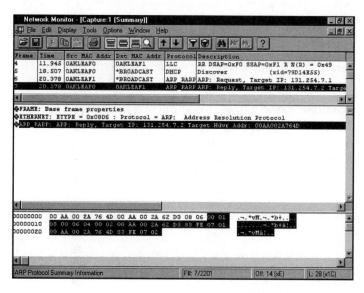

Fig. 1.17   Displaying information for a specific frame in the Capture Detail and Capture Hex panes.

You can apply Network Monitor's Display Filter by clicking the Edit Display Filter toolbar button (with the funnel symbol) to display the Display Filter dialog, shown in figure 1.18. You can use Boolean logic to create a custom filter with the AND, OR, and NOT buttons. Creating custom filters is useful in isolating network problems, such as cross-router traffic, that degrade overall network performance.

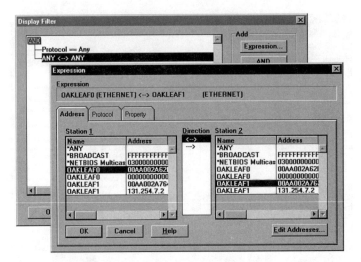

Fig. 1.18 Designing a capture filter in the Display Filter dialog.

Internet, Intranet, and Remote Access Services

A substantial percentage of the new installations of Windows NT Server 4.0 are likely to be devoted to delivering Web pages via the Internet or, more likely, a private intranet. Later, the section "Embracing and Extending the Internet" discusses Microsoft's Internet and intranet strategy. Meanwhile, the following sections describe the new features of Windows NT Server 4.0 that are of specific to Internet and intranet services, plus a related topic—Remote Access Services (RAS).

Internet Information Server 2.0. Microsoft Internet Information Server (IIS) 2.0, which now is built into Windows NT 4.0, is fully integrated with Windows NT Server 4.0's security and administrative features. IIS supplies Web, Gopher, and FTP services, and uses the Secure Sockets Layer (SSL) to provide the security necessary for communication privacy and simple implementations of online Internet shopping services. New features of IIS version 2.0 are as follows:

■ Installation of IIS now is incorporated into the Windows NT Server 4.0 Setup application.

■ You can administer IIS 2.0 with any Web browser, running either on the server or from a client. Microsoft Internet Explorer 2.0 is included on the Windows NT Server 4.0 distribution CD-ROM.

■ Other administrative tools include System Management Server 1.2 and Simple Network Management Protocol (SNMP).

■ NCSA- and CERN-style map files help you port Web pages from UNIX systems to IIS 2.0.

■ The Create New Key and Certificate Request dialog of the new Key Manager tool (see fig. 1.19) generates the key pair required to obtain a SSL certificate from VeriSign. (For further information on SSL certificates for IIS 2.0, visit **www.verisign.com**.)

Fig. 1.19 Generating a key pair to obtain a Secure Sockets Layer certificate from VeriSign.

- Improvements to IIS 2.0 and Windows NT Server 4.0 increase performance by more than 40 percent, compared with IIS 1.0 running on Windows NT Server 3.51.

- IIS 2.0 uses the Point-to-Point Tunneling Protocol (PPTP) built into Windows NT Server 4.0 to create secure private intranets that users can access via public data networks, including the Internet. (PPTP is the subject of the following section.)

- The Internet Database Connector (IDC) now can send multiple queries from a single HTML page and correctly format the query result sets.

- Internet Services Application Programming Interface (ISAPI) programming is improved by exposing several server variables to IF %variable% statements in template (.HTX) files and by supporting nested IF statements.

- IIS 2.0 supports Microsoft Proxy Server (codenamed *Catapult* when this book was written) for creating software-based security firewalls with Windows NT 4.0 servers. Catapult isn't included on the Windows NT Server 4.0 CD-ROM; you can download the Catapult files from **http://www.microsoft.com/infoserv/catapult/step1.htm**.

- You can add the Microsoft Index Server (originally codenamed *Tivoli*) to Windows NT Server 4.0 for content indexing and full-text searching of HTML and Microsoft Office documents. (Like Proxy Server, Index Server isn't included on the Windows NT Server 4.0 distribution CD-ROM; you can download the required files from **http://www.microsoft.com/ntserver/search/step1.htm**.)

Point-to-Point Tunneling Protocol (PPTP). PPTP provides data security when you are connecting clients to servers via public data networks, such as the Internet, by using dial-up connections. You can use PPTP to create a virtual private network (VPN) at a very low cost if you're willing to live with the data rates provided by Integrated Services Digital Network (ISDN) or 28.8kbps modems.

> **Note**
>
> Your Internet service provider must have PPTP installed for remote clients to connect using PPTP.

PPTP uses protocol encapsulation to support multiple protocols via TCP/IP connections and encrypts data to assure privacy. Although PPTP isn't as secure as the protocols under development for Internet commerce using bank cards and other credit instruments for payments, it's more secure than today's face-to-face transactions during which the merchant or waiter has temporary possession of your credit card.

RAS Multilink Channel Aggregation. RAS Multilink Channel Aggregation allows dial-in clients to combine multiple modem or ISDN lines to gain faster communication with Windows NT 4.0 servers. This feature is primarily of interest for fixed sites with the need for periodic connections, not to mobile users who seldom have access to multiple lines. Most of today's low-cost digital ISDN modems for the Basic Rate Interface (BRI) automatically bridge two ISDN B (bearer) channels to achieve data rates of 112kbps or 128kbps. You can aggregate one or more conventional modems with ISDN modems, but this is unlikely to become a conventional practice. Multilink Channel Aggregation is most useful to bridge from two to all 23 B channels of the ISDN Primary Rate Interface to achieve a data rate close to that of a North American T-1 trunk (1.544mbps). Multilink Channel Aggregation is one of the subjects of Chapter 18, "Managing Remote Access Service."

FrontPage 1.1. Late in the beta testing cycle, Microsoft announced that Windows NT Server 4.0 would include a copy of FrontPage 1.1, Microsoft's first integrated Web page authoring and management tool. FrontPage 1.1's Web server management component, FrontPage Explorer, provides outline and link views of individual Internet or intranet sites (see fig. 1.20). FrontPage 1.1 also includes an integrated HTML editor for creating Web pages (see fig. 1.21). The bundled FrontPage 1.1 comes with single-server and single-client licenses. You must buy the retail version if you want to support additional servers or clients.

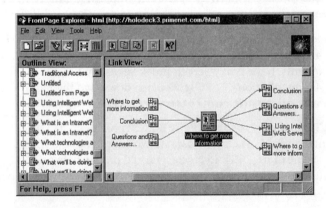

Fig. 1.20 The Outline View and Link View panes of the FrontPage Explorer application.

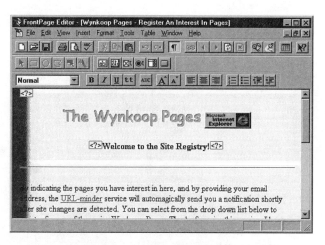

Fig. 1.21 FrontPage 1.1's WYSIWYG Web page editing application.

Distributed Component Object Model (DCOM)

The Component Object Model (COM) is Microsoft's specification for creating reusable application components that developers can combine into custom applications to fulfill specific objectives. Microsoft's Object Linking and Embedding (OLE) specification 2+, which includes OLE Automation (now simply called Automation), is an extension to COM. Automation is the foundation on which three-tier client/server applications are built. Three-tier applications consist of the following components:

- *User services*, which run on the client and provide the user interface to the application, communicate with business services.

- *Business services*, also called *business rules*, implemented by Automation servers, communicate with data services.

- *Data services* provided by relational database management systems (RDBMSs) run on an application server, such as Windows NT Server.

Original OLE Controls (OCXs) and the new, lightweight ActiveX controls also are built on COM. The original implementation of COM required that Automation clients and servers run on the same PC.

Both the Server and Workstation versions of Windows NT 4.0 support Distributed COM (DCOM), which allows stand-alone components (called *out-of-process OLE or Automation servers*) written to the DCOM specification to communicate across networks. Microsoft expects to provide DCOM capability for Windows 95 and Macintosh clients by the end of 1996. DCOM allows developers to implement three-tier architecture with Automation server applications located on a server, which don't need to be the server running the RDBMS that provides data services. DCOM competes with IBM's Distributed Systems Object Model (DSOM). You register remote Automation servers (also called *Remote Automation Objects*) with the Remote Automation Connection Manager shown in figure 1.22.

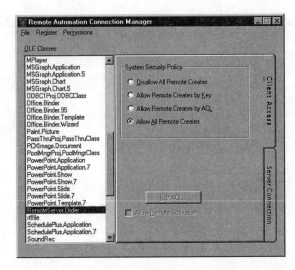

Fig. 1.22   Setting up client access to a Remote Automation Object created with Visual Basic 4.0.

Note

During its development, Microsoft referred to Distributed COM as *NetworkOLE*, and you might continue to see references to NetworkOLE even by Microsoft employees. The Enterprise Edition of Visual Basic 4.0 implemented what Microsoft called "NetworkOLE 0.9" to support Remote Automation Objects created with Visual Basic running under Windows NT Server 3.51. If you now run Visual Basic 4.0 Remote Automation Objects on a Windows NT 3.51 server, you should upgrade from NetworkOLE 0.9 to DCOM—both the server and the clients—when migrating to Windows NT Server 4.0. According to Microsoft's Questions and Answers for the future Visual Basic for Applications (VBA) version 5.0 at **http://www.microsoft.com/vba/vba5qa.htm**, VBA 5.0 will include built-in programming support for DCOM.

Telephony API (TAPI) 2.0

TAPI 2.0 is an updated Win32 service that provides in Windows NT 4.0 the basic functionality of Windows 95's TAPI 1.4. TAPI employs Microsoft and third-party Telephony Service Provider (TSP) products to implement communication services. Windows NT 4.0 includes Microsoft's 32-bit Unimodem (Universal Modem) driver, which first appeared in Windows 95, as a built-in TSP.

TAPI 2.0 is backwardly compatible with TSPs and other TAPI 1.4 telephony applications that run on Windows 95. TAPI 2.0 supports 16-bit TAPI applications through a thunking layer (Tapi.dll) that supplies 32-bit addresses to Windows NT 4.0's Tapi32.dll. Tapi32.dll provides the marshaling layer, using lightweight remote procedure calls (LRPCs), to transfer function requests to Tapisrv.exe and to load and invoke required TSP DLLs.

Windows NT 4.0's TAPI 2.0 components support symmetrical multiprocessing, multithreaded applications, and preemptive multitasking on Intel and RISC processors. According to Microsoft, TAPI 2.0 enhances call center management with modeling of predictive dialing ports and queues, provides call and data association, and offers music on hold features. Applications can negotiate and renegotiate quality-of-service (QOS) parameters to request a specific bandwidth. You must purchase TAPI 2.0-enabled third-party TSPs and application software to take advantage of these new TAPI features.

The Unimodem TSP of Windows NT 4.0 provides substantially improved performance compared with the relatively limited telecommunications features of Windows NT 3.5+. Windows NT 4.0 provides much better support for large modem banks used by RAS (Remote Access Service) servers, and comes with many more modem-definition files. The RAS features of TAPI 2.0 are one of the subjects of Chapter 18, "Managing Remote Access Service."

> **Note**
>
> The data/voice features of the upgraded Unimodem/V for Windows 95, which Microsoft released in late 1995, isn't included in the retail release of Windows NT Server 4.0 or Workstation 4.0. It's likely that you'll be able to download the TAPI 2.0 Unimodem/V driver for Windows NT 4.0 from the Microsoft Web site in late 1996.

Understanding Windows NT Marketing and Pricing Strategies

No book on Windows NT Server is complete without a few observations on Microsoft's marketing strategy and product pricing. Clearly, Microsoft's primary objectives are to eradicate IBM's OS/2 on the client side with Windows 95 and Windows NT Workstation 4.0, and to subsume the NetWare, UNIX, and OS/2 LAN Server NOS markets with Windows NT Server 4.0.

A secondary objective is to constrain Apple computers to their present share (about 6 percent) of the PC market by making Windows 95 as appealing and as easy to use as Apple's System 7.x operating system (renamed Mac OS in 1995). Offering Windows NT Workstation 4.0 and its successors as an alternative to Apple's oft-delayed Copeland operating system also is likely to constrain Apple's role in future high-end workstation markets.

Microsoft hopes to supplant high-priced UNIX workstations with Intel and reduced instruction set computer (RISC) PCs running Windows NT Workstation 4.0 by enhancing Silicon Graphic's Open GL three-dimensional graphics features with DirectDraw on Windows NT Workstation 4.0. To accomplish its objectives, Microsoft is counting on rapidly declining prices of Pentium and Pentium Pro chips and is hedging its processor bets by supporting new RISC platforms, such as the PowerPC.

It remains to be seen whether Microsoft can achieve its objectives for Windows NT 4.0 and successors on all fronts, but the following marketing factors point to the ultimate dominance of Windows NT Server 4.0 as an "enterprise-wide" network operating system:

- The Intel Pentium Pro is designed specifically for fully 32-bit Windows NT. Windows 95 doesn't gain significant performance advantages from the Pentium Pro because Windows 95 contains a substantial amount of 16-bit code to achieve backward compatibility with existing 16-bit applications. Despite problems in early 1996 with Intel motherboards that support up to four Pentium Pros, scalable server hardware that supports incremental symmetrical multiprocessing (SMP) upgrades is likely to dominate the high-end server market in 1997.

- The components of Microsoft's new BackOffice server suite—SQL Server, Exchange Server, System Management Server, and SNA Server—run only on Windows NT Server. (Technically, IIS 2.0, Index Server, and Proxy Server also are BackOffice components.) Windows NT Server 4.0's support for both Intel and popular RISC platforms, however, makes Windows NT at least as "open" a system as UNIX with its myriad proprietary flavors.

- Major publishers of relational database systems (RDBMSs), such as Oracle and Informix, supply versions for Windows NT Server. These RDBMSs traditionally have run only on relatively high-priced UNIX systems and can involve licensing costs in the hundreds of thousands of dollars. The relatively low licensing cost of Microsoft SQL Server has caused other RDBMS vendors to drastically reduce their prices for scaled-down "workgroup" versions that run on Windows NT. Microsoft SQL Server, however, is an enterprise-category RDBMS, not a scaled-down product.

- Virtually all of the most popular third-party Internet server applications are designed to run on Windows NT Server. In many cases, the first release of these Internet servers is for Windows NT, followed by successive versions for various proprietary flavors of UNIX.

- At prices in effect when this book was written, Windows NT Server has a significant cost-benefit advantage over Novell NetWare 4.x. The advantage is more pronounced if such features as Macintosh connectivity, Remote Access Service, and full TCP/IP support are factored into the equation. These features are included in Windows NT Server but are extra-cost options for NetWare users.

- Suppliers of sophisticated administration tools for UNIX networks are porting their products to Windows NT Server. Examples are Digital's Polycenter NetView for Windows NT and Computer Associates' UniCenter for Windows NT.

- An increasing number of well-known hardware and software firms are forming development partnerships with Microsoft to add advanced features, such as server clustering, to Windows NT Server. Later, the section "Forging Alliances for Scalable Windows NT Server Hardware" describes several of the most important contributors to Microsoft's Windows NT Server development and marketing efforts.

- Windows NT was the only operating system other than AIX (a UNIX flavor) offered by IBM for its PowerPC product line when this book was written. That IBM doesn't supply OS/2 Warp for the PowerPC product line is indicative of the market clout of Windows NT.

This list of factors that point to increasing acceptance of Windows NT Server by corporations and institutions doesn't mean that OS/2 will disappear, UNIX is doomed, and

Apple's market share will continue to drop to insignificance. The IDC report, quoted earlier in this section, projects an 8 percent annual growth rate for NetWare, 11 percent for UNIX, and 12 percent for OS/2. (The Mac OS isn't included in IDC's projections because the Mac OS isn't considered a network operating system.) According to a story in the April 22, 1996, issue of *InfoWorld Electric* (the Internet version of *InfoWorld* magazine), Apple has licensed Windows NT code from Microsoft and is likely to port Windows NT to the PowerPC Reference Platform that's due in late 1996.

The article "NT Server Rollout" in the May 20, 1996, issue of *Information Week* described the "largest-ever" Windows NT Server deployment at 8,400 General Motors dealerships. When completed, GM's Access Common Dealership Environment (CDE) will link a Compaq server running Windows NT Server 4.0 at each dealership with GM's PulSat satellite communications network. The article quotes a Sentry Market Research report indicating that half of the information system (IS) buyers at the 700 large companies surveyed plan to install Windows NT Server in the next few years—up from less than 40 percent with similar plans during 1995. Simultaneously, the percentage of IS buyers planning to base their server strategies on UNIX dropped from about 75 percent in 1995 to 50 percent in 1996. You can read additional details of the General Motors Windows NT Server 4.0 rollout at **http://www.microsoft.com/ntserver/customers.htm**.

An order for 8,400 servers is unusual, to say the least. Most of the early 1996 announcements of major migrations to Windows NT by large North American and European firms range from 25 to 100 servers, but also involve the sale of large numbers of Windows 95 or, more commonly, Windows NT Workstation client licenses—often numbering in the thousands. As an example, Intel is reported to be standardizing on Windows NT 4.0 desktop PCs for the firm's worldwide operations and expects to have installed more than 15,000 copies of Windows NT Workstation 4.0 by the time the migration is complete.

Another article in the same issue of *Information Week*, "Windows NT Servers Will Soon Get Cheaper," quotes a Gartner Group market estimate that projects dollar sales of server hardware for Windows NT will climb from about $4 billion in 1996 to about $18 billion in 2000, slightly under the $20 billion estimated 1996 sales of UNIX boxes. Further, the Gartner Group estimates that during this period, sales of hardware for NetWare servers will remain at about $2 billion. Thus, it's not surprising that the largest manufacturers of server hardware are concentrating on the Windows NT market.

Datamation magazine (the "granddaddy" of computer periodicals) published "The Datamation Cowen Report: Enterprise Computing Drives IS Spending" in its May 1, 1996, issue. Cowen & Co. paints an equally upbeat future for Windows NT Server in the 1996–97 time frame, estimating that Windows NT comprised 18 percent of the network operating systems in use in early 1996. Cowen's survey disclosed that users' installations plans for 1996–97 call for 51 percent Windows NT Server, 21 percent NetWare, 17 percent UNIX, and 11 percent for all other systems. According to Cowen, close to 50 percent of all users surveyed said that Windows NT Server will be their "primary application server operating system."

> **Tip**
>
> *Information Week* and *Datamation* magazines are good sources of information on the latest developments in client/server computing and how Windows NT Server fits into the IS programs of large organizations. These two publications have Web sites at **http://techweb.cmp.com/iw/current** and **http://www.datamation.com/**, respectively, with searchable content. The *Datamation* site also includes a list of feature stories up to six months in advance of publication.

Good press and optimistic market-share predictions might not determine whether your organization adopts Windows NT Server 4.0 as its primary network operating system. Glowing reviews of any software product are suspect and deservedly suspect; all software contains bugs of varying severity, or at least a few warts. There is, however, comfort as well as strength in numbers. *Fortune* magazine's "Give It Away & Get Rich!" article in the June 10, 1996, issue explains the software numbers game: "Software is subject to what economists call 'network externalities.' This essentially means that the more widely used something is, the more people value it." The increasing acceptance of Windows NT Server by large firms as an organization-wide network operating system lends credence to Microsoft's claims for the capabilities of Windows NT Server 4.0.

Embracing and Extending the Internet

In early 1995, while Microsoft was readying Windows 95 for its long-delayed release and enticing content providers to augment The Microsoft Network online service, other firms were making a beeline to the Internet. Prodigy—then owned by IBM and Sears, Roebuck and Co.—was the first commercial online service to offer access to the World Wide Web, soon to be followed by CompuServe and America Online. Although several software startups offered Web browsers, Netscape's Navigator quickly gathered the lion's share of the browser market. Sun Microsystems was the initial favorite in the UNIX-based Web server category, and Apple gained a substantial share (estimated at as much as 30 percent) of the Web server business for its PowerMacs. Netscape and O'Reilly Associates were among the leaders in supplying Web server software for Windows NT 3.5+. Microsoft, it appeared, was asleep at the Internet switch.

On December 7, 1995, the "sleeping giant" woke up. Microsoft announced that it would "embrace and extend" the Internet. In a flurry of press releases, Microsoft announced the availability of a beta version of Internet Explorer (IE), which is based on technology developed by Spyglass; a stripped-down version of Visual Basic for Applications for programming interactive Web pages; ActiveVRML for adding virtual reality features; and agreements with several other firms to foster use of Microsoft's new Web browser, including negotiations with Sun Microsystems to license the Java programming language for inclusion within IE.

 On its Web site, Microsoft unveiled its Web server strategy, based on Windows NT Server 3.51+ and the Internet Services API (ISAPI) for writing server-based extensions to Internet Information Server. Both IE 1.0 and IIS 1.0 were free and downloadable from **http://www.microsoft.com**. All you needed to use these free products, of course, were

Windows 95 and Windows NT 3.51, respectively. IE 2.0 and IIS 2.0 are included with Windows NT Server 4.0.

On June 13, 1996, Microsoft held its Intranet Strategy Day at the San Jose (California) Convention Center, accompanied by a media blitz of gargantuan proportion. Bill Gates and two Microsoft vice presidents, Paul Maritz and Pete Higgins, described how Microsoft intended to divert the lion's share of the lucrative intranet server business from industry-leader Netscape. (Despite the Internet hype, corporate intranets are what's generating real income today for most software vendors.) If you missed the press accounts, check out **http://www.microsoft.com/intranet/default.htm** for transcripts and PowerPoint slides of the Intranet Strategy Day presentation. In July 1996, Microsoft launched its SiteBuilder Workshop at **http://www.microsoft.com/ workshop/**. Although primarily directed to authors and designers of Web pages using ActiveX technologies, one section of the Workshop is devoted to site administration, availability, security, and other network administrator duties.

One of Microsoft's more remarkable transformations, aside from giving away extraordinary quantities of "free" software, is the candor with which the company now discusses forthcoming Internet- and intranet-related products. The vast majority of Microsoft's alpha- and beta-testing programs historically have required participants to sign nondisclosure agreements (NDAs) in order to participate in the testing process, thereby getting an early look at forthcoming new products or upgraded versions of existing products. With the exception of ActiveMovie, Microsoft's replacement for the aging Video for Windows system, and the forthcoming Microsoft Media Server, alpha and beta versions of most Internet-related products are open to all comers.

From the start, the Shell Update Release for Windows NT has been an open, public beta program without an NDA requirement. Microsoft distributed more than 200,000 free copies of the second beta version of Windows NT 4.0. (The Beta 2 release was used to write the first draft of the manuscript for this book; Release Candidate 2.3 was used to complete the writing.) Microsoft's new openness in disclosing the technical details behind its Internet strategy is a welcome change for users and developers alike.

Note

The term *open* or *open systems*, when used by Microsoft's competitors, means *doesn't require Windows*. In the Internet browser business, the term means *not from Microsoft* because it's likely that 90 percent of all browsers run under some version of Microsoft Windows. By no stretch of the imagination does *open* mean *non-proprietary*.

The competition is intense between Microsoft and Netscape to create proprietary extensions to HTML and their respective browsers that become *de facto* Internet standards by virtue of market dominance. So far, Netscape (with an estimated 80 percent of the browser market) has been the hands-down winner of market share. Whether Microsoft can overcome Netscape's lead in the browser market remains to be seen.

Intranetworking and Internet Information Server 2.0

The conventional definition of an *intranet* is any private network running TCP/IP. This book uses the term *intranet* to mean a private TCP/IP network with an Internet server that can distribute HTML-encoded documents. Intranets mesh well with current organizational buzzwords, such as downsizing, re-engineering, horizontal management, empowering employees, workgroup collaboration, and real-time information distribution.

Many organizations now are using intranets to distribute human resources policy manuals, hortatory messages from upper management, white papers, and other information that would ordinarily require printing and physical distribution. HTML conversion add-ons for word processing applications, such as the Internet Assistant for Microsoft Word, ease the process of moving from the printed page to a *"Company* Wide Web." Figure 1.23 shows a 12-page Word 7.0 document converted to a single HTML-encoded Web page with the Internet Assistant for Microsoft Word, which also converts figures embedded in Word documents to .GIF files for browser compatibility.

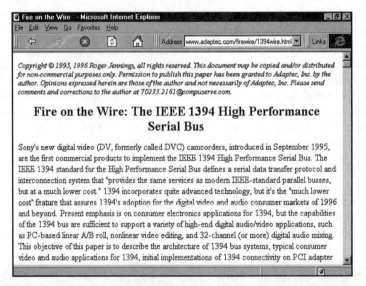

Fig. 1.23 A Word 7.0 document converted to HTML and displayed in the Beta 2 version of Internet Explorer 3.0.

Note

For an example of a large-scale collection of hyperlinked Web pages created with Word 7.0 and converted to HTML format with Internet Assistant for Microsoft Word, visit **http://www.adaptec.com/firewire/1394main.html**. The embedded Visio 4.0 diagrams of **http://www.adaptec.com/firewire/1394wire.html** and **http://www.adaptec.com/firewire/1394dvcs.html** are .GIF files rendered by the Internet Assistant for Microsoft Word. You can download the free Assistant and a tutorial for its use from **http://www.microsoft.com/msword/internet/ia/**.

Intranets also offer a foundation on which to build work-flow and project-management applications and, when well implemented, foster collaboration, cooperation, and information sharing among employees. You can connect a private intranet to the Internet through a firewall that lets mobile employees dial into the intranet through an Internet service provider (ISP) without compromising confidential information. Thus, telecommuters and field sales personnel can communicate with the home office at very low hourly cost, compared with toll-free telephone lines.

One of the major applications for intranets is distributing, in real time, information stored in various corporate databases. Microsoft's Internet Database Connector (IDC), included with IIS 1.0 and 2.0, allows you to quickly create Web pages that return to an HTML table the result set of a user-specified query against a Microsoft SQL Server or Access database, or any other RDBMS that supports Microsoft's 32-bit Open Database Connectivity (ODBC) API. The SQL Server 6.5 Web Assistant lets you create entire Web pages from database query result sets with minimum effort.

One of the primary drawing cards of intranets is the ease with which users can connect to and navigate a well-designed private Web site. When you install IIS 2.0, the Setup program installs a temporary home page (see fig. 1.24) at \inetsrv\wwwroot\ default.htm. Launching IE 2.x on any client with a TCP/IP connection to the server and simply typing the DNS server name or the TCP/IP address in the Address text box displays DEFAULT.HTM. (You simply replace DEFAULT.HTM with your own version of that file with hyperlinks to your other HTML pages.) IIS 2.0, together with the Internet Assistant for Microsoft Word, makes it a quick-and-easy process to create a demonstration intranet site for review and testing by your organization's management.

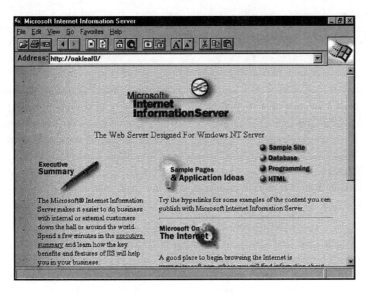

Fig. 1.24 Displaying the default Web page included with IIS 2.0 in Internet Explorer 2.0.

Managing Internet Information Server 2.0

Internet Information Server 2.0 includes the Internet Service Manager for setup and maintenance of World Wide Web (WWW), Gopher, and FTP sites, which the Windows NT Server 4.0 Setup program installs by default in separate subfolders—\inetsvr\ wwwroot, \inetsvr\gophroot, and \inetsvr\ftproot, respectively. Figure 1.25 shows the opening window of Internet Service Manger with the Web, Gopher, and FTP services installed and running.

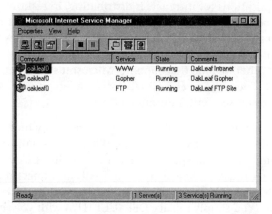

Fig. 1.25 The opening window of the Internet Service Manger in Report view.

Note

The Internet Peer Server included with Windows NT Workstation 4.0 includes a copy of Internet Service Manager for remote administration of Internet Information Server 2.0. The Internet Peer Server allows you to test newly created Web pages locally, and then transfer the pages to the desired location within the \inetsvr folder for distribution. You also can use the Workstation version to host a Web site using several third-party Web server applications.

Double-clicking an item in the Computer column displays the Service Properties for *ServerName* sheet for the service. The default Service page allows you to specify the connection timeout, maximum number of simultaneous connections, and anonymous logon and/or password authentication for the default Internet Guest account, IUSR_*SERVERNAME* (see fig. 1.26). User Manager for Domains allows you to alter user group membership for this account; the default user groups for the Internet Guest account are Domain User and Guest.

An alternative is to establish a new Internet user group with specific permissions, and then make the Internet Guest account a member of the Internet group. You can use Server Manager to set permissions for the \inetsvr folder and its subfolders; if \inetsvr is installed on an NTFS volume, you also can set permissions for individual files.

Fig. 1.26 The Service page of the WWW Service Properties sheet of Internet Service Manager.

In addition to the Service page, Internet Service Manager's Service Properties sheet includes Directories, Logging, and Advanced pages. (Microsoft hasn't replaced *directory* with *folder* in all instances.) The Directories page displays Web-related subfolders of the \inetsvr folder, including Web-style share names, such as /Scripts, in the Alias column (see fig. 1.27). The Logging page allows you to log user statistics to a text file or to a SQL Server 6.x database (see fig. 1.28) or any other ODBC-compliant RDBMS. Before specifying the logging database in the Logging page, you need to create the ODBC database and add a System data source for the database with Control Panel's ODBC tool. The Advanced page allows you to specify TCP/IP clients to be excluded from intranet access; alternatively, you can specify the TCP/IP address of each client with intranet access.

Fig. 1.27 Displaying the Web-related folders page of the WWW Service Properties sheet of Internet Service Manager.

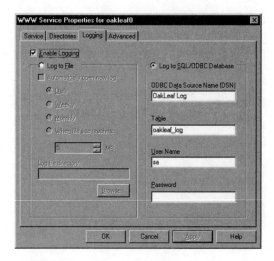

Fig. 1.28 Setting up user activity logging to a SQL Server 6.x database.

Forging Alliances for Scalable Windows NT Server Hardware

It's possible to run Windows NT Server 4.0 on a garden-variety PC with an 80486DX processor and 16M of RAM, but you're not likely to be satisfied with the performance of such a server in a production networking environment. Today's trend is to high-performance multiprocessor servers with two to four 200 MHz Pentium Pros on an Intel motherboard, a minimum of 64M of RAM, and RAID arrays of 4G+ SCSI-3 (Ultra-SCSI wide) fixed-disk drives.

Fortunately, the cost of DRAM declined drastically in early 1996. Moderately priced 4.3G, 9G, and even 23G SCSI-3 drives that use embedded-servo technology, and thus don't require thermal recalibration, are expected from several suppliers by the end of 1996. The price of 100mbps PCI adapter cards that support 100BaseT Ethernet connections also is dropping into the affordable range. If you have enough hardware savvy, you can assemble a very high-performance server from off-the-shelf components at a moderate cost.

Most organizations are reluctant to "roll their own" server hardware and instead look to established suppliers of high-end hardware to deliver servers preconfigured for a particular purpose, often with Windows NT Server and one or more BackOffice components installed and tested. This is especially the case for RISC-based systems using Alpha, MIPS, or PowerPC processors. It's the most common practice (often a necessity) in the UNIX world to purchase server hardware and its proprietary UNIX operating system from the same supplier. Microsoft doesn't supply server hardware, so the availability of packaged servers from name-brand suppliers is critical to the ultimate success of Windows NT Server.

Scalability through clustering of individual Windows NT servers is one of the hottest topics for late 1996 and 1997. At the Windows Hardware Engineering Conference (WinHEC) in the spring of 1996, Microsoft announced the future availability of its Wolfpack clustering technology, initially for enabling two server PCs to share a group of fixed-disk drives to achieve fault tolerance through simple redundancy. Microsoft expects to release this scaling architecture, called *failover clustering*, for Windows NT in early 1997.

In the interim, several manufacturers have announced new, scalable server systems based on Windows NT Server 4.0, either independently or by technology-sharing agreements with Microsoft. The following sections describe some of the more important of these new products that extend the reach of Windows NT Server 4.0 to organization-wide networking.

Digital Equipment Corporation

DEC announced in May 1996 its clustering software called Failover Manager, which connects Alpha- and Intel-based servers through SCSI adapters sharing a SCSI-3 bus, as part of an overall DEC program called Digital Clusters for Windows NT. Two Windows NT servers, each with their own system fixed disk and a SCSI host adapter, connect via external SCSI cables to a set of fixed disks housed in an expansion cabinet.

The connected computers appear to users as a single Windows NT server. The two servers share the production load when both are operational; if one server fails, the other server takes over while the dead server undergoes repair. At $995 per server, the software-based Failover Manager was the lowest-cost fault-tolerance solution available for Windows NT Server when this book was written. For more details on Digital Clusters for Windows NT, visit **http://www.windowsnt.digital.com/clusters/**.

DEC's Alliance for Enterprise Computing, announced in April 1996, supplies hardware, services, field support, and networking assistance for Windows NT Server installations under a multimillion-dollar agreement with Microsoft. Microsoft is covering a substantial share of DEC's cost of setting up and training personnel for the Alliance. Microsoft's objective is to provide the same level of support for Windows NT that customers have come to expect from higher-priced mini- and mainframe computers and software. DEC expects to employ 2,300 Microsoft Certified Professionals by the end of 1997. Details on the Alliance are at **http://www.alliance.digital.com/**.

Tandem Computers, Inc.

Tandem—best known for its fault-tolerant parallel servers—entered into an agreement with Microsoft in May 1996 to develop fault-tolerant, scalable Windows NT servers. Tandem will license its NonStop ServerWare and ServerNet cluster interconnect technology to Microsoft for use with Windows NT Server and the forthcoming Wolfpack system in return for a $30 million payment.

Microsoft gains the benefit of Tandem's reputation for the fault tolerance that's considered critical by financial institutions, airlines, and others who need 100 percent, 24-hour-per-day server reliability. Tandem claims that its computers and software manage

90 percent of the world's security transactions, 66 percent of credit-card transactions, and 80 percent of all ATM transactions. Additional information on the agreement is available from **http://www.tandem.com/msoft/index.html**.

Compaq Computer, Inc.

Compaq is expected to release a line of Pentium Pro-based Windows NT servers in late 1996 that use a subset of Tandem's NonStop ServerNet technology as early as September. According to published reports, Compaq will offer a low-cost, fault-tolerant model for branch office workstations and a high-end version, based on the Intel chipset, for corporate data centers. Details on Compaq's agreement with Tandem are available at **http://www.compaq.com/newsroom/pr/pr161095a.html**.

In addition to Intel-based servers—a market in which Compaq is a major player—the firm supplies network interface cards (NICs), repeaters, switches, and management software. Compaq acquired these products, which make up its Netelligent product line, when it purchased Thomas-Conrad and NetWorth in 1995. Netelligent products are aimed at branch and remote offices, workgroups, and department and small-business networks.

Amdahl Corporation

Amdahl, best know for its IBM-plug-compatible mainframes and large-scale data storage systems, announced in mid-May 1996 its EnVista line of servers that use the Pentium Pro Quad (Orion) architecture and Windows NT Server 4.0. Amdahl claims that the EnVista Central system is scalable to eight clustered nodes of one- to four-processor servers. The EnVista Availability Manager, similar to DEC's Failover Manager, works with a new line of high-capacity data storage systems. You can get more details on the EnVista product line at **http://www.amdahl.com/doc/products/summary.htm**.

Amdahl also provides the EnVista Channel for ESCON, which connects the EnVista servers to IBM System/390 mainframes running MVS using Microsoft SNA Server 2.11. Amdahl reports that EnVista Channel for ESCON achieves a 4.8M/sec rate when transferring data from an IBM System/390 mainframe through Polaris Communications' ESCON PCI adapter card. Bringing Amdahl into the fold adds the prestige of a major mainframe manufacturer to the ranks of Windows NT server suppliers.

From Here...

The objective of this chapter was to provide an overview of Windows NT Server 4.0 with emphasis on the new features Microsoft added to version 4.0. Microsoft's marketing strategy for Windows NT Server and establishing Internet and intranet servers with Microsoft Internet Information Server 2.0 (included with Windows NT Server 4.0) also were covered. The chapter concluded with a brief description of the latest developments in hardware for Windows NT Server, including new clustering initiatives.

The balance of Part I of this book, "Networking with Windows NT Server 4.0," is organized in the sequence typical of a new network server installation. The following chapters provide the background you need before you install Windows NT Server 4.0:

■ Chapter 2, "Planning Your Windows NT Network Installation," details the steps required to plan and budget for the hardware and software needed to establish your Windows NT Server 4.0 network.

■ Chapter 3, "Understanding the Windows NT Operating System," introduces the technical foundation of Windows NT and the Windows NT File System (NTFS).

■ Chapter 4, "Choosing Network Protocols," explains how to select one or more of the three principal networking protocols supported by Windows NT based on your network configuration.

■ Chapter 5, "Purchasing Networking Hardware," provides guidance in the selection of the adapter cards, cabling, hubs, routers, and related equipment required to complete the physical network installation.

If you're upgrading an existing Windows NT Server installation, you might want to skip ahead to Chapter 6, "Making the Initial Server Installation."

Networking

Chapter 2

Planning Your Windows NT Network Installation

The most important element of a successful PC network installation is thorough planning. To be successful, a network needs to be efficient and effective. *Efficient* means that the network is technically elegant, is installed within budget, and is maintainable and expandable with minimum staff time. *Effective* means that the network fully serves the needs of its users.

This chapter presents the 11 key issues you must consider to plan your network properly. Depending on your particular environment and the scale of your network, some of these issues take precedence over others. Regardless of priority, each issue is important and deserves consideration in the planning process. Considering each planning issue in turn helps you develop a framework for your network, prevents you from overlooking important needs, and avoids common stumbling blocks along the way to implementation.

Developing the Network Implementation Plan

Traditionally, most Windows NT Server installations occur within a corporate or institutional environment. Windows NT Server is particularly appealing to small to mid-sized organizations because of its relatively low acquisition cost, moderately priced client licenses, ease of installation, and simplicity of maintenance. Although Microsoft proudly points to "buys" of hundreds of Windows NT Server installations, plus thousands of Windows NT Workstation licenses from well-known Fortune 500 firms, single-server installations with 10 to 100 clients fuel much of the momentum of the Windows NT market.

> **Note**
>
> You can download the current version of Microsoft's *Enterprise Planning Guide* (for large organizations) and the *Deployment Guide for Windows NT Server and NetWare Integration* from **http://www.microsoft.com/ntserver/epds.htm**. When this book was written, these two guides had not been updated to Windows NT Server
>
> (continues)

This chapter explains how to

- Use the 11 key network planning issues to develop a network that meets user, maintainability, and manageability needs

- Establish a working budget and use it as a tool to manage purchases and to get the most network for your money

- Use project-management software for managing personnel resources and deadlines

- Use outside help from vendors and consultants to plan and design your network, and how to choose those sources

---

(continued)

4.0. The basic concepts outlined in these two publications, however, apply equally to versions 3.51 and 4.0 of Windows NT Server.

Regardless of the size of the organization adopting a Windows NT 4.0 network, the following 11 topics are critical to the planning process:

- Meeting business objectives

- Determining user and workgroup needs

- Establishing security

- Determining fault-tolerance requirements

- Incorporating existing infrastructure

- Connecting to the outside world

- Developing an implementation schedule

- Considering network management needs

- Providing for future growth

- Working within a budget

- Training users

The sections that follow describe these planning elements in detail.

Meeting Business Objectives

It's easy to focus so much attention on the technical issues of planning a network that you lose sight of the primary goal, which is to meet your organization's strategic and tactical business objectives. These objectives may be stated broadly—for instance, "To improve corporate-wide communications among all employees." The objectives may be stated more narrowly: "To provide access to Internet mail and the World Wide Web for executive and administrative staff members." In many cases, the objectives may not be explicitly stated. Whatever the case, you can be sure that before management approves the funds to implement your network installation or upgrade, management must see that the plan will meet a perceived objective or solve a problem.

Talk to upper management to discover the rationale for the project, keeping in mind that the stated reasons aren't always the real reasons why such a project has been initiated. Find out what results upper management foresees. Ask what management expects to be accomplished when the project is complete, or what should be done more quickly, inexpensively, or efficiently as a result of the project.

Sometimes the real motivation behind the project doesn't originate with upper management at all, but instead derives from a particular department head or group within the organization. It's up to you to uncover the true objectives of the network installation, and to make sure that the network you design and install meets the objectives, solves the problems, and fulfills the expectations of your executive management.

The planning stage also is the time to consider proposing that the scope of the project be expanded beyond that originally requested. Upper management focuses on the big picture and, as a result, is typically unaware of all the implications and possibilities inherent in networking technology. It often happens that planning a network project to solve stated needs also offers you the opportunity to address other pressing computer-related problems with minimum additional money and effort. Upper management may not even realize that the organization is missing such an opportunity, unless you describe the opportunity. Often, by spending a bit more money, you can kill two birds with one stone; sometimes you can even nail an entire flock.

Determining User and Workgroup Needs

You want to keep upper management happy, because it controls the size of your paycheck. But you also want to keep users happy, because unhappy users can make your life miserable. Take the time early in the planning process to find out what users expect from the network; then modify your plan, as needed, to give them as much as possible of what they asked for. If management requirements determine the strategic thrust of the network, user needs determine the tactical direction.

The core unit of network planning, a workgroup comprises a group of people who share related job functions. Workgroups are typically—although by no means always—formally defined units of the organization. Members of a workgroup often not only use specialized software not used elsewhere in the organization, but they also have a common need to access the same data. A workgroup can range in size from one or two people in a small firm's accounting department to hundreds or even thousands of people in the outbound telemarketing group of a large firm. Figure 2.1 illustrates a network comprising three workgroups—Personnel, Engineering, and Finance—each of which has at least one workgroup server, connected by switched Ethernet. The key to determining what comprises a workgroup is to discover shared job functions, plus similarities in the software used and the data accessed.

After you analyze the workgroup makeup within your organization and determine which workgroup will be affected by the project, the next step is to talk to workgroup leaders to find out their views on the project. Depending on the workgroup's size and how much time you have available, you may find it worthwhile to talk to each staff member in the group, either individually or in a group meeting. It's during this process that you discover the detailed information about user needs that will allow you to make the network more useful to the people who actually use it. No one is in a better position to know the real day-to-day problems than the folks in the trenches. All you have to do is ask them.

Workgroup members are likely to tell you where shared printers should be located, that they can't read accounting Excel worksheets because they have only Quattro Pro, that having Internet mail would let them deal with customers more efficiently, or that their 486SX PCs are too slow to run the new version of the inventory software. All of this is useful information that you never discover unless you ask. You'll also hear a lot of requests that you can't possibly grant, so don't make the mistake of letting workgroup members believe they'll automatically get everything they want.

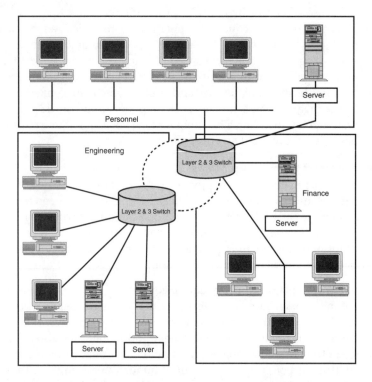

Fig. 2.1 Personnel, Engineering, and Finance workgroups connected by switched Ethernet.

Tip

Ask specific questions, such as "Where would be the best place to locate the network laser printer for your workgroup?" as well as more general questions, such as "What two or three things could we do to make your life easier?" After you go through this process with each workgroup, you have a much better idea of how to configure your network and what minor changes and additions you can make that have a big payoff. You also become a hero to the users, simply by asking the questions.

Now is also the time to consider whether workgroups not a part of the original plan can be added to the plan at little or no additional cost. For example, the original project might cover connecting the accounting workgroup to a server that shares an accounting database. During the planning phase, you might discover that the human resource management (HRM) group located on the other side of the wall could also be connected within budget and run its HRM application on the same server. Often, all that stands in the way of providing a major benefit to an overlooked workgroup is a few Ethernet cards and an additional hundred feet or so of cable.

> **Note**
>
> Workgroups often are provided with a server dedicated to specific workgroup activities, such as accounting, purchasing, production, and marketing. The constantly decreasing cost of server hardware makes distributing the server workload among workgroups economically feasible. The workgroup servers are organized as members of a common domain serving a single geographic site. Chapter 16, "Distributing Network Services with Domains," describes the topology of Windows NT Server domains. You also can download a copy of the Microsoft white paper "Windows NT Server Domain Planning for Your Enterprise" from **http://www.microsoft.com/ntserver/ enter.htm**.

Establishing Security

Security means protecting your hardware, software, and data. The time to start thinking about security is during the network planning process. Security is made up of the following four elements:

- *Server security* consists of assigning passwords, granting access rights to server volumes and directories, and other explicit permissions to use shared data. This aspect of security is covered fully in Chapter 12, "Managing User and Group Accounts," and Chapter 13, "Sharing and Securing Network Resources."

- *Backup security*, discussed in Chapter 8, "Installing File Backup Systems," is absolutely necessary to ensure that data stored on a server or servers isn't lost due to operating system or hardware failures.

- *Physical security* means protecting your servers, hubs, and other active network components by placing them behind locked doors.

- *Data communication security* means protecting your data while it's "on the wire" (in transit between two locations), as well as protecting data resident on local hosts from crackers attempting to gain access from outside your network.

Physical Security. Although your environment may make it difficult or impossible to physically secure all your components, strive to put all server-related hardware behind locked doors. Physical security for network servers is especially important today because of the recent trend toward burglary of server-grade PCs. Servers have the latest Pentium or Pentium Pro chips, large amounts of memory, high-speed disk drives, and other costly components bringing top dollar from PC fences.

Even more important for most organizations is the possibility of their data being stolen. This is a two-edged sword:

- Catastrophic loss of company data is one of the major causes of business failures. Even with a good backup strategy in place, you may find it difficult or impossible to reconstruct all your data in a timely manner.

- You have to consider where your stolen data may end up. Your data may be sold to an unscrupulous competitor, providing that company with your customer lists, accounting information, and other confidential company data. Secure your server well.

All servers and active network components should be situated in equipment rooms or wiring closets, and only you and your network administrative staff should have the keys to these locations. This can be a hard battle to win because, invariably, some users and managers feel they have the right to gain unrestricted access to "their" equipment. These folks will resort to everything from quoting fire codes to lobbying senior management to obtain such access. Stake out your claim early and fight to keep it. After all, you're responsible for maintaining the equipment and assuring its online availability; such responsibilities require that the network administration team have absolute control of the server(s).

If you do secure your equipment rooms, also be sure to establish a key-control policy to ensure that those on the approved list can always gain access when necessary. Designate backup staff, and make sure that each backup person is provided with a key or with access to the key box. Otherwise, if the primary person is sick, on vacation, or simply unreachable, the backup person may be unable to effect repairs simply because he can't get through a locked door.

Here's an example of what can happen if you lose the server access battle: A workgroup is down. Your staff expert appears, determines that the problem is caused by a misbehaving router, and decides to reboot the router—not a trivial decision. He notifies users in other affected workgroups throughout the building, shuts the network down in an orderly fashion, and reboots the router. The problem is solved and your expert returns covered in glory. Now consider what the users observed. Their workgroup was down, and the expert rebooted the router by pressing a big red button. A week, a month, or a year later, that workgroup goes down again. They call the expert for help, wait for 15 minutes with their arms crossed, and then decide that no one will show up any time soon. One bright person remembers the last time that this happened, the expert pushed the big red button on the box in the corner. The person pushes the button and takes the entire network down without notice. Guess who takes the blame?

In addition to securing access to your active network components, one step you can take to avoid such problems is to establish and post clear policies concerning how and to whom problems should be reported. Be sure to post this information where it's readily accessible to users, and not locked up in the server room. Put them instead over the coffee machine, where the users may actually notice them.

Unless your IS department or help desk is open around the clock, pay particular attention to how users should report problems after hours. Someone working desperately in the evening or on a weekend to meet a deadline may feel he has no alternative but to attempt repairs himself. Simply designating an on-call person and posting his pager number can potentially avoid a lot of grief.

Data Communication Security. Unlike physical security, which is primarily concerned with protecting your network hardware from unintentional abuse by employees, data communications security focuses primarily on protecting your data from being compromised by outside intruders. Managers of most local area networks (LANs), which are self-contained within a building or campus, don't need to be too concerned about

Networking

over-the-wire data communications security. If your LAN is connected to the outside world in any fashion, however, you must take steps to prevent unauthorized access to your data by outside parties.

One important aspect of security is protecting your data from viruses. Most of today's viruses propagate via online data communication, usually as a result of downloading infected files from the Internet or bulletin-board services. Windows NT 4.0 virus-scanning programs are available now from several vendors (including McAfee, Intel, and Symantec), and more are on the way. Figure 2.2 shows the main window of McAfee VirusScan for Windows NT after finding no infected files on the server drive. Any of these scanning products will detect any virus you're at all likely to see in the real world. Don't be too impressed by how many viruses each claims to detect or pay too much attention to the comparative claims. All of them are good; none of them is perfect.

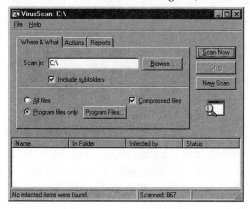

Fig. 2.2 The main window of McAfee Virus Scan for Windows NT, with no viruses detected.

The burgeoning of wide area networks (WANs) and the use of the Internet to carry corporate traffic brings the data communications security issue to the forefront. Banks and other financial institutions long ago established private secure data communications networks to avoid the danger of their data being intercepted or otherwise compromised. Even private, secure networks have been compromised by determined hackers. If your environment requires you to establish links between networks at multiple locations, or if you plan to provide remote access services to mobile users, you should plan to provide at least some data communications security. Depending on your particular needs, ensuring data communications security may be easy and relatively inexpensive, or it may be quite complex and extremely expensive.

If your security needs are modest, you have only two or three locations in close proximity to link, and you don't need dial-up network access, leased lines from the telephone company (telco) may be the solution. Because leased lines provide a hard-wired dedicated link from one location to another rather than go through a telephone company switch, leased lines are inherently secure. This security stems not from any special efforts made to secure the link, but simply from the fact that the link is inaccessible to would-be eavesdroppers.

If, on the other hand, you need to link many widely geographically dispersed locations, you may have a greater problem. The cost of leased lines—especially lines providing high link speeds—mounts very quickly, and even leased lines may not provide an adequately high level of security for your needs. Because you pay for the dedicated bandwidth of a leased line 24 hours a day, 365 days a year, whether you're using the line or not, most companies use packet-switching networks, which charge on a usage basis. Packet switching has brought the cost of providing high bandwidth links to multiple locations within reason. From a security standpoint, the down side of packet switching is that, by its nature, packet switching combines the data from many companies and places all the data on a common carrier, thus making data vulnerable to interception and compromise at many points along the way.

 Until a year or two ago, using packet switching usually meant contracting with AT&T, MCI, H&R Block, or a similar provider of specialized data delivery services. During the last two years, organizations have increasingly turned to the Internet to provide low-cost packet-switched data delivery. In theory, the Internet is an insecure means of data delivery. In practice, the Internet is probably at least as secure as your telephone. Just as your voice telephone conversations can be intercepted by anyone with a reasonable degree of technical competence and the motivation to do so, your Internet traffic can also be intercepted.

You can avoid having your data compromised by using data encryption, either at the application level or at the packet level. Encryption doesn't prevent your data from being intercepted—it simply garbles the data, making it useless to the eavesdropper. How you implement encryption determines what level of security encryption provides for your data.

Application-level encryption depends on the software you're running to perform the encryption. This can be a workable method as long as it occurs without requiring user intervention. For example, a client/server database application may be designed so that the client- and server-side software both encrypt outgoing traffic and decrypt incoming traffic transparently to the user, leaving the would-be eavesdropper watching a stream of random garbage characters.

Application-level encryption that depends on user intervention can't be considered a reliable means of protecting data. For example, although your e-mail package may allow you to encrypt outgoing messages on demand by taking certain manual steps, the likelihood that individual e-mail users will remember how to encrypt their message—not to mention the likelihood that they'll go to this extra trouble—is small. Depend on application-level encryption only in specialized circumstances, and even then only when the encryption is invisible to the users.

Note

Microsoft's Internet Information Server 2.0, included with Windows NT Server 4.0, provides Point-to-Point Tunneling Protocol (PPTP) for secure communication over the Internet. PPTP is discussed in Chapter 18, "Managing Remote Access Services," and Chapter 19, "Setting Up the Internet Information Server."

Packet-level encryption occurs at the hardware level, typically in the boundary router or in a specialized device designed to handle it. Packet-level encryption encrypts the data portion of each outbound packet, but leaves unchanged the packet and frame header and trailer data, including the source and destination addresses. This means that the encrypted packets can be handled by standard devices along the way to the destination. At the destination, a similar device strips the packet and frame header and trailer information, decrypts the data portion of the packet, and delivers the decrypted data to the addressee.

Packet-level encryption devices can be configured to allow you to designate that only specific networks require that packets sent to them be encrypted, allowing data destined for other networks to go out unencrypted. Thus, for example, you can designate each company network site as requiring encrypted data, while allowing users to access other sites normally. This is particularly useful if you plan to use the Internet to deliver your data securely. Figure 2.3 illustrates the use of encrypting routers to assure privacy of communication over the Internet.

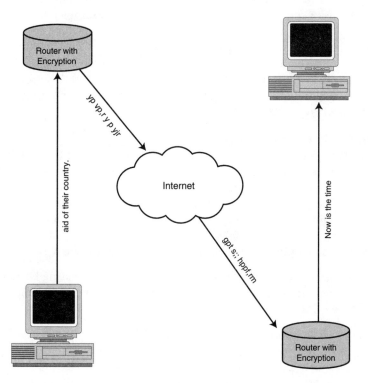

Fig. 2.3 Using router-based encryption to ensure communication privacy on the Internet.

Firewalls are another tool in the datacomm security arsenal. Unlike encryption, which is concerned with protecting data in transit, a firewall is designed to control access to your network. A firewall filters out inbound traffic unless that traffic originates from an approved source. Likewise, a firewall can be configured to filter outbound traffic, thereby allowing internal users to access only approved external hosts.

Like any technology, firewalls aren't a complete guarantee. It's possible for a technically knowledgeable person to spoof an authorized host and get past your firewall. Still, firewalls are becoming extremely popular as a means to isolate secure internal networks from the anarchy of the Internet. Microsoft's Internet Proxy Server for Windows NT—in the beta-test stage and code-named *Catapult* when this book was written—is an example of a firewall that you can implement at moderate cost.

Everything has its price, and security is no exception. Assigning long, randomly generated passwords makes it much more difficult for a hacker to guess a password, but at the same time makes life more difficult for authorized users. Securing all your equipment behind locked doors limits the chance that the equipment will be damaged accidentally or maliciously, but it also makes it more difficult for your staff to maintain the equipment. Installing over-the-wire encryption hardware and firewalls minimizes the likelihood that your data will be compromised in transit, but it also requires expensive equipment and scarce staff time to install and maintain.

Too much security can be counterproductive—not only in terms of time, money, and effort, but in terms of compromising the security itself. For example, many organizations mandating long, random, frequently changed passwords simply did it because it seemed to be a "good idea at the time." They've been surprised to find a blizzard of yellow sticky notes posted on each monitor with the users' passwords written on them. Don't attempt to establish security features that require extraordinary user effort. Instead, determine what data must be protected, and at what level of security. Plan for as much security as you really need, where you need it, and no more.

Determining Fault-Tolerance Requirements

Fault tolerance is a system's capability to continue to function after the failure of one or more critical components. The key to fault tolerance is the use of redundancy to eliminate single points of failure. Most networks provide at least some fault tolerance, although it may be limited to installing an uninterruptible power supply (UPS) to protect against power failures, and perhaps a RAID (redundant array of inexpensive disks) subsystem to guard against fixed-disk failures. Some networks are fully fault tolerant, achieved by providing online backup spares for each device on the network.

UPSs and RAID systems are briefly discussed in Chapter 5, "Purchasing Networking Hardware." RAID systems are covered in detail in Chapter 7, "Setting Up Redundant Arrays of Inexpensive Disks (RAID)."

Building a fault-tolerant network is expensive, and the more fault tolerance you build in, the more expensive it becomes. The cost of providing a backup bridge for each working bridge, a backup router for each working router, a backup server for each working server, and so on escalates quickly. As a result, most networks use redundancy only at those points that are either most critical or most likely to fail. Power failures are both common and critical, so nearly all networks use UPSs to protect against them. Disk failures are less common, but because they're critical, many network servers are equipped with RAID disk subsystems. Hubs, bridges, and routers fail very infrequently, so it's uncommon to see full redundancy implemented for these components.

> **Note**
>
> One means of providing server fault tolerance is to implement a *fail-over system,* in which duplicate servers are connected to a single RAID system by a SCSI adapter in each server. Microsoft announced at the Windows Hardware Engineering Conference (WinHEC) in the spring of 1996 the intention to support fail-over redundancy as the first step in the company's plan to implement clustering technology for Windows NT servers. Fail-over clustering is expected to arrive in early 1997, as an extension of Windows NT Server 4.0.
>
> To learn more about the future of clustering, download the white paper "Microsoft Windows NT Server Cluster Strategy: High Availability and Scalability with Industry-Standard Hardware" from **http://www.microsoft.com/BackOffice/reading/clusterwp.htm**.

To determine fault-tolerance requirements, you must determine the answers to the following questions about each component of the network:

- What happens if a component fails, both in terms of immediate effects and in terms of lasting damage?

- How likely is that component to fail?

- If the component fails, is there an alternative method—less expensive than duplicating the component—that will acceptably substitute for the failed component until it can be repaired or replaced?

- What does it cost to provide full, or partial, redundancy for that component? Is the tradeoff of additional cost versus increased reliability justified?

When most people think about fault tolerance, they think only about hardware. A commonly overlooked fault-tolerance issue is data communications reliability. If your network is connected to remote branch offices, vendor and customer sites, or to the Internet, you must consider the reliability of each such link and determine the criticality of the data carried on the link. If the data is high-volume, real-time, and critical to your organization's operations, you may need to duplicate the high-speed links to each remote site. If the data is lower volume or less critical, you may be able to get by with a dial-up link as a backup to the main high-speed link (see fig. 2.4). In the case of batch-mode data transfer, you may be able to dispense with a backup link completely.

Another issue to consider is designing for fault tolerance by location. For example, your internetwork may comprise a main office in Chicago, plants in Pittsburgh and Winston-Salem, North Carolina, and both national and international sales offices. Consider designing your networks and siting your data storage so that, in the event of a data communications link failure, each site is self-supporting to the greatest extent possible. That way, when the link from the Cleveland sales office to corporate headquarters goes down, Cleveland can continue to sell and service accounts, albeit perhaps without real-time inventory data or delivery schedules. Similar results can be achieved on the local level by loading software locally on workstations rather than centrally on the server, replicating databases to multiple servers, having at least some locally attached printers, and so forth. Replication of information stored in relational databases is one of the subjects of Chapter 22, "Running Microsoft SQL Server 6.5."

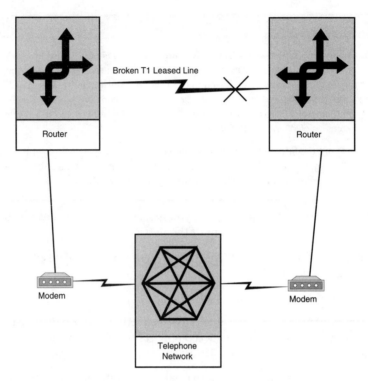

Fig. 2.4 Substituting analog modem connections over the switched telephone network for a failed T1 leased line.

Hardly any organization (except, perhaps, the military) builds fully fault-tolerant networks. Doing so can double, triple, or even quadruple network costs, both in terms of initial cost and in terms of ongoing monthly charges for things such as datacomm lines, maintenance agreements, and so on. At the same time, hardly anyone builds networks without at least some degree of fault tolerance.

The key, as usual, is to balance cost versus performance. Install just as much fault tolerance as you really need. If you can't afford even that much, install as much as you can afford, focusing your efforts on the items most likely to break and on those that will cause the most trouble when they do break. If this means that all you can afford is to install a UPS on the server, do so. Don't worry about what you haven't been able to do. Doing anything to increase fault tolerance is better than doing nothing. You might be better off putting some of the fault-tolerance money into a faster server or a network management application package.

Incorporating Existing Infrastructure

In the best of all worlds, you can plan your new network from the ground up, choosing the best components to fit each requirement and integrating the whole into a smoothly functioning system. In the real world, however, you seldom have this luxury. The year-old server in accounting can't be thrown away. The folks in marketing are running NetBEUI on a peer LAN and would rather fight than switch networking protocols. Administration is running IPX/SPX on a Novell NetWare 3.12 server, using a critical application that runs only as a NetWare loadable module. Engineering is running TCP/IP on UNIX workstations. The graphic designers in the publications department have Macintoshes connected by an AppleTalk network. Office politics alone prevent you from changing any of this, even if you had the budget to replace everything (which you don't). Welcome to the real world.

In one sense, the presence of these legacy systems can work to your advantage by providing you with information about user needs, throughput requirements, and so on. The down side is that existing equipment may be outdated, expensive, or impossible to maintain; use protocols incompatible with those you plan to use; or lack support for the network management software you intend to install. One of the hardest aspects of planning a new LAN or a substantial upgrade to an existing LAN is taking these legacy situations into account. Legacy problems can be divided into the software- and protocol-related issues and the hardware issues described in the next two sections.

Software-Related and Protocol-Related Planning Issues. Fortunately, Windows NT Server gives you most of the tools needed to resolve software- and protocol-related problems. Unlike server software from Novell, IBM, and other vendors, Windows NT Server was designed from the ground up to work in a heterogeneous environment. Windows NT Server provides native support for IPX/SPX, NetBEUI, and TCP/IP, thereby eliminating many of the problems of dealing with a mixed-protocol environment. Various add-on products are also available from Microsoft and third parties to provide extended functionality for TCP/IP and NetWare integration, making your job just that much easier. See Chapter 17, "Integrating Windows NT with Heterogeneous Networks," for a complete discussion of these software- and protocol-related issues.

If your network will be connected to the Internet, the network must provide TCP/IP support at the server and at the workstations. Now is the time to begin planning for the Internet connection. There are three main points to consider:

- *Reserving your domain name and address blocks.* If you don't plan to connect to the Internet immediately, you should contact the InterNIC to obtain legal network addresses and, optionally, a domain name. The advantage to reserving your domain name as soon as possible is to increase the possibility of obtaining a desirable name that's not already in use (domain names are allocated on a first-come, first-served basis).

  There isn't much of an advantage in obtaining a legal block of addresses anymore, because most ISPs require that their customers use addresses allocated to the ISP. In fact, many people who change ISPs have to deal with the often difficult task of renumbering their network.

- *Planning Internet address allocations.* Unless you work for a huge multilocation enterprise, the chance of obtaining anything larger than a block of Class C addresses is slim to none. With the "shortage" of IP addresses, the InterNIC and your service provider will require that you subnet your network to take full advantage of the IP address space. Although subnetting is not rocket science, it requires a solid background in mathematics—primarily in binary logic operations.

■ *Planning for DNS, WINS, and DHCP.* The DHCP server that's bundled with NT Server is a very good tool for managing IP addresses on client machines. The DHCP will "lease" an IP address to a client for a predetermined amount of time (from one minute to infinity), and is an excellent way to handle situations such as a notebook computer moving from location to location. If your network is composed of multiple LANs, you need either to have a DHCP server on each LAN, or to use a router that forwards DHCP requests to a DHCP server.

WINS is Microsoft's preferred method for NT Server clients to resolve machine (NetBIOS) names to IP addresses. WINS servers require very little maintenance and, unlike DHCP servers, can be configured to replicate with each other for automatic fail-over. WINS also can be configured to work with the NT DNS server to update the DNS server automatically when a new host IP host is added to the network.

DNS is the Internet Protocol's standard method for mapping IP host names with IP addresses, and also for mapping an IP address to a host name. Windows NT Server clients can be configured to use DNS to resolve the machine name, but Windows NT's DNS has some limitations—most notably, the hosts must be in the same DNS domain. The Windows NT DNS server, new to Windows NT 4.0, can be configured to automatically and dynamically import host names and addresses from a WINS server into a DNS subdomain, greatly reducing IP address management.

Hardware-Related Planning Issues. Hardware-related integration issues can be thornier than software issues, especially because candidates for replacement are usually hubs, routers, and similar active network components. These hardware devices seldom are seen by upper management, who almost never understand their function. Deciding what legacy networking hardware to keep and work around versus what hardware to replace may be easily accomplished in isolation, but explaining to upper management why it makes sense to replace a recently purchased and expensive piece of networking equipment can be a tough sell. Sometimes you can successfully explain matters to management and convince them of the necessity; sometimes the "Trust-me-we-just-have-to-do-this" method works; and sometimes you just have to buy the replacement hardware quietly, put the older component on the shelf as a "spare," and hope that no one ever inquires too pointedly about it.

You typically replace existing networking hardware for at least one of these reasons:

■ *Compatibility* is usually the easiest sell. If you absolutely need to route TCP/IP and IPX/SPX but your existing router supports only TCP/IP and can't be upgraded to support both, it's easy to make clear to everyone that the old router must be replaced.

■ *Capacity* is another easy sell. If you have an existing 12-port dumb hub but your new network requires more than 12 ports at a particular location, it's easy to point out that you can't plug a workstation into a port you don't have.

■ *Reliability* is a tougher point to make. Everyone wants the network to be operational 24 hours per day, seven days per week, and everyone understands that sometimes the network will be down. No one outside your department, however, understands exactly why the network goes down. Replacing older and less reliable components can greatly increase the reliability and uptime of the network as a whole, and it's certainly a valid issue to consider in your network design.

Getting this point across to upper management can be difficult, particularly if you've been doing your job well and if, as a result, you haven't had any major network outages recently. Still, it's you (the network administrator) who takes the heat when things fail, and it's you who gets the calls at 4 a.m. to come fix the problem.

- *Manageability* is usually the hardest sell of all. For all but the smallest networks, using manageable active network components can make the difference between having a reliable network run by a productive, proactive network staff, and spending all your time putting out network fires and killing router snakes. Manageability means the capability to remotely monitor and control components such as bridges and routers, usually by a standard protocol such as SNMP (Simple Network Management Protocol). Manageability is discussed later in the section "Considering Network Management Needs."

> ### Note
>
> A network built with fully managed components can often operate with half the network staff required to operate an unmanaged network, and can do so more efficiently and more effectively. Still, upper management often doesn't fully appreciate the efficiencies of using managed components. You can tell management all day long that managed network components make the difference between making a five-minute change from your desk and having someone spend four hours driving out to a site and making the change manually. Management often still sees only the direct additional costs involved in installing managed components, and ignores the indirect costs associated with using your staff inefficiently. If your network will be medium-size or larger—particularly if you'll have equipment installed at multiple sites—fight for managed components.

Connecting to the Outside World

Few networks these days are pure LANs. The proliferation of remote access servers, fax servers, branch office connectivity, and connections to the Internet give a WAN aspect to most so-called LANs. Unless your network has no connections to the outside world, you must understand wide-area connectivity issues in order to plan your network installation properly. The days when the "phone people" and "data people" were separate groups reporting to separate department heads are long gone. If you don't know what a hunt group is or how a BRI ISDN line varies from a T1 connection, find out before you plan your network infrastructure, not afterward. Data communications line charges are becoming an increasingly large portion of monthly IS costs as more and more LANs are extended into WANs. Competition between common data communication carriers has resulted in a bewildering array of alternative services with a wide range of installation, monthly, and usage charges.

The best place to start learning about data communication is your local telco. Ask to talk to the telco's data communications group and set up a meeting. After you understand the basic issues, you're in a much better position to compare the alternatives available for data communications, along with the telco's installation costs and monthly service charges. Understanding the basics also lets you make informed decisions regarding competitive services available from various sources, including your local telco, AT&T, MCI, Sprint, and other common-carrier service providers. After you understand the fundamentals of packet switching, for example, you're in a much better position to judge whether frame relay or ATM makes sense for your WAN.

Data communications is a rapidly changing area of technology. Its terminology is confusing and changes constantly. Sometimes it seems that the price and availability of a particular service vary with which clerk happens to answer the phone. Nevertheless, planning your network properly requires that you have at least a working knowledge of data communications technology.

Developing an Implementation Schedule

Is the most frequent question you hear, "How much is this going to cost?"? If so, bringing up a strong second place has to be, "How long is this going to take?" Although some elements of timing are within your control, in many cases you're at the mercy of outside parties, over whom you have little or no control. Purchasing delays, hardware vendor lead times, and data communications line installation delays conspire to prolong the process.

Making matters worse is the interdependency of some elements. Having a necessary hardware component show up one day late can cause a two- or three-week delay, if the result is the telco rescheduling line installations. You may find that everything necessary shows up just when your staff is 100 percent committed to some other activity that can't wait. You may be ready to proceed, only to find that accounting is processing payroll, preventing you from doing that department's upgrade when planned. Julius Caesar's law says that nothing comes in on time and under budget, and nowhere is this more true than in a network installation.

For all the preceding reasons, develop a detailed implementation schedule, and then do your best to stick to it if you want to have your network installed in a timely fashion. The best way to do this is to purchase and use a project-management software package, discussed in more detail later in the section "Using Project-Management Software to Manage Resources and Schedules."

Considering Network Management Needs

Network management protocols have been developed to allow the network administrator to manage connected devices, track resource usage and trends, and detect and correct critical errors and problems, all from a central management workstation. For all but the smallest networks, having remote management installed can mean the difference between a network easily maintained with minimum staff time, and a network occupying your staff full time just to make routine changes and repairs.

Network operating-system-level utilities intended to ease user administration, track disk space allocations, administer password policies, and so forth provide useful functions, and certainly fall under the umbrella of network management. So, too, do application metering programs, backup utilities, and LAN hardware inventory programs. Packet-level analysis tools such as sniffers, protocol analyzers, and cable meters are invaluable in tracking down physical problems on the cable, misbehaving components, and the like.

More important by far to the task of keeping the network up and running efficiently on a day-to-day basis, however, are the standards-based applications designed to monitor and manage your active network components remotely by using protocols such as SNMP and Management Information Base (MIB). These applications function by using a central management station to query and control management agents installed on various critical system components, such as hubs and routers. Proxy agents installed on managed components also can be used to monitor components that aren't themselves manageable. For example, a proxy agent running on a managed router may be used to monitor a dumb hub, which otherwise wouldn't be manageable.

These applications monitor your network by allowing you to set threshold levels, referred to as *traps*, for various criteria on the management agent for critical system components. When one threshold level is exceeded, the management agent informs the software running on the central management station, allowing you to take action to correct the problem. Another function of network management applications is remote management. A managed component can be controlled from the central management workstation, eliminating the need to make an on-site visit to make programming changes.

Although the underlying network management protocols used by these applications are standards-based, the implementations aren't. Although the standards-based protocols offer all the basic tools needed for network management, they pay little heed to interface requirements and ease of use. Also, standards-based protocols, by their nature, must use the least-common denominator, making no provision for managing extended features and enhanced functions specific to a particular brand and model of component. As a result, major vendors have developed proprietary network management software that's specific to their own components. These products, many of which are Windows-based, provide graphic representations of the installed components, allowing monitoring and management simply with a mouse click.

Figure 2.5 shows a UNIX-based network management system displaying a diagram of traffic over a wide-area internetwork. The downside is that all but the very high-end management software products work only with the manufacturer's components, providing little or no management capabilities for components from other manufacturers.

Installing network management isn't inexpensive. In addition to the cost of the components themselves, a central management station and management software must be purchased. Management software normally starts around $5,000 for element managers, and escalates rapidly to $20,000 and above for full-function enterprise managers. The cost of the management station itself isn't insignificant, because most of these products specify a minimum of a high-end Pentium with 16M or 32M of RAM and a 21-inch monitor. Some of them require a $30,000 Sun or Hewlett-Packard workstation. Still, all these costs pale in comparison to the usual alternative—hiring additional skilled staff to maintain the network as it expands and extends to remote sites.

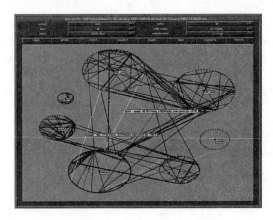

Fig. 2.5 A diagram of traffic over a wide-area internetwork (courtesy of Hewlett-Packard Company).

For most medium-size and larger networks—particularly those that support multiple sites—the cost of installing network management is quickly repaid in increased productivity and in a reduced need to expand staff as the network grows and extends to other sites. At the same time, given the relatively high cost of purchasing the central management workstation and software, you certainly don't want to duplicate these costs to provide additional stations. Because network management software is proprietary, the only way to avoid doing so is to make sure that all your managed components are provided by the same manufacturer.

> **Note**
>
> Microsoft's System Management Server (SMS), a component of the BackOffice server suite, provides many of the features of large-scale network management systems at moderate cost. The primary advantage of SMS is that it's fully integrated with Windows NT Server 4.0 and is designed specifically for managing Windows clients, as well as providing automated installation of application software for client workstations. A dedicated SMS server usually serves a single domain. Installing SMS is the subject of Chapter 24, "Administering Clients with System Management Server."

Providing for Future Growth

All organizations have short-term tactical goals and long-term strategic objectives, all of which must be supported by the network if they're to be successful. As you plan and design your network and internetwork, keep constantly in mind that you're aiming at a moving target. Storage requirements increase as time passes. The total number of employees and workstations served by the network are likely to increase, as well as the number of sites to be connected. Newer technologies, such as client/server applications and document imaging, may be implemented in the future, placing increased demands on your servers and on network bandwidth. A properly planned and designed network must have the scalability needed to support future growth, both that of a predictable nature and that due to unforeseeable changes in the technology and the way your organization does business.

Begin planning for future growth by examining trends for the past few years. Have employee counts been increasing, decreasing, or remaining stable? Has the number of installed PCs increased, or are most newly purchased PCs simply replacing older models? Have all departments and sites been fully computerized, both in terms of hardware and applications, or is computerization an ongoing process? Have some functions of your organization been outsourced? If so, is this outsourcing likely to occur for other functions? Examine each such historical trend and discover whether a trend will likely continue or change over time.

Turn next to examining expected changes for the near future. What projects are in the planning stage that could affect network resource requirements? Perhaps your paper archives are due to be converted to magneto-optical storage. Your organization may plan to establish a major Web site on the Internet. A new branch office may be in the cards a year or so down the road.

After you consider all these issues and come up with your best guess for what your network will need to support a year, two years, or further in the future, design your network around components that will support its expected future size. Following are four keys to designing your network for future growth:

- *Design your network to comply with industry standards.* The networking landscape is littered with failed attempts by various vendors to propose proprietary components and protocols as industry standards. By sticking with mature and broadly supported standards such as Ethernet, TCP/IP, and SNMP, you ensure that your network will be easily expandable down the road.

- *Provide the network management capabilities needed to monitor traffic and loading, and develop trend analyses.* You need to know where the bottlenecks are now and where bottlenecks are likely to develop in the future, if you're to take action to eliminate them.

- *Design for modularity.* A properly planned and designed network or internetwork can be expanded by incremental additions and upgrades over the years. A poorly designed network may require wholesale replacement of components as needs change. Break down the project into subprojects, treating each site, workgroup, or major department group as an individual element of the network as a whole. Choose components for that group that will support its current size and expected future growth. That way, if unforeseen increases in demand occur, you make changes only to those components that directly support the affected group.

- *Build in overcapacity.* For example, if a particular workgroup currently requires 11 network ports, don't buy a 12-port dumb hub to service that workgroup. If you do, you'll find yourself replacing it two months later when the workgroup adds an employee and decides that it needs to convert one of its stand-alone laser printers to a network printer. Don't even buy the 16-port stand-alone hub. Instead, choose the 24-port stackable hub.

If you can't afford to buy the managed version now, make sure that the version you do buy is upgradable to include management. You'll pay somewhat more for your hubs and end up with a lot of unused ports. You'll find that as the network grows, however, this small additional cost will be more than offset by the money you don't have to spend to tear out the original component and replace it with what you should have purchased in the first place. A year from now, when you finally convince your boss that you can't live without network management, you'll find it an easier sell if it involves only inexpensive incremental upgrades to existing components rather than a wholesale replacement of all your existing hubs.

Spending 5 percent or 10 percent more than needed to provide a bare-bones network infrastructure pays off in the following ways:

- Spending this small additional sum now eliminates the need to spend more later.

- The expenditure greatly reduces the staff time needed to maintain and upgrade the network, perhaps even delaying or eliminating the need to hire additional network staff.

- The investment allows you to be much more responsive to changing user needs— for example, it lets you add a new workstation in minutes or hours, instead of the days or weeks it might take if the existing infrastructure is inadequate.

- Adding a bit of slack to the network frees your time to take care of users, rather than spend all your time taking care of the network itself.

Working Within a Budget

The key to working within a budget is to plan exactly what to buy before you spend a cent. Buying networking products on a piecemeal basis is a great temptation but is almost always a mistake. When the project is approved and the budgeted funds are transferred to your account, there's often an impetus to show progress quickly. Vendors encourage this behavior by offering limited-duration specials and promotions. The inevitable result of falling into the trap of piecemeal purchasing is that you either overbuy on the early items and find yourself scrambling later on—perhaps settling for much less than you really need on the later items—or that you take a more conservative approach to spending early and later find that you spent less than you should have on the items purchased first. In either case, you haven't optimized the allocation of funding for the project.

The alternative to network-purchasing anarchy is to sit down at the start of the project to map out exactly what needs to be done and what items need to purchased to accomplish the task. The benefit to this approach is that it gives you the flexibility to prioritize needs and allocate funds accordingly before any money is committed. You may find that the budgeted amount is totally inadequate to do the job at even a minimum level. You may find that the budgeted funds are adequate to do the job, but that a small additional amount would allow you to do a much better job. If you're very fortunate, you may find that you can buy everything you need to do the job right and still have funds left over, which you may be able to apply to a guerrilla upgrade to an orphaned project. Whatever the result, this preliminary planning step puts you in a stronger position to go back to management and negotiate either the funding level or the scope of the project, before you find yourself committed. If you don't know the numbers, you can't present a convincing case.

After you establish this baseline budget, you can begin actually purchasing items, doing so first for the more expensive and more critical components. As purchase orders come back, you can compare your budgeted costs with the real costs, adjusting later purchases to take into account any overages or shortfalls in purchasing the earlier items. Buy less important and optional items late in the purchasing process to make sure that any compromises needed to meet budget are made on these less critical items.

A good way to go about the process is to create a master purchasing spreadsheet with one line item for each individual item to be purchased. If designed properly, this spreadsheet can be an invaluable tool not only for establishing the initial budget, but for tracking receipt of components as they arrive and flagging overdue items.

The following list provides a good starting point for the columns of a purchasing spreadsheet:

- *Item description.* A brief name or description of the item.

- *Estimated cost.* Approximate cost for the line item, used for preliminary budgeting and pulled from *Computer Shopper* or a similar publication.

- *Purchase requisition number.* Useful information to have ready when you follow up with the purchasing department.

- *Purchase requisition date.* Used to flag purchase orders that are slow in arriving.

- *Purchase order number.* Again, useful information to have easily available when you need to follow up with purchasing or with vendors. This also provides an easy visual clue to the status of your orders. If this column is blank, it hasn't been ordered yet.

- *Purchase order date.* The date the purchase order was issued—again, useful when following up with purchasing or vendors.

- *Purchase order amount.* The real dollar amount you'll pay for this line item.

- *Cost differential.* The difference between your estimated cost and the cost on the purchase order. This number tells you how well you budgeted costs initially and how closely you're keeping to budget, allowing you to make adjustments to later purchases to keep to budget.

- *Delivery date.* The requested or promised delivery date for each item. A quick scan of this column will tell you which items are late in arriving and allow you to quickly take follow-up action to resolve the problem.

- *Received.* A simple check-off column that allows you to mark which items have arrived. Again, this provides a quick visual clue to developing delivery problems.

- *Vendor name, contact person, and phone.* Useful information to have readily at hand.

- *Notes.* Miscellaneous information that doesn't fit elsewhere.

Note

The columns in this spreadsheet will vary, depending on your purchasing policies and procedures. If you have the luxury of being able to do your own purchasing directly instead of working through a purchasing department, for example, many of the columns listed aren't needed.

In addition to this master budgeting spreadsheet, you're likely to find that it's useful to develop supporting spreadsheets for various purposes. Some line items on the master spreadsheet may require more detail than is appropriate, such as server configurations and options. Other related items, such as configuration planning by site or department, can have a separate spreadsheet, with summary totals linked to the master budgeting spreadsheet. This methodology keeps the master to a manageable level of detail.

Tip

One final item that's often overlooked in setting up a project budget is establishing a contingency reserve to cover unexpected requirements. If your budgeted amount seems likely to be adequate to complete the project, or if this is your first such project, 10 percent of the total budgeted amount is a reasonable contingency reserve. If the budgeted amount is stingier, or if you have considerable experience in doing similar projects, 5 percent may suffice. Guard this reserve jealously, releasing it only very late in the project. It's better to return unspent funds than to run out of money with purchases still to be made.

Training Users

The importance of user training and its impact on your planning and budgeting vary widely, depending on your particular situation. If your networking project is simply an upgrade or a replacement of an existing network, and your users continue to use the same applications, training may have a negligible impact on planning and budgeting. If your network is a completely new installation intended to serve users who aren't currently computerized, you may have major planning and budgeting issues to consider, perhaps including a computer training classroom with equipment and instructors. If your network links users who previously used stand-alone PCs, at the very least you must make provision for training these users to use e-mail and other network-specific applications.

You must balance the need for user training against the funds, space, and other resources available, keeping in mind that users being trained can't to do their usual jobs simultaneously. If you decide to provide training, you must decide whether to conduct the training in-house, conduct it at a commercial training center, or pay an independent trainer to give classes at your site. Unless you live in a major metropolitan area or decide to train only on the most common Windows productivity applications, you're likely to find that there's no alternative but to train in-house, because no one offers classes on the software you're using. Many organizations compromise by providing a "train the trainer" program, where one or more chosen individuals from each department or location undergo training and then return to their groups where they, in turn, train the other users.

Managing the Project

After the basic planning and budgeting issues are resolved, you must initiate and manage the installation of the network. The following sections describe how to use commercial project-management software to determine the schedule of the work and to allocate the resources required to complete the installation and startup of the network, including acquiring the services of vendors, value-added resellers, and independent network consultants.

Using Project-Management Software to Manage Resources and Schedules

In the course of planning, purchasing, and implementing your network, you accumulate vast amounts of information: scores of specific user requests, hundreds of to-do items, dozens or hundreds of individual items to be purchased, vendor lead times to be coordinated, and data communications line installation schedules. Throughout the course of the project, many changes occur. Item prices actually quoted may be higher or lower than you initially estimated. Key components may be backordered. Managers suddenly discover a desperate need for something they didn't bother to mention during your initial interviews, and upper management backs up the new requests. Winter storms result in delayed deliveries. All this information must be recorded, updated as changes occur, and kept organized if you're to have any hope of staying on schedule and within budget.

Installation of a PC network is, in fact, a construction project, and deserves to be treated as such. Project-management software, which is critical to construction projects, runs the gamut in features and functionality from Schedule+'s to-do lists to mid-range project management software, such as Microsoft Project. Figures 2.6 and 2.7 illustrate Gantt and PERT (Program Evaluation and Review Technique) charts, respectively, for NetWare to Windows NT network migration using a Microsoft Project template included in the Windows NT 3.51 Resource Kit. Simple to-do lists lack the capability to handle a project of this scale. High-end project-management applications, such as Primavera, are intended for people who manage multimillion-dollar construction projects for a living. High-end packages are very expensive, quite difficult to learn, and are overkill for this type of project.

Buy Microsoft Project (or one of the competing mid-range project-management applications) and spend a half day or so learning the basics. You don't need to master every feature of the software to obtain useful results. After you learn to enter and edit tasks and resources, set milestones, track critical paths, and print Gantt charts, you have most of the tools you need to manage your resources and schedules successfully.

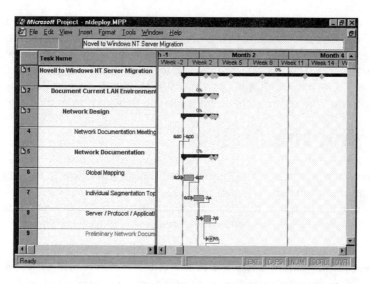

Fig. 2.6 A Gantt chart created by the Network Planning template for Microsoft Project.

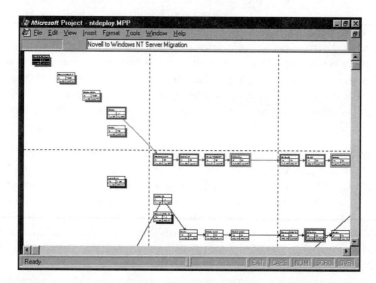

Fig. 2.7 A PERT chart created by the Network Planning template for Microsoft Project.

In most situations, the major resource you must manage is your own time and that of your staff. The availability of resources affects schedules, because completing any given task requires commitment of a certain period of time by a staff member with a particular skill. While that staff member is occupied with a particular task, he's unavailable to work on another task requiring similar skills. You'll likely find that one or two key people form a bottleneck, with more demand for their services than can be fulfilled. As a result, the time line stretches out, even though other resources may be standing idle. Following are three keys to maintaining a schedule from a resource point of view:

- *Estimate, as accurately as possible, the time that will be needed to complete each task.* This step is critical. If you greatly underestimate the time needed for too many steps, your entire schedule will collapse. Everyone is an optimist when it comes to estimating how long an activity will take, so make your best guess and then double it. As the project proceeds, update these estimates based on your experience to date. You may be surprised to see the effect of a minor change in one aspect of your schedule on the project as a whole.

- *Marshal your resources carefully.* Most organizations have a diverse information systems staff, with each member having a mix of skills. One person may be able to fill in for another in one area, but not in another. Determine which one or two key staff members are likely, because of their special skills, to be in great demand; then schedule other staff members to do as many of the tasks as they possibly can, freeing up the time of the persons with critical skills.

- *Don't try to manage activities that you don't control.* This seems obvious, but it doesn't always work out the way it should. People can't be two places at the same time, nor can they effectively serve two masters simultaneously. If you're the head of your information systems department, you have no problem in directing your staff to do what needs to be done when it needs to be done. If, on the other hand, you're somewhere lower in the organizational hierarchy, you may find yourself pleading for help from other staff members that have conflicting demands on their time, because you don't have the authority to direct their activities. Managing a project properly requires that you have control of participants' schedules, or at least that you have a solid commitment of a certain percentage of their time over the course of the project. You must be provided with vacation schedules for each staff member. If you don't have the authority to schedule staff resources, your schedule will collapse.

One of the many benefits of using project-management software is the reports it provides. These reports can tip you off early to potential budget overruns, resource conflicts, and deadlines unlikely to be met. These reports, in summary or consolidated form, are also useful for keeping management informed of progress, one often-overlooked aspect of successful project management. Giving management weekly or even daily updates—depending on the size and scope of the project—allows managers to become active participants in the project and accomplishes three things:

- It makes management aware early of potential budget problems and delays, allowing managers to take action while there's still time to do so.

- Because management has been following the project closely, if you find it necessary to ask for more money or more time, you more likely will have your request granted because management understands the reasons for the request.

- By involving management early and often in the project, managers are more likely to "sign on" and become active advocates for what you're trying to accomplish.

Getting Outside Help

Few organizations have in-house all the skills needed to plan and implement a major networking project, particularly a project that involves internetworking. Even those organizations that do have such staff often find that other demands on staff time make it impractical to take on a major project while continuing to meet day-to-day obligations for existing networks. As a result, it's often necessary to look outside the organization for help in implementing such a project. Such outside help falls into two categories: manufacturers and value added resellers (VARs) of networking components, and consultants.

Using Vendors and Resellers. Vendors and VARs can be very useful sources of advice in configuring your network. Vendors and VARs are obviously intimately familiar with the capabilities of their equipment and have probably installed many similar networks for organizations much like your own.

Balanced against these advantages is the obvious conflict of interest. The vendor or VAR wants to sell specific brands of equipment, so more than likely that person won't recommend competing gear that may be a better or more cost-effective solution for your particular needs. Another negative factor is that the vendor or VAR focuses on just one part of the total picture, leaving you to worry about integrating the system as a whole. On balance, although vendors and VARs often provide a surprisingly high level of commitment to helping you plan and implement your network, you're usually better off to first select a vendor or VAR, and then later use whatever services are available from the vendor or VAR to help you implement your chosen design.

Using Consultants. The second source of outside help is an independent consultant. True consultants bill you only for their time and expenses and, therefore, are an unbiased source of advice—at least in theory. In practice, many individuals and companies who represent themselves as consultants are, in fact, thinly disguised VARs who make some or most of their income from reselling hardware and software. A properly qualified independent consultant can help you with all aspects of your project, from the initial planning through the implementation phase.

Consultants have two drawbacks:

- They can be very expensive. Depending on your location, a good networking consultant will probably charge at least $125 per hour, with specialists in internetworking often getting two to three times that amount. Hours can mount very quickly, unless you keep a tight rein on what the consultant is and isn't expected to do.

  Hiring consultants is often worthwhile, if only in an advisory role. Because consultants have "seen it all before," one hour of their time may save you a day or even a week of your own time. Even more important, recommendations by consultants may save you from making a multithousand-dollar mistake. After you plan and design your network, it's almost always worthwhile to hire a good consultant for a half day or day to sit down with you and go over your plan. He often can point out alternative methods you may not have considered, or better or less expensive sources for components.

■ Even a consultant with wide experience has personal preferences for particular manufacturers and specific ways of doing things. A consultant who is, for example, an expert on Cisco routers seldom has as much depth of experience in working with competing routers from DEC or HP. It's human nature to stick with what you know works, and consultants are no exception to this rule. There are many right ways of addressing a problem, although there are many more wrong ways of solving the problem. What you care about is that the route you choose is one of the right ways, and a consultant can help make sure that this happens.

Choosing a consultant can be difficult. There are no state licensing boards for computer consultants; as a result, anyone can call himself a computer consultant, regardless of his qualifications (or lack thereof). To make matters worse, even a consultant who has done good work for you in the past or is highly recommended to you by your peers may not be qualified for your particular project. Even worse, the consultant may not be aware that he isn't qualified for your project and, thus, not disclose this fact.

When you speak to someone for whom the candidate consultant has done work, ask that person whether the project was completed successfully, on time, and under budget. Ask what problems have developed since that time and if the consultant was responsive to the problem. Focus not on personalities, but on results.

A more objective method of assessing a consultant's qualifications is to find what industry certifications he holds and what those certifications imply. Networking hardware and software vendors long ago realized that, in the absence of formal state licensing boards for consultants, it was up to them, the vendors, to provide some mechanism for assuring would-be clients that consultants had achieved at least some minimum level of competence with their products.

> **Note**
>
> Microsoft has developed a certification program for Windows NT Server called the Microsoft Certified System Engineer, or MCSE. The youth of this program and the still relatively small market share of Windows NT Server, compared with Novell NetWare, means that relatively few people have completed the requirements for the MCSE. (As of early 1996, there were about 7,500 MCSEs in North America.) This situation likely will change, as many Novell Certified NetWare Engineers (CNEs) are adding MCSE certifications to their resumes. Unless the consultant you plan to hire is a specialist in a particular product area, such as data communications, make sure that the consultant you employ holds an MCSE certification.

Balancing Resources and Requirements

Before you purchase the components to build your network, balance the resources you have available with your requirements. Unless you are in the enviable and unlikely position of being given an unlimited budget, you must make compromises in some areas to get what you need in other areas. It does little good to have the best server on the market if purchasing the server leaves you without enough money to buy network cards for your workstations. Chapter 5, "Purchasing Networking Hardware," is devoted to the hardware acquisition process, but advance planning is required to assure that you can complete the network installation without exceeding your budget.

Establishing a Minimum Configuration

Begin the purchase planning process by establishing a minimum acceptable configuration for each component. Don't compromise in terms of quality, but rather in terms of features and function. Stick to brand names, but work from the low end of the product line rather than the high end. Determine the minimum server configuration in terms of processor, disk storage, RAM, and other features that will do the job. Even if you would prefer to install 100Mbps 100BaseT network cards, instead determine the cost for 10Mbps 10BaseT cards for each workstation. Calculate the cost of installing a cabling system with only enough horizontal runs to meet your immediate needs. Plan on unmanaged hubs and other active components rather than the latest and greatest in managed equipment.

If you're lucky, you'll find at the end of this process that you have money left in your budget. If you're very lucky, it may be a significant amount. If you're already over budget, it's time to go to management and state that the job can't be done with the funds available. Don't make the mistake of trying to install a network with inadequate funding.

Allocating Remaining Funds

After you establish a baseline via the process described in the preceding section, carefully consider how the remaining funds, if any, can best be spent.

Server memory can always be upgraded easily later, but Category 3 wire in the wall remains Category 3 wire in the wall forever. If you have to choose between an expensive managed hub, an inexpensive dumb hub that isn't upgradable, or a moderately priced hub that's configured initially as dumb but later can be upgraded to managed, pick the moderately priced hub. You're likely to find the money to upgrade the moderately priced hub in the future, but if you buy the non-upgradable hub, you probably will be stuck with it into the next century.

Maximize the number of free adapter card slots, free drive bays, and memory sockets in the server. For example, if you choose to equip your server with 64M of RAM, specify two 32M SIMMs (single in-line memory modules) in preference to four 16M SIMMs. Later, you won't have to replace all your memory to upgrade the server because it has no free SIMM sockets. Although, in principle, your server may be better off having as many drive spindles running as possible, in practice you're better served by buying fewer larger disks in preference to more smaller ones, leaving drive bays available for future expansion. Substantial improvement in the reliability of large (4G and bigger) fixed-disk drives has occurred in the past two years.

Favor a few expensive items rather than many inexpensive ones. It's always easier to obtain subsequent approval for inexpensive upgrades to many small items than it is to acquire funding for a single expensive upgrade. Upgrading all your workstation NICs from 10Mbps to 100Mbps is a much harder sell than is a request to add another 32M of RAM or a few more gigabytes of disk space to the server.

Buy now what you may not be able to buy later. If expanding the memory on your server requires an expansion card, and that card doesn't come with the server, buy the card now. You may not be able to obtain the card when you're ready to add memory.

Similarly, pay close attention to the type of fixed-disk drives supported by your RAID controller. Many RAID controllers support only a few specific drive models. Some controllers require that all drives be identical. You don't want to find in a year or two that your only alternative is to replace all of your drives just because the drive you need is no longer available.

Dealing with Vendors

A good vendor is a godsend and can be very helpful in the initial planning process. A bad supplier can make your life miserable. Good vendors deliver what you ordered at the price they quoted, and do so on time. Bad vendors are usually a day late and a dollar short. Good vendors have the expertise and take the time to advise you on your purchases. Although you obviously must take into account suppliers' vested economic interest, their close relationship with manufacturers benefits you in terms of timely information and advice.

Unfortunately, good vendors are seldom the lowest bidder. Depending on your environment, you may be forced to buy only from low bidders, or you may have the luxury of choosing vendors based on factors other than simply lowest price. Do everything you can to select a good vendor and direct purchases his way. You'll find that the small additional cost is more than made up for by the services that the vendor provides, not only in terms of good advice, but also in delivery preference for items in short supply, generous interpretation of warranty terms, and/or provision of equipment on loan. Don't hesitate to use lower prices quoted by other vendors as a bargaining tool, but realize that good vendors incur additional costs to provide additional services and thus are entitled to a moderate price premium.

Decide first what you consider to be commodity items. This decision is determined by the level of in-house expertise and by where you choose to focus your efforts. All shrink-wrapped 3Com 3C509 Ethernet cards are the same, so you can safely treat this type of item as a commodity and simply shop for the best price. On the other hand, a Hewlett-Packard NetServer LM2 network server is not a commodity item. If you have a dozen other NetServers installed and have a network staff to configure them to your way of doing things, adding one more LM2 should be easy, and you can probably safely shop for the lowest price.

Otherwise, you can probably use, and should be willing to pay for, the advice a good vendor will give you. Don't make the mistake of trying to get the best of both worlds by soliciting extensive pre-purchase help from a knowledgeable vendor, and then turn around and price-shopping the configuration with others.

From Here...

This chapter outlined the overall process of planning a network installation, with emphasis on establishing a new network or upgrading an existing PC network to Windows NT Server 4.0. Much of the content of this chapter is applicable to planning the installation of any network operating system and isn't specific to Windows NT Server 4.0. The intent of this chapter is to provide you with a planning framework before you delve into the details of Windows NT networking architecture. The remaining three chapters in Part I are devoted to Windows NT 4.0:

- Chapter 3, "Understanding the Windows NT Operating System," describes the architecture of Windows NT with emphasis on Windows NT 4.0 networking features.

- Chapter 4, "Choosing Network Protocols," discusses Windows NT Server 4.0's support for multiple protocols and how to determine the protocol(s) to use for your network.

- Chapter 5, "Purchasing Networking Hardware," describes the process of acquiring the hardware you need to set up or upgrade your Windows NT 4.0 network.

Chapter 3

Understanding the Windows NT Operating System

Windows NT is, first and foremost, a general-purpose computer operating system for business use. Although this book concentrates on the networking features of Windows NT Server 4.0, Windows NT is equally at home running heavy-duty workstation applications, such as computer-aided design of aircraft components or non-linear video editors and animated graphics applications for producing broadcast television programs.

The Workstation and Server versions of Windows NT 4.0 share a common source code base; the network management and application server features of Windows NT Server 4.0 are modular components added to the basic operating system modules of Windows NT Workstation 4.0. Thus, the underlying architecture of Windows NT differs markedly from dedicated network operating systems, such as Novell NetWare and Banyan VINES, that concentrate on file and printer sharing.

Windows NT was designed from the ground up as an application server for 32-bit Windows programs; this contrasts with NetWare, which initially gained application services in the form of an add-in to support custom-programmed NetWare Loadable Modules (NLMs). The architecture of Windows NT closely resembles that of UNIX, with some added features derived from Digital Equipment's VMS operating system.

Unlike other versions of Windows (including Windows 95), Windows NT isn't encumbered with the baggage of backward compatibility obligations to the installed base of low-end PCs designed to run 16-bit Windows and DOS applications. Windows NT 4.0 doesn't accommodate 16-bit device drivers for adapter cards and other hardware accessories, nor does it support the Plug-and-Play hardware standard of Windows 95.

Windows NT 4.0 also isn't optimized for mobile PCs and isn't designed to run computer games; Microsoft has positioned Windows 95 as the operating system of choice for laptop and notebook PCs, as well as personal entertainment applications. Microsoft explicitly designed Windows NT from the ground up for use in corporate and institutional computing environments ranging from small-business LANs to global WANs.

This chapter covers the following topics:

- The history of Windows NT development
- A summary of Windows NT operating features
- Objects, subsystems, and virtual memory
- The NT File System (NTFS)
- Remote Procedure Calls (RPCs)
- Windows NT networking

An understanding of the internal complexities underpinning the Windows NT operating system isn't an absolute necessity in order to plan, budget, set up, and administer a Windows NT network. Windows NT's server-related application programming interfaces, as an example, primarily are of interest to programmers writing specialized server-based applications, such as tape backup utilities. On the other hand, gaining a working knowledge of Windows NT architecture is quite useful when evaluating tradeoffs between software and hardware implementations of Windows NT Server functions, such as Remote Access Services and Multiprotocol Routing. If you're familiar with Windows NT architecture and terminology, you're also better prepared to discern between facts and propaganda in vendor specifications and consultant recommendations. Thus, this chapter appears immediately before the chapters related to choosing network protocols and buying networking hardware.

Gaining a Historical View of Windows NT

Windows NT is the result of a schism between Microsoft and IBM in their joint development program for OS/2 Presentation Manager. In October 1988, Microsoft hired David N. Cutler, the architect of Digital's VMS operating system for its VAX minicomputer, to create a 32-bit portable operating system to replace DOS. Coincidentally, IBM and Microsoft introduced OS/2 Presentation Manager in October 1988 (see fig. 3.1). Underlying the "sweetness and light" in the joint press releases of the day was Microsoft's desire to exercise control over the future direction of the design of OS/2. Dave Cutler put together a team to develop a "New Technology" operating system, while Microsoft continued to work with IBM to improve OS/2, which was required to run Microsoft's LAN Manager network operating system and the PC version of Sybase's SQL Server relational database management system, introduced in 1988 as Microsoft SQL Server.

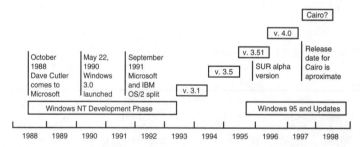

Fig. 3.1   The development timeline for Windows NT.

> **Note**
>
> Microsoft's LAN Manager and IBM's LAN Server products derived from Microsoft's original MS-NET peer-to-peer networking product for DOS, sold by IBM as PC-NET. LAN Manager, which used the NetBEUI protocol, never became a major player in the network operating systems (NOS) market. Industry reports in the early 1990s indicated that LAN Manager then had about a 10 percent share of the NOS market; NetWare was the undisputed NOS leader with 60 percent to 70 percent of the installed base.

Microsoft launched Windows 3.0 on May 22, 1990. Windows 3.0 was an instant success, overwhelming IBM's nascent market for OS/2 on the desktop. On September 17, 1990, Microsoft and IBM announced a division of responsibility for the continued development of OS/2. IBM alone would work on the 1.x and 2.x versions, while Microsoft was to be responsible for the advanced 3.x versions. OS/2 3.0 was specified to be a 32-bit, portable, multiprocessing, preemptive multitasking operating system with advanced security features.

In the fall of 1991, with Windows assured a dominant role on the world's desktop PCs, Microsoft played its Windows NT hand. Steve Ballmer, Microsoft's vice president of marketing, stated that OS/2 "was dead" if IBM didn't agree to use the Windows NT kernel as the foundation for OS/2 3.x. IBM, which even in 1991 was calling its beta version of OS/2 2.0 "better DOS than DOS, better Windows than Windows," wasn't about to adopt the kernel of a Windows-centric operating system for OS/2 3.0. On its own, IBM began to develop what ultimately became the first version of OS/2 Warp, a 32-bit operating system that primarily ran 16-bit (only) Windows applications and offered neither portability nor multiprocessing capabilities.

Windows NT 3.1

Microsoft released Windows NT 3.1 and Windows NT 3.1 Advanced Server for Intel and MIPS processors in August 1993. The version number came from Windows 3.1, whose graphical user interface (GUI) Microsoft grafted to Windows NT. The Advanced Server version, designed to replace LAN Manager running under Microsoft's OS/2, supported the NetBEUI protocol and included a primitive TCP/IP stack.

Prospective users were put off by what were then considered to be Windows NT's humongous resource requirements: 16M of RAM and 100M or so of fixed-disk space just to run the operating system. Windows NT required hardware vendors to write new 32-bit device drivers for their products, which limited support for existing adapter cards and peripherals. Sales of Windows 3.1 continued to boom, but the market for Windows NT 3.1 failed to meet Microsoft's optimistic projections. According to industry reports, total sales of both versions of Windows NT 3.1 were in the low hundred thousands, most of which were for evaluation, not production use.

> **Note**
>
> The Windows NT driver dilemma for hardware vendors isn't over yet. At the Windows Hardware Engineering Conference (WinHEC) in April 1996, Microsoft announced the Windows Driver Model (WDM), which lets Windows NT and Windows 95 share common 32-bit drivers. Windows NT 4.0 and Windows 95 are expected to be updated to support the WDM in late 1996 or early 1997.

Windows NT 3.5 and 3.51

The cost of PCs capable of running Windows NT declined dramatically during 1994. The price of dynamic RAM (DRAM) plummeted, as did the price per megabyte of fixed-disk storage, minimizing the hardware cost penalty for adopting Windows NT. During this period, Dave Cutler's Windows NT development group labored to reduce the minimum

RAM requirement, enhance networking features, improve overall performance, and port Windows NT to Digital's Alpha AXP RISC (Reduced Instruction Set Computing) processor. The result of this effort was the September 1994 introduction of Windows NT 3.5, which reduced RAM requirements by about 4M.

The most significant improvements in version 3.5, however, were the addition of NWlink (Microsoft's IPX/SPX stack for NetWare), and substantial improvements to the TCP/IP stack and TCP/IP administration tools. Microsoft changed the default network protocol from NetBEUI to IPX/SPX, but it was the inclusion of TCP/IP features, such as WINS (Windows Internet Naming Service), DNS (Domain Name Service), DHCP (Dynamic Host Configuration Protocol), and support for PPP (Point-to-Point Protocol) and SLIP (Serial Line Internet Protocol) over RAS (Remote Access Service) that made corporate network administrators take Windows NT 3.5 seriously as a production network server, as well as a database server. Windows NT 3.5 also included remote server administration tools that ran under Windows for Workgroups 3.1.

> **Note**
>
> Microsoft announced its BackOffice 1.0 suite simultaneously with the release of Windows NT 3.5. BackOffice 1.0 included Windows NT Server 3.5, SQL Server 4.21a, SNA Server 2.1, System Management Server 1.0, and Microsoft Mail Server 3.2. Like the Microsoft Office productivity software suite, the BackOffice bundle offered a substantial discount on the license fees for the individual server components. The chapters in Part V, "Windows NT Server and Microsoft BackOffice," discuss Microsoft's licensing policies and describe the individual BackOffice components.

Microsoft announced the Windows NT Workstation and Server 3.51 update on June 12, 1995. The primary objective of version 3.51 was to support Windows 95's common controls and common dialogs in order to run forthcoming 32-bit "Designed for Windows 95" applications under Windows NT. Windows NT 3.51 also supplied selective NTFS data compression and limited support for PC Card (then PCMCIA) adapters. Windows NT 3.51 added minor enhancements to OLE, including support for "NetworkOLE 0.9" (the precursor of Windows NT 4.0's Distributed COM), which lets developers with the Visual Basic 4.0 Enterprise Edition deploy Remote Automation Objects (RAOs) for three-tier client/server database applications.

The Shell Update Release and Windows NT 4.0

Press hoopla surrounding the release of Windows 95 relegated Windows NT to bit-player status during the latter half of 1995. Windows 95 greatly enhanced usability and made network installation a snap, but required at least 8M to run most applications reasonably well and 16M for 32-bit mega-apps, such as Access 95. (Microsoft recommends 12M for Access 95, but you need 16M to achieve satisfactory performance with large applications.) Direct-mail and retail PC suppliers preinstalled Windows 95 on virtually all of their systems destined for the home and small-business markets.

Most corporate and institutional buyers, however, shunned Windows 95 for a variety of reasons, not the least of which were the costs of adding needed RAM, user training, 32-bit software upgrades, and lost productivity during the migration to a new operating system. The perception that Windows 95 was a 16-bit/32-bit kluge and was less robust than Windows NT contributed to lack of short-term success of Windows 95 in the corporate environment. The vast majority of people who tried Windows 95, however, agreed that the Windows 95 UI was a substantial improvement over that of Windows 3.1+.

Microsoft correctly assumed that after a person used Windows 95 for any length of time, he or she would consider the Windows 3.1+ UI of Windows NT Workstation 3.51 to be klutzy, at best. To answer this problem, Microsoft released an unsupported alpha version of the Shell Update Release (SUR) for Windows NT 3.51 in late 1995. The alpha SUR had a variety of problems but demonstrated the feasibility of grafting the Windows 95 UI to Windows NT 3.51. (Fortunately, you could uninstall the UI update easily.) Microsoft's initial plan was to provide the SUR in the form of a Service Pack (maintenance release) for Windows Workstation and Server 3.51+. Even though a 4.0 version number appeared when the alpha SUR was installed, Microsoft representatives insisted that version 4.0 was reserved for the "next major release of Windows NT" (a.k.a. Cairo).

Note

It's relatively uncommon for administrators to work at the server console, which usually is located in a closet or other confined and secure space, unless absolutely necessary. You can perform the most common server administrative duties remotely from Windows NT 4.0 or Windows 95 clients. Thus, the Windows 95 UI currently is of more importance to users of the Workstation version than to administrators responsible for the Server version of Windows NT 4.0. Grafting the Windows 95 UI to Windows NT Server 4.0 is a necessity for the transition to a common object model for future versions of Windows NT and Windows 95.

Microsoft released the first beta version of the SUR—now officially named Windows NT 4.0—in early 1996. Beta 1 had the Windows 95 UI in place but lacked many of the promised features described in Chapter 1, "Placing Windows NT Server in Perspective." Microsoft distributed Beta 2, a full-featured version, to more than 200,000 testers in late May 1996. According to Microsoft, the Windows NT 4.0 beta program was the most widespread in the firm's history of Windows NT beta testing. The final version of Windows NT 4.0 was released to production on July 31, 1996. The first recipients of Windows NT Server 4.0 were to manufacturers for preinstallation on server PCs.

◀◀ See "What's New in Windows NT Server 4.0," p. 20

Cairo and 64-Bit Windows NT

Microsoft's early 1995 goals for Cairo centered primarily on substitution of the Object File System (OFS) for NTFS. OFS was to be a distributed, object-oriented file system that incorporated a directory repository. (A *directory repository* is a database that contains records for the directory trees of all the servers in a domain. The repository provides a logical view of the network that doesn't depend on its physical implementation.) Entries in the directory repository were to be based on the OFS file-naming system using object names and property values (such as author and creation date), rather than on conventional Uniform Naming Convention syntax (\\Servername\Sharename\Filename).

Files created by today's 32-bit Windows applications, such as Microsoft Word 7.0, let you add property values as attributes of documents (see fig. 3.2). The objective is to enable searching not only by file name, but on property values and indexed file content. The plan was to use OLE DB (an OLE Automation database interface) and OLE DS (OLE directory services) to query and manipulate the repository entries. The Windows 95 UI also was scheduled for the Cairo release, originally planned for release in early 1996.

> **Note**
>
> Windows 95, Explorer, and the Macintosh use the term *folder* in place of *directory*. Elsewhere in the book, use of *folder* predominates. This chapter uses the term *directory* when it's part of a specific compound term, such as *directory repository* or *directory services*.

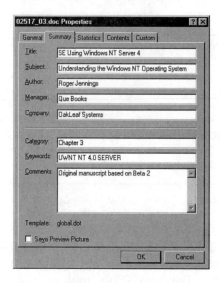

Fig. 3.2   Setting property values in Word 7.0 for an OLE document file.

> **Note**
>
> Setting property values of document files becomes increasingly important as Windows NT Server moves toward an object-oriented file system. The property sheets for files created with members of the Microsoft Office suite let you add custom properties to files in the Custom page of the *File Properties* sheet. For example, a magazine publisher might add Issue (date or number format) and Section (text format) properties for article manuscripts. By querying custom property values, the Cairo Explorer would display only those files meeting specified criteria.

Microsoft's December 1995 "Internet initiative" resulted in a change of plans for the implementation of OFS and the directory repository. At the March 1996 Windows Professional Developer's Conference (PDC), Microsoft announced that OFS features will be incorporated within NTFS and that the repository (directory services) will be implemented in a database derived from the message store architecture of Exchange Server 4.0. Also, Cairo will support DNS naming conventions, allowing the use of DNS names (such as marketing.com) to specify directory trees and to enable inclusion of intranet and Internet URLs in the repository.

◀◀ See "Embracing and Extending the Internet," p. 44

The upshot of Microsoft's change of strategy for Cairo and OFS means a further delay in the release of the next major version of Windows NT. Microsoft, however, is incrementally adding features originally planned for the Cairo version, such as the Windows 95 UI and Distributed COM. Although Cairo probably won't arrive until very late 1997 or (more likely) early 1998, you're likely to find many new Internet-related features added to Windows NT 4.0 in the form of periodic Service Packs, rather than in point releases such as Windows NT 3.51.

Summarizing Windows NT Operating System Features

Dave Cutler's Windows NT development team achieved Microsoft's basic objectives of 1988 in the first release of Windows NT. These objectives were as follows:

■ *Reliability* by protecting the core operating system from malfunctioning applications and by isolating the operating system and applications from direct operations on hardware. Structured exception handling handles processing of application and low-level errors. NTFS provides increased reliability for file operations by a built-in transaction logging system.

■ *Extensibility* by adopting a client/server model using a base operating system (kernel, the client) extended by application programming interfaces (APIs, the servers). In this case, the term *client/server* is used in its UNIX context, not that of the client/server model applied to networks and database applications.

■ *Portability* across different processor platforms, including RISC systems, through the use of a processor-specific Hardware Abstraction Layer (HAL) that provides the isolation layer between the operating system and hardware. Portability of Windows NT is provided by writing the source code for the operating system, with a few exceptions, in an ANSI-standard C programming language.

■ *Security* by compliance with at least the U.S. Department of Defense C2 standard, which provides "need-to-know" protection and auditing capability. Security in Windows NT primarily is implemented through ACLs (Access Control Lists).

■ *Compatibility* with existing 16-bit DOS and Windows applications, plus the most common PC hardware devices and peripherals. Windows NT also provides the capability to execute applications written to the POSIX.1 standard, a requirement of the federal government's software procurement policies. Early versions of

Windows NT supported NTFS, HPFS (OS/2's High-Performance File System), and FAT file systems. Windows NT 4.0 no longer handles HPFS volumes.

Note

POSIX is a specification for an interface to an operating system, which need not be (but usually is) UNIX. Microsoft has contracted with a third-party developer, Softway Systems, Inc. to develop a POSIX.2 shell and utilities, which Softway markets as OpenNT. OpenNT replaces the POSIX.1 subsystem of Windows NT and provides case-sensitive file naming (files named File1 and file1 can coexist), file links (a single file can have multiple names), background processing, and job control, plus file user and group access, and file ownership. Additional information on OpenNT is available at **http://www.softway.com/OpenNT/ datasht.htm**.

■ *Scalability* for better performance through the use of multiple CPUs with a Symmetrical Multiprocessing (SMP) architecture. To take advantage of SMP, 32-bit Windows applications must be written to use multiple threads of execution.

◀◀ See "Forging Alliances for Scalable Windows NT Server Hardware," p. 50

Windows NT universally receives high marks for reliability, extensibility, portability, and security. However, many DOS and 16-bit Windows applications—particularly those that write directly to hardware—don't run under Windows NT, and Windows NT requires specially written 32-bit device drivers for adapter cards and peripherals. Windows NT's scalability has limitations; although Windows NT 4.0 supports up to 32 processors, you begin to receive diminishing returns when you install more than four to six processors in a single server.

Note

You have little or no reason to run 16-bit Windows or any DOS applications on a Windows NT 4.0 server. Furthermore, the vast majority of the hardware devices that you need to implement servers are supported by 32-bit Windows NT drivers, either built into Windows NT 4.0 or available from the hardware manufacturer. Software and hardware incompatibilities—especially with sound cards, digital video capture boards, and other multimedia equipment—are barriers to use of Windows NT Workstation 4.0, not the Server version.

The "Designed for Windows 95" logo on a product doesn't guarantee that it works with Windows NT. Microsoft removed the Windows NT compatibility requirement for the Windows 95 logo about the time Windows 95 reached the market. Many industry experts question the wisdom of this decision, which apparently was motivated by Microsoft's desire to gain a large number of third-party Windows 95 applications as quickly as possible.

The following sections describe the basic elements of the Windows NT operating system from a bottom-up perspective.

The Windows NT Executive

The Windows NT executive consists of a collection of system (also called *native*) services, the kernel, and a hardware abstraction layer (HAL), organized as shown in figure 3.3. Operations that run entirely within the Windows NT executive are called *kernel mode* services. The HAL, plus code in the kernel and the Virtual Memory Manager, is specific to the category of processor used; Windows NT 4.0 has HALs for Intel 80486 and higher CISC (Complex Instruction Set Computing) processors, and for three RISC processors: MIPS, Alpha AXP, and PowerPC. A replacement HAL is supplied by a computer manufacturer whose design departs from the reference design for a particular processor. In addition to creating a new HAL for each processor family and implementation, Windows NT and 32-bit Windows applications must be recompiled for each processor family. Thus, for example, there are separate versions of the 32-bit Microsoft Office applications for Intel, MIPS, Alpha, and PowerPC systems. Existing 16-bit Windows and DOS applications run on an 80x86 emulator unique to each RISC processor.

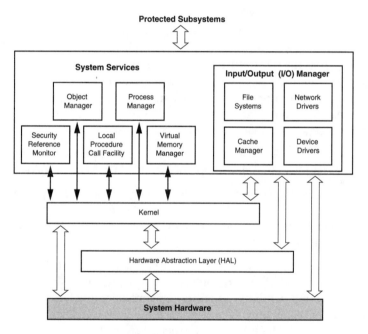

Fig. 3.3   The components making up the Windows NT executive.

The Windows NT executive consists of the following components:

■ The *Security Reference Monitor* (SRM) provides basic security features, such as tracking user account privileges, managing ACLs, auditing, protecting objects, and limiting access to system resources. User logon is directed to the SRM, which creates an access token for each authenticated user. An *access token* is an object whose properties include the user's Security ID (SID), the SIDs of groups to which the user belongs, and special privileges of the user.

- *Object Manager* (OM) is responsible for creating objects to represent (abstract) system resources, such as files, hardware devices, and shared memory. Objects expose to the operating system a consistent interface to properties (data) and methods (behavior) of the particular resource. OM manages objects during their lifetime and destroys (deletes) an object when it's no longer needed.

- The *Local Procedure Call* (LPC) *Facility*, which provides communication between applications (clients) and protected subsystems (servers), is a localized version of the Remote Procedure Call (RPC) feature of Windows NT. RPCs are the subject of the later section "Calling Remote Procedures."

- *Process Manager* (PM) is responsible for managing processes (executable applications) and threads (executable subcomponents of applications). PM handles the allocation of threads to processors when Symmetric Multiprocessing is in use.

- *Virtual Memory Manager* (VMM) allocates protected memory to each process. When memory requirements exceed the amount of available RAM, VM stores part of the RAM contents to the fixed-disk paging file and then retrieves the contents when needed (a process also called *swapping*). Paging is very slow compared to direct RAM operations; servers ordinarily have large amounts of RAM (64M or more) to minimize paging operations. Some vital operating system objects and data structures are held in a *non-paged pool* that's never swapped to disk.

- *Input/Output Manager* (IOM) acts on files and devices that manipulate files, including networking components. A description of each IOM component follows this list.

- The *kernel* is a low-level component responsible for processor interrupt and software exception handling, synchronizing multiple processors, and scheduling threads for execution. The system services of the executive rely on a variety of low-level objects supplied by the kernel.

- The *Hardware Abstraction Layer* (HAL) consists of a layer of code between the processor and the kernel that translates processor-specific features—such as stack operations, input/output handling, and interrupt controller functions—to a uniform set of interfaces for kernel functions. The HAL (Hal.dll) is relatively small; for example, Windows NT 4.0's HAL for Intel processors is 52K in size.

The Windows NT executive is a self-contained, low-level operating system, lacking only a user interface. The UI for the executive is provided by the Win32 subsystem that's discussed in the next section.

For Windows NT network administrators, the Input/Output Manager is the most important component of the executive, because most network operations occur within the IOM. IOM implements device-independent input/output services for all hardware components except the processor(s). The I/O system of Windows NT is *asynchronous*—that is, when an I/O request is issued, the operating system continues with other tasks until the device involved completes the requested operation. (Protected subsystems also can request synchronous I/O but usually pay a performance penalty for doing so.) The IOM is unique among the executive components, because IOM communicates with the kernel, with the HAL, and directly with hardware components through device drivers (refer to fig. 3.3).

The IOM is comprised of these elements:

- *File systems* support multiple file architectures through layered drivers—thus, new or improved file systems can be added to Windows NT. Windows NT 4.0 supports 16-bit FAT and NTFS file systems; OS/2's HPFS, which was supported in prior versions of Windows NT, can't be used with Windows NT 4.0. For servers, the FAT file system is used only for accessing diskettes and CD-ROMs. (You can use the FAT file system for a Windows NT server, but doing so is strongly discouraged.) Windows NT 4.0 does *not* support the 32-bit FAT file system included with Service Pack 2 for the OEM (original equipment manufacturer) version of Windows 95 that computer assemblers preinstall on their PCs. NTFS is the subject of the later section "Handling Files with NTFS."

- *Cache Manager* stores the most recently accessed fixed-disk data in system memory to improve the performance of sequential reads. Cache Manager supplements the built-in cache of high-performance SCSI fixed-disk and CD-ROM/WORM drives. Cache Manager also improves write performance by using VMM to perform asynchronous writes in the background.

- *Network drivers* consist of the network server and network redirector. The server receives network I/O requests, and the redirector transmits network requests. The term *redirector*, which originated in the early days of MS-NET and PC-NET, is derived from the process of intercepting file operation requests on the local PC (interrupt int13h for Intel processors) and rerouting (redirecting) the operations over the network to the server.

- *Device drivers* consist of a 32-bit code layer between the preceding three elements and hardware, such as SCSI host adapters for drives, network interface cards (NICs), keyboards, mice, and graphic adapter cards. Windows NT treats network drivers as device drivers.

Note

As noted earlier in this chapter and elsewhere, the lack of device drivers for the wide variety of hardware devices used with 16-bit Windows and Windows 95 has hampered the acceptance of Windows NT Workstation. All of today's hardware devices that are designed for use with production servers have Windows NT drivers. These devices are listed in the current version of the Windows NT Hardware Compatibility List (HCL) that's included with the Windows NT 4.0 documentation and periodically updated by Microsoft. You can obtain the current HCL from **http://www.microsoft.com/backoffice**.

Clients and Protected Subsystem Servers

The layers above the Windows NT executive provide *user-mode* services. These layers consist of the environmental subsystems (servers) for 32-bit and 16-bit Windows applications, DOS, OS/2, and POSIX applications, plus client applications in each of these five categories. The Win32 subsystem provides the user interface (graphic display, mouse, and keyboard handlers) for all servers and for those system services of the executive that involve interaction with the user via, for instance, the User Manager for Domains, Server Manager, and the Virtual Memory settings in the Performance page of the System Properties sheet. Thus, the Win32 subsystem is the only component of Windows NT that's visible to the user.

> **Note**
>
> There's a distinction between the user-mode and kernel-mode services that are components of Windows NT and the term *services* used elsewhere in this book. Unless otherwise noted, *services* refer to executable applications that are startable when Windows NT boots. These services appear in the Service list of Control Panel's Services tool, and may be started automatically or manually, or be disabled. The members of Microsoft BackOffice, for example, run as services under Windows NT, as do the Server and Workstation services. (Microsoft implemented Windows NT's Server services as a device driver for various reasons, a description of which is beyond the scope of this book.)

Figure 3.4 shows the relationship of the environmental subsystems and client applications. Local procedure calls (solid lines) provide all communication between subsystems and between clients and subsystems. Subsystems also can request native services by a system trap, shown as a dashed line in figure 3.4. Each subsystem has its own protected memory space.

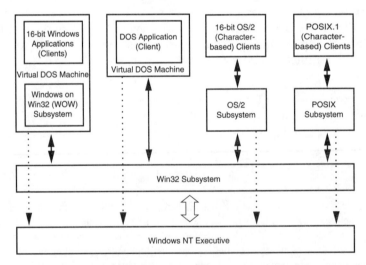

Fig. 3.4 The environmental subsystems and client applications that provide user-mode services.

> **Note**
>
> Messages between client applications and environmental subsystems pass through the Windows NT executive, which establishes a separate message queue for each instance of a client application or virtual DOS machine (VDM). For clarity, the trip to and from the executive doesn't appear in figure 3.4.

Figure 3.4 shows these environmental subsystems:

- *Virtual DOS machines* (VDMs) provide a protected environment for individual 16-bit DOS applications. The Win32 subsystem provides a character-based window (called a *console*) for interaction with the user. One VDM is created for each instance of a DOS application.

- *Windows on Win32* (WOW) runs all 16-bit Windows 3.1+ applications in a single instance of a VDM with common protected memory. Thus, if one unruly Windows 3.1+ application crashes the VDM, all other running 16-bit Windows applications crash with it. Each 16-bit Windows application is assigned its own thread of execution to provide multitasking capability.

- *The OS/2 subsystem* runs character-based OS/2 applications in a console. The paucity of character-based OS/2 applications that don't have Windows NT equivalents means that system and network administrators seldom need be concerned with using the OS/2 subsystem.

- *The POSIX.1 subsystem* can run POSIX-compliant applications, which is required for government purchase of "open systems." Windows NT survived a recent appeal by UNIX bidders of an award of a Coast Guard workstation contract to Unisys that proposed to use Windows NT as the operating system. Microsoft's funding of development of the POSIX.2 shell and utilities of OpenNT, mentioned earlier in this chapter, is related to one of the Coast Guard contract requirements. It's likely that Cairo will substitute POSIX.2 for the POSIX.1 subsystem.

Handling Files with NTFS

One of the most important new features of Windows NT 3.1 was NTFS, an outgrowth of HPFS that Microsoft and IBM developed for OS/2. Following are Microsoft's design objectives for NTFS, with a brief description of how the objectives were achieved:

- *Support for large fixed-disk drives.* The original version of HPFS had a maximum volume size of 4G. Windows 95's 16-bit FAT file system is limited to 2G volumes with 64K clusters; the large cluster sizes makes storing small files very inefficient because each file requires a minimum of one cluster. Windows NT uses 64-bit addresses for clusters of physical storage sectors that range from 512 bytes to 4K, depending on the size of the disk and its sector size. (Most fixed disks have a sector size of 512 bytes.) The maximum volume size for NTFS is 2^{64} bytes (16,777,216 terabytes) and files can be up to 2^{64} bytes long. Large volume and file sizes are especially important for storing full-screen, full-motion video for editing and broadcast applications.

- *Recoverability.* NTFS stores two copies of its equivalent of DOS's file allocation table (FAT), called the *master file table* (MFT). Thus, if the original version of the disk's system data becomes corrupted due to a hardware failure (typically, a bad disk sector), the copy automatically is used on bootup, and the operating system creates a new original from the copy. NTFS uses a transaction log to maintain file consistency in the event of a hardware problem (such as a power failure) or system failure during the write process. NTFS uses the transaction log to return the disk to a consistent state during the next disk access.

■ *Fault-tolerance through redundancy*. Windows NT Server can create a software RAID (Redundant Array of Inexpensive Disks) for NTFS volumes. If you choose RAID 1 (*disk mirroring* or *duplexing*) or RAID 5 (*disk striping with parity*), you store two copies of all server files. In case of disk hardware failure, NTFS uses the file copies. If the system detects a bad disk sector, NTFS marks the sector as bad, and then creates a replacement sector from data stored on the other disk. Chapter 7, "Setting Up Redundant Arrays of Inexpensive Disks (RAID)," describes RAID levels and the tradeoffs between implementing RAID arrays in hardware or by software.

■ *Security*. Windows NT treats disk files, like processes, as objects. A NTFS file object has properties (also called *attributes*) such as name, creation date, date last updated, archive status, and a security descriptor. A file object also has a set of methods, including open, read, write, and close. A user, including networked users, can't invoke a method of a file object until the Security Reference Monitor determines that the user has permission for a particular method.

■ *Data compression*. Selective data compression made its first appearance in Windows NT 3.51. Data compression saves disk space at the expense of somewhat slower file access. Unlike the DriveSpace compression utility of DOS 6+ and Windows 95, NTFS lets you selectively compress a folder (and its subfolders) or individual files. On servers, compression usually is reserved for infrequently accessed files or very large files, such as large Windows bitmap (.BMP) files, that aren't already compressed. Compressing and decompressing frequently accessed files reduces server performance by a significant margin.

■ *Multiple data streams in a single file*. NTFS permits subdividing the data in a file into individual *streams* of data. The most common application of multistream files is for storing Macintosh files on Windows NT servers. Macintosh files have two streams (called *forks*): the data fork and the application fork. The application fork contains information on the program that created or can edit the file. (In Windows NT and Windows 95, the Registry associates applications with file extensions, serving a purpose similar to that of the Macintosh's application fork.) The default data stream has no name; additional streams have names. Developers address a particular stream in a file by a suffix preceded by a colon, as in *Filename.ext:streamname*.

■ *Localization with Unicode*. NTFS supports Unicode file names. Unicode uses 16 bits to specify a particular character or symbol, rather than the 7 or 8 bits of ASCII and ANSI characters. 16 bits accommodate 64K characters and symbols, so Unicode doesn't depend on changing code pages for national language support (NLS).

Note

One recurrent theme in this book is, "Use NTFS, not FAT, for servers." In the early days of Windows NT, some network administrators were reluctant to abandon FAT in favor of NTFS because they

wanted to be able to boot a server with a DOS diskette and gain access to files in case of a problem booting Windows NT. The emergency repair disk you create when you install Windows NT
and the Windows NT Setup program's Repair facility is much more effective than booting from
DOS to recover from a system failure.

▶▶   See "Repairing the Windows NT Server Operating System Installation," p. 213

The next two sections describe the features of NTFS that are of the most significance to
Windows NT Server 4.0 network administrators.

Understanding the Master File Table

The structure of DOS's FAT is relatively simple—FAT stores the DOS 8.3 file or folder
name, a set of standard attributes (read-only, hidden, system, and archive bits), size of
the file in bytes, and a pointer to (physical location of) the cluster that holds the first
byte of file data. The master file table (MFT) of NTFS is much larger and more complex
than the FAT for a drive having the same directory structure and file complement. The
MFT, and its mirror-image redundant copy, is similar in structure to a table of a database,
with fixed-length and variable-length records. (The boot sector contains pointers to the
location of the MFT and its mirror copy; file control blocks, or FCBs, point to a particular
record in the MFT.)

The MFT of a volume that contained only directories and very small files would comprise
the entire contents of the volume. Storing the data of small files within a MFT record
makes access much faster and minimizes unused cluster space (slack). If the data won't
fit in the MFT record, the NTFS driver creates pointer(s) to non-resident data stored in
runs. A run, also called an *extent*, is a contiguous block of disk space; non-resident data
may be stored in one or more runs, which are a maximum of 16 disk clusters.

Microsoft provides only a small amount of "official" information on the MFT in the
Windows NT Resource Kit and in Helen Custer's *Inside the Windows NT File System* monograph. Figure 3.5 is a simplified diagram of the MFT record structures for files and folders.
(The HPFS Extended Attributes field isn't shown in fig. 3.5, because Windows NT 4.0
doesn't support HPFS volumes.) The first 16 records of the MFT contain what Microsoft
calls "special information," also called *metadata*.

◀◀   See "Print and CD-ROM Publications," p. 11

> **Note**
>
> Custer's monograph states that MFT is a relational database, apparently because the MFT consists
> of records with attributes in columns. The rules of normalization for relational databases, however,
> require that all records in a table represent a single entity set and have a consistent set of attributes
> (columns). Mixing of records for files and directories isn't, in itself, a serious violation of relational
>
> (continues)

Networking

(continued)

database theory because NTFS treats directories as files. However, the Index Root, Index Allocation, and Bitmap attributes of directory records aren't consistent with the Data attribute of file records. Further, the first 16 records contain metadata in fields that vary from the file and index records. Relational database theorists wouldn't consider MFT a properly normalized relational table.

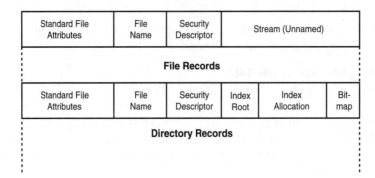

Fig. 3.5 The simplified structure of the file and directory records of the Master File Table for an NTFS volume.

Table 3.1 lists the attributes (fields or columns) of the MFT and describes the content of each attribute, including three attributes that don't appear in figure 3.5. The terms *attribute*, *property*, *field*, and *column* are interchangeable in discussions of database tables. Similarly, *row* and *record* refer to the same element of a table. A *volume* is a collection of fixed-disk clusters that's identified by a single logical drive letter; a NTFS volume may consist of contiguous clusters on two or more drives, which need not be elements of a RAID array. NTFS lets you combine contiguous free space on two or more disks into a single volume.

Table 3.1 Attributes of the NTFS Master File Table (MFT)	
Attribute (Field)	**Description**
Standard Attributes (Standard Information)	Contains standard file attributes, such as time stamps, archive status, and linkage data, plus an attribute list for large files.
Filename	Contains the Unicode file name (up to 255 characters) and the DOS 8.3 file name, created from the Unicode file name. For POSIX, contains additional names for the same file (called *links* or *hard links*).
Security Descriptor	Contains information on ownership, access rights, and other security-related information used by the Security Reference Monitor.
Data	Contains file data for files up to about 1.5K long; otherwise, a pointer to the data. The default data is an unnamed stream; NTFS provides for additional named streams.
Index Root	Contains relative location of directory information (index records only).
Index Allocation	Contains the size and location of directory index (index records only).
Bitmap	Contains a bitmapped image of the directory structure (index records only).

Attribute (Field)	Description
Volume Information	Contains the version number and name of a volume (volume system record only, not shown in fig. 3.5).
Extended Attributes	Previously used for HPFS files, which are no longer supported in Windows NT 4.0 (not shown in fig. 3.5).
User-Defined Attributes	Will contain special attributes for custom searches (not shown in fig. 3.5); reserved for implementation in future versions of Windows NT and NTFS, presumably Cairo.

For additional details of the low-level organization of MFT records, check out **http:// www.c2.org/hackmsoft/ntfs/doc/**.

> **Note**
>
> Bitmaps are a very efficient way to index records in tables, especially where indexes on multiple fields are required. An index dramatically speeds the location of an individual record in a table with a large number of records. Bitmapped indexing, not to be confused with bitmapped graphics, speeds access to the index itself. FoxPro was the first desktop database to take full advantage of bitmapped indexing in its Rushmore technology. After acquiring FoxPro, Microsoft adapted the Rushmore indexing method to Access .mdb files (commencing with Access 2.0). The Windows NT 4.0 version of NTFS indexes only the file name field. Cairo is expected to include the capability to create indexes on user-defined attributes for faster searching.

Implementing Recoverability with Transactions

Relational database management systems, such as Microsoft SQL Server and Access, use transactions when adding, updating, or deleting records from tables. A transaction assures that *all* operations affecting records of related tables take place; if a problem prevents completion of the entire transaction, the database tables are restored to their original status before the transaction. For example, if an orders database contains Orders and LineItems tables, adding or deleting an Orders record requires simultaneous addition or deletion of the related LineItems record(s). LineItems records without a corresponding Orders record are called *orphan records*, which you don't want in a database. SQL Server uses the reserved words COMMIT TRANS(ACTION) and ROLLBACK TRANS(ACTION) to attempt and reverse a transaction, respectively. Records in a temporary transaction log record the progress of the transaction; information in these records is used to roll back the transaction, if necessary.

> **Note**
>
> A temporary transaction log, such as that used by Microsoft Access, varies from the persistent transaction log maintained by client/server RDBMSs, such as Microsoft SQL Server. The persistent transaction log records all successful database transactions since the last backup of the database. After restoring the backup copy of a damaged database, the transaction log is executed to bring the restored copy of the tables back to the status of the instant when the damage occurred, less any transactions in progress at that point.

I

Networking

▶▶ See "Setting Up Transaction Logging," p. 828

NTFS uses a similar transaction logging process to recover from a system failure during a disk write operation. Following is a brief description of the process of recoverable writing to an NTFS file:

1. The NTFS file I/O driver initiates the write process, including an instruction to the Log File Service to log the transactions involved.

2. The data is written to cache memory under control of Cache Manager.

3. Cache Manager sends the data to the Virtual Memory Manager for background writing to the disk file, a process called *lazy writes*, achieved by periodic flushing of the cache to the disk drive.

4. The Virtual Memory Manager sends the data back to the NTFS driver, which passes the data through the Fault Tolerant driver (when using a software RAID array) to the disk driver.

5. The disk driver sends the data to the host controller (usually a SCSI host controller for servers), which passes the data to the destination fixed disk(s).

6. If write caching is enabled on the fixed-disk drive(s), the data is written to on-drive memory, and then transferred locally to the disk. Otherwise, the data is written directly to the disk.

7. If the write operation proceeds without an error, the transaction log record is deleted.

8. If an error occurs, the transaction log record remains in the transaction table. On the next disk access, the Log File Service detects the log record and restores the corresponding MFT record to its original condition before the write attempt.

This transaction logging process takes care of problems associated with operations that affect the directory structure—such as creating, copying, and deleting files—to maintain directory consistency. Errors that occur only when altering the data in the file aren't recoverable unless you have a RAID 1 or RAID 5 array. Contents of the self-contained write cache of a disk drive that aren't written to the disk before a power or hardware failure are lost, and the failure may not be reflected in transaction log records. For this reason, most SCSI drives with read/write caches are shipped with write caching turned off.

Calling Remote Procedures

Remote Procedure Calls (RPCs) permit applications to be executed by individual components that reside on other networked PCs, a process often called *distributed computing*. The RPC facility of Windows NT conforms to the Open Software Foundation's RPC standards incorporated in its Distributed Computing Environment (DCE) specification, with which virtually all flavors of UNIX comply.

Figure 3.6 is a diagram of a 32-bit Windows application that uses RPCs to connect to functions contained in three Windows DLLs (dynamic link libraries) that reside on three PCs running Windows NT Server or Workstation 4.0. If the library functions perform very processor-intensive tasks (such as rendering 3-D animated computer graphics for movies), using RPCs for distributed processing rivals the performance of Symmetrical Multiprocessing with two or more processors. Fast network connections, such as 100BaseT or Fiberchannel, are needed if large amounts of data must be passed between the executable program and the library function.

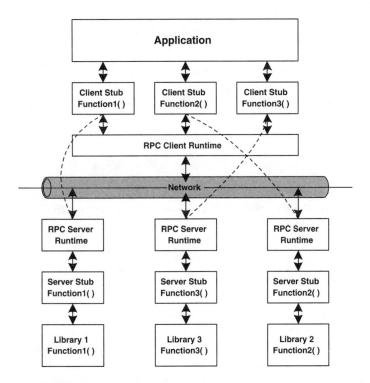

Fig. 3.6 Calling three library functions on remote computers with RPCs.

Following is a brief description of each layer shown in figure 3.6:

- *Application* is the program that calls library functions. Data sent to and re-turned by the function are implemented as function call arguments, as in RenderFrame(DrawingOut, FrameIn). RenderFrame is the name of the function, DrawingOut is an output parameter, and FrameIn is an input parameter.

- *Client function stubs* have parameters that correspond to the function call argu-ments. The client stubs marshal the parameter values over the network; *marshaling* processes the parameter values for transmission over the network. Client function stubs take the place of the corresponding functions that ordinarily would be con-tained in local DLLs.

■ *RPC client runtime* is responsible for determining the network location of the called function and the transport protocol required, and connects to the appropriate network driver of the I/O manager.

■ *RPC server runtime* receives RPCs and directs each call to the appropriate server function stub. Both the server and client runtime use Windows NT's transport provider interface (TPI) to communicate with the network driver.

■ *Server function stubs* unmarshal the function parameters and call the corresponding functions of the local DLL(s).

■ *Library function* contains the code that does the work. Remote DLLs are identical to local versions.

Using conventional RPCs requires the developer to create and compile an interface definition language (IDL) file, which creates the client and server stubs for the function. The IDL file also creates header files (function prototypes), which must be added to the calling client application. Thus, C and C++ applications that use RPCs must be recompiled to incorporate the RPC header information.

Note

RPCs running over NetBEUI networks use the named pipes interface for transferring data. *Named pipes* is an extension to NetBIOS that provides a persistent data conduit between networked processes. Microsoft and IBM first implemented named pipes, which provide a self-contained security mechanism, in LAN Manger. SQL Server, as an example, uses named pipes for receiving SQL statements from clients and returning query result sets and other database information to clients. Named pipes, implemented as a file I/O device, primarily are used for streaming data transport. In addition to named pipes over NetBEUI, Windows NT provides built-in RPC facilities for TCP/IP, IPX/SPX, and DECnet.

Distributed COM (DCOM), a new feature of Windows NT 4.0, adapts the RPC facility to permit communication between Microsoft COM (Common Object Model) objects over networks. DCOM makes distributed computing simpler by eliminating the need to rewrite client applications to accommodate RPCs through the use of OLE Automation techniques. (Microsoft's Object Linking and Embedding is built on COM.) DCOM substitutes OLE client and OLE proxy stubs for client and server function stubs, respectively. For example, a 32-bit OLE Automation client application written in Visual Basic 4+ easily can be adapted to use Remote Automation Objects (RAOs), which are out-of-process OLE servers (executable OLE applications). The Automation Manager supplied with the Enterprise Edition of Visual Basic 4+ takes the place of the RPC client and server runtimes.

 ◄◄ See "Distributed Component Object Model (DCOM)," p. 39

> **Note**
>
> In early 1996, with its "Internet incentive," Microsoft began substituting the term *ActiveX* for *OLE* in situations where linking and embedding of objects within other objects either wasn't involved or was only of minor importance. *OLE Controls*, for instance, became *ActiveX controls*. Now you're likely to see *OLE Automation* replaced by *Automation*. Microsoft didn't change OLE Automation to ActiveX Automation, because COM's Automation interface also is used for ActiveX objects, as well as linked and embedded OLE objects. The use of the term *OLE* for linking and embedding documents created with the components of Microsoft Office is expected to continue.

Networking with Windows NT

Windows NT networking processes make extensive use of the RPC facility, which provides a consistent set of methods by which local processes and remote processes communicate. The Server and Workstation versions of Windows NT 4.0 both support RPC networking, allowing users of the Workstation version to share files, printers, and other peripherals. A group of Windows NT Workstation users that share files and peripherals among one another (usually on an *ad hoc* basis) usually is called a *workgroup*. The workgroup (also called *peer-to-peer*) networking capabilities of Windows NT Workstation 4.0 are quite similar to those of Windows 95, except that there's a limit of 10 simultaneous inbound connections to a PC running Windows NT 4.0. (There's no limit on outbound connections.)

Helen Custer's 1993 book, *Inside Windows NT*, describes NetBEUI as "Windows NT's primary local area network transport protocol." The book contains many references to LAN Manager, which was then Microsoft's only network operating system offering. Microsoft designed Windows NT 3.1 to be fully compatible with LAN Manager servers running OS/2 and LAN Manager clients running on DOS/Windows, Macintosh, and UNIX platforms. LAN Manager compatibility was essential for integrating Windows NT 3.1 into the existing Microsoft networking infrastructure. NetBEUI remains the most common protocol for workgroup networking with Windows NT 4.0 and Windows 95, because it's simple for users to set up and is fast.

Peer-to-peer networking isn't limited to NetBEUI; you also can set up workgroups that use TCP/IP or IPX/SPX network transports. You don't need client licenses for Windows NT 4.0 peer-to-peer networking. Peer-to-peer networking receives only cursory coverage in this book because of the limited number of connections permitted to a client running Windows NT Workstation 4.0. You can't use members of the BackOffice server suite on peer-to-peer networks; with the exception of the single-user Workstation (Developer) version of SQL Server, BackOffice applications must be installed on Windows NT Server.

The primary difference between the Server and Workstation versions of Windows NT 4.0 (other than price) is the capability to create and manage network domains. LAN Manger 2.x provided an early version of domain-based networking. (Microsoft originally planned to supply domain networking features to Windows NT as an add-on called LAN Manager for Windows NT.) The most important advantage of the use of domains is the capability to use a single-user logon to multiple servers and services (such as SQL Server and Exchange Server). Network administrators need to create only a single account for the user in his or her primary domain. Trust relationships between domains determine whether secondary domains accept the authentication provided by the user's primary domain.

 ▶▶ See "Understanding Domain Architecture and Security," p. 567

The use of multiple domains in large networks allows distributing management of the network among individual facilities. Setting up and administering Windows NT domains is the subject of Chapter 16, "Distributing Network Services with Domains." The downside of domains is that you must license Windows NT Server 4.0 and purchase a client license for each client (called a *per-seat* license) or for a specific number of simultaneous clients connecting to a server (a *per-server* license.)

From Here...

This chapter briefly overviewed the history and the features of Windows NT, with emphasis on Windows NT networking capabilities. The history of Windows NT included a discussion of the relationship between Microsoft's LAN Manager and IBM's LAN Server, both of which are based on OS/2, and Windows NT Server. A full description of all the unique features of the Windows NT operating system would require a multivolume set of books, so only brief coverage of the topics of primary interest to network administrators appears in this chapter. The chapter concluded with a discussion of Windows NT's implementation of RPCs and the differences between the Server and Workstation versions of Windows NT 4.0.

The following chapters provide detailed explanations of the topics discussed in this chapter:

■ Chapter 4, "Choosing Network Protocols," explains how to select one or more of the three principal networking protocols supported by Windows NT based on your network configuration.

■ Chapter 12, "Managing User and Group Accounts," describes how to use Windows NT Server 4.0's User Manager for Domains, take advantage of the new Add User Accounts and Group Management Wizards, and utilize Windows NT's built-in user groups.

■ Chapter 16, "Distributing Network Services with Domains," covers Windows NT Server's trusted domains and other distributed networking features that allow single-user logon for multiple network servers and server-based applications running on LANs and WANs.

Chapter 4

Choosing Network Protocols

One of the greatest strengths of the Windows NT Server operating system is the variety of networking protocols it supports. But that variety can be a source of confusion when it's time to choose the protocol(s) to use for your network.

This chapter describes the transport protocols compatible with Windows NT. A *protocol* is a set of rules, implemented in software, that govern communication between two computers. Not all operating systems support all protocols, so you must select the appropriate networking protocols that you set up for Windows NT Server to accommodate all the client computers connected to the network, plus other servers now in use, if any. If this computer will connect to a larger network, such as the Internet or a WAN, you must accommodate this in your protocol choice as well.

Chapter 5, "Purchasing Networking Hardware," covers the various physical networks (Ethernet, Token Ring, and others) and provides a detailed discussion of the network cards, cables, and other hardware components that connect the computers. Making these hardware choices doesn't automatically determine the network protocol(s) you use, but your choice of network protocol(s) is likely to determine the network-related peripheral components you purchase, such as routers.

Understanding the OSI Seven-Layer Model

Communication over a network is a complex task. To simplify the task of discussing and building networks, the OSI (Open Systems Interconnection) seven-layer networked model was developed by the International Standards Organization (ISO), a branch of the United Nations headquartered in Geneva. OSI applies to a great variety of networking situations. At the heart of OSI is the diagram shown in figure 4.1. The seven layers, numbered from the bottom to the top, represent the seven different aspects of networking. Layer 1, the physical layer, is the most concrete, consisting of components that can

This chapter shows you the following:

- How a transport protocol interacts with a physical network and with the operating system

- How Windows NT 4.0 makes it possible to use more than one protocol simultaneously

- The kinds of clients that might attach to your server

- The kinds of other servers to which your server might need to connect

- The most popular network protocols and the characteristics that distinguish them

- Guidelines for choosing protocols

actually be touched. On the other hand, layer 7, the application layer, is the most abstract, consisting of high-level software.

The OSI model doesn't correspond precisely to commercial networking software products, some of which span several levels or break a level into several tasks. Instead, the model provides a useful way of discussing the complex task of arranging communication between computers.

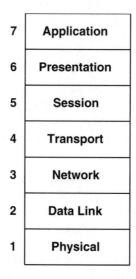

7	Application
6	Presentation
5	Session
4	Transport
3	Network
2	Data Link
1	Physical

Fig. 4.1   The seven layers of the Open Systems Interconnection (OSI) model.

The Physical Layer

The physical layer sends bits over the wire or over another connection, such as a fiber-optic cable or wireless connection, between computers. It deals with the electrical signals that represent the 0 (off) or 1 (on) state of a bit traveling over the network cabling. The decision to use a particular type of network interface card or a choice between twisted-pair and coaxial cable is a decision about the physical layer, which is implemented in networking hardware.

The Data-Link Layer

The data-link layer deals with *frames*, groups of bits that are transmitted over the network. It relies on the physical layer to actually send the bits. The data-link layer ensures that frames sent over the network are received and, if necessary, resends them. Ethernet is an example of a data-link layer, as is Token Ring, and each has a different layout for a frame.

> **Note**
>
> In the official terminology of the OSI model, the group of bits sent by the data-link layer is called a *physical layer service data unit*. In practice, people call it a *frame* or a *data frame*.

The IEEE networking model divides this layer into two sublayers: Logical Link Control (LLC) and Media Access Control (MAC), as shown in figure 4.2. The MAC sublayer handles interaction with the physical layer below, and the LLC sublayer handles interaction with the network layer above. The MAC layer provides standard interfaces for Carrier Sense Multiple Access with Collision Detection (CSMA/CD, Ethernet) networks, token-passing bus networks (similar to ArcNet), and Token Ring networks.

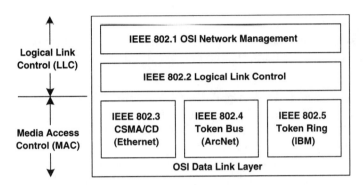

Fig. 4.2   The IEEE 802 series standards for Logical Link Control and Media Access Control within the OSI data-link layer.

The Network Layer

The network layer deals with *packets*, which may be larger or smaller than frames. If the packets are larger than frames, the network layer breaks the packet into frames to send them, and reassembles them on receipt. If the packets are smaller than frames, the network layer bundles frames into packets to send them and breaks them apart on receipt.

In either case, the network layer relies on the data-link layer to transmit the frames themselves. The network layer also deals with routing packets between computers (*hosts*) on the network, and it knows the addresses of the hosts on the network. Typically, the network layer can adjust the routing of packets to deal with network traffic and congestion. The network layer doesn't keep track of whether packets arrived at their destination or whether any errors occurred during transmission—that job is handled by the transport layer.

The Transport Layer

The transport layer deals with *messages*, which may be larger or smaller than packets. This layer ensures that messages travel between hosts without data loss and, if necessary, arranges for packets to be re-sent. The transport layer relies on the network layer to transmit the frames.

NetBEUI, TCP/IP, IPX/SPX, and other transport protocols handle the duties of the network layer and the transport layer. It's quite common for these two layers to be combined into a single protocol, and it is protocols that this chapter discusses.

> **Note**
>
> Some people argue that TCP/IP, the transport protocol of the Internet, isn't a single protocol, but rather a suite of protocols that includes TCP, IP, UDP, and others. In the near future, IP will be changed to accommodate more addresses, but TCP probably won't need to change. Most ordinary users and network administrators tend to think of TCP/IP as a single element.

The Session Layer

The session layer establishes and maintains a session between applications running on different computers. It knows the names of other computers on the network and handles security issues.

The session layer relies on the transport layer to transmit messages between the two computers. NetBIOS, the session-layer for the Windows network, and Sockets, the session layer for TCP/IP, are examples of typical session-layer software. Windows NT uses the 32-bit Windows Sockets (Winsock) session layer.

> **Note**
>
> Winsock is the specification developed by more than 20 cooperating vendors that describes implementations of sockets on Windows machines. The first release of the specification was for TCP/IP protocols only, but it was designed to work over other protocols in the future. Different vendors release their own DLLs that implement the Winsock specification; a 32-bit Winsock DLL is included with Windows NT and Windows 95.

The Presentation Layer

The presentation layerprovides services that a number of different applications use, such as encryption, compression, or character translation (PC ASCII to IBM's EBCDIC, for example, or PC/Intel's little-endian to Macintosh and Motorola's big-endian byte-ordering). The presentation layer relies on the session layer to pass on the encrypted, compressed, or translated material. One implementation of a presentation layer is XDR (External Data Representation) under RPC (Remote Procedure Call).

> **Note**
>
> RPC is a service that allows programmers to create applications that consist of multiple procedures; some procedures run locally, whereas others run on remote computers over a network. RPC is especially useful because it takes a procedural, rather than transport-centered, view of network operations. RPC simplifies the development of distributed or client/server applications. RPC is used extensively by Microsoft BackOffice applications, such as Microsoft Exchange Server, and for communication between Automation client and Automation server applications.

The Application Layer

The application layer handles requests by applications that require network communication, such as accessing a database or delivering e-mail. This layer is directly accessible to applications running on networked computers. It relies on the presentation layer to manipulate and transmit the communication. RPC is an example of an application-layer implementation.

Many important protocols span the presentation and application layers—for example, named pipes and FTP (the File Transfer Protocol, not the application itself). Clients use named pipes, for example, to communicate with Microsoft SQL Server. FTP is familiar to all UNIX and Internet users.

Comparing Windows NT and OSI Network Layers

The networking architecture of Windows NT is built of layers that don't fully correspond to the layers of the OSI model. Windows NT's layers are shown in figure 4.3, which includes the OSI layers for reference.

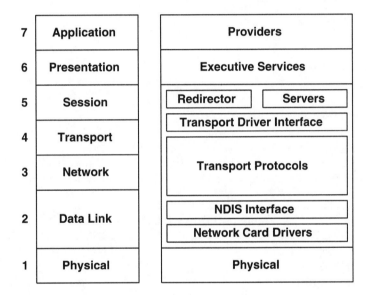

Fig. 4.3 A comparison of the Windows NT networking model (right) and the OSI model (left).

The keys to figure 4.3 are Windows NT's two new layers: the Transport Driver Interface (TDI) and the Network Device Interface Specification (NDIS). These layers allow Windows NT to use simultaneously a number of different transport protocols in the layer between TDI and NDIS, and to make the choice of transport protocol transparent to the session and data-link layers.

TDI sits between the transport protocols and the session layer, which may be NetBIOS, Winsock, RPC, or some other session layer, no matter what the transport protocol chosen. TDI isn't so much a program as it is a specification—that is, a set of rules for writing the layers above and below it.

The NDIS interface, which sits between network adapter cards and transport protocols, allows any of the transport protocols to run over any of the adapter cards, as long as the protocols are written to the NDIS interface and the adapter card supports NDIS. NDIS also allows multiple protocols to be used at the same time on the same network adapter card.

Whether you think of the protocols discussed in this chapter as spanning two levels of the OSI model, or as the thick central layer of the Windows NT model, the protocols serve the same purpose—to move chunks of information around the network based on the network address of the destination.

Networking with Windows NT's Protocols

Windows NT Server provides built-in support for seven networking protocols:

- NetBEUI and NetBEUI Frame (NBF)
- NWLink (IPX/SPX)
- TCP/IP
- Data Link Control (DLC)
- AppleTalk
- Remote Access Services (RAS)
- Streams

Figure 4.4 shows how each protocol fits into the Windows NT network layer diagram shown earlier in figure 4.3. The following sections detail each of the seven protocols.

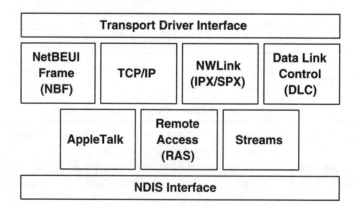

Fig. 4.4 Windows NT's transport protocols between the Transport Driver Interface and the NDIS interface.

NetBEUI and NetBEUI Frame

The NetBIOS Extended User Interface (NetBEUI) protocol, introduced in 1985, is an extension of the NetBIOS data-link layer. IBM developed NetBEUI to handle LANs of 20 to 200 workstations, such as those that a company might set up for a single department. IBM's assumption was that gateways between LANs would provide large-scale networking capability.

NetBEUI is a compact, fast protocol, but it's more than 10 years old and doesn't scale well to larger networks. NetBEUI isn't a routable protocol; routable protocols let you create a wide area network (WAN) by interconnecting LANs. A routable protocol is vital if your LAN is to be connected to anything but a small cluster of client PCs.

The NetBEUI Frame (NBF) protocol builds on NetBEUI to overcome some of these difficulties. In particular, NBF overcomes the session limit, which is 254 in NetBIOS. This makes it operable for larger networks that must retain compatibility with existing NetBEUI networks.

If you now have a NetBEUI network in operation, the commercial implementation of NetBEUI running on the PCs you plan to connect to your Windows NT server is likely one of the following:

- Microsoft LAN Manager, which uses a server that runs on Microsoft's implementation of OS/2

- IBM LAN Server, which uses a server running under IBM OS/2

- Microsoft MS-Net, an early DOS peer-to-peer networking system similar to IBM's original PC-Net

NetBEUI networks are very simple to implement but are difficult to expand because the NetBEUI protocol isn't routable. To a great extent, the limitations of NetBEUI are responsible for the success of Novell NetWare in the network operating system market. If you're starting from scratch to build a network around a Windows NT Server machine, avoid NBF in favor of TCP/IP or, if you also must support NetWare, IPX/SPX (NWLink).

TCP/IP

Transmission Control Protocol/Internet Protocol (TCP/IP) is the protocol of choice for WANs and is rapidly being adopted for LANs. TCP/IP, used for decades on the Internet and its predecessors, has been fine-tuned to maximize performance in extraordinarily large networks. Unlike NetBEUI, which is a proprietary IBM and Microsoft protocol, TCP/IP is in the public domain. The Internet Engineering Task Force (IETF) is the standards body that coordinates extensions and improvements to TCP/IP through a mechanism known as Requests for Comments (RFCs).

> **Note**
>
> A number of Internet standards describe the TCP/IP protocol and related protocols. These are accessible using FTP in the directory **ftp://ftp.merit.edu/documents/std/**. An index to the Internet standards is at **ftp://ftp.merit.edu/documents/std/INDEX.std**.

TCP/IP is an incredibly robust and reliable protocol. It was designed to keep the Department of Defense's Advanced Research Projects Agency's network (ARPANET, the precursor to the Internet) functioning, even if many of the cities it connected had been wiped out in a nuclear war. During the early history of ARPANET, only defense contractors and university research facilities were connected. To encourage expansion of the network, commercial users were admitted; today, the vast majority of traffic on the Internet is commercial, not government-related.

> **Note**
>
> The term *commercial*, in this case, includes individual users who connect to the Internet through commercial SPs or ISPs. SPs (service providers) lease high-speed connections to the Internet backbone and provide modem banks for individual dial-up access to the Internet. ISPs (Internet service providers) sell dial-up access and other Internet-related services (such as hosting Web pages) to individuals and small companies that don't need an intranet.

▶▶ See "Choosing an Internet Service Provider," p. 691

TCP/IP is a very flexible protocol that you can deploy in a small-scale LAN and later expand to accommodate hundreds or thousands of users. TCP/IP requires more knowledge to manage than other networks, because each machine must have a unique IP address and subnet mask. Tools (DHCP, WINS) are available in Windows NT Server to simplify these tasks, and experienced TCP/IP administrators are relatively easy to find and hire. If you're setting up a simple TCP/IP LAN with fewer than 100 or so client PCs, it's a reasonably simple job to administer the LAN if you learn how to use Windows NT Server's built-in administrative tools for TCP/IP.

The most important advantage of TCP/IP over NetBEUI is that TCP/IP is a *routable* protocol. A *router* is a device that forms a connection between a LAN and a WAN, or between two LANs. The router intercepts network packets and leaves the packets on the LAN if they are for a machine on the LAN; if not, the router passes the packets to another LAN or WAN. The structure of IP network addresses is designed specifically for efficient routing, and the price of dedicated routing hardware has decreased dramatically over the past few years.

▶▶ See "Routers," p. 156

IP Addresses. Every machine on a TCP/IP network has an IP address, such as 205.210.40.3. An IP address—sometimes referred to as a *dotted quad*—consists of four numbers, each in the range of 0-255, separated by dots. When an entire LAN joins the Internet, it's common to assign IP addresses to the machines on the LAN that are easily distinguished from IP addresses on the rest of the Internet. Groups of related addresses are referred to as Class A, B, or C addresses:

- A *Class C address* is actually about 250 IP addresses, each with the same values (for example, 205.210.40) for the first three components. The last component is different for each machine on the LAN. (A LAN with a Class C address can't have 255 machines, because some values for each component are reserved.)

■ A *Class B address* is actually about 60,000 IP addresses, each with the same values (for example, 130.105) for the first two components. Each of the last two components can vary. The owners of Class B addresses typically have far fewer than 60,000 machines on their internal networks, but more than 250.

■ A *Class A address* is about 15 million IP addresses, all with the same first component (for example, 47) and with three different components at the end.

Only a limited number of these classes are available. For example, first components with values between 1 and 126 are reserved for Class A addresses (in practice, fewer than 50 Class A addresses have been assigned, primarily to Internet builders such as the U.S. military and telecommunications companies). First components between 128 and 191 are available for Class B addresses, and between 191 and 223 for Class C addresses. First components above 223 are reserved; if your installation requires only a single IP address, it will be assigned from the Class B or C address of your ISP.

This structure makes routing simple to arrange. If you have a Class C address, for example, traffic destined to an IP address that varies in the first three components from that of your LAN is to be routed out to the rest of the Internet; traffic with the same first three components as your LAN stays on the LAN. This is coded in a value called a *subnet mask*. The subnet mask 255.255.255.0 codes this routing pattern for a Class C address.

You can split a single Class C address into several smaller pieces, each piece on its own LAN. The subnet mask is a bit-by-bit mask of the IP address, with each component representing eight bits. For example, the subnet mask 255.255.255.224 defines a 31-address subnet with the following properties:

■ All traffic for machines with first three components that vary from the routing machine is headed off the LAN.

■ Of the remaining traffic, that for machines where the first three bits of the last component match those of the routing machine stays on the LAN. Since only the last five bits can vary, 31 (16+8+4+2+1) machines are on this subnet.

■ The remaining traffic is headed off the LAN.

A Class C address could be split into seven such subnets, allowing for great flexibility in combining small LANs. If large LANS are involved, a Class B address can be split in a similar manner.

The job of managing and assigning IP addresses and subnet masks can involve substantial effort. The Dynamic Host Configuration Protocol (DHCP) included with Windows NT Server reduces this effort significantly. To do it by hand, administrators must use Control Panel's Network tool; on the Protocols page select the TCP/IP protocol and click Properties, choose the IP Address page, and then fill in the IP address and subnet mask as shown in figure 4.5.

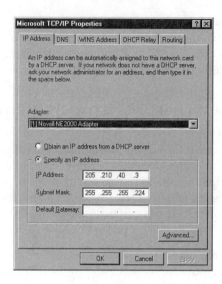

Fig. 4.5 Setting the IP address and subnet mask manually.

Internet Domain Names. Whereas administrators need to be comfortable with IP addresses, most users are not. The Domain Name System was introduced in the early 1980s to cope with the Internet's growth, which was considered to be very rapid then but has been eclipsed by the growth rates of the 1990s. Machines on the Internet have domain names such as que.mcp.com or ftp.merit.edu, made up of two or more short strings of letters and numbers separated by dots.

Domain names are far less structured than IP addresses but are easier for humans to interpret. For example, the domain names csri.utoronto.ca and psych.utoronto.ca are obviously related (in fact, they identify the Computer Science Research Institute and the psychology department, both at the University of Toronto).

▶▶ See "Name Resolution and the Domain Name System," p. 698

A computer running Windows NT Server that's on the Internet can have two names: one that it's known by on the Internet, and one that it's known by on the local network (the NetBIOS name defined during Setup). The job of managing names is made easier by the Windows Internet Name Service (WINS), which is included with Windows NT Server.

Commercial Implementations. TCP/IP implementations are available for UNIX systems, the Macintosh, and Windows 3.x, and are included in Windows 95 and Windows NT Server and Workstation 4.0. TCP/IP supports many session-layer implementations, including NetBIOS (called NetBIOS over TCP/IP), Sockets (Winsock), Streams, and RPC. TCP/IP is the most commonly used protocol to provide dial-up network access (RAS) for mobile users.

NWLink (IPX/SPX)

The Internetwork Packet Exchange/Sequenced Packet Exchange (IPX/SPX) protocol is the heart of Novell NetWare. Microsoft's implementation of the IPX/SPX protocol is called NWLink. The IPX/SPX protocol is based on the Xerox Network System (XNS) protocol developed by Xerox Corp. XNS, which is no longer in use, had two components: IDP (Internet Datagram Protocol) and SPP (Sequenced Packet Protocol). IPX is based on IDP; SPX is based on SPP.

▶▶ See "Integrating Windows NT Server with Novell NetWare," p. 599

IPX/SPX is a high-performance protocol for local area networking and is easier than TCP/IP to implement and administer. Like TCP/IP, IPX/SPX is a routable protocol, so it can be used to establish a WAN. Because of NetWare's commercial success, IPX/SPX is now the default network protocol installed when you set up Windows 95. Unless you're installing Windows NT Server within an existing NetWare environment, however, TCP/IP is a better protocol choice, especially if you intend to provide Internet or related intranet services to client PCs. To conserve resources, you should uninstall IPX/SPX if you won't be using it. Using Windows NT Server with Novell NetWare servers is one of the primary subjects of Chapter 17, "Integrating Windows NT with Heterogeneous Networks."

DLC

IBM's DLC (Data Link Control) protocol is used to communicate with mainframes as a component of IBM's System Network Architecture (SNA). On some LANs, DLC is used to communicate with printers that are connected directly to the LAN, rather than to a workstation or server. Several high-end Hewlett-Packard LaserJet printers offer DLC interfaces as an option.

AppleTalk

AppleTalk is the primary network protocol used by Macintosh computers. It's supported by Windows NT Server's Services for Macintosh, which allows Macintosh users to share Mac-format files stored in Windows NT Server folders and use printers connected to a Windows NT server. Shared Windows NT folders appear to Mac users as conventional Mac folders. Mac file names are converted to FAT (8.3) and NTFS standards, including long file names (LFNs), as required. DOS and Windows client applications that support Mac file formats can share the files with Mac users.

Windows NT server supports the Mac application fork, so Mac users can double-click a file stored on a Windows NT server and launch the associated application. The application fork of a Mac file serves the same purpose as Windows file extension associations. Mac users can drag and drop their files from a Mac folder directly to a Windows NT server folder.

▶▶ See "Setting Up Macintosh Clients," p. 403

RAS

Windows NT Server provides RAS (Remote Access Service) to enable temporary connections to systems that aren't on your LAN—typically, dial-up connections over a conventional telephone line. Windows NT Server includes built-in support for Integrated Services Digital Network (ISDN) modems. A single Windows NT server supports up to 255 simultaneous RAS connections. Chapter 18, "Managing Remote Access Service," covers the subject of dial-up RAS in more detail.

 The RAS connection can use SLIP (Serial Line Internet Protocol) or, preferably, PPP (Point-to-Point Protocol) over a dial-up or dedicated phone line, or via the X.25 network communications protocol. When a PPP connection is made, your LAN and the remote site can communicate by using NetBEUI, TCP/IP, or IPX/SPX. PPP with TCP/IP is the most common protocol for connecting mobile users to intranets. The Microsoft Network Client included with Windows 95 uses dial-up PPP with TCP/IP to connect to MSN's bank of Windows NT servers and, through MSN, to the Internet.

The new PPTP (Point-to-Point Tunneling Protocol)—announced by Microsoft, 3Com Corp., Ascend Communications, ECI Telematics, and U.S. Robotics in March 1996—allows users to "tunnel" through the Internet to reach their secure networks from a local dial-up connection.

 ▶▶ See "Using the Point-to-Point Tunneling Protocol," p. 685

> **Note**
>
> RAS clients are available for DOS and Windows 3.1+ and are included with Windows for Workgroups, Windows 95, and Windows NT. Windows 95 supports a single dial-in RAS connection if you buy the Windows 95 Plus! pack to obtain the Windows 95 RAS server upgrade.

Streams

Streams is a protocol specification that enables Windows NT to support third-party communications protocols. In effect, the third-party protocol is enclosed by an upper Streams layer and a lower Streams layer (see fig. 4.6). The upper Streams layer talks to the session layer and the third-party protocol; the lower Streams layer talks to the third-party protocol and the data-link layer.

> **Note**
>
> Streams also is the name of a UNIX session-layer protocol that was developed by AT&T in 1984. AT&T's Streams was intended to serve the same purpose as Sockets, but Sockets and Winsock have been so successful that Streams is no longer implemented in most UNIX systems. It's not at all related to the Windows NT Streams protocol.

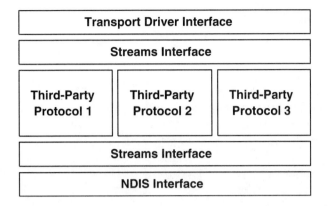

Fig. 4.6 Supporting third-party transport layers with the Streams layer.

Supporting a Variety of PC Clients

It's possible that you're installing an entire office full of computers, and you can choose the client PCs and operating systems that fit best with Windows NT Server. In this case, Windows NT Workstation 4.0 for desktop PCs and Windows 95 for laptop PCs (and desktop PCs with less than 16M of RAM) are the logical choices. It's more likely, however, that you're integrating a server into an environment that's now running one or more operating systems. The optimum protocol choice allows all your machines to talk to your server without spending large amounts of money and/or time.

> **Note**
>
> Theoretically, any protocol can be implemented for any operating system. If you discover an obscure piece of third-party software that lets all the machines in your environment use the same protocol, such a product might seem a likely candidate. In this chapter, the assumption is that you're choosing from the generally available and popular implementations—and that means not every operating system can run every protocol. Integrating obscure third-party software into a network is a chancy proposition, at best.

It's possible for your server to support a number of different protocols at once; but to keep your workload to a minimum, choose your protocol(s) carefully so that you use as few as possible. In addition to making administration more complicated, running several protocols simultaneously consumes more memory on the server and client computers, and can have a deleterious effect on system performance. The following sections describe the types of clients commonly connected to Windows NT servers and the networking protocols individual clients support.

Windows NT Workstations

Not surprisingly, using clients running Windows NT Workstation 4.0 allows you to use almost any of the networking protocols supported by Windows NT Server, including

- NetBEUI Frame (NBF)

- NWLink (IPX/SPX)

- TCP/IP

In many cases, your choice of protocol under Windows NT is determined not by your operating system, but by the software your Windows NT clients run. For example, most Windows Internet software (including Web browsers) runs over TCP/IP using Winsock, but not over NetBEUI.

▶▶ See "Connecting Windows NT Workstation 4.0 Clients," p. 395

PCs running Windows NT Workstation 4.0 can participate in peer-to-peer (workgroup) networks, which operate independently of the Windows NT server(s) that support the primary (client/server) network. A maximum of 10 workgroup members can connect simultaneously to a Windows NT client that shares the workgroup files. NetBEUI (the Windows network) is the most common method of establishing peer-to-peer workgroups. Most network administrators discourage peer-to-peer file sharing because of security issues, including lack of coordinated access control to sensitive information and centralized backup procedures.

Windows 95

Windows 95 offers the same suite of 32-bit network protocols as Windows NT Workstation. One primary advantage of Windows 95 is the ease in which Plug-and-Play network adapter cards install. In general, software that runs under Windows NT Workstation also can run under Windows 95, thus users can choose their operating system without being concerned about networking issues. Another is that many new PCs are shipping with Windows 95 installed, saving the cost of another operating system. Windows 95 has been designed for less powerful PCs, but you should be aware of limitations (memory or disk space) on the client machines that preclude running Windows 95 efficiently. Chapter 10, "Configuring Windows 95 Clients for Networking," is devoted to optimizing the networking performance of Windows 95 PCs.

Windows for Workgroups 3.1x

Because it's an older product than Windows NT or Windows 95, Windows for Workgroups (WfWg) 3.1x doesn't support as many protocols. WfWg 3.1x limits the workstation to running only two networks at once. You connect to a Microsoft network and one other network by running one of the following protocols:

- IPX/SPX

- NetBEUI

- TCP/IP

Again, the software you're running will play a major part in your choice among these options. Some software runs only over certain network protocols; check your documentation.

▶▶ See "Connecting Windows for Workgroups 3.11 Clients," p. 387

Networking

Windows 3.1+

Windows versions before Windows for Workgroups don't support networking directly; instead, early releases of Windows used DOS-based networking. Like the DOS clients mentioned in the next section, Windows 3.1+ clients attached to your Windows NT server can use one of the following protocols:

- NetBEUI

- IPX/SPX

- TCP/IP (with a third-party Winsock DLL like the one from Trumpet software, available at **http://www.trumpet.com.au**)

It's not possible for one Windows 3.1+ client to use more than one network protocol at a time.

▶▶ See "Connecting Windows 3.1 Clients," p. 378

> **Note**
>
> Sometimes two applications on the same computer talk to each other by using a standard protocol as though they were running over a network. Choosing to install that protocol and to run those applications doesn't affect your choice of protocol for your actual network. If a developer on a NetBEUI LAN is testing an Internet (Winsock) application, for example, two Internet applications may be running on the developer's machine using Winsock to communicate. The developer isn't on a TCP/IP LAN.
>
> Similarly, if you form a temporary connection to another workstation or server by using a networking protocol, the temporary connection doesn't imply that you're networked to that machine, and it doesn't affect your protocol choice. If the Internet developer dials up to an ISP by using a third-party stack such as Trumpet, that single machine is communicating with the ISP using TCP/IP but isn't connected to a TCP/IP LAN.

DOS-Only PCs

MS-DOS clients have a rather limited set of protocols available but can be connected to your Windows NT server by using one of these protocols:

- NetBEUI

- IPX/SPX

- TCP/IP (with a third-party stack)

It's not possible for one MS-DOS PC to run more than one network protocol simultaneously.

OS/2 Clients

Just as Microsoft has improved PC networking capabilities with each new version of Windows, IBM has increased the networking features of OS/2, generally providing with the operating system access to protocols that in the past could be accessed only with third-party add-ons. OS/2 versions 1.x, 2.x, and Warp can all use any of these protocols:

- NetBEUI

- IPX/SPX

- TCP/IP

Apple Macintosh Computers

You can connect PCs that don't run DOS or Windows to a Windows NT server. The protocols supported for Macs are

- AppleTalk

- TCP/IP

Choosing AppleTalk will make your life difficult if there are any non-Macintosh machines (other than your Windows NT server) on your network, and if you want the Macs to have peer-to-peer access to the files on non-Macintosh workstations. If possible, all Macs connected to a network served by Windows NT should use the TCP/IP protocol.

    ▶▶ See "Connecting Macintosh Clients," p. 400

UNIX Workstations

UNIX systems have even less in common with Windows and DOS systems than Mac systems do. However, TCP/IP is a protocol that was designed for use with various operating systems. Using TCP/IP lets UNIX workstations talk to your Windows NT server without difficulty. Interconnecting with UNIX networks is one of the subjects of Chapter 17, "Integrating Windows NT with Heterogeneous Networks."

Supporting Multiple Servers

Arranging for one or more client PCs to be networked to your server may be all you need on a relatively small network. On the other hand, there may be other servers in your installation that must be connected to your new Windows NT server. Each additional server can communicate by using one or more of the protocols supported by Windows NT.

Other Windows NT Servers

As usual, when the machines to be connected are using the same operating system, you have the most flexibility in choosing a protocol. Interconnected Windows NT servers support the full range of protocols:

- NetBEUI Frame (NBF)

- Data Link Control (DLC)

- NWLink (IPX/SPX)
- TCP/IP
- Streams
- AppleTalk

It wouldn't be wise to choose DLC, Streams, or AppleTalk in this case, because they're limited protocols that might not be supported by other clients on your network, but such a choice is technically possible.

Novell NetWare Servers

To Windows NT Server, talking to a NetWare server isn't very different from talking to a NetWare client—you simply use the SPX/IPX protocol. Novell offers an implementation of TCP/IP for NetWare 3.x and 4.x; if you plan to install the TCP/IP protocol, using TCP/IP to interconnect NetWare and Windows NT servers is preferred.

UNIX Servers

UNIX servers, like UNIX clients, should be part of a TCP/IP network. Microsoft's version of TCP/IP is fully compatible with the UNIX implementations of TCP/IP.

Local Intranet Servers

One of the hottest developments in the networking world is *intranetworking*, using Internet software and protocols to communicate within a company. Intranetworking is discussed fully in Chapter 19, "Setting Up the Internet Information Server," and Chapter 20, "Administering Intranet and World Wide Web Sites." People within the company use Internet tools such as e-mail, Web browsers, and FTP file-transfer programs to deliver information over their own internal intranet. Typically, TCP/IP is the transport protocol of choice.

Microsoft Internet Information Server (IIS) 2.0 is a Web server for Windows NT Server 4.0. IIS builds on the strong background of third-party Internet servers previously available for Windows NT, including FTP, Gopher, and Web servers. IIS is fast, secure, and free, thus making it very popular for creating both intranet and Internet sites. Internet Information Server 2.0 is included with Windows NT Server 4.0.

The Internet

Connecting to the Internet can be a very simple or very complex project, as discussed in Chapter 19, "Setting Up the Internet Information Server." Connecting one machine to the Internet through a PPP connection is a very different project from connecting an entire LAN through one server machine. If there are security issues that require that the connection pass through a firewall, it's an even more complex job. Chapter 18, "Managing Remote Access Service," addresses some of these issues.

The Internet greatly simplifies the choosing of network protocols. The I in TCP/IP stands for Internet, and TCP/IP is the only protocol that you can use on the Internet.

Mainframes

There are many different mainframes, but one of the most important players is the IBM AS/400, which uses System Network Architecture (SNA). SNA relies on DLC as its transport protocol. If you use the SNA Server component of Microsoft BackOffice, you can connect to a number of different mainframes, including

- IBM AS/400s

- All IBM mainframes

- IBM plug-compatible mainframes running IBM host software (such as Amdahl, Fujitsu, or Hitachi)

- Tandem

- Fujitsu (using FNA)

- Hitachi (using HNA)

- OS/2 Comm Manager or Extended Services (using APPC)

- UNIX-based SNA gateway products (using APPC)

- IBM RS/6000 RISC computers

Planning for Network Interoperability

If all the workstations you plan to connect to your Windows NT server use the same protocol, life is simple. Assuming that you have a collection of machines to connect to your Windows NT server and that the collection uses two different protocols, the following options are available:

- You can run two or more different protocols on the Windows NT server.

- You can change the protocol that one set of workstations is using, so that all are using the same protocol.

- You can replace one set of workstations with a set that runs the same protocol as the others.

- You can gather the workstations into two or more LANs with gateways to handle translation and interconnection.

Setting up Windows NT Server to use one protocol to talk to one set of machines and a different protocol for the rest involves the fewest changes to the workstations, the smallest investment, and the least disruption to your users. This approach has some performance penalties; network processes consume more of your system memory and might even cause paging, which slows your system down. There will be cases where you gladly accept these relatively minor performance penalties to connect previously incompatible workstations.

Changing the protocols the workstations run might allow you to keep the same workstations while running only one protocol. This approach simplifies administration and improves the performance of your server, but it likely will be costly to buy new licenses for the protocol to be implemented on the client workstations. Also, there may be disruption to your users as you change the software that joins them together in a network. If some of your workstations are using a specific protocol for significant security or performance reasons, it may not be wise to change the protocol.

You may think it's unlikely that two sets of workstations would use different protocols if it's so simple to make them the same, but it's a matter worth investigating. For example, a wide variety of systems can run TCP/IP, and TCP/IP is a good solution when combining Macintosh and Windows workstations. However, many administrators automatically assume that the protocol is NetBEUI or IPX/SPX for the Windows machines and Apple-Talk for the Macs. Another approach for machines that use NetBIOS over NetBEUI is the simple change to running NetBIOS over IPX/SPX.

The most drastic solution, if the workstations can't switch to a common protocol, is to replace one set of workstations and their application software. The mildest version of this approach is to move to a more recent version of the operating system while keeping the same applications, such as upgrading from Windows for Workgroups to Windows 95 or to Windows NT Workstation. The more dramatic approach is to change the systems completely, such as replacing Macintosh workstations with Windows 95 machines. Changing from Macs to PCs is very likely to meet with strong resistance from your users, but many firms are eliminating Macs in order to standardize user support on a single client platform. Remember, it's not enough for the operating systems themselves to support the transport protocol; the software that your users utilize must also support the protocol, either by trusting the operating system to handle all networking or by supporting the protocol directly.

If none of these solutions seems palatable, perhaps the two sets of workstations should be on two separate LANs. A gateway can transfer traffic between the two LANs while making any necessary translations between the network transport formats.

Note

There's often some confusion about the name for a device (a combination of hardware and software) that sits between two networks. Here are some definitions:

- *Bridge.* Connects two similar LANs, usually running the same protocol, and passes the data on essentially unchanged.

- *Gateway.* Connects dissimilar networks and translates frame format, byte order for addresses, or similar low-level protocols.

- *Router.* Sits between networks and directs traffic to the appropriate network. If the networks are dissimilar, they need a gateway as well as a router.

- *Proxy server.* As part of a firewall, intercepts requests between networks and refuses them or passes them on according to the proxy server's own security rules.

Bear in mind that decisions can change with time. For example, you might choose to run two protocols at first, and then slowly migrate to a single protocol as new workstations replace the old ones. Be sure to choose a solution that will work with your future needs as well as your current requirements. These issues, and the mechanics of setting up a network of different workstations, are covered in more detail in Chapter 5, "Purchasing Networking Hardware," and Chapter 17, "Integrating Windows NT with Heterogeneous Networks."

Making the Final Protocol Choice

Perhaps as you've read this chapter, it has become clear that only one protocol fills the bill. You may be combining Macintosh and UNIX workstations and have chosen TCP/IP, so only one protocol is necessary. Or you may have an existing network that uses IPX/SPX and see no reason to change protocols.

But if you're building a network from scratch, or need to change the protocol of one of two sets of workstations and aren't sure which one to change, the following are some important issues to consider:

- How big is your LAN? NetBEUI can't handle more than 200 or so workstations. Even NBF isn't the best choice for a large LAN.

- Are there WANs or other LANs you want to connect to? A routable protocol (TCP/IP or SPX/IPX) is vital in that case.

- If you're not connected to a WAN, do you plan someday to connect to the Internet (an enormous WAN running TCP/IP)? The Internet is becoming vital to many businesses for research, advertising, and customer support, and the Internet or an intranet should be included in your networking plans.

- What software are your users running? What protocols does it support?

This may make it sound as though TCP/IP is the one-size-fits-all solution to all your networking needs. Of course, it's not that simple. Managing a TCP/IP server and assigning IP addresses to each machine on the network aren't simple tasks. If your organization has a staff of experienced SPX/IPX administrators, their knowledge and experience are assets that might sway you to choose SPX/IPX for your Windows NT 4.0 servers. Otherwise, choose TCP/IP.

From Here...

Having chosen a network transport protocol or protocols, you must get the protocol(s) installed and working, and then manage the resulting network. Not surprisingly, a large part of the rest of this book covers these tasks. The following chapters relate directly to networking protocols:

- Chapter 10, "Configuring Windows 95 Clients for Networking," discusses connecting Windows 95 workstations to your server.

- Chapter 11, "Connecting Other PC Clients to the Network," discusses connecting DOS, Windows 3.x, Windows for Workgroups, and Macintosh workstations to your server.

- Part III, "Administering a Secure Network," contains chapters 12 through 15 and covers all the details of how to be a network system administrator.

- Part IV, "Wide Area Networking and the Internet," contains chapters 16 through 20 and covers issues such as heterogeneous networks, the Internet, and intranets.

- Chapter 24, "Administering Clients with System Management Server," shows you how to make your administration tasks easier.

Networking

Chapter 5

Purchasing Networking Hardware

Windows NT Server 4.0 is a stable and robust network operating system, equally well suited to environments ranging from small offices to multinational corporations. Choosing the proper hardware to operate it will ensure that your network works reliably and is easy to maintain and expand. Spending some time planning your installation will pay off down the road in fewer problems and easier growth.

Compared with other modern network operating systems, such as Novell NetWare 4.1, Windows NT Server makes surprisingly modest hardware demands. Microsoft's specified minimum requirements, however, are unrealistically low for most situations. Fortunately, Windows NT Server scales very well. Whereas Novell NetWare requires adding substantial amounts of memory to support additional disk storage, Windows NT Server has no such direct correlation between RAM requirements and the amount of disk storage supported. A Windows NT server that's properly configured initially with adequate processor power and RAM will support substantial growth before requiring replacement or significant upgrading of the server.

Selecting a Media Access Method

The first important decision you must make is which media access method to use. This decision is comparable in importance to a railroad's choice of which gauge to use (how far apart do you put the tracks?). Everything devolves from this decision, including your choice of active network components, the type of cabling that you'll install, and ultimately the performance, reliability, and cost of your network.

In Chapter 4, "Choosing Network Protocols," you learn about the OSI Model and the purpose of its various layers. Media access methods are addressed primarily in the second layer, or data-link layer, with some overlap into the first, or physical layer. The data-link layer is the subject of an Institute for Electrical and Electronic Engineers (IEEE) standard.

In this chapter, you learn how to

- Choose the best media access method and cabling topology for your environment

- Select appropriate active network components to optimize network performance and to allow for future growth

- Configure and specify server hardware to meet your immediate and future needs

- Work with vendors to take advantage of their expertise and to obtain the hardware you need at the best price

◀◀ See "Understanding the OSI Seven-Layer Model," p. 107

The IEEE is a standards body that codifies and publishes official standards documents. Among these standards are the IEEE 802 series, which cover media access methods for local area networks and other related issues. The IEEE develops these standards in cooperation with various industry bodies. When a standard is adopted and promulgated, all manufacturers of equipment addressed by that standard ensure that their products fully comply with the standard in question. This is why, for example, you can freely mix different manufacturers' Ethernet cards and be assured that they'll all talk to each other properly.

ARCnet

One of the oldest media access methods still in use is ARCnet. Developed in 1977 by DataPoint Corporation, ARCnet (for Attached Resource Computer Network) was deservedly popular in the early and mid-1980s. Its combination of simplicity, low cost, and reasonable performance made it a good choice at a time when Ethernet was extremely expensive and Token Ring didn't yet exist.

Thousands of Novell NetWare 2.x networks were installed using ARCnet, many of which are still running today. ARCnet is an obsolete media access method. If you happen to have an ARCnet network in place, you may choose to run a Windows NT server on it. Otherwise, you shouldn't consider ARCnet.

Token Ring

Introduced by IBM in 1986, Token Ring has a lot going for it, balanced by a few negatives. Token Ring is fast, reliable, and well supported by IBM in both the PC and mainframe environments. Balanced against this are the following factors:

■ Token Ring is extremely expensive when compared with Ethernet alternatives. The price of one name-brand Token Ring card can buy between three and five name-brand Ethernet cards. This cost disparity holds true across the range of networking hardware you need, such as hubs, routers, and so forth.

■ Token Ring hasn't achieved wide industry acceptance, due initially to IBM's restrictive licensing policies and subsequently to the market dominance of Ethernet. As a result, your choice of network interface cards (NICs) and other active network components is restricted to only a handful of vendors with Token Ring, whereas with Ethernet you can choose among scores of vendors.

Like ARCnet, Token Ring uses a token-passing access method, but with a somewhat different mechanism. In Token Ring, a station with data to be transmitted first waits for an idle token. It changes the status of the token to busy (called a *burdened busy token*), appends a destination address, attaches data to the token, and passes the burdened busy token to the next station in the ring. Each station functions in Token Ring as a unidirectional repeater, receiving data from the downstream station, regenerating it, and passing it to the upstream station. This next station regenerates the burdened busy token and passes it to the next station in sequence. This process continues until the burdened busy token reaches its destination. At the destination, the recipient extracts the data from the token and sends an acknowledgment (ACK) to the originating station. On receipt of this ACK, the originating station generates an idle token and passes it to the next station. Figure 5.1 illustrates a token passing between four computers in the ring.

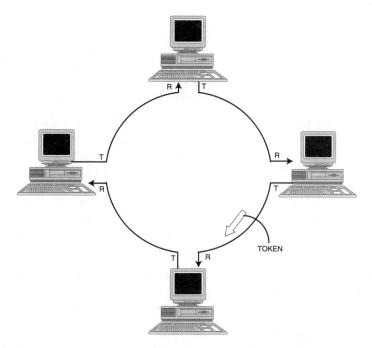

Fig. 5.1   Passing a token between four computers in a Token Ring network.

Because only one token can exist on the ring at any given time, one station is designated an *active monitor*. The responsibility of this station is to monitor the ring for out-of-norm conditions, including the absence of a token, a damaged token, or multiple tokens coexisting. When such a condition is found, the active monitor corrects the problem and returns the ring to normal operating conditions.

Token Ring uses a star-wired ring topology in which each station is connected by an individual cable run to a concentrator called a *multistation access unit* (MAU). Token Ring originally operated on 150-ohm shielded twisted-pair (STP) cable arranged in a star-wired ring with data throughput of 4mbps. Newer Token Ring equipment can operate on unshielded twisted-pair (UTP) cable and fiber-optic cable, as well as the original STP cable. The throughput has also been upgraded to 16mbps. Many newer Token Ring components can operate at either 4mbps or 16mbps to ease transition from the older technology to the newer. A ring must be exclusively 4mbps or 16mbps; the two speeds can't coexist on the same ring.

Token Ring, including its enhancements, has been adopted as standard 802.5 by the IEEE. Its market share is second only to Ethernet, although the growth of new Token Ring networks has slowed as Ethernet has increased its dominance. Although large numbers of Token Ring networks are installed, Token Ring remains in essence a niche product. It's primarily limited to exclusive IBM shops and to those locations with a need to interconnect their networks to IBM minicomputers and mainframes. Although IBM's commitment to Token Ring remains strong, even IBM has been forced to bow to market realities and begin offering Ethernet as an option.

Ethernet

Invented by Bob Metcalfe in 1973 and developed as a commercial product by Digital Equipment Corporation, Intel, and Xerox (DIX), Ethernet is the media access method of choice for most new networks being installed today. Ethernet is inexpensive, performs well, is easily extensible, and is supported by every manufacturer of network equipment. Ethernet has become the networking standard by which all others are judged.

Ethernet is based on a contention scheme for media access known as CSMA/CD, or Carrier Sense Multiple Access with Collision Detection. *Carrier Sense* means that each Ethernet device on the network constantly monitors the carrier present on the cable and can determine when that carrier is idle and when it's in use. *Multiple Access* means that all Ethernet devices on the cable have an equal right to access the carrier signal without obtaining prior permission. Ethernet is called a *baseband system* because only one transmission can be present on the wire at any one time. *Collision Detection* means that if two or more Ethernet devices transmit simultaneously and thereby corrupt all the data, the collision is detected and is subsequently corrected.

Unlike token-based schemes, any Ethernet station is permitted to transmit any time it has data to be sent. When a station needs to transmit, it first listens to make sure that the carrier is free. If the carrier is free, the station begins transmitting the data.

The original Ethernet specification, referred to as 10Base5, operated on 50-ohm thick coaxial cable in a bus topology with a data throughput of 10mbps and a maximum segment length of 500 meters. Concerns about the cost and difficulty of working with thick coax cable brought about the 10Base2 specification, which runs the same data rate over thinner and cheaper RG-58 coaxial cable, but limits segment length to only 180 meters. 10Base2 also is called *thin Ethernet* or *thinnet*. Figure 5.2 illustrates 10Base2 cabling to two Ethernet NICs.

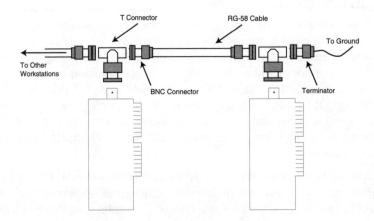

Fig. 5.2   Connections between 10Base2 cabling and Ethernet NICs.

With the introduction of the 10BaseT specification, Ethernet was extended from the original physical bus topology to a physical star topology running on inexpensive UTP cable, again with a data rate of 10mbps. Unlike 10Base2, 10BaseT requires a hub (described later in the "Simple Hubs" section) to interconnect more than two PCs (see fig. 5.3). You can create a two-PC 10BaseT network with a special cross-connect cable. 10BaseT uses RJ-45 modular connectors, shown in figure 5.4, which were originally designed for commercial telephone applications.

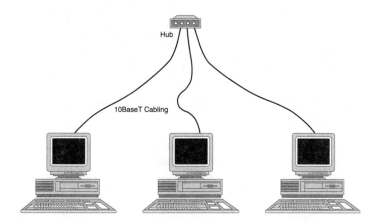

Fig. 5.3   Three PCs connected by 10BaseT to a hub.

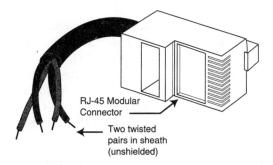

Fig. 5.4   An RJ-45 modular connector.

High-Speed Ethernet Variants

As the load on an Ethernet cable increases, the number of collisions increases and the cumulative throughput begins to fall. The traditional solution to this problem has been to divide a heavily loaded network into multiple segments by using bridges, which are described later in the "Bridges" section. The use of bridges to create additional segments essentially breaks the network into multiple neighborhoods. Local traffic within a neighborhood is kept local, and only traffic that needs to cross segment boundaries does so.

To address these perceived Ethernet performance problems, three contending high-speed challengers have arisen. The first, Full Duplex Ethernet, doubles bandwidth to 20mbps.

The remaining two, 100BaseT and 100VG–AnyLAN, compete at the 100mbps level. All these competitors propose to achieve their bandwidth increases using existing cable in at least one of their variants.

Full Duplex Ethernet. Full Duplex Ethernet is one recent scheme for increasing bandwidth beyond the 10mbps available with standard Ethernet. An Ethernet device may be transmitting or receiving, but it can't do both simultaneously. Full Duplex Ethernet devices, on the other hand, transmit and receive data simultaneously, thereby doubling effective bandwidth to 20mbps.

Full Duplex Ethernet devices are designed to work on 10BaseT networks using UTP cabling, and achieve their higher data rates simply by placing data on the transmit pair and receive pair simultaneously. Although Full Duplex Ethernet can coexist with standard 10BaseT Ethernet on the same cabling system, implementing Full Duplex Ethernet requires that NICs, hubs, bridges, routers, and other active network components be upgraded or replaced to support it.

Full Duplex Ethernet is likely to disappear as superior high-speed alternatives become available to replace it. Don't consider it for your network.

100BaseT. Of the two competing 100mbps proposed standards, 100BaseT was first out of the starting gate. 100BaseT remains conceptually close to Ethernet roots, using CSMA/CD media access combined with one of two signaling methods. 100BaseT signaling combines CSMA/CD and FDDI Physical Layer specifications and runs on two pairs of a Category 5 cable. 100BaseT can also run on STP or fiber. The 4T+ signaling method runs CSMA/CD on four pairs of Category 3 cable.

At the data-link layer, the major change involves timing. CSMA/CD-based systems function on the assumption that all collisions are detected. The maximum cabling length in an Ethernet network is limited by Round Trip Delay (RTD) time. The RTD of the entire network must be small enough that the two devices located farthest from each other can detect a collision in progress. The much higher signaling speed used by 100BaseT means that such collisions are present on the cable and detectable for a much shorter span. As a result, the maximum end-to-end cabling length for a 100BaseT network is 250 meters, or one-tenth that of a 10BaseT network.

100VG–AnyLAN. The second of the 100mbps proposed standards is 100VG–AnyLAN. Although it's often considered to be an extended version of Ethernet, 100VG–AnyLAN is really not Ethernet at all. It replaces Ethernet's CSMA/CD media access method with a demand-priority method more similar conceptually to that used by Token Ring, although access to the cable is arbitrated by a centralized controller rather than by possession of a token. In fact, the 100VG–AnyLAN specification permits using Token Ring frames as well as Ethernet frames.

100VG–AnyLAN is named for a composite of its 100mbps transmission rate, its capability to run on four pairs of Category 3 Voice Grade (VG) cable, and its support for both Ethernet and Token Ring frame types. 100VG–AnyLAN also can be run on two pairs of Category 5 cable, on STP, and on fiber.

With 100VG–AnyLAN, all stations constantly transmit an IDLE signal to the hub. When a station has data to transmit, it sends a request to transmit to the hub. When a request arrives at the hub, the hub transmits an incoming (INC) signal to the other stations. These stations then cease transmitting the IDLE signal, which frees the line for traffic. After the hub receives the frame from the source station and forwards it to the destination, it sends an IDLE signal to all stations that didn't receive the frame, and the cycle begins again.

A request can be either a Normal Priority Request (NPR) or a High Priority Request (HPR). An NPR arriving at the hub is serviced immediately if no HPRs are outstanding. HPRs are always given initial priority in processing over NPRs. However, if HPRs exist when an NPR arrives at the hub, a timer is started on the NPR. After a certain period passes, the NPR is promoted to an HPR and processed. This priority-demand system allows high priority traffic such as real-time video and audio frames to be processed isochronously.

The major drawback to 100VG–AnyLAN is that the complexity and processing power required at the hub is similar to that required for a switching hub but doesn't provide the benefits of switching. For the cost of the required 100VG–AnyLAN network cards and hubs, you can instead install switched Ethernet with much less effort and superior results.

Other High-Speed Media Access Methods

Several other high-speed Ethernet alternatives exist. Each of these has, at one time or another, been proposed as a desktop standard, and each has failed to become such a standard because of the high cost of NICs and hub ports. As a result, each has been largely relegated to use in network backbones.

Fiber Distributed Data Interface (FDDI). Developed by the ANSI X3T9.5 Committee, the FDDI specification describes a high-speed token-passing network operating on fiber-optic cable (see fig. 5.5). In its original incarnation, FDDI was intended to operate on dual counter-rotating fiber rings with a maximum of 1,000 clients and a transmission rate of 100mbps. FDDI can support a large physical network. Stations can be located as far as 2 kilometers apart, and the total network can span 200 kilometers. Like Token Ring, FDDI is deterministic and offers predictable network response, making it suitable for isochronous applications such as real-time video or multimedia.

Two classes of FDDI stations exist. Class A stations, also called *dual-attached stations*, attach to both rings using four fiber strands. This offers full redundancy, because failure of one ring simply causes traffic to shift to the other, allowing communication to continue uninterrupted. Class B stations, also called *singly attached stations*, connect only to the primary ring and do so via a star-wired hub. During a ring failure, only Class A stations participate in the automatic ring reconfiguration process.

FDDI is commonly seen in network equipment rooms, providing the network backbone used to link hubs and other active network components. FDDI to the client is rarely seen, appearing primarily in U.S. government and large corporate locations, where the resistance of fiber-optic cable to electronic eavesdropping outweighs the large additional cost of installing FDDI.

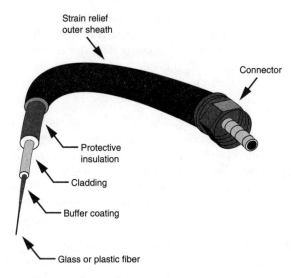

Fig. 5.5 A fiber-optic cable with a typical FDDI connector.

Copper Distributed Data Interface (CDDI). The FDDI specification actually makes provision for two physical-layer Physical Media Dependencies (PMDs). Traditional FDDI operates on a fiber PMD. CDDI, more properly referred to as Twisted-Pair Physical Media Dependent (TP-PMD), is exactly analogous to FDDI, but runs on Category 5 UTP cable rather than fiber.

The high cost of buying and installing fiber-optic cable was the original motivation for the development of TP-PMD. As fiber installation costs have decreased dramatically, the justification for TP-PMD has become more difficult due to other advantages of fiber-optic cable. By its nature, fiber-optic cable doesn't generate electrical interference, nor is it subject to being interfered with. Also, because FDDI is often used to link separate buildings on a campus, the fact that fiber is an electrical insulator allows you to use it without considering issues such as lightning protection and building grounds. Don't consider using TP-PMD in your network.

Asynchronous Transfer Mode (ATM). ATM competes with FDDI for the network backbone. Although it's usually thought of as running at 155mbps on fiber media, ATM hardware is in fact available running at data rates ranging from 1.544mbps T1 through IBM's 25mbps implementation up through the telephone company's OC-48 multigigabitper-second rates and on various media, including fiber-optic cable and unshielded twisted pair. Although ATM to the desktop has from time to time been proposed as a standard, the extremely high cost of ATM adapters and hub ports has limited ATM to use as a network backbone technology.

ATM is defined at the physical and data-link layers of the OSI Reference Model. It's a high-bandwidth, low-latency transmission and switching methodology similar in concept to traditional packet-switching networks. It combines the high efficiency and bandwidth usage of packet-switching networks with the guaranteed bandwidth availability of circuit-switching networks. ATM uses fixed-length 53-byte cells, each of which contains

48 bytes of data and 5 bytes of header information. Fixed cell length reduces processing overhead and simplifies the design and construction of the very high-speed switches required for ATM speeds.

The speed and switching capabilities of ATM were major factors in its selection by the ITU (formerly CCITT) as the methodology of choice for broadband Metropolitan Area Networking. ATM is a demand-priority isochronous technology, and therefore suitable for real-time applications such as voice, video, and multimedia.

Media Access Recommendations

If you have an existing ARCnet, Token Ring, or Ethernet network in place that's adequate for your needs, there's no question—use what you have. All of these are supported by Windows NT Server 4.0, and all will provide at least adequate performance.

If you'll be installing a new network or substantially upgrading and expanding an existing one, give strong consideration to using Ethernet. The performance and expandability constraints of ARCnet make it a strong candidate to be replaced when your network needs to grow. Most firms replacing ARCnet networks choose Ethernet over the newer high-performance ARCnet variants. Similarly, many firms considering large-scale expansions of an existing Token Ring network, particularly one running at 4mbps, find that the limited selection and high cost of 16mbps Token Ring NICs and active network components make it possible to replace the entire Token Ring network with 10BaseT Ethernet and still spend less than they would simply to upgrade the Token Ring network.

Consider installing a new Token Ring network only if you find yourself in one of the following two special situations:

- If your business depends heavily on IBM mainframes and minicomputers, you may find that a Token Ring environment makes sense for you. Even then, you should balance carefully the costs of upgrading your mainframes and minicomputers to Ethernet versus the cost of installing a full Token Ring network for all your PCs.

- If you have real-time process control or numeric control systems that require a deterministic network to offer predictable response times, you may also find that a Token Ring environment makes sense for you. Even then, don't rule out running Token Ring only where required and using Ethernet for the rest of your network.

Consider installing 100BaseT if you're planning a large network. Dual 100/10mbps NICs are standardized and are available now for little more than 10BaseT 10mbps cards. Although 100BaseT hub ports are still quite expensive, you may want to consider installing 100/10mbps-capable cards with the intent of upgrading your hubs and other active network components later as needed.

In the end, most organizations find 10BaseT Ethernet is the way to go. A properly designed Ethernet network offers high performance and reliability, and does so at a price much lower than that of the alternatives. With a properly designed cabling system, Ethernet networks are easily upgradable by replacing hubs and other central components as needed while leaving most of the network, including client NICs, in place. Also,

Ethernet's market dominance ensures that you always have many competing products to choose from. In a competitive market such as Ethernet, manufacturers are constantly improving performance and reliability, and reducing prices.

Designing a Network Cabling System

The importance of cabling to the performance and reliability of your network can't be overstated. The cabling system is to your network what your circulatory system is to your body. Experienced network managers tell you that the majority of problems in most networks are due to cabling and connector problems. A properly designed, installed, documented, and maintained cabling system allows you to avoid these problems and to concentrate on running your network. Craftsmanship is the single most important factor in the reliability of a cabling system.

Another issue addressed by a well-designed and properly documented cabling system is that of maintainability. If your cabling system is a rat's nest, adding a station can turn into an all-day affair as you attempt to locate spare pairs, determine in which equipment closet they terminate, and so forth. By contrast, adding a station on a properly structured cabling system takes only a few minutes. If your company is like most, you probably don't have enough skilled network staff to do all that needs to be done. In terms of time saved, the presence of a good cabling system can be just like having one more full-time staff member.

The question of installing the cabling system yourself versus contracting it out often doesn't receive the attention it deserves. Many companies make the mistake of pricing only the cable and connecting hardware needed to do the job and forgetting that cable installation is a very labor-intensive process. When quotes arrive from the cabling contractors, they're shocked at the price difference between the raw materials cost and the quoted prices, and decide on that basis to do it themselves. For most companies, this is a major mistake. Unless your company is large enough to have staff members dedicated to installing LAN cabling, you should probably contract it out. Don't expect the voice guys in the telecommunications division to install LAN cabling. They don't have the equipment or the experience to do the job properly.

> **Note**
>
> When this chapter was written, professionally installed LAN cabling started at about $50 per run. The price can be much greater, depending on the type of cable required, the number of runs to be made, the difficulty of installation, and so forth. Obviously, you can expect to pay more if you live in New York City than if you live in Winston-Salem.

Having made the decision to contract your LAN cabling out, don't make the mistake of deciding on the installer purely on the basis of price. If you put your cabling contract out to bid, as you should, you'll probably find that most of the low-priced responses come from companies that specialize in business telephone systems. Although these types of contractors may appear to know how to install LAN cabling, many don't.

Probably the best approach to make when deciding on a bid to install cable is to focus on those companies that specialize in installing LAN cabling. When making the final decision, use the following guidelines to help you choose the right cabling company for you.

Network Topologies

You can arrange your cabling in many ways. These are referred to as *topologies*. *Physical topology* describes the way in which the physical components of your cabling are arranged. *Electrical topology* describes the way in which it functions as an electrical circuit. *Logical topology* describes the way in which the system functions as a whole. Physical and logical topologies don't necessarily go hand in hand. It's possible to have a physical topology of one type supporting a logical topology of another. You also can have a hybrid physical topology.

Only three of the many possible physical and logical topologies are commonly used in LAN cabling—the bus, the star, and the ring:

■ *Bus* topology, illustrated by figure 5.6, uses a straight piece of cable to which clients are connected along its length, either directly or by means of drop cables. A bus has two ends, each of which is physically terminated with a resistor of the appropriate value, to prevent signal reflection and standing waves.

The main advantage of a physical bus topology is that it's simple to run and typically uses less cable than any other physical topology. The main disadvantage of a physical bus is that a break anywhere on the cable results in all clients being unable to communicate.

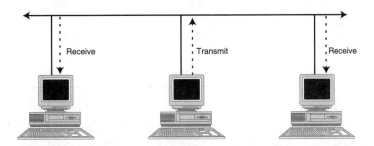

Fig. 5.6 Three PCs connected by a bus, such as 10Base2 Ethernet.

> **Note**
>
> Ethernet runs on a bus topology. The older 10Base5 and 10Base2 Ethernet implementations use a logical bus running on a physical coaxial cable bus. The newer 10BaseT Ethernet implementation uses a logical bus running on a physical UTP cable star. ARCnet also runs on a logical bus. Early ARCnet implementations ran a physical bus on RG-62 coaxial cable. Later ones use a logical bus running on a physical UTP star.

■ *Star* topology uses a central concentrator, or hub, as illustrated by figure 5.7. Each client is connected directly to the hub with a cable to which nothing else is connected. Each end of each cable run in a star is terminated, but this termination is internal at the hub and the client NIC.

The main advantage of a physical star topology is ease of maintainability and troubleshooting. A cable problem affects only the single device to which that cable is connected; isolation problems are easier than on bus topologies. The only real disadvantage of a physical star is that it typically requires somewhat more cable and labor to install, which is a minor issue in the overall scheme of things. The physical star has become the topology of choice for most new network cabling installations.

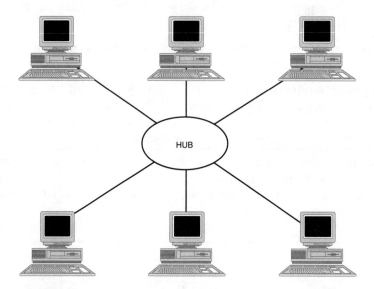

Fig. 5.7   Six PCs connected to a hub in a star network.

> **Note**
>
> 10BaseT Ethernet and newer implementations of ARCnet run a logical bus on a physical star. Token Ring runs a logical ring on a physical star. No common networking method uses a logical star topology.

■ *Ring* topology is simply a bus topology in which the terminators are eliminated and the ends of the cable connect to form a closed ring (see fig. 5.8). In a ring, each device connects to exactly two other devices, forming a closed circle. A physical ring topology shares the advantages and disadvantages of a bus. It requires less cable than the star but, like the bus, is difficult to troubleshoot and is subject to complete failure if a break occurs in the ring.

> **Note**
>
> FDDI runs a logical ring on a physical ring. Token Ring runs a logical ring on a physical star.

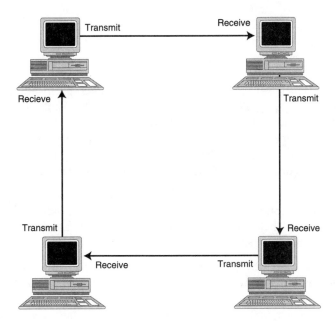

Fig. 5.8   Four PCs connected in a ring network.

Cable Types

Cable is available in thousands of varieties, but only a few of these are suitable for connecting a LAN. You don't need to know everything about cable to install a LAN successfully, but you should know at least the basics. The following sections describe the main types of cable used for LANs, and explain how to select the cable that's most appropriate for your environment.

Coaxial Cable. Coaxial cable, called *coax* for short, is the oldest type of cable used in network installations. It's still in use and is still being installed today. Coax comprises a single central conductor surrounded by a dielectric insulator surrounded by a braided conducting shield (see fig. 5.9). An insulating sheath then covers this assemblage. Coaxial cable is familiar to anyone with cable television.

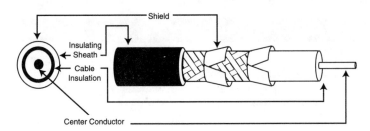

Fig. 5.9   Construction of a doubly shielded coaxial cable.

Coax has a lot going for it. It's a mature technology, is inexpensive, offers high data throughput, and is resistant to electrical interference. These advantages are balanced by a few disadvantages. Coax is difficult to terminate properly and reproducibly. Because coax is typically used in a physical bus topology, many connections are required, increasing the chances of a bad connection taking down the entire network.

The following three types of coax cable are commonly seen in network installations:

■ *Ethernet coax* (Thick Net). The original Ethernet 10Base5 specification uses Ethernet coax. Ethernet coax, usually called Thick Net, is a 50-ohm cable about as big around as your thumb. It's inflexible and therefore difficult to run, and is by far the most expensive type of coax treated in this section, typically costing $1 or more per foot. Connections are made to Thick Net using piercing tap transceivers, whereby an actual hole is drilled through the sheath, shield, and dielectric to reach the center conductor.

Thick Net is most common now as a network backbone in older installations. The sole advantage of Thick Net is that it allows a maximum cabling run of 500 meters. Almost no Thick Net is being installed today.

■ *Ethernet 10Base2 coax* (thinnet). The difficulty and expense of working with Thick Net resulted in the Ethernet 10Base2 specification, which uses RG-58 coax. RG-58 is a 50-ohm cable that's also called *thinnet* or *Cheapernet*. Thinnet is less than a quarter inch in diameter, is flexible (and therefore easy to install), and typically costs 15 cents per foot. Thinnet cables terminate in a barrel nut connector (BNC). A thinnet network is run as a daisy chain, with each client using a T-connector to allow connection of one cable coming in to the client and another going out. The end stations have only a single cable with the other connection terminated.

An Ethernet network running on thinnet has all the advantages of Thick Net, except that maximum cable length is limited to 180 meters. Thinnet cabling is still very commonly found connecting Ethernet clients and is still being installed new today, although there are better alternatives. Thinnet is also used at many sites as a backbone media to connect hubs and other active network components together.

■ *RG-62 coax*. ARCnet networks were originally installed using RG-62 coax. RG-62 is a 93-ohm cable also used to connect some types of IBM mainframe devices. Except for the different impedance and types of devices it's used to connect, RG-62 is similar to Thick Net and thinnet cable. Like them, it must be terminated at each end.

> **Tip**
>
> If the network you're building is very small—fewer than 10 clients all located in close physical proximity—you may be tempted to use thinnet coax to avoid the cost of buying a hub. If you insist on doing so, at least buy premade cables in the appropriate lengths to connect each device rather than try to terminate the coax yourself. For any larger network, don't even consider using coax.

Shielded Twisted-Pair Cable. Shielded twisted-pair (STP) cable comprises insulated wires twisted together to form pairs. These pairs are then twisted with each other and enclosed in a sheath. A foil shield protects the cable against electrical interference. Depending on the type of cable, this shield may lie immediately beneath the sheath, protecting the cable as a whole, or individual pairs may be shielded from other pairs. Figure 5.10 shows the construction of a typical STP cable.

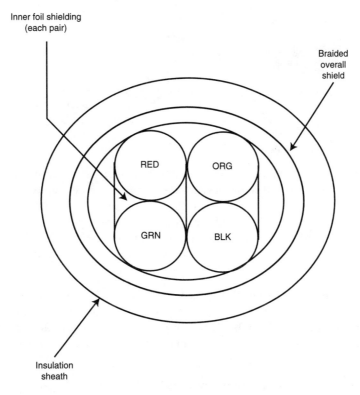

Inner foil shielding
(each pair)

Braided
overall
shield

RED

ORG

GRN

BLK

Insulation
sheath

Fig. 5.10   Construction of a typical shielded twisted-pair cable.

The sole advantage of STP cable relative to UTP cable is the greater resistance of STP cable to electromagnetic interference. STP cable is very expensive, typically costing from two to five times as much as equivalent UTP cable. IBM Token Ring was originally designed to run on STP cable, and that's still about the only place where you're likely to see it installed. Most new Token Ring installations are done using UTP cable. Don't consider using STP cable for your network.

Unshielded Twisted-Pair Cable. Unshielded twisted-pair (UTP) cable dominates network cabling installations today. Like STP cable, UTP cable is constructed from twisted pairs of wire, which are then in turn twisted with each other and enclosed in a sheath (see fig. 5.11). The UTP cable normally used for client cabling includes four such twisted pairs, although UTP cable is available in pair counts ranging from two to more than 1,000. The twist reduces both spurious emissions from the cable and the effects of outside electromagnetic interference on the signal carried by the cable. UTP cable is available in thousands of varieties, differing in pair count, sheath type, signal-carrying capability, and other respects. UTP cable used for network wiring has a nominal impedance of 100 ohms.

Networking

I

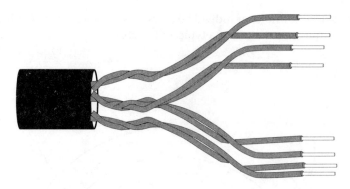

Fig. 5.11   A UTP cable with four pairs.

UTP cable is now the *de facto* and *de jure* standard for new network cabling installations. It's inexpensive, easy to install, supports high data rates, and is reasonably resistant to electrical interference, although less so than the other types of cable discussed here. Typical four-pair UTP cable ranges in price from 3 cents to 50 cents per foot, depending on the signal-carrying capability of the cable and the type of sheath. Don't consider using anything but UTP cable for your network. Even small networks benefit from the advantages of UTP cable.

On casual examination, a piece of UTP cable appears to be a simple item. Nothing is further from the truth. A quick glance at just one manufacturer's catalog reveals hundreds of different types of UTP cable. Only a few of these are appropriate for any given task, and one is probably exactly right. The following sections discuss some of the variables to consider when specifying UTP cable.

Conductor Size. UTP cable is commonly available in 22, 24, and 26 AWG (American Wire Gauge) using either solid or stranded conductors. Although 22 AWG cable has some advantage in terms of the distance a signal can travel without degradation, this is primarily of concern in analog phone systems and is outweighed by the additional cost and other factors for data wiring. Data station cabling should be done using 24 AWG solid conductor cable. Use stranded cable only for patch cords and similar jumpers, in which the flexibility of stranded conductors is needed.

Pair Count. UTP cable is available in pair counts ranging from two to more than a thousand. UTP cable runs made to the client are almost universally four-pair cables. High pair-count cables—25-pair, 50-pair, 100-pair, and greater—are used primarily in voice wiring as riser cables to concentrate station runs and link floors within a building. Pair count is inextricably linked to the signal-carrying capability of the cable, with higher signaling rates being limited to smaller cables.

Until 1994, not even 25-pair cable was available that met the minimal Category 3 data standards. Although such 25-pair cable is now available from AT&T, you should still avoid using riser cables to carry data. When you find yourself wanting a riser cable, it probably means that you should instead install a hub at that location and use fiber or another backbone media to link that hub to the rest of the network.

Sheath Material. You can buy UTP cable, designed for inside wiring, with either general-purpose sheathing or plenum-rated sheathing. The sheath of general-purpose cable is usually constructed of polyvinyl chloride (PVC). PVC sheathing is acceptable for wiring that runs inside conduit or in spaces not used to route HVAC source and return. Plenum cable uses sheathing constructed of Teflon or a similar compound. Its use is mandated by law and by the National Electrical Code (NEC) if the cable is exposed within an HVAC (Heating, Ventilation, and Air Conditioning) plenum. When exposed to flame, PVC sheath produces toxic gases, whereas plenum sheath doesn't.

Unfortunately, plenum sheathing is extremely expensive. The same box of Category 5 cable that costs $130 with PVC sheathing may cost nearly $400 with plenum sheathing.

Don't even think about using PVC cable where you're required by the NEC to use plenum. First, doing so breaks the law. Second, if an inspector finds PVC cable where you should have used plenum, you're required to remove and replace it. Third, if a fatal fire ever does occur at your site, you would hate to wonder for the rest of your life whether your decision to save a few bucks on cable cost someone his life.

Quality Grades. UTP cable varies widely in terms of how fast a signaling rate it supports and over what distance. The terms Type, Level, and Category are used and often misused interchangeably. The IBM Cabling System defines a variety of cables, each of which is designated a *Type*. Underwriters' Laboratories (UL) runs a LAN cabling certification plan that assigns *Level* ratings to various qualities of UTP cabling. The Electronic Industry Association/Telephone Industry Association (EIA/TIA) has a similar program that rates UTP cables by *Category*.

To offer just one example, IBM Type 3 is a UTP cable used in the IBM Cabling System, and is, in fact, the only UTP cable defined within that system. Type 3 cable is intended to carry analog telephone signals and low-speed data traffic—1mbps and 2mbps terminal traffic and 4mbps Token Ring. In terms of electrical characteristics and signal-carrying capability, Type 3 cable corresponds roughly to UL Level 2 cable. The lowest Category assigned by the EIA/TIA system is Category 3, which is substantially superior to Type 3. UL rates cable at levels 1 through 5, with levels 3, 4, and 5 corresponding to the EIA/TIA categories 3, 4, and 5. So although you may hear someone refer to Category 2 cable, no such thing exists.

You can spend a long time learning everything there is to know about UTP cable. Fortunately, you don't need to. The EIA/TIA has developed minimum specifications (categories) for grades of cable appropriate for various uses. All you have to do is pick a cable category that meets your requirements and your budget.

Category 3 cable (Cat 3, for short) is the minimum level you should consider for any new cable installation. Using the standard two pairs of the available four pairs, Cat 3 cable supports data rates as high as 10mbps Ethernet, and can be used over short runs for 16mbps Token Ring. Cat 3 can support the newer 100mbps technologies such as 100BaseT and 100VG–AnyLAN, but only by using all four pairs. Cat 3 typically costs about $60 per 1,000 foot spool in PVC sheathing, and about $125 per spool in plenum sheathing. Cat 3 is used almost exclusively now for voice cabling, with only about 10 percent of new data cabling being done using Cat 3.

> **Note**
>
> Consider very carefully before you decide to install Category 3 cable. Although you can certainly save a few dollars now by installing Cat 3 instead of a higher grade cable, that wire is going to be in your walls for a long time. In five or 10 years, you may rue the decision to install Cat 3. Do so only if your budget is such that using Cat 3 is your only option.

Category 4 (Cat 4) cable is obsolete. Its reason for existing was simply that it was marginally better than Cat 3, allowing 16mbps Token Ring networks to operate over greater distances than are supported on Cat 3. It's now stuck in the middle—not much better than Cat 3 and not much cheaper than Cat 5. Don't consider Category 4 cable for your network.

Category 5 (Cat 5) cable is the cable of choice for most new network installations. Cat 5 cable supports 100mbps data rates using only two pairs, and offers the potential for carrying data at gigabit rates. Cat 5 typically costs about $130 per 1,000 foot spool in PVC sheathing, and about $350 per spool in plenum sheathing. About 80 to 85 percent of all new data cabling installed is done using Cat 5 cable. The huge demand for Cat 5 cable has resulted in the manufacturer of the sheathing material being unable to meet demand, particularly for the plenum variety, so Cat 5 cable can be hard to come by.

For flexibility, some organizations have gone to the extent of specifying Cat 5 cable for all their cabling, including voice. You should specify Cat 5 cable for your network. Because the majority of the cost to run cable is in labor, you'll likely pay only a 10 to 20 percent overall premium to use Cat 5 rather than Cat 3. This additional cost can easily be justified for most organizations by the additional flexibility Cat 5 offers over the 15- to 25-year life of a typical cabling plant.

Fiber-Optic Cable. Fiber-optic cable (usually called *fiber*) has become increasingly common in network installations. Just a few years ago, fiber was an esoteric and expensive technology. Although fiber-optic cable was initially positioned for use as a network backbone, most networks continued to use coax to carry backbone traffic. Fiber itself was expensive, the active components were costly and in short supply, and even something as simple as putting a connector on a fiber-optic cable was a difficult and expensive process. In recent years, large reductions in the cost of the fiber media itself, improvements in the means used to terminate it, and the widespread availability of inexpensive fiber-based active network components have made fiber-optic cable a realistic alternative for use as a network backbone.

Fiber-optic cable offers the highest bandwidth available of any cable type. It has very low signal attenuation, allowing it to carry signals over long distances. The complete absence of crosstalk allows multiple high-bandwidth links to exist within a single sheath. Fiber-optic cable is completely immune to electromagnetic interference and conversely, because it doesn't radiate, is secure against eavesdropping.

Fiber-optic cable is much smaller in diameter and lighter than copper cables capable of carrying the same bandwidth, and is therefore easier to install. Lastly, because many fiber-optic cables have no metallic components, they are electrical insulators and can therefore be used to link buildings without concerns about lightning protection and grounding issues.

Set against all these advantages are a few disadvantages. The installed cost of fiber-optic cable is still somewhat higher than that of copper, and the active network components designed to work with it also cost more. Also, fiber-optic cable is typically more fragile than copper cable, requiring careful attention to bend radii limits and handling requirements during installation.

Structured Cabling Systems

The Electronic Industries Association and Telephone Industries Association (EIA/TIA) recognized the need for a truly standards-based wiring specification. In cooperation with IBM, AT&T, DEC, and other vendors, the EIA/TIA developed the EIA/TIA 568 Commercial Building Telecommunications Wiring Standard. This specification incorporated the best features of each competing standard to develop a composite standard that supported any vendor's equipment and at the same time ensured backward compatibility with existing cabling systems installed using the propriety cabling standards of each participating vendor. The vendors, in turn, updated their own specifications to full compliance with EIA/TIA 568. As a result, you can buy a cabling system from many vendors with the assurance that, as long as it's EIA/TIA 568 compliant, it will support any industry-standard networking scheme.

If you buy an installed cabling system, you should specify full compliance with both the EIA/TIA 568 Wiring Standard and the EIA/TIA 569 Pathways and Spaces Standard. If you design and install the cabling system yourself, you should pay close attention to the provisions of both the EIA/TIA 568 and 569 specifications, even if you don't intend your cabling system to achieve full compliance.

Both of these specifications can be purchased from Global Engineering Documents at 800-854-7179. Order these documents if you plan to design and install the cabling system yourself. If you intend to contract the installation, you probably don't need to buy the documents.

Cabling System Recommendations

Whether your cabling system needs to support five clients in a small office or 500 clients in a multibuilding campus, you should adhere to several guidelines to ensure that your cabling system provides the service that you expect:

- Design and install your cabling system in full compliance with the EIA/TIA 568 Commercial Building Telecommunications Wiring Standard, using a star topology running on UTP cable. To the extent that your floor plan allows, adhere closely to the EIA/TIA 569 Pathways and Spaces Standard.

- Pay careful attention to the quality of even the smallest components used. Just as a chain is no stronger than its weakest link, your cabling system is no better than the quality of the worst component that's a part of it. Good installations are often spoiled by using substandard small components. Don't scrimp on patch cords and drop cables.

■ Have your cabling installed by LAN cabling specialists. Using the highest quality components means nothing if the craftsmanship of the installer isn't up to par. Use the expertise of your cabling vendor.

■ Install new voice cabling at the same time you're cabling for data. It's a great temptation to make do with existing voice cabling, but you may find that the advantages of having a single integrated cabling system more than make up for the small additional cost.

■ Install Category 5 cable exclusively for data, and install lots of it. Install at least Category 3 cables for voice, and consider carefully using Category 5 for voice as well as data. Make sure that you specify different color cable sheaths for voice and data runs. Consider the EIA/TIA 568 requirement for two runs to each office to be an absolute minimum. Run a voice cable, a data cable, and a spare cable to each wall box, and leave the spare cable unterminated, with sufficient slack on each end to allow you to terminate later as needed. Consider putting three such cable runs into wall boxes on at least two walls of each office. You'll bless your foresight in the coming years.

■ Make absolutely certain that your cable installer fully documents the cabling system, from every conductor to every single cable installed. Horizontal cables, riser cables, and punchdown blocks should be numbered and pin assignments provided. You should be able to trace any conductor from the wall jack through punchdown blocks and patch panels to the final termination. If your cabling plant is large, consider buying a cable management software package to record this information initially and then keep up-to-date with changes and additions to the cabling. Assign one person the responsibility for making changes to the cabling plant, and then make it known that making physical changes to the cabling system without recording them is a serious offense.

Designing for Expandability and Ease of Maintenance

The first principle here is to overwire your station runs. It costs just a little more to run two cables than it does to run only one. If you have a location that you're absolutely positive never needs more than one cable run, go ahead and run a spare anyway, leaving the spare unterminated with enough slack on both ends for future use. Although you may end up with several $10 pieces of cable left unused in the wall for eternity, the first time you need one of those cable runs will more than pay for every extra run you made. Don't scrimp on cable runs. They're cheap and easy to make when the cabling system is being installed. They're expensive and difficult or impossible to make later on.

The second principle is to overwire your backbone and riser runs. If a 25-pair riser does the job now, put in a 50-pair or even a 100-pair riser. If a six-fiber cable carries your present traffic, install a 12-fiber cable instead. The cable itself is cheap. What costs money is labor, and most of the labor is spent terminating the cable. By installing more pairs than you need and leaving them unterminated, you have the best of both worlds. Having the extra pairs in place costs next to nothing, but they are there and can be terminated if and when you need them.

The third principle is to pay close attention to the physical environment of your wiring closets and equipment rooms. Nothing is more miserable than trying to maintain a cabling system in an overheated or freezing closet while holding a flashlight in your teeth. Make sure that your wiring closets and equipment rooms are well-lighted, properly ventilated, and provided with more electrical receptacles than you think you'll ever need. Your equipment will be much happier, and so will you when you need to make changes to the cabling.

Selecting Active Network Components

If the cabling system is the arteries and veins of your network, the active network components are its heart. By itself, the cabling system is just dead wire. Active network components bring that wire to life, putting data on it and allowing the various parts of your network to communicate with each other.

If you remember only one thing from this section, make it this: The single most important factor in choosing active network components is to *maintain consistency*. Having chosen one manufacturer as your supplier, it's easy to be seduced by another manufacturer's component that's a bit cheaper or has a nice feature or better specifications. Don't fall into this trap. You'll pay the price later in dollars, time, and aggravation when you find that you can't solve a problem related to the interaction of the two manufacturers' components because neither will take responsibility, or that you have to buy a second $5,000 network management software package because neither manufacturer's management software will work with the other's product.

Network Interface Cards

A network interface card, commonly referred to as a NIC, is used to connect each device on the network to the network cabling system. NICs operate at the physical and data-link layers of the OSI Reference Model. At the physical layer, a NIC provides the physical and electrical connection required to access the network cabling and to use the cabling to convey data as a bit stream. At the data-link layer, the NIC provides the processing that assembles and disassembles the bit stream on the cable into frames suitable for the media access method in use. Every device connected to the network must be equipped with a network interface, either by means of a peripheral NIC or by means of similar circuitry built directly into the component.

A NIC is media-dependent, media-access-method-dependent, and protocol-independent. *Media-dependent* means that the NIC must have a physical connector appropriate for the cabling system to which it's to be connected. *Media-access-method-dependent* means that even a card that can be physically connected to the cabling system must also be of a type that supports the media access method in use. For example, an Ethernet card designed for UTP cable can be connected to but doesn't function on a Token Ring network wired with UTP cable. *Protocol-independent* means that a particular NIC, assuming that appropriate drivers are available for it, can communicate using a variety of higher-level protocols, either individually or simultaneously. For example, an Ethernet NIC can be used to connect a client simultaneously to a LAN server running IPX/SPX and to a UNIX host running TCP/IP.

It's common in the industry to differentiate between NICs intended for use in clients and those intended for use in servers. Conventional wisdom says that inexpensive NICs are fine for use in a client where performance is less of an issue, but that for your server you should buy the highest-performance NIC you can afford. In fact, although you can use any NIC in any computer system it fits (client or server), you should pay close attention to selecting NICs for both your clients and your servers. Installing high-performance NICs in your server and using low-performance NICs in your clients is actually counter-productive. In this situation, because the server NIC can deliver data so much faster than the client NIC can accept it, the network is flooded with retransmissions requested by the client NIC. These constant retransmissions greatly degrade network performance. The solution is simple. Balance the performance of the NICs you use in your clients with the performance provided by the server NIC.

The following sections provide guidance on choosing the right NIC for clients and servers.

NIC Bus Types for Client PCs. The first consideration in choosing a client NIC is the client's bus type. There are two schools of thought on this issue:

- You should install a NIC that uses the highest performance bus provided by that client. For example, if the client has both ISA and VLB slots, choosing a VLB NIC rather than an ISA NIC will result in better performance.

- The advantages of standardization outweigh the incremental performance benefits of matching the card to the client. Members of this school of thought, faced with a mixed client environment of ISA, PCI, and VLB systems, would choose ISA NICs for all clients.

There's something to be said for each of these positions, but, on balance, standardizing on ISA NICs for 10mbps clients usually makes sense. Clients using 100BaseT NICs, however, are likely to have PCI buses; thus, you're likely to need to support both ISA and PCI NICs.

> **Caution**
>
> For clients running Windows NT Workstation 4.0, make sure that your server NIC is listed on the Windows NT Hardware Compatibility List (HCL) described later in the "Conformance to the Microsoft Windows NT Hardware Compatibility List" section.

Software-Configurable or Jumper-Configurable NICs. A NIC has various settings that usually need adjustment before you can use the card. Nearly all cards are configurable for IRQ. Many require setting DMA, base address, and media type. All ARCnet cards and some Token Ring cards allow the network address to be set by the user.

One important factor that contributes to the usability of a NIC is whether these settings are made using physical jumpers or by using a software utility. A card that requires setting physical jumpers is inconvenient. Making a change involves disassembling the computer, removing the card, setting the jumpers, and then putting everything back together. It's often necessary to go through this process just to examine how the card is now set. A software configurable card, on the other hand, can be both examined and set simply by running a program. Fortunately, most cards shipping today are configurable with software. Don't consider buying one that isn't.

Remote Boot Clients. Some NICs support remote boot. *Remote-boot* capability simply means that the NIC itself contains all the files needed to boot the client and connect it to the network. These files are generated by the network administrator and stored on a ROM chip installed on the NIC.

Several years ago, diskless workstations had a brief vogue based on a two-fold justification:

- *The lower cost of clients not equipped with hard disks and floppy drives.* This issue has faded in importance with the plummeting cost of drives, as well as the emergence of Microsoft Windows as a corporate standard and the desirability of using a local hard disk to host Windows swap files.

- *Security.* A client that has no drives protects against theft of company data by making it impossible for a dishonest employee to copy information to a floppy disk. It also makes protecting the network against viruses much easier. Because client users can't boot their computers or run programs from a floppy disk, this potential source of infection is removed and only the server must be protected.

Note

The Network Computer (NC), proposed by Larry Ellison of Oracle Corp. and other competitors of Microsoft, is similar in concept to a diskless workstation. The NC contains sufficient software in read-only memory (ROM) to boot the operating system and connect to a TCP/IP network. NCs download applications, such as a Web browser, from the network and run the applications in RAM. There's no reason, however, that an NC can't be designed to boot from the network.

Name-Brand NICs vs. Clone NICs. The best reason to pay the premium for a name-brand NIC is that part of that premium goes to pay for better quality control and reliability. In working with thousands of name-brand and clone NICs over the years, many experienced network administrators seldom see name-brand NICs that were damaged out of the box, and almost never experience a failure of a name-brand NIC that wasn't due to some easily explained problem such as a lightning strike. The choice is yours, but most LAN administrators recognize that the relatively small amount of money saved by buying clone NICs can be rapidly swamped by the costs of just one network failure attributable to using cheap cards.

Server NICs. All the same factors that apply to choosing client NICs also apply to choosing server NICs, with a few more. Whereas a client NIC is responsible for handling only the traffic of its own client, a server NIC must process traffic from many clients in rapid sequence. Doing so demands a high-speed link to the I/O system of the server. Accordingly, NICs intended for use in servers are universally designed to use a high-speed bus connection.

Until recently, the requirement for speed meant that server NICs were either EISA or MCA cards. The advent of PCI, which transfers 4 bytes at a time on a 33 MHz mezzanine bus for a total throughput of 132mbps, has made both EISA and MCA obsolete. The pending extension of PCI to 64 bits will allow it to transfer 8 bytes at a time, doubling throughput to 264mbps. All newly designed servers are PCI-based. If they offer EISA or MCA slots, it's only for compatibility with legacy expansion cards. Even IBM, the originator and long the sole champion of MCA, has begun offering PCI-based servers.

Another factor that's of little concern in client NICs, but more important in server NICs, is that of processor usage. All NICs require some assistance from the system processor, but a properly designed server NIC should minimize this dependence. This issue is of particular concern with 100BaseT server NICs. In some cases, for instance, one server equipped with four such NICs may lose more than 50 percent of the processor just in handling the overhead for the NICs. Find out what level of processor usage your proposed server NICs require, and favor those with low usage.

Deciding which NIC to install in your server is straightforward. If you have a PCI server (as recommended in the later section "Choosing a Bus Type"), install a name-brand PCI NIC. In choosing the brand of NIC, simplify global network management issues by giving first preference to a card made by the manufacturer of your other active network components. Alternatively, choose a card made by the server manufacturer to simplify server management.

> **Caution**
>
> Make sure that your server NIC is listed on the Windows NT Hardware Compatibility List (HCL) described later in the "Conformance to the Microsoft Windows NT Hardware Compatibility List" section.

One of the most valuable pieces of real estate in your network is a server expansion slot. Even though a typical server has many more slots than a client, the competition for these slots is intense. Multiport NICs combine the function of more than one NIC onto a single card. They're available in dual- and quad-NIC versions from a variety of suppliers. If your LAN runs Ethernet, and if you segment it, consider carefully how many server slots you have available and whether you should buy a dual-port or quad-port NIC.

Repeaters

Repeaters are used to clean up, amplify, and rebroadcast a signal, extending the distance that the signal can be run reliably on a particular type of cable. They function exclusively at the physical layer of the OSI Reference Model. Repeaters are media-dependent and protocol-independent. As purely electrical devices, repeaters are unaware of the content of the signals that they process. They simply regenerate the signal and pass it on. Figure 5.12 illustrates, in the context of the OSI Model, a repeater between two network segments.

Local repeaters are used to extend signaling distance within the confines of a LAN. Remote repeaters are used to extend a LAN segment, often by means of fiber-optic cable, to a remote location without requiring installation of a bridge or router. The clients at the remote site appear logically to be on the same local segment as that to which the remote repeater is attached.

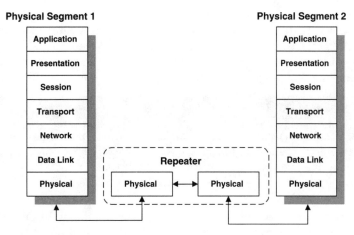

Fig. 5.12 Connecting two network segments with a repeater.

Hubs, bridges, routers, gateways, and all other active network components include basic repeater functionality. Use stand-alone local repeaters as needed to manage cable length limitations within your network, or to extend your LAN to remote locations that don't justify installation of a bridge or router.

Simple Hubs

Hubs are used as concentrators to join multiple clients with a single link to the rest of the LAN. A hub has several ports to which clients are connected directly, and one or more ports that can be used in turn to connect the hub to the backbone or to other active network components.

A hub functions as a multiport repeater. Signals received on any port are immediately retransmitted to all other ports on the hub. Hubs function at the physical layer of the OSI Reference Model. They're media-dependent and protocol-independent. Hubs come in a wide variety of sizes, types, and price ranges.

Stand-Alone Hubs. Stand-alone hubs are simple and inexpensive devices, intended primarily to serve a self-contained workgroup in which the server is connected to one port and the clients to other ports, and no interconnection to a larger network exists. They range in size from four to 24 ports. Depending on port count, stand-alone hubs vary from about the size of a modem to about the size of a pizza box. They normally operate on low voltage supplied by a power brick similar to that used to power external modems and consume little power.

Stand-alone hubs offer little or no expandability. This isn't usually a problem because these hubs are inexpensive and can simply be purchased in a size appropriate for your needs. Stand-alone hubs usually offer no provision for management, although high-end stand-alone hubs may have management features standard or as an option. Manageability—the ability to control the hub from a remote management station—isn't normally a major issue in the small workgroup environment for which these hubs are intended.

A typical name-brand, eight-port, stand-alone, unmanaged hub has a street price of less than $200, or less than $25 per port. Hubs with higher port counts may cost somewhat more on a per-port basis. Hubs that include management features may approach $100 per port. If your network comprises only a few clients that are all located in close proximity, a stand-alone hub is an excellent and inexpensive way to connect these systems.

> **Tip**
>
> Make sure that any stand-alone hub you buy has *jabber protection*. This feature monitors each port for constant uncontrolled transmission that will flood the network. If this condition is detected, jabber protection temporarily shuts down the offending port while allowing the remainder of the ports to continue functioning.

Stackable Hubs. Stackable hubs are a fairly recent development. In the past, you had to choose between a stand-alone hub, which provided little functionality but at a low price, and an enterprise hub—also called a *chassis hub*—which provided enterprise-level functionality but at a very high cost. Stackable hubs do a good job of blending the best characteristics of both other types of hub. They offer much of the expandability and management capabilities of enterprise hubs at not much greater cost than stand-alone hubs.

What distinguishes a true stackable hub is that it possesses a backplane used to link it directly to a similar hub or hubs, melding the assembled stack into a single hub running a single Ethernet bus. Although stand-alone hubs can be physically stacked and joined simply by connecting a port on one to a port on the next, the result isn't a true stack. To understand why, you need to understand that Ethernet places a limit on the maximum number of repeaters that are allowed to separate any two stations. A device connected to any port of any hub in a stack of stackable hubs is connected directly to the single bus represented by that stack. As a result, any two devices connected to that stack can communicate while going through only the one repeater represented by that stack. The *stack* of stand-alone hubs, on the other hand, results in two stations connected to different hubs within that stack going through at least two repeaters to communicate.

Stackable hubs are commonly available in 12-port and 24-port versions. Some manufacturers also offer 48-port versions. The street price of stackable hubs ranges from about $75 to $250 per port, depending on port density and what, if any, management options are installed. For most organizations, these hubs offer the best combination of price, features, and expandability available.

Hub Manageability. Manageability is another consideration in choosing stand-alone or stackable hubs. This is simply a hub's capability to be configured and monitored from a remote client running specialized software. Although protocols such as Simple Network Management Protocol (SNMP) and Remote Monitoring (RMON) are standardized, their implementations aren't. This means that it's unlikely that you'll be able to manage one manufacturer's hub with remote software intended for use with another manufacturer's hub. (This is yet another reason to stick with one manufacturer for your active network components.)

Although hub manufacturers attempt to represent *dumb* or unmanaged hubs as a separate category from *smart* or manageable hubs, the reality is that manageability is just one more feature that may be standard, optional, or unavailable on a particular hub. Most low-end stand-alone hubs aren't manageable and can't be upgraded. High-end stand-alone hubs and most stackable hubs either come with management standard, or at least offer it as an option. Unless yours is a very small network, you should buy manageable hubs, or at least ones that can be upgraded to manageability.

Bridges

Bridges are used to divide a network into mutually isolated segments while maintaining the whole as a single network. Bridges operate at the data-link layer of the ISO Reference Model (see fig. 5.13). They work with frames, which are organized assemblages of data rather than the raw bit stream on which hubs, repeaters, and other physical-layer devices operate.

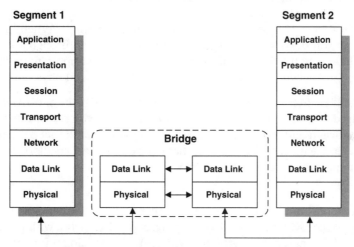

Fig. 5.13 Connecting two network segments with a bridge.

Bridges are media-dependent. A bridge designed to connect to UTP cabling can't connect to a coax cable, and vice versa. Bridges are protocol-independent above the data-link layer. It doesn't matter to an Ethernet frame or to the bridge that directs it whether that frame encapsulates an IP packet, an IPX packet, or some other type of packet at the logical level. A bridge simply sees that the frame originated from a particular hardware address and needs to be sent to another hardware address.

Frames include, in addition to the raw data itself, a header that identifies the address of the source station and the address of the destination station. Frames use physical rather than logical addresses. When a client transmits an Ethernet frame to the server, the source address is the MAC or hardware address of the client's Ethernet card, and the destination address is the MAC address of the Ethernet card in the server.

A bridge divides a single network cable into two or more physical and logical segments. The bridge listens to all traffic on all segments and examines the destination hardware address of each frame. If the source and destination hardware addresses are located on the same segment, the bridge simply discards that frame because the destination can hear the source directly. If the source and destination addresses are located on different segments, the bridge repeats the frame onto the segment where the destination address is located. Traffic with both source and destination addresses on the same segment is kept local to that segment and isn't heard by the rest of the network. Only traffic whose source and destination addresses are on different segments is broadcast to the network as a whole.

When used properly, bridges can significantly reduce the total volume of traffic on the network. This is particularly important on Ethernet networks, because as the network grows and the traffic volume increases, collisions become more frequent and the overall performance of the network degrades.

Another important characteristic of bridges is that they negate the impact of repeaters. Ethernet allows a maximum of four repeaters to intervene between the source and destination stations. By using a bridge, a frame on the source segment may pass through as many as the legal limit of four repeaters before reaching the bridge. When the bridge places that frame on the destination segment, it may again pass through as many as four repeaters on its way to the destination station. This can be an important design consideration in Ethernet networks, particularly those that are large and physically widespread.

Defined in the IEEE 802.1 specification, the Spanning Tree Algorithm (STA) detects loops within a bridged network. STA allows a bridge to determine which available alternative path is most efficient and to forward frames via that path. Should that path become unavailable, a bridge using STA can detect that failure and select an alternate path to prevent communications from being severed.

Routers

Routers are used to connect one network to another network. Routers operate at the network layer of the ISO Reference Model (see fig. 5.14). They work with packets, which are composed of a frame encapsulated and with logical addressing information added.

Routers are similar to bridges but are media-independent. A router designed to process IP packets can do so whether it's physically connected to UTP cabling or to a coax cable. Routers are protocol-dependent above the data-link layer. A router designed to process IP packets can't process IPX packets and vice versa, although multiprotocol routers do exist that are designed to process more than one type of network-layer packet.

Packets are encapsulated within a data-link layer frame. Packets include a header, which identifies the addresses of the source station and the destination station. Packets use logical rather than physical addresses. Unlike bridges, which require the source and destination address to be on the same network, router addressing allows the destination address to be on a different network than the source address.

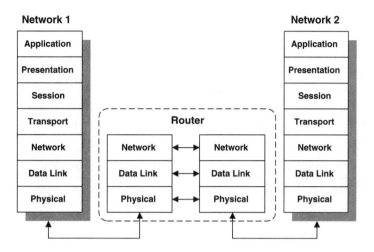

Fig. 5.14   Connecting two network segments with a router.

Routers are much more complex than bridges and are accordingly more expensive and require more configuration. A bridge makes a simple decision. If the destination address is on the same segment as the source address, it discards the frame. If the two addresses are on different segments, it repeats the frame. A router, on the other hand, must make a complex decision about how to deliver a particular packet to a distant network. A router may have to choose the best available route from a variety of alternatives.

Routers work with the logical addressing information contained in network-layer packets, and not all upper-layer protocols provide this information. Windows NT Server includes native support for TCP/IP, IPX/SPX, and NetBEUI. TCP/IP and IPX/SPX packets include the network-layer logical addresses needed by routers and are referred to as *routed* or *routable* protocols. NetBEUI packets don't include this network-layer information, and accordingly are referred to as *non-routed* or *non-routable*. This means that if you're using TCP/IP or IPX/SPX transport, you have the choice of designing your network around bridges, routers, or both. If instead you're using NetBEUI, bridging is your only alternative, because routers can't handle NetBEUI packets.

Routing vs. Bridging

A great deal of confusion exists about the differences between bridges and routers and about when the use of each is appropriate. This confusion is increased by the availability of *brouters*, which simply combine the functions of bridges and routers.

The differences between routers and bridges are the differences between a single network and an internetwork. A group of connected devices that share a single common network layer address are defined as a single network. Bridges are used to join segments within a single network. Routers are used to join separate networks.

Bridges function at the data-link layer and work with hardware addresses, which provide no information about the geographical location of the device. Routers function at the network-layer and work with logical addresses, which can be mapped to geographical locations.

Gateways

A gateway is used to translate between incompatible protocols, and can function at any one layer of the OSI Reference Model, or at several layers simultaneously (see fig. 5.15). Gateways are most commonly used at the upper three layers of the OSI Model. For example, if you have some users using the Simple Mail Transfer Protocol (SMTP) for e-mail and others using the Message Handling System (MHS) protocol, a gateway can be used to translate between these two protocols so that all users can exchange e-mail.

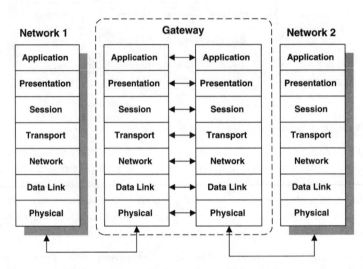

Fig. 5.15   Connecting two networks using dissimilar protocols with a gateway.

Because of the work they must do to translate between fundamentally incompatible protocols, gateways are usually very processor-intensive and therefore run relatively slowly. In particular, using a gateway to translate transport protocols, such as TCP/IP to and from IPX/SPX, usually creates a bottleneck. Use a gateway only if it's the only solution available, and then only on an interim basis while you migrate to common shared protocols. Gateways typically are difficult to install and maintain, and the translations they provide are often imperfect at best, particularly at the upper ISO layers.

Note

The Internet community uses the term *gateway* to refer to a *router*.

Enterprise Hubs, Collapsed Backbones, Ethernet Switches, and Virtual LANs

Simple networks use hubs, bridges, and routers as building blocks. As networks become larger and more complex, performance and manageability requirements often make it necessary to make fundamental changes to the network architecture. The following sections describe how you can use enterprise hubs, collapsed backbones, Ethernet switches, and virtual LANs to accommodate the demands of large and complex networks.

Enterprise Hubs. Enterprise hubs are in fact more than hubs. These devices are based on a wall-mounted or rack-mounted chassis that provides two or more passive backplanes into which feature cards are inserted to provide the exact functionality needed (see fig. 5.16). Cards are available to provide hubs for Ethernet, Token Ring, FDDI, and ATM networks. Other cards can be installed to provide routing, bridging, gateway, management, and other functions.

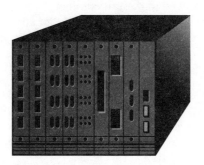

Fig. 5.16   A typical enterprise hub with plug-in cards.

An enterprise hub is something you buy only if you have to. The unpopulated chassis alone can cost more than $10,000. The cards used to populate an enterprise hub are likewise expensive, both in absolute terms and on a per-port basis. Why, then, would anyone buy an enterprise hub instead of a pile of stackables? For three reasons: to establish a collapsed backbone, to implement Ethernet switching, and to build a virtual LAN.

Collapsed Backbones. Collapsing the backbone simply means to move all active network components into a single physical cabinet and then to link them by using a very high-speed bus. Rather than locate hubs and other active network components in equipment rooms near the clients, these components are reduced to cards contained in a single chassis sited centrally. This scheme has certain perceived advantages both in terms of management and in terms of implementing technologies such as switching and virtual LANs.

Ethernet Switches. To understand Ethernet switches, you need to understand the progression in hub design and functionality from simple stand-alone hubs and stackables to the modern full-featured enterprise hub:

- Stand-alone hubs are simple repeaters. All devices connected to any port on a stand-alone hub are connected to the single segment represented by that hub.

- At the entry level, enterprise hubs and a few stackables provide a backplane that supports multiple segments. Each hub card is, in effect, a stand-alone hub operating on its own segment. A station's segment is determined by which physical hub card it's connected to. Using multiple hub cards segments traffic, but does nothing to interconnect the separate segments. Moving traffic between two or more of these segments requires a bridge or router.

■ At the next step up, an enterprise hub replaces physical assignment of ports to segments with a switched matrix, which allows logical assignment of any port to any segment. This is a static rather than dynamic assignment. A port is assigned to a particular segment until the network manager intervenes to change the assignment. At this level, the enterprise hub still provides no interconnectivity between ports located on different segments. The only real difference between this arrangement and the one described in the preceding bullet point is that you can change port assignments programmatically rather than go out and physically move a jumper cord. Adding a management card to the chassis provides the capability to make these changes programmatically. This is the level at which many installed enterprise hubs are working.

■ The next logical step is to provide self-contained bridging and routing functions within the enterprise hub. This is accomplished by adding a card or cards to the chassis to provide these connectivity functions—in effect combining your hubs, bridges, and routers into a single box. Many installed enterprise hubs and nearly all newly purchased ones function at this level.

■ The final step in the evolution of the hub is to provide a switching backplane, which can connect any port to any other port dynamically and under control of the hub itself. Rather than link a port to a segment, the hub links a port directly to another port via building up and tearing down (as needed) dedicated logical channels on its high-speed backplane—in effect assigning each port to its own segment. It's at this level that your enterprise hub essentially becomes a switch.

The single characteristic that distinguishes a hub from a switch is that, on the hub, all traffic generated by any port is repeated and heard by all other ports on the hub, while a switch instead establishes virtual circuits that connect the two ports directly (see fig. 5.17). Traffic on this virtual circuit can't be heard by ports not a part of the virtual circuit. In essence, the hub resembles a CB radio conversation, whereas the switch resembles a telephone conversation. To look at it another way, each device attached to a switch port is to all intents and purposes connected to its own dedicated bridge or router port.

Switches use one or both of two methods to process traffic. *Store-and-forward* processing receives and buffers the entire inbound frame before processing it, whereas *cut-through* begins processing the inbound frame as soon as enough of it has arrived to provide the destination address. A cut-through switch therefore never has possession of the entire frame at any one time. The advantage of cut-through is raw speed and increased throughput. The advantage of store-and-forward is that because the entire frame is available at once, the switch can perform error checking, enhanced filtering, and other processing on the frame. Both methods are used successfully and, in fact, many switches incorporate elements of both types of processing.

The first and most common type of switch is the segment switch, which is conceptually similar to a bridge or a router. Functioning as a switched learning bridge, the segment switch provides basic filtering and forwarding between multiple segments.

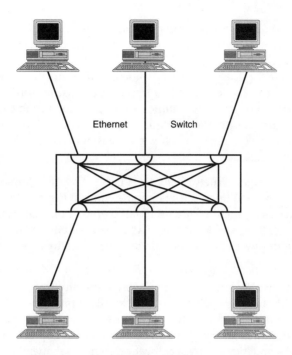

Fig. 5.17   Traffic between six PCs with a switched Ethernet hub.

The next step up in switches is the private LAN switch, in which each port can connect to any other port via a dedicated virtual segment built up and torn down as needed by the switch itself. As long as the software is properly written and the backplane has sufficient cumulative bandwidth, every pair of ports can, in theory, communicate with each other at full network bandwidth without contention or collision. In practice, of course, some ports (such as servers) are more popular than others, so the theoretical cumulative throughput of any switch can never be reached. A private LAN switch simply extends the concept of bridging multiple segments to reduce traffic to its ultimate conclusion of providing each device with its own segment.

You also can add routing functionality to a switch. The switches discussed previously filter and forward frames and otherwise function as bridges at the data-link layer of the OSI Reference Model. Routing switches extend this functionality to working with the network layer of the OSI Model. The level of routing functionality varies by manufacturer and model, from those on the low end (which provide barrier routing) to those on the high end (which essentially provide each device with a dedicated router port). Routing switches are expensive components, and as the level of routing functionality increases, so does the price.

Virtual LANs. Switching is itself the logical conclusion of the use of segmenting to reduce traffic. However, reducing traffic to the extent that a particular frame or packet is received only by the designated port raises a fundamental problem.

Until now, the discussion has focused only on user traffic, those frames and packets that contain user data. There is, however, another type of traffic on a LAN. Overhead or administrative traffic comprises frames and packets used by the network to maintain itself. Novell servers generate Service Advertising Protocol (SAP) traffic to inform all devices on the LAN of the services available from that server. Routers use Routing Information Protocol (RIP) and other protocols to communicate routing information to each other. All of this administrative traffic is essential. Without it, the LAN doesn't run. For switching to reach its ultimate utility, you must somehow ensure that this overhead traffic is heard by all devices that need to hear it.

The solution to this problem is the *virtual LAN* (VLAN). A VLAN allows any arbitrary group of ports to be clustered under programmatic control. Just as all the users attached to a traditional Ethernet segment hear all the traffic present on that segment, all the users on a VLAN hear all the traffic on the VLAN. The difference is that VLAN users can be located on different physical networks and scattered broadly geographically.

With a traditional hub, the physical port into which a client is connected determines which network that client belongs to. With a switch, the physical port no longer determines which network the client belongs to, but the client must still belong to a network physically located on that switch. With a VLAN, any client plugged into any port located on any switch can be logically configured to be a member of any network. This feature of VLANs breaks the dependency of physical location to network membership, allowing users to be relocated anywhere within the internetwork and still remain a member of the same network.

Some of the building blocks of VLAN technology have been around for several years, but the technology as a whole hasn't yet been fully implemented. The high cost of fast data links has also contributed to the slow adoption of VLANs. As the technology continues to mature and the cost of high-speed data links continues to drop, VLANs will become an increasingly common part of the network landscape.

Summary Recommendations for Active Network Components

The following list summarizes the recommendations for active network components discussed in the preceding sections, with additional suggestions for power conditioning and spares:

- Scale the infrastructure to your needs, keeping in mind that most networks grow. In a typical network, installed components should have at least 25 percent of their capacity unused, and should be easily expandable to at least 100 percent additional capacity. If your initial configuration puts you at or near capacity on a particular component, install the next level up.

- Choose one manufacturer for your active network components and then buy all the components you can from that one manufacturer. Standardize as much as possible, even to the extent of using the same model within the manufacturer's line when possible.

- Consider purchasing only manageable components, or those that can be upgraded to manageability. If your entire network can run from only one hub and is likely to remain small, you can safely avoid the extra expense of manageability. Otherwise, look to the future.

- Understand fully the differences between bridges and routers and use them appropriately to control network traffic.

- Provide a standby uninterruptible power supply (UPS) in each equipment room and make sure that each active network component is connected to the UPS. UPSs are the subject of the later section "Uninterruptable Power Supplies and Power Protection."

- Provide full lightning protection to supplement that provided by the UPS. Protect all wires connected to the network, including AC power, telephone lines, and leased lines. Ideally, you should provide such protection for each client as well. If you don't do so, at least protect key active network components such as bridges, routers, and servers by installing data line protectors.

- Purchase standby spares for critical network components. Even if your system is under a maintenance contract, having a spare hub available can make the difference between being down for 15 minutes and being down for a day.

Specifying Server Hardware

The most important computer on your network is the server. The server runs Windows NT Server software to provide shared access to programs, data files, and printers. On many Windows NT Server networks, programs actually run centrally on the server itself. For small networks, the server represents the majority of the cost of the network. On larger networks, the cost of the server becomes a correspondingly smaller part of the total cost, but the server is no less important for this fact.

Many Windows NT Server installations use a standard PC with upgraded memory and disk storage as their server. Others are designed around a true purpose-built server. Although using an upgraded PC as a server can be viable for a very small network, purpose-built servers have many advantages in architecture, performance, and redundancy features. Using a purpose-built server benefits any network, and should be considered mandatory if your network will have more than a handful of users.

Installing a standard PC system board in a tower case with a lot of RAM and some large high-performance SCSI disk drives doesn't make a server. Many mail-order vendors have done just this and represent the result as a true server. The system may even be certified by Microsoft to run Windows NT Server 4.0. Think twice before choosing such a system as your server. Look instead at servers from the large, well-established computer companies offering on-site maintenance performed by locally resident technicians. You'll find that such systems may cost a bit more than servers from mail-order PC companies, but purpose-built servers offer a host of advantages in performance, reliability, and maintainability.

General Types of Servers

For convenience and marketing reasons as much as anything else, true servers are usually classified by the size of network they're intended to support. There's a great deal of overlap in these categories, and a fully configured entry-level server may, in fact, exceed a minimally configured mid-range server in both price and capability.

Workgroup Servers. *Workgroup servers* are the entry-level server. These servers are designed to support up to 25 or so users running primarily file and print sharing, but can function as light-duty application servers as well. Workgroup servers cost little more than an equivalently configured PC, running from about $4,000 on the low end to perhaps $8,000 or $9,000 when fully expanded. They're usually based on a single Pentium processor and usually can't be upgraded to multiple processors. Disk arrays and Error Checking and Correcting (ECC) memory are optional items, if they're offered at all. Workgroup servers are usually built in a mini- or mid-tower case, although some use a full-tower case. Examples of this class of server are the Compaq ProSignia 300 and ProLiant 1000, the DEC Prioris LX, the Hewlett-Packard NetServer LC/LF lines, and the IBM PC Server 320.

Departmental Servers. Departmental servers are the mid-range servers, supporting from 20 to 150 users. These servers can do double duty as both file and print servers, and as moderate-duty application servers. The price of departmental servers ranges from about $15,000 on the low end to perhaps $40,000 on the high. At this level, disk arrays, ECC memory, and redundant power supplies are often standard equipment, or are at least available as options. Departmental servers are based on 133-MHz or faster Pentium processors.

Although they may be offered at the entry level with a single processor, these servers are designed to support symmetrical multiprocessing (SMP) with at least two processors. Cases are always at least full-tower, and may be double-wide cubes or rack-mountable. Examples of this class of server are the Compaq ProLiant 2000, the DEC Prioris HX and Prioris XL, the Hewlett-Packard NetServer LH/LM lines, and the IBM PC Server 520.

Enterprise Servers. Enterprise servers are the high-end products. These servers can provide file and print sharing services for 100 to 500 users, and at the same time support heavy-duty application server functions in a transaction processing environment. Enterprise servers range in price from perhaps $30,000 to $100,000 and more. At this level, fault tolerance and redundancy elements, such as disk arrays, ECC memory, and duplicate power supplies, are standard.

Enterprise servers available today are based on 133-MHz and faster Pentium processors, and offer SMP support for at least four and often more processors. Cases are monsters, providing as many as 28 drive bays. Examples of this class of server are the Compaq ProLiant 4000, the DEC Prioris HX/5100, the HP LS, and the IBM PC Server 720.

Server Type Recommendations. General server types don't really end with the enterprise server. Companies such as TriCord and NetFrame produce Intel-based servers in the $100,000 to $1 million price range, equipped with scores of processors and gigabytes of RAM. DEC, Hewlett-Packard, IBM, and other traditional minicomputer and mainframe manufacturers produce equally powerful servers based on non-Intel processors. These extremely high-end servers have very limited application. Most companies can rule them out based on cost alone. Even if you can afford one, the question becomes whether it makes sense to buy one.

File and print sharing services can be handled for any reasonable number of users, such as fewer than 250, by an enterprise or even a departmental server. Even if your user count exceeds the capabilities of one of these servers, it usually makes more sense to organize your users into workgroups and provide each workgroup with its own smaller server than it does to put all your users on a single huge server. About the only place a very large server makes sense is as an application server in a heavy transaction processing environment accessing huge databases. Such large-scale client/server software development is problematic, so it makes sense at this level to consider traditional multiuser minicomputer and mainframe solutions, thus rendering the very large server a solution in search of a problem.

Conformance to the Microsoft Windows NT Hardware Compatibility List

Make sure that any server you consider, with all its peripheral components, appears on the Microsoft Windows NT Server Hardware Compatibility List. A printed booklet with this information ships with the Windows NT Server software. However, the list is updated frequently to account for rapid changes within the industry, and you should download the most recent version when you're ready to place the order for your server. You can retrieve the most recent version of the Hardware Compatibility List from **http://www.microsoft.com/BackOffice/ntserver/hcl** or via anonymous FTP from **ftp://ftp.microsoft.com\bussys\winnt\winnt-docs\hcl**. It can also be found in Library 1 of the WINNT forum or Library 17 of the MSWIN32 forum on CompuServe Information Service.

Warranties, Maintainability, and Local Service

Server downtime can cost your company hundreds or even thousands of dollars per hour. More important, it can cost the LAN manager his job. When the LAN is down, employees still draw salaries, queries go unanswered, orders go unfilled, and work backs up. The issues of reliability and service are therefore an important aspect—some would say the most important aspect—of choosing a server.

You can configure your server with every fault-tolerant and redundancy feature offered by the manufacturer. Despite every precaution you take, the day will still come when your server goes down. What happens then can make the difference between an unpleasant episode and a disaster. The time to consider this problem is when you buy your server.

Choosing the Server Components

As you read earlier, the most critical part of your network is the cabling and active network components. This isn't to say, however, that the decision of which server to buy is a trivial one. This section discusses the most important factors to consider when deciding on the right server for your installation.

Know what role your server will play and the tasks it will be required to perform. Older generation network operating systems, such as Novell NetWare, focus almost exclusively on providing shared file and print services, a use that Windows NT Server also supports admirably. However, unlike Novell NetWare, Windows NT Server is also a stable and reliable application server platform.

Providing only file and printer sharing puts a relatively light load on a server. Raw processor speed is much less important than disk subsystem performance and network I/O. Although any server operating system likes memory, a file server has relatively modest RAM requirements.

An application server needs more of everything than a file server:

- More processor power by far, because user programs are actually running on the server.

- More memory to support the user programs running on the server.

- Better disk performance, because an application server is usually running disk-intensive database applications. In theory, an application server should require less network I/O performance because most of the data is manipulated internally, and data on the network is limited to requests and queries from the clients and results being sent back to them. In practice, most client/server applications—particularly in-house designs—are written so poorly that network I/O jumps drastically when they're implemented.

There's no hard-and-fast dividing line between file servers and application servers. Any computer that can run Windows NT Server 4.0 can function as an application server. What distinguishes the two server types is what you run on them and what hardware you provide to support what you choose to run. There's a great deal of overlap between configurations appropriate for each. Following are common configurations for file/printer sharing and application servers:

- A typical Windows NT server configured as a file and printer server might have one 133-MHz Pentium processor, 32M or 64M of RAM, and a few gigabytes of disk storage.

- A typical Windows NT server configured as an application server might have two or four 166-MHz Pentium processors, 128M or 256M of RAM, and 10G of RAID disk storage.

The first system might be a perfectly adequate application server in a small network with light application server demands, whereas the second configuration might not even be an adequate file server in a large location with hundreds of clients using it to share files and printers.

The second factor to consider is how much fault tolerance you need and how much you're willing to pay to get it. If your server will be supporting mission-critical applications, you would do well to place fault tolerance, redundancy, and maintenance issues at the top of your list of priorities. Modern purpose-built servers are designed to minimize single points of failure, and have many fault-tolerance features built in, including RAID disk subsystems, ECC memory, and redundant power supplies. If your application is truly critical, weigh the costs versus the benefits of providing complete redundancy, including one or more hot standby servers, standby power generators, and so forth.

> **Note**
>
> Because components with moving parts—disk subsystems, power supplies, and so on—are by far the most likely to fail, purpose-built servers typically address these components first by using redundant disk subsystems and overbuilt or duplicated power supplies. For most users, this provides an adequate level of fault tolerance at a reasonable price. When you get into the realm of standby servers, SCSI switches, and so forth, costs begin to mount rapidly.

The third factor to consider is whether to buy a new server or to convert an existing machine to run Windows NT Server 4.0. Particularly at smaller locations, the latter choice often seems attractive. Although it may seem that you can save money by just adding some memory and disk to an existing system, the reality is almost always that attempting to do so results in a server that costs nearly as much as a new purpose-built server and is substantially inferior to it.

Deciding on the Processor(s). The fundamental nature of a server is determined by the type of processor it uses—and how many. Windows NT Server gives you a wide range of flexibility in making this choice. Windows NT Server runs on popular processors from Intel, DEC, IBM, and other manufacturers. The following sections examine the issues involved in selecting the processor that your server will use.

RISC-Based Servers. Windows NT Server 4.0 was designed from the ground up to be a processor-independent operating system. In addition to running on the Intel x86 series of processors, Windows NT Server is available for several RISC processors from other manufacturers, including the DEC Alpha, the MIPS, and the PowerPC.

CISC stands for Complex Instruction Set Computer and RISC for Reduced Instruction Set Computer. Intel processors, including the Pentium and Pentium Pro, are considered to be CISC processors. Processors such as the DEC Alpha, the MIPS, and the PowerPC are considered to be RISC processors. In fact, this line is nowhere near as clearly defined as many believe it to be. Intel processors incorporate many RISC elements, and many RISC processors have instruction sets that can be difficult to differentiate from a CISC instruction set.

In theory, RISC processors are designed with relatively few simple processor instructions. These simple instructions are used as building blocks to accomplish more complex tasks. CISC processors have a larger selection of basic instructions, many of which are more complex than RISC instructions and accomplish more in a single instruction.

Comparing the current crop of RISC and CISC processors in a real-world environment shows that all of them are very fast. They have similar performance on integer operations, with RISC showing somewhat better performance on floating-point operations. Judged purely on performance benchmarks, then, RISC would seem to be the way to go. This turns out not to be the case.

Intel's market dominance ensures that software is written first, and possibly only, for Intel processors, greatly limiting both the breadth and depth of your choices on RISC-based competitors. Even if the database server or other software you intend to use is available today on a particular RISC platform, updates are likely to be slower in coming to this platform than to Intel. Also, a real risk exists that sales for a specific RISC platform may not meet expectations, and support for it may be dropped entirely, leaving your hardware and software orphaned.

Choosing Intel Processors. The Pentium is the mainstream processor for Windows NT Server 4.0. It's available in versions running at 75 MHz, 90 MHz, 100 MHz, 120 MHz, 133 MHz, 150 MHz, and 166 MHz. The 90-MHz and 100-MHz versions are closely related, as are the 120-MHz and 133-MHz versions. When this book was written, most purpose-built servers used one or two 133-MHz or faster Pentium processors.

The Pentium Pro offers some significant architectural and performance advantages over the Pentium when running 32-bit software, such as Windows NT Server. It shows up to 50 percent greater performance compared with the Pentium of the same clock speed. The Pentium Pro was designed from the ground up to be used in multiple-processor systems, and allows the use of up to four processors without the additional complex and expensive multiprocessing circuitry required by the Pentium.

There's little doubt that the Pentium Pro will become the processor of choice for servers. When this book was written, single-processor versions of Pentium Pro systems were beginning to appear. Release of multiprocessor Pentium Pro servers has been delayed by problems Intel encountered with support for SMP systems based on the Pentium Pro. Multiple Pentium Pro servers are expected to become available in late 1996.

If your server is to be a single-processor one, it makes sense to consider the Pentium Pro for its superior performance with Windows NT Server. If you need the additional power of symmetrical multiprocessing, your only choice at the moment is the standard Pentium.

Sizing Processor Cache Memory. Processor cache memory (usually just called *cache*) consists of a relatively small amount of very high-speed memory interposed between the processor and the main system memory. Cache buffers the very high-speed demands of the processor against the relatively modest speed of the main system's dynamic RAM.

All modern Intel processors have processor cache memory built in. This internal cache is called Level 1, or L1, cache. Pentium processors have 8K of L1 cache. Pentium Pro processors come with 256K or 512K of L1 cache. L1 cache is essential; without it, the processor would spend most of its time waiting for the slower main memory to provide data. 8K of L1 cache isn't enough to provide adequate performance.

The key determinant of the value of a cache is its *hit rate*, which is simply a percentage expressing how often the required data is actually present in the cache when it's needed. Hit rate can be increased either by increasing the size of the cache itself or by improving the efficiency of the algorithms used to determine which data is kept in cache and which is discarded.

Increasing the cache hit rate to improve performance must be done by adding a second level of cache externally. This external cache is called Level 2, or L2, cache. Following are the three types of external L2 cache:

- Asynchronous (async) cache is the least expensive and least desirable of the three. Async cache uses relatively slow and inexpensive cache RAM and provides the least caching benefit. However, everything is relative, and a system equipped with L2 async cache greatly outperforms no L2 cache at all.

- Pipeline burst cache is in the middle. Somewhat more expensive than async cache and considerably more efficient, pipeline burst cache is most commonly found on low-end and mid-range servers. Upgrading from async cache to pipeline burst cache for very little money is often possible. Doing so is worth the expense.

- Synchronous (synch) cache is by far the best-performing technology. Because it requires very high-speed cache RAM chips, synch cache is quite expensive and is likely to be found on mid-range and high-end servers.

The question of how much L2 processor cache to get and of what type may be resolved by the server you choose. You may find that the amount and type of cache is fixed, or you may find that you have alternatives as to size and type. In general, prefer quality to quantity. A system with 128K of synchronous cache usually outperforms a system with four times as much asynchronous cache. If you're given the option, consider 128K of pipeline burst cache as a minimum for your single-processor Pentium server, but get 256K or 512K if you can.

Deciding on a Multiprocessor System. As demands for processor power increase, it might seem apparent that one solution is to simply add more processors. Doing so is not the quick fix that it first appears to be, however. Broadly speaking, there are two methods to use multiple processors:

- *Asymmetric multiprocessing* (AMP) is a design in which processors are dedicated to particular tasks. This scheme is common in mainframe architectures where, for example, a Pentium class processor under control of the mainframe operating system is dedicated to providing communications I/O. AMP isn't common in smaller systems and isn't germane to Windows NT servers.

- *Symmetric multiprocessing* (SMP) is where the action is in Intel-based servers. In an SMP system, each processor is a full peer of every other processor and is interchangeable as far as applications are concerned. SMP servers are especially effective as application servers for Microsoft BackOffice components, such as SQL Server and Exchange Server.

Windows NT Server 4.0 has native support for up to 32 processors in an SMP arrangement, although commonly available servers usually support only two or four processors, with a few servers offering support for eight. Adding processors doesn't scale linearly—that's to say, a system with two processors isn't twice as fast as the same system with only one. This is because overhead is involved in managing work assigned to multiple

Networking

processors and in maintaining cache coherency. Experience has shown that a system with two processors is perhaps 70 or 80 percent faster than the system with only one processor. Equipping a system with four Pentium processors can be expected to result in a server about three times faster than the same server with only one processor.

You should, therefore, give some weight to a server's capability to handle more than one processor. Dual-processor motherboards carry a modest price premium over the single-processor variety. Even if your current requirements are fully met by a single processor server, being able to add a second processor can mean the difference between having to upgrade the server and having to replace it.

Determining Memory Requirements. Servers run on memory. Every time Windows NT Server has to swap data from RAM to disk, you take a big performance hit. A server using a slow processor with lots of memory outperforms a server with a fast processor and less memory every time. Memory makes up a relatively small percentage of the overall cost of a typical server. The drastic price reduction for dynamic RAM that occurred in early 1996 has made additional memory very affordable.

Memory comes in a variety of physical forms, densities, and types. The Single Inline Memory Module (SIMM) has become the standard packaging in the last few years, taking over from the Dual Inline Package (DIP) chips used formerly. The Single Inline Pin Package (SIPP) was an early attempt to package memory more densely, but has since disappeared because of the physical and other advantages of SIMM packaging. Almost any server you buy uses SIMM memory, with the exception of a few that use the newly introduced Dual Inline Memory Modules (DIMMs). DIMMs are uncommon and often are of a proprietary design. SIMMs, on the other hand, are the industry standard and therefore are preferred.

SIMMs were originally manufactured in 30-pin packages. Nearly all 30-pin SIMMs are 1 byte wide and must therefore be added four at a time to a 32-bit wide system bus. Newer SIMMs are manufactured in 72-pin packages and are 4 bytes wide, allowing them to be added one at a time to most systems. Some systems, particularly servers, have a memory architecture that requires adding 72-pin SIMMs two at a time. Even this, however, gives you substantially more flexibility than the older 30-pin SIMMs. No current server worthy of that name uses 30-pin SIMMs.

Memory can be designed with one or more extra bits that are used to increase its reliability. Parity memory has one such extra bit. A 30-pin parity SIMM is actually 9 bits wide rather than 8, with the extra bit assigned as a parity check bit. Similarly, a 72-pin parity SIMM is actually 36-bits wide rather than 32 bits, with the extra 4 bits used as a parity check. Parity can detect on single-bit errors. When it detects such an error, the result is the infamous `Parity Check Error--System Halted` message.

> **Tip**
>
> For clients, the future is no doubt non-parity memory. In fact, the Intel Triton chip set used by most Pentium system boards doesn't even support parity memory; the Triton chip set ignores the

ninth bit if it's present. That's a clue, by the way. If the server you're considering for purchase uses the Triton chip set, you can be assured that the system board wasn't intended for use in a server.

Memory reliability is so important in a server that even parity memory isn't a sufficient safeguard. Borrowing from mainframe technology, manufacturers of Intel-based servers have begun using Error Checking and Correcting (ECC) memory. ECC memory usually is 11 bits wide, dedicating 3 error-checking bits for each 8 data bits. ECC memory can detect *and correct* single-bit errors transparently. Single-bit errors are the vast majority, so ECC memory avoids nearly all the lockups that would otherwise occur with parity memory. Just as important, ECC memory can at least detect multiple-bit errors and, depending on the type of ECC memory, may also be able to correct some of these errors. Although ECC memory may lock the system on some multiple-bit errors, this is far preferable to allowing data to be corrupted, which can occur with simple parity memory.

Although ECC memory is 11 bits wide or wider, its implementations normally use standard SIMMs and simply allocate an extra SIMM to providing the ECC function. This allows the system to use standard SIMM memory rather than proprietary and costly memory designed especially as ECC memory. ECC memory is usually standard on enterprise-level servers, standard or optional on departmental-level servers, and may be optional or not available on workgroup-level servers. You should install ECC memory if possible.

Although Windows NT Server loads in 16M of system memory, you won't have much of a server with only that amount. As with any network operating system, the more memory, the better the performance. Following are recommendations for the initial amount of RAM you need to install for different server environments:

■ If you're configuring your Windows NT server to provide only file and print sharing, consider 24M the absolute minimum. 32M is a better starting point, and if your server supports many users, you should probably consider equipping it with 64M to start.

■ If your Windows NT server provides application server functions, consider 64M as the bare minimum and realize that some products may not run in this little memory. 128M is usually a safer bet, and many choose to start at 256M.

■ As a general rule of thumb, calculate what you consider to be a proper amount of memory given your particular configuration and the software you plan to run, and then double it as your starting point. Monitor your server's performance, and add more memory as needed.

Consider the availability of SIMM sockets when you're configuring memory. Buy the densest SIMMs available for your server to conserve SIMM sockets. Choose two 32M SIMMs in preference to four 16M SIMMs. Bear in mind that the day may come when you have no more room to add memory without swapping out what you already have installed.

Choosing a Bus Type. All newly designed servers use the PCI bus; make sure that the server you buy uses PCI. All other bus designs for servers are obsolete, including EISA and VLB buses. PCI still places a limit on the number of slots available on a single PCI bus, so larger servers use either dual PCI or bridged PCI buses. These systems simply use supporting circuitry to double the bus or to extend a single PCI bus to provide additional PCI slots.

Disk Subsystems. The disk subsystem comprises the disk controllers and fixed-disk drives of your server. Choosing a good disk subsystem is a key element in making sure that your server performs up to expectations. The following sections discuss fixed-disk drives, with emphasis on SCSI-2 devices and SCSI-2 host adapter cards, and introduce you to clustering technology. Tape backup systems, which almost always are SCSI-2 devices, are the subject of Chapter 8, "Installing File Backup Systems."

Enhanced Integrated Drive Electronics (EIDE) Drives. The Enhanced Integrated Device Electronics (EIDE) specification, developed by Western Digital, has gained wide industry support, although Seagate and some other manufacturers have proposed a competing standard called Fast ATA. These two standards are very similar and are merging as this is written.

EIDE supports as many as four drives. It allows a maximum drive size of 8.4G. It increases data-transfer rates of between 9mbps and 13mbps, similar to those of SCSI-2. It makes provision under the ATA Packet Interface (ATAPI) Specification for connecting devices other than hard drives. ATAPI CD-ROM drives are now common, and ATAPI tape drives are becoming more so.

Small Computer System Interface (SCSI). Small Computer System Interface (SCSI, pronounced *scuzzy*) is a general-purpose hardware interface that allows the connection of a variety of peripherals—hard-disk drives, tape drives, CD-ROM drives, scanners, printers, and so forth—to a host adapter that occupies only a single expansion slot. You can connect up to seven such devices to a single host adapter and install more than one host adapter in a system, allowing for the connection of a large number of peripheral devices to a system.

SCSI is the dominant drive technology in servers for the following two reasons:

■ SCSI supports many devices, and many types of devices, on a single host adapter. Expansion slots are precious resources in a server. SCSI's capability to conserve these slots by daisy-chaining many devices from a single host adapter is in itself a strong argument for its use in servers.

■ SCSI provides request queuing and elevator seeking. Other drive technologies process disk requests in the order in which they're received. SCSI instead queues requests and services them in the order in which the data can be most efficiently accessed from the disk. This isn't a particular advantage in a single-user, single-tasking environment because requests are being generated one at a time by a single user.

In Windows NT Server's multiuser, multitasking environment, however, queuing and elevator seeking offer major performance advantages. Rather than service disk requests in the order in which they're received, SCSI determines the location of each requested item on the disk and then retrieves it as the read head passes that location. This method results in much greater overall disk performance and a shorter average wait for data to be retrieved and delivered to the requester.

SCSI is a bus technology. In fact, it's convenient to think of SCSI as a small LAN contained within your server. Up to eight devices can be attached to a standard SCSI bus. The SCSI host adapter itself counts as one device, so as many as seven additional devices can be attached to a single host adapter. Any two of these devices can communicate at any one time, either host to peripheral or peripheral to peripheral.

SCSI can transfer data using one of two methods. Asynchronous SCSI, also referred to as *Slow SCSI*, uses a handshake at each data transfer. Synchronous, or Fast, SCSI reduces this handshaking to effect a doubling in throughput.

SCSI uses a variety of electrical connections, differing in the number of lines used to carry the signal. Single-ended SCSI uses unbalanced transmission, where the voltage on one wire determines the line's state. Differential SCSI uses balanced transmission, where the difference in voltage on a pair of wires determines the line's state. Single-ended SCSI allows a maximum cable length of three meters for Fast SCSI and six meters for Slow SCSI. Differential SCSI allows cable lengths up to 25 meters. Single-ended SCSI is intended primarily for use within a single cabinet, whereas Differential SCSI allows the use of expansion cabinets for disk farms.

You need to be aware of the following terminology used to refer to SCSI subsystems:

- SCSI-1 uses an 8-bit bus connection and 50-pin D-Ribbon (Centronix) or D-Sub (DB50) external device connectors. (25-pin DB25 connectors also are used.) SCSI-1 offers a maximum data transfer rate of 2.5mbps asynchronous and 5mbps synchronous. SCSI-1 is obsolete.

- SCSI-2 uses an 8-bit, 16-bit, or 32-bit bus connection. The data-transfer rates range from 2.5mbps for 8-bit asynchronous connections to 40mbps for 32-bit synchronous connection.

- Fast SCSI is a SCSI-2 option that uses synchronous transfers to double the data transfer rate compared with systems using Asynchronous or Slow SCSI. Fast SCSI requires a 50-pin Micro-D external device connector, which is considerably smaller than the D-Sub connector.

- Wide SCSI is a SCSI-2 option that uses a 16-bit or 32-bit wide connection to double or quadruple the data-transfer rate compared with the 8-bit wide connection used by SCSI-1. 16-bit Wide SCSI uses a 68-pin Micro-D connector for external devices. Fast and Wide SCSI-2 quickly is becoming the standard for server fixed-disk drives.

> **Note**
>
> Wide SCSI lets you connect 15 SCSI devices to a single host adapter. Dual host adapters, such as the Adaptec AHA-3940UW Ultra Wide adapter, consist of two host adapters on a single PCI card, letting you connect up to 30 devices to two internal and one external SCSI cables.

■ Ultra SCSI is a subset of the SCSI-3 specification, which was pending approval when this book was written. Ultra is Fast SCSI with a doubled clock rate, which provides twice the potential throughput. Ultra and Ultra Wide SCSI host adapters are readily available, but delivery of large quantities of Ultra SCSI and Ultra Wide SCSI drives isn't likely to occur until late 1996.

EIDE vs. SCSI Drives for Servers. Although EIDE has addressed many of the theoretical drawbacks of IDE versus SCSI for use in servers, actual EIDE implementations continue to lag SCSI. Maximum supported drive size is becoming similar, although current EIDE drives top out at 4.3G versus 23G for Ultra Wide SCSI. Similarly, drive rotation rates, which are an important factor in determining real-world throughput, top out at 5,400 rpm in current EIDE drives, versus 7,200 rpm for SCSI drives. Theoretical throughput is similar, but Fast and Wide SCSI-2 drives, such as Seagate's ST15150W 4.3G Barracuda drive, have greater throughput than any currently available EIDE drive.

The key advantage of SCSI for servers remains its support for queued requests and elevator seeking, along with its support for daisy-chaining many devices. Its sole drawback relative to EIDE is its somewhat higher cost. Although EIDE drives can be used successfully in a small server with very light demands on its disk subsystem, you should use SCSI if your server will do anything more than provide file and printer sharing for perhaps four or five users.

SCSI Bus Termination. Proper bus termination is essential for successful data transfer from SCSI devices to the SCSI host adapter card. You must terminate both the internal (ribbon cable) and external SCSI buses. If you're using only internal or only external devices, the adapter card's built-in termination circuitry must be enabled. Internal termination must be disabled if you connect a combination of internal and external devices. In most cases, you determine whether on-card termination is enabled by setting the adapter's BIOS parameters during the hardware boot process. Figure 5.18 illustrates SCSI termination for internal devices; figure 5.19 shows termination of a combination of typical internal and external SCSI devices.

> **Note**
>
> Internal devices include termination circuitry, which usually is enabled or disabled with a jumper. Drives that conform to the SCAM (SCSI Configured AutoMagically) specification don't require setting a jumper. You terminate external devices with a connector that contains the termination circuitry. Active (rather than passive) termination is necessary for Fast, Wide, and Ultra SCSI devices.

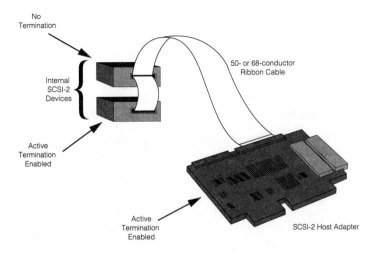

Fig. 5.18 SCSI termination for internal devices.

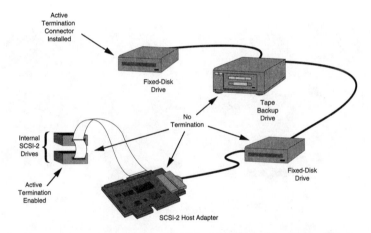

Fig. 5.19 SCSI termination for a combination of internal and external devices.

Disk Controllers. If you buy a purpose-built server, the choice of host adapter is straightforward. Low-end servers normally are equipped with a standard SCSI-2 host adapter and offer few options, except perhaps the amount of cache RAM on the adapter. High-end servers normally ship with a host adapter, which provides various hardware RAID options. Mid-range servers usually offer a choice between a standard host adapter and an upgraded adapter with hardware RAID support. In each case, your options are limited to those offered by the server manufacturer. This is really no limitation at all, because server manufacturers carefully balance their systems to optimize throughput with the chosen adapter.

When you choose a disk subsystem, you must consider how much disk redundancy you want to provide. At the simplest level, a Windows NT server may have a single host adapter connected to one or more disk drives. Disk redundancy increases the safety and performance of your disk subsystem at the cost of requiring additional disk drives and more complex host adapters. Windows NT's built-in support for software RAID (Redundant Array of Inexpensive Disks) and hardware RAID controllers are the subject of Chapter 7, "Setting Up Redundant Arrays of Inexpensive Disks (RAID)."

If you're assembling your own server, following are recommendations for purchasing PCI SCSI-2 host adapters to be used as conventional (independent) drives or with Windows NT 4.0's built-in software RAID system:

- If you must support both conventional (narrow) and Wide SCSI-2 devices with a single adapter, buy an adapter with both 50-pin and 86-pin connectors. Don't try to mix narrow and Wide SCSI devices on a single cable. The Adaptec AHA-2940UW adapter, shown in figure 5.20, provides both internal and external Wide SCSI-2 connectors for high-performance disk drives, plus an internal narrow SCSI-2 connector for CD-ROM and conventional SCSI-2 drives.

Fig. 5.20 A single Ultra SCSI adapter with a narrow and Wide internal connector and a single Wide external connector (courtesy of Adaptec Inc.).

- If you don't need to support existing narrow SCSI-2 devices, consider using a dual Fast and Wide SCSI-2 host adapter, such as the Adaptec AHA3940UW shown in figure 5.21. Your Pentium or Pentium Pro motherboard must support PCI bridging to use the AHA3940UW. You gain a significant speed advantage by connecting drives in pairs to the two internal SCSI cables.

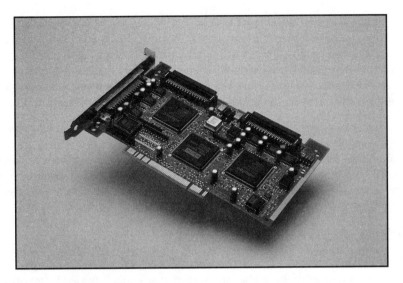

Fig. 5.21 A dual Ultra Wide SCSI adapter with two Wide internal connectors and a single Wide external connector (courtesy of Adaptec Inc.).

Clustering. A *cluster* is defined as an interconnected group of two or more servers that appear transparently to a user as a single server. Clustering uses a combination of specialized high-speed connectivity hardware with software running on each server to link the servers into a cluster and provide this transparent access.

◀◀ See "Forging Alliances for Scalable Windows NT Server Hardware," p. 50

Although clustering is common in the minicomputer environment—particularly with the Digital Equipment Corporation line of VAX minicomputers—clustering for PC servers is just beginning to appear. Microsoft is committed to a clustering strategy for Windows NT Server, which uses industry-standard hardware components to provide inexpensive clustering functionality.

Uninterruptable Power Supplies and Power Protection. All this expensive hardware does you no good whatsoever unless you keep it supplied with clean, reliable AC power provided by an uninterruptable power supply (UPS). A UPS performs the following two functions:

■ It supplies auxiliary power to keep your network components running when the mains power fails. UPSs vary in how much power they supply, the quality of that power, and for how long they can supply it.

■ It conditions the mains power to protect your equipment against spikes, surges, drops, brownouts, and electrical noise, all of which can wreak havoc with your servers, clients, and active network components.

Understanding Power Protection Issues. Power companies do a remarkably good job of supplying consistent power in most areas of the United States. Still, when the power leaves the power plant—more particularly, when it leaves the distribution transformer near you—the electric utility ceases to have complete control. Voltage is subject to variations due to loads placed on a circuit and to the higher voltage circuit that supplies it. Following are some of the problems that commonly affect your power:

■ A sudden and complete loss of power for an extended period is called a *blackout* or *outage*. Blackouts can be caused by something as common as a cable being cut or a drunk hitting a power pole, or by something as unusual as load-shedding, where at times of peak demand the power company intentionally cuts service to whole areas to protect the rest of the grid. Blackouts are what causes most firms to consider purchasing UPSs.

■ A high-voltage, high-current device, such as an elevator motor starting, can cause the voltage to drop significantly on all 110-volt circuits supplied by the same high-voltage circuit. This drop, called a *brownout*, is noticeable as a dimming of incandescent lights. Brownouts can last up to several seconds if caused by an overload. Short-term brownouts are referred to as *sags*. At times of peak demand, the electric utility may intentionally reduce the delivered voltage, thereby causing a long-term brownout. Brownouts are potentially more destructive to your equipment than any other common electrical problem.

■ A short-duration absence of voltage is called a *drop*. Drops are common but aren't often noticed. No dimming is seen in incandescent lamps because the filament doesn't have a chance to cool down. PC power supplies have large capacitors, giving them enough electrical momentum to cover the drop.

■ A sudden drop in load, such as an elevator motor coming off line, can cause a *surge*. A surge is a temporary sustained overvoltage condition in which the delivered voltage is substantially higher than the nominal 108 volt to 125 volt. Surges can last from a fraction of a second to several seconds, and are much less dangerous to equipment than are extended brownouts. Most equipment can deal successfully with any surges likely to occur. Still, surges shouldn't be discounted as a potential problem.

■ A sudden peak in voltage which lasts for only a fraction of a second is called a *spike* or a *transient*. Spikes are produced by a variety of sources, including motors, lightning-induced voltages, and transformer failures. Although spikes can have extremely high voltage, they're also usually of very short duration, and accordingly the total power delivered is normally quite small. The switching power supplies common in computer equipment are actually quite good at suppressing transient voltages, but they make expensive surge protectors.

One factor often overlooked in considering electrical protection is that damage to components can be incremental and cumulative. It's easy to spot the damage after an overvoltage event, such as a lightning strike. Chips are charred and may literally be smoking. It isn't as easy to spot the damage after a less severe event. The component may pass all diagnostics and run flawlessly, but be damaged nonetheless.

Most chips are designed to work at 5 volts. A spike at 100 or even 1,000 times that voltage may leave the chip apparently undamaged, but may in fact have done near-fatal damage to delicate circuitry and traces. Because silicon doesn't heal itself, this damage is cumulative. The next minor overvoltage event may be the straw that breaks the camel's back, leaving you with a dead network and no idea what caused it. Choosing and using good UPSs will ensure that this doesn't happen to you.

Understanding UPS Types. The original UPS designs comprised a battery, charging circuitry, and an inverter. The load—your equipment—is never connected directly to mains power but is instead powered at all times by the inverter, driven by battery power. The battery is charged constantly as long as there's mains power (see fig. 5.22). This type of UPS is called a *true UPS* or an *online UPS*.

Fig. 5.22   Power flow in an online UPS.

An online UPS has several advantages. First, because the load is driven directly by battery power at all times rather than switched to battery when mains power fails, there's no switch-over time. Second, because there's no switch, the switch can't fail. Third, full-time battery operation allows the equipment to be completely isolated from the AC mains power, thereby guaranteeing clean power.

Balanced against these advantages are a few drawbacks. First, an online UPS is expensive, often costing 50 to 100 percent more than alternatives. Second, because an online UPS constantly converts mains AC voltage to DC voltage for battery charging and then back into AC to power the equipment, efficiencies are often 70 percent or lower, compared to near 100 percent for other methods. In large installations, this may noticeably increase your power bill. Third, battery maintenance becomes a more important issue with a true UPS, because the battery is in use constantly.

The high cost of online UPS technology led to the development of a less expensive alternative that was originally called a *standby power supply* (SPS). Like an online UPS, an SPS includes a battery, charging circuitry, and an inverter to convert battery power to 120-volt AC. Unlike the online UPS, the SPS also includes a switch. In ordinary conditions, this switch routes mains power directly to the equipment being powered (see fig. 5.23, top). When the mains power fails, the switch quickly transfers the load to the battery-powered inverter, thus maintaining power to the equipment (see fig. 5.23, bottom).

Five or ten years ago, the switching time of an SPS was a major concern. For example, IBM used power supplies from two different manufacturers in the PC/XT. One of these had sufficient "inertia" to continue powering the system for between 8 and 15 milliseconds (ms) after power failed, while the other allowed only 2 ms or 3 ms grace. Systems that used the first type of power supply worked just fine with SPSs of that era. Systems using the second type of power supply crashed immediately when power failed, because the switching time required by the SPS was longer than the power supply could stand.

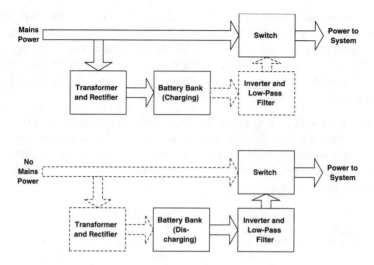

Fig. 5.23 A standby power supply with mains power (top) and powering the server during a power outage (bottom).

Switching time is of much less concern today for two reasons. First, SPSs have been improved to reduce switching times from the 5 ms to 8 ms range common several years ago to the 1 ms range today. Second, PC power supplies have also been improved. A typical PC power supply today can continue to operate without power for a substantial fraction of a full 60 ms cycle. These two factors combined make it unlikely that the short switching time required by a modern SPS will cause the PC to lose power.

A simple SPS functions in only two modes. When mains power is at or above the minimum threshold voltage required, it's passed directly to the computer. When mains power voltage falls below the threshold, the SPS switches to battery power. This means that each time a sag or brownout occurs, your systems are running on battery power. A typical simple SPS may switch to battery if the incoming voltage drops below 102 volts—a relatively common occurrence.

A line-interactive SPS adds power-conditioning functions to monitor and correct the voltage of the incoming mains power. When a sag or brownout occurs, the line-interactive SPS draws more current at the lower voltage in order to continue providing standard voltage to your equipment without using battery power. A typical line-interactive SPS may continue to provide standard AC voltage to your equipment without using battery power when mains power voltage drops as low as 85 volts, thereby reserving its battery for a true blackout situation.

Understanding UPS Specifications. The three critical elements of a UPS are how much power it can provide, of what quality, and for how long. The first two are determined by the size and quality of the inverter circuitry. The third is determined by the size of the battery connected to the UPS.

The VA (volt-ampere) rating of a UPS determines the maximum amount of power that the UPS can supply and is determined by the rating of the components used in the inverter circuitry of the unit. For example, an SPS rated at 600 VA can supply at most 5 amps of current at 120 volts. Trying to draw more than 5 amps overloads and eventually destroys the inverter circuitry.

The second essential issue in choosing a UPS is the quality of power it provides, which is determined by the design of the inverter circuitry. Nearly all online UPSs and the better grade SPSs provide true sine wave output from their inverters. Less expensive units with lower-quality inverters provide only an approximation of sine wave output, using square wave, modified square wave, or sawtooth waveforms. Any of these departures from true sine wave put an additional burden on the power supply of connected components, causing overheating of the component power supply and making its failure more likely. Don't settle for less than true sine wave output in your UPS.

The third essential issue in choosing a UPS is how long it can continue to provide backup power for a given load. This is determined by the type and amp-hour rating of the battery. The amp-hour rating is simply the product of how many amps of current the battery is rated to provide, times the number of hours it can provide that current.

Unfortunately, the total amp-hours deliverable by a given battery depend on the load. For example, you might expect that a battery capable of delivering 5 amps for 12 minutes, or 1 amp-hour, could instead deliver 10 amps for six minutes, also 1 amp-hour. This isn't the case, however. High current draws reduce the total amp hours deliverable, while low draws increase them. The battery described might provide 10 amps for only three minutes, or 0.5 amp-hour, whereas it might allow a draw of 1 amp for 120 minutes, or two amp-hours.

What this means in real terms is that you can't assume that a UPS that powers two servers for 10 minutes can power four servers for five minutes, even if the load is within the VA rating of that UPS. For example, the author's 600 VA unit is rated to supply a full 600 VA for only five minutes, but can supply 300 VA for 22 minutes. In other words, cutting the load in half more than quadruples the runtime.

With most small UPSs, you take what you're given with respect to batteries. The batteries are built-in, and you have few or no choices about battery type or VA rating. Some larger UPS models—typically starting at 1,000 VA or more—use external batteries, allowing you to choose both the type and number of batteries to be used. Some modular systems allow you to add batteries in a daisy-chain arrangement, allowing whatever runtime you're willing to pay for.

Sizing a UPS. Calculating UPS loads and runtimes is imprecise at best. Servers and other components, even when fully configured, usually draw considerably less power than the rating of their power supplies, which are rated for the maximum load the system can support. Even nominally identical components can vary significantly in their power draw. Loads vary dynamically as tape drives, Energy Star compliant monitors, and other components come on- and offline.

Although you can use commercially available ammeters in an attempt to determine exactly what each of your components really draws and size your UPS accordingly, few system managers do so. Most elect to simply sum the component wattages (applying the power factor correction for components with switching power supplies), add a fudge factor for safety, and then buy the next size up.

UPS Manageability. Manageability is another issue you need to consider when choosing a UPS. There are two aspects to UPS manageability, as follows:

- Any but the most inexpensive UPS makes provision for interaction with the network operating system, allowing the UPS to signal the server to shut down gracefully when backup power is about to run out, and thereby avoiding disk corruption and other problems that result from a sudden unexpected loss of power.

  Windows NT Server provides this function directly, but only for supported UPS models. Check the latest version of the Hardware Compatibility List to verify that your UPS is supported. Even if it isn't, the UPS manufacturer may provide software that runs on Windows NT Server 4.0 to add this functionality.

- True remote management is provided by an SNMP agent included with the UPS. This allows the UPS to be monitored, tested, and controlled from a remote management client. If you're running such a remote management package to control other aspects of your network, make sure that the UPS model you choose is supported by your management software package.

From Here...

This long chapter covered the three primary categories of hardware required to set up a Windows NT network: network cabling, active network components, and server systems. Ethernet was recommended as the media access method, 10BaseT and/or 100BaseT for cabling, ISA NICs for 10BaseT clients, and PCI NICs for 100BaseT clients and servers running either 10BaseT or 100BaseT. Guidelines for choosing Pentium- and Pentium Pro-based servers, along with recommendations for SCSI-2 drives and host adapter cards, were included. The chapter concluded with a description of the two basic types of uninterruptible power supplies.

The following chapters provide further information on the topics discussed in this chapter:

- Chapter 6, "Making the Initial Server Installation," guides you through Windows NT Server 4.0's setup application, with emphasis on preparing you to answer the questions posed in the setup dialogs.

- Chapter 7, "Setting Up Redundant Arrays of Inexpensive Disks (RAID)," describes how to choose between software and hardware RAID implementation and how best to take advantage of Windows NT Server 4.0's software RAID capabilities.

- Chapter 8, "Installing File Backup Systems," explains the tradeoffs between different types and formats of backup systems, and how to manage server backup operations to ensure against lost data in case of a fixed-disk failure.

- Chapter 18, "Managing Remote Access Service," explains how to select and install modems, and configure Windows NT Server 4.0's RAS component to support dial-in access to shared network resources by mobile users.

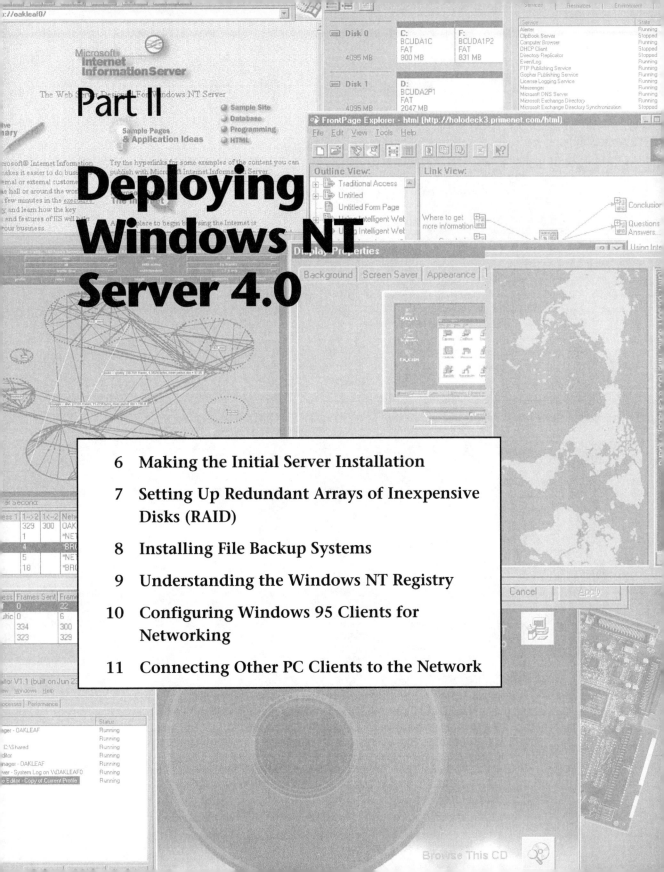

Part II

Deploying Windows NT Server 4.0

6   Making the Initial Server Installation

7   Setting Up Redundant Arrays of Inexpensive Disks (RAID)

8   Installing File Backup Systems

9   Understanding the Windows NT Registry

10   Configuring Windows 95 Clients for Networking

11   Connecting Other PC Clients to the Network

Chapter 6

Making the Initial Server Installation

One of the primary selling points of Windows NT Server 4.0 is its ease of installation. A "standard" installation, using default values, on a new server computer takes less than 30 minutes. Windows NT Server 4.0 is such a powerful and flexible operating system that a one-size-fits-all "standard" installation procedure is sure to shortchange some users or, in the worst case, deprive all users of the potential capabilities of Windows NT Server 4.0.

The process of installing a network operating system starts long before you put the distribution CD-ROM into the drive. This is especially true for Windows NT Server 4.0, because you have a number of decisions that shouldn't be made while staring at an installation question that you must answer in the dialog on-screen. If your server is now running another operating system, you have many more decisions to make than if you're installing Windows NT on a brand-new computer. If you're installing Windows NT Server 4.0 for the first time, you should read this chapter thoroughly before touching the door of the CD-ROM drive.

This chapter covers the following topics:

■ What you need to know before starting the installation

■ The preinstallation backup process

■ Installing Windows NT Server 4.0

■ Operations after installation

Deploying Windows NT

II

Gathering Information and Making Decisions

You must consider several major issues before you start to install Windows NT Server 4.0. Are you installing Windows NT Server over another operating system? Are you familiar with all the hardware contained in or attached to your server? Is your computer already connected to a network (perhaps in a peer-to-peer configuration), or are you installing Windows NT Server 4.0 and a new network at the same time? The following sections cover each issue.

> **Note**
>
> If you're upgrading Windows NT Server 3.5+ to Windows NT Server 4.0, the installation process is very close to automatic. All your existing settings—including Registry entries, users, groups, and services—are preserved. Thus, much of the advice in the following sections doesn't apply to a Windows NT upgrade. The most important change involves the new hardware device drivers required for version 4.0. Be sure to review the "Knowing Your Hardware" section before upgrading.

Preparing to Upgrade from Another Version of Windows

If you're running Windows 3.1, Windows for Workgroups 3.11, or Windows 95 on your server, it's a reasonably good bet that you plan to continue to use the files (and possibly applications) installed there after Windows NT is installed. For example, you may be running a shared-file database server that you plan to use under Windows NT Server 4.0 until upsizing to a client/server relational database management system, such as Microsoft SQL Server 6.5, that runs under Windows NT Server. In this case, you must tread very carefully during the installation procedure.

> **Note**
>
> It's an uncommon practice to run conventional end-user Windows applications on a Windows NT server. If you're upgrading a PC used as a peer-to-peer server in a Windows 95 or Windows for Workgroups 3.1+ environment, it's recommended that you devote the server PC to entirely to Windows NT Server. Uninstall Windows 95 applications, such as Microsoft Office 95, before installing Windows NT to conserve disk space. (You must reinstall Office 95 applications to run them under Windows NT Server or Workstation.) If you're upgrading from 16-bit Windows or Windows 95, install Windows NT in its own folder (\Winnt), not your existing \WINDOWS directory or \Windows folder. By doing so, you can easily delete the old operating system files after completing the Windows NT Server installation.

In addition to accessing existing files, do you want to be able to continue to use the existing operating system? As a rule, running two operating systems on a server (called *dual-booting*) is very dangerous. You don't want people to be able to boot the server into DOS/Windows or some other operating system, bypassing all the security procedures that you've instituted under Windows NT Server. If someone with access to the room that holds the server can boot it into another operating system, they can access (read and change) any file that operating system can read. Further, dual-booting precludes the use of NTFS (NT File System) for volumes that other Windows versions must be able to access.

Assuming that you want to keep all the old files but not use the old operating system, do you want your old settings preserved and used in Windows NT Server? You need to know the answers to these questions before you begin the installation procedure.

Note

Some decisions you make during installation, such as deciding whether the computer will be a domain controller or a server, can't be undone without completely reinstalling Windows NT Server. If you're installing Windows NT Server 4.0 in an existing Windows domain, you must know the role that the new server plays in the domain—Primary Domain Controller (PDC), Backup Domain Controller (BDC), or plain server. If you're installing Windows NT Server over an existing version, the server role is predefined. Before you start an upgrade, make sure that the server is connected to the network and the network connection is active. Later, the "Choosing to Install as a Domain Controller" section explains these roles.

Before proceeding with the Windows NT Server installation on a PC that shares folders, back up at least the shared folders to tape or to another PC with adequate disk space. Backing up to tape and to another PC is the best insurance against tape drive or media failure. Backing up to another PC is particularly important if you have a backup tape drive that isn't supported with a new Windows NT 4.0 driver. Later, the section "Backing Up Data on an Existing Computer" discusses backup operations in greater detail.

Knowing Your Hardware

The Setup program that installs Windows NT Server provides automatic hardware detection, but you need to answer questions about your hardware and make decisions before you start the installation process. The most important question about any hardware component you plan to use is this: Is the hardware component supported by Windows NT Server? If it isn't supported, you may have to install custom Windows NT drivers provided by your hardware manufacturer. The product documentation that accompanies the retail version of Windows NT Server 4.0 includes the Hardware Compatibility List (HCL) booklet. Updates to the HCL are provided at regular intervals at the following locations:

- On CompuServe, in the **WINNT** forum, Library 1

- On CompuServe, in the **MSWIN32** forum, Library 17

- On the Web at **http://www.microsoft.com/ntserver/hcl/hclintro.htm**

- By FTP, on **ftp.microsoft.com**, in the directory /bussys/winnt/winnt-docs/hcl

Be sure to check all the hardware in your system against this list before you begin to install Windows NT Server. If a hardware component you plan to use isn't on the list, you must obtain a 32-bit Windows NT driver. If such a driver isn't supplied with the hardware, contact the vendor or manufacturer to obtain a Windows NT driver.

Caution

Don't assume that because your current hardware is supported by an earlier version of Windows NT that it's supported by Windows NT 4.0. The device driver architecture has been substantially changed in version 4.0. Check the Hardware Compatibility List and obtain a driver, if you need one, before you begin the installation process.

Drivers for Legacy SCSI Host Adapters. Some less common hardware that was fully supported in earlier versions of Windows NT is now slightly less supported. You need a driver disk for older SCSI host adapters, but you can build the driver disk from files supplied on the Windows NT Server 4.0 CD-ROM. The following SCSI host adapters require you to create a driver disk:

- Always IN-2000

- Data Technology Corporation 3290

- Maynard 16-bit SCSI Adapter

- MediaVision Pro Audio Spectrum-16

- Trantor T-128, T-130B

- UltraStor 124f EISA Disk Array Controller

To create the driver disk, format a diskette and copy all the files from the driver folder to this diskette. The CD-ROM driver folder is one of the following:

- \drvlib\storage\retired\X86 for 486, Pentium, or Pentium Pro machines

- \drvlib\storage\retired\MIPS for machines with a MIPS RISC processor

- \drvlib\storage\retired\ALPHA for machines with a Digital Alpha processor

- \drvlib\storage\retired\PPC for IBM/Motorola PowerPCs

Label the diskette as the driver diskette for retired storage drivers for Windows NT Server 4.0, and keep the diskette ready to use during the installation.

Fixed-Disk Drive(s). Windows NT Server supports SCSI and IDE devices (primarily fixed-disk drives, CD drives, and tape drives), as well as other mass-storage devices, including the SCSI RAID drive arrays discussed in Chapter 7, "Setting Up Redundant Arrays of Inexpensive Disks (RAID)." Windows NT Server automatically detects mass storage devices during the installation processes and assigns these devices logical drive letters, beginning with C.

As part of the installation process, you can partition your fixed-disk drives, or ask Windows NT Server to respect the partitioning you've already done. After the drives are partitioned, you install a file system on each partition. When you partition a drive, it appears to the operating system as two or more smaller drives, usually called *volumes*. The first partition of each physical fixed disk is assigned a drive letter in sequence; the remaining partitions are then assigned drive letters.

There are two main reasons for partitioning a drive: it's to be accessed by more than one operating system, or you want to use drive letters as a convenient way to organize the drive. Partitioning a server drive for dual-boot operation is uncommon, because dual-booting servers isn't a recommended practice.

Some examples of partitioning for organizational reasons include the following:

- *Network access permissions*. Rather than assign these on a folder-by-folder basis, you might find it more convenient to partition the drive to permit access to all the folders of one partition and deny access to others.

- *Backups*. Different partitions, each accessed by its own drive letter, might be on a different backup schedule.

- *Controlling disk space use*. Put a folder or group of folders that should be restricted to a limited size on a relatively small partition. Disk full messages automatically limit users' ability to store additional files. One application for limiting file space is a partition where you allow anonymous incoming FTP, which allows Internet users to upload files to your drive.

If your drive is already partitioned and you plan to use the files that are kept on it, maintain the existing partitions. You can't repartition a drive without losing the information stored in the partition. If the first partition is smaller than 150M or the volume is compressed, you won't be able to maintain the existing partitions and will have to back up the files, repartition the disk, and then restore the files into the new partitions.

Each partition has an assigned *file system*, a method of storing and organizing files. The following two file systems can be used with Windows NT Server 4.0:

- *NTFS*, the Windows NT File System, allows long file names and handles security well. The files will be accessible to DOS, 16-bit Windows, or Windows 95 programs if they're run under Windows NT, but won't be accessible to such programs if the machine is running DOS, Windows 3.x, or Windows 95.

    Your server shouldn't be running two operating systems, so NTFS is your file system of choice. There's no practical limit to the size of an NTFS partition. NTFS minimizes the amount of slack (unusable space due to the use of large clusters to store small files) and lets you compress drives, folders, or individual files to conserve disk space.

- *FAT*, the 16-bit File Allocation Table, works with various operating systems (primarily MS-DOS) but isn't as robust or secure as NTFS. 16-bit FAT partitions are limited to a size of 2G. If, as an example, you use a Seagate ST15150W 4.3G Barracuda drive with the FAT file system, you must create a minimum of three partitions to gain access to all the drive's capacity. You would use a FAT file system on a dual-boot system, which isn't recommended for servers.

> **Note**
>
> Microsoft has announced that a 32-bit version of the FAT file system, called FAT32, will be available for installation by suppliers of PCs that preload Windows 95 by late 1996. When this book was written, Microsoft stated that FAT32 wasn't intended for retail distribution with Windows 95 and won't be supported by Windows NT. The primary reason for providing FAT32 is to overcome the 2G partition size barrier and to allow the use of a smaller cluster size in order to reduce the percentage of slack on large fixed-disk drives. NTFS has neither the 2G partition limit nor the slack problem.

II

Deploying Windows NT

The C: volume, the active system partition on the first internal hard disk, is the Windows NT system partition. The system partition contains a specific set of files used to start Windows NT Server and can't be compressed. The system partition can't be part of a volume set or a stripe set. If this restriction poses a problem for you, set aside a 150M system partition; the rest of the drive can be partitioned more flexibly.

If you won't be using any other operating system and don't have any organizational reasons for partitioning a single drive, make each drive one partition that uses NTFS. If your drive contains files you want to use after the installation, don't change the partitioning or the file system, but convert the file system to NTFS after the installation.

> **Note**
>
> It's possible to convert the file system to NTFS as part of Setup and preserve all your existing files. However, if you quit Setup without completing all the steps, the conversion won't be done. It's less confusing—and usually quicker—to leave the file system alone until Setup is complete, and then convert it to NTFS.
>
> To convert a FAT (DOS, Windows 3.x) or HPFS (OS/2) partition to NTFS and preserve all the files on it, open a Command Prompt window (sometimes called a *DOS box*) from the Start menu by choosing Programs and MS-DOS Prompt. Type the command **convert *d*: /fs:ntfs** (where *d*: is the drive you want to convert) in the text box and press Enter. If you try to convert the system partition (typically C), you'll be warned that the Convert program can't get exclusive access, but that the conversion can be scheduled as part of the next restart. Choose Yes, and then restart Windows NT Server to proceed with the conversion. Several additional restarts are required before the conversion completes.

CD-ROM Drive. Installing Windows NT Server 4.0 requires access to a CD-ROM drive, preferably with a SCSI interface. You don't need one of the high-speed 6X or 8X drives designed for multimedia applications; a 2X drive is quite adequate for installing server software, including Microsoft BackOffice components. It's possible to install Windows NT Server 4.0 over the network from a CD-ROM drive of another machine, but such a process is cumbersome.

Printer. You must know the make and model of your printer, and the port to which it's connected. Check the hardware compatibility list to verify that Windows NT includes a driver for your printer. If you aren't ready to install your printer during Setup, you can add it later by using the Printers tool under My Computer.

Network Adapter. The Setup software detects network adapter cards automatically, but it asks you to confirm the IRQ number, I/O base port address, memory buffer address, and other network card settings. If you installed the network card yourself, you have the required information that you need to accept the proposed values or enter new values. If you didn't install the network card, be sure to obtain the required network card settings from your computer vendor or the technician who installed the card.

If the PC has a network card, you can use Control Panel's Network tool or Windows Setup to display the current IRQ and I/O address range settings for your network card.

Figure 6.1 shows the Resources page of the property sheet for an Intel EtherExpress 16/16TP network card. Click the Advanced tab to display additional settings for the network adapter. Windows 3.1+'s Network Setup dialog leads to dialogs that display similar information.

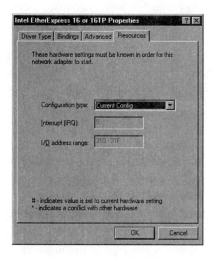

Fig. 6.1 The Resources page of the property sheet for a typical network adapter displaying the current IRQ and I/O address range.

Providing Names and Identification

During the installation process, you must provide the following names and numbers:

- Your name, or the name of the corporate contact responsible for this copy of Windows NT Server 4.0

- The name of the organization

- The product ID from the inside back cover of the Windows NT Server Installation Guide or from a sticker on the case of the CD-ROM

- The computer name assigned to the server

The computer name must be unique on your network—it must not match a group or domain name on your network. The computer name also can't be longer than 15 characters. Make sure that you know the names of the computers, domains, the groups on your network, and the way that names are assigned. In some environments, computers are named for the person or department using them, for the function they serve, or according to a more whimsical pattern, such as names of flowers or precious stones. Make sure that the name for this server makes sense in your environment. If you aren't sure about it, contact the person who named the other machines to confirm your choice of a server name. If your entire network is new, take a moment to think of a logical scheme for naming machines on the network.

Choosing to Install as a Domain Controller

A *domain* is a group of computers that have the same administrative rules—for example, all the computers that belong to one department. There may be several domains on a network. Using domains makes administration much easier, because you don't need to set up an account for each user on each server. One machine, the *Primary Domain Controller* (PDC), maintains the domain account database. Other machines on the network that don't have copies of the account database are *domain servers*, also called *plain servers*. Computers with copies of the account database are called *Backup Domain Controllers* (BDCs). Chapter 16, "Distributing Network Services with Domains," discusses in detail the architecture of Windows NT Server domains.

If you plan to set up multiple Windows NT servers, you must decide which server acts as the PDC, which server(s) act as the BDC(s), and which server(s) act as the domain servers. (This decision isn't easily reversible—in fact, making some changes of domain status requires a full reinstallation of Windows NT Server.) For new installations, you install Windows NT Server 4.0 as the PDC first, and then add BDCs and domain servers while the PDC is operating and connected to the network.

When you install Windows NT Server on the first server of a domain, you must create a PDC and name the domain. Choose a name that isn't being used by any existing domain. Users of all client computers connected to the network must know the name of the domain controller(s) to which each client connects.

Backing Up Data on an Existing Computer

Before you undertake a step as significant as changing the operating system (or reinstalling your current operating system), you must back up the data on your system. Chapter 8, "Installing File Backup Systems," shows you how to organize backups and use the Windows NT backup system with tape drives. If the machine stores vital data, the safest approach is to make two backups, each on different media. For example, back up to tape, and then copy the crucial files over the network to a different hard drive in case the tape is unreadable. In many instances, backup tapes are found to be unreadable, either because of a defect in the tape or tape drive, or because the format of the tape is specific to the prior operating system. Another problem, mentioned earlier in the chapter, is the current lack of Windows NT 4.0 drivers for many low-end backup tape drives. If your computer is already running Windows NT and is a Primary Domain Controller, make sure that the Backup Domain Controller has an up-to-date copy of the domain account database.

After the backup, if the drive is compressed, you must decompress it. Whether the drive is compressed with Stacker, DoubleSpace for DOS 6, or DriveSpace for Windows 95, you must undo the compression before you try to install Windows NT Server 4.0 on the drive. Don't try to decompress before the backup; one of the disasters the backup ensures against is data loss during decompression. After you decompress the drive, however, back up the decompressed files that you want to preserve.

If the drive is compressed, it's because not all the files fit without compression. Thus, it's likely that the first step in the decompression process is to remove some of the files temporarily, preferably by moving the files to another server. Moving files without inconveniencing users of vital data isn't a simple task and requires advance planning. For example, users must be warned to save and close files by a certain time, and the files must be unavailable for a short time after that. Don't forget to clear at least 148M (preferably 200M) of free drive space to install Windows NT Server 4.0.

In addition to the 148M of free drive space, you need a blank 3 1/2-inch diskette that's labeled *NT Server Emergency Repair Disk* and is further identified with the name of the Windows NT server. You don't need to format the diskette; the Setup program formats the diskette for you. If your A drive accommodates 2.88M diskettes, use an unformatted diskette or a diskette formatted to 1.44M (don't use a diskette preformatted at 2.88M).

Starting the Basic Installation

After you make your decisions, gather the necessary information, and prepare your computer, you're ready to run Setup. The setup process involves many steps and a substantial number of Press Enter to Continue prompts. Most of the decisions don't need detailed explanations, but some steps are critical for a satisfactory installation. Following is a summary of steps that comprise the installation process:

1. Create boot diskettes, if necessary.

2. Start Setup from the boot diskettes, a network share, or from an existing operating system.

3. Choose to install or repair.

4. Detect mass storage.

5. Choose to upgrade or install from scratch.

6. Confirm basic system information.

7. Set up your fixed-disk drive(s).

8. Watch the copying process.

9. Identify the user, company name, and licensing terms.

10. Choose the type of domain controller.

11. Select the locale.

12. Set the administrator password.

13. Check for the Pentium floating-point division bug.

14. Fine-tune the installation.

15. Join the network.

16. Finish Setup.

17. Configure virtual memory.

18. Install IIS.

19. Set the time and date.

20. Configure your display.

21. Create the emergency repair disk.

22. Restart the computer for the last time.

The following sections describe each of these steps in detail.

Running the Setup Program

If you're installing Windows NT Server 4.0 on a computer with a CD-ROM drive supported by Windows NT Server, insert the first Setup diskette, labeled *Setup Boot Disk*, in the A drive; insert the Windows NT Server CD-ROM in the CD-ROM drive; reboot the computer; and skip to the section "Choosing to Install or Repair." Setup uses diskettes for the first part of the installation procedure, and then detects the CD-ROM drive automatically and uses the CD-ROM drive for the rest of the installation.

The following sections pertain to installing Windows NT Server over the network from another server or from a CD-ROM drive that isn't supported by Windows NT Server but is supported by DOS or Windows 95.

Creating Setup Boot Disks. The Windows NT Server 4.0 distribution CD-ROM is bootable, but relatively few CD-ROM drives and/or system BIOSes support bootable CD-ROMs. To install Windows NT Server 4.0 on most PCs with a supported CD-ROM but no operating system installed, you must use Setup boot disks to install a minimal version of Windows NT on the PC. If you have the distribution CD-ROM but no boot disks, have three formatted, blank 3 1/2-inch diskettes ready and follow these steps to create the required boot disks:

1. Insert the distribution CD-ROM in the CD-ROM drive of a PC running DOS, Windows NT, or Windows 95. If the Setup splash screen appears, close it.

2. At the command prompt, log on to the CD-ROM drive and change to the \I386 folder (or the folder for the appropriate platform).

3. Type **winnt /ox** (DOS or Windows 95) or **winnt32 /ox** (Windows NT) and press Enter to start the Setup program.

4. Accept or correct the path to the CD-ROM files, and then press Enter or click Continue. Windows NT displays the dialog shown in figure 6.2.

5. Insert a diskette labeled *Windows NT 4.0 Server Setup Disk #3* in the A drive and click OK to continue.

6. When prompted, insert the remaining two diskettes, *Windows NT 4.0 Server Setup Disk #2* and *Windows NT 4.0 Server Setup Boot Disk*, and press Enter or click OK.

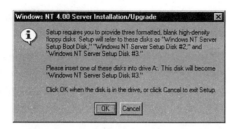

Fig. 6.2 The Windows NT 4.00 Server Installation/Upgrade dialog for creating Setup boot disks.

The diskettes are necessary if your Windows NT installation becomes corrupt, requiring use of the emergency repair disk created later in the installation process. Leave the Setup boot disk in the A drive and restart your computer, booting from the A drive. Skip to the "Choosing to Install or Repair" section to continue with the description of the setup process.

Installing from a Network Server. Installing over the network is more common for workstations, which may not all have CD-ROM drives, than for servers. You must have an operating system installed and a functional network connection to install Windows NT Server from a network server. To install Windows NT Server 4.0 over the network, you need another machine on the network with either the Windows NT Server CD-ROM in a shared CD-ROM drive, or a prepared Windows NT Server installation folder with a copy of one of the three folders from the CD-ROM:

- \I386 contains all the files needed to install to computers using Intel 80486 and Pentium processors. These processors are members of the Intel I386 family.

- \Mips is for RISC machines using Silicon Graphics MIPS processor(s).

- \Alpha is for RISC machines using Digital Equipment Corporation's Alpha processor family.

- \Ppc is for PowerPCs from Apple, IBM, and others using the PowerPC RISC processor.

To prepare an installation folder for network setup of Windows NT Server, follow these steps:

1. Create a folder on the server with an appropriate name, such as Installnt.

2. Share the folder, giving the Administrator group at least Read access.

3. Create a subfolder with the same name as the one you copy from the CD-ROM—for example, \I386.

4. Copy the installation files from the CD-ROM's subfolder to the new installation subfolder.

II

Deploying Windows NT

To start Setup from the new computer after the Windows NT installation folder is created, or to run from an unsupported CD-ROM drive, you follow almost identical steps:

1. Label four blank 3 1/2-inch diskettes as *Setup boot disk*, *Setup disk 2*, *Setup disk 3*, and *NT Server Emergency Repair Disk*. Add the name of the computer to the emergency repair diskette. You can use the other three diskettes for installation on other computers; the emergency repair diskette is specific to the computer on which the installation is made.

2. Start the machine where Windows NT Server is to be installed by using the existing operating system, which must either support an attached CD-ROM drive or have a connection to the network.

3. If the machine is using DOS, change to the network drive and directory or to the CD-ROM drive and directory that holds the installation files. If the machine is using Windows 95, open an Explorer window for the network or CD drive. If the machine is using a previous version of Windows NT, open a File Manager window for the network or CD drive. (If the machine runs Windows 3.1x, exit Windows, if necessary, and perform the installation from DOS.)

4. From DOS, run WINNT.EXE by typing `winnt` and pressing Enter. From earlier versions of Windows NT, run Winnt32.exe by double-clicking the file in File Manager. From Windows 95, run Winnt.exe by choosing Run from the Start menu, typing `winnt`, and then pressing Enter.

5. When requested, provide the drive and directory name for the location of the installation files.

6. Insert each formatted setup diskette when prompted. The WINNT or WINNT32 program copies the required setup files to the diskettes.

7. Continue the setup process as described later, starting with the section "Choosing to Install or Repair."

Installing from an Existing Operating System. If you have a compatible CD-ROM drive and a compatible operating system, you can start the Setup program from DOS or Windows as follows:

■ For Windows NT 3.5+ or DOS/Windows 3.1+, use the method described earlier in the "Creating Setup Boot Disks" section, but omit the /ox command-line parameter.

■ For Windows 95, inserting the CD-ROM in the drive uses AutoPlay to display the splash screen shown in figure 6.3. (This splash screen also appears if you insert the CD-ROM into a PC running Windows NT 4.0, which also supports AutoPlay.)

Fig. 6.3   The Windows 95 and Windows NT splash screen for installation from the operating system.

In either case, you're prompted to confirm the location of the files on the CD-ROM; then Setup copies all the setup files to a temporary folder, requests you to reboot, and begins the installation process. You need approximately 250M of free disk space to store the installation copies and the working copies of the files. When the files are copied, remove the CD-ROM from the drive (and the diskette, if any, in your A drive), and reboot the computer. On restarting, the Boot.ini file automatically starts the Windows NT setup process.

Choosing to Install or Repair

If you use the setup diskettes, Setup runs from the setup boot diskette, requests a second diskette, and then displays a blue (DOS) screen titled Windows NT Server 4.0 Setup: Welcome to Setup, which asks whether you want to repair an existing Windows NT Server installation or continue with a full installation.

> **Tip**
>
> At any point in the setup process where you're prompted for input, pressing F1 provides Help. Pressing F3 exits Setup. Input options are summarized at the bottom of the screen.

The first part of this chapter covers installing Windows NT Server 4.0 for the first time, so press Enter to continue the installation process. You're requested to insert Setup Disk #2 and press Enter.

> **Note**
>
> One of the last setup steps is building the emergency repair diskette, which you use to repair a damaged or corrupted installation of Windows NT Server. The repair process is described in the "Repairing the Windows NT Server Operating System Installation" section near the end of this chapter.

Detecting Mass Storage

The mass storage devices (SCSI and IDE adapters) on your system ordinarily are detected automatically during the setup process, and Setup automatically installs the required driver(s). You have the option of skipping the automatic detection process and selecting the driver yourself. The automatic detection process is somewhat slow, so if you're installing Windows NT Server on a number of similar machines, you might want to select the mass storage driver manually.

> **Note**
>
> If your device isn't on the supported hardware list, the automatic detection process won't find it. Also, some hardware combinations cause the automatic detection to hang the Setup program. If Setup hangs, reboot the computer, start Setup again, and bypass the automatic detection process. Allow the automatic detection at least five minutes before assuming it has hung.

Press Enter to proceed or S to skip the automatic detection process. After Setup detects hardware and loads drivers, you're given an opportunity to confirm the hardware that was detected and to add more mass storage devices, if necessary. If you press S to add devices manually, a list of drivers known to Windows NT appears; choose a driver from the list. If you have a driver disk, choose Other and insert the disk when prompted. When all the drivers are loaded, press Enter to continue.

> **Note**
>
> IDE and ESDI drives are detected at this point too, but not shown to you. You set up your fixed-disk drives later in the Setup process.

After selecting mass storage devices, the Windows NT End-User License Agreement (EULA) appears. To read the license agreement, press Page Down 13 times, and then press F8 to accept the terms of the agreement. If you don't press F8, installation terminates.

You're then requested to insert the distribution CD-ROM into the drive and press Enter.

Choosing to Upgrade or Install from Scratch

If an earlier version of Windows NT is detected on your hard drive, you have the opportunity at this point to upgrade, preserving as many of your old settings as possible. If you choose to upgrade by pressing Enter, skip to the "Watching the Copying Process" section. If you choose to install from scratch by pressing N, or if a previous version wasn't installed on your hard drive, the installation continues as described in the following section.

Confirming Basic System Information

Setup reports the basic computer hardware it has detected and asks for your confirmation of its findings. You may want to change the keyboard layout at this point (if, for example, you're using a Dvorak or other alternative layout), but the balance of the reported information is almost invariably correct. To change an entry, use the up and down arrows to highlight it, and then press Enter. A list of choices appears; choose the one you want with the up and down arrows and the Enter key. When the hardware summary is correct, highlight No Changes and press Enter to continue.

Setting Up Your Fixed-Disk Drives

After you watch the detection of mass storage devices, add more drivers if needed, and then confirm your hardware, you next must make Windows NT Server work with your fixed-disk drive(s). This involves the following basic steps:

1. Partition the drive(s).

2. Format with the right file system.

3. Specify the installation folder.

The following sections describe each of the preceding steps in detail.

Partitioning the Drive(s). The first partition is the system partition. On x86-based machines, the system partition is drive C. If you have more than one partition, make sure that the first one (the C partition) has sufficient room for the system files (about 148M).

Setup shows the partitions that already exist on your fixed-disk drive. Use the up and down arrow keys to highlight a partition or the unpartitioned space; then press D to delete it, C to create a partition in unpartitioned space, or Enter to choose it as the system partition.

Formatting with the Right File System. Next, you choose a file system and optionally format the partition with that system. You can choose to format the partition with FAT or NTFS; keep in mind, however, that these two options destroy the data stored on the partition. If the partition is already formatted, you can elect to convert the partition to NTFS or retain the existing format. As noted earlier in the chapter, unless you have a compelling reason to use the FAT format, choose NTFS.

Use the up and down arrows to highlight your choice (for example, Convert to NTFS) and press Enter to continue.

Specifying the Install Folder. Setup now needs to know where to put the Windows NT and system files. The default suggestion, C:\WINNT, ordinarily is satisfactory. You can, however, install these files in a folder of any name on a partition of the first physical (boot) drive. To change the folder name, use the Backspace key to remove the suggested name and type your chosen name.

At this point, Setup looks for previous versions of Windows on your machine. (If you formatted your system partition in the previous step, you wiped out any previous

II

Deploying Windows NT

versions that were on the machine.) Rather than ask you to choose whether to upgrade or dual boot, Setup determines the answer based on whether you use the same folder. Following are your options when you choose the same or a different installation folder:

- If you had a previous version of Windows NT, installing in the same folder causes your old settings to be used in this new installation and the old version to be removed. Installing in a different folder allows you to dual-boot between the older version and Windows NT Server 4.0.

- If you had Windows 95, you can't migrate your settings and aren't allowed to use the same folder. You can dual-boot between Windows 95 and Windows NT Server 4.0.

- If you had Windows 3.x, you dual-boot regardless of the folder choice you make. If you use the same folder, your settings are migrated; if you use a different folder, you must specify new settings throughout the rest of Setup.

Tip

You don't want to dual-boot a server machine, so be sure to remove Windows 95 or Windows 3.x before reaching this step. If you want to remove an existing operating system at this point, exit Setup, delete Windows 95 or Windows 3.x, and restart the installation process.

Watching the Copying Process

Now that Setup can access your partitioned and formatted drive(s), and has established where the system files are to go, it's time to copy the files to the fixed disk. Before doing so, Setup offers to examine your fixed-disk drive for defects. Press Enter to allow the examination to proceed, or Esc to skip it. (If you're having trouble installing Windows NT Server and find yourself at this point in the install repeatedly, it's not necessary to repeat the examination every time.) After the examination is performed or skipped, Setup copies files to the folder chosen in the previous step. The time required to create the copies depends on the speed of the CD-ROM or network connection, and the performance of your fixed-disk drive.

Note

An error message during the copying process that indicates a checksum error between the file on the CD-ROM and that of your fixed-disk drive indicates a hardware problem. The most likely source of the problem is a damaged CD-ROM surface, dirt on the CD-ROM drive's optical components, a defective fixed disk, or a defective disk controller. Another less likely source of checksum errors is improper termination of a chain of SCSI devices. Improper SCSI termination usually results in an installation failure before the copying process starts.

Recovery from such an error depends on what happened and why. You may be able to correct the problem and choose Retry; more than likely you'll have to begin the Setup process again. If the CD is damaged, you must replace it.

When the copying process is complete, Windows NT Server is ready to run, but additional configuration information is required to finalize the installation process. At this point, you're prompted to remove a diskette still in the A drive. Also remove the CD-ROM. Press Enter to restart the system.

After the computer restarts, the rest of the process proceeds under the operating copy of Windows NT Server. Setup's simple character-based interface is replaced with Windows NT-style dialogs, and you indicate choices by clicking dialog buttons instead of pressing keys. The Help and Exit Setup options remain available, but they're activated by dialog command buttons. Also, you use the Back and Next buttons to move through the Setup Wizard (as Microsoft calls this next stage of Setup). You're requested to insert the CD-ROM into the drive indicated in the Copy Files From text box, and then click OK to copy the additional files. After the files are copied, click Next to continue.

Identifying the User, Company Name, Licensing Terms, and Computer Name

Provide the full (first and last) name of the main user (usually you) and the company name, as discussed earlier in this chapter, if you aren't upgrading an existing Windows NT installation. Click Next to continue.

You must type the product ID from the inside back cover of the installation guide or from the sticker on the Windows NT Server 4.0 CD-ROM's case. Click Next to continue. If you're upgrading an existing Windows NT Server installation, Setup copies files; skip to the "Specifying Creation of an Emergency Repair Disk" section later in this chapter.

The next step asks you to choose your licensing method—Per Server or Per Seat. Per Server licensing requires you to have a client license for every simultaneous connection to this server; Per Seat requires you to have a client license for every client machine in your installation. Which is better for you depends on how many clients and servers you have, and how many servers each client connects to at once. Here are some examples:

- If you have 100 clients but they mostly run stand-alone and connect to a server only 10 at a time, you would need 100 client licenses using the Per Seat method, but only 10 using the Per Server method. Choose Per Server.

- If you have 100 clients and four servers, and every machine is connected to at least two servers at all times, you would need 200 or more licenses using the Per Server method but only 100 using the Per Seat method. Choose Per Seat.

After selecting the licensing method, click Next to enter the computer name for the server, which is limited to a maximum of 14 characters. The name you assign at this point appears to all other computers on the network. Press Next to continue.

▶▶ See "Licensing BackOffice Components," p. 779

Choosing the Type of Domain Controller

The Server Type dialog offers you three options:

- Primary Domain Controller

- Backup Domain Controller

- Stand-Alone Server

You must install the Primary Domain Controller before any other domain servers; this decision is difficult to reverse. The first Windows NT server you install in a network always is a Primary Domain Controller. Click Next to continue.

If this is the first server on your network, you're creating a new domain, so you name the domain at this point. (You should have already picked out a unique domain name.) If the domain already has a Primary Domain Controller, you can join the domain as a Backup Domain Controller. Make sure that the Primary Domain Controller is operational and that you know the administrator password for the domain. If you choose to install this server as a stand-alone server, the domain name is simply the domain you join.

No matter what server type you choose, Setup searches the network for existing domain names. For a Primary Domain Controller, Setup searches to verify that the new name is unique. For a secondary domain controller or a stand-alone server, Setup ensures that the domain name you supply exists.

Setting the Administrator Password

The Administrator account is used to manage this installation of Windows NT Server. Someone who knows the Administrator password can add and delete users, install and remove applications, and make any other system changes that might be required. When you install a Primary Domain Controller, you set this password. Choose a sensible password that's hard to forget yet difficult to guess. You enter it twice in this dialog; both entries must be the same, to rule out a slip of the fingers as you type it.

Dealing with the Pentium Floating-Point Division Bug

If your machine is an Intel Pentium-based computer, Setup checks for the known floating-point division bug. If you have a faulty chip, you're given the option of turning off the Pentium's floating-point operations and simulating them within NT instead. Although the simulated calculations are much slower, they're always right, so you should choose to disable the hardware floating-point calculations. If your Pentium chip doesn't have a faulty floating-point module, you won't see this screen.

Specifying Creation of an Emergency Repair Disk

At the end of a successful setup, Windows NT Server saves the computer's configuration information to the disk so that if your fixed-disk drive becomes corrupted, you can recover your configuration information. At this point in the Setup process, you're asked whether you want to make an emergency repair disk later. Doing so is *strongly* recommended. Using the emergency repair disk is covered later in the "Repairing the Windows NT Server Operating System Installation" section.

Fine-Tuning the Installation

If the computer is to be a dedicated server rather than a workstation, you can save disk space by skipping the installation of accessories such as CD Player, games, screen savers, wallpaper, and so on.

> **Note**
>
> If you've installed Windows NT Server 4.0 on another computer, you can eliminate the Readme files from this installation. Before making this election, however, make sure that you have access to the Windows NT Server 4.0 Readme files on at least one computer.

Choose the components you want installed or not installed in the Select Components dialog. If you want part of a component, such as Multimedia, installed, click the Details button to select individual applications. Click OK on the Details dialog to return to the list of components. When that list has each component selected, unselected, or partially selected as you prefer, click Next to move to the next stage of Setup.

Joining the Network

Now all of Setup is complete, except for setting up the network. You confirm you want to go on to the network portion of Setup by clicking Next. You can't get back to earlier screens after moving to the network portion. You perform the following general steps for the network installation:

1. Describe your connection to the network.

2. Choose to install the Internet Information Server.

3. Choose and configure a network adapter.

4. Choose protocols.

5. Choose services.

6. Confirm network bindings.

7. Start the network and join a domain.

Describing Your Connection to the Network. The first question Setup asks is how you connect to your network. If your machine has a network adapter card (as it almost certainly does), choose Wired to the Network. If you dial up to a network (an unlikely choice for Windows NT Server), choose Remote Access to the Network.

Choosing to Install the Internet Information Server. The Internet Information Server makes your information available over the Internet or a corporate intranet, and is discussed fully in Chapter 19, "Setting Up the Internet Information Server." At this point in the Setup process, you specify only whether you intend to install it.

Choosing and Configuring a Network Adapter. Assuming that you have one or more network adapters, in the next step Setup detects them automatically. A functioning network adapter card is required for installation of a Primary Domain Controller or a Backup Domain Controller, but the network doesn't need to be operational at this point in the installation process.

Click Start Search to find the first adapter. If a second adapter is to be found, click Find Next to search for it. If you have an adapter that wasn't found, click Select from list to specify the card yourself. Click Next to move on.

II

Deploying Windows NT

Choosing Protocols. Next, choose one or more network protocols: IPX/SPX, TCP/IP, or NetBEUI. (This decision is discussed in detail in Chapter 4, "Choosing Network Protocols.") You can configure multiple protocols by checking more than one box in this dialog. The most common combination is NetBEUI and TCP/IP, unless you have an existing Novell NetWare network, in which case you should select all three protocols at this point. You can add or remove network protocols with Control Panel's Network tool after installing Windows NT Server.

Choosing Services. You can choose to install any of these five network services:

- Internet Information Server

- RPC Configuration

- NetBIOS Interface

- Workstation

- Server

Adding new services after the fact is harder than adding them now, and you can use Control Panel's Services tool later to disable services you don't want to run. You also can add or remove network services with the Services page of Control Panel's Network tool (see fig. 6.4). For most server installations, it's best to install all the preceding services at this point.

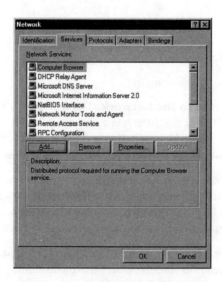

Fig. 6.4   Adding or removing network services in the Services page of the Network property sheet.

Even more services are available if you click Choose From List:

- DHCP Relay Agent

- Gateway (and Client) Services for NetWare

- Microsoft DHCP Server

- Microsoft DNS Server

- Microsoft Internet Information Server

- Microsoft TCP/IP Printing

- Network Monitor Agent

- Network Monitor Tools and Agent

- Remote Access Service

- Remoteboot Service

- RIP for Internet Protocol

- RIP for NWLink IPX/SPX compatible transport

- RPC support for Banyan

- SAP Agent

- Services for Macintosh

- Simple TCP/IP Services

- SNMP Service

- Windows Internet Name Service

Network Settings. Setup confirms that you're ready to install the adapters, protocols, and services that were selected over the previous few dialogs. Click Next, and you have the opportunity to confirm adapter settings, such as the interrupt (IRQ) number and I/O port address (see fig. 6.5). As discussed earlier in the chapter, you should know these settings before you start the installation procedure.

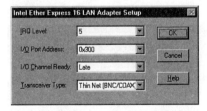

Fig. 6.5 Setting the interrupt number, I/O port address, and other properties for your network adapter.

The Network Settings property sheet is next. You can display the same properties by using the Protocols page of Control Panel's Network tool (see fig. 6.6) after you install Windows NT Server 4.0. To configure a protocol, select it from the list on the Protocols page and click the Properties button. If you're not sure how to use this property sheet, you can leave it for now and bring it up again after Windows NT Server is completely installed.

II

Deploying Windows NT

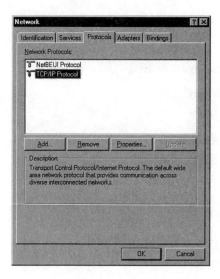

Fig. 6.6 The Protocols page of the Network property sheet for adding and configuring networking protocols.

Each network protocol is configured separately. Figure 6.7 shows the configuration dialog for TCP/IP, the Microsoft TCP/IP Properties sheet.

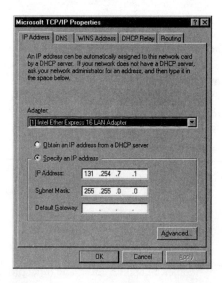

Fig. 6.7 The IP Address page of the Microsoft TCP/IP Properties sheet.

On the IP Address page, set the IP address and subnet mask for your machine, or tell Windows NT to use DHCP (Dynamic Host Configuration Protocol) to assign an IP address dynamically. If you didn't establish these settings during your network planning process, get them from the person who did.

> **Note**
>
> IP addresses uniquely identify machines on TCP/IP networks, such as the Internet, and are specifically assigned. You can't just arbitrarily choose an IP address; you must use an address that makes sense both within your network and, if applicable, on the Internet. The subnet mask is used to distinguish between IP addresses on your network and those that aren't. Like the IP address, the subnet mask is determined during the network planning process. The default gateway, if specified, must also be determined by a network administrator.

The DNS (Domain Naming System) page is used to control the way the server looks up domain names of other computers on a LAN or WAN (see fig. 6.8). You enter the IP addresses of one or more DNS servers accessible to your server. DNS servers translate a fully qualified domain name such as **www.mcp.com** into an IP address. You can get these addresses from the same person who provided your server's IP address. Some networks use multiple DNS servers, checking the local one first and then asking a remote DNS server if the name wasn't found in the local one. To change the priority of an IP address within the list, click the Up↑ or Down↓ buttons.

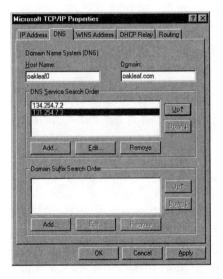

Fig. 6.8 The DNS page of the Microsoft TCP/IP Properties sheet.

▶▶ See "Understanding WINS and DNS Name Resolution," p. 570

The WINS Address page describes the way that WINS (Windows Internet Naming Service) looks up the domain names of other computers (see fig. 6.9). Enter the IP addresses of your primary and secondary WINS servers as provided by the person who told you your own IP address. For machines that are local to your network, you may want to use DNS and LMHOSTS services; if so, select their check boxes. The Scope ID is usually left blank; provide a Scope ID only if you're told to by your network administrator.

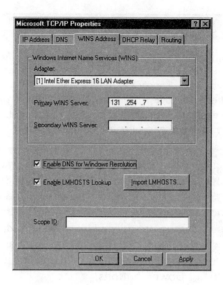

Fig. 6.9   The WINS Address page of the Microsoft TCP/IP Properties sheet.

The DHCP Relay page identifies your DHCP servers. These servers manage IP addresses within your internal network, and you get their addresses from the person who told you to use DHCP rather than specify the IP address of your machine. If you need to adjust the other parameters on this page rather than accept the defaults, this person will tell you so.

The Routing page is relevant only to machines with more than one network adapter with more than one IP address. If you turn on IP forwarding, your server can route traffic between the two networks.

Confirming Network Bindings. Setup gives you the opportunity to adjust your network bindings at this point. If you aren't sure what network bindings are or why you might want to adjust them, leave them alone. The default bindings usually are adequate for installation and network startup.

You can enable and disable communications between services and adapters or protocols by double-clicking the service name, clicking the adapter or protocol, and then clicking the Enable or Disable button.

Starting the Network and Joining a Domain. After Windows NT is configured for your network hardware, Setup loads the network software and establishes a connection to the network. Confirm that you've made all the choices by clicking Next, and then wait while the network starts. Setup asks for a domain name. Provide the same domain name you used earlier, and wait while Setup searches the network. If you're joining a domain but not installing a Primary Domain Controller, provide the Administrator name and password here.

Finishing Setup

Click the Finish button to move to the final Setup steps. Setup creates Program menu groups and desktop icons, if you had an earlier version of Windows installed. Adding groups and icons doesn't install the applications or make any changes to the settings and configurations stored in Windows 3.1+'s .INI or REG.DAT files, or in Windows 95's Registry. You must rerun the application's Setup program if the application must be reconfigured for Windows NT or if you're upgrading from Windows 95.

To finish up the Setup process, you need follow these general steps:

1. Install Internet Information Server 2.0.

2. Set the time and date.

3. Configure your display.

4. Create the emergency repair disk.

5. Restart the server for the last time.

Installing Internet Information Server

The dialogs and decisions involved in installing IIS are covered in detail in Chapter 19, "Setting Up the Internet Information Server." To install only World Wide Web services, clear the Gopher Service and FTP Service check boxes. Click OK to continue. Accept the default folders for the service(s) you install, unless you have a specific reason to do otherwise. Click OK to continue and then click OK again when asked to confirm your choices. Setup copies a number of files to your drive. Click OK when advised that you must establish an Internet domain name for the server.

In the Install Drivers dialog, select SQL Server in the Available ODBC Drivers list and click OK to continue.

Setting the Time and Date. You now get a chance to set the time, date, and time zone. On the Time Zone page, select your time zone from the drop-down list. This list is arranged numerically according to the time difference from Universal Time (UT, formerly known as Greenwich Mean Time, GMT). Zones east of Greenwich, England, appear above it in the list. After you choose your time zone, the map of the world in this dialog scrolls so that your time zone is in the center. Windows NT Server knows the rules for use of Daylight Savings Time; make sure that the Automatically Adjust for Daylight Savings Time box is marked or cleared, as appropriate for your location.

On the Date & Time page, set the current date and time with the spin controls.

After Setup is complete and Windows NT Server is running, you can bring up this property sheet again with the Control Panel's Date/Time tool (see fig. 6.10).

II

Deploying Windows NT

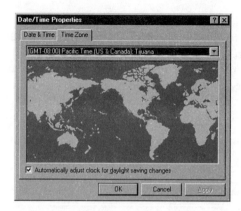

Fig. 6.10   Using the Date/Time tool to set the time zone, and the current time and date.

Configuring Your Display. Until now, the setup program has used standard VGA resolution (640×480 pixels) with 16 colors. Windows NT attempts to detect the type of chip on your graphics adapter card. If you're using an adapter with a popular Windows graphics accelerator chip for which a DirectDraw driver is included with Windows NT, click OK when the Detected Display message box appears. Otherwise, you must install a driver from a diskette provided by the graphics card supplier.

The Settings page of the Display Properties sheet (see fig. 6.11) lets you set a resolution and color depth suited to the combination of your graphics adapter card and video display unit (VDU). Some adapter cards provide additional features and controls on the Settings page. For a simple adapter, follow these steps to set your display properties:

1. Click the Display Type button to confirm that the correct graphics adapter card has been detected, and change the selection, if necessary.

Fig. 6.11   Configuring the color depth and resolution of your display.

2. Adjust the number of colors, resolution, and refresh frequency. For servers, a resolution of 800×600 pixels and a color depth of 256 colors is adequate. If you have a 15-inch or smaller display, the Large Fonts selection improves readability in 800×600 resolution.

3. Click the Test button to examine the results of the settings you choose.

4. Click OK to close the Display Properties sheet.

Creating the Emergency Repair Disk

At this point, Windows NT Server 4.0 is installed, configured, and ready to act as a network server. The final step is to create an emergency repair disk to use in case of a catastrophic failure. Any 3 1/2-inch diskette will suffice, because Setup formats the diskette before copying the files. Label the emergency repair disk with the server name you assigned, and store it in a safe location.

Be sure to update your emergency repair diskette frequently to keep the configuration data up-to-date. Your server's configuration is likely to change appreciably during the first few hours of use as you install applications, change users, and groups, and so on. The pace of change slackens with time, but you should make a habit of updating your emergency repair disk regularly. To create an updated emergency repair disk, follow these steps:

1. Insert your original emergency repair disk or a new diskette in drive A. From the Start menu choose Run, type **rdisk** in the Open text box, and click OK to open the Repair Disk Utility dialog (see fig. 6.12).

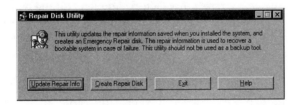

Fig. 6.12   The Repair Disk Utility dialog.

2. Click Update Repair Info to update the diskette's content. (If you've lost your emergency repair disk, insert a blank diskette and choose Create Repair Disk.)

3. Confirm your intent to update the existing emergency repair diskette (see fig. 6.13). Click OK when asked if you want to create an emergency repair disk, and then click OK to format the diskette and create the updated version.

4. After the updated emergency repair disk is created, click Exit to close the Repair Disk Utility dialog.

It's a generally accepted practice to create a duplicate of the emergency repair diskette for off-site storage, along with duplicates of driver disks you used during Setup. Driver diskettes also are needed during the repair process.

II

Deploying Windows NT

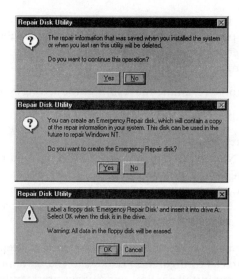

Fig. 6.13 Confirming the update operation.

> **Tip**
>
> Add an entry to the Administrative Tools Program menu for Rdisk.exe to make the program easier to run after every significant configuration change.

Restarting the Server for the Last Time

After you make the emergency repair disk, Setup completes all the tasks required to install and configure Windows NT Server 4.0 and automatically restarts the server. Remove the emergency repair disk from the A drive and remove the CD-ROM to allow the system to boot from the fixed-disk drive. (The boot process takes more time if you converted a FAT partition to NTFS as part of the setup process, because it's at this point the format conversion occurs.) After Windows NT loads, press Ctrl+Alt+Delete to log on, and use the administrative account name and password you created earlier to log on to Windows NT Server. Your installation is complete.

Preparing the Server for Use

If you installed Windows NT Server onto a machine that was running Windows 3.1x, and you installed Windows NT into the same directory as before (typically, \WINDOWS), the Program Manager settings for a user (other than the administrator) are initialized. In this case, the Programs menu choices are based on the Windows 3.1+ settings that were present before Windows NT Server was installed. For example, if there was a program group called Invoices under Windows 3.1+, each new user sees a Programs menu group called Invoices with the same program items in it. Groups with names such as Main aren't migrated in this manner, because new Windows NT Server equivalents of these Programs menu groups were created earlier in the Setup process.

If the machine is to be a dedicated server, with no access by ordinary users, running existing applications is of no consequence. If the server is also used as a workstation (not a recommended practice), create local accounts for the workstation users. Log on to the other users' local accounts to oversee the migration of Windows 3.1+ applications and fix any problems that appear before releasing the computer for others to use.

▶▶ See "Managing User Accounts," p. 421

Repairing the Windows NT Server Operating System Installation

You can ruin your Windows NT Server software in various ways, and in some cases there's no way to recover. Making complete backups frequently is one way to reduce the recover work involved; having an emergency repair diskette is another. This section assumes that you have a problem that prevents your server from booting successfully. It further assumes that the Last Known Good choice during the boot process is of no assistance, and that you can't edit the Registry remotely from another computer to adjust your settings. The last resort is to reinstall Windows NT Server from scratch—but first try using your emergency repair disk.

Gather together (from off-site storage, if necessary) the emergency repair disk, originals or copies of the three Setup diskettes, any driver disks you used during the original installation, and the original CD-ROM used for installation. If any of these are missing, the repair process may be impossible. Follow these steps to attempt to repair the server:

1. Correct hardware problems, if any, and install replacement hardware as needed.

2. Boot from the Windows NT Server 4.0 boot diskette, switch to Setup Disk 2 when prompted, and select Repair at the first prompt. You can select one or more of these choices:

   - Inspect Registry Files

   - Inspect Startup Environment

   - Verify Windows NT System Files

   - Inspect Boot Sector

   Move the highlight up and down through this list with the arrow keys, and press Enter to select or deselect the highlighted item. If you have no idea what's wrong, leave all the items selected. When your list is complete, highlight Continue (perform selected tasks) and press Enter.

3. Repair checks for mass storage devices using the same process as Setup. The steps and keystrokes involved are identical to those discussed in the "Detecting Mass Storage" section earlier in this chapter.

4. When asked if you have the emergency repair disk, press Enter if you do and Esc if you don't.

5. You're prompted for the original installation media (the CD-ROM) so that installed files can be compared to the originals.

6. After a partial file examination process, you have a chance to restore Registry files. You should try at least one repair attempt without restoring Registry files. If that doesn't make the system bootable, and no backups are available, repeat the repair process and restore the Registry files. All changes made since the emergency repair disk was created, whether the installation of an entire application suite or a change to a user's desktop settings, will be lost.

7. Repair examines the remaining files on your fixed-disk drive and compares them to files on the installation media. If a file is found that varies from the original, you're given four choices:

   • Press Esc to skip this file—that is, leave the version Repair thinks is corrupted on your fixed-disk drive.

   • Press Enter to repair this file—that is, copy the original file from the CD-ROM to your fixed-disk drive.

   • Press A to repair this file and all additional files Repair thinks are corrupted, with no more prompts.

   • Press F3 to stop the repair attempt.

8. When the Repair process is complete, you're prompted to remove any diskette still in the drive. Press Enter to restart the computer.

When a reboot is successful, you have the following problems to tackle:

■ You must establish the cause of your catastrophic problem and make sure that it has been solved.

■ You'll likely need to perform some reconfiguration, because some of your configuration information might be lost or reverted to old values.

■ You must restore data from backup tape(s) if data files were lost.

■ You must notify users of the problem and let them know whether they need to update their own configurations.

If the Repair process doesn't work after several tries, you must reinstall Windows NT Server from scratch, and then reinstall applications as needed. In the event of serious corruption, you may lose all the user and group information for your server. A successful Repair operation takes about half as long as an install; always try a Repair first.

> **Note**
>
> If you have another Windows NT server acting as a Backup Domain Controller, you can regain your user and group settings by promoting the BDC to a Primary Domain Controller, reinstalling Windows NT Server as a BDC, and resynchronizing the two domain controllers.

▶▶ See "Understanding the Roles of Domain Controllers," p. 570

From Here...

After you have your server up and running, more work needs to be done before your server can be considered completely installed. The remaining chapters of this part of the book cover other aspects of setting up your server and the clients that connect to the server:

- Chapter 7, "Setting Up Redundant Arrays of Inexpensive Disks (RAID)," explains how the RAID approach can make your system more reliable.

- Chapter 8, "Installing File Backup Systems," explains how to protect the users on your network from personal mistakes, as well as from hardware trouble.

- Chapter 9, "Understanding the Windows NT Registry," introduces you to the database that stores all the settings and configuration information you provide.

- Chapter 10, "Configuring Windows 95 Clients for Networking," tackles the work involved in connecting Windows 95 workstations to your server.

- Chapter 11, "Connecting Other PC Clients to the Network," describes the process of attaching machines running other operating systems to your server.

Two chapters in Part III, "Administering a Secure Network," and two chapters in Part IV, "Wide Area Networking and the Internet," also are relevant to a network administrator performing Windows NT Server 4.0 installations:

- Chapter 12, "Managing User and Group Accounts," covers setting up users and groups on your server to make it usable.

- Chapter 13, "Sharing and Securing Network Resources," describes some of the setting up that a successful network requires.

- Chapter 18, "Managing Remote Access Service," covers the Remote Access Service, including installing it and getting it working.

- Chapter 19, "Setting Up the Internet Information Server," describes the installation process to create a private intranet or to connect your server to the Internet.

II

Deploying Windows NT

Chapter 7

Setting Up Redundant Arrays of Inexpensive Disks (RAID)

A *redundant array of inexpensive disks* (RAID) uses multiple fixed-disk drives, high-speed disk controllers, and special software drivers to increase the safety of your data and to improve the performance of your fixed-disk subsystem. All commercial RAID subsystems use the Small Computer System Interface (SCSI, pronounced "scuzzy"), which now is undergoing a transition from high-speed SCSI-2 to ultra-fast SCSI-3 (also called *ultra-wide SCSI*). Virtually all network servers now use narrow (8-bit) or wide (16-bit) SCSI-2 drives and controllers. Ultra-wide SCSI host adapters for the PCI bus can deliver up to 40M per second (40M/s) of data to and from the PC's RAM.

RAID protects your data by spreading it over multiple disk drives and then calculating and storing parity information. This redundancy allows any one drive to fail without causing the array itself to lose any data. A failed drive can be replaced and its contents reconstructed from the information on the remaining drives in the array.

RAID increases disk subsystem performance by distributing read tasks over several drives, allowing the same data to be retrieved from different locations, depending on which location happens to be closest to the read head(s) at the instant the data is requested.

There are different levels of RAID, each of which is optimized for various types of data handling and storage requirements. RAID can be implemented in hardware or as add-on software. Modern network operating systems, such as Windows NT Server, provide native support for one or more RAID levels.

The various component parts of RAID technology were originally developed for mainframes and minicomputers. Until recently, the deployment of RAID systems was limited by its high cost to those environments. In the past few years, however, RAID has become widely available in the PC LAN environment. The cost of disk drives has plummeted. Hardware RAID controllers have become, if not mass-market items, at least reasonably priced. The cost objections to implement RAID systems are now disappearing. Your server deserves to have a RAID system; don't even consider building a server that doesn't use RAID.

In this chapter you learn how to

- Use RAID to increase the security of your data and the performance of your server

- Balance the benefits and drawbacks of the various RAID levels and how to choose a RAID level to match your specific data storage requirements

- Decide between hardware-based RAID implementations and the native software RAID support provided by the Windows NT Server operating system

II

Deploying Windows NT

> **Note**
>
> Most of the chapters of this book use the term *fixed-disk drive* to distinguish these drives from other data-storage devices, such as removable media devices (typified by Iomega's Zip and Jaz products), CD-ROM, magneto-optic, and other storage systems that use the term *drive*. In this chapter, the term *drive* means a fixed-disk (Winchester-type) drive.

Understanding RAID Levels

Although the various component parts of RAID have been used in the mainframe and minicomputer arenas for years, the RAID model was originally defined in a white paper published in 1987 by the University of California at Berkeley. This paper set the theoretical framework on which subsequent RAID implementations have been built.

The paper defines five levels of RAID, numbered 1 through 5. RAID levels aren't indicative of the degree of data safety or increased performance—they simply define how the data is divided and stored on the disk drives comprising the array, and how and where parity information is calculated and stored. In other words, the higher number isn't necessarily better.

Disk drives do only two things: write data and read data. Depending on the application, the disk subsystem may be called on to do frequent small reads and writes; or the drive may need to do less frequent, but larger, reads and writes. An application server running a client-server database, for example, tends toward frequent small reads and writes, whereas a server providing access to stored images tends toward less frequent, but larger, reads and writes. The various RAID levels vary in their optimization for small reads, large reads, small writes, and large writes. Although most servers have a mixed disk access pattern, choosing the RAID level optimized for the predominant environment maximizes the performance of your disk subsystem.

The various RAID levels are optimized for various data storage requirements, in terms of redundancy levels and performance issues. Different RAID levels store data bit-wise, byte-wise, or sector-wise over the array of disks. Similarly, parity information may be distributed across the array or contained on a single physical drive.

RAID levels 1 and 5 are very common in PC LAN environments. All hardware and software RAID implementations provide at least these two levels. RAID level 3 is used occasionally in specialized applications, and is supported by most hardware and some software RAID implementations. RAID levels 2 and 4 are seldom, if ever, used in PC LAN environments, although some hardware RAID implementations offer these levels.

> **Note**
>
> Although RAID really has only levels 1 through 5 defined, you'll commonly see references to RAID 0, RAID 0/1, RAID 6, RAID 7, and RAID 10, all of which are *de facto* extensions of the original RAID specification. These uses have become so common that they're now universally accepted. Because RAID is a model or theoretical framework (rather than a defined protocol or implementation), manufacturers continue to market improved RAID technology with arbitrarily assigned RAID levels.

The following sections describe the RAID Advisory Board, which sets the standards for RAID systems, and the features that distinguish the RAID levels from one another.

The RAID Advisory Board

The RAID Advisory Board (RAB) is a consortium of manufacturers of RAID equipment and other interested parties. RAB is responsible for developing and maintaining RAID standards and has formal programs covering education, standardization, and certification. Supporting these three programs are six committees: Functional Test, Performance Test, RAID-Ready Drive, Host Interface, RAID Enclosure, and Education.

RAB sells several documents, the most popular of which is *The RAIDbook*, first published in 1993. *The RAIDbook* covers the fundamentals of RAID and defines each RAID level. It's a worthwhile acquisition if you want to learn more about RAID.

The RAB Certification Program awards logos to equipment that passes its compatibility- and performance-testing suites. The RAB Conformance Logo certifies that the component so labeled complies with the named RAID level designation as published in *The RAIDbook*. The RAB Gold Certificate Logo certifies that a product meets the functional and performance specifications published by RAB.

Note

For more information about the RAID Advisory Board and its programs, contact Joe Molina, RAB Chairman, at the RAID Advisory Board, affiliated with Technology Forums Ltd., 13 Marie Lane, St. Peter, Minnesota 56082-9423, (507) 931-0967, fax (507) 931-0976, e-mail **0004706032@mcimail.com**. The RAID Advisory Board can also be reached via the Web at **http://www.andataco.com/rab/**.

RAID 0

RAID 0 is a high-performance, zero-redundancy array option. RAID 0 isn't properly RAID at all. It stripes blocks of data across multiple disk drives to increase the throughput of the disk subsystem, as shown in figure 7.1, but it offers no redundancy. If one drive fails in a RAID 0 array, the data on all drives on the array is inaccessible. RAID 0 is used primarily for applications needing the highest possible reading and writing data rate.

Nevertheless, there's a place for RAID 0. Understanding RAID 0 is important because the same striping mechanism used in RAID 0 is used to increase performance in other RAID levels. RAID 0 is inexpensive to implement for two reasons:

- No disk space is used to store parity information, eliminating the need to buy either larger disk drives or more of them for a given amount of storage.

- The algorithms used by RAID 0 are simple ones that don't add much overhead or require a dedicated processor.

RAID 0 offers high performance on reads and writes of short and long data elements. If your application requires large amounts of fast disk storage and you've made other provisions for backing up this data to your satisfaction, RAID 0 is worth considering.

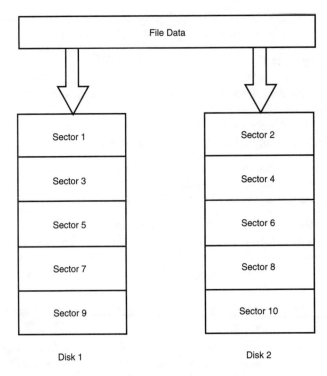

Fig. 7.1   A diagram of RAID 0 (Sector Striping) with two drives.

RAID 0 uses striping to store data. *Striping* means that data blocks are alternately written to the different physical disk drives that make up the logical volume represented by the array. For instance, your RAID 0 array might comprise three physical disk drives that are visible to the operating system as one logical volume. Suppose that your block size is 8K and that a 32K file is to be written to disk. With RAID 0, the first 8K block may be written to physical drive 1, the second block to drive 2, the third to drive 3, and the fourth and final 8K block again to drive 1. Your single 32K file is thus stored as four separate blocks residing on three separate physical hard disk drives.

This block-wise distribution of data across multiple physical hard disks introduces two parameters used to quantify a RAID 0 array. The size of the block used—in this case, 8K—is referred to as the *chunk size*. The chunk size determines how much data is written to a disk drive in each operation. The number of physical hard disk drives comprising the array determines the *stripe width*. Both chunk size and stripe width affect the performance of a RAID 0 array.

When a logical read request is made to the RAID 0 array (fulfillment of which requires that an amount of data larger than the chunk size be retrieved), this request is broken into multiple smaller physical read requests, each of which is directed to and serviced by the individual physical drives on which the multiple blocks are stored. Although these multiple read requests are generated serially, doing so takes little time. The bulk of the time needed to fulfill the read request is used to transfer the data itself. With sequential reads, which involve little drive head seeking, the bottleneck becomes the internal transfer rate of the drives themselves. Striping lets this transfer activity occur in parallel on the individual disk drives that make up the array, so the elapsed time until the read request is completely fulfilled is greatly reduced.

Striping doesn't come without cost in processing overhead, and this is where chunk size affects performance. Against the benefit of having multiple spindles at work to service a single logical read request, you must weigh the overhead processing cost required to write and then read this data from many disks rather than just one. (*Spindle* is a commonly used synonym for a physical drive.) Each SCSI disk access requires numerous SCSI commands to be generated and then executed, and striping the data across several physical drives multiplies the effort required accordingly.

Reducing the block size too far can cause the performance benefits of using multiple spindles to be swamped by the increased time needed to generate and execute additional SCSI commands. You can actually decrease performance by using too small a block size. The break-even point is determined by your SCSI host adapter and by the characteristics of the SCSI hard disk drives themselves, but, generally speaking, a block size smaller than 8K risks performance degradation. Using block sizes of 16K, 32K, or larger offers correspondingly greater performance benefits.

Sequential reads and writes make up a small percentage of total disk activity on a typical server disk subsystem. Most disk accesses are random; by definition, this means that you're probably going to need to move the heads to retrieve a particular block of data. Because head positioning is a physical process, relatively speaking it's very slow. The benefit of striping in allowing parallel data transfer from multiple spindles is much less significant in random access because all the system components are awaiting relatively slow head positioning to occur. Therefore, striping does little to benefit any particular random-access disk transaction. Strangely, however, it does benefit random-access disk throughput as a whole, as explained in the following paragraphs.

Imagine a scene at your local hardware store. There's only one checkout line, and the owner is considering opening more. The single existing checkout line works well when the store isn't busy, but at peak times customers have to stand in line too long. Some customers pay cash, whereas others use credit cards.

The owner opens four additional checkout lines, but decides to dedicate particular lines to particular items—one line for garden supplies, one for paint, one for tools, and so forth. He notices that, although this scheme reduces the average wait, sometimes one checkout line has people waiting in it while other lines are free. His next step is to allow any of the five lines to process any type of item. He immediately notices a big drop in average wait time and is satisfied with this arrangement until he notices that the queues haven't completely disappeared. Because some individual transactions take longer than others, any given line may move unpredictably more slowly than others, leaving customers standing in line while other checkout lines are free. His final modification is to install a serpentine queue ahead of the checkout lines to allow each customer in turn to use whichever checkout line becomes free first.

In this example of a branch of mathematics called *queuing theory*, the checkout lines are analogous to the physical hard drives in the array, and the customers are analogous to disk transactions. Customers who pay cash are analogous to disk reads, and those who use a credit card are analogous to disk writes. Just as a checkout clerk can ring up only so many items in a given amount of time, even a very fast hard drive is limited in the number of disk transactions per second it can execute. Just like many people can show up at the checkout line almost simultaneously, a server can generate many more disk requests in a short period of time than the disk can process. Because server requests tend to be bursty—many requests occurring nearly simultaneously followed by a period with few or no requests—the disk subsystem must buffer or queue outstanding requests at times of peak demand and then process these requests as demand slackens.

Because striping distributes the single logical volume's data across several physical drives, each of which can process disk transactions independently of the other drives, striping provides the equivalent of additional dedicated checkout lines. Requests are routed to the physical drive that contains the data needed, thereby dividing a single long queue into two or more shorter queues, depending on the number of drives in the array. The number of drives over which the data is distributed is called the *stripe width*. Because each drive has its own spindle and head mechanism, these requests are processed in parallel, shortening the time required on average to fulfill any particular disk request.

In most servers with a disk subsystem bottleneck, the problem is found to be an unequal workload distribution among the physical disk drives. It's not uncommon to see servers with several physical hard drives in which 90 percent or more of the total disk activity is confined to just one of these drives. RAID 0 and striping addresses this problem by distributing the workload evenly and eliminating any single drive as a bottleneck. RAID 0 improves read and write performance for both random small block I/O and sequential large block I/O. What RAID 0 doesn't do is protect your data. There's no redundancy, and the loss of any single drive in a RAID 0 array renders the contents of the remaining drives useless.

Note

One of the primary applications for RAID 0 is the capture and playback of high-quality digital video and audio data. By adding multiple wide-SCSI 2 drives, such as the 4.3G Seagate Barracuda ST15150W, to a chain of devices connected to an Adaptec AHA-3940UW SCSI host adapter, you can obtain sustained data-transfer rates up to almost the 40M/s rating of the host adapter. Such data rates can support the 270Mbps (megabits per second) data rate of decompressed, component digital video that conforms to the international ITU-R BT.601 (D-1) standard used for broadcast television. This application for RAID 0 pertains to high-performance Windows NT Workstation 4.0 installations, but not to conventional network servers.

RAID 1

What do you do to make sure that you don't suffer by losing something? The obvious answer is to make a copy of it. RAID 1 works this way, making two complete copies of everything to mirrored or duplexed pairs of disk drives. This 100 percent redundancy means that if you lose a drive in a RAID 1 array, you have another drive with an exact duplicate of the failed drive's contents. RAID 1, shown in figure 7.2, offers the greatest level of redundancy, but at the highest cost for disk drives.

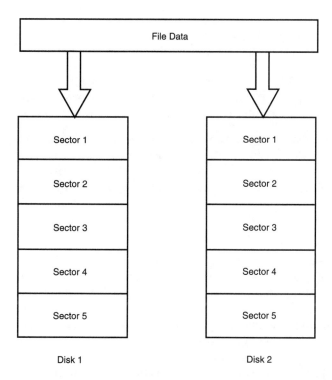

Fig. 7.2 A diagram of RAID 1 (mirroring or duplexing) with two drives.

Mirroring means that each disk drive has a twin. Anything written to one drive is also written to the second drive simultaneously. Mirroring is 100 duplication of your drives. If one drive fails, its twin can replace it without loss of data.

Mirroring has two disadvantages:

- The most obvious is that you must buy twice as many disk drives to yield a given amount of storage.

- The process of writing to both drives and maintaining coherency of their contents introduces overhead, which slows writes.

Mirroring has two advantages:

- Your data is safely duplicated on two physical devices, making catastrophic data loss much less likely.

- Read performance is greatly increased because reads can be made by the drive whose heads happen to be closest to the requested data.

Duplexing is similar to mirroring, but it adds a second host adapter to control the second drive or set of drives. The only disadvantage of duplexing, relative to mirroring, is the cost of the second host adapter—although duplex host adapters, such as the Adaptec AHA-3940W, are less costly than buying two AHA-2940W or AHA-2940UW single-host adapters. Duplexing eliminates the host adapter as a single point of failure.

RAID 1 is the most common level used in mainframes, where cost has always been a low priority relative to data safety. The rapidly dropping cost of disk storage has made RAID 1 a popular choice in PC LAN servers as well. Conventional wisdom says that RAID 1 is the most expensive RAID implementation, due to the requirement for buying twice as many disk drives. In reality, RAID 1 may be the most expensive way to implement RAID, or it may be the least expensive, depending on your environment.

In a large server environment, the cost of duplicating every disk drive quickly adds up, making RAID 1 very expensive. With smaller servers, however, the economics can be very different. If your server has only one SCSI hard disk drive installed, you may find that you can implement RAID 1 for only the relatively small cost of buying another similar disk drive. When this book was written, the cost of 1G of high-performance SCSI-2 storage was about $250, based on the $1,150 street price of a 4.3G Seagate ST15150W drive.

RAID 1 is provided as a standard software feature with most network operating systems, including Windows NT Server 4.0. You may also find that your SCSI host adapter offers RAID 1 support—although it may be called something else. If the host adapter manual doesn't mention RAID 1, check for references to hardware support for mirroring or duplexing. If you find that your SCSI adapter does support hardware mirroring, you have what you need to implement RAID 1 mirroring in hardware. Simply install another drive similar to the existing one (or identical, depending on the host adapter requirements), reconfigure it in accordance with the directions in the manual, and you're running RAID 1. If you have a choice between using either Windows NT Server 4.0 native software RAID 1 support or that provided by your SCSI host bus adapter, choose the hardware solution. Implementing RAID in hardware offers better performance and doesn't put any additional load on the server.

RAID 1 Read Performance. RAID 1 reads are usually faster than those of a stand-alone drive. To return to the hardware store analogy, there are now multiple checkout lines, each of which can handle any customer. With RAID 1 reads, any given block of data can be read from either drive, thereby shortening queues, lowering drive usage, and increasing read performance. This increase occurs only with multithreaded reads. Single-threaded reads show no performance difference, just as though all but one of the checkout lines were closed.

Most RAID 1 implementations offer two alternative methods for optimizing read performance. The first is referred to as *circular queue* or *round-robin scheduling*. Using this method, read requests are simply alternated between the two physical drives, with each drive serving every second read request. This method equalizes the read workload between the drives and is particularly appropriate for random-access environments, where small amounts of data—record or block sized—are being accessed frequently. It's less appropriate for sequential-access environments, where large amounts of data are being retrieved. Most disk drives have buffers used to provide read-ahead optimization, and the drive hardware itself reads and stores the data immediately following the requested block on the assumption that this data is most likely to be requested next. Alternating small block requests between two physical drives can eliminate the benefit of this read-ahead buffering.

The second method used in RAID 1 to increase read performance is called *geometric*, *regional*, or *assigned cylinder scheduling*. This method depends on the fact that head positioning is by far the slowest activity that a disk drive engages in. By giving each of the two drives comprising the RAID 1 array responsibility for covering only half of the physical drive, this head positioning time can be minimized. For example, by using mirrored drives, each of which has 1,024 cylinders, the first drive might be assigned responsibility for fulfilling all requests for data that's stored on cylinders 0 through 511, with the second drive covering cylinders 512 through 1,023.

Although this method is superficially attractive, it seldom works in practice. First, few drives have their data distributed in such a way that any specific cylinder is equally likely to be accessed. Operating system files, swap files, user applications, and other frequently read files are likely to reside near the front of the disk. In this situation, your first disk may be assigned literally 90 percent or more of the read requests. Second, even if the data were to be distributed to equalize access across the portion of the disk occupied by data, few people run their drives at full capacity, so the second drive would have correspondingly less to do. This problem can be addressed by allowing a user-defined split ratio, perhaps assigning disk 1 to cover the first 10 percent or 20 percent of the physical drive area and disk 2 to cover the remainder. In practice, no known RAID 1 systems allow user tuning to this extent.

RAID 1 Write Performance. RAID 1 writes are more problematic. Because all data has to be written to both drives, it appears that there's a situation where customers have to go through one checkout line to complete a transaction. They then have to go to the back of the other checkout line, wait in the queue, and then again complete the same transaction at the other register. RAID 1, therefore, provides a high level of data safety by replicating all data, an increase in read performance by allowing either physical drive to fulfill the read request, and a lower level of write performance due to the necessity of writing the same information to both drives.

Overall RAID 1 Performance. It might seem that RAID 1 would have little overall impact on performance, because the increase in read performance would be balanced by the decrease in write performance. In reality, this is seldom the case.

First, in most server environments, reads greatly outnumber writes. In a database, for example, any particular record may be read 10 times or 100 times for every single time it's written. Similarly, operating system executables, user application program files, and overlays are essentially read only. Any factor that benefits read performance at the expense of write performance will greatly increase overall performance for most servers most of the time.

Second, although it may seem reasonable to assume that writing to two separate drives would halve write performance, in reality the performance hit is usually only 10 percent to 20 percent for mirrored writes. Here's why: Although both physical writes must be executed before the logical write to the array can be considered complete, and the two write requests themselves are generated serially, the actual physical writes to the two drives occur in parallel. Because it's the head positioning and subsequent writing that occupy the bulk of the time required for the entire transaction, the extra time needed to generate the second write request has just a small impact on the total time required to complete the write.

RAID 2

RAID 2 is a proprietary RAID architecture patented by Thinking Machines Inc. RAID 2 distributes the data across multiple drives at the bit level. RAID 2 uses multiple dedicated disks to store parity information and, thus, requires that an array contain a relatively large number of individual disk drives. For example, a RAID 2 array with four data drives requires three dedicated parity drives. RAID 2 has the highest redundancy of any of the parity-oriented RAID schemes.

The bit-wise orientation of RAID 2 means that every disk access occurs in parallel. RAID 2 is optimized for applications such as imaging, which requires transfer of large amounts of contiguous data.

RAID 2 isn't a good choice for random-access applications, which require frequent, small reads and writes. The amount of processing overhead needed to fragment and reassemble data makes RAID 2 slow, relative to other RAID levels. The large number of dedicated parity drives required makes RAID 2 expensive. Because nearly all PC LAN environments have heavy random-disk access, RAID 2 has no place in a PC LAN. However, RAID 2 does have some specific advantages for special-purpose digital video servers.

RAID 3

RAID 3, shown in figure 7.3, stripes data across drives, usually at the byte level, although bit-level implementations are possible. RAID 3 dedicates one drive in the array to storing parity information.

Like RAID 2, RAID 3 is optimized for long sequential disk accesses in applications such as imaging and digital video storage, and is inappropriate for random-access environments such as PC LANs. Any single drive in a RAID 3 array can fail without causing data loss, because the data can be reconstructed from the remaining drives. RAID 3 is sometimes offered as an option on PC-based RAID controllers, but is seldom used.

RAID 3 can be considered an extension of RAID 0, in that RAID 3 stripes small chunks of data across multiple physical drives. In a RAID 3 array that comprises four physical drives, for example, the first block is written to the first physical drive, the second block to the second drive, and the third block to the third drive. The fourth block isn't written to the fourth drive, however; it's written to the first drive to begin the round-robin again.

The fourth drive isn't used directly to store user data. Instead, the fourth drive stores the results of parity calculations performed on the data written to the first three drives. This small chunk striping provides good performance on large amounts of data, because all three data drives operate in parallel. The fourth, or parity, drive provides the redundancy to ensure that the loss of any one drive doesn't cause the array to lose data.

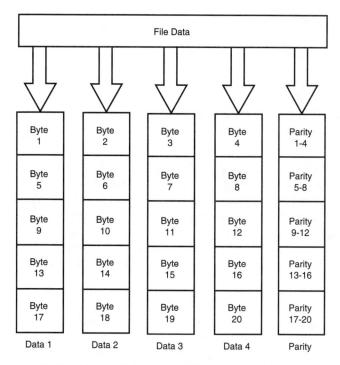

Fig. 7.3   A diagram of RAID 3 (byte striping with dedicated parity disk) with three drives.

For sequential data transfers, RAID 3 offers high performance due to striping, and low cost due to its reliance on a single parity drive. It's this single parity drive, however, that's the downfall of RAID 3 for most PC LAN applications. By definition, no read to a RAID 3 array requires that the parity drive be accessed unless data corruption has occurred on one or more of the data drives. Reads, therefore, proceed quickly. However, every write to a RAID 3 array requires that the single parity drive be accessed and written to in order to store the parity information for the data write that just occurred. The random access typical of a PC LAN environment means that the parity drive in a RAID 3 array is overused, with long queues for pending writes, whereas the data drives are underused because they can't proceed until parity information is written to the dedicated parity drive.

To return to the hardware store analogy, RAID 3 allows multiple checkout lines, all but one of which accept only cash. The sole remaining checkout line accepts only credit cards. As long as most of your customers pay cash, this scheme works well. If, instead, many customers decide to pay by credit card, the queue for the single checkout line that accepts credit cards grows longer and longer while the checkout clerks in the cash lines have nothing to do. In the same way, RAID 3 works well in read-intensive environments, but it breaks down in the random-access read/write environments typical of PC LANs.

Deploying Windows NT

II

> **Note**
>
> RAID 3 is a common option on hardware RAID implementations. In practical terms, RAID 5 is a universally available option and is usually used in preference to RAID 3, because it offers most of the advantages of RAID 3 and has none of the drawbacks. Consider using RAID 3 only in very specialized applications where large sequential reads predominate—for example, a dedicated imaging server or for distributing (but not capturing) digital video data. Otherwise, use RAID 5.

RAID 4

RAID 4 is similar to RAID 3, except RAID 4 stripes data at the block or sector level rather than at the byte level, thereby providing better read performance than RAID 3 for small random reads. The small chunk size of RAID 3 means that every read requires participation from every disk in the array. The disks in a RAID 3 array are, therefore, referred to as being *synchronized*, or *coupled*. The larger chunk size used in RAID 4 means that small, random reads can be completed by accessing only a single disk drive instead of all data drives. RAID 4 drives are, therefore, referred to as being *unsynchronized*, or *decoupled*.

Like RAID 3, RAID 4 suffers from having a single, dedicated parity disk that must be accessed for every write. RAID 4 has all the drawbacks of RAID 3 and doesn't have the performance advantage of RAID 3 on large read transactions. About the only environment for which RAID 4 would make any sense at all is one in which nearly 100 percent of disk activity is small random reads. Because this situation isn't seen in real-world server environments, don't consider using RAID 4 for your PC LAN.

RAID 5

RAID 5, shown in figure 7.4, is the most common RAID level used in PC LAN environments. RAID 5 stripes both user and parity data across all the drives in the array, consuming the equivalent of one drive for parity information.

With RAID 5, all drives are of the same size, and one drive is unavailable to the operating system. For example, in a RAID 5 array with three 1G drives, the equivalent of one of those drives is used for parity, leaving 2G visible to the operating system. Adding a fourth 1G drive to the array, the equivalent of one drive is still used for parity, leaving 3G visible to the operating system.

RAID 5 is optimized for transaction processing activity, in which users frequently read and write relatively small amounts of data. It's the best RAID level for nearly any PC LAN environment, and is particularly well-suited for database servers.

The single most important weakness of RAID levels 2 through 4 is that they dedicate a single physical disk drive to parity information. Reads don't require accessing the parity drive, so they aren't degraded. This parity drive must be accessed for each write to the array, however, so RAID levels 2 through 4 don't allow parallel writes. RAID 5 eliminates this bottleneck by striping the parity data onto all physical drives in the array, thereby allowing both parallel reads and writes.

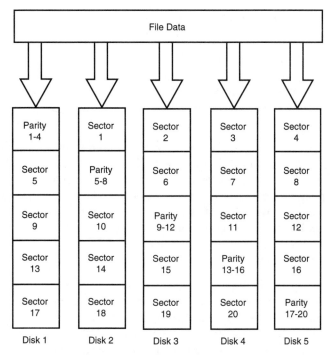

Fig. 7.4 A diagram of RAID 5 (sector striping with distributed parity) with five drives.

RAID 5 Read Performance. RAID 5 reads, like RAID levels 2 through 4 reads, don't require access to parity information unless one or more of the data stripes is unreadable. Because both data and parity stripes are optimized for sequential read performance where the block size of the requested data is a multiple of the stripe width, RAID 5 offers random read performance similar to that of RAID 3. Because RAID 5 allows parallel reads (unlike RAID 3), RAID 5 offers substantially better performance on random reads.

RAID 5 matches or exceeds RAID 0 performance on sequential reads because RAID 5 stripes the data across one more physical drive than does RAID 0. RAID 5 performance on random reads at least equals RAID 0, and it's usually somewhat better.

RAID 5 Write Performance. RAID 5 writes are more problematic. A RAID 0 single-block write involves only one access to one physical disk to complete the write. With RAID 5, the situation is considerably more complex. In the simplest case, two reads are required—one for the existing data block and the other for the existing parity block. Parity is recalculated for the stripe set based on these reads and the contents of the pending write. Two writes are then required—one for the data block itself and one for the revised parity block. Completing a single write, therefore, requires a minimum of four disk operations, compared with the single operation required by RAID 0.

The situation worsens when you consider what must be done to maintain data integrity. The modified data block is written to disk before the modified parity block. If a system failure occurs, the data block may be written successfully to disk, but the newly calculated parity block may be lost. This leaves new data with old parity and thereby corrupts the disk. Such a situation must be avoided at all costs.

Transaction Processing with RAID 5. RAID 5 addresses the problem of keeping data blocks and parity blocks synchronized by borrowing a concept from database transaction processing. Transaction processing is so named because it treats multiple component parts of a related whole as a single transaction. Either the whole transaction completes successfully, or none of it does.

For example, when you transfer money from your checking account to your savings account, your savings account is increased by the amount of the transfer and, at the same time, your checking account is reduced by the same amount. This transaction obviously involves updates to at least two separate records, and possibly more. It wouldn't do at all to have one of these record updates succeed and the other fail. On the one hand, you'd be very upset if your checking account was decreased without a corresponding increase in your savings account. Similarly, the bank wouldn't like it much if your savings account was increased but your checking account stayed the same.

The way around this problem is a process called *two-phase commit*. Rather than simply write the altered records individually, a two-phase commit first creates a snapshot image of the entire transaction and stores it. It then updates the affected records and verifies that all components of the transaction completed successfully. After this is verified, the snapshot image is deleted. If the transaction fails, the snapshot image can be used to roll back the status of the records that had already been updated, leaving the system in an unmodified and coherent state.

RAID 5 uses a two-phase commit process to ensure data integrity, further increasing write overhead. It first does a parallel read of every data block belonging to the affected stripe set, calculating a new parity block based on this read and the contents of the new data block to be written. The changed data and newly calculated parity information are written to a log area, along with pointers to the correct locations. After the log information is written successfully, the changed data and parity information are written in parallel to the stripe set. When the RAID controller verifies that the entire transaction completed successfully, it deletes the log information.

Caching RAID 5 Data. The two-phase commit process obviously introduces considerable overhead to the write process, and in theory slows RAID 5 writes by 50 percent or more, relative to RAID 0 writes. In practice, the situation isn't as bad as might be expected. Examining the process shows that the vast majority of extra time involved in these overhead operations is consumed by physical positioning of drive heads. This brings up the obvious question of caching.

On first glance, caching might appear to be of little use for drive arrays. Drive arrays range in size from a few gigabytes to the terabyte range. (A *terabyte* is 1,024 gigabytes.) Most arrays service mainly small random read requests; even frequent large sequential reads can be—in this context at least—considered random relative to the overall size of the array. Providing enough RAM to realistically do read caching on this amount of disk space would be prohibitive simply on the basis of cost. Even if you were willing to buy this much RAM, the overhead involved in doing cache searches and maintaining cache coherency would swamp any benefits you might otherwise gain.

Write caching, however, is a different story. Existing RAID 5 implementations avoid most of the lost time by relocating operations, where possible, from physical disk to non-volatile or battery-backed RAM. This caching, with deferred writes to frequently updated data, reduces overhead by an order of magnitude or more and allows real-world RAID 5 write performance that approaches that of less-capable RAID versions.

To return to the hardware store analogy, RAID 5 allows multiple checkout lines, all of which accept both cash (disk reads) and credit cards (disk writes). Because each checkout line is equipped with a scanner, it doesn't take much longer to process many items (large sequential disk access) than it does to process only a few items (small random disk access). As long as most customers pay cash, this scheme works well. The queues are short, transactions are completed quickly, and nobody has to wait long. Even though some customers pay by credit card, the queues remain relatively short because most transactions in any given queue will be cash. If, instead, many customers decide to pay by credit card, the queues at each checkout line grow longer because checkout clerks take much longer to process credit-card transactions than they do to accept cash. In the same way, RAID 5 works well in environments such as typical PC LANs, which involve mostly reads with less frequent writes.

Proprietary and Non-Standard RAID Levels

RAID is the hottest topic in mass storage today. Only a year or two ago, articles on RAID were seen only in magazines intended for LAN managers. Today, you find RAID systems discussed in mass-market computer magazines such as *PC Computing*. Inevitably, the first discussions of using RAID in workstations, rather than only in servers, are beginning to appear.

As is usually the case with a "hot product" category, manufacturers push the envelope to develop their own proprietary extensions to the standards-based architectures. And, as usual, some of these extensions originate with the engineering folks and represent real improvements to the genre. Others come from the marketing department and represent nothing but an attempt to gain a competitive advantage with vaporware.

RAID 6. The term *RAID 6* is now being used in at least three different ways. Some manufacturers simply take a RAID 5 array, add redundant power supplies and perhaps a hot spare disk, and refer to this configuration as RAID 6. Others add an additional disk to the array to increase redundancy, allowing the array to suffer simultaneous failure of two disks without causing data loss. Still others modify the striping method used by RAID 5 and refer to the result as RAID 6.

Any of these modifications may yield worthwhile improvements. Be aware, however, that when you see the term *RAID 6* used, you must question the vendor carefully as to exactly what's meant by the vendor's interpretation of RAID 6.

RAID 7. RAID 7 is patented by Storage Computer Corporation. From published documents, it appears that RAID 7, architecturally, most resembles RAID 4, with the addition of caching. RAID 7 uses a dedicated microprocessor-driven controller running an embedded propriety real-time operating system called SOS. Storage Computer equips its arrays with dual fast SCSI-2 multiple channel adapters, allowing one array to be simultaneously connected to more than one host, including mainframes, minicomputers, and PC LAN servers.

Storage Computer claims that RAID 7 provides performance equal to or better than RAID 3 on large sequential reads, while at the same time equaling or bettering RAID 5 on small random reads and writes. Anecdotal reports claim performance increases of between three and nine times, compared with traditional RAID 3 and RAID 5 arrays.

The claimed benefits of RAID 7 have been hotly debated on the Internet since RAID 7 was introduced. Some of those posting comments have reported significant increases in performance, whereas others have questioned the benefits and even the safety of RAID 7, particularly in a UNIX environment. The jury is still out on RAID 7.

Stacked RAID

One characteristic of all RAID implementations is that the array is seen as a single logical disk drive by the host operating system. This means that it's possible to *stack* arrays, with the host using one RAID level to control an array of arrays, in which individual disk drives are replaced with second-level arrays operating at the same or a different RAID level. Using stacked arrays allows you to gain the individual benefits of more than one RAID level while offsetting the drawbacks of each. In essence, stacking makes the high-performance RAID element visible to the host while concealing the low-performance RAID element used to provide data redundancy.

One common stacked RAID implementation is referred to as *RAID 0/1*, which is also marketed as a proprietary implementation called *RAID 10* (see fig. 7.5). This method combines the performance of RAID 0 striping with the redundancy of RAID 1 mirroring. RAID 0/1 simply replaces each individual disk drive used in a RAID 0 array with a RAID 1 array. The host computer sees the array as a simple RAID 0, so performance is enhanced to RAID 0 levels. Each drive component of the RAID 0 array is actually a RAID 1 mirrored set; thus, data safety is at the same level you would expect from a full mirrored set.

Other stacked RAID implementations are possible. For example, replacing the individual drives in a RAID 5 array with subsidiary RAID 3 arrays results in a RAID 53 configuration.

Another benefit of stacking is in building very large capacity arrays. For reasons described earlier, RAID 5 is the most popular choice for PC LAN arrays. However, for technical reasons described later, a RAID 5 array should normally be limited to five or six disk drives. The largest disk drives available when this book was written for PC LANs hold about 9G, placing the upper limit on a simple RAID 5 array at about 50G. Replacing the individual disk drives in a simple RAID 5 array with subsidiary RAID 5 arrays allows extending this maximum to 250G or more. In theory, it's possible to use three tiers of RAID—an array of arrays of arrays—to further extend capacity to the terabyte range.

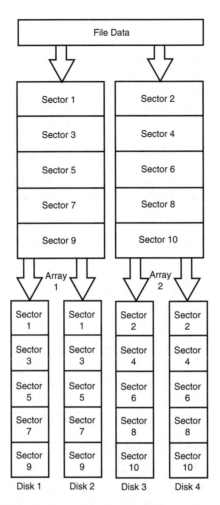

Fig. 7.5 A diagram of RAID 0/1 (sector striping to mirrored target arrays) with four drives.

> **Note**
>
> Seagate has announced a 23G version of its 5 1/4-inch Elite product line, which increases the practical upper size limit of a simple RAID 5 array to about 150G.

Sizing the Array

So far this chapter has discussed redundancy, but it hasn't explained in detail what happens when a drive fails. In the case of RAID 0, the answer is obvious. The failed drive contained half of your data, and the half remaining on the good drive is unusable. With RAID 1, the answer is equally obvious. The failed drive was an exact duplicate of the remaining good drive, all your data is still available, and all your redundancy is gone until you replace the failed drive. With RAID 3 and RAID 5, the issue becomes much more complex.

Because RAID 3 and RAID 5 use parity to provide data redundancy rather than physically replicate the data as does RAID 1, the implications of a drive failure aren't as obvious. In RAID 3, the failure of the parity drive has no effect on reads, because the parity drive is never accessed for reads. For RAID 3 writes, failure of the parity drive removes all redundancy until the drive is replaced, because all parity information is stored on that single drive. When a data drive fails in a RAID 3 array, the situation becomes more complicated. Reads of data formerly stored on the failed drive must be reconstructed using the contents of the other data drives and the parity drive. This results in a greatly increased number of read accesses and correspondingly lowered performance.

With RAID 5, the situation is similar to a failed RAID 3 data drive. Because every drive in a RAID 5 array contains data and parity information, the failure of any drive results in the loss of both data and parity. An attempt to read data formerly residing on the failed drive requires that every remaining drive in the array be read and parity used to recalculate the missing data. In a RAID 5 array containing 15 drives, for example, a read and reconstruction of lost data would require 14 separate read operations and a recalculation before a single block of data could be returned to the host. Writes to a RAID 5 array with one failed drive also require numerous disk accesses.

To make matters worse, when the failed drive is replaced, its contents must be reconstructed and stored on the replacement drive. This process, usually referred to as *automatic rebuild*, normally occurs in the background while the array continues to fulfill user requests. Because the automatic rebuild process requires heavy disk access to all the other drives in an already crippled array, performance of the array can degrade unacceptably. The best way to limit this degradation is to use a reasonably small stripe width, limiting the number of physical drives in the array to five or six at most.

Specifying a RAID Implementation

Up to this point, the discussion of RAID levels has been limited to theoretical issues, such as relative performance in read and write mode. The following sections offer concrete recommendations to implement a RAID subsystem for your Windows NT Server 4.0.

Picking the Best RAID Level for Your Needs

In theory, there are two important considerations in selecting the best RAID implementation for your particular needs.

The first consideration is the type of data to be stored on the array. The various RAID levels are optimized for differing storage requirements. The relative importance in your environment of small random reads versus large sequential reads and of small random writes versus large sequential writes, as well as the overall percentage of reads versus writes, determines—in theory, at least—the best RAID level to use.

The second consideration is the relative importance to you of performance versus the safety of your data. If data safety is paramount, you may choose a lower performing alternative that offers greater redundancy. Conversely, if sheer performance is the primary issue, you may choose a higher performing alternative that offers little or no redundancy and instead use backups and other means to ensure the safety of your data.

Always lurking in the background is also, of course, the real-world issue of cost.

These issues can be summarized for each RAID level as follows:

■ RAID 0 striping offers high performance, but its complete lack of redundancy and concomitant high risk of data loss makes pure RAID 0 an unrealistic choice for nearly all environments, although it makes sense in applications that generate large transitory temp files. RAID 0 is inexpensive because it's supported by many standard SCSI host adapters and requires no additional disk drives.

■ RAID 1 mirroring provides 100 percent redundancy for excellent data safety and, at the same time, offers reasonably good performance. RAID 1 is often an excellent choice for small LANs, offering decent performance and a high level of safety at a reasonable cost. Because RAID 1 is supported by most standard host adapters and requires that each data drive be duplicated, it's inexpensive to implement in small arrays and very expensive for large arrays.

■ RAID 3 byte striping with dedicated parity offers good data safety and high performance on large sequential reads, but its performance on random reads and writes makes it a poor choice for most LANs. The growth of imaging applications is revitalizing RAID 3 to some extent, because these applications fit well with RAID 3 strengths. If you're doing imaging, consider implementing RAID 3 on the logical volume used to store images.

RAID 3 is moderately expensive to implement. Although it requires only one additional disk drive to store parity information, RAID 3 isn't commonly available on standard disk adapters or as a software implementation; therefore, it requires a special—and moderately expensive—host adapter.

■ RAID 5 sector striping with distributed parity offers good data safety, good read performance for small random reads and large sequential reads, and reasonable write performance. RAID 5 usually turns out to be the best match for the disk access patterns of small and mid-size LANs. RAID 5 can be inexpensive to implement because it requires only a single additional disk drive and can be implemented in software. Various RAID 5 hardware implementations are also available, offering better performance than software versions but at a correspondingly higher price. If your server has only one array, RAID 5 is almost certainly the way to go.

■ Stacked RAID is useful when performance and data safety are high priorities relative to cost. In particular, RAID 0/1, when properly implemented, can combine the high performance of RAID 0 with the complete redundancy of RAID 1. At the same time, RAID 0/1 eliminates the drawbacks of both—except, of course, the cost. Stacked RAID is also useful if your total array capacity must exceed 50 gigabytes or so.

■ Multiple arrays are worth considering if your data storage requirements are large and diverse. Rather than try to shoehorn all your data into a single array running a compromise level of RAID, consider installing multiple arrays, each of which runs the RAID level most appropriate for the type of data being stored and the patterns of access to that data.

Understanding RAID Product Features

You can implement RAID in various ways. The SCSI host adapter in your current server may provide simple RAID functionality. You can replace your current SCSI host adapter with a host adapter that offers full RAID support. Software RAID support is provided natively by most network operating systems, including Windows NT Server 4.0. If you're buying new server hardware, chances are that the vendor provides hardware RAID support standard or as an option. If you need to upgrade your existing server, you can choose among various external RAID arrays that provide features, functionality, and performance similar to that provided by internal server RAID arrays.

Each method has advantages and drawbacks in terms of cost, performance, features, and convenience. Only you can decide which method best suits your needs. The following sections describe the most important features of various RAID implementations and the tradeoffs involved with each implementation.

Hot Swappable Disks and Hot Spare Disks. Most external RAID subsystems, and many servers with internal RAID subsystems, allow hard disk drives to be removed and replaced without turning off the server. This feature, known as *hot swapping*, allows a failed disk drive to be replaced without interrupting ongoing server operations.

A similar method, known as *hot sparing*, goes one step further by providing a spare drive that's installed and powered up at all times. This drive can automatically take the place of a failed drive on a moment's notice. Most systems that provide hot sparing also support hot swapping, to allow the failed drive to be replaced at your leisure.

Obviously, the drive itself and the system case must be designed to allow hot swapping and/or hot sparing. Most internal server RAID arrays and nearly all external RAID arrays are designed with front external access to hard drives for this reason. Hot swapping is a necessity for production servers; hot sparing is a very desirable option.

Automatic Rebuild. With either hot swapping or hot sparing, the integrity of the array itself is restored by doing a rebuild to reconstruct the data formerly contained on the failed drive and to re-create it on the replacement drive. Because rebuilding is a very resource-intensive process, a well-designed RAID subsystem gives you the choice of taking the array down and doing a static rebuild, or of allowing the rebuild to occur dynamically in the background while the array continues to service user requests. Ideally, the array should also let you specify a priority level for the background rebuild, allowing you to balance users' need for performance against the time needed to re-establish redundancy.

In practice, performance on an array with a failed drive—particularly on a RAID 5 array—may already be degraded to the extent that trying any sort of rebuild while users continue to access the array isn't realistic. The best solution in this case is usually to allow the users to continue to use the array (as is) for the rest of the day and then to do the rebuild overnight. Your choice in this situation is a static rebuild, which is far faster than a dynamic background rebuild.

Disk Drive Issues. In the scramble to choose the best RAID level, fastest RAID controller, and so forth, one issue that's frequently overlooked is that of the disk drives themselves.

The RAID implementation you select determines how much flexibility you have in choosing the drives to go with it.

External RAID arrays and internal server RAID arrays typically offer the least flexibility in choice of drives. Although these subsystems use industry-standard disk drives, the standard drives are repackaged into different physical form factors to accommodate custom drive bay designs as well as the proprietary power and data connections needed to allow hot swapping. Because these proprietary designs fit only one manufacturer's servers or even just one particular model, they're made and sold in relatively small numbers. This combination of low volume and a single source makes the drives quite expensive.

Another related issue is that of continuing availability of compatible drives. Consider what might happen a year or two from now when you want to upgrade or replace drives. The best designs simply enclose industry-standard drives in a custom chassis that provides the mechanical and electrical connections needed to fit the array. These designs allow the user to upgrade or replace drives simply by installing a new supported standard drive in the custom chassis. Beware of other designs that make the chassis an integral part of the drive assembly. You'll pay a high price for replacement drives, if you can find them at all.

Third-party hardware RAID controllers offer more flexibility in choosing drives, at the expense of not providing hot swapping. These controllers simply replace your existing standard SCSI host adapter and are designed to support standard SCSI disk drives. The situation isn't quite as simple as it seems, however. You might reasonably expect these controllers to be able to use any standard SCSI drive. The reality is different. Most of these controllers support only a very limited number of disk drive models, and they often specify the exact ROM revision level required on the drive. Before you buy such a controller, make sure that the drives you intend to use appear on this compatibility list. Also, make sure that the controller's drive tables can be easily updated via flash ROM (or similar means), and that the manufacturer has a history of providing such updates.

Software-based RAID offers the most flexibility in selecting drives. Because software-based RAID subsystems are further isolated from the disk drives than are hardware-based RAID implementations, most software-based RAID implementations—both those native to NOSs and those provided by third parties—care little about the specifics of your disk drives. Software RAID depends on a standard SCSI host adapter to communicate with the disk drives. As long as your host adapter is supported by your software and your drives are in turn supported by the host adapter, you're likely to find few compatibility problems with software-based RAID. Typical software-based mirroring, for example, doesn't even require that the second drive in a mirror set be identical to the first, but simply that it's at least as large as the first drive. Windows NT Server's implementation of software-based RAID is described later in the section "Understanding Windows NT Server 4.0 Software RAID."

Power Supplies. Most external RAID arrays and some internal server RAID arrays use dedicated redundant power supplies for the disk drives. The arrangement of these power supplies significantly affects the reliability of the array as a whole. Some systems provide a dedicated power supply for each individual disk drive. Although this seems to increase redundancy superficially, in fact it simply adds more single points of failure to the drive component. Failure of a power supply means failure of the drive that it powers. Whether the failure is the result of a dead drive or a dead power supply, the result is the same.

A better solution is to use dual load-sharing power supplies. In this arrangement, each power supply can power the entire array on its own. The dual power supplies are linked in a harness that allows each to provide half of the power needed by the array. If one power supply fails, the other provides all the power needed by the array until the failed unit can be replaced. Another benefit of this arrangement is that because the power supplies normally run well below their full capacity, their lives are extended and their reliability is enhanced when compared with a single power supply running at or near capacity. Power supplies also can be hot swappable (although this feature is more commonly called *hot pluggable* when referring to power supplies).

Stacked and Multiple-Level Independent RAID Support. Some environments require a stacked array for performance, redundancy, or sizing reasons. Others may require multiple independent arrays, each running a different RAID level or mix of RAID levels. If you find yourself in either situation, the best solution is probably either an external RAID array or a high-end internal server RAID array.

The obvious issue is whether a given RAID implementation offers the functionality needed to provide stacks and multiple independent arrays. The not-so-obvious issue is the sheer number of drives that must be supported.

External RAID arrays support many disk drives in their base chassis, and they usually allow expansion chassis to be daisy-chained, extending the maximum number of disks supported even further. High-end servers support as many as 28 disk drives internally, and again often make provision for extending this number via external chassis. Mid-range servers are typically more limited, both in the number of drives they physically support and in their provisions for stacking and multiple independent arrays. A typical mid-range server RAID array doesn't support multiple independent arrays, but it may offer simple RAID 0/1 stacking.

Manageability. Look for a RAID implementation that provides good management software. In addition to providing automatic static and dynamic rebuild options, a good RAID management package monitors your array for loading, error rates, read and write statistics by type, and other key performance data. The better packages even help you decide how to configure your RAID array for optimum performance.

Implementing RAID in Hardware

Hardware-based RAID implementations usually offer the best performance for a given choice of RAID level and drive performance. Another advantage of hardware RAID is that server resources aren't devoted to calculating parity and determining which drive is to receive which block of data. The following sections offer recommendations for the specification of hardware-based RAID subsystems for your server.

RAID as a Server Option. If you're buying a new server, by all means consider the RAID options offered by the server manufacturer. Any system seriously positioned for use as a server offers RAID as an option, if not as standard equipment. Low-end servers may offer

RAID as an option. Mid-range and high-end servers come standard with RAID and often offer optional external enclosures to expand your disk storage beyond that available in the server chassis alone.

Purchasing RAID as a part of your server has the following advantages, most of which are related to single-source procurement:

- One manufacturer supplies the server and the RAID hardware, so the RAID hardware can be tweaked to optimize performance.

- Internal server RAID offers the best chance to avoid ROM revision-level issues and other nasty compatibility problems. If you do have a problem, you can complain to one source and not have to worry about finger-pointing by different vendors.

- Driver updates are available from a single source, relieving you of having to play the systems integrator game the next time you want to upgrade your network operating system or replace disk drives.

- Single-source warranty and maintenance is a definite benefit. If you buy a combination server and RAID array from a major manufacturer, you make only one phone call when your server breaks. Large server manufacturers have trained service personnel located near you, and can provide service 24 hours a day, seven days a week.

- Availability of known-compatible disks at upgrade time provides scalability insurance. Server manufacturers realize that you aren't likely to buy their servers unless you can be certain that parts for them will continue to be available for some reasonable time.

Upgrading an Existing Server to Hardware RAID. If your current server is otherwise suitable, upgrading the server to hardware RAID may be a viable alternative to buying a new server. This upgrade can range from something as simple and inexpensive as adding another disk drive and enabling mirroring on your SCSI host adapter, to a process as complex, and potentially expensive, as adding an external RAID array cabinet. Somewhere in the middle (in cost and complexity) is replacing your existing SCSI host adapter with a dedicated RAID controller.

Each solution provides the basic reliability and performance benefits of hardware RAID. Each solution varies in the level of the features, convenience, and extended RAID functionality it provides.

Mirroring with Your Current SCSI Host Adapter. The SCSI host adapter in your current server may support RAID 0, RAID 1, or both. Even if it doesn't support simple RAID, replacing the host adapter with one that offers RAID 0 or RAID 1 support is an inexpensive alternative. If your server has only one or two SCSI hard drives, this method allows you to implement mirroring at the cost of simply buying a matching drive for each existing drive.

This approach buys you 100 percent redundancy and decent performance, and does so inexpensively. What it doesn't provide are other features of more expensive hardware RAID implementations, such as hot swappable drives and redundant power supplies.

Still, for smaller servers, this is a set-and-forget choice. If your server is small enough that buying the extra disk drives is feasible, and if you don't care that you'll need to take down the server to replace a failed drive, this method may well be the best choice. It gives you about 95 percent of the benefits of a full-blown RAID 5 implementation for a fraction of the cost.

Adding a Dedicated RAID 5 Controller Card. The next step up in hardware RAID, in terms of cost and performance, are the dedicated RAID controller cards. These cards replace your existing SCSI host adapter and include a dedicated microprocessor to handle RAID 5 processing. They range in price from less than $1,000 to perhaps $2,500, depending on their feature sets, the number of SCSI channels provided, the amount and type of on-board cache supplied, and other accouterments.

All of these cards support at least RAID 1 and RAID 5, and most offer a full range of RAID levels, often including various enhanced non-standard RAIDs. The Adaptec AAA-130 host adapter, as an example, is a low-cost (about $500 street price) host adapter that supports RAID 0, 1, 5, and 0/1 (10) with hot-swappable drives in the RAID 5 configuration. The AAA-130 is designed for entry-level servers, which Adaptec Inc. defines as serving 60 or fewer clients. Figure 7.6 shows the Adaptec AAC-330 host adapter designed for mid-range servers. The AAC-330 uses an Intel i960 RISC microprocessor for improved performance when serving a large number of clients.

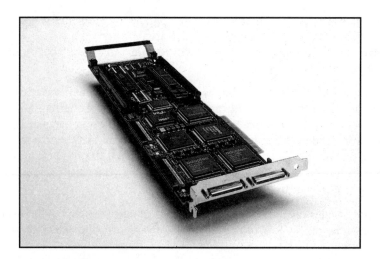

Fig. 7.6   The Adaptec AAC-330 RAIDport host adapter, which uses an Intel i960 RISC processor to provide mid-range server capabilities. (Courtesy of Adaptec Inc.)

The price of dedicated RAID controller cards has been coming down rapidly, both due to increasing sales volume and to competition from RAID software alternatives. The best examples of these cards offer RAID functionality and performance comparable to internal server RAID arrays and external RAID array enclosures. In terms of convenience features, these adapter cards suffer an inherent disadvantage, because they don't provide hot-swap capabilities, redundant power supplies, and other high-end features.

> **Note**
>
> Most RAID controller cards are sold through original equipment manufacturer (OEM) arrangements with server vendors. For instance, the Mylex DAC960—one of the better examples of this type of adapter—is used by Hewlett-Packard to provide RAID support in its NetServer line of servers. HP modifies the BIOS and makes other changes to optimize the DAC960 for use in the company's servers. The Adaptec AAC330 is sold through OEM and VAR (value-added reseller) channels; the Adaptec AAA130 is available from distributors and some computer retailers.

Think long and hard before you decide to buy one of these cards as an individual item, rather than as a part of a packaged solution. Although the card itself appears to be inexpensive relative to the quoted price for an external RAID enclosure, you usually find that after adding up the cost of disk drives, cabling, and possibly an external enclosure, you meet or exceed the price of the turnkey solution. It's still up to you to do the systems integration, locate and install the appropriate disks and drivers, and maintain the subsystem. If you decide to use one of these cards, budget for two of them. Few organizations accept having their LAN down for an extended period if the RAID controller fails. On-site maintenance is the exception rather than the rule for these cards. Even doing a swap via overnight courier usually means that your LAN will be down for at least a day or two.

Using an External RAID Enclosure. External RAID enclosures are the high end of hardware RAID. They offer all the features of internal server arrays and more. Hot-pluggable, load-balancing dual power supplies are a common feature, as are hot-swappable drives, extensive management capabilities, a full range of RAID options, and provision for stacked RAID. Most of these units support multiple independent RAID arrays, and some allow connection of more than one host. Most units also allow you to add additional slave enclosures to expand your disk capacity. As you might expect, all of this functionality substantially increases the acquisition cost.

External RAID subsystems are of two types. The first is based on one of the dedicated RAID controller cards described in the preceding section. In this type of unit, called a *dumb external array*, all the RAID intelligence is contained on the card installed in the server cabinet, and the external enclosure simply provides mounting space and power for the disk drives. The enclosure makes provision for hot-swapping and redundant power supplies, but the actual RAID functionality remains with the server. RAID configuration and management is done at the server. Although such subsystems physically resemble more sophisticated external arrays, in concept these units are really just simple extensions of the dedicated RAID controller card method, and accordingly are relatively inexpensive. They're usually priced in the $3,000 to $5,000 range for the enclosure and controller, before being populated with disk drives.

Dumb external arrays are often created from their component parts by mail-order and second- and third-tier computer companies to permit offering a RAID solution for their servers. These arrays suffer from most of the same drawbacks as the dedicated RAID controller cards—limited drive type support, infrequent driver updates, lack of on-site maintenance, and the possibility of vendor insolvency.

II

Deploying Windows NT

The second type of unit, called a *smart external array*, relocates RAID processing to the external enclosure and provides one or more SCSI connectors by which the host server (or servers) is connected to the array. The host server sees a smart external array as just another standard SCSI disk drive or drives.

With this type of smart array, RAID configuration and management are done at the array itself. Because these arrays are intended for use in diverse environments—including Novell NetWare, Microsoft Windows NT Server, and UNIX—these arrays usually offer various methods for setup and programming. A typical unit might be programmable in a UNIX environment by connecting a dumb terminal to a serial port on the external array or by using Telnet. In a Windows NT Server 4.0 environment, you use provided client software for the network operating system. These arrays have available full software support—drivers and management utilities—for several operating systems, although they often come standard with support for only one operating system of your choice. Support for additional operating systems and for extended functionality with your chosen operating system is often an extra-cost option. Smart external RAID arrays start at around $8,000 or $10,000, without drives, and go up rapidly from there.

Smart external arrays offer everything you might want in a RAID unit, including support for stacked RAID, multiple independent arrays, and multiple host support. Because manufacturers realize that these are critical components, on-site maintenance is available, provided either by the manufacturer or by a reputable third-party service organization. The construction of these units resembles minicomputer and mainframe practices rather than typical PC peripherals.

The first major concern when you use smart external arrays is drive support. Some units allow you to add or replace drives with any SCSI drive of the appropriate type that's at least as large as the old drive. Other units require that you use only drives that exactly match the existing drives by make, model, and sometimes even by ROM revision level. Still other units can use only drives supplied by the array manufacturer, because the drives themselves have had their firmware altered. These manufacturers tell you that these firmware changes are required for performance and compatibility reasons, which may be true. However, the net effect is that you can then buy new and replacement drives only from the array manufacturer, which is usually a very expensive alternative.

The second major concern is software support. With smart external arrays, you're at the mercy of the array manufacturer for NOS support, drivers, and management utilities. Make absolutely certain before buying one of these arrays that it has software support available for Windows NT Server 4.0. It does you no good to accept a vendor's assurance that the array supports Windows NT, only to find later that the array supports only versions 3.5 and earlier.

Check the array manufacturer's history of providing support for Windows NT upgrades immediately after release of the upgrade. Although this isn't a perfect means of prediction—companies can, and do, change—a history of frequent updates for Windows NT Server is a reasonable indicator that the company is committed to providing continuing support for its users.

External RAID enclosures can be your best choice, particularly if you require large amounts of disk storage, have multiple servers, or use more than one NOS. Don't rule out external RAID enclosures simply on the basis of sticker shock. Examine the true cost involved in acquiring, maintaining, and managing one of these units versus the cost involved, including increased staff time, of providing similar functionality using other means.

Understanding Windows NT Server 4.0 Software RAID

All the RAID implementations examined so far are implemented by specialized hardware. It's possible, however, to use the server CPU to perform RAID processing, thereby avoiding buying additional hardware. Microsoft Windows NT Server 4.0 includes as a standard feature RAID 0, RAID 1, and RAID 5 functionality built into the NOS software, allowing you to build a RAID subsystem using only standard SCSI host adapters and drives. Windows NT Server 4.0 provides these RAID options, so you might wonder why anyone would purchase expensive additional hardware to accomplish the same thing.

The first reason is performance. In theory, at least, using software RAID can have scalability performance advantages. Because software RAID runs as another process on the server, upgrading the server processor or increasing the number of processors simultaneously upgrades RAID processing. In practice, this potential advantage usually turns out to be illusory. Although Microsoft has done a good job of incorporating RAID functionality into Windows NT Server 4.0, a well-designed hardware RAID solution always offers better performance, particularly on larger arrays. Benchmark tests nearly always show software RAID bringing up the rear of the pack in performance relative to hardware RAID, and even Microsoft admits that its software RAID solution is outperformed by a well-designed hardware RAID. Also, although using the server CPU to perform RAID processing can be acceptable on a small or lightly loaded server, doing so on a more heavily loaded server—particularly one running as an application server—steals CPU time from user applications and, therefore, degrades overall server performance.

The second reason that may mandate against using Windows NT Server software RAID is that of flexibility, convenience, and server uptime. In terms of reliability, Windows NT Server software RAID secures your data just as well as hardware RAID does. What it doesn't do, however, is provide redundant power supplies, hot swapping of disks, background rebuild, and other hardware RAID features designed to minimize server downtime. As a result, a server running Windows NT software RAID is no more likely to lose data than a server running hardware RAID, but is considerably more likely to be down for extended periods while failed disk drives are repaired and rebuilt. Unless you're running Windows NT Server on a system equipped with hot swappable drives and other RAID amenities—which would usually be equipped with a hardware RAID controller anyway—this lost ability to hot swap drives and otherwise maintain the array without taking down the server may be unacceptable.

The three primary advantages of a RAID subsystem are increased data security, increased disk performance, and decreased server downtime. Windows NT Server 4.0 native software RAID, with its full support for RAID 1 and RAID 5, does an excellent job of securing your data. It does a reasonably good job of increasing disk subsystem performance, although not to the extent that a well-designed hardware RAID does. It's only in terms of decreasing server downtime that Windows NT Server software RAID falls short, and this is characteristic of any pure software RAID solution. If yours is a small array on a server supporting a limited number of users, the drawbacks of Windows NT Server software RAID may be an acceptable tradeoff for reduced costs. For larger arrays and critical environments, buy the appropriate RAID hardware solution.

Windows NT Server RAID Options. On the reasonable assumption that software RAID is better than no RAID, using Windows NT Server 4.0 to provide RAID functionality makes sense, particularly for small servers that wouldn't otherwise be equipped with RAID functionality. Following are the RAID options available with Windows NT Server:

- RAID 0 is referred to by Microsoft as *Disk Striping*, or the use of stripe sets. Like any RAID 0 arrangement, stripe sets increase disk subsystem performance but do nothing to provide data redundancy. The failure of any disk drive in a stripe set renders the data on the remaining drives in the stripe set inaccessible. Windows NT Server allows a stripe set to comprise from two to 32 individual disks. Increasing the number of disks in a stripe set increases the probability of data loss, because failure of a single drive results in a failure of the entire stripe set. If the disks assigned to a stripe set vary in size, the smallest determines the common partition size of the stripe set. The remaining space on other drives in the stripe set may be used individually or assigned to a volume set.

- RAID 1, referred to by Microsoft as *Disk Mirroring*, or the use of mirror sets, is supported directly by Microsoft Windows NT Server for any hardware configuration with at least two disk drives of similar size. Windows NT Server doesn't require that the mirrored drive be identical to the original drive, but only that the mirrored drive be at least as large. This considerably simplifies replacing failed drives if the original model is no longer available. RAID 1 duplexing is supported directly for any hardware configuration with at least two disk drives of similar size and two disk controllers. As with any duplex arrangement, this removes the disk controller as a single point of failure. As with mirrored drives, Windows NT Server doesn't require duplexed drives to be identical.

- RAID 5, referred to by Microsoft as *Disk Striping with Parity*, is also supported natively by Windows NT Server for any hardware configuration with at least three disk drives and one or more disk controllers. Windows NT Server allows as many as 32 drives in a striping set, although to maintain acceptable performance when a single drive fails, it's a better idea to limit the RAID 5 array to five or six drives.

Configuration Considerations: Volume Sets, Extensibility, and Booting. In addition to mirror sets and stripe sets, Microsoft Windows NT Server provides a similar disk-management function called a *volume set*. Volume sets, although often confused with RAID, provide neither the data safety of RAID 1 or RAID 5, nor the performance benefits of RAID 0. A volume set simply allows a single logical volume to span more than one physical disk drive. With a volume set, data isn't striped to multiple disk drives, but instead is written sequentially to each disk drive in the volume set as the preceding drive is filled. A volume set allows you to combine the capacity of two or more smaller disk drives to provide a single larger volume. Because volume sets are accessed as a single logical unit, the failure of any single drive in a volume set renders the data on the remaining drives inaccessible.

Because volume sets provide neither data redundancy nor performance benefits, and because by their nature they increase the chances of data loss due to drive failure, volume sets are normally a poor choice for configuring your disk storage. If your data storage requirements exceed the capacity of the largest disk drives available to you, a far better choice is to use RAID 5 to provide a single large volume with data redundancy. The chief advantage of volume sets is that, unlike stripe sets and mirror sets, they are dynamically extensible. If a volume set begins to fill up, you can increase the capacity of the volume set simply by installing another physical disk drive and adding its space to the existing volume set. If, on the other hand, a stripe set or mirror set approaches its total capacity, your only option is to tear down the existing set, add drive capacity, build a new set, and restore your data.

One final issue to consider before you decide to implement Windows NT Server software RAID is that of system booting. Windows NT Server doesn't allow the system to boot from either a stripe set or a stripe set with parity. It does allow the system to boot from a mirror set. This means that to implement a stripe set, your server must have at least three disk drives—one boot drive, and at least two drives to comprise the stripe set. Similarly, implementing a stripe set with parity requires at least four drives, one from which the system boots and at least three more drives for the volume of the stripe set with parity. It's therefore common for small Windows NT Server systems to have five disk drives, the first two of which comprise a mirror set from which the system boots and on which applications reside, and the final three of which comprise a stripe set with parity on which most of the data is stored.

Creating Windows NT Server Stripe and Mirror Sets

After you install a sufficient number of drives and make sure that your SCSI host adapter recognizes each drive, you can create one or more of the three levels of RAID supported by Windows NT Server 4.0. The following sections provide the instructions for implementing Windows NT 4.0's software RAID 0, 1, and 5. RAID 0 and 1 require two physical drives; RAID 5 requires three physical drives. Each drive must have unused space in which to create the stripe set or mirror volume.

◄◄ See "Setting Up Your Fixed-Disk Drives," p. 199

Note

The computer used in the following example is OAKLEAF3, a 133MHz Pentium server that dual boots Windows 95 for digital video editing and Windows NT Server 4.0 for network test purposes. OAKLEAF3 is equipped with two Seagate ST15150W 4.3G Barracuda Wide SCSI drives (Bcuda1, Disk 0, and Bcuda2, Disk 1); a 1G Micropolis narrow SCSI drive (Microp1, Disk 2); and a Toshiba

(continues)

Deploying Windows NT

II

(continued)

4X SCSI CD-ROM drive connected to an Adaptec AHA-2940UW host controller. Bcuda1 has five 800K FAT partitions (Bcuda1p1 through Bcuda1p5), and Bcuda2 has two 4G FAT partitions (Bcuda2p1 and Bcuda2p2). Microp1 is divided into 800K (Microp1p1) and 200K (Microp1p2) partitions. The Bcuda1p4, Bcuda2p2, and Microp1p2 partitions were deleted (converted to free space) before performing the steps described in the following sections.

Creating RAID 0 Stripe Sets. Creating a RAID 0 stripe set is the simplest of the three processes offered by Windows NT 4.0's Disk Administrator. To create a RAID 0 stripe set, proceed as follows:

1. Log on as an administrator and run Disk Administrator by choosing Programs, Administrative Tools, and Disk Administrator from the Start menu.

2. Click to select an unused area on the first disk drive.

> **Note**
>
> Physical drives commonly are called *spindles* to avoid confusion with logical drives created by multiple partitioning of a single physical drive.

3. Pressing and holding the Ctrl key, click to select additional unused areas on other disk drives, up to a total of as many as 32 disk drives. You may select only one area on each disk drive. Figure 7.7 shows 800M and 2G areas of free space selected on Disk 0 and Disk 1, respectively.

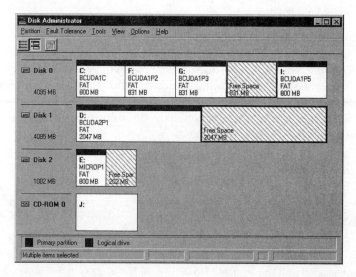

Fig. 7.7 Selecting free space areas on two physical drives to create a RAID 0 stripe set.

4. From the Partition menu, choose Create Stripe Set to open the Create Stripe Set dialog, which displays in the Create Stripe Set of Total Size box the default total

size of the stripe set spanning all selected drives (see fig. 7.8). This total size takes into account the smallest area selected on any disk drive, adjusting (if necessary) the sizes of the areas on the other selected drives to set all to identical size. The total size value is approximately the size of the smallest disk area multiplied by the number of drives in the stripe set.

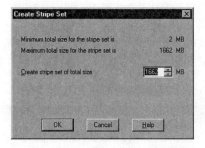

Fig. 7.8 Setting the total size of the stripe set in the Create Stripe Set dialog.

5. Click OK to accept the default size. Windows NT Server prepares to create the stripe set and assigns the stripe set a single default drive letter (see fig. 7.9). At this point, no changes have been made to the drives.

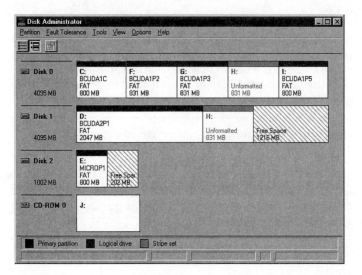

Fig. 7.9 The stripe set before making the changes to the selected partitions.

6. From the Partition menu choose Commit Changes Now. A dialog appears to inform you that changes have been made to your disk configuration (see fig. 7.10). Click Yes to accept and save the changes.

II

Deploying Windows NT

Fig. 7.10 Committing changes to your drives for the RAID 0 stripe set.

7. A second message box appears to notify you that the update was successful (see fig. 7.11) and that you should save the disk configuration information and create a new emergency repair disk. (These steps are performed at the end of this procedure.) Click OK.

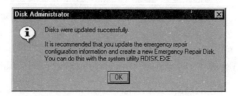

Fig. 7.11 Disk Administrator's confirmation of changes to your drive configuration.

> **Note**
>
> If another message box appears, to inform you that you must restart the computer for the changes to take effect, click OK to begin system shutdown. After Windows NT Server is restarted, again log on as an administrator and run Disk Administrator. The need to shut down and restart Windows NT depends on the status of the selected disk regions before the beginning of this process.

8. Click to select the newly created but unformatted stripe set (see fig. 7.12). From the Tools menu choose Format to open the Format Drive *D*: dialog.

9. Type a name for the volume in the Label text box (see fig. 7.13). You're given the opportunity to choose an NTFS or FAT file system; select NTFS (the default). Marking the Quick Format check box bypasses drive sector checking during the formatting process. Click OK to continue.

> **Note**
>
> If you haven't previously formatted the free space used for the stripe set, clear the Quick Format check box. A full format tests for bad sectors during the formatting process and marks bad sectors unusable in the drive's sector map.

10. A confirmation dialog appears, to warn you that continuing overwrites the contents of the volume (see fig. 7.14). Click Yes to continue formatting.

11. If you marked the Quick Format check box, the Quick Format progress indicator appears only briefly. For a conventional formatting operation, the progress indicator shown in figure 7.15 appears for a minute or more, depending on the size of the volume.

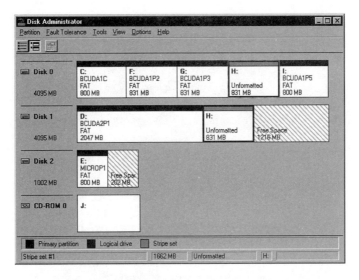

Fig. 7.12 Selecting the unformatted stripe set.

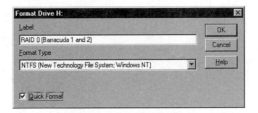

Fig. 7.13 Adding a volume label and selecting the file system type.

Fig. 7.14 Confirming the formatting step.

Fig. 7.15 The format progress indicator for a full format (Quick Format not selected).

12. When formatting is complete, a dialog informs you of the total available disk space on the new volume (see fig. 7.16). Click OK. The new volume is ready for use (see fig. 7.17).

Fig. 7.16 The Format Complete dialog displaying the size of the stripe set volume.

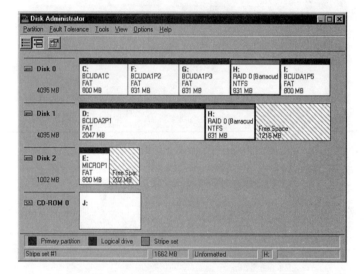

Fig. 7.17 Disk Administrator displaying the newly created RAID 0 stripe set.

> **Note**
>
> The status bar at the bottom of Disk Administrator's window isn't updated at the completion of the formatting process. To update the status bar, select another volume, and then reselect the newly created set.

Creating Drive Configuration and Emergency Repair Diskettes. After making permanent changes to your drive configuration, always save the configuration changes, replace the repair information on the fixed disk, and create a new emergency repair disk. Follow these steps to assure that you can restore your existing configuration in the event of a system failure:

1. To save the current drive configuration, choose Configuration and then Save from the Partition menu to display the Insert Disk dialog (see fig. 7.18). Insert a formatted diskette and click OK to save the configuration. In the event of a major catastrophe, you can use the diskette to restore the current drive configuration by choosing Configuration and then Restore from the Partition menu.

Fig. 7.18   Creating a drive configuration diskette.

   2. Choose Run from the Start menu, type **rdisk** in the Open text box, and click OK to open the Repair Disk Utility dialog (see fig. 7.19).

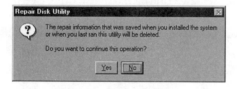

Fig. 7.19   The opening dialog of the Repair Disk Utility.

   3. Click the Update Repair Info button. The confirmation dialog shown in figure 7.20 appears. Click OK to continue the update process. The progress meter displays the status of the update (see fig. 7.21), which takes a minute or two.

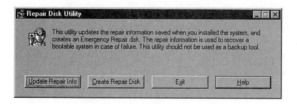

Fig. 7.20   Confirming the update of locally stored repair information.

Fig. 7.21   Metering the progress of updating the locally stored repair information.

   4. After the local repair information is updated, a message box appears, asking whether you want to create an emergency repair diskette (see fig. 7.22). After up-dating local repair information, it's *imperative* that you create a new emergency repair diskette. Insert a diskette, which doesn't need to be formatted, in the diskette drive and click Yes.

   5. Replace your existing emergency repair diskette with the new emergency repair diskette, which should be stored in a safe location. (Consider making two emer-gency repair diskettes, storing one diskette off site.) The old diskette is unusable with the new repair information stored on the local fixed disk.

II

Deploying Windows NT

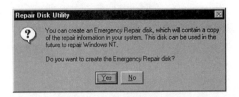

Fig. 7.22 Creating the updated emergency repair diskette.

> **Caution**
>
> If you don't create an emergency repair diskette after updating local repair information, it's likely that the repair diskette won't work when used in the event of a major system failure. In this case, your only alternative is to reinstall Windows NT Server 4.0.

Creating RAID 1 Mirror Sets. Mirror sets differ from stripe sets; whereas stripe sets may span as many as 32 drives, mirror sets are created on a paired drive basis. You must first create a standard formatted volume, and then create the mirror drive.

Creating and Formatting a New Standard Volume. To create and format a new separate volume from the free space available on a single drive, follow these steps:

1. Log on as an administrator and run Disk Administrator by choosing Programs, Administrative Tools, and Disk Administrator from the Start menu.

2. Click to select an unused area on the fixed disk drive (see fig. 7.23).

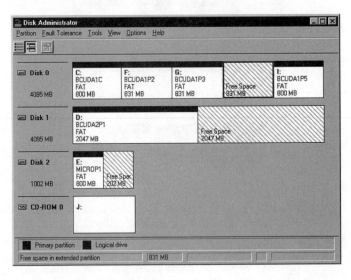

Fig. 7.23 Selecting an unused area of a drive in which to create a new standard volume.

3. From the Partition menu, choose Create to open the Create Logical Drive dialog, which displays in the Create Logical Drive of Size box the default total size of the free space of the selected drive (see fig. 7.24). Accept the default size unless you want to create a volume of a smaller size.

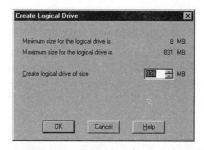

Fig. 7.24   Setting the size of the volume in the Create Logical Drive dialog.

4. Click OK. Windows NT Server prepares to create the stripe set, assigning the volume a single default drive letter. At this point no changes have been made to the drive and the drive (H in fig. 7.25) is disabled.

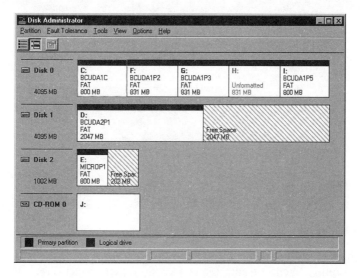

Fig. 7.25   The proposed volume, before making the changes to the selected partition.

> **Note**
>
> You can't format the inactive volume shown in figure 7.25. The Tools menu's Format option is disabled at that point. You must commit the changes to create the new volume's partition, and then format the partition.

5. From the Partition menu choose Commit Changes Now. A dialog informs you that changes have been made to your disk configuration (refer to fig. 7.10). Click Yes to accept and save the changes. A second message box appears, to notify you that the update was successful, and that you should save the disk configuration information and create a new emergency repair disk (refer to fig. 7.11). These two steps are performed after you complete the drive reconfiguration process. Click OK.

> **Note**
>
> If another message box appears, to inform you that you must restart the computer for the changes to take effect, click OK to begin system shutdown. After Windows NT Server is restarted, again log on as an administrator and run Disk Administrator. The need to shut down and restart Windows NT depends on the status of the selected disk regions before the beginning of this process.

6. Click to select the newly created but unformatted volume (H in fig. 7.26). From the Tools menu choose Format to open the Format Drive D: dialog.

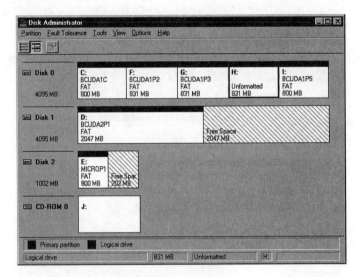

Fig. 7.26 Selecting the active but unformatted volume.

7. Type a name for the volume in the Label text box (refer to fig. 7.13). You're given the opportunity to choose an NTFS or FAT file system; select NTFS (the default). Marking the Quick Format check box bypasses drive sector checking during the formatting process. Click OK to continue.

> **Note**
>
> As recommended in the preceding section on RAID 0 stripe sets, don't use Quick Format if you haven't previously formatted the free space used for the new volume. A full format tests for bad sectors during the formatting process and marks bad sectors unusable in the drive's sector map.

8. A confirmation dialog warns you that continuing overwrites the contents of the volume (refer to fig. 7.14). Click Yes to continue formatting. If you marked the Quick Format check box, the Quick Format progress indicator appears only briefly. For a conventional formatting operation, the progress indicator shown earlier in figure 7.15 appears.

9. When formatting is complete, a dialog informs you of the total available disk space on the new volume (refer to fig. 7.16). Click OK. The new volume is ready for use as an independent volume or as a member of a mirror set.

Note

If your new volume is intended as an independent volume (not a member of a mirror set), update the configuration and repair information as described earlier in the section "Creating Drive Configuration and Emergency Repair Diskettes."

Creating the Mirror of the Standard Volume. Mirroring creates a formatted volume of the same size as the new standard volume, but on another physical drive. To create the mirror partition, follow these steps:

1. From Disk Administrator, select the newly formatted standard volume.

2. Pressing and holding the Ctrl key, select an unused area on another disk drive that's at least as large as the newly created volume (see fig. 7.27).

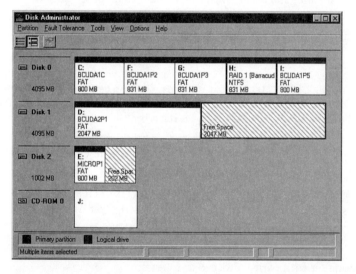

Fig. 7.27 Selecting the formatted volume and the free space on another physical drive to create the mirror set.

3. From the Fault Tolerance menu choose Establish Mirror.

4. From the Partition menu choose Commit Changes Now. Windows NT Server creates the mirror set and assigns the drive letter of the first drive of the set (H in fig. 7.28).

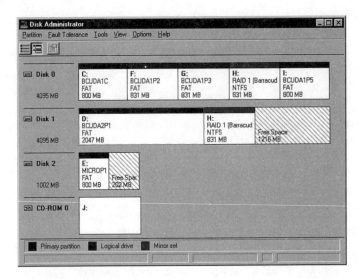

Fig. 7.28 Disk Administrator displaying the newly created mirror set (drive H).

Note

The mirror set is not created immediately on completion of step 4. Setting up the mirror partition and formatting the partition occurs as a background task. Disk Administrator's status bar displays INITIALIZING during the process. To determine when the process is complete, periodically select another volume, and then reselect the mirror set. The process is complete when you see HEALTHY on the status bar.

---

5. Update the configuration and repair information as described earlier in the section "Creating Drive Configuration and Emergency Repair Diskettes."

Creating RAID 5 Stripe Sets with Parity. The process of creating a stripe set with parity is very similar to that used to create a RAID 0 stripe set. While a RAID 0 stripe set can be created on only two physical drives, a RAID 5 stripe set with parity requires a minimum of three drives—one for parity information and at least two for data.

To create a stripe set with parity, proceed as follows:

1. Log on as an administrator and run Disk Administrator by choosing Programs, Administrative Tools, and then Disk Administrator from the Start menu.

2. Click to select an unused area on the first disk drive.

3. Pressing and holding the Ctrl key, select at least two additional unused areas on other disk drives, up to a total of as many as 32 disk drives. You may choose only one area on each disk drive. Figure 7.29 shows three unused areas selected on drives 0, 1, and 2.

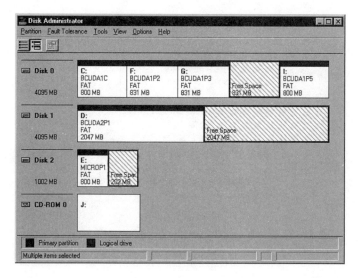

Fig. 7.29   Selecting a minimum of three areas of free space to create a RAID 5 stripe set with parity.

4. From the Fault Tolerance menu choose Create Stripe Set with Parity. The Create Stripe Set with Parity dialog appears, displaying the total size of the stripe set with parity spanning all selected drives (see fig. 7.30). This total size takes into account the smallest area selected on any disk drive, adjusting if necessary the sizes of the areas on the other selected drives to set all to identical size.

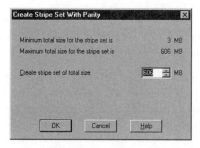

Fig. 7.30   Setting the size of the RAID 5 stripe set in the Create Stripe Set with Parity dialog.

5. Click OK to accept the default. Windows NT Server prepares to create the stripe set with parity and assigns a drive letter (see fig. 7.31). The stripe set with parity must now be prepared for use.

6. From the Partition menu choose Commit Changes Now. A dialog appears, to tell you that changes have been made to your disk configuration. Click Yes to accept and save the changes. A message box appears, to notify you that the update was successful. Click OK.

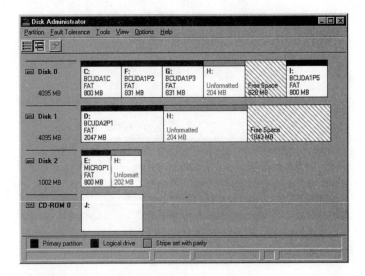

Fig. 7.31 The three partitions proposed for the RAID 5 stripe set.

> **Note**
>
> If another message box appears, to inform you that you must restart the computer for the changes to take effect, click OK to begin system shutdown. After Windows NT Server is restarted, again log on as an administrator and run Disk Administrator. The need to shut down and restart Windows NT depends on the status of the selected disk regions before the beginning of this process.

7. Select the newly created but unformatted stripe set with parity, and from the Tools menu choose Format to open the Format Drive *D*: dialog.

8. Type a name for the volume in the Label text box (see fig. 7.32). You're given the opportunity to choose an NTFS or FAT file system; select NTFS (the default). The Quick Format check box is disabled when you create a RAID 5 stripe set. Click OK to continue.

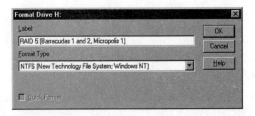

Fig. 7.32 Adding a label to the RAID 5 volume and selecting the file system.

9. When formatting is complete, a dialog appears, to inform you of the total available disk space on the new volume.

The size shown in figure 7.33 (409M) varies from that shown earlier in figure 7.30 (606M); 409M is the correct volume size.

Fig. 7.33 Disk Administrator confirming the correct size of the RAID 5 volume.

10. Click OK. The new RAID 5 volume is ready for use (see fig. 7.34).

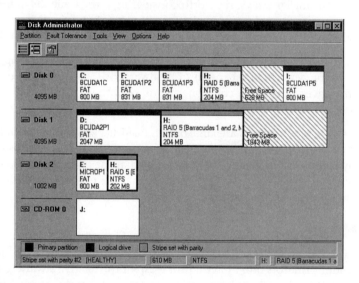

Fig. 7.34 The formatted RAID 5 volume ready for use.

> **Note**
>
> As is the case with mirror sets, RAID 5 volumes aren't ready for use until the background process-ing to create the additional partitions and format the partitions completes. This process may take several minutes when creating large RAID 5 volumes. The process is complete and you can use the drive when HEALTHY appears on the status bar, as shown in figure 7.34.

Summarizing RAID Recommendations

Given the wide diversity of RAID products available and the equally broad range of needs and budgets, it's difficult to make hard-and-fast recommendations for the most appropri-ate means of implementing RAID. However, the following observations serve as useful guidelines:

■ If your disk storage requirements are small, consider using your existing SCSI host adapter to implement mirroring. If your host adapter doesn't support hardware mirroring, consider replacing it with one that does. Purchase an additional disk drive to mirror to each existing drive. The result will be greatly increased data safety and better performance at minimal cost. Choose this hardware method in preference to the RAID 1 software functions of Windows NT Server on the basis of performance and minimizing load on the server.

■ If your disk storage requirements are moderate—and particularly if you need RAID 5—consider using either Windows NT Server software RAID or one of the hardware alternatives. Windows NT Server RAID 5 support appears to be rock solid, and performs well on smaller arrays. It's worth considering if the tradeoffs in flexibility, ease of maintenance, and server loading are of minor importance to you. If any or all of these factors concern you, choose a hardware RAID implementation.

■ If you're buying a new server, buy one with built-in hardware RAID support. In addition to the performance benefits of hardware RAID, the presence of hot swappable drives and similar components will contribute to increased uptime for your server.

■ If your storage requirements are large or you need stacked RAID, multiple independent arrays, or support for multiple hosts, a good external RAID enclosure is the only way to go. Give preference to those units that use industry standard components as widely as possible, rather than those that use proprietary hardware modifications to squeeze out the last ounce of performance.

From Here...

Although RAID arrays are found on virtually every production server, many network designers and administrators don't have a firm grasp of the relative advantages and disadvantages of RAID levels and implementation strategies. Thus, this chapter provides a detailed description and comparison of these two subjects of major importance to server performance and reliability.

The remaining chapters of Part II cover the other basic elements of setting up Windows NT Server, and connecting Windows 95 and other clients to your network:

■ Chapter 8, "Installing File Backup Systems," describes how to choose and set up backup systems for your RAID array. Although server RAID arrays are relatively secure, periodic backup to tape or other storage media is an absolute necessity to ensure against data loss in the event of a catastrophe.

■ Chapter 9, "Understanding the Windows NT Registry," takes you inside the Registry files used by Windows NT Server 4.0 through the use of the new Registry Editor that you use to inspect Registry values and, under very specific conditions, to modify these values.

■ Chapter 10, "Configuring Windows 95 Clients for Networking," provides the information you need to optimize the network functions of Windows 95 client PCs.

■ Chapter 11, "Connecting Other PC Clients to the Network," describes how to connect computers running Windows 3.1+, DOS, and the Macintosh operating system to your Windows NT Server 4.0 network.

II

Deploying Windows NT

Chapter 8

Installing File Backup Systems

Disk drives fail, taking critical data with them. People accidentally delete the wrong file. Databases become corrupt, sometimes for no apparent reason. As the network administrator, it's your job to protect against these and other causes of data loss by maintaining backup copies of your important data.

Backing up your data to tape or other removable storage media serves these purposes:

- Backups provide a copy of your data to protect against the catastrophic data loss that occurs when a disk drive fails and your RAID subsystem can't regenerate the data.

- They provide an offline copy of data that can be recovered if the working copy of a file is deleted or improperly modified.

- They provide a data archive that can be preserved for historical or legal purposes.

- They allow you to maintain a copy of your data, off premises, to protect against fire or other natural disasters.

In addition to these reasons for backing up data, proper data backup contributes to a network administrator's employment security. Many organizations have a policy of immediately terminating any network administrator responsible for an unrecoverable data loss. Even without such a policy, failure to properly back up data may result in the need of the responsible person to seek alternative employment.

The advent of RAID and other redundancy options has made some LAN administrators more casual about backing up critical data. In reality, RAID addresses only the first of the four preceding reasons for backing up. The other three reasons make backing up just as crucial as it was before RAID subsystems became a common feature of servers running Windows NT.

In this chapter, you learn

- The types of backup available and how each type of backup can best be used to ensure the safety of your data

- How to choose a tape-rotation method that stores multiple copies of your data for safety, while allowing fast and easy retrieval of backup data when needed

- How to select the best backup hardware for your server, taking into account cost, speed, reliability, and storage capacity

Understanding Backup Types

Windows NT Server 4.0 provides built-in support for various backup devices, primarily tape backup drives. The Microsoft Hardware Compatibility List for Windows NT, current when this book was written, identifies 145 individual makes and models of backup devices that are compatible with Windows NT Server 4.0. Before you choose backup hardware and software for your Windows NT Server 4.0 installation, however, it's important to understand how Windows NT Server 4.0 handles the file backup process. The following sections explain the purpose of the file archive bit and the types of backup operations supported by Windows NT Server 4.0 and third-party device drivers for backup devices.

> **Note**
>
> You can obtain the current version of the Hardware Compatibility List for Windows NT from Microsoft's Web site at **http://www.microsoft.com/ntserver/hcl/hclintro.htm** or by FTP from **ftp.microsoft.com**, in the /bussys/winnt/winnt-docs/hcl folder.

The Archive Bit

To manage a backup strategy, it's essential that your backup software has a way of knowing when a file has been created or modified since the last normal backup was done. One way to do this is to examine the date/time stamp on each file, and compare it with the time that the last backup was done to determine whether the file has changed. This method, used by the backup applet bundled with Windows 95, is simple in concept but unreliable in use. Using date/time stamps to determine the files to back up is unreliable, because many programs alter the contents of a file but don't change the date/time stamp when doing so. As a result, a better method of determining backup currency is needed. Fortunately, such a method has been available since the early days of MS-DOS.

Like MS-DOS, Windows NT stores with each file an attribute called the *archive bit*. The archive bit is set to on (a value of 1) when a file is created or modified to indicate that the file hasn't been backed up since the last change to it occurred. Because the archive bit is set to on whenever a file has been written to, it provides a completely reliable means of knowing when a file has changed. Windows NT Server 4.0 backup functions, like all modern full-featured backup programs, uses the archive bit to manage backup.

Normal Backups

A *normal backup* copies all selected files, regardless of the state of their archive bits, to the tape drive or other backup media, and then turns off the archive bit on all files that have been copied (see fig. 8.1). Most third-party backup software refers to this process as a *full backup*.

> **Note**
>
> A normal backup doesn't necessarily copy all files from a particular volume or disk drive, but it may simply copy a file or set of files from a specified folder or folders on the selected volume or disk drive. What determines a normal backup is that all *selected* files are copied without regard to the state of their archive bit.

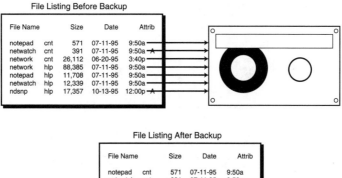

Fig. 8.1 A normal or full backup, which copies all selected files to tape and turns off the archive bit.

Re-creating a failed hard drive from a normal backup set of the entire drive is straightforward. If the system drive has failed, you must replace the drive and reinstall Windows NT Server before proceeding. If the system drive is operable, after replacing the data drive, use the Windows NT Server backup application, NTBACKUP, to do a full restore of the tape to the new drive. Partial restores, such as those of accidentally deleted files, are equally straightforward. NTBACKUP is described later in the section "Using the Windows NT Server 4.0 Backup Application."

Copy Backups

A *copy backup* is identical to a normal backup, except that copy backups skip the final step of resetting all the archive bits on backed up files to off (see fig. 8.2). Most third-party backup software refers to this process as a *full copy backup*. The resulting backup tape is identical to what would have been created by a normal backup, but the archive bit status of the files on the disk remains unchanged. The main purpose of a copy backup is to allow you to create an archive or off-site backup set without affecting your main backup set's rotation process.

Because the contents of a copy backup set are indistinguishable from those of a normal backup set, restore procedures are identical for these two types of backups.

Incremental Backups

An *incremental backup* copies to the backup media all selected files that have their archive bit turned on, and then turns the archive bit off for the files that have been copied (see fig. 8.3). The tape from the first incremental backup done after a normal backup contains only those files altered since the last normal backup. Subsequent incremental backup tapes contain only those files that changed since the last incremental backup. After completing each incremental backup, all files have their archive bits turned off, as though a normal backup were done.

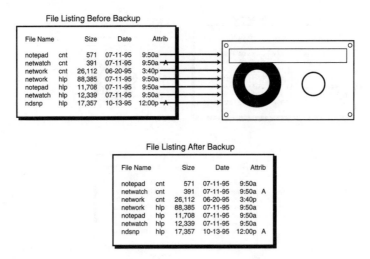

Fig. 8.2 A copy backup, which copies all selected files to tape but leaves the archive bit unchanged.

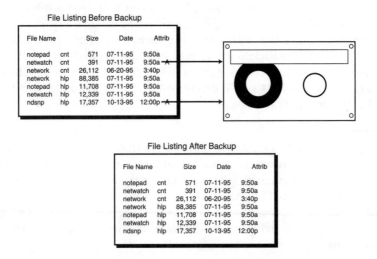

Fig. 8.3 An incremental backup, which copies only changed files to tape and sets the archive bit off.

Re-creating a failed hard drive from incremental backup sets is a bit more involved than using a normal backup set, because each incremental backup tape contains only some of the changed files, and different incremental backup tapes may contain different versions of the same file. To re-create a failed disk drive, you first restore the most recent normal backup set to the replacement disk. Then you restore all incremental backup sets created after the normal backup set, beginning with the earliest, and proceeding sequentially to the latest incremental backup set.

Restoring an accidentally deleted file is a more complex process. To ensure that you get the latest version of the file, you must start by examining the most recent incremental backup set and work backward until you locate the most recent occurrence of the file on an incremental backup set. If the file in question hasn't changed since the last normal backup, you may have to work all the way back to the last normal backup set before you locate the file. Fortunately, most backup software makes this process somewhat easier by allowing you to search backup logs to locate the file so that you can load the proper tape directly.

> **Tip**
>
> The incremental backup is best suited to environments where a relatively large number of different files change each day. Because the incremental backup sets the archive bit off after each of these files is backed up, each file is backed up only on the day that it's changed. This may reduce the number of tapes needed for each daily tape set, and also cuts down on the time required for daily partial backups.

Differential Backups

A *differential backup* copies to the backup media all selected files that have their archive bits turned on, but then leaves the archive bits unchanged on the files that have been copied (see fig. 8.4). This means that each differential backup set contains all files changed since the last normal backup. It also means that each differential backup set is larger than the preceding set, because later sets contain all the files previously backed up, plus all files changed since that last backup.

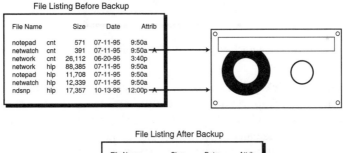

Fig. 8.4 A differential backup, which copies only changed files to tape and leaves the archive bit unchanged.

Re-creating a failed hard drive using a differential backup set is relatively straightforward. As with an incremental backup set, you begin by restoring the last normal backup set. Because each differential backup set contains all files changed since the last normal backup, however, you need to restore only the most recent differential backup set. Restoring an accidentally deleted file is similarly straightforward. If the file is listed on your

II

Deploying Windows NT

most recent differential backup log, restore from the latest differential backup set. Otherwise, restore from the last normal backup.

Daily Copy Backups

A *daily copy backup* copies all selected files that have been modified that day, but leaves the archive bits unchanged on the files that are copied (see fig. 8.5). Like the Windows 95 backup mentioned earlier in the section "The Archive Bit," the daily copy backup uses file date stamps to determine their eligibility for backup, rather than examine the status of the archive bit.

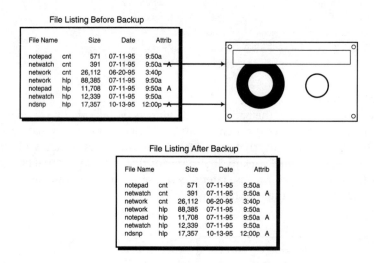

Fig. 8.5   A daily copy backup, which copies only changed files to tape, based on the file date, and leaves the archive bit unchanged.

Unlike the incremental backup, which copies all files changed since the last normal backup or incremental backup was done, the daily copy backup must be run at least once each day if it's to be successfully used to archive files changed since the last normal backup. If you fail to run the daily copy backup on one particular day, none of the files changed on that day is written to tape until the next normal, copy, incremental, or differential backup is done. Because it ignores the state of the archive bit, the daily copy backup also fails to back up changed files if the file date stamp wasn't altered at the time the file was changed.

Choosing Among the Backup Types

A normal backup has the considerable advantages of thoroughness and simplicity. Each normal backup set contains all the selected files on your hard drive. No juggling of tapes is required to locate a particular file. If a problem occurs, simply retrieve the last normal backup tape and do a full or partial restore, as appropriate. The primary problem with normal backups is that they consume large numbers of backup tapes and take a long time to complete.

> **Note**
>
> Doing a proper backup requires that the contents of the server disk be static—that is, that files not be in use and subject to change by users while the backup process proceeds. For many organizations, this means that the best time to do backups is during evening hours and on weekends. Assuming that the server can be taken down for backup at 7 p.m. and must be back in service by 7 a.m., the backup must be completed within 12 hours.
>
> The fastest 4mm DAT tape drives commonly used for Windows NT Server backup can transfer data at a sustained rate of perhaps 30M/minute, or about 1.8G/hour, allowing time to back up a little more than 20G overnight on weekdays. Even the larger 8mm tape drives with automatic tape changers top out at 60M/minute or so, extending the maximum to perhaps 40G or 50G for an overnight backup. If your server disk "farm" is larger than 40G or 50G, if you have multiple servers to back up to a single tape drive, or if your company's hours of operation are longer, you don't have time to complete a normal backup each night.

Although most servers today aren't a size that causes the time required to do a backup to be an insurmountable problem, this situation will change as larger server disk storage subsystems become the norm. Only a few years ago, 1G was considered a large amount of disk storage for a PC server. Today, 10G arrays are common and 50G servers are available. The increasing use of multimedia and document imaging, plus the decreasing cost of disk storage, means that most server disk farms will continue to grow over the next few years. Because tape drive throughput isn't likely to keep pace, you're likely to find, ultimately, that you no longer have time to do a normal backup overnight.

The second reason that it may not be feasible to use only normal backup sets is tape capacity. Unless your IS department or computer room is staffed 24 hours a day, 7 days a week (24×7), overnight backups require either that the size of the backup set not exceed the capacity of a single tape, or that expensive "jukebox" tape changers are used to do unattended backups.

It's for these reasons that the concepts of incremental and differential partial backups were developed. Using either incremental or differential backups with less-frequent normal backups allows only changed files to be backed up routinely, whereas the unchanged bulk of the disk contents are backed up only weekly, or monthly, typically over the course of a weekend. Because only a subset of the full disk is copied to tape each night, the time and tape capacity factors become lesser issues.

The choice between using incremental backup or differential backup for your partial backups depends on how many files are changed, how frequently the files are changed, the size of the files, and how frequently you expect to need to do restores. If most of your files are large and change infrequently, choosing incremental backup minimizes the total amount of data that must be written to tape, because this data is written only once each time the file changes when using incremental backup (instead of each time a backup is done with differential backup). Conversely, if you have many small files that change frequently, the storage economy of incremental backup is likely to be outweighed by the ease of file retrieval with differential backup.

If the daily copy backup has any valid application, it's to run quick, supplementary "snapshot" backups during the course of the working day. If your main backup rotation does a normal backup each day, you can use either incremental or differential backup to make snapshot backups, because the state of the archive bit doesn't matter to the normal backup run each night. If instead your main backup rotation uses either incremental or differential backup on some nights, any partial backup you do during the day must not alter the archive bits of any files. Incremental backups reset the archive bit and are, therefore, unusable for snapshot backups in this environment. Differential backups don't reset the archive bit; however, using differential backups defeats the purpose of a quick snapshot backup, because the process backs up not just the day's work, but all preceding work as well. If your main backup rotation uses partial backups and you need to do snapshot backups during the course of the day, the daily copy backup may be a useful tool, provided that you keep its limitations in mind. Otherwise, don't consider using daily copy backup.

If you're fortunate enough to have a tape drive large enough to do a normal backup on a single tape, and you have the time each night to complete a normal backup, then do so. Using only normal backups makes it much easier to manage the backup process and much less likely that you might accidentally overwrite the wrong tape or otherwise compromise the integrity of your backup sets. If—as is more common—you must depend on less frequent normal backups and daily partial backups, decide whether using incremental backup or differential backup better suits your data; then use the method that best matches your needs. For typical Windows NT servers, a program using normal backups, with differential backups, is the best choice.

Developing a Backup Strategy

Developing a coherent backup strategy that reliably safeguards your data requires more than simply deciding to do a normal backup each weekend and a partial backup every night. You must also consider several other factors, discussed in the following sections, that bear on data integrity and managing the backup process.

Organizing Disk Storage

The first issue to consider when developing a backup strategy is how you arrange the data on your server's fixed-disk drives. If you have only a single disk volume on your server, there's nothing to decide. If, however, you have multiple volumes, you can decide what type of data resides on each volume. Figure 8.6 shows one possible arrangement of data on volumes intended to make backup easier. Making the correct data organization decisions eases the entire backup process; making the wrong decisions can complicate backup operations needlessly.

A satisfactory organization places user home directories and other areas with files that frequently change on one or more volumes but segregates system files and other files that change infrequently in a separate volume of their own. Depending on the number of volumes you've created and the types of data you must store, you can extend this file segregation process. For example, if you have a large database that's updated infrequently, you may decide to place it on a dedicated volume, thereby minimizing or obviating entirely the need for backup of that volume. Similarly, if you have large imaging files that change frequently, you may allocate a volume to them and then use incremental backup for only that volume, using differential backup for other volumes where its use is more appropriate. Always manage your volumes with backup issues in the back of your mind.

Fig. 8.6   Organizing disk volumes to optimize backup operations.

> **Note**
>
> Client/server relational database management systems (RDBMSs), such as Microsoft SQL Server 6.5, present special difficulties in backing up data because their files remain open whenever the RDBMS is running. Most RDBMSs therefore provide a backup system independent of the backup application supplied with Windows NT Server 4.0.
>
> RDBMS backup procedures use a periodic *database dump*, which is equivalent to a normal backup. Incremental backups save the content of a *transaction log*, which lists all modifications to the database since the last dump. On completion of a database dump, the transaction log file is deleted. RDBMS transaction logs vary from the transitory transaction logs created by Windows NT's Log File Service for NTFS volumes.

Ensuring Backup Integrity

The second issue to consider when developing a backup strategy is how you verify the integrity of your backups. Many LAN administrators have found, to their sorrow, that the backup tape they relied on to restore a failed drive is unreadable. You don't want to find this out when it's too late to recover your data. The way to avoid this problem is to perform a *compare operation* to verify that the contents of the backup tape correspond to the contents of the disk drive.

Inexpensive tape drives use a single head to perform both read and write operations. Doing a compare with these tape drives requires a second complete pass of the tape through the drive, doubling backup time. More expensive tape drives have separate read and write heads, accommodating a process called *read-after-write*. With these drives, the write head records the backup data to tape, which is then read immediately by the second read head and compared with the data stream coming from the fixed-disk drive. Read-after-write tape drives definitely are preferred, because such drives can perform both a backup and compare during a single tape pass, assuming that read-after-write is supported by the backup software.

If you find yourself forced to use a tape drive that requires a second pass to compare files, take the extra time to do the compare. Otherwise, you may find yourself with a failed disk drive and no backup from which to restore your data. Many network administrators with low-cost tape drives compromise between running a compare after every backup and never running a compare operation. A common procedure is to run a compare after each normal backup but run partial backups without doing the compare. Another, somewhat riskier, method is to do the compare on partial backups, where a compare runs more quickly, and not run the compare on the larger, multitape normal backups. Whichever method you choose, make sure that you do a compare at least occasionally, to verify that your tape drive is really writing readable data to your tapes.

Tip

Periodically reading backup tapes created by one tape drive on another tape drive that accommodates the same format is a necessity to ensure that you don't have tape interchange problems. If you have an undiscovered interchange problem and your source tape drive fails or is destroyed in a calamity, you can't restore your backup by using another tape drive. Interchange problems usually occur as a result of mechanical changes in the tape path or head alignment that don't affect compare operations on the same drive. Interchange problems are more likely to occur with high-density tape formats, such as 4mm DAT and 8mm.

Backing Up Open Files

The third major issue to consider when developing a backup strategy is how to handle the backup of open files. Open files on the network pose a difficult problem for network administrators who want to make sure that all files are successfully backed up. Most backup programs, including the Windows NT Server 4.0 backup application, let you specify how to handle open files on the network. You can elect to bypass open files during the backup operation, or return to open files at the end of a backup session to determine whether the open files have been closed and can therefore now be backed up.

Backing up an open file also isn't practical because the file may be written to and closed while being written to the tape drive. This results in a corrupted file stored to tape. Consider the result of backing up an open database file that has related index files open. The main database file is successfully written to tape in its current state, and the backup software continues to read other files from the disk. A user saves data, modifying both the main database file and one or more index files. (Separate data and index files are used by desktop database systems such as dBASE, FoxPro, and Paradox.) Because the main database file has already been written but the index files haven't, the resulting backup tape contains an older version of the main database file and newer versions of the index files. If you then restore this database and its associated index files, the index files don't match the database files, and applications can't access the database files.

Note

Clearly, it's preferable to perform backups when all files are closed and you're the only user logged on to the server. This may not always be possible, however—particularly if your server must be operational 24 hours a day, 7 days a week. Many firms that operate Internet servers don't want to discourage connection to their Web site by taking the server out of service for backups.

The only way to handle the open file backup problem is to use a RAID subsystem (described Chapter 7, "Setting Up Redundant Arrays of Inexpensive Disks (RAID)") to provide built-in redundancy for your disk storage. Other than the additional cost, RAID has two drawbacks:

- When a drive does fail, your data is completely vulnerable until that drive has been replaced and the parity information rebuilt. This problem can be solved—albeit at significant expense—by building an array of arrays to give you two levels of redundancy.

- Of the four main reasons for backing up—protecting against drive failure, allowing recovery of accidentally deleted files, providing a historical archive copy, and allowing you to store a copy of your data off site—RAID addresses only the first problem.

Matching Backup Media Capacity to Disk Size

Before purchasing a tape drive or other means of backup, carefully consider the size of the largest backup you're likely to need. Ideally, the capacity of the tape drive you select should exceed by a comfortable margin the size of the largest backup data set you make during the life of the tape drive. The goal is to ensure that any backup set, regardless of its size, can be written to a single tape. Avoiding backup sets that span multiple tapes makes backup administration and tape rotation considerably easier and minimizes the chance for using the wrong tape by mistake.

When selecting a tape drive, keep in mind that the disk storage on your server is likely to grow larger as time passes. Remember also that the nominal capacities stated for tape drives assume 2:1 compression of the data being backed up. A tape drive rated at 14G capacity may have only a 7G native capacity, depending on file compression to gain the remaining 7G. If you back up a typical mix of files on a server used primarily for office automation tasks, you may find that the drive achieves the estimated 2:1 compression ratio. If you're backing up a disk drive dedicated to fixed images or video files, which usually are stored in a compressed format, you may find that you achieve compression ratios of 1.1:1 or less.

Organizing Rotation Methods

Tapes should be rotated in an organized manner to satisfy the following five goals:

■ The tape containing the most recent backup of that data is quickly available so that the server can be restored to use with minimum delay.

■ Older copies of the current data can be archived for the period necessary to ensure that damage or deletion of important data, which isn't noticed immediately, can be retrieved from the most recent archived backup where the data still exists in a usable form.

■ A backup copy of critical data can be stored off site to guard against catastrophic damage to the server and on-site backup copies.

■ The integrity and usability of the backup sets is preserved if one or more tapes break or are lost.

■ Wear on tapes is equalized, avoiding continuous use of some tapes and infrequent use of others.

Various tape-rotation schemes has been developed. Some are quite simple in concept, at the expense of inadequately meeting one or more of the preceding goals. Others are quite complex and meet all the goals for a good rotation scheme, but are difficult to administer on a day-to-day basis.

Some tape-rotation methods use normal backups exclusively; others use less frequent normal backups with daily incremental or differential backups; still others can be used either way. You may be forced to use a rotation that includes partial backups if your tape drive can't store a normal backup set to a single tape, or if time constraints don't allow daily normal backups. If neither condition applies, you're better served by a rotation that uses normal backups exclusively.

The following sections describe five different types of rotation methods. Each method assumes that a normal backup can be done to a single tape and that your organization operates on a five-day-per-week schedule. The methods may be modified if one or both of these conditions can't be met.

Weekly Normal Backup with Daily Differential Backup (Four-Tape Method). The four-tape rotation method, shown in figure 8.7, is very commonly used for small servers. The backup tape set comprises at least four tapes, labeled *Weekly A*, *Weekly B*, *Daily A*, and *Daily B*. The rotation begins with a normal backup to Weekly A on Friday of Week 1, followed by a daily differential backup to Daily A on Monday through Thursday of Week 2. On Friday of Week 2, a normal backup is done to Weekly B, followed by daily differential backups to Daily B on Monday through Thursday of Week 3. On Friday of Week 3, a normal backup is done to Weekly A, and the cycle begins again.

Although the four-tape method is simple to administer and uses a minimum number of tapes, it suffers the following drawbacks:

■ Retrieval of historical copies of your data is limited to a two-week span.

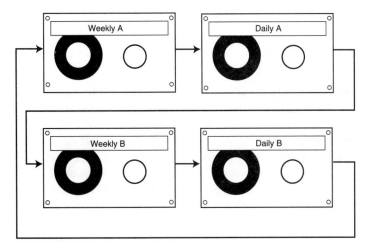

Fig. 8.7 A weekly normal backup with daily differential backup using four tapes.

■ You're faced with the choice of either storing the normal backup off site, where it's not quickly accessible, or having the normal backup readily available for use, but at risk.

■ All daily backups are written to a single tape over the course of a week, so you must return to the last weekly tape if the daily tape in use fails.

■ Daily tapes are used four times more often than are weekly tapes, making the daily tapes much more likely to fail.

You can make the following minor modifications to this rotation scheme to address the preceding problems without substantial complication of the backup administration process:

■ A copy backup can be processed monthly to a tape that's then stored off site, addressing the first two problems of the preceding list. Depending on your need for historical data, this set can comprise 12 tapes labeled *January* through *December*, cycled on a yearly basis, or three tapes labeled *Month 1* through *Month 3*, cycled on a quarterly basis.

■ By adding two tapes to the set, you can provide two daily differential backups tapes in each set and alternate using them. Using this method, label tapes *Weekly A*, *Weekly B*, *Daily A—Odd*, *Daily A—Even*, *Daily B—Odd*, and *Daily B—Even*. You make weekly normal backups as above but alternate using daily tapes—use the Odd tape if the day of the month is odd, and the Even tape if the day of the month is even. This way, when you run a differential backup, the tape you're writing to is never the one containing the most recent backup set. This eliminates the third problem described earlier. Because it alternates daily backups between two tapes, it also reduces uneven tape wear.

■ You can extend the preceding method to use eight tapes labeled *Monday A* through *Thursday A* and *Monday B* through *Thursday B* for daily differential backups. At the small cost of six additional tapes, you eliminate the third and fourth problems of the preceding list. If a daily tape fails, you lose only that day's backup, rather than have to return to the last prior full weekly backup. Each tape is used once every two weeks, equalizing wear, although the daily tapes from later in the week and (in particular) the weekly tapes will still be used somewhat more heavily due to the larger size of the backup sets written to them.

Weekly Normal Backup with Daily Incremental Backup (10-Tape Method). This version of the 10-tape rotation method, shown in figure 8.8, uses 10 tapes, labeled *Weekly A*, *Weekly B*, *Monday A* through *Thursday A*, and *Monday B* through *Thursday B*. The rotation begins with a normal backup to Weekly A on Friday of week 1, followed by a daily incremental backup to the appropriately labeled daily A tape on Monday through Thursday of week 2. On Friday of week 2, a normal backup is done to Weekly B, followed by daily incremental backups to the appropriately labeled daily B tape on Monday through Thursday of week 3. On Friday of week 3, a normal backup is done to Weekly A, and the cycle begins again.

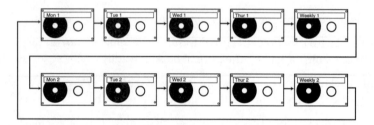

Fig. 8.8 A weekly normal backup with daily incremental backup using 10 tapes.

This version of the 10-tape method shares the first two drawbacks of the four-tape method, allowing only two weeks of historical data and making no provision for off-site storage. These problems can be addressed by making a copy backup each month, which is stored off site and rotated on a quarterly or annual basis. The third problem, loss of a daily tape, is more difficult to address. Because a daily incremental backup tape contains only a subset of the files changed during that week, loss of one daily incremental backup tape may require you to return to the last normal backup to retrieve a copy of a particular file. Also, if you need to restore a failed hard drive, loss of one incremental backup tape, which happens to contain critical or interdependent files, may force you to roll your restore back to the last preceding normal backup. The only way to protect against this problem is to run the incremental backup twice each day to different daily tapes, defeating the purpose of using a partial backup rotation scheme.

Although this version of the 10-tape method is commonly used, it offers the worst of all worlds. This version of the 10-tape method puts your data at risk, uses no fewer tapes than other methods, and saves very little time compared to using differential backups. Don't consider using this version of the 10-tape method.

Daily Full Backups with Two Set Rotation (an Alternate 10-Tape Method). This alternate 10-tape method, shown in figure 8.9, is the simplest tape-rotation system in common use that uses normal backups exclusively. It uses 10 tapes, labeled *Monday A* through *Friday A* and *Monday B* through *Friday B*. A normal backup is done each day to the appropriate tape, and the full set is cycled every two weeks. The major drawback to this method is that it limits historical data to a two-week span. Again, the historical problem can be addressed simply by doing a biweekly or monthly normal backup to a separate tape and archiving the tape. The archive tapes can be rotated on a quarterly or annual basis.

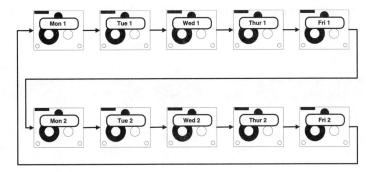

Fig. 8.9   A daily full backup with two-set rotation using 10 tapes.

Grandfather-Father-Son Rotation (21-Tape Method). The grandfather-father-son (or GFS) method, shown in figure 8.10, is probably the most commonly used tape-rotation method. It's relatively easy to manage, fairly efficient in terms of the number of tapes required, and is supported by almost every backup software package on the market. A GFS rotation can use normal backups exclusively, or can use a combination of normal backups and partial backups.

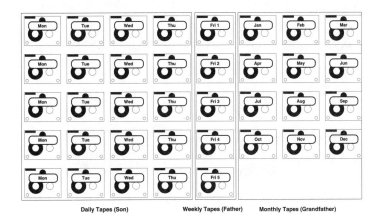

Daily Tapes (Son)   Weekly Tapes (Father)   Monthly Tapes (Grandfather)

Fig. 8.10   A grandfather-father-son tape rotation using 10 tapes.

GFS is nearly always an acceptable, if not optimum, choice for a small- or medium-size Windows NT server. The two primary drawbacks to GFS are that it uses some tapes more heavily than others and that, in its unmodified form, makes no provision for balancing off-site storage needs with quick retrieval requirements.

A typical GFS rotation scheme requires 21 tapes to be used over the course of a year, although this number can be altered depending on your particular archiving needs. Four daily tapes are labeled *Monday* through *Thursday*. Five weekly tapes are labeled *Friday 1* through *Friday 5* (the fifth Friday tape accommodates months with five Fridays). Twelve monthly tapes are labeled *January* through *December*.

The daily tapes are used on the day corresponding to the tape label, and are overwritten every week. Each Friday, the correspondingly numbered Friday tape is used, meaning that Friday tapes are overwritten only once each month. On the last day of each month, a normal backup is done to the corresponding monthly tape, which is therefore overwritten only once per year.

> **Tip**
>
> Depending on your needs, you can alter the time span between archival backups. Firms for which archiving is less critical can substitute quarterly tapes for monthly ones. Firms for which archiving is very important may choose to substitute biweekly or even weekly archive tapes for the monthly tapes described here.

Tower of Hanoi Rotation (TOH). The Tower of Hanoi (TOH) rotation method, shown in figure 8.11, is named for a game that uses three posts and several rings of various diameters. The object of the game is to relocate the rings by using a minimum number of moves so that the rings are placed in sequence on a post, with the largest ring on the bottom and the smallest on the top. The TOH backup model introduces new tapes to the backup set periodically, using the newly introduced tape every other rotation. TOH doubles the time before the previous tape comes back into the rotation, consequently doubling the time before earlier tapes are introduced back into the rotation.

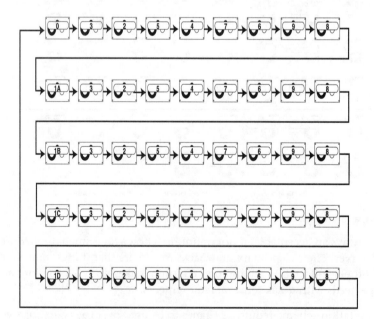

Fig. 8.11 The Tower of Hanoi tape rotation.

The TOH rotation has many advantages, but at the cost of considerable complexity in terms of managing the tape rotation. Wear on individual tapes is distributed relatively evenly over time using this method, but the real advantage of TOH versus GFS and other methods is that TOH saves many versions of each file, allowing you to selectively retrieve different versions of the file.

Note

The TOH rotation originated for mainframe and minicomputer backup, and has since migrated to the PC LAN environment. For a long time, Palindrome's PC Backup software was the only product supporting this rotation, although TOH rotation is now becoming more common. Backup software from Symantec and other third parties offer automated TOH implementation.

If the backup software you select supports a Tower of Hanoi rotation, consider using it for its many advantages, particularly if yours is a medium or large LAN. If your software doesn't provide TOH, don't even consider an attempt to implement TOH rotation manually. You will almost certainly use the wrong tape at one time or another, destroying the integrity of the rotation.

Using Hierarchical Storage Management (HSM)

A concept called *Hierarchical Storage Management* (HSM) was originally developed in the mainframe arena and is beginning to migrate to PC LANs. HSM is based on the fact that, although fixed-disk drives offer fast access to data, they are an expensive commodity of finite capacity on real-world LANs. Tape and other backup media offer much slower access, but can be extended to essentially unlimited capacity simply by adding more tapes. HSM uses fast but limited-capacity fixed-disk drives to store backup data that's needed quickly, plus tapes to store an unlimited amount of data that doesn't need to be retrieved as quickly.

HSM categorizes storage devices as online, near-line, and offline:

- *Online* storage devices offer immediate high-speed access to real-time data, with typical access times on the order of 10 milliseconds. Online storage devices offer relatively small storage capacity on the order of 1G to 10G. Online storage is the most expensive type per byte stored, costing from $250 to $2,500 per 1G stored, depending on configuration. Disk drives and RAID arrays are online storage devices.

- *Near-line* storage devices also offer immediate access to data, but with much slower access times and correspondingly lower costs per byte stored. The fastest near-line devices—that is, magneto-optical and WORM (write-once, read-many) drives and arrays—may offer access times of 50 milliseconds or better, nearly as fast as a standard disk drive, but not quite fast enough to serve as a primary storage medium. Slower near-line devices, such as optical and tape jukeboxes, may have access times measured in seconds or tens of seconds, allowing on-demand access of archived data with short delays acceptable for occasional use. Near-line storage devices typically range in cost from $50 to $1,000 per 1G stored, depending on type and total capacity. Capacities of near-line devices, such as jukeboxes, range from 50G to 1,000G (1 terabyte), and more.

■ *Offline* storage usually means tape cartridges sit on the shelf. Offline storage is used for data needing to be accessed very infrequently, if at all, but too valuable to be discarded. Retrieving data stored offline requires human intervention—someone has to locate the appropriate tape and physically place it in the tape drive. Offline storage is very inexpensive per byte stored. A $20 tape may hold more than 20G, putting the cost at less than $1 per 1G stored.

The key to HSM systems is that files are automatically migrated from the faster (and more expensive) online storage devices to near-line storage and eventually to offline storage, based on the usage patterns of the particular file. This process is managed by the HSM software itself, without the need for routine intervention by the LAN administrator. Infrequently used files, which must nevertheless remain available, can be designated as near-line.

> ### Note
>
> HSM has become a hot topic during the last 18 months or so, and HSM-based products for Windows NT Server are shipping from (or have been announced by) most major backup software suppliers, including Seagate/Palindrome, Conner/Arcada, Cheyenne, and others. If your storage requirements can benefit from HSM, examine the capabilities and costs of these products before deciding on a final backup solution.

Considering Enterprise Backup Solutions

Simple backup solutions, both hardware and software, focus on the needs of relatively small server backup in a single-server environment. If your LAN includes multiple servers, multiple sites, huge amounts of server disk storage, or the need to back up user workstations running diverse operating systems, consider acquiring an enterprise backup solution.

Enterprise backup systems combine sophisticated backup software, often including HSM capabilities, with hardware designed to offer an integrated, centralized backup solution for the entire enterprise. Although enterprise backup systems aren't cheap, the alternative is replicated software and hardware on multiple servers.

Palindrome's Backup Director and Legato's Network Archivist products historically have been the leaders in the enterprise backup market, although competing products from Arcada, Cheyenne, Symantec, and others are now beginning to appear. Used with high-capacity tape drives or tape auto-changers, these products automate the backup process for a large multiserver network, allowing administration from a central location.

One unique product deserves mention in the enterprise storage category. The Intel Storage Express system is a turnkey software and hardware solution to enterprise backup. Intel Storage Express handles multiple servers running different network operating systems, including Windows NT Server and Novell NetWare. Storage Express can back up drives of individual workstations running DOS, Windows 3.x, Windows NT, OS/2, and several flavors of UNIX. Storage Express is expandable on a modular basis to provide as much as 144G of tape capacity, using either 4mm DAT or 8mm drives.

Storing Data Off Site

The issue of off-site storage of backup tapes presents a conundrum. Although you want to keep your data stored safely off site to guard against catastrophic damage to your LAN, at the same time you want backup copies of your data to be readily accessible when you need them.

> **Note**
>
> There are at least two good reasons to maintain an off-site set of backup tapes. Most obviously, doing so protects against catastrophic data loss due to fires and natural disasters, which may claim your on-site backup tapes at the same time they destroy your server.
>
> Less obvious but just as important to many companies is the need to maintain archival sets of backup data for legal or other reasons. It may be necessary to keep several years' worth of data relating to tax issues, personnel files, and so on. Space constraints alone often make it necessary to keep these archives off site.

The best available fire-safe storage units can't guarantee that fragile tapes will survive a major fire. Many businesses suffering a catastrophic data loss find themselves out of business shortly thereafter; thus, there's no substitute for off-site storage. It's obviously preferable that the contents of the tapes stored off site be as up-to-date as possible. However, because the off-site tapes are a last-ditch defense that are never likely to be used, some currency sacrifice may be acceptable.

The opposite side of the safety issue is the need for backup data to be quickly accessible. If a hard drive fails on a production LAN, you need to restore as soon as possible, and you need to do the restore from the most recent backup. Having the LAN down can cost your company hundreds, thousands, or even tens of thousands of dollars per hour in lost productivity and orders. Having to wait several hours or longer to get your hands on the most recent backup is unacceptable.

How you manage this problem depends on how recent you require your off-site backup to be, versus how quickly the most recent backup must be accessible. Organizations that demand the best of both worlds have no real alternative but to use duplicate normal backups, cycling one copy off site each day and keeping the other available for local use. If your requirements are less demanding, you can simply keep the most recent normal backup on site and cycle the next-most-recent normal backup to off-site storage on a rotating basis. If you require only minimal off-site protection, you can simply perform a monthly archive backup and move it off site.

Regardless of how frequently you rotate backups off site, the issue arises of where to store the tapes. Although various services offer secure storage of off-site backups, most organizations work on a less formal basis. Short of nuclear war, it's very unlikely that both an on-site backup and an off-site backup stored at an unprotected location, such as your home, would be destroyed simultaneously. Giving up the marginal added safety of using a commercial off-site storage facility pays dividends, not only in terms of costs not incurred but in terms of ease of rotating the off-site backup sets. Keep your off-site sets at home, and develop a rotation scheme to keep the tapes refreshed frequently.

Developing a Restore Plan

It's easy to focus on backing up to the extent that you lose sight of the real purpose of backing up data, which is to restore the data when necessary. The objective is to back up frequently and restore very seldom, if ever. More fundamentally, the goal of backing up is to ensure that if the server crashes, you can get the server back up and running quickly.

Most network administrators back up dozens or hundreds of times for each episode requiring a full restore. Network administrators may perform partial restores of accidentally deleted files on a weekly or even daily basis, but full restores are rare, usually occurring only when the server disk storage system is upgraded, the operating system is changed, or a disk drive crashes. You don't get much practice doing full restores. To make matters worse, when you do need to do a full restore, you're often working under the gun, with a crashed hard drive and many upset users waiting for the server to return to life. Accordingly, it's worthwhile to spend some time to develop a plan to make sure that when you do need to do a full restore, you can do so easily and quickly. Following are the four items necessary to assure a successful data-restore process:

- *Maintain the integrity of your backup sets.* There's no worse feeling for LAN administrators than attempting to do a full restore of a crashed drive, only to find that the backup set(s) are corrupted or otherwise unusable. Running a comparison on your backup can help ensure against this happening, but the only real way to make sure that your backup set is usable is to try to restore from it. You obviously don't want to test the integrity of a backup set by restoring to a production server, lest you find that the backup set was corrupt and that by restoring you've also corrupted the live data on the server. If you have a test-bed, development, or standby server available, periodically try to restore your production backup to that server. If the spare server doesn't have enough disk space to do a full restore, at least make sure that you can restore to the extent of the available disk space. If your backup sets span multiple tapes, make sure that at least the change from restoring tape 1 to restoring tape 2 succeeds. Otherwise, you may find that you can restore only the first tape from each set.

- *Make sure that spare hardware is available immediately.* Tape drives are relatively reliable devices; they die only when you really need them. Although there's no scientific basis for the preceding statement, a corollary to Murphy's Law is, "When something really bad (such as a disk crash) occurs, other bad happenings are likely to follow in its wake." Whatever tape drive you choose, make sure that you have at least two drives of the same make and model on site. Also, make sure that you have whatever hardware is needed to install to the failed drive from scratch, including a spare SCSI host adapter and cables.

- *Prepare and maintain an emergency repair kit.* If the C drive fails, it does you no good to have a functioning tape drive and a good backup tape if you have no way to boot the server. Your emergency repair kit must contain everything needed to rebuild your server from scratch. You need a boot disk, diagnostic software, the Windows NT Server 4.0 distribution CD, a copy of your backup program, any drivers that you have installed or updated yourself, and so on. The emergency repair kit also should include the tools needed to open the server and replace failed components.

It's also critical that this kit be kept up-to-date. Many network administrators take the first step of building such a kit, but then ignore the fact that every change made to the production server renders this kit increasingly obsolete. You don't want to find that your emergency kit contains version 4.2 of your backup program but that it won't restore the backup you did with version 4.3. Build an emergency restore kit and keep it up-to-date.

■ *Plan to minimize server downtime in the event of a failure.* Even if you have everything you need readily at hand when a drive fails, the process of running the restore can take several hours. Every minute of this time increases the users' level of aggravation and costs your company money in salaries and lost sales.

Tip

Even carefully planned backup and restore policies and procedures are of little use unless a qualified person is present to implement them when needed. A LAN administrator will sometimes be sick, on vacation, at a conference, or otherwise away when a restore needs to be done.

Make sure that at least one, and preferably several, of your staff members have been trained to follow the backup and restore procedures you've implemented. An untrained person who tries to restore data to your network server may do more harm than good. Also make sure that each of these "pinch hitters" is fully informed of where tapes are stored and can get to them, if needed.

You can do little to make the restore run faster, but one step guaranteed to save time is having a prebuilt C system disk sitting on the shelf, ready to use. This disk should be bootable and should include a full installation of Windows NT Server 4.0, along with all special drivers needed to support the peripherals on your server. It should also include an installed copy of your backup software. If your system drive fails, you can plug this spare drive into the server and avoid wasting an hour or two tracking down distribution disks, reinstalling Windows NT Server 4.0 and its drivers, and getting your backup software installed and running.

Choosing Backup Hardware

Backup and tape drives traditionally are considered synonymous. Although tape is the overwhelming choice of backup media for most network administrators, various optical storage technologies are beginning to nip at its heels. These technologies are still niche products, insofar as the backup market is concerned, both because they're largely proprietary in nature and because their cost per byte stored is still relatively high in most cases. Still, it's worth examining some of these alternatives briefly, both for their current value in fitting specific needs and their possible future value as an alternative to tape. The following sections describe the relative merits of common tape backup formats and alternative optical storage systems for backup and archiving data.

Tape Drives and Formats

Tape drives are the traditional method for backing up data. In terms of reusability and cost per byte stored, the tape drive is now—and is likely to remain—the best choice for backing up Windows NT Server 4.0s. The following sections describe the most common types of tape drives in use today.

Quarter-Inch Cartridge (QIC) Drives. Most tape drives sold today are quarter-inch cartridge or QIC-compatible. The following form factors are used for QIC cartridges:

- Full-size cartridges are about the size of a small paperback book and are commonly referred to as a DC-600, although various versions of this cartridge exist.

- Smaller cartridges are the familiar 3 1/2-inch minicartridge commonly called a DC-2000, but many versions of this cartridge exist.

QIC-80 minicartridges originally stored 80M on a 205-foot tape, but they have since been expanded. 120M capacity is achieved by the use of 307 1/2-foot tapes, and 250M is achieved by the use of data compression. The newer cartridges with 350M capacity use an even longer tape. QIC-80 drives are controlled by the diskette controller and are too small and too slow for serious consideration as a backup solution for all but the smallest servers.

In response to the rapid growth in the size of disk drives, the Quarter-Inch Cartridge Standards Committee approved the QIC-3010 standard in 1991 and the QIC-3020 standard in 1993. The QIC-3010 standard specifies a 3 1/2-inch minicartridge tape with a native capacity of 340M and a compressed capacity of 680M. The QIC-3020 standard specifies a 3 1/2-inch minicartridge tape with a 680M native capacity and a 1.36G compressed capacity.

Sony recently introduced the QIC-Wide cartridge, using 0.315-inch (8mm) wide tape, rather than the 0.250-inch tape used in earlier QIC cartridges. QIC-Wide expands native storage capacity from 120M to 210M, usually advertised as 420M compressed. QIC-Wide drives can read and write both QIC-Wide and standard QIC-80 tapes, but standard drives can't read QIC-Wide tapes.

Note

The QIC-Wide cartridge seems destined to die an early death, due to its marginal increase in capacity and that Sony is the sole source of tapes, which are rather costly compared with standard QIC tapes.

Another scheme to extend the usefulness of the QIC-80 format is 3M's recently introduced DC-2120XL tapes. Usually sold in a kit containing two DC-2120XL tapes and a copy of Arcada Backup 4.1, these tapes increase the native QIC-80 capacity to 175M, again usually advertised as 350M with compression. These tapes have the advantage of working in an unmodified 120/250M QIC-80 drive. (It's interesting that the Arcada backup software included in the kit can't format a tape, thereby presumably ensuring a continuing market for preformatted 3M brand tapes.)

The most recent activity on the QIC-80 front has been the introduction of Travan technology by Hewlett-Packard's Colorado Memory Systems subsidiary, which manufactures the drives, and 3M, which produces the tapes. First shipped in the summer of 1995, Travan drives use tapes that look like a lop-sided QIC-80 minicartridge. The drives, compatible with QIC-80, QIC-3010, and QIC-3020 media, can read from and write to standard QIC-3010 and QIC-3020 cartridges.

The initial Travan media, designated TR-1, provide 400M native capacity, with compression achieving 800M per tape. Travan levels TR-2 and TR-3 began shipping in the fall of 1995, and TR-4 was released in mid-1996. The TR-2 tape uses a modified QIC-3010 cartridge to provide 800M native capacity, yielding 1.6G with compression. The TR-3 tape provides 1.6G native capacity, using a modified QIC-3020 cartridge, yielding a nominal 3.2G of storage using compression. The TR-4 tape stores 4G natively, or 8G with compression.

TR-1, TR-2, and TR-3 cartridges each contain 750 feet of 0.315-inch-wide tape. The TR-1 uses 550-Oersted media to record at 14,700 flux transitions per inch (ftpi), whereas the TR-2 and TR-3 cartridges use higher coercivity 900-Oersted media to record at 22,125 ftpi and 44,250 ftpi, respectively. Because Travan technology is patented by 3M, tapes are available only from 3M and are quite expensive, about $35 each (street price).

These QIC minicartridge drives share two failings, both due to the desire of tape drive manufacturers to supply inexpensive drive mechanisms:

- QIC mini-cartridge drives depend on the diskette controller. Standard "floppy disk" controllers transfer data at only 500kbps, which translates to backup speeds of only about 3M per minute.

- QIC mini-cartridge drives have only a single head, used for reading, writing, and erasing. Thus, a backup and compare requires two passes of the tape through the drive, essentially doubling already slow backup times.

Tape-drive manufacturers realize that with workstations commonly equipped with 1G or larger fixed-disk drives, the slow data transfer rates of QIC drives are becoming unacceptable. The manufacturers have tried to address the problem by introducing accelerator cards that double data transfer rates to 1mbps, the same as that of 2.88M diskette drives. QIC-3020 drives support 2mbps transfer rates with special controller cards. Even at best, 2mbps translates to only about 12M/minute. At this rate, backing up 6G of server disk takes more than eight hours and requires changing tapes at least five times. When you remember that these inexpensive drives also require a second pass to do a compare, it becomes obvious that server backup needs a better solution.

Some newer QIC-3020 drives use the ATAPI IDE interface, so backup speeds will be constrained by the tape-drive mechanism rather than by diskette data transfer rate. Given that media capacities are increasing—particularly with Travan TR-2, TR-3, and TR-4—it remains to be seen whether these faster QIC drives will provide adequate performance and capacity for low-end servers. The drives' lack of separate read and write heads precludes read-after-write, requiring a second compare pass.

Digital Linear Tape (DLT). The newest technology in tape backup is called Digital Linear Tape, or DLT. Because it's very fast, offers large capacities, and is extremely reliable, DLT is beginning to replace DAT and 8mm tape drives in large server environments. Current DLT tape drives have capacities of 40G compressed, or 20G uncompressed, so even a very large disk subsystem can be backed up to a single tape.

DLT divides the tape into multiple parallel horizontal tracks. While the single write head remains stationary, the DLT drive streams the tape past it, allowing the DLT tape drive to record information to tape as fast as the server can supply it. This removes the tape drive as the bottleneck restricting backup speed and limits backup performance only by the maximum throughput available from the server.

DLT tape drives and their tapes are also extremely robust. A typical DLT drive is rated at 15,000 in-use hours MTBF (mean time between failures). The tapes themselves are rated at 500,000 hours, so the average tape should outlast the technology itself.

Helical Scan Tapes. Originally developed for use in video recording, helical scanning works by running a tape past a head that rotates at an angle relative to the motion of the tape. The resulting tracks, shown in figure 8.12, resemble diagonal lines running from one edge of the tape to the other, repeating this pattern from end to end on the tape.

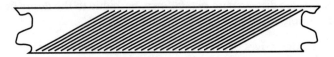

Fig. 8.12   A helical scan tape drive, which uses a head angled relative to the direction of tape movement to record diagonal tracks on the tape.

The advantage of helical scanning is that information can be packed more densely on the media. The most common application of helical scan recording is the consumer VCR; both VHS and 8mm VCRs, as well as the new Digital Video (DV) camcorders and VCRs, use helical scanning. Helical scan recording is a mature technology, although it's more expensive to implement than the linear recording used in QIC-80 drives.

The following helical scan tape backup technologies were available when this book was written:

- Digital Audio Tape (DAT) is also called 4mm for the width of its tape. DAT drives comply with standards set by the Digital Data Storage (DDS) Group. The original 1991 DDS specification provided 2G natively and 4G with compression on a 90-meter tape. The DDS-2 standard, released in 1993, doubled this capacity to 4G native and 8G compressed on a 120-meter tape, doubling transfer rates. DDS-3, adopted in late 1994, specifies capacities of 12G native and 24G compressed. DDS and DDS-2 drives are available now. DDS-3 drives should be readily available by the time you read this book.

  DAT drives use a minicartridge tape that costs less than $20. The best DAT drives provide data-transfer rates of about 30M per minute, or 10 times that of a standard QIC-80 drive. Internal DAT drives have a street price of under $1,000 for the 2G/4G

DDS versions, and perhaps $200 more for the 4G/8G DDS-2 versions. The 12G/24G DDS-3 versions will probably be priced, initially, in the $2,000 range.

- 8mm, also named for the width of its tape, is derived from the 8mm videotape format and is an alternative to DAT drives. (8mm is commonly called DAT, although properly that term is reserved for the 4mm format.) 8mm drives are available at street prices of about $1,200 for internal drives with capacities of 3.5G native and 7G compressed, and about $1,500 for similar drives with capacities of 7G native and 14G compressed. Jukebox changers are available for applications in which a single 8mm tape isn't large enough. Exabyte offers a typical changer, holding up to 10 14G tapes, for a total capacity of 140G. 8mm drives use minicartridge tapes that cost about $20 each. 8mm drives offer data transfer rates up to twice those of 4mm DAT.

The best backup solution for most Windows NT Server environments is either 4mm or 8mm tape. Both drive types are available only with a SCSI-2 interface. The drives are fast, inexpensive, and reliable; the tapes are small and inexpensive.

Writable Optical Drives

Writable optical drives today are used primarily for archiving data, rather than backup. Various new technologies include erasable CD-ROMs (CD-E) and writable digital video discs (DVDs, also called *digital versatile discs*), which store up to 4.7G. Even farther in the future are exotic writable disc technologies, based on cholesteric liquid crystals (CLCs), which promise up to 280G of storage per side.

The following sections describe currently available drives that use lasers to write to and read from discs that, for the most part, have the same dimensions as conventional audio CDs and CD-ROMs.

CD-Recordable Drives. Recordable CD (CD-R) technology has been around for a few years, but it's just now joining the mainstream. With prices on drives dropping below the magic $1,000 point, CD-R drives are poised to take off. CD-R drives are similar to standard CD-ROM drives, but CD-R drives use a higher powered laser that can write to specially designed CDs. These CDs can then be read in any standard CD-ROM drive.

CD-R's relatively low capacity of 680M, its use of relatively expensive media (about $7 per disc), and its lack of rewritability make CD-R a poor choice for routine backup. The first two issues are likely to be addressed at least incrementally as the technology improves, although revolutionary improvements are unlikely. The read-only nature of a CD-R disc can be an advantage for applications such as data archiving.

> **Note**
>
> The ubiquity of CD-ROM drives makes CD-R a useful means of transferring large amounts of data between systems, because anyone with a reasonably modern PC is likely to have a drive capable of reading the disc.
>
> (continues)

II

Deploying Windows NT

(continued)

You can use a CD-R drive to produce relatively small runs of CD-ROM discs with large amounts of data that need to be transported to clients, customers, or branch offices. However, the CD-R media is relatively expensive (at $7 or so each), and recording a CD takes a considerable amount of time (several minutes to perhaps an hour, depending on your drive). These factors realistically limit data distribution via CD-R to perhaps a few dozen copies at a time. If you need larger numbers—say, 250 copies of your product catalog for distribution to customers—use a commercial CD duplication service.

Magneto-Optical Drives. Magneto-optical (MO) disks are another technology sometimes considered for use as a backup media. Magneto-optical disks use a combination of a high-power laser and a magnetic head to write to their media. The laser heats the media, allowing the magnetic head to realign the magnetic particles. Because this action is repeatable, MO disks are read-write like a traditional disk drive, rather than write-once like CD-R and WORM drives.

MO drives now have performance more similar to that of hard-disk drives than the performance usually associated with optical drives. However, MO drives have relatively low capacity and high media costs, making them inappropriate as backup devices for most situations.

WORM Drives

Write-once, read-many (WORM) technology has been available longer than either CD-R or MO devices. WORM drives are available in various platter sizes up to 12 inches and in capacities of up to 6G per disc. WORM jukeboxes can provide near online storage capacity in the terabyte range. WORM drives are incrementally rewritable (data can be added incrementally), allowing backup of multiple versions of the same file or folder to a WORM disk.

WORM is an excellent—if expensive—archiving medium. For applications that require storing huge amounts of data, such as document imaging, the nearly online performance of WORM can be considered adequate for online use.

Using the Windows NT Server 4.0 Backup Application

The Windows NT Server 4.0 backup application, NTBACKUP, has two obvious advantages: it's included with Windows NT 4.0 (so it's free), and, as a bundled application, compatibility and reliability problems are less likely to occur. Balanced against these advantages are NTBACKUP's paucity of high-end features and limited options. If your LAN is relatively small, the LAN's architecture is simple, and your backup requirements are modest, NTBACKUP suffices. For single-server environments that use a simple tape-rotation method and have no need to backup workstations from the server, NTBACKUP is more than adequate.

NTBACKUP can back up files stored on a drive using either the NTFS or FAT file systems, and it can restore the files backed up from a drive using one file system to a drive using the other file system. NTBACKUP does only file-by-file backups, and it makes no provision for doing a disk-image backup. NTBACKUP supports only tape drives as destination devices. You can't, for example, back up from one hard drive to another using NTBACKUP.

Setting Up NTBACKUP for Use with Your Tape Drive

The NTBACKUP program files are installed when you install Windows NT Server itself. Before using NTBACKUP, however, you must first install support for your tape drive. Do so by following these steps:

1. From Control Panel, double-click the Tape Devices tool to display the Tape Devices property sheet (see fig. 8.13). The Devices page shows installed tape devices. You highlight a displayed tape device and click the Properties button to display the properties for that device. You also can click the Detect button to attempt to automatically detect and install a driver for a physically installed tape device that's not shown in the list.

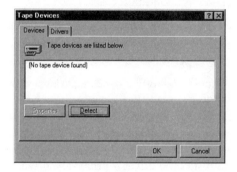

Fig. 8.13   The Devices page of the Tape Devices property sheet.

2. To install a new tape device manually, click the Drivers tab. Windows NT builds a driver list for several seconds, and then displays the Drivers page (see fig. 8.14). The Drivers page shows a list of installed tape device drivers.

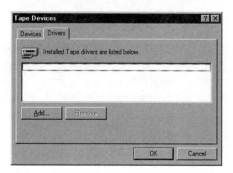

Fig. 8.14   The Drivers page of the Tape Devices property sheet.

II

Deploying Windows NT

3. You can click the Remove button to remove a currently installed driver. If no driver is shown for the tape drive you want to install, click the Add button. Windows NT 4.0 again creates a driver list. After a few seconds, the Install Driver dialog appears (see fig. 8.15).

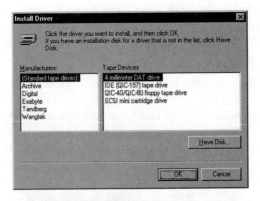

Fig. 8.15   The Install Driver dialog listing manufacturers and tape device types.

> **Note**
>
> Click the Have Disk button of the Install Driver dialog to install a new or updated driver provided by your tape drive's manufacturer.

4. Select the manufacturer of your tape drive in the Manufacturers list and then select one of the supported tape devices made by that manufacturer from the Tape Devices list. Click OK to install the driver for that tape drive, or Cancel to abort the process.

5. You're prompted to insert the Windows NT 4.0 distribution CD-ROM disk into your CD-ROM drive (see fig. 8.16). You can type the path where the files are located, select the location from the drop-down list, or browse for the proper location. The distribution files for a server running an Intel processor are located in the \i386 folder of your CD-ROM drive.

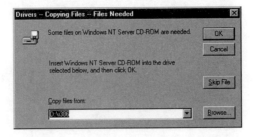

Fig. 8.16   The Files Needed dialog for installing tape backup drivers.

6. After the Copy Files From text box is completed properly, click OK to begin installing the new tape device driver.

7. When the files are copied, you're prompted to restart Windows NT 4.0 for the changes to take effect.

Backing Up Using NTBACKUP

Using NTBACKUP to back up your files requires several steps. You must prepare and label the media; select the volumes, folders, and files to be included in the backup set; choose the appropriate backup options to use; and then run the backup itself. Optionally, you may choose to run a comparison pass after completing the backup to verify the integrity of your backup set.

Preparing and Labeling Media. Depending on the type of tape drive you use, there may be little—or quite a lot—of preparation needed. QIC tape drives require that tapes be formatted before use and that they be periodically retensioned to avoid breakage. The QIC formatting process takes considerable time, but such time consumption can be avoided by purchasing preformatted tapes. Like VCR tapes—the other technology that uses helical scanning—DAT and 8mm tapes require neither formatting before use nor periodic retensioning.

NTBACKUP gives you several tape tools, most of which you'll seldom need to use. NTBACKUP allows you to erase tapes by using either a standard erase (which simply deletes the header information) or a secure erase (which actually overwrites the data on the tape). NTBACKUP allows you to retension tapes that require such maintenance, and allows you to eject a tape if your tape drive supports software-controlled ejection. (Now *there's* a useful feature!)

Note

If your labeling habits are poor, now is the time to fix them. The last thing you need is poorly labeled backup tapes. Inadequate tape labels make it much more likely that you'll eventually back up to the wrong tape. Also, poorly labeled backup tapes make it nearly impossible to find the correct tape days or weeks later when you need to do a restore. Make it a standard practice to label your tapes legibly and indelibly. Otherwise, you'll sooner or later regret not doing so.

How you label a tape depends on several factors, including the tape rotation method you use and the practices particular to your site. Make sure that the label is permanently affixed, and includes at least the server name, the volume ID (if appropriate), the set to which the tape belongs, and the tape number. For example, you might label a tape as follows:

> Admin Server
> SYS volume
> Set A
> Tape 1 of 1

to indicate that that tape is number 1 of 1 from Set A, used to back up the SYS volume of the Administration server. Alternatively, if you are of a minimalist bent, something like the following might do as well:

> \\ADMIN\SYS
> A-1

II

Deploying Windows NT

> **Tip**
>
> Always maintain a manual backup log, indicating the date that each backup was done, the contents of that backup, the type of backup, and the tape set to which the data was written. That way, if the server crashes, you won't find yourself trying to retrieve the software-generated backup log from a crashed hard disk drive.
>
> Many people record this information on a label attached to the tape itself. A better practice is to keep a spiral-bound notebook nearby and record the details of each backup session in this notebook. This makes it easy to retrieve the information when needed without sorting through a pile of tapes.

Selecting Drives, Folders, and Files to Be Backed Up. After you prepare and label your tapes, the next step is to run Windows NT Backup and select the drives, folders, and files to be backed up. Proceed as follows:

> **Note**
>
> Before trying to run a backup, make sure that you're logged on as either an Administrator or as a Backup Operator. Otherwise, you may not have the necessary permissions to access all files that need to be backed up, and the resulting backup tape will be incomplete.

1. From the Start menu, choose Programs, Administrative Tools (Common), and Backup to open the Backup – [Tapes] window (see fig. 8.17). If a blank formatted tape is in the tape drive, it's shown in the left pane as `Blank Tape`. If the tape contains data, the left pane displays the creation date and other particulars of the tape, and the right pane displays a brief summary of the tape's contents.

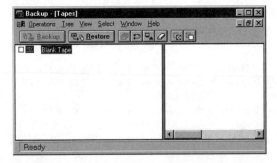

Fig. 8.17   The Backup – [Tapes] window, with a blank tape inserted in the tape drive.

> **Tip**
>
> If you have more than one tape drive installed, now is the time to verify that you have the correct tape drive selected. To do so, from the Operations menu choose Hardware Setup. The Hardware Setup dialog appears, presenting you with a drop-down list of installed tape devices. Select the tape drive you want to use and click OK to select that drive.

2. To begin selecting the drives, folders, and files to be backed up, from the <u>W</u>indow menu choose Drives. The Backup – [Drives] window appears (see fig. 8.18).

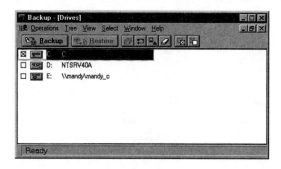

Fig. 8.18 The Backup – [Drives] window, displaying drives accessible to NTBACKUP.

3. To select an entire drive to be backed up, mark the check box to the left of that drive's icon. To back up only some of the folders and files on a particular drive, double-click the icon for that drive to view a folder tree for that drive (see fig. 8.19). The folder tree view is similar to Windows NT Explorer, showing folders in the left pane and the files contained in a selected folder in the right pane. Single-clicking a folder name in the left pane displays the files contained in that folder in the right pane.

Fig. 8.19 NTBACKUP's folder view displaying folders and files available for backup.

4. Select folders to be backed up by marking the check box to the left of the folder, which selects all files contained in that folder and its subfolders. Alternatively, you select individual files within a folder by marking the check box for that file or files in the right window pane and leaving the folder name in the left pane unmarked (see fig. 8.20).

II

Deploying Windows NT

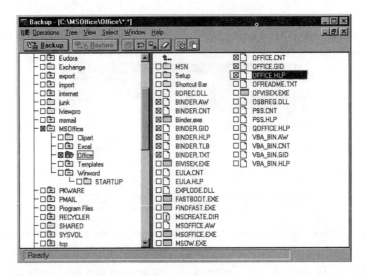

Fig. 8.20   Selecting specific folders and files for backup.

> **Note**
>
> The check box for folders that aren't selected for backup are empty. The check box for folders in which all files and subfolders are selected for backup are marked with an × on a white background. The check box for folders in which only some files and/or subfolders are selected for backup are marked with an × on a gray background.

> **Tip**
>
> If you want to back up many, but not all, of the files on a particular drive, you *can* select those folders and files individually by marking their check boxes. An easier way, however, is simply to mark the check box for the drive itself, which appears at the extreme top left of the folder tree pane. Doing so marks all folders and files on the drive to be backed up. You can then clear the check boxes for those folders and files that you don't want to back up.

5. Repeat steps 3 and 4 for any other drives to be backed up.

Choosing Options and Running the Backup. After you select the drives, folders, and files to be backed up, the next step is to choose backup options. To do so, click the Backup button in the Backup window to display the Backup Information dialog. The Backup Information dialog is divided into three sections (see fig. 8.21). The first section presents several items about the currently mounted tape, including its name, owner, and creation date. The first section also allows you to specify various options that determine how the backup job is run.

The following list describes the first set of backup options:

■ The *Tape Name* text box allows you to enter a descriptive name for this tape.

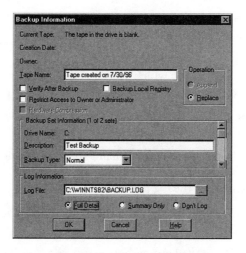

Fig. 8.21   Setting backup options in the Backup Information dialog.

- The *Verify After Backup* check box allows you to specify whether you want to do a second comparison pass after the backup is complete. Leaving this option selected ensures that the backup data is written to tape successfully, but it nearly doubles the time needed to complete the backup.

- The *Backup Local Registry* check box lets you specify whether the Registry is backed up. The Registry, described fully in Chapter 9, "Understanding the Windows NT Registry," is a critical component of Windows NT. You should back up the Registry as a matter of course. Don't clear this check box unless you have a very good reason for doing so.

- The *Operation* section lets you choose whether the current backup data is added to the end of the current tape or overwrites the current contents of the tape. Append adds and Replace overwrites.

- The *Restrict Access to Owner or Administrator* check box lets you secure the contents of the tape against unauthorized access. When this check box is marked, the contents of the tape can subsequently be accessed only by the tape's owner or by a member of the Administrators or Backup Operators group. This check box remains disabled (gray) unless you select the Replace option in the Operation section.

- The *Hardware Compression* check box determines whether hardware compression is used on drives that support it. If your drive doesn't provide hardware compression, this check box is disabled.

The second section of the Backup Information dialog, Backup Set Information, lets you specify information about particular backup sets, using a scroll bar to allow you to view one such set at a time. (The scroll bar appears only if you have selected more than one drive to be backed up.) Each backup set includes the following information:

II

Deploying Windows NT

- *Drive Name* is the drive (for example, C) that you picked during the selection process described earlier. If you selected files or folders on more than one drive, use the scroll bar to view the desired drive.

- *Description* is a free text area in which you can enter a brief meaningful description of the contents of the backup set, or choose from existing stored descriptions.

- *Backup Type* is a drop-down list from which you can select Normal, Copy, Incremental, Daily Copy, or Differential to do your backup.

The third section of the Backup Information dialog, Log Information, lets you specify logging information for the backup session, including the log file name and location, and the level of detail you want the log to contain:

- The *Log File* text box allows you to enter the drive, folder, and name of the file to which session information is to be logged as an ASCII text file.

- When selected, the *Full Detail* option button causes all transaction detail to be logged, including the names of all files and folders that are backed up. Although this level of detail can be useful at times, the resulting log files can be huge.

- When selected, the *Summary Only* option button logs only critical exception information, such as tape mounting information, start time of the backup, and files that were selected for backup but couldn't be opened.

- When selected, the *Don't Log* option button disables all logging functions.

After you select the options desired, click OK to begin the backup. The backup then begins, unless you have chosen the Replace option and the target tape already contains data. If so, you'll be prompted to make sure that you really want to overwrite the tape. When the backup completes, a compare pass begins, if you chose that option.

Note

Regardless of the setting for Log Information, if NTBACKUP encounters corrupted files, it displays the problem in the status area of the Backup Status dialog and records this problem in the file CORRUPT.LST. If this happens, you first should determine the reason for it. After you do so to your satisfaction, delete CORRUPT.LST before trying to restore from that or any other tape. Failing to delete CORRUPT.LST results in error messages informing you of corrupt files each time you try to restore from that or any other tape.

As the backup begins, the Backup Status dialog appears (see fig. 8.22). The Backup Status dialog displays the progress of your backup until it completes.

Tip

The backup applet bundled with Windows NT Server 4.0 is a trimmed-down version of Arcada Backup Exec for Windows NT. If you like NTBACKUP but would prefer a product with more power and flexibility, consider purchasing Arcada Backup Exec. Arcada was recently acquired by Seagate Software Storage Management Group, and can be reached at **http://www.arcada.com**.

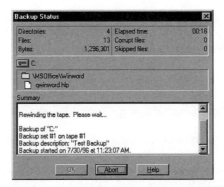

Fig. 8.22 Displaying backup progress and status messages in the Backup Status dialog.

Note

Unlike most third-party backup software, NTBACKUP has weak automation features. The biggest shortfalls are the absence of both a comprehensive macro language and the absence of built-in support for tape-rotation algorithms. NTBACKUP has no native scheduler, but it can be run from the command line by using the Windows NT scheduler service, AT commands, and batch files.

You can invoke all NTBACKUP options from the command line. This allows you to build an automated backup scheduling system of sorts, leaving you only with the problem of managing tape rotations manually. For a complete list of available commands and syntax, see the topic "Using Batch Files to Do Backups" in the NTBACKUP help file. If you need scheduling and other automation features, you're far better off buying a commercial backup software package instead of spending a lot of time trying to make NTBACKUP do things it really wasn't designed to do.

Restoring Using NTBACKUP

Restoring with NTBACKUP is relatively straightforward. NTBACKUP allows a backup set to be restored to the same system from which it was made, or to a different system. NTBACKUP also allows backup sets made from either of the supported file systems to be restored to a disk, using any of the three file systems. The following steps show you how to use NTBACKUP to restore files to your system:

1. Insert the tape that contains the data to be restored into your tape drive.

2. From the Start menu, choose Programs, Administrative Tools (Common), and Backup to run NT Backup. The Backup – [Tapes] window appears (see fig. 8.23). The left pane of this window displays the name and creation date of the tape. The right pane displays the folder backed up to the root level of the tape, the set number, and the number of the tape within that set.

3. Double-click the folder name in the right pane of the Backup – [Tapes] window. NTBACKUP loads the catalog from tape and displays the folder tree contained on the tape (see fig. 8.24).

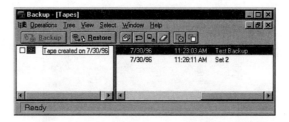

Fig. 8.23   The Backup – [Tapes] window, displaying the tape date and the folder backed up.

Fig. 8.24   NTBACKUP displaying tape contents in folder tree format.

4. Select the drives, folders, and files to be restored in the same manner as you specified them earlier in the section "Selecting Drives, Folders, and Files to Be Backed Up."

5. After you select all the drives, folders, and files you want to restore, click the Restore button to begin restoring. The Restore Information dialog appears (see fig. 8.25).

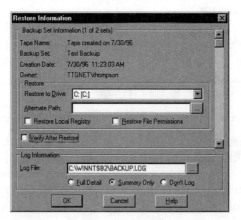

Fig. 8.25   Selecting restore options in the Restore Information dialog.

The Restore Information dialog is divided into two sections. The Backup Set Information section displays properties of the mounted tape, including its name, the backup set of which it is a member, its creation date and its owner. The Backup Set Information section also allows you to set the following options:

- The *Restore to Drive* drop-down list allows you to choose the drive to which the backup set is to be restored. NTBACKUP can restore to any drive visible to Windows NT, including those on other servers.

- The *Alternate Path* text box allows you to restore to a different path than that from which the files were originally backed up.

- When selected, the *Restore Local Registry* check box causes NTBACKUP to restore Registry information if it's present on the backup tape.

- The *Restore File Permissions* check box determines whether ACL (Access Control List) information will be restored with the file. If this box is selected, the original ACL information is re-created as the file is restored. If the box is deselected, the restored file instead inherits the ACL information of the directory to which it's restored. If you're restoring to a FAT or HPFS partition, this check box remains grayed out, because Windows NT Server doesn't support permissions on file systems other than NTFS.

- When selected, the *Verify After Restore* check box causes NTBACKUP to perform a comparison pass after completing the restore to verify that restored files correspond to those stored on tape. Exceptions are written to the log file.

The second section of the Restore Information dialog, Log Information, allows you to specify logging information for the restore session, including the log file name and location, and the level of detail you want the log to contain:

- The *Log File* text box allows you to enter the drive, folder, and name of the file to which session information is to be logged as an ASCII text file. Figure 8.26 illustrates a typical log file opened in Windows Notepad.

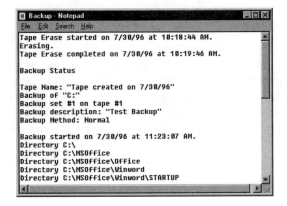

Fig. 8.26 Windows Notepad displaying records created by a typical backup log.

- The *Full Detail* option button, when selected, causes all transaction detail to be logged.

- The *Summary Only* option button, when selected, logs only critical exception information—for example, files selected for restore that couldn't be read from tape.

- The *Don't Log* option button, when selected, disables all logging functions.

After you select the options desired, click OK to begin the restore. The restore then begins and runs to completion, with a message that tells you the process is complete. When the restore completes, a compare pass begins (if you selected that option).

Looking Beyond NTBACKUP

Choosing the right backup software is as important as choosing the right backup hardware. Windows NT Server 4.0's NTBACKUP is a quite competent application, but it's a bit Spartan. NTBACKUP provides fundamental backup features, but you won't find the bells and whistles on it like those provided by third-party backup software.

If you have multiple servers, plan to use Tower of Hanoi or other complex tape-rotation methods, or must back up workstations running diverse operating systems, you need to consider purchasing one of the commercial backup programs available from numerous third parties. Third-party software is needed if you must back up multiple servers in a heterogeneous network, such as a network that includes both Windows NT and Novell NetWare servers.

The rapid market growth for Windows NT Server 4.0 has backup software vendors scrambling to release versions of their products for Windows NT. Just a year or two ago, third-party backup choices for Windows NT were very limited, both in number and in feature sets. That situation has changed for the better and continues to improve with every passing month. Nearly all the big-name backup software publishers that previously concentrated their efforts exclusively on Novell NetWare have now released Windows NT Server versions; in some cases, the Windows NT version appears to have more features than the original version for NetWare.

Most of these software products, in addition to the complete selection of basic backup features you might expect, offer extensive customization options, powerful macro languages to automate the entire backup process, automated databases to support sophisticated tape-rotation algorithms, and the capability to back up workstations running diverse operating systems. Describing these third-party offerings is beyond the scope of this book and, because of the rapid pace of development of backup software, current products are likely to be upgraded for Windows NT Server 4.0. Vendor sites and magazine reviews on the Web are the best source of current information on third-party backup software.

From Here...

Backing up critical data and assuring the ability to restore data when required are a network administrator's primary responsibility. Thus, this entire chapter is devoted to backup methodology, hardware, and software. If you're upgrading a network from an earlier version of Windows NT Server or from another network operating system, now is an ideal time to re-examine your data backup and restore practices, and to consider upgrading your backup hardware to greater capacity and faster data-transfer rates.

The following chapters contain material relating to data backup operations:

■ Chapter 5, "Purchasing Networking Hardware," discusses the SCSI-2 interface used by the majority of backup drives.

■ Chapter 20, "Administering Intranet and World Wide Web Sites," explains the backup issues specific to this growing market for Windows NT Server 4.0.

■ Chapter 22, "Running Microsoft SQL Server 6.5," includes sections describing how to use disk dumps and log copies to back up and restore SQL Server databases.

II

Deploying Windows NT

Chapter 9

Understanding the Windows NT Registry

If you've used Windows 95 or previous versions of Windows NT, you've already seen the Registry at work. When you double-click a file on your Windows 95 desktop or in Windows NT 3.5+'s File Manager to launch an application, entries in the Registry enable Windows NT Server to launch the correct application. One category of Registry entries creates associations between file extensions and the application that can display and, in most cases, edit a particular type of file. But the Registry does much more than launch the appropriate application for a particular document type.

Tracking Configuration Settings in the Registry

The Registry keeps track of everything you can imagine it keeps track of, and much more. Most of the administrative tools you use to configure Windows NT Server and keep it running smoothly alter Registry entries. The following sections briefly describe how Windows NT uses the Registry.

What Types of Information Are Registered?

The Registry is the one place that stores virtually everything that needs to be known about your hardware, operating system, and the users who may log on to the system. The Registry stores the following types of information:

- Information about your hardware.

- Network information.

- OLE and ActiveX information.

- File association information—what application launches what kind of file, and vice versa.

- The time zone and local language.

- For each user, program groups and other Program Manager settings.

- For each user, desktop settings such as colors and wallpaper.

This chapter covers the following:

- What the Registry is

- How the Registry is organized

- The type of information the Registry contains

- How to view and edit the Registry

- How the Registry replaces entries in CONFIG.SYS and .INI files

- For each user, all preferences in all user applications, unless the applications are older 16-bit applications that use .INI files. Preferences include the "recent files" list on the File menu.

- All user profiles.

- Your user and group security information.

The Importance of the Windows NT Registry

Under Windows 3.x, the settings described in the preceding section were maintained in many different files. System-wide settings were kept in one of the following files:

- AUTOEXEC.BAT

- CONFIG.SYS

- WIN.INI

- SYSTEM.INI

- REG.DAT

If you're an administrator or a power user of a Windows 3.1x machine, you probably use the SysEdit application to open the first four of these files at once. SysEdit provides a convenient editing environment for text-based system configuration files.

Also, 16-bit Windows applications often have a configuration (also called an *initialization*) file. Most applications use *APPNAME*.INI for this purpose, but some applications use alternative file names and extensions. For example, REG.DAT provides OLE server information and file extension associations. You use the RegEdit application to edit REG.DAT. When you need to change or view the settings for an application, the first task is to guess what file the settings might be in and then what utility to use to edit the file.

Windows NT's Registry keeps everything in one place. You can view any and all of these settings by using one tool—the Windows NT 4.0 Registry Editor, which is derived from the Windows 95 RegEdit application. The Registry is arranged in a logical and straightforward way that clearly distinguishes among the following three classes of settings:

- System-wide, for all applications and all users (for example, your computer's microprocessor type)

- System-wide, for one user (for example, your color scheme)

- For one application for one user (for example, the last four files you opened in Excel)

Although you continue to use a variety of different tools to change Registry values in Windows NT 4.0, don't underestimate the value of using just one tool to view any of the settings. It can be a bit intimidating to navigate such a large collection of settings and configuration information, but understanding the structure and content of the Registry is very important when administering Windows NT Server 4.0.

Note

Both Windows NT 4.0 and Windows 95 use Registry files, but the internal (binary) structure of the Registry files varies between the two operating systems. The difference in file structure is the primary reason that Microsoft couldn't provide an automatic upgrade utility from Windows 95 to Windows NT 4.0 when Windows NT 4.0 was released, although upgrading from Windows 3.1+ to Windows NT 4.0 is supported. (Upgrading creates or preserves the Registry information for installed applications.) The capability to automatically upgrade from Windows 95 to Windows NT 4.0 is more important for the Workstation than the Server version, because servers seldom are required to run various desktop applications.

The Danger of Changing Registry Values

Changing values of entries in the Registry can cause your server to be unstartable. Rather than change Registry entry values directly, you should use one of the following tools to change these values:

- Most hardware settings are handled by the hardware recognition process when you start your computer. (That's how Plug and Play works, in part, but Windows NT Server 4.0 doesn't implement Plug and Play.)

- Many system configuration and application settings are set when you run the appropriate setup program.

- The Administrative Tools program group (see fig. 9.1) contains User Manager, Disk Administrator, Performance Monitor, Backup, Event Viewer, and Windows NT Diagnostics tools. These dedicated tools are far safer and more intuitive ways to interact with the Registry than the Registry Editor.

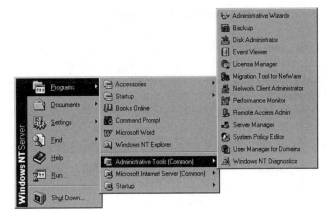

Fig. 9.1 Applications in the Administrative Tools program group that manipulate Registry values.

- Control Panel (see fig. 9.2) contains the Accessibility Options, Add/Remove Programs, Console, Date/Time, Devices, Display, Fonts, Internet, Keyboard, Licensing, Modems, Mouse, Multimedia, Network, ODBC, PC Card (PCMCIA), Ports, Printers, Regional Settings, SCSI Adapters, Server, Services, Sounds, System, Tape Devices,

Telephony, and UPS tools, in addition to any tools that are added by applications you install (typically, other servers run as services). Control Panel tools interact with a small part of the Registry—for example, the Keyboard tool changes the user's keyboard settings in the Registry.

Fig. 9.2   Control Panel tools that make changes to the Registry.

- Using desktop applications changes the Registry. For example, the list of recent files is generated automatically as you open files in the application.

- OLE servers and ActiveX controls register themselves when they're installed or run for the first time.

How the Windows NT and Windows 95 Registries Vary

In many important ways, the Windows NT Registry is the same as the Windows 95 Registry. Certainly, the concepts are the same. The same tools and applications read from and write to the Registry, and the Registry Editor is similar. However, the names for specific collections of information stored within the Registry aren't identical. Nonetheless, experience with the Windows 95 Registry is readily transferable to Windows NT Server 4.0's Registry.

Viewing the Registry's Organization

Understanding the Registry requires you to learn another new vocabulary. The Registry is made up of *keys*, some of which have *subkeys*. Keys have *value entries*, and groups of keys and their value entries are gathered into a *hive*.

Keys

A *key* is a named collection of information, just as a folder is a named collection of files. The Registry is arranged in a hierarchy quite similar to a folder tree. At the top of the hierarchy are the following five keys (also see fig. 9.3):

- *HKEY_LOCAL_MACHINE* contains system-wide hardware information and configuration details.

- *HKEY_CLASSES_ROOT* contains OLE and ActiveX information and file associations.

- *HKEY_CURRENT_CONFIG* contains startup information that's also kept in HKEY_LOCAL_MACHINE.

- *HKEY_CURRENT_USER* contains all the settings specific to the current user.

- *HKEY_USERS* contains all the settings for all users, including the current one and a default.

Each key is discussed in individual sections later in this chapter.

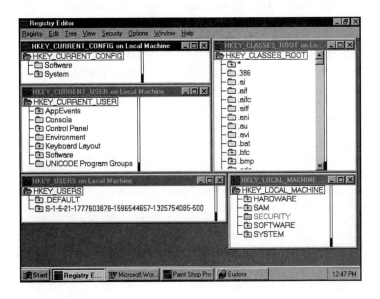

Fig. 9.3 The five top-level Registry keys.

Subkeys

Just as a folder in a file system can have subfolders, a key can have *subkeys*; and, just as a subfolder is itself a folder, a subkey is a key, another named collection of information. Each key can have many subkeys, each of which can have many subkeys, and the hierarchy can be many levels deep.

By convention, key and subkey names are gathered into full names and separated with backslashes that appear like folder path names. An example is a key called HKEY_LOCAL_MACHINE\HARDWARE\DESCRIPTION\System\MultifunctionAdapter\0\DiskController\0\FloppyDiskPeripheral. The FloppyDiskPeripheral key is a subkey of the 0 key, which is a subkey of the DiskController key, and so on, up to the top-level key, HKEY_LOCAL_MACHINE. Key names, by the way, can contain spaces, just as spaces are permissible in Windows 95 and Windows NT 4.0's long file names (LFNs).

Value Entries

To continue the analogy of a file structure further, a key can contain both value entries and subkeys, just as a folder can contain both files and subfolders. *Value entries* in keys resemble files in folders. A value entry contains the information to examine or change, just as a file contains the data you display or edit. A key can (and often does) support more than one value entry.

A value entry has three components:

- The name of the value entry

- The type of information it contains (numerical or character data, for instance)

- The value of the information (c:\program.exe or 0, for example)

The following sections describe each of these components.

Value Entry Names. Microsoft chose names for most value entries that are reasonably comprehensible; you probably can guess what CurrentUser, InstallDate, LogFilePath, and DiskCacheSize contain without any need for documentation. Much of the information is added to the Registry when you install programs on the system, and application vendors may not choose sensible or easy-to-understand names.

When there's only one value entry in a key, it's possible—but not necessarily wise—that the programmer who added the key left the name unassigned. When omitting a single value name, the Registry Editor shows (Default) in place of the missing value entry name. This practice is quite common in the file association entries of the HKEY_CLASSES_ROOT key. Use the name of the key to understand the information in the value entry.

Data Types. The data type must be one of the following five allowable data types:

- *REG_BINARY*. Raw binary data, which is displayed by the Registry Editor in hexadecimal format.

- *REG_DWORD*. Exactly 4 bytes of binary data. The Registry Editor can display these values as binary, decimal, or hexadecimal numbers.

- *REG_SZ*. A string of characters terminated by a NULL character.

- *REG_MULTI_SZ*. Several strings of characters separated by NULL characters, and terminated by two NULL characters.

- *REG_EXPAND_SZ*. A string of characters that contains a symbol to be expanded when the value is used. The symbol begins and ends with a % character.

The REG_EXPAND_SZ symbols correspond to environment variables—for example, %PATH% expands to the value of the PATH environment variable. Most environment variables also are stored in the Registry, but they aren't all under the same key. Some environment variables are in the HKEY_LOCAL_MACHINE\SYSTEM\CurrentControlSet\Control\Session Manager\Environment key, and others appear under HKEY_CURRENT_USER\Environment. Environment settings in AUTOEXEC.BAT aren't stored in the Registry, but some applications modify both AUTOEXEC.BAT and the Registry during installation, so many of your environment variables are accessible from the Registry.

The value of the value entry is a number or a string according to the type. Binary numbers are almost impossible to read in the Registry Editor, but specific tools, such as Windows NT Diagnostics (discussed in its own section later in this chapter), can display these value entries in a more meaningful format.

Hives

A *hive* is a single key with all its subkeys and value entries. Six keys, each discussed later in this chapter, are the six standard hives in the Windows NT 4.0 Registry:

■ HKEY_LOCAL_MACHINE\SAM

■ HKEY_LOCAL_MACHINE\SECURITY

■ HKEY_LOCAL_MACHINE\SOFTWARE

■ HKEY_LOCAL_MACHINE\SYSTEM

■ HKEY_CURRENT_USER

■ HKEY_USERS\DEFAULT

A hive is a collection of keys, subkeys, and values stored in a single file. Each hive file has an associated log file that's used to ensure that the hive file isn't corrupted by a partial update.

Hive files and their associated log files are stored in the \Windows\System32\Config folder, except for user information, which is in \Windows\Profiles*username,* one folder for each user. The hive and log file names are as follows:

■ SAM and SAM.LOG

■ SECURITY and SECURITY.LOG

■ SOFTWARE and SOFTWARE.LOG

■ SYSTEM and SYSTEM.ALT

■ NTUSER.DAT and NTUSER.DAT.LOG, in the *username* folder mentioned earlier

■ DEFAULT and DEFAULT.LOG

The reason for pairing hive and log files, as mentioned earlier, is to ensure that the Registry can't be corrupted. For example, if a power failure should occur as your change to a value entry is written, the value might be changed, but the date stamp might still contain the old date and time, or the size of the entry might not be correct. The hive and log approach guarantees that these types of errors don't happen.

When it's time to write out changes to a hive file, Windows NT inserts a few extra steps. First, Windows NT writes to the log file the new data and instructions for where the data

II

Deploying Windows NT

goes. After this data is safely written to the disk, Windows NT writes a special mark at the beginning of the hive file to indicate that the file is being changed. The changes are written to the hive file and, on completion, the mark is removed. If a power failure or other serious problem occurs during the process, Windows NT notices when opening the file that the "being changed" mark exists, re-creates the changes from the log file, and then removes the mark. This process maintains the consistency of the hive file.

Note

The relationship between the hive and log files is similar to that between SQL Server's device and log files. Log files record all transactions (operations that modify database values) since the last backup. In the event of a failure that requires restoration of the backup copy, the backup copy is loaded, and then the transaction log is run against the database to add the post-backup entries. In the case of SQL Server, log files are stored on a physical device (disk drive) separated from the device containing the database(s). Windows NT hive and log files are stored on the same disk.

The SYSTEM hive is loaded so early that a simpler process is needed. SYSTEM.ALT is just a copy of the SYSTEM hive file. The changes to SYSTEM aren't logged, but the "being changed" mark is still used. After SYSTEM is written, SYSTEM.ALT is written in the same way. If a power failure occurs while writing SYSTEM, Windows NT will notice the "being changed" mark and use SYSTEM.ALT as a safe backup. Of course, the changes that were being made when the failure occurred are lost.

Understanding Some Important Keys

It's not possible to list all the keys in your Registry, because every time you install hardware or software, keys are added. It's not even possible to list all the keys in the Registry of a typical machine running Windows NT Server and no applications; publication limits on page count preclude such a listing. It's also not useful to provide a list of all Registry keys; once you know roughly where to look, it's quicker to use the Registry Editor to search for the exact key or value entry. Thus, this section doesn't attempt to describe all Registry keys, but it suggests appropriate locations to search for particular classes of Registry entries.

HKEY_LOCAL_MACHINE

As mentioned earlier in this chapter, HKEY_LOCAL_MACHINE contains system-wide hardware information and configuration details. This key has five important subkeys, four of which are so important that they are located in the standard hive list you've already seen. In addition to SAM, SECURITY, SOFTWARE, and SYSTEM (the standard hive subkeys of HKEY_LOCAL_MACHINE), there's also a HARDWARE key.

SAM. SAM is an acronym for *Security Account Manager*. This key contains the database of user and group information, as well as security information for the domain.

SAM has one subkey, again called SAM, which contains two subkeys—Domains and RXACT. RXACT doesn't ordinarily contain anything, but Domains has two subkeys—Account and Builtin.

Caution

Don't attempt to change any value in the SAM key or its subkeys with the Registry Editor. You could leave a user's account unusable. Utilize User Manager to make the changes, as described in Chapter 12, "Managing User and Group Accounts."

▶▶ See "Working with User Manager for Domains," p. 416

The entire HKEY_LOCAL_MACHINE\SAM key is also accessible as HKEY_LOCAL_MACHINE\SECURITY\SAM. Changes you make in one key are immediately reflected in the other key.

SECURITY. This key contains policies as well as a link to the SAM database. The subkeys are Policy, RXACT, and SAM. This material is discussed in more detail in Chapter 13, "Sharing and Securing Network Resources."

▶▶ See "Understanding NTFS Permissions," p. 468

SOFTWARE. This key is where system-wide configuration information is stored for each software product installed on the computer. For example, if you install Visual C++ 4.0, there's a key called HKEY_LOCAL_MACHINE\SOFTWARE\Microsoft\Developer\ Directories with two value entries. One value entry, Install Dirs, holds the name of the directory the program was installed into. The other value entry, ProductDir, holds the name of the main directory to be used by the product.

Nothing in the Developer subkey contains any user-specific settings; user-specific entries are stored elsewhere in the Registry, under HKEY_CURRENT_USER\SOFTWARE, discussed later. For example, user-specific Developer Studio settings would be in the HKEY_CURRENT_USER\SOFTWARE\Microsoft\Developer key.

Tip

The Registry must be updated if you move software from one location to another—for example, between fixed-disk drives in the same machine. Thus, it's usually quicker and easier to uninstall the software, and then reinstall the software in the new location. Depending on the application, many different keys may need to be modified to point to the new drive or folder. Let the uninstall and reinstall software do the work, and heed the general rule: *never change the Registry by hand.*

The SOFTWARE key is organized by the name of the company that makes the software. Several keys are present, even if you haven't installed any applications. They include the following:

- *Classes.* Another name for the HKEY_CLASSES_ROOT key, discussed in its own section later in this chapter.

- *Description.* Names and version numbers of installed software. Don't change these.

- *Microsoft.* Information related to products from Microsoft, including many that are installed automatically with Windows NT Server.

- *Program groups.* The information for all the Common Program Groups. Change these only with Program Manager.

- *Secure.* Just a handy place to keep keys that need more security.

SYSTEM. This key contains information used during startup that can't be fully determined by Windows NT Server until startup is over. All but two of the subkeys of SYSTEM are called *control sets.* The Select and Setup subkeys are not control sets, but rather are used by Windows NT to choose which control set to use on startup.

A control set is all the information needed to start the system. Two to four control sets are kept in SYSTEM, with names such as ControlSet001 and ControlSet002. There's also a CurrentControlSet, which is linked to one of the other control sets. This allows you to switch back to a control set that works if you (or an application you run, or a system crash) make changes to the Registry that prevent the computer from starting.

Fortunately, during startup, you have a chance to press the space bar to use the Last Known Good menu, a specific control set. The subkey that implements the Last Known Good feature, called Select, has four value entries:

- *Default.* The number of the control set (a value of 002 means use ControlSet002) that will be used at the next startup unless the user chooses Last Known Good.

- *Current.* The number of the control set that was used this time at startup.

- *LastKnownGood.* The number of the control set that represents the values that succeeded most recently.

- *Failed.* The number of the control set that was used during a failed startup. When you choose Last Known Good, this control set is no longer current. By storing the number of a bad control set as the Failed value, Windows NT lets you know where to look for the bad setting that caused startup to fail.

You may sometimes see a Clone subkey in the SYSTEM key. This subkey is used to build that LastKnownGood value. During startup, the current control set is copied into Clone. If the startup succeeds, Clone is copied into LastKnownGood.

If your Registry is corrupted, choosing the Last Known Good menu during startup makes it possible to bring Windows NT Server up so that you can (or might be able to) correct the problem that caused the corruption. Your Registry might become corrupted for various reasons, but bad sectors on your fixed disk or (far more frequently) user errors are usually the culprits. If you edit your Registry by hand and make a serious mistake, you may leave your server unbootable. Using Last Known Good saves you from a complete reinstall.

Although every boot problem is different, here's a typical pattern:

1. A power failure or hardware error requires a reboot, or you perform a routine reboot after changing Registry entries with the Registry Editor or some other tool.

2. The system doesn't boot into Windows NT Server.

3. You power down, and on powerup watch for the Last Known Good prompt.

4. You press Space to use the Last Known Good control set.

5. You examine both the current control set and the failed one to see what's different, and what changes you need to make to your current configuration (if any) that will achieve the effect you originally wanted without preventing a successful boot.

Caution

If you make changes to any of the control sets discussed in this section (other than CurrentControlSet) within the Registry Editor, you can void the insurance that these keys provide for you. Use Server Manager or Control Panel's Devices, Network, Server, or Services tool. Use the Registry Editor to *look* at entries, not *change* them.

Each control set contains two subkeys—Control and Services. The exact subkeys in each key vary, but the typical subkeys in the Control subkey are as follows:

- *BootVerificationProgram.* Use this key to tell the system how to define "succeeded" if you don't want to use the default definition. *Be sure you know what you're doing before you alter this key value.*

- *ComputerName.* This subkey contains the ComputerName and ActiveComputerName subkeys. Change the values of these subkeys only with Control Panel's Network tool.

- *ServiceGroupOrder.* This lists the order in which groups of services should be started.

- *GroupOrderList.* This subkey lists the order to start services within a group.

- *HiveList.* This subkey contains the location of the hive files, usually \WINDOWS\SYSTEM32\Config. *Do not change.*

- *Keyboard Layout.* With its subkeys, this subkey defines the keyboard language layout. You change it with Control Panel's Regional Settings tool.

- *Lsa.* This is used by the local security authority. *Do not change.*

- *NetworkProvider.* This subkey defines the network provider. You change it with Control Panel's Network tool.

- *Nls.* This subkey defines national language support. Change it with Control Panel's Regional Settings tool.

- *Print.* With its subkeys Environments, Monitors, Printers, and Providers, the Print subkey defines the printers and printing environment for the system. You can change it with Print Manager.

- *PriorityControl.* This subkey defines the priority separation. Change it with Control Panel's System tool.

- *ProductOptions.* This shows the product type (for example, Winnt). *Do not change.*

- *SessionManager.* This subkey contains global and environment variables. Its Environment and MemoryManagement subkeys can be changed with Control Panel's System tool; *do not change the others.*

- *Setup.* This contains hardware choices. Change it with Windows NT Setup.

- *TimeZoneInformation.* This subkey contains time zone settings. You change it with Control Panel's Date/Time tool.

- *Virtual device drivers.* This contains information about virtual device drivers. *Do not change.*

- *Windows.* This subkey contains various paths needed by the system. *Do not change.*

- *WOW.* This contains options for running 16-bit applications. *Do not change.*

The Services subkey of each control set has a hundred or so subkeys, so these subkeys aren't listed here. The Services subkeys describe device drivers, file system drivers, service drivers, and other hardware drivers. Use Windows NT Diagnostics to view the information in these subkeys. Utilize User Manager or Control Panel's Devices, Network, or Services tool to change the information in these subkeys.

Finally, the Setup subkey of HKEY_LOCAL_MACHINE\SYSTEM is used by Windows NT Setup. Don't change the Setup subkey values.

HARDWARE. All the information in the HARDWARE key is written into the Registry during startup, disappears when you shut down the machine, and then is recalculated and rewritten during the next startup. That makes it meaningless to change HARDWARE values in an attempt to solve a system problem, and that's also why the HARDWARE key isn't stored in a hive. To view HARDWARE key values in a more readable format, use Windows NT Diagnostics.

The HARDWARE key contains the following subkeys:

- *Description.* Describes the hardware recognized automatically by the system.

- *DEVICEMAP.* Points to the location in the Registry where the driver for each device is located. Typically, this is in the Services subkey of one of the control sets.

- *RESOURCEMAP.* Points to the location in the Registry where the driver for each resource is located. Typically, this is in the Services subkey of one of the control sets.

HKEY_CURRENT_CONFIG

Windows NT implements *hardware profiles*, which make it simple for users to switch a number of settings related to hardware at once. For example, a laptop user might have "docked" and "mobile" profiles, with the mobile profile using a lower density screen, different color scheme, and so on. This is unlikely to be of interest on a server, which usually keeps the same hardware configuration at all times. To implement this feature, Windows NT no longer assumes that there's only one set of hardware settings; this new key holds the current settings. Behind the scenes, changing your hardware profile from mobile to docked involves copying the docked profile into this HKEY_CURRENT_CONFIG key. Hardware profiles primarily are of interest to users of Windows NT Workstation 4.0.

HKEY_CLASSES_ROOT

This key, which is linked to HKEY_LOCAL_MACHINE\SOFTWARE\Classes, contains file association and OLE and ActiveX server information. The file association keys all have a name that starts with a period (.) and represents a file extension, such as .BMP or .TXT. Each key has one value entry, typically with no name, that contains the name of a key for the application that will launch files with that extension. To change file association keys, use the File Types page of Explorer's Options property sheet by choosing Options from the View menu (see fig. 9.4).

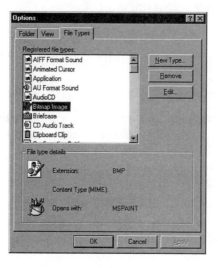

Fig. 9.4 Associating file types with applications.

The OLE-related keys have names that don't start with the period character. The subkeys vary from application to application, but all have a CLSID subkey for the OLE Class ID. One important value entry is shell\open\command, which contains the command line to be used when a file of this type is opened by double-clicking a file in Explorer. For example, the value item HKEY_CLASSES_ROOT\Word.Document.6\shell\ open\command has the value c:\MSOFFICE\WINWORD\WINWORD.EXE /w on those few installations of Windows NT Server that run desktop applications. Other subkeys cover the behavior of the application as an OLE server. For example, HKEY_CLASSES_ROOT\Word.Document.6\protocol\StdFileEditing\Verb\0 has the value Edit, an OLE verb.

> **Caution**
>
> Don't edit these values unless specifically directed to do so by your application vendor or Microsoft. You could leave the application unusable.

HKEY_CURRENT_USER

This key stores all the profile information that's current to the user who's logged on to the server at the moment. A *user profile* is a collection of keys that contains all the information about one user. The current user profile information overrides prior user profile settings in HKEY_LOCAL_MACHINE. The subkeys of HKEY_CURRENT_USER, none of which you should change with Registry Editor, are as follows:

- *Console*. Defines the base options, window size, and so on for character-based applications such as Telnet.

- *Control Panel*. All the user-specific information set by Control Panel (colors, wallpaper, double-click rate, and much more).

- *Environment*. Environment variables set with Control Panel's System tool.

- *KeyboardLayout*. This user's keyboard layout. Change with Control Panel's Keyboard tool.

- *Printers*. The printers installed for this user. Change with Print Manager.

- *Software*. All the settings (options, preferences, customizations, recently opened files, window sizes, and more) for all the software that this user has access to. The structure of this subkey is the same as the HKEY_LOCAL_MACHINE\SOFTWARE key, but the names of the keys under the product name and of the value entries are different. These entries are all changed by the applications that use them.

When a user logs on, his profile is copied from HKEY_USERS into HKEY_CURRENT_USER. If the correct profile for the user isn't found, the default profile (discussed in the next section) is used.

HKEY_USERS

The HKEY_USERS key contains all the active user profiles, each under a key with the same name as the user's Security ID string. HKEY_USERS also contains a .DEFAULT subkey with all the default settings for a new user. The subkeys under each user and under .DEFAULT are the same as those listed in the preceding section for HKEY_CURRENT_USER.

Using the Windows NT Diagnostics Utility

In many of the preceding subkey sections, you read warnings against modifying Registry values. Sometimes, however, you need to know the value of a Registry setting, particularly a hardware setting. One way to look at all your hardware-related Registry settings at once is to use WINMSD, the Windows NT Diagnostics utility. As the name implies, this utility helps you diagnose the behavior of your system by examining a variety of settings at once. To run WINMSD, from the Start menu choose Programs, Administrative Tools, and Windows NT Diagnostics. WINMSD gathers various settings into nine pages (see fig. 9.5):

- *Version.* Operating system information, including version number, build number, serial number, and registered owner.

- *System.* Processor and BIOS information.

- *Display.* Display type, settings, and drivers.

- *Drives.* All fixed, removable, and remote drives, arranged by type (floppy, local hard drive, CD-ROM, remote hard drive) or drive letter.

- *Memory.* System memory and paging files.

- *Services.* Running or Stopped status for all system services or devices.

- *Resources.* Ports, mouse, floppy drives, and other system resources.

- *Environment.* Environment variables.

- *Network.* Domain, workgroup, access level, and what user is logged on now. Network settings and statistics are also available.

Fig. 9.5 Checking Windows NT version data in the Windows NT Diagnostics utility.

If you aren't sure which Control Panel tool or Registry key to use to check a Registry value, use WINMSD. WINMSD is quick, and you can't accidentally change a value. If you want to keep a record of the settings described in the preceding list, use the printed reports from WINMSD rather than compile a written list from values displayed by the Registry Editor.

Backing Up the Registry

It's very important to back up the Registry often, and especially before you change anything to try to fix a problem. Some of the Registry information is saved on the emergency repair disk, but not all. The following are four different ways to back up the Registry:

- From within the Registry Editor, choose Save Key from the Registry menu and save the key to alternate media (diskette, tape, or a drive elsewhere on the network). To restore from this backup, choose Restore Key from the Registry Editor's Registry menu.

- If you back up to tape using Windows NT Backup, mark the Backup Local Registry check box in the Backup Information dialog, and the Registry will be backed up to tape with regular files. To restore from this backup, use Windows NT Restore.

- Use REGBACK.EXE or REPAIR.EXE, programs included in the Windows NT Resource Kit, to back up Registry files. To restore the Registry, use REGREST.EXE or REPAIR.EXE.

- From another operating system, copy the files in the C:\Winnt\System32\Config folder (if you didn't install into C:\Winnt, adjust this folder name accordingly) to alternate media. Also copy the user information hives from each C:\Winnt\Profiles*username* folder. To restore the Registry, use that other operating system to copy the backups into those folders again.

Using the Registry Editor

The Registry Editor is the best way to get a feel for the hierarchical nature of the Registry. Experienced users can also utilize the Registry Editor to edit the Registry, when there's no other way to accomplish certain changes. It's not available from the Start menu, directly. From the Start menu, choose Run (or use an MS-DOS prompt), and then type **regedt32** to run the Registry Editor. When it first starts, the Registry Editor displays the five topmost keys, as shown earlier in figure 9.3.

Working with Keys and Value Entries

In figure 9.3, the subkeys under each key are collapsed, and each is represented by a single line in the right pane. Figure 9.6 shows an expanded subkey.

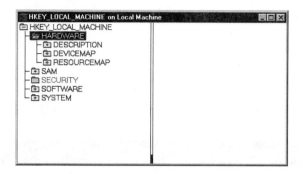

Fig. 9.6 Expanding a Registry key to display subkeys.

To expand a collapsed key or to collapse an expanded one, perform one of the following four actions:

- Double-click the name of the key.

- Single-click the + sign (for a collapsed key) or – sign (for an expanded key) in the file folder to the left of the key name, if present.

- With the key name selected, press Enter.

- With the key name selected, choose Expand One Level or Collapse Branch from the Registry Editor Tree menu.

The right pane of each window displays the value entries. For each value entry, three pieces of information, separated by colons, are provided: name, type, and value. Figure 9.7 shows the value entries for Notepad, the simple text editor supplied with Windows NT. Some of the value entries (such as lfFaceName) are strings, whereas others (such as lfPitchAndFamily) are binary numbers. If the value of a value entry hasn't yet been set, the Registry Editor displays (value not set).

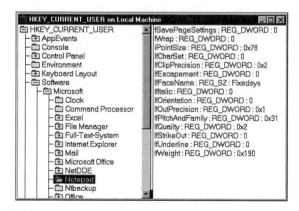

Fig. 9.7 Displaying some primary settings for Notepad in the HKEY_CURRENT_USER\Software\ Microsoft\Notepad key.

II

Deploying Windows NT

As mentioned earlier in the chapter, an entry of (Default) in the name column means that the value entry doesn't have a name. A (Default) entry is always displayed, so every key appears to have at least one value entry.

To adjust the relative sizes of the panes, click the border between the panes and drag the border left or right. To change the value of a value entry, double-click somewhere on its line; this action is the same as choosing Binary, String, DWord, or MultiString (as appropriate) from the Edit menu, described in a later section.

Caution

Be very careful when deleting or editing value entries. There is no undo for these operations.

Using the Registry Editor Menus

In addition to the mouse manipulations described in the preceding section, you can move through the Registry with commands arranged into eight menus: Registry, Edit, Tree, View, Security, Options, Window, and Help. These menus are familiar to experienced Windows users. The following sections describe Registry Editor's menus.

The Registry Menu. The Registry menu handles the tasks normally found on a File menu. Because a Registry spans more than one file, it's inappropriate to name this menu File.

Following are the Registry menu's 11 commands:

- *Open Local* opens the five top keys of the Registry on this computer.

- *Close* closes the Registry. If you have two Registries open (one for this computer and one for a remote computer), the Registry that owns the key that is in the top window is closed.

- *Load Hive* brings a saved hive into the HKEY_USERS or HKEY_LOCAL_MACHINE key. One of these keys must be the top window to enable this command.

- *Unload Hive* removes the hive that was loaded by the Load Hive command.

- *Restore* loads key values from a saved hive. They can't be unloaded afterwards.

- *Save Key* saves a hive for later use by the Load Hive or Restore commands.

- *Select Computer* opens a remote Registry.

- *Print Subtree* prints one key and all its subkeys and value items. Some keys can generate hundreds of pages of printout, so use this menu item with care.

- *Printer Setup* brings up the usual Printer Setup dialog.

- *Save Subtree As* saves a selected key or subkey and all its subkeys and value entries into a text file. This may be more convenient than printing a paper copy of the subtree.

- *Exit* closes the Registry Editor application.

The Edit Menu. The commands on the Edit menu let you change Registry values. *(Exercise extreme caution when changing Registry values.)* If possible, use the appropriate specific tool to make the change after using the Registry Editor to determine what value change must be made.

The Edit menu has the following seven commands:

- *Add Key* lets you create a new key under the currently selected key.
- *Add Value* lets you create a String Value, Binary Value, or DWORD Value under the currently selected key.
- *Delete* deletes the selected key or value entry.
- *Binary* brings up a dialog for editing a binary (REG_BINARY) value.
- *String* brings up a dialog for editing a string (REG_SZ or REG_EXPAND_SZ) value.
- *DWord* brings up a dialog for editing a double word (REG_DWORD) value.
- *Multi String* brings up a dialog for editing a multiline string (REG_MULTI_SZ) value.

The Tree Menu. The Tree menu controls the way in which the tree of keys and subkeys is displayed. The four commands are as follows:

- *Expand One Level* shows the subkeys directly under the selected key or subkey.
- *Expand Branch* shows all the subkeys under the selected key or subkey.
- *Expand All* shows all the subkeys under all the keys in the top window.
- *Collapse Branch* hides all the subkeys under the selected key or subkey.

The View Menu. The View menu gives you control of the appearance of the Registry Editor interface. The View menu offers the following eight commands:

- *Tree and Data* shows the tree of keys and subkeys in the left pane, and the value entry names, types, and values in the right pane.
- *Tree Only* shows only the tree of keys and subkeys.
- *Data Only* shows only the value entry names, types, and values.
- *Split* moves the mouse pointer to the border between the panes and lets you adjust their relative sizes without having to hold the mouse button down.
- *Display Binary Data* brings up a dialog that displays binary data in a more readable form.
- *Refresh All* redraws both panes in all windows to reflect changes that may have been made in other applications.
- *Refresh* redraws both panes in the top window to reflect changes that may have been made in other applications.
- *Find Key* brings up a dialog to search for a key or subkey by name.

II

Deploying Windows NT

The Security Menu. The $\underline{S}$ecurity menu controls access to Registry keys. Use of these menu items to restrict access to Registry keys is discussed later in the section "Restricting Access to Registry Keys." The following are the three choices of the $\underline{S}$ecurity menu:

- *Permissions* brings up a dialog to set permissions on the selected key and its subkeys.

- *Auditing* brings up a dialog to arrange monitoring of access to certain keys and subkeys.

- *Owner* is used to change the ownership of a key.

The Options Menu. The $\underline{O}$ptions menu controls various options and settings within Registry Editor. The following are the five menu items:

- *Font* allows you to change the font in which the information is displayed.

- *Auto Refresh* toggles the automatic refreshing of key information. This can be useful if a lot of other applications are running that might change the Registry, but it slows the Registry Editor considerably.

- *Read Only Mode* prevents changes to the Registry and is a useful safety feature when you're using the Registry Editor to examine values you don't plan to change.

- *Confirm on Delete*, another useful safety feature, toggles the confirmation of all deletions.

- *Save Settings on Exit* toggles the saving of all these settings when you leave the editor.

The Window Menu. The $\underline{W}$indow menu controls which window is the top one and how the windows are arranged. The number of menu items varies with the number of open windows, but always includes one item for each open window, plus the following three items:

- *Cascade* resizes and moves all the open windows into a cascade of equal-sized windows.

- *Tile* resizes and moves all the open windows so that they are all the same size and cover the Registry Editor window without overlapping each other.

- *Arrange Icons* aligns the icons of minimized windows at the bottom of the Registry Editor window.

The Help Menu. Registry Editor help isn't extensive. The $\underline{H}$elp menu has only the following four choices:

- *Contents* lets you look through the contents of the Help file.

- *Search for Help On* is used to search the Help file or its index for keywords.

- *How to Use Help* explains the Help subsystem.

- *About Registry Editor* displays the usual product information and some system information, such as amount of free memory.

Inspecting Another Computer's Registry

Occasionally, you may need to view or change a setting on another computer that's not located with your Windows NT Server computer. Fortunately, Windows NT Server can view and edit Registry entries of other computers running Windows NT or Windows 95. As well, you can edit the Registry of your server from another Windows 95 or Windows NT machine.

Choosing to Edit Remotely

Rather than travel to the computer with the problem or tell the user to make the change with another tool, you might choose to edit the Registry remotely from your computer in at least the following situations:

- The user can't tell you what's wrong and can't search through the Registry to report what settings have been changed.

- The user doesn't have the authority or the skill to change a Registry value, even when you can dictate the necessary keystrokes by telephone.

- The problem is so quick to fix, and the remote computer is so far away (in another building or another city), that it's not worth the time for you to go to the computer.

- The problem is one that makes the remote computer very hard to use. An example is when the background and foreground text colors have been set to the same color so that no one can read the text in dialogs.

Preparing for Remote Registry Editing

Of course, you can't just take over the Registry of any other computer on your network and start changing values. Preparation is involved, especially if the remote computer is running Windows 95.

Editing a Windows 95 Registry from Windows NT. If the remote computer is running Windows 95, you must enable user-level security and remote administration from that computer's Control Panel. First, use the Network tool's Access Control page, and select User-Level Access Control. Then use the Password tool's Remote Administration page and mark Enable Remote Administration of This Server. Finally, on the Network tool's Configuration page, mark Add the Microsoft Remote Registry Services.

> **Note**
>
> The details of this process are covered in Chapter 10, "Configuring Windows 95 Clients for Networking," and in the Windows 95 Resource Kit Help, included with the CD-ROM version of Windows 95.

Editing a Windows NT Registry from Windows 95. If you're trying to manipulate a Windows NT Registry from a Windows 95 machine (perhaps to fine-tune the departmental server from your desktop), you must add the Microsoft Remote Registry services and arrange user-level access; however, you don't need to enable remote administration of the Windows 95 machine. No preparation is required on the Windows NT Server machine.

Editing a Windows NT Registry from Windows NT. If you need to manipulate the Registry of one Windows NT machine from another (any combination of Windows NT Server and Windows NT Workstation), no preparation is required.

Opening the Remote Registry

To edit from an NT machine, start Registry Editor, and use the Registry menu's Select Computer command to open windows with the HKEY_LOCAL_MACHINE and HKEY_USERS keys of the remote computer to the left pane. Then inspect or change the keys and value entries of the remote computer. The changes take effect immediately, so use extra care—especially if the remote computer is in use while you are changing the Registry. You might want to save this task for a time when the remote machine is not in use, or arrange such a time with your users.

From a Windows 95 machine, start Registry Editor and choose Connect Network Registry from the Registry menu to open the remote Registry. You can then inspect or change the keys and value entries of the remote computer. As mentioned earlier, take great care. This is especially true when changing settings on a departmental server—a large number of users could be inconvenienced with a single keystroke.

Maintaining Registry Security

You can restrict users' ability to change Registry values in a number of ways. Such restrictions should be part of an overall security plan that allows users to access only those administrative features they need.

First, don't provide Administrator access to non-administrators. You can restrict the access of non-administrator users to the Registry. You also should consider deleting Registry Editor and Policy Editor from client computers. (On Windows NT machines, delete the files Regedit.exe and Poledit.exe from the C:\Winnt folder, and the file Regedt32.exe from the C:\Winnt\System32 folder. If Windows NT wasn't installed into C:\Winnt, use the folder name into which it was installed.) You can administer clients from the server, which usually is in a location with more physical security than the rest of the network.

> **Note**
>
> Regedit.exe is the Windows 95-style Registry Editor. It has less functionality than Regedt32, the Registry Editor discussed in this chapter.

To control access to individual keys, you can add or remove names from the Access Control List (ACL) for each key. If you care enough about a particular key's value to restrict access, you should audit access to the key, or audit failed access attempts.

> **Caution**
>
> Excessive access restrictions can make applications unusable or the system unbootable. Always make sure that the administrator has access to all keys. Always back up the Registry before implementing any security restrictions.

Restricting Access to Registry Keys

The process of restricting access involves several different administrative tools. Follow these steps:

1. In User Manager for Domains, choose Policies Audit, and make sure that Audit These Events is selected. Select Success or Failure, or both, for File or Object Access.

2. Within Registry Editor, select the key for which you want to restrict access, and then choose Owner from the Security menu. Figure 9.8 shows the Owner dialog. If you aren't the owner of a key, you can't change permissions for that key. As administrator, you can change the owner to yourself, but you can't return ownership unless the original owner gives you Full Control permissions on the key.

Fig. 9.8 Displaying the owner of a Registry key with the Owner dialog.

3. After you confirm or take ownership of the key, choose Permissions from the Security menu. The Registry Key Permissions dialog is used to assign permissions to the groups listed (see fig. 9.9). To add another group, click Add; to remove a group, click Remove. When the permissions for this key are correct, click OK.

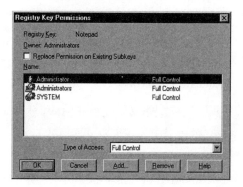

Fig. 9.9 Setting access permission with the Registry Key Permissions dialog.

The available permissions are as follows:

- *Full Control.* Users in the group can view, change, take ownership, and change permissions. Administrators and the System group should have Full Control on every key.

- *Special Access.* Users in the group can view and change the key.

- *Read.* Users in the group can only read the key.

II

Deploying Windows NT

4. Choose Auditing from the Security menu to arrange auditing of key access. This brings up the Registry Key Auditing dialog (see fig. 9.10).

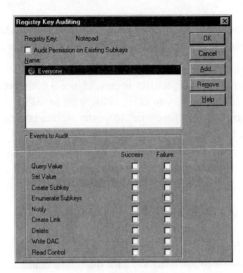

Fig. 9.10 Setting auditing choices in the Registry Key Auditing dialog.

5. From the Registry Key Auditing dialog, select the types of accesses you want to be logged for each group.

You may not want to log successful accesses at all because there may be a large number of accesses. For example, many keys are updated every time a user runs an application, and each update may generate several log entries. Logging failed accesses allows you to discover applications that are no longer working for users, or users who are trying to change keys for which they have no permission.

The types of access audits are as follows:

- *Query Value*. An attempt to learn the value of the key.

- *Set Value*. An attempt to change the value of the key.

- *Create Subkey*. An attempt to make a subkey within the key.

- *Enumerate Subkeys*. An attempt to list the subkeys of this key.

- *Notify*. Notification events from the key.

- *Create Link*. An attempt to create a link within a key.

- *Delete*. An attempt to delete the key.

- *Write DAC.* An attempt to change the permissions (Discretionary Access Control) on a key.

- *Read Control.* An attempt to learn the permissions on a key.

Viewing an Audit Log

To view the audit logs, from the Start menu, choose Programs, Administrative Tools, and Event Viewer. From the Log menu, choose Security to see a list of the logged events. Figure 9.11 shows a sample list. These entries aren't very helpful beyond the user name; double-click one to see details like those in figure 9.12. These entries were generated as follows:

1. Auditing was turned on in User Manager for Domains.

2. In Registry Editor, auditing was turned on for both success and failure for any access to keys under HKEY_USERS*the-SID-of-the-account-in-use-at-the-time*\\Software\\Microsoft\\Notepad.

3. In Notepad, the font was changed, and then Notepad was closed.

4. In the Event Viewer, the menu item Log Security was chosen.

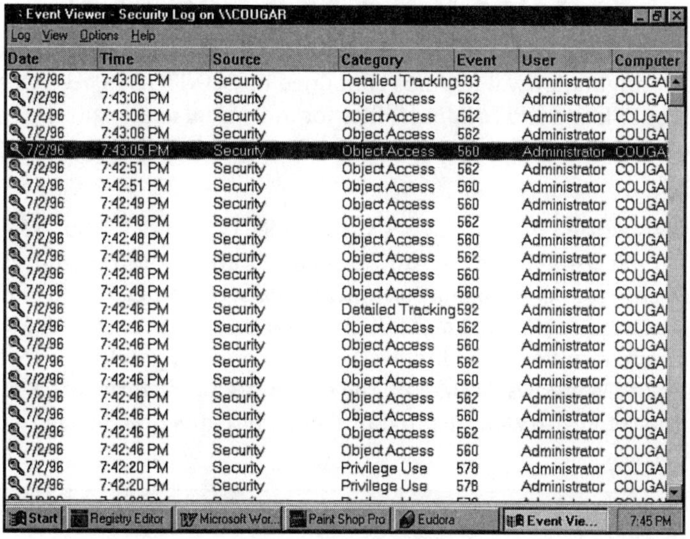

Fig. 9.11 Event Viewer's Security log listings for Registry events.

Even at a cursory glance, figure 9.12 shows that the Notepad key was changed. Further investigation could narrow down the source of a user's trouble quite easily. For example, if you're logging only failures, you might relax security restrictions so that the operation no longer fails.

II

Deploying Windows NT

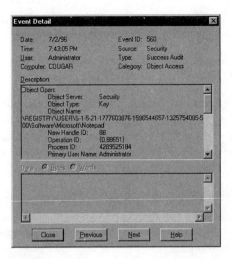

Fig. 9.12 Viewing Security log entry detail for opening a Registry key object.

Understanding the Interaction of .INI and CONFIG.SYS Files with the Registry

At the beginning of this chapter, you learned that the Registry is a place to store the sort of settings and configuration values once contained in CONFIG.SYS, AUTOEXEC.BAT, WIN.INI, SYSTEM.INI, and *APPNAME*.INI files for individual applications. Applications written for Windows NT or Windows 95 use the Registry to determine settings and configuration values.

16-bit applications written for Windows 3.x run under Windows NT but, obviously, such applications aren't Registry-aware. To run, 16-bit applications need their *APPNAME*.INI files to contain settings and configuration values. The setup programs of Windows 3.x applications often modify WIN.INI and SYSTEM.INI, and create an *APPNAME*.INI file for the application. As a result of the Windows NT Setup process, you find WIN.INI and SYSTEM.INI files in \Windows\System32, the system root directory. These files don't affect the behavior of Registry-aware programs at all, but affect the behavior of older 16-bit applications.

> **Note**
>
> As a rule, 16-bit applications don't need to reside on a Windows NT 4.0 Server, unless the server shares these applications with client PCs. If you must run 16-bit Windows applications on the server, you need to be aware of the interaction of Registry and .INI file entries.

A developer can access the information in an .INI file in two ways. If the programmer has chosen the "brute-force" method of opening the file and reading through it, the application operates completely independently of the Registry. However, Microsoft provides a set of Windows API functions to look up values in an .INI file, and most developers use these Windows API .INI file functions because they simplify programming. Under

Windows NT, these .INI file functions have the same name as under Windows 3.x, but for certain specific keys the functions operate on the Registry rather than on an .INI file. This means that 16-bit programs, written by developers before the Registry existed, store their configuration entries in the Registry.

The HKEY_LOCAL_MACHINE\Software\Microsoft\WindowsNT\CurrentVersion\ IniFileMapping key maps .INI file entries to Registry keys. Figure 9.13 shows the win.ini subkey and its value entries. The value for each value entry is the Registry key to which it's mapped (note that each key may have a number of value entries). The strings USR and SYS stand for the keys HKEY_CURRENT_USER and HKEY_LOCAL_MACHINE\Software, respectively. Also, three symbols—!, #, and @—may be present as the first character of the value.

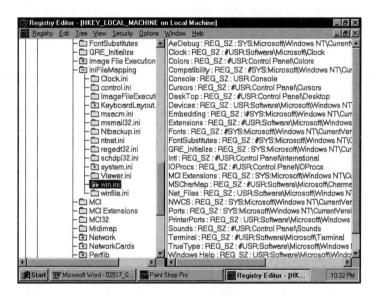

Fig. 9.13   Displaying the mapping of WIN.INI entries to Registry keys.

In all cases, a request to read from or write to the .INI file is translated into a request to read or write a Registry entry, but if one of these characters is present, the connection is made even tighter. The meaning of each of the three symbols is as follows:

■ ! means that, as well as write the value to the Registry, the value should be written to the .INI file.

■ # means that when a user first logs on to Windows NT, the value should be initialized from the .INI file.

■ @ means that if the mapped key doesn't contain the value entry being requested, the request fails rather than goes to the .INI file.

From Here...

It's possible to use Windows NT Server 4.0 with only a vague idea of the Registry and the purpose it serves—at least until a Registry-related problem arises. As a network administrator, you must know what information is stored in the Registry and how to change Registry entries when necessary. It's important to understand how dangerous it can be to edit Registry values with the Registry Editor, and why, despite the danger, you occasionally must use the Registry Editor to alter values.

Many of the remaining chapters in this book touch on the Registry from time to time, but the following chapters elaborate on Registry entries:

■ Chapter 8, "Installing File Backup Systems," explains the tradeoffs between different types and formats of backup systems, and how to manage server backup operations to ensure against lost Registry data in case of a fixed-disk failure.

■ Chapter 12, "Managing User and Group Accounts," covers the issues of user administration and security that affect the user-related keys of the Registry.

■ Chapter 16, "Distributing Network Services with Domains," covers additional Registry-related security issues.

Chapter 10

Configuring Windows 95 Clients for Networking

An ideal workstation operating system installs and configures the network client software and interface cards automatically, supports a wide variety of network transport protocols, provides a single unified logon to servers running different network operating systems, and accommodates virtually all existing hardware and software for Intel-based PCs. Microsoft Windows 95 meets all of these criteria. Although Windows 95 is not yet perfect, it's the most versatile operating system now available for networked PC clients, especially laptop and notebook PCs, as well as desktop PCs equipped with legacy adapter cards. (Microsoft defines legacy devices as hardware components that don't support Windows 95's Plug-and-Play standards.)

With multisite, multiplatform internetworks becoming common, and user demands for Internet access increasing, network administrators increasingly find that they must deal with multiple network transport protocols. The Internet and most private intranets run over TCP/IP, your legacy NetWare servers understand only IPX/SPX, and the peer-to-peer network down the hall uses NetBEUI. Your NetWare servers run NetWare Core Protocol (NCP), and your Windows NT servers run Server Message Block (SMB). The folks in sales need PPP dial-up networking. Tying all these diverse systems and protocols together requires a client operating system that allows you to support all these protocols simultaneously and still have enough memory left to run applications. Windows 95 fulfills this requirement.

Windows 95 Networking Features

Many network managers eagerly anticipated the retail release of Windows 95 on August 24, 1995. Windows 95 promised to eliminate most of the client-side problems that have plagued LAN administrators for years. Its built-in support for many networks and its extensible architecture provided these important networking features:

- *Multiple client support.* With earlier-generation client operating systems, installing software for more than one type of network operating system was problematic at best. The client software was provided by the

In this chapter you learn how to

- Set up Windows 95 to provide network support, including installing network adapter drivers

- Install and configure network client software, including the Client for NetWare Networks

- Install and configure network transport protocols

- Install and configure shared resources using file and printer sharing for Microsoft Networks and for NetWare Networks

- Install and configure Windows 95 on your network server

II

Deploying Windows NT

network operating system (NOS) vendor, and conflicts often occurred when installing a second network protocol. Even if you could install and configure support for a second protocol successfully, the additional memory required often made it difficult to run applications on the client. Sane LAN managers didn't even think about trying to install support for a third protocol.

These problems disappeared when Microsoft released Windows 95, with its built-in support for multiple clients. Out of the box, Windows 95 provides native support for Novell NetWare, Artisoft LANtastic, Banyan VINES, DEC PATHWORKS, and SunSoft PC-NFS. Of course, it also fully supports Microsoft networking systems, including LAN Manager, Windows 3.11 for Workgroups, Windows NT Workstation, and Windows NT Server.

■ *Multiple protocol support.* Windows 95 has built-in support for TCP/IP, IPX/SPX, and NetBEUI, which collectively are the transport protocols used on the vast majority of networks. Windows 95 handles the two major network core protocols, with full support for Microsoft SMB and nearly full support for Novell NCP. Windows 95 supports both Microsoft Network Driver Interface Specification (NDIS) and Novell Open Datalink Interface (ODI) for network interface cards (NICs), also called network adapters. Windows 95 supports a wide variety of standard communications protocols, such as named pipes and Remote Procedure Calls (RPCs). In short, Windows 95 includes every network protocol you'll likely need. In the unlikely event that a building block you need is missing, the extensible, 32-bit architecture of Windows 95 means that a third-party product may be written to fill the void.

 ▶▶ See "Calling Remote Procedures," p. 102

■ *Simultaneous connection to multiple networks.* Whereas Windows 3.1 allows you to connect to only one network and Windows 3.11 for Workgroups to only two networks simultaneously, Windows 95 imposes no limitation on the number of types of simultaneous network protocols in use.

■ *Single network logon.* If your network runs more than one NOS, Windows 95 lets you connect to all servers simultaneously at logon, provided that you establish identical user names and passwords on the various servers. Windows 95 automatically processes logon scripts on Windows NT and NetWare servers.

■ *Automatic server reconnection.* When a downed server returns to service, Windows 95 reconnects to that server automatically, remapping drive letter assignments and printer connections as established before the failure.

■ *Automatic client setup.* Windows 95 makes installing and configuring network clients easy. During setup, Windows 95 detects the network interface card in the workstation and automatically installs the appropriate 32-bit protected mode drivers for the NIC. Windows 95 may be installed locally to the client's fixed disk or run as a shared copy on the network server. (Running shared copies of Windows 95, however, isn't a recommended practice.)

Windows 95 provides full scripting support to allow automated installation and configuration. It automatically detects and configures Plug-and-Play and PC Card (formerly PCMCIA) devices. Setup and configuration are performed from Control Panel's Network tool, with setup information stored in the Registry, thus eliminating the need for manual maintenance of configuration files. System policies and user profiles may be established to automate installation and to control user access to resources.

■ *Peer-to-peer networking.* When Microsoft shipped Windows for Workgroups 3.11 with built-in peer networking, many wondered whether third-party peer networks, such as LANtastic and PowerLAN, could survive. With Windows 95, Microsoft has made life much more difficult for third-party peer-to-peer NOS vendors. Any Windows 95 PC running either the Client for Microsoft Networks or the Client for NetWare Networks can share its disk and printer resources with other Windows 95 PCs on the network. Windows 95 provides user-level security on Windows NT Server and NetWare server-based networks using the existing server's security system for user verification and authentication. Windows 95 also provides share-level security on Microsoft networks.

■ *Dial-up networking.* Windows 95 comes equipped for remote access to networks. The dial-up networking client supports connection to TCP/IP and IPX/SPX networks via Point-to-Point Protocol (PPP), Serial Line Internet Protocol (SLIP), and NetWare Connect. For additional information on dial-up networking with Windows NT Server 4.0, see Chapter 18, "Managing Remote Access Service."

■ *Long file-name support.* Windows 95 finally eliminates the antiquated DOS 8.3 file-naming convention. Windows 95 allows a file name to be as long as 255 characters, or 260 characters including the path.

■ *Improved network performance.* Windows 95 uses 32-bit protected-mode client software, drivers and protocols implemented as VxDs, and virtual "anything" drivers, offering significantly better performance than that provided by older 16-bit real-mode drivers. Network performance is further enhanced by the use of VCACHE to cache network data, allowing frequently accessed network data to be read from a local cache rather than be transferred repeatedly across the network. In addition to offering faster data access, VCACHE also reduces network congestion by cutting traffic.

■ *Minimal conventional (DOS) memory usage.* Windows 95 provides all the preceding networking features with a near-zero conventional memory footprint. Installing multiple 16-bit clients and protocol stacks under DOS and Windows 3.x consumed a substantial amount of the 640K of conventional memory available to DOS. Windows 95 eliminates this conventional memory problem by using Windows (extended) memory to run network client software, drivers, and protocols.

Installing Network Support

If Windows 95 is installed on a client PC that already has a network interface card installed and is connected to an active network, the Setup program recognizes the situation and makes the decisions necessary to automatically install and configure Windows 95 to

II

Deploying Windows NT

provide network services. If you need to convert a stand-alone PC running Windows 95 to a network workstation, you can easily modify your existing Windows 95 configuration to provide network services. Adding network support to a Windows 95 client is done from Control Panel's Network tool, and requires the following steps:

1. Install a network adapter in the workstation and configure Windows 95 to recognize it. If both the workstation BIOS and the network adapter are Plug-and-Play compliant, Windows 95 will recognize the newly installed adapter and configure itself and the adapter automatically. Otherwise, you may have to install and configure the appropriate drivers manually.

2. Install the client software for one or more network operating systems.

3. Fill out the information required in the Identification page of the Network property sheet, providing a unique name for the workstation, identifying the workgroup to which it belongs, and providing a description for the workstation.

4. Fill out the information required in the Access Control page of the Network property sheet, if the workstation shares file or print resources on the network.

When you've completed these steps, you've installed basic network support for Windows 95. The following sections describe each step in detail. Customizing the client software, installing and configuring protocols, and enabling other network services are covered later in this chapter.

Installing Network Interface Cards

When you install Windows 95, you can choose to have Setup locate installed network adapter cards. Windows 95 includes a large database of information about hundreds of popular NICs and their default settings. If a NIC is installed in the client, chances are that Windows 95 can automatically locate the NIC and load the proper drivers for it during the installation process.

If automatic identification fails, if you need to change settings for an installed adapter, or if you need to install a new adapter, you can do so from Control Panel's Network tool. Unlike earlier Windows versions, which required that some network settings be changed by manually editing text files in various locations, Windows 95 centralizes all network installation and configuration functions within Control Panel's Network tool.

To install a NIC manually, proceed as follows:

1. Double-click Control Panel's Network tool. The Network property sheet appears with the Configuration page active (see fig. 10.1).

2. Click the Add button. The Select Network Component Type dialog appears (see fig. 10.2) from which you can add a client, an adapter, a protocol, or a service.

3. Select Adapter and click the Add button to display the Select Network Adapters dialog (see fig. 10.3). From the Manufacturers list on the left, select the manufacturer of the adapter you're installing. A list of supported network adapters from the selected manufacturer appears in the Network Adapters list on the right. Select the appropriate adapter and click OK to install the drivers for the selected adapter.

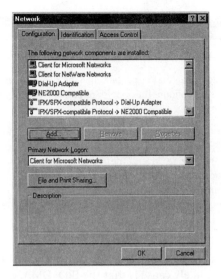

Fig. 10.1 The Configuration page of Control Panel's Network property sheet.

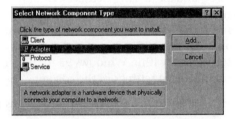

Fig. 10.2 Selecting the network adapter in the Select Network Component Type dialog.

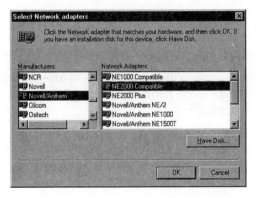

Fig. 10.3 Installing the drivers for a NIC in the Select Network Adapters dialog.

Tip

If your network adapter doesn't appear in the list, you have two alternatives:

■ Refer to your NIC's documentation to determine whether it can emulate a NIC that does appear on the list. If so, configure the adapter to emulate the supported adapter and try to install it.

■ You can install drivers provided by the adapter manufacturer using the Have Disk button in the Select Network Adapters dialog. Use this method as a last resort if the manufacturer provides only 16-bit real-mode drivers. These real-mode drivers occupy conventional memory and are much slower than the 32-bit protected-mode drivers supplied with Windows 95. If the manufacturer supplies a driver specifically for Windows 95, you may want to consider using the manufacturer's driver instead of that supplied with Windows 95.

Changing NIC Settings

If Windows 95 appears to identify your NIC correctly but you still can't communicate with the network, the most likely cause is that the IRQ, DMA, or base address of the adapter doesn't match the settings used by Windows 95. This situation doesn't arise if you're using both a PNP BIOS and a PNP NIC, because Windows 95 automatically changes NIC settings as needed. If you're using an older BIOS and/or a legacy NIC, however, Windows 95 may install the NIC using the manufacturer's default settings, which may or may not correspond with the NIC's current settings. You can correct this mismatch by altering the settings from within Windows 95 for IRQ, DMA, or base address as needed to correspond to the actual settings of the adapter.

To view and change settings for your network adapter, proceed as follows:

1. From Control Panel, double-click the System tool to open the System Properties sheet.

2. Click the Device Manager tab to display the Device Manager page (see fig. 10.4).

3. Click the + icon next to the Network Adapters item to show installed network adapters. Highlight the adapter to be viewed or changed (see fig. 10.5).

4. Click the Properties button to display the property sheet for that adapter (see fig. 10.6). The General page shows basic information about the adapter, including type, manufacturer, and version.

   It also shows status information in the Device Status section. This section should always display the message This device is working properly. If another message appears here, your network adapter may be inoperable or misconfigured.

   If you use multiple hardware configurations, the Device Usage section allows you to select one or more boxes to indicate which configuration(s) this device should be used for.

5. Click the Resources tab to display information about the IRQ, base memory address, and other resources used by the network adapter (see fig. 10.7). If your network adapter was detected automatically when you installed Windows 95, the Use

Automatic Settings check box is marked, and the settings for each resource type are disabled. You must clear this check box before making any changes to the resource settings.

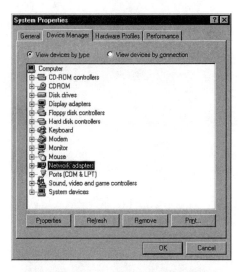

Fig. 10.4   The Device Manager page of the System Properties sheet.

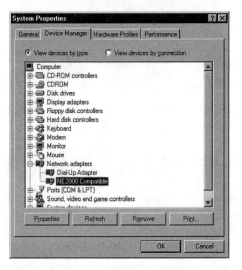

Fig. 10.5   The Installed Network Adapters page of the System Properties sheet.

Deploying Windows NT

II

Note

At the bottom of the adapter's property page is the Conflicting Device List. If there are no conflicts, you may safely leave the settings as they are. If the Conflicting Device List shows one or more devices whose settings conflict with those of your network adapter, you must change settings for either the network adapter or the conflicting device in order to eliminate the conflict.

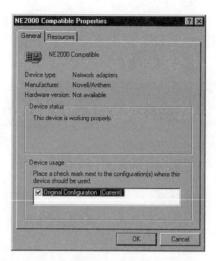

Fig. 10.6 The network adapter property sheet for an NE2000-compatible NIC.

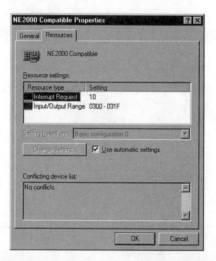

Fig. 10.7 The network adapter resources page for an NE2000-compatible NIC.

Tip

Using the same settings for all network adapters makes it easier to maintain your network. Many network adapter manufacturers and many users have standardized on using IRQ 10 and Base Memory Address 300H for just this reason. On most computer systems, these values aren't already in use by other devices. For this reason, if a conflict arises between a network adapter set to these values and another device, it's usually better to change the settings for the other device and leave the network adapter as is.

Installing and Removing Network Clients

Windows 95 makes several default choices for a NIC, whether the NIC is automatically installed during Windows 95 installation or installed manually later. IPX/SPX (NWLink) and NetBEUI transport protocols are both installed, allowing the client workstation to operate with Windows NT Server, Novell NetWare, and Microsoft peer-to-peer (workgroup) networks. The Client for Microsoft Networks is installed as the Primary Network Logon. The Client for NetWare Networks is installed as a secondary client. These default choices are designed for the most common network environments.

There are two common reasons to change these default selections:

- You may need client software that isn't installed by default.

- For performance reasons, you may want to remove support for an unused client.

The following sections describe how to add and remove network client drivers.

Installing a Network Client. In addition to the Client for Microsoft Networks and the Client for NetWare Networks, Windows 95 provides client drivers forBanyan VINES, FTP Software NFS Client (InterDrive 95), Novell 16-bit ODI NetWare, and SunSoft PC-NFS. Additional client driver packages and updates are also available on diskette from third parties. To install one of these additional network clients, follow these steps:

1. From the Network property sheet, click Add to open the Select Network Component Type dialog (see fig. 10.8).

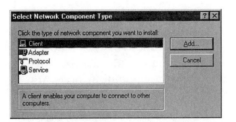

Fig. 10.8   Selecting a network client in the Select Network Component Type dialog.

2. Highlight Client and click Add. In the Select Network Client dialog, highlight the client you want to install and click OK (see fig. 10.9). Alternatively, you may install a third-party network client from disk by clicking Have Disk and following the prompts. In either event, you're returned to the main Network property sheet, where you continue setup and configuration.

Tip

The NetWare client software supplied with Windows 95 works well in a Novell NetWare 3.1x environment, but lacks support for NetWare Directory Services (NDS) used with NetWare 4.x servers. Until recently, if you needed NDS support, your only alternative was to run 16-bit real-mode Novell drivers under Windows 95, with additional memory consumption and performance pen.alties.

Better alternatives are now available. Novell supplies a native 32-bit Windows 95 NetWare client that includes NDS support. Microsoft supplies Service for NetWare Directory Services, an update that's installed as a service.

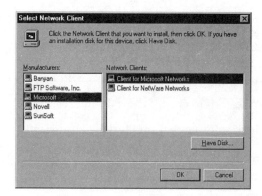

Fig. 10.9   Selecting a network client to add.

Novell released in mid-February 1996 the NetWare Client 32 for Windows 95. This full-featured client software is available in two versions. The first version, a 4.6M file named c3295n_1.exe, is intended for installations from a local or network hard drive. The second version, a 5.6M file named c3295d_1.exe, can be used to create a diskette installation set. Both files are dated February 5, 1996. An 800K supplemental update file named c3295d.exe and dated July 19, 1996, is also available in the same folder.

You can download either version of the NetWare Client 32 for Windows 95 from CompuServe (GO NWCL32). The two versions also are available on the Web at **http://netwire.novell.com/**, or via anonymous FTP at ftp.novell.com in the /pub/updates/nwos/nc32w952/ folder. A supporting 43K file named c32faq.exe includes a list of frequently asked questions and the corresponding answers. You also can purchase the client software on diskette for $99 from authorized Novell resellers.

Tip

Some users of the Novell NetWare Client 32 for Windows 95 dated February 5, 1996, have reported stability and compatibility problems with this release. Novell has acknowledged the problems.

The Microsoft Service for NetWare Directory Services is installed as a service that enhances the functionality of the original Client for NetWare Networks included with Windows 95. You can download the required files from the Web at **http://www.microsoft.com/windows/software/msnds.htm**.

Note

Microsoft's Service Pack 1 for Windows 95 includes an update to Shell32.dll that lets you browse NetWare Directory Service printers from the Add Printer wizard. This update is applicable only if you've installed Microsoft's Service for NetWare Directory Services.

Service Pack 1 also fixes a potential security problem when using Windows 95's file and printer sharing that's described later in the "File and Printer Sharing for Microsoft Networks" section. You can download Service Pack 1 from **http://198.105.232.5/windows/software/servpak1/**

---

sphome.htm. A complete list of the fixes in Service Pack 1 is included in the "Updating Shared Files with Service Packs" section near the end of this chapter.

Removing a Network Client. You should remove a network client that's not being used, because extra clients consume resources and slow performance. To remove an extra network client in the main Network property sheet, highlight the unused network client and click Remove. The unused network client driver is removed immediately.

Completing the Identification Page

The Identification page of the main Network property sheet contains information about the client and the workgroup to which the client belongs (see fig. 10.10).

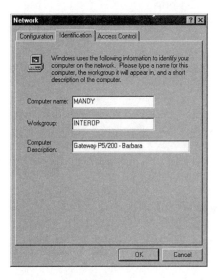

Fig. 10.10 The Identification page of the Network property sheet, including the computer name and description, and the workgroup to which it belongs.

The Identification page consists of these elements:

- *The Computer Name text box* specifies the network name of the computer. It must be unique on the network and may include up to 15 alphanumeric characters. It may not include spaces, but may include the following characters:

    ! @ # $ % ^ & ( ) _ ' { } . ~

    During installation, Windows 95 generates a default ComputerName using the first eight characters of the user name.

- *The Workgroup text box* specifies the workgroup to which the computer belongs. Like the Computer Name, the Workgroup may include up to 15 alphanumeric characters, including the following characters but excluding spaces:

    : ! @ # $ % ^ & ( ) _ ' { } . ~

During installation over Windows 3.1+, Windows 95 by default uses the previously defined workgroup name. If no workgroup has been defined, Windows 95 generates a default workgroup name using the first 15 characters of the organization name.

■ *The Computer Description text box* is a free-text description of the computer. The text box is used primarily to identify the client to other clients using peer-based services. The text box may include up to 48 alphanumeric characters, but may not include commas. During installation, Windows 95 by default inserts the licensing information user name in this text box.

Completing the Access Control Page

If a client shares its local file and print resources with other workstations on the network, the Access Control page of the Network property sheet is used to specify how permission to access these resources is determined (see fig. 10.11).

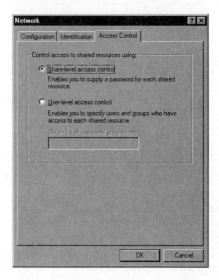

Fig. 10.11   The Access Control page of the Network property sheet, which lets you specify share-level access control or user-level access control to determine which network users can access shared resources on your computer.

Share-Level Access Control. Share-level access control allows each shared resource on the workstation to be protected by a workgroup password. Using Explorer, you right-click a local folder name and choose Sharing to specify whether that folder is to be shared. If the folder is shared, you may specify the following access security options:

■ *Read-Only access* lets you enter the Read-Only Password for that resource. Another user that has this password may view but not alter the contents of the shared folder.

■ *Full access* lets you enter the Full Access Password for that resource. Another user that possesses this password may view and alter the contents of the shared folder.

■ *Depends on Password access* lets you enter a Read-Only Password and a Full Access Password for that resource. Another user that possesses either password may view the contents of the shared folder. Only a user with the Full Access Password may alter the contents.

Access to shared local printers is specified in a similar manner. Share-level access control may be used with file and printer sharing for Microsoft Networks. This feature isn't available if you're using file and printer sharing for NetWare Networks.

User-Level Access Control. User-level access control allows a user seeking access to shared resources to be validated using the account information stored for that user on a Windows NT domain or on a Novell NetWare server.

When you select User-Level Access Control, the Obtain List of Users and Groups From text box is enabled. If you're using file and printer sharing for Microsoft networks, enter the name of a Windows NT domain or an individual Windows NT server here. If you're using file and printer sharing for NetWare Networks, enter the name of a NetWare 3.1x server, or the name of a NetWare 4.x server running in bindery emulation mode.

When a user attempts to access a shared resource on the local system, Windows 95 first validates that user with the specified server. If the user has no account on the specified server, he is refused access to the shared resource. If the user has an account on the server, Windows 95 then determines that user's access rights to the local shared resource.

Granting access with user-level access control is done in similar fashion as the preceding method for share-level access control, but with a further refinement. Share-level access control limits access based solely on a user's possession of the password for that shared resource. User-level access control adds an access control list (ACL), which allows access to a shared resource to be specified by individual user name and by groups. Either full or read-only access to a particular shared resource can be granted, with the access method determined separately for each user and group. User-level access control also allows you to refine access levels by defining custom access for specific users or groups.

Unlike share-level access control, user-level access control may be used with both file and printer sharing for Microsoft Networks or file and printer sharing for NetWare Networks.

Configuring Network Clients

By default, Windows 95 installs both the Client for Microsoft Networks and the Client for NetWare Networks. For most networks, these clients operate properly when installed with the default settings. Common configuration items can be changed by using Control Panel's Network property sheet for the client in question. Changes that affect the low-level operation of the client aren't usually needed. When low-level changes are needed, you make the modifications by using the System Policy Editor or by altering values in the Windows 95 Registry.

Configuring the Client for Microsoft Networks

The Client for Microsoft Networks Properties sheet contains a single page with the following sections (see fig. 10.12):

II

Deploying Windows NT

■ The Logon Validation section allows you to specify whether to log on to a Windows NT domain. To do so, select this check box and type the domain name in the Windows NT Domain text box.

■ The buttons in the Network Logon Options section let you specify Quick Logon or Logon and Restore Network Connections. The Quick Logon option connects you to the network but doesn't attempt to verify the availability of network resources that you've mapped as logical drives until you try to access the mapped drive. The Logon and Restore Network Connections option verifies that each mapped resource is accessible before completing the logon process.

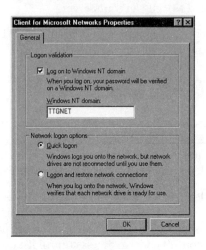

Fig. 10.12 Configuring the Client for Microsoft Networks.

Configuring the Client for NetWare Networks

The Client for NetWare Networks uses the NWLink IPX/SPX compatible transport protocol exclusively, and normally requires little configuration. Compared with using native Novell client software, the biggest change that most users will notice is that the Client for NetWare Networks doesn't support the Novell NWPOPUP utility. Microsoft supplies WINPOPUP as a substitute. Like NWPOPUP, WINPOPUP allows users to send messages to and receive them from each other. Unlike NWPOPUP, WINPOPUP doesn't respond to NetWare system messages, such as new mail notifications, by popping up a message box over the running application.

The General page of the Client for NetWare Networks Properties sheet lets you set logon parameters for the NetWare server (see fig. 10.13).

Specify the following items on the General page:

■ *The Preferred Server drop-down list* lets you specify which NetWare server the Windows 95 workstation connects to when Windows 95 starts. You also can leave this box empty, in which case Windows 95 at startup connects to the "nearest" NetWare server—that is, the server that responds fastest. If the client PC is running

NetWare client software when Windows 95 is installed, Preferred Server defaults to the setting in the Novell NET.CFG file.

■ *First Network Drive* lets you specify the lowest drive letter assigned to a network drive. Early versions of DOS reserved drives A through E as local drives, and drive F was assigned as the first network drive. Larger hard drives partitioned into multiple volumes have become common, consuming more local drive letters. CD-ROM drives and other drives using removable media have also proliferated, consuming still more drive letters.

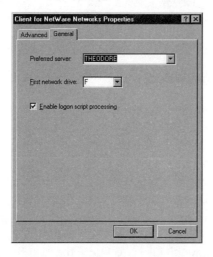

Fig. 10.13 The General page of the Client for NetWare Networks Properties sheet.

> ### Tip
>
> To ensure that workstations with various hardware configurations can use consistent network drive letter assignments, you should leave room for additional local drives by setting this parameter to a higher drive letter than F. Many organizations use H as the first network drive letter, assigning it to the user's Home folder as a mnemonic. Using H as the first network drive provides room for three or four local fixed-disk drive volumes, a CD-ROM drive, and a removable disk drive.

■ *The Enable Logon Script Processing check box,* if selected, causes Windows 95 to run the NetWare logon script for the user logging on.

The Advanced page of the Client for NetWare Networks Properties sheet lets you select a Value from a drop-down list for each Property displayed (see fig. 10.14).

Setting the Primary Network Logon

The Primary Network Logon determines which client software handles startup functions, such as user authentication and running logon scripts. By default, Windows 95 sets the Client for Microsoft Networks as the Primary Network Logon. You can set one of the other installed network clients as your Primary Network Logon if you prefer your startup functions to be performed by that client. You also can select Windows Logon as your Primary Network Logon, if you prefer not to connect automatically to the network each time you start Windows 95.

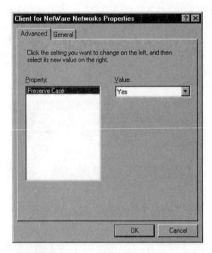

Fig. 10.14 The Advanced page of the Client for NetWare Networks Properties sheet.

To specify your preferred Primary Network Logon, select the client in the Primary Network Logon drop-down list of the Network property sheet (see fig. 10.15) and click OK. The Network property sheet closes and the System Settings Change message box appears, informing you that changes don't take effect until the next time you start Windows. Click Yes to restart Windows immediately and put your changes into effect.

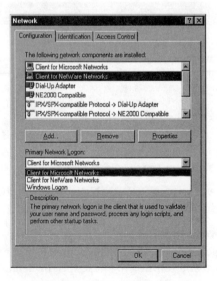

Fig. 10.15 Setting the Primary Network Logon with the Network property sheet.

Configuring Network Protocols

One of Microsoft's objectives for Windows 95 was to minimize the need for user intervention to configure network protocols. In most cases, Windows 95's default configuration for the protocols you choose are satisfactory. If not, the following sections describe how to configure Windows 95's network protocols manually.

Configuring NetBEUI

NetBIOS Extended User Interface (NetBEUI) is a fast and simple transport protocol used by Windows for Workgroups 3.1+ and other DOS and Windows peer-to-peer LANs. NetBEUI packets don't contain network header information, so NetBEUI isn't routable; thus, NetBEUI is inappropriate for large networks. If Windows 95 detects the presence of NetBEUI on the network during installation, the Setup program automatically installs NetBEUI support. You normally don't need to make changes to the NetBEUI configuration.

To display the NetBEUI Properties sheet for the network, select the NetBEUI entry that's bound to your NIC and click the Properties button. (Alternatively, double-click the NetBEUI entry.) The NetBEUI Properties sheet displays the Bindings page (see fig. 10.16). If you don't plan to share your files or a printer attached to your computer with other members of your workgroup using NetBEUI, click the File and Printer Sharing for Microsoft Networks entry to clear the check box.

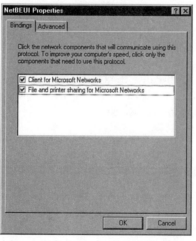

Fig. 10.16   The Bindings page of the NetBEUI Properties sheet.

The Advanced page of the NetBEUI Properties sheet (see fig. 10.17) lets you specify values for Maximum Sessions and NCBS for the real-mode NetBEUI driver. These tuning parameters affect only the real-mode driver, which Windows 95 normally doesn't use. The protected-mode NetBEUI driver is configured dynamically.

The Set This Protocol to Be the Default Protocol check box, if selected, sets NetBEUI as the default protocol. This option should always be deselected if your network includes Windows NT Server or NetWare servers. It should be selected only if you're running a peer-to-peer network, and only then if that network includes workstations that aren't running Windows 95.

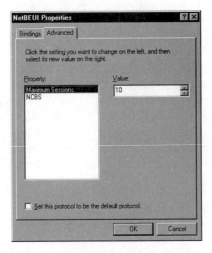

Fig. 10.17   The Advanced page of the NetBEUI Properties sheet.

Configuring NWLink

NWLink is Microsoft's implementation of the IPX/SPX transport protocol originally developed by Novell for NetWare. The default transport protocol used by Windows NT Server, NWLink is fully interoperable with IPX/SPX running on NetWare servers and clients. Windows 95 installs the NWLink protocol automatically when the Client for NetWare Networks is installed, because the Client for NetWare Networks uses the NWLink protocol exclusively. NWLink can also be used to support other client software, including the Client for Microsoft Networks.

Most client PCs require few or no changes to the default settings for NWLink. If the client is running Novell client software when Windows 95 is installed over an existing Windows 3.x installation, the setup program configures Windows 95 NWLink settings to correspond to the settings specified in the Novell NET.CFG configuration file.

The Bindings page of the IPX/SPX-Compatible Protocol Properties sheet lets you specify which clients and services use NWLink transport (see fig. 10.18). For better performance, clear the check boxes for network components that don't need to use NWLink.

The Advanced page of the IPX/SPX-Compatible Protocol Properties sheet lets you specify parameters that affect the low-level functioning of the NWLink protocol (see fig. 10.19). With one exception (Frame Type), these values are set dynamically and shouldn't be changed.

> **Note**
>
> If an otherwise functional Windows 95 network workstation can't see a NetWare server on an Ethernet network, the problem is almost certainly a frame type mismatch. NetWare can use any of

four Ethernet frame types: Ethernet_802.2, Ethernet_802.3, Ethernet_II, and Ethernet_SNAP. The frame types being used by the server and the workstation must be identical for communication to take place.

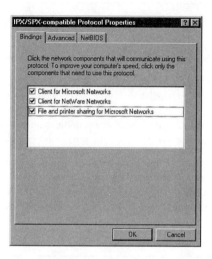

Fig. 10.18   The Bindings page of the IPX/SPX-Compatible Protocol Properties sheet.

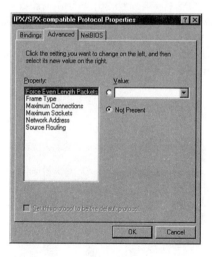

Fig. 10.19   The Advanced page of the IPX/SPX-Compatible Protocol Properties sheet.

The Windows 95 IPX/SPX protocol defaults to frame type Auto, which usually succeeds in detecting the frame type being used by the NetWare server. If auto detection fails, you must explicitly set the frame type in the Advanced page of the IPX/SPX-Compatible Protocol Properties sheet. You can set the frame type to the following values: Auto, Ethernet 802.2, Ethernet 802.3, Ethernet II, Token Ring, or Token Ring SNAP.

NetWare 3.11 and earlier servers default to the Ethernet_802.3 frame when using Ethernet. The corresponding Windows 95 frame type is Ethernet 802.3. NetWare 3.12 and higher servers default to Ethernet_802.2 frames, for which the corresponding Windows 95 frame type is Ethernet 802.2.

Note

For an Ethernet network, Novell recommends using the Ethernet_802.2 frame type, and Microsoft recommends that Windows 95 be set to frame type Auto. Both recommendations are *wrong*.

Ethernet 802.2, which is the most recent standards-based Ethernet frame, uses the OSI 802.2 LLC specification. Ethernet II is an older specification, which was originally developed by Digital Equipment, Intel, and Xerox. Newer isn't always better, however. The majority of Ethernet traffic worldwide still uses Ethernet II frames. All active components understand how to handle Ethernet II frames. On the Internet, Ethernet II always works. The same can't be said for Ethernet 802.2.

If your workstations need Internet access, if your network includes a UNIX host, or if you plan to use SNMP management on your NetWare servers, run Ethernet II. Even if you have no current need for these services, using Ethernet II now makes the transition to these services easier. There are no performance penalties or other drawbacks to using Ethernet II instead of Ethernet 802.2. Set your Windows 95 frame type to Ethernet II and add Ethernet_II frame support to each of your NetWare servers.

The NetBIOS page of the IPX/SPX-Compatible Protocol Properties sheet lets you enable the use of NetBIOS over IPX/SPX (see fig. 10.20). Windows 95 workstations can communicate with each other, and with Windows NT Server and NetWare servers directly, by using only the NWLink protocol. However, some network applications, such as IBM/Lotus Notes, require NetBIOS to communicate. Disable NetBIOS over IPX/SPX support unless you have applications that specifically require NetBIOS.

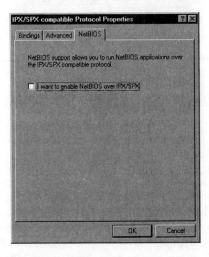

Fig. 10.20 The NetBIOS page of the IPX/SPX-Compatible Protocol Properties sheet.

Configuring TCP/IP

Windows 95 doesn't install support for the TCP/IP transport protocol by default. If your network includes UNIX hosts, or if your clients need access to the Internet, you must install TCP/IP support as described earlier in the "Installing a Network Client" section. After TCP/IP is installed, you must configure the protocol. TCP/IP is designed for use in internetworks and requires that the administrator have both a deeper understanding of the protocol and the willingness to configure and manage the protocol.

▶▶ See "Integrating Windows NT Server with UNIX," p. 632

The following sections describe how to configure the TCP/IP protocol by using the six pages of the TCP/IP Properties sheet.

Allocating an Internet Protocol Address. The IP Address page of the TCP/IP Properties sheet lets you specify how your workstation is allocated an Internet Protocol (IP) address (see fig. 10.21).

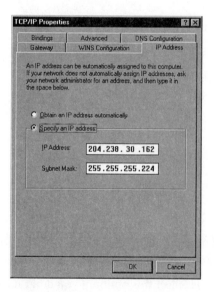

Fig. 10.21   The IP Address page of the TCP/IP Properties sheet.

Following are the parameters that you can specify in the IP Address page:

- *Obtain an IP Address Automatically.* If your network includes a Windows NT Server running the Dynamic Host Configuration Protocol (DHCP) service, select this option. The DHCP server allocates an IP address to the workstation automatically at startup. For more information about DHCP, see Chapter 17, "Integrating Windows NT with Heterogeneous Networks."

- *Specify an IP Address.* If your network doesn't include a DHCP server, or if you simply want to specify the IP address for this workstation manually, select this option.

II

Deploying Windows NT

Enter the appropriate IP Address and Subnet Mask in the text boxes provided. Chapter 17 also discusses assignment of IP addresses.

Caution

Use extreme care when you enter the IP Address and Subnet Mask values. If either value is entered incorrectly, problems ranging from subtle address conflicts to a network crash will result.

Using the Windows Internet Naming Service. The WINS Configuration page of the TCP/IP Properties sheet (see fig. 10.22) lets you specify whether this client uses the Windows Internet Naming Service (WINS) and, if so, which server or servers provide WINS. For more information about WINS, see Chapter 17, "Integrating Windows NT with Heterogeneous Networks."

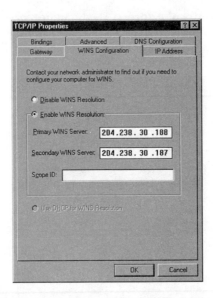

Fig. 10.22 The WINS Configuration page of the TCP/IP Properties sheet. You can set the following parameters in the WINS Configuration page:

- *Disable WINS Resolution.* Select this option if you don't have a WINS server running on your network or don't want the client to use WINS.

- *Enable WINS Resolution.* Select this option if you have a WINS server running on your network and want this client to use the service. If you choose this option, enter the appropriate IP addresses for the primary WINS server and, if applicable, for the secondary WINS server. Enter also the scope ID.

- *Use DHCP for WINS Resolution.* Select this item if you have a DHCP server running on your network and have enabled DHCP on this client.

Specifying a TCP/IP Gateway. The Gateway page of the TCP/IP Properties sheet lets you add and remove gateways used by the Windows 95 client (see fig. 10.23). The term *gateway* can be used in two ways: In the OSI Reference Model, *gateway* refers to a device that translates upper-level protocols. In the Internet community, *gateway* refers to a router. (Microsoft uses *gateway* to refer only to a router.)

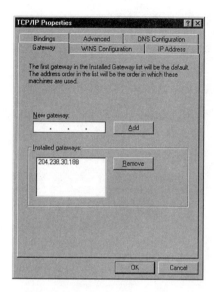

Fig. 10.23 The Gateway page of the TCP/IP Properties sheet.

◀◀ See "Routers," p. 156

> **Note**
>
> Enter the IP address of the gateway and click the Add button to add a gateway to the Installed Gateways list. To remove an installed gateway, highlight the entry and click the Remove button.
>
> The first gateway appearing in the Installed Gateways list is the default, which is used when available. If the default gateway is unavailable, Windows 95 attempts to access other installed gateways in the order in which they appear in the Installed Gateways list.

Binding the TCP/IP Protocol to Clients and Services. The Bindings page of the TCP/IP Properties sheet lets you specify which clients and services use the TCP/IP transport protocol (see fig. 10.24). For better performance, clear the check box next to clients and services that don't need to use TCP/IP transport.

The Client for Microsoft Networks normally should be bound to TCP/IP. File and printer sharing for Microsoft Networks should be bound to TCP/IP only if you plan to use these services across a TCP/IP-based internetwork.

Setting Low-Level TCP/IP Parameters. The Advanced page of the TCP/IP Properties sheet lets you alter low-level TCP/IP configuration parameters and specify TCP/IP as your default protocol (see fig. 10.25).

Selecting the Set This Protocol to Be the Default Protocol check box causes Windows 95 to use TCP/IP transport as the default. Most installations that support TCP/IP use TCP/IP as the default protocol.

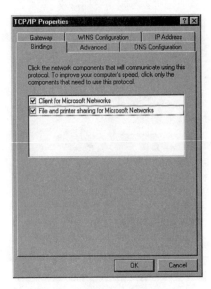

Fig. 10.24 The Bindings page of the TCP/IP Properties sheet.

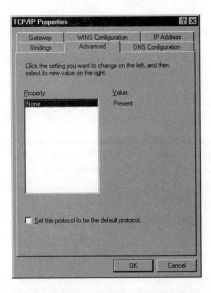

Fig. 10.25 The Advanced page of the TCP/IP Properties sheet.

Using the Domain Name Service to Resolve IP Addresses. The DNS Configuration page of the TCP/IP Properties sheet (see fig. 10.26) lets you enable or disable the use of Domain Name Service (DNS) to resolve IP addresses and, if DNS is enabled, to provide

DNS configuration information to the client. DNS translates character-based addresses, such as server names, to numeric IP addresses.

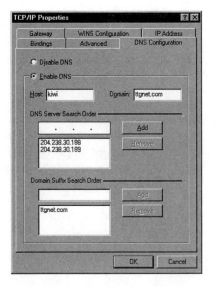

Fig. 10.26 The DNS Configuration page of the TCP/IP Properties sheet.

The DNS Configuration page offers the following settings:

- *Disable DNS*, if selected, causes the client not to use DNS to resolve IP addresses.

- *Enable DNS*, if selected, causes the client to use DNS to resolve IP addresses.

- *Host* is the name of the client computer system—for example, AR_1.

- *Domain* is the Internet domain—not to be confused with the Windows NT domain, of which the client is a member. In figure 10.26, the client is a member of the ttgnet.com Internet domain.

- *The DNS Server Search Order section* lets you add and remove the IP addresses for one or more servers that provide DNS services. The IP address that appears first in this list is the primary DNS and is used whenever the device at the address is available. The IP address that appears second in the list is the secondary DNS and is used only if the primary DNS device is unavailable.

- *The Domain Suffix Search Order section* lets you add and remove Internet domains to be searched. This feature allows partially qualified names to be resolved. For example, if your primary Internet domain is widget.com but you frequently access a host named NTS that belongs to the domain gadget.com, specifying gadget.com as a secondary search domain allows that host to be resolved when specified simply as NTS rather than as NTS.gadget.com.

Installing File and Printer Sharing

Windows 95 offers two ways to share your local files and printers with other clients on the network. If the client runs the Client for Microsoft Networks, you can install the Server Message Block (SMB) file and printer sharing for Microsoft Networks. If the client runs the Client for NetWare Networks, you can install the NetWare Core Protocol (NCP) based file and printer sharing for NetWare Networks. Only one of these services can be installed on a client. The following sections describe how to set up file and printer sharing on both types of networks.

File and Printer Sharing for Microsoft Networks

File and printer sharing for Microsoft Networks lets you share the local disk and printer resources of a client with any other computer on the network that supports SMB services, including systems running Windows NT Server and Workstation, Windows for Workgroups 3.11, LAN Manager, and DEC PATHWORKS. Using file and printer sharing for Microsoft Networks requires that the client run the Client for Microsoft Networks service. If you're using user-level security, a Windows NT Server domain controller must be used to provide authentication.

 ▶▶ See "Understanding Domain Architecture and Security," p. 567

To install file and printer sharing for Microsoft Networks, follow these steps:

1. From Control Panel, double-click the Network tool.

2. In the Configuration page of the Network property sheet, click the Add button.

3. In the Select Network Component Type dialog, double-click Service.

4. In the Select Network Service dialog, select Microsoft in the left list. Then select File and Printer Sharing for Microsoft Networks on the right, as shown in figure 10.27. Click OK to close the open dialogs.

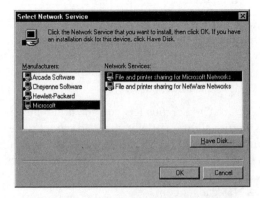

Fig. 10.27 Installing file and printer sharing for Microsoft Networks.

After you install file and printer sharing for Microsoft Networks, you must enable file sharing, printer sharing, or both. To enable one or both of these services, follow these steps:

1. From Control Panel, double-click the Network tool to open the Network property sheet.

2. Click the File and Print Sharing button to open the File and Print Sharing dialog (see fig. 10.28).

3. Select either or both of the check boxes of the File and Print Sharing dialog to enable file sharing, printer sharing, or both.

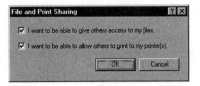

Fig. 10.28   Enabling file and print sharing services.

Note

The preceding process only enables the client to provide File and Print Sharing services. You must determine which files and printers you want to share, if any, and explicitly specify sharable resources as described earlier in the "Share-Level Access Control" section. Shared resources are visible to any Microsoft Networking client that browses the network.

Caution

In October 1995, Microsoft announced that a potentially serious security problem existed for users running file and printer sharing for Microsoft and NetWare Networks. A fix for this and other problems is included in Windows 95 Service Pack 1, mentioned earlier in the chapter. Service Pack 1 is now available as a 1.2M file named Setup.exe from Microsoft's Web site at **http://www.microsoft.com/windows/software/servpak1/enduser.htm** or from the Microsoft Download Service BBS. Before you install and enable file and printer sharing for Microsoft Networks or for NetWare Networks, make sure that you first install Windows 95 Service Pack 1 on the client. A complete list of the fixes in Service Pack 1 is included in the "Updating Shared Files with Service Packs" section near the end of this chapter.

File and Printer Sharing for NetWare Networks

File and printer sharing for NetWare Networks lets you share the local disk and printer resources of a client with other computers on networks that support Novell NetWare Core Protocol (NCP) services, including Novell NetWare for DOS and Windows-based clients, other clients running Windows 95 that use the Client for NetWare Networks, and systems running Windows NT. Using file and printer sharing for NetWare Networks requires that the client run the Client for NetWare Networks instead of the Novell-supplied client software. Share-level security isn't available with the Microsoft implementation of this service. If you're enabling user-level security, a NetWare server must be used to provide authentication.

To install file and printer sharing for NetWare Networks, follow these steps:

1. From Control Panel, double-click the Network tool to open the Network property sheet.

2. On the Configuration page of the Network property sheet, click the Add button.

3. In the Select Network Component Type dialog, double-click Service.

4. In the Select Network Service dialog, select Microsoft in the left list. Then select File and Printer Sharing for NetWare Networks in the right list and click OK to close the dialogs.

As is the case for file and printer sharing for Microsoft Networks, after you install file and printer sharing for NetWare Networks, you must enable file sharing, printer sharing, or both. To enable one or both of these services, follow these steps:

1. From Control Panel, double-click the Network tool to open the Network property sheet.

2. Click the File and Print Sharing button to open the File and Print Sharing dialog.

3. Select either or both of the check boxes to enable file sharing, print sharing, or both.

A client that's sharing resources using file and printer sharing for NetWare advertises its availability as a peer-to-peer server and the availability of the shared resources using either Workgroup Advertising or Novell Service Advertising Protocol (SAP). The visibility of shared resources to other clients browsing the network depends both on what client software the remote computer uses and which of the two advertising methods is used by the peer server, in accordance with the following rules:

■ Another client running the Client for NetWare networks sees shared resources provided by a peer server exactly as any other shared resources on the network. If the peer server is using Workgroup Advertising, it appears in a workgroup. A peer server running SAP isn't presented as a member of a workgroup, but instead appears only when you view the entire network.

■ Another client running the Novell NETx shell or VLM redirectors sees shared resources on a peer server only if the peer server is running SAP advertising. Shared directories appear as volumes on the server, and shared printers appear as Novell print queues. If the peer server runs Workgroup Advertising, its shared resources aren't visible to clients running Novell-provided clients.

Caution

A potentially serious security problem exists for users running file and printer sharing for NetWare Networks. Refer to the caution in the earlier "File and Printer Sharing for Microsoft Networks" section for details.

Managing Windows 95 on the Network

Windows 95's network installation and administration features are a significant improvement over Windows 3.x. Like Windows 3.x, Windows 95 can be installed to a local client fixed-disk drive from distribution files stored on a network drive, or can be installed as a shared copy to run from the network server. (Using a shared copy of Windows 95 isn't a recommended practice due to the amount of network traffic-sharing Windows 95 generates.) Unlike Windows 3.x, Windows 95 provides a wealth of features intended to ease management of client configurations and of the network itself.

Installing Windows 95 from the Network

You can install Windows 95 to the network server by using Server-Based Setup. This process copies the Windows 95 distribution files to the network server, and allows Windows 95 clients to be installed directly from the server. After the files are installed to the server, Machine Directory Setup allows you to create machine directories, which contain files specific to the hardware configurations of particular workstations.

Installing Windows 95 to the Server Using Server-Based Setup. In Windows 95, the Server-Based Setup program, Netsetup.exe, prepares the server for installing Windows 95 clients from the network. Netsetup.exe replaces the Administrative Setup procedure (SETUP /A) used in Windows for Workgroups 3.1+. The Server-Based Setup program creates and maintains shared machine directories on the server and creates setup scripts to automate the client installation process. After the Windows 95 distribution files are installed and configured on the server using Netsetup.exe, clients can run Windows 95 Setup.exe from the server to complete the local installation.

> **Note**
>
> Before beginning this procedure, make sure that you have at least 80M of free disk space on the server volume to which the Windows 95 distribution files are to be installed.

To install a setup copy of Windows 95 on Windows 4.0 NT Server from a Windows 95 client, follow these steps:

1. From the Start menu, click Run and browse the Windows 95 CD-ROM for the program \win95\admin\NETTOOLS\NETSETUP\Netsetup.exe. Double-click Netsetup.exe and then click OK to run the program. The Server Based Setup dialog appears (see fig. 10.29).

2. In the Set Server Install Path section, click the Set Path button. Type the path name for the server folder in which to install the Windows 95 setup files. If the specified folder doesn't exist, you're asked whether you want to create the folder.

3. After entering the installation path, the Install button is enabled. Click Install to open the Source Path dialog (see fig. 10.30).

4. Decide where you want shared files to be installed and indicate your choice in the Install Policy section by selecting Server, Local Hard Drive, or User's Choice:

- If you choose Server, shared files are always run from the server, saving disk space on clients at the expense of creating substantial additional network traffic.

- Choosing Local Hard Drive means that the shared files are installed to each client's local hard disk, occupying additional drive space but reducing network traffic.

- Choosing User's Choice lets you decide each time Windows is installed from the network whether to run the shared files from the server or from the local hard disk.

Unless you have a very compelling reason to allow users to run Windows 95 shared files from the server, choose Local Hard Drive.

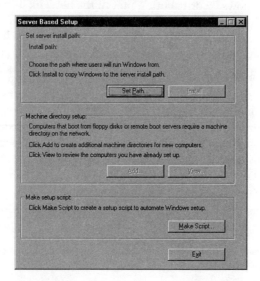

Fig. 10.29 Setting the server install path, performing machine directory setup, and making setup scripts in the Server Based Setup dialog.

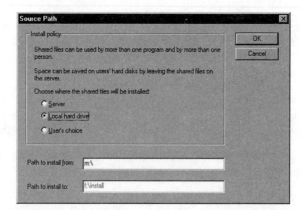

Fig. 10.30 Selecting the type of network installation and specifying the installation path in the Source Path dialog.

5. Verify that the Path to Install From entry is correct, changing the path if necessary. The Path to Install To is displayed in a text box but can't be changed at this point. (If you must change the installation path, click Cancel to return to the previous dialog and then click Change Path to respecify the path.) After verifying that all the information is correct, click OK.

6. The Create Default dialog lets you choose to accept a default setting of options that the Server-Based Setup program uses to create batch setup scripts to automate the installation process (see fig. 10.31). Unless you have a specific reason for doing otherwise, click the Create Default button.

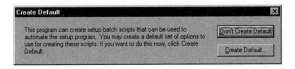

Fig. 10.31   Specifying the default option settings for server-based setup in the Create Default dialog.

7. If you choose to create defaults, the Server Based Setup Default Properties sheet appears (see fig. 10.32). This sheet displays a hierarchical listing of all policy items that can be edited for use as defaults during automated installation. After you finish editing these items, click OK to close the property sheet.

Fig. 10.32   Editing default setup values in the Server Based Setup Default Properties sheet.

8. A dialog appears with a prompt to enter your product identification number. Enter the number that appears on the case of the Windows 95 CD-ROM and click OK.

The copy process begins (see fig. 10.33). This process copies more than 80M of files to your server drive, so make sure that you have adequate disk space available before beginning the installation. After all files are copied to the installation directory, the setup

II

Deploying Windows NT

program marks the files as read-only. The program then tells you that installation is complete.

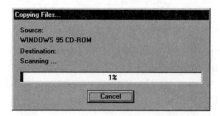

Fig. 10.33 Progress of the copying process shown by the Copying Files message box.

Performing a Machine Directory Setup. After the files are installed to the network server, you're returned to the Server Based Setup dialog. The next step is to create any needed machine directories. Although only a small subset of the Windows 95 files are specific to a particular client, these files are too large to fit on a floppy disk. If a particular client boots from a floppy drive, or is diskless and uses Remote Initial Program Load (RIPL), that client's files can be stored in a specific machine directory on the server. Files stored in a machine directory are specific to an individual client configuration. To install a machine directory, proceed as follows:

1. In the Machine Directory Setup section of the Server Based Setup dialog, click the Add button to add a machine folder using the Set Up Machine dialog.

   > **Note**
   >
   > At any time during this process, you can click the View button to display existing machine directories.

2. In the Set Up Machine dialog, select Set Up One Machine to create a machine directory for a single client (see fig. 10.34). Type the name of the client in the Computer Name text box.

3. Type the path name for the machine directory in the Path to Machine Directory text box.

   > **Note**
   >
   > Attempting to use mapped drive letter syntax, such as f:*folder*, causes an error. Use UNC syntax for the directory name: *Servername**Foldername*.

4. If you want to generate a setup script for this client, select the Generate Setup Script check box.

5. To change default policy values, click Edit Script to display the *Computername* Properties sheet (see fig. 10.35). Edit the policies as needed for this client. When your changes are complete, click OK to return to the Set Up Machine dialog.

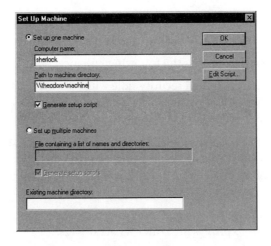

Fig. 10.34   Creating a folder for computer-specific installation in the Set Up Machine dialog.

Fig. 10.35   Editing computer-specific setup policies in the Computername Properties sheet.

6. Click OK to create the machine directory, save the information, and close the Set Up Machine dialog.

You can select Set Up Multiple Machines in the Set Up Machine dialog to create machine directories for several similar clients simultaneously. In this case, type the path and name of a file that contains the names and directories for the group of clients for which machine directories are to be set up. The Set Up Multiple Machines selection is useful primarily for a large number of identically configured clients.

Updating Shared Files with Service Packs. Microsoft has committed to releasing Windows 95 updates periodically. The first such update, Windows 95 Service Pack 1, was released in early 1996. As noted earlier in the chapter, this 1.2M update may be downloaded from **http://www.microsoft.com/windows/software/servpak1/**

enduser.htm. For complete instructions on installing the service pack in a network environment, refer to the ADMIN.DOC file included with the distribution file, SETUP.EXE.

Windows 95 Service Pack 1 includes the following enhancements and fixes:

- *OLE32 Update* fixes a potential security hole with Microsoft Office 95 applications using OLE. Previously, slack space in the application data files could contain data from deleted files, which could be viewed using Notepad or another editor.

- *Shell Update* fixes a file-copy problem that could result in zero-length files when copying a file onto itself using two views of the same network resource. If you've installed the Service for NetWare Directory Services update, the Shell Update also makes it possible to browse NDS printers from the Add Printer wizard.

- *Common Dialog Update for Windows 3.1 Printer Drivers* fixes problems when using 32-bit applications to print with Windows 3.1 drivers.

- *File and Printer Sharing for Microsoft Networks* fixes a security hole that exists when using file and printer sharing for Microsoft Networks on a network using Samba SMBCLIENT. It also fixes a security hole when using user-level security.

- *Samba* fixes a situation in which the different file-naming conventions used by Windows 95 and UNIX could cause problems. This update to Vredir traps file names that are legal UNIX file names but not legal Windows 95 file names.

- *File and Printer Sharing for NetWare Networks* fixes a security hole that might have allowed unauthorized users to access restricted data.

- *Password List* fixes a potential security hole that occurred when connecting to a password-protected resource and saving the password. The original distribution used an easily broken encryption method to store the passwords. This update makes the stored encrypted password almost impossible to recover by illicit means.

- *System Agent* fixes SAGE.DLL to correct problems with floating-point calculations performed while System Agent was running.

- *Exchange* updates the version of the Microsoft Exchange client shipped with Windows 95 to add various enhancements and fixes.

- *Printer Port* adds support for ECP ports used by newer laser printers and fixes some minor timeout problems.

Setting Up User Profiles on the Server

Many companies need to accommodate roving users—those who may log on at different workstations—by making sure that a user's personal profile is used at whatever workstation he uses to log on. This need is accommodated by storing user profile information on the network server, where it's accessible from any connected workstation. After user profiles are enabled, Windows 95 handles this process automatically, synchronizing user profile information between the server and the local hard disk.

If your network server is running Windows NT Server, the only special requirement for handling roving users is that a home directory must exist for each such user on the server. If the server is running Novell NetWare, a mail directory must exist for the user.

When a roving user logs into a Windows 95 client workstation, Windows 95 first examines the local hard drive and that user's home directory on the server to locate a User.dat file for that account. If a User.dat file exists for that user in both places, the most recent copy is used. If it exists in only one place, that copy is used, but is then saved to both the local and network drives. If it exists in neither place, the default is used and is then saved under that logon name to both the local hard drive and to the home directory on the server.

If that same roving user then logs into a different Windows 95 client workstation, the process is repeated. If a User.dat exists on both the local hard drive and the server, the latest version is used, and is then saved to both the local hard drive and the server.

Because Windows 95 always checks for multiple copies of User.dat in different locations, uses the latest version for the current session, and then saves the latest version to all locations where a User.dat was found for that user, a roving user will always be using the latest version of his User.dat. All of these processes occur automatically and transparently to the user. It's simply the way Windows 95 is designed to work. The only requirements for it to occur are as follows:

- The user has an account and a home directory on the Windows NT server or a mail directory on the NetWare server, and

- User profiles are enabled on the User Profiles page of the Password Properties sheet (see fig. 10.36), and either

- Client for Microsoft Networks is the primary network logon if the profiles are to be stored on the NT Server

  or

  Client for NetWare Networks is the primary logon if the profiles are to be stored on a Novell server.

Note

A user profile is stored in the user's home directory on a Windows NT Server. Creating a user account on a Windows NT server doesn't automatically create a home directory for that user, so you must manually create the directory if that user roves.

A user profile is stored in the user's mail directory on a Novell server. This directory is created automatically when the NetWare user is created, so no further action is needed.

The Windows 95 Registry comprises two files—User.dat and System.dat. User.dat contains information about user settings and preferences. System.dat contains information about system hardware configuration and settings. Using user profiles allows more than one user to use the same Windows 95 system while maintaining individual settings for each user. Windows 95 updates and maintains user profile information automatically after user profiles are enabled. You can use mandatory user profiles to limit users' ability to alter desktop settings and to provide a consistent interface throughout the network, making training and client-management issues considerably easier to deal with.

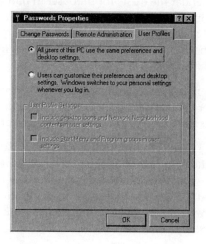

Fig. 10.36 The Passwords Properties sheet's User Profiles page.

User profile information can be stored either locally on the client or on the network server. If the user profile information is stored locally, Windows 95 uses the settings for a specific user when that user logs on to that client, allowing each user of the client to have his own desktop settings and other preferences available at logon. If the user profile information is instead stored on the network server, a user can log on to any Windows 95 client running a 32-bit protected-mode client and still be presented with his preferred settings.

Because user profiles store only user information and not system information, various client hardware configurations are each handled by the local System.dat file specific to the individual client, whereas desktop settings and other user-specific information are retrieved from the user profile information of User.dat stored on the server's home directory for the user.

Using System Policies
System policies are defined in a policy file stored on the network server. When a user logs on, local Registry values are superseded by those stored in the system policy file. Using system policies lets you enforce mandatory system configurations and control what users are permitted to do and change on the desktop. You can use system policies to standardize such network settings as client and protocol configurations and peer-based resource sharing.

You can create and change system policies by using the System Policy Editor, Poledit.exe (more commonly called PolEdit). You can use PolEdit to change Registry settings on either a local or remote computer. You can create a standardized set of Registry settings, store them in a system policy file, and then use this to standardize the Registry on many systems. You can apply these system policy settings individually or to groups already defined on a Windows NT Server or a NetWare server.

Installing the System Policy Editor. PolEdit isn't installed by default when you install Windows 95. To install PolEdit on a Windows 95 management client, proceed as follows:

1. Double-click Control Panel's Add/Remove Programs tool to open the Add/Remove Programs Properties sheet.

2. Click the Windows Setup tab to show the Windows Setup page (see fig. 10.37).

3. Click the Have Disk button to open the Install From Disk dialog (see fig. 10.38).

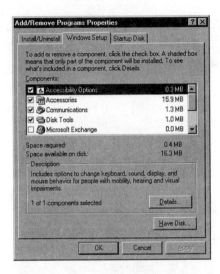

Fig. 10.37   The Windows Setup page of the Add/Remove Programs Properties sheet.

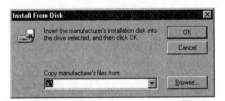

Fig. 10.38   Using the Install From Disk dialog for installing Poledit.exe.

4. Click Browse and locate the admin\apptools\poledit directory of the Windows 95 CD-ROM. Two .INF files appear: grouppol.inf and poledit.inf (see fig. 10.39).

5. Select grouppol.inf and click OK. You're returned to the Install From Disk dialog with \admin\apptools\poledit\grouppol.inf specified as the Copy Manufacturer's Files From location (see fig. 10.40).

II

Deploying Windows NT

6. Click OK to display the Have Disk dialog (see fig. 10.41) and to choose the Components to be installed. Select Group Policies to install group-based support for system policies. Select System Policy Editor to allow setting system policies for your network. Click Install to begin installing the software.

7. When the Add/Remove Programs Properties sheet reappears, click OK to complete the installation. You're prompted to restart your computer for the changes to take effect.

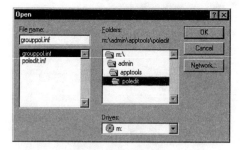

Fig. 10.39   The Open dialog for installing Poledit.exe from a network drive.

Fig. 10.40   Specifying the location of Poledit.exe in the Copy Manufacturer's Files From text box.

Using the System Policy Editor. You can use PolEdit in the following modes:

■ *Registry mode* lets you edit the Registry of a local or remote computer directly. Any changes you make to the Registry take effect immediately.

■ *Policy File mode* lets you create and modify .POL system policy files that can subsequently be used on other clients. Changes you make to a policy file take effect only when the policy file is invoked during the user's next network logon.

To use Registry mode to make changes to a local Registry, run PolEdit. From the File menu choose Open Registry. Two icons appear—Local User and Local Computer. Clicking Local User, which corresponds to data contained in the User.dat portion of the Registry, displays a hierarchical tree showing user items that may be edited. Clicking Local Computer similarly lets you edit items contained in the System.dat part of the Registry.

Fig. 10.41 The completed Have Disk dialog with Group Policies and System Policy Editor added.

> **Caution**
>
> Configuration changes are stored in the Registry. Using Control Panel tools to make Registry changes is far safer than other methods and conceals the intricacies of the Registry from the person making the changes. PolEdit permits direct editing of a subset of the Registry. The Registry Editor, Regedit.exe (also known as RegEdit), permits direct editing of the entire Registry and is the most powerful—as well as most dangerous—choice. Use the least powerful Registry editing tool that accomplishes your editing objective.

To use Registry mode to make changes to a remote Registry, run PolEdit. From the File menu choose Connect. When prompted, enter the name of the remote computer to open that computer's Registry for editing. If you have administrative privileges on that computer, if user-level access control is enabled on the remote computer, and if the Remote Registry service is enabled on both the local and remote computers, you can edit the remote Registry as though it were local.

To use Policy File mode to create and modify system policy files, run PolEdit. From the File menu, choose New File to create a new system policy file, or Open File to open an existing system policy file. Changes that you make to the System Policy file are saved when you exit PolEdit but take effect only when the policy file is invoked during the user's next network logon.

Managing Windows 95 Clients Remotely

Windows 95 provides several tools designed to allow you to manage networked clients running Windows 95 from a central management client rather than make on-site visits to the client. These remote management tools include the following:

- *System Policy Editor*, described in the preceding section, lets you make direct changes to remote clients on an individual basis and to create system policy files that control the behavior of multiple clients on the network.

- *Registry Editor* is another tool that you can use to make direct changes to the Registry of a remote client. Unlike the Policy Editor, which can change only a subset of Registry entries, Registry Editor has full access to the Registry.

- *System Monitor* reports performance information across the network, using virtual device drivers to monitor many aspects of system performance. System Monitor is a much simpler version of the Simple Network Management Protocol (SNMP).

- *Net Watcher* lets you manage shared resources across the network when you're using the peer-to-peer LAN features of Windows 95.

- *Backup agents* are provided for Cheyenne ARCserve and Arcada Backup Exec to allow you to back up client files from a central server that uses Cheyenne or Arcada backup software, respectively.

The following sections describe how to enable remote management of clients over the network and how to use the System Policy Editor, Registry Editor, System Monitor, and Net Watcher with remote clients.

Enabling Remote Management

Before you can use the remote management features provided by Windows 95, you must first enable some functions on the remote clients to be managed and on the central management client. Although the specific requirements vary with the remote management features you want to use, making the following changes on the remote client provides full remote management access:

- *Enable user-level security,* as discussed earlier in this chapter. Although some remote management functions are available with only share-level security enabled on the remote client, enabling user-level security gives you access to all remote management functions.

- *Enable remote administration,* if necessary. If the remote client has user-level security enabled, remote administration is enabled automatically. If the remote client uses share-level security, remote administration must be enabled manually. To do so, double-click Control Panel's Passwords tool and select the Enable Remote Administration of This Server check box. For share-level security, enter a password to control access to remote administration. For user-level security, add specific users as administrators.

- *Grant remote administration privileges* to the administrator. With user-level security enabled, certain users are automatically granted remote administration privileges, as follows:

  - On a Windows NT Server network, members of the DOMAIN ADMINISTRATORS group

  - On a Novell NetWare 3.1x network, the user SUPERVISOR

  - On a Novell NetWare 4.x network, the user ADMIN

- *Install file and printer sharing,* as detailed earlier in this chapter.

■ *Install Microsoft Remote Registry service.* From Control Panel, double-click the Network tool. Click Add and choose Service. Click the Have Disk button and specify the \admin\nettools\remotreg directory on the Windows 95 distribution CD. Select Microsoft Remote Registry (see fig. 10.42) and click OK to install the remote Registry service.

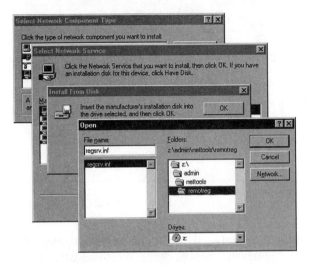

Fig. 10.42   Installing Microsoft Remote Registry service from the Windows 95 CD-ROM.

In addition to the items in the preceding list, the following changes are needed on the central management client:

■ Install Remote Registry services, as described earlier.

■ Verify transport protocol support to ensure that the management client has at least one protocol (NWLink, TCP/IP, or NetBEUI) in common with each remote client to be managed.

Using Remote Management

After you enable remote management, you can use the System Policy Editor, Registry Editor, and other tools to manage remote clients, as described in the following sections.

Using Policy Editor Remotely. You can use Policy Editor to make changes to the Registry on a remote client. Most of these changes take effect immediately, but some require that the remote client be restarted for them to take effect.

To use Policy Editor remotely, follow these steps:

1. Run Policy Editor and choose Connect from the File menu to open the Connect dialog.

2. In the Connect dialog, type the name of the remote client with the policy to be edited. If the proper services are installed and enabled on both your client and the remote client, and if you have the necessary permissions, the Registry of the

Deploying Windows NT

II

remote client is loaded into Policy Editor. The title bar of Policy Editor shows the name of the remote client whose Registry is being edited (see fig. 10.43).

3. Make the necessary changes and save them.

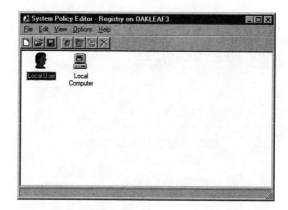

Fig. 10.43 Policy Editor displaying the Local User and Local Computer icons for a remote Windows 95 computer (OAKLEAF3).

Using Registry Editor Remotely. Like Policy Editor, the Registry Editor can be used to make changes to the Registry of a remote client. To use Registry Editor remotely, follow these steps:

1. Run Registry Editor. From the Registry menu, choose Connect Network Registry.

2. In the Connect Network Registry dialog, type the name of the remote client to be edited. If you have the proper services loaded and permissions granted, the Registry of the remote client is loaded into Registry Editor, appearing as a branch below the existing Registry information for the local machine (see fig. 10.44).

3. Make the necessary changes and save them.

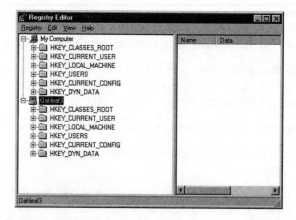

Fig. 10.44 Registry Editor displaying the Registry keys of the local (OAKLEAF1, My Computer) and a remote (OAKLEAF3) Windows 95 computer.

Using System Monitor Remotely. You can use the System Monitor to view performance statistics of a remote system. Using System Monitor remotely requires that the remote client have Remote Registry service installed.

To use System Monitor to view performance statistics on a remote system, do the following:

1. Run System Monitor. From the File menu choose Connect.

2. In the Connect dialog, type the name of the remote client to be monitored and then click OK. If the necessary services are installed on both computers and if you have the appropriate permissions, System Monitor displays parameters for the remote system (see fig. 10.45).

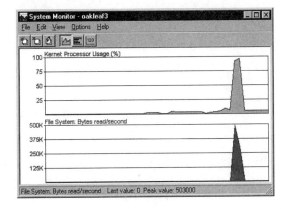

Fig. 10.45 Monitoring processor usage and file system bytes read of a remote Windows 95 computer (OAKLEAF3).

Using Net Watcher Remotely. Net Watcher lets you monitor and control shared resources on the network. By using Net Watcher, you can add and delete shared resources on remote clients, display shared resources and connected users, close files left open by users, and disconnect users. Using Net Watcher to control remote clients requires that the remote clients have File and Print Sharing enabled. With File and Print Sharing enabled, a client can share resources with other clients on the network, and is referred to as a *peer-to-peer server*, *peer server*, or simply a *server*.

To use Net Watcher to connect to a remote client, follow these steps:

1. Run Net Watcher and choose Select Server from the Administer menu.

2. In the Select Server dialog, type the name of the remote client (peer server) you want to control. Alternatively, click the Browse button to browse a list of available servers.

3. Type the password for the peer server you select, if necessary. You're connected to the remote client, and Net Watcher displays the default shares for the selected client in the right pane (see fig. 10.46).

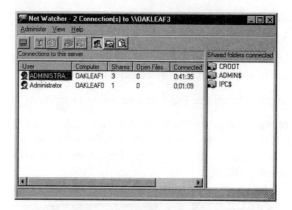

Fig. 10.46 Using Net Watcher to display the users sharing folders of a remote Windows 95 computer (OAKLEAF3).

To use Net Watcher to add shared folders on a remote client, do the following:

1. After you connect to the remote client as described in the preceding steps, choose Shared Folders from the View menu to display the Shared Folders dialog.

2. Click Add Shared Folder to display the Enter Path dialog.

3. Type the name of the folder to be shared. Alternatively, click the Browse button to browse for the folder to be shared and select the drive or folder you want to share. When you click OK, the *Sharename* property sheet appears, with the Not Shared option selected.

4. Select the Shared As option, complete the share information (see fig. 10.47), and click OK to close the dialog. The information you supply here depends on whether you're using share-level access or user-level access, as described earlier in this chapter. (Fig. 10.47 shows the entries for user-level access.) After you complete this step, the newly shared folder is added to the Shared Folder view and is accessible to other users (see fig. 10.48).

To use Net Watcher to remove shared folders on a remote client, follow these steps:

1. After you connect to the remote client (as described earlier in this section), choose Shared Folders from the View menu to display the Shared Folders dialog.

2. Select the folder that's no longer to be shared; click Stop Sharing Folder; and, when prompted, confirm that you want to stop sharing that folder. The shared folder is removed from the Shared Folder view and is no longer accessible to other users.

Fig. 10.47 Setting up a share on a remote Windows 95 computer (OAKLEAF3) with user-level access.

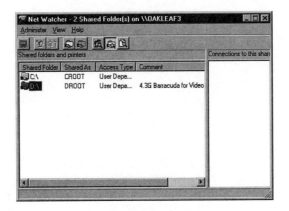

Fig. 10.48 The additional server share (DROOT) displayed by Net Watcher.

From Here...

One of the primary responsibilities of Windows NT 4.0 Server network administrators is to assure that Windows 95 clients, whether desktop or portable PCs, gain the maximum possible benefit from Windows NT networking. This chapter described how to set up and administer Windows 95 clients to accommodate NetBEUI, TCP/IP, and IPX/SPX protocols. If you're migrating from Novell NetWare to a Windows NT 4.0 Server environment, Windows 95's capability to run multiple network protocol stacks without consuming

Deploying Windows NT

II

conventional DOS memory is an important consideration. Combinations of NetBEUI for high-speed network communication in departmental Windows NT networks and TCP/IP for wide area networking, including access to intranets and the Internet, also is common.

The following chapters contain information related to or complementing the content of this chapter:

■ Chapter 11, "Connecting Other PC Clients to the Network," describes how to set up Windows 3.1, Windows for Workgroups 3.1+, Windows NT 3.5+ and 4.0 Workstation, and Apple Macintosh clients for networking with Windows NT 4.0 Server.

■ Chapter 12, "Managing User and Group Accounts," describes how to optimize the structure of and manage client accounts on Windows NT 4.0 servers.

■ Chapter 17, "Integrating Windows NT with Heterogeneous Networks," discusses how to optimize the use of Windows NT 4.0 Server with Novell NetWare and UNIX networks, with emphasis on TCP/IP connectivity.

Chapter 11

Connecting Other PC Clients to the Network

One of Windows NT Server's strengths is its capability to provide file, print, and application services to a number of different Windows and Macintosh clients.

Windows 3.1+ is the least functional of the client platforms, from a networking viewpoint. Windows for Workgroups (WfWg) incorporates the network components that Windows 3.1+ lacks, making WfWg Windows NT Server-aware and providing additional flexibility in its support of other Windows NT Server 4.0 features, such as multiple networking protocols. For these reasons, WfWg is the most common 16-bit client platform in use by today's Windows NT Server networks. The prevalence of WfWg clients is beginning to decline as 32-bit Windows 95 and Window NT Workstation become the standard operating systems for mobile and desktop PCs, respectively. Much of the information in Chapter 10, "Configuring Windows 95 Clients for Networking," applies to connecting both Windows 95 and Windows NT 4.0 clients to the network.

Windows NT Workstation 4.0 provides the greatest functionality, flexibility, and stability of all the Windows clients. Accordingly, Windows NT Workstation requires more PC resources than Windows 3.1+ and WfWg. Windows NT takes full advantage of the new Intel Pentium Pro processors and provides symmetrical multiprocessing (SMP) for 32-bit threaded applications. An increasing number of organizations are equipping their power users with dual-processor workstations with the 32M or more of RAM required to take advantage of SMP with high-end graphics applications, such as Adobe PhotoShop.

Macintosh client support is provided as part of Windows NT Server 4.0. In essence, your Windows NT server becomes an AppleShare server to provide file and print services to your Mac clients.

In this chapter, you learn the steps required to enable Windows NT Server 4.0 client connectivity for the following environments:

- Windows 3.1
- Windows for Workgroups 3.11
- Windows NT Workstation 4.0
- Apple Macintosh System 6.0.7 or higher

II

Deploying Windows NT

Connecting Windows 3.1 Clients

Microsoft designed Windows 3.1+ as, primarily, a stand-alone product with networking capability added as an extension to the underlying MS-DOS operating system. The easiest way to provide Windows 3.1+ clients with connectivity to Windows NT 4.0 servers is to upgrade the client PCs from Windows 3.1+ to Windows for Workgroups 3.11. If you have a reason not to upgrade Windows 3.1+ clients to WfWg 3.11, the following sections describe how to install the Microsoft Client for DOS and Windows that's included with Windows NT Server 4.0.

Note

If your Windows 3.1 clients currently connect to one or more Novell NetWare 3.x or 4.x servers, you can avoid the installation of additional network client software by setting up Windows NT Server 4.0 to provide the IPX/SPX transport, in addition to NetBEUI and/or TCP/IP. Chapter 17, "Integrating Windows NT with Heterogeneous Networks," describes how to add the IPX/SPX protocol to a Windows NT 4.0 server.

Windows 3.1, unlike WfWg 3.11, requires you to choose a single network protocol. It's possible, but inconvenient, to use a multi-boot DOS technique so that Windows 3.1 clients can change network protocols.

Creating Client Installation Diskettes

You need the Windows NT Server 4.0 CD-ROM and two high-density diskettes to create the DOS setup disks for installing the Network Client v3.0 for MS-DOS and Windows. You install from the diskettes the DOS-based drivers on each computer running Windows 3.1 that connects to your Windows NT server. Follow these steps to create the installation diskettes:

1. If you haven't previously copied the client installation files to a \clients folder of a server drive for server-based installation, insert the Windows NT Server 4.0 CD-ROM into your CD-ROM drive.

2. From the Windows NT Server 4.0 Start menu, choose Programs, Administrative Tools, and then Network Client Administrator to open the Network Client Administrator dialog.

3. Select Make Installation Disk Set (see fig. 11.1) and click OK to display the Share Network Client Installation Files dialog.

Fig. 11.1   Selecting the Make Installation Disk Set option of the Network Client Administrator dialog.

4. In the Path text box of the Share Network Client Installation Files dialog, type the path to the \clients folder. If you use the CD-ROM, type or browse to the *d:*\clients folder, where *d:* is the drive letter for your CD-ROM drive. Select the Use Existing Path option (see fig. 11.2) and click OK to open the Make Installation Disk Set dialog.

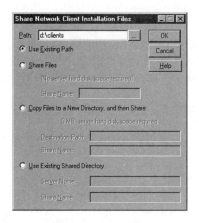

Fig. 11.2   Setting the path to the Windows NT Server 4.0 distribution CD-ROM.

5. The Network Client or Service list box of the Make Installation Disk Set dialog lets you choose the client drivers to copy. Select Network Client v3.0 for MS-DOS and Windows (see fig. 11.3). Make sure that the diskette destination drive is correct, and click OK to create the two diskettes. If the diskettes aren't formatted, mark the Format Disks check box.

Fig. 11.3   Selecting the Network Client v3.0 for MS-DOS and Windows in the Network Client or Service list of the Make Installation Disk Set dialog.

Tip

If you anticipate the need to create additional sets of network install diskettes, copy the files from the *d:*\clients folder to a \clients folder on your server. Creating a \clients folder is one of the options of the Share Network Client Installation Files dialog.

Installing the MS-DOS and Windows Client

Now that you've created the installation diskettes, the next step is to install the network drivers on your Windows 3.1 client. As part of the diskette creation, a Setup program is provided to facilitate this process. The following steps describe how to install the Network Client v3.0 for DOS and Windows on a Windows 3.1 client PC:

1. You must install the client software from DOS, so exit Windows to the DOS prompt.

2. Insert client diskette #1 and type **a:\setup** at the command line. Press Enter to run the Setup application and display the initial Setup screen.

3. Press Enter to continue to display the screen where you select the path to which to install the network drivers. The default is C:\NET (see fig. 11.4). Choose a different drive or directory, if desired, and press Enter to continue.

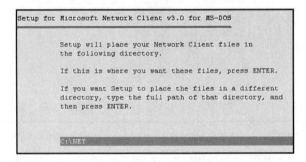

Fig. 11.4 Specifying the path to the client's network files.

4. Setup first prompts you select a network card driver. Scroll the list and choose the correct driver for your network card. If your card isn't listed, choose the Network Adapter Not Shown on List Below option, which lets you load an adapter driver from diskette. The network card manufacturer usually provides a diskette with drivers for popular operating systems. In this case, Setup looks for the OEMSETUP.INF file to load the driver for the Microsoft Network Client.

5. Setup next examines your system and proposes to allocate memory to network buffers for best performance (see fig. 11.5). Press Enter to accept the buffer allocation, or press C to continue without optimizing buffer memory.

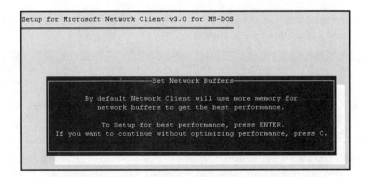

Fig. 11.5 Specifying allocation of network memory buffers to optimize network performance.

> **Note**
>
> You can have the network drivers allocate part of your system's RAM as a packet buffer. This provides for fewer packet drops if your network card can't process packets fast enough, but consumes additional system RAM. In most cases, you can accept the default buffer allocation.

6. Setup prompts you for a user name that identifies the client to the network. This name also becomes your computer name. Type the computer name in the User Name text box (see fig. 11.6), and press Enter to continue.

```
Setup for Microsoft Network Client v3.0 for MS-DOS


        User Name is the name that identifies you in your workgroup.
        Choose a name that is unique in your workgroup.

        A user name can have up to 20 characters, and can contain
        letters, numbers, and these characters:

             !  #  $  %  &  ( )  ^  _  `  { }  ~

        User Name:    TestClient
```

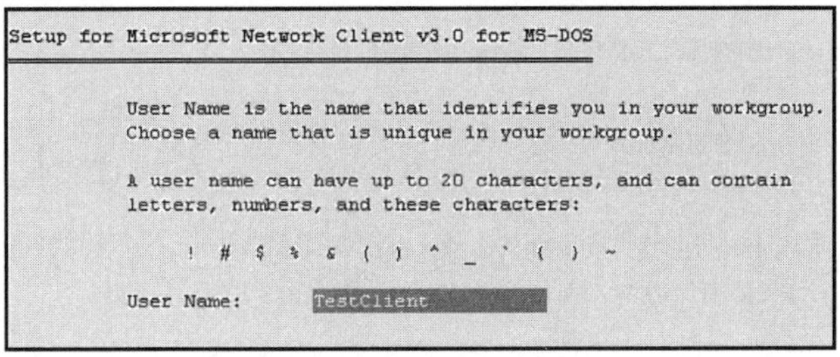

Fig. 11.6   Specifying the User Name for the client.

7. The screen displays a list of the default values for Names, Setup Options, and Network Configuration. Use the arrow keys to select Change Network Configuration (see fig. 11.7), and press Enter to continue.

```
Setup for Microsoft Network Client v3.0 for MS-DOS


        Names:
                Your User Name is TestClient

        Setup Options:
                Use the Full Redirector.
                Run Network Client.

        Network Configuration:
                Modify your adapter and protocols with this option.

        ┌─────────────────────────────────────────────────┐
        │  Change Names                                   │
        │  Change Setup Options                           │
        │  Change Network Configuration                   │
        │                                                 │
        │  The listed options are correct.                │
        └─────────────────────────────────────────────────┘
```

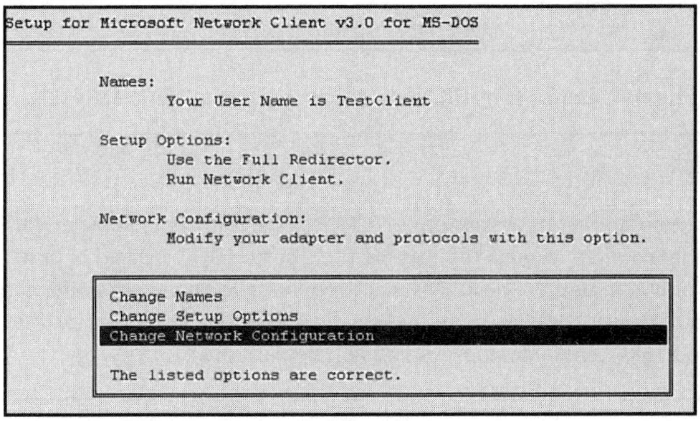

Fig. 11.7   Preparing to change the network configuration.

8. Assuming that Setup has correctly detected your network adapter, it's identified as the Installed Network Adapter. By default, NWLink IPX is the default network protocol.

To change to NetBEUI, the most common protocol for small Windows NT networks, press Tab and use the arrow keys to select the NWLink IPX Compatible Transport in the upper box. Press Tab to return to the configuration options, select Remove (see fig. 11.8), and press Enter.

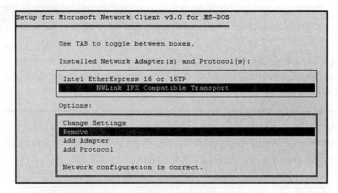

Fig. 11.8   Removing the NWLink IPX Compatible Transport.

 ◀◀ See "NetBEUI and NetBEUI Frame," p. 112

9. From the list of protocols, select Microsoft NetBEUI (see fig. 11.9) and press Enter. Select Network Configuration Is Correct and press Enter again.

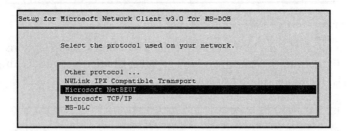

Fig. 11.9   Selecting the Microsoft NetBEUI protocol in place of NetWare's IPX.

> **Note**
>
> Many large organizations are adopting TCP/IP as the primary or sole network protocol for client/server communication. You can elect to install TCP/IP, instead of or in addition to NetBEUI or IPX, in step 9. The TCP/IP stack requires additional conventional memory. Consumption of conventional memory may be a problem for clients that load several device drivers and TSRs (terminate-and-stay-resident applications).

 ◀◀ See "TCP/IP," p. 113

10. Select Setup Options and press Enter to view your Microsoft Client setup options (see fig. 11.10).

11. If you want to validate your Windows 3.1 client to your Windows NT Server domain, select Change Logon Validation and press Enter. In the next screen, select Logon to Domain, press Enter, select The Listed Options Are Correct, and press

Enter again (see fig. 11.11). If you plan to use Domain Logon Validation, you must make sure to use the Full Redirector (the default).

```
Setup for Microsoft Network Client v3.0 for MS-DOS

          This screen enables you to change your redirector,
          startup, logon, and net pop-up options.

      Change Redir Options     : Use the Full Redirector.
      Change Startup Options   : Run Network Client.
      Change Logon Validation : Do Not Logon to Domain.
      Change Net Pop Hot Key   : N

      The listed options are correct.
```

Fig. 11.10   Preparing to set up domain logon during the boot process.

```
Setup for Microsoft Network Client v3.0 for MS-DOS

          This screen enables you to change your redirector,
          startup, logon, and net pop-up options.

      Change Redir Options     : Use the Full Redirector.
      Change Startup Options   : Run Network Client.
      Change Logon Validation : Logon to Domain.
      Change Net Pop Hot Key   : N

      The listed options are correct.
```

Fig. 11.11   Verifying the Setup options for the client installation.

12. If you plan to log on to a Windows NT domain, highlight the Names option and press Enter. Change the DomainName text to correspond to your Windows NT Server domain name. After entering the domain name, use the tab and arrow keys to accept changes.

13. Select The Listed Options Are Correct (see fig. 11.12) and press Enter to complete installation of the files required for the client.

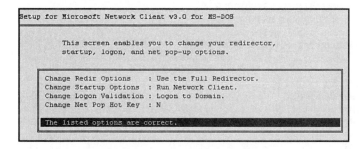

```
Setup for Microsoft Network Client v3.0 for MS-DOS

      Names:
              Your User Name is TestClient

      Setup Options:
              Use the Full Redirector.
              Run Network Client.

      Network Configuration:
              Modify your adapter and protocols with this option.

      Change Names
      Change Setup Options
      Change Network Configuration

      The listed options are correct.
```

Fig. 11.12   Verifying all your client software installation options in the final installation screen.

II

Deploying Windows NT

Viewing Changes Made to Windows 3.1 Configuration and Initialization Files

The Setup program adds the following line to the client's CONFIG.SYS file:

```
Device=c:\net\ifshelp.sys
```

The client's AUTOEXEC.BAT file is modified to include the following additional instruction:

```
c:\net\net start
```

The Microsoft client software uses the PROTOCOL.INI file to store network adapter and protocol configuration. Following are typical entries in PROTOCOL.INI for NetBEUI with a NE2000-compatible network adapter:

```
[network.setup]

version=0x3110
netcard=ms$ne2clone,1,MS$NE2CLONE,1
transport=ms$ndishlp,MS$NDISHLP
transport=ms$netbeui,MS$NETBEUI
lana0=ms$ne2clone,1,ms$netbeui
lana1=ms$ne2clone,1,ms$ndishlp
[MS$NE2CLONE]
IOBASE=0x300
INTERRUPT=3
DriverName=MS2000$
[ndishlp$]
DriverName=ndishlp$
Bindings=
[protman$]
DriverName=protman$
[data]
version=v4.00.950
netcards=
[protman]
DriverName=PROTMAN$
PRIORITY=MS$NDISHLP
[MS$NDISHLP]
DriverName=ndishlp$
BINDINGS=MS$NE2CLONE
[MS$NETBEUI]
DriverName=netbeui$
SESSIONS=10
NCBS=12
BINDINGS=MS$NE2CLONE
LANABASE=0
```

The SYSTEM.INI file contains information about your NetBIOS computer name, the default user name, workgroup and/or domain, and the location of the password file for that user name. The password file (*.PWL) is stored on the local machine in an encrypted format; Windows NT clients use password files stored on the server. The first time the user logs on to Windows NT, he or she is prompted to create the password file for the user name specified in the SYSTEM.INI file. The following are typical SYSTEM.INI networking entries:

```
[network]
sizworkbuf=1498
```

```
filesharing=no
printsharing=no
autologon=yes
computername=WINDOWS1
lanroot=C:\NET
username=USER1
workgroup=WORKGROUP
reconnect=yes
dospophotkey=N
lmlogon=1
logondomain=MASTER
preferredredir=full
autostart=full
maxconnections=8

[network drivers]
netcard=ne2000.dos
transport=ndishlp.sys,*netbeui
devdir=C:\NET
LoadRMDrivers=yes
[Password Lists]
*Shares=C:\NET\Share001.PWL
```

> **Note**
>
> The preceding .INI files are created during the client networking setup process. If you need to edit the entries in these files, use DOS's EDIT.EXE, or Windows SYSEDIT.EXE or Notepad. For instance, if you want to change the name of the Windows NT domain to which you log on during client startup, you edit the `logondomain` entry in the SYSTEM.INI file. Changes you make take effect when you reboot the client PC.

Setting Up Windows to Use the Network Drivers

After the DOS network drivers are in place, you must tell Windows 3.1 which network drivers you're using. Start Windows, and follow these steps to install the Windows network drivers:

1. From the Main group, double-click the Windows Setup icon to open the Windows Setup window. From the Options menu choose Change System Settings to open the Change System Settings dialog.

2. In the Network list, select Microsoft Network (or 100% Compatible), as shown in figure 11.13. Click OK to continue.

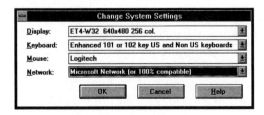

Fig. 11.13 Installing Microsoft Networking in Windows 3.1.

3. You're prompted for your original Windows 3.1 disk 2. Insert the diskette in the drive and press Enter. After the drivers are loaded, choose Restart Windows to make the changes effective.

Connecting to Windows NT File and Printer Resources

After installing the client network drivers and setting up Windows 3.1 for networking, you're ready to connect to Windows NT Server 4.0 resources. To connect a Windows 3.1 client to a Windows NT server, follow these steps:

1. Open File Manager.

2. From the Disk menu choose Network Connections to open the Network Connections dialog.

3. Using the standard Universal Naming Convention (UNC) notation, *SERVERNAME**SHARENAME*, type the network path to a Windows NT server share. In the Drive drop-down list, select the drive letter to which you want to map the share (see fig. 11.14).

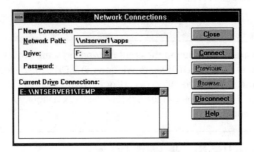

Fig. 11.14   Setting the path to a Windows NT server share.

4. Click Connect to map the server share to the selected drive letter. The next time you open the Network Connections dialog, your mapped drive appears in the Current Drive Connections list.

You connect to printers shared by Windows NT servers by following these steps:

1. Open Print Manager from the Main program group.

2. From the Options menu choose Network Connections to open the Printers–Network Connections dialog.

3. Type the network path of the server and printer share to which you want to connect. Select a local LPT port (LPT1 if you don't have a local printer) to redirect to the shared printer, as shown in figure 11.15. Leave the Password text box empty, unless you want to restrict access to the printer. (Some organizations restrict access to color laser printers because of the high cost per page.)

4. Click the Connect button to connect to the Windows NT server's printer queue.

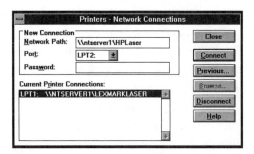

Fig. 11.15 Connecting to a printer shared by a Windows NT server.

Note

Unlike Windows NT clients, which download the required printer driver from the server, you must install the appropriate printer driver for your networked printer on the local workstation. In most cases, you need either the Windows 3.1+ installation diskettes or a Windows 3.1+ printer driver from the printer supplier to make the shared printer operable from the client.

If you have problems connecting to your Windows NT server's resources, following are a number of potential areas for troubleshooting:

■ If you're using NetBEUI as your network protocol, make sure that your Windows NT server is on the same physical network segment as your client, or at least bridged to your client segment. Also make sure that your server is running the network protocol that you've installed on your client.

■ When your client boots, make sure that you provide the correct password and receive confirmation of your connection to the Windows NT domain. The Command Completed Successfully message appears if all is well.

■ If you receive an Access Denied message when trying to connect to a Windows NT server resource, make sure that the network administrator for the server has given your Windows 3.1 client user account appropriate permissions to the resource.

Connecting Windows for Workgroups 3.11 Clients

Windows for Workgroups 3.11 offers greatly improved networking connectivity compared with Windows 3.1. Because the network drivers for WfWg are Windows-based, you can install multiple network drivers, and the NetWare and NetBEUI drivers don't consume conventional (DOS) memory. The TCP/IP stack for WfWg 3.1+ includes TSR drivers that run in conventional memory. WfWg 3.11 includes the TCP/IP protocol stack, which Microsoft developed after the release of the original 3.1 version of WfWg.

The following sections describe how to install the TCP/IP network drivers from the Windows NT Server 4.0 CD-ROM on a WfWg client PC, how to upgrade existing networking files, and how to connect to a Windows NT 4.0 server using the TCP/IP protocol.

Installing the 32-bit TCP/IP Network Protocol

Installing or updating the TCP/IP protocol for WfWg 3.1+ requires one high-density diskette and the Windows NT Server 4.0 CD-ROM. You'll also likely need the distribution diskettes for the version of WfWg 3.1+ installed on the client and, if not supported by WfWg 3.1+, a network adapter driver diskette.

To create the required installation diskette, install the TCP/IP protocol on clients running WfWg 3.1+, and update your WfWg configuration to allow connectivity to Windows NT Server resources, follow these steps:

1. Follow steps 1 through 4 of the procedure for creating network setup diskettes described earlier in the section "Creating Client Installation Diskettes." Only one of the two diskettes is required for installation of TCP/IP. In step 4, select TCP/IP 32 for Windows for Workgroups 3.11, rather than Network Client v3.0 for MS-DOS and Windows.

2. Create \WIN and \SYSTEM directories on the second diskette. By using Explorer, copy NET.EXE and NET.MSG from the \Clients\update.WfW folder of the CD-ROM to the \WIN directory of the diskette. Copy all the remaining files in \Clients\update.WfW to the \SYSTEM directory. The second diskette is used to update the WfWg network files after you set up the TCP/IP protocol.

3. Start WfWg 3.1+ and, from the Network program group, click Network Setup to open the Network Setup dialog.

4. Click Networks to open the Networks dialog, select the Install Microsoft Windows Network option (see fig. 11.16), and then click OK to close the Networks dialog and return to the Network Setup dialog.

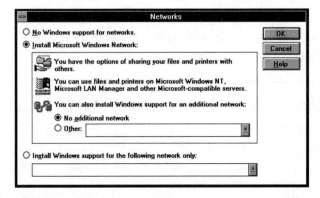

Fig. 11.16   Installing network drivers for a WfWg client with no network installed.

5. Click Drivers in the Network Setup dialog to open the Network Drivers dialog. Click Add Adapter to open the Add Network Adapter dialog, and select the adapter driver installed in the client PC (see fig. 11.17). Click OK to close the Add Network Adapter dialog and return to the Network Drivers dialog.

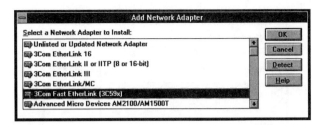

Fig. 11.17   Selecting the client PC's network adapter card.

6. Click Add Protocol in the Network Drivers dialog to open the Add Network Protocol dialog. Select Add Protocol, and double-click Unlisted or Updated Protocol to install the updated version of TCP/IP from the diskette (see fig. 11.18).

> **Note**
>
> Although WfWg 3.11 has TCP/IP, NWLink, and NetBEUI, it's a good idea to load the latest driver versions.

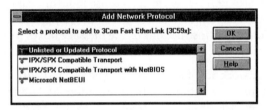

Fig. 11.18   Selecting installation of the client PC's network protocol from a diskette.

7. At the prompt, insert the diskette with the network protocol update and click OK. A message box confirms that you're installing Microsoft TCP/IP-32 3.11b. Click OK to install the protocol files on the client's drive and then return to the Network Drivers dialog.

8. By default, NetBEUI and NWLink are installed by WfWg 3.1+. You can remove these protocols by selecting the unneeded protocol in the Network Drivers list of the Network Drivers dialog and then clicking Remove. After you're done configuring the adapter drivers, click Close to close the Network Drivers dialog, and then click OK in the Network Setup dialog to end the network setup operation and open the Microsoft Windows Network dialog.

9. You're prompted to provide your computer name, workgroup name, and default logon name (see fig. 11.19). For authentication by your Windows NT server, the default logon name is the user name of your server account. The workgroup name is *not* the name of the Windows NT domain to which you connect, and it shouldn't duplicate the name of any domain on the network.

II

Deploying Windows NT

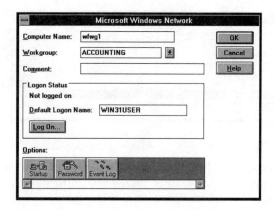

Fig. 11.19 Providing the user name, workgroup name, and computer name.

10. After entering user and machine information, you might be asked to supply your network adapter driver diskette(s) and/or some of your original WfWg diskettes. In some cases, you may have trouble finding the correct driver files on your network adapter driver diskette. Look for a directory such as \NDIS or \WFW, which contains an OEMSETUP.INF file. On the PC used for this example, which has a 3Com Etherlink III adapter, the correct driver files happened to be located in \NDIS\WFW. Follow the instructions of the message boxes to add or update the network adapter driver(s).

11. After updating network adapter drivers, the Microsoft TCP/IP Configuration dialog prompts you to enter in the TCP/IP information, including IP address, default gateway, and other TCP/IP-specific parameters (see fig. 11.20). Although the appearance of the TCP/IP Properties sheet of Windows 95 varies from the TCP/IP Configuration dialog of WfWg 3.1+, you specify the same values for TCP/IP parameters in both environments.

◄◄ See "Configuring TCP/IP," p. 351

12. After completing the TCP/IP configuration, click OK to exit the network setup operation, and then exit to DOS.

13. Insert the second diskette with the \WIN and \SYSTEM directories. Locate the client's existing NET.EXE and NET.MSG files (usually in c:\windows) and overwrite the existing versions with the copies in the diskette's \WIN directory. Next, copy the .DLL and .386 files in the diskette's \SYSTEM directory to the \WINDOWS\ SYSTEM subdirectory, also overwriting the existing versions.

14. Restart WfWg to load the updated network applications and drivers.

When WfWg starts, you're prompted for the user name that you specified in step 9 and for a password. Enter the password to be used for the Windows NT server account. The first time you log on after setting up networking, a message box asks whether you want to create a password file. As with the MS Network Client for DOS, the .PWL file is created locally and contains an encrypted version of the password. The .PWL file is used for Windows NT domain account authentication during the logon process.

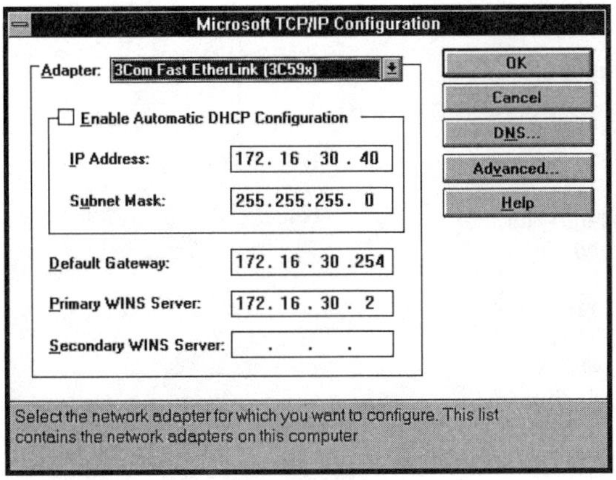

Fig. 11.20   TCP/IP Configuration options in WfWg.

Viewing Changes Made to WfWg 3.1+ Configuration and Initialization Files

The Setup program adds the following line to the client's CONFIG.SYS file:

```
Device=c:\windows\ifshelp.sys
```

where c:\windows is the directory containing the WfWg system files.

The client's AUTOEXEC.BAT file is modified to include the following additional instruction:

```
c:\windows\net start
```

The Microsoft Network Client for DOS/Windows 3.1 stores network protocol information in the PROTOCOL.INI and SYSTEM.INI files, located in the c:\net subdirectory. Most of the network driver components in WfWg load when you start WfWg, so the preceding network installation process puts all of its changes into the SYSTEM.INI file in the WfWg system subdirectory, usually c:\windows\system.

The following additions are made to SYSTEM.INI as part of the network installation:

```
[boot]
network.drv=wfwnet.drv
[boot.description]
network.drv=Microsoft Windows Network (version 3.11)
secondnet.drv=No Additional Network Installed
[386Enh]
network=*vnetbios,*vwc,vnetsup.386,vredir.386,vserver.386
[Network]
FileSharing=No
PrintSharing=No
winnet=wfwnet/00025100
multinet=nonet
LogonDisconnected=Yes
EnableSharing=no
```

Deploying Windows NT

II

```
UserName=WIN31USER
Workgroup=ACCOUNTING
ComputerName=wfw1
Comment=wfw workstation
logonvalidated=yes
reconnect=yes
LogonDomain=NEWDOMNT
AutoLogon=Yes
StartMessaging=Yes
LoadNetDDE=Yes
LMLogon=1
DomainLogonMessage=Yes
cachethispassword=yes
[tcm$el59x0]
NameServer1=172.16.30.2
DefaultGateway=172.16.30.254
IPMask=255.255.255.0
IPAddress=172.16.30.40
Description=3Com Fast EtherLink (3C59x)
Binding=tcm$el59x

[MSTCP]
EnableRouting=0
Interfaces=tcm$el59x0
deadgwdetect=1
pmtudiscovery=1

[DNS]
DNSServers=
HostName=wfw1
DomainName=
DNSDomains=

[NBT]
NameServer1=172.16.30.2
LANABASE=0
EnableProxy=0
EnableDNS=0

[Password Lists]
*Shares=C:\WINDOWS\Share000.PWL
WIN31USER=C:\WINDOWS\WIN31USE.PWL
[network drivers]
devdir=C:\WINDOWS
LoadRMDrivers=No
netcard=el59x.dos
transport=ndishlp.sys
```

All protocol configuration information, including this client's TCP/IP configuration information, is kept in the SYSTEM.INI file, rather than the PROTOCOL.INI file used by DOS/Windows 3.1+-based clients. You can use a text editor, such as Notepad or SysEdit, to change your network settings for WfWg in the SYSTEM.INI file. Be sure to restart WfWg after you make changes to SYSTEM.INI.

Logging On and Connecting to Windows NT Server 4.0 Resources

To access Windows NT Server resources, you must set up the domain logon process for the client. Follow these steps:

1. From WfWg's Control Panel, double-click the Network icon to open the Microsoft Windows Network dialog.

2. Click the Startup button to open the Startup Settings dialog. Accept the default settings in the Startup Options group, making sure that the Log On at Startup check box is marked.

3. Mark the Log On to Windows NT or LAN Manager Domain check box and type the name of your Windows NT server domain in the Domain Name text box (see fig. 11.21). Click OK twice to close the Start Up Settings dialog and exit the Microsoft Windows Network dialog.

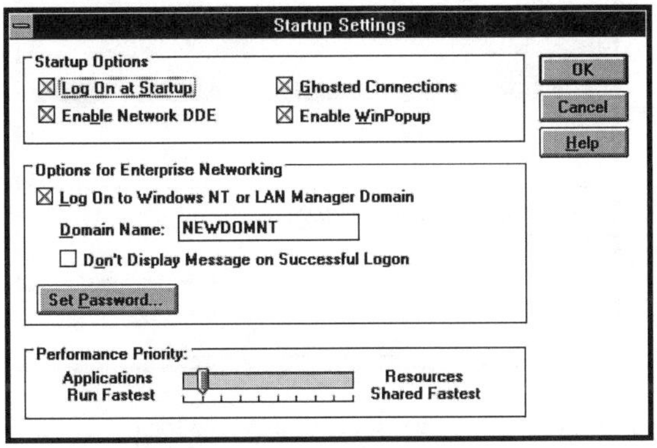

Fig. 11.21 Setting domain logon options in the Startup Settings dialog.

4. Exit and restart WfWg. On startup, the Welcome to Windows for Workgroups dialog appears, requesting entry of the user name for this client and that user's password.

5. You're prompted for a domain logon. If you use the same user name for the domain as for the workgroup, enter the same password as for the workgroup. Make sure that the Create Password File check box is marked.

Note

The next time you start WfWg, you log on to the workgroup. If the domain user name and password are the same as that for the workgroup, you log on to the Windows NT domain without the additional prompt.

Tip

If you don't want to see the workgroup logon prompt at startup, delete the workgroup user name password so that the logon process skips the workgroup logon dialog and proceeds directly to the domain logon.

After you log on to the domain, a logon script you've defined for the client's domain user name on Windows NT Server is processed by the WfWg client. You need to create a logon script for WfWg clients only if you want to automate additional logon operations.

II

Deploying Windows NT

After the WfWg client is authenticated by the Windows NT Server domain, it's easy to share the Windows NT server's resources. To share files, start File Manager on the client. From the Disk menu choose Connect Network Drive to open the Connect Network Drive dialog. Browse network shares to find the share that you want to connect to, and then double-click the entry to map the drive to the selected drive letter (see fig. 11.22).

Fig. 11.22   Mapping a Windows NT Server share to a WfWg logical drive.

To connect to printer resources, open Print Manager from the Main program group. From the Printer menu choose Connect Network Printer; from the Connect Network Printer dialog, select the Windows NT server that shares a printer; and double-click the share name of the printer you want to use (see fig. 11.23).

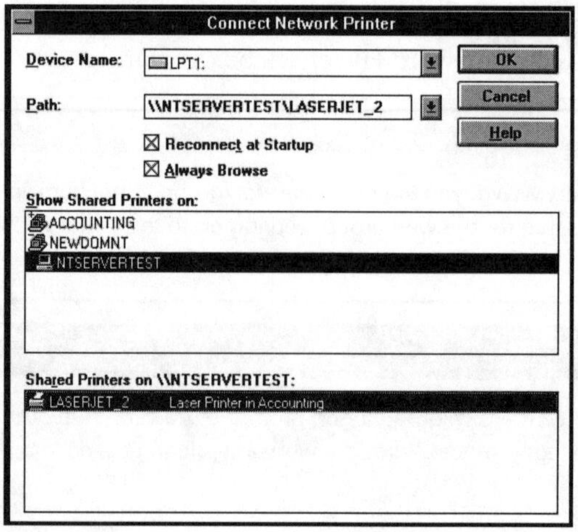

Fig. 11.23   Using a printer shared by a Windows NT server.

If you have problems connecting to your Windows NT server resources, following are a number of potential areas for troubleshooting:

- If your client is having trouble connecting to Windows NT Server, you may see a Network Name Not Found message. This message means that your client can't find the Windows NT server to which you're trying to connect. If you're using the TCP/IP stack and trying to access Windows NT Server resources in a routed network environment, make sure that you've specified a WINS server address in the client's TCP/IP Configuration dialog.

- If you can't browse Windows NT network resources with File Manager or Print Manager, make sure that you've installed the most recent network drivers available from Microsoft. (You can obtain updated drivers from Microsoft's Web site, **http://www.microsoft.com**.) Older versions of the network drivers for WfWg cause browsing problems.

Connecting Windows NT Workstation 4.0 Clients

Connecting Windows NT Workstation 4.0 clients to a Windows NT 4.0 server is similar to the process for connecting Windows 95 clients, which is described in Chapter 10, "Configuring Windows 95 Clients for Networking." Connecting a Windows NT workstation to a Windows NT server involves setting up the client's network adapter and protocol(s), and then using Windows NT Workstation 4.0's built-in tools to connect to the server's shared folders and printers. The differences between connecting clients running Windows NT Workstation 3.51 and 4.0 to a Windows NT 4.0 server primarily involve changes to the user interface. The following sections describe how to connect a Windows NT Workstation 4.0 client to a Windows NT Server 4.0 domain.

Installing the Network Software

On a Windows NT workstation, you first need to choose the network protocol you want to use, and then install it. You must choose a protocol based on what the server is running. TCP/IP is the preferred protocol for Windows NT 4.0 networks, so the following steps describe how to install and configure TCP/IP on a client running Windows NT Workstation 4.0:

1. From the Start menu choose Settings and Control Panel, and then double-click the Network tool to open the Network properties sheet.

2. Click the Protocols tab to display the Protocols properties page; then click Add to open the Select Network Protocol dialog.

3. Select the TCP/IP Protocol item and click OK (see fig. 11.24).

4. A TCP/IP Setup dialog appears, asking whether you want to configure your client's TCP/IP stack for use with DHCP. If you plan to use DHCP, click Yes.

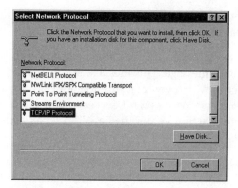

Fig. 11.24 Adding the TCP/IP protocol in Windows NT Workstation 4.0 .

5. A Windows NT Setup dialog appears, prompting you to enter the location of the Windows NT Workstation distribution files. These files are located on the Windows NT Workstation CD-ROM. For example, if your CD-ROM drive is F: and your Windows NT client uses a Pentium processor, you type **F:\i386** and click Continue.

6. Windows NT Setup copies the TCP/IP files to your client. When the copy operation is complete, click Close.

7. Windows NT then proceeds to bind the new protocol to your client's network adapter. When the binding process completes, the Microsoft TCP/IP Properties sheet appears (see fig. 11.25). The IP Address page displays by default, and gives you the opportunity to enter the IP address, subnet mask, and default gateway for the client. Click the Advanced button to enter additional IP addresses or default gateways for the client's network adapter.

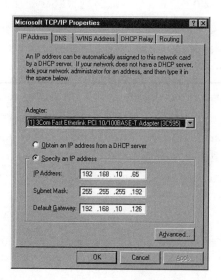

Fig. 11.25 Setting Windows NT 4.0 TCP/IP configuration options.

> **Note**
>
> If you want to access a Windows NT server on a different network segment from your Windows NT 4.0 workstation, you need to enter a default gateway and then enter either a WINS server address or create an LMHosts file. You can install the WINS configuration and LMHosts file on your Windows NT client by selecting the WINS Address tab of the Microsoft TCP/IP Properties sheet.

8. After you enter all the TCP/IP configuration information, click OK. Windows NT prompts you to restart the system for the changes to take effect. After the system restarts, you must decide whether you want to install the client into the Windows NT domain, or whether to make it a member of a workgroup.

> **Note**
>
> Domain client users can log on to Windows NT servers in their domain and seamlessly authenticate by a single logon to all resources for which they have permission. Workgroup users log on to their local machines, just as in Windows for Workgroups, and then authenticate explicitly to the needed Windows NT Domain resources. If you want the clients to take advantage of all of Windows NT's features (including centralized security and logon scripts), install Windows NT 4.0 clients into the domain. The next two steps describe this process.

9. To install the workstation into the domain, start Control Panel's Network tool as described in step 1. On the Network property sheet, select the Identification tab. On the Identification page, you see your client's current machine name and the name of the workgroup to which your client belongs.

10. Click the Change button to open the Identification Changes dialog and enter the new domain name you want to join (see fig. 11.26).

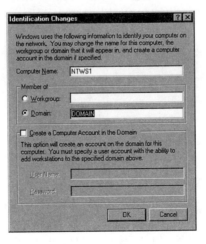

Fig. 11.26 Joining the Windows NT Server domain in Windows NT Workstation 4.0.

11. You need to create for the client a *machine account*, which uniquely identifies your machine to the domain. To do so, you must have Administrator access to the domain. If you're a member of the Domain Administrators group, select the Create a Computer Account option in the Domain check box, and then enter your administrator name and password. Then click OK to join the domain. You see a message welcoming you to the domain if the join succeeded.

> **Note**
>
> If you aren't a member of the Domain Administrators group, a network administrator must create a machine account for the client with the Server Manager utility. The account must exist before you can log on to the domain, and is in addition to the user account in the domain. The process for joining the domain is the same as in step 11, except that you don't need to enter an administrative account name at the time you join the domain.

12. After you join the domain, you're asked to restart the workstation to have the changes take effect. The next time the Windows NT logon prompt appears, the Domain text box shows the domain you belong to, plus your workstation name. To log on to the domain, make sure that the domain name appears when you enter your user name and password. If the domain name is missing, type the name in the Domain text box.

Attaching to Domain Resources

After you log on to the domain, you connect to Windows NT Server resources by the same process as Windows 95 or WfWg. Connecting to Windows NT Server 4.0 file and print shares from Windows NT Workstation 4.0 involves the following steps:

1. From the Start menu, choose Programs and Windows NT Explorer to launch Explorer. Double-click the Network Neighborhood icon to display the available servers and their network resources (see fig. 11.27). When you open Network Neighborhood, Explorer displays all the computers in your network domain.

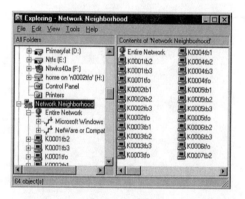

Fig. 11.27   Windows NT Explorer displaying computers on the network.

2. Select the name of the server with the share to which you want to connect. The shares for the server appear in Explorer's right pane. Figure 11.28 shows the shared Export, NETLOGON, profiles, and Printers folders of the N0001tfo server share.

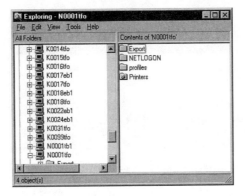

Fig. 11.28 Windows NT Explorer displaying server shares in the left pane and share subfolders in the right pane.

3. From the Tools menu choose Map Network Drive, or click the Map Network Drive button on the toolbar to open the Map Network Drive dialog (see fig. 11.29).

Fig. 11.29 Mapping a server file share to a Windows NT Workstation 4.0 logical drive.

4. If you can't connect to the share with your current user name, type the required user name in the Connect As text box. Mark the Reconnect at Logon check box if you want this share connection to be automatically re-established the next time you log on. Click OK to make the connection.

5. To make a connection to a printer share, from the Start menu choose Settings and Printers to open the Printers window. Double-click the Add Printer icon to start the Add Printer Wizard. Click the Network Printer Server option and then click the Next button to display the Connect to Printer dialog (see fig. 11.30).

6. Browse the available printer resources, and double-click the printer share you want to use. Then click Finish to end the Add Printer Wizard.

If you've followed the steps in this section and are still having difficulty connecting your Windows NT 4.0 workstation to Windows NT Server 4.0, the following troubleshooting tips are likely to help you make the connection:

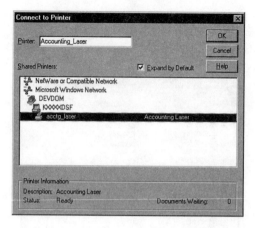

Fig. 11.30   Connecting to printers from Windows NT Workstation 4.0.

■ If you're trying to connect to Windows NT Server shares from Explorer and you receive a The Network Path wasn't found message, you have a name resolution problem. If you're using the TCP/IP network protocol, make sure that you have an LMHosts or WINS entry for your Windows NT server in your client's TCP/IP Configuration dialog. You can verify that name resolution isn't the problem by issuing the following command from the Start menu's Run command line: net view\\ servername. This command tells you, regardless of network protocol, whether your client can find the server on the network.

■ If you receive access-denied messages to a share or printer resource, make sure that you have the correct permissions to access those resources or files. Windows NT allows user permissions to be placed on shares and printers, as well as files on an NTFS partition. You must have explicit rights, granted by the network administrator, to use the resources.

Connecting Macintosh Clients

Windows NT Server 4.0 includes the Services for Macintosh (SfM), which allow users of Apple Macintosh computers running System 6.0.7 or higher to use folders and printers shared by Windows NT domains. File services for Macintosh, which let Mac users store and retrieve files on the Windows NT server, are provided only from partitions formatted as NTFS.

The following sections describe how to install SfM on a Windows NT 4.0 server and how to use SfM with Macintosh clients.

Adding Services for Macintosh on Windows NT Server

Following are the steps for installing Services for Macintosh on a Windows NT 4.0 server:

1. Insert the Windows NT Server 4.0 CD-ROM in the server's CD-ROM drive.

2. From the Start menu, open the Control Panel.

3. Double-click the Network tool to open the Network property sheet, and then click the Services tab.

4. On the Services page of the Network property sheet, click the Add button to display the Select Network Service dialog. In the Network Server list, scroll to and select the Services for Macintosh item (see fig. 11.31). Click OK to close the dialog and open the Windows NT Setup dialog.

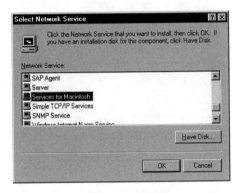

Fig. 11.31 Starting installation of Services for Macintosh.

5. Type the path to the installation files for your processor type on the CD-ROM in the text box of the Windows NT Setup dialog. For Intel-based servers, the location is *d:*\i386, where *d:* is the CD-ROM drive letter. Click Continue to copy the files.

6. After copying is complete, click the Close button of the Network property sheet. Windows NT starts the AppleTalk network protocol and opens the Microsoft AppleTalk Protocol Properties sheet (see fig. 11.32). The default adapter displays the network adapter in your server to which AppleTalk is bound. If you have Macintosh clients connected to the specified network adapter, Windows NT finds and uses the default AppleTalk zone. If not, follow the directions in step 7 to install the Windows NT Server as a seed router, and provide the router with your zone information.

7. Selecting the Routing properties page lets you enable AppleTalk routing (see fig. 11.33). You must enable routing if you have multiple network adapters in your server, each of which is running AppleTalk for individual network segments; there's no other seed router for that segment; and you want to enable AppleTalk communication between the segments.

   For each network interface that appears in the Adapter drop-down list, you choose the AppleTalk Phase 2 network number and the default zone. Mark the Use This Router to Seed the Network check box to enable AppleTalk route seeding. Usually, there's one seed router per AppleTalk segment, and all other AppleTalk routers listen for the seed; the seed tells that segment what AppleTalk Phase 2 network address and zone to use.

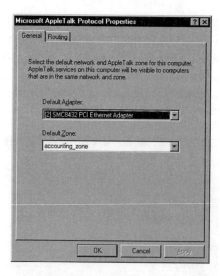

Fig. 11.32 The General page of the Microsoft AppleTalk Protocol Properties sheet.

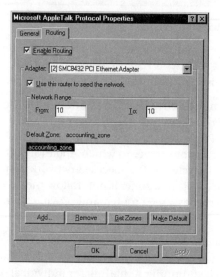

Fig. 11.33 The Routing page of the Microsoft AppleTalk Protocol Properties sheet.

8. After you complete configuration of AppleTalk network options and click OK, you're prompted to restart your system. Click Yes to shut down and restart.

9. After the server starts up, two new services—File Server for Macintosh and Print Server for Macintosh—are installed. You can verify installation of these services by using the Control Panel's Services tool.

> **Note**
>
> AppleTalk Phase 2 network addresses are expressed as a range, such as 10–12. Each number in the range supports up to 253 nodes, so a range of 10–12 supports 3×253, or 759 AppleTalk clients. Range values must be unique and can't overlap. Accepted range values are 1 to 62579.
>
> When you assign a range, choose the minimum number of networks you need. If a given segment has only 10 Mac clients, for example, choose a network range of 20–20, which supports up to 253 clients on a single segment.

Setting Up Macintosh Clients

Clients must run Macintosh System 6.0.7 or higher to access Windows NT Server resources. You don't need to install special software for basic file and printer sharing on the Windows NT network.

From the Macintosh client's Chooser, select AppleShare; any Windows NT server running Services for Macintosh (SfM) and containing a Mac-accessible volume appears (see fig. 11.34). Click OK and provide a user name and password, which is passed to the Windows NT Server domain account database for authentication. When authenticated, the client can access available volumes based on the user's permissions.

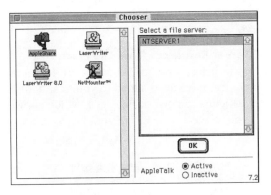

Fig. 11.34 Viewing available Windows NT servers running SfM from the Macintosh Chooser.

When you log on to the Windows NT server running SfM from a Macintosh client, the Apple User Authentication Module (UAM) handles network security. Microsoft provides a UAM that supports Windows NT 4.0 authentication and encryption. The Microsoft UAM provides greater security and recognizes the Windows NT domain name as a preface to the user logon name (for example, *ntdomain*\joesmith instead of joesmith). This allows a Macintosh client to connect to Windows NT servers that are running SfM and exist in multiple Windows NT domains. Figure 11.35 shows an example of a Macintosh installed with the Microsoft UAM.

The Microsoft UAM is installed on your Windows NT server drive when you install the Services for Macintosh. By default, SfM creates a Macintosh-accessible folder in your system partition named *d:*\Microsoft UAM Volume, and a subfolder named AppleShare Folder. Follow these steps to install the Microsoft UAM on your Macintosh clients:

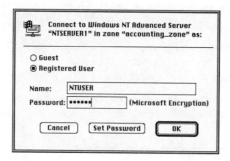

Fig. 11.35 The logon screen of a Macintosh with the Microsoft UAM installed.

1. From the Macintosh Chooser, select AppleShare. When the Windows NT server running SfM appears, log on using the default Apple UAM by providing an existing domain user name.

2. Mount the Windows NT Server's Microsoft UAM Volume on the Macintosh client. Open the volume's folder to display the AppleShare folder. Open the AppleShare folder, and drag the Microsoft UAM file from the Windows NT Server volume to the AppleShare folder on your Macintosh's System Folder. If you don't find an AppleShare folder within the System Folder, drag the whole AppleShare folder from the Windows NT Server to the System Folder. Restart the Macintosh client for the changes to take effect.

Accessing Windows NT Server Resources from the Macintosh

After installing Services for Macintosh on your Windows NT 4.0 server, a number of new services, tools, and menu choices have been added to your standard Windows NT utilities. For example, Control Panel has a new MacFile tool, which allows you to view and control the use of SfM on your server. The MacFile tool has four buttons: Users, Volumes, Files, and Attributes (see fig. 11.36).

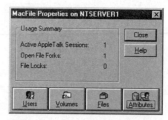

Fig. 11.36 The opening dialog of Control Panel's MacFile tool.

The following list describes the purpose of the buttons:

■ *Users* displays the Macintosh Users on *SERVERNAME* dialog, which lets you view the Macintosh clients connected to a server, disconnect them, or send them a message (see fig. 11.37).

■ *Volumes* opens the Macintosh-Accessible Volumes on *SERVERNAME* dialog, which lets you view the current Mac-accessible volumes defined on your server and which clients are connected to the volumes (see fig. 11.38).

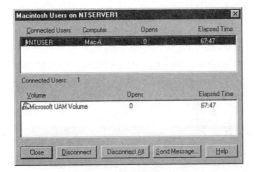

Fig. 11.37 The Macintosh Users on *SERVERNAME* dialog of the MacFile tool.

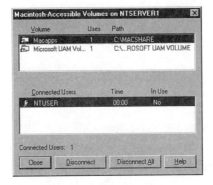

Fig. 11.38 The Macintosh-Accessible Volumes on *SERVERNAME* dialog.

- *Files* displays the Files Opened by Macintosh Users dialog, showing you which files are open on your server, by whom, and whether the files are locked.

- *Attributes* opens the MacFile Attributes of *SERVERNAME* dialog, which lets you control parameters of SfM, such as whether the Macintosh clients see a logon message, whether the clients are required to use Microsoft Authentication, and how many sessions a particular user can run (see fig. 11.39).

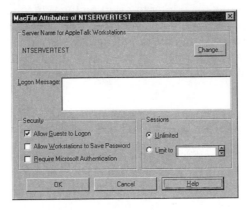

Fig. 11.39 The MacFile Attributes of *SERVERNAME* dialog.

After loading SfM, Server Manager now contains a new MacFile menu choice (see fig. 11.40). From the MacFile menu, you can create new Macintosh-accessible volumes, set permissions, and assign associations. Associations for the Macintosh are similar to File Manager associations in Windows; for instance, .DOC files are associated with the Microsoft Word application. You provide a similar association for Macintosh files stored on your Windows NT server.

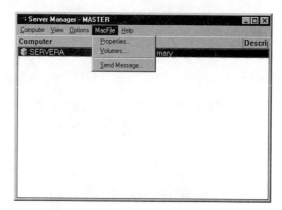

Fig. 11.40   Server Manager's MacFile menu commands.

Macintosh files have two "forks"—the *data fork* contains the data part of the file, and the *resource fork* contains information about the associated application and the application's icon. To set up Macintosh associations, you must start the familiar File Manager. From the Start menu, choose Run and type the command **winfile**. Next, choose <u>A</u>ssociate from the MacF<u>i</u>le menu to associate resource fork information with Windows NT file extensions, so that files with extensions have the proper appearance and application association when viewed on the Macintosh client.

To provide printing services to your Mac users, you have two options: connecting a printer to the Windows NT server's parallel or serial port, or connecting an AppleTalk-compliant printer directly to your network.

In the first case (connecting the printer to a port on the Windows NT server running SfM), you can use any type of printer. The Print Service for Macintosh converts incoming Macintosh client PostScript jobs to the print language supported by the printer. The Macintosh clients connect to the network printer through the Chooser, as is the case for all Macintosh printing operations. Both Macintosh and PC clients share the same printer(s).

The second case requires an AppleTalk-based, network-attached printer. Such printers are connected to the network via LocalTalk, Ethernet, or Token Ring connections.

Windows NT Server's SfM provides support for networked AppleTalk printers. Normally, Macintosh clients printing to network-attached Macintosh printers spool the print job on a local Macintosh print spooler, which runs on the client. If you must support printing to networked AppleTalk printers on Windows NT Server 4.0, you must disable print spooling on the Macintosh client.

Caution

Make sure that you disable spooling on the Macintosh client by running Chooser, selecting the LaserWriter or appropriate printer driver, and turning off background printing. If you don't disable background printing—and more than one client is accessing the Windows NT Server-based AppleTalk printer—print jobs spooled locally will conflict with those spooling on the server. The result will be chaos at the printer.

Note

LocalTalk is the native MAC-Layer protocol that came standard for many years on the early Macintoshes. You can get ISA bus-based LocalTalk cards for your Intel-based Windows NT server if you need to connect clients using LocalTalk to your server running SfM. As an example, Daystar Digital makes a LocalTalk adapter that's compatible with a Windows NT server. Check the Windows NT 4.0 Hardware Compatibility List for other supported LocalTalk cards.

After you disable background printing, your Macintosh clients share the Windows NT server's print queue with PC clients. To set up a Windows NT Server 4.0 print queue for an AppleTalk printer, follow these steps:

1. From the Start menu, choose Settings and Printers to bring up the Printers window (see fig. 11.41).

Fig. 11.41   Adding a new AppleTalk printer from the Printers window.

2. Double-click the Add Printer icon to start the Add Printer Wizard; select the My Computer button; and click Next.

3. In the next Add Printer Wizard dialog, you see a list of printer ports to use (see fig. 11.42). If you're adding a printer that's connected to your Windows NT server via a parallel or serial port, mark the check box next to the appropriate port, click Next, and skip to step 5.

4. If you're adding a network-attached AppleTalk printer, click Add Port to open the Printer Ports dialog. Highlight AppleTalk Printing Devices and click OK. The Available AppleTalk Printing Devices dialog appears (see fig. 11.43), listing all AppleTalk zones available on your Widows NT server. Select the AppleTalk printer you want to use by double-clicking the zone and the printer name; then click OK to close the dialog.

II

Deploying Windows NT

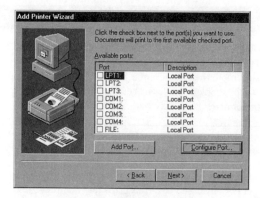

Fig. 11.42   Selecting a printer port from the Add Printer Wizard.

Fig. 11.43   Selecting a network-attached AppleTalk printer.

   5. The next Add Printer Wizard dialog (see fig. 11.44) prompts you to specify the make and model of printer you're creating and click Next.

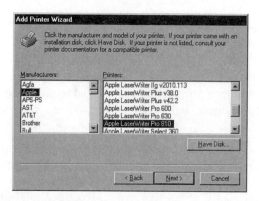

Fig. 11.44   Specifying the make and model of your AppleTalk printer.

6. The next Add Printer Wizard dialog asks you to enter the printer name. This should be a descriptive name that your users will see when they browse printer resources (for example, *8th floor LaserWriter*). Click Next after entering a name.

7. The next dialog lets you set up the printer to be shared by Microsoft Windows clients as well as Macintosh. Unless you plan on supporting these Windows clients on this printer, select the Not Shared button and then click Next.

8. The final dialog asks whether you want to print a test page after the printer is set up. Choose Yes or No and click Finish.

9. The Copying Files – Files Needed dialog appears next, prompting you for the path to the Windows NT Server CD-ROM. On Intel-based systems, enter *d:\i386*, where *d:* is the CD-ROM drive letter.

10. After the appropriate printer drivers have been copied from the CD-ROM, the properties sheet appears for your new printer (see fig. 11.45). Here is where you can add comments, change configuration, set security on the printer, or modify the printer scheduling properties. Click OK to complete the printer's configuration.

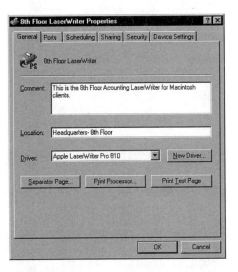

Fig. 11.45 Displaying the Macintosh printer's properties sheet.

11. The Print Server for Macintosh service is installed with the System account as the Startup user name. If you print to a network printer, you need to change the System account to a domain account that has network access. From the User Manager for Domains utility, create a new user account for use with the Print Server for Macintosh service (you might call the account MacPrintUser).

▶▶ See "Managing User Accounts," p. 421

12. Use the newly created account to assign permissions to your network-attached AppleTalk printer(s). From the Start menu, choose Settings and then Printers; then highlight your AppleTalk printer in the Printers window. Then choose Properties from the File menu, click the Security tab, and then click the Permissions button to assign your new user account access to this printer through the Printer Permissions dialog (see fig. 11.46).

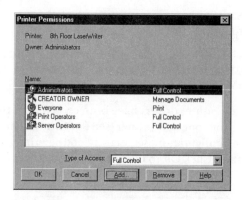

Fig. 11.46   Adding user permissions to the AppleTalk printer.

13. From the Printer Permissions dialog, click the Add button; from the Add Users and Groups dialog, click Show Users, and then scroll to your new user account defined in step 11. Assign the user Full Control rights to the printer in the Type of Access pull-down list (see fig. 11.47). Click OK three times to eventually close the property sheet.

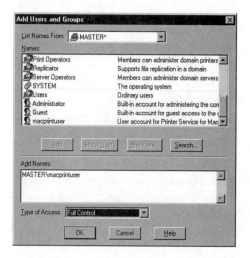

Fig. 11.47   Assigning user MacPrintUser Full Control rights to the printer.

14. You need to assign the new user account to the Print Server for Macintosh Service. From the Start menu, choose Settings and Control Panel, and then double-click the Services tool. In the Services dialog, scroll to Print Server for Macintosh, click Startup, click the This Account option, and then type the user account name you created in the preceding step in the This Account text box. Enter and confirm the password for the account (see fig. 11.48), and then click OK to complete the change.

Fig. 11.48 Modifying the account for the Print Server for Macintosh service.

If you've installed Macintosh support on a Novell NetWare server, you're certain to find that Windows NT Server's SfM is much easier and more intuitive than Novell's approach. If you follow the steps described in this section, you can quickly and painlessly add file and print service for your Macintosh clients. If you do have problems after SfM is installed, however, here's a list of common problems you might encounter, and their possible solutions:

- Perhaps the most common area of confusion is AppleTalk network numbering and zones. If your Windows NT server isn't the only AppleTalk router on a given segment, make sure that the network configurations you apply to the Windows NT Server adapter corresponds with those already defined on your AppleTalk router. For example, if an Ethernet segment contains an AppleTalk router that's configured with AppleTalk network number 10–10 and a zone called Accounting, make sure that your Windows NT server's Ethernet adapter connected to that segment has the same network number and zone.

- Although it's an optional step, it's a good idea to install Microsoft's UAM that's provided with SfM on your Macintosh clients. If you're having problems authenticating from your Macintosh client to your Windows NT server, it's likely that installing the MS-UAM will provide a solution to the problem.

- If printer jobs from your Macintosh clients overwrite jobs from PC clients printing to the same printer, make sure that you've disabled Background Printing on all your Macintosh clients that are using the AppleTalk printers defined in Windows NT Server.

■ If print jobs get to the Windows NT spooler and stop there, ensure that you've set up the Print Server for Macintosh service with a Startup user account defined in your Windows NT domain. Also make sure that the user account has been granted permission to the printer (see steps 11 through 14 earlier in this section).

From Here...

This chapter discussed connecting a variety of client computers to a Windows NT Server 4.0 network. Windows 3.1+, which uses the DOS-based Microsoft Network Client that comes with Windows NT Server 4.0 to provide network access to Windows NT Server resources, is limited in networking capability and flexibility. Windows for Workgroups 3.11, which uses Windows-based drivers, provides more networking flexibility to the client, including support for logon scripts and integrated resource-sharing options. Clients running Windows NT Workstation 4.0 provide the greatest networking flexibility and robustness by better integrating with the Windows NT Server 4.0 network.

The chapter closed with a description of the support provided by Windows NT Server 4.0 for Macintosh file and print services, including the steps to install Services for Macintosh on Windows NT 4.0 servers. Also discussed were the configuration options for printer setup on a Windows NT 4.0 server, to allow both Mac and PC clients to use AppleTalk-based networked printers.

The following chapters contain information relating to or complementing the contents of this chapter:

■ Chapter 10, "Configuring Windows 95 Clients for Networking," describes how to specify the parameters required for clients that use the TCP/IP protocol to connect to Windows 4.0 servers.

■ Chapter 12, "Managing User and Group Accounts," describes how to optimize the structure of, and manage, client accounts on Windows NT 4.0 servers.

■ Chapter 17, "Integrating Windows NT with Heterogeneous Networks," discusses how to optimize the use of Windows NT Server 4.0 with Novell NetWare and UNIX networks, with emphasis on TCP/IP connectivity.

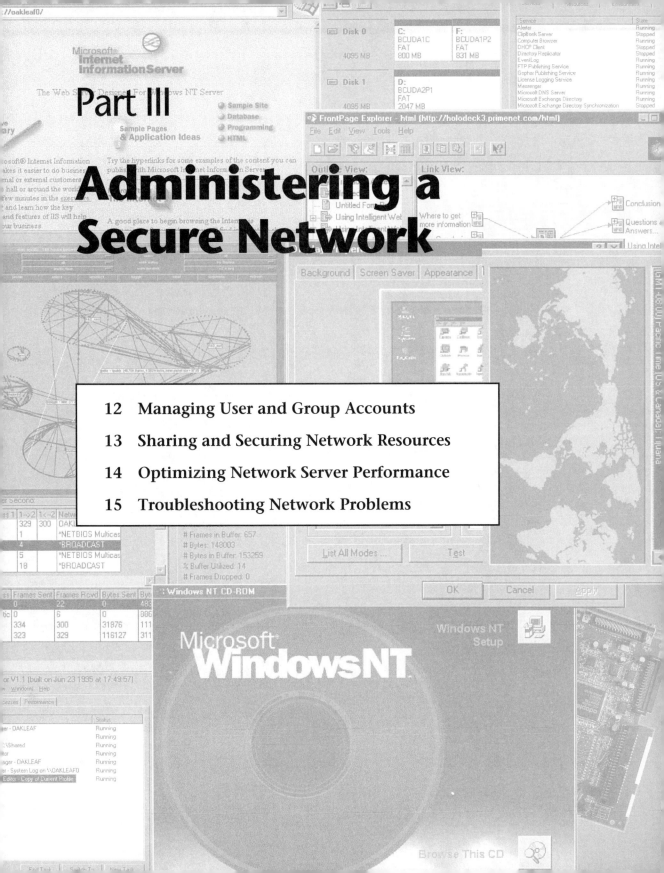

Part III

Administering a Secure Network

12 Managing User and Group Accounts

13 Sharing and Securing Network Resources

14 Optimizing Network Server Performance

15 Troubleshooting Network Problems

Chapter 12

Managing User and Group Accounts

The fundamental purpose of a network operating system (NOS) is to create a productive environment for users while maintaining a high level of security. This also is the primary goal of all network administrators.

Windows NT Server 4.0 qualifies as an advanced NOS because it not only provides file directory and print services to its users, but also functions as an application server for Microsoft BackOffice and other server-based applications that run as services on Windows NT. The advanced security features of Windows NT Server have the potential to make network administration a very complex and demanding occupation. Fortunately, Microsoft provides a powerful and flexible tool, User Manager for Domains, for managing the users of a Windows NT Server network. User Manager for Domains lets network administrators create and manage individual user accounts and user groups, and manage the security policies that affect the user accounts and groups.

Defining Account and Group Terminology

User accounts are the foundation on which network security is built; groups define collections of users. The following terms are basic to managing user and group accounts:

- A *user account* defines all the information necessary for the user to connect to the Windows NT network. The user account includes the user name and password required to log on to the network. An account also defines the user groups to which the user belongs and, most importantly, the rights and permissions to access system resources granted to the user. The user account contains additional information, such as the user environment profile, a list of logon workstations, and a schedule of logon hours.

- A *user group* is a management tool that collects user accounts into a named group. You assign rights and permissions to a user group in a manner similar to that for a user account. You can grant user accounts

This chapter explains how to

- Effectively add and administer user accounts on a Windows NT Server network

- Employ user groups to manage the rights and privileges for a large number of users

- Manage the security policies for user accounts and user groups

- Take advantage of Windows NT Server 4.0's default set of groups and user accounts

- Use Windows NT Server 4.0's Administrative Wizards for adding new users and user groups

III

Administering a Network

membership in a user group. When you grant a user account membership in a user group, the user account inherits all the rights and privileges of that user group. The overall concept of Windows NT's user groups is similar to the group security implemented by database management systems, such as Microsoft SQL Server and Microsoft Access.

■ A *domain* is a network concept that defines a collection of shared resources—such as file and application servers, printers, CD-ROM drives, modems, and other devices—that are centrally managed and advertised to potential users. Only users who've successfully logged on to the domain and been granted access to the resources by means of a set of permissions can use the resources. Individual domains usually are defined by geographic location (such as North America) or by function (such as accounting).

■ A *global group* is a collection of user accounts within a single domain. A global group can't contain other groups and can include only user accounts from the domain in which the group was created. Global groups can be assigned privileges in domains that trust the domain in which the group was created. This allows global groups to be assigned privileges anywhere on the network. Trusted domains are one of the subjects of Chapter 16, "Distributing Network Services with Domains."

■ A *local group* can be assigned privileges only in the domain in which the local group was created. Unlike a global group, a local group can contain users and global groups. Local groups allow the administrator to collect groups from several domains and manage them as a single group in the local domain. When privileges are assigned to a local group, all users and global groups in the local group inherit these privileges.

Working with User Manager for Domains

You can employ User Manager for Domains to manage accounts within any domain to which the user has administrative access. Individual users have administrative access if they are members of any of the three Windows NT user groups shown in Table 12.1.

Table 12.1   Windows NT User Groups That Have Permission to Administer User Accounts and Groups

Windows NT User Group	Group Description
Administrators	A local group whose members can perform all user and group management functions.
Domain Admins	A global group that, in most cases, is a member of the Administrators local group. As a member of the Domain Admins group, the user is automatically given local Administrator privileges.
Account Operators	A restricted account whose members can manage most properties of user accounts and groups. A member of this group *can't* manage the following Windows NT Server groups: Administrators, Domain Admins, Account Operators, Server Operators, Print Operators, and Backup Operators. Members of this group also can't manage the account of domain administrators and can't alter domain security policies.

The following sections describe how to take full advantage of the User Manager for Domains application.

Starting the User Manager for Domains

You can start User Manager for Domains (called *User Manager* from here on for brevity) from the taskbar or from the command line.

To start User Manager from the taskbar's Start menu, choose Programs, Administrative Tools, and User Manager for Domains to open User Manager's window. By default, information for the domain where your user account is defined appears in the window (see fig. 12.1).

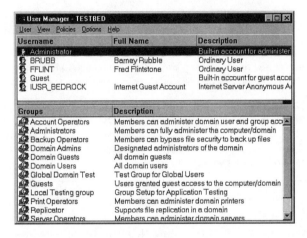

Fig. 12.1 Viewing user information for the default domain in User Manger's main window.

To start User Manager from the Run dialog, follow these steps:

1. From the Start menu, choose Run to open the Run dialog.

2. In the Open text box, type `usrmgr` to open User Manager in the domain in which your user account is defined.

With the addition of a command-line argument, you can optionally start User Manager with a connection to a specific domain or server. Usrmgr.exe accepts either a specified domain or server as the command-line argument:

- To start User Manager in a specific domain, include the domain name as a command-line argument. For example, to start User Manager in the domain BEDROCK, type `usrmgr bedrock` in the Open text box (see fig. 12.2).

- To start User Manager for a specific server, provide the server name in place of the domain name. For example, to start User Manager for the computer FRED, type `usrmgr \\fred` in the Open text box.

3. Click OK to execute the command.

Fig. 12.2   Starting User Manager from the command line with a specific domain name.

Alternatively, you can run User Manger from the Windows NT command prompt by typing the same commands as those shown in step 2.

Note

All Microsoft Network products, including Windows for Workgroups, Windows NT Workstation, and Windows NT Server, use the Universal Naming Convention (UNC) to indicate a specific server. This requires that the server name to be prefaced by two backslashes, as in \\fred.

You can display a specific server in User Manager only if the computer maintains its own security database. Otherwise, the domain information for your user account is displayed. If the specified server is a primary or backup domain controller, the domain information is displayed instead of that for the specific server. For more information on domains and security databases, see Chapter 16, "Distributing Network Services with Domains."

Starting Multiple Instances of User Manager

Unlike applications that are limited to a single instance, such as Explorer, User Manager allows multiple simultaneous instances. Multiple instances of User Manager is a valuable time-saving feature for administrators of large networks or multiple domains.

The most effective method for running multiple instances of User Manager is to create program icons for each domain or computer that you administer. Each program icon contains the name of the domain or computer as the command-line argument to the program command line. By creating multiple instances of User Manager in this manner, you can administer each domain simply by double-clicking the program icon.

The easiest method for creating multiple copies of User Manager with assigned domains is to follow these steps:

1. From the Start menu choose Programs and then Explorer to open an instance of the Windows NT Explorer.

2. Open the Administrative Tools folder by moving to \Winnt\profiles\All Users\Start Menu\Programs, and then double-clicking the Administrative Tools folder.

3. Select the User Manager shortcut icon (see fig. 12.3).

4. From Explorer's Edit menu, choose Copy.

5. Select the destination folder. To create an additional Start menu item in the Administrative Tools folder, don't change folders.

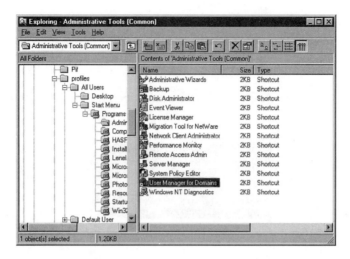

Fig. 12.3   Selecting the User Manager shortcut in the Administrative Tools folder.

6. From the Edit menu choose Paste to add a second User Manager shortcut to the selected folder.

7. Right-click the new User Manager shortcut icon. From the popup menu, choose Properties to open the User Manager for Domains Properties sheet.

8. Edit the command-line entry in the Target text box by adding a space and the domain name or the computer name to the end of the command line, as in `%SystemRoot%\system32\usrmgr.exe domainname` (see fig. 12.4).

Fig. 12.4   Modifying the properties of the new User Manager shortcut to open to a specified domain.

Selecting a New Domain with User Manager

If you choose to manage multiple domains of computers from the same instance of User Manager, changing domains is an easy task. To select a new domain or server, follow these steps:

1. From the <u>U</u>ser menu, choose <u>S</u>elect Domain to open the Select Domain dialog (see fig. 12.5).

Fig. 12.5 Choosing the domain with the Select Domain dialog.

2. Select a new domain from the Select Domain list by clicking the domain name item. Optionally, you can type a domain or server name in the Domain text box. If you enter a server name, remember to follow the UNC naming convention and precede the server name with two backslashes.

> **Note**
>
> The following section describes when to specify a Low Speed Connection for connecting to servers on a wide area network (WAN).

3. Click OK to display the user and group information for the selected domain or server.

Using a Low-Speed Connection to Connect to a Domain

If you're administering a domain or a server through a low-speed connection such as Switched-56, partial T1, or a modem, you achieve better performance and response if User Manager's Low Speed Connection setting is enabled. When you administer a domain, the lists of user accounts, groups, or computers are displayed. The low bandwidth of some WAN connections impedes the speed at which the lists can be produced and managed. Marking the Low Speed Connection check box of the Select Domain dialog improves the management of remote domains by restricting the operation of User Manager in the following ways:

- The list of user accounts isn't displayed in User Manager's main window, and the Select Users choice of the User menu is disabled. You can manage all user accounts and create new accounts, but you must specify the name of the account.

- The list of user groups isn't displayed in User Manager's main window. You can create and manage local groups by making the appropriate choice from the User menu. You *cannot* create or manage global groups. You can manage global group memberships indirectly by setting the group memberships through the individual user accounts.

- All View menu items are disabled.

User Manager remembers the last 20 domains or servers previously administered. The Low Speed Connection setting is set or reset automatically when one of the last 20 domains or computers is selected. The last connection speed setting is applied regardless of whether the Low Speed Connection check box of the Select Domain dialog is marked or cleared.

To start User Manager in a low- or high-speed mode, you can include the command-line parameter /1 (low speed) or /h (high speed) in the Open text box of the Run dialog, from the command prompt, or in the command-line entry of a User Manager shortcut.

Managing User Accounts

Every user of a Windows NT Server network must have a user account, which consists of all the information that defines a user to the Windows NT network. The user account defines the resources on Windows NT computers and domains that can be accessed by the user.

A user account consists of the typical user name and password, as well as how, when, and where a user can attach to the network; what resources the user can access; and what security rights the user has for the accessible resources. The user account also defines the local and global groups of which the user is a member.

> **Note**
>
> When upgrading an existing Windows NT 3.x server, the user accounts and groups are preserved during the upgrade. For example, a clean Windows NT 4.0 installation does *not* contain the group Power Users. When upgrading an existing server, this group is preserved and migrated into the new Windows NT Server 4.0 installation.

The following sections describe the built-in user accounts, how to add new accounts, and how to modify account properties to take full advantage of Windows NT Server 4.0's support for networked users.

Managing the Built-In User Accounts

When you install Windows NT, two built-in accounts—Administrator and Guest—are established when a domain is created. Unlike named user accounts, the Administrator

III

Administering a Network

and Guest accounts can't be deleted. These two accounts are installed on the primary domain controller.

The Administrator Account. The Administrator account is set up by default to allow the installer to manage and configure the Windows NT Server 4.0 software immediately after installation. The user who manages the domain's overall configuration uses the Administrator account. The Administrator account has more control over the domain and its servers than any other user account on the Windows NT network.

During installation of the primary domain controller, the Windows NT Server 4.0 Setup program prompts for the password of the built-in Administrator account. Remember and protect this password. If you forget or lose the Administrator password, the Administrator account is unusable.

> **Note**
>
> After you install the primary domain controller, it's good practice to create another account that contains administrative-level privileges. After you create this account, use it to manage the domain, and reserve the built-in Administrative account for emergency purposes.

The Administrator account is added as a member of the following built-in user groups:

- Administrators (local group)
- Domain Admins (global group)
- Domain Users (global group)

The Administrator account can't be removed from these built-in groups. Detailed descriptions of these user groups appear later in the "Managing User Groups" section.

> **Note**
>
> The Administrator account is the most powerful user on the network, having total access to and control over all resources within the domain for which the account is created. To create a user account with the same power as an Administrator, the user account must be included in all three of the groups of which the Administrator is a member.
>
> One strategy that's often used in large networks is to assign two user accounts to network administrators—one with administrative permissions and one with only user permissions. The administrative account is used only when performing network management, and the user account is utilized at all other times. The objective is to prevent inadvertent changes to network configuration as a result of conventional user activities.

Some of the Administrator capabilities include managing security policies; establishing domain trust relationships; creating, modifying, and deleting user accounts; creating shared directories and printers; modifying operating system software; and installing and updating devices and partition disks. This is only a small sample of the capabilities available to an administrative account with full Administrator privileges.

The Guest Account. The Guest account is at the opposite end of the permissions spectrum from the Administrator account. The Guest account is provided for occasional or one-time users. The built-in Guest account is a part of the Domain Guests built-in group and inherits a very limited set of permissions from that group.

Note

The Guest account isn't the same as the Internet Guest account, IUSER_*SERVERNAME*, that's created when you install Internet Information Server (IIS) 2.0. The Internet Guest account allows anonymous logon to the server on which IIS is installed and, by default, includes membership in the Domain Users and Guests groups. If you're using IIS for a private intranet, you can delete the Internet Guest account. Additional information on Internet and intranet accounts is provided in Chapter 19, "Setting Up the Internet Information Server," and Chapter 20, "Administering Intranet and World Wide Web Sites."

Although the Guest account can't be removed from the system, the account is disabled by default during installation. This means that the administrator must explicitly enable the account for the Guest account to be used. In practice, this account usually is enabled only if there are resources on the network that must be accessible by individuals who don't have formal accounts that enable file and other resource sharing. As an example, persons without the need to access server files might be allowed to use the Guest account to use a shared printer.

Note

The Guest account initially contains an empty password. An empty password allows users from untrusted domains to log on to your domain as Guest and access any resources that are accessible to the Guest account. The Guest account can be changed by an administrative account to add a password, if desired.

Adding New User Accounts

Your network isn't useful without users, and your network is equally unsecure and unproductive if you use only the two built-in accounts. This means that new user accounts must be added for each network user, with the possible exception of Guest users. Following are the two methods for adding a new user account:

- The administrator can create a new user account.

- A new user account can be copied from an existing user account and the appropriate changes made to specify information specific to the new user.

Creating a New User Account with User Manager. Add a new user by choosing New User from User Manager's <u>U</u>ser menu to open the New User dialog. To add a new user account, fill in the dialog's text boxes, mark the appropriate security check boxes, and click the <u>A</u>dd button to create the user account. Figure 12.6 shows the New User dialog with text box entries, before security options are selected.

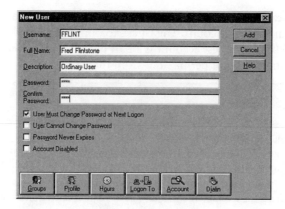

Fig. 12.6 Creating a new account with the New User dialog.

The New User dialog contains many controls that the network administrator must assign values to. The New User dialog contains the following controls:

■ *Username.* Each network user must have a unique user name. The user name can contain up to 20 characters. You can use any combination of upper- and lower-case letters, numbers, or punctuation in the user name, except for the following characters:

= + [ ] / \ ; : < > ? * " '

> **Note**
>
> The user name entered in the New User dialog is used whenever the user logs on to a Windows NT computer or a Windows NT network. The user name is case-sensitive and must be entered with the exact spelling as when the account was created. Establishing a consistent naming policy for all users benefits network administrators and network users.
>
> There are several common naming conventions, such as using the first initial of the first name with the last three letters of the last name (for example, Fred Flintstone would have a user name of ffli). Microsoft uses the first name, followed by as many letters of the last name as are required to create an unique user name, which also is used as the employee's Internet e-mail alias (*firstlast*@microsoft.com). Whatever naming scheme you choose, make sure that it's consistent.

■ *Full Name.* This optional text box is used to enter the full descriptive name of the user for which the account is being created—for example, Fred Flintstone. As with the user name, the full name serves the network administrator better if a consistent method of full names is used, such as first name, last name, or last name, first name.

■ *Description.* The Description text box also is optional and can be used to further identify the user of this account. An example is adding a user's department or title to this text box.

■ *Password and Confirm Password.* The Password text box is used with the Username when users log on from a PC running Windows NT Workstation or Windows 95 with Windows NT Server authentication. You can leave the Password text box empty until users enter their password, but this leaves the network temporarily in a very unsecure state. If you leave the Password text box empty, be sure to select the User Must Change Password at Next Logon check box.

The Password text box is limited to 14 characters and is case-sensitive. It displays encrypted text as a row of asterisks (*) when you type in this field. To make sure that the password is entered correctly, you must fill in the Confirm Password text box with the identical password as the Password text box before the account can be added.

■ *User Must Change Password at Next Logon.* If this check box is marked, users must change their password the first time that the account is used or the next time they log on to the domain. This check box, marked by default, should be used if the users aren't present when the accounts are being created for them or you can't give them a password directly.

When you mark the User Must Change Password at Next Logon check box, the initial password must be either blank or something very intuitive to the user, such as the company name or the word *password.* This option allows users to customize their own passwords without administrative assistance. Be sure to verify that users immediately log on and change their password to avoid a potential security breach.

■ *User Cannot Change Password.* The User Cannot Change Password option is primarily used when the passwords for user accounts are administered centrally by the network administrator. This option is used primarily if several users share the same account or in very secure networks. This option also is specified for the Internet Guest account, if present.

Select the User Cannot Change Password option only if the users aren't allowed to enter their own password and the network administrator assigns passwords to users.

■ *Password Never Expires.* When this option is selected, users aren't required to change passwords periodically. Enabling this option isn't a good security practice, however; users should change their passwords on a regular basis, such as quarterly or even monthly. In certain cases, such as a rarely used account like the Administrator, you might want to use this option to avoid forgetting the password.

The Password Never Expires option is also used when security isn't a high priority compared to user convenience. Most users like to keep one password to avoid forgetting a new password. When this option is used, the check box User Must Change Password at Next Logon is cleared.

■ *Account Disabled.* In certain instances, a user account must be disabled. Selecting this check box prevents a user from logging on to the network until the check box is cleared.

III

Administering a Network

Some of the reasons for disabling a user account are as follows:

- Creating a template account that's used only to create new accounts by copying (a process explained in the following section)

- Disabling an account temporarily while a person is on vacation or extended leave

Understanding the Additional Account Properties. When adding a new user, a set of five buttons appears at the bottom of the New User dialog (refer to fig. 12.6). These buttons allow the account administrator to specify additional properties for a user account. The buttons that control these properties are Groups, Profile, Hours, Logon To, Account, and Dialin. These properties are explained later in the "Managing User Account Properties" section.

Copying a User Account. To ease the task of setting up new user accounts, User Manager allows you to copy an existing user account as a template to create a new account. In large networks, a system administrator creates template accounts that contain all the attributes of a user in a particular department. When a new user account must be created, the appropriate template account is copied and the appropriate account information is changed to reflect the details pertinent to the new user.

Note

As noted earlier, template accounts usually are disabled so that users can't access the network or network resources through template accounts.

To copy a user account, perform the following steps:

1. From User Manager's window, select the user account to be copied.

2. Choose Copy from the User menu to display the Copy of *Username* dialog.

3. Enter the appropriate account information for the new user account (see fig. 12.7).

4. Click the Add button to create the new user account.

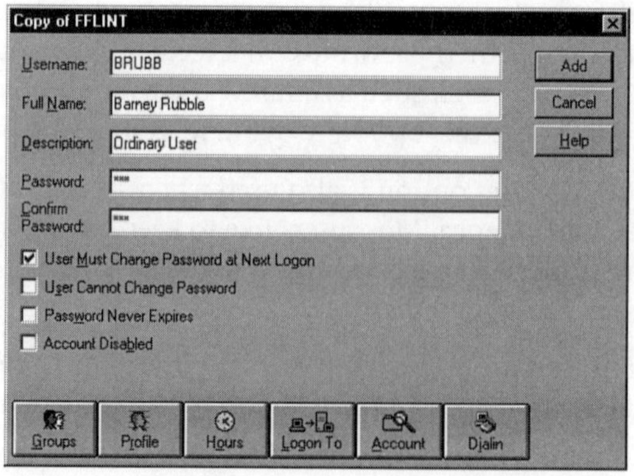

Fig. 12.7 Copying an existing user account to a new user account.

Modifying User Accounts

User Manager allows account administrators to modify user accounts individually or modify multiple accounts simultaneously.

An individual user account can be modified by

■ Double-clicking a user account item in the Username list of User Manager's window

■ Selecting a user account in User Manager's window, and then either pressing Enter or choosing the Properties command from the User menu

Either method displays the User Properties sheet (see fig. 12.8), which looks similar to the New User dialog. The only significant difference between the User Properties sheet and the New User dialog is the addition of an Account Locked Out check box. This check box is disabled unless the account is now locked out because of an excessive number of incorrect logon attempts. This check box is used to clear a locked-out account.

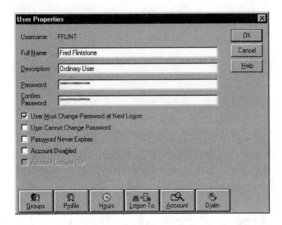

Fig. 12.8 The User Properties sheet for modifying individual user accounts.

You can modify multiple user accounts simultaneously by any one of the following methods:

■ Select a range of accounts by selecting a starting point in the list of user accounts and dragging the mouse pointer over the accounts to select.

■ Select a range of accounts by selecting a starting point in the list of user accounts and, while holding the Shift key down, selecting the last account in the range.

■ Select individual accounts by pressing the Ctrl key and then individually selecting each account to modify.

■ Choose Select Users from the Users menu to open the Select Users dialog (see fig. 12.9). The Select Users dialog lets you select or deselect all the users assigned to a particular group within the domain you're administering. Multiple groups can't be simultaneously selected or deselected in this dialog.

Fig. 12.9 Selecting users belonging to a particular group.

After the user accounts to be modified are selected, press Enter or choose Properties from the Users menu to display the User Properties sheet (see fig. 12.10).

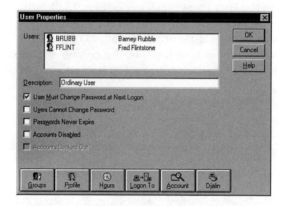

Fig. 12.10 The User Properties sheet for selected user accounts.

When modifying multiple accounts, only the options common to all the users are displayed. The additional account property buttons located at the bottom of the dialog allow the administrator to assign common attributes to all the selected user accounts.

Managing User Account Properties

Additional user account properties are accessed and managed through the set of buttons located at the bottom of the New User and Copy of *Username* dialogs and the User Properties sheet described in the preceding sections.

These property buttons allow the account administrator to specify additional properties for a user account. The buttons that control these properties are Groups, Profile, Hours, Logon To, Account, and Dialin. The dialogs that appear when you click each button are described in the following sections.

Assigning Group Membership to a User Account

A user account is assigned to group membership by clicking the Groups button to display the Group Memberships dialog (see fig. 12.11). This dialog allows the account administrator to assign and revoke group membership privileges.

The Group Memberships dialog shows all the groups that the account belongs to in the Member Of list. All the groups to which the account does *not* belong appear in the Not Member Of list.

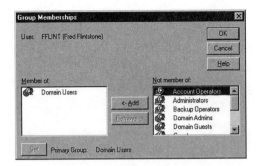

Fig. 12.11   Assigning users to groups with the Group Memberships dialog.

To assign a user to one or more groups, take one of the following actions:

- Double-click the group to which to add the user account in the Not Member Of list.

- Select one or more groups in the Not Member Of list and click the Add button.

To remove a group membership from the user account, take one of the following actions:

- Double-click the group to be removed from the user account in the Member Of list.

- Select one or more groups in the Member Of list and click the Remove button.

In the Group Memberships dialog, the setting for the user account's primary group applies only to users accessing a Windows NT network through Services for Macintosh. To set the primary group, select a group from the Member Of list and click the Set button.

◀◀ See "Connecting Macintosh Clients," p. 400

> **Note**
>
> A group that's set as the user account's primary group may not be removed from the account's membership list. To remove the group from the user account, another group must be set as the primary group before the previously selected primary group can be removed.

Defining and Managing User Profiles

To further define a user's profile, the Profile button lets you select custom settings for one or more users. Clicking the Profile button displays the User Environment Profile dialog, shown in figure 12.12.

User profiles provide power and flexibility for system administrators and users when configuring a network environment. User profiles are typically stored in a common folder on a Windows NT server. Windows NT Workstation clients also can have individual user profiles to supplement the user profile stored on the Windows NT server.

III

Administering a Network

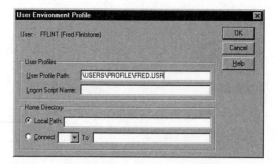

Fig. 12.12 Setting user environment parameters in the User Environment Profile dialog.

> **Note**
>
> Windows NT Server 4.0's user profiles apply to Windows 3.1, Windows for Workgroups 3.1+, Windows NT 3.5+ and 4.0, and Windows 95 clients. Windows 95, however, provides its own mechanism for establishing networked user profiles and system policies, which offer several features not included in Windows NT Server 4.0's user profiles.

◀◀ See "Setting Up User Profiles on the Server," p. 364, and "Using System Policies," p. 366

User profiles specify the startup information when individual users log on to Windows NT. This information includes the user environment (environment variables, paths, and mapped drives), program groups, and available applications. When a user profile is stored on a central NT server, the user environment is the same regardless of the computer the user logs on from. When the user profile is stored on individual NT machines, the environment reflects the settings stored on each machine.

User profiles also can contain mandatory settings that you assign; users aren't allowed to alter these settings. This procedure ensures a standard working environment for each user and relieves the problems that result from erroneous changes made to a user profile, such as deleting a Start menu folder or shortcut.

Specifying the User Profile Path. The user profile is specified in the User Profile Path text box, which contains the location of a user profile located on a Windows NT server. If the text box is empty, the profile is stored locally on each machine that the user logs on to.

Two types of user profiles are available:

- *Personal User Profiles.* This profile type is assigned to each user and can be altered by the user. Each user has his own private profile file with the file extension .USR.

- *Mandatory User Profiles.* This type of profile is assigned by the system administrator and can't be changed by the user. A mandatory user profile has the file extension.man.

To assign a profile to a user account, type the profile path and file name in the User Profile Path text box. Be sure to follow the UNC naming convention. For example, to store a profile named Profile.usr on the computer BEDROCK in the folder Users, type **bedrock\users\profile.usr**.

You can create the profile file ahead of time by using the User Profile Manager. If the specified profile file doesn't exist when the user first logs on, the file is created automatically by using the default profile that exists on the workstation the user logs on from. Any changes are saved automatically to the profile file.

Note

When using mandatory user profiles, the following rules apply:

■ Mandatory profiles are added in the same manner, with the exception of the file extension (.MAN).

■ Unlike an individual user account, a mandatory user account must be created by the account administrator with User Profile Manager. This account must then be placed in the location specified in the profile path. If a profile isn't created, users with mandatory profiles aren't permitted to log on to Windows NT.

Setting a Logon Script Name. *Logon scripts* are optional batch files that are run whenever a user logs on to a Windows NT network. Logon scripts are tailored to the client operating system that's used to log on to the network. All client operating systems for Intel PCs, except OS/2, use the .BAT extension for the script file (OS/2 uses the .CMD extension).

Logon scripts aren't as flexible as user profiles but can be used instead of user profiles or with user profiles. By default, all logon scripts are stored in the folder *SERVERNAME*\ Winnt\system32\Repl\Import\Scripts, where *SERVERNAME* is the UNC server name of the primary domain controller for the domain you're administering. Because all scripts are stored in a central spot, only the name of the script file needs to be entered in the Logon Script Name text box. You can change the location of the Scripts folder by using Server Manager.

If a relative path is entered in the Logon Script Name text box, such as \Users\ Logon.bat, it's appended to the stored folder path. Using the preceding example, the logon script is run from the folder *SERVERNAME*\Winnt\system32\Repl\Import\ Scripts\Users\Logon.bat.

Logon scripts can be assigned on an individual basis, or the same logon script can be assigned to multiple users.

Specifying a Home Folder. The home folder is the default folder in which a user is placed when starting a DOS-command session.

> **Note**
>
> Windows NT 4.0, like Windows 95, has adopted the term *folder* to replace *directory*; thus, this chapter uses the term *home folder*, which is likely to be adopted by most users of Windows 95 client PCs.

The home folder also is used as a repository for user files. The home folder can be a folder located on the client's local fixed disk or on a network drive.

To set up a home folder on a local machine, perform the following steps:

1. In the User Environment Profile dialog (accessed by clicking the Profile button), select the Local Path option.

2. Type the local path (for example, `c:\users\default`) in the Local Path text box.

In a network environment, where a user can log on from multiple machines, the home folder should be located on a networked drive so the user can have access to it from any machine. A system administrator can set up shared network drives for users to log on to. To set up a home folder on a networked drive, perform the following steps:

1. In the User Environment Profile dialog, select the Connect option.

2. From the drop-down list box, select the drive letter of the client machine to contain the home folder.

3. In the To text box, type a complete path for the home folder using the UNC naming convention (for example, `\\bedrock\home\fred`). This makes the home folder available to the user on any machine that the user logs on from.

If the home folder doesn't exist, Windows NT creates the folder. Also, the folder is protected so that only the specified user (and administrators) have access to the folder contents.

Managing Profiles for Multiple Users. When multiple users are selected in User Manager's window, the User Environment Profile dialog changes to reflect the selection of multiple users within groups (see fig. 12.13). If all the user profiles to be modified are to share the same profile file name, logon script, and home folder, you make the same dialog entries as for individual accounts, as described in the preceding section.

You can streamline the process for creating individual user profiles based on a single profile for multiple users by utilizing the environment variable, %USERNAME%. Windows NT Server 4.0 automatically replaces %USERNAME% with the user's logon ID. Assume that each user is to have an individual user profile with the file name derived from the user's first name. For the user names FFLINT, WFLINT, and BRUBBLE, supplying the path \\BEDROCK\Profiles\%USERNAME%.usr has the same effect as creating three individual user profiles—\\BEDROCK\Profiles\FFLINT.usr, \\BEDROCK\Profiles\WFLINT.usr, and \\BEDROCK\Profiles\BRUBBLE.usr. The variable %USERNAME% is expanded and replaced with the actual user name when any of the multiple users specified in the Users list of the User Environment Profile dialog log on to the Windows NT network. The %USERNAME% environmental variable can be used in any of the text boxes of the User Environment Profile dialog.

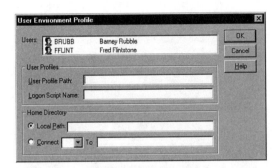

Fig. 12.13 The User Environment Profile Dialog for multiple user accounts.

Caution

Take care when using the %USERNAME% variable with long file names—the variable name is replaced with the actual user name. This may cause problems when DOS, Windows 3.1+, and Windows NT 3.5 clients log on to the network. DOS, Windows 3.1+ (including Windows for Workgroups 3.1+), and Windows NT 3.5 are limited to 8.3 DOS file names. If your network includes clients other than Windows 95 and Windows NT 3.51+, make sure that the folder and profile names follow the 8.3 naming convention. In particular, the user name must not exceed eight characters in length.

Managing Logon Hours

When administering a large network, you might want to restrict the hours during which an account has access to the network. For example, certain workers may be able to access network resources only during normal business hours—Monday through Friday from 8 a.m. to 5 p.m.—whereas other users have unrestricted network access.

You manage logon hours for a user account by clicking the Hours button at the bottom of the New User and Copy of *Username* dialogs and the User Properties sheet to display the Logon Hours dialog (see fig. 12.14).

The Logon Hours dialog displays a weekly schedule of times allowed for user logon. The dark areas indicate valid logon times. Logon hours are permitted by selecting the desired hours and clicking Allow. Similarly, restricted hours are specified by selecting the hours and clicking Disallow.

You can use any of the following four methods to select logon times in the Logon Hours dialog:

■ Clicking the day of week label—for example, Sunday—selects the entire day.

■ Clicking the top of an hour column selects that hour every day of the week.

■ Clicking the column square above Sunday selects the entire week.

■ Clicking a specific hour selects that hour.

After the logon hours are set, click OK to save the logon hours for that account.

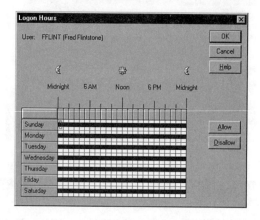

Fig. 12.14 Managing user logon time limitations with the Logon Hours dialog.

Setting Logon Hours for Multiple Users. When managing logon hours for multiple users, select the desired users from User Manager's window and click the Hours button from the User Properties sheet. The Logon Hours dialog changes slightly from the single-user version, as shown in figure 12.15.

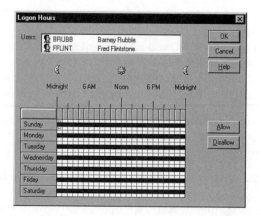

Fig. 12.15 Managing logon hours for multiple users.

If all the selected users don't have the same logon hours, a message box appears with the warning The selected users have different Logon Hours settings. If you continue the operation, all the user logon hours are reset and new logon hours are set in the same manner previously described for setting the logon hours for an individual user account.

Logging Off Users Who Are Logged On When Logon Hours Expire. Although logon hours restrict when users can log on to a Windows NT network, users may be logged on when their logon time expires. The action that occurs in this situation is determined by the Account Policy set up by the domain administrator. (Setting up account policies for terminating after-hour connections is discussed later in the section "Removing Users from the Network When Logon Hours Expire.")

The following two actions can occur when a logged-on user's logon time expires:

- Typically, logged-on users remain logged on, but they're denied the ability to make any new connections or to access additional network resources.

- The domain administrator can choose to forcibly disconnect logged-on users on expiry of their specified logon times. When you choose this option, all logged-on users receive a warning to log off the connected resource before the expiry time. Any users who don't log off before the logoff time are automatically disconnected.

> **Note**
>
> The option to forcibly log off applies only to users of client PCs running Windows NT Workstation or Windows 95. All non-Windows NT or Windows 95 computers are *not* disconnected when the logoff time expires. Non-Windows NT/95 computers can't access any new network resources but can continue to use without restriction the resources to which they're then connected.

Restricting Logon Privileges to Assigned Workstations

You can restrict which clients on the network users can log on. This is accomplished by clicking the Logon To button from the New User and Copy of *Username* dialogs and the User Properties sheet to display the Logon Workstations dialog shown in figure 12.16.

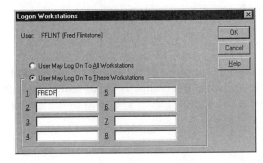

Fig. 12.16 Restricting client logon access through the Logon Workstations dialog.

> **Note**
>
> The workstations from which a user is permitted to log on is restricted to clients running Windows NT Workstations or Windows 95. Users of non-Windows NT or Windows 95 clients aren't affected by these settings.

By default, all new accounts—unless the account is a copied account and the account being copied has restricted access—can log on from all clients. If client logon access needs to be restricted, follow these steps:

1. Select the User May Log On To These Workstations option.

2. Type up to eight client computer names in the text boxes.

3. Click OK to establish the restriction.

When multiple users are selected from User Manager's window, the Logon Workstations dialog displays information that applies only to all selected users. By selecting the option User May Log On To All Workstations or by restricting client access, all selected users are affected.

Managing Account Information

You assign specific user account information by clicking the Account button at the bottom of the New User and Copy of *Username* dialogs and the User Properties sheet to display the Account Information dialog shown in figure 12.17.

Fig. 12.17 Altering user accounts through the Account Information dialog.

The Account Information dialog lets the you determine the expiration date of the account and the type of account.

By default, a user account never expires. In situations where an expiration date is needed (such as when an employee leaves the company or for temporary employees), the account becomes inactive at the end of the day specified in the End Of date edit box.

The Account Type section specifies whether the account is global or local according to the following rules:

■ Select Global Account if the user account must be recognized by other domains that trust the user logon domain.

■ Select Local Account if the user logs on to the domain from an untrusted domain or if user access is to be restricted to the logon domain.

The Account Information dialog can be invoked for multiple users. When multiple users are selected, only the properties common to all accounts are selected. Setting any of the options changes all selected accounts.

Setting User Dial-In Permissions

Windows NT Server 4.0 has eased the burden of granting dial-in permissions to users. In previous versions, dial-in permissions had to be assigned from the Remote Access Administration utility. Now dial-in permissions can be assigned directly from the User Manager by selecting the Dialin button in the New User and Copy of *Username* dialogs or the User Properties sheet.

By default, users do *not* have dial-in permission. Dial-in permission must be granted to each user. Figure 12.18 shows the Dialin Information dialog.

Fig. 12.18 Setting callback properties in the Dialin Information dialog.

If your network's users need dial-in permission, simply mark the Grant Dialin Permission to User check box. Next, the Call Back options must be set. Three choices are available:

- No Call Back
- Set By Caller
- Preset To

If you select Set By Caller, the user is prompted to enter an optional number that the server can use to call back the user. This option is very valuable for users who travel a great deal, need to access the network for information while on the road, and want to minimize telephone charges.

The Preset To option is limited because the server calls back to a specific number each time the user dials into the network. This option should be used only for strict security purposes where the user, usually a telecommuter, is always at a specific location.

Using the Add User Account Wizard

Wizards are Microsoft's approach to automating multistep operations necessary to achieve a specific objective. Wizards, which originated in Microsoft Access and later migrated to all members of the Microsoft Office suite, are intended primarily to aid new users of Microsoft productivity applications.

Windows NT Server 4.0 offers eight Administrative Wizards of varying usefulness to Windows NT network administrators. The Add User Account Wizard guides you through the

III

Administering a Network

4.0

addition of a new user account. To use the wizard properly, however, you must have a fundamental understanding of Windows NT's implementation of user accounts and groups. Thus, the Add User Account Wizard is likely to play a limited or non-existent role in the day-to-day administration of Windows NT Server 4.0s.

To give the Add User Account Wizard a trial run, which requires that you have Domain Administrator privileges, follow these steps:

1. From the Start menu choose Programs, Administrative Tools, and then Administrative Wizards to open the Getting Started with Windows NT Server window (see fig. 12.19).

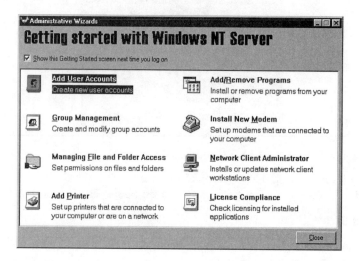

Fig. 12.19 Selecting the Add User Account Wizard from the Administrative Wizards window.

2. Double-click the Add User Accounts icon to open the first dialog of the Add User Account Wizard, which displays the server's domain name (see fig. 12.20). Use the Domain Name drop-down list if you want to add the new user to another domain with which your server has a trust relationship. Click the Next button.

▶▶ See "Implementing Domains and Trusts Between Domains," p. 580

3. Type the full name of the user, the user's logon ID, and an optional user description in the three text boxes (see fig. 12.21). Click the Next button.

4. Assign and confirm a password for the new user in the Password and Confirm Password text boxes (see fig. 12.22). Use the default option, which requires users to change their password at the next logon, unless you have a specific reason for doing otherwise. Click the Next button.

Fig. 12.20 Selecting the domain for the new user in the first Add User Account Wizard dialog.

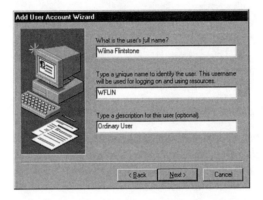

Fig. 12.21 Adding user account information in the second Add User Account Wizard dialog.

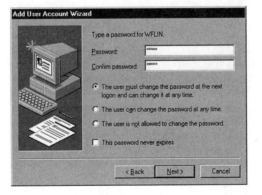

Fig. 12.22 Specifying a temporary user password in the third Add User Account Wizard dialog.

5. By default, the new user is added to the Domain Users group. To add the user to another group, select the group in the Available Groups list, and then click the Add button (see fig. 12.23). You can remove a user from an added group by selecting the entry in the Selected Groups list and clicking the Remove button. (The Wizard won't let you remove the user from the Domain Users group.) Click the Next button.

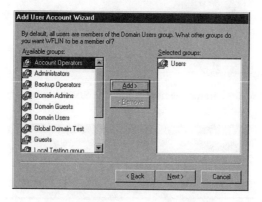

Fig. 12.23   Adding the new user to an additional user group in the fourth Add User Account Wizard dialog.

6. Mark the check boxes to set up one or more of the options shown in figure 12.24. Options not available are disabled. The option to set up a Microsoft Exchange Server account for the user is enabled only if you have Microsoft Exchange Server installed. Click the Next button.

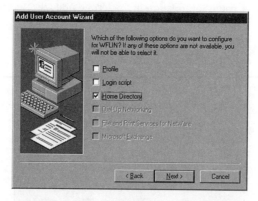

Fig. 12.24   Selecting user account options in the fifth Add User Account Wizard dialog.

7. The options you specified in step 6 determine the sequence of wizard dialogs. As an example, if you selected Home Directory in step 6, the dialog shown in figure 12.25 appears. Click the On Another Computer option button, specify the user's drive letter mapping in the Connect Drive list for the user's home folder on the server, and type the UNC path to the server share for the home folder in the To text box.

(You receive an error message if the share doesn't exist.) Click the Next button. If you selected more than one option in step 6, additional dialogs appear to aid you in setting up the additional options.

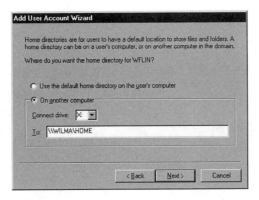

Fig. 12.25 Specifying a home directory and its user share mapping.

> **Note**
>
> You must have previously created the share for the user's home folder and assigned appropriate permissions for the share. The usual location for home folders is in the \Users folder of the server. Ordinarily, only domain administrators and the user have permissions to users' home folders.

8. You can add restrictions to the user's account by selecting The Following Restrictions option to enable the four check boxes shown in figure 12.26. If you specify one or more restrictions, additional dialogs appear to help you define the restrictions. Click the Next button.

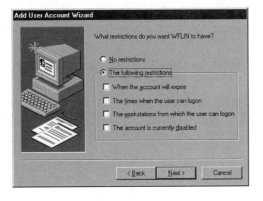

Fig. 12.26 Specifying user account restrictions, if applicable.

9. When you complete the dialogs for user restrictions (if any), the last dialog that appears indicates that the wizard is about to complete the task (see fig. 12.27). Click the Finish button to create the account.

Fig. 12.27 Confirming the completion of account information entry in the last Add User Account Wizard dialog.

> **Note**
>
> The account for the new user isn't created until you click the Finish button. You can use the Back button to review your prior steps or cancel the account entry at any point in the process by clicking the Cancel button.

10. A message box (see fig. 12.28) confirms the creation of the new user account. Click No to exit the Add User Account Wizard or Yes to add another account.

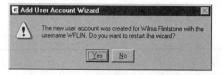

Fig. 12.28 The message box that confirms the addition of the new user account.

Administering the Domain Account Policy

The domain account policy determines password and lockout restrictions for all users in the domain. Choose Account from User Manager's Policies menu to open the Account Policy dialog (see fig. 12.29). The following sections describe how to set domain-wide policies for passwords and account lockout.

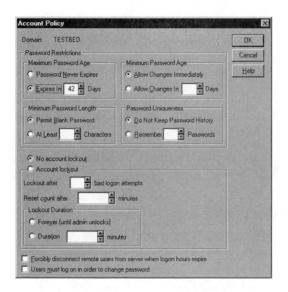

Fig. 12.29 Setting account policies for all domain users with the Account Policy dialog.

Setting the Account Policy for Passwords

The domain administrator can define the following types of password restrictions:

- *Maximum Password Age* determines how long account passwords are in effect before they expire. The options are Password Never Expires or Expires In *n* Days (the default).

- *Minimum Password Age* determines how long a user account is forced to retain a new password. The objective is to prevent users from entering a dummy password when their password expires and then immediately changing it back to the old password. The options available are Allow Changes Immediately (the default) or Allow Changes In *n* Days.

- *Minimum Password Length* determines the minimum allowable length for all passwords. The options available are Permit Blank Password (the default) or At Least *n* Characters. To maintain a secure network, require passwords of at least six (preferably at least eight) characters.

- *Password Uniqueness* tells Windows NT Server whether to keep a history of previously used passwords. The objective is to prevent users from reusing the same password when a password expires. The available options are Do Not Keep Password History (the default) or Remember *n* Passwords. For maximum security, set *n* to 8 or greater.

At the bottom of the Account Policy dialog is a Users Must Log On in Order to Change Password check box. If this option is selected and a user's password expires, the user of the account must ask the account administrator to change the password.

III

Administering a Network

Setting the Account Lockout Policy

The Account Lockout Policy setting determines the actions that are taken if a user forgets his password, or illegal attempts are made to access the network, as evidenced by multiple failed attempts to log on. In this event, either of the following actions can be chosen:

- *No Account Lockout.* If this option is selected, any user can try an unlimited number of times to log on to the network.

- *Account Lockout.* If this option is selected, the domain administrator sets up lockout parameters to deter repeated illegal logon attempts. The following sections explain the lockout parameters.

Setting Account Lockout Options. One of following two options applies to the Account Lockout setting:

- *Lockout After* n *Bad Logon Attempts* locks out the user account after *n* failed logon attempts occur. This option forces the account user to wait until the account is unlocked, either through administrative or automatic intervention.

- *Reset Count After* n *Minutes* automatically resets the number of bad logon attempts to zero after *n* minutes of account inactivity since the last bad logon attempt.

Setting Lockout Duration Options. One of following two options applies to the Lockout Duration setting:

- *Forever (Until Admin Unlocks).* When this option is selected, the account is locked out indefinitely until the administrator manually resets the account.

- *Duration* n *Minutes.* When this option is selected, the account automatically unlocks after *n* minutes of locked time.

Removing Users from the Network When Logon Hours Expire. When users are logged on to a Windows NT network and their logon hours expire, the domain administrator can either continue to let them access the network resources to which they're already logged on, or forcibly disconnect all users running Windows NT Workstation or Windows 95 from the network. This option is the same as the option described earlier in the section "Logging Off Users Who Are Logged On When Logon Hours Expire," except that all domain users are affected by this option.

If the option Forcibly Disconnect Remote Users from Server When Logon Hours Expire is selected in the Account Policy dialog, remote users whose logon hours expire are prompted to disconnect from the network. If users don't log off, the server will disconnect them automatically.

Managing User Groups

The preceding sections of this chapter make many references to user groups. User groups define the rights and privileges that are assigned to the users in those groups. At the bottom portion of User Manager's window is a scrollable, alphabetically sorted list of the standard (built-in) groups of Windows NT Server 4.0 (see fig. 12.30).

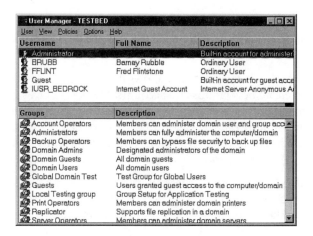

Fig. 12.30 Built-in user groups available in User Manager's window.

Two types of groups are shown in the Groups list—global groups and local groups. A global group is depicted with a world globe in the background. A local group is depicted with a workstation in the background.

User Manager lets domain administrators create, modify, and delete groups; assign user accounts to groups; and remove user accounts from groups. The following sections describe the 11 built-in user groups of Windows NT Server 4.0 and explain the management of user groups.

Examining the Built-In Groups of Windows NT Server 4.0

The actions that a user account can perform depends on the group memberships assigned to the user account, the rights and privileges the user account inherits from the group(s), plus specific permissions assigned to the account by the account administrator. Windows NT Server 4.0 has 11 built-in user groups, each with a pre-established set of permissions for use of network resources. Descriptions of a few of these groups, by necessity, appear earlier in this chapter but are repeated here for completeness. Following is a brief description of each built-in user group, in the approximate order of decreasing privilege:

- The *Administrators* group is the most powerful local group in the domain. The administrators are responsible for the overall configuration of the domain and the domain's servers.

- *Domain Admins* is a global group that's a member of the Administrators group. By default, members of the Domain Admins group are as powerful as the Administrators group. The Domain Admins group can be removed from the Administrators group, if necessary, to restrict the group's authority.

- *Users* is a local group that provides the capabilities that most users need to perform normal tasks. Members of this group have no rights to administer servers running Windows NT Server 4.0.

III

Administering a Network

- *Domain Users* is a global group that's a member of the local Users group. By default, all new accounts are automatically added to this group, unless the account is specifically removed by the account administrator.

- *Account Operators* is a local group that allows its members to use the User Manager application to create new groups and accounts. Members of this group have limited capabilities to administer accounts, servers, and groups in the domain. Members of this group can't modify or delete accounts or groups belonging to the Administrators, Domain Admins, Account Operators, Backup Operators, Print Operators, or Server Groups. Account operators can't administer account policies.

- *Backup Operators* is a local group that can back up and restore files on the domain's primary and backup controllers. Members of this group also can log on to a server and shut down the server, presumably for backup operations.

- *Print Operators* is a local group that allows its members to create and manage printer shares in the domain. These members also can log on to a server and shut down the server.

- *Server Operators* is a local group that allows its members to manage the domain's primary and backup controllers. This group's members also can manage folder and print shares, as well as administer server functions such as setting system time for the entire domain.

- *Replicator* is a local group that supports the capability to perform folder replication functions. Only accounts needed to log on to the Replicator services of the primary and backup domain controllers should be members of this group.

- *Domain Guests* is a global group that's a member of the local Guests group. This group is intended for user accounts that have more limited rights than a member of the Domain Users group.

- *Guests* is a local group with very limited capabilities. This group is used for occasional or one-time users.

> **Note**
>
> The Power Users group of Windows NT 3.51 isn't included as a built-in group of Windows NT 4.0. When upgrading a Windows NT 3.x server to Windows NT 4.0, the Power Users group is migrated to 4.0.

Adding Local Groups

The built-in user groups are adequate for most Windows NT Server 4.0 networks. If you have a large, complex network, you might want to define your own user groups by, for example, organizational function or department. As an example, members of the Finance, Marketing, Sales, and Production departments might have their own group. Similarly, vice presidents, directors, managers, and supervisors might be assigned to their own group.

To add a local group to the domain, follow these steps:

1. From User Manager's <u>U</u>ser menu, choose New <u>L</u>ocal Group to display the New Local Group dialog (see fig. 12.31).

Fig. 12.31   Adding a new local group with User Manager.

2. In the Group Name text box, type a group name that's no longer than 20 characters. A Group Name is required.

3. Type a group description in the Description text box. Although this is optional, a meaningful description is useful as your network grows and more groups are added.

To add user accounts to the new group, click the Add button to display the Add Users and Groups dialog (see fig. 12.32). To add users to the local account, follow these steps:

1. Select the account entry in the Names list and click the Add button, or double-click the entry in the Names list to add the account to the Add Names list. (A description of each option in the Add Users and Groups dialog follows.)

2. Repeat step 1 for each additional account you want to add to the new group.

3. Click OK to add the accounts to the new group and close the Add Users and Groups dialog.

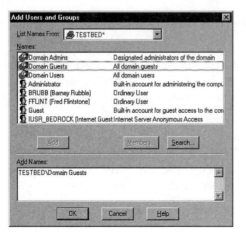

Fig. 12.32   Adding new user accounts and global groups to a local group.

Local groups can include users and global groups from the domain of the local group. Local groups also can include global users and global groups from other domains that are trusted by the local groups' domain.

The purpose of the options in the Add Users and Groups dialog is as follows:

- *List Names From.* This drop-down list lets you select the domain from which to add names or groups. The default setting is the domain for the local group.

- *Names.* This list displays all the users and global groups of the domain that's being viewed. The items in this list are candidates for inclusion in the new local group.

- *Members.* To view the members of a global group, select the global group from the Names list and click the Members button.

- *Search.* This button is used to find a domain name—a useful feature if your network contains many domains.

Adding Global Groups

The process for adding a new global group is identical to adding a local group, except that rather than choose New Local Group, you choose New Global Group from the User menu to display the New Global Group dialog (see fig. 12.33). Unlike local groups, which can contain global groups and users, a global group can contain only users.

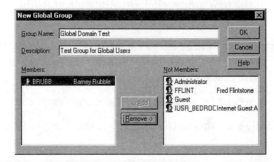

Fig. 12.33   Adding a new global group with User Manager.

Copying a Group

If a new group needs to be created, and the group will have similar rights and members as another group, it's easier to copy a group than to add a new group and manually set up the group's attributes. To copy a group, follow these steps:

1. Select a group to copy in User Manager's window.

2. From the User menu choose Copy.

3. The Add New Local Group or Add New Global Group dialog appears, depending the type of group you selected in step 1.

4. Type a new name and description for the group.

5. Modify the group's membership, as necessary.

6. Click OK to create the new group and close the dialog.

Deleting Groups from the Domain

Only user-defined groups may be deleted from the domain. The built-in groups of Windows NT Server 4.0 can't be deleted.

> **Caution**
>
> Be careful when deleting groups from a domain. A deleted group can't be restored by an undo process.

Each group you create receives a unique security identifier (SID). If you delete a group and re-create a group with the identical name, the new group receives a different SID and doesn't inherit the original group's attributes.

To delete a group from a domain, follow these steps:

1. Select the group to delete from the Groups list of User Manager's window.

2. From the User menu choose Delete. A warning message appears (see fig. 12.34).

Fig. 12.34 Warning shown when deleting a group from a domain.

3. Click OK to proceed with the transaction, or click Cancel to abort the operation.

4. If you click OK, a second message asks the operator to confirm the decision. Click Yes to delete the group.

Deciding When to Use Local Groups or Global Groups

Determining when to add a local group or a global group to a domain can often be difficult. Use the following guidelines to determine whether to create a new global or local group:

■ Use global groups when user accounts from this domain need to access resources of this domain and other domains.

■ Use local groups when user accounts from this domain or other domains need to be used in resources of this domain. A local group should also be used when global groups from this domain or other domains need to be used in resources from this domain.

Providing Users in Trusted Domains Access to Resources in Trusting Domains

Although one domain trusts another domain, the trust relationship doesn't grant users access to resources in the trusting domain. The easiest method for allowing users from other domains access to your resources is to add a global group from the outside domain to a local group in your domain.

User Manager lets you create global groups in other domains if the other domain trusts your domain. You can set up a global group in the external domain, select the user accounts needed from the outside domain, and then assign that global group to a local group in your domain.

Using the Group Management Wizard

The Group Management Wizard is a tool for creating new groups and adding users to the new group. You also can use the Group Management Wizard to change the membership of or delete existing groups.

The Group Management Wizard makes entering information into the New Global User or New Local User dialog a multistep process. Thus, it's questionable whether this wizard is of significant benefit to Windows NT network administrators.

To decide for yourself whether use of the Group Management Wizard is worthwhile, follow these steps:

1. From the Start menu choose Programs, Administrative Tools, and then Administrative Wizards to open the wizard selection dialog; then double-click the Group Management icon to display the first Group Management Wizard dialog.

2. The wizard lets you create a new group and add members or modify the membership roster of an existing group. To create a new group, accept the default Create a New Group and Add Members option (see fig. 12.35). Click the Next button.

Fig. 12.35 Choosing between creating a new group and working with an existing group in the first Group Management Wizard dialog.

> **Note**
>
> If you choose to modify an existing group, you select the computer on which the group was created, and then select the group to modify. You can delete the group or, in a succeeding dialog, modify the membership of the group.

3. Type the name of the new group (spaces are allowed in the group name) and an optional description in the two text boxes (see fig. 12.36). Click the Next button.

Fig. 12.36 Naming and describing a new group in the second Group Management Wizard dialog.

4. If you're working at the server on which the group is to be created, accept the default option, On My Computer (see fig. 12.37); otherwise, select On Another Computer. Click the Next button.

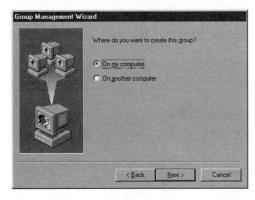

Fig. 12.37 Specifying the location of the new group in the third Group Management Wizard dialog.

5. If you select a computer that's a domain controller, the message shown in figure 12.38 appears. Click OK to continue.

Fig. 12.38 The message that notifies you the computer on which the group is to be created is a domain controller.

6. You can choose between creating a Global Group (the default) and a Local Group (see fig. 12.39). Unless you have a specific reason for creating a Local Group, accept the default and click Next.

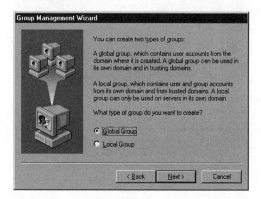

Fig. 12.39 Choosing between a new Global Group or Local Group in the fourth Group Management Wizard dialog.

7. All users appear in the Available Members list. Select each user you want to join to the new group and click the Add button to add the user to Selected Members list (see fig. 12.40). When you've added all the members, click Next.

Fig. 12.40 Adding users to the new group in the fifth Group Management Wizard dialog.

8. The last dialog (see fig. 12.41) confirms the name and the domain for the new group. Click Finish to add the new group to the domain.

Fig. 12.41 Confirming the addition of the new group in the last Group Management Wizard dialog.

9. A message confirms addition of the new group (see fig. 12.42). If you've had enough group management wizardry for the moment, click No. If you want to give the Group Management Wizard another try, click Yes.

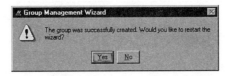

Fig. 12.42 The message indicating that, at last, the group has been created.

Managing User Rights Policy

Each user's capabilities are determined by the rights and privileges assigned to the user. A user's *rights* refer to the entire system or domain. All rights are assigned by User Manager. The rights assigned to a user directly affect the tasks that a user can perform on the network.

> **Note**
>
> *Permissions* assigned to a user refer to the specific files, folders, and hardware devices that are accessible to a user. For additional information on user permissions, see Chapter 13, "Sharing and Securing Network Resources."

Determining User Rights

A Windows NT network has two categories of rights: basic and advanced. Table 12.2 lists the user rights of Windows NT Server 4.0 and the built-in groups that receive these rights.

Table 12.2 Basic Rights for the Built-In Windows NT Groups

User Rights	Groups Rights Are Assigned To
Access this computer from network	Administrators, EVERYONE
Add workstations to domain	Administrators, Backup Operators, Server Operators
Backup files and directories	Administrators, Backup Operators, Server Operators
Change the system time	Administrators, Server Operators
Force shutdown from a remote system	Administrators, Backup Operators, Server Operators
Load and unload device drivers	Administrators
Log on locally	Account Operators, Administrators, Backup Operators, Print Operators, Server Operators
Manage auditing and security log	Administrators
Restore files and directories	Administrators, Backup Operators, Server Operators
Shut down the system	Account Operators, Administrators, Backup Operators, Server Operators
Take ownership of files or other objects	Administrators
Bypass traverse checking	EVERYONE
Log on as a service	Replicators
Assign user rights	Administrators
Create and manage local groups	Administrators, Users
Create and manage user accounts	Administrators
Create common groups	Administrators
Format computer's hard disk	Administrators
Keep local profile	Administrators, EVERYONE
Lock the computer	Administrators, EVERYONE
Manage auditing of system events	Administrators
Override the lock of the computer	Administrators
Share and stop sharing directories	Administrators
Share and stop sharing printers	Administrators

Note

The term EVERYONE is not a group, but a Windows NT convention for indicating that all users in all groups have this right.

Assigning New User Rights

When you create a new user group, the user rights can be added and removed from the group to customize the set of rights received by members of the new group. To add or delete rights from group membership, follow these steps:

1. In User Manager's window, choose <u>U</u>ser from the <u>P</u>olicy menu to display the User Rights Policy dialog (see fig. 12.43).

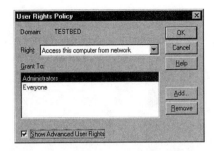

Fig. 12.43 Assigning user rights to groups and accounts in the User Rights Policy dialog.

2. The Right drop-down list at the top of the dialog displays rights that you can assign to or remove from Windows NT Server 4.0 groups. By default, only basic rights are listed in the list. To see advanced rights, mark the Show Advanced User Rights check box at the bottom of the dialog, and then select the right you want to examine.

When you select a user right from the Right drop-down list, the Grant To list changes to reflect the groups to which the right is assigned.

3. To add new groups to the right, click the Add button to display the Add Users and Groups dialog with a list of users and groups in the domain. Select the groups and users to which you want to assign the right.

To remove a user right from a group or user, select the right, select the user or group to be removed in the Grant To list, and then click the Remove button.

4. When all your changes are complete, click OK to effect the changes and close the dialog.

From Here...

In this chapter, you learned to utilize User Manager to configure user accounts and groups. The administrator of a Windows NT Server 4.0 network has total control of all users and network resources. You can tailor each user group and user account to meet the operational need of each user, department, or division, commensurate with the required level of security for the network. This chapter also described how to use the Add User Account Wizard and Group Management Wizard as alternatives to direct manipulation of user accounts and groups with User Manager for Domains.

For more information related to the content of this chapter, see the following chapters:

- Chapter 10, "Configuring Windows 95 Clients for Networking," describes how to implement Windows 95's unique networked user logon and system policies.

- Chapter 13, "Sharing and Securing Network Resources," describes user permissions for the common types of networked resources.

- Chapter 16, "Distributing Network Services with Domains," describes how Windows NT Server 4.0 domains are used in wide area networking.

III

Administering a Network

Chapter 13

Sharing and Securing Network Resources

The fundamental purpose of any network operating system (NOS) is to give users access to shared network resources such as folders, files, and printers. Just as important as the capability to share these resources is the capability to control which users have access to each resource.

Windows NT Server 4.0 provides all the tools you need to share and secure folders and files. You can control access to folders and files on a very broad level. For example, folder shares function like a blunt instrument. They allow you to share a folder on the Windows NT Server computer, but they allow access control only at the group level, and only then to the folder and all subfolders as a group. NTFS folder access permissions and NTFS file access permissions, on the other hand, function more like scalpels. They allow you to control access very finely, down to the level of deciding whether one particular user can access one particular file in one particular subfolder.

Windows NT Server 4.0 also provides all the tools you need to share and secure network printers. You can share printers that are physically connected to the computer running Windows NT Server. You can also share printers that are physically connected to other Microsoft Networking clients on the network, configuring them to appear as shared resources on the Windows NT Server computer.

Sharing and Securing Folders and Files

Windows NT Server makes it easy for you to share folders and files. Behind this ease of use lurks the power needed to control which users can access which resources. In the following sections, you learn how to share folders and files and how to control access to them. The extent to which you can secure your folders and files depends on the file system you decide to use.

In this chapter, you learn how to

- Create shared folders on the server

- Use share permissions to control global access to shared folders

- Use NTFS folder permissions and NTFS file permissions

- Use the Add Printer Wizard to share a printer attached directly to the computer running Windows NT Server 4.0

- Configure a remote network printer server and print queue as a shared server resource

- Install and configure printer auditing

III

Administering a Network

> **Note**
>
> Windows NT 4.0, like Windows 95, has adopted the term *folder* to replace *directory*; thus, this chapter uses the term *folder*, which is likely to be adopted by most Windows NT users. (Similarly, this chapter uses the term *subfolder* in place of the term *subdirectory*.) Some Windows NT dialogs and help screens still use the term *directory*. When one of these screen elements is explicitly referred to in the text, this chapter uses the term *directory* to correspond to Microsoft usage and to avoid confusion.

Windows NT Server File Systems

Windows NT Server lets you choose among three supported file systems. The first two of these file systems are supported largely for historical and backward-compatibility reasons. The third was designed to provide the performance, security, and features needed by a modern network operating system.

The three supported file systems of Windows NT Server 3.x and 4.0 are as follows:

- The *FAT file system* is marginally faster than the other file systems on small servers, but provides none of the data integrity features available with the HPFS and NTFS file systems. Access control is limited to share-level security. Don't consider using the FAT file system on a production server.

- The *High Performance File System (HPFS)*, originally developed by IBM for its OS/2 operating system, is fast and provides good data integrity features, but offers only share-level security. However, all features of HPFS are matched or bettered by NTFS, so there's no reason to use HPFS. Unlike prior versions of Windows NT, Windows NT 4.0 doesn't support HPFS, although you can access HPFS files and folders running on networked Windows NT 3.x servers.

- The *NT File System* (NTFS) is the native file system designed by Microsoft for Windows NT Server. It's fast, offers excellent security, and provides rock-solid data integrity functions.

Although Microsoft offers you a choice of file systems, don't spend too long thinking about which to pick. Using NTFS provides the best mix of speed, security, and protection for your data.

 ◀◀ See "Handling Files with NTFS," p. 97

Understanding Folder Shares

Until a folder is shared, no user can access it across the network. Even the system administrator, who has full access to all server folders and files, can't access a folder across the network until a share has been created for that folder.

Folder shares provide the first level of security by controlling which folders on the server are visible to—and therefore accessible by—logged-on users. As a means of securing access, folder shares have the following drawbacks:

■ Sharing a folder automatically shares all files contained in that folder and in its subfolders. If you need finer control of which subfolders and files are accessible to which users, you must use folder access permissions and file access permissions, which are available only if you're using the NTFS file system.

■ A folder share controls access only for those users who log on to the server from a remote workstation. Any user with physical access to the server can log on locally and bypass share-level security.

Note

Sharing works with all three file systems supported by Windows NT Server—FAT, HPFS (Windows NT Server 3.x only), and NTFS. Shares are the only form of access control available with the FAT and HPFS file systems. This means that any user who has physical access to the server can log on locally and bypass security on FAT and HPFS volumes.

Creating, Modifying, and Removing Folder Shares. To create a folder share, you must be logged on locally to the computer running Windows NT Server, and your account must be a member of the Administrators, Server Operators, or Power Users group. Follow these steps to create a new folder share:

1. Double-click the My Computer icon to display a list of drives available on your server.

2. Double-click one of the available drives to display a list of folders contained on that drive. If the folder you want to share isn't at the root level, click the + symbol to the left of the parent folder name to display a list of subfolders for that folder.

3. Right-click a folder to display the context-sensitive menu.

4. Click Sharing to display the Sharing page of the property sheet for that folder (see fig. 13.1).

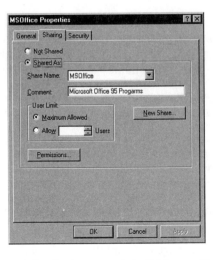

Fig. 13.1 Creating a share with the Sharing page of the *Foldername* Properties sheet.

5. By default, the folder is marked Not Shared. Select the Shared As option button to activate the remaining controls of the dialog and to let you enter information for the share.

6. Type a descriptive name for the share into the Share Name combo box. This is the name by which users access the shared folder. Optionally, type a more complete description of the resource into the Comment text box.

7. Specify User Limit information. By default, the new share is set to Maximum Allowed, which allows any number of users to access the share simultaneously, up to the limit of the number of users for which the server is licensed.

   Select the Allow option button and select a specific number of allowable simultaneous users, if you want to limit the number of users who are permitted to access this share at any one time. Do this if you're concerned about performance degradation when a large number of users contend for a single resource.

By default, the new share provides Full Control to the group Everyone. This means that any user with an account on the server can add, modify, or delete files contained in this folder. The following section, "Working with Share Permissions," describes how to restrict access to the new share.

> **Caution**
>
> Although Windows NT Server 4.0 converts long file and folder names to a form usable by clients running DOS and Windows versions before Windows 95, it doesn't perform a similar conversion for share names. So although Windows NT Server 4.0 allows you to use share names that exceed the MS-DOS 8.3 naming conventions, doing so makes these shares inaccessible to some clients.

To remove a folder share, perform the preceding first four steps to display the Sharing page of the *Foldername* Properties sheet. Select the Not Shared option button and then click the Apply button.

To modify the share, specify a new Share Name, Comment, or User Limit, as described in the preceding steps. You also can create an alias for this shared resource by clicking the New Share button and completing the dialog. Doing so allows the same shared resource to be accessed by more than one share name.

Clicking the Permissions button allows you to determine which users and groups have access to this shared resource, and at what level. The following section describes how to restrict access in this manner.

Working with Share Permissions. Share permissions control which users and groups can access a share, and at what level. You can add, modify, view, or remove the following share permissions for each folder you have shared on the server:

- *No Access (None)* permission restricts all access to the shared folder.

- *Read* permission allows the user to view file names and subfolder names within the shared folder. You can change to a subfolder, and you can open a file in the shared folder or in a subfolder in read-only mode, but you can't write to that file or delete it. You can execute program files for which you have only Read permission.

■ *Change* permission grants all the rights provided by Read permission, and adds the rights to create new files and subfolders, modify the contents of new or existing files, and delete files and subfolders.

■ *Full Control (All)* permission grants all the rights provided by Change permission, and adds the rights to create and modify NTFS file permissions and folder permissions, as well as take ownership of NTFS files and folders.

You can modify, view, and remove share permissions by using the following procedure:

1. Perform the first four steps in the preceding section to display the Sharing page of the *Foldername* Properties sheet.

2. Click the Permissions button to display the Access Through Share Permissions dialog (see fig. 13.2). The Name list displays the users and groups authorized to access this share. By default, the group Everyone is assigned the Full Control permission to the share.

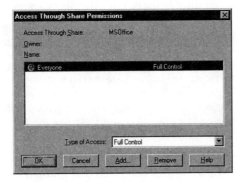

Fig. 13.2 Setting share permissions in the Access Through Share Permissions dialog.

3. To modify the share permission for an existing user or group, highlight that user or group and select a Type of Access from the drop-down list.

To remove the share permission for an existing user or group, highlight that user or group and click the Remove button.

4. Click OK to accept the changes and return to the *Foldername* Properties sheet.

Adding a share permission requires a few more steps. To add a share permission, display the Add Through Share Permissions dialog by following steps 1 and 2 in the preceding list. Then proceed as follows:

1. Click the Add button to display the Add Users and Groups dialog (see fig. 13.3).

2. Select the domain or computer from which the new users or groups are to be added by highlighting a choice in the List Names From drop-down list. Groups that are members of the selected domain or computer are displayed in the Names list.

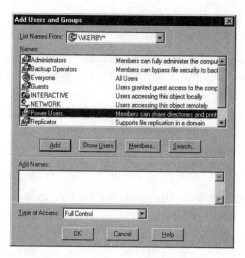

Fig. 13.3 Granting share permissions to users and groups in the Add Users and Groups dialog.

  3. Select one of the displayed groups by clicking its name. (By default, only the groups are displayed. To display users, click the Show Users button.)

> **Tip**
>
> You can add several users and groups to the share in a single step by selecting multiple users and groups using standard Windows selection conventions. Hold down the Ctrl key and click to add additional individual users or groups to the selected list. Hold down the Shift key and click to add a contiguous range of users or groups to the selected list. As you select each user or group to be added, its name appears in the Add Names list.

  4. After you select all users and groups to be added to the share, use the Type of Access drop-down list to select the access type to be granted to the selected users and groups.

  5. Click the Add button and then click OK to add the selected users and groups to the share. The Access Through Share Permissions dialog appears, with the new users and groups added to the share and their access type displayed.

> **Caution**
>
> If you're using share permissions to restrict access to a shared folder, remember to remove the default share permission that grants the group Everyone the Full Control share permission for that folder. Share permissions are cumulative, so any user has *all* share permissions granted to *any* group of which he is a member.

  6. In the Access Through Share Permissions dialog, click OK to return to the *Foldername* Properties sheet. Click OK to accept the changes you've made to the share.

Note

Share permissions specify the maximum level of access available within the shared folder tree. Any subsequent restrictions you add with NTFS folder permissions and NTFS file permissions (described in the following section) can only further restrict access. They can't grant an access level above that allowed by the share permission.

Administrative Shares. In addition to the shares that you create, Windows NT Server automatically creates several shares for administrative purposes. These administrative shares include at least the following:

■ *ADMIN$* points to the location of the shared Windows NT Server folder on the server. For example, if you install Windows NT Server to the C:\Winnt folder on your server, the ADMIN$ share points to this folder.

■ *[drive letter]$* points to the root folder of each drive on the server. For example, if your server has three drives, designated C, D, and E, these drives are each represented by an administrative share, named C$, D$, and E$, respectively.

The most common administrative shares are the drive and folder shares. However, administrative shares can also represent a named pipe for Remote Procedure Calls, a communication-device queue (only on LAN Manager servers), or a shared printer.

◄◄ See "Calling Remote Procedures," p. 102

Tip

If you want to create a share that isn't visible to users browsing the network, make the final character of the share name a $. A share so named doesn't appear to a user browsing network resources. To access the share, the user must know the exact share name and must explicitly type it.

Displaying All Shares and Disconnecting Shares. Shared folders are indicated by a distinctive icon in Windows NT Explorer and the My Computer window. However, sometimes it's useful to see a comprehensive list of shares displayed in one place. To see a list of all active shares on your server, proceed as follows:

1. From Control Panel, double-click the Server icon to display the Server dialog (see fig. 13.4).

2. Click the Shares button to display the Shared Resources dialog (see fig. 13.5). For each share, this dialog displays the Sharename, Uses (the number of current active sessions for the share), and Path associated with the share name.

3. To disconnect one share, highlight the share name and click the Disconnect button. You can disconnect all shares in one step by clicking the Disconnect All button.

III

Administering a Network

Fig. 13.4   The initial dialog of Control Panel's Server tool.

Fig. 13.5   The Shared Resources dialog, displaying share names and number of connected users.

Using the Managing Folder and File Access Wizard

The Managing Folder and File Access Wizard provides a quick and easy way to create and manage folder shares.

> **Note**
>
> During each major step of the Managing Folder and File Access Wizard, you can click the Next button to proceed to the next step, click the Back button to return to the preceding step, or click the Cancel button to abort the process.
>
> During subsidiary dialogs in the Managing Folder and File Access Wizard process, you use the standard Windows dialog buttons. Clicking OK accepts the changes you've made and proceeds to the next step in the process. Clicking Cancel returns you to the previous dialog without making changes. In the interest of brevity, the following steps assume that you click the appropriate button to proceed with each step of the process.

To use the Managing Folder and File Access Wizard, follow these steps:

1. From the Start menu, choose Programs, Administrative Tools, and Administrative Wizards to display the Administrative Wizards menu.

2. Click the Managing File and Folder Access icon to display the first dialog of the Managing Folder and File Access Wizard (see fig. 13.6).

Fig. 13.6 The opening dialog of the Managing Folder and File Access Wizard.

  3. Select On My Computer to create or manage shares on the server, or select On Another Computer to manage shares on another computer on the network. In this example, a new share is created on another server. The Managing Folder and File Access Wizard displays the dialog shown in figure 13.7.

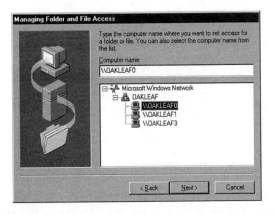

Fig. 13.7 Selecting the computer where the share is to be created.

  4. Select the computer where you want to create or manage the share and click Next. The Managing Folder and File Access Wizard displays the dialog shown in figure 13.8. In the example, a new share name is entered into the To Create a New Folder, Type a New Name text box to create a new share named SHARED.

  5. Click Next to display the Managing Folder and File Access confirmation message shown in figure 13.9. Click Yes to create the new folder. The Managing Folder and File Access Wizard displays the message box shown in figure 13.10 to confirm that the new folder has been created successfully. Click OK.

III

Administering a Network

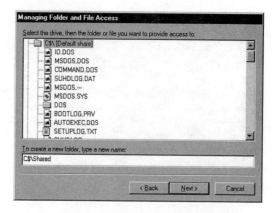

Fig. 13.8 Selecting an existing folder or creating a new folder.

Fig. 13.9 Confirming the creation of the new folder for the share.

Fig. 13.10 Confirming that the new folder has been created.

6. Click Next to display the next Managing Folder and File Access Wizard dialog (see fig. 13.11). This dialog allows you to set permissions for the folder to determine who has access to it, and at what level. By default, the original permissions for the share are retained, and these permissions flow down to affect the files and subfolders contained within this folder.

To change these default permissions, click Change Permissions and choose one of the three options presented:

- Only I Have Access and Full Control

- I Have Access and Full Control, Everyone Else Can Only Read It

- Everyone Has Access and Full Control

Mark the Apply These Permissions to All Folders and Files Within This Folder check box if you want the permissions you set here to apply to all subfolders and files contained within this folder. Unmark the check box if you want these permissions to apply only to this folder.

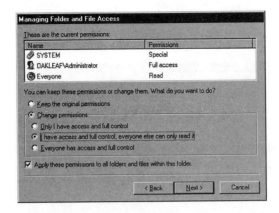

Fig. 13.11 Assigning permissions to the shared folder.

7. Click Next to display the Managing Folder and File Access message box (see fig. 13.12). This message box allows you to specify whether the folder will be shared with network users. Click Yes to allow network users to access the folder.

Fig. 13.12 Specifying whether you want to share this folder with network users.

8. The Managing Folder and File Access Wizard displays the dialog shown in figure 13.13. You may rename the share, provide a brief description of the share, and specify which types of network users may access the share. Make any changes necessary and click Next.

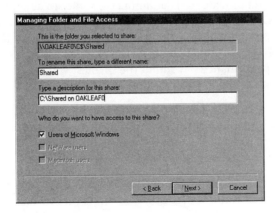

Fig. 13.13 Renaming the share, adding a description, and selecting the type of network users who have access to the share.

9. The Managing Folder and File Access Wizard displays the summary shown in figure 13.14. Click Finish to complete creating the share.

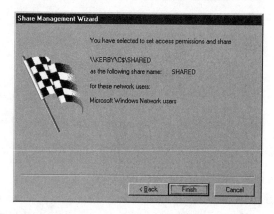

Fig. 13.14   The summary displays the choices you've made for the new share.

10. The message box shown in figure 13.15 lets you exit the Managing Folder and File Access Wizard or continue managing shares. Click No to exit or Yes to manage another share.

Fig. 13.15   The final message of the Managing Folder and File Access Wizard.

Understanding NTFS Permissions

Share-level access control provides only a limited capability to determine which users can access which files. The FAT and HPFS file systems offer only share-level access control. If you need to control access down to subfolders and individual files, your only choice is to use the NTFS file system. Doing so is no sacrifice at all, because NTFS offers more features, better performance (on all but the smallest volumes), and better security than the other file systems supported by Windows NT Server.

In addition to the file name, file size, and date/time stamp, NTFS stores extended attributes with each file and folder entry. One of these extended attributes, named *permissions*, determines which users and groups have access to the shared resource. NTFS has the following types of permissions:

■ *File access permissions* store information about which users and groups are permitted to access a specified file and the level of access they're allowed. For example, the user Admin and the group Programmers might have full read/write access to a particular database file; the group Marketing might have read-only access; and the group Accounting might have no access at all.

■ *Folder access permissions* store information about which users and groups are permitted to access a specified folder and the level of access they're allowed. For example, the user Webmaster and the group Administrators can have full read/write access to the Web server folder on your server (which contains your private company intranet), the group Everyone can have read-only access, and the user Guest can have no access at all.

By default, a user inherits file and folder permissions from the group of which that user is a member. For example, if a newly created user is assigned to the group *marketing*, that user is automatically granted all file- and folder-access permissions possessed by the group. If a user is a member of more than one group, that user has *all* permissions owned by *any* group of which he is a member.

Paying careful attention to how you assign file and folder permissions to groups allows you to reduce or eliminate the time-consuming and error-prone process of assigning permissions on a user-by-user basis.

> **Note**
>
> NTFS file and folder permissions can be used only to further restrict share-level permissions established when the original share was created or modified. NTFS permissions can't grant something that was taken away by the share-level permission in effect. For example, if the share-level permission restricts users to read-only access, setting NTFS file or folder permissions to a higher level of access does nothing to increase the users' level of access. Conversely, if the share-level permission allows full access but an NTFS permission further restricts access to read-only, users affected by the NTFS permission are limited to read-only access.

Working with NTFS File Access Permissions. NTFS file access permissions control which users and groups can access a file, and at what level. Remember that NTFS file access permissions can further restrict the access level granted by share permissions, but they can't extend access beyond that granted by share access permissions. You can add, modify, view, or remove the following file access permissions for each file:

■ *No Access (None)* permission restricts all access to the shared file.

■ *Read (RX)* permission allows you to view the file name and open the file in read-only mode, but you can't write to the file or delete it. Because read (R) permission implies execute (X) permission, if the file is an executable program file, read permission allows you to execute it.

■ *Change (RWXD)* permission grants all the rights provided by Read permission, and adds the rights to write (W) and delete (D) the file, create new files and subfolders, modify the contents of new or existing files, and delete files and subfolders.

■ *Full Control (All)* permission grants all the rights provided by Change permission, and adds the rights to change NTFS file access permissions and folder permissions, and to take ownership of NTFS files and folders.

III

Administering a Network

■ *Special Access* permission allows you to customize the file access permissions for a particular file. You can specify any combination of read (R), write (W), execute (X), delete (D), change permissions (P), and take ownership (O). For example, you can use Special Access file access permissions to allow a specified user or group to have read, write, and execute permissions for the file, but not to have delete permission.

Modifying, Viewing, and Removing NTFS File Access Permissions. You can modify, view, and remove NTFS file access permissions by following these steps:

1. In Windows NT Explorer, highlight the file or files for which permissions are to be added, modified, viewed, or removed.

2. Right-click to display the context-sensitive menu, and choose Properties to display the *Filename* Properties sheet.

3. Click the Security tab to display the Security page (see fig. 13.16).

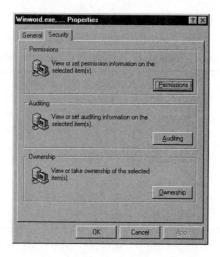

Fig. 13.16 The Security page of the *Filename* Properties sheet.

4. Click the Permissions button to display the File Permissions dialog (see fig. 13.17).

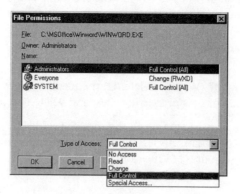

Fig. 13.17 Granting permissions to groups with the File Permissions dialog.

5. Select a type of access from the Type of Access drop-down list. You can choose one of the standard types of access—No Access, Read, Change, or Full Control—or you can select Special Access to customize file access permissions for this file or group of files.

6. If you've selected one of the standard types of access, click OK to apply the selected file access permissions. You then return to the *Filename* Properties sheet. Click OK again to accept the changes and exit the *Filename* Properties sheet.

If you select Special Access, the Special Access dialog shown in figure 13.18 appears. Mark the check boxes to select the types of access to be granted for the selected file(s). The example shows a file for which all permissions except Take Ownership (O) have been granted. This custom set of permissions falls between the standard file access types Change (RXWD) and Full Control (RXWDPO).

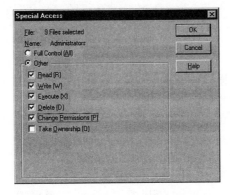

Fig. 13.18 Setting specific permissions for a group in the Special Access dialog.

7. After you select the permissions for the file, click OK to accept these settings and return to the File Permissions dialog.

8. In the File Permissions dialog, click OK to apply the selected file access permissions and return to the *Filename* Properties sheet. Click OK again to accept the changes and exit the *Filename* Properties sheet.

Adding NTFS File Access Permissions. You can add NTFS file access permissions by following these steps:

1. Follow steps 1 through 4 from the preceding section to display the File Permissions dialog.

2. Click the Add button to display the Add Users and Groups dialog (see fig. 13.19).

3. Select the domain or computer from which the users and groups are to be added from the List Names From drop-down list. Available groups are displayed in the Names list. You also can display individual users from within these groups by clicking the Show Users button.

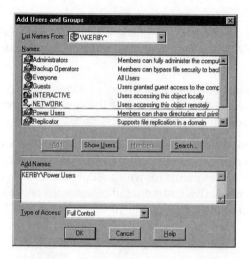

Fig. 13.19   Granting the Power Users group file access in the Add Users and Groups dialog.

4. Select individual users or groups for which you want to add file access permissions by double-clicking the name in the Names list. Each of these is displayed in the Add Names list as you select it.

   You can also select multiple users and groups in the Names list by using standard Windows conventions for making multiple selections. After you finish making selections, click the Add button to transfer all selected names to the Add Names list.

5. Select the type of access to be granted to the selected users and groups from the Type of Access drop-down list.

   > **Note**
   >
   > Only the standard types of access—No Access, Read, Change, and Full Control—are available in the Add Users and Groups dialog. If you need to assign special file access permissions for the users or groups being added, simply choose any one of the standard permissions here and modify your selection in the File Permissions dialog in the following step.

6. Click OK to accept your changes and return to the File Permissions dialog. The newly added users or groups are displayed in the Names list. If you need to assign special file access permissions to the newly added users or groups, highlight them now and assign these special file access permissions using the steps described in the preceding section.

7. After you properly assign all permissions, return to the File Permissions dialog and click OK to return to the *Filename* Properties sheet. Click OK to accept the changes and exit the *Filename* Properties sheet.

Working with NTFS Folder Access Permissions. NTFS folder access permissions control which users and groups can access a folder and its files, and at what level. Remember that NTFS folder access permissions can further restrict the access level granted by share permissions, but they can't extend access beyond that granted by share access permissions.

You can add, modify, view, or remove the following folder access permissions for each folder. Each named permission affects the folder in question and the files contained within it. The first parenthetical item after each folder access permission name lists the effect of that permission on the folder; the second parenthetical item lists the effect of that permission on files contained within the folder.

- *No Access (None) (None)* permission restricts all access to the shared folder. Specifying No Access for a user eliminates that user's access to the folder, even if the user is a member of a group or groups that have access to the folder.

- *List (RX) (Not Specified)* permission allows the user to view a list of files and sub-folders contained within the folder, and to change to a subfolder, but it doesn't grant permission to access the files.

- *Read (RX) (RX)* permission grants all the rights provided by list permission. It allows the user to open a file in read-only mode, but not to write to the file or delete it. Because read (R) permission implies execute (X) permission, if the file is an execut-able program file, read permission allows you to execute it.

- *Add (WX) (Not Specified)* permission allows the user to create new files and new subfolders within the folder, but doesn't grant permission to access the files, in-cluding those newly created.

- *Add & Read (RWX) (RX)* permission combines the rights granted by the Read and Add folder permissions described in the preceding items.

- *Change (RWXD) (RWXD)* permission grants all the rights provided by the Add & Read permission, and adds the rights to write (W) to and delete (D) files and to delete (D) subfolders.

- *Full Control (All) (All)* permission grants all the rights provided by the Change per-mission, and adds the rights to change NTFS file access permissions and folder permissions, as well as take ownership of NTFS files and folders.

- *Special Directory Access* permission allows you to customize folder access permis-sions. You can specify any combination of read (R), write (W), execute (X), delete (D), change permissions (P), and take ownership (O). For example, you can use special directory access folder access permissions to allow a specified user or group to have list and read permissions for files within the folder, but not to have the execute permission.

- *Special File Access* permission allows you to customize file access permissions. You can specify any combination of read (R), write (W), execute (X), delete (D), change permissions (P), and take ownership (O). Special file access permission works in the same way as the special directory access permission described in the preceding item, but affects only specified files contained within the folder rather than the folder itself.

> **Note**
>
> NTFS folder access permissions supersede restrictions placed on files by NTFS file access permissions. For example, if a user has the Full Control folder access permission in a folder that contains a file with file access permissions set to read (R), that user can modify or delete the file.

Modifying, Viewing, and Removing NTFS Folder Access Permissions. You can modify, view, and remove NTFS folder access permissions by following these steps:

1. In Windows NT Explorer, highlight the folder or folders for which permissions are to be added, modified, viewed, or removed.

2. Right-click to display the context-sensitive menu, and choose Properties to display the *Foldername* Properties sheet.

3. Click the Security tab to display the Security page (refer to fig. 13.16).

4. Click the Permissions button to display the Directory Permissions dialog (see fig. 13.20).

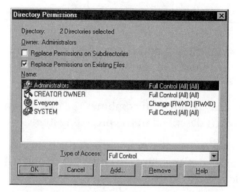

Fig. 13.20 Granting file permissions for two NTFS folders in the Directory Permissions dialog.

5. Select an access type from the Type of Access drop-down list. You can choose one of the standard types of access—No Access, List, Read, Add, Add & Read, Change, or Full Control. You also can choose Special Directory Access to specify a custom set of access rights for the affected folders, or Special File Access to specify a custom set of access rights for the files contained within those folders.

> **Note**
>
> The Directory Permissions dialog includes two check boxes—Replace Permissions on Subdirectories and Replace Permissions on Existing Files—that allow you to specify which files and folders within the selected folder tree are affected by the permissions you set. Marking both check boxes causes the permissions you set to affect the selected folder, the files it contains, the subfolders of that folder, and the files contained in these subfolders.

Marking only the Replace Permissions on Subdirectories check box causes the permissions you set to affect only the selected folder and its subfolders, but not the files contained within them. Marking only the Replace Permissions on Existing Files check box causes the permissions you set to affect only the selected folder and the files contained within it, but not the subfolders or their files. Clearing both check boxes causes the permissions you set to affect only the selected folder, but not the files contained within it or the subfolders and their files.

6. If you've selected one of the standard access types, click OK to apply the selected folder access permissions. You then return to the *Foldername* Properties sheet. Click OK again to accept the changes and exit the *Foldername* Properties sheet.

If you select Special Directory Access, the Special Directory Access dialog appears (see fig. 13.21). Mark the check boxes to select the types of access to be granted for the selected folder or folders. The example shows access being set for two folders for which all permissions except Take Ownership (O) have been granted. This custom set of permissions falls between the standard folder access types Change (RXWD) and Full Control (RWXDPO).

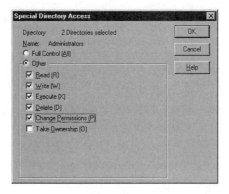

Fig. 13.21 Granting specific permissions for two NTFS folders in the Special Directory Access dialog.

7. After you select the permissions for the folder, click OK to accept these settings and return to the Directory Permissions dialog.

8. In the Directory Permissions dialog, click OK to apply the selected folder access permissions and return to the *Foldername* Properties sheet. Click OK again to accept the changes and exit the *Foldername* Properties sheet.

9. If you select Special File Access, the Special File Access dialog shown in figure 13.22 appears. Mark the check boxes to select the types of access to be granted for files contained within the selected folder or folders. The example shows access being set for two folders for which all permissions except Take Ownership (O) have been granted. This custom set of permissions falls between the standard folder access types Change (RXWD) and Full Control (RWXDPO).

III

Administering a Network

Fig. 13.22 Granting specific file permissions in the Special File Access dialog.

> **Note**
>
> The Special File Access dialog is almost identical to the Special Directory Access dialog but includes one additional item. Selecting the Access Not Specified option button in the Special File Access dialog prevents files in the affected folder or folders from inheriting folder permissions.

10. After you select special file access permissions for the affected folder or folders, click OK to accept these settings and return to the Directory Permissions dialog.

11. In the Directory Permissions dialog, click OK to apply the permissions and return to the *Foldername* Properties sheet. Click OK again to accept the changes and exit the *Foldername* Properties sheet.

Adding NTFS Folder Access Permissions. You can add NTFS folder access permissions by following these steps:

1. Follow steps 1 through 4 from the preceding section to display the Directory Permissions dialog.

2. Click the Add button to display the Add Users and Groups dialog (see fig. 13.23).

3. Select the domain or computer from which the users and groups are to be added from the List Names From drop-down list. Available groups are displayed in the Names list. You can also display individual users from within these groups by clicking the Show Users button.

4. Select individual users or groups for which you want to add file access permissions by double-clicking the name in the Names list. Each of these is displayed in the Add Names list as you select it. You can also select multiple users and groups in the Names list by using standard Windows conventions for making multiple selections. After you finish making selections, click the Add button to transfer all selected names to the Add Names list.

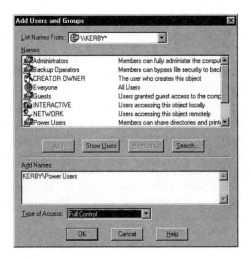

Fig. 13.23 The Add Users and Groups dialog with the Power Users group added.

5. Select the access type to be granted to the selected users and groups from the Type of Access drop-down list.

> **Note**
>
> Only the standard types of access—No Access, List, Read, Add, Add & Read, Change, and Full Control—are available in the Add Users and Groups dialog. If you need to assign special directory access permissions or special file access permissions for the users or groups being added, simply choose any one of the standard permissions here and modify your selection in the Directory Permissions dialog in the following step.

6. Click OK to accept your changes and return to the Directory Permissions dialog. The newly added users or groups are displayed in the Name list. If you need to assign special directory access permissions or special file access permissions to the newly added users or groups, highlight them now and assign these special access permissions using the steps described in the preceding section.

7. After you properly assign all permissions, return to the Directory Permissions dialog and click OK to return to the *Foldername* Properties sheet. Click OK to accept the changes and exit the *Foldername* Properties sheet.

Replicating Folders

Windows NT Server 4.0 allows you to replicate, or copy, folders to other computers or domains to maintain identical copies of folders and files on more than one computer. The folder from which data is copied is called the *export folder* and is located on the *export server*; the folder to which data is copied is called the *import folder* and is located on the *import computer*. The export and import folders can be located on the same computer or on different computers.

III

Administering a Network

> **Note**
>
> A server running the Windows NT Server 4.0 replication service can be either an export server or an import computer, or both. A client running Windows NT Workstation 4.0 can participate in folder replication, but only as an import computer.

Folder replication does more than simply copy data from the export folder source to the import folder destination. The Windows NT Server replication service functions much like an FTP mirror program. It monitors the export folder for changes to existing files and newly created files and subfolders, and replicates these changes and additions to the import folder. The replication service also deletes files in the import folder that have been deleted from the export folder. By doing so, it synchronizes the contents of the two folders.

Folder replication is most commonly used for the following two purposes:

■ *Replicating logon scripts from one domain controller to other domain controllers.* This allows users of any domain controller to log on locally, and reduces server load and network traffic.

■ *Replicating a database from one server to another.* This allows users who access the database to be distributed among two or more servers in order to share the workload among multiple servers.

You can also use folder replication to keep a frequently updated backup copy of a heavily used database file, which would otherwise be difficult to back up.

Creating a Replication User

Before you can configure the replication service, you must first create a special user for that service. Create a new user, as described in Chapter 12, "Managing User and Group Accounts." This new special user must have the following properties:

■ The user must be assigned to the Backup Operators group.

■ The Password Never Expires check box must be marked.

■ The Logon Hours settings must allow this user access at all times.

You won't be able to name the new user Replicator because a group already exists with that name. Choose another similar name, such as Replicate.

Starting the Replication Service

After you create the special user, you must then configure and start the Directory Replicator service before folder replication can occur. To do so, proceed as follows:

1. From Control Panel, double-click the Services tool to display the Services dialog, shown in figure 13.24 with the Directory Replicator service shown highlighted. The Status is shown as blank, indicating that the Directory Replicator service isn't running. Startup is shown as Manual, indicating that this service won't be started unless you do so manually.

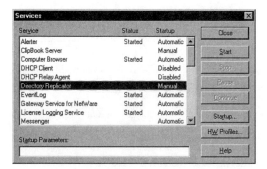

Fig. 13.24   Selecting the Directory Replicator service in the Services dialog.

   2. With the Directory Replicator service highlighted, click the Startup button to display the Service dialog (see fig. 13.25).

Fig. 13.25   Setting the Startup Type and Log On As account in the Service dialog.

   3. In the Startup Type section, select the Automatic option to indicate that the Directory Replicator service should start automatically each time Windows NT Server is started.

   4. In the Log On As section, select the This Account option, and enter the domain and user account name that you created in the preceding section. You can also click the ... button to display a list of available accounts to choose from.

   Type the password for this account in the Password and Confirm Password fields.

   5. Click OK to accept the changes. You're prompted to restart Windows NT Server.

   6. After Windows NT Server is restarted, double-click Control Panel's Services tool to verify that the Directory Replicator service has been started successfully. You should see a display similar to figure 13.26, with the Directory Replicator service shown with Status as Started and Startup as Automatic.

III

Administering a Network

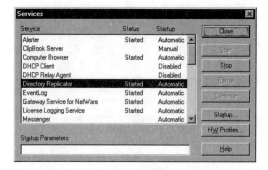

Fig. 13.26 Confirming startup of the Directory Replicator in the Services dialog.

Configuring Folder Replication

After you successfully configure the Directory Replicator service, you must then configure an export server and an import computer.

To configure the export server, you must provide the following pieces of information:

- The export folder designates the source folder from which files and subfolders are exported.

- The Export To list designates computers and domains to which files and subfolders are exported. If you designate a domain here, exported data is replicated on all computers in the export to domain that have replication enabled.

To configure the import computer, you must also provide two pieces of information, as follows:

- The import folder designates the destination folder in which imported files and subfolders are stored.

- The Import From list designates computers and domains from which data to be imported is accepted.

To configure the export server and the import computer, proceed as follows:

1. From Control Panel, double-click the Server tool to display the Server dialog (refer to fig. 13.4).

2. Click the Replication button to display the Directory Replication dialog (see fig. 13.27).

3. In the export section, select the Export Directories option to enable exporting. Then complete the From Path text box to designate which folder is to be exported. Click the Add button to add domains or computers to the To List to designate a target or targets to which data are exported.

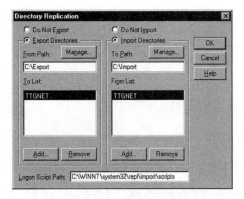

Fig. 13.27 Setting replication paths, lists, and script location in the Directory Replication dialog.

> **Note**
>
> Windows NT Server 4.0 creates default import and export directories when you install it. The default import directory is C:\Winnt\System32\Repl\Import. The default export directory is C:\Winnt\System32\Repl\Export.

4. Click the Manage button to display the Manage Exported Directories dialog (see fig. 13.28). You can use the controls in this dialog to add and remove exported directories and to add and remove locks on managed directories.

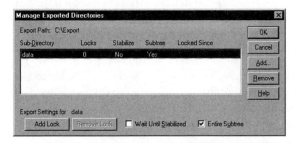

Fig. 13.28 Setting export subdirectory parameters in the Manage Exported Directories dialog.

5. If this server will also be an import computer, select the Import Directories option in the import section of the Directory Replicator dialog to enable importing. Then complete the To Path text box to designate which folder is to receive the imported data. Click the Add button to add domains or computers to the From List to designate computers and domains from which imported data is to be accepted.

6. Click the Manage button in the import section to display the Manage Imported Directories dialog (see fig. 13.29). You can use the controls in this dialog to add and remove imported directories and to add and remove locks on managed directories.

III

Administering a Network

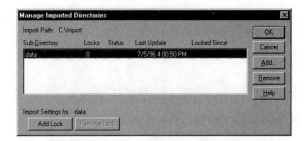

Fig. 13.29   Setting import subdirectory parameters in the Manage Imported Directories dialog.

Sharing and Securing Network Printers

Beyond sharing folders and files, the most common purpose of most networks is to share printers. One justification for early local area networks was their capability to share expensive laser printers among many users. In the past few years, the prices of laser printers have plummeted; it's now economically feasible for many companies to provide sub-$1,000 personal laser printers, such as the Hewlett-Packard LaserJet 5L and 5P, to any client that needs one.

Still, in all, the original justification for sharing expensive printers on the network holds true. Ten years ago, you might have been sharing a $3,500 LaserJet that printed eight letter-size pages per minute at 300 dpi. Today, you might instead be sharing a laser printer that prints 20 11-by-17-inch pages per minute at 600 dpi, but that printer still costs $3,500, and budget realities still demand that it be shared. Just as it always did, the network allows you to share scarce and expensive resources, such as high-speed laser printers and color printers.

Windows NT Server makes it easy to share printers on the network. Printers attached directly to the computer running Windows NT Server can be shared as a network resource and used by any network client authorized to do so. Network clients running Windows 3.11 for Workgroups, Windows 95, or Windows NT Workstation can also function as printer servers, sharing their attached printers with other network users.

> **Note**
>
> Any Windows Networking server or client can share an attached printer as a network resource. Windows NT Server also supports sharing of directly network connected Hewlett-Packard network printers, using the HP JetDirect network interface. A *directly network connected printer* is one that contains its own network adapter card and connects directly to the network cable, rather than to a network client that provides printer server functions for that printer. Directly network connected printers are also called DLC printers, from the Data Link Control protocol that must be installed to support them.
>
> You can use directly network connected printers in locations that are too far removed from the network server to be cabled directly to the server, but where you don't want to put a network client computer. High-speed laser printers, color printers, and other output devices designed to be used as shared network resources are often connected directly to the network in this fashion.

Configuring Locally Attached Server Printers as Shared Resources

After you physically install the printer to be shared and connect it to the computer running Windows NT Server, you can use the Add Printer Wizard to configure it and make it available as a shared printer. To do so, proceed as follows:

1. From My Computer, double-click the Printers icon to display available printers in the Printers window. (If you haven't yet installed any printers, only the Add Printer icon appears in the Printers window.)

2. Double-click the Add Printer icon to invoke the Add Printer Wizard (see fig. 13.30). You can select the My Computer option to add a printer to the local computer, or the Network Printer Server option to add a network printer that's physically connected to a different computer. This section describes adding a locally connected printer, so select the My Computer option button and click Next.

Fig. 13.30 Specifying the printer location in the first Add Printer Wizard dialog.

3. The next dialog, shown in figure 13.31, allows you to specify the port to which the printer is connected, to add a port, and to modify the properties for a port. Mark the check box that corresponds to the port to which your new printer is connected.

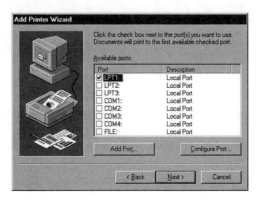

Fig. 13.31 Selecting the printer port in the second Add Printer Wizard dialog.

III

Administering a Network

4. If you need to add a port to the Available Ports list, click the Add Port button to display a list of available printer ports (see fig. 13.32). When you add a printer port and accept the change by clicking OK, you return to the preceding Add Printer Wizard dialog, where the newly added printer port appears as an available selection.

Fig. 13.32   Adding a new printer port in the Printer Ports dialog.

5. In the second Add Printer Wizard dialog (refer to fig. 13.31), you can click the Configure Port button to display and modify port settings. If the selected port is a parallel port, the Configure LPT Port dialog appears (see fig. 13.33).

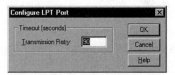

Fig. 13.33   Setting the printer timeout in the Configure LPT Port dialog.

> ### Tip
>
> The only configuration item available for a parallel port is Transmission Retry, which should ordinarily be left at the default setting. If the server to which the printer is connected is very busy, other workstations can have difficulties in completing a print job to this shared printer. If so, try increasing the value for Transmission Retry a little at a time until the problem disappears.

If the selected port is a serial port (also called a *COM port*), the Ports dialog appears (see fig. 13.34). Highlight the COM port to which the printer is connected and click the Settings button to display the Settings for COM*x* dialog (see fig. 13.35). Select the settings for Baud Rate, Data Bits, Parity, Stop Bits, and Flow Control from the drop-down lists that correspond to the settings of the printer being installed.

Fig. 13.34 Choosing between available COM (serial) ports in the Ports dialog.

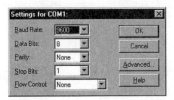

Fig. 13.35 Selecting standard COM port parameters Settings for COMx dialog.

6. Click the Advanced button to display the Advanced Settings for COM*x* dialog (see fig. 13.36). In this dialog, you can adjust settings for COM Port Number, Base I/O Port Address, and Interrupt Request Line (IRQ). The FIFO Enabled check box, when marked, allows Windows NT to use the buffering provided by 16550 and higher UARTs to improve Windows printing performance. If an advanced UART was detected during Windows installation, this check box is marked by default and should be left marked. If Windows NT didn't detect an advanced UART on this port during installation, the check box is disabled (grayed out).

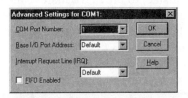

Fig. 13.36 Specifying the I/O memory address and interrupt level in the Advanced Settings for COM*x* dialog.

> **Caution**
>
> The settings for COM Port Number, Base I/O Port Address, and Interrupt Request Line (IRQ) should almost always be left at their default values. Alter these settings only if you've changed the standard COM port settings for your hardware. Otherwise, Windows won't be able to locate the COM port.

III

Administering a Network

7. After you finish selecting the printer port, click OK to advance to the Add Printer Wizard printer selection dialog (see fig. 13.37). Begin by highlighting the manufacturer of your printer in the Manufacturers list. When you highlight a manufacturer, the Printers list displays supported printer models for that manufacturer. Highlight the model of your printer and click Next.

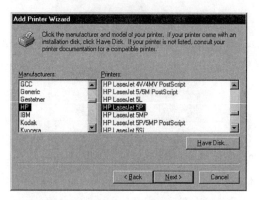

Fig. 13.37 Selecting the printer manufacturer and model in the third Add Printer Wizard dialog.

> **Note**
>
> If you have an updated printer driver supplied by the printer manufacturer, click the Have Disk button and follow the prompts to load the updated driver.

8. The fourth Add Printer Wizard dialog, shown in figure 13.38, allows you to specify whether this printer is shared, to provide a share name for the printer, and to load support for other operating systems that will be printing to this printer. After you complete this dialog, click Next. If you've specified that support for operating systems other than Windows NT 4.0 is to be loaded, you're prompted to insert driver disks for those operating systems.

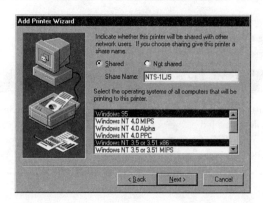

Fig. 13.38 Assigning a share name and specifying types of client PCs in the fourth Add Printer Wizard dialog.

> **Caution**
>
> Be careful when you choose a share name for the printer. If this printer will be accessed by clients running MS-DOS or Windows 3.1+, the share name you select must conform to the MS-DOS 8.3 naming conventions, or the printer won't be visible to these clients. If all your clients are running Windows 95 or Windows NT 4.0, you can select a share name that conforms to Microsoft's long file name conventions.

9. The next step in the Add Printer Wizard allows you to print a test page (see fig. 13.39). You should always allow the wizard to print the test page to verify that your printer has been installed successfully and is performing as expected. After you print the test page and verify that it printed correctly, click the Finish button to complete the Add Printer Wizard.

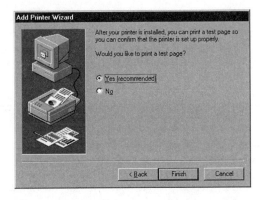

Fig. 13.39 Printing a test page in the fifth Add Printer Wizard dialog.

10. The Copying Files –– Files Needed dialog (see fig. 13.40) prompts you to insert the Windows NT Server CD-ROM so that the necessary files can be copied from it. Specify the drive and path name for these files, or click the Browse button to browse for the location. Make sure that the CD-ROM disk is inserted in the drive, and click OK to proceed with copying files.

Fig. 13.40 Specifying the location of the required printer driver in the Copying Files –– Files Needed dialog.

11. When all needed files are copied from the Windows NT CD-ROM, the Add Printer Wizard prompts you to insert the distribution media for the other operating

III

Administering a Network

systems you've elected to provide printing support for. Insert the media and specify the location of these files as described in the preceding step.

After all needed files are copied, the Add Printer Wizard takes you directly to the Printer Properties sheet to allow you to configure the newly installed printer. This process, used both to configure newly installed printers and to reconfigure printers that are already installed, is described in the following section.

Configuring Network Printer Servers as Shared Resources

The preceding section described how to configure a printer that's physically attached to the computer running Windows NT Server as a shared printer. The Add Printer Wizard also allows you to configure a network printer server as a shared resource on the server. A *network printer server* is a print queue that services a printer that's physically connected to a different computer on the network.

In this section, you learn how to configure a printer queue serviced by a Novell NetWare printer server as a Windows NT Server shared resource. You can use the same procedure to associate a Windows Networking printer queue with a share name on your Windows NT server, allowing you to present printers connected to Windows Networking clients as a server shared resource.

To install and configure a network printer server as a shared server resource, proceed as follows:

1. From My Computer, double-click the Printers icon to display available printers in the Printers window.

2. Double-click the Add Printer icon to invoke the Add Printer Wizard (see fig. 13.41). You can select the My Computer option button to add a printer to the local computer (as described in the preceding section), or the Network printer server option button to add a network printer that's physically connected to a different computer. This section describes adding a network printer server, so select the Network printer server option and click the Next button.

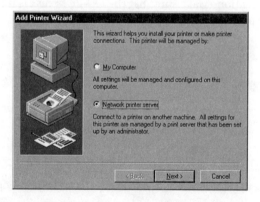

Fig. 13.41 Specifying a networked printer as a shared resource in the first dialog of the Add Printer Wizard.

3. The Connect to Printer dialog appears, displaying the available networks and network printer queues that are visible to Windows NT Server.

4. Highlight and double-click the printer server name to display the print queues associated with that printer server (see fig. 13.42). In the example, a Novell NetWare printer server named Theodore is servicing a print queue named \\THEODORE\\LASER_QUE. If more than one print queue exists on that server, double-click the print queue you want to select to insert it in the Printer text box. (If only one print queue exists on the printer server, it's inserted into the Printer text box automatically when you select the printer server.) Click OK to select that print queue.

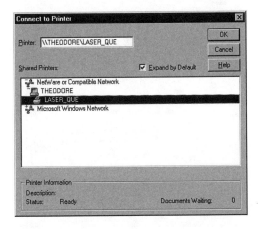

Fig. 13.42 Selecting a printer on a NetWare server from the second dialog of the Connect to Printer dialog.

5. If the selected print queue doesn't have a printer driver installed, you're prompted to install an appropriate printer driver locally on the Windows NT Server computer (see fig. 13.43). Click OK to install the printer driver locally.

Fig. 13.43 The message box that indicates the local server is missing the required printer driver.

6. The Add Printer Wizard moves next to selecting a printer manufacturer and model (refer to fig. 13.37). Begin by highlighting the manufacturer of your printer in the Manufacturers list. When you highlight a manufacturer, the Printers list displays supported printer models for that manufacturer. Highlight the model of your printer and click the Next button to proceed to the next step.

7. The Connect to Printer –– Copying Files –– Files Needed dialog prompts you to insert the Windows NT Server CD-ROM so that the necessary files can be copied from it. Specify the drive and path name for these files, or click the Browse button to browse for the location. Make sure that the CD-ROM disk is inserted in the drive, and click OK to proceed with copying files.

8. When the necessary files are copied, the Printer Properties sheet appears (see fig. 13.44). The example shows a Hewlett-Packard LaserJet 5P printer. The exact contents of this dialog vary, depending on the capabilities of the particular printer you're installing. Configure these settings appropriately, and then click OK to proceed to the next step.

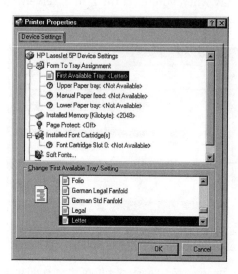

Fig. 13.44   Setting the printer configuration in the Printer Properties sheet.

9. The Add Printer Wizard default printer dialog (see fig. 13.45) asks you whether this printer should be set as the default printer. Select the appropriate option and click Next.

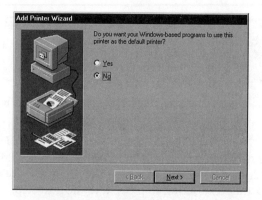

Fig. 13.45   Selecting between default and non-default local printer status in the fourth Add Printer Wizard dialog.

10. The final Add Printer Wizard dialog appears (see fig. 13.46). Click Finish to complete installation of your network print queue printer and return to the Printers window.

Fig. 13.46 Indication of successful addition of the remote printer in the final Add Printer Wizard dialog.

Configuring Printer Properties

The following procedure is automatically invoked as the final step in installing a local printer, described earlier in the section "Configuring Locally Attached Server Printers as Shared Resources." When used in this fashion, the Add Printer Wizard places you at step 3 in the following procedure. This procedure can also be used to reconfigure an existing printer, beginning with step 1:

1. From My Computer, double-click the Printers icon to display available printers in the Printers window.

2. Highlight the printer you want to configure, and right-click to display the context-sensitive menu. Choose Properties to display the General page of the *Printername* Properties sheet (see fig. 13.47).

3. On the General page, supply the following information:

- *Comment* allows you to enter a short comment that can be viewed by users of the printer. For example, if the printer is available only during normal business hours, you might note that in the Comment text box.

- *Location* allows users to view the physical location of the printer to make sure that they know where to pick up their print jobs.

- *Driver* allows you to select from a drop-down list of available drivers for the printer.

- *New Driver* allows you to install a new or updated driver for the printer. To do so, click the New Driver button and follow the prompts.

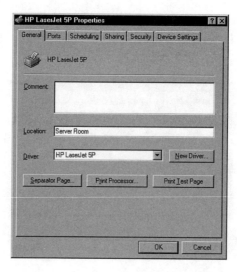

Fig. 13.47 Specifying printer properties in the General page of the *Printername* Properties sheet.

- *Separator Page* allows you to specify options for separator pages, used to keep print jobs separate.

- *Print Processor* allows you to select different methods of processing the incoming byte stream. The default WinPrint processor should be used unless you have specific reasons for changing it.

- *Print Test Page* allows you to print a test page to verify printer functioning.

4. After you complete the General page, display the Ports page (see fig. 13.48). You can use the Add Port, Delete Port, or Configure Port buttons to modify the port configuration for your printer, as described in the preceding section. The Enable Bidirectional Support check box is marked by default if your printer supports this function. If it doesn't, this selection is disabled (grayed out) to prevent you from selecting bidirectional support on a printer that doesn't have that capability.

5. After you finish configuring the port, display the Scheduling page (see fig. 13.49). The Scheduling page allows you to specify when the printer is available to users, at what priority print jobs are to be handled, and the various options to control how spooled documents will be processed.

The following options are available from the Scheduling page:

- *Available* defaults to Always, allowing users to access this printer at any hour. You can select the From option and specify From and To times if you want to restrict availability of the printer to specified hours.

- *Priority* allows you to specify what priority level Windows NT Server assigns to this printer.

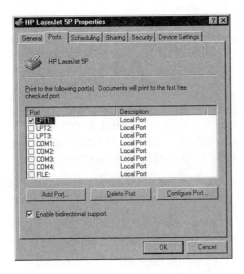

Fig. 13.48 Selecting a parallel port in the Ports page of the *Printername* Properties sheet.

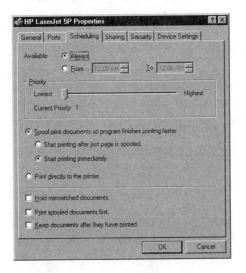

Fig. 13.49 Specifying spooler properties in the Scheduling page of the *Printername* Properties sheet.

- *Spool Print Documents so Program Finishes Printing Faster* allows you to specify that incoming print jobs are written to a temporary file and processed from that file. If you select this option, you can choose between Start Printing After Last Page Is Spooled and Start Printing Immediately. In the first case, Windows NT Server waits until the entire print job has been written to a temporary spool file before it begins printing the document. In the latter case, Windows NT Server begins printing as soon as it has received enough data to complete the first page. The latter selection is marked by default, because

Start Printing Immediately almost always provides better printing performance. If your network is very heavily loaded, you may need to specify Start Printing After The Last Page Is Spooled to prevent pages from different print jobs from being interleaved, and other printing problems.

- *Print Directly to the Printer* allows you to specify that incoming print jobs are sent directly to the printer without first being queued. Never choose this option for a shared printer on a Windows NT server. Doing so can cause pages printed directly to the printer to be interleaved with pages from a print job that are being despooled from the printer queue.

- *Hold Mismatched Documents*, if marked, retains documents in the queue that couldn't be printed successfully because of mismatched pages.

- *Print Spooled Documents First*, if marked, gives preference to printing documents contained in the spool before printing other documents.

- *Keep Documents After They Have Printed*, if marked, retains documents in the print queue even after they print successfully. Windows NT Server ordinarily removes documents from the print spool after they are printed. Marking this check box results in all documents being retained in the spool, which causes a rapid growth in disk space consumed for spooled documents. Mark this check box only as a part of diagnosing printing problems.

6. After you finish setting scheduling options, display the Sharing page (see fig. 13.50). The upper section of the Sharing page allows you to specify that the printer be Not Shared or Shared. If it's set as Shared, you can modify the share name in the Share Name text box.

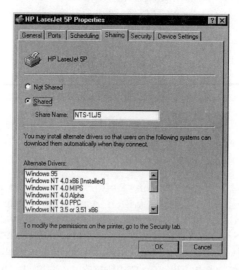

Fig. 13.50 Specifying a share name and alternate drivers, if required, in the Sharing page of the *Printername* Properties sheet.

The bottom section of the Sharing page allows you to specify alternate drivers that allow users of other operating systems to use the shared printer. In the example shown in figure 13.50, the Alternate Drivers list shows that support is installed only for Windows NT 4.0 running on the x86 processor family. You can install support for additional operating systems by highlighting them in this list. Later, when you finally accept changes to all pages of the *Printername* Properties sheet by clicking OK, you're prompted to insert the disks containing the printer drivers needed.

7. After you finish setting sharing options, display the Security page (see fig. 13.51). The Security page has three sections, each of which is accessed by clicking that section's button. The Permissions section allows you to specify which groups are permitted to access the printer. The Auditing section allows you to specify by user and by group which actions are recorded to an audit log. The Ownership section allows you to specify which user or group owns the printer.

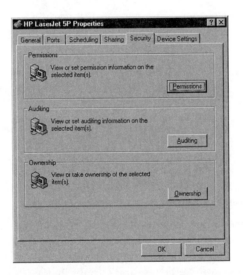

Fig. 13.51   The Security page of the *Printername* Properties sheet.

8. Click the Permissions button to display the Printer Permissions dialog (see fig. 13.52). The Name list displays the name of each group that's now authorized to access the printer on the left, with that group's level of access specified on the right. You can add a group by clicking the Add button and responding to the prompts. You can remove a group by clicking the Remove button.

You can change the access level associated with a group or groups by highlighting the group or groups and selecting the type of access to be allowed from the Type of Access drop-down list. You can assign one of the following types of access:

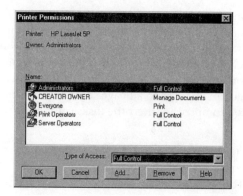

Fig. 13.52 Setting printer permissions for user groups in the Printer Permissions dialog.

- *No Access* allows the group so assigned no access whatsoever to the printer.

- *Print* allows the group so assigned to print documents, but not to manage the printer or to modify its properties. This is the access level you should assign to ordinary users of the printer.

- *Manage Documents* allows the group so assigned to print documents and to manage the printer. Manage documents is normally assigned to the creator/ owner of the printer.

- *Full Control* allows the group so assigned to print documents, manage the printer, and modify its properties. Full control should normally be assigned to the groups Administrators, Print Operators, and Server Operators.

After you set permissions as necessary, click OK to return to the Security page of the *Printername* Properties sheet.

9. In the Security page of the *Printername* Properties sheet, click the Auditing button to display the Printer Auditing dialog (see fig. 13.53). By default, no auditing is assigned for the printer. To add auditing for specified users and groups, click the Add button to display the Add Users and Groups dialog (see fig. 13.54). You can add users and groups to the Add Names list by either double-clicking the user or group name, or by highlighting the name and clicking the Add button. Each user or group name is added to the Add Names list as you add it.

After you finish adding users and groups, click OK to return to the Printer Auditing dialog, which shows Domain Users added for auditing in figure 13.55. The example shows auditing configured to report only Print Failure for the selected group. After you specify the desired level of auditing for each selected group, click OK to accept the changes and return to the Security page of the *Printername* Properties sheet.

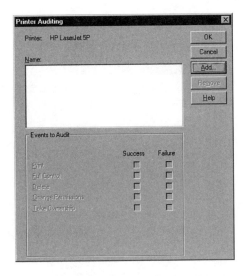

Fig. 13.53 Audit log options disabled in the Printer Auditing dialog.

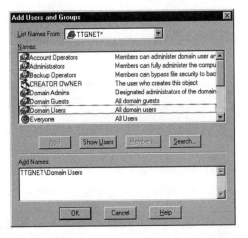

Fig. 13.54 Selecting groups for printer auditing in the Add Users and Groups dialog.

> **Caution**
>
> Be careful about assigning auditing for printers. If you assign too many auditing triggers to too many groups, the audit log file soon grows out of control. Not only does it occupy disk space that can otherwise be used for storing user data, but the large number of audit entries makes it impossible to notice the really important ones. If you decide to use auditing at all, limit it to logging attempts at unauthorized activities or with problems that occur during normal operations.

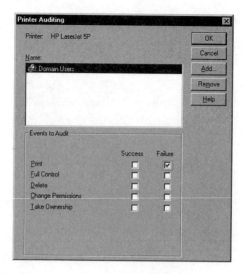

Fig. 13.55 The Printer Auditing dialog with the Domain Users group added for auditing.

10. In the Security page of the *Printername* Properties sheet, click the Ownership button to display the Owner dialog (see fig. 13.56). You can take ownership of this printer by clicking the Take Ownership button, or close the dialog by clicking Close. In either case, you return to the Security page of the *Printername* Properties sheet.

Fig. 13.56 Taking ownership of the printer in the Owner dialog.

11. In the *Printername* Properties sheet, display the Device Settings page. The appearance of this page varies depending on the characteristics of the printer for which you're setting properties. After you configure the device settings to your satisfaction, click OK to save the properties settings for all pages.

From Here...

This chapter covered how to share the three primary server resources—folders, files, and printers. Although Windows NT Server 4.0's new Managing Folder and File Access Wizard provides a step-by-step approach to sharing files and folders, most network administrators are likely to use the Windows NT Explorer's file or folder property sheets to manage server shares.

The chapter also described how to use the Add Printer Wizard to share a printer connected to an LPT or COM port of the server, as well as how to create a Windows NT shared resource (print queue) from a printer connected to a NetWare server. The chapter concluded with a description of how to change properties of a printer previously set up as a shared Windows NT resource.

The following chapters provide additional information on topics discussed in this chapter:

- Chapter 10, "Configuring Windows 95 Clients for Networking," shows you how to set up PCs running Windows 95 to take maximum advantage of Windows NT 4.0 networks, including the use of printers shared by Windows NT servers.

- Chapter 11, "Connecting Other PC Clients to the Network," provides the details on setting up Windows 3.1+, Windows for Workgroups 3.1+, Windows NT Workstation 4.0, and Macintosh clients to communicate with Windows NT 4.0 server and use printers shared by Windows NT servers.

- Chapter 12, "Managing User and Group Accounts," describes how to use Windows NT Server 4.0's User Manager for Domains, take advantage of the new Add User Accounts and Group Management wizards, and utilize the built-in user groups of Windows NT.

III

Administering a Network

Chapter 14

Optimizing Network Server Performance

Although it's a relatively easy task to set up a Windows NT 4.0 server and connect printers and workstations to form a network, it's not as easy to tune your network for maximum performance. Because Windows NT Server 4.0 is not only a file server but also an application server, you must monitor many performance parameters to ensure that your network doesn't grind to a halt.

Fortunately, Microsoft now includes a very powerful tool, Performance Monitor (PerfMon), with Windows NT Server 4.0. Performance Monitor, which originated in Microsoft System Management Server 1.0, lets an administrator view the workings of virtually every component of your Windows NT 4.0 server and network. Performance Monitor also is included with Windows NT Workstation 4.0.

This chapter is divided into two principal sections. The first section, "Using Performance Monitor," helps you understand how Performance Monitor works and how to use the options available to the network administrator. The second major section, "Optimizing Windows NT 4.0 File and Print Servers," illustrates how to monitor specific characteristics of your network and computers using Performance Monitor and provides tips to obtain better network performance.

Using Performance Monitor

Performance Monitor monitors the operating characteristics, such as system memory consumption and processor usage, of a computer running Windows NT. The data gathered can be displayed as charts, used to generate alerts, and saved in files for later analysis.

To start Performance Monitor, choose Programs, Administrative Tools, and then Performance Monitor from the Start menu. The Performance Monitor program window appears (see fig. 14.1). By default, no objects are monitored.

In this chapter, you learn to

■ Understand and use Performance Monitor to view the characteristics of a Windows NT 4.0 server

■ Generate charts, alerts, logs, and reports from the data gathered by Performance Monitor

■ Tune a Windows NT 4.0 server for use primarily as a file server

■ Tune a Windows NT 4.0 server for use primarily as an application server

III

Administering a Network

4.0

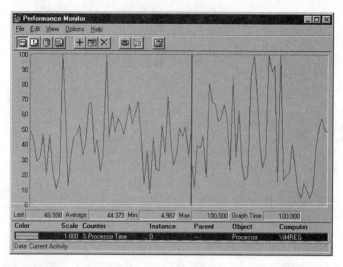

Fig. 14.1 Performance Monitor's opening window displaying % Processor Time.

> **Note**
>
> Figure 14.1 shows the Processor object being monitored. Later in this chapter, the "Creating a New Chart" section shows you how to monitor objects such as the Processor.

Using Objects and Counters in Performance Monitor

Performance Monitor records the behavior of objects in the system by the use of counters. In Windows NT, an object is a standard entity for identifying and using a system resource. Examples of objects are individual processes, shared memory, and physical devices. Like programming objects, Windows NT objects usually have data (properties) and behavior (methods); most counters record the rate (or a related unit) at which a particular method executes. As an example, a counter displays the number of fixed-disk read operations (methods) per second.

Performance Monitor provides a specific set of counters for each object type. The counters provide statistical information for each of the object types. Table 14.1 lists the most important objects of Windows NT (memory, the paging file, the physical disk, and the processor), the counters associated with each object, and the significance of each counter.

Table 14.1   The Most Important System Objects and Counters of Windows NT 4.0

Counter	Description	Significance
Memory		
Available Bytes	The amount of virtual memory now available	When the value falls below a threshold, Windows NT gradually takes memory from running applications to maintain a certain minimum of available virtual memory.

Counter	Description	Significance
Pages/Sec	The number of pages that had to be written to or read from the disk and placed in physical memory	This counter indicates whether more physical memory is needed in your system. A value greater than 5 for a single disk could indicate a memory bottleneck.
Page Faults/Sec	The number of page faults in the processor	This value indicates that the data needed wasn't immediately available on the specified working set in memory.

Paging File

Counter	Description	Significance
% Usage	The amount of the paging file (Pagefile.sys) that's in use	This counter indicates whether you should increase the size of Pagefile.sys. If this value is near 100 percent, increase the size of the paging file.
% Usage Peak	The peak usage of system paging	This value also indicates whether the paging file is of the appropriate size. If this value nears the maximum age-file size, increase the size of the paging file.

Physical Disk

Counter	Description	Significance
Avg. Disk Bytes/Transfer	The average number of bytes transferred to or from disk during read/write operations	Low values of this counter indicate that applications are accessing the disk inefficiently. If this value is greater than 20K, the disk drive is performing well.
Avg. Disk Sec/Transfer	The amount of time a disk takes to fulfill requests	A high value can indicate that the disk controller is continually retrying the disk because of read or write failures. A high value is greater than 0.3 second.
Disk Queue Length	The number of disk requests outstanding at the time the performance data is collected	This value relates to the number of the spindles that make up the physical disk. A single disk has one spindle. RAID drives have multiple spindles but appear as a single drive. A typical value is up to two times the number of spindles making up the physical disk.
% Disk Time	The percentage of time that the disk is in use	If this value consistently is above 85 percent active, consider moving some files to an additional server or upgrading the disk drive.

Processor

Counter	Description	Significance
% Processor Time	The percentage of elapsed time that a processor is busy executing a non-idle thread	This counter indicates how busy a processor is. If this value is very high, the system may benefit from a processor upgrade or multiple processors.

(continues)

III

Administering a Network

	Table 14.1 Continued	
Counter	**Description**	**Significance**
Processor		
Interrupts/Sec	The rate of service requests from I/O devices	This indicates the number of requests processed from device drivers. If this value increases without corresponding increases in system activity, it could indicate a hardware problem in the system.

You can monitor multiple instances of some of the objects listed in table 14.1. For example, you can view the performance of each processor in a multiprocessor system. You also can monitor each Physical Disk object in a system with multiple fixed-disk drives.

> **Note**
>
> Multiple instances of an object can be opened, even if multiple physical devices don't exist in the system. For example, multiple Processor objects can be monitored on a single-processor system; in this case, each instance of the processor displays the same data.

One of the most important capabilities of Performance Monitor is the capability to monitor the performance of Windows NT objects on remote machines. For example, from a client running Windows NT Workstation 4.0, a system administrator can monitor the performance of objects on all the Windows NT servers in a domain. This feature is very useful for detecting load-balancing problems in the network.

You monitor behavior of a remote computer's objects by following these steps:

1. If Performance Monitor isn't displaying a chart, choose Chart from the View menu.

2. Choose Add to Chart from the Edit menu to open the Add to Chart dialog (see fig. 14.2).

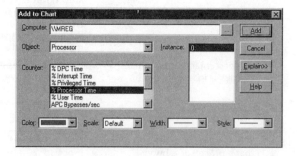

Fig. 14.2 Adding a chart to Performance Monitor with the Add to Chart dialog.

3. In the Add to Chart dialog's Computer text box, type the computer name of the Windows NT computer to monitor. Alternatively, click the button to the right of the text box to display the Select Computer dialog, which displays a list of all computers on the network (see fig. 14.3).

If you use the Select Computer dialog, double-click the name of the domain or workgroup to display a list of servers and workstations in that entity. Select the name of the server or workstation to monitor, and then click OK to close the dialog.

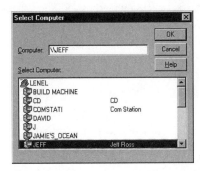

Fig. 14.3 Using Performance Monitor's Select Computer dialog to select other computers on the network.

4. In the Add to Chart dialog, a new chart is added to Performance Monitor by selecting an object from the Object drop-down list, selecting a counter for the object from the Counter list, and then clicking the Add button. Figure 14.2 shows the Processor object and % Processor Time counter selected.

5. Click Cancel to close the Add to Chart dialog. The line chart begins to display % Processor Time (refer to fig. 14.1).

Charting Performance Characteristics

Performance Monitor typically creates line charts, but histograms or bar charts are alternatives for certain types of data. When using charts, Performance Monitor displays the collected statistical data near the bottom of the window in the value bar.

The value bar contains the following information:

■ *Last* shows the most recent reading that was taken.

■ *Average* displays the average of all data readings taken since the chart was created.

■ *Min* shows the lowest reading that was taken.

■ *Max* displays the highest reading that was taken.

■ *Graph Time* shows the amount of time that one chart on-screen covers.

Creating a New Chart. Creating a new chart requires that you select a computer, object, and counter to monitor. The following example illustrates creating a new chart using the Processor object and % Processor Time counter. Monitoring the percentage of processor time consumed indicates whether the server's CPU is overworked. Such a

III

Administering a Network

condition indicates that the server needs a faster processor or that some of the work performed by this server should be distributed to another server.

To create a new line chart for monitoring % Processor Time, follow these steps:

1. Choose Chart from the View menu or click the View a Chart button on the toolbar.

> **Note**
>
> If a chart already exists, you can clear it by choosing New Chart from the File menu.

2. A new line representing the object being monitored is added to the chart by choosing Add to Chart from the Edit menu or by clicking the Add Counter button in the toolbar. The Add to Chart dialog appears. (You must complete the rest of the steps before the new line appears in Performance Monitor.)

3. In the Computer text box, type the computer name of the system to monitor, or click the button to the right of the text box to open the Select Computer dialog, which shows all computers on the network (refer to fig. 14.3).

4. In the Add to Chart dialog, select the object you want to monitor from the Object drop-down list. In this example, choose the Processor object. When you select an object, the Counter list box fills with the appropriate counters for that object.

5. Select the counter that you want to monitor from the Counter list. In this example, select the % Processor Time counter. When you select a counter, you can see a explanation of what the counter represents by clicking the Explain button.

6. If the computer has more than one CPU, the Instance list box fills with an instance for each CPU. Select the instance to monitor. In this example, select 0 for the first CPU.

7. You can choose the Color of the object, the Scale factor, the line Width, and the line Style. These options enable you to identify more distinctly each counter when the same chart is monitoring more than one counter.

8. Click the Add button to add the new performance characteristic to be monitored to the chart.

9. You can add more performance characteristics to the chart by repeating steps 3 through 8.

10. After you add all the objects that you want to monitor, click the Cancel button to return to the Performance Monitor window. Performance Monitor now begins monitoring the chosen objects.

> **Note**
>
> To obtain the most realistic readings from your system, make sure that tasks such as screen savers are disabled. Depending on the object being monitored, an active screen saver distorts the readings.

Editing a Chart. When your chart is running, you can edit any of the counters being monitored. As shown in figure 14.1, a legend of all counters being monitored appears at the bottom of Performance Monitor's window. To edit any counter, follow these steps:

1. Select the counter to be edited from Performance Monitor's legend at the bottom of the window.

2. From the Edit menu choose the Edit Chart Line command, or double-click the counter in Performance Monitor's legend. The Edit Chart Line dialog appears (see fig. 14.4).

3. The Edit Chart Line dialog looks similar to the Add to Chart dialog but doesn't allow for Computer, Object, Counter, or Instance changes. The only changes that you can make are to the Color, Scale, Width, and Style of the line representing the object being edited. Make the appropriate changes and click OK.

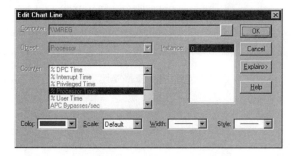

Fig. 14.4   Using the Edit Chart Line dialog to modify a counter.

Deleting Monitored Objects from a Chart. It often becomes necessary to delete objects from the chart during the course of monitoring system performance. You may need to delete an object due to inconclusive results obtained from the object, or simply to clear a chart that's monitoring many performance characteristics. Any counter being monitored can be deleted by following these steps:

1. Select the counter to be deleted from Performance Monitor's legend.

2. Choose the Delete From Chart command on the Edit menu, or press the Delete key.

Customizing the Chart Options. Several options are available for Performance Monitor charts that modify the presentation of the chart display. To modify the chart options, choose Chart from the Options menu. The Chart Options dialog appears (see fig. 14.5). Table 14.2 describes all the available chart options.

Table 14.2 Options for Modifying Charts	
Chart Options	**Description**
Legend	If this option is selected, the legends for each chart line appear at the bottom of Performance Monitor.

(continues)

III

Administering a Network

Table 14.2 Continued	
Chart Options	**Description**
Value Bar	If this option is selected, the value bar shows the values of Last, Average, Min, Max, and Graph Time.
Gallery	The Gallery setting determines how the data is displayed. The options are Graph, which is the default and most useful method, or Histogram, which displays the data as a bar graph.
Update Time	The Periodic Update setting, the most commonly used method, tells Performance Monitor to read new data at the time interval specified in the Interval (Seconds) text box. Manual Update tells Performance Monitor to update on user request.
Vertical Grid	This option displays grid lines on the vertical axis.
Horizontal Grid	This option displays grid lines on the horizontal axis.
Vertical Labels	This option displays labels for the vertical (y) axis.
Vertical Maximum	This option specifies the maximum value for the vertical axis. This value should be changed to reflect the counter being monitored. For example, set Vertical Maximum to 100 when using a percentage counter.

Fig. 14.5 Customizing the presentation of Performance Monitor charts using the Chart Options dialog.

Using Performance Monitor to Set Alerts

One of the useful features of Performance Monitor is the capability to define alerts, which can be sent to any station on the network when a monitored counter reaches a critical value. An *alert* is a method of monitoring any counter and performing a specified action when the counter exceeds or falls below a predetermined threshold value. You can choose to log the alert, send a notification message to a user on the network, or run an application.

You can view the alerts defined by Performance Monitor by either

■ Choosing Alert from the View menu

■ Clicking the View the Alerts button of Performance Monitor's toolbar

Figure 14.6 shows alerts generated at five-second intervals for % Processor Time counter values in excess of 5 percent.

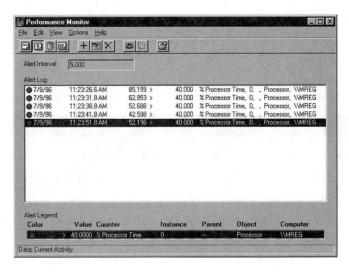

Fig. 14.6   Viewing alerts in Performance Monitor's alert view.

Adding an Alert. You add alerts to Performance Monitor by performing steps similar to the steps used for adding charts to Performance Monitor. To add a new alert to the view, follow these steps:

1. To create a new alert view, choose <u>A</u>lert from the <u>V</u>iew menu, or click the Alert toolbar button.

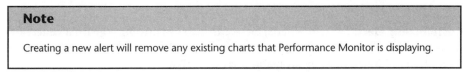

> **Note**
>
> Creating a new alert will remove any existing charts that Performance Monitor is displaying.

2. Choose <u>A</u>dd to Alert from the <u>E</u>dit menu, or click the Add button, to add a new alert to the view. The Add to Alert dialog appears (see fig. 14.7).

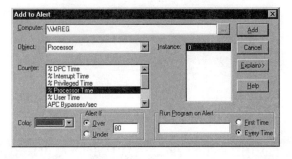

Fig. 14.7   Adding alerts with the Add to Alert dialog.

3. Type the computer name of the system to monitor in the Computer text box, or click the button to the right of the text box to open the Select Computer dialog, which shows all computers on the network (refer to fig. 14.3).

4. From the Object drop-down list, select the object that you want to monitor. In this example, choose the Processor object. When an object is selected, the Counter list box fills with the appropriate counters for that object.

5. Select the counter that you want to monitor from the Counter list box. In this case, select the % Processor Time counter.

> **Tip**
>
> When you select a counter, you can see an explanation of what the counter represents by clicking the Explain button.

6. If the computer has more than one CPU, the Instance list box fills with an instance for each CPU. Select the instance to monitor. In this example, select instance 0 for the first CPU.

7. Select a Color for the alert.

8. Enter the alert threshold in the Alert If section, and specify whether the alert is to run if the value is Under the threshold or Over the threshold.

9. When the alert triggers and if an application is supposed to run, specify the application name in the Run Program on Alert text box. Indicate whether the alert is to be run the First Time the alert triggers or Every Time the alert triggers.

10. When the options are set, click the Add button to add the alert to Performance Monitor.

Customizing Alerts. As with charts, alerts can also be customized with a variety of options. Choosing Alert from the Options menu opens the Alert Options dialog (see fig. 14.8). Table 14.3 describes the available alert options.

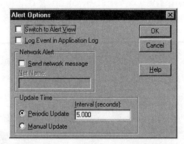

Fig. 14.8 Setting alert options with the Alert Options dialog.

Table 14.3 Actions That Can Be Performed When an Alert Is Triggered	
Alert Option	**Description**
Switch to Alert View	Performance Monitor switches to alert view when an alert is triggered.
Log Event in Application Log	Performance Monitor generates an entry in the Application Log when the alert is triggered. You can view the Application Log from Event Monitor.

Alert Option	Description
Send Network Message	Performance Monitor sends a network message to the machine specified in the Net Name text box. Don't enter double backslashes (\\) before the machine name.
Update Time	Two options are available here. The first and most used is Periodic Update, which tells Performance Monitor to read new data at a time interval specified in seconds in the Interval (Seconds) text box. Manual Update tells Performance Monitor to update on user request.

Performance Monitor uses NetBIOS as the transport protocol for network messages. If your alerts are sending network messages, you must ensure that NetBIOS is available as a transport protocol and that the NetBIOS service is running. The NetBIOS messenger service must be running for alerts to send network messages. The NetBIOS messenger service is alerted of the intended recipients.

You can determine whether the NetBIOS messenger service is started by using Control Panel's Services tool. The service name Messenger appears in the list box of all services, along with the current status of the service. If this service doesn't appear, you must install the NetBIOS Interface protocol by using Control Panel's Network tool.

The following two methods start the Messenger service:

- From the Command prompt, type **net start messenger**.

- In Control Panel, double-click the Services tool. Then select the Messenger service from the list box displaying all services and click the Start button. You can change the startup properties of the service to have it start automatically when the computer boots.

After the Messenger service starts, make sure that the alert recipient is added by typing **net name** *machinename* **add**, where *machinename* is the name you typed in the Net Name text box in the Alert Options dialog.

Using Performance Monitor Log Files

You use log files to provide a history of how your network is operating. You can set up Performance Monitor to keep a log for the results of running charts and of alerts that occur.

Maintaining log files can ease the burden of network administrators as the network grows and performance begins to degrade. You can examine log files to determine the source and location of bottlenecks and devise plans for correcting the problems.

Recording Data to a Log File. To record data to a log file, follow these steps:

1. Select the log view by choosing Log from the View menu or by clicking the View Output Log File Status toolbar button. Performance Monitor displays a new log view window (see fig. 14.9).

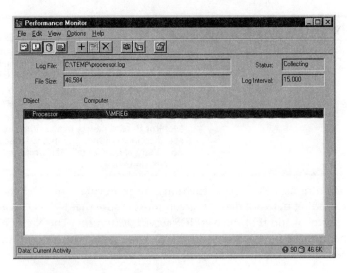

Fig. 14.9 Displaying current log activity in log view.

2. From the File menu, choose New Log Settings to clear existing log settings.

3. A new log file is added by choosing Add To Log from the Edit menu or by clicking the Add toolbar button. The Add To Log dialog appears (see fig. 14.10).

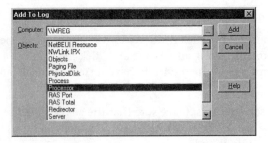

Fig. 14.10 Adding objects to be logged through the Add To Log dialog.

4. Type the computer name of the system to monitor in the Computer text box, or click the button to the right of the text box to open the Select Computer dialog, which shows all computers on the network (refer to fig. 14.3).

5. From the Objects list box, select the object that you want to monitor. In this example, choose the Processor object. Unlike in chart view, when an object is selected, all instances of the object are logged.

6. After you select the object you want to log, click the Add button to add the object to the log.

7. To log multiple objects, repeat steps 5 and 6 for each object. Then click Cancel to close the dialog.

8. Now that the objects to log are selected, the log file needs to be set. This is done through the Log Options dialog (see fig. 14.11), which you can open by choosing Log from the Options menu.

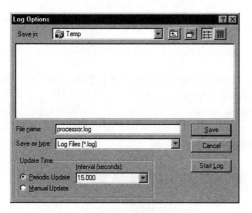

Fig. 14.11   Setting log options in the Log Options dialog.

9. Enter a new log file name, or select an existing log file to overwrite from the Log Options dialog.

10. In the Update Time section, either select Periodic Update and set a time interval in seconds, or select Manual Update for user intervention. These selections determine when data is written to the log file.

11. Click the Start Log button to start logging data. Performance Monitor's window changes to the log view.

To stop data logging, open the Log Options dialog and click the Stop Log button.

Viewing Recorded Data. Logged data, unlike chart data, doesn't appear in Performance Monitor's window. You can open for viewing only log files that aren't currently opened (in the process of logging). If the log you want to view is in use, you must first stop the log by choosing Log from the View menu. Then choose Log from the Options menu to open the Log Options dialog and click Stop Log.

To view the log data, follow these steps:

1. Choose the Data From command from the Options menu to open the Data From dialog (see fig. 14.12).

2. Select the Log File option.

3. Type the path and name of the log file to view in the text box, or click the button to the right of the text box to find the log file.

4. Click OK to close the Data From dialog.

Fig. 14.12 Changing where the viewed data is retrieved from in the Data From dialog.

5. To specify a time frame to view within the log file, choose Time Window from the Edit menu to open the Input Log File Timeframe dialog (see fig. 14.13). The bar above the Bookmarks section indicates the time line for logging events in the file. The Bookmarks section lists events when data was logged. The default is the entire time span for the log file.

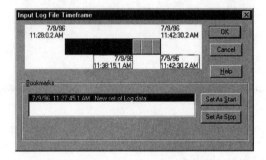

Fig. 14.13 Altering the time span for viewing logged data in the log file.

6. To set a new start time, select a bookmark and click the Set As Start button.

7. To set a new end time, select a bookmark and click the Set As Stop button.

8. Click OK to close the Input Log File Timeframe dialog and display the logged data.

To resume viewing current activity, you must open the Data From dialog and select the Current Activity option.

Optimizing Windows NT 4.0 File and Print Servers

Microsoft's developers made an appreciable improvement in Windows NT Server 4.0's file and print services compared with Windows NT 3.5x, especially for high-speed networks using 100BaseT NICs. However, various hardware and software bottlenecks can still reduce the performance of Windows NT 4.0 file and print servers. The following sections describe the process of optimizing a Windows NT Server 4.0 used primarily for file and print sharing.

Minimizing Disk Bottlenecks

Fixed-disk drives contribute more than their share of performance problems. You use Performance Monitor's Physical Disk object to check for drive bottlenecks.

Unlike the other objects in Performance Monitor, the disk subsystem must be initialized before disk activity can be monitored. To activate the monitoring of the disk subsystem, follow these steps:

1. From the Start menu, choose Programs and Command Prompt to open the Command Prompt window.

2. On the command line, type `diskperf -y`.

3. Exit the command line by typing `exit` or by closing the Command Prompt window.

4. Shut down and restart Windows NT.

If the DiskPerf driver isn't started by performing the preceding steps, the Physical Disk's counters don't work. Failure to start DiskPerf becomes evident when a chart is selected for the physical disk, and the graph doesn't indicate activity during disk operations.

One of the most obvious counters of the Physical Disk object is the % Disk Time counter, which is the equivalent to monitoring the computer's disk activity LED. When the % Disk Time approaches 80 percent or higher, the server has a disk-usage problem and is said to be disk-bound.

Another useful counter is Disk Queue Length, which counts the number of processes waiting to use the physical disk. When more than two processes are regularly waiting to access the disk, the server is disk-bound.

The following sections describe hardware and software solutions for disk-bound file and print servers.

Hardware Solutions for Reducing Disk Bottlenecks. Buying SCSI-2 or, better yet, SCSI-3 fixed-disk drives with fast seek times is the most straightforward solution for increasing data throughput. Many disk drives are available with 4M/sec (4M per second) sustained data transfer rates or greater and 9 ms seek times or less. For example, 4.3G Seagate ST15150W Wide SCSI-2 Barracuda drives can provide a sustained data rate in the range of 6M/sec, which is several times more data than you can transport over 10BaseT media. A large read cache on high-speed drives also improves performance, and enabling a drive's write cache provides a performance boost, but at the expense of data security. The primary advantage of high-speed drives in relatively low-speed networks is that the system devotes less time to reading and writing data, which is only a part of the processor and network workload.

◄◄ See "RAID 5," p. 228

III

Administering a Network

> **Note**
>
> If your Avg. Disk Sec/Transfer rate is significantly below that calculated for your drive/controller combination, you might have a SCSI termination problem that results in multiple reads or writes as a result of data errors. Active termination is a requirement for high-speed SCSI drives. If the last device on your SCSI chain uses passive termination, it's likely to reduce the effective data rate. If you mix Wide and conventional (narrow) SCSI devices on a host adapter that supports both cable types, such as the Adaptec AHA-2940UW, be sure to follow the manufacturer's recommendation for mixed-SCSI device address settings. Using the wrong addresses for low-speed devices can slow high-speed devices dramatically.

SCSI host controllers represent another potential hardware bottleneck. Attaching a high-performance drive to a legacy SCSI controller (such as an 8-bit SCSI controller) doesn't make economic sense. PCI bus-mastering controllers, such as the Adaptec AHA-2940UW and AHA-3940UW, provide synchronous data access at burst rates of up to 40M/sec and 80M/sec, respectively. You can attach up to 15 devices to a Wide SCSI-2 bus. Replacing Windows NT Server 4.0's software RAID implementation with a controller that implements hardware RAID also improves disk subsystem performance.

 ◀◀ See "Implementing RAID in Hardware," p. 238

Some SCSI host adapters can perform asynchronous I/O, which allows drives to perform operations in parallel. If your host adapter can perform asynchronous I/O, you can use *stripe sets* to maximize the server's performance. A stripe set allows data to be distributed across several drives, making disk operations very fast because the physical drives work in parallel.

> **Note**
>
> When buying a SCSI host adapter, make sure that it supports asynchronous I/O; most host adapters don't support this feature, nor do any IDE drives.

The cost of high-performance fixed-disk drives has declined rapidly in 1996 and is expected to drop further in 1997 as larger drives that use magneto-resistive heads and embedded servo positioning tracks become common. PCI bus-mastering host controllers range in street price from about $350 to $500, and low-cost hardware RAID controllers should hit the market by the end of 1996.

> **Caution**
>
> If you plan to change SCSI host adapters, make a full, known-good backup (or two) before doing so. Low-level and high-level drive formats aren't identical for all SCSI host adapters. Changing from one SCSI adapter to another may require you to reformat all your disk drives.

Software Solutions for Reducing Disk Bottlenecks. If your Windows NT 4.0 server is used as a print server in addition to a file server, an option is to increase priority of the thread that handles file services and reduce the priority of the thread that handles print services. Boosting the priority of the file-server thread causes file requests to be handled more quickly, at the expense of print services.

By default, the print-server thread is set to 2 and the file-server thread is 1. The larger the number, the higher the priority assigned to the thread. To change the priority of the file-server thread with Registry Editor, follow these steps:

1. From the Start menu, choose Run to open the Run dialog.

2. In the text box, type **regedt32** and click OK to launch Registry Editor (see fig. 14.14).

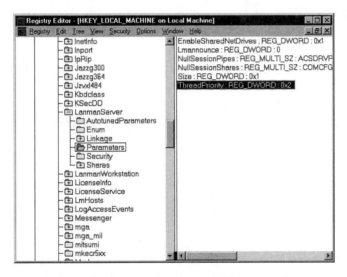

Fig. 14.14 Using the Registry Editor to change Windows NT system values.

3. Select the HKEY_LOCAL_MACHINE view.

4. Expand the SYSTEM\CurrentControlSet\Services\LanmanServer\Parameters key.

5. Select the ThreadPriority entry.

> **Note**
>
> Not all systems have a ThreadPriority entry. If your system doesn't have this entry, it can be added through the Edit menu. Set the initial value to 2.

6. Change the value from 1 to 2 to increase the file server thread priority.

> **Note**
>
> Server threads run at foreground process priority by default. Other threads in the system service (such as the XACTSRV thread, which is used for processing print requests) run at foreground process priority, plus 1. Thus, a file server that's also a print server may suffer from server thread starvation because the server threads are running at a lower priority than the print threads. Increasing the ThreadPriority value to 2 places a server thread in the same priority class as a print thread. The maximum value for ThreadPriority is 31. Don't increase the ThreadPriority value above 2; a value greater than 2 can cause other undesired system side effects.

7. Close the Registry Editor.

If your network consists of multiple Windows NT servers, you can use a technique called *load balancing*, which distributes the workload across multiple servers. Load balancing lets all the servers operate at a similar capacity, rather than heavily tax certain servers and underutilize other servers.

To load balance a system, each server must be evaluated to determine where the most activity occurs. Once this is established, the most heavily used files and folders can be replicated across other servers to balance the network load. *Replicating* is a method of duplicating the content of folders, files, or even entire disks onto another disk drive on another machine. Although this technique is primarily used for providing an online path to information in case of a system crash of a primary server, it can be used for load balancing also. Users that need to view information can be sent to the replicated data, thus reducing the traffic to the primary server.

 ◀◀ See "Replicating Folders," p. 477

Eliminating Unneeded Network Protocols

One advantage of the Windows NT operating system is its support for all commonly used network protocols. Although multiprotocol capability is a major selling point, a server doesn't benefit by having all available protocols loaded if some protocols aren't used or aren't necessary.

When a network runs multiple protocols, the performance of the network suffers. For example, if your network includes NetWare file servers, you're running the NWLink protocol with IPX/SPX support. It may not be necessary to run the NetBEUI or TCP/IP protocols in this instance. Alternatively, if your network must run TCP/IP, you should consider changing the NetWare servers to use TCP/IP.

The number of bindings that a network contains also affects network performance. By changing the binding order, you can obtain significant gains in network performance. For example, NetBIOS is the binding interface for the NT file server. The problem is that NetBIOS has binding interfaces to three protocols—NetBEUI, TCP/IP, and NWLink—presenting the server software with multiple choices when trying to satisfy a network request.

Changing the Binding Order of Multiple Protocols

If you can't reduce the number of network protocols in use, you can alter the order of binding to satisfy the most network requests on the first attempt. To view and alter the order of network bindings, follow these steps:

1. From the Start menu, choose Settings and then Control Panel.

2. Double-click Control Panel's Network tool to open the Network property sheet.

3. Click the Bindings tab to display the Bindings properties page. Select the All Protocols entry from the combo box, if it's not already selected.

4. In the list box, you can change the order of the protocol bindings for each service. Double-click the entry for the service for which you want to change the binding priority to display the underlying bindings for the service (see fig. 14.15).

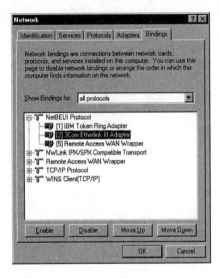

Fig. 14.15 Using the Bindings page of the Network properties sheet to rearrange network protocol bindings.

5. If most users use TCP/IP, for example, select this binding and click the Move Up button until TCP/IP is at the top of the list. (The Move Up and Move Down buttons are disabled until you select a protocol for a particular service.)

6. Click OK to accept the changes or Cancel to abort the changes.

7. If you click OK and have made changes, Windows NT re-creates the bindings and asks that you shut down and restart the server. On restart, the new binding priorities are effective.

Overcoming Network Media Limitations

You also can use Performance Monitor to view network characteristics that affect file server performance. Select the Server object and view the Bytes Total/sec counter (see fig. 14.16); compare this number to the rated media speed of your network, such as 4mbps or 16mbps Token Ring or 10mbps Ethernet. If the number of Bytes Total/sec is near the media speed of your network, your network is overworked. In this case, you must separate the network into multiple segments to ease the burden. Fortunately, Windows NT Server 4.0 lets you install multiple network cards for segmenting.

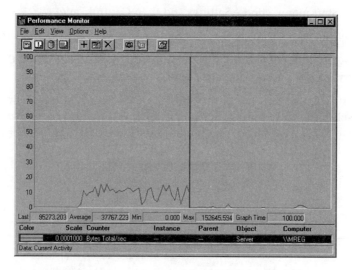

Fig. 14.16 Monitoring the network performance of a Windows NT server.

Some additional tips for fine-tuning the network performance of your Windows NT Server are as follows:

- If your server uses WINS (Windows Internet Name Service) and TCP/IP, you can reduce the number of system broadcasts by binding the NetBIOS interface to TCP/IP.

- If your network contains Windows for Workgroups (WfWg) clients and you use TCP/IP, be sure to update the WfWg clients with the version of Windows for Workgroups included on the Windows NT Server 4.0 CD-ROM. The new WfWg TCP/IP driver increases the server's performance.

Reducing File Fragmentation

It's a common misconception that Windows NT Server's NTFS eliminates problems with file fragmentation. Fragmentation—defined as files stored in multiple, non-contiguous clusters—slows file read and write operations, especially with large files.

Although Windows 95 includes a built-in defragmentation utility, Disk Defragmenter, Windows NT 4.0 doesn't provide such an application. Commercial products are available to help correct and reduce the amount of disk fragmentation for your Windows NT systems. Symantec's Norton Utilities for Windows NT contains a utility similar to the Windows 95 Disk Defragmenter.

One unique product available is Diskeeper for Windows NT from Executive Software (**http://www.execsoft.com**). Diskeeper is a Windows NT service that runs constantly in the background and controls disk fragmentation as it occurs. By having Diskeeper work in real time, you never have to take the server offline to perform defragmentation, and your drive is optimized for the fastest disk access possible.

Note

When purchasing any third-party accessory software for Windows NT 4.0, make sure that the supplier warrants that the product is designed for Windows NT 4.0. Changes between versions 3.x and 4.0 of Windows NT affect many applications that use Windows NT's lower-level services.

Optimizing Windows NT 4.0 as an Application Server

Windows NT gained its initial reputation as a high-performance application server, primarily running client/server relational database management systems (RDBMSs), such as Microsoft SQL Server. The Microsoft BackOffice server suite adds Exchange Server, System Management Server (SMS), and SNA (Systems Network Architecture) Server as server-based applications. Other firms, such as Oracle and IBM, offer server-based RDBMSs and messaging systems that run under Windows NT Server 4.0.

Running on the same system, several client/server applications that service large numbers of users can tax the capabilities of even the highest-performance computer platforms. When dealing with application servers, the most obvious place to look for bottlenecks is the CPU and memory systems.

Examining an Application Server's CPU Usage

Performance Monitor is a valuable tool for detecting overuse of a server's CPU(s). Select the Processor object and watch the % Processor Time counter during periods of the heaviest network traffic. By examining the % Processor Time counter, you can determine CPU loading and how often your CPU is being "maxed out." When % Processor Time reaches 85 percent or more on a regular basis, you should consider upgrading your processor to a higher speed (if supported by your server's motherboard) or add an additional processor (if you have a multiprocessing system). If your server does double duty—acting as a file server and an application server—consider adding a new server to take over application services.

Tip

Multithreaded server applications take much better advantage of multiprocessor systems than file servers. If you intend to add an application server, invest in a system that can support up to four CPUs, even if you install only one processor initially. An application server should be equipped with a minimum of 64M of RAM. Use the largest single-inline memory modules (SIMMs) or dual-inline memory module (DIMMs) that the motherboard supports to maximize the amount of RAM that you can install in the future. Depending on the usage of your server-based applications, adding RAM may be more cost-effective than increasing the number of CPUs. Memory usage is the subject of the next section, "Examining Memory Usage in an Application Server."

III

Administering a Network

Another area of concern is the number of Interrupts/Sec with which the processor must contend. The number of interrupts per second is not a CPU problem, but the values of the Interrupts/Sec and % Interrupt Time counters can point out potential server hardware problems. A typical Windows NT server handles about 100 to 150 interrupts per second on the average. If the Interrupts/Sec counter displays 600 or more interrupts per second, the problem is likely to be a faulty or failing hardware component (often an adapter card).

You can detect poorly written device drivers by viewing the value of the System object's Context Switches/Sec counter. If the rate of context switching is more than 500 per second, it's possible that a device driver has built-in critical sections that take too long to process. (A *critical section* is a Win32 synchronization object that ensures that only one thread can execute a particular block of code at a time.)

A less obvious problem is screen savers running on the server. A screen saver is a relatively small task that runs after a period of inactivity, but some screen savers can be CPU killers. Examples of killer screen-savers are the Bezier Curves and 3-D Pipes screen savers that are part of Windows NT. (The CPU burden is caused by the 3-D graphics used by these screen savers.) Windows NT 4.0 has a simple built-in screen saver that's operational before an operator logs on at the server console. You remotely monitor most servers, which usually are in a relatively inaccessible location, so turning the monitor off when not in use is the most effective screen saver.

Examining Memory Usage in an Application Server

One of the most effective methods for achieving better system performance is through the addition of more physical (DRAM or dynamic RAM) memory. Within reasonable limits, the performance of Windows NT Server 4.0's operating system and the server-based applications improves with the addition of more memory. Just adding more RAM, however, isn't the entire solution to optimizing application server performance; you must correctly use the available memory.

 ◀◀ See "The Windows NT Executive," p. 93

Experience shows that no matter how much memory exists in a Windows NT Server system, the operating system and server-based applications always find ways to use additional RAM. Windows NT Server uses most memory as a disk cache.

You use the Memory object's counters in Performance Monitor to check memory usage. The number of Committed Bytes should be less than half of the physical memory available, leaving the other half or more of RAM for disk caching. The number of Available Bytes should be at least 1M—preferably much more. If Performance Monitor displays less than the preceding values, you need more RAM.

Examining Virtual Memory. Virtual memory supplements RAM with disk files that emulate RAM, a process called *swapping* or *paging*. Virtual memory is defined as the amount of physical memory (RAM) available in the system *plus* a pre-allocated amount of memory on the system's fixed disk. Windows NT allocates the disk-based component of virtual memory in Pagefile.sys, which by default resides in the root folder of the disk drive on which you install Windows NT.

Pagefile.sys is unique because Windows NT creates the file as a series of contiguous clusters during installation. This structure lets the operating system issue a special set of disk I/O calls to read and write from Pagefile.sys, rather than use the conventional file system for disk I/O. The disk I/O calls to Pagefile.sys are much faster than Windows NT's normal disk operations but are much slower than memory I/O operations. To achieve maximum system performance, your objective is to minimize paging.

Note

The amount of paging performed is directly related to the how virtual memory is used. Windows NT reserves about 4M of RAM for its own use and allocates up to half of the remaining RAM as a disk cache, so running large server applications is likely to involve paging operations. Check the Memory object's Pages/sec counter during periods of maximum activity of your server-based applications, such as SQL Server and Exchange Server. The Pages/sec counter's value should be 5 or less. If the number of Pages/sec is greater than 5, the server is performing too many paging operations, and you need to increase the amount of server RAM.

Virtual memory operations become very slow if the amount of virtual memory needed by Windows NT and running applications exceeds the amount of space allocated to Pagefile.sys. When this situation occurs, Windows NT dynamically expands the size of Pagefile.sys. The expansion process is slowed as Windows NT searches the disk for free disk space. Additional disk space is not in the contiguous-sector block of the original Pagefile.sys, a condition that slows read and write operations.

Maximizing Network Throughput. For application servers, network throughput is extremely important. The following steps help to maximize network throughput:

1. From the Start menu, choose Settings and Control Panel.

2. Double-click Control Panel's Network tool to open the Network property sheet.

3. Click the Services tab to make the Service properties page active, and select Server from the Network Services list (see fig. 14.17).

4. Click the Properties button to open the Server Configuration dialog (see fig. 14.18).

5. Select the Maximize Throughput for Network Application option.

6. If you don't have LAN Manager 2.x clients on the network, clear the Make Browser Broadcasts to LAN Manager 2.x Clients check box.

7. Click OK to accept the changes, or click Cancel if you haven't made changes. If you have made changes, you must shut down and restart Windows NT to make the change effective.

III

Administering a Network

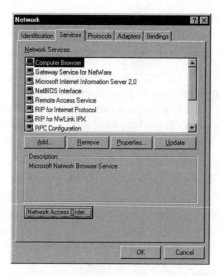

Fig. 14.17 Configuring the server network software for better system performance.

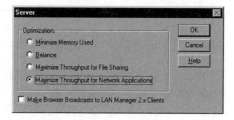

Fig. 14.18 Maximizing network throughput for Windows NT Server applications.

You can control the amount of virtual memory allocated to Pagefile.sys by following these steps:

1. From the Start menu, choose Settings and then Control Panel.

2. Double-click Control Panel's System tool to open the System Properties sheet.

3. Click the Performance tab to make the Performance properties page active, and click the Virtual Memory button to open the Virtual Memory dialog (see fig. 14.19).

4. To change the amount of disk space consumed by Pagefile.sys, alter the settings in the dialog.

5. Click OK if you've made changes or Cancel if you haven't made changes. You must shut down and restart the server if you make changes to Pagefile.sys.

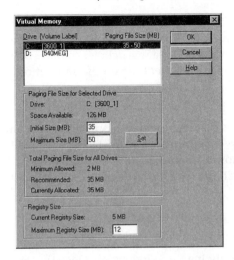

Fig. 14.19 Altering the amount disk space used for virtual memory with Control Panel's System tool.

Note

When Windows NT allocates memory for Pagefile.sys, it tries to allocate contiguous space on the hard disk equal to the size specified for virtual memory. If contiguous space equal to the specified size is not available, the largest amount of contiguous space available is allocated and the remaining amount is allocated from the closest available clusters on the disk. When contiguous space is allocated, Windows NT is much faster at swapping memory to and from disk. Whenever increasing the size of your virtual memory, it would be beneficial to defragment your hard disk in order to maximize the possibility of allocating contiguous disk space for Pagefile.sys.

Viewing Virtual Memory with Performance Monitor. The Commit Limit counter of Performance Monitor's Memory object shows the amount of memory in Pagefile.sys plus the amount of RAM that can be swapped to disk. In a system with 32M of RAM and a 57M Pagefile.sys file, the Commit Limit is 82.5M. When the number of Committed Bytes exceeds the Commit Limit, Windows NT attempts to expand Pagefile.sys. To view the amount of memory that can't be paged from RAM, view the Pool Non-Paged Bytes counter.

There are four recommendations to reduce the amount of page swapping:

- Add more RAM to the system.

- Remove unneeded services to lower operating system memory consumption.

- Remove unneeded device drivers.

- Install a faster fixed disk to reduce paging response time.

Two Windows NT Server 4.0 services consume large amounts of memory: DHCP (Dynamic Host Configuration Protocol) and WINS (Windows Internet Name Service). If you need these services, you might find it a wiser choice to place DHCP and WINS on another server, such as a file server, rather than on the application server.

From Here...

This chapter demonstrates that Performance Monitor is an extremely valuable tool for tracking network and server performance characteristics. By analyzing the data obtained from the Performance Monitor combined with the knowledge of how the servers in your network are being used, all the tools are available to achieve optimum network performance.

The following chapters provide additional information useful when optimizing Windows NT Server 4.0's performance:

■ Chapter 3, "Understanding the Windows NT Operating System," briefly describes the Virtual Memory Manager that is responsible for allocating memory resources.

■ Chapter 4, "Choosing Network Protocols," shows you how to add and delete the network protocols supported by Windows NT 4.0.

■ Chapter 5, "Purchasing Networking Hardware," includes advice on determining server hardware and RAM requirements.

Chapter 15

Troubleshooting Network Problems

Troubleshooting network problems is by no means an easy task. There are numerous areas where network problems can arise. Bad wiring causes problems at the physical layer. A failed network card results in trouble at the data-link layer. Routing errors arise at the network layer. Worse yet, the network operating system or applications may cause problems at the transport, session, presentation, or application layer.

As this litany of potential woes indicates, it's important to have a good understanding of the OSI model (one of the subjects of Chapter 4, "Choosing Network Protocols") when you troubleshoot network problems. Finding a network problem often involves deciding which OSI layer is *not* the culprit. You need good troubleshooting tools and intimate familiarity with the networking protocols in use before you can be an effective network troubleshooter.

This chapter concentrates on solving the most common networking problems associated with Windows NT Server 4.0. Fortunately, Windows NT Server provides several tools (such as Control Panel) and utilities (such as Network Monitor) for configuring and troubleshooting network problems.

Relating Network Protocols and Troubleshooting Issues

Windows NT and its predecessor, LAN Manager, rely on NetBIOS protocols—including Server Message Blocks (SMBs), named pipes, and mailslots—for all native file and print services, plus many of Windows NT Server's application services. Most NetBIOS-based protocol stacks, such as Windows NT's NetBEUI Frame (NBF), rely on broadcasting network packets to every client and server on the network.

Each NetBIOS device on the Windows NT network has a *NetBIOS name*, which uniquely identifies the device and contains information about the NetBIOS-related services the device provides. *Broadcasting* is the means by which a

This chapter covers the following primary troubleshooting topics:

- Examining how Windows NT's multiple protocols affect your troubleshooting tasks

- Using Windows NT Server 4.0 tools for solving networking problems

- Troubleshooting problems with WINS, browsing, domain trusts, static and dynamic routing, and other connectivity mechanisms

NetBIOS device advertises its NetBIOS name and capabilities to other network devices. Broadcasting is also how a NetBIOS device can locate another device or capability on the network.

Broadcasting is ideal for services that require real-time distribution to multiple clients, such as real-time stock-market data. Broadcasting is well suited to small networks because it reduces network response time. Broadcasting, with reduced packet overhead, is responsible for NetBEUI's excellent performance on small networks. On larger networks, broadcasting creates a substantial amount of network traffic and adds to the difficulty of identifying a network device that's causing a problem. Much of your network troubleshooting time—if you have a large network—is likely to be devoted to overcoming problems related to excessive broadcasts.

NetBEUI Broadcasting

All NetBEUI traffic is broadcast-based. If you install only the NetBEUI protocol on your Windows NT server, the server responds only to broadcast requests from other NetBEUI devices. NetBEUI isn't routable; if you have two Ethernet segments separated by a router (see fig. 15.1), NetBEUI broadcasts aren't forwarded across the router. The only way to overcome this limitation is to enable bridging on the router, so that both segments appear as one physical segment. In this case, the router bridges the traffic between the two segments using MAC (Media Access Control) layer addresses. Bridging eliminates the advantages of a segmented network. As you can imagine, maintaining a bridged network in a large LAN installation quickly grows unmanageable, especially if you also must maintain routed protocols, such as TCP/IP, on the same segments.

 ◀◀ See "NetBEUI and NetBEUI Frame," p. 112

If you must troubleshoot problems with a broadcast-based protocol, most of the tools for a directed protocol, such as TCP/IP, are ineffective. This is because many conventional network analysis tools rely on analyzing the interaction of source-destination network addresses to determine the flow of communication and where a connection is failing. Broadcast-based systems simply flood packets to every network device, whether or not the device is involved in the connection.

The best way to troubleshoot problems on a broadcast network is to connect a protocol analyzer to the network, and then filter MAC addresses to determine who transmitted what to whom. Protocol analyzers are one of the subjects of the later section "Using Windows NT's Troubleshooting Tools."

> **Note**
>
> The best way to troubleshoot broadcast-based network problems with a protocol analyzer is to filter out all traffic except those devices you're interested in. For example, with Microsoft's Network Monitor, you can filter on a given source and destination MAC address pair if you know those devices are having network problems.

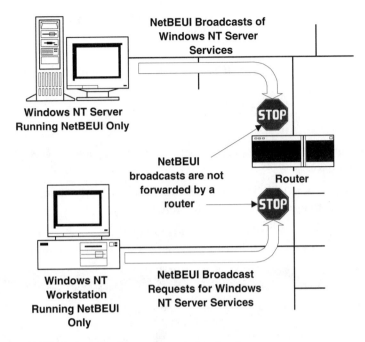

Fig. 15.1 NetBEUI broadcast blocking on a routed network.

IPX/SPX

Windows NT 4.0's IPX/SPX support is similar to that for NetBEUI, except that IPX implements the OSI network layer, whereas NetBEUI doesn't. The addition of the network layer makes IPX routable. Windows NT's NWLink stack supports the IPX protocol with the NetBIOS session layer. This means that you can run your NT network using only IPX for file, print, and application services, if you choose.

◀◀ See "NWLink (IPX/SPX)," p. 117

In this case, although the IPX/SPX protocol is routable, NetBIOS-over-IPX is broadcast-based. NetBIOS service announcement functions, such as browsing, aren't forwarded across subnets in a routed network. This means that devices running only NWLink and separated by a router won't normally be able to browse or connect to each other's resources. You must have a mechanism on your dedicated routers, such as that provided by Cisco Systems' IPX Helper feature, to forward broadcasts to the desired destination.

TCP/IP

TCP/IP is a directed protocol that eliminates most of the broadcast traffic associated with NetBEUI and IPX protocols. A directed protocol usually involves point-to-point communication between two or more networked devices. Integration of NetBIOS and TCP/IP, which Microsoft calls *NetBT* (or, more commonly, *NBT*) follows two established Request For Comments (RFCs), defined by the Internet Engineering Task Force (IETF) as RFCs 1001 and 1002. From these RFCs, Microsoft built an entire suite of services to facilitate the use of TCP/IP with NetBIOS.

◄◄ See "TCP/IP," p. 113

The RFCs for NBT specify three TCP/IP service ports, which perform the following functions:

- *NetBIOS Name* uses UDP (User Datagram Protocol) port 137 for name-resolution requests.

- *NetBIOS Datagram* uses UDP port 138 for authentication, name registration, and browsing services.

- *NetBIOS Session* uses TCP (Transport Control Protocol) port 139 for Server Message Blocks (SMBs) that perform file transfers and print jobs.

By using these three ports, Windows NT provides all its native services over TCP/IP. Windows NT also supports more traditional TCP/IP services, such as FTP and Telnet.

> **Tip**
>
> For a list of all the TCP/IP services Windows NT supports, view the *%systemroot%*\system32\ drivers\etc\Services file. This file, like its UNIX counterpart, contains service names and port numbers for most TCP/IP services. Services is a simple text file, so you can view it with a text editor, such as Notepad.

Windows Internet Naming Service (WINS). Use of TCP/IP requires traditional NetBIOS functions such as network browsing, name lookups, and user messaging to be mapped to the network addresses used by TCP/IP. Microsoft developed the Windows Internet Naming Service (WINS) as its method for mapping IP addresses to NetBIOS machine names. The function of WINS is similar to the Domain Name Service (DNS) provided by most UNIX-based systems, but WINS provides additional NetBIOS-related services, including the capability to associate different NetBIOS functions for a given machine name to a single IP address and to register Windows NT domain names to an IP address that represents a domain controller in the specified domain.

Machines running Windows NT Server and Workstation with the TCP/IP protocol stack use WINS to register their NetBIOS names and IP addresses. WINS registration occurs dynamically when the device starts up, or statically to guarantee that a certain machine name is registered to a certain IP address. WINS also registers Windows users based on the IP address of the machine from which each user logs on. This feature is used by services that must determine the IP address for a given user. For instance, the net send command queries WINS to find the IP address for the message destined for a specified user name.

After all servers and clients are registered with WINS, subsequent NetBIOS-related operations such as browsing, messaging, authentication, and file and print services use the WINS database, located on a Windows NT server, to perform name resolution between NetBIOS names and IP addresses. Using the WINS database eliminates the need for broadcast name resolution, thus decreasing network traffic and easing troubleshooting tasks.

The WINS database is a Jet (Access) database, WINS.MDB, and uses a Jet system database with the default name, SYSTEM.MDB, both of which are located in the \%*systemroot*%\ system32\wins folder. Figure 15.2 shows an example view of a WINS database that includes entries for workstations, users, and domains. Assuming that you've installed WINS, follow these steps to view the WINS database:

1. From the Start menu, choose Programs, Administrative Tools, and WINS Manager to open the WINS Manager window.

2. From the Mappings menu choose Show Database to display the Mappings dialog.

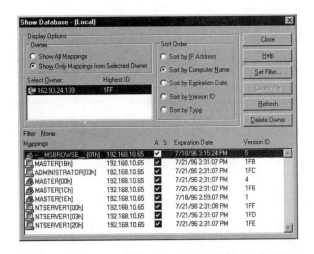

Fig. 15.2   A WINS database viewed in WINS Manager's Mappings dialog.

The hexadecimal value (indicated by the suffix h) in square brackets ([ ]) after each name shown in figure 15.2 indicates the type of service the entry provides. This value is called the *16th Byte* of the name. Table 15.1 defines each device name type and 16th Byte value you're likely to encounter.

Table 15.1   WINS 16th Byte Values for Domain, User, and Machine Names

Device Name and 16th Byte Value	Usage
Domain Names	
<domain_name>[1Dh]	The name of the Domain Master Browser.
<domain_name>[1Eh]	The name used by browsers to elect a Master Browser.
<domain_name>[00h]	The name registered by the Workstation service on the domain controller to receive browser broadcasts from LANMan servers.
<domain_name>[1Bh]	The name registered by all domain controllers in a domain.
<domain_name>[1Ch]	The name registered by all domain controllers, which can contain up to 25 IP addresses of other domain controllers. This group is used to provide a client with a list of domain controllers that can authenticate its logon request.
User Names	
<user_name>[03h]	The name that registers logged-on users for net send operations.
Machine Names	
<computer_name>[00h]	The name registered by the Workstation or Redirector service on this computer.
<computer_name>[03h]	The name registered by the Messenger service on this computer, which is used to issue a net send command to a machine name.
<computer_name>[+++*nn*h]	The name used by the Network Monitoring agent when it's installed on this computer (*nn* indicates any hexadecimal value).
<computer_name>[1Fh]	The name registered by the NetDDE service on this computer.
<computer_name>[20h]	The name registered by the Server service on this computer.

Note

In Windows NT 4.0, you can now specify your own 16th Byte value (in addition to those shown in table 15.1) by using the Internet Group type Static Mapping. Each Internet Group type you define can contain up to 25 IP addresses. For example, you might create an Internet Group of printers called PRINTERS, with a 16th byte of [EFh]. An application could then query WINS for a list of all [EFh] type printers and perform some operation based on the list WINS returns.

When troubleshooting WINS problems, it's important to keep in mind the different 16th Byte values (also called *types*). If the WINS database becomes corrupted, certain machine functions might be disabled because a 16th Byte entry for the service is missing or has the wrong value. Later, the section "Understanding WINS and DNS Name Resolution" provides assistance in troubleshooting WINS name-resolution problems.

> **Tip**
>
> Be sure to back up your WINS.MDB file periodically. Jet database files aren't immune from corruption. WINS attempts to recover a corrupted WINS.MDB file from data stored in .LOG files, but full recovery isn't always successful. Choose Backup Database from WINS Manager's Mappings menu to create a backup for your WINS.MDB file.
>
> You can also enable automatic backup of the WINS database each time the WINS service is stopped. From WINS Manager, choose Configuration from the Server menu, click Advanced, and mark the Backup on Termination check box.

NetBIOS Node Types. Part of RFCs 1001 and 1002 calls for defining NetBIOS over TCP/IP devices based on the method(s) by which they access NetBIOS services. (The methods are called *nodes*.) For example, if a Windows NT server doesn't use WINS, all name-resolution requests are via IP broadcasts. In most cases, the broadcast is a name-resolution packet sent to IP broadcast address 255.255.255.255. If the server is configured to use WINS, the server issues a directed request to the WINS database, and then follows with an IP broadcast if the requested name isn't registered with WINS, called *h-node resolution*. The four sequences of name resolution are as follows:

- *b-node* uses only broadcasts to resolve NetBIOS names.

- *p-node* uses only point-to-point communication (for example, directed packets) to resolve NetBIOS names.

- *h-node* uses p-node operation first to resolve names, and then b-node, if needed.

- *m-node* uses b-node operation first to resolve names, and then p-node, if needed.

By default, a Windows host configured with a static IP address and specifying a particular WINS server is an h-node device. If you want to force another node type, you can use DHCP (Dynamic Host Configuration Protocol) to automatically assign client IP addresses and specify the node type.

Using Windows NT's Troubleshooting Tools

Windows NT provides a variety of built-in tools for troubleshooting network problems. Using Windows NT tools is important because traditional network troubleshooting tools don't always support the NetBIOS implementation of network protocols that NT requires. It's particularly important that the hardware or software protocol analyzers you use recognize the unique nature of Windows NT-specific operations such as DHCP, WINS, and SMBs.

Using Protocol Analyzers

Protocol analyzers are invaluable tools for discovering problems on a network or simply understanding the flow of packets between servers and clients. The advantage of a dedicated (hardware) protocol analyzer is the capability to capture problems from the

OSI physical layer up to the application layer. If you have a Token Ring segment that's *beaconing*—that is, generating an excessive number of beacon tokens because of some problem on the ring—you can see what device is responsible. If your network is experiencing intermittent loss of connectivity, a protocol analyzer might show you that a specific server or client workstation is generating a large number of malformed packets, in which case you can remove and repair the offending device.

The best known hardware-based protocol analyzer is Network General's Expert Sniffer. The Sniffer usually comes bundled with a portable PC and includes a specialized network interface card that's designed to capture and decode packets. Network General also supplies PCMCIA cards and software for use in specific notebook PCs, which let you build your own Sniffer. Network General also produces the Distributed Sniffer, which is a specialized box that lets you plug into and capture packets on multiple segments simultaneously.

Devices such as the Expert Sniffer not only allow you to capture and decode packets, but also provide help with diagnosing problems by analyzing the data and suggesting possible causes for detected problems. Further information on Network General's Sniffer product line is available from **http://www.ngc.com/product_info/ product_info.html**.

Software-only protocol analyzers are less costly than hardware devices but provide less functionality. Examples of popular software-based analyzers are Novell's LANalyzer for Windows (see **http://corp.novell.com/market/apr96/mm000109.htm** for more information) and Microsoft's Network Monitor, which is part of Microsoft System Management Server (SMS) and now is included with Windows NT Server 4.0. Both applications provide the capability to decode network packets and support various types of pre- and post-packet filtering for several protocols. Network Monitor (NetMon) is ideal for troubleshooting Windows NT networking problems because NetMon is designed to identify the NetBIOS elements specific to Windows NT networks.

All protocol analyzers, regardless of whether they're hardware- or software-based, must be connected to each segment you want to monitor. You need an analyzer agent on each segment of a routed network to capture packets for analysis. The agent is necessary because routers don't forward some packets that may be of interest, such as broadcast packets. Figure 15.3 shows a two-segment network with hardware and software protocol analyzers.

Note

If you use a software agent such as Novell's LANalyzer, you must make sure that the server is using a network interface card that supports *promiscuous mode*. In normal operating mode, a NIC captures a packet on the wire only long enough to test whether the destination MAC address is its own. If not, it sends the packet back onto the wire. In promiscuous mode, a NIC captures each packet, regardless of whether the packet is meant for its address, and passes the packet to the analyzer agent. Modern NICs support promiscuous mode, but if you have older NICs, such as the original IBM 4/16 Token Ring card, you must upgrade the NIC.

Promiscuous mode operation, however, can induce at least 30 percent more load on the CPU in the PC where the NIC is installed. As a result, Windows NT 4.0's Network Monitor agent now supports Microsoft's NDIS 4.0 specification. This means that any NIC—even those that don't support promiscuous mode—can capture packets to NetMon, as long as the NIC is using NDIS 4.0 drivers.

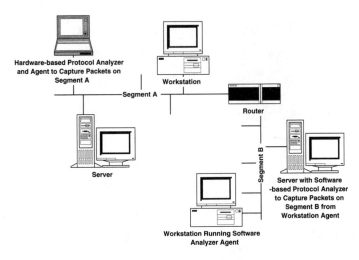

Fig. 15.3 A two-segment network with a hardware and software protocol analyzer.

Using Windows NT 4.0's Network Monitor

The Network Monitor tool that comes with Windows NT Server 4.0 is very handy for troubleshooting Windows NT-related network problems. Because it's a software-based tool, you can use it to view packets going to and from your Windows NT server. The Network Monitor Agent Service comes with Windows NT Server and Workstation 4.0, and must be installed and running before you can use Network Monitor. You need only one device running the Network Monitor agent per routed segment, and that device can be running on either Windows NT Server or Workstation 4.0.

Note

The version of the Network Monitor application that's included with Windows NT Server 4.0 is limited in its capabilities, compared with the version that now ships with Microsoft System Management Server (SMS) 1.2. Specifically, for security reasons, Windows NT Server 4.0 doesn't let you connect to remote NetMon agents running on Windows NT systems across a routed network. You must run the SMS version of NetMon to gain this functionality.

Installing Network Monitor and Its Agent Service. You have two options when installing NetMon components on Windows NT Server 4.0. The first option lets you install just the Network Monitor agent. The second option installs both the NetMon GUI tool and the agent. You choose the agent-only install if you have the SMS version of the NetMon application and want to enable monitoring across a routed network. In this case, the agent-only option is installed on one Windows NT Workstation or Server per segment.

III

Administering a Network

To install the Network Monitor Tools and the Agent Service, follow these steps:

1. From Control Panel, double-click Network to open the Network property sheet, and then click the Services tab.

2. Click Add to open the Select Network Service dialog (see fig. 15.4).

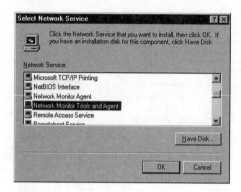

Fig. 15.4   Installing the Network Monitor Tools and Agent.

3. In the Network Service list, select Network Monitor Tools and Agent; then click Have Disk to open the Insert Disk dialog.

4. You're prompted for the path to your Windows NT Server distribution CD-ROM. Enter the path to the CD-ROM drive and the appropriate subfolder for your processor. For instance, if your CD-ROM drive is E on an Intel-based server, type `e:\i386` and click OK.

5. After Windows NT finishes copying files, you return to the Network property sheet. Click Close to cause Windows NT Server to reconfigure network bindings and request a system restart. You must restart the server for the changes to take effect.

6. By default, the Network Monitor Agent Service is installed for manual startup. To start the Agent Service, type `net start "Network Monitor Agent"` at the command prompt; or from Control Panel's Services tool, select Network Monitor Agent and click Start.

Using Network Monitor. If you're using the NetMon version that comes with Windows NT Server 4.0, you can trace packets flowing to and from the server on which you've installed the NetMon application. To use the NetMon application, follow these steps:

1. From the Start menu, choose Programs, Administrative Tools, and Network Monitor to launch NetMon (see fig. 15.5).

2. Choose Networks from the Capture menu to open the Select Capture Network dialog (see fig. 15.6). You must connect to the Network Monitor agent bound to your server NIC before using NetMon. If you have more than one NIC in the server, you'll be able to bind to one or the other to trace packets.

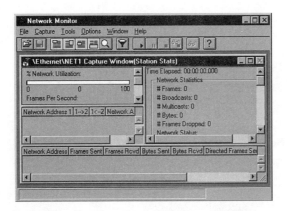

Fig. 15.5   Network Monitor's window on initial startup.

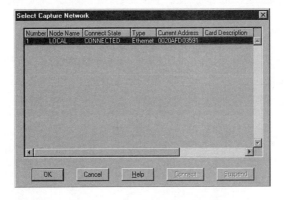

Fig. 15.6   Connecting to the Network Monitor Agent.

3. Select the desired adapter to connect, if you have more than one NIC, and click OK to close the dialog.

4. Choose <u>S</u>tart from the <u>C</u>apture menu to open the Capture window and begin capturing packets (see fig. 15.7).

By default, the Capture window is broken into four panes: Total Statistics, Session Statistics, Station Statistics, and Graph. You can toggle which panes you want to see by clicking the four pane toggle buttons of the toolbar. Alternatively, you can mark or unmark the appropriate checked item of the <u>W</u>indow menu.

5. After you finish capturing, from the <u>C</u>apture menu choose <u>S</u>top or Stop and <u>V</u>iew. If you choose Stop and <u>V</u>iew, the Capture Summary window appears (see fig. 15.8). This window displays summary information about each packet you've captured, including the frame number, the time since the start of the capture (in seconds and milliseconds), and source and destination MAC addresses or device names, protocol used, and a description of the packet.

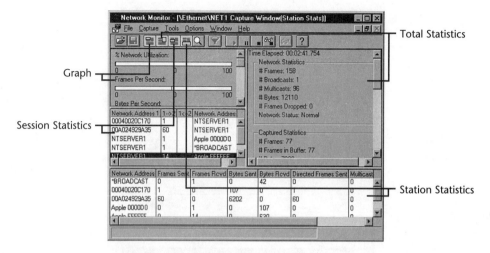

Fig. 15.7 Capturing packets with Network Monitor.

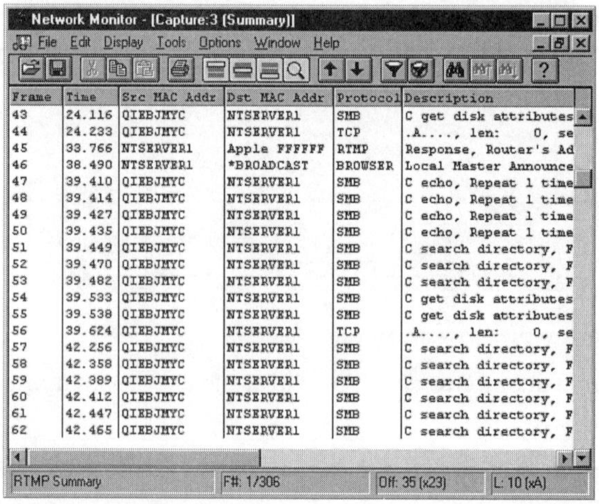

Fig. 15.8 Viewing all packets captured in the Capture Summary window.

Note

NetMon keeps a database of names that correspond to a given MAC address. You can view the entries in this database by choosing Addresses from the Capture window's Capture menu or from the Capture Summary window's Display menu.

In figure 15.9, the address database contains some default entries for broadcasts on Ethernet, Token Ring, and FDDI, as well as a special MAC address used by NetBIOS. Also, a Windows NT Server called NTSERVER1 and a Windows 3.1 client called QIEBJMYC have been discovered and automatically added to the database. In the Address Database dialog, you can click Save to save these entries to the default address database, DEFAULT.ADR.

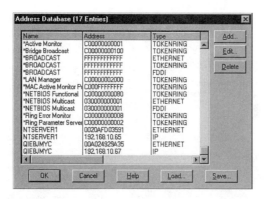

Fig. 15.9   Viewing NetMon's address database.

6. Choose Filter from the Display menu of the Capture Summary window to open the Display Filter dialog (see fig. 15.10), which lets you create filters for the captured packets. You can filter by protocol, by station address, or by a protocol property. For an example, double-click the Protocol == Any entry to enable all protocols and open the Expression dialog. (Whether or not you filter on protocol, address, or property, the Expression dialog appears, to let you define the parameters of your filter.)

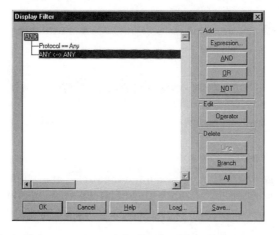

Fig. 15.10   The default filter expressions of the Display Filter dialog.

If you want to set up a filter so that only IP packets appear, click Disable All in the Expression dialog; then from the Disabled Protocols list, scroll down to select IP:. Click Enable to display only IP packets (see fig. 15.11). Click OK twice, to close the Expression and Display Filter dialogs, and to engage the filter.

7. Double-click a packet item in NetMon's list to display additional information about the packet. The Capture Summary window opens with three panes that provide summary, detail, and hexadecimal information about the selected packet (see fig. 15.12).

III

Administering a Network

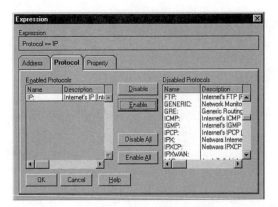

Fig. 15.11 Setting up a display filter to show only IP packets.

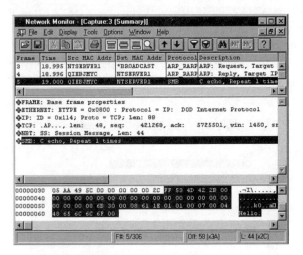

Fig. 15.12 Viewing detailed information on a captured packet.

8. Click the middle (detail) pane to examine the packet at each protocol layer. Each OSI layer is represented by an entry, including Physical (Frame), MAC (Ethernet, Token Ring, and so on), Network (IP, IPX, AppleTalk, and so on), Transport (TCP), and Session (NBT).

A plus symbol to the left of each layer item indicates that there is more detail available under that heading. Double-click one such entry to display detailed information for that portion of the frame. Figure 15.13 shows an IP layer entry that has been expanded to show all the fields of the IP header, including source and destination IP addresses for that packet, and the packet's size. The content of the selected location of the packet appears in hexadecimal format in the pane at the bottom of the Capture Detail window.

Network Monitor is useful in troubleshooting various network-related problems, such as name resolution by a WINS server. You can use NetMon to capture packets coming into the WINServer to determine whether a client's name-resolution requests reach the server, and whether the server responds to the requests. By using NetMon's trace capability, you can verify that the client makes a WINS request to the server and the server returns a packet indicating that the name wasn't found. You then use WINS Manager to determine whether the name exists in the server's WINS database or whether the WINS database is corrupted.

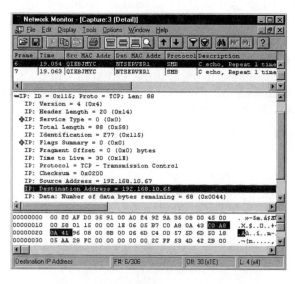

Fig. 15.13   Viewing packet detail within the IP header.

Using Performance Monitor as a Network Troubleshooting Tool

Windows NT's Performance Monitor (PerfMon) is a valuable tool for monitoring the operation of Windows NT servers and workstations, including their network components. PerfMon lets you monitor network interfaces on a server to determine bandwidth usage, rates of errors and broadcasts, and protocol-specific counters. Figure 15.14 shows PerfMon's Add to Chart dialog listing some of the counters available for the Network Segment object.

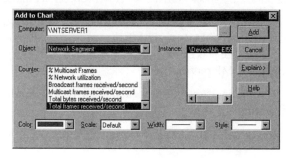

Fig. 15.14   Performance Monitor's Network Segment counters.

III

Administering a Network

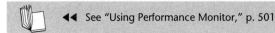

◄◄ See "Using Performance Monitor," p. 501

The % Network Utilization counter gives a running snapshot of current network usage on the segment you're monitoring. This counter is a valuable tool for performing a quick analysis of a segment where you suspect problems are occurring. You can launch PerfMon and do a quick check without having to install a protocol analyzer or software agent.

Installing the SNMP Service. You need to install the SNMP (Simple Network Management Protocol) service to obtain all the available TCP/IP and/or IPX statistics for your network interface. Without SNMP, PerfMon can't see some of the network objects. To install SNMP service, follow these steps:

1. From Control Panel, double-click the Network tool to open the Network property sheet, and then click the Services tab.

2. Click Add to open the Select Network Service dialog.

3. In the Network Service list, select SNMP Service (see fig. 15.15), and then click Have Disk to open the Insert Disk dialog.

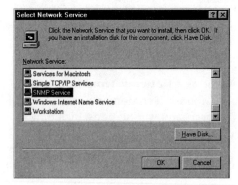

Fig. 15.15   Installing the SNMP service from the Select Network Service dialog.

4. You're prompted for the path to your Windows NT Server distribution CD-ROM. Enter the path to the CD-ROM drive and the appropriate subfolder for your processor. For instance, if your CD is drive E on an Intel-based server, type `e:\i386` and click OK to copy the SNMP service files.

5. The Microsoft SNMP Properties sheet appears, to let you customize the SNMP agent on your system (see fig. 15.16).

Following is a brief description of each page of the Microsoft SNMP Properties sheet:

   • The default Agent page lets you enter contact and location information, as well as specify the services provided by the server. The service selections— Physical, Applications, Datalink/Subnetwork, Internet, and End-to-End—let you specify which SNMP statistics this server should collect. The selection is based on the services that the server provides. For example, marking the Datalink/Subnetwork check box provides MAC-layer statistics on the server's network interfaces. The Internet check box provides information on the network-layer protocol, such as IP or IPX, and is useful if you're running routing services on your server.

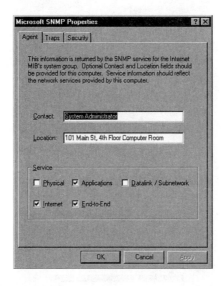

Fig. 15.16   Setting SNMP Agent configuration options.

- The Traps page lets you select a community name to be used by all trap messages and specify a trap destination, using either IP or IPX protocol (see fig. 15.17). *Traps* are SNMP messages that get sent from your server whenever a significant event occurs. A significant event can be a NIC that has been disconnected or is reconnected, or a user-initiated server shutdown. Traps are sent to an SNMP management console running at the trap destination you specify.

- The Security page lets you set up SNMP security for the service (see fig. 15.18). Options include whether the service should send a trap each time an SNMP manager authenticates with the service, the accepted community names for use by SNMP managers, and whether any SNMP device can communicate with the service or only specified IP or IPX hosts.

6. After you complete the setup of the SNMP agent for your server, click OK to close the Microsoft SNMP Properties sheet and click Close in the Network property sheet. You'll be required to restart your system for the changes to take effect.

As part of the installation of the SNMP service, Microsoft provides a number of Management Information Bases (MIBs). These MIBs contain the various attributes that the SNMP service tracks. SNMP managers monitor the MIB attributes of servers, routers, and other SNMP-compliant network devices.

III

Administering a Network

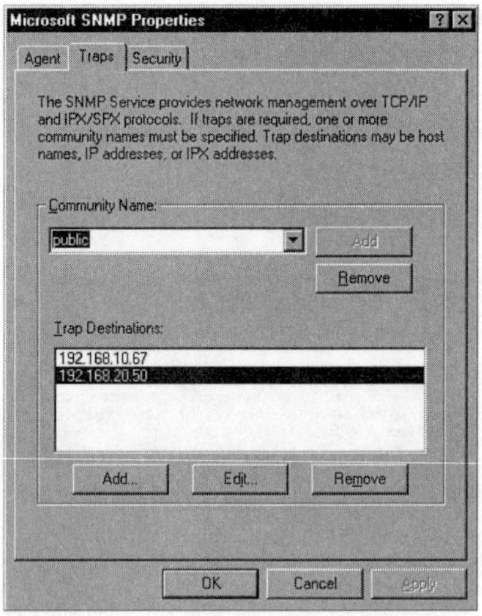

Fig. 15.17 Setting the Trap properties for the SNMP service.

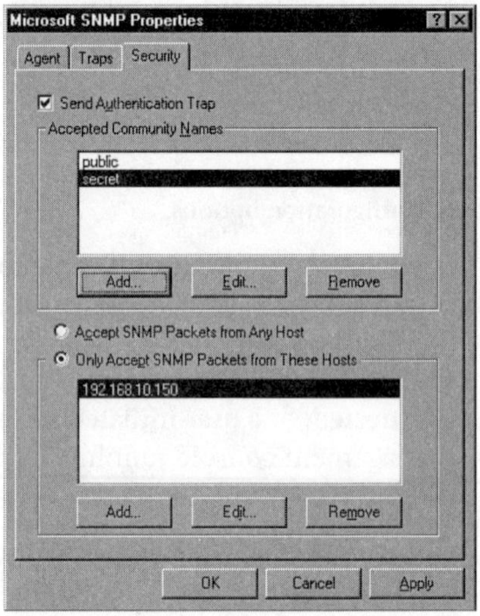

Fig. 15.18 Setting Security properties for the SNMP service.

If you're familiar with the SNMP MIB specification, Windows NT provides two trees in the private MIB section. 1.3.6.1.4.1.77 is the LANManager tree that provides information on shares, sessions, and users. 1.3.6.1.4.1.311 is the Microsoft tree that provides statistics on WINS and DHCP. A *tree* in the MIB, as represented by the Object ID (OID) 1.3.6.1.4.1.77, is really an "address" where an SNMP manager that's connected to Windows NT Server's SNMP service can attach to find SNMP information about a specific attribute on the server. Under each tree are *leaf objects* corresponding to individual characteristics for that device. For example, under the 1.3.6.1.4.1.311 tree for WINS and

DHCP, an SNMP Manager can find what entries are contained in the WINS database on that server, or who the WINS service's replication partners are.

Using Performance Monitor with TCP/IP Networks. After installing the SNMP service on your Windows NT server, you can use PerfMon to gather IP- and/or IPX-related statistics about your system. The most useful application of PerfMon as a network troubleshooting tool is tracking protocol-related information over time with PerfMon's logging function. By using the IP object in PerfMon, for example, you can track datagram errors, packets received, or packets discarded over time (see fig. 15.19).

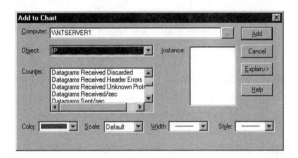

Fig. 15.19 PerfMon's Add to Chart dialog showing IP-related counters.

PerfMon also includes counters for ICMP, TCP, and UDP objects that provide similar information to IP. Tracking these counters over time provides valuable information about network performance on your Windows NT server, especially when you must troubleshoot TCP/IP or IPX network problems.

Using Windows NT's Network-Related Commands and Utilities

Windows NT 4.0 and the Windows NT Resource Kit provide many useful command-line tools for troubleshooting network problems. The following sections describe the most important tools included with Windows NT Server 4.0 and the additional command-line utilities provided in the Windows NT Resource Kit.

Windows NT Server 4.0's Built-In Networking Tools. You can use the command-line tools that come with Windows NT 4.0 to help solve many basic networking problems. Most of the tools are for TCP/IP and are likely to be familiar to UNIX users.

Address Resolution Protocol. The arp (address resolution protocol) command lets you view the current contents of the arp cache on a server or workstation. arp -a displays the contents of the arp cache; arp -d and arp -s let you manually remove and add entries to the arp cache. With ping, you can use arp to determine whether a device is communicating on the network. If you ping a device in question, you should see a corresponding entry in the arp cache of either the device you're pinging, or that of the default gateway if the device isn't on your local subnet (see fig. 15.20).

Hostname. The hostname command returns the name of the system on which the command is executed. The name returned is the name specified in the DNS setup section of the TCP/IP configuration of the system, rather than the NetBIOS name.

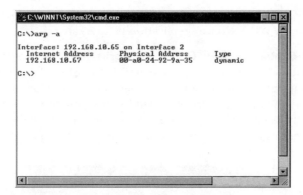

Fig. 15.20   Using the arp command to view the arp cache.

Ipconfig. The ipconfig command returns all the current TCP/IP, DNS, and WINS information for the system. Use ipconfig /all to display all the information, and just ipconfig to obtain abbreviated information (see fig. 15.21).

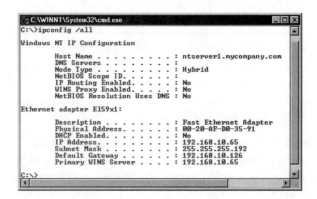

Fig. 15.21   Viewing the output of the ipconfig command.

The ipconfig command is also a quick way to get the MAC address of the NIC installed in the device. If you're using DHCP, you can also use the ipconfig command to renew a DHCP address reservation, or release an address on a DHCP client using the /renew and /release parameters.

Nbtstat. The nbtstat command is one of the most useful Windows NT networking tools, because it provides various information about NetBIOS names and their addresses. For example, if you know the NetBIOS name of a workstation and want to know its IP address, follow these steps:

1. Type **net view *machinename*** at the command prompt, where *machinename* is the NetBIOS name of the device. You receive a list of shares available on that machine, or the message There are no entries in the list.

2. Type **nbtstat -c** to display the name and IP address of the machine specified in step 1. You don't need to specify the machine name because the result of the

preceding name resolution is cached in the NetBIOS Name Cache, which you can view with the -c parameter.

You also can use the nbtstat -A ip_address command to determine what machine is registered to a given IP address (see fig. 15.22). Note that this command requires an *uppercase* A parameter. When you issue this command, the server or workstation sends a name request to the IP address of the primary WINS server specified in the issuing device's TCP/IP WINS configuration page. The returned information is the contents of the WINS database for ip_address. This command is useful if you're trying to troubleshoot WINS problems.

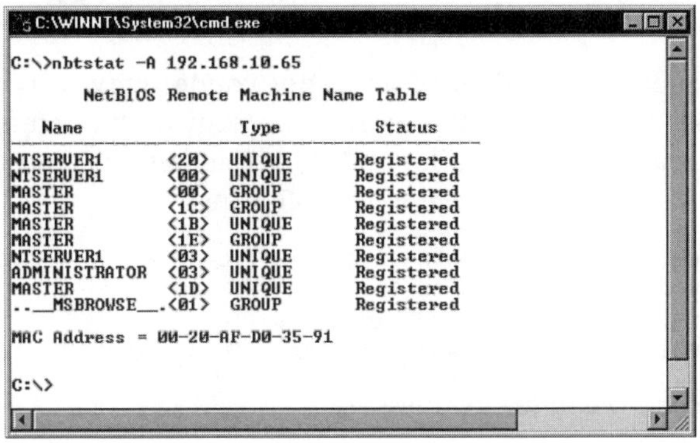

```
C:\WINNT\System32\cmd.exe                          _□×

C:\>nbtstat -A 192.168.10.65

        NetBIOS Remote Machine Name Table

   Name              Type         Status

NTSERVER1     <20>  UNIQUE     Registered
NTSERVER1     <00>  UNIQUE     Registered
MASTER        <00>  GROUP      Registered
MASTER        <1C>  GROUP      Registered
MASTER        <1B>  UNIQUE     Registered
MASTER        <1E>  GROUP      Registered
NTSERVER1     <03>  UNIQUE     Registered
ADMINISTRATOR <03>  UNIQUE     Registered
MASTER        <1D>  UNIQUE     Registered
.._MSBROWSE_.<01>  GROUP      Registered

MAC Address = 00-20-AF-D0-35-91

C:\>
```

Fig. 15.22 Viewing the output of the nbtstat -A command.

Netstat. The netstat command performs many of the same functions as its UNIX counterpart. The netstat -a command displays all current TCP and UDP connections from the issuing device to other devices on the network, as well as the source and destination service ports, and—in the case of TCP—the current state of the connection (for instance, Established or Time-Wait). You also can use netstat -r to post a listing of the routing table on a given machine (see fig. 15.23).

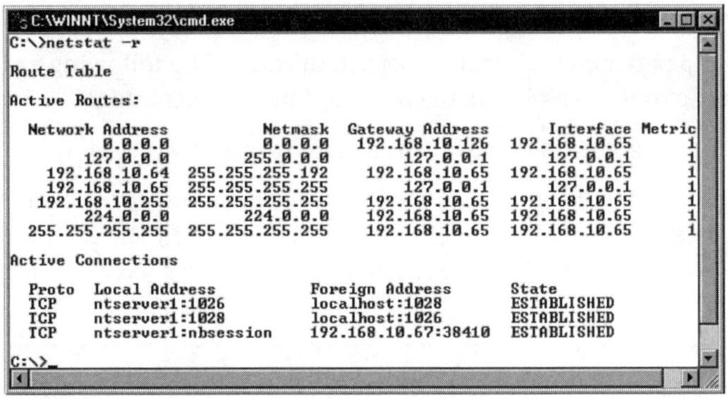

```
C:\WINNT\System32\cmd.exe                                              _□×
C:\>netstat -r

Route Table

Active Routes:

  Network Address          Netmask  Gateway Address        Interface Metric
        0.0.0.0          0.0.0.0  192.168.10.126    192.168.10.65     1
      127.0.0.0          255.0.0.0        127.0.0.1        127.0.0.1     1
  192.168.10.64  255.255.255.192    192.168.10.65    192.168.10.65     1
  192.168.10.65  255.255.255.255        127.0.0.1        127.0.0.1     1
 192.168.10.255  255.255.255.255    192.168.10.65    192.168.10.65     1
      224.0.0.0        224.0.0.0    192.168.10.65    192.168.10.65     1
255.255.255.255  255.255.255.255    192.168.10.65    192.168.10.65     1

Active Connections

  Proto  Local Address          Foreign Address        State
  TCP    ntserver1:1026         localhost:1028         ESTABLISHED
  TCP    ntserver1:1028         localhost:1026         ESTABLISHED
  TCP    ntserver1:nbsession    192.168.10.67:38410    ESTABLISHED

C:\>_
```

Fig. 15.23 Using netstat -r to view the routing table of a Windows NT server.

The `netstat -e` command gives you statistics on your network interface. When combined with an interval parameter—for example, `netstat -e 10`—the following information is updated every 10 seconds:

```
Interface Statistics          Received          Sent
Bytes                           184763        125248
Unicast Packets                    304           437
Non-unicast Packets               1419          1419
Discards                             0             0
Errors                               0             0
Unknown Protocols                  313
```

The preceding information is useful if you're troubleshooting suspected network problems and want to determine whether the network interface is generating errors.

Ping. The `ping` command is widely used for testing connectivity. This command sends an ICMP echo packet to the host or IP address you specify on the command line. For example, `ping 200.200.1.1` sends an echo packet to IP address 200.200.1.1. If `ping` is successful, you see a series of replies similar to the following:

```
Reply from 200.200.1.1: bytes=32 time=10ms TTL=32
Reply from 200.200.1.1: bytes=32 time=10ms TTL=32
Reply from 200.200.1.1: bytes=32 time=10ms TTL=32
Reply from 200.200.1.1: bytes=32 time=10ms TTL=32
```

If `ping` fails, you receive the following message:

```
Request timed out.
```

You can test whether a server's TCP/IP subsystem is working correctly with the `ping 127.0.0.1` command, also known as the *loopback address*. This is the *localhost* address, or the default hostname for that machine; this address and hostname is installed by default when you install Windows NT's TCP/IP stack. A successful ping indicates that this virtual address is alive, and that your TCP/IP stack is functioning correctly.

Route. The `route` utility lists a server's TCP/IP routing table and can add or delete static routes. You also can add persistent (static) routes that are maintained through shutdown and startup. To view the current routing table, type **route print**.

You can use the -p parameter to create a persistent route. The following example shows how to add a static route to a remote network and make it persistent:

```
route -p add 192.168.20.0 MASK 255.255.255.0 200.200.1.255 1
```

The trailing 1 indicates that the remote network is one router *hop* (one pass through a router) away. The example routes to the remote network 192.168.20.0 using the gateway/router address of 200.200.1.255. The remote network has a subnet mask of 255.255.255.0.

Note

Persistent routes are stored in the HKEY_LOCAL_MACHINE\System\CurrentControlSet\Services\Tcpip\Parameters\PersistentRoutes of the Registry.

Tracert. The `tracert` command lets you trace the path to a destination IP address, identifying all the intermediate hops between the source and destination. You can use the `tracert` command—a very powerful tool for determining how packets are traversing your network—to troubleshoot routing loops or down routers, as well as discover timeout problems across the network.

The `tracert` command uses ICMP to find the path to the end station you specify. The following example, `tracert EndStation`, traces a path to a client called EndStation at IP address 172.16.12.1:

```
Tracing route to EndStation [172.16.12.1]
over a maximum of 30 hops:
  1    181 ms    130 ms    130 ms  172.16.4.254
  2    160 ms    131 ms    120 ms  routera.mycompany.com [172.16.5.254]
  3    151 ms    120 ms    120 ms  routerb.mycompany.com [172.16.6.254]
  4    160 ms    140 ms    140 ms  172.16.8.254
  5    161 ms    140 ms    140 ms  routerc.mycompany.com [172.16.9.254]
  6    170 ms    141 ms    130 ms  EndStation [172.16.12.1]
Trace complete.
```

In this example, the path to the EndStation client is six hops from the device where the command is initiated. The first hop is to the default gateway (172.16.4.254) on the subnet where the command was issued. Along the way, `tracert` does a DNS *reverse-address lookup* of each hop (unless you specify the `-d` parameter) to resolve IP addresses of intermediate hops to host names. If your router interfaces aren't configured in DNS, all you see are the addresses in lines 1 and 4 of the example.

> **Note**
>
> A DNS reverse lookup is exactly as it sounds. Rather than resolve a known host name to an IP address, a reverse lookup resolves a known IP address to a host name.

In the following example, the EndStation client is unreachable from the source. The trace stops after the third hop. This could mean that either the end station is down, or the destination subnet isn't accessible from the source. The latter problem can be due to router problems or to an intermediate route filter of some type. The best way to approach solving these kinds of problems is to determine what part of the path *does* work, and narrow the possible suspects as you go. A good troubleshooting technique with `tracert` is to connect to the last successful step along the path—in this case, routerb.mycompany.com—and determine whether you can get to the destination from there. If not, your problem is likely to be in a destination device or an intermediate router. You might need to run another trace from routerb to determine whether intermediate hops to the destination are failing.

```
Tracing route to 172.16.80.1
over a maximum of 30 hops
  1    140 ms    120 ms    130 ms  172.16.4.254
  2    131 ms    120 ms    120 ms  routera.mycompany.com [172.16.5.254]
  3  routerb.mycompany.com [172.16.6.254]  reports:
  ➡Destination host unreachable.
Trace complete.
```

Windows NT Resource Kit Utilities. The Windows NT Resource Kit includes several useful tools for troubleshooting network problems. Many are easy-to-use GUI-based tools, but others are cryptic, not very well documented, and require trial-and-error experimentation to use correctly. Microsoft provides product support (including bug fixes) for the Resource Kit utilities, but doesn't respond to requests for enhancements. You also can send questions by e-mail to **rkinput@microsoft.com**; someone at Microsoft might get back to you, if only to tell you that the information you need is available somewhere else.

> **Note**
>
> The Windows NT 4.0 Resource Kit wasn't available when this book was written. The descriptions that follow apply to the tools included in the Windows NT 3.51 Resource Kit, few of which worked with Windows NT Server 4.0.

Following is a description of the utilities in the Resource Kit that are most useful for network troubleshooting.

Browser Monitor. Browmon.exe is the Browser Monitor, the 3.51 version of which is incompatible with Windows NT 4.0. BrowMon is very useful when you need to troubleshoot browser problems. You can check the contents of the Master Browser on each subnet in question to determine whether your missing device is actually contained in the browser list for that segment.

> **Note**
>
> When you run BrowMon, you see only browser information for the local network segment. If you want to know what's contained on the Domain Master Browser (almost always the Primary Domain Controller, or PDC), you must run BrowMon from a machine on the same segment as the PDC.

Browser Status. Browstat.exe is the Browser Status command-line utility that's useful for retrieving general browser information, such as statistics and domain information. The 3.51 version of BrowStat is incompatible with Windows NT 4.0. You can also use BrowStat to force a browser election, force a master browser to stop, and find out if you have any Windows for Workgroups workstations acting as Master Browsers on a network segment.

Domain Monitor. Dommon.exe, the Domain Monitor utility, displays the current status of a given domain's Domain Controller, including whether its Security Accounts Manager (SAM) databases are synchronized. DomMon also shows the current trust status of any domains with which the current domain has a trust relationship. The 3.51 version of DomMon is incompatible with Windows NT 4.0.

DomMon is useful for troubleshooting problems with trust relationships, because it allows you to see which remote domain controller the current domain uses for the trust. From this point, you can verify connectivity between the two servers as part of your troubleshooting process.

GetMac. Getmac.exe is a simple utility that returns the MAC address of the machine on which it's run. The 3.51 version of GetMac works with Windows NT 4.0. GetMac is useful if you're having problems with ARP and need to know MAC addresses. GetMac returns the MAC address of each network protocol loaded on your machine, similar to the following:

```
E:\ getmac
Transport Address   Transport Name
-----------------   --------------
20-4C-4F-4F-50-20   \Device\NetBT_NDISLoop1
00-00-00-00-00-00   \Device\NetBT_NdisWan5
20-4C-4F-4F-50-20   \Device\Nbf_NDISLoop1
20-4C-4F-4F-50-20   \Device\NwlnkNb
```

NetWatch. Netwatch.exe is a GUI-based utility, similar to Windows 95's Net Watcher, that lets you monitor user connections to shares on servers and clients. The 3.51 version of NetWatch works with Windows NT 4.0. As figure 15.24 shows, you also can see what files a user has open on a given share.

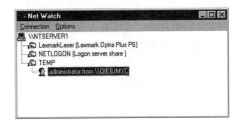

Fig. 15.24   Using the NetWatch utility to view users logged on to a Windows NT Server 4.0 share.

Windows NT doesn't have the NetWare 3.x concept of user logon connections into each server; Windows NT attaches to domain resources as needed. This utility, however, tells you who's connected to which share on a given server or client, and which files they have open.

◀◀ See "Using Remote Management," p. 371

NSLookup. Nslookup.exe serves the same function as its UNIX equivalent. The 3.51 version of Nslookup.exe works with Windows NT 4.0. You can use NSLookup to query DNS servers to determine the IP address of a specified host name, or the host name of a specified IP address. The `nslookup` command sends the request to the address and subdomains defined in the DNS configuration portion of Windows NT's TCP/IP configuration screen (see fig. 15.25). `nslookup` takes no parameters. When you enter the command, you're placed at the > prompt, where you enter the name or address you want to resolve (see fig. 15.26).

SMBTrace. The Smbtrace.exe command-line utility is similar to the UNIX `etherfind` command, except that `smbtrace` tracks Server Message Block packets only. The 3.51 version of Smbtrace.exe works with Windows NT 4.0. SMBTrace is a real-time packet tracer that shows the SMB packets that are flowing to and from your system, which is useful for

III

Administering a Network

understanding the flow of SMB packets during file transfers and print jobs. By default, smbtrace captures incoming packets only. The /slow parameter captures both incoming and outgoing, and the /rdr parameter captures only outgoing packets. You can change the amount of information smbtrace displays with each packet by using the /verbosity:*n* parameter, where *n* is a number between 1 and 5, 5 being most verbose.

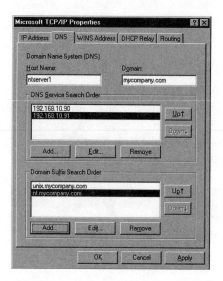

Fig. 15.25 Setting DNS Configuration options in the Microsoft TCP/IP Properties sheet.

Fig. 15.26 Using nslookup to resolve DNS names and addresses.

WNTIPcfg. The Windows NT IP configuration tool, Wntipcfg.exe, lists all the TCP/IP configuration information for the system on which WNTIPcfg runs. WNTIPcfg provides the same information as ipconfig -a in a graphical format. The 3.51 version of DomMon is incompatible with Windows NT 4.0.

Taking Advantage of Other Resources

In addition to the tools described in the preceding sections, the following resources also include network troubleshooting advice and tools:

- Microsoft Knowledge Base (**http://www.microsoft.com/kb/**) is an online repository of known problems and their fixes.

- The Microsoft Technet CD is a monthly subscription that combines fixes, driver updates, and the Knowledge Base, as well as other useful information.

- The Windows NT Resource Center, run by BHS Software of Beverly Hills (**http://www.bhs.com**), is perhaps the most popular Web site for Windows NT-related files, information, and problem resolution. Check out the BHS Tech Center if you have a networking problem you can't resolve.

- Internet newsgroups, such as **comp.os.ms-windows.nt.admin.networking** and **comp.os.ms-windows.nt.misc**, also are good sources of troubleshooting information.

You can find useful NT-related information in many other places on the Internet. Just choose your favorite search engine and search on `Windows NT`.

Solving Windows NT Server Network Problems

Windows NT Server is similar to other operating systems when troubleshooting basic network problems. If there are connectivity problems, you check the cabling, the network interface card, and the network protocol configuration. Windows NT, however, includes a number of additional network-related components (such as browsing, trusts, and WINS) that can compound basic network problems. An understanding of some of the common problems related to Windows NT's special networking features helps you become a more accomplished network administrator. The following sections explore some of the more common problems and suggest possible solutions.

Understanding and Solving Connectivity Problems

Connectivity problems manifest themselves in different ways. In Windows NT, a connectivity problem can cause trust relationships to fail or cause drive mappings to time out.

You were introduced to a number of tools in the preceding sections for testing connectivity. In the following sections, the utilities are applied to help solve connectivity problems that arise in Windows NT environments.

Solving Basic Connectivity Issues. Utilities such as ping allow you to test connectivity from point A to point B. The ping utility may succeed, but success verifies only that TCP/IP is working. If you must verify Windows NT Server's file, print, and application service availability, you must be able to verify connectivity at the NetBIOS level.

The `net view` command is the NetBIOS equivalent of ping. A `net view \\`*servername* command might result in the following message:

III

Administering a Network

```
System error 53 has occurred.
The network path was not found.
```

This message usually means that either the *servername* system is down, or the device's name can't be resolved. You may find the case where ping succeeds but net view fails. An example of such a situation is when a NetBIOS device, such as a server, has found a name conflict on startup. While the server was shut down, WINS may have registered another name at the server's IP address, or the same server name may have been registered at a different network address. You can use the nbtstat -n command to determine whether there's a conflict. In either case, the network subsystem might start, but the NetBIOS services don't. You can check for this situation by searching the system log with the Event Viewer application on the device in question.

If you receive system error 53 and have verified that the system's NetBIOS subsystem isn't in conflict, you likely have a name-resolution problem. In this case, verify on a TCP/IP network that you have an entry in WINS or an LMHosts file to resolve the name in question.

Identifying Router Problems. If you suspect your connectivity problems are related to routing—that is, you've verified that both source and destination are up and can access devices on their local segment—use tracert to determine where in the path you have a problem.

Identifying Default Gateway Problems. If you're in a networked environment where each segment has multiple, redundant routes to reach a specified destination, you should be aware of an idiosyncrasy in Windows NT's TCP/IP stack. Windows NT Server 4.0's Advanced IP Addressing dialog provides the capability to specify multiple default gateways to reach remote segments (see fig. 15.27). If the first gateway in the list fails, however, any subsequent User Datagram Protocol (UDP) packets fail to search the list for the next gateway. When the first TCP packet finds the primary gateway down, the packet goes down the list to the next gateway and makes it the active gateway. Thus, subsequent UDP packets use the new gateway to reach their destination. You may never notice use of an alternative gateway unless the primary gateway is down when you're first powering up a system.

The Netlogon Service, which is responsible for domain authentication, uses UDP to authenticate a client and user to a domain. As a result, when a server that is a backup domain controller (BDC) starts up with its primary default gateway down, the BDC can't contact other servers that aren't on the same physical network segment—that is, across a router. The result is the following message:

```
A Domain Controller could not be contacted
```

In this case, until the first TCP packet goes out, the BDC can't authenticate—and therefore synchronize—to the domain. Although this is a specialized problem of redundant routing, it's significant, especially on the workstation side.

Browsing

Browsing is a feature unique to Windows NT and its predecessor, LAN Manager. Browsing is solely a function of NetBIOS and slightly parallels Novell's SAP service announcements. Troubleshooting browsing problems, especially in a NetBEUI or IPX-NetBIOS environment, is downright difficult. You're limited to the BrowMon and BrowStat tools (discussed earlier in this chapter). Troubleshooting browsing problems is a bit better in the TCP/IP environment, where browsing is broken up by logical subnets and browser advertisements are broadcast-based, thus not forwarded by the routers.

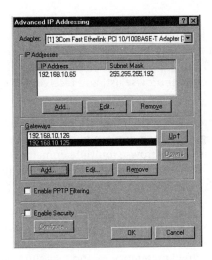

Fig. 15.27 Setting multiple default gateways with the Advanced IP Addressing dialog.

The best way to troubleshoot browsing is first to understand the browsing process. A domain environment has three types of browsers, as follows:

- *Domain Master Browser.* By default, the primary domain controller (PDC) is the Domain Master Browser for a particular domain.

- *Master Browser.* Each network segment contains at least one Master Browser. In the case where you have only one segment, the PDC is also the Master Browser.

- *Backup Browser.* Each network segment has at least one backup browser, which is responsible for holding elections to pick a new Master Browser if the Master Browser goes away.

Following is a step-by-step description of the election process to determine a new Master Browser:

1. When a client or server starts up, it sends a broadcast browser announcement that identifies the device's presence.

2. The Master Browser on the segment responds by adding the client or server to its browse list and sends back a list of the backup browsers.

3. When a client or server wants to browse the network, it sends a NetServerEnum request to the master or backup browsers to retrieve the browse list.

4. Every 12 minutes, each client or server that isn't a browser reannounces itself to the Master Browser. If a client or server doesn't reannounce for three consecutive 12-minute intervals, it's dropped from the Master Browser's list.

5. Every 15 minutes, the backup browser contacts the Master Browser to update its browse list. If the Master Browser doesn't respond, this triggers the backup browser to hold an election.

6. The Master Browser also must contact the Domain Master Browser, which contains the entire browse list for the domain, including devices announced by other master browsers. Every 15 minutes, the Master Browser contacts the Domain Master Browser, provides its current browse list, and receives the current full domain browse list.

7. Master browsers also announce their domain every 15 minutes. If you have multiple domains on a segment, each domain populates the other domains' Master Browser lists so that users can browse multiple domains. In a TCP/IP environment, browsers use WINS to determine the identity of the domain master browsers, which are indicated by the 16th Byte type: *<domain_name>*[1Bh].

8. If at any time during the preceding steps the Master Browser goes down, the backup browser forces an election. Alternatively, a client can force an election if it discovers the Master Browser failure before the backup browser does. The election proceeds using a predefined preference method. NetBIOS systems have an order of preference for browsability: Windows NT Server, followed by Windows NT Workstation, then by Windows for Workgroups, and Windows 95. If there's a tie among recipients, other criteria, such as how long the system has been up and the name of the system, can be used to break the tie.

Browser operations use NetBIOS mailslots to perform tasks such as announcements, elections, and updates. Windows NT Server's mailslots are second class. First-class mailslots provide guaranteed delivery; second-class mailslots are connectionless, so delivery of messages isn't guaranteed.

If you're having browser problems, the first thing to check with BrowMon is the contents of the Master Browser on your network segment. If the computer in question isn't in the list, a possible cause is a Windows for Workgroups client on the segment that has the MaintainServerList parameter of its SYSTEM.INI [386Enh] section set to something other than No.

Another possible problem is that the browser service on a Windows NT server or workstation isn't running. You can check this with Windows NT's Control Panel's Services tool, or issue the net start command to see which services are running.

Finally, you can prevent a Windows NT workstation or server from announcing itself to the Master Browser by issuing the following command:

```
net config server /hidden:yes
```

If someone has set the /hidden parameter, you don't see the server on the browser, but you can connect to the server by using its UNC name.

Routing

By default, Windows NT Server doesn't support dynamic routing. That is, if you have two NICs in a server, you can't send routing updates between the two NICs. You can set up routing between the two cards by selecting the Enable IP Forwarding check box in the Routing page of the Microsoft TCP/IP Properties sheet (see fig. 15.28), accessed from Control Panel's Network tool.

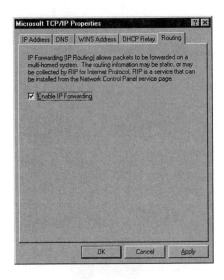

Fig. 15.28   Enabling IP routing in the Routing page.

Microsoft includes with Windows NT Server 4.0 support for dynamic routing with the RIP for NWLink IPX/SPX service and RIP for Internet Protocol Service. Unless you run these services, you must configure routing with the static `route` command described earlier in the chapter. Most problems with routing in Windows NT relate to this static routing concept. Specifically, if you're trying to communicate from a segment connected to a NIC in a Windows NT server to another segment connected to a second NIC, also installed in that server, you need a static route.

In the example shown in figure 15.29, if you're trying to communicate from Client A on Network B to Server B on Network C, Windows NT Server C needs a static route to tell traffic how to get to Network C. The persistent route statement is

```
route -p add 172.16.42.0 MASK 255.255.255.0 172.16.40.2 1
```

where 172.16.42.0 is the destination network Client A is trying to get to, and 172.16.40.2 is the router interface on the far end of Network A that forwards the packet to the correct network.

Troubleshooting Trusts

Trust relationships allow resources and user accounts to be shared between domains. The major network problems that arise as a result of trusts are in a WAN using TCP/IP. Domain controllers use WINS to determine names and IP addresses of trusted domain

III

Administering a Network

controllers in remote domains. As a result, if there are problems with WINS, trust relationships break down.

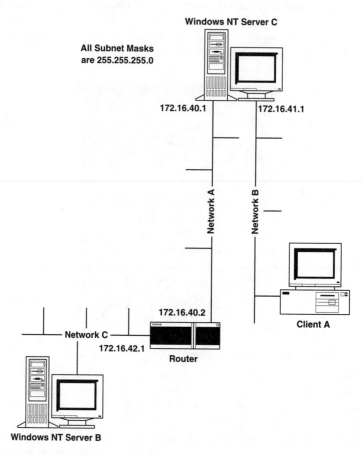

Fig. 15.29 An example of a configuration that requires a static route.

If you're replicating your WINS databases so that all domain controllers in each domain can resolve each other, establishing and maintaining a trust relationship should be easy. Domain controllers, by default, register their domain names in WINS using the [1Ch] 16th Byte type. However, if this replication has failed or has become corrupted, you can statically map domains in WINS so that each side of the trust can resolve the other—in effect, statically adding the [1Ch] entries. Figure 15.30 shows an example of static mapping of trust domains in the Static Mappings dialog of WINS Manager. To access the WINS Manager, use the Start menu and choose Programs, Administrative Tools, and then WINS Manager. When you click Add Mappings in the Static Mappings dialog, you see a place to type your static entries, and a number of choices for entry type (see fig. 15.31).

If you're establishing a trust relationship and dynamic registrations in WINS don't seem to be functioning correctly, you can statically map both the remote domain and its domain controllers in your WINS database. Doing so guarantees that your domain controller always has the correct information on how to reach the remote domain, even if the remote domain's WINS database is corrupted and doesn't provide the proper dynamic registrations to other domain controllers.

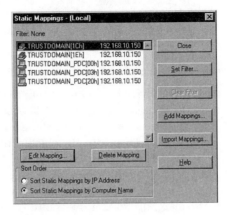

Fig. 15.30   Displaying WINS static mappings with WINS Manager.

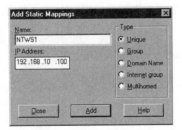

Fig. 15.31   Setting static mapping options in the Add Static Mappings dialog.

To statically map a remote domain in your WINS database, follow these steps:

1. From the WINS Manager utility, choose Static Mappings from the Mappings menu. Click Add Mappings to display the Add Static Mappings dialog (refer to fig. 15.31).

2. Select the Group option button, and enter the name of your trusted domain in the Name text box. Enter the IP address of the trusted domain's PDC in the IP Address text box and click Add to add the address.

3. Repeat step 2 to create a Domain Name type entry for the Remote Domain Name. A scrollable list appears that allows multiple IP addresses to be entered in the field (see fig. 15.32). To this list, add the IP addresses of all the Domain Controllers in the Remote Domain.

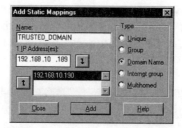

Fig. 15.32   Adding a Domain Name type static mapping from the Add Static Mappings dialog.

You can verify that your static entries have been entered into the WINS database by choosing Show Database from the Mappings menu in WINS Manager. Figure 15.33 shows the contents of a WINS database after adding the static domain mappings. This example shows a remote domain called TrustDomain, which contains a server called TrustDomain_PDC. The [1Eh] value indicates the Group entry for the remote domain. The [1Ch] value indicates the Internet Group entry, and the three Unique type values ([00h], [03h], and [20h]) are for the PDC itself. If you have a two-way trust between domains, create these static WINS mappings so that they point to each domain on either side of the trust.

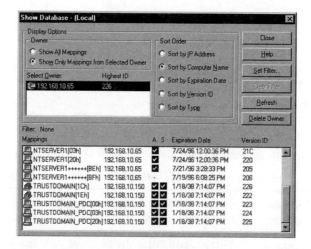

Fig. 15.33   Creating a static mapping set for a remote domain.

Understanding WINS and DNS Name Resolution

As noted at the beginning of this chapter, name resolution is the source of many networking problems with Windows NT Server. This is especially true if you're using the TCP/IP stack, because you may also have to contend with DNS as a potential name service for NetBIOS name lookups. Windows NT Server offers the following places where you can store names for resolution in a TCP/IP environment:

- WINS
- LMHosts

- Hosts

- DNS

Depending on the network function being performed, the path that name resolution follows varies. When you issue a net *view* command to a *servername*, for example, Windows NT first determines the node type of the device (h-node, p-node, m-node, or b-node). Based on the determination, NetBIOS name resolution follows these steps:

1. Regardless of node type, Windows NT checks the contents of the local NetBIOS name cache, which you can view by using nbtstat -c. If the name is in the cache, name resolution is complete.

2. If the name isn't in the name cache, this step depends on node type. For h-node and p-node systems, the WINS server defined in the TCP/IP configuration is queried. For m-node and b-node, a name-resolution broadcast request is sent on the local segment.

3. If either WINS lookup or broadcast lookup fails, h-node broadcasts on the local segment for name resolution, whereas m-node queries WINS.

4. If each of the preceding steps fails for the specified node type, this step depends on the device's configuration. In the WINS Address page of the Microsoft TCP/IP Properties sheet, you can choose to use DNS for NetBIOS name lookup and/or use an LMHosts file (see fig. 15.34).

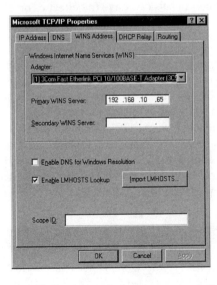

Fig. 15.34   Setting advanced configuration options for name resolution.

If you've elected to use an LMHosts file, all node types consult LMHosts for name resolution.

If you're not using LMHosts (or if LMHosts fails) and you've checked to use DNS for NetBIOS Name Lookup, all node types proceed to use the local hosts file that's located in the *%systemroot%*\system32\drivers\etc folder. If you haven't selected to use DNS, the name-resolution sequence fails, and you see the message The Network Path was Not Found.

If you've elected to use DNS and the local hosts file fails, Windows NT queries the DNS servers you've configured in your TCP/IP DNS configuration for your NetBIOS name. If this fails, name resolution fails and again you see the message The Network Path was Not Found.

The process Windows NT uses for name resolution when performing non-NetBIOS operations varies. For Winsock-based (Winsock is the Windows Sockets standard) operations such as ping, Telnet, FTP, or any other function or service that doesn't require name resolution of NetBIOS resources, Windows NT uses the following steps:

1. Regardless of node type, the local hosts file is checked.

2. If hosts fails, the device queries DNS according to its TCP/IP configuration.

3. If DNS fails, name resolution uses WINS as a last resort. If WINS resolution fails, you receive a failed name lookup message. For example, if you ping a host name and name resolution fails, you receive the message Bad IP Address.

Solving name-resolution problems requires an understanding of the process, and then troubleshooting each step of the process. A good tool for determining where the flow stops is a protocol analyzer, which also tells you whether significant delays in name resolution are occurring. Such delays can have the effect of breaking an application that depends on the timeliness of name resolution. If you can detect delays with a protocol analyzer, you can move name entries to guarantee that they occur more quickly.

For example, a DNS lookup for a given host may take more time than the calling application allows. In that case, you might move that hostname address mapping into the local *%systemroot%*\system32\drivers\etc\hosts file for faster resolution. Alternatively, if WINS is taking too long to resolve a name, or you experience delays in reaching a WINS server, you can increase the timeout of the NetBIOS name cache on your server. By default, name-resolution responses from WINS are cached in the name cache for 10 minutes. If your environment is fairly stable—that is, Windows NT devices don't change addresses often—you can increase the value of the name cache timeout. NetBIOS name resolution looks to the name cache first, so you go to WINS less often for name resolution.

Tip

You can increase the timeout value for the NetBIOS name cache by editing the Registry on your Windows NT Server. The Cache Timeout value is stored in HKEY_LOCAL_MACHINE\System\CurrentControlSet\Services\NetBT\Parameters\CacheTimeout. The value in this key is in milliseconds, and defaults to 600000 (600 seconds). You can change the value from 60000 to about 4 million milliseconds. Change the value in small increments either direction, depending on your network environment. Too small a value results in excessive requests to WINS. If you set the value too large, devices whose addresses have changed might never be found.

From Here...

This chapter discussed how the different network protocols that Windows NT supports for file, print, and application services affect network troubleshooting. NetBEUI and IPX are broadcast-based protocols that require a bridged network or special router forwarding and aren't very scalable. Windows NT's NetBIOS-over-TCP/IP support, also called NetBT, uses a centralized name service (WINS) to avoid the need to broadcast between subnets. Using TCP/IP and NetBT simplifies network troubleshooting.

The chapter also described the utilities that come with Windows NT 4.0 for interrogating and checking network-related services, such as ping, nbtstat, and tracert, and programs included in the Windows NT Resource Kit.

The chapter concluded with a discussion of common Windows NT-specific network problems, such as browsing and name resolution, and how you can use the tools and utilities to aid troubleshooting network problems.

The following chapters contain information related to network troubleshooting:

- Chapter 4, "Choosing Network Protocols," explains how to select one or more of the three principal networking protocols supported by Windows NT, based on your network configuration.

- Chapter 14, "Optimizing Network Server Performance," describes the Windows NT Server 4.0 Performance Monitor and explains tuning methodology to help you maintain optimum network throughput as your network usage grows.

- Chapter 17, "Integrating Windows NT with Heterogeneous Networks," shows you how to set up and administer Windows NT Server within a Novell NetWare or a UNIX networking environment.

- Chapter 24, "Administering Clients with System Management Server," covers the basics of planning, administration, and management for Microsoft SMS 1.x.

III

Administering a Network

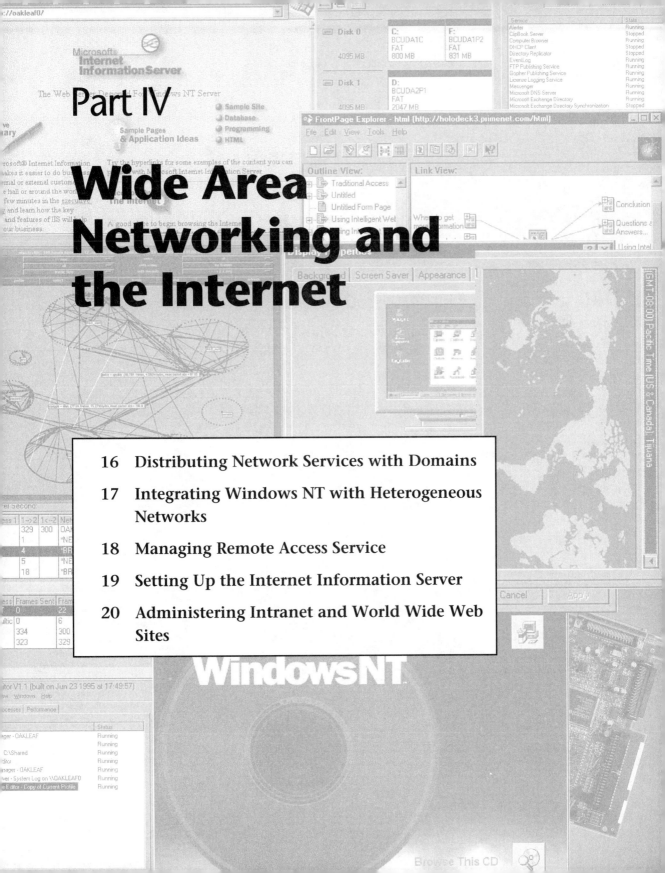

Part IV

Wide Area Networking and the Internet

16 Distributing Network Services with Domains

17 Integrating Windows NT with Heterogeneous Networks

18 Managing Remote Access Service

19 Setting Up the Internet Information Server

20 Administering Intranet and World Wide Web Sites

Chapter 16

Distributing Network Services with Domains

One primary strength of Windows NT Server is its domain facility for providing access to and control of network resources wherever needed. Windows NT Server provides file, print, and application services to a variety of clients in various environments. Access to these services doesn't need to be limited by geography or network bandwidth. More importantly, control and administration of these services can be distributed to fit either a centralized or decentralized support model. Windows NT Server uses domains to provide unified access to and administration of resources in large, distributed networks.

This chapter emphasizes the value domains bring to your Windows NT network environment, and how to take best advantage of domains in LANs and WANs. The chapter also shows you how to use the Domain Planner tool of the Windows NT 4.0 Resource Kit to establish the architecture of your domains.

Understanding Domain Architecture and Security

In the simplest terms, a Windows NT *domain* is a logical grouping of servers, workstations, users, groups, and printers within a physical network. The architecture of Windows NT domains is quite complex, involving security issues, different types of user groups, and trust relationships. For this introductory discussion, you can consider a domain to be a group of *resources* (Windows NT objects) that are bound by a common membership into a single administrative unit. The purpose of domains is to permit distributed network management by segmenting the resources of large networks into sets of manageable sizes.

If you've used Windows for Workgroups, you're familiar with the concept of small groupings of users who need access to common resources, such as files and printers, which reside either on members' PCs or on a central peer-to-peer file server. Domains are extensions of workgroups designed to support

This chapter covers the following :

■ What constitutes a domain, and how domains vary from workgroups

■ The roles of domain controllers and how they communicate

■ The mechanics of creating and changing domains

■ The various domain models you can use

■ How to use trust relationships to assign resources

■ How to position domain controllers for best network performance

larger sets of users who may be located at geographically distant sites. Figure 16.1 illustrates the concept of a domain named SalesCo, which consists of two servers (HQ and Regional), plus client PCs for UserA through UserF. The Regional server for the Sales user group and the HQ server for the Accounting user group are connected by a telecommunications link. The HQ server, a Primary Domain Controller (PDC), is the administrative site for the domain. The Regional server is a Backup Domain Controller (BDC). The relationships between PDCs and BDCs is the subject of the later section "Understanding the Roles of Domain Controllers."

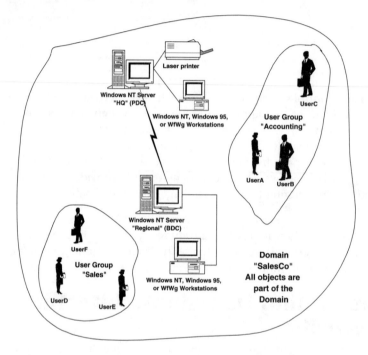

Fig. 16.1 A domain containing servers, printers, client PCs, users, and groups.

Windows NT Server authenticates users when they log on to a server in a domain (*authentication* is the process by which users gain access to the resources for which they have rights). Unlike earlier network operating systems, such as Novell NetWare 3.x, users log on once to the domain, rather than log on to each server they want to access. Likewise, administrators can assign rights to a Domain User or Domain Group, and these rights are applied universally to any domain resource users want to access.

> **Note**
>
> Windows NT Server's single-logon approach extends to server-based applications, such as the members of Microsoft's BackOffice suite. If you install BackOffice applications with Windows NT Server's integrated security feature, users aren't required to separately log on to SQL Server, Exchange Server, System Management Server, or SNA Server. All BackOffice products use Windows NT's built-in security model to authenticate users to these BackOffice services.

IV

Understanding Windows NT Security Identifiers

Beyond the concept of grouping user, machine, and server resources into logical domains, Windows NT provides a mechanism to secure a resource's right to the domain. That is, when a server or client joins a domain, or when a user or user group is created within a domain, Windows NT Server provides a mechanism to guarantee that the new resource is uniquely associated with the domain. From a security standpoint, this mechanism also assures that a user or machine that isn't properly identified to the domain can't access resources in the domain. Windows NT uses a SID (Security Identifier), in addition to a name, to identify each domain resource, group, or user. The SID is generated at the time of creation of the resource and is unique. You can't duplicate a SID, because the SID is based on a variety of CPU information at the instant of the SID's creation.

When you establish a new domain by installing Windows NT Server as the Primary Domain Controller, which is the default for your first Windows NT Server installation, the domain receives its own SID. As you add servers, clients, groups, and users to the domain, their unique SIDs include a reference to the original domain SID. If you move a client PC from one domain to another, the client's SID references the wrong domain and can't use the resources of the new domain. Figure 16.2 illustrates this situation with Server Manager; WORKSTATION1's SID doesn't refer to Primary Domain Controller SERVERA's SID, so WORKSTATION1 appears with its icon disabled (grayed). Overcoming problems with SIDs that reference the wrong domain is one of the subjects of the later section "Moving Machines Between Domains and Renaming Domains."

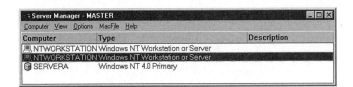

Fig. 16.2   Server Manager displaying invalid domain client PCs.

The advantages of a secure logical grouping of resources become apparent when you must manage large groups of users and machines. Network security is paramount in Windows NT Server's domain architecture. Fortunately, Windows NT Server's administrative tools, such as User Manager for Domains and Server Manager, shield network administrators from most (but not all) of the complexity of SIDs. One of Microsoft's guiding principles in the design of Windows NT is that features to make network administration more convenient must not compromise network security in any way.

Note

Users of clients running Windows for Workgroups 3.1+, Windows 95, and Windows NT can create independent peer-to-peer workgroups within a Windows NT domain. Workgroup members share files, printers, and other resources independently of Windows NT's domain security services. Most Windows NT network administrators discourage the establishment of peer-to-peer workgroups because of their lack of security.

Understanding the Roles of Domain Controllers

Windows NT Server supports the following two types of domain controllers, both of which are network servers:

- *Primary Domain Controller* (PDC). Only one PDC server can exist within a domain.

- *Backup Domain Controller* (BDC). You can have any number of BDCs in a domain. The number of BDCs in a domain depends on the number of users in a domain and the structure of your network.

Setting Up a Primary Domain Controller. The PDC is by default the first server you install in a new Windows NT network. When you install a new Windows NT server in an existing network and choose to create a new domain, the Setup program scans your network for a domain controller with the name you specified. If no PDC with the same name is found, the server becomes the PDC.

Caution

When installing a new server in an existing domain, make sure that the server has network access to the existing PDC. You can install a BDC only if you have a functioning network connection to the PDC. If you install the unconnected server as a second PDC with the same domain name and later connect the original PDC to the network, you have two PDCs in the same domain with different domain SIDs. Any clients or servers can't authenticate to the domain. In this situation, you must reinstall Windows NT Server 4.0 on the new server while the PDC is connected to the network. If you reinstall Windows NT Server 4.0 as a BDC, the PDC replicates user and group information to the new BDC.

The PDC's role is critical to Windows NT networking. The PDC is the keeper of all user, group, and machine account information for the domain. This information is stored in the SAM (Security Accounts Manager) database, which resides in files in the %*systemroot*%\system32\config folder on the PDC's fixed disk. The PDC is responsible for maintaining the master version of the domain SAM. When you change user passwords, add or remove user and group accounts, or add or remove machines in the domain, the PDC's SAM records these changes.

Note

You can use the Getsid.exe command-line application included in the Windows NT Resource Kit to determine the SID for a specified user account. Getsid.exe is useful for troubleshooting user authentication problems. You can't, however, change the user account SID with Getsid.exe. Use the `getsid` command as follows:

```
getsid \\servername accountname \\servername accountname
```

`getsid` requires two account names because part of its function is to compare the SIDs of each to determine whether they're the same. Figure 16.3 shows an example of the output of `getsid`.

Fig. 16.3 Comparing and displaying SID information with `getsid`.

Configuring Backup Domain Controllers. If the PDC is the only domain controller in your domain, the PDC is responsible for maintaining the domain SAM, plus performing routine domain tasks, such as authenticating user logon requests and maintaining user accounts. If you have a large number of users in a domain, routine domain management tasks can occupy a substantial percentage of server resources, slowing normal file, printer, and application server operations.

If servers and clients are connected to a remote PDC by a low-speed network connection, such as Switched-56 or ISDN lines, authentication by the PDC can become very slow. To avoid problems that arise from overload or remote PDCs, Windows NT supports the concept of Backup Domain Controllers (BDCs). A BDC is a Windows NT server installed into a domain after the PDC is installed. The BDC's function is to offload some of the routine domain-related tasks from the PDC and provide redundancy in the event that the PDC becomes unavailable. The BDC contains a copy of the domain SAM, which is replicated (copied) from the PDC on a periodic basis.

The BDC has a local copy of the SAM, so the BDC also can authenticate users. If you have a geographically dispersed network, you assign a BDC to serve remote users. If a user wants to change his password or an administrator wants to create a new user group, the BDC handles the change, and then passes the new password or user account to the PDC during the synchronization process. If the PDC is shut down or otherwise unavailable, you aren't allowed to make changes, such as user passwords or new accounts, to the domain SAM. Even if the PDC isn't available, you can authenticate existing users, and access resources on the BDC and other servers in the domain.

Promoting a Backup Domain Controller to a Primary Domain Controller. When the PDC fails or is unavailable for an extended period of time, or if you want to change PDC machines, you can promote any BDC in the domain to the PDC. The promoted PDC takes over the role of maintaining the master copy of the SAM database, and the old PDC becomes a BDC just as any other. To promote a BDC to a PDC, follow these steps:

1. Launch Server Manager from the Start menu by choosing Programs and then Administrative Tools.

2. If the PDC is operational, highlight the BDC you want to promote and choose Synchronize with Primary Domain Controller from the Computer menu to assure that the BDC's SAM copy and PDC's SAM are identical. Click OK to acknowledge both messages you receive during the synchronization process.

> **Note**
>
> Although Windows NT 4.0 performs this step automatically during the promotion process, it's a good idea to synchronize the BDC with the PDC to verify that the synchronization process succeeds. To verify the success of the synchronization process, check the NETLOGON 5711 event in the System Log for a `... completed successfully` message.

3. Highlight the BDC you want to promote (see fig. 16.4) and choose Promote to Primary Domain <u>C</u>ontroller from the <u>C</u>omputer menu.

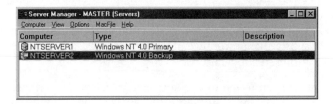

Fig. 16.4   Selecting a BDC to promote to a PDC.

4. If the current PDC is operating, you're prompted to acknowledge that you're promoting a BDC in place of the PDC. Click Yes if you want to promote the BDC. If the current PDC isn't up (the icon is grayed in Server Manager), you're warned that the PDC can't be contacted, and that promoting the BDC will conflict with the original PDC, if it becomes operational. Click Yes if you're willing to accept this condition.

> **Caution**
>
> When you promote a BDC to PDC, the NetLogon service is stopped, and all connections to those two servers are broken temporarily. If either server is a RAS server, remote connections will be broken as well. Any users attached to the servers lose their connections to the BDC (and to the PDC, if it's running). If you must perform a BDC promotion, make sure that you warn your users before doing so. From Server Manager, highlight the BDC you're promoting, choose Send <u>M</u>essage from the <u>C</u>omputer menu to open the Send Message dialog, type a warning message, and click OK to send the message. Windows 3.1+ and Windows 95 clients must be running the WinPopup application, and Windows NT clients must have the Messenger service running to receive network messages.

5. You see a series of dialogs indicating that the NetLogon service is stopping and restarting on each of the two servers. When the promotion completes, the previous BDC indicates that it's now a Primary Domain Controller, and the prior PDC becomes a Backup Domain Controller (see fig. 16.5).

Using Non-Domain Servers. You can choose to add servers to your network that aren't domain controllers. To do so, select the Server option during installation of Windows NT Server 4.0 on the machine. Non-domain servers use Windows NT Workstation security, one of the subjects of the later section "Adding Windows NT Clients to the Domain." You install non-domain servers primarily for the following reasons:

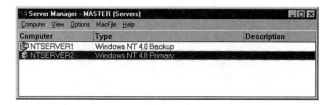

Fig. 16.5   The BDC of figure 16.4 promoted to a PDC.

- The server is used for heavy-duty applications, such as a database or messaging server, and you want to devote all the server's resources to application serving, not domain administrative duties.

- It's certain (or likely) that the server will be installed in a domain other than the domain in which it's originally set up.

Understanding the Domain Synchronization Process

To spread the load of authentication across BDCs that may reside anywhere on your network, including WANs with slow or unreliable links, Windows NT performs a periodic domain synchronization process. By default, every five minutes a Backup Domain Controller sets up a connection with the PDC, sends all SAM changes that originated on the BDC during the interval, and receives changed information from the PDC's SAM. The PDC keeps track of the *revision level* (the current version) of the SAM for each BDC in the domain; thus, the PDC sends only the incremental changes needed to keep the SAMs in synchronization. If the BDC loses communication with the PDC for an extended period, the PDC performs a full synchronization by copying the BDC's changes to the PDC's SAM and sending a complete copy of the PCD's SAM to the BDC; this process ensures that the BDC's database is complete and up-to-date.

Manually Synchronizing Domain SAMs. If you make a large number of changes to the domain SAM, or make changes that must take effect immediately (such as unlocking a user's account), you can perform a full or partial manual synchronization with Server Manager. Server Manager's Computer menu offers the following synchronization options:

- *Synchronize the entire domain.* For a PDC selected in Server Manager's Computer list, choose Synchronize the Entire Domain to cause the PDC to contact each BDC and, depending on the BDC's revision level, send the appropriate records to ensure that the BDC has a complete copy of the current SAM database. A full synchronization is called a *push process*.

- *Synchronize a single BDC with the PDC.* For a selected BDC, choose Synchronize with Primary Domain Controller to force that BDC to contact the PDC and request all changes since the last synchronization (a *pull process*). Figure 16.6 shows the message you receive when using Server Manager to synchronize a BDC with a PDC. This pull process guarantees only that a selected BDC is synchronized; it doesn't affect any other BDC in the domain.

Fig. 16.6 The message you receive when using Server Manager to synchronize a BDC with a PDC.

> **Note**
>
> As a rule, it's best to synchronize the entire domain from the PDC. Doing so ensures that all changes are pushed to the entire domain. Only changes get pushed, not the entire SAM, so in most cases (less than a 100 changes), network traffic due to domain synchronization is insignificant.

Changing Automatic Synchronization Intervals. If you're concerned that a large number of SAM changes might affect network performance, you can change Registry values on each BDC to control the replication frequency and the percentage of system resources assigned to perform synchronization.

◄◄ See "The Danger of Changing Registry Values," p. 305

You add the following new values to the \HKEY_LOCAL_MACHINE\SYSTEM\ CurrentControlSet\Services\NetLogon\Parameters key of a BDC or PDC to control how much data is sent from the BDC to the PDC and how often SAM replication from the PDC is performed:

■ ReplicationGovernor is a BDC value that governs how much data and for how long a BDC communicates with the PDC while synchronizing. The value uses the REG_DWORD data type and is expressed as a percentage. If the ReplicationGovernor value is missing, the default is 100 (percent). A value of 100 specifies that the buffer the BDC allocates for SAM changes is 128K (the maximum) and the call to the PDC for synchronization occupies 100 percent of the available time to complete the transfer. With a 128K buffer, the BDC can hold about 4,000 SAM changes. If you want to limit the size of the SAM buffers (and, thus, the time a synchronization requires to complete), you can adjust the ReplicationGovernor value for each BDC. For example, on a slow link where few domain changes occur, you might be able to tune the ReplicationGovernor value down to 50. If the value is too low, however, the BDC may never be able to complete the synchronization process.

■ Pulse is a PDC value that governs how often the PDC automatically sends SAM changes to the BDCs. Pulse is a value of type REG_DWORD (see fig. 16.7) for the PDC only and defaults to 300 seconds (five minutes). You can change the value to suit the frequency of SAM updates that occur on your network. Any changes made to the SAM between pulse intervals are sent to BDCs with out-of-date revision levels.

■ PulseConcurrency is a PDC value of type REG_DWORD that specifies how many BDCs a PDC can contact concurrently for updates. This entry defaults to 20 concurrent updates sent to the BDCs. (If you have less than 20 BDCs, you don't need to add this value.) The maximum value is 500. The higher the number, the less time it takes to synchronize the entire domain, because the PDC sends more concurrent synchronizations. High numbers put a much greater load on the PDC and prevent it from performing other tasks during the synchronization process, such as user authentication or user account maintenance.

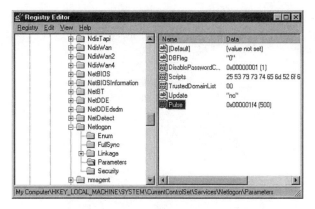

Fig. 16.7   Adding a `Pulse` value to the PDC's NetLogon\Parameters key with the Registry Editor.

Adding Backup Domain Controllers to a New Domain

Even in a small, self-contained domain, you should have at least one BDC to accommodate user logons in the event of failure of the PDC. If you're building a large domain, you must determine the number of BDCs needed to accommodate all your users. Microsoft recommends a maximum of 2,000 users per BDC, but your network architecture is more likely to determine this number. For instance, if you have a branch office that connects to the rest of your network with a slow link, it makes sense to place a BDC in the remote office for local authentication, as well as file and printer sharing. Fortunately, it's a relatively simple matter to add BDCs as required to handle the authentication load. Later in this chapter, the section "Deciding on the Right Design" provides recommendations for distributing BDCs within one or more domains.

> **Tip**
>
> If you're building a number of BDCs to be placed on remote networks with slow links, it's a good idea to start the BDC with a local network connection to the PDC. The initial SAM replication occurs quickly and completely over the LAN. You then move the BDCs (as quickly as possible) to your remote network locations and resynchronize the BDC SAMs to the PDC during the startup operation. This process ensures that only incremental changes to the SAM occur over the WAN link.

Adding Windows NT Clients to the Domain

After you install the PDC and one or more initial BDCs, you add the network clients to your domain. When a Windows client is added to the domain, Windows NT Server creates a domain *machine account* for the client. The machine account is a unique SID assigned to the client name to identify the client to the PDC and BDC(s) so that users logging on to the client can access domain resources. Before a client running Windows NT Workstation 4.0 is installed to a domain, it's part of its own workgroup. Figure 16.8 illustrates the NTWS1 client installed to the workgroup WORKGROUP. NTWS1 maintains its own local SAM database of user and group accounts, which you can view by running User Manager (see fig. 16.9) from the Start menu by choosing Programs and then Administrative Tools.

◄◄ See "Connecting Windows NT Workstation 4.0 Clients," p. 395.

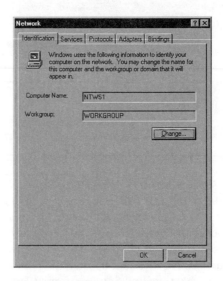

Fig. 16.8 A Windows NT 4.0 client installed as a member of a workgroup.

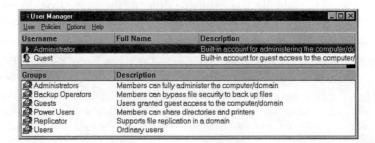

Fig. 16.9 Viewing the local SAM database of a Windows NT 4.0 client with User Manager.

When you join a PC client running Windows NT Workstation to the domain, the client's local SAM database is "hooked" into the domain SAM database of the BDC or PDC. The Domain Administrators global group automatically is made a member of the client's Administrators local group so that Domain Administrator members have access to the client's resources. When you log on to the client, the local SAM authenticates the logon name and password for access to the client's resources. Next, the logon name and password is passed to the BDC or PDC for domain authentication and access to domain resources. This process, called *workstation security*, permits logging on to the client without the need to join the domain.

> **Note**
>
> Windows NT Workstation is the only Microsoft client that uses the concept of machine accounts. Windows 3.1+ and Windows 95 clients don't create machine accounts in a Windows NT domain. When you want to authenticate to resources in a domain from these clients, you're simply using your domain user ID for authentication. The machine account provides an additional level of security for Windows NT Workstation. That is, a valid machine account enables an administrator to restrict access to domain resources based on a user authenticating from a specific domain workstation.
>
> Also, workstations with machine accounts can be administered from Server Manager. From Server Manager, you can view a workstation's shares, files in use, or where to send alerts generated by that workstation.

Moving Machines Between Domains and Renaming Domains

The unique SID of the machine account contributes to Windows NT security, but the SID creates problems when you want to move devices into and out of domains, or to rename a domain. The following sections describe the issues involved with reconfiguring clients and servers for use in different domains.

Moving Clients Between Domains. You may find a need to move a client from one domain to another. For example, a user in the Accounting domain may be relocating to the Sales domain. Moving a client to the new domain means changing that client's domain SID to match that of the new domain.

When you move a client running Windows NT Workstation to a new domain, you connect to the new domain by changing the domain's name in the Identification page of Control Panel's Network property sheet. If you log on to the client as a member of the Domain Administrators group, you can change the domain to which the client is assigned and receive a new SID for its machine account when you connect it to the new domain. To let users change domains on their own, a member of Domain Administrators must choose <u>A</u>dd Computer to Domain from Server Manager's <u>C</u>omputer menu to create a new account for the client in the other domain.

If you have a Windows NT Workstation client in DomainA that you want to move temporarily to DomainB, you must re-create a machine account for that machine when reconnecting it to DomainA. The DomainA SID originally assigned to the client can't be re-created on re-entering DomainA.

> **Note**
>
> Windows 3.1+ and Windows 95 clients don't use machine accounts, so moving a client from one domain to the other is simply a matter of providing that client a user ID in the new domain.

Moving a Domain Controller to Another Domain. Moving a domain controller from one domain to another isn't a step to be taken lightly. If you want to rename a domain, all domain controllers must be renamed. You can change the domain name of a PDC or BDC to a new, unique domain name (as described in the next section), but changing the domain name doesn't change the domain SID. Thus, you can't move a PDC or BDC to a new domain simply by changing its domain name; a truly new domain requires a new SID, which requires a new installation of Windows Server NT 4.0. After you reinstall Windows NT Server 4.0, you also must reinstall as upgrades other applications running on the server, such as SQL Server or Exchange Server.

> **Note**
>
> The need to reinstall server applications when moving a PDC or BDC to a new domain is one of the reasons for running BackOffice and other server-based applications on a non-domain (plain) Windows NT 4.0 server. Moving a plain server to a new domain follows the same process as moving a client running Windows NT Workstation 4.0. The plain server receives a new machine account SID, but the new SID is transparent to clients that access the server-based applications.

 ◄◄ See "Choosing the Type of Domain Controller," p. 201

If you *must* move a server that's now functioning as the PDC from DomainA to existing DomainB, follow these general steps:

1. Verify that the Domain Administrators group has full access to all drives, folders, and files on the PDC to be moved. The Domain Administrators group exists in all domains.

2. Promote a BDC in DomainA to PDC. The PDC to be moved becomes a BDC.

3. Perform an independent full backup of the PDC in DomainA, including the Registry. You can restore the full backup in case you reconsider moving the PDC and want to reinstall it as a BDC in DomainA.

4. Perform a *new* Windows NT Server 4.0 installation on the old PDC into DomainB as a BDC, if the domain exists, or as a PDC if the domain is new. Run winnt32 from the Windows NT Server 4.0 CD-ROM and install a *new* version of Windows NT Server 4.0 to a different directory, such as winnt41, in an existing partition with sufficient free space for the installation.

> **Note**
>
> The word *new* is emphasized here because a repair/upgrade installation doesn't alter the existing domain SAM database. If you don't choose a new installation during the Setup process, the server retains the original domain SID without regard to a change of domain names.

5. Start the newly installed BDC. The BDC synchronizes with DomainB's PDC on startup; after synchronization is complete, you can promote the new BDC to the PDC.

6. Reinstall as upgrades any server-based applications on the new BDC or PDC.

7. Remove and re-create all file, folder, and printer shares using the local copy of Explorer on the server, or a local or remote copy of Server Manager.

When you move a Primary Domain Controller from one domain to another, all references to user and group accounts that existed in DomainA (such as file and folder permissions for NTFS volumes) are lost. File and folder permissions for the server in the new domain appear as Account Unknown. Groups and users in the new domain are identified with the new domain's SID as a prefix to the group and user SID.

Renaming a Domain. As noted in the preceding section, the original DomainA SID remains as the DomainB SID when you rename a PDC from DomainA to DomainB. Renaming a domain requires you to change the domain names of all devices installed in the renamed domain. Changing the domain name of every device, including BDCs and clients, may be a huge task if you've installed Windows NT to many servers and clients across a dispersed network. If DomainA participates in trust relationships with other domains, renaming the domain breaks the trust relationships, and you must re-create them. (Windows NT trust relationships are the subject of the next section.)

If you *must* change a domain name, follow these steps:

1. First, in Server Manager, highlight the PDC and select Synchronize Entire Domain from the Computer menu.

2. Beginning with the PDC, start Control Panel's Network tool. Select the Identification page of the Network property sheet. Click the Change button to open the Identification Changes dialog (see fig. 16.10).

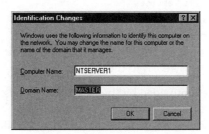

Fig. 16.10 Renaming a domain on the PDC in the Identification Changes dialog.

3. Type the new domain name in the Domain Name text box, and click OK. The warning shown in figure 16.11 appears. Click Yes to confirm the name change. You're required to restart your server after the change is confirmed.

4. Repeat steps 1 through 3 to rename the rest of your domain controllers.

5. Rename all your Windows NT Workstation machine accounts for the new domain name.

See the earlier section "Moving Clients Between Domains" for instructions on how to change domain names for clients running Windows NT Workstation.

Fig. 16.11 The warning you receive before changing your PDC's domain name.

Implementing Domains and Trusts Between Domains

The objective of Windows NT Server's domains and trusts is to provide users with a single logon to authenticate them to Windows NT Server resources, no matter where these resources are physically and logically located. An understanding of the authentication process is necessary to take maximum advantage of Windows NT Server 4.0's domain and trust architecture. Familiarity with the authentication process also is necessary to optimize the logical topology of your network to balance logon speed with the performance of applications running on your Windows NT 4.0 servers.

> **Note**
>
> This book uses the term *logon* to include the authentication process. Technically, authentication precedes logon, because users can't log on to the network until they're authenticated. Unless otherwise indicated in the text, *logon* includes both authentication and logon operations.

Distributing Authentication Services

One of the principal roles a PDC and BDC(s) provide in a domain is authentication of Windows NT client and server machines, and all users, including users of Windows 3.1+ and Windows 95 clients. Domain controllers verify that a particular user or machine running Windows NT has valid access to the domain.

The authentication process is provided by the NetLogon service, which runs on Windows NT servers and clients using Windows NT Workstation. The NetLogon service provides a secure channel for messages associated with authentication and domain synchronization. A *secure channel* is a connection between the NetLogon services on two machines that's established and maintained internally by Windows NT's security subsystem, using its own set of user names and passwords. Administrators have no access to this connection.

Authenticating Windows NT Clients. When a client running Windows NT Workstation is powered up, the client goes through a series of steps to authenticate to the domain in which the client is installed. The authentication process depends, in part, on the network protocol in use. TCP/IP, the recommended protocol for new Windows NT networks, takes the following steps to authenticate a Windows NT client when the Windows Internet Naming Service (WINS) is installed:

1. The Windows NT client—installed as a p-node or h-node type WINS client—stores its domain name locally and queries the WINS server database first for all domain name entries of 16th Byte type <1C> for the client's domain.

2. The WINS server responds with a list of up to 25 domain controllers in its 1C listing for the client's domain. This list is dynamic and represents the last 25 domain controllers for the client's domain that have registered with the WINS server, regardless of the domain controller's location on the network.

3. The client sends a NetLogon mailslot packet to each domain controller in the WINS list. The packet, in effect, asks, "Can you authenticate me to the domain?" For h-node type clients, after the mailslot packet is sent to each 1C type server, a broadcast packet is sent out on the local segment, asking the same question.

4. All domain controllers that receive the request packet respond, if able, and the first affirmative response to arrive at the workstation handles the authentication request. A domain controller that resides on the same physical network segment as the requesting client is likely to respond the fastest.

After the machine is authenticated to the domain by the fastest-responding domain controller, any user that logs on to that machine uses the responding domain controller's domain SAM database to verify his identity by means of a user name and password.

> **Tip**
>
> You can view which server a client uses for authentication by inspecting the value of the HKEY_LOCAL_MACHINE\SOFTWARE\Microsoft\WindowsNT\CurrentVersion\Winlogon\CacheLastController Registry entry.

The process a client uses to choose an authentication domain controller is based on the fact that the controller responding most quickly to the request provides the authentication service to the client. There's no simple means to specify particular domain controllers to provide authentication to a set of workstations. If you have domain controllers across a slow link, there's an off chance that those domain controllers might respond first to client requests, and provide authentication services across that slow link. This is an undesirable situation if the link is very slow. The goal is to prevent unwanted responses from remote domain controllers. In a routed TCP/IP environment, where WINS provides the list of candidate domain controllers, the challenge is to remove the remote domain controller from the 1C list for that domain. You can restrict candidate domain controllers by creating a static mapping in WINS of a domain name type with a list of only those domain controllers that you want to respond for authentication services.

In the case of a network that's broadcast-based, such as NetBEUI or NWLink, you can control where the broadcasts go by using bridge filters and limiting broadcast forwarding between network segments. Any DCs that reside on the same physical network segment as a client, however, always receive the broadcast request for authentication.

Optimizing the Placement of Domain Controllers. Deciding where to place your domain controllers depends on the network protocol you're using and the topology of your network. In a heavily segmented, routed TCP/IP environment, it makes sense to put all your domain controllers and other servers in a centralized server farm. A *server farm* consists of one or more network segments wherein all servers reside (see fig. 16.12). Each workstation segment has an equal opportunity to access both authentication and file and print services provided by the server farm.

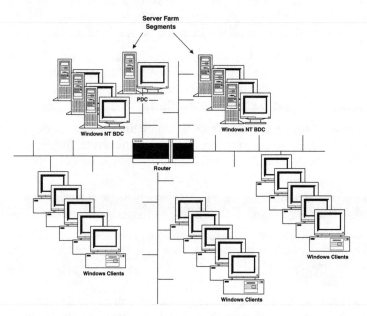

Fig. 16.12 Domain controller placement in a highly segmented network.

In a less-segmented (flat), bridged, or broadcast-based environment such as that illustrated by figure 16.13, it's more efficient to place one or more domain controllers, plus associated file and print services, on the same client segment. In this configuration, the domain controllers and other servers can quickly service large numbers of workstations, regardless of the network protocol used.

If you're designing a domain to support remote offices that access your corporate network over slow links, such as ISDN or Switched-56 lines, install a BDC in each remote office (see fig. 16.14), especially if the office has more than one or two users that need to access domain resources. The BDC also provides file and printer sharing services for the remote office.

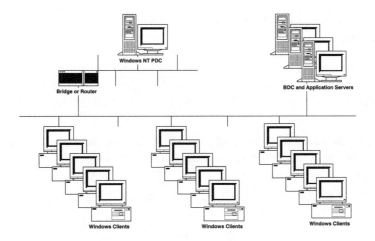

Fig. 16.13   Domain controller placement in a flat network.

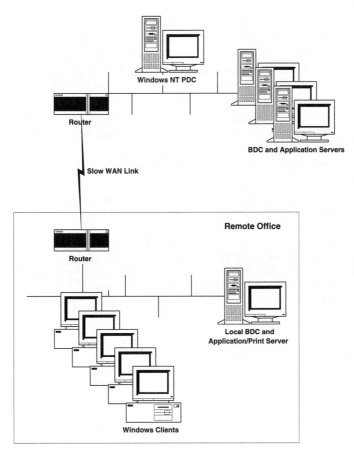

Fig. 16.14   Installation of Backup Domain Controllers in remote offices.

The majority of traffic on Windows NT networks isn't authentication, domain synchronization, or name and browser requests, which occur relatively infrequently. File and print services provided to users probably account for 80 percent or more of network usage. Where the extra traffic related to authentication and synchronization becomes a problem is in remote offices with low-bandwidth links. Twenty percent more traffic can mean the difference between a reliable connection to the corporate LAN and many dropped packets.

Understanding Memory Requirements for and Loads on Domain Controllers. Microsoft recommends the following amounts of RAM for PDCs running Windows NT Server 4.0:

- For up to 8,000 user accounts, at least 32M of RAM is needed.

- From 8,000 to 20,000 users, 64M of RAM is the minimum.

- Beyond 20,000 users and up to about 40,000 users, 148M to 182M of RAM is required.

Memory requirements increase if most of your BDCs also must perform other tasks, such as file and printer sharing, or application serving. Using the PDC and BDC(s) for ordinary network services is common in smaller networks serving 100 or fewer users. As the number of users increases, bursts of authentication and domain synchronization activity temporarily affect the performance of other services provided by PDCs and BDCs. Users may notice a significant performance drop in client/server applications, such as database front ends to SQL Server or the Exchange client for Exchange Server, during these bursts. Fortunately, it's relatively easy to add a new BDC to the domain to distribute the server load and to back up the existing BDC, in the event you must promote the existing BDC to a PDC. If you have multiple BDCs, consider demoting the BDC running server-based applications to a "plain" (non-domain) server.

> **Note**
>
> You can use relatively low-cost configurations for added BDCs, because a second BDC doesn't need to have RAID drives or other high-end server features. (RAID for backing up a backup is overkill.) You can assign BDCs relatively low-priority tasks, such as printer sharing and fax server duties. Similarly, a low-end BDC is an ideal server for CD-ROM jukeboxes, because the data rate of even 8X CD-ROM drives (about 1,200kbps) is low compared with fixed-disk drives and the network's capacity.

Understanding Trust Relationships

If you support a large organization with multiple departments or divisions that want to manage their own resources, use Windows NT Server's trust relationships. A *trust relationship* connects two or more domains and lets users in one domain access resources in another domain. A single logon provides user access to domains having the appropriate trust relationship.

You often see domain diagrams depicting one-way or two-way trust relationships (with arrows pointing in one or two directions, respectively, between domains, as in fig. 16.15).

> **Note**
>
> There's also a trust relationship between a client and the domain, and between domain controllers and the domain. When this trust relationship becomes corrupted—usually by problems with the domain SAM database—you're likely to receive a message indicating that the trust relationship between a client or a server and the domain has failed. Trust relationships between domain resources and their domain are different from the domain-to-domain trusts that are the subject of this section.

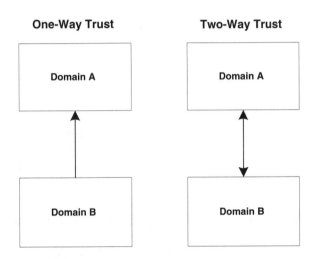

Fig. 16.15 A diagrammatic view of one-way and two-way trusts.

Domains are described as either *trusted by* or *trusting* another domain. Resources in the trusting domain (also known as the *resource domain*) are accessed by user accounts residing in the trusted domain (also called the *account domain*). Figure 16.16 illustrates the one-way trust relationship between a trusted and a trusting domain.

> **Tip**
>
> When discussing trusts, it's difficult to remember which domain is trusted and which is trusting. A good mnemonic is to picture the diagram of a one-way trust, indicated by an arrow pointing from one domain to the other. The trusting domain is at the base of the arrow and the trusted domain at the arrowhead.

A two-way trust between two domains, indicated by a two-headed arrow, permits users and groups in either domain to access resources in the other domain. In this case, the two domains are both trusted and trusting.

One-Way Trust

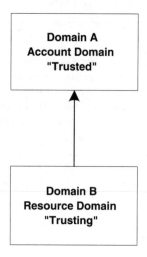

Fig. 16.16 A one-way relationship between trusted and trusting domains.

A trust lets an administrator in the resource domain assign, for example, file permissions to users or groups in the account domain from a file utility such as Explorer. A trust provides only the connectivity between two domains. You must explicitly grant access to resources in the trusting domain for users in the trusted (account) domain, in the same manner you grant access for users in their own domain.

Trusts allow you to distribute management of resources between multiple domains. For example, your IS department may want to manage creation of all user accounts and certain centralized server resources in the IS-MASTER domain, while providing users and administrators in the Accounting department the ability to manage resources in their own domain, called Accounting. A one-way trust relationship—with Accounting as the trusting domain and IS-MASTER as the trusted domain—accomplishes this objective. The accounting users log on to the IS-MASTER domain but are permitted to access and manage resources in Accounting by means of the trust relationship.

> **Note**
>
> In most account-resource domain relationships, a Windows NT client's machine account is installed to the resource domain, not the account domain. This approach allows all workstation resources to be managed in the resource domain, while the user accounts that log on to the workstations are managed in the account domain. Managing of the account domain is simpler, because the domain contains only user and group accounts, plus the domain's servers.

Establishing Trusts. Establishing trusts is a relatively simple process. By using the User Manager for Domains utility, you can create one- and two-way trusts between domains. As an administrator, you'll need to have access to a Windows NT Server Domain Controller in each domain that's part of the trust in order to establish the trust relationship.

Follow these steps to create a one-way trust relationship between the account and re-source domains:

1. From the account (trusted) domain, launch User Manager for Domains by choosing Programs and then Administrative Tools from the Start menu.

2. Choose Trust Relationships from the Policies menu.

3. From the Trust Relationships dialog, click the Add button next to the Trusting Domains list to open the Add Trusting Domain dialog.

4. Enter the name of your resource domain in the Trusting Domain text box; then provide and confirm a password in the Initial Password and Confirm Password text boxes (see fig. 16.17). This password must be supplied when you configure the resource domain's trust relationship to the account domain. Click OK to confirm the trusting domain.

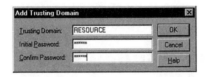

Fig. 16.17 Adding a trusting domain from the account domain with User Manager for Domains.

5. Repeat steps 1 and 2 on a Windows NT Server in the resource domain. Then, from the Trust Relationships dialog, click the Add button next to the Trusted Domain list. Enter the name of the account domain here, and enter the password you speci-fied in step 4 in the Password text box to establish the trust (see fig. 16.18). Click OK to confirm the trust.

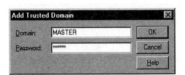

Fig. 16.18 Adding a trusted Domain from the resource domain with User Manager for Domains.

Windows NT Server then attempts to contact the trusted domain in order to establish the trust. If the trust fails, refer to Chapter 15, "Troubleshooting Network Problems," for a discussion of troubleshooting trust problems.

◄◄ See "Troubleshooting Trusts," p. 557

If you're creating a two-way trust, repeat steps 1 through 5. However, starting on the resource domain, define the account domain as the trusting domain. Then from the resource domain, add the account domain to the resource domain's trusted domain list.

> **Note**
>
> You can use the Domain Monitor utility of the Windows NT 4.0 Resource Kit to monitor the status of your trust relationships.

When the trust is established, you have access to users and groups in the account domain from any domain utility you run in the resource domain, such as Explorer, User Manager for Domains, or Print Manager.

Limitations of Trusts. As useful as trusts are, they have limitations. In Windows NT Server 3.51, a single domain could be trusted by only up to 128 trusting domains. In Windows NT Server 4.0, this number is much larger but still limited. There's also the issue of trying to manage large numbers of trusts. If you're supporting a large environment with many one-way or two-way trusts between domains, the complexities associated with setting up and maintaining a large number of trust relationships aren't trivial. Obviously, you must balance the benefits of providing resources anywhere to anyone against the complexity of the domain design required to provide these resources.

Understanding Windows NT's Domain Models

When you begin the design of your Windows NT network environment, you have a choice of four standard domain models to use for your organization, as well as hybrids of the standard models. Before you decide on a specific model, carefully analyze how the model matches the business methods of your organization. When you've installed a large network infrastructure, changing your domain design requires a major effort. Thus, careful up-front planning is a must.

> **Note**
>
> If you must change your domain structure, it's much easier to build trust relationships between domains than take them away. In the latter case, you're likely to be forced to reinstall user accounts and groups, and reassign permissions to resources when you move account information from a resource domain into an account domain, as in the case of moving from a two-way trust environment to a one-way trust model.

The Single Domain Model

The Single Domain model is the simplest. As its name implies, it involves only a single domain, which holds all account information and resources (see fig. 16.19). The Single Domain model doesn't use trust relationships, because there's only one domain.

The Single Domain model is best suited for an organization with centralized administration, a homogeneous user population, and less than 5,000 users. Beyond 5,000 users, it makes sense to start breaking up domains into resource and account domains.

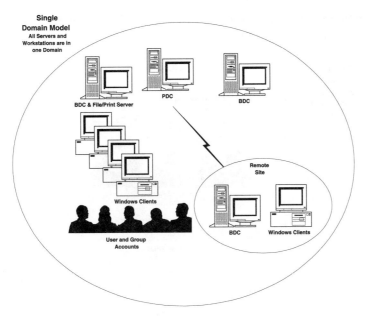

Fig. 16.19   The simple Single Domain model.

The Single Master Model

The Single Master model (see fig. 16.20) uses a single master account domain to provide user and group access to multiple resource domains. This model is best suited to an organization with centralized corporate support and a number of departmental or regional groups that want to manage their own resources.

Users log on to the single account domain, so you need to provide account domain BDCs in close proximity to resource domains, especially if the resource domains are spread out across your network and across slow links. In the case where you have remote offices across slow links, and those offices are part of the resource domains, you must have a resource domain server and a BDC from the account domain in the remote office. If you don't have a local account domain BDC, users must authenticate across the slow link to the closest account domain BDC.

> **Note**
>
> In any one-way trust model, users logging on to the account domain from clients in the resource domain are *pass-through authenticated* to the account domain. That is, the BDC or PDC that authenticates a resource domain workstation passes a user logon to a BDC or PDC in the account domain using the trust relationship.

The Multiple Master Model

The Multiple Master model is similar to the Single Master, but seeks to provide load-balancing of the Master account domain by providing for multiple account domains, which are two-way trusted with each other (see fig. 16.21). Users in one account domain can access resources of another account domain if the users have been granted permissions in the other account domain.

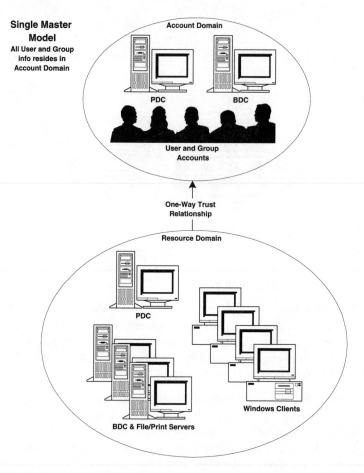

Fig. 16.20 The Single Master model, with multiple resource domains.

The Multiple Master is a good choice for large organizations, and organizations where either a centralized or decentralized support structure is used. The Multiple Master model lets you distribute responsibility for each account domain to a separate support organization, with each support organization administering its own set of resource domains.

Complete Trust

A Complete Trust between multiple domains is one where all domains are two-way trusted with every other (see fig. 16.22). In the Complete Trust model, all users and groups potentially can access resources in every other domain. This model is best suited to a fully distributed support organization. The Complete Trust model also assumes that you have some level of trust in administrators from each domain, because they potentially have administrator access to all accounts and all resources in every domain.

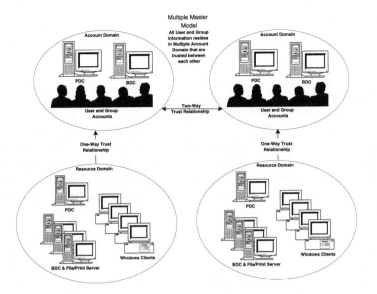

Fig. 16.21   The Multiple Master model, with multiple account domains.

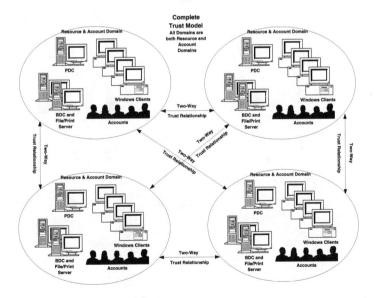

Fig. 16.22   The Complete Trust model implemented by a network of trusts.

Another advantage to the Complete Trust model is that users from one domain can log on to a workstation in any other domain and access their resources as though they were at their home workstation. This is valuable for organizations where employees frequently travel from office to office.

A disadvantage of the Complete Trust model, however, is that for each additional domain you add, you need to establish a two-way trust with every other domain. As you increase the number of two-way domains, the number of two-way trusts you manage quickly grows to unmanageable proportions.

Hybrid Domain Models

In addition to the preceding four models, there's opportunity to combine two or more of the standard models to create a hybrid model that best fits your organization. For example, you might like the concept of the Multiple Master domain model, but you don't want the Master Account Domains to trust each other. Instead, you want to create a number of Single Master Domains, each with its own resource domains. You also want to give a subset of users in your organization, such as network administrators, access to all domains everywhere, as in the Complete Trust.

You can build a new Master Account Domain, called Shared, for users requiring cross-resource access (see fig. 16.23). In this case, all your existing resource domains also are trusting to the cross-resource domain. Users requiring cross-resource access log on to the Shared domain, and are granted access to as many resource domains as needed.

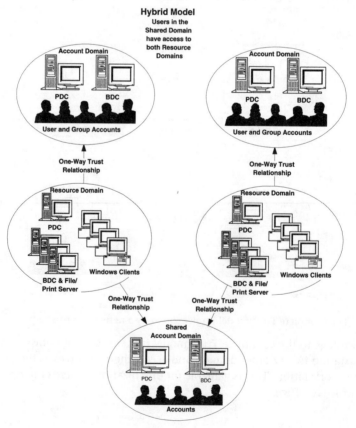

Fig. 16.23 An example of a hybrid domain model.

There are many other options for domain models. The only caveat is that one-way trust relationships aren't transitive. That is, if DomainA resources are trusting DomainB users, and DomainB resources are trusting DomainC users, there's no relationship between DomainA resources and DomainC users (see fig. 16.24).

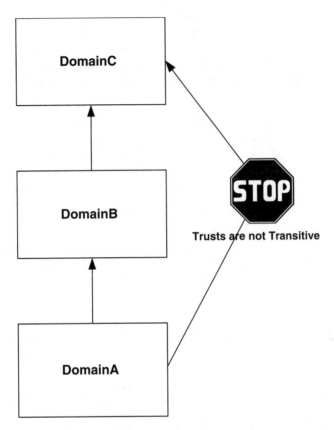

Fig. 16.24   An example of one-way trusts that lack a transitive relationship.

Deciding on the Right Design

The right design for your organization depends on the following factors:

- The size of your user base

- The nature of your network topology, including LANs, WANs, and remote offices

- Your support organization—centralized or decentralized

- The needs of your users

In the real world, it's the "soft" needs, such as requirements of your end users and the role your support organization plays, that drives the domain design. You can develop creative strategies to accommodate limited bandwidth or large numbers of users, but if the environment can't be supported or doesn't provide the flexibility end users want or need, you may as well not even install the infrastructure. Given the nature of Windows NT domain designs and the difficulty of changing established domain models, it's important to choose the right domain model from the beginning.

If you have a decentralized but centrally coordinated support team with users whose needs are flexible, the Multiple Master model is the best choice, followed by the Complete Trust model. Some network administrators argue that the Complete Trust "leaves the barn door wide open," but if your support organization is disciplined and communicates well between support units, the complete trust model provides the maximum flexibility.

If your organization has centralized support but end users demand the flexibility to do what they want with their resources, either the Single Master or the Multiple Master model is a good choice. In a large organization with 5,000 or 10,000 users, make sure that you have a well-defined group in charge of user accounts and resource access. Otherwise, maintaining such a large SAM quickly becomes an overwhelming task.

Using the Windows NT Resource Kit's Domain Planner
The Windows NT Resource Kit includes a tool called Domain Planner that, while limited in its creativity, provides a mechanism for planning the actual details of your domain. The facility it provides lets you specify the number of users, locations, and support characteristics, and provides you with an inventory of domain controllers and servers needed for your environment.

Domain Planner is fairly simple in its methodology, applying one of the four domain models based on the information you provide. Domain Planner is a good first step toward understanding domain design and can help you create an effective domain plan for your environment.

> **Note**
>
> The "Domain Planning for Your Enterprise" white paper, available from **http:// www.microsoft.com/ntserver/enter.htm**, and the "Microsoft Windows NT Server Directory Services" white paper, available from **http://www.microsoft.com/backoffice/techbriefs/ tech5000.htm**, are useful documents to aid the domain planning process.

Implementing Resource Sharing
After you install your domains and the trusts are in place, you must assign user and group accounts access to resources in your resource domains. As noted earlier in this chapter, creating a trust relationship in and of itself doesn't provide users with immediate access to resources. You must explicitly permit users or groups from the Account Domain access to the Resource Domain, using tools such as User Manager for Domains and Explorer. Generally, the best way to do this is by assigning permissions by groups. Chapter 12, "Managing User and Group Accounts," and Chapter 13, "Sharing and Securing Network Resources," discuss creating global groups and sharing resources with groups, respectively.

From Here...

This chapter explained the concept of Windows NT domains, a logical grouping of servers, client workstation, users, and groups. The chapter also described the role of Primary and Backup Domain Controllers, and discussed how BDCs can help take the load off the PDC for authentication services. The BDC synchronizes with the PDC to keep the domain SAM database up-to-date on all domain controllers. The difficulties of moving and renaming domains was a major topic of this chapter.

The balance of the chapter dealt with trust relationships and domain models, including the differences between trusted account domains and trusting resource domains, and one-way and two-way trusts. Suggestions for criteria to apply when deciding on a Domain Model also were provided. The chapter concluded with a brief description of how to implement resource sharing after you establish a trust relationship between domains.

For further information about the topics covered in this chapter, see the following:

- Chapter 12, "Managing User and Group Accounts," describes how to use Windows NT Server 4.0's User Manager for Domains, take advantage of the new Add User Accounts and Group Management Wizards, and utilize the built-in user groups of Windows NT.

- Chapter 13, "Sharing and Securing Network Resources," explains Windows NT Server's security system for shared file, folder, and printer resources and how to use the new Managing File and Folder Access Wizard and the Add Printer Wizard to simplify sharing Windows NT Server 4.0's resources.

Chapter 17

Integrating Windows NT with Heterogeneous Networks

Network managers in the real world seldom have the luxury of working in a homogeneous network operating system (NOS) environment. If your organization runs Windows NT Server as its only NOS, consider yourself lucky. If instead, like many system administrators, you must contend with an installed base of mixed NetWare 3.1x and 4.x servers, a UNIX host here and there, and perhaps a System Network Architecture (SNA) host lurking in the glass house, then read on.

Spanning Multiple Network Protocols

Windows NT Server 4.0 uses a protocol-independent networking architecture, which allows it to interoperate with a wide range of NOSs and protocols. With its support for standard network application interfaces, Windows NT Server easily accommodates simultaneous interoperability with Novell NetWare, UNIX, and IBM SNA networks.

NetWare historically has dominated the NOS market, and now holds about two-thirds of both the number of servers installed and the number of workstations using it. Although Windows NT Server is closing this gap quickly, many network managers will find it necessary to support both NOSs on a temporary basis as their organizations transition to Windows NT Server. Others will need to provide such support on a more or less permanent basis in organizations that plan for both NOSs to coexist on a long-term basis. Fortunately, Windows NT Server provides excellent tools for both migration and long-term coexistence.

UNIX is a fact of life in most medium and large organizations, and again Windows NT Server provides many of the tools you need to allow UNIX workstations and hosts to coexist with Windows NT Server. Microsoft has also recognized the continuing importance of mainframe connectivity to the enterprise and has accordingly provided SNA connectivity tools and services with Windows NT Server.

In this chapter, you learn how to

■ Integrate Windows NT Server into an existing Novell NetWare environment

■ Provide Microsoft Windows NT Server clients with access to UNIX hosts and provide UNIX clients with access to Windows NT Server services

■ Use SNA Server for Windows NT Server to connect DOS, Windows, Mac, OS/2, and Windows NT clients to IBM SNA networks

■ Build universal clients using Windows 3.11 for Workgroups and Windows 95

Integration Feuds

Microsoft's chairman, Bill Gates, and Novell's former chairman, Ray Noorda, didn't much like each other or, at least, so it appeared to most observers in the early 1990s. Each seemed determined to make life as difficult as possible for the other, causing much unnecessary suffering among users of Microsoft and Novell NOSs. This disagreement, played out in the trade press over the years, took on the characteristics of an elementary school yard spat.

Client-side support promised by Novell for Windows NT was late in arriving and seemed to many to be a conscious action on the part of Novell to cripple acceptance of Windows NT. For its part, Microsoft promoted the use of Gateway Services for Windows NT Server as a means to allow hundreds of clients to access a Novell server running only a five-user NetWare license. Novell broadsides were answered in turn by Microsoft, culminating when Novell threatened suit against Microsoft for bundling Novell client software with Windows, and Microsoft subsequently withdrawing that software. To this day, configuring a Windows 3.x client to access a Novell server requires installing client software acquired separately from Novell.

Ray Noorda's departure from Novell and Bob Frankenberg's ascension to the helm appear to have resulted in an uneasy truce in this duel of the Titans, although border skirmishes continue. Microsoft and Novell appear to have realized that neither firm is likely to disappear anytime soon as a key player in the NOS market, and that coexistence better serves both their customers and their own interests. Novell recognizes that Windows NT Server will increasingly appear in heretofore exclusively Novell shops and, accordingly, is improving NetWare's integration with Windows NT, including plans to port NetWare Directory Services (NDS) to the Windows NT platform. On its part, Microsoft has implicitly recognized the current dominance of NetWare and now provides excellent tools for coexistence and migration.

Windows NT Network and Transport Protocols

Until recently, the fundamental problem with integrating Microsoft, Novell, and UNIX networks has been that each used a different and incompatible transport protocol. Microsoft networks historically have used NetBEUI, whereas Novell networks depended on IPX/SPX, and UNIX networks used TCP/IP. As observed in Chapter 4, "Choosing Network Protocols," each network and transport protocol is fast and reliable, and each has advantages and drawbacks:

- NetBEUI requires minimal setup and is easy to administer. Because NetBEUI packets contain no network layer header information, however, they can be bridged only and can't be routed, making NetBEUI usable only for LANs. Microsoft is de-emphasizing NetBEUI for enterprise networking, relegating it to peer networking only.

- IPX/SPX was originally designed for local area networking. Like NetBEUI, IPX/SPX is easy to set up and administer. Unlike NetBEUI, however, IPX/SPX can be routed. Because IPX/SPX was originally designed as a LAN protocol rather than a WAN protocol, it lacks subnetting support, variable packet lengths, and other technical features that make it a less-than-ideal choice as a foundation on which to build an internetwork, at least when considered in isolation. Still, because it combines the ease of use of NetBEUI with much of the flexibility and power of TCP/IP, IPX/SPX can be a good choice as the shared network and transport protocol for a heterogeneous network, particularly one that heavily depends on Novell NetWare servers. Microsoft refers to its IPX/SPX implementation as NWLink.

■ TCP/IP was designed from the ground up for internetworking. As the *lingua franca* of the Internet, TCP/IP provides in abundance all the tools needed to build an internetwork. The sole drawback to TCP/IP is that it can be extremely complex to administer, both on the server side and on the client side. If your environment includes UNIX hosts or workstations, or if you want to set up a corporate intranet or connect to the Internet, you must run TCP/IP.

The Novell-centric view is that everyone should speak IPX/SPX. Although Novell has made some half-hearted, expensive, and poorly received attempts to provide native TCP/IP support—for example, NetWare/IP—the Novell world continues to revolve around IPX/SPX. Similarly, in the UNIX universe, you either speak TCP/IP, or no one listens to you. Many networks, particularly those growing from smaller peer-based environments, depend on NetBEUI, so this protocol, too, needs to be accommodated.

> **Note**
>
> Windows NT Server 4.0 installs only NWLink IPX/SPX transport by default, but allows additional transport protocols to run simultaneously. If your network includes NetWare servers, you should leave NWLink installed. If your network includes UNIX hosts, spans multiple sites, or connects to the Internet, you should also load TCP/IP transport when you install Windows NT Server.

Fortunately, Microsoft has realized the importance of all three of these protocols to those who need to build heterogeneous networks and has provided support for each of the three protocols in Windows NT Server 4.0. You can run one, any two, or all three of these protocols simultaneously to provide the fundamental network and transport layer support you need to build your network. This broad network and transport layer support provides the foundation for linking heterogeneous networking components.

Integrating Windows NT Server with Novell NetWare

The almost seamless integration of Windows NT Server 4.0 with NetWare is one of the major reasons for the phenomenal growth of Windows NT Server sales. In less than two years, Windows NT Server has grown from an also-ran product, which barely appeared in sales charts, to a major competitor to NetWare. Windows NT Server, in contrast to NetWare, provides a superior application server platform. The Microsoft BackOffice suite (the subject of the chapters in Part V, "Windows NT Server and Microsoft BackOffice") provides a solid foundation for developing client/server applications, and competing client/server application development tools from other vendors increasingly are being ported to the Windows NT Server environment.

All these applications can be accessed natively by Microsoft clients, as well as by NetWare clients, by using either the Novell NETx network shell or the VLM (Virtual Loadable Module) requester. The IPX/SPX protocol (NWLink) provided with Windows NT Server (see fig. 17.1) lets NetWare clients communicate with a server application using Novell NetBIOS, Winsock, and Remote Procedure Calls (RPCs).

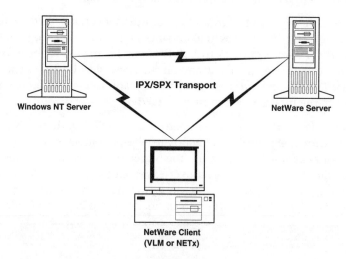

Fig. 17.1   Connecting Windows NT and NetWare servers to a NetWare client with NWLink.

Although Windows NT Server's support for diverse network and transport layer protocols has eliminated one problem, still remaining is the issue of what core protocol is used for communication between servers and workstations. Microsoft uses the Server Message Block (SMB) protocol for this purpose, whereas NetWare uses NetWare Core Protocol (NCP). If NetWare clients are to be able to access Windows NT servers, and if Windows NT clients are to be able to access NetWare servers, something must be done to translate between these two fundamental but incompatible protocols. Microsoft provides the following two utilities to bridge this gap:

- *Gateway Service for NetWare* (GSNW) allows clients running Microsoft client software to access shared files on a NetWare server and to print to NetWare printers. GSNW translates the upper layer SMB calls to and from NetWare NCP calls. GSNW is included with Windows NT Server 4.0.

- *File and Print Services for NetWare* (FPSN) allows Windows NT Server to emulate a NetWare 3.12 server. Novell clients can access shared files and printers in the same way that they would access shared resources on any NetWare 3.12 server. FPSN avoids the translation between SMB and NCP by simply dealing with NetWare clients directly as NCP devices.

With a market share that now stands at about 65 percent and is gradually declining, Novell has little motivation to provide tools to make it even easier for Windows NT Server to coexist with or replace NetWare. On the other hand, with market share now at about 10 percent and growing explosively, Microsoft Windows NT Server has everything to gain from readily making available such tools to ease coexistence and migration. Fortunately, Microsoft, recognizing its second-place position in the networking business, has taken responsibility for bridging the core protocol gap by providing a set of tools designed to facilitate integration of Windows NT Server with NetWare servers.

Accessing Novell NetWare Servers Using Microsoft Clients

Clients running Microsoft Networking client software can access shared files and printers on a Novell NetWare server in one of the following three ways:

- Use a client operating system, such as Windows NT Workstation or Windows 95, that provides built-in support for both Microsoft Networking and NetWare. As supplied, these clients provide full access to NetWare 3.1x servers. They allow you to access NetWare 4.x servers using bindery emulation mode, but don't provide NDS support. You can update your Windows 95 clients to provide full NDS support by installing the Service for NetWare Directory Services, available in Windows 95 Service Pack 1, which you can download from **www.microsoft.com**.

- Add a Novell NetWare client protocol stack to a client to provide full access to NetWare services. The Novell NetWare client coexists with the Microsoft Networking client and supports full NDS access on NetWare 4.x servers. You can download the 32-bit client for Windows 95 from **ftp.novell.com/pub/updates/nwos/ nc32w952** and for DOS/Windows 3.1+ from **ftp.novell.com/pub/updates/ nwos/cl32dw21**.

- Install Gateway Service for NetWare (GSNW) to let clients running only Microsoft Networking client software access NetWare server resources via gateway services provided by Windows NT Server.

The method you use for a particular client depends on both the operating system that client is running and the level of NetWare connectivity you need to provide to that client.

Using a Client Operating System with Built-In NetWare Support. Windows 95 and Windows NT 4.0's Workstation and Server versions include the Windows NT Multiple Provider Router (MPR) API, which isn't to be confused with the Multi-Protocol Routing Service, described later in this chapter. The MPR API provides a consistent application interface to the local file system, remote Windows network servers, and NetWare servers.

Any workstation running either of these 32-bit operating systems has access internally to all services needed to use NetWare resources without the need for a separate NetWare-specific protocol stack. NDS isn't supported, although any of these clients can access a NetWare 4.x server running in bindery emulation mode. Installing NetWare support for a Windows 95 client is described fully in Chapter 10, "Configuring Windows 95 Clients for Networking." Installing NetWare support for Windows NT Workstation is described in Chapter 11, "Connecting Other PC Clients to the Network."

Adding a Novell Protocol Stack. If your clients' operating system doesn't include native NetWare support, or if you require extended access to NetWare 4.1 services, you have no alternative but to install Novell NetWare client software on that client. Novell supplies full-function NetWare client software for numerous workstation operating systems, including DOS, Windows 3.x, Windows 95, Windows NT, OS/2, UNIX, and the Macintosh.

The primary drawbacks to installing Novell client software are as follows:

- Additional effort is required to configure each workstation initially.

- Additional ongoing maintenance is required to support a more complex client environment.

- Additional conventional or base memory is needed for the second protocol stack.

> **Note**
>
> The preceding problems are likely to disappear in the long run, as Microsoft improves NetWare support in its client operating systems. Both Microsoft and Novell are now shipping 32-bit NetWare clients for Windows 95 that provide NDS support.

Adding NetWare client support to coexist with an existing Microsoft Networking client is relatively straightforward, but doing so successfully requires that you first understand the fundamentals of how a Novell NetWare client accesses a NetWare server.

Novell clients require an IPX driver to provide network and transport layer services, and a shell to provide network redirection. Novell clients can use one of two methods for meeting each of these requirements:

- The original Novell client software used a monolithic IPX driver with the NETx shell. The monolithic IPX driver, IPX.COM, is generated for each client using the Novell program WSGEN. The resulting IPX.COM file is specific to the individual client because it's hard-coded for the address and IRQ of the NIC, and so forth. The monolithic IPX.COM drivers are a nightmare to administer; each change to a client configuration requires that the IPX.COM for that client be created anew. More important from an interoperability aspect, IPX.COM supports only a single IPX protocol stack.

- The NetWare shell was originally provided in versions specific to the version of DOS being used. NET2.COM, for example, was used with MS-DOS 2.x; NET3.COM was used with MS-DOS 3.x; and so forth. With the advent of MS-DOS 5.0, Novell shipped a version called NETx, which could be used with any version of DOS. Variants of NETx called EMSNETx and XMSNETx were also provided to take advantage of expanded and extended memory, respectively.

With the advent of NetWare 4.0, Novell altered its client software support. The NETx shell was replaced by the Virtual Loadable Module (VLM) requester. More important from an interoperability standpoint, the monolithic IPX.COM was replaced by the Novell Open Datalink Interface (ODI), which breaks down the services formerly provided by IPX.COM into separate layers:

- The link support layer is loaded first by running the program LSL.COM provided by Novell. The link support layer provides a standardized low-level hardware interface and handles routing of frames to the correct protocol service.

- The Multiple Link Interface Driver (MLID) is loaded next. The MLID is specific to the model of network interface card being used. For example, if you use a 3Com 3C509 Ethernet card, run the MLID 3C5X9.COM. If instead you're using a Novell NE2000 Ethernet card, run NE2000.COM. The MLID provides an interface to the link support layer running below it and to the protocol stack(s) running above it.

- The protocol support layer is the last ODI layer to be loaded. It provides services for one or more network protocols. For example, IPX services are provided by the program IPXODI.COM, which is often the only protocol support to be found on NetWare clients. However, LSL and the MLID can simultaneously load and service additional protocols—for example, TCPIP.EXE.

Clients that use ODI to provide protocol support can use either the NETx shell or the VLM requesters to provide redirection services. Although the VLM requester provides superior services and reduced memory usage, many NetWare clients continue to use the NETx shell. In some cases, this is due to incompatibilities between the VLM requester and a few older network applications. In others, it's simply a matter of inertia. Clients that run the monolithic IPX.COM are limited to using NETx because the monolithic drivers don't support the VLM requester.

Whether you choose to install NETx NetWare shell or the VLM NetWare requester, ensure that your NICs are using Novell ODI drivers. The older monolithic drivers are no longer supported by Novell, are much harder to maintain, and—most importantly—don't let you run other protocols. As mentioned earlier, Windows NT Server is protocol independent. Windows NT Server is bundled with the NWLink protocol, so many NetWare system managers will be happy to learn that they don't have to install a second protocol stack on their clients. Other NetWare administrators may opt to load the Microsoft TCP/IP protocol stack supplied on the Windows NT Server 4.0 CD-ROM, giving their clients simultaneous access to NetWare, Windows NT, UNIX, and the Internet.

Microsoft Networking software uses a methodology similar to but incompatible with ODI to communicate with NICs. This method, called the Network Device Interface Specification (NDIS), offers functionality similar to ODI. Fortunately, both Microsoft and Novell provide *shim drivers* (or *shims*) that allow interoperability between ODI and NDIS. Microsoft PC-client software uses the NetWare ODI driver, automatically installing the NDIS-to-ODI shim.

Using Gateway Service for NetWare. The Gateway Service for NetWare (see fig. 17.2) is bundled with Windows NT Server 4.0. Running as a service on Windows NT Server 4.0, GSNW lets one or more Microsoft Networking clients access NetWare resources. Used with Client Service for NetWare and the NWLink protocol, GSNW allows Windows NT Server clients to access shared files on a NetWare server and to print to NetWare printers. Microsoft Networking clients don't need to run the IPX/SPX protocol because the GSNW translates the upper layer SMB calls to and from NetWare NCP calls.

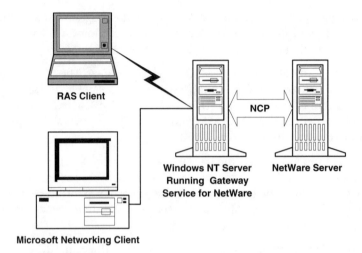

Fig. 17.2 Microsoft Networking clients accessing shared resources on a Novell NetWare server with the Gateway Service for NetWare.

> **Note**
>
> An added benefit of using GSNW is that it can be deployed with Remote Access Service to allow remote Microsoft Networking clients to access NetWare file and print services transparently. For more information on Remote Access Service, see Chapter 18, "Managing Remote Access Service."

Before implementing GSNW, the Windows NT Server administrator and the NetWare administrator should consider the following issues:

- *NDS support.* GSNW is intended primarily for use in a NetWare 2.x/3.x environment and doesn't support Novell NDS. Although a GSNW client can access a NetWare 4.x server, it can do so only through bindery emulation mode.

- *Performance.* The GSNW uses a single NetWare connection through which all requests are routed to the NetWare server from GSNW clients. On the one hand, this is an advantage because additional NetWare user licenses beyond the single license needed by GSNW don't need to be purchased for each user logging on to a NetWare server from GSNW. The down side of GSNW is that traffic from all GSNW users is routed through a single NetWare connection, so performance can degrade noticeably under a heavy load.

- *Shared rights.* GSNW uses a single connection to the NetWare server, so all GSNW clients use the same NetWare account. This means that all GSNW clients have identical trustee rights and other permissions, which are determined by the settings for that one account. All GSNW users are assigned to the NetWare group NTGATEWAY.

- *Logon scripts.* Microsoft networking clients don't execute NetWare logon scripts.

- *Backup.* The backup software bundled with NetWare doesn't back up GSNW clients.

■ *Account management.* Whether a particular Windows NT client is granted access to GSNW, as well as global restrictions placed on GSNW users that have been granted access, are determined by the Windows NT Server system administrator.

Configuring a NetWare Server to Use Gateway Service for NetWare. Little needs to be done on the NetWare server to prepare it for use with GSNW, but Supervisor access on the NetWare server is required to use the Novell SYSCON utility to make these changes. To prepare the NetWare server, follow these steps:

1. Log on to the NetWare 3.1x server as supervisor (or supervisor equivalent) and run SYSCON.EXE (see fig. 17.3).

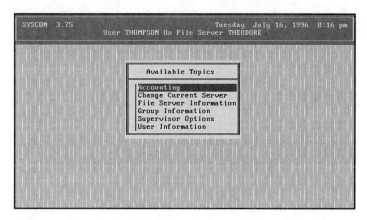

Fig. 17.3 Using Novell's SYSCON.EXE to prepare the NetWare 3.1x server for the Gateway Service for NetWare.

2. Create a new NetWare group with the mandatory name NTGATEWAY (see fig. 17.4). Grant this group the file, directory, and printer rights that you want available to all users of the shared gateway.

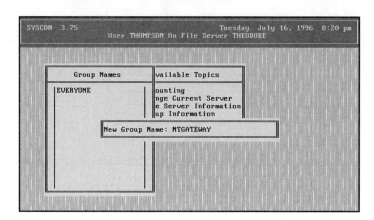

Fig. 17.4 Creating the NetWare group NTGATEWAY and granting all file, directory, and printer rights to be shared.

3. Create a new NetWare user with the same name and password as that used to log on to the Windows NT Server running GSNW (see fig. 17.5). This user is granted NetWare Supervisor Equivalent rights. This account is used by the system manager for maintenance and can also be used by the Migration Tool for NetWare, which requires full access to the NetWare server. With this account, logging on to the NetWare server from the computer running Windows NT Server allows you to run NetWare utilities, in addition to using NetWare files and printers.

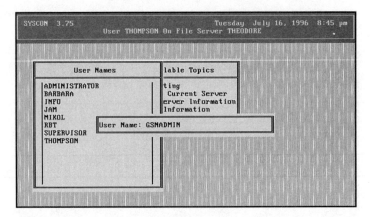

Fig. 17.5   Creating a supervisor equivalent user for system maintenance and to run NetWare utilities.

4. Create one or more new NetWare user accounts (see fig. 17.6) to be used by GSNW users, and assign each of these accounts to the NTGATEWAY group. Each account inherits the rights granted to the NTGATEWAY group and can also be assigned additional file and directory access rights of its own.

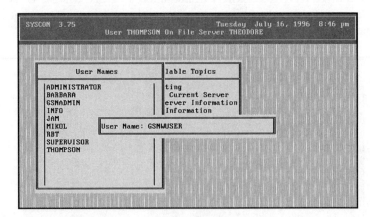

Fig. 17.6   Creating NetWare user accounts for shared access to the NetWare server, and assigning them to the NTGATEWAY group.

Installing Gateway Service for NetWare. After you make the necessary changes to your NetWare server, the next step is to install the GSNW on your Windows NT Server. Proceed as follows:

1. In Control Panel, double-click the Network tool to display the Network property sheet. Click the Services tab to display installed network services (see fig. 17.7).

2. Click Add to display the Select Network Service dialog (see fig. 17.8).

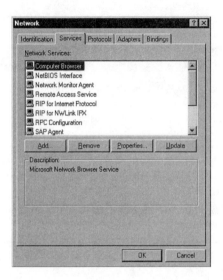

Fig. 17.7   Displaying installed Network Services in the Network property sheet.

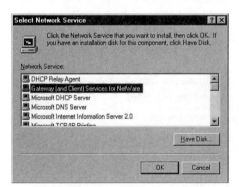

Fig. 17.8   Selecting Gateway (and Client) Services for NetWare in the Select Network Service dialog.

3. Select Gateway (and Client) Services for NetWare and click OK to display the Windows NT Setup dialog (see fig. 17.9).

4. In the text box, type the drive and path name where the GSNW distribution files are located, and then click Continue to begin copying files. Windows NT Setup displays the progress of the file copying operation.

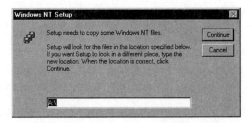

Fig. 17.9   Specifying the location of the Gateway Service for NetWare distribution files in the Windows NT Setup dialog.

Note

At this point, the NWLink IPX/SPX Protocol Configuration dialog may appear if you have more than one NIC installed in your server, or if Windows NT can't automatically configure the protocol. If so, specify which NIC is to be used to link to the NetWare server. Windows NT Server normally detects the correct frame type needed by this NIC to communicate with the NetWare server and installs it as a default, showing the Frame Type as Auto Detected. If for some reason you need to change the frame type, choose one from the Frame Type list box. Other tunable parameters are stored in the Registry and can be changed by clicking the Advanced button.

There's usually no reason to alter these settings. Make sure that you have good reason before you attempt to do so.

 ◄◄ See "Using the Registry Editor," p. 318

5. After all files are copied, the Network property sheet reappears, with Gateway Service for NetWare now visible as an installed network service (see fig. 17.10).

Fig. 17.10   The Network property sheet displaying Gateway Service for NetWare as an installed network service.

6. Click Close to complete the installation of Gateway Service for NetWare. Windows NT Server then configures and stores the affected bindings.

When the bindings review is complete, the Network Settings Change dialog appears to notify you that you must restart Windows NT Server before the changes will take effect.

Choosing a Preferred NetWare Server. If more than one NetWare server exists on your network when GSNW is first run, the Select Preferred Server for NetWare dialog displays to prompt you to choose one of these servers as the default server to which GSNW should connect. You can either choose one of the servers as the default preferred server for that logon account, or choose none. Based on your selection, the preferred server is determined as follows:

■ If you specify a server, that server remains your preferred server until you explicitly change it. Because the server that you first attach to performs the logon validation that's then used to determine user access to server resources, specifying a server is normally preferable.

■ If you specify no preferred server, GSNW locates the *nearest* NetWare server each time you log on. Understand that *nearest* means the NetWare server that responds the fastest at the moment you log on, so if you choose the None option, you can't predict to which server you'll connect.

Enabling the Gateway and Activating Shares. After you create the necessary group and user accounts on the NetWare server and install GSNW, the next step is to enable GSNW. Follow these steps:

1. From Control Panel, double-click the GSNW tool to display the Gateway Service for NetWare dialog (see fig. 17.11).

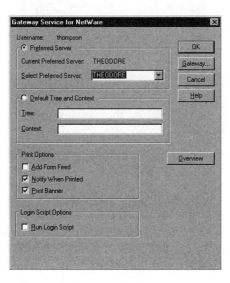

Fig. 17.11 Setting the preferred server and other options in the Gateway Service for NetWare dialog.

2. Click Gateway to display the Configure Gateway dialog. Mark the Enable Gateway check box, and fill in the Gateway Account, Password, and Confirm Password text boxes, as shown in figure 17.12.

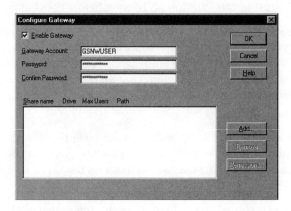

Fig. 17.12 Enabling the gateway and entering account name and password information in the Configure Gateway dialog.

3. Choose Add to display the New Share dialog (see fig. 17.13). Enter a Share Name by which the resource will be known. Next, enter the Network Path associated with the share. Optionally, enter a Comment to further describe the shared resource. Finally, select a drive letter from the drop-down list to be assigned to the share.

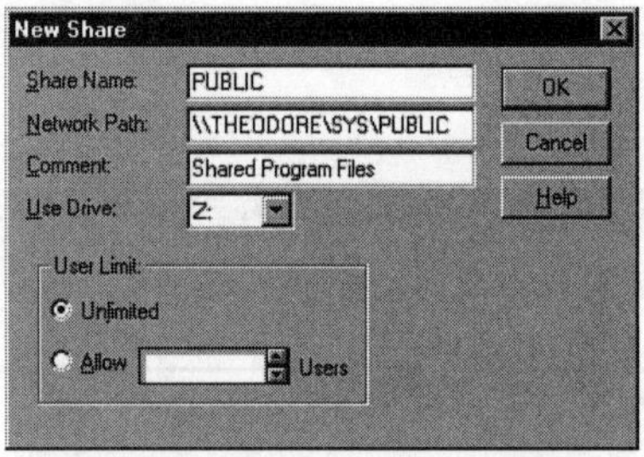

Fig. 17.13 Entering a share name, specifying the associated network path, and designating a drive letter by which the share can be accessed.

The User Limit section allows you to specify the maximum number of users who can access the share concurrently. Select either Unlimited, or select Allow and use the arrow keys to specify a maximum allowable number of concurrent users.

After you complete all this information, click OK to accept your changes.

4. The Configure Gateway dialog reappears, with the new share visible (see fig. 17.14). Use the Add button to create additional shares as needed. Use the Remove button to remove unneeded shares.

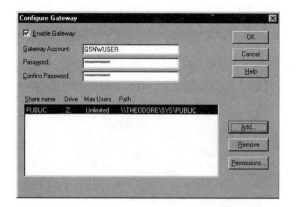

Fig. 17.14   The completed Configure Gateway dialog, showing the newly created share.

5. To set permissions for the shares you've just created, choose Permissions to display the Access Through Share Permissions dialog (see fig. 17.15). Use this dialog to set permissions as described in Chapter 13, "Sharing and Securing Network Resources."

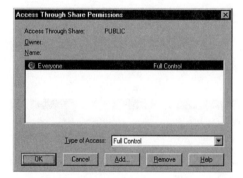

Fig. 17.15   Assigning permissions for the newly created share in the Access Through Share Permissions dialog.

Installing and Configuring a GSNW Print Gateway. Installing a GSNW print gateway lets Microsoft Networking users print to NetWare printers. After Gateway Service for NetWare is installed and enabled, and a print gateway is configured, a NetWare printer appears on the Windows NT Server computer simply as another shared printer. Access to and control of shared NetWare printers is determined by setting the properties for the shared printer from within the Printers folder on the Windows NT server. Print jobs sent to the gateway are redirected to the NetWare print queue to which the gateway is mapped.

To install and configure the GSNW print gateway, follow these steps:

1. From the Start menu, choose Settings and then Printers to display the Printers folder. Double-click the Add Printer icon to display the Add Printer Wizard (see fig. 17.16).

Fig. 17.16 Setting up a shared network printer with the Add Printer Wizard.

 ◄◄ See "Configuring Locally Attached Server Printers as Shared Resources," p. 483

2. Select the Network Printer Server option, and click Next to display the Connect to Printer dialog (see fig. 17.17).

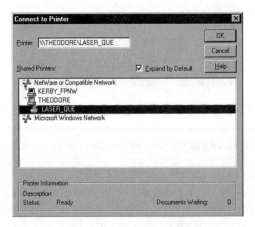

Fig. 17.17 Displaying available print queues for a Windows NT server.

3. In the Shared Printers list, double-click NDS tree names and NetWare 3.1x server names to expand the display and list the shared printers available with each server. When you've located the printer to be shared, select it and click OK.

4. The Add Printer Wizard next prompts you to specify whether you want this printer to be the default printer for Windows applications (see fig. 17.18). Select Yes or No and then click Next.

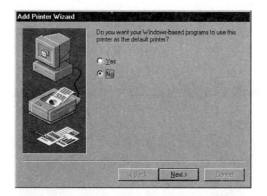

Fig. 17.18 Specifying that the printer won't be the default printer for Windows applications.

5. The Add Printer Wizard informs you that the printer has been installed successfully (see fig. 17.19). Click Finish to complete the installation and return to the Printers folder. At this point, the shared printer is installed but not yet enabled.

Fig. 17.19 The Add Printer Wizard's final step in adding a print queue for a NetWare printer.

6. To enable the newly created shared printer, right-click its icon to display the context-sensitive menu, and choose Properties to display the print queue property sheet.

7. Select the Shared option button and enter a name for the shared printer (see fig. 17.20). The rest of the printer configuration process is described step by step in Chapter 13, "Sharing and Securing Network Resources."

◄◄ See "Sharing and Securing Network Printers," p. 482

8. Choose OK to accept your changes and return to the Printers folder. Close the Printers folder. The shared printer is now available for use by authorized GSNW users.

Microsoft Networking clients now see the shared NetWare printer as they would any shared printer available on the Windows NT server.

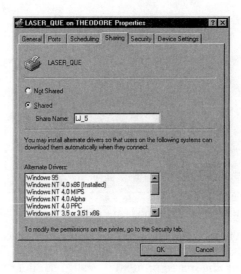

Fig. 17.20 Specifying a Share Name for the printer.

Accessing Microsoft Windows NT Servers Using NetWare Clients

Many LAN administrators are faced with integrating a new Windows NT server into an existing network that includes a large installed base of NetWare clients. You may have scores or hundreds of clients, each already running Novell client software to access the existing NetWare servers. Visiting each workstation to install and configure new network client software is expensive, time-consuming, and disruptive. Fortunately, Microsoft offers a way to avoid this effort and cost by using the existing NetWare client software to access the new Windows NT server.

File and Print Services for NetWare, shown diagrammatically in figure 17.21, is a $100 utility available from Microsoft that runs on Windows NT Server. Running File and Print Services for NetWare causes the Windows NT 4.0 server to appear to Novell clients as a NetWare 3.12 server. Unlike GSNW, the performance of File and Print Services for NetWare is very good and doesn't degrade under heavy load. Microsoft positions File and Print Services for NetWare as a product that not only eases integration of Windows NT into a NetWare environment, but one that also serves as an excellent transition tool.

> **Note**
>
> It's easy to confuse the purposes of Gateway Service for NetWare versus File and Print Services for NetWare. They're exactly opposite. Gateway Service for NetWare allows Microsoft clients to access a Novell NetWare server. File and Print Service for NetWare allows Novell clients to access a Windows NT server.

File and Print Services for NetWare uses as its foundation Windows NT Server's NWLink, GSNW, and an enhanced version of the bundled Migration Tool for NetWare. With Directory Service Manager for NetWare (described in a later section), an administrator can centrally manage user accounts for both NetWare and Windows NT servers.

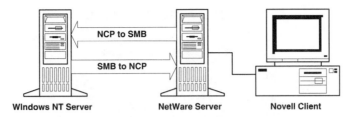

Fig. 17.21 Emulating a NetWare 3.12 server with Windows NT 4.0's File and Print Services for NetWare.

NetWare clients can access a Windows NT server running File and Print Services for NetWare by using either the NetWare NETx shell or the VLM requester. Installing File and Print Services for NetWare creates a NetWare volume called :SYSVOL, which has a directory structure analogous to a NetWare SYS: volume, including the LOGIN, PUBLIC, MAIL, and SYSTEM directories. Clients can continue to use NetWare-compatible utilities, including ATTACH, LOGIN, LOGOUT, SETPASS, MAP, SLIST, CAPTURE, and ENDCAP to access shared files and printers.

File and Print Services for NetWare also includes an enhanced version of the basic Migration Tool for NetWare bundled with Windows NT Server. The Migration Tool for NetWare, covered more fully later in the section "Migrating from Novell NetWare to Windows NT Server," translates NetWare account information to Windows NT Server, re-creating NetWare user and group information, files and directories, security and permissions, and logon scripts.

> **Note**
>
> Although File and Print Services for NetWare allows workstations running Novell client software to access the Windows NT server without using Microsoft client software, you must still provide each such client with a Windows NT Server user access license.

Installing File and Print Services for NetWare. To install File and Print Services for NetWare (FPNW), follow these steps:

1. From Control Panel, double-click the Network tool to display the Network property sheet, and then click Add to display the Select Network Service dialog.

2. Click Have Disk to display the Insert Disk dialog. Enter the drive and path where the FPNW distribution files are located, and then click OK to continue.

3. The Select OEM Option dialog appears (see fig. 17.22). You're installing FPNW, so select File and Print Services for NetWare. Click OK to continue. Windows NT Setup copies the distribution files from the diskette.

4. After all files are copied, the Install File and Print Services for NetWare dialog appears (see fig. 17.23). Use this dialog to specify the location of the NetWare SYS: volume, enter the supervisor account information, and tune server performance. Set the following values:

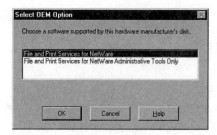

Fig. 17.22 Installing File and Print Services for NetWare from the distribution diskette.

- *Directory for SYS Volume* is completed with the default value of C:\SYSVOL. Accept this location, or specify an alternate drive and directory name. The location you specify must reside on an NTFS partition if you want to set NTFS file access permissions and NTFS directory access permissions to control access to the volume.

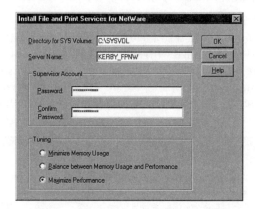

Fig. 17.23 Specifying volume location, supervisor account information, and performance tuning in the Install File and Print Services for NetWare dialog.

- *Server Name* is completed with the default value of *SERVER_NAME*_FPNW. Accept this name or specify an alternate server name that users will use to access this server. The name you specify can't be the Microsoft computer name for the server.

- *Password* and *Confirm Password* requires that you enter and re-enter the supervisor account password for the NetWare server.

- The options in the Tuning section allow you to determine server performance and resource usage:

Option	Description
Minimize Memory Usage	Uses minimal memory at the expense of slower FPNW performance. This selection is most appropriate for a server that's used primarily for purposes other than sharing files and printers—for example, an application server.

Option	Description
Balance Between Memory Usage Performance	Provides moderately high server performance with moderate memory usage. This choice is most appropriate for a general-purpose server that will share files and printers as well as run applications.
Maximize Performance	Provides the highest server performance at the expense of increased memory usage. This choice is most appropriate for a server that will be dedicated to sharing files and printers.

5. After you fill in all required values, click OK to accept your changes. The File and Print Services for NetWare dialog appears (see fig. 17.24).

Fig. 17.24   Entering the password for the account to be used to run File and Print Services for NetWare.

6. Enter and confirm the password to be used to run File and Print Services for NetWare and click OK. Windows NT Setup copies the FPNW distribution files to your server.

7. After all files are copied, the Network property sheet appears (see fig. 17.25), with File and Print Services for NetWare visible as an installed network service.

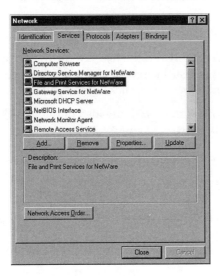

Fig. 17.25   The Network property sheet, displaying File and Print Services for NetWare as an installed network service.

8. Click Close to complete the installation. Windows NT Server begins Bindings Configuration. After configuring the bindings, it stores the bindings and then finally reviews the bindings.

9. After Windows NT Server finishes configuring, reviewing, and storing the bindings, it displays the NWLink IPX/SPX Properties sheet (see fig. 17.26). Enter the Internal Network Number and specify parameters for each NIC. Use the Adapter drop-down list to select each adapter, and specify a frame type. Leave the frame type set at Auto Frame Type Detection unless you're experiencing problems connecting to the NetWare server.

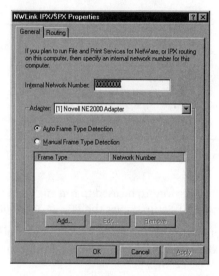

Fig. 17.26 The NWLink IPX/SPX Properties sheet's General page, which allows you to specify protocol properties for each adapter.

10. Click the Routing tab (see fig. 17.27). If you want your Windows NT server to act as an IPX/SPX router, mark the Enable RIP Routing check box. After you complete the NWLink IPX/SPX Properties sheet, click OK to continue.

11. If the internal network number you provided in step 10 is invalid, the NWLink IPX/SPX message box shown in figure 17.28 appears. When you click OK to return to the NWLink IPX/SPX Properties sheet, Windows NT Server generates a random internal network number for you (see fig. 17.29). Accept this randomly generated number, or enter a correct internal network number of your own. Choose OK to continue.

12. Windows NT again configures, stores, and reviews the bindings. The Network Settings Change message box appears to warn you that you must restart Windows NT Server before the changes take effect. After the server restarts, FPNW is available.

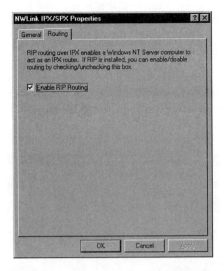

Fig. 17.27   Enabling IPX/SPX RIP routing on the Routing page of the NWLink IPX/SPX Properties sheet.

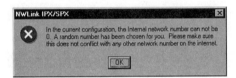

Fig. 17.28   The NWLink IPX/SPX message box that warns you that the internal network number is invalid.

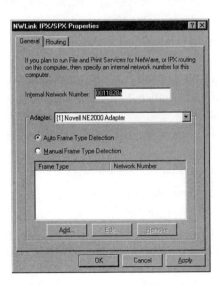

Fig. 17.29   The random internal network number generated by Windows NT Server.

Configuring and Managing File and Print Services for NetWare. After you install File and Print Services for NetWare, you must configure it before Novell NetWare resources are available to users. Follow these steps to configure FPNW:

1. From Control Panel, double-click the FPNW tool to display the File and Print Services for NetWare on *Servername* dialog (see fig. 17.30). The File Server Information section displays various statistics about the associated NetWare file server and the FPNW gateway to that server.

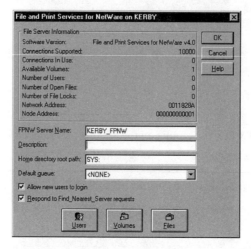

Fig. 17.30 Displaying statistics and configuration parameters for the FPNW gateway in the File and Print Services for NetWare on *Servername* dialog.

2. The FPNW Server Name text box displays the default name assigned to the FPNW gateway when it was installed. You can assign another name or accept the name as is.

3. Enter a short description of the FPNW gateway in the Description text box, if needed.

4. The Home Directory Root Path text box displays the NetWare volume assigned to this gateway when it was installed. You can assign another volume, or accept the volume displayed.

5. The Default Queue drop-down list is initially set to <NONE>. The list displays all NetWare print queues available on the server. Select one of these queues to specify it as the default print queue for FPNW users.

The Users, Volumes, and Files buttons in the File and Print Services for NetWare on *Servername* dialog allow you to manage the FPNW gateway, as follows:

■ Click Users to display the Users on *Servername* dialog (see fig. 17.31). The Connected Users list displays the name, Network Address, Node Address, and Login Time for each user. You can use this list to Disconnect a user, to Disconnect All users, or to Send Message to a user or users. The Resources list displays the Drives and Opens for each resource.

After you finish managing users, click Close to return to the File and Print Services for NetWare on *Servername* dialog.

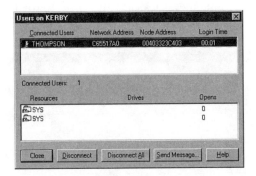

Fig. 17.31   Displaying user statistics and managing users with the Users on *Servername* dialog.

■ Click Volumes to display the Volumes Usage on *Servername* dialog (see fig. 17.32). The Volume list displays available volumes. For each volume, Users lists the current number of users accessing that volume; Max Users lists the maximum number of concurrent users allowed; and Path lists the Windows NT Server drive and folder associated with the NetWare volume.

Fig. 17.32   Displaying volume statistics and managing volumes in the Volumes Usage on *Servername* dialog.

The Connected Users list displays the name of each Connected User, Connection Time, and Opens for the volume highlighted in the Volume list. You can disconnect a specific user by highlighting that user and choosing Disconnect, or disconnect all users by choosing Disconnect All. After you finish managing volumes, click Close to return to the File and Print Services for NetWare on *Servername* dialog.

■ Click Files to display the Files Opened by Users on *Servername* dialog (see fig. 17.33). The Opened By list displays the name of the user who opened each listed file. For each open file, For displays the permissions associated with that open; Locks displays the number of Locks on that file; and Volume and Path display the location of the file. Click Close File to close a selected file. Click Close All Files to close all files listed. Click Refresh to update the list of displayed files.

After you finish managing files, click Close to return to the File and Print Services for NetWare on *Servername* dialog.

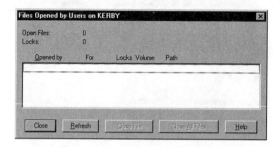

Fig. 17.33   Displaying file statistics and managing files with the Files Opened by Users dialog.

After you finish configuring and managing the FPNW gateway, click OK to accept the changes and close the File and Print Services for NetWare on *Servername* dialog.

Other Windows NT Server Integration Tools for NetWare

In addition to GSNW and the File and Print Service for NetWare, two other tools are available for Windows NT Server to aid integration with Novell NetWare environments. The Directory Service Manager for NetWare allows you to manage user accounts on Windows NT servers and NetWare servers using a single integrated database. The Multi-Protocol Routing Service allows your Windows NT server to provide software routing to link networks.

Directory Service Manager for NetWare. If, in addition to one or more Windows NT servers, your network includes Novell NetWare 2.x/3.x servers or NetWare 4.x servers running bindery emulation, you might consider buying Directory Service Manager for NetWare. Directory Service Manager for NetWare (see fig. 17.34) is used initially to export NetWare user account information into Windows NT Directory Services and to subsequently maintain all Windows NT Server and NetWare Server user account information in a common database.

During the initial transfer of NetWare user account information, the administrator has the option of creating a Map File to re-create the NetWare accounts' passwords, assign a single password to all accounts, or set the password to the user name. The *Directory Service Manager for NetWare Administrators Guide* lists the necessary steps involved to import the NetWare servers user account information. The initial setup process is complicated, so Directory Service Manager for NetWare includes a Trial Run option that creates a log file containing the account information that would be migrated to the Windows NT Server.

After you select the user and groups to be propagated to and from the NetWare servers, any changes to those accounts on Windows NT Server are replicated automatically to the NetWare servers. The replication process isn't bi-directional, so all subsequent changes must be made using Directory Service Manager for NetWare. When the initial migration is complete, the Directory Service Manager for NetWare database doesn't reflect any changes made directly to a NetWare server. Once installed, Directory Service Manager for NetWare provides a single network logon (see fig. 17.35).

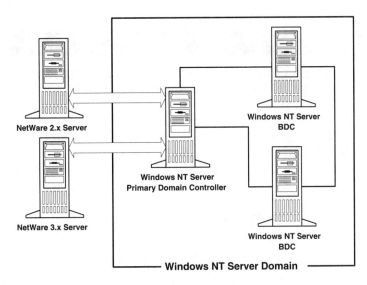

Fig. 17.34 Directory Service Manager for NetWare connecting NetWare 2.x/3.x servers to a Windows NT 4.0 domain.

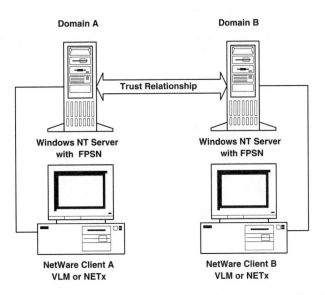

Fig. 17.35 Creating a single network logon for NetWare clients across two Windows NT domains.

Installing Directory Service Manager for NetWare. To install Directory Service Manager for NetWare, follow these steps:

1. From Control Panel, double-click the Network tool to display the Network property sheet. Click the Services tab.

2. Choose Add to display the Select Network Service dialog. Windows NT Server 4.0 builds a list of available services and displays them in the Network Service list box.

> **Caution**
>
> If an older version of Directory Service for NetWare is already installed on the computer, it appears in the Network Service list box. Don't select the older version. Instead, choose Have Disk to install the current version.

3. Click Have Disk to display the Insert Disk dialog. In the text box, type the drive and path name where the DSMN distribution files are located, and then choose OK. The Select OEM Option dialog appears (see fig. 17.36). You're installing the full service, so select Directory Service Manager for NetWare and click OK.

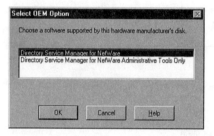

Fig. 17.36   Choosing the full Directory Service Manager for NetWare in the Select OEM Option dialog.

> **Note**
>
> If you're installing directly from the distribution CD, the DSMN distribution files are located in *d*:\dsmn\nt40*processor*, where *d* is the drive letter assigned to your CD-ROM drive, and *processor* is the type of processor installed in your server, such as i386 for Intel computers.

4. After Setup installs the files, the Install Directory Service Manager for NetWare dialog appears (see fig. 17.37). Enter and confirm a password of your choice for the service account, and click OK.

5. Windows NT Server returns to the Network property sheet, displaying DSMN as an installed network service (see fig. 17.38).

6. Click Close to complete the installation. Windows NT Server configures, stores, and reviews bindings. The Network Settings Change dialog notifies you that you must restart the server before the changes take effect.

Fig. 17.37 Entering and confirming the password for the account to be used for DSNW.

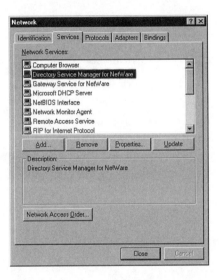

Fig. 17.38 The Network property sheet displaying DSMN as an installed network service.

Configuring and Managing Directory Service Manager for NetWare. After you install DSMN, follow these steps to configure and manage it:

> **Note**
>
> This procedure makes changes to the bindery on your NetWare server. Before you begin, be sure to back up the bindery. To do so, log on to the NetWare server as supervisor or supervisor equivalent from a DOS, Windows 3.1x, or Windows 95 client (you can't run the Novell system utilities from Windows NT). Notify all connected NetWare clients to log off. After they do so, run BINDFIX.EXE. Store the resulting three bindery backup files (NET$OBJ.OLD, NET$PROP.OLD, and NET$VAL.OLD) in a safe place before continuing.

1. From the Start menu, choose Programs, Administrative Tools, and Directory Service Manager for NetWare to run the Synchronization Manager. The title bar displays the domain name you're managing. When first run, the Synchronization Manager displays an empty NetWare Server list box, shown in figure 17.39.

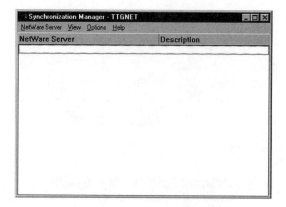

Fig. 17.39 The initial status of DSMN's Synchronization Manager.

2. From the <u>N</u>etWare Server menu, choose <u>A</u>dd Server to Manage to display the Select NetWare Server dialog (see fig. 17.40). The Select NetWare Server list displays available NetWare servers.

3. Select one of the servers listed and click OK to display the Connect to NetWare Server dialog (see fig. 17.41). Enter a user name and a password. This account must be either the supervisor or another account with supervisor equivalent privileges on the NetWare server.

4. Click OK to display the Propagate NetWare Accounts to Windows NT Domain dialog (see fig. 17.42).

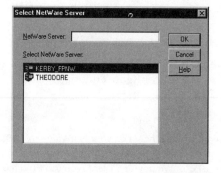

Fig. 17.40 Displaying available NetWare servers in the Select NetWare Server dialog.

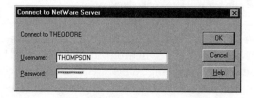

Fig. 17.41 Specifying a user name in the Connect to NetWare Server dialog.

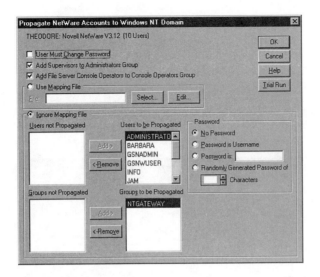

Fig. 17.42   The default NetWare users and groups propagated to Windows NT Server by DSMN synchronization.

5. By default, all NetWare users are placed in the Users to Be Propagated list box, and all NetWare groups are placed in the Groups to Be Propagated list box. Use the Add and Remove buttons to move users and groups between the list boxes. Also specify the following settings:

   - *User Must Change Password*, if marked, specifies that when a user first logs on, he must immediately change his password.

   - *Add Supervisors to Administrators Group*, if marked, specifies that Novell supervisor and supervisor equivalent users will be added as members of the Windows NT Administrators group.

   - *Add File Server Console Operators to Console Operators Group*, if marked, specifies that Novell File Server Console Operators will be added as members of the Windows NT Console Operators group.

   - *Use Mapping File*, if selected, specifies that individual user propagation parameters are based on the contents of an ASCII mapping file.

   - The *Password* section allows you to specify how passwords will be assigned on the newly created Windows NT accounts. Select one of the option buttons to determine password assignments. No Password specifies that the new account won't be assigned a password. Password is Username specifies that the password will be set to the user name for each account. Password Is allows you to specify a single password that will be used for all newly created accounts. Randomly Generated Password Of specifies that each newly created account will have a randomly generated password with the number of characters specified by the Characters spinner box.

6. After you complete the Propagate NetWare Accounts to Windows NT Domain dialog as shown in figure 17.43, click Trial Run to test your settings. If a problem occurs during the trial run, a message box displays the problem and gives you the opportunity to correct it. Fix any problems reported and rerun the trial run until it completes successfully.

7. When the trial run completes successfully, the Synchronization Manager message box (see fig. 17.44) tells you so. Click Yes to display the trial run log file (see fig. 17.45).

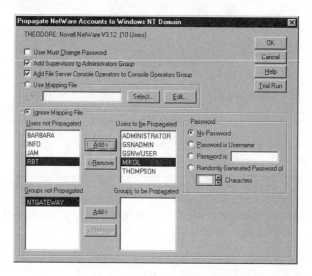

Fig. 17.43 Specifying changes to the default settings of the Propagate NetWare Accounts to Windows NT Domain dialog.

Fig. 17.44 The Synchronization Manager's message after a trial run succeeds.

8. Review the log file to make sure that synchronization will take place as expected. When you're satisfied that everything is correct, close the log file to return to the Propagate NetWare Accounts to Windows NT Domain dialog.

9. Click OK to complete the synchronization. The Synchronization Manager message box (see fig. 17.46) notifies you that you should back up your NetWare bindery before proceeding.

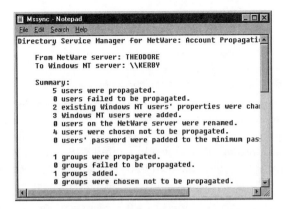

Fig. 17.45 Displaying the trial run log file in Notepad.

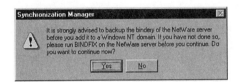

Fig. 17.46 Synchronization Manager's warning to back up your NetWare bindery before proceeding.

10. When you're satisfied that your NetWare bindery is safe, click Yes to display the Set Propagated Accounts on *Servername* dialog (see fig. 17.47).

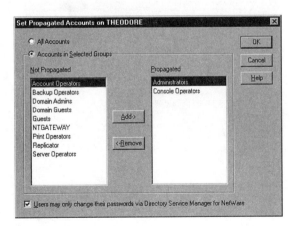

Fig. 17.47 The Set Propagated Accounts on *Servername* dialog specifies which accounts will be propagated, based on group membership.

> **Note**
>
> By default, the Users May Only Change Their Passwords via Directory Service Manager for NetWare check box is marked. If you want users to be able to change their passwords by using standard Novell utilities, unmark this check box.

11. Use the Add and Remove buttons to specify the users to be propagated. After you complete this process, click OK to propagate the accounts and display the Synchronization Manager message box shown in figure 17.48. Click Yes to remove the users and groups that weren't selected to be propagated from the NetWare server; click No to leave those users and groups on the NetWare server.

12. The Synchronization Manager appears, with the newly propagated NetWare server visible. Select that server and use the NetWare Server menu to manage the server (see fig. 17.49).

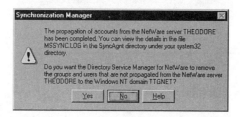

Fig. 17.48 Synchronization Manager's message that the selected accounts have been propagated.

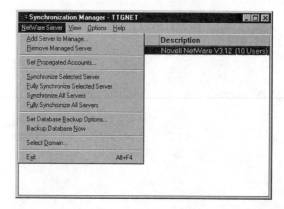

Fig. 17.49 Synchronization Manager displaying the newly propagated NetWare server, allowing you to manage it.

Multi-Protocol Routing Service. The Multi-Protocol Routing (MPR) Service (see fig. 17.50) allows a Windows NT server to provide a low-cost, software-based LAN-to-LAN routing solution, allowing small companies to avoid buying an expensive hardware router. The Microsoft MPR Service is analogous to and a direct replacement for the Novell Multi-Protocol Router. MPR is intended primarily for use by small organizations whose only server runs Windows NT Server, as well as by organizations that are replacing NetWare with Windows NT and need a software-based router to replace the Novell MPR.

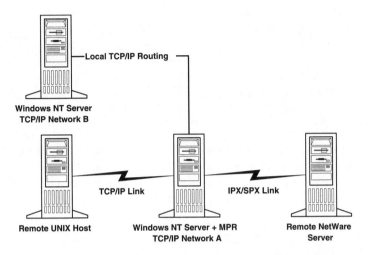

Fig. 17.50   The Multi-Protocol Routing Service providing software-based routing between a remote UNIX host and a remote NetWare server.

Windows NT Server provides standard software-based routing support for remote users via its Remote Access Service (RAS), as well as for local users running AppleTalk networks. The optional MPR Service extends this software-based routing support to provide enhanced support for IPX/SPX and TCP/IP networks.

> **Note**
>
> Like other software-based routing products, MPR Service can be used to link networks into a WAN using dial-up or leased lines. Unlike some commercial products, MPR Service doesn't directly support dial-up links using an asynchronous serial port and modem. Instead, all communications links must be made using either NICs or communications support cards that emulate NICs. MPR Service supports a variety of such cards from several manufacturers. These cards can be used to establish links using frame relay, ISDN, x.25, and other telecommunications protocols. Check the latest version of the Windows NT Hardware Compatibility List before buying interface cards to use with MPR Service.

Companies of any size are likely to find Windows NT Server 4.0's MPR Service useful in the following ways:

- Used with an ISDN or frame-relay communications interface, MPR can provide an efficient, low-cost, and high-speed Internet gateway using your existing Windows NT Server.

- Used with one or more high-speed communications interfaces, MPR can provide an inexpensive method to connect branch office networks to the main network without requiring the purchase of expensive dedicated hardware routers for each end.

Integrating Windows NT Server with UNIX

UNIX, in one of its many variants, is commonly found as a host operating system in medium and large companies, often as an application server. Although Windows NT Server is an excellent application server platform, which may eventually supplant UNIX for that function in many organizations, you may need to provide client support for UNIX hosts on a temporary basis, if not permanently. If your organization uses UNIX as a client operating system, perhaps on engineering workstations, you might also be faced with providing client support to allow these UNIX workstations to access the Windows NT server.

Integrating UNIX and Windows NT Server means working with TCP/IP. Although Windows NT Server doesn't implement the full TCP/IP protocol suite, it does include both the basic TCP/IP protocol support and most of the TCP/IP utilities you need to allow Windows NT Server and UNIX to interoperate. You can use available third-party products to fill most of the gaps. Windows NT Server 4.0 includes the following core TCP/IP protocols, utilities, and services:

- *Core protocols.* TCP, IP, UDP, ARP, and ICMP. Remote Access Service (RAS) also provides SLIP and PPP support.

- *Application interfaces.* Winsock or Windows Sockets (based on the Berkeley Socket API), Remote Procedure Calls (RPCs), NetBIOS, and Network DDE.

- *Basic Utilities.* `finger`, `ftp`, `lpr`, `rcp`, `rexec`, `rsh`, `telnet`, and `tftp`.

- *Diagnostic tools.* `arp`, `hostname`, `ipconfig`, `lpq`, `nbtstat`, `netstat`, `ping`, `route`, and `tracert` (traceroute).

- *Servers.* `ftp`, `lpd`, `snmp`, `chargen`, `daytime`, `discard`, `echo`, `quote`, DHCP, and WINS.

The TCP/IP protocol suite evolves continuously. The TCP/IP standards are maintained and published primarily by the Internet Engineering Task Force (IETF). The actual standards documents, called Requests For Comments (RFCs), can be downloaded via the Internet from **http://www.internic.net**. It's crucial for any TCP/IP implementation to comply with the various RFCs if the implementation is to interoperate with other TCP/IP systems. Table 17.1 lists the RFCs to which the TCP/IP implementation supplied with Windows NT Server 4.0 adheres.

Table 17.1 InterNIC RFCs Supported by Windows NT Server 4.0			
RFC	**Title**	**RFC**	**Title**
0768	User Datagram Protocol	1122	Requirements for Internet Hosts—Communication Layers
0783	TFTP Protocol Revision 2	1123	Requirements for Internet Hosts—Application and Support
0791	Internet Protocol	1134	Point-to-Point Protocol: A Proposal for Multi-Protocol Transmission of Datagrams over Point-to-Point Links
0792	Internet Control Message Protocol	1144	Compressing TCP/IP Headers for Low-Speed Serial Links

RFC	Title	RFC	Title
0793	Transmission Control Protocol	1157	A Simple Network Management Protocol (SNMP)
0826	Ethernet Address Resolution Protocol: Or Converting Network Protocol Addresses to 48-bit Ethernet Address for Transmission on Ethernet Hardware	1179	Line Printer Daemon Protocol
0854	Telnet Protocol Specification	1188	A Proposed Standard for the Transmission of IP Datagrams over FDDI Networks
0862	Echo Protocol	1191	Path MTU Discovery
0863	Discard Protocol	1201	Transmitting IP Traffic over ARCNET Networks
0864	Character Generator Protocol	1231	IEEE 802.5 Token Ring MIB
0865	Quote of the Day Protocol	1332	The PPP Internet Protocol Control Protocol (IPCP)
0867	Daytime Protocol	1334	PPP Authentication Protocols
0894	Standard for the Transmission of IP Datagrams over Ethernet Networks	1533	DHCP Options and BOOTP Vendor Extensions
0919	Broadcasting Internet Datagrams	1534	Interoperation Between DHCP and BOOTP
0922	Broadcasting Internet Datagrams in the Presence of Subnets	1541	Dynamic Host Configuration Protocol
0959	File Transfer Protocol	1542	Clarifications and Extensions for the Bootstrap Protocol
1001	Protocol Standard for a NetBIOS Service on a TCP/UDP Transport: Concepts and Methods	1547	Requirements for an Internet Standard Point-to-Point Protocol
1002	Protocol Standard for a NetBIOS Service on a TCP/UDP Transport: Detailed Specifications	1548	The Point-to-Point Protocol (PPP)
1034	Domain Names—Concepts and Facilities	1549	PPP in HDLC Framing
1035	Domain Names—Implementation and Specification	1552	The PPP Internetwork Packet Exchange Control Protocol (IPXCP)
1042	Standard for the Transmission of IP Datagrams over IEEE 802 Networks	1553	Compressing IPX Headers over WAN Media (CIPX)
1055	Nonstandard for Transmission of IP Datagrams over Serial Lines: SLIP	1570	PPP LCP Extensions
1112	Host Extensions for IP Multicasting		

Windows NT Server Integration Tools for UNIX

Windows NT Server 4.0 provides two important tools for integrating Windows NT with UNIX:

- Dynamic Host Configuration Protocol (DHCP) allows IP addresses to be pooled and assigned as needed to clients. DHCP is an Internet standard protocol.

- Windows Internet Naming Service (WINS) maps easily remembered Windows machine names to the corresponding IP addresses. WINS is a Microsoft proprietary protocol.

Dynamic Host Configuration Protocol (DHCP). One of the most labor-intensive and error-prone aspects of managing a TCP/IP network is assigning IP addresses to each host and workstation on the network. IP addresses must be unique. Unintentionally assigning the same IP address to two different computers can cause problems ranging from subtle workstation errors to a complete network crash. In the past, IP addresses had to be assigned manually, with all the difficulties that task implies. Installing a new workstation or relocating an existing one required that a technician make an on-site visit to configure the workstation with the appropriate IP address.

Windows NT Server greatly simplifies IP address management by using the Dynamic Host Configuration Protocol (DHCP). A DHCP server running on Windows NT Server is allocated a block of IP addresses, which are then available to be assigned automatically to workstations as needed. When a workstation running a DHCP client is booted, it requests an IP address from the DHCP server. The DHCP server assigns, or leases, an IP address to that workstation for the duration of its lease period, which is set by NTADMIN.

Using DHCP has the following advantages:

- The DHCP server allows centralized management of IP addressing information. If the DHCP server is set up properly, no address conflicts or TCP/IP configuration errors can occur on connected DHCP clients. Centralized management also means that your IP address management workload is greatly reduced.

- Because workstations are assigned an IP address at boot time, they can be moved freely from location to location without manually reconfiguring the IP address information each time a workstation is moved. This is a particularly useful feature as notebook computers become more prevalent, along with the need to simply plug them into whatever network port happens to be available without further ado.

> **Note**
>
> If a workstation is removed and then reconnected to the same subnet before the lease period has expired, that workstation is assigned its previous IP address, based on the MAC (or hardware) address of the NIC. If the workstation is connected to a different subnet or to the same subnet after the lease period expires, the next available IP address is assigned to it.

The DHCP server is assigned a block of IP addresses, referred to as a *DHCP scope*. For example, if InterNIC assigns your company the IP C block ranging from 207.104.167.1 to 207.104.167.255, you might choose to subnet this block using a net mask of 224 into six subnets, each supporting 30 hosts. You might then assign the subnet containing the IP addresses 207.104.167.33 through 207.104.167.62 as your DHCP scope, keeping the other subnet addresses for other uses. These 30 available IP addresses can then be assigned to DHCP clients automatically as needed. In addition to the pooled addresses assigned on a first-come, first-served basis to DHCP clients, the DHCP server can reserve specific IP addresses for use by servers and other systems for which a static IP address is necessary or desirable.

If your routers support RFC 1542, which defines forwarding of BOOTP and DHCP broadcasts, only one DHCP server is required to support your entire IP internetwork. If they don't, a DHCP server can serve only DHCP clients located on the same IP subnetwork, and you'll need to install a DHCP server on each subnet for complete coverage of your internetwork.

To be assigned an IP address automatically by the DHCP server, each workstation must have DHCP client software installed and enabled. Windows NT Server and Workstation versions 3.5 and higher have DHCP clients built in, as does Windows 95. You can DHCP-enable Windows 3.11 for Workgroups by installing Win32s and the Microsoft 32-bit TCP/IP VxD supplied with the Windows NT Server CD-ROM. DOS workstations can use DHCP if you install the Microsoft Network Client for MS-DOS 3.0 or higher real-mode TCP/IP driver supplied on the Windows NT Server distribution CD-ROM.

Non-DHCP clients can coexist on the same network with DHCP clients and can use TCP/IP and Windows networking services, but at the expense of requiring some manual intervention. IP addresses for non-DHCP clients must be assigned manually in the old manner, and IP addresses so assigned must be excluded from the DHCP scope to avoid duplication of IP address assignment.

Installing Dynamic Host Configuration Protocol (DHCP). To install DHCP, follow these steps:

1. From Control Panel, double-click the Network tool to display the Network property sheet. Click the Services tab, and then click Add to display the Select Network Service dialog.

2. Select Microsoft DHCP Server and click OK to begin installing DHCP.

3. The Windows NT Setup dialog prompts you for the location of the DHCP distribution files. Enter the location and click Continue to begin copying the files. Windows NT displays a message saying that any adapters now using DHCP must be assigned a static IP address (see fig. 17.51). Click OK to continue.

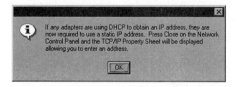

Fig. 17.51 The warning that adapters now using DHCP must be assigned a static IP address before installation can proceed.

4. Windows NT displays the Network property sheet, shown in figure 17.52 with DHCP installed. Click Close to complete the installation of DHCP.

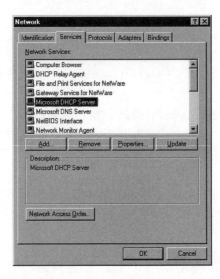

Fig. 17.52   The Services page of the Network property sheet, with the Microsoft DHCP Server installed.

Windows NT Server analyzes the changes you've made to your network configuration. It first configures the bindings, then stores the bindings, and finally reviews the new bindings configuration.

Configuring and Managing DHCP.   After you install DHCP, follow these steps to configure it:

1. From the Start menu, choose Programs, Administrative Tools, and then DHCP Manager to run the DHCP Manager (see fig. 17.53).

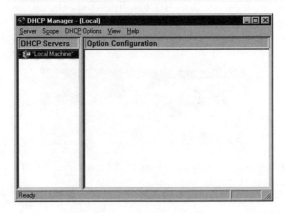

Fig. 17.53   Using the DHCP Manager to configure and manage DHCP.

2. From the Scope menu choose Create to display the Create Scope dialog (see fig. 17.54). Enter the range of IP addresses you want to comprise the scope. You can exclude specific addresses and ranges of addresses from the scope. Specify the lease duration as either Unlimited or as Limited to a specific number of Days, Hours, and Minutes.

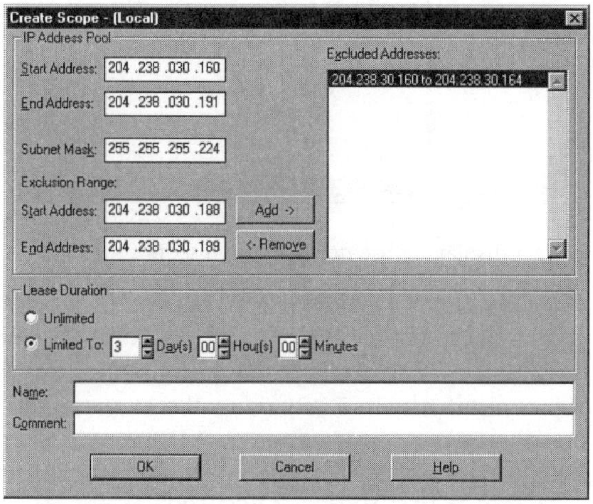

Fig. 17.54 Entering a range of IP addresses to comprise the DHCP scope and configuring DHCP lease durations.

> **Tip**
>
> It's a good idea in general—and in particular if the demand for IP addresses in your organization outstrips the supply—to limit the DHCP lease duration to a reasonable time to prevent an idle client from holding an unused IP address. Many organizations find that two or three days is reasonable, although if IP addresses are in short supply, setting this parameter to one day or less is acceptable. Avoid setting it to too short a period, or clients will constantly be "churning" IP addresses.

3. After you complete all fields in the Create Scope dialog, click OK. In the DHCP Manager message box that appears (see fig. 17.55), click No to leave the DHCP scope inactive, or Yes to activate the newly defined DHCP scope. When the scope is activated, the newly defined scope appears in DHCP Manager (see fig. 17.56). When you're finished adding DHCP scopes, close DHCP Manager.

Fig. 17.55 The DHCP Manager message that lets you activate your newly defined DHCP scope.

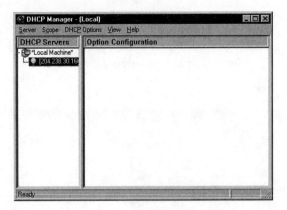

Fig. 17.56 DHCP Manager displaying the newly defined scope.

Windows Internet Naming Service (WINS). A Windows NT Server running TCP/IP and the Windows Internet Name Service (WINS) server software is called a *WINS server*. A WINS server provides a lookup table to map computer names to IP addresses, allowing users to refer to another computer by its easily remembered name rather than by its numeric IP address. In the Windows NT environment, WINS provides a service analogous to the use of Domain Name Service (DNS) in the Internet Protocol suite. WINS uses NetBIOS over TCP/IP, defined in RFC 1001 and RFC 1002 as p-node.

Using WINS offers the following advantages:

- *Simplified management.* The WINS server maintains a dynamic lookup table to map computer names to Internet addresses, allowing centralized management of this information. The alternative—maintaining static LMHOSTS files on each client—requires a great deal of manual intervention. Each client must be altered individually each time a host is to be added or an address changed. WINS also centrally manages replication of WINS data, eliminating the need to copy changed host files to multiple servers.

- *Reduced network traffic.* The data maintained by the WINS server allows a client to perform a single lookup to resolve the IP address of a destination computer, greatly reducing IP broadcast traffic that would be transmitted on the network in the absence of WINS or another address resolution method.

- *NetBIOS support.* DNS provides address resolution services only to IP clients. WINS supports NetBIOS clients as well.

- *WAN support.* According to Microsoft, clients on a LAN with a WINS server present can browse domains located beyond the boundary router, even if the destination domain has no local domain controller present. (The prerelease version of Windows NT Server 4.0 used to write this book didn't support the feature.)

The WINS Server software is bundled with Windows NT Server. Installing the WINS Server software is described in the following section.

To use WINS server services, a client must first have WINS software installed. Windows NT Workstation and Windows 95 are both supplied standard with a WINS client, as is the Microsoft Windows client software provided with the Windows NT Server distribution. Clients running Windows 3.11 for Workgroups can use the WINS client software supplied with the TCP/IP add-on for Windows 3.11 for Workgroups, available as TCP32B.EXE from the Microsoft Download Service (206-936-6735) or via Internet anonymous FTP from **ftp.microsoft.com**. Although DOS workstations can participate in WINS, equipping them to do so requires buying the Workgroup Add-On for DOS from Microsoft.

Installing Windows Internet Naming Service (WINS). To install WINS, take the following steps:

1. From Control Panel, double-click the Network tool to display the Network property sheet. Click the Services tab, and then click Add to display the Select Network Service dialog.

2. Select Windows Internet Name Service and click OK to display the Windows NT Setup dialog. Type the location of the files and click Continue to copy the files.

3. After all files are copied, Windows NT returns you to the Network property sheet, showing Windows Internet Name Service installed (see fig. 17.57). Click Close to continue the installation process.

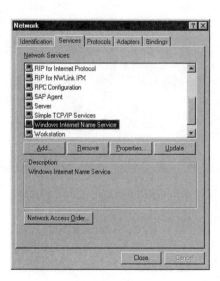

Fig. 17.57   The Services page of the Network property sheet, showing Windows Internet Name Service installed.

4. Windows NT Server analyzes the changes you've made to your network configuration. It first configures the bindings, then stores the bindings, and finally reviews the new bindings configuration. When this process is complete, the Network Settings Change dialog notifies you that you must restart your computer for the changes to take effect.

Configuring and Managing WINS. After you install WINS, follow these steps to configure it:

1. From the Start menu, choose Programs, Administrative Tools, and then WINS Manager to run WINS Manager (see fig. 17.58).

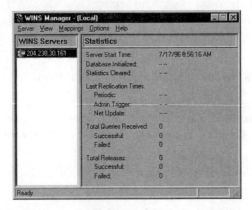

Fig. 17.58   The opening window of WINS Manager.

2. From the Server menu choose Configuration to display the WINS Server Configuration dialog (see fig. 17.59).

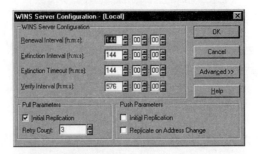

Fig. 17.59   The WINS Server Configuration dialog.

3. Set WINS configuration parameters as follows:

   - *Renewal Interval* specifies how frequently a client re-registers its name. Keep this value set to 4 days or more to minimize network traffic and the load on the WINS server.

   - *Extinction Interval* specifies what period must elapse between the time that an entry is marked as *released* (available for reuse) and the time it's marked as *extinct* (marked for deletion from the WINS database).

   - *Extinction Timeout* specifies what period must elapse between the time that an entry is marked as extinct and the time that it's actually scavenged from the database. The maximum permissible value is 4 days.

- *Verify Interval* specifies the period after which the WINS server must verify that old names not owned by that server are still active. The maximum permissible value is 24 days.

- In the Pull Parameters section, the *Initial Replication* check box, if marked, causes the WINS server to pull replica information from partner WINS servers when WINS is initialized, or when a replication parameter is changed. The *Retry Count* spinner box specifies how many retries will be made to pull the replica.

- In the Push Parameters section, the *Initial Replication* check box, if marked, causes this WINS server, when initialized, to notify its partner WINS servers of database status. The *Replicate on Address Change* check box, if marked, causes this WINS server to notify its partner WINS servers when an address changes in its database.

4. After you set the parameters in the WINS Server Configuration dialog, choose Advanced to expand the dialog to display the Advanced WINS Server Configuration items (see fig. 17.60).

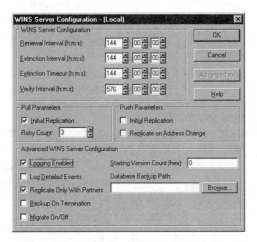

Fig. 17.60 The advanced options of the WINS Server Configuration dialog.

5. Set the advanced WINS configuration parameters as follows:

- The *Logging Enabled* check box, if marked, causes the WINS server to log database changes to the JET.LOG file.

- The *Log Detailed Events* check box, if marked, causes this WINS server to record full detail to the log file. Marking this box can result in substantial performance degradation on your server.

- The *Replicate Only With Partners* check box, if marked, causes this WINS server to perform push and pull database replication functions only with partner WINS servers.

- The *Backup On Termination* check box, if marked, causes this WINS server to back up the WINS database when the WINS service is stopped, except when the server itself is shut down.

- The *Migrate On/Off* check box, if marked, causes this WINS server to treat static records in its database as dynamic when these static records conflict with information received from a new registration or a replication from a partner WINS server. Mark this check box if you're upgrading to Windows NT on systems that previously ran another operating system.

- The *Starting Version Count (Hex)* box specifies the highest version ID number (in hexadecimal) for the WINS database. Increase this value if your WINS database becomes corrupted. If this WINS server is partnered with other WINS servers, use a value higher than the version number associated with replicas of this WINS server database on the partner servers.

- The *Database Backup Path* text box allows you to enter or browse for a drive and path where the backup copy of the WINS database is to be stored. Specify a local server drive rather than a network connection for this item. If you enter a valid path here, WINS automatically backs up its database to this location every three hours. When WINS is started, it verifies the integrity of its database. If it finds that the database is corrupted, WINS restores the database from this location.

6. After you complete all fields, click OK to close the WINS Server Configuration dialog. When you're finished configuring WINS, close the WINS Manager.

Sharing Windows NT Files with UNIX

The Windows NT TCP/IP core protocols and utilities provide only FTP as a means to share files between Windows NT and a UNIX or other TCP/IP host. Windows NT Server implements FTP in both client and server versions. Similarly, virtually every UNIX implementation includes both an FTP client and an FTP server. It's common, however, for workstations running operating systems other than UNIX to have only FTP client software.

Although FTP is the primary method for copying files between TCP/IP hosts, problems can occur when transferring files between systems with dissimilar file systems. The FTP protocol has built-in translation schemes that work well for common text and unstructured binary files. However, some systems, such as minicomputers and mainframes, have complex file systems and use file formats that might not successfully transfer between unlike systems.

Although FTP can be used to copy files between UNIX and Windows NT Server hosts, this manual process does nothing to provide a shared file system between the hosts. Clearly, something more is needed if Windows clients are to have real-time access to files stored on a UNIX host. Three methods are available for such access:

- *Network File System* (NFS), a Sun Microsystems product, is complicated to administer and requires that you buy additional software for your Windows NT server. NFS, however, does provide bi-directional access, allowing UNIX clients to access files stored on a Windows NT server as well as allow Microsoft clients to access files stored on UNIX hosts.

■ *Microsoft LAN Manager for UNIX* (LMU) adds the protocol support needed to allow UNIX hosts to participate in Microsoft Networking using the SMB protocol. Using LMU adds another complex product to administer, and LMU is relatively expensive.

■ *SAMBA* is a free product that runs on your UNIX host, allowing it to emulate a Microsoft LAN Manager server. Microsoft clients see a UNIX host running SAMBA as just another Microsoft Networking server and can access files stored on the UNIX file system as though the files were located on an actual Microsoft Networking server. SAMBA is essentially unidirectional, however, and provides only limited batch-mode access using SMBCLIENT for UNIX clients to files that reside on a Windows NT Server volume. The SAMBA home page is located at **http://lake.canberra.edu.au/pub/samba/samba.html**.

Network File System. Sun Microsystems, a leading supplier of UNIX workstations and servers, developed the NFS specification and published it in RFC 1094. NFS is now the *de facto* file server protocol implemented on UNIX systems. Since its original inception, NFS has evolved into NFS version 3 as detailed in RFC 1813. The NFS architecture is designed to be independent of the operating system, file system, and transport protocol used. NFS is built on top of the Remote Procedure Call (RPC) API described in RFC 1057. RPC, an interprocess network messaging protocol, allows networking software developers to port NFS to a wide variety of hardware platforms and operating system environments.

NFS, like FTP, is a client/server protocol. Unlike FTP, NFS provides transparent shared access to remote files across a network. A primary design consideration of an NFS server is to have the minimum possible impact on the host machine. In contrast to a NetWare server, an NFS server uses *stateless* protocols. (Stateless means that an NFS server maintains no information about the NFS clients it serves.) The NFS protocol burdens the client with maintaining the connection to the NFS server and also requires that the client ensure the integrity of the transactions. If, for example, an NFS server crashes, the NFS client must remount the shared files after the NFS server is rebooted.

Microsoft doesn't supply NFS software for Windows NT Server. Several third-party NFS products are available from companies such as Hummingbird Communications, Intergraph, NetManage, and Process Software. These and other NFS products provide NFS services only to the Windows NT host. Windows NT Server clients can't access NFS imported file systems unless NFS software is first installed on the individual clients.

Using Microsoft LAN Manager for UNIX to Add Microsoft Networking Support to UNIX Hosts. LMU allows UNIX hosts to participate in a Microsoft Networking environment. Microsoft licensed LMU to AT&T, which has in turn relicensed LMU to other UNIX vendors. LMU implementations are available for different varieties of UNIX, both directly from UNIX vendors (for example, SCO Microsoft LAN Manager for SCO Systems) and from third-party vendors (for example, Unipress Software Microsoft LAN Manager for UNIX).

LMU adds support for the SMB protocol to UNIX hosts. The SMB protocol, developed by Microsoft, IBM, and Intel, is the foundation used for interoperability by all Microsoft Networking products. SMB corresponds in function to the NetWare Core Protocol (NCP) used by Novell NetWare. In addition to Windows NT Server, LMU is compatible with Microsoft OS/2 LAN Manager, Microsoft Windows for Workgroups, IBM LAN Server, MS-DOS LAN Manager, DEC PATHWORKS, 3Com 3+Open, and MS-NET.

Installing the SMB protocol on a UNIX host allows interoperability between UNIX and Windows NT Server and its clients. It's possible to install LMU on just one UNIX host, which then shares NFS imported file systems with a Windows NT server and its clients. This process incurs additional overhead for the NFS-to-SMB gateway and slows perfor-mance, although doing so may be a cost-effective alternative to buying multiple copies of LMU for lightly accessed UNIX hosts.

Using SAMBA to Allow UNIX Hosts to Emulate Windows NT Server. An alternative to purchasing LMU is to install the freely available SMB software SAMBA. Installing the SAMBA suite of programs on your UNIX host allows your Microsoft Networking clients to access UNIX files and printers as though they were resources on a Windows NT server. Originally developed by Andrew Tridgell, SAMBA has since been enhanced and extended using input from "net gurus" all over the world. SAMBA includes the following major components:

- *smbd* is the SMB server itself, which provides the core SMB support needed to handle client connections.

- *smbclient* is the client program run on the UNIX host.

- *smb.conf* is the SAMBA configuration file.

- *nmbd* is the NetBIOS name server, used to allow clients to locate servers.

SAMBA is officially supplied in source code form only, although user-contributed com-piled versions (binaries) for most UNIX platforms can be found on the Internet. SAMBA is freely modifiable and may be distributed under the GPL. Make files are available for compiling binaries for a large number of UNIX variants, detailed in table 17.2. SAMBA source code can be downloaded via anonymous FTP from **nimbus.anu.edu.au**, in the directory /pub/tridge/samba.

Table 17.2 SAMBA-Supported UNIX Implementations		
SunOS	HP-UX	SCO
A/UX 3.0	Intergraph	SEQUENT
AIX	ISC SVR3V4 (POSIX mode)	SGI
Apollo Domain/OS sr10.3 (BSD4.3)	Linux	SOLARIS
BSDI	Net BSD	SunOS
Data General UX	NeXT	SVR4
Free BSD	OSF1	ULTRIX

Building Universal Clients for Microsoft Windows NT, Novell NetWare, and UNIX

As this chapter demonstrates, PCs running Microsoft client software can be provided with access to NetWare server resources, but with some limitations. Similarly, workstations running Novell NetWare client software can be provided with access to Windows NT Server resources by running the GSNW or the File and Print Service for NetWare on your Windows NT server. Here again, some restrictions apply, particularly for those who run NetWare 4.x servers.

The explosion of the Internet and of the use of TCP/IP for internetworking also makes TCP/IP client support very desirable. As a result, what many organizations need is a standardized PC client software configuration that simultaneously provides full support for Windows NT Server, NetWare, and UNIX, and does so with a high degree of stability while consuming minimum conventional workstation memory.

As discussed in Chapter 10, "Configuring Windows 95 Clients for Networking," using Windows 95 as your client operating system minimizes or eliminates the problems of dealing with base memory limitations. Windows 95 used with a supported NIC provides protocol support and redirection services using 32-bit drivers, which eliminate the base memory footprint while providing client services for Microsoft Networking, NetWare, and TCP/IP. Although Windows 95 as shipped doesn't support NDS on NetWare 4.x servers, both Microsoft and Novell have 32-bit client software that does support NDS available for free downloading via the Internet, MSL, or NetWire.

Another alternative is to use more than one redirector or shell with multiple protocol stacks on the clients. NetWare and Windows NT Server both support DOS, Windows, Windows for Workgroups, Windows 95, Windows NT, OS/2, and Macintosh clients. Some NetWare system managers have an almost religious aversion to implementing multiple protocol stacks on their client workstations, let alone multiple redirectors.

These NetWare administrators had good reason to be wary in the past. The 640K limitation on base memory inherent to Intel-based PCs running in real mode made for a tight fit. When DOS, the network protocol drivers, and the NetWare shell were loaded, often not enough memory was left to run large applications, let alone enough to consider adding one or more additional protocol stacks and network shells. Modern client operating systems such as MS-DOS 6.x, Windows 3.11 for Workgroups, and Windows 95 have dramatically simplified the problem of cramming the network software into base memory and have made running dual protocol stacks and redirectors a realistic alternative.

The quest for such a universal client continues, and a perfect solution doesn't yet exist. If, however, like most LAN administrators, you find that most of your clients are running Windows 3.11 for Workgroups or Windows 95, it's straightforward to configure either of these client operating systems to provide simultaneous support for Windows NT Server, TCP/IP, and NetWare.

Configuring Windows 3.11 for Workgroups as a Universal Client

Windows 3.11 for Workgroups provides native networking support only for Windows Networking. It can, however, be used as a foundation on which to build a universal network client using inexpensive or free utilities for TCP/IP and NetWare connectivity. Configuring Windows 3.11 for Workgroups as a universal client requires the following:

- *Windows Networking support* enabled within Windows 3.11 for Workgroups.

- *NetWare support* provided by installing the ODI drivers and NetWare client software available from Novell, and then enabling NetWare support within Windows 3.11 for Workgroups.

- *TCP/IP support* provided by installing a Winsock-compliant stack, available from Microsoft or third parties.

- *Windows Packet Driver support* provided by installing ODIPKT.COM and WINPKT.COM, available via anonymous FTP from **ftp.cica.indiana.edu** in the /pub/pc/win3/winsock directory.

Installing Windows Network Support. Installing Windows Networking support for Windows 3.11 for Workgroups is fully described in Chapter 11, "Connecting Other PC Clients to the Network."

> ### Caution
>
> Remember that although Windows 3.11 for Workgroups provides the client software needed to access your Windows NT Server, you must still purchase a client access license for each computer that does so.

Installing Novell NetWare Support. To add support for NetWare, use the client software provided by Novell. The client software, packaged as several self-extracting archive files named VLMKIT*.EXE, can be downloaded via Internet anonymous FTP from **ftp.novell.com** or from the CompuServe NetWire forum, or can be purchased on disk directly from Novell. The VLM client software is free if your Novell server is version 3.12 or higher. It's available at a nominal charge for those using NetWare 3.11 servers.

Installing TCP/IP Support. Adding a TCP/IP protocol stack to Windows 3.11 for Workgroups is done by installing software written to the Windows Sockets specification, commonly referred to as Winsock. Following are some Winsock implementations available from various sources, ranging in cost from free to quite expensive:

- Microsoft distributes a free Winsock implementation for Windows for Workgroups in an archive named TCPIP32B.EXE, which can be downloaded from the Microsoft Download Service (206-936-6735) or via anonymous FTP at **ftp.microsoft.com**. Earlier versions of this product experienced compatibility and stability problems, but the version now posted for download works reliably. Microsoft's Winsock implementation is unique in its support for both DHCP and Microsoft Networking over TCP/IP.

- Various inexpensive shareware Winsock implementations—most notably, Peter Tattam's Trumpet Winsock—can be downloaded via anonymous FTP at **ftp.trumpet.com.au** in the /ftp/pub/winsock directory, as well as from many BBSs. These shareware implementations vary widely in quality, features, and bundled applications. The best of them, like Trumpet, are both inexpensive—at $20 a seat or so—and reliable.

- Many commercial Winsock implementations are available, although this market appears to be rapidly shrinking due both to the availability of inexpensive shareware versions and the bundling of TCP/IP support in Windows 95. Commercial Winsock vendors have tried to fight back by bundling various TCP/IP applications with their products—FTP clients, newsreaders, and so forth—but better applications are available for free on the Internet, and these products remain expensive at $50 to $200 per seat.

Pick one Winsock implementation and use it for all your Windows 3.11 for Workgroups clients. There's seldom any reason to look further than Microsoft's free Winsock software. Consider Trumpet Winsock and similar products only if you need telephone dialer support. Consider commercial Winsock implementations only if you need specialized features not available with the free or inexpensive products.

Installing Packet Driver Support. The next step is to install packet driver support to enable the ODI NIC drivers and Windows itself to handle packets properly. Two programs are universally used to provide these functions in Windows 3.1x installations: ODIPKT handles the ODI packet interface tasks, and WINPKT allows handles the Windows packet interface duties.

ODIPKT. ODIPKT is used to provide packet driver support to the Novell ODI NIC drivers. The current version of ODIPKT.COM can be downloaded via anonymous FTP from **ftp://hsdndev.harvard.edu/pub/odipkt/odipkt.com** or from any Web site or BBS that has a Winsock area.

ODIPKT allows a single NIC running ODI to service multiple packet driver protocol stacks, including IPX/SPX and TCP/IP. ODIPKT supports Ethernet, Token Ring, and ARCnet frames.

ODI supports multiple frame types simultaneously on a single physical NIC. Because the frame types typically used with NetWare to transport IPX/SPX packets aren't appropriate to transport TCP/IP packets, it's common to see a single NIC in a NetWare workstation bound to two frame types, such as Ethernet II for TCP/IP, and Novell Ethernet 802.3 or 802.2 for IPX/SPX. One or more frame types are specified for each physical NIC in the NET.CFG file. Each frame type is seen by ODI as a separate logical NIC. The following NET.CFG fragment illustrates a typical configuration:

```
Link Driver NE2000
port 300
int 10
FRAME Ethernet_II
FRAME Ethernet_802.3
```

The first three lines name the link driver and specify that the physical Ethernet card is located at address 300 and interrupt 10. The final two lines bind the Ethernet_II frame type appropriate for UNIX as logical board 0 and the Ethernet_802.3 frame type used for IPX/SPX as logical board 1.

ODIPKT depends on buffers supplied by the ODI link support layer (LSL). Make sure that your NET.CFG specifies enough buffers of a size large enough to support your NIC. For example, using 1,514-byte Ethernet frames on a NIC that supports multiple buffers, your NET.CFG may contain the following:

```
Link Support
            BUFFERS 2 1600
```

This instructs LSL to reserve two buffers, each of 1,600 bytes.

ODIPKT.COM is typically loaded by STARTNET.BAT and requires only two command-line arguments. The first specifies the logical board number; the second specifies the software interrupt, or vector, to be used, which is specified as a decimal number. A typical STARTNET.BAT fragment might look something like the following:

```
lsl
3c5x9
odipkt 0 96
winpkt 0x60
ipxodi
vlm /mx
```

The first line loads the LSL portion of ODI. The second loads the packet driver version of the 3Com 3C509 Multiple Link Interface Driver (MLID). The third loads ODIPKT to support logical board 0 using software interrupt 96 decimal. The fourth line loads WINPKT (described in the following section) and specifies software interrupt 0x60 hexadecimal. (Note that 96 decimal corresponds to 0x60 hexadecimal.) The fifth line loads IPX support for NetWare, and the sixth line loads the NetWare VLM client software into extended memory. ODIPKT must be loaded after LSL.COM and the MLID, but it must be loaded before WINPKT.

WINPKT. WINPKT is a shim that provides packet support for Windows. The current version of WINPKT.COM can be downloaded via Internet anonymous FTP from **ftp.cica.indiana.edu** in the /pub/pc/win3/winsock directory, or from any Web site or BBS that has a Winsock area.

WINPKT takes only one command-line argument, which is the software interrupt used by ODIPKT. Make sure that both ODIPKT and WINPKT are using the same software interrupt.

Note
ODIPKT uses decimal notation and WINPKT uses hexadecimal notation.

Using Windows 95 as a Universal Client

Windows 95 is an ideal universal network client. Used with a supported NIC, Windows 95 can provide simultaneous connectivity to Windows NT Server, NetWare, UNIX, and SNA servers, using supplied 32-bit drivers and occupying nearly no conventional memory. The only drawback to using Windows 95 as a client is that, as shipped, the NetWare client software doesn't support NDS. When this book was written, beta versions of 32-bit NetWare drivers with NDS support were available from both Microsoft and Novell. For full information on how to configure Windows 95 as a universal network client, see Chapter 10, "Configuring Windows 95 Clients for Networking."

> **Note**
>
> Although Windows 95 provides client functionality for Windows NT Server, you must purchase a client access license for each computer that uses Windows 95 to access your Windows NT server.

Integrating Windows NT in IBM SNA Environments

Windows NT is bundled with the Data Link Control (DLC) protocol that allows communication with IBM SNA machines and other network devices, such as Hewlett-Packard laser printers with network interfaces. The Windows NT DLC protocol binds with either a Token Ring interface card (TIC) or an Ethernet NIC that supports the Ethernet Version 2 (DIX) framing format.

> **Note**
>
> The order of the bindings section when installing the DLC protocol is very important. If you have more than one NIC (Windows NT supports up to 16), you must ensure that the DLC protocol is bound to the appropriate NIC. By default, the DLC protocol binds to adapter number 0, the first network adapter installed into the system.

The DLC protocol provides the foundations for communication with SNA mainframes and midrange hosts, such as an IBM AS/400. The DLC protocol supports SNA LLC type 2 and type 1 frames. Windows NT doesn't include any user applications that utilize the DLC protocol. Third-party SNA products, such as Wall Data's Rumba for Windows NT, works with the DLC protocol to provide IBM 3270 terminal emulation to a Windows NT system. Rumba is one of the few third-party SNA products that doesn't require the SNA Server for Windows NT.

SNA Server for Windows NT, a component of the Microsoft BackOffice suite, is sold separately from Windows NT Server. Unlike Rumba's relatively simple terminal emulation, SNA Server for Windows NT provides a client/server architecture that allows as many as 2,000 users, or clients, to have 10,000 simultaneous connections to 250 different SNA hosts.

SNA Server for Windows NT provides Windows NT, Windows 95, Windows 3.x, MS-DOS, OS/2, and MAC clients 3,270 and 5,250 terminal and printer emulation, file transfer, and Emulator High Level Language (EHLLAPI) sessions on SNA Hosts. SNA Server for Windows NT also supports the following SNA APIs and protocols:

- *Advanced Program to Program Communications* (APPC) using the LU 6.2 protocol

- *Common Programming Interface for Communications* (CPI-C) using the LU 6.2 protocol

- *Common Service Verbs* (CSV) as defined by the NetView API

- *Logical Unit APIs* (LUA) using either LUA/Request Unit Interface or LUA/Session Level Interface over LU 0, 1, 2 & 3

Microsoft SNA Server is the only system on the network that uses the SNA protocols. Client systems can run Microsoft Networking (SMB), IPX/SPX, Vines, AppleTalk, or TCP/IP to communicate with SNA Server that translates the communication to the SNA host or hosts.

SNA Server also provides a platform for third-party vendors to develop SNA-based applications for both the clients and the SNA Server for Windows NT.

Migrating from Novell NetWare to Windows NT Server

Windows NT Server includes a superb set of tools to help it coexist with Novell NetWare servers, but Microsoft wants you to replace your NetWare servers with servers running Windows NT. Having seen other NOSs, including some of their own earlier efforts, fall by the wayside as a result of trying to compete head-on with NetWare, Microsoft wisely has avoided attempting the brute-force method with Windows NT Server 4.0. Instead, Microsoft has cleverly positioned Windows NT Server 4.0 as a product that easily coexists with NetWare.

Few independent analysts question that Windows NT Server 4.0 is an even match for NetWare 4.1. Although Novell continues to trumpet the advantages of its NetWare Directory Services over the domain-based directory services model used by Windows NT Server, the reality is that either method works well for most organizations. Also, the method by which Windows NT Server provides application server functions is recognized by most observers as being superior both in concept and in execution to the NLM-based method used by Novell.

What has kept other NOSs, some with unquestionable advantages, from replacing NetWare on a wholesale basis is NetWare's installed base. No one seriously questions that NetWare 3.1x is an obsolescent NOS, eclipsed in power and features by Windows NT Server and other modern NOSs, including NetWare 4.x. Yet the fact remains that only recently have new shipments of NetWare 4.x licenses exceeded those of new NetWare 3.12 licenses. The installed NetWare 3.1x base predominates and is expected to continue its dominant role for some time to come. Even NetWare 2.x has a substantial and continuing presence.

The reason for the continuing dominance of earlier versions of NetWare is quite simple. Like an old shoe, NetWare 2.x/3.x is comfortable. For every NetWare 4.x expert available, a dozen technicians and consultants know the earlier versions of NetWare inside and out. For every true Windows NT Server expert, you find perhaps 100 NetWare gurus. Although this situation is starting to change, many network administrators still find comfort in using the old familiar NetWare 2.x/3.1x.

Recognizing this inertia factor, Microsoft has taken an intelligent approach by positioning Windows NT Server as a product that can coexist peacefully in a NetWare shop and do useful things well that NetWare does poorly or not at all. This guerrilla marketing strategy is beginning to pay off, as LAN administrators, bringing up their first Windows NT Server, quickly realize that Windows NT Server was never anything to be afraid of in the first place.

Whether you plan incremental replacement of NetWare servers with Windows NT Server 4.0, wholesale replacement, or simply continuing coexistence, you should become familiar with the Microsoft Migration Tool for NetWare (see fig. 17.61). This tool automates the process of moving files, directories, file attribute and rights, and user and group account information from an existing NetWare server to a Windows NT server. A basic version of this tool is bundled with Windows NT Server itself. A more advanced, full-function version is included with the optional File and Print Service for NetWare. If you plan to do a migration, do yourself a favor and buy File and Print Service for NetWare to get the advanced version. Its capability to migrate logon scripts alone is worth the $100 price of the File and Print Service for NetWare product.

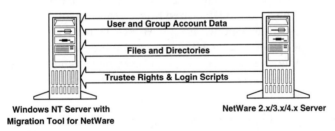

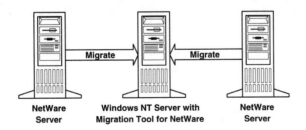

Fig. 17.61 The Migration Tool for NetWare, which allows you to migrate Novell NetWare users and groups to Windows NT Server.

The Migration Tool for NetWare can be used in several ways. Following are some of the things you can do:

- Migrate the contents of a single NetWare server to a single Windows NT server

- Migrate the contents of two or more NetWare servers to a single Windows NT server, combining and merging the contents of the NetWare servers during the process

- Migrate the contents of two or more NetWare servers to two or more Windows NT servers, relocating and distributing the contents of the NetWare servers as you choose among the Windows NT servers

Using the Migration Tool for NetWare results in no changes whatsoever to the NetWare server and can be done without taking down either the NetWare server or the Windows NT server. All services on both the NetWare server and the Windows NT server continue to be available to users during the migration process.

The Migration Tool for NetWare offers the option to do a trial migration, allowing you to test the results of a migration before actually making any changes to either server. Potential conflicts, such as duplicate user names, are highlighted during this trial migration process, allowing you to resolve them before doing the actual migration.

From Here...

If you're integrating Windows NT Server 4.0 into an existing PC network, the odds are that your present network is running Novell NetWare. Thus, the first part of this chapter covered Windows NT's Gateway Services for NetWare, File and Print Services for NetWare, and Directory Services Manager for NetWare. UNIX networks running TCP/IP are commonly used by medium- to large-sized firms, so a substantial part of this chapter was devoted to integrating Windows NT 4.0 with UNIX networks. The chapter closed with detailed recommendations for creating universal Windows 3.1+ and Windows 95 clients for Microsoft Windows NT, NetWare, and UNIX networking, as well as a brief discussion of integration with IBM SNA networks and migrating from NetWare to Windows NT networking.

The following chapters contain information related to the content of this chapter:

- Chapter 4, "Choosing Network Protocols," explains how to select one or more of the three principal networking protocols supported by Windows NT based on your network configuration.

- Chapter 10, "Configuring Windows 95 Clients for Networking," shows you how to set up PCs running Windows 95 to take maximum advantage of Windows NT 4.0 networks, including the use of server-based desktop configurations and policies.

- Chapter 11, "Connecting Other PC Clients to the Network," provides the details on setting up Windows 3.1+, Windows for Workgroups 3.1+, Windows NT Workstation 4.0, and Macintosh clients to communicate with Windows NT 4.0 servers.

Chapter 18

Managing Remote Access Service

Rising sales of laptop and notebook computers for mobile computing, combined with continuing growth in the number of telecommuting workers, makes remote access to computer networks a necessity. Most of today's mobile PC users are limited to dial-up networking over a 28.8kbps modem connection, which can be agonizingly slow. Future implementation of wireless Personal Communication Services (PCS) promises to deliver increased bandwidth without the need for a wired POTS (plain old telephone service) connection. Telecommuters now can take advantage of the increased bandwidth of relatively low-cost ISDN connections. Those lucky enough to participate in trials of cablemodems and xDSL (various high-speed digital subscriber line systems) implementations get dial-up networking at T-1's 1.44mbps or better, at least in the downstream (receiving) direction.

Windows NT Server 4.0's Remote Access Service (RAS) and dial-up networking (DUN) represents a substantial improvement over the Windows NT 3.51 implementation. Windows NT 4.0 finally supports 32-bit TAPI (Telephony API) 2.0 and the Unimodem driver, both of which originated in Windows 95. TAPI 2.0 brings a client/server architecture to Windows telephony, which makes setting up and administering RAS and DUN a relatively easy task. Even in otherwise NetWare-only environments, Windows NT Server 4.0 is likely to carve a niche as a dedicated RAS server as a result of its relatively low cost and capability to support up to 255 simultaneous RAS connections.

Windows 95 is likely to remain the client operating system of choice for most mobile PC users because of Windows 95's better support for PC Cards and its battery-saving power management features. Most telecommuters will continue to use Windows 95 at home because of Plug-and-Play modem installation, legacy hardware support, and lesser resource requirements than Windows NT Workstation 4.0. The emphasis of this chapter is on conventional analog modem and ISDN connections for RAS; a brief description of new digital technologies for telecommuters appears near the end of this chapter.

This chapter covers the following topics:

- Remote access architectures

- 32-bit TAPI in Windows NT 4.0

- Installing RAS Dial-Up Networking

- Installing and testing RAS clients

- Monitoring RAS connections

- Using PPTP to create virtual private networks

Touring the New Communications Features of Windows NT Server 4.0

Windows NT Server 4.0 provides the following new telecommunications features, most of which are derived from earlier Windows 95 implementations:

- *TAPI* is one of Microsoft's recent additions to WOSA, the Windows Open Services Architecture. TAPI 2.0's architecture is based on 32-bit telephony service providers, such as Unimodem, that plug into the TAPI framework. (Windows NT 4.0 now doesn't support the voice features of Windows 95's Unimodem/V upgrade.) Later, the "Understanding TAPI 2.0" section describes the structure and technical features of TAPI 2.0.

- *Autodial and Log-on Dial* are client features that let you map an association between a DUN entry and a network address for access to files. As in Windows 95, when you double-click a file icon in Explorer and the file isn't accessible on the network, a popup window asks whether you want to connect via DUN.

- *Restartable file copy* eliminates the frustration of having to start file downloads from scratch after interruption of a RAS connection. Restartable file copy remembers the status of an interrupted file transmission; when you reconnect, RAS sends only the missing part of the file.

- *Idle disconnect* automatically terminates a RAS connection after a specified period of time of no communication activity.

- *PPP Multilink*, combined with *RAS Multilink*, lets you combine (bond) two or more physical communications links to increase RAS throughput when using TCP/IP to connect to the Internet or a private intranet. This feature primarily is useful for supporting multiple simultaneous ISDN connections. If you have a limited number of inbound ISDN lines, remote users can combine two B (bearer) channels for a 112kbps connection when traffic is light and drop back to a single B channel as more remote users connect.

- *Point-to-Point Tunneling Protocol* (PPTP) lets you connect to your network via the Internet to save long-distance telephone charges. PPTP running on Windows NT Server 4.0 adds virtual private networking (VPN) support for Windows NT Workstation 4.0 clients. PPTP provides a secure connection through encryption of TCP/IP, IPX, and NetBEUI protocols. To take advantage of PPTP, your Internet service provider (ISP) must support PPTP.

With the exception of TAPI 2.0, which benefits Server and Workstation RAS implementations, the new communication features of Windows NT 4.0 primarily are directed to client-side communication. Microsoft's objective is to bring Windows NT 4.0's communication features up to the ease-of-use level of Windows 95. PPP Multilink and PPTP are Internet-specific technologies that are expected to play a more important role as the use of ISDN increases and more ISPs support PPTP.

Deciding on a Dial-Up Networking Architecture

Before you implement DUN via Windows NT RAS on a production basis, you must decide on the system architecture. Hardware and software requirements depend on the number of inbound lines you intend to support, as well as the method of connection of the hardware to your network. Following are the most common types of RAS architecture:

■ *Single or multiple internal modems.* If you have enough ISA slots available on your RAS server and have a built-in PS/2 mouse port, you can install up to a total of four internal modems on COM1, COM2, COM3, and COM4, sharing interrupts IRQ4 (COM1 and COM3) and IRQ3 (COM2 and COM3). Users also can connect to individual modem-equipped client PCs on the network; the Windows 95 Plus! pack adds RAS server capabilities to clients. Figure 18.1 illustrates a Windows NT RAS server with two external modems and a Windows 95 client providing DUN services.

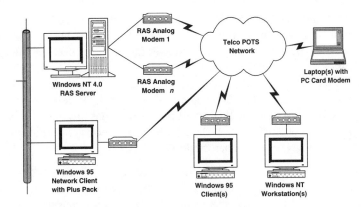

Fig. 18.1 A small dial-up networking installation with Windows NT and Windows 95 RAS servers communicating with analog modems.

> **Tip**
>
> Reliable interrupt sharing by modems depends on the make and model of the modems you install, plus the server's system BIOS and motherboard. (It's seldom practical to install more than two internal modems in a server.) Some Plug-and-Play modems are difficult to install under Windows NT. Before you buy three or four modems, test two modems sharing IRQ3 or IRQ4 with simultaneous inbound connections.

■ *Multiple external modems with multiport serial cards.* Multiport serial cards are the safest choice for providing more than two inbound connections. Relatively low-cost serial cards are available in four-port and eight-port versions. The modem configuration is the same as that shown in figure 18.1. Some multiport serial cards have built-in microprocessors to minimize server CPU resources devoted to handling multiple connections.

You can use some multiport serial cards to connect to a combination of analog modems and external ISDN devices. Make sure that the supplier includes software that supports Windows NT 4.0 RAS.

> **Tip**
>
> Make sure that the modems you buy support the new V.34 standard, which provides 33.6kbps bandwidth. To take advantage of V.42-bis MNP 5 hardware data compression offered by most V.34 modems, be sure to buy modems for both ends of the connection from the same supplier. Hardware compression, which can increase data transmission rates by a factor of two or more, seldom works properly between modems from different vendors. U.S. Robotics Sportster V.34+ 28.8kbps modems are used for the examples in this chapter. These modems usually (but not always) provide a 57.6kbps connection, equivalent to a 1-B ISDN connection with an external ISDN adapter.

- *Internal or external ISDN adapters*. External ISDN adapters emulate analog modems, so you simply connect one or two external ISDN adapters to the server's serial port(s). External ISDN adapters provide slower connections because the serial protocol includes stop and start bits, which consume 20 percent of the available bandwidth. Internal ISDN adapters, which don't require stop and start bits, provide connections at the maximum ISDN data rate. Internal ISDN adapters installed in Intel-based servers can use the ISDN miniport driver that originated in Windows NT 3.5. Regardless of the type of ISDN adapter you select, verify that the device supports Windows NT 4.0 RAS before purchasing.

- *ISDN Ethernet adapters*. Simple ISDN Ethernet adapters have an NT-2 ISDN and a 10BaseT Ethernet connector. You assign a NetBIOS name to the adapter, which emulates a server. Multiple users can share a single ISDN Ethernet adapter (with bridging) for outbound connections to an ISP offering ISDN service. As an example, the Ascend Pipeline-25Fx supports up to four users and has analog connections for a telephone and fax machine. One Ethernet adapter can support two 1-B inbound connections to a single telephone line provisioned as a hunt group.

- *ISDN Routers*. ISDN routers provide IP and IPX routing in addition to bridging. Some ISDN Ethernet adapters offer IP and/or IPX routing as an option. The Ascend Pipeline-50, for instance, provides bridging for an unlimited number of users and supports IP and IPX routing, including PPP Multilink. ISDN routers are the best choice for handling high volumes of inbound ISDN traffic. High-end ISDN routers handle multiple BRI lines or a single PRI line, which provides 23 B channels and one D channel. U.S. Robotics' Total Control Enterprise Network Hub supports a combination of analog modems (in groups of four), ISDN adapters, switched-56 lines, and T-1 connections for up to a total of 64 simultaneous connections. Figure 18.2 illustrates an Ethernet router that accommodates both ISDN adapters and analog modems.

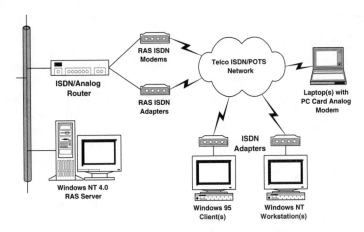

Fig. 18.2   A combination ISDN and analog Ethernet router for dial-up networking for telecommuters and mobile PC users.

Note

Ascend Communications, Inc., which claims to have more than 40 percent of the market for ISDN networking bridges and routers, offers an extensive glossary of ISDN terminology at **http:// www.ascend.com/techdocs/glossary.html**. A U.S. Robotics' white paper, "The Shape of the ISDN Market: 1996 and Beyond," at **http://www.usr.com/business/3022.html** offers an overview of ISDN technology for Internet and telecommuting applications.

Unless you need to support only a few mobile users or telecommuters, choose a multiple-port serial card and external modems for analog connections. You can add external 28.8kbps modems and phone lines as traffic warrants. For ISDN connections, the trend is to ISDN routers because of their rapidly decreasing cost. If you plan to provide users with outbound ISDN connections to your ISP, be sure to install another line to support your telecommuters' inbound calls.

> **Note**
>
> Microsoft's Get ISDN program for Windows 95 provides a simplified ordering system for instal-lation of ISDN lines in North America. The details of the program are available at **http://www.microsoft.com/windows/getisdn/**. Windows 95 clients using internal ISDN modems require the ISDN Accelerator Pack, which you can download from **http://www.microsoft.com/windows/getisdn/dload.htm**, and compatible drivers for your adapter. The ISDN Accelerator Pack isn't required for external ISDN adapters.

Understanding TAPI 2.0

TAPI 2.0 is a 32-bit Windows NT service derived from TAPI version 1.4 introduced by Windows 95. TAPI 2.0 supports Intel and RISC symmetrical multiprocessing with multithreaded operation and preemptive multitasking. TAPI 2.0 supports Windows 95 32-bit TAPI 1.4 and Windows 3.1+ 16-bit TAPI 1.3 applications. TAPI 2.0 includes addi-tional features for managing communications applications that run in the background. TAPI 2.0 is designed to support various telephony services, including call-center manage-ment and quality of service (QOS) negotiation. The discussion in this chapter is limited to TAPI 2.0's RAS features.

Figure 18.3 illustrates the basic architecture of TAPI 2.0. TAPI.DLL provides core 16-bit telephony services for Windows 95 and Windows 3.1+. In Windows NT 4.0, TAPI.DLL is only a 16-bit thunking layer that converts 16-bit to the 32-bit addresses required by Win-dows NT 4.0's Tapi32.dll. Tapi32.dll uses LRPCs (lightweight remote procedure calls) to pass function requests to Tapisrv.exe. Tapisrv.exe runs as a service process; all telephony service providers (TSPs) run in Tapisrv.exe's context, improving performance by elimi-nating context switching. Figure 18.3 shows the Unimodem TSP (Unimodem.tsp, a DLL) connected to Unimodem.sys, a kernel mode component that provides access to serial ports and internal modems. The Unimodem.tsp and Unimodem.sys components support analog modems and external ISDN adapters that emulate modems. Support for internal ISDN adapters is provided by the ISDN miniport driver that originated in Windows NT 3.5.

Tapi32.dll also supports user interface elements, such as talk/hangup dialogs, designed by third-party TSP suppliers. Many independent software vendors (ISVs) provide fax, call center, and other TAPI services. A brief technical paper, "Windows Telephony (TAPI) Support in Windows NT 4.0," available at **http://www.microsoft.com/win32dev/netwrk/tapiwp.htm**, provides additional technical details on TAPI 2.0.

> **Note**
>
> If you update Windows NT Server 3.5x to Windows NT Server 4.0, installed internal or external modem(s) use the existing Modem.inf file and don't use TAPI 2.0's Unimodem driver. You must remove and reinstall the modem(s) to gain TAPI 2.0 and Unimodem support.

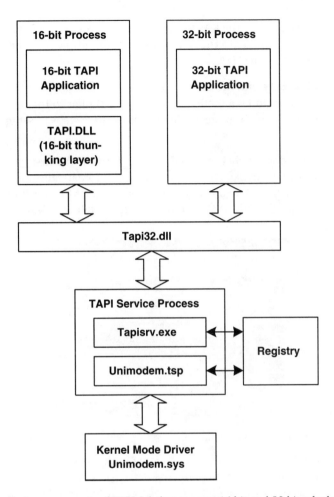

Fig. 18.3   The basic components of TAPI 2.0 that support 16-bit and 32-bit telephony services.

Setting Up Windows NT Server 4.0 Remote Access Service

Setting up Windows NT Server 4.0 RAS involves the following overall steps:

- Install the modem(s)
- Configure RAS for dial-up networking
- Enable dial-in connections for users with the Remote Access Admin application

The following sections describe the RAS setup process for a single analog modem shared by multiple DUN users. Changes to the setup process for multiple modems and ISDN adapters are noted where applicable.

Installing Internal or External Modems

Windows NT Server 4.0 includes a modem setup process similar to that of Windows 95. After physically installing one or more modems, follow these steps to set up the modem for use with RAS:

1. In Control Panel, double-click the Modem tool. If this is the first modem installed on the server, the first Install New Modem dialog automatically appears (see fig. 18.4). If you're installing an additional modem, the Modems Properties sheet appears; click the Add button to display the Install New Modem dialog.

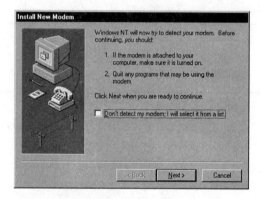

Fig. 18.4   The first Install New Modem dialog.

2. Click Next with the Don't Detect my Modem check box cleared to see whether Windows NT can detect your modem. The detection process may fail, even for modems with drivers included on the Windows NT Server 4.0 distribution CD-ROM, resulting in the dialog shown in figure 18.5. (Failure to detect supported modems might be the reason that Microsoft doesn't append "Wizard" to the Install New Modem dialog's caption.)

3. Click Next to display the dialog for selecting a modem manually. First, select the vendor in the Manufacturers list, and then locate the product in the Models list (see fig. 18.6). If you can't find the model, click Have Disk to use the vendor's driver disk if it includes Windows NT 4.0 drivers. Otherwise, select (Standard Modem Types) in the Manufacturers list and your modem's speed in the Models list. In most cases, the Standard Modem driver works, but it may not implement special features of your modem, such as hardware data compression.

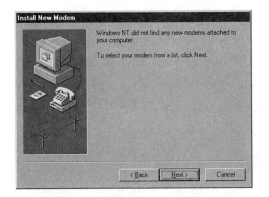

Fig. 18.5 A common response to Windows NT 4.0's attempt to detect a modem.

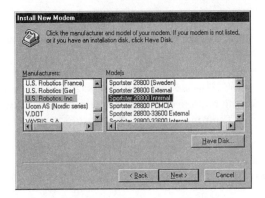

Fig. 18.6 Selecting a modem vendor and product from Windows NT 4.0's list of supported modems.

> ### Tip
>
> Some external ISDN adapters, such as the Motorola BitSURFR, are supported with drivers included on the Windows NT Server 4.0 distribution CD-ROM. Vendors frequently update drivers for internal and external ISDN adapters, so the versions supplied with Windows NT Server 4.0 may not be the latest. Always check the vendor's Web site for recently updated drivers before installing an ISDN adapter.

4. Click Next to specify the COM port on which to install the modem. Most modems are factory-configured for installation on COM2, so select the default COM2 entry in the list (see fig. 18.7). If you've specified a different COM port when configuring the modem, click the All Ports button to make a selection.

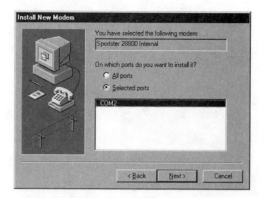

Fig. 18.7   Specifying the COM port on which to install the modem.

> **Note**
>
> You add more COM ports and specify IRQ and base address settings with Control Panel's
> Port tool.

5. Click Next to continue. The Modem Setup message box advises that you must restart the system for the modem to become operational. Click OK, but ignore the
message; Windows NT automatically restarts during the RAS configuration process.

6. The final Install New Modem dialog indicates that modem installation is complete.
Click Finish to display the Modems Properties sheet (see fig. 18.8), which supports
entries for as many modems as you can install in the PC or connect to a multiport
serial card.

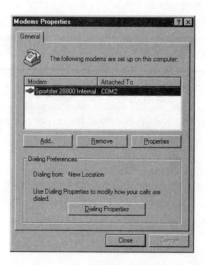

Fig. 18.8   The Modems Properties sheet, with an entry for a single modem.

7. Click Properties to display the *Modem_Name* Properties sheet. The General page lets you determine the speaker volume (usually off for RAS use) and the Maximum Speed in bps (see fig. 18.9). Accept the default value for the modem (usually 57,600bps) unless instructed otherwise.

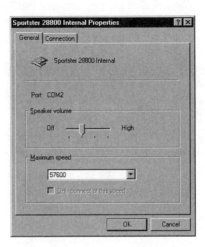

Fig. 18.9 The General Page of the property sheet for the selected modem.

8. Click the Connection tab to display the Connection property page. The standard serial protocol for RAS is 8N1—8 data bits, no parity, and 1 stop bit (see fig. 18.10). Call preferences relate only to dial-out operations. RAS settings override the Disconnect a Call if Idle for More Than… setting specified in this dialog.

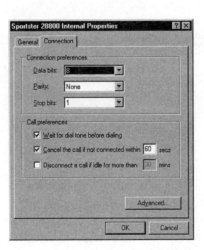

Fig. 18.10 The Connection page of the property sheet for the selected modem.

9. Click the Advanced button of the Connection page to display the Advanced Connection Settings dialog. If the modem supports V.42 MNP 2 through MNP 4 error control, the Use Error Control check box is enabled and marked by default. The

Compress Data check box also is enabled and checked for modems that support V.42-bis MNP 5 data compression (see fig. 18.11). The default Use Flow Control setting and Hardware (RTS/CTS) option are satisfactory for all RAS connections to clients with modems manufactured during the last five years or so. To create a modem log file for troubleshooting purposes, mark the Record a Log File check box. Click OK to close the dialog, and then click OK to close the specified modem's property sheet and return to the Modems Properties sheet.

Fig. 18.11 The Advanced Connection Settings dialog for a V.34 modem supporting hardware error correction and data compression.

10. Click Dialing Properties to display the Dialing Properties sheet (see fig. 18.12). You need to set up these properties only if you plan to use the server to dial out. (Dialing out to an ISP or other remote server sometimes is useful for troubleshooting modem problems.) Click OK to close the property sheet.

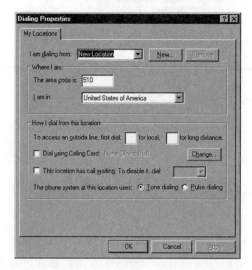

Fig. 18.12 Supplying dial-out information in the Dialing Properties sheet.

11. Click Close to close the Modems Properties sheet. A Modem Setup message box asks whether you want to configure Dial-up Networking, the subject of the next section (see fig. 18.13). Click Yes.

Fig. 18.13 The message box leading to the configuration process for Dial-up Networking.

Configuring Dial-Up Networking

Before you can use the first or additional modems, you must configure DUN parameters. Any major changes to a modem's configuration require that you repeat the setup process. To set DUN parameters for a modem or ISDN adapter, follow these steps:

1. In the Remote Access Setup dialog, which lists all modems installed on the server (see fig. 18.14), select the modem to configure and click Configure to open the Configure Port Usage dialog.

Fig. 18.14 The Remote Access Setup dialog with a single modem installed.

2. In most cases, the default Port Usage option, Receive Calls Only, is satisfactory for a RAS server (see fig. 18.15). If you want to test your modem by dialing out, select the Dial Out and Receive Calls option. Click OK to close the dialog.

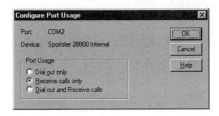

Fig. 18.15 Configuring the usage of the COM port on which the selected modem is installed.

IV

WANs and the Internet

3. Click Network in the Remote Access Setup dialog to open the Network Configuration dialog for the selected modem. By default, RAS supports each of the basic networking protocols (NetBEUI, TCP/IP, and IPX) installed on your server. If you don't use the modem for dial-out, the Dial Out Protocols check boxes are disabled (see fig. 18.16). To provide secure transmission of passwords, accept the default Require Microsoft Encrypted Authentication option if all your clients run Windows and support MS-CHAP (Microsoft Challenge Handshake Authentication Protocol) authentication; otherwise, select Require Encrypted Authentication. You also can specify that data be secured with the RSA Data Security RC4 encryption algorithm by marking the Require Data Encryption check box. If you're installing an ISDN adapter that supports bonding of ISDN B-channels, mark the Enable Multilink check box.

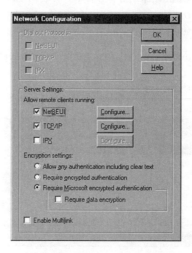

Fig. 18.16 Setting allowable network protocols, encryption, and multilink options in the Network Configuration dialog.

4. To configure NetBEUI services, click the Configure button next to the NetBEUI check box to open the RAS Server NetBEUI Configuration dialog. The default option is to allow dial-in clients to connect to the Entire Network (see fig. 18.17). Click OK to close the dialog.

Fig. 18.17 Setting the extent of network access for the NetBEUI protocol.

5. To configure TCP/IP services, click the adjacent Configure button to open the RAS Server TCP/IP Configuration dialog. Most RAS clients are configured to obtain a temporary TCP/IP address from the server. If you have DHCP (Dynamic Host Configuration Protocol) installed, select the Use DHCP to Assign Remote TCP/IP Client Addresses option. If you haven't installed DHCP, select the Use Static Address Pool option and specify beginning and ending addresses that provide a sufficient number of addresses to support the maximum number of inbound connections to the server plus a connection for the server itself (see fig. 18.18). The server occupies the first address—131.254.7.10 in figure 18.18. The rest of the address range, 13.254.7.11 through 131.254.7.20, provides for a maximum of 10 simultaneously connected RAS/DUN clients.

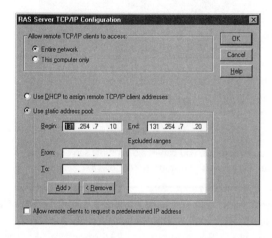

Fig. 18.18 Setting options for the TCP/IP protocol and assigning a static pool of TCP/IP addresses for RAS clients.

> **Caution**
>
> Marking the Allow Remote Clients to Request a Predetermined IP Address check box requires that you specify a fixed TCP/IP address for clients' dial-up adapters. Doing so prevents the client from connecting to ISPs, such as The Microsoft Network, that assign temporary TCP/IP addresses to connected users.

6. Click OK to close the RAS Server TCP/IP Configuration dialog, click OK to close the Network Configuration dialog, and then click Continue in the Remote Access Setup dialog to install bindings for RAS services (see fig. 18.19, top). If you don't have DHCP installed, you receive the Error – Unattended Setup message box shown in figure 18.19 (middle); click No to continue. When the binding process is complete, the Network Settings Change message box appears (see fig. 18.19, bottom). Click Yes to restart Windows NT Server with RAS operational.

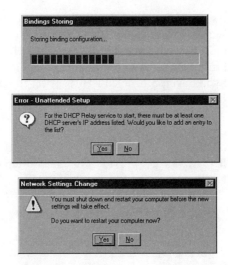

Fig. 18.19 RAS binding progress (top), a message received if DHCP isn't running (middle), and the message indicating the binding process is complete (bottom).

> **Note**
>
> If you're installing multiple modems, you can avoid multiple server restarts by setting up all the modems, and then shutting down and restarting Windows NT Server.

Granting Client Access with the Remote Access Admin Application

After you set up RAS for DUN, you use the Remote Access Admin application to specify the users who can connect via RAS and control RAS operation. Follow these steps to enable clients to connect to your RAS server:

1. From the Start menu choose Programs, Administrative Tools, and Remote Access Admin to open the Remote Access Admin application, which connects to all RAS servers in your domain. Figure 18.20 shows the OAKLEAF domain with the OAKLEAF0 RAS server set up in the preceding section.

> **Note**
>
> If you have a large number of services, such as the entire BackOffice suite, running on your RAS server, it might take up to a few minutes after rebooting for RAS to start.

2. From the Users menu choose Permissions to open the Remote Access Permissions dialog. Select a user in the Users list, which includes all domain and local users, and mark the check box to grant the user dial-in permission (see fig. 18.21). Alternatively, you can click the Grant All button to grant permission to all users, and then remove the permission from specific users, such as Guest. If you want to enable call-back for security or telco billing purposes, select the Set By Caller or Preset To option. If you select Set By Caller, a dialog appears when the client logs on,

requesting a call-back number. If you select Preset To, type the client's telephone number (with area code) in the text box. You can add parentheses, hyphens, and spaces to make the entry more legible; the dialer ignores punctuation and white space.

3. Click OK to close the dialog. Before you can test the RAS server, you must set up one or more DUN clients. Setting up Windows 95 and Windows NT clients for DUN is the subject of the following sections.

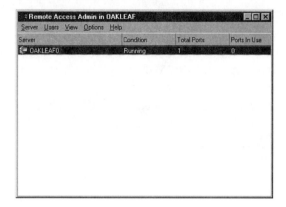

Fig. 18.20   The Remote Access Admin application's window, with a single RAS server in the default domain.

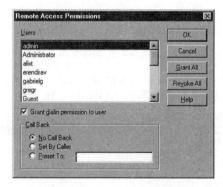

Fig. 18.21   Granting dial-in permission to individual Windows NT Server users.

Installing and Testing Dial-Up Networking on Clients

Setting up DUN for Windows 95 and Windows NT clients, with a few exceptions, is a relatively straightforward process. Windows 95 offers the advantage of supporting Plug and Play for simplified modem installation, plus hot-swapping of modems and other PC Cards for laptops. The following sections assume that the clients have a modem installed and operating, but no entries for dial-up networking.

> **Note**
>
> You install modems in Windows NT Workstation 4.0 by using the same method as that described earlier for Windows NT Server 4.0 in the "Installing Internal or External Modems" section, except that you specify the Dial-Out Only option in the Configure Port Usage dialog.

Windows 95 Clients

Setting up and testing DUN on Windows 95 clients with a modem installed and tested involves the following steps:

1. From the Start menu choose Programs, Accessories, and Dial-Up Networking to open the Dial-Up Networking window (see fig. 18.22). Double-click the Make New Connection entry to open the first Make New Connection dialog.

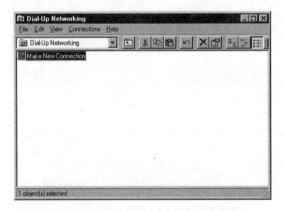

Fig. 18.22 Windows 95's Dial-Up Networking window with no DUN connections specified.

2. Type a name for the client connection in the text box and select the modem to use, if more than one modem is installed (see fig. 18.23).

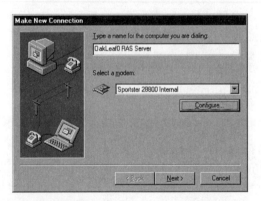

Fig. 18.23 Naming a connection and selecting a modem in the first Make New Connection dialog.

3. To gain a slight improvement in performance, click the Configure button to display the *Modem_Name* Properties sheet, and then display the Connection page (see fig. 18.24). Click Port Settings to open the Advanced Port Settings dialog, and set the Receive Buffer slider to High (see fig. 18.25). Click OK twice to close the dialog and the *Modem_Name* Properties sheet.

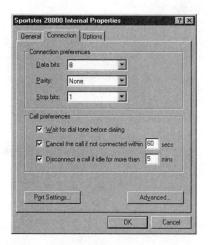

Fig. 18.24 The property sheet for a specific modem.

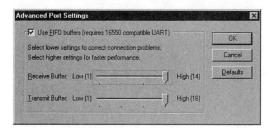

Fig. 18.25 Setting the Receive Buffer to maximum capacity to improve inbound data performance.

4. Click Next to display the second Make New Connection dialog. Type the area code and telephone number of the RAS server's modem, and select the country code, if necessary (see fig. 18.26). If the RAS server has multiple analog modems or ISDN adapters in a hunt group, use the first number of the hunt group.

5. Click Next to display the last Make New Connection dialog to confirm the connection name (see fig. 18.27). Click Finish to add the connection to the Dial-Up Networking list.

IV

WANs and the Internet

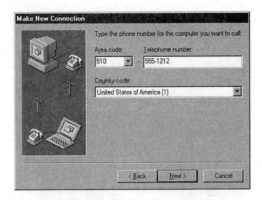

Fig. 18.26 Entering the dialing parameters.

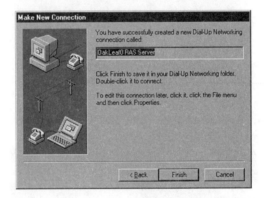

Fig. 18.27 The last step in the Make New Connection sequence for Windows 95.

6. Right-click the new entry in the Dial-Up Networking list and choose Properties from the popup menu to display the *ConnectionName* Properties sheet. Click the Server Types button to display the Server Types dialog. Accept the default PPP: Windows 95, Windows NT 3.5, Internet entry in the Type of Dial-Up Server drop-down list. Mark all Advanced Options check boxes, and clear the Allowed Network Protocols check box for any protocol not supported by the server (see fig. 18.28).

7. Click the TCP/IP Settings button to display the TCP/IP Settings dialog. Make sure that the Server Assigned IP Address and Server Assigned Name Server Address options are selected. (Specifying a TCP/IP address or a name server prevents connection, unless the RAS server is specifically set up to accommodate these client settings.) The Use IP Header Compression and Use Default Gateway on Remote Computer check boxes are marked by default (see fig. 18.29).

8. Click OK to close the TCP/IP Settings dialog, click OK to close the Server Types dialog, and then click OK again to close the *ConnectionName* Properties sheet.

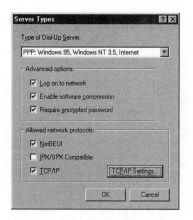

Fig. 18.28 Setting additional connection properties in the Server Types dialog.

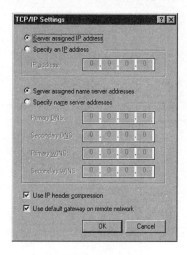

Fig. 18.29 Specifying conventional TCP/IP settings for DUN.

9. If you must specify special dialing parameters, such as dialing 9 for an outside line, double-click the connection entry in the Dial-Up Networking window to display the Connect To dialog (see fig. 18.30). Click the Dial Properties button to open the Dialing Properties sheet (see fig. 18.31). Make any necessary changes and click OK to return to the Connect To dialog.

> **Note**
>
> If you're setting up a client that's connected to the network, it's a good idea to log off the network at this point. Although you can maintain a simultaneous network and RAS connection using the same account, testing RAS with only a dial-up connection is a more foolproof process.

Fig. 18.30   The Connect To dialog with the setting specified in the Make New Connection sequence.

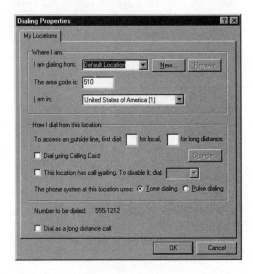

Fig. 18.31   Setting special dialing parameters for the RAS connection.

   10. Type your user name, if necessary, and password in the Connect To dialog. The Save Password check box is disabled when the client isn't logged on to the network. Click Connect to start the DUN process. A series of windows displays the connection progress (see fig. 18.32). The first time you make a connection, the standard Windows 95 network logon dialog appears, and you must enter your password for verification.

   11. Click the Details button of the Connected to *ConnectionName* window to show the protocol(s) in use (see fig. 18.33).

Fig. 18.32 The sequence of dialogs during the RAS logon process.

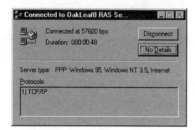

Fig. 18.33 Displaying network protocol(s) in use in the detailed version of the Connect To window.

12. Launch Network Neighborhood, and then expand the display of shares for the server to which you're connected (see fig. 18.34).

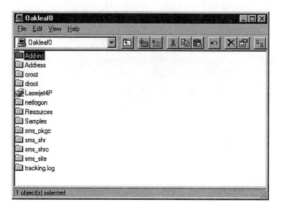

Fig. 18.34 Using Network Neighborhood to display DUN shares on the OAKLEAF0 server.

13. To terminate the connection, click the Disconnect button in the Connected to *ConnectionName* window.

> **Note**
>
> The notorious "could not negotiate a compatible set of protocols" Dial-Up Networking message (see fig. 18.35) indicates a problem with your Windows 95 networking protocol(s). If you've selected only NetBEUI as your protocol and the client is connected to the server on the network, two attempts to register the same NetBEUI computer name creates the problem. This message also appears on a relatively small percentage of Windows 95 clients that attempt to connect with TCP/IP. Although a client with this problem can't connect to a Windows NT 4.0 RAS server, it likely can connect via TCP/IP to a Window NT 3.5+ RAS server. The only currently known solution to this problem is to remove all the network protocols on the client, reboot the client, and then reinstall the protocols from scratch with the Windows 95 distribution CD-ROM.

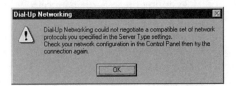

Fig. 18.35   The message that indicates a problem with Windows 95's currently installed networking protocols.

Windows NT Clients

Installation and operation of Dial-Up Networking on a Windows NT 4.0 client varies significantly from Windows 95's approach. The following steps describe how to install the RAS software from the Windows NT 4.0 distribution CD-ROM, and then set up and test Windows NT 4.0 DUN:

1. From the Start menu choose Programs, Accessories, and Dial-Up Networking. The Dial-Up Networking dialog indicates that DUN isn't installed (see fig. 18.36). Click the Install button.

Fig. 18.36   The dialog indicating that Windows NT 4.0 Dial-Up Networking hasn't been installed.

2. The Files Needed dialog vaguely indicates that Some files on (Unknown) are needed (see fig. 18.37) if you didn't specify RAS when you installed Windows NT 4.0. If you previously installed the files, skip to step 4.

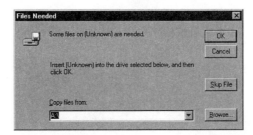

Fig. 18.37 The dialog that indicates you need to install RAS files from the distribution CD-ROM or a network installation share.

3. Click Browse and specify the \I386 (or other processor) folder of the distribution CD-ROM. The file needed is Rascfg.dl_ (see fig. 18.38). Click Open to return to the Files Needed dialog (see fig. 18.39). Click OK to install the RAS files.

Fig. 18.38 Specifying the \I386 folder of the distribution CD-ROM for RAS installation.

Fig. 18.39 The Files Needed dialog with the path to the files on the CD-ROM.

4. The Add RAS Device dialog has a list of RAS Capable Devices (see fig. 18.40). If you have only one modem installed, accept the default; otherwise, choose the modem to use with RAS/DUN. Click OK to continue.

Fig. 18.40   Selecting a RAS-capable modem.

   5. In the Configure Port Usage dialog, select the Dial Out Only option unless you
   want to configure the client as a RAS server (see fig. 18.41). Windows NT Workstation 4.0 supports a single RAS/DUN connection, similar to the RAS server feature
   installed by the Windows 95 Plus! pack. Click OK to continue.

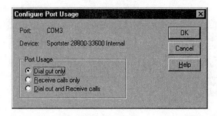

Fig. 18.41   Selecting the RAS operating mode(s) in the Configure Port Usage dialog.

   6. The Dial-Up Networking message box indicates that The phonebook is empty (see
   fig. 18.42). Windows NT 4.0 uses a phonebook metaphor, rather than Windows
   95's Dial-Up Connection, for selecting a RAS/DUN connection. Click OK to launch
   the New Phonebook Entry Wizard.

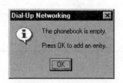

Fig. 18.42   The message that appears when you haven't added an entry to the DUN phonebook.

   7. Type the name of the RAS connection in the Name the New Phonebook Entry text
   box (see fig. 18.43). Click Next to continue.

   8. The Server dialog offers connection options for the Internet, plain (clear) text passwords, and non-Windows NT RAS servers (see fig. 18.44). None of these options
   apply when using Windows NT Server 4.0 DUN, so click Next to open the Phone
   Number dialog.

   9. You can type the phone number directly in the text box (see fig. 18.45), or mark
   the Use Telephony Dialing Properties check box to make the extended dialing parameters appear. Select the Country Code and Area Code, and type the Phone
   Number for the connection (see fig. 18.46).

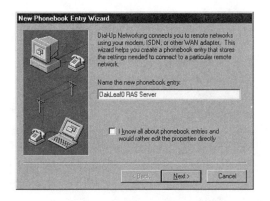

Fig. 18.43 Naming a new RAS connection in the first New Phonebook Entry Wizard dialog.

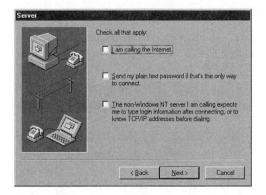

Fig. 18.44 Choosing options for connecting to the Internet, with unencrypted passwords, and to RAS servers other than Windows NT.

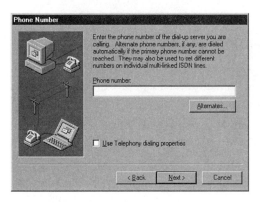

Fig. 18.45 The default version of the Phone Number dialog.

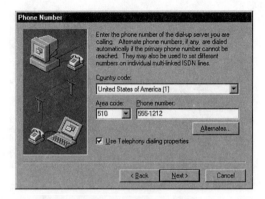

Fig. 18.46 The TAPI version of the Phone Number dialog.

10. If you want to add alternate numbers to dial, in case the main number is busy, click Alternates to display the Phone Numbers dialog (see fig. 18.47). To add another number, type it in the New Phone Number text box and click the Add button. Click OK to close the dialog.

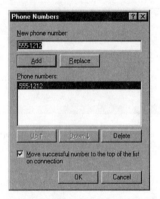

Fig. 18.47 Displaying current RAS server phone numbers.

11. In the final New Phonebook Entry Wizard dialog, click Finish to add the entry to the phonebook and open the Dial-Up Networking dialog with the first phonebook entry selected (see fig. 18.48).

12. Click Dial to start the RAS connection. A series of dialogs monitors the connection progress (see fig. 18.49).

13. If the client you're testing is directly connected to the network and you use NetBEUI as one of your network and RAS protocols, you receive the error message shown in figure 18.50. Click Accept to accept a connection via TCP/IP.

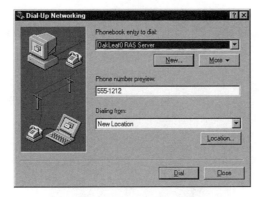

Fig. 18.48 The DUN phonebook entry for dialing a Windows NT 4.0 RAS server.

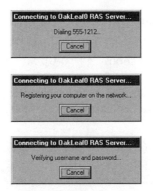

Fig. 18.49 Dialogs that monitor the progress of your DUN connection.

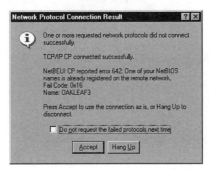

Fig. 18.50 The error message that occurs if you're logged on to the network and attempt a RAS connection with NetBEUI protocol.

14. When the connection succeeds, the Connection Complete dialog appears (see fig. 18.51). After making the first connection, mark the Do Not Display This Message Again check box, and then click OK.

Fig. 18.51 The final step in completing the first DUN connection.

15. You can monitor the status of the connection by right-clicking the DUN icon at the right of the taskbar and choosing Dial-Up Monitor to open the Dial-Up Networking Monitor property sheet (see fig. 18.52). Two of the more interesting statistics of the Status page are the Compression In and Compression Out percentages, which indicate the efficiency of hardware compression.

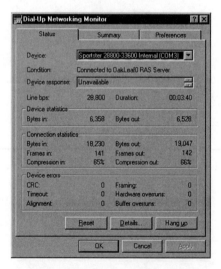

Fig. 18.52 Using the Dial-Up Networking Monitor tool to check the performance of the DUN connection.

16. To terminate the connection, right-click the DUN icon of the task bar and choose Hang Up, and then click Yes when requested to confirm the disconnect.

You also can start DUN by double-clicking the Dial-Up Networking icon in My Computer (see fig. 18.53).

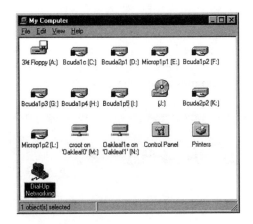

Fig. 18.53 Starting Dial-Up Networking from My Computer.

Monitoring Connections with Remote Access Admin

In addition to enabling RAS for users, described earlier in the section "Granting Client Access with the Remote Access Admin Application," Remote Access Admin also lets you supervise RAS connections to the server. To use Remote Access Admin to monitor RAS connections, follow these steps:

1. Launch Remote Access Admin, if necessary. Remote Access Admin's window displays all the servers in the domain set up as remote access servers, and the number of active connections of each (see fig. 18.54).

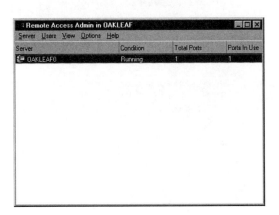

Fig. 18.54 Remote Access Admin displaying a single RAS server with one connected user.

2. Double-click an active server entry in the list to display the Communication Ports dialog. An entry for each COM port of the server set up for RAS appears in the list, along with the user name and the time the connection started (see fig. 18.55). You can disconnect the user or, if messaging service is enabled on both ends of the connection, send a popup message to the user.

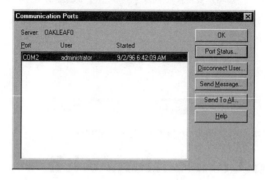

Fig. 18.55 Displaying the entry for the RAS server's COM port.

3. Click Port Status to display the Port Status dialog (see fig. 18.56). The Port Status dialog is similar to the Status page of the Dial-Up Networking Monitor property sheet for an outbound RAS connection (refer to fig. 18.52). If the server has more than one COM port assigned to RAS, you can select the port from the drop-down Port list.

Fig. 18.56 The Port Status dialog for a TCP/IP RAS connection immediately after user logon.

> **Note**
>
> If you haven't enabled dial-out RAS on the server, the Dial-Up Networking icon doesn't appear in the taskbar. In this case, you launch Dial-Up Networking Monitor from the Dial-Up Networking tool of Control Panel.

Using the Point-to-Point Tunneling Protocol

Microsoft's Point-to-Point Tunneling Protocol (PPTP) is an encryption system that provides secure communication between computers over the public Internet. Microsoft has submitted PPTP to the Internet Engineering Task Force (IETF) for incorporation into the IP-Sec (Secure IP) service standard. PPTP uses MS-CHAP for authentication and allows NetBEUI and IPX protocols to "piggyback" on TCP/IP packets.

> **Note**
>
> When this book was written, PPTP's status was that of a proprietary Microsoft protocol available only in Windows NT Server and Workstation 4.0. Microsoft promised that PPTP would be available for Windows 95 and Windows 3.1+ by the end of 1996. Microsoft's brief white paper, "Virtual Private Networking Using the Point-to-Point Tunneling Protocol (PPTP)," is available at **http:// www.microsoft.com/ntserver/communications/pptp.htm**, which provides links to PPTP FAQs (Frequently Asked Questions) and the Internet Draft Standard for PPTP.

Using the Internet to provide remote access services for mobile users and telecommuters minimizes time-based telecommunications costs by providing network access through a local call to an ISP. VPNs created with PPTP also can replace costly telco-leased lines. PPTP is especially cost-effective for international connections to remote sites and overseas workers.

Another advantage of PPTP is that it eliminates the banks of modems needed to service multiple simultaneous RAS connections. You create a multihomed server by adding another network card to the server, enabling PPTP on the added card, and connecting the card to a PPTP router. The PPTP router can share existing T-1 or ISDN line(s) to the ISP.

You enable PPTP on Windows NT 4.0 clients and servers by marking the Enable PPTP Filtering check box on the Advanced IP Addressing dialog (see fig. 18.57), which you access from the IP Address page of the TCP/IP Properties sheet. The initial incarnation of PPTP is based on server-to-server connections to create virtual WANs. Windows NT Server 4.0's built-in routing capabilities are useful for isolating PPTP traffic from conventional TCP/IP traffic on the LAN. You can also use PPTP for dial-up networking over POTS or ISDN lines. A POTS or ISDN line is generally regarded as a secure channel, but such lines aren't immune from physical wiretaps or interception of a wireless segment of the connection. Windows NT Server 4.0's Network.wri file in your \Winnt folder provides additional guidelines for dial-up networking with PPTP in the "Dial-Up Networking Notes" section.

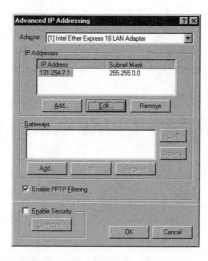

Fig. 18.57 Enabling PPTP filtering for a specified network adapter.

To implement PPTP, all participants in the communication path must have routers equipped to handle PPTP. Networking hardware suppliers, including Ascend, U.S. Robotics, and 3Com, were beta-testing PPTP in the fall of 1996 and should have software upgrades available for their remote-access products by the end of 1996. The extent to which ISPs upgrade their gateways and routers for PPTP depends on the initial demand by Windows NT 4.0 users.

From Here...

This chapter described the architecture of various types of remote access systems, ranging from simple analog modems to high-end RAS routers that combine multiple analog modems and ISDN adapters. Setting up Windows NT Server 4.0 as a RAS server with an internal or external modem, and configuring Windows 95 and Windows NT 4.0 RAS clients also was covered. The chapter concluded with a brief description of PPTP and its use for creating virtual private networks using the Internet as a backbone.

The following chapters include information related to the topics covered in this chapter:

- Chapter 4, "Choosing Network Protocols," explains how to select one or more of the three principal networking protocols supported by Windows NT based on your network configuration.

- Chapter 17, "Integrating Windows NT with Heterogeneous Networks," describes how to set up DHCP services for assigning TCP/IP addresses to DUN clients.

- Chapter 19, "Setting Up the Internet Information Server," describes the basics of ISDN and includes other useful information relating to telco connections between LANs and ISPs.

Chapter 19

Setting Up the Internet Information Server

The explosive growth of the Internet in the mid-1990s creates an opportunity as well as a challenge for Windows NT network administrators. Organizations that for years have relied on Novell NetWare servers now are adopting Windows NT Server to create private intranets and to connect to the public Internet. A recent market study conducted by Cognitive Communications and reported in the August 5, 1996, issue of *Newsbytes* indicates that 85 percent of the firms surveyed either have set up or are planning to implement an organization-wide intranet. The use of the Internet as a marketing tool for a wide range of products and services is increasing at a furious pace. Substituting an Internet connection for 800-number dial-up connections for network access by mobile employees can save a substantial part of a firm's monthly telephone charges.

This chapter provides an introduction to Microsoft's Internet product line, the linchpin of which is Internet Information Server (IIS) 2.0, a component of Windows NT Server 4.0. Its primary topics are planning for Internet services, connecting to an Internet service provider, how IIS services work, and installing IIS 2.0. IIS HTTP (World Wide Web), FTP (File Transfer Protocol), and Gopher services are fully integrated with Windows NT Server 4.0 and, if installed, Microsoft SQL Server 6.5. Thus, installation and startup of IIS 2.0 is a relatively simple process, especially for a private intranet. Planning and connectivity issues require far more attention than simply starting up IIS; thus, much of this chapter is devoted to these two subjects.

Viewing Microsoft's Internet Product Line

Microsoft is pursuing an aggressive strategy to gain the position of premier provider of Internet operating systems, applications, and development tools. Microsoft is betting heavily on the company's ability to succeed in a field that historically has been dominated by UNIX servers and Netscape browsers. Integrating a no-charge copy of Internet Information Server (IIS) 2.0 with

In this chapter, you learn how to

- Set up Internet Information Server 2.0 for Web publishing, either on the Internet or for a private intranet

- Bring an FTP server online to allow users to download files

- Understand Internet Information Server 2.0's security matrix

- Provide your users a variety of content with a single browser

Windows NT 4.0 is certain to accelerate the adoption of Windows NT and IIS as the most popular Internet server platform. Microsoft's dominance of the client-side operating system market, combined with free distribution of its Internet Explorer 3.0 browser, portends trying times for Netscape and its Navigator product line.

On December 7, 1995, Microsoft jumped headlong into the Internet arena and quickly provided the software that network administrators and Webmasters need, ranging from developer tools to client-side components. If a piece of its Internet software puzzle is missing, Microsoft either licenses the needed technology or acquires the firm that developed it. Microsoft intends this comprehensive (and acquisitive) approach to put the company in the enviable position of providing an all-around, one-stop solution for participants in what Bill Gates calls the "Internet gold rush."

Microsoft's Internet product offerings, as of mid-1996, include the following browsers, content authoring tools, and servers:

- *Internet Explorer 3.0*, a browser that includes native support for HTTP, FTP, and Gopher protocols, and provides extensibility through Microsoft's ActiveX technology

- *FrontPage 1.1*, Microsoft's high-end Web site management tool, which provides WYSIWYG Web page content editing and the server extensions required to deliver the content

- *Internet Assistant for Word*, which converts documents between the Word .DOC and HTML environments, and also serves as a rudimentary Web browser

- *Internet Assistant for Excel*, to save your Excel worksheets as HTML pages, complete with formatting and tables

- *Internet Assistant for PowerPoint,* which lets you save PowerPoint presentations for easy viewing on the Web

- *Internet Assistant for Access*, to provide a means of exporting information in Access databases to Web pages

- *Internet Information Server 2.0*, the core component of the Microsoft Internet strategy, the suite of services that provide the HTTP, FTP, Gopher server capability, plus other Internet and intranet support

- *Search Server*, code-named Tripoli, which indexes documents in HTML, Word, and other common formats to provide a local search service for users

- *Proxy Server*—commonly known by its code name, *Catapult*—which is a firewall that gives your users desktop access to the Internet while maintaining network security

- *Merchant Services,* a suite of applications for conducting Web-based commerce, including Secure Electronic Transactions (SET), electronic storefronts, and several other tools for retailing operations

- *Normandy,* the code name for the extensions to Merchant Services that create a "Service Provider in a Box" software suite based on Microsoft's technology developed for The Microsoft Network

Microsoft also supplies the following APIs and development tools for programmers of the company's Internet client and server platforms:

- *ActiveX controls* (formerly OLE Controls), for enhancing the appearance and automating the behavior of Web pages

- *Internet Server API* (ISAPI) applications and filters, to extend the server software by creating routines that can be called from those accessing your site in order to complete database or other processing functions

- *Internet Database Connector* (IDC), an ISAPI extension, to provide dynamic access from special Web pages to ODBC data sources

- *ActiveX Scripting,* also called Visual Basic Script (VBS), for manipulating Web pages with a Visual Basic-like programming language

- *ActiveX Server Scripting,* code-named *Denali,* which brings VBS to Internet Information Server for back-end application development

- *Virtual Reality Markup Language* (VRML) extensions, to provide users with an interactive 3-D experience

- *Java and JavaScript* support, by means of ActiveX technology, and a fast just-in-time (JIT) compiler to speed execution of Java applets, plus a Java development environment, Visual J++

Tip

What's remarkable about the items in the two preceding lists is that most of the products described are available at no charge, except for the cost of downloading time. For a list of products available from the Microsoft Web site, visit the Microsoft Free Product Downloads page at **http://www.microsoft.com/msdownload/**.

Planning Your Site

It's important to create a comprehensive plan before you start bringing up your site. The plan should include the services you intend to offer, and how you plan to provide user access to those services. Following are the issues to resolve before you start the installation of IIS:

- If you want to provide inbound and/or outbound Internet connectivity, what type of telecommunications link should you use?

- What services are needed? World Wide Web services are a given, but you might also want to provide FTP access and Gopher service.

■ Does the information you offer from the Web site need to be accessible from FTP and Gopher services?

■ What types of security should you implement? Security means more than "everyone should have a password." Decide—down to the folder level, at a minimum—groups that have resource access and groups barred from access.

■ Do you want to provide Internet e-mail services from the same server running IIS?

■ Who's responsible for creating the design of and content for your site, as well as routine maintenance of the site? Larger organizations usually use independent Web design firms to establish the graphic and navigational features of the site, and use a full-time Webmaster to maintain the site.

> **Note**
>
> The Microsoft SiteBuilder Workshop at **http://microsoft.com/workshop/** provides a wide range of information and software for developing Web sites, including sections on planning and production, as well as site administration.

■ Do you intend to provide custom Web pages created from database information? If your data source is Microsoft SQL Server, you must have the SQL Server Internet Connector license for an Internet server or, if you don't have the required client licenses, for an intranet installation.

■ What type of server audit logging, if any, do you want to use? If you use SQL Server 6.x to store audit logs, you also must have the required server and connection licenses.

> **Note**
>
> Microsoft's BackOffice Family Licensing and Pricing page at **http://www.microsoft.com/ BackOffice/det4.htm** provides details on Microsoft SQL Server licensing policies.

The rest of this chapter helps you determine the answers to the first five of these questions, with emphasis on getting started with Internet Information Server 2.0. Chapter 20, "Administering Intranet and World Wide Web Sites," covers logging, database connectivity, and content creation for Web sites.

Connecting to the Internet

The first issue to settle is how you connect to the Internet. Even if you intend to establish only an intranet, you might want to consider using the Internet to provide low-cost inbound access to your Web site for telecommuters and mobile employees. Your company's link to the Internet will be provided by an Internet service provider (ISP). The ISP assigns your site a domain name (*companyname*.com) and an IP address, which is registered with InterNIC, an organization responsible for assuring that all Internet sites have globally unique domain names. The selection of an ISP is a critical step in setting up your Web site.

> **Note**
>
> If you want to provide public access to your Web site and private dial-up networking via the Internet, you need a firewall to maintain network privacy. A firewall also is necessary to provide security if your Web server is connected to your organization's LAN. Microsoft offers its Proxy Server (code-named *Catapult*) as a software firewall for providing network users safe access to the Internet; you also can buy third-party hardware firewalls. Visit **http://www.microsoft.com/ infoserv/catapult/** for more information on the Proxy Server.

Choosing an Internet Service Provider

Choosing an ISP used to be easy, because there were very few. As the popularity of the Internet has grown, so too has the number of businesses vying for your connectivity dollars. Some of the names will be familiar: MCI, Sprint, GTE, and so forth. Your local phone system carrier may have joined the game as well. Other ISPs are literally run out of an enterprising person's basement.

Some of the important points to consider while choosing an ISP include the following:

- *Price.* Pricing for Internet services is becoming less of an issue. Increasing competition continues to narrow the gap between the low and high ends of the ISP price spectrum.

- *Type of connections offered.* Not all ISPs provide all the different services that you may need. Make sure that you have a complete understanding of what you need and use this as a critical determining factor in selecting the ISP you use.

- *Capacity.* Be sure to ask what capacity connection your ISP has to the Internet backbone. If the ISP has a 56kbps connection and hundreds of users, response time may not be acceptable during times of peak loads. Most ISPs have at least a T-1 Internet connection.

- *Fault tolerance.* High-end providers have multiple T-1 or other connections to the Internet backbone. If one circuit fails, another takes over to provide connectivity.

- *Service.* What kind of service agreement is standard for a particular company? Does the ISP guarantee a minimum bandwidth or minimum downtime? Does the ISP have 24-hours-a-day, 7-days-a-week coverage by support staff?

- *Reputation.* References are desirable when entering into an agreement for a service on which your business will depend.

- *Stability.* Small ISPs may offer customized services, but new competition from long-distance carriers and regional telephone companies makes the long-term viability of small ISPs questionable.

- *Other services.* An ISP should be able to provide domain name services, electronic mail, and Usenet news services, if you need them. Your ISP should also be able to help you secure IP addresses for your internal network and register your domain name.

Understanding Connection Types

Just as important as your choice of an ISP is the technology you use to make the Internet connection. Table 19.1 lists the more common telecommunications technologies and their capacities in raw bits per second, approximate number of users supported, approximate monthly cost, and interface type.

Table 19.1	The Different Types of Available Connections to the Internet			
Connection Type	**Data Rate**	**Simultaneous Users**	**Approximate Monthly Cost**	**Local-Loop Interface**
Dial-up	28.8kbps	1-2	$40-100	2 wire twisted pair
56k	56kbps	10-20	$300-800	2 or 4 wire twisted pair
ISDN	144kbps	10-40	$60-250	2 wire twisted pair
Frame Relay	Up to 1.544mbps	5-250	$200-1,000	2 or 4 wire twisted pair or fiber
T-1	1.544mbps	50-250	$100-3,000	4 wire twisted pair or fiber
T-3	44.736mbps	250-4,000	$50,000-150,000	Fiber or coax

Table 19.1 shows that you can approach getting connected to the Internet in many different ways. Your decision must be based primarily on anticipated traffic, which services are available from your ISP, and your local telephone carrier's ability to provide the service to your site. The costs shown in table 19.1 are the approximate combined monthly rates of ISP and local carrier charges. These costs don't include hook-up fees or the necessary hardware, such as CSU/DSUs (Channel Service Unit/Data Service Unit) and routers. Of course, the costs in your area may vary, but table 19.1 should give you a good idea of what expenses to expect.

Selecting a Dial-Up Access Method. The most familiar and popular way to gain access to the Internet is simply a modem and ordinary voice line to dial into an ISP. This is an inexpensive and relatively pain-free method for a few users to gain Internet access. Typically, each computer has its own modem and a dedicated POTS (plain old telephone service) line; access is available only to the user of that computer. The problem with individual Internet access is the cost of installing dedicated lines and the monthly charge for them.

It's possible, using Windows NT Remote Access Server or a hardware router, to provide multiuser access with a single POTS line. The performance of this type of connection is acceptable for only a few simultaneous users. More than about two simultaneous users slows response to an unacceptable level. Although dial-up access may be sufficient for a few internal users occasionally "surfing the Net," it's unlikely that external customers would visit your Web site if a 28.8kbps modem is your primary means of connection.

> **Note**
>
> Most modem manufacturers tout compatibility with various hardware compression technologies. One manufacturer claims an 8:1 compression ratio, turning its 28.8kbps modem into a 230.4kbps speedster. Although this compression is possible using certain types of text data, don't count on throughput being anything near this value for real-life information. Web site content often is heavily graphical in nature. Graphic files are particularly difficult to compress; in the case of JPEG and GIF files, compression has already taken place, and little or no additional hardware compression is likely.

Selecting a 56kbps Connection. If you plan to host a Web server on your local premises and/or have several users that need to access the Internet, a dedicated 56kbps connection is a good place to start. Your carrier may call the 56kbps connection 56k, DDS, Digital Data Service, Dataphone Digital Service, or some other variation on the same theme. The 56kbps digital circuits have been around for a long time and were the first commonly available high-speed technology to move information between remote sites. Although 56kbps communication doesn't seem all that fast by today's standards, users considered it a blistering data rate in the days when 300- and 1,200-baud modems were the standard.

In telecommunications terminology, a 56kbps circuit is known as a DS0 (pronounced "dee-ess-zero") circuit. A DS0 circuit is one of the basic building blocks used by telecommunications companies. A fully digital circuit is being used, so no digital-to-analog conversion is necessary and, accordingly, many problems inherent in analog circuits and modems—primarily noise—are removed from the equation.

The additional bandwidth and reliability don't come free. The cost of a 56kbps circuit often is an order of magnitude higher than that of a voice circuit. You also need more hardware to set up the link; a router and CSU/DSU is required at each end of the circuit. Figure 19.1 shows the physical configuration of using a 56kbps circuit to connect your LAN to the Internet through an ISP.

In addition to a router to direct the TCP/IP traffic, you need a CSU/DSU to connect to your carrier's circuit. The CSU is used to terminate the digital circuit in a method acceptable to the phone company. The CSU usually has LEDs on the front of the unit to indicate the status of the link and for loopback testing. The DSU, located between the CSU and your router, is responsible for converting the electrical signal from your router into a signal acceptable by your CSU.

> **Note**
>
> The disadvantage of using 56kbps lines lies in their point-to-point operation. Although this obviously isn't a problem if you have a single site, the setup and equipment expenses can become significant if you're connecting multiple sites. If you have several sites to connect, you should investigate frame-relay services.

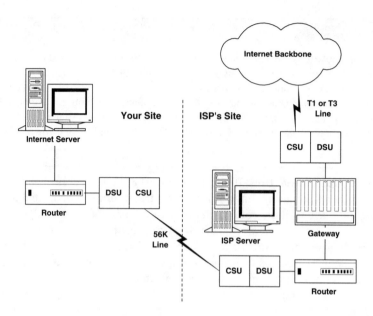

Fig. 19.1   A typical configuration for a dedicated 56kbps circuit to an ISP that connects to the Internet.

Selecting an ISDN Connection. Although your telephone cable may struggle with a 28.8kbps analog modem connection, it probably can carry a 144kbps digital ISDN signal. ISDN (Integrated Services Digital Network) has been hailed as the ideal service for telecommuters and small businesses. Due to real and imagined political and technological problems, however, the ISDN promise only recently has become a reality in North America. (ISDN has been widely available in Europe for many years.) If anything, ISDN's recent North American popularity has proven that consumers and telecommuters were starved for its advanced capabilities.

The "Integrated" part of ISDN refers to the capability to handle voice and data simultaneously over the same twisted-pair cable that currently provides your voice or modem service. ISDN is a switched, point-to-point, connection-based system that's purely digital. ISDN's digital nature allows it to dial, handshake, and connect in only a second or two. The average modem can take nearly a minute to perform the same task.

The standard ISDN circuit is called BRI (Basic Rate Interface) service. BRI consists of two 64kbps data channels and one 16kbps signal channel. The 64kbps channels are called B, or bearer, channels. (In some locations, the B channels are 56.1kbps.) The 16kbps channel, called the D or data channel, is used for circuit signaling and management. BRI service is also referred to as 2B+D service. The two 64kbps channels can be used for voice or data in parallel or combination. You can use one channel for data and the other for voice, or both channels for data and voice. You can't make direct use of the D channel.

Through a technique called *bonding*, both B channels can be combined to form a single 128kbps data connection channel. The most popular type of bonding is called

Multi-Link PPP (Point-to-Point Protocol), or MLPPP. Currently, no standards for bonding exist, but industry groups are working on a standard. In some cases, you need the same brand of ISDN equipment on each end of the circuit to enable bonding.

Figure 19.2 shows the typical ISDN setup. The service termination point is called the NT-1 (Network Terminator, type 1). The NT-1 is provided by your carrier or, more commonly, is built into your ISDN equipment. The NT-1 terminates a single twisted-pair cable from the central office (called a *local loop,* or U interface), and converts the data on the local loop to an S/T interface. The T signal connects to an NT-2 network terminator, which is responsible for breaking the signal into its B and D channels, and connecting to non-ISDN devices, such as a voice telephone, through an optional terminal adapter (TA).

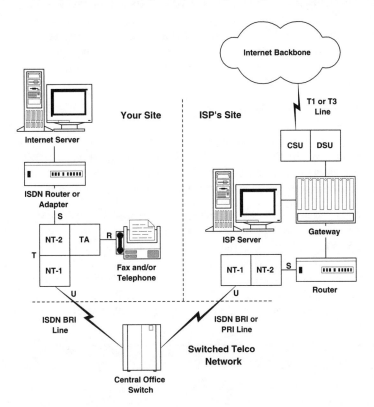

Fig. 19.2   The hardware components for an ISDN BRI connection to an ISP.

Typical ISDN equipment contains the NT-1, NT-2, and a TA, and is often referred to as an *ISDN adapter.* An ISDN adapter is roughly analogous to the CSU/DSU used by 56kbps connections. Your terminal equipment, such as your PC or your router, connects to external ISDN adapters, such as Motorola's BitSURFR Pro, with an RS-232 (serial port) connection. The ISDN adapter appears to Windows NT as a very fast modem. Internal ISDN adapters, such as the US Robotics Sportster 128K, also includes the NT-1 and NT-2 components.

> **Note**
>
> In addition to the R, S/T, and U ISDN interfaces is a V interface at the central office (CO) that connects the Line Termination (LT) function for the local loop to the Exchange Termination (ET) function for connecting the CO to other exchanges. The V interface usually resides in the CO switch.

An alternative to ISDN adapters that emulate analog modems is an ISDN router. All the major manufacturers of TCP/IP routers, such as Cisco Systems and Ascend Communications, produce ISDN routers. An ISDN router makes the connection between the U channel and your Ethernet LAN, usually with 10BaseT media. Some ISDN routers support dial-on-demand. If idle for a preset period of time, the line disconnects. When a packet needs to be forwarded over the ISDN link, the router reconnects to the specified ISDN telephone number and forwards the traffic. ISDN connects very quickly, so the user notices little or no delay. The cost saving from using a dial-on-demand configuration can be significant if your carrier charges for connect time.

Availability of ISDN service varies considerably. In many areas of the United States, ISDN's popularity has pushed its demand beyond the supply. You may have to wait several months for your carrier to provide you with service. Also, you may have to wait for ISDN service to be available in your area. Many smaller or rural municipalities don't have ISDN service. Carriers in many states realized the benefits of ISDN years ago and, like Pacific Bell in California, have built substantial infrastructure to handle the demand.

ISDN's cost varies just as much as its availability; monthly service charges range from $30 to $180 per month and may depend on usage. ISDN modems range in cost from about $300 to $500. Many carriers charge a substantial installation fee, especially if the customer's premises are a long distance from the central office. If timed usage charges apply and your site generates substantial traffic, ISDN can become more expensive than a dedicated 56kbps or T-1 circuit. ISDN, however, is well suited for providing Windows NT's Remote Access Service and dial-up networking to mobile users, as well as outbound connections to the Internet.

> **Note**
>
> If your Web server is hosted on the ISP's computer rather than on a server at your facility, an ISDN line is likely to be your most economical choice for managing the site. The speed of ISDN—roughly five times that of a 28.8kbps modem connection—greatly speeds the process of sending updates to the off-site server.

Selecting Frame Relay Connectivity. Currently, frame relay is a hot topic in the wide area networking industry, partly because a mid-1996 decision by the Federal Communications Commission requires carriers to publish tariffs for frame relay services.

(Previously, the price of frame relay service was negotiable.) *Frame relay* is a switch-based technology developed by the local telephone companies (telcos). Local exchange carriers (LECs) have developed a network of frame-relay switches. Any point in the frame-relay network can access any of the other frame-relay switches. A company with multiple locations can communicate across the frame-relay network, with each location having to maintain only a single WAN connection.

A frame-relay connection point is called an *access link*. Access links are 56kbps or T-1 interfaces. The maximum data rate at each access link is called the *port speed* and is equal to or less than the interface link. For example, you may have a 56kbps access link but only a 32kbps port speed. Customers with a T-1 access link might have a 128kbps, 512kbps, or 1.544mbps port speed. The primary advantage of frame relay is that you pay only for the bandwidth you need and the time you use that bandwidth.

> **Note**
>
> Routes across the frame-relay network are determined by a *permanent virtual circuit* (PVC). PVCs connect frame-relay devices, and a single access link can support multiple virtual circuits.

Your guaranteed bandwidth across a frame-relay network is called the *committed information rate* (CIR). The CIR is always less than the port speed and will be the biggest decision you make when ordering a frame-relay circuit. One highly promoted feature of frame relay is its capability to burst above the CIR. *Bursting* allows network traffic to take advantage of a period of lower activity in the frame-relay network to grab some extra bandwidth. The bursting capacity is available up to the port speed. However, the total bandwidth available within the network is finite, and each PVC is given a percentage based on its CIR.

Because the popularity of frame relay has grown, many carriers are finding their networks running at close to maximum throughput. Don't count on operating in burst mode very often. In fact, packets that go above the CIR are eligible to be discarded if the burst bandwidth isn't available at that particular instant. Needless to say, the delays caused by packets being discarded and the protocol recovery mechanism can result in long transmission delays and unhappy users.

One scenario for ISP connection is a T-1 access link with a 512kbps port speed and a 256kbps CIR. With this configuration, you always have at least 256kbps of throughput. Under ideal conditions, the circuit can temporarily burst up to 512kbps. If you determine that a bigger pipe is needed, you can increase the port speed and the CIR. Figure 19.3 shows an example configuration for a frame-relay installation.

Selecting Connections at T-1 Speeds and Above. T-1 connections are used by organizations with large numbers of employees accessing the Internet or large numbers of Internet users accessing their servers. T-1 connections are very similar in concept and functionality to 56kbps lines. The obvious difference between 56kbps and T-1 is a 24-fold increase in bandwidth. T-1 circuits have a data rate of 1.544mbps in a dedicated, point-to-point configuration.

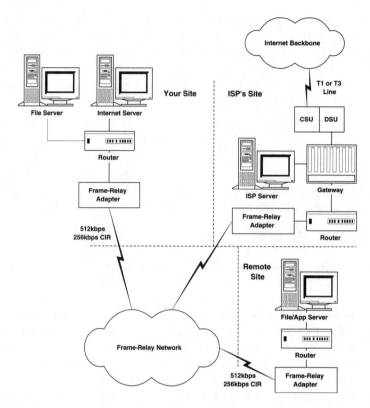

Fig. 19.3   Using frame relay to connect several sites to each other and to the Internet.

A T-1 circuit is another major building block for telecommunications networks. Also known as a DS1, a T-1 consists of 24 DS0s. Some carriers offer a variation on T-1, called Fractional T-1 (FT1). FT1 offers speeds from DS0 to DS1 usually in two, four, or six DS0 multiples. Fractional T-1 isn't always financially advantageous. For a slight increase in cost, you may be able to use a full T-1 circuit. Check with your carrier and ISP for price differentials.

Firms with truly huge bandwidth requirements (and very deep pockets) should investigate T-3 services. A T-3 service provides a data rate of 44.736mbps. T-3, also known as a DS3 circuit, is equivalent to 28 DS1s. Microsoft uses multiple T-3 circuits to support The Microsoft Network. If you're in the market for T-1 or higher speed circuits, plan on spending some time negotiating with your local carriers and ISP.

Name Resolution and the Domain Name System

Names on the Internet are critical to its ease of operation, and the system that ties all the names together is the Internet's Domain Name Services (DNS). DNS is a hierarchical naming system used for Internet navigation and within many organizations that use TCP/IP. Like the Windows Internet Naming Service (WINS), DNS maps readable (friendly) names, such as microsoft.com, to numeric IP addresses, such as 207.68.137.35 (the IP address of microsoft.com).

The Internet started as a simple network of a few systems. Each system was responsible for maintaining a hosts file, which mapped every system's name to its IP address. The drawbacks of maintaining a static hosts text database become apparent when considering a network of more than a few dozen systems. DNS was developed to overcome these limitations and to provide name services dynamically as the Internet grew and evolved. Although the original designers of DNS had no idea the Internet would grow to millions of systems internationally, the DNS system has, with a few enhancements along the way, scaled quite well.

The DNS name space is a tree. Domain names are nodes, and systems are leaves on the tree (see fig. 19.4). A fully qualified domain name is constructed by concatenating the domain names to the system name from left to right as you climb the tree. Each component is separated by a dot. The root domain is .com for most Web sites, although .org (organization), .gov (government), and country codes (.ca for Canada) also are common. The organization name (microsoft, corp, and company) in figure 19.4 is prepended to the root domain, as in microsoft.com, corp.com, and company.com, forming a fully qualified domain name that corresponds to a particular IP address. Association of a domain name with an IP address is called *name resolution*. Finally, a service prefix (typically www, ftp, or news) is added, as in www.microsoft.com. The http:// prefix used by Web browsers identifies the hypertext transport protocol for HTML. For e-mail, the service prefix typically is the person's e-mail alias, separated from the domain name with an ampersand, as in *anyone*@company.com.

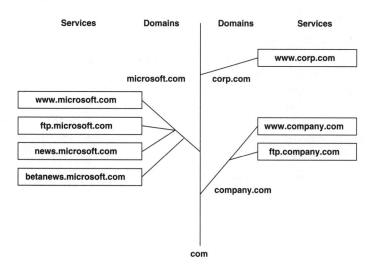

Fig. 19.4 Hierarchical view of the domain name system.

New to Windows NT 4.0 is a native DNS service with a graphical user interface. Previously, you had to buy third-party DNS packages or, more likely, DNS services were provided by UNIX systems on the network. Windows NT Server 4.0's DNS service can integrate with WINS (Windows Internet Name Service). You're likely to be using WINS with DHCP (Dynamic Host Configuration Protocol) to dynamically manage your IP addresses on your internal networks. In this case, DNS handles name resolution at the upper layers and passes the request to WINS for final resolution. This capability is particularly important for those shops that use DNS and DHCP. You need to have either WINS or DNS running for intranet users to use friendly Internet-style names, rather than numeric IP addresses, to reach your IIS services.

> **Note**
>
> If you publish only Web pages and your users have Microsoft Internet Explorer 2+, you don't need to install WINS or DNS. Typing only the server name (such as **oakleaf0**) in the browser's Address text box delivers Default.htm, the default (home) page of your Web site. Later in this chapter, the "Configuring the Directories" section describes how to change default page names.

An Overview of IIS and Its Components

Internet Information Server includes the three basic components you need to create a full-fledged intranet or Internet site: a Web service, an FTP server, and a Gopher server. Combining these services into IIS 2.0 lets you install, manage, and use them in a suite of applications.

Understanding World Wide Web Service

The World Wide Web server component of IIS is Microsoft's answer to the core technology of today's Internet. Web servers deliver content to Web browsers as text-based documents. The documents contain special formatting called HyperText Markup Language (HTML) that's derived from the Standardized General Markup Language (SGML). *Tags*—embedded HTML codes enclosed by < and > characters—indicate to the browser exactly how a document should be displayed to the user. Following is an example of the HTML code for a simple Web page:

```
<!doctype html public "//IETF//DTD HTML//EN">
<HTML>
<HEAD>
<TITLE>HTML Sample pages</TITLE>
</HEAD>
<BODY BACKGROUND="../images/backgrnd.gif" BGCOLOR="FFFFFF">
<TABLE>
<TR>
<TD><IMG SRC="../images/SPACE.gif" ALIGN="top" ALT=" "></TD>
<TD><A HREF="/samples/IMAGES/mh_html.map">
    <IMG SRC="/SAMPLES/images/mh_html.gif" ismap BORDER=0
    ALIGN="top" ALT=" "></A></TD>
```

```
</TR>
<TR>
<TD><IMG SRC="../images/SPACE.gif" ALIGN="top" ALT=" "></TD>
<TD><HR> <font size=+3>HTML</font> <font size=+3>S</font>
   <font size=+2>tyle</font> <font size=+3>E</font>
   <font size=+2>xamples</font>
<P>
<font size=2>Below are links to several pages that demonstate styles
that are built into the HTML language. While looking at these pages,
try using the View Source menu item in your browser to see the HTML
that defines each page. You can copy text from that view to use in
your own Web pages you are authoring.
</font>
</TD>
</TR>
<P>
<TR>
<TD><IMG SRC="../images/space.gif" ALIGN="center" ALT=" "></td>
<td>
<UL>
<IMG SRC="../images/bullet_H.gif" ALIGN="center" ALT=" ">
   <A HREF="/samples/htmlsamp/styles.htm">Very basic HTML styles</A>
<P><IMG SRC="../images/bullet_H.gif" ALIGN="center" ALT=" ">
   <A HREF="/samples/htmlsamp/styles2.htm">A few additional
   HTML styles</A>
<P><IMG SRC="../images/bullet_H.gif" ALIGN="center" ALT=" ">
   <A HREF="/samples/htmlsamp/tables.htm">Basic HTML tables</A>
</UL></font>
<P>
</td>
</tr>
</TABLE>
</BODY>
</HTML>
```

In addition to plain text that you see in a typical HTML document, there usually are placeholders for graphics and other elements, including video clips, sound clips, and other non-text objects contained in binary (non-text) files. Binary files, such as backgrnd.gif in the preceding HTML example, are stored in files whose relative location from the Web root folder is specified in the tags. The virgule (forward slash, /) is used as the path separator, rather than the DOS backslash (\), because of the use of / by UNIX.

Displaying a Web page requires a series of conversations between the Web browser and other components of the Internet or a Windows NT server. The process consists of the following steps:

1. In the Address text box of a browser, type http://www.*domainname*.com, the URL (Uniform Resource Locator) that you want to view. The http part of the address tells the browser that the type of connection you're trying to make is to a Web server. The www component points to the site's Web server. (Some sites substitute another prefix for www.) The com suffix indicates a commercial site; other common suffixes are org (organization) and net (network).

2. The browser looks up the address on the Internet by referencing the DNS server specified by InterNIC for that domain. The address that's returned—say, 198.105.232.5—is then used to connect to the Web server.

3. The browser contacts the specified Web server and requests a document—either the default document specified by the server or a document specified by appending \document.htm[l] to the URL.

4. The server sends the page to the Web browser for display and review, a process called *loading*.

5. When the browser encounters a tag for a binary file, the browser requests transfer of the file's data as a separate and distinct data stream. This process allows the browser to control whether the object is transferred, as well as the timing of the transfer.

Many browsers, including Microsoft's Internet Explorer (IE), let you turn off images altogether, making pages load substantially faster. Figure 19.5 shows The Internet Properties sheet of IE 3.0, in which you can control whether the browser processes still image, sound, and/or video files by marking or clearing the check boxes in the Multimedia section. Images and other binary types requested by the browser usually are sent with the MIME (Multipurpose Internet Mail Extensions) protocol.

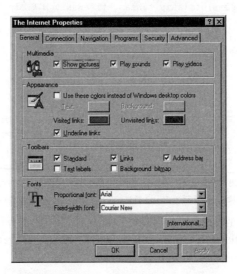

Fig. 19.5 Specifying whether to display multimedia elements of Web pages with Internet Explorer's The Internet Properties sheet.

Note

Image and other binary file loading time is less of an issue with intranets because network speeds generally support much higher throughput than modems or ISDN adapters. Leave the option to load pages/view images selected to display intranet Web pages with graphics.

Understanding the File Transfer Protocol Service

File Transfer Protocol offers a means of transferring binary files with tolerance for speed difference between systems, varying network traffic, and divergent system platforms. With FTP, users can upload, download, or manage files on your network, on the Internet, or on your intranet server with the support of a proven protocol.

The FTP service is installed on your system when you install IIS, unless you specify otherwise, so you can provide this service to your users. FTP lets you make binary, document, and other types of files available to your users by the following means:

- From within a Web browser

- With a command-line FTP utility

- With a Windows FTP utility

Many Web pages supply links to download graphics, audio, executable, and other types of files to your system. One way Web pages handle file downloads is to provide a link to an FTP address for the file you request. When your browser encounters an FTP address, it uses the FTP protocol to download the file. FTP addresses in Web documents have the following syntax:

```
ftp://ftp.sitename.site extension/[folder/...]filename.ext
```

As an example, **ftp://ftp.intellicenter.com/reality/sitelist.zip** specifies that the file SITELIST.ZIP is found at the IntelliCenter site in the Reality folder. By recognizing the URL as one that necessitates file transfer, your browser enables downloading the file without leaving the browser environment.

Note

When you access a URL that refers to an FTP site, your browser indicates that it's signing into the site, sending commands, and—if successful—receiving a file. The browser changes into FTP emulation mode and begins an electronic conversation with the FTP server to retrieve the item you've requested.

The other two options for accessing an FTP site include a command-line, character-based solution and a dedicated Windows FTP utility. When you install Windows 95 or Windows NT, you're automatically provided with a character-based FTP utility. To access a remote site manually with the Ftp.exe utility, follow these steps:

1. From the Start menu choose Run, type **ftp** in the Open text box, and press Enter to run Ftp.exe.

2. Type **open ftp.domainname.com** at the prompt and press Enter.

3. Your Internet dialer appears to establish an Internet connection. Click Connect, if you're using The Microsoft Network or a similar dialer.

4. When the connection is made to the FTP server, you're prompted for a user name. If the site supports anonymous FTP, type **anonymous**; otherwise, type your user name. Press Enter.

5. Enter your password. Anonymous FTP sites often request your Internet e-mail address as the password. Press Enter.

6. The site responds with a logon confirmation and displays the `ftp>` prompt (see fig.
   19.6). Type any valid FTP command at the prompt. To download a file, type **get**
   filename.ext and press Enter; the file is downloaded to the Desktop folder. Many
   FTP commands are the same as DOS commands; examples are `dir` (read the direc-
   tory/folder) and `cd` (change directory/folder).

7. When you're through with the session, type **bye**, **quit**, or **disconnect** to log off the
   FTP server.

Fig. 19.6 Using the command-line version of FTP included with Windows NT and Windows 95.

> **Note**
>
> At a vast majority of FTP sites, you rarely can upload files or other information unless you're a
> known user to the system. Downloading files is an option that's often left in a more anonymous
> state, allowing downloads from users that aren't directly known to the system. Anonymous users
> can download publicly accessible files.
>
> In many cases, if you retrieve sensitive files or other protected information, you must sign into the
> FTP site with a specific user ID and password, just as you do when you log on to a network.

Most Windows FTP utilities, such as WS_FTP (a shareware utility), store configurations
for multiple sites. When you start the utility, you're prompted to select the site to which
you want to connect. Figure 19.7 shows an example of configuration selection with
WS_FTP.

> **Note**
>
> To log on from a browser to an intranet FTP site with anonymous access, type **ftp://**
> **anonymous@*servername*** in the Address text box. Your browser displays a list of the folders and
> files in the designated FTP root folder.

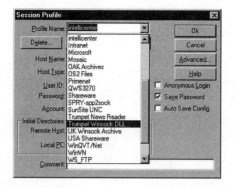

Fig. 19.7   Selecting a configuration for an FTP site in the WS_FTP utility.

Understanding the Gopher Service

The Gopher server, also installed when you install IIS, lets you publish conventional text documents for user review. A Gopher server excels in working with ASCII or ANSI documents, and provides extensive search and retrieval options. Gopher is one of the simplest interfaces to your server. The Gopher approach to information retrieval provides a way for a client system to make a request of a server, get the results quickly, and disconnect until the next request is ready to be processed. Gopher was created to address the world of the Internet, where millions of documents are available, and, at any given time, an extremely large number of users are searching for some bit of information.

Gopher's capability to connect, to get what it needs, and to disconnect is optimal for this type of situation. Gopher relies primarily on standard text files, although it supports other file types. In practice, Gopher has become a victim to the popularity of the Web and Web-based search services, such as Yahoo and AltaVista. Microsoft's Search Server (called *Tripoli* during its beta-test period) gives your users a much easier method of searching for content in text and some types of binary files.

Understanding How IIS Interacts with the Windows NT Domain Model

You set up all access rights with the Windows NT Server's User Manager for Domains. Groups and users are the foundation for the security of IIS server processes and their components. If you don't observe the proper security policies when setting up an Internet server connected to your LAN, it's possible for hackers to obtain access to shared directories containing highly confidential information.

◀◀ See "Working with User Manager for Domains," p. 416

The Windows NT domain in which your Internet or intranet server resides controls all aspects of who can access your system, how they access it, when they access it, and more. The domain controls all these different aspects, so it's important to understand how to set up your intranet user base, assign rights, and control your users' access privileges. It's equally important to restrict permissions of the account used by visitors to your Internet site.

 ◄◄ See "Understanding Domain Architecture and Security," p. 567.

> **Caution**
>
> Never grant administrative rights to users you're about to set up for your IIS server processes. Be sure to set up separate and distinct accounts for anonymous Web, FTP, and Gopher access, if you support more than a Web publishing service.
>
> If you use the account with domain administrative privileges for logging on to the Internet services, you create a serious security breach. It's only a matter of time before your system is threatened by a user's ability to manipulate the content of the site, and possibly destroy the site. Only the network administrator, Webmaster, and designers should have administrative privileges for IIS.
>
> If you use the same account for FTP, Web, and Gopher services, determining where a problem lies is more difficult if you need to track logons, accesses, and other user-specific questions, such as comments and problem reports.
>
> Although you don't have to predefine these user accounts, you should plan for them and be sure to validate user rights on all services before making the Internet services available to users at any level.

Installing the Internet Information Server

Before you install IIS, make sure that you have enough disk space to store the documents and supporting objects (such as graphics) you intend to bring online. A complete installation of IIS 2.0 requires about 3.8M, including the sample files. Multimedia content consumes extraordinary amounts of disk space. If you aren't sure about the amount of content that you must store, prepare now to move user folders and other files to another server. Alternatively, consider adding another disk drive of 2G or greater capacity to your server.

> **Note**
>
> Microsoft recommends that you install IIS 2.0 on an NTFS partition. This book recommends that all server partitions be formatted as NTFS for heightened security and improved performance. If you've installed Windows NT Server 4.0 in a FAT partition and don't want to convert that partition to NTFS, consider installing the content folders and files to another partition or drive that's formatted with NTFS. It's possible, but not easy, to store additional content on another server in the domain. IIS 2.0 doesn't recognize server shares mapped to logical drive letters, so you must use UNC in HTML tags if the content is located on a remote server. You'll find life much easier if you keep all your content (publishing) files on the same logical drive. Windows NT's Disk Manager lets you create volume sets of multiple drives that share the same logical drive letter, so you can expand the volume capacity later as capacity requirements increase.

Preparing to Install the Gopher Service

Before you install the Gopher service, you must establish a domain (friendly) name for your server on the network to permit intranet users to access Gopher. If you don't intend to provide Gopher service, skip this section. You can use WINS or DNS to establish the friendly name. To use DNS to establish the name for your server, you must be running the Windows NT DNS service. If you haven't installed the DNS service, follow these steps:

1. From Control Panel, open the Network property sheet and click the Services tab.

2. Click the Add button to open the Select Network Service dialog, which displays a list of the network services available for Windows NT Server 4.0.

3. Select Microsoft DNS Server and click OK.

4. When prompted, enter the path to the CD-ROM distribution files for your processor type, and then click OK to copy the required files and install the DNS Server.

To establish the local domain name, follow these steps:

1. From Control Panel, open the Network property sheet and click the Protocols tab.

2. Double-click the TCP/IP Protocol entry in the Network Protocols list to open the Microsoft TCP/IP Properties sheet, and select the DNS page.

3. The NetBIOS name of your computer appears in the Host Name text box. Enter the domain name you want to use (*company*.com) in the Domain text box.

4. Click the Add button to open the TCP/IP DNS Server dialog. Type the IP address of your server in the text box and click the Add button to close the dialog. You can specify a maximum of three DNS servers for the list (see fig. 19.8 for an example).

5. Click OK twice, to close the Microsoft TCP/IP Properties sheet and the Network property sheet.

Making an Initial Installation or Upgrading a Prior Version of IIS

When you first install Windows NT Server 4.0, you're offered the opportunity to install IIS 2.0 during the latter part of the setup process. In this case, make sure that you mark the Install Microsoft Internet Information Server check box when specifying setup options during the initial installation process. If you aren't installing IIS 2.0 with a new or upgrade installation of Windows NT Server 4.0, you have the following options for launching the IIS 2.0 Setup program:

■   If the Install Internet Information Server icon appears on your desktop, insert the Windows NT Server 4.0 distribution CD-ROM and double-click the icon.

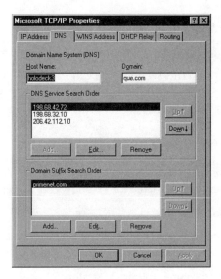

Fig. 19.8   Defining a host name, domain name, and DNS server address in the DNS page of the Microsoft TCP/IP Properties sheet.

■ From Explorer, browse the distribution CD-ROM's \i386\Inetsrv folder (or the folder appropriate to your processor type) and double-click the Inetstp.exe file icon. The CD-ROM uses AutoPlay, new to Windows NT 4.0, so as an alternative you can click the Browse This CD button of the AutoPlay splash screen to open an instance of My Computer and browse to Inetstp.

■ From the Start menu choose Run, type *d:*\i386\inetsrv\inetstp (where *d:*/ is your CD-ROM drive designator) in the Open text box, and click OK.

Note

If you have existing content files, be sure to back up the files before installing IIS 2.0. Although removing a prior version of IIS doesn't remove existing directories or content files, a full backup of the existing IIS folders (*d*:\inetsrv is the default main folder for prior IIS versions) is recommended in case problems occur during the upgrade.

When the Internet Information Server Setup program starts, follow these steps:

1. Close all running applications; then click OK to proceed to the next Microsoft Internet Information Server 2.0 Setup dialog.

2. If you have a prior version of IIS installed, a dialog appears with three buttons: Add/Remove, Reinstall, and Remove All. Click the Remove All button to delete the prior installation. Click Yes when asked to confirm removal. If you haven't stopped the Internet services, you receive message boxes asking whether you want to stop the services. Click Yes in each instance. When you're notified that the services have been removed, click OK and then restart Inetstp.exe to open the Microsoft Internet Information Server 2.0 Setup dialog.

3. Select the services you want to install by marking or clearing the check box for the service (see fig. 19.9). For safety, don't install the WWW Service Samples if you have existing content. You must install the ODBC Drivers & Administration (tool) if you want to use Microsoft SQL Server for logging or to provide content. The default installation folder for IIS 2.0 executable and helper files is \WINNT\System32\inetsrv, but you can locate these files elsewhere by clicking the Change Directory button and specifying a different folder. Click OK to open the Publishing Directories dialog.

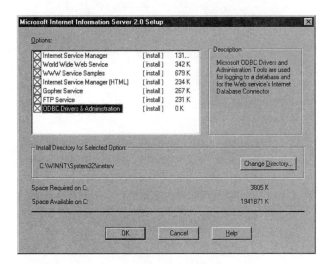

Fig. 19.9 Selecting the Internet services to install in the Microsoft Internet Information Server 2.0 Setup dialog.

> **Note**
>
> If the disk space requirement for the ODBC Drivers & Administration selection is 0, ODBC drivers are already installed. Even in this case, you should mark the ODBC check box to ensure that the latest ODBC 2.5 drivers are installed.

4. The default content (publishing) folder for IIS 2.0 installed from the Windows NT Server 4.0 CD-ROM is \InetPub. (Prior versions of IIS used the \inetsrv folder.) Each service you specify stores its default content in root subfolders: \InetPub\wwwroot, \InetPub\ftproot, and \InetPub\gophroot (see fig. 19.10). You can locate \InetPub and its subfolders on any local volume. Unless you have existing content in another set of folders, accept the default locations. Click OK to continue with the installation and start the IIS 2.0 services.

5. If you selected installation of the ODBC Drivers & Administration in step 3, the Install Drivers dialog appears. Only the SQL Server driver is included with Windows NT Server 4.0, so select this driver (see fig. 19.11). Verify that version checking is in use by clicking the Advanced button to open the Advanced Installation Options dialog. Mark the Install Selected Driver(s) with Version Checking check box to assure that other applications that install ODBC drivers don't overwrite a later version. (You can check the version number of ODBC components by clicking the Versions button.) Click OK to return to the Install Drivers dialog. Click OK again to proceed with the installation.

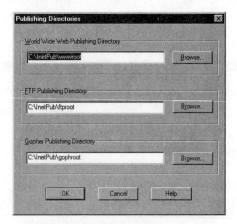

Fig. 19.10 Specifying the location of content files in the Publishing Directories dialog.

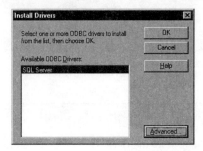

Fig. 19.11 Selecting installation of the 32-bit ODBC 2.5 driver for Microsoft SQL Server in the Install Drivers dialog.

6. When a message appears that IIS 2.0 setup has completed successfully, click OK to exit the Setup program. You now have a new program group, Microsoft Internet Server, which includes Internet Server Setup, Internet Service Manager, Internet Service Manager (HTML), Key Manager, and Product Documentation choices. Setup also installs Internet Explorer 2.0 and adds the IE 2.0 icon to your desktop.

Using the Internet Service Manager

The three components of IIS run as Windows NT services. You use Internet Service Manager to check the status of IIS services. There are two versions of Internet Service Manager:

■ The conventional, executable version (Inetmgr.exe), which you launch from the Start menu by choosing Programs and Internet Service Manager. Internet Service Manager displays the status of each installed service (see fig. 19.12). You can start and stop IIS services by selecting the service in the list and clicking the VCR buttons of the toolbar. You use Internet Service Manager in the following sections to configure each service.

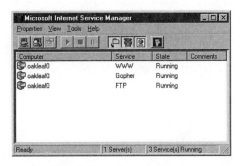

Fig. 19.12 Displaying the status of installed IIS services in the executable version of Internet Service Manager.

■ The Web page version (\WINNT\System32\inetsrv\iisadmin\default.htm), which you launch from the Start menu by choosing Programs and Internet Service Manager (HTML). The HTML version, which runs in a browser, lets you remotely administer IIS services, with the exception of stopping and starting services. You open the page in your browser by typing *servername*/**iisadmin** in the Address text box of your browser. Figure 19.13 shows the HTML version of Internet Service Manager open in Internet Explorer 3.0 on a PC running Windows 95. You click the WWW, FTP, or Gopher button to open a page that includes an administration dialog for the service. You also can read the documentation for IIS 2.0 remotely from the default page.

> **Note**
>
> You must have administrative privileges to run either version of Internet Service Manager. The HTML version isn't located in the \InetPub\wwwroot subfolders to which, by default, the anonymous Internet or intranet user has access.

Testing the Default IIS 2.0 Installation

As a quick test of the installation, double-click the Internet Explorer icon on the desktop to start the newly installed browser, which automatically displays a default home.htm file. To verify that the IIS demonstration files are installed correctly, type *servername* (such as **oakleaf0**) in the Address text box of the browser to open the InetPub\ wwwroot\default.htm page (see fig. 19.14). Internet Explorer automatically prepends http:// to *servername*.

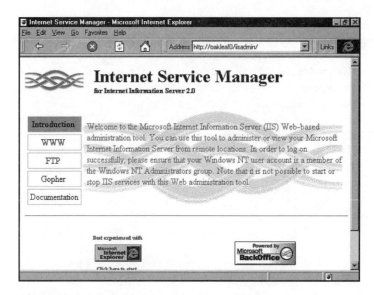

Fig. 19.13 Using the HTML version of Internet Service Manager to administer IIS 2.0 remotely.

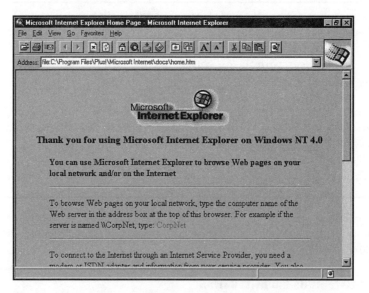

Fig. 19.14 The default home page for the IIS 2.0 demonstration files displayed in Internet Explorer 2.0.

To verify accessibility to your Internet server by networked users, at a remote client type *servername* or `http://servername` in your browser's Address text box. Experiment by navigating to the sample site, Volcano Coffee Company, to test the speed of your network connection and IIS 2.0. Volcano's home page, shown in the Windows 95 version of Internet Explorer in figure 19.15, includes several small graphics, a waveform audio file, and an animated marquee ("Get on The Great Taste Tour").

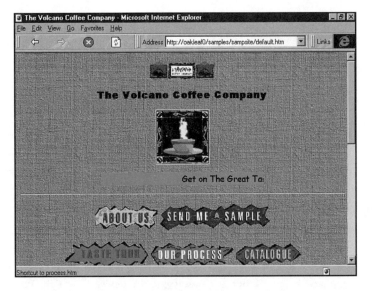

Fig. 19.15 The home page of the Volcano Coffee Company sample Web site displayed in the Windows 95 version of Internet Explorer 3.0.

Setting Audit and Logging Options

Although auditing and logging of your Internet services might appear to be related only to security issues, auditing and logging have many other benefits. You should know who is accessing the various services and content offered by your server. User access information helps you recognize the need for additional services, better ways to service users, and emerging trends in usage and server loading.

Always enable logging. You can set up logging to maintain only a limited history. If you worry about the size of history files, consider setting options to keep only five days or less of history. You begin to spot trends, and simultaneously use the logs to help in case of any problems that may arise.

WWW Server Options and Logging Parameters

To set Web server options and logging parameters, open Internet Service Manager and double-click the icon for the WWW service to open the WWW Service Properties sheet. The following sections describe how to set server options and logging parameters for your Web service in the four pages of the WWW Service Properties sheet.

Configuring the Service Options. The Service page of the WWW Service Properties sheet (see fig. 19.16) includes two very critical items that specify the privileges of users of your Web server. The Anonymous Logon section specifies the default logon name and password for your system users. The Password Authentication section lets you indicate the type of authentication used for secure access to the service.

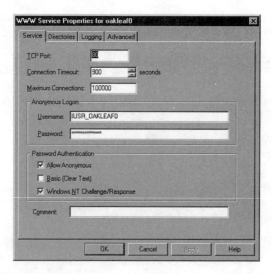

Fig. 19.16 Setting service options for the Web server in the Service page of the WWW Service Properties sheet.

Note

The remaining default option values of the Service page usually are satisfactory for Web sites with moderate traffic. It's seldom necessary to change the default TCP Port value (80). You might want to decrease the Connection Timeout to less than the default 15 minutes.

Web browsing is typically an anonymous service, unless your site includes confidential information. You can secure your entire Web site by clearing the Allow Anonymous check box. However, it's more common to assign an anonymous logon account for access to non-confidential information while simultaneously securing other areas for protected access. You must allow anonymous logon if your server is connected to the Internet for public access.

When you install IIS 2.0, a new user is automatically added to your Windows NT user database. The user, given a name of IUSR_ plus the name of your system (OAKLEAF0 in this case), has sufficient rights to access your server's services and browse your server's content. This new user is created with the same basic rights as a user that might be considered "average."

The anonymous user is created as a member of the Domain Users group and the Guest group. Of course, the user also belongs to the Everyone group when allowed or disallowed access to a given resource. IIS creates a random password for the anonymous user account. A very important facet of the IUSR_OAKLEAF0 account is that it's granted the Log On Locally right, as shown in the User Manager for Domains User Rights Policy dialog (see fig. 19.17).

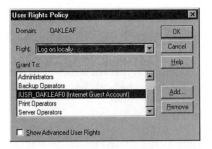

Fig. 19.17 The User Rights Policy dialog displaying the Log On Locally right granted to the IUSR_OAKLEAF0 account.

All users of the Web service must be able to log on locally because the logon request is made to the WWW Server process. That process takes the name provided by the user and logs on through Windows NT's standard security model. By doing so, Windows NT assigns appropriate security rights and permissions to the logon account, providing a solid security model that's fully integrated with the Windows NT domain model.

In situations where you want every user to log on to the server, deselect the Allow Anonymous option in the WWW Service Properties sheet (refer to fig. 19.16). This assures that everyone using your Web site provides a user name and password when accessing the server. Intranet users are authenticated by their current credentials—their user name and password. Internet users are prompted for a user name and password before being granted access to your site. The advantage of requiring password access is that your logging of resource usage reflects the people who are really using the system.

As mentioned earlier, the other important setup option is the type of authentication to be used. Two different authentication types are used to secure all or part of your site. The mix of browsers used on your intranet dictates your decision of authentication type. As of this writing, the only browser supporting the Windows NT Challenge/Response option is Microsoft Internet Explorer 2.0 or later. If you have a mixed browser community—for example. if you have users with Netscape's Navigator browser—you must also enable Basic (Clear Text) authentication in the Service page of the WWW Service Properties sheet (refer to fig. 19.16). Otherwise, you block such users from access to your site.

The NT Challenge/Response option works in the following manner:

1. If a user requests a secured Web page but isn't currently signed in with sufficient rights, the server fails the request and closes the connection to the browser.

2. The browser is informed of the failure by the server's response.

3. The browser prompts the user for user name and password credentials, passing this information to the server along with another attempt to access the secured resources.

4. The server uses the new credentials to log on to Windows NT and attempts access to the resource. The renewed attempts generally occur up to three times, but depend on the browser used.

5. The user ID and password move across the link encrypted, protecting them from being "stolen" in transit by someone with less-than-noble intentions.

With the Basic (Clear Text) option, the User ID and password move across the link encoded, but still decipherable by a determined hacker. The browser keeps a channel to the server open as it attempts to access the shared resource. If you enable the Basic (Clear Text) option, the Internet Service Manager warns you that you're enabling a less secure method of sending passwords over the network and asks you to confirm your choice (see fig. 19.18).

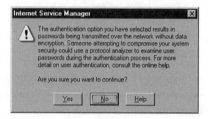

Fig. 19.18 Internet Service Manager's warning when you enable the Basic (Clear Text) authentication option.

> **Note**
>
> Most of the configuration options for the three IIS services are largely identical. Thus, this chapter provides limited coverage in the FTP and Gopher sections for completing the basic configuration options. The differences between the standard configuration with the Web server options, and the FTP and Gopher services, are covered in the sections devoted to these two services.

Configuring the Directories. At first glance, the Directories page of the WWW Service Properties sheet might seem an unimportant feature, and the default folders might appear adequate for your foreseeable needs. As time goes on and you provide more services to your users, however, you will find that the folder options are a central component of your system, and are especially helpful in Web and FTP services.

> **Note**
>
> The Internet Service Manager is another example of Microsoft's failure to make a full transition to substitution of the term *folder* for *directory*. For consistency with the rest of this book, *folder* is used except in cases where *directory* is part of a proper name for a dialog or dialog object.

Figure 19.19 shows the default folders created when you install IIS 2.0. The C:\WINNT\System32\inetsrv\iisadm folder, which contains the Web pages for the HTML version of the Internet Service Manager, is aliased to the virtual folder /iisadm.

You access virtual folders by appending the folder name to the server address, as in [http://]oakleaf0/iisadm for intranet access. Marking the Enable Default Document check box and specifying the name of an existing default document is the equivalent of the [http://]oakleaf0/iisadm/default.htm address. Unless you want to make the user enter the name of a specific document, each virtual folder should include a default document.

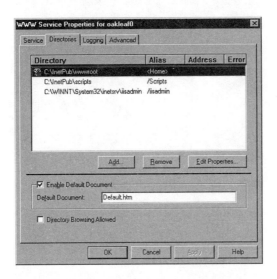

Fig. 19.19 The default folders and virtual folder aliases set up by IIS 2.0.

Note

You can have only a single folder specified as the home folder for your entire Web server. If you specify a different home folder, IIS prompts you to save the change.

You can establish any number of folder aliases by clicking the Add button to display the Directory Properties sheet. As an example, you can create a virtual folder, named demo, for the C:\InetPub\wwwroot\samples folder (see fig. 19.20). Intranet users can access the default.htm document with the [http://]oakleaf0/demo address. If you specify a folder on a remote server, you must enter the UNC path to the server share and type valid credential entries for the share in the User Name and Password text boxes in the Account Information section (shown disabled in fig. 19.20). Figure 19.21 shows the demo virtual folder added to the Directory list of the WWW Service Properties sheet. Folder aliases aren't visible to users browsing your FTP service. To use FTP's cd *aliasname* command to change folders, the user must have prior knowledge of the name of the folder alias.

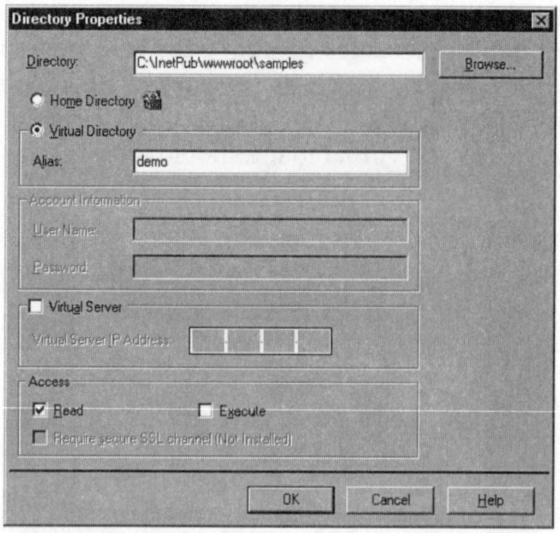

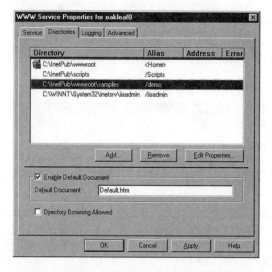

Fig. 19.20 Adding a new virtual folder to the Directories page.

Fig. 19.21 The new virtual demo folder added to the Directory list.

> **Note**
>
> If you want to implement a system following the UNIX standard for default pages, change your default document name from default.htm to index.html. Index.html is the default starting page on the vast majority of Web servers, so setting the default to the standard makes it easier for an experienced UNIX Webmaster to maintain pages on the server.

The final option in establishing a virtual folder is to specify the access rights in the Directory Properties sheet. To enable viewing content, mark the Read check box. Read access means read-only access; users can't make any changes to the folder. To enable a program folder that has executable files that add functionality to your Web pages, mark the Execute check box. Execute access does not allow users to scan folder contents.

> **Caution**
>
> Never grant Read access to any of your application or script subfolders. If you do, users may not only browse the folders, seeking programs that "look interesting," but they also can run the programs to see what they do. By providing Execute rights, users can execute applications and scripts, but can't perform blind folder listings or copy files from the location. This means that you should not mix scripts and applications with Web pages in a single folder.

The primary use of the Directories page of the WWW Service Properties sheet is to manage the content you provide to the users of your system. By placing different categories of content in different folder trees, you accomplish the following objectives:

- You place the information in physically different areas, potentially even on a different server.

- You limit the scope of a search engine, such as Microsoft Index Server, incorporated at your site. You usually can limit the scope of the search engine to a particular folder structure. By separating content into different areas, you speed search time for your users.

- You can move static content to a folder tree that may be backed up less frequently, perhaps only on a monthly basis. If you have content that's more dynamic, such as pages for an online magazine or other constantly changing source, keep this content in a folder tree that's backed up daily.

Virtualizing Remote Server Shares. Placing content on a remote server share is tricky, because when the remote server is accessed, the share is accessed using the name and password you provide in all cases. If the user name and password you provide doesn't have access to the share, the user can't access the pages the share contains, whether or not the user has permissions for the share itself.

Consider the following scenario to help explain this approach:

- Your main Web server is located on Holodeck3. For your standard default intranet connections, users specify either holodeck3 or http://holodeck3 to access your default.htm page, located in the \InetPub\wwwroot folder. This works fine, because the user logs on to the system as your standard Internet Guest account, IUSR_HOLODECK3.

- Suppose that you place some material on a server named Twinkie. This server has a share, Secret, to which you want to connect. Only one user, Julie, has access to \\TWINKIE\SECRET.

- To make the connection to the share, you specify the full UNC path in the Directory text box and use Julie's user name and password.

- You provide Read access to the folder and call it SECRET. After this is done, users can access the share.

There's one problem with this scenario: Anyone accessing your server can access the new folder by typing its virtual folder URL, http://holodeck3/secret, which provides access to the default.htm file. Bear in mind that you initially set the folder for very limited access (only by the user named Julie). By providing the name and password in the property sheet for the folder mapping, you bypass the security on the folder entirely, making the information available to any user on your network who can launch Internet Service Manager. In essence, you hard-code the folder name and password.

This apparent security bypass happens because you provide Windows NT's security layer with a valid user name and password. The remote server doesn't provide the same level of security that you have when attempting to access a secured folder or file physically located on the IIS server.

For this reason, carefully architect your server to provide secure and non-secure access to the information you want to make available. Never put information on a remote server if the information needs to be protected from some users and available to other users. Put public, widely available information on the remote server.

In cases where you have secure information, always put the information on the IIS server, allowing Windows NT's security management to step in, protecting the information.

This same approach also applies to virtual server configurations. When you indicate a virtual server, the provided user name and password is used to connect to the remote server. If secure information resides at that remote location, move it to the local system and allow Windows NT to manage the secure access to the information.

Configuring Logging Options. The log files created by the Internet Information Server include the IP address for the incoming request, the type of request made, and information about the success or failure of the request. Logs also provide information about access to individual pages. In the case of your Web server, this information is very valuable when determining what content to revise, keep, or remove from the system. You set standard logging options in the Logging page for the WWW Service Properties sheet (see fig. 19.22).

Most of the logging options shown in figure 19.22 are self-explanatory, but following are recommendations for starting up your Web site:

- Use the Log to File option when you bring up your system, rather than set up an ODBC database connection. This removes one more variable from your installation when tracking down any odd behavior seen in system startup. When your system is firmly in place, and if you're comfortable with it, implement the logging to a database. You can log to a SQL Server table or, if you have the ODBC driver for Microsoft Access, to a Jet 2+ table.

- Accept the Automatically Open New Log and Daily defaults. When the service runs, the current log file is open, which denies access to the file for review purposes. To provide information in a timely manner when first bringing up your site, you want recent information as quickly as possible. By selecting the Daily option, you have to wait only until just after midnight to open the previous day's log.

■ Consider changing the default value of the Log File Directory from the default \WINNT\System32\LogFiles folder. You may want to change this value to a more logical location, such as an\InetPub\LogFiles folder.

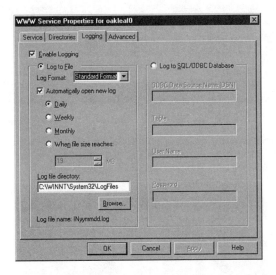

Fig. 19.22 Setting options in the Logging page of the WWW Service Properties sheet.

▶▶ See "Logging to an ODBC Data Source," p. 729.

You can import the text version of the log into Microsoft Excel to perform quick checks on system performance. The fields of the log file are comma-separated (Excel .csv format). Excel's Text Import Wizard makes the process easy, but you must manually select Delimited in step 1 of the Wizard and specify Comma in step 2 to achieve the desired result. Figure 19.23 shows a typical log file imported into Excel 7.0, with a few of columns compressed to display the Web pages viewed. During startup, it's easier to analyze usage with Excel than to write a database front end that does the analysis automatically. You can use Access 95 to import the text file and view the log in table datasheet view. Access 95's Text Import Wizard is quite similar to Excel 7.0's.

Configuring Advanced Options. The Advanced options, which are common to all three IIS server processes, let you exclude computers with specific IP addresses or specify the IP address of each computer allowed access to your site. Figure 19.24 shows settings that allow only three specified computers to gain access to the site. Alternatively, you can use a subnet mask to let a group of computers within a subnet access the site.

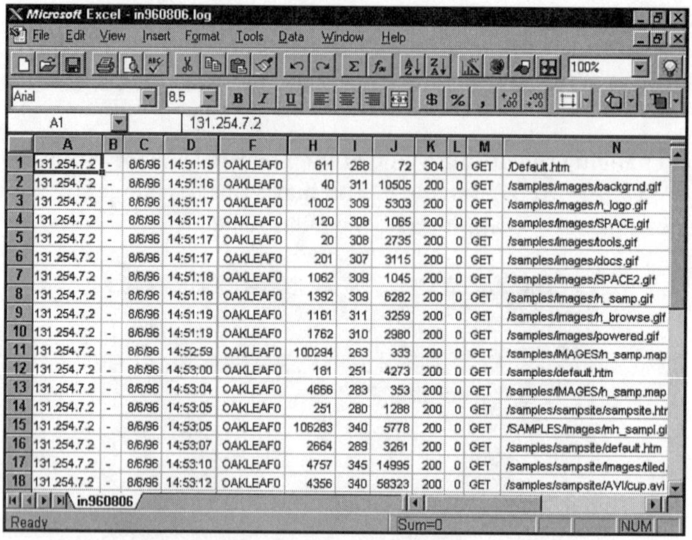

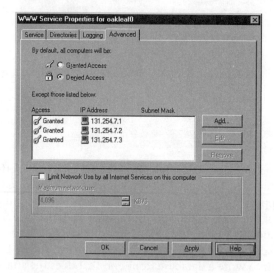

Fig. 19.23 A Web service log imported into an Excel 7.0 worksheet.

Fig. 19.24 Specifying the IP address of individual computers that have access to your site.

The alternative is to indicate that everyone has access to the system except for those IP addresses in the list. In cases where you have a confirmed attempt or attempts to compromise your system, you can remove the offending person's access rights. Figure 19.25 shows a group of computers having IP addresses beginning with 131.254.7 locked out of the site.

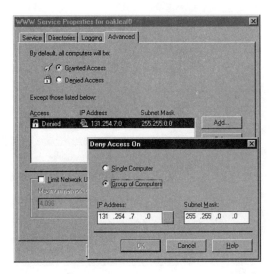

Fig. 19.25 Denying access to a group of computers based on their IP address range.

To enter an address, click the Add button of the Advanced page to open the Permit Access On or Deny Access On dialog. When you enter the address, you can use "wild cards" by selecting the Group of Computers option and providing the part of the IP address that's constant for the systems addressed. When entering a single computer's address, you can click the ellipsis button at the right of the IP Address text box to enter a computer name based on DNS entries. The ellipsis button is disabled in figure 19.25 because manual entry of a group of computer names is selected.

The Limit Network Use check box of the Advanced page lets you limit the total throughput on your server that's devoted to the service. The default value, 4,096KB/S, is a substantial percentage of a 10BaseT or 10Base2 network connection. If you need to limit total throughput of all your site's services, you can type any reasonable value (between, say, 1,000 to 5,000) into the text box.

Setting FTP Server Options

The FTP service options are quite similar to those for the Web service described in the preceding sections. The differences lie in the first two pages of the FTP Service Properties sheet, Service and Messages. The Service page (see fig. 19.26) adds a Current Sessions button, but doesn't include the Password Authentication options of the WWW Service Properties sheet.

The Current Sessions button opens the FTP Users Sessions dialog to show you who's on the system, when they connected, and how long they've been on. Don't turn off the FTP server as long as users appear on the display. If you turn off the FTP server, you not only close the user connection, but also terminate their download operation in progress.

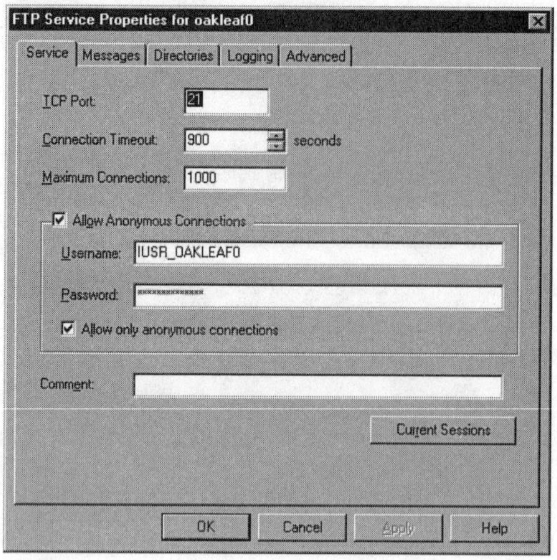

Fig. 19.26 The Service page of the FTP Service Properties sheet.

The Messages page (see fig. 19.27) lets you personalize your FTP site with Welcome, Exit, and Maximum connections messages. If you have an index for the content of your FTP site, it's a common practice to suggest that users read the index before proceeding. When you connect to an FTP site with a browser, the Welcome message appears below the FTP Root at *Servername* title (see fig. 19.28).

Fig. 19.27 Specifying the messages that appear when a user logs on and off an FTP site, and when the maximum number of connections is reached.

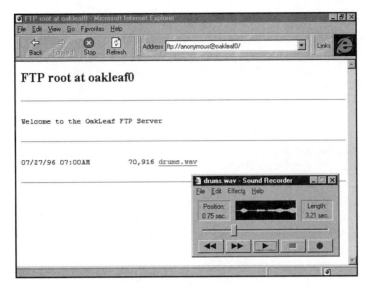

Fig. 19.28   Internet Explorer 3.0 playing a waveform audio (.WAV) file from an FTP site.

Setting the Gopher Server Options

When you set up the Gopher server options, the Logging and Advanced options are identical to those for the other services, and the Directories option is quite similar. However, the Service page (see fig. 19.29) varies slightly from the Service page of the other two services. You enter the name or title and an e-mail address to which to report problems in the Service Administrator section.

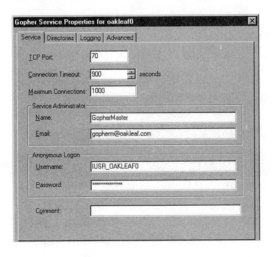

Fig. 19.29   Setting up Gopher options in the service.

> **Note**
>
> At this writing, no Gopher client has been found that recognizes an intranet address for the URL other than that of the Microsoft Internet Explorer. The Gopher protocol, one of the first cross-server protocols to let users skip around the Internet, is a legacy technology superseded by other protocols and new navigation technologies. With Internet search servers, such as Digital's AltaVista and Microsoft's Search Server for intranets, there's little incentive to implement IIS 2.0's Gopher service.
>
> If you use Internet Explorer and want to access the Gopher server, preface the URL with the URL identifier of Gopher.

Gopher uses a series of indexes and content information files, called *tag files*, to access your site. You use the GDSSET command-line utility, located in the \WINNT\system32 and \WINNT\system32\inetsrv folders, to create these tag files. GDSSET creates a small, hidden file that contains information about the files. Following is a simple tag file for a text file named crack.txt created with GDSSET:

```
0
GdsPriv=Gs1.0;04/03/96;22:37:37
Type=0
Name=Demonstration Information
```

The command line to create this file is

```
gdsset -g0 -f "Demonstration Information" -d crack.txt
```

This command line includes a set of options, plus the description and name of the file. When you run the utility, you receive a simple display of the result, as in the following example:

```
Gopher Object Type = 0
 Gopher FriendlyName = Demonstration Information
 Tag information for C:\inetsrv\gophroot\crack.txt
    Object Type = 1
    Friendly Name = crack.txt
    Admin Name = Default Admin Name
    Admin Email = Default Admin Email
```

Table 19.2 lists the options that are commonly used with GDSSET.

Table 19.2 Common GDSSET Command-Line Options

Option	Description
-g	The type of file being indexed
-f	"Friendly" description to be displayed instead of the file name
-d	The file name of the file being referenced (case-sensitive)
-c	For updating, or changing, an existing tag file
-D	Indicates the folder (case-sensitive)
-a	Administrator's name
-e	Administrator's e-mail address

The easiest way to tag files is simply to use the file name parameter,

```
GDSSET filename.ext
```

where *filename.ext* is the name of the file you want to index. GDSSET prompts you for the file's friendly name and then saves the tag file. Saved tag files are hidden in the folder from which you run the GDSSET utility. These tag files save with the same file name as the original file indexed, but a new extension, .GTG, is appended to the file name to specify a Gopher tag file.

The type of source file is specified in accordance with the codes shown in table 19.3.

Table 19.3 Common Gopher File Types for Tag Files	
Code	**Type of Gopher Tag File**
0	Standard text file
1	Folder of additional Gopher files
9	A binary file, the default
g	A GIF graphic file
h	An HTML page

The file type codes shown in table 19.3 are the most common for intranet and Internet installations. The tag file defaults to type 9, a binary file, indicating to the server that it should MIME-encode the file. The browser examines the file type and determines whether to download the file to the local hard drive or to display it in the browser.

Understanding URLs

The URL prefixes listed in table 19.4 are supported by most mainstream browsers.

Table 19.4 Common URL Prefixes	
Prefix	**Purpose**
File:	Opens a local or network drive file for browsing. *Example:* File://c:\mydir\ myfile.htm
Http:	Opens an HTML document for viewing. *Example:* http://holodeck3/ or http:// www.microsoft.com/ie/ie.htm
Https:	Opens a secure HTML document for viewing, requiring the establishment of a Secure Socket Layer conversation with the server. *Example:* https://holodeck3
Gopher:	Opens a Gopher session. *Example:* gopher://holodeck3
FTP:	Opens an FTP session. *Example:* ftp://www.intellicenter.com/myfile.zip

You may encounter other prefixes, but the prefixes listed in table 19.4 are the most common on the Internet. Other prefixes include telnet: (which establishes a Telnet session to the address you indicate) and news: (which attempts to attach to a Usenet News service). Many of these less commonly implemented protocols execute locally stored utility applications to support these protocols.

From Here...

Microsoft's IIS 2.0 is intended primarily to be a high-performance Web server for private intranets and the public Internet. This chapter explained how to set up and connect to each service offered by IIS 2.0. World Wide Web, FTP, and (to a lesser degree) Gopher services combine to provide comprehensive sources of information for intranet and Internet users.

The following chapters provide additional information related to the topics discussed in this chapter:

- Chapter 12, "Managing User and Group Accounts," describes how to use Windows NT 4.0 Server's User Manager for Domains, take advantage of the new Add User Accounts and Group Management wizards, and utilize the built-in user groups of Windows NT.

- Chapter 13, "Sharing and Securing Network Resources," explains Windows NT Server's security system for shared file and folder resources and how to use the new Managing File and Folder Access Wizard to simplify sharing Windows NT 4.0 server resources.

- Chapter 17, "Integrating Windows NT with Heterogeneous Networks," shows you how to set up and administer Windows NT Server's WINS and other TCP/IP-related services.

- Chapter 20, "Administering Intranet and World Wide Web Sites," describes key elements of maintaining a Web site that reliably distributes the content of HTML-encoded documents, outlines a Webmaster's duties, and briefly describes the integration of popular HTML authoring tools with an intranet or Internet server.

Chapter 20

Administering Intranet and World Wide Web Sites

Bringing your intranet or Internet site online after installing and setting up Internet Information Server (IIS) 2.0 is only the first step toward making your new system a success. You must consider many factors in order to achieve the objective of providing accurate and timely information to your site's users. As the site administrator or Webmaster, you need up-to-date details on your site's activity and its demands on your system. This chapter concentrates on two basic areas: Activity logging and distribution of activity reports, and generating Web pages with tools that are included with IIS 2.0 or available for no-charge downloading from Microsoft's Web site.

Logging to an ODBC Data Source

Chapter 19, "Setting Up the Internet Information Server," describes how to set up logging for your intranet or Internet server to a text file. As you amass information on the usage of your site, log files in text format become increasingly difficult to analyze. Although you can import text log files into an Excel worksheet or Access table, appending log records directly to a database table is a simpler and less error-prone process.

Following are the basic steps to create a logging database and query the IIS 2.0 log files to find the information you want:

1. Create a database devoted to logging operations.

2. Add a table with the structure required for IIS 2.0 logging.

3. Establish an ODBC system data source to connect to the database.

4. Change the logging option for each of your services to the ODBC data source.

5. Write SQL queries that return the information required to analyze usage of your site.

This chapter shows you how to

- Change activity logging on your system to use an ODBC database

- Display data from Internet Information Server 2.0's counters with Performance Monitor

- Add dynamic database capabilities to your Web pages with the Internet Database Connector

- Use Microsoft dbWeb for enhanced Web-based query features

- Set up and use Microsoft FrontPage 1.1 for Web management and content creation

The following sections describe these steps in detail, or provide references to information in previous chapters that relate to these steps. Microsoft SQL Server 6.5 and Access 95's Jet 3.0 databases are used as examples, but you can use any client/server or desktop database system for which you have a 32-bit ODBC 2.5 driver. The examples assume that you have at least some familiarity with SQL Server 6.x and/or Microsoft Access.

Creating the Logging Database

Following are brief recommendations for creating the logging database:

- For SQL Server databases, create a new device, such as Logging.dat, to contain the database. Don't install user databases in the Master.dat device. Unless you plan to accumulate data over long periods of time, a device size of 10M to 25M should suffice. If you expect a very active Web site, allocate 100M to save a week or so of data. You can use the entire capacity of Logging.dat for your logging database. Be sure to turn off transaction logging for the database. You can use your SQL Server administrator account to create the device and database, but it's a good idea to add a new database user account and a password for the logging operation. Chapter 22, "Running Microsoft SQL Server 6.5," describes how to create new SQL Server devices and databases (with and without transaction logs), and to add SQL Server user accounts.

- For Jet 3.0 databases, you must install Access 95 or Visual Basic 4.0 on your server to provide the Jet libraries. If you want to implement Jet 3.0 database security, Access 95 is required to provide the System.mdw file that provides security features. Don't turn on Jet security until you prove the logging system is operational. Create an Access database, such as Logging.mdb, in a separate subfolder of InetPub. You also must install the 32-bit ODBC driver for Jet 3.0, which is a component of Microsoft Office 97. Make sure that you have the required license for each component you install.

Adding the Logging Table

Internet Information Server 2.0 requires a logging table with a specific structure corresponding to the fields of the text version of the log described in Chapter 19, "Setting Up the Internet Information Server." A single logging file includes records for all IIS 2.0 services.

Table 20.1 lists the column information for the logging table for SQL Server and Jet data types. The Integer size in the table applies only to the Jet Number data type. Null values are allowed in each column. IIS 2.0 returns Null values in the LogDate field; the LogTime field includes date and time information in string format.

Table 20.1 · Table Structure for Logging Table

Column	SQL Data Type	Jet Data Type	Size
ClientHost	Char	Text	255
UserName	Char	Text	255
LogDate	Char	Text	255
LogTime	Char	Text	255

Column	SQL Data Type	Jet Data Type	Size
Service	Char	Text	255
Machine	Char	Text	255
ServerIP	Char	Text	255
ProcessingTime	Int	Number	Integer
BytesRecvd	Int	Number	Integer
BytesSent	Int	Number	Integer
ServiceStatus	Int	Number	Integer
Win32Status	Int	Number	Integer
Operation	Int	Number	Integer
Target	Char	Text	255
Parameters	Char	Text	255

Tip

Don't create indexes on the table; indexes slow appending of new records. The improved query performance delivered by indexes doesn't warrant the impact of multiple indexes on your Web site's performance.

Creating a SQL Server Table. Listing 20.1 shows the SQL Server query to create the LogTable table used in the following sections. The four lines of listing 20.1 beginning with if exists delete an existing version of the table before creating the new table.

Listing 20.1 The SQL Server Query to Create the Logging Database

```
/****** Object: Table dbo.LogTable ******/
if exists (select * from sysobjects where id =
    object_id('dbo.LogTable') and sysstat & 0xf = 3)
    drop table dbo.LogTable
GO

CREATE TABLE LogTable (
    ClientHost char (50) NULL ,
    UserName char (50) NULL ,
    LogDate char (12) NULL ,
    LogTime char (21) NULL ,
    Service char (20) NULL ,
    Machine char (20) NULL ,
    ServerIP char (50) NULL ,
    ProcessingTime int NULL ,
    BytesRecvd int NULL ,
    BytesSent int NULL ,
    ServiceStatus int NULL ,
    Win32Status int NULL ,
    Operation char (200) NULL ,
    Target char (200) NULL ,
    Parameters char (200) NULL
)
GO
```

Note

The logtemp.sql query that IIS 2.0 setup installs in \WINNT\system32\inetsrv is a simplified version of the query of listing 20.1. The logtemp.sql query creates a table named inetlog with the varchar, rather than fixed-width char, data type for text columns. Fixed-width fields provide better performance than variable-width fields at the expense of table size.

To execute the query of table 20.1, follow these steps:

1. Launch SQL Enterprise Manager, if necessary, and select the Logging database in the Server Manager window by expanding the tree for your SQL Server, expanding the Databases tree, and then clicking the Logging item.

2. From the Tools menu, choose SQL Query Tool to open the Query window. Alternatively, click the SQL Query Tool toolbar button. The Query tool opens with the Query page displayed for the selected database.

3. Type the content of table 20.1 into the Query text box (see fig. 20.1). You can omit the lines preceding CREATE TABLE, if you want. Alternatively, choose Open from the File menu and browse to the logtemp.sql file to use the query supplied with IIS 2.0.

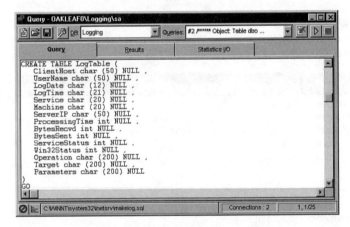

Fig. 20.1 Typing the makelog.sql query into SQL Enterprise Manager's query text box.

4. From the Query menu choose Execute, or click the Execute Query button (with the VCR play symbol) of the Query toolbar. Assuming there are no typographical errors, the Results window displays the message This command didn't return data, and it didn't return any rows.

5. Verify the structure of the newly created table by choosing Tables from the Manage menu to open the Manage Tables window. Select LogTable (dbo) from the Table drop-down list (see fig. 20.2).

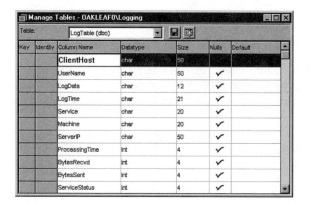

Fig. 20.2 Verifying the structure of the LogTable table created by executing makelog.sql.

6. Choose <u>M</u>anage from the <u>L</u>ogins menu to open the Manage Logins dialog. Select <New User> from the Login Name drop-down list, and then type the user name for the logging account, such as logging. Type a password for the account in the Password text box.

7. Click the Permit column for the Logging database, which automatically makes the Logging database the default for the logging user (see fig. 20.3).

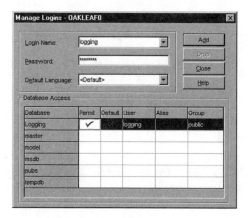

Fig. 20.3 Verifying the structure of the LogTable table created by executing makelog.sql.

8. Click the Add button to add the logging user, confirm the password when requested, and then click the Close button to close the Manage Logins dialog.

After you verify that logging of user activity succeeds, you can use SQL Server's security system to assure that only authorized persons can access the Logging database.

▶▶ See "Establishing Database Permissions," p. 830

> **Note**
>
> You can use Access 95 to create a Jet 3.0 LogTable in an .MDB file (as described in the following section), and then use Access's Save As/Export command on the File menu to export the table structure to the SQL Server database. Before exporting the table, you must create an ODBC data source for the SQL Server database, as described later in the section "Creating ODBC Data Sources for SQL Server Databases."

Creating a Jet 3.0 Table. Using a Jet 3.0 table eliminates the need to license and administer SQL Server. To create a Jet 3.0 database with a LogTable table, follow these steps:

1. Launch Access 95, preferably with a new System.mdw file, and choose New Database from the File menu to open the New dialog. Click OK to accept the default Blank Database and to open the File New Database dialog.

> **Note**
>
> If you've assigned a password to the Access Admin account, the new database you create has security applied. The System.mdw file that contains account information must also be located on the server. If you use a new System.mdw file, the default Admin user has an empty password, which eliminates the need for the System.mdw file to open the database. You can create a new System.mdw file with Access 95's Workgroup Administrator application.

2. Name the file Logging.mdb, and then click the Create button to close the File New Database dialog and create the database. (The file location isn't important at this point, because you can copy Logging.mdb to the server after you create it.)

3. With the Table page of the Database Container active, click the New button to display the New Table dialog. Select Design View in the list and click OK to open the new table in design mode.

4. Assign Field Name, Data Type, and Size values for each column according to table 20.1. You set the Size value in the General field property page (see fig. 20.4). Accept the default No value for the Required and Indexed field attributes. For text fields, set Allow Zero Length to Yes.

5. Click the Table View toolbar button, and then click Yes when you're asked whether you want to save the table.

6. Type the table name (Logging) in the Save As dialog and click OK to continue.

7. When asked whether you want to create a primary key field, click No. Your new table appears in Datasheet view.

8. Close Access and copy Logging.mdb to a logging subfolder of the \InetPub folder on the server. If you created or want to create a secure database, copy System.mdw to the same folder.

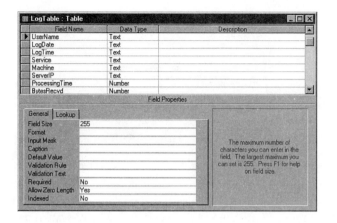

Fig. 20.4 Specifying the field attributes of a Jet 3.0 logging table.

Setting Up ODBC System Data Sources

The ODBC data source is one of the most common source of problems with logging databases, as is the Internet Database Connector (IDC) described later in the "Using the Internet Database Connector" section. Problems with ODBC data sources are common to SQL Server and other client/server or desktop databases having 32-bit ODBC drivers. Thus, it's important to understand the details of setting up ODBC data sources for access by IIS 2.0 and server applications that run with IIS 2.0.

IIS runs as a Windows NT service, which starts automatically after Windows NT loads. In most cases, the server runs with no local user logged on. In Windows NT 4.0 and Windows 95, conventional ODBC data sources are associated with a specific user profile. Thus, a conventional ODBC data source isn't accessible to IIS 2.0 or IIS server applications until the user who created the data source logs on to Windows NT Server.

To solve this problem, Microsoft added ODBC system data sources for 32-bit ODBC 2.5. An ODBC system data source is accessible as soon as Windows NT Server (and SQL Server, if used) starts. ODBC system data sources don't depend on a user logging on to the server. You use ODBC system data sources for logging and for most of the dynamic Web pages you create from information stored in databases.

To create an ODBC system database on the server, follow these initial steps:

1. From the server's Control Panel, double-click the ODBC tool to launch the ODBC Administrator, which displays the Data Sources dialog. Figure 20.5 shows data source names (DSNs) set up by the installation of Microsoft Office 95 Professional Edition, plus a SQL Server data source for the pubs demonstration database. The data sources that appear when launching the ODBC Administrator are user databases, not system databases.

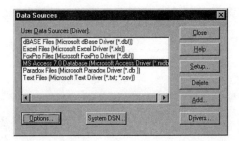

Fig. 20.5 ODBC user data sources displayed by the opening dialog of the ODBC Administrator.

2. Click the System DSN button to open the System Data Sources dialog (see fig. 20.6). If you haven't previously defined a system data source, the System Data Sources (Driver) list contains only the LocalServer default ODBC system data source installed by SQL Server.

3. Click the Add button to open the Add Data Source dialog.

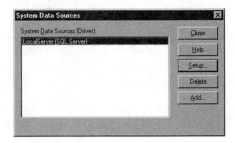

Fig. 20.6 The System Data Sources dialog displaying the default SQL Server ODBC system data source.

At this point, the steps to create SQL Server and Jet data sources diverge, as described in the next two sections.

Creating ODBC Data Sources for SQL Server Databases. To continue creating an ODBC system database for SQL server, follow these steps:

1. In the Add Data Source dialog, select the SQL Server driver in the Installed ODBC Drivers list (see fig. 20.7). Click OK.

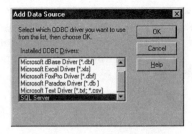

Fig. 20.7 Selecting the SQL Server driver in the Add Data Source dialog.

2. In the ODBC SQL Server Setup dialog, type the name of the data source—in this case, **SQLLogging**—in the Data Source Name text box.

3. Type an optional brief description of the data source in the Description text box.

4. In the Server combo box, select (local) if SQL Server is installed on the same server as IIS 2.0. Otherwise, select the server name on which SQL Server is installed, or type the server name in the text box. Accept the (Default) entries for Network Address and Network Library. Leave the Use Trusted Connection check box unmarked, unless SQL Server is installed in another (trusted) domain.

5. Click the Options button to expand the ODBC SQL Server Setup dialog.

6. Type the name of your logging database—in this case, **Logging**—in the Database Name text box (see fig. 20.8). Specifying the database name is *very* important to proper operation of your logging system.

Fig. 20.8   Completing the entries in the expanded version of the ODBC SQL Server Setup dialog.

7. Click OK to close the dialog and add the new system data source to the System Data Sources dialog (see fig. 20.9). Click Close to exit the ODBC administrator.

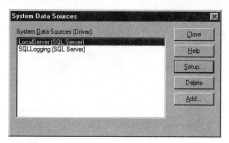

Fig. 20.9   The SQLLogging data source added to the System Data Sources list.

Creating ODBC Data Sources for Jet Databases. The process for creating an ODBC system data source for a Jet database is similar to that for SQL Server, but the Access 95 (7.0) ODBC driver presents a different dialog for specifying the database. To create an ODBC system database for Jet 3.0 tables, starting from the open Add Data Source dialog, follow these steps:

1. In the Add Data Source dialog, select the Microsoft Access (*.mdb) driver, and then click OK to display the ODBC Microsoft Access 7.0 Setup dialog.

2. Type the DSN—in this case, `JetLogging`—in the Data Source Name text box and add an optional description of the data source.

3. Click the Options button to expand the dialog. You don't need to change the defaults for Page Timeout and Buffer Size. Make sure that the Exclusive and Read Only check boxes are cleared (see fig. 20.10).

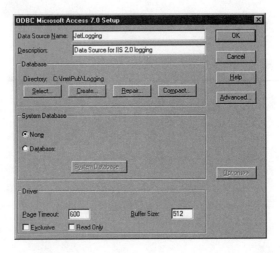

Fig. 20.10 Entering the DSN and Description in the ODBC Microsoft Access 7.0 Setup dialog.

4. Click Select to open the Select Database dialog. Browse to the \InetPub\Logging folder and select logging.mdb (see fig. 20.11). Click OK to close the dialog and return to the ODBC Microsoft Access 7.0 Setup dialog.

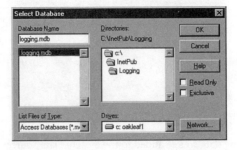

Fig. 20.11 Specifying the logging .mdb file in the Select Database dialog.

5. If you want to secure your logging database and have copied System.mdw to the \InetPub\Logging folder, select the Database option in the System Database section, and then click the System Database button to open the Select System Database dialog.

If you don't plan to secure the database, skip to step 8.

6. Select All Files (*.*) in the List Files of Type list, select system.mdw, and click OK to close the dialog, as shown in figure 20.12. (The Access 95 ODBC driver specifies the earlier .mda extension for system files, rather than .mdw for Access 95's workgroup file.) Click OK to close the dialog.

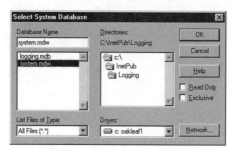

Fig. 20.12 Specifying the Access system (workgroup) file in the Select System Database dialog.

7. Click Advanced in the ODBC Microsoft Access 7.0 Setup dialog to open the Set Advanced Options dialog. The default admin user appears in the Login Name text box with an empty Password text box. You change the Login Name and Password entries after using Access 95 to secure the database. Optionally, enter the default folder for the file in the New value for DefaultDir text box (see fig. 20.13). Click OK to close the dialog and return to the ODBC SQL Server Setup dialog.

Fig. 20.13 The security settings of the Set Advanced Options dialog.

8. The ODBC Microsoft Access 7.0 Setup dialog displays the specified .mdb and .mdw files (see fig. 20.14). Click OK to close the dialog and add the JetLogging ODBC system data source.

9. In the System Data Sources dialog, click Close to exit the ODBC Administrator.

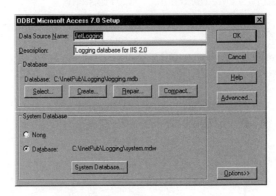

Fig. 20.14 The completed ODBC Microsoft Access 7.0 Setup dialog.

Specifying the ODBC System Data Source for Logging

Now that you've created the table and the ODBC system data source for logging informa-tion, you change the logging instructions for each service. Follow these steps to imple-ment the changes:

1. Launch Internet Service Manager, and then double-click the entry for the WWW Service to open the WWW Service Properties sheet.

2. Select the Logging properties page and type the name of your logging data source (**SQLLogging** or **JetLogging**) in the ODBC Data Source Name (DSN) text box.

3. Type the name of the table you created—in this case, **LogTable**—in the Table text box.

4. Leave the User Name and Password text boxes empty; the user name and password you entered in the ODBC Microsoft Access 7.0 Setup dialog for the data source provide this information (see fig. 20.15). Click OK to close the WWW Service Prop-erties sheet.

5. Repeat steps 1 through 4 for each of the other services your server runs.

6. Test for proper setup of your logging database by displaying Web pages, download-ing files by FTP, and using the Gopher service, if installed.

Note

If a user accesses your server by using the file: protocol, the user's actions aren't logged. The client handles this type of URL by conventional network file sharing. Be sure to test your logging data-base with the appropriate URL prefix for each service.

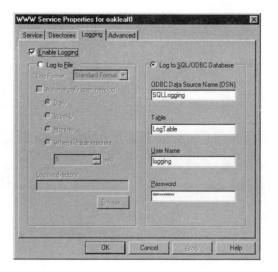

Fig. 20.15 Changing logging to a SQL Server ODBC system data source on the Logging page of the property sheet for a service.

Writing Sample Queries for Reviewing Logs

The log data can quickly become overwhelming unless you write meaningful queries for analysis. Following are some of the questions that queries against the database can answer:

- What time of day are most people accessing the server?

- What pages are most popular?

- Who is accessing the server (by IP address)?

The sample SQL Server query of listing 20.2 returns summary information for hits against the server, and displays the relative popularity of Web pages. Figure 20.16 shows SQL Enterprise Manager displaying the result set returned by the last three queries of listing 20.2 against entries created by two brief testing sessions.

Listing 20.2 A Sample Transact-SQL Query That Returns Information on Usage and Web Page Popularity

```
SELECT 'Total hits' = COUNT(*),'Last Access' = MAX(LogTime)
FROM LogTable

SELECT 'Hit summary' = Count(*), 'Date' = SUBSTRING(LogTime,1,8)
FROM LogTable
GROUP BY SUBSTRING(LogTime,1,8)

SELECT 'Time of day' = (SUBSTRING(LogTime,13,2) + ' ' +
SUBSTRING(LogTime,18,2)), 'Hits' = COUNT(SUBSTRING(LogTime,10,2))
FROM LogTable
GROUP BY (SUBSTRING(LogTime,13,2) + ' ' + SUBSTRING(LogTime,18,2))
```

(continues)

Listing 20.2   Continued

```
SELECT 'Page' = SUBSTRING(Target,1,40), 'Hits' = COUNT(Target)
FROM LogTable
WHERE   (CHARINDEX('HTM',target) > 0)
GROUP BY Target
ORDER BY 'Hits' DESC
```

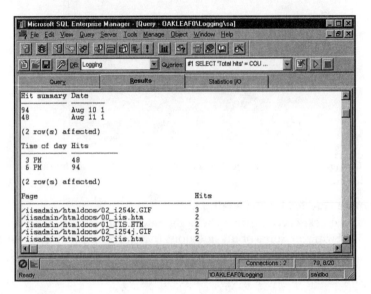

Fig. 20.16   The result set of the last three queries of listing 20.2, displayed by SQL Enterprise Manager's Query tool.

You can create queries similar to those shown in listing 20.2 for FTP and Gopher services. If you log to a Jet database, you can use Access 95's graphical query-by-design tool to create analytical queries. Access 95's built-in graphing capability also is useful for analyzing usage of your site.

Using SQL Server Web Assistant to Distribute Activity Reports

If you want to distribute usage information for your site, SQL Server 6.5's Web Assistant automates the process. The SQL Web Assistant automatically creates formatted Web pages that contain query result sets formatted as tables. A single page can display the result set from one or more queries. You also can specify the frequency at which the page is updated by a SQL Server 6.5 scheduled task. If you use a scheduled task, you can add a DELETE query after the SELECT queries to maintain records only for a specified period in the logging table. You must have system administrator privileges to use the Web Assistant.

The following steps use the SQL Server Web Assistant to create a Web page, WWWPages.htm, that displays the result of the last query in listing 20.2:

1. From the Start menu, choose Programs, Microsoft SQL Server 6.5, and SQL Server Web Assistant to open the first dialog of the Assistant.

2. In the Login dialog, type the SQL Server Name, Login ID (`logging` for this example), and the Password (see fig. 20.17). Alternatively, you can use SQL Server's integrated security feature to log on to SQL Server by marking the check box labeled Use Windows NT Security to Log In Instead of Entering a Login ID and/or a Password. Click the Next button to continue.

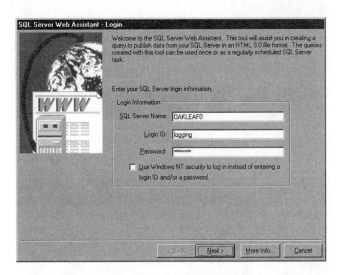

Fig. 20.17 Entering required information in the Login dialog of the SQL Server Web Assistant.

3. In the Query dialog, select the Enter a Query as Free-Form Text option to open the Type Your Query text box. Select your logging database (Logging for this example) in the Which Database Do You Want to Query? drop-down list.

4. Type one or more consecutive SELECT queries in the text box. Figure 20.18 shows the last query of listing 20.2 pasted into the Type Your Query text box. Multiple SELECT queries are allowed; the result of each SELECT query appears in a separate table on the Web page. Click Next to continue.

> **Tip**
>
> It's a good idea to copy and paste a previously tested query into the Type Your Query text box to avoid typographical or syntax errors.

5. In the Scheduling dialog, select the frequency at which you want to update the log by choosing On a Regular Basis from the drop-down list and specifying the update interval in the Every text box and interval drop-down list (see fig. 20.19). Intervals include hours, days, and weeks.

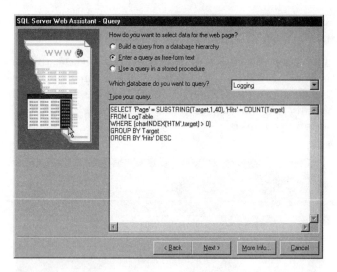

Fig. 20.18   Specifying the query to create the content for the Web page.

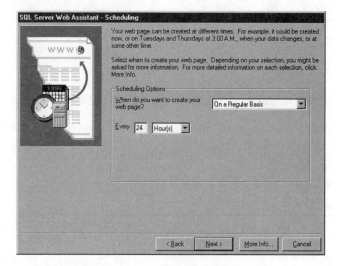

Fig. 20.19   Specifying the refresh interval for the Web page.

Alternatively, you can choose Now in the When Do You Want to Create Your Web Page? drop-down list to generate a Web page immediately. If you specify Now, you create only a single instance of the page. (Running a scheduled task immediately is described later in this section.) Click Next to continue.

6. In the File Options dialog, type the full path to and the name of the file in the top text box. The file must be located in the \InetPub\wwwroot folder or subfolder. If

you want to restrict access to the activity report page, specify a subfolder with the appropriate Windows NT group permissions.

7. Select the option button labeled The Following Information. Type the title of the page, which appears in your browser's title bar, and the title for your query result, which appears at the top of the page, in the two associated text boxes (see fig. 20.20). Alternatively, you can specify use of a pre-existing template file to display the result. Click Next to continue.

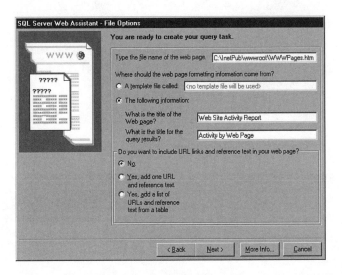

Fig. 20.20 Specifying file options for the Web page.

Tip

The File Options dialog lets you add URLs and descriptions, either as a single line or as rows of a table. Additional URLs are useful for linking to other pages, if your report offers multiple pages.

8. In the Formatting dialog, select how you want the text to appear (see fig. 20.21). In most cases, the options labeled Insert an Update Date/Time Stamp at the Top of the Page, and Include Column or View Column Names with the Query Results are adequate for the report. Click Finish to display the Finished dialog, and then click Close to close the dialog and terminate the Web Assistant.

If you specified Now in step 5, you can check your Web page by opening the *Pagename*.htm file with the **file://*path*/*Pagename*.htm** URL in the browser on your server, or from a client with the **http://*servername*/*Pagename*.htm** URL if the file is in the \InetPub\wwwroot folder. Figure 20.22 shows the page created with the values specified in the preceding steps. If you use a multiple SELECT query, each query result set appears in separate tables, separated by a bar.

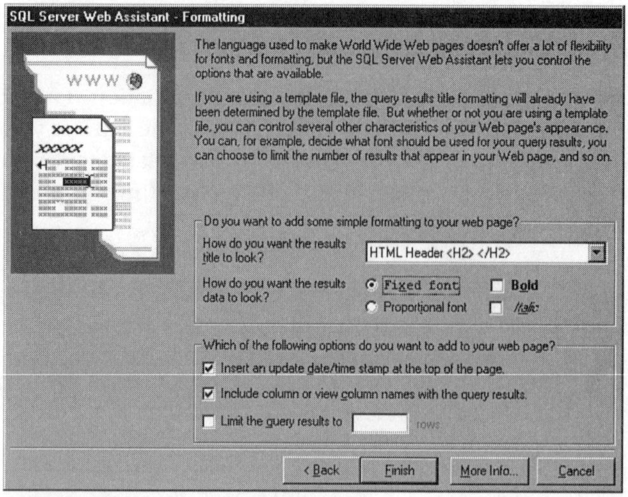

Fig. 20.21 Setting query text and page formatting options.

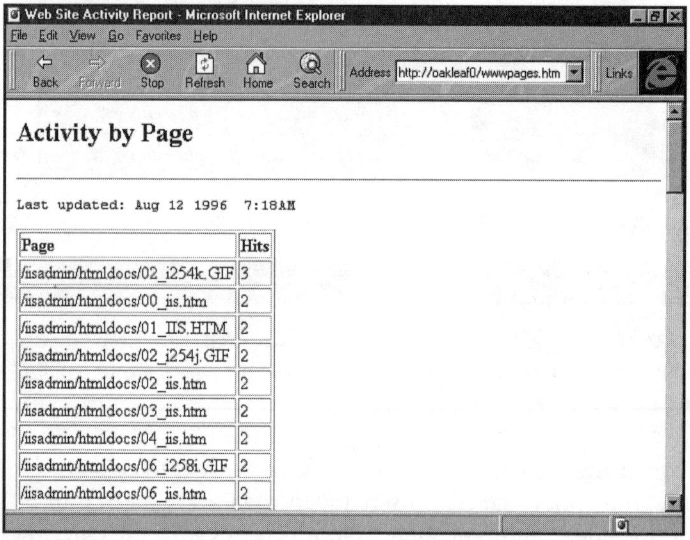

Fig. 20.22 The single-query report page created by using the example values of this section.

If you specified a scheduled task in step 5, Web Assistant creates an encrypted stored procedure in the logging database named Web_*yymmddhhmmsscc*, based on your computer's system time when creating the stored procedure. (The last two digits, *cc*, are hundredths of seconds.) You must take the following steps to run SQL Enterprise Manager's Managed Scheduled Tasks tool to generate a test copy of your Web activity report:

1. From the Start menu, choose Programs, Microsoft SQL Server, and SQL Enterprise Manager.

2. In the Server Manager window, expand the server item; then expand the Databases item and select the logging database.

3. From the Server menu, choose Scheduled Tasks to open the Manage Scheduled Tasks window. Select the Web_*whatever* entry for the activity report you just created (see fig. 20.23).

Fig. 20.23 Selecting the task to execute immediately in the Manage Scheduled Tasks window of SQL Enterprise Manager.

4. Click the Run Task toolbar button (with the clock and the small green arrow), or choose Run Task from the File menu. Click Yes in the confirmation message box to run the task and create the page.

Using Performance Monitor

As the use of your intranet or Internet server grows, it's useful to determine the extent to which user activity taxes your server's resources. Installation of IIS 2.0 adds to Windows NT Server's Performance Monitor (PerfMon) the counters shown in table 20.2.

Table 20.2   Counters Added by IIS 2.0 to Performance Monitor

Counter	Purpose
Aborted Connections	Total unintended disconnects
Bytes Received/sec	The instantaneous rate of incoming bytes from all users
Bytes Sent/sec Rate	The instantaneous rate of outgoing bytes sent to all users
Bytes Total/sec Rate	The total of Bytes Received/sec and Bytes Sent/sec
CGI Requests	The accumulated number of Common Gateway Interface (CGI) requests from the Web service
Connection Attempts	The accumulated number of connections, successful or not
Connections/sec	The instantaneous number of requests for Web pages
Connections in Error	The accumulated number of failed connections
Current Anonymous Users	The instantaneous number of users who are logged on via the Internet
Current CGI Requests	The instantaneous number of CGI operations being processed

(continued)

Table 20.2 Continued	
Counter	**Purpose**
Current Connections	The sum of Current Anonymous Users and Current NonAnonymous Users
Current ISAPI Extension Requests	The instantaneous number of ISAPI operations being processed
Current NonAnonymous Users	The instantaneous number of users who are logged on via an intranet
Files Received Total	The accumulated number of files uploaded by users
Files Sent Total	The accumulated number of files downloaded by users
Files Total	The sum of Files Received Total and Files Sent Total
Get Requests	The accumulated number of GET requests received by the Web service
Gopher Plus Requests	The accumulated number of Gopher Plus requests
Head Requests	The accumulated number of queries to determine whether a user needs to refresh a Web document
ISAPI Extension Requests	The accumulated number of requests for services using ISAPI, such as the Internet Data Connector
Logon Attempts	The accumulated number of logons, successful or unsuccessful
Maximum Anonymous Users	The peak number of Internet users
Maximum CGI Requests	The peak number of CGI operations
Maximum Connections	The peak number of Internet plus intranet users (Maximum Anonymous Users plus Maximum NonAnonymous Users)
Maximum ISAPI Extension	The peak number of operations that use Requests ISAPI
Maximum NonAnonymous	The peak number of intranet users Users
Not Found Errors	The accumulated number of requests that resulted in an HTTP 404 error code being returned to the requester
Other Request Methods	The accumulated number of requests, other than GET, POST, or HEAD
Post Requests	The accumulated number of POST operations
Total Anonymous Users	The accumulated number of Internet users
Total NonAnonymous Users	The accumulated number of intranet users

In table 20.2, the accumulation of totals begins at system startup.

◄◄ See "Using Performance Monitor," p. 501

PerfMon's graph views let you display any of the counters in the table 20.2, but most of the counters deserve only occasional checking. Figure 20.24 shows a PerfMon configuration that displays the most important instantaneous and accumulated values for a Web and FTP site. Table 20.3 lists the counters and scaling factors used to create the graph of figure 20.24. Scaling factors are not the defaults; to maintain a readable scale, for example, you must scale the Bytes/sec values by 0.001 to display kBytes/sec. If your site traffic is heavy, change the scaling factors to suit expected full-scale values.

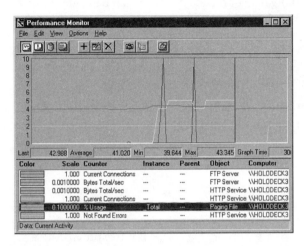

Fig. 20.24 Monitoring server activity.

Table 20.3 Performance Monitor Key Indicators		
Counter	**Scaling Factor**	**Counter Object**
FTP Current Connections	1.0	FTP Service
HTTP Current Connections	1.0	HTTP Service
FTP Total Bytes/Sec	0.001	FTP Service
HTTP Total Bytes/Sec	0.001	HTTP Service
% Usage, Page File	0.1	Paging File
Not Found Errors	1.0	HTTP Service

Figure 20.24 shows, in relative terms, the activity on your server at a glance. You can see very quickly the number of connections and other important parameters. If you observe the % Usage of the page file growing steadily, check the types of access being completed. If you have an ISAPI application running, the application might have a memory-management problem.

An increasing % Usage of the paging file over time indicates that more virtual memory (the paging file) is being consumed. Typically, additional resources are required to handle the load as more users connect to the server. If the % Usage of your page file is above 80 percent, increase the size of the file. If % Usage continues to rise and you're certain you don't have a resource problem with a CGI executable or an ISAPI extension, consider adding more memory to the system.

Enhancing Your Site with Dynamic Database Access

One of the attractions of intranet and Internet servers for large organizations is that information stored in organization-wide databases can be made easily available on Web pages. A standard Web browser, such as Internet Explorer 3.0, can eliminate the need for most custom decision-support and even some transaction-processing front ends to client/server database back ends. Although sending a fully formatted Web page creates more network traffic than returning query result sets to a custom database front end, you gain the following benefits with Web database techniques:

- Most database users are likely to be familiar with Internet browsing and thus require little or no training to navigate a well-designed set of data-driven Web pages.

- Many browsers operate on Windows, Mac, and UNIX machines, eliminating the need to create three versions of every client/server front end in a multiplatform environment.

- Mobile users easily can access Web pages, either by Windows NT's Remote Access Service (RAS) or, if you choose, via the Internet. Access via the Internet saves the cost of long-distance calls or charges for toll-free phone lines.

You can provide two basic types of database services with the tools included with Windows NT Server 4.0 and SQL Server 6.5:

- *Static pages* that provide lists in tabular format. Static pages are better suited to intranets, where users expect hard-core information, not entertainment. You can use SQL Server 6.5's Web Assistant, described earlier in the "Using SQL Server Web Assistant to Distribute Activity Reports" section, to create and automatically update static lists.

- *Dynamic pages*, in which users easily can choose the information they want and obtain more detailed information about a choice. In the database front-end business, this process is called *drilling down*. Dynamic pages are equally suited for delivery by intranets and the Internet.

You can provide access to databases in several ways—from using the Internet Database Connector (included with Windows NT Server 4.0) to using ISAPI to directly manipulate the database with custom applications. In this chapter, the focus is on the IDC, how it works, and how you use it to create dynamic Web pages.

Using the Internet Database Connector

The IDC uses the Internet Services API (ISAPI) and an ISAPI DLL, Httpodbc.dll, to make the connection between Web pages and ODBC data sources in order to create Web pages based on parameterized (user-defined) queries. Query parameter(s), which determine the content of the resulting Web page, originate in a Web page that includes text boxes or lists for entering query constraints. A *Filename*.idc file contains the query's SQL statement and parameters to access the ODBC data source. A *Filename*.htx file provides the template into which the query result is inserted. Figure 20.25 shows the relationship between the components of the IDC.

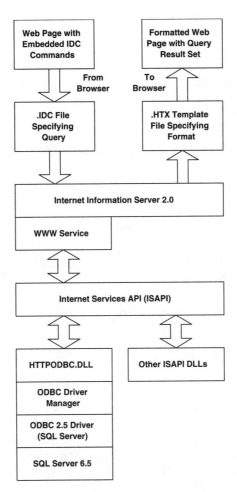

Fig. 20.25 The server-side components required to implement the Internet Database Connector.

Note

ISAPI is an extension to IIS 2.0 that provides services similar to CGI executables. The advantage of ISAPI over CGI is that ISAPI DLLs run in IIS 2.0's process space, rather than in the separate process space required for executable applications. Using DLLs rather than EXEs provides a substantial improvement in performance and minimizes Windows NT Server resource requirements.

The following sections are based on the three IDC-based examples supplied with IIS 2.0, which query the pubs database supplied with SQL Server. You must have SQL Server 6.x installed to try these examples, which are located in the \InetPub\wwwroot\samples\ dbsamp folder.

Creating an ODBC System Data Source for IDC Files. Before you can run the three IDC examples, you must create an ODBC system data source with the data source name Web SQL, and specify pubs as the default database. (Creating an ODBC data source is the subject of the section "Setting Up ODBC System Data Sources" near the beginning of this chapter.) Figure 20.26 shows the ODBC SQL Server Setup dialog for the Web SQL data source. You must be logged on to SQL server with the default sa (system administrator) account with no password for the example to work correctly.

Fig. 20.26 Creating the Web SQL ODBC system data source.

To test your data source, type servername/samples/dbsamp/dbsamp2.htm in your browser's Address text box to display the example that uses a form to provide a user-entered parameter. The parameterized query returns the names of authors and year-to-date sales amounts that exceed the entered value. Figure 20.27 shows dbsamp2.htm, which includes the reference to the IDC file, sample.idc, open in Internet Explorer 3.0.

Accepting the default value, 5,000, for year-to-date royalties results in the sample2.idc page shown in figure 20.28. What appears isn't the content of the sample.idc file, but a page named sample2.idc created by the sample.htx template file. The .IDC and opening .HTM files usually—but not necessarily—share the same file name. The .IDC and .HTX files for the IDC examples are located in the \InetPub\scripts\samples folder.

Specifying IDC Query Parameters in Web Page Forms. You use the HTML <FORM ...> tag with the <INPUT ...> tag to create a text box into which you enter the parameter value for the query parameter specified in the .idc file. Listing 20.3 shows the HTML code of the dbsamp2.htm page that lets you enter a minimum yearly sales amount to serve as the query parameter.

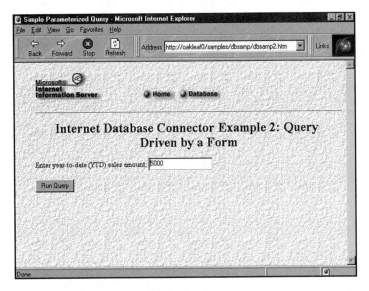

Fig. 20.27   The IIS 2.0 database example page that uses a form to pass a parameter to the Filename.idc file.

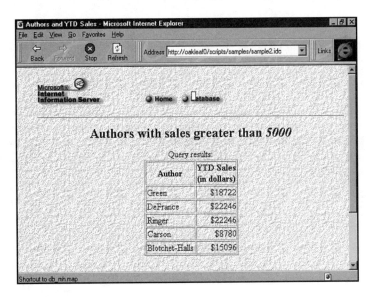

Fig. 20.28   The sample2.idc Web page returned with the query result set constrained by the sales amount entered in dbsamp2.htm.

Listing 20.3   The HTML Code of dbsamp2.htm That Implements a Parameterized Query

```
<HTML>
<HEAD><TITLE>Simple Parameterized Query</TITLE></HEAD>
<BODY BACKGROUND="/samples/images/backgrnd.gif">
<BODY BGCOLOR="FFFFFF">
<TABLE>
<TR>
<TD><IMG SRC="/samples/images/SPACE.gif" ALIGN="top" ALT=" "></TD>
<TD><A HREF="/samples/IMAGES/db_mh.map"><IMG SRC="/SAMPLES/images/db_mh.gif"
ismap BORDER=0 ALIGN="top" ALT=" "></A></TD>
</TR>
<tr>
<TD></TD>
<TD>
<hr>
<font size=2>

<CENTER>
<H2>Internet Database Connector Example 2: Query Driven by a Form</H2>
</CENTER>

<FORM METHOD="POST" ACTION="/scripts/samples/sample2.idc">
<P>
Enter year-to-date (YTD) sales amount: <INPUT NAME="sales" VALUE="5000" >
<P>
<INPUT TYPE="SUBMIT" VALUE="Run Query">
</FORM>
</font>
</td>
</tr>
</table>
</BODY>
</HTML>
```

The `<FORM METHOD="POST" ACTION="/scripts/samples/sample2.idc">` line specifies the name and location of the .IDC file, relative to the \InetPub\wwwroot folder. The `"sales"` element of the `Enter year-to-date (YTD) sales amount: <INPUT NAME="sales" VALUE="5000" >` line is the name of the parameter, the value of which is returned by `%sales%` in the .IDC file and by `idc.sales` in the .HTX template file.

Examining the IDC Source File. Listing 20.4 shows the content of the sample2.idc file, which has the minimum entries necessary to specify the DSN, log on to SQL Server, specify the .HTX template file to use, and provide the query to return a result set. The parameter that sets the minimum year-to-date sales is `%sales%`; user-supplied parameters in .IDC files are enclosed by percent signs. You can add a `Password: password` line after `Username:`, but the password is clear text and is visible to anyone with access to the folder in which the .IDC file is stored. If you use integrated security to log on to SQL Server, the Username: and Password: entries are ignored. The user ID and password of the anonymous user applies for Internet connections; for an intranet connection, the user's credentials apply. If you must supply a Password: entry to log on to SQL Server, be sure to secure access to the folder in which you store the .IDC file. Security issues are the subject of the later section "Considering User Rights and Database Security."

Listing 20.4   A Simple IDC Source File

```
Datasource: Web SQL
Username: sa
Template: sample.htx
SQLStatement:
+SELECT au_lname, ytd_sales
+ from pubs.dbo.titleview
+ where ytd_sales > %sales%
```

Note

The + symbol in the SQL Statement line is the line-continuation character for .IDC files. Elements of SQL statements not on a single line with SQLStatement: must be preceded with the + symbol. Httpodbc.dll parses .IDC files by looking for the ASCII/ANSI carriage return (CR) code, which has a decimal value of 13.

When IIS 2.0 loads an .IDC file, IIS examines the extension and determines the application used for the source file. One of the very powerful capabilities and features of IIS is its capability to use extension resolution to determine how to handle a given request. Files with a .GIF extension, for example, are graphic images, and files with an .IDC extension are IDC source files that associate with Httpodbc.dll. Associations for IIS 2.0's Web service are set up in the following Registry tree location:

```
HKEY_LOCAL_MACHINE
        SYSTEM
                CurrentControlSet
                        Services
                                W3SVC
                                        Parameters
                                                ScriptMap
```

If you add a new association entry with the Registry Editor, make it of the data type REG_SZ and type the associated extension. To correctly map the association, include the period before the extension, as in .idc. For the value, specify the path and file name executed when the extension loads. Provide the path from the root to ensure that IIS can locate the application regardless of the current working folder. Figure 20.29 shows the Registry entry for the .IDC extension in the Windows NT 4.0 Registry Editor.

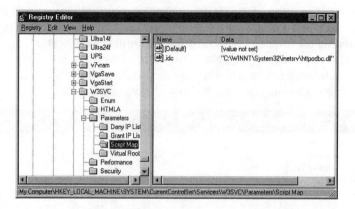

Fig. 20.29 Windows NT 4.0's Registry Editor displaying the associated DLL for .IDC files, Httpodbc.dll.

Understanding the Template File. Listing 20.5 is the HTML code for the simple template file, sample.htx, that's used by the example dbsamp1.htm and dbsamp2.htm files.

Listing 20.5   HTML Source Code to Create the Query Result Page Returned to the User

```
<HTML>
<HEAD><TITLE>Authors and YTD Sales</TITLE></HEAD>
<BODY BACKGROUND="/samples/images/backgrnd.gif">
<BODY BGCOLOR="FFFFFF">
<TABLE>
<TR>
<TD><IMG SRC="/samples/images/SPACE.gif" ALIGN="top" ALT=" "></TD>
<TD><A HREF="/samples/IMAGES/db_mh.map">
<IMG SRC="/SAMPLES/images/db_mh.gif" ismap BORDER=0 ALIGN="top"
ALT=" "></A></TD>
</TR>
<tr>
<TD></TD>
<TD>
<hr>
<font size=2>
<CENTER>
<%if idc.sales eq ""%>
<H2>Authors with sales greater than <I>5000</I></H2>
<%else%>
<H2>Authors with sales greater than <I><%idc.sales%></I></H2>
<%endif%>
<P>
<TABLE BORDER>
<%begindetail%>
<%if CurrentRecord EQ 0 %>
<caption>Query results:</caption>
<TR>
<TH><B>Author</B></TH><TH><B>YTD Sales<BR>(in dollars)</B></TH>
```

```
</TR>
<%endif%>
<TR><TD><%au_lname%></TD><TD align="right">$<%ytd_sales%></TD></TR>
<%enddetail%>
<P>
</TABLE>
</center>
<P>
<%if CurrentRecord EQ 0 %>
<I><B>Sorry, no authors had YTD sales greater than </I><%idc.sales%>.</B>
<P>
<%else%>
<HR>
<I>
The web page you see here was created by merging the results
of the SQL query with the template file SAMPLE.HTX.
<P>
The merge was done by the Microsoft Internet Database Connector and
the results were returned to this web browser by the Microsoft
Internet Information Server.
</I>
<%endif%>
</font>
</td>
</tr>
</table>
</BODY>
</HTML>
```

Sample.htx is a standard HTML document. The formatting is Spartan, and most of the HTML tags should be familiar to those of you who have experience with HTML tables. The %au_lname% and %ytd_sales% parameters in the <TR><TD><%au_lname%></TD> <TD align="right">$<%ytd_sales%></TD></TR> line specify the field names of the pubs.dbo.titleview view that populate the table columns.

The page is created based on the information that is, or isn't, returned from the query. For example, the following section of code performs conditional testing, examining for an empty set. The dbsamp1.htm page doesn't return a value for the IDC parameter (idc.sales eq ""), whereas the dbsamp2.htm page returns either the default value (5000) or a user-entered value.

```
<%if idc.sales eq ""%>
    <H2>Authors with sales greater than <I>5000</I></H2>
<%else%>
    <H2>Authors with sales greater than <I><%idc.sales%></I></H2>
<%endif%>
```

Considering User Rights and Database Security

If you don't implement database security, access via the IDC or any other Web-based application that delivers information from databases can be a wide-open door to your entire database system. Obviously, you must avoid giving any Internet or intranet user system administrator access to your databases. Potential security breaches arise from exposing your databases to users, not through security loopholes in IDC or other Web-based Internet applications. You must protect your databases against unauthorized access by hackers, either on-site or connected via the Internet. Following are basic recommendations for securing your databases for Internet and intranet connections:

- If you allow anonymous Internet connections to your site, grant appropriate (read-only) database permissions to the anonymous user (usually IUSR_*servername*). Also grant the anonymous user read-only access to the \InetPub\wwwroot folder and its subfolders that contain public information. You also must grant execute rights to scripts folders that contain executable files. Anonymous users who try to access pages for which they have no rights automatically receive an error message.

- For intranet users, enable Windows NT's integrated security for SQL Server. With integrated security, users log on to SQL Server with their network logon credentials, usually as members of the Domain Users group. You assign read-only permissions for database access to the Domain Users group. Jet databases don't offer integrated security, so you must provide a System.mdw file with a user name and password that you specify in the ODBC system data source Setup dialog. System.mdw files are one of the subjects of the "Creating a Jet 3.0 Table" section earlier in the chapter.

 ▶▶ See "Establishing Database Permissions," p. 830

Using Microsoft dbWeb

Microsoft's dbWeb 1.1 combines many of the features of SQL Server's Web Assistant and the IDC, and works with any RDBMS or desktop database for which 32-bit ODBC 2.5 is available. dbWeb eliminates the need to write .IDC and .HTX files, and handles graphic images well. dbWeb also makes it easy to create Web pages that include drop-down lists and text boxes for parameterized queries.

The dbWeb application consists of a server-side ISAPI component and the dbWeb Administrator, a Visual Basic 3.0 application that you use to create Web pages containing formatted database reports. Like most other Microsoft Internet-related applications, dbWeb 1.1 is free and downloadable as a 7.7M self-extracting setup file, dbWeb11.exe, from **http://www.microsoft.com/intdev/dbweb/dbwins-f.htm**. You also can download a dbWeb tutorial in Word 6.0 .doc format from **http://www.microsoft.com/intdev/dbweb/**.

To install dbWeb 1.1 from dbWeb11.exe, follow these steps:

1. In Explorer, double-click the dbWeb11.exe icon to start the InstallShield setup process. Click Yes when asked whether you want to install dbWeb, click Next in the initial installation dialog, read the license agreement, and then click Accept to open the Choose Destination Location dialog.

2. Accept the default folder for the dbWeb administrative files, C:\dbWeb, or click the Browse button to use a different folder (see fig. 20.30). Click Next.

Fig. 20.30   Specifying the directory for dbWeb 1.1's administrative files.

3. The 32-bit ODBC 2.5 drivers are the latest version, so clear the Microsoft ODBC 2.5 check box of the Select Components dialog (see fig. 20.31). You need the remaining components to run and administer dbWeb, as well as to try the sample databases, which are supplied in Jet 2.0 (16-bit) .MDB format. Click Next.

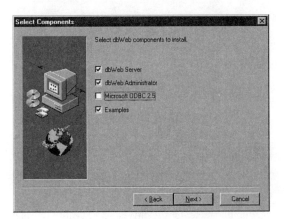

Fig. 20.31   Selecting for installation all the components of dbWeb 1.1 except the ODBC 2.5 components.

4. In the Microsoft Internet Information Server Configuration dialog, accept the values in the HTML Document Directory, Script Directory, and Logical Script Path text boxes, as shown in figure 20.32. (Microsoft hasn't yet adopted the term *folder* in all of its applications.) Click Next to complete the installation.

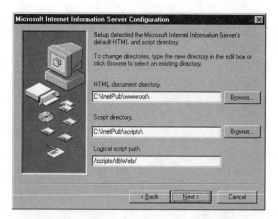

Fig. 20.32   Specifying the directory locations for dbWeb 1.1, with the version of Internet Information Server 2.0 included with Windows NT Server 4.0.

5. Click OK to close the Information message box; then click Yes when asked whether you want to start the dbWeb service (see fig. 20.33). Setup automatically adds three new ODBC system data sources for Jet databases and a dbWeb Administrator choice to the Start menu's Programs group.

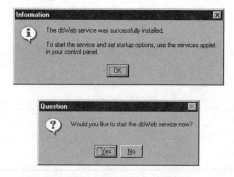

Fig. 20.33   The final two message boxes for the installation of dbWeb 1.1.

Note

You must change the Startup parameter for the dbWeb service with Control Panel's Services tool from Manual to Automatic, if you want dbWeb to run as a Windows NT service when you run dbWeb as a production service.

If you installed IIS 2.0 using the default Internet publishing directory, \InetPub, you must modify the DBX files that dbWeb uses to specify the location of its sample documents. Follow these steps to make the changes required to run the sample applications:

1. From the Start menu, choose Programs and dbWeb Administrator to launch the dbWeb Administrator application.

2. Double-click the dbnwind icon in the Data Sources window to display the eight individual dbnwind data sources, each of which has one or two Web page(s). The dbnwind data source connects to NWIND.MDB, the venerable sample database of Microsoft Access.

3. Double-click the Category_Products data source to open the editing dialog for the data source. Click the DBX tab to display the page for custom file formats.

4. Replace the \INETSRV\ element of the path statement with \InetPub\, as shown in figure 20.34, and then click OK.

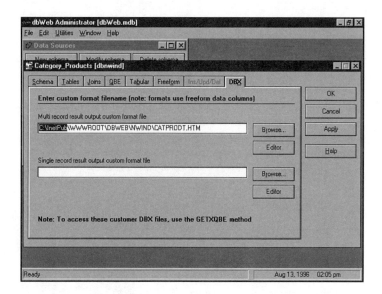

Fig. 20.34 Changing the directory for dbWeb HTML pages in the DBX page of the data source editing dialog.

5. Repeat steps 3 and 4 for each data source of the dbnwind database. (The dbpubs data sources don't use DBX entries.) Many of the dbnwind data sources require that you correct entries for multirecord and single-record versions of the data source.

6. Close the dbWeb Administrator application.

You access the dbWeb sample pages from a networked browser with the URL **http://servername/dbweb/dbwtest.htm**. Scroll down to the links to Pubs Examples and Northwind Examples to try the examples (see fig. 20.35). Figure 20.36 shows the page for the Northwind Category_Products data source displaying the first of four Categories table records and part of the Products table for the Beverages category. The Products list corresponds to an Access subform. The Category Listing page is static; no user-entered criteria is accepted.

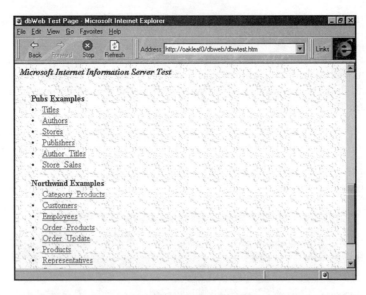

Fig. 20.35 Links to the sample dbWeb data sources for the dbpubs and dbnwind databases.

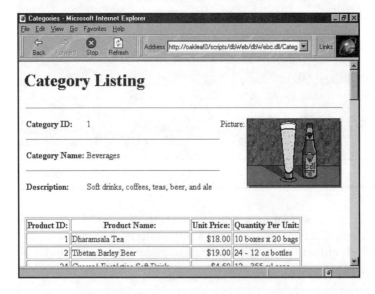

Fig. 20.36 The dbWeb Categories page created by the Category_Products data source.

Figure 20.37 illustrates a more complex, dynamic query page for the pubs database. You enter query constraints in text boxes with modifiers chosen from standard drop-down lists. Figure 20.38 shows the result of the query of figure 20.37. (The pubs database hasn't been updated for the 510 area code of the San Francisco East Bay region.) If you click a City link, a list of all authors in the same city appear, illustrating the drill-down capabilities of dbWeb pages.

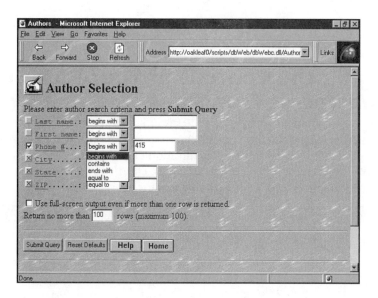

Fig. 20.37   A dbWeb query page with a user-entered search parameter.

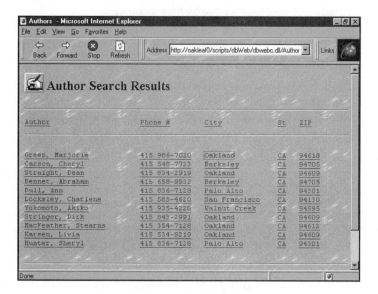

Fig. 20.38   The result set of the dbWeb query of figure 20.37.

All the sample applications are relatively simple decision-support front ends, some of which offer drill-down capabilities. One of the benefits of using dbWeb is the capability to easily create Web pages for transaction processing, such as adding orders and line items to the Orders and Order_Details table. The dbtutor.doc file describes how to design a dbWeb order-entry form. It's not likely that you'd use dbWeb to establish an electronic commerce Web site, but dbWeb is a remarkably useful tool for demonstrating the database capabilities of IIS 2.0 to members of management who may not be up-to-date on the latest Web technology.

Managing the Content of Your Web Site with Microsoft FrontPage

Windows NT Server 4.0 includes a copy of Microsoft FrontPage 1.1 for IIS 2.0 with a single client license. Like dbWeb, FrontPage 1.1 has two components: a server-side FrontPage Explorer for maintaining the organization of your Web pages, and a client-side WYSIWYG Web page editor for creating HTML files. FrontPage's ease of use makes it a logical tool to create the initial set of custom pages for your Web site.

> **Note**
>
> The initial retail version of FrontPage 1.1 didn't include the ISAPI extension to connect to IIS 2.0. You needed to download a beta version of the IIS 2.0 extension from the Microsoft Web site. The version of FrontPage included with Windows NT Server includes the IIS 2.0 extension, but you must install the extension manually.

Installing FrontPage 1.1 and the IIS 2.0 Server Extension

The Windows NT Server 4.0 setup program doesn't offer an option to install FrontPage 1.1. To install FrontPage from the distribution CD-ROM onto your Web server, follow these steps:

1. After inserting the Windows NT Server distribution CD-ROM and waiting for the splash screen to appear, click the Browse This CD button and double-click the Frontpg folder icon. Print Fpiis.doc, which contains some important information regarding security and other issues when using FrontPage 1.1 with IIS 2.0.

2. Click the Frontpg folder icon (in the Frontpg folder) and review the Fpreadme.txt file, which contains primarily information related to upgrading FrontPage 1.0 installations. Then double-click Setup.exe to begin the setup process.

3. Click the Next button of the first setup dialog to open the Destination Path dialog to set the folder to contain the FrontPage administrative files. Accept the default location, \Program Files\Microsoft FrontPage, or click the Browse button to choose a different location (see fig. 20.39). Click the Next button.

4. In the Setup Type dialog, you can select the Typical option, which installs the FrontPage Personal Web Server and the standard extensions (not including the IIS 2.0 extension). To save disk space, select the Custom option (see fig. 20.40) and click Next to display the Select Components dialog.

5. You need only the Client Software, because you install the IIS 2.0 extensions to use IIS 2.0, rather than the Personal Web Server, later in this procedure. Clear the Personal Web Server and Server Extensions check boxes (see fig. 20.41); then click Next.

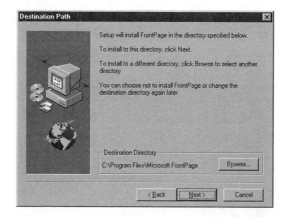

Fig. 20.39 Specifying the location of the FrontPage 1.1 administrative files.

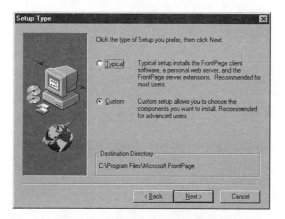

Fig. 20.40 Choosing between Typical and Custom installation options for FrontPage 1.1.

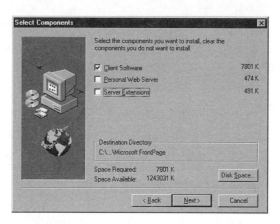

Fig. 20.41 Selecting only the Client Software for an IIS 2.0 installation.

6. In the Select Program Folder dialog, accept the default Microsoft FrontPage program folder or select an existing program folder for the FrontPage menu (see fig. 20.42). Click Next.

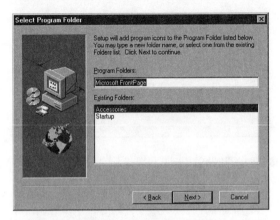

Fig. 20.42 Selecting the program folder for the FrontPage menu.

7. The Start Copying Files dialog (see fig. 20.43) confirms your prior choices. Click Next to complete the installation. When InstallShield has completed copying files, click Finish to close the last installation dialog.

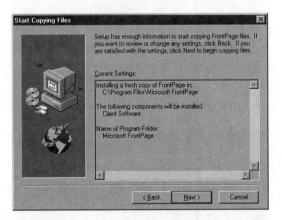

Fig. 20.43 Confirming your installation choices in the Start Copying Files dialog.

8. Navigate with Explorer to the \Frontpg\Iisext folder and double-click Iisext.exe to start the setup program for the IIS 2.0 extensions. Click Next to close the Welcome dialog and open the Ready to Transfer Files dialog that confirms the installation path (see fig. 20.44). Click Next to install the files.

9. When the Setup Complete dialog appears, make sure that the Run Server Administrator Now check box is marked, and click Finish to launch Server Administrator. Click OK when each message box shown in figure 20.45 appears.

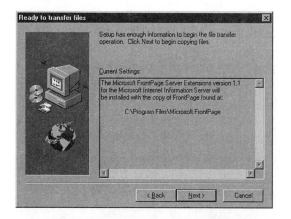

Fig. 20.44 Confirming the installation location for the IIS 2.0 extensions for FrontPage 1.1.

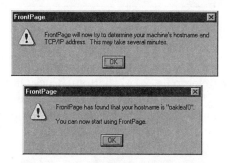

Fig. 20.45 Determining the server name and TCP/IP address the first time you start FrontPage's Server Administrator.

10. In the Server Administrator dialog, click the Install button to open the Configure Server Type dialog. Select MS Internet Information Server from the list, as shown in figure 20.46. (If you selected the Custom configuration, the other extensions shown in fig. 20.46 aren't available.) Click OK to open the first of two Server Configuration dialogs.

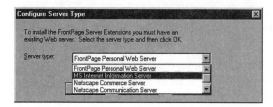

Fig. 20.46 Selecting IIS 2.0 as the FrontPage server type.

11. In the first Server Configuration dialog, click the Browse button and navigate to the location of the servsupp (server support) subfolder of the folder in which you installed the FrontPage administration files. The default value for the location of the required servers.cnf file is C:\Program Files\Microsoft FrontPage\serversupp\ (see fig. 20.47, top). Click OK to open the second Server Configuration dialog.

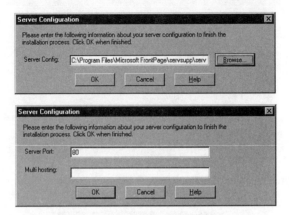

Fig. 20.47 The Server Configuration dialogs for setting the location of the server configuration file (top) and the TCP/IP port number for IIS 2.0 (bottom).

12. In the second Server Configuration dialog, type the TCP/IP port for IIS 2.0, usually **80**, the default value (refer to fig. 20.47, bottom). Click OK to display the Confirmation Dialog shown in figure 20.48. Click OK to install the IIS 2.0 extension. The FrontPage Server Administrator dialog appears as shown in figure 20.49.

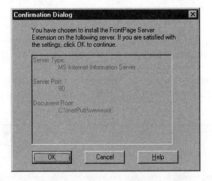

Fig. 20.48 Confirming the settings for Server Type, Server Port, and Document Root for the IIS 2.0 extension.

13. Click the Security button to add your Windows NT user ID to the list of Administrators for the default Web, <Root Web>, in the Administrator Name and Password dialog. Type and confirm your password (see fig. 20.50), and then click OK to return to the FrontPage Server Administrator dialog.

14. Click OK when a message confirms your addition to the Administrators list, and then close the Server Administrator dialog.

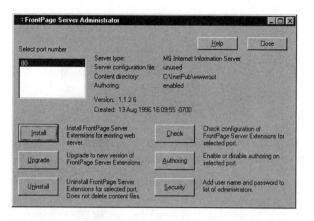

Fig. 20.49   The Server Administrator dialog after setting up the IIS 2.0 extension.

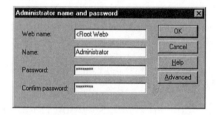

Fig. 20.50   Adding a password for your user ID to enable administration of the FrontPage Web site.

15. FrontPage 1.1 requires Basic (Clear Text) authentication. If you haven't specified Basic authentication in the Services page of Internet Service Manager's WWW Service Properties sheet, you receive the message shown in figure 20.51.

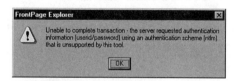

Fig. 20.51   The message indicating that you haven't enabled the Basic (Clear Text) authentication required by FrontPage 1.1.

16. Run Internet Service Manager and open the WWW Service Properties sheet. Verify that the Basic (Clear Text) password check box is marked. If you mark the Basic check box, the message shown in figure 20.52 explains the security consequences of your action. Click OK to close the WWW Service Properties sheet, and then exit Internet Service Manager.

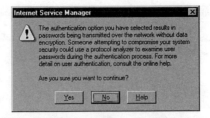

Fig. 20.52 The message that explains that enabling the Basic (Clear Text) authentication option may compromise the security of password transmission.

Experimenting with FrontPage Explorer and Editor

The organization of Web sites and the generation of Web content is beyond the scope of this book, but you can gain an idea of the capabilities of the FrontPage Explorer by using it to map the .HTM files supplied with IIS 2.0 and those added by any other Web applications you've installed, such as dbWeb. FrontPage automatically organizes your Web pages into a hierarchy based on their contained hyperlinks to other pages at your site, as well links to other sites. The FrontPage Editor lets you edit existing Web pages and create new pages in a graphical context.

To create a view of the sample IIS 2.0 Web pages in FrontPage Explorer and run the FrontPage Editor, follow these steps:

1. From the Start menu, choose Programs, Microsoft FrontPage, and FrontPage Explorer to open the Explorer application.

2. Choose Open Web from the File menu to display the Open Web dialog. Click List Webs to display the <Root Web> entry in the Webs list (see fig. 20.53).

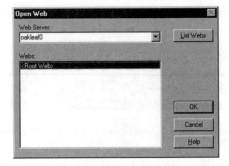

Fig. 20.53 Displaying existing FrontPage Webs in the Open Web dialog.

3. With the <Root Web> entry selected, click OK to open the Name and Password Required dialog. Type your administrator name and password, assigned in step 13 of the preceding section (see fig. 20.54). Click OK to open the <Root Web> in FrontPage Explorer (see fig. 20.55). A list of pages appears in the Outline View

pane, and a map of the hyperlink relationships of the pages appears in the Link
View pane.

Fig. 20.54 Logging on to FrontPage Explorer as an administrator.

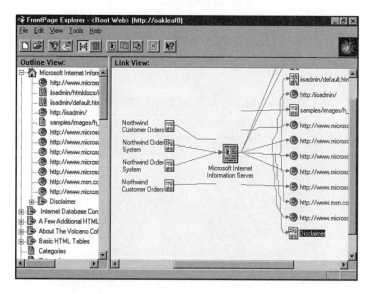

Fig. 20.55 FrontPage Explorer's view of the <Root Web> with IIS 2.0 and dbWeb sample pages.

   4. Double-click one of the icons for a local Web page, such as Disclaimer, to open the
   FrontPage Editor (see fig. 20.56).

   5. From the editor's window, choose HTML from the View menu to display the HTML
   code for the page in the View HTML dialog (see fig. 20.57). You can't edit the
   HTML code in this dialog; the FrontPage editor generates all HTML code.

FrontPage provides a set of templates that you can use to learn the basics of Web content
generation, as well as to provide a starting point for the design of production pages. The
list of templates shown in figure 20.58 appears when you choose New Web from Front-
Page Explorer's File menu. Select the Learning FrontPage template if you want to try the
tutorial included in the FrontPage help file.

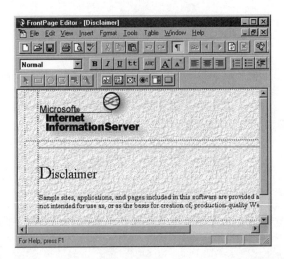

Fig. 20.56 FrontPage Editor displaying a Web page from the IIS 2.0 sample site.

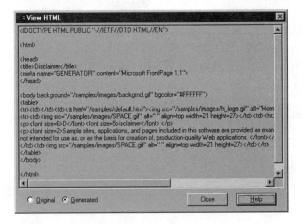

Fig. 20.57 Displaying HTML code in FrontPage Editor's Generated format.

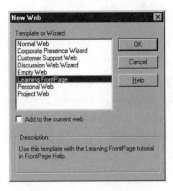

Fig. 20.58 A list of the templates and wizards included with FrontPage 1.1.

From Here...

This chapter provided an introduction to the techniques used by professional Webmasters to establish and distribute activity logging data using SQL Server 6.5 and its Web Assistant add-in. The Internet Database Connector and Microsoft dbWeb examples demonstrated that you can automatically create Web pages from existing information stored in your organization's databases. The chapter closed with instructions on how to install Microsoft FrontPage 1.1 and the required IIS 2.0 extensions, plus a brief description for getting started with FrontPage.

For content related to the subjects discussed in this chapter, see the following chapters:

- Chapter 18, "Managing Remote Access Service," explains how to configure Windows NT Server 4.0's RAS component to support dial-in access to Web pages by mobile users.

- Chapter 19, "Setting Up the Internet Information Server," covers the initial installation and configuration of the Internet Information Server and its services.

- Chapter 22, "Running Microsoft SQL Server 6.5," describes how to install and set up SQL Server 6.5 and establish database security applicable to Web sites.

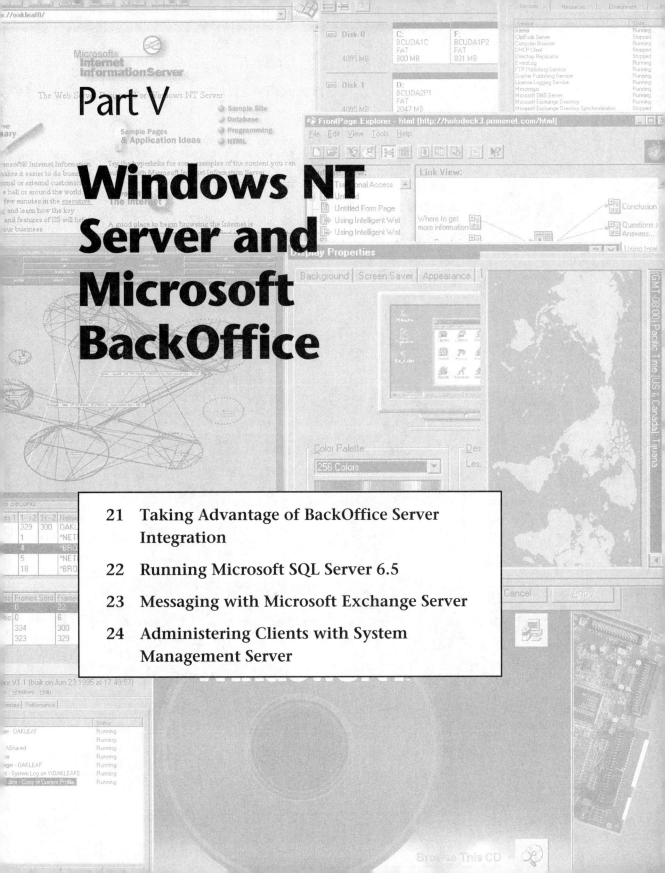

Part V

Windows NT Server and Microsoft BackOffice

21 Taking Advantage of BackOffice Server Integration

22 Running Microsoft SQL Server 6.5

23 Messaging with Microsoft Exchange Server

24 Administering Clients with System Management Server

Chapter 21

Taking Advantage of BackOffice Server Integration

Microsoft has acquired about 90 percent of the market for Windows productivity application suites with Microsoft Office. The success of the bundled Office applications led the firm to take a similar approach to market its server-based products. Microsoft announced the BackOffice "Integrated Information System" on September 21, 1994, with the release of Windows NT 3.5. Press reports credit Steve Ballmer, Microsoft's executive vice president, as the originator of the BackOffice name. An ebullient Ballmer decreed 1995 to be the "Year of BackOffice." In retrospect, Ballmer missed the mark by about a year; BackOffice didn't gain real marketing momentum until 1996.

> **Note**
>
> Robert McDowell, Microsoft's vice president for enterprise systems, said in the spring of 1996 that the BackOffice suite of products was selling at a rate of $1 billion per year, more than tripling sales in the preceding six months. Annualizing Microsoft's $2.2 billion in sales achieved during the first calendar quarter of 1996 (Microsoft's third fiscal quarter), sales of the BackOffice suite are running at about 11.5 percent of Microsoft's gross income. The growth rate of BackOffice sales, however, exceeds that of Microsoft's overall sales, which grow roughly 40 percent per year. Thus, Ballmer's 1994 goal of a 25 percent contribution by BackOffice components to Microsoft's 1999 total income appears realistic.

Microsoft offers BackOffice as a "full package product," also called an SKU (stock-keeping unit), but BackOffice is better categorized as a concept. The BackOffice bundle, version 2.0 when this book was written, has limited utility in production environments due to its single-server licensing restriction. The BackOffice concept uses Windows NT Server's built-in domain architecture, security system, and application server capabilities to support various integrated back-end services. Full integration of each component with Windows NT Server, including providing a single user logon for all services, is what has made the BackOffice concept a commercial success.

This chapter covers the following topics:

- The components of Microsoft BackOffice

- New Internet-related server components

- Licensing methods for BackOffice components

- Licensing costs for BackOffice

- Using Control Panel's License tool and License Manager

V

Microsoft BackOffice

Aiming at a Moving BackOffice Target

The current version of Microsoft BackOffice is a suite consisting of the following bundled components:

- *Windows NT Server 4.0*, replacing version 3.51 in BackOffice 2.0

- *Internet Information Server 2.0*, included with Windows NT Server 4.0, replacing version 1.0 in BackOffice 2.0, plus a single-user version of Microsoft FrontPage 1.1, also included with Windows NT Server 4.0

- *SQL Server 6.5*, a client/server relational database management system (RDBMS)

- *Exchange Server 4.0*, the first version (despite the 4.0 version number) of the belated client/server replacement for Microsoft Mail Server 3.5

- *System Management Server (SMS) 1.2* for managing Windows clients, distributing software, and tracking client software, replacing version 1.1 in BackOffice 2.0

- *SNA Server 2.11*, to provide connectivity to IBM mainframes and AS/400 series minicomputers via IBM's System Network Architecture

The preceding list demonstrates that BackOffice, as a retail product, is in a constant state of flux. Synchronizing the release of updated BackOffice components for a specific product version number appears to be a difficult, if not impossible, task. Component synchronization problems plagued users of early versions of Microsoft Office; release problems finally appear to be overcome in Office 97. Most users don't want to wait for simultaneous upgrades to every BackOffice component before being able to take advantage of the features offered by a new release of System Management Server or SNA Server. Complex business issues, such as incremental upgrade pricing for server and client licenses, impede administration of sites using the BackOffice bundle.

> **Note**
>
> Internet Information Server 2.0 is the subject of Chapter 19, "Setting Up the Internet Information Server," and Chapter 20, "Administering Intranet and World Wide Web Sites." SQL Server 6.5 is covered in Chapter 22, "Running Microsoft SQL Server 6.5." Chapter 23, "Messaging with Microsoft Exchange Server," introduces you to Microsoft Exchange Server 4.0, and Chapter 24, "Administering Clients with System Management Server," describes how to use SMS 1.1 and 1.2.
>
> SNA Server is a specialized server application and is beyond the scope of this book, which is limited to conventional PCs. A brief discussion of SNA Server 2.11 appears in Chapter 17, "Integrating Windows NT with Heterogeneous Networks."

 ◄◄ See "Integrating Windows NT in IBM SNA Environments," p. 649

The frequent changes to BackOffice components and Microsoft's Byzantine upgrade licensing policies make buying a Microsoft "software insurance policy" (described later in "The Annuity Model for BackOffice Upgrades" section) a wise investment for most BackOffice users.

In addition to the standard BackOffice components of the preceding list, the following Internet-related Windows NT Server applications were in various stages of development and testing when this book was written:

- *Proxy Server* (code-named Catapult) for connecting intranets to the Internet, providing control of users' outbound access to Internet sites (**http:// www.microsoft.com/proxy/default.htm**)

- *Index Server* (code-named Tripoli) for providing search services on the content of Web sites and intranets (**http://www.microsoft.com/ntserver/search/**)

- *Media Server* (code-named Cougar, formerly Tiger) for distributing real-time streaming video and audio content over intranets and the Internet, using Microsoft ActiveMovie to render the content on 32-bit Windows clients

- *Merchant Services* for establishing electronic storefronts on the Web (**http:// www.microsoft.com/ecommerce/content.htm**)

- *Normandy*, the code name for a Windows NT Server-based platform for Internet service providers and commercial Web sites, much of the technology of which is based on that of The Microsoft Network (**http://www.microsoft.com/ internet/normandy/entry.htm**)

Several of the components in the preceding list are likely to gain official status as full-fledged members of the BackOffice suite. Although Catapult was in beta test in the fall of 1996, Microsoft's BackOffice Web page (**http://www.microsoft.com/backoffice/**) already sported a Proxy Server tab. Index Server, like Internet Information Server, is likely to be included as a component of a future version of Windows NT. Media Server, Merchant Services, and Normandy, which have a much narrower market than Proxy Server and Index Server, probably will remain outside the mainstream BackOffice server suite.

Licensing BackOffice Components

Microsoft sells Windows NT Server 4.0 and other BackOffice components through authorized Microsoft resellers, which include virtually all major software distributors. Large firms qualify to buy directly from Microsoft. Microsoft and its resellers offer quantity discounts, as well as discounted competitive upgrades for current users of NetWare and Banyan VINES. Academic licenses are available at about 60 percent of the commercial price. Microsoft commercial pricing examples shown in the following sections were effective for U.S. purchasers in mid-1996, and may vary depending on the reseller you choose and your negotiation skills.

> **Note**
>
> For a referral to an authorized Microsoft reseller, call Microsoft at (800) 426-9400.

V

Microsoft BackOffice

Per-Seat vs. Per-Server Licensing

Before the introduction of BackOffice, Microsoft priced Windows NT Advanced Server 3.1 and Microsoft SQL Server 4.21 by the number of client connections. Both server products offered "Enterprise" versions that allowed connection of an unlimited number of clients, without the requirement to buy individual client licenses. With the introduction of BackOffice 1.0, however, Microsoft adopted a per-seat licensing system with a per-server option available for some components. The difference between per-seat and per-server licensing is as follows:

- *Per-seat* licensing requires that each client connected to the network have a Client Access License for Windows NT, if the client uses Windows NT's networking services. Each client also must have a Client Access License for each BackOffice service it uses. A per-seat client may connect simultaneously to any number of Windows NT servers with a single Client Access License. There's no built-in server connection limit; the network administrator is responsible for assuring licensing compliance.

- *Per-server* licensing requires that the number of Client Access Licenses must equal the number of PCs simultaneously using Windows NT's networking or BackOffice services. The license is associated with a single server. If one PC is simultaneously connected to two Windows NT servers, two Windows NT Client Access Licenses are consumed. When the Windows NT server's connection limit is reached, no more connections are possible. Per-server licensing often is called *license pooling* or *multiplexing*. Per-server licensing isn't available for System Management Server.

Per-seat licensing is the most common choice for larger organizations running multiple Windows NT servers. Per-seat licensing also is the easiest to administer; you count the number of client PCs and buy that many Client Access Licenses for Windows NT Server and each BackOffice server application you run.

Per-server licensing is advantageous under the following circumstances:

- You use Windows NT Server 4.0 only as a remote access server (RAS) to provide mobile personnel with network services. In this case, you need to purchase only Client Access Licenses for the maximum number of simultaneous inbound connections you support.

- You use Windows NT Server 4.0 and Internet Information Server 2.0 as an Internet server, with periodic LAN connection by the Webmaster or others for updates and maintenance. You need Windows NT Client Access Licenses for a Windows NT intranet server if clients use Windows NT networking to connect to the server. See **http://www.microsoft.com/ntserver/det3.htm** for specific details on Internet licensing.

- You're making a test installation that involves sequential evaluation of BackOffice components by various sets of users. You have the one-time option of installing Windows NT Server and the other BackOffice components (except System Management Server) in per-server mode, and then changing the licensing method to per-seat. You can't change from per-seat to per-server mode.

> **Note**
>
> You don't need a Client Access License to remotely administer another computer with Performance Monitor, Server Manager, or User Manager for Domains. Local logon to the server through the built-in Workstation service doesn't require a Client Access License.

The preceding scenarios assume that you use NetWare or another network operating system for file and printer sharing. If you use Windows NT Server only for hosting SQL Server, Exchange Server, and/or SNA Server, and use another network operating system for communication with the service, the Windows NT server is called an *application server* and doesn't require Windows NT Client Access Licenses. You must have a Client Access License, either per-seat or per-server, for each service you run.

> **Note**
>
> A Client Access License isn't software; it's a document. Windows for Workgroups, Windows 95, and Windows NT Workstation each include the required client software to connect to Windows NT Server. The distribution CD-ROMs for BackOffice components include the required client software for the service.

BackOffice Server and Client Access Licenses

BackOffice server and BackOffice Client Access Licenses are sold as separate full-package products (SKUs) at a substantial discount (in the range of 30 percent to 40 percent) from the combined prices of the individual components. The full value of the discount, however, is attained only if each of your clients uses every component of BackOffice. For most users, the BackOffice bundle discount is illusory.

Like Microsoft Office, all the BackOffice server components are licensed to run only on a single machine and are restricted to per-seat licensing. Similarly, the BackOffice Client software is licensed for installation on one PC. You aren't permitted to pool BackOffice client licenses among client PCs on your network. Detailed information on licensing terms and conditions, as well as prices, for BackOffice server and Client Access Licenses is available at **http://www.microsoft.com/backoffice/howtobuy.htm**.

Microsoft recommends BackOffice for the following types of customers:

- Small businesses
- Branch offices within organizations running BackOffice components at a central location
- Sites that run Exchange Server and any other BackOffice component
- Sites that use System Management Server with SQL Server
- Client-server development

The WAN-connected branch office scenario is the most likely to show a potential saving by implementing BackOffice. Small businesses seldom have need for SNA Server and

V

Microsoft BackOffice

aren't likely to devote the administrative resources necessary to implement System Management Server. For client/server development, the Microsoft Developer Network (MSDN) offers a yearly Enterprise Subscription (formerly Level 2) that includes quarterly releases of BackOffice (the BackOffice Test Platform) with licenses for five simultaneous connections. The subscription includes special Premium Shipments for BackOffice upgrades between the quarterly releases. The $1,499 for the Enterprise Subscription represents a substantial discount from the ERP (estimated retail price) for BackOffice with five Client Access Licenses. More information on MSDN subscriptions is available from **http://www.microsoft.com/msdn/msdnprog.htm**.

Buying BackOffice to achieve savings resulting from the use of only two BackOffice services on a single server is a marginal proposition, at best. The value of your time spent analyzing such potential savings is unlikely to be recovered by the actual reduction in licensing cost.

Windows NT 4.0 License Packages and Cost

Windows NT Server 4.0 is available in five-user and 10-user versions. Table 21.1 lists the theoretical licensing costs for typical numbers of clients connected to a single Windows NT Server 4.0 installation. Volume discounts available through Microsoft Open Licensing Pack (MOLP) purchases aren't applied to the amounts shown in table 21.1. Total and per-client costs for 50 or more clients are approximate. Further licensing details are available at **http://www.microsoft.com/ntserver/howbuy.htm**.

Table 21.1   Approximate Licensing Cost and Cost per Client for Typical Windows NT Server Installations

License	Number of Clients 5	10	25	50	100	250
Server	$809	$1,129	$809	$1,129	$809	$1,129
Clients	N/A	N/A	659	1,318	3,130	7,198
Total	809	1,129	1,468	2,447	3,939	9,037
Per Client	162	113	59	49	39	36

> **Note**
>
> There's no explanation for the $320 cost difference between the five-client and 10-client versions of Windows NT Server 4.0. This difference represents a cost of $64 each for the additional five clients. Single-quantity client licenses are priced at $39.95, about $120 less than the incremental licensing of five clients. There's also no obvious explanation for Microsoft's fascination with the number nine as the terminal digit for pricing its BackOffice components. The $39.95 price for a single Client Access License suggests that consumer product price-pointing may have crept into the process.

SQL Server 6.5 Licensing

Microsoft SQL Server 6.5 is available in five-user, 10-user, and 25-user versions. Table 21.2 lists Microsoft's published costs (May 1996) for typical numbers of clients connected to a single SQL Server. Microsoft Open Licensing Pack (MOLP) purchases and volume discounts are applicable for 50 clients or more. For the latest information on SQL Server 6.5 licensing, check **http://www.microsoft.com/sql/howbuy.htm**. Microsoft also offers SQL Workstation that runs on Windows NT Workstation and provides only a single connection.

Table 21.2   Approximate Total Licensing Cost and Cost per Client for SQL Server 6.5*

License	Number of Clients					
	5	10	25	50	100	250
Server	$1,399	$1,999	$3,999	$1,399	$1,399	$1,399
Clients	N/A	N/A	N/A	6,200	11,780	30,380
Total	1,399	1,999	3,999	7,599	13,179	31,779
Per Client	280	200	160	152	132	127

*Amounts shown were published by Microsoft in May 1996.

Note

The $2,999 Internet Connector License Pack for SQL Server is required if a Web server (Microsoft Internet Information Server or any other Web server) is populated from SQL Server data. Population includes the use of the Internet Database Connector, dbWeb, or the SQL Server Web Assistant with SQL Server.

Exchange Server 4.0 Licensing

Microsoft Exchange Server 4.0, like SQL Server 6.5, comes in five-user, 10-user, and 25-user versions. Table 21.3 lists Microsoft's published costs (May 1996) for typical numbers of clients connected to a single Exchange server. Microsoft Open Licensing Pack (MOLP) purchases and volume discounts are applicable for 50 clients or more. For pricing details on all versions of Exchange Server, check **http://www.microsoft.com/Exchange/howbuy/pricing1.htm**.

Table 21.3   Approximate Total Licensing Cost and Cost per Client for Microsoft Exchange Server 4.0*

License	Number of Clients					
	5	10	25	50	100	250
Server	$999	$1,369	$2,139	$999	$999	$999
Clients	N/A	N/A	N/A	2,700	5,130	13,230
Total	999	1,369	2,139	3,699	6,129	14,229
Per Client	200	137	85	74	61	57

*Amounts shown for 10 through 250 units were published by Microsoft in mid-1996.

> **Note**
>
> Microsoft offers the Internet Mail Connector for $377 per server and the X.400 Connector for $757 per server. You must license the Connector for each Exchange server in your system. An alternative to individual Connector licenses is the Enterprise Edition of Exchange Server ($1,970 without Client Access Licenses, $4,039 with 25 Client Access Licenses), which includes both the Internet and X.400 Connectors.

System Management Server 1.2 Licensing

System Management Server isn't priced with bundled client licenses. Table 21.4 lists Microsoft's published costs (May 1996) for typical numbers of clients connected to a single SMS 1.1 installation. (Pricing for version 1.2 is expected to be similar or identical.) SMS is the only BackOffice component that requires per-seat licensing. Microsoft Open Licensing Pack (MOLP) purchases and volume discounts are applicable for 50 clients or more. System Management Server price details are at **http://www.microsoft.com/BackOffice/det5.htm**.

Table 21.4   Approximate Total Licensing Cost and Cost per Client for System Management Server 1.1*

| License | Number of Clients | | | | | |
	5	10	25	50	100	250
Server	$649	$649	$649	$649	$649	$649
Clients	275	550	1,074	1,850	3,700	9,250
Total	924	1,199	1,723	2,499	4,349	9,899
Per Client	185	120	69	50	43	40

Amounts shown were published by Microsoft in June 1996.

> **Note**
>
> At least one SQL Server 6.5 license is required for use of System Management Server. Client Access licenses for the SQL Server installation used with SMS aren't required unless SQL Server is accessed by clients for other purposes. Access to SQL Server for administration of SMS doesn't require a SQL Server Client Access License.

SNA Server 2.11 Licensing

SNA Server, like System Management Server, isn't priced with bundled client licenses. Table 21.5 lists Microsoft's published costs (May 1996) for typical numbers of clients connected to a single SNA Server 2.11 installation through an application that accesses SNA services, such as Attachmate Extra or WallData Rumba. Microsoft Open Licensing Pack (MOLP) purchases and volume discounts are applicable for 50 clients or more. An SNA Workstation version, similar in concept to SQL Workstation, also is available. Get SNA Server pricing details from **http://www.microsoft.com/sna/howbuy.htm**.

SNA Server requires a mainframe or IBM AS/400 System Network Architecture connection; installing and using SNA Server is beyond the scope of this book.

Table 21.5 Approximate Total Licensing Cost and Cost per Client for SNA Server 2.11*

| License | Number of Clients | | | | | |
	5	10	25	50	100	250
Server	$409	$409	$409	$409	$409	$409
Clients	325	650	1,294	2,250	4,500	11,250
Total	734	1,059	1,703	2,659	4,909	11,659
Per Client	147	106	68	53	49	47

Amounts shown are based on published Microsoft pricing as of June 1996.

Licensing Costs for All BackOffice Components

Table 21.6 summarizes and averages the data of tables 21.1 through 21.5 to provide an example of the total cost for all BackOffice components installed on a single Windows NT server for various numbers of client licenses. As mentioned earlier in the chapter, running all BackOffice services on a single Windows NT server for more than about 10 or 20 clients is likely to be impractical. As an example, a single-server configuration doesn't provide for a Backup Domain Controller, which is necessary for installations with more than 10 or 20 users. Adding Windows NT Server 4.0 licenses at the 25, 50, 100, and 250 client level, however, adds less than 10 percent to total cost per client.

Table 21.6 Approximate Total Licensing Cost and Cost per Client for All BackOffice Components

| Component | Number of Clients | | | | | |
	5	10	25	50	100	250
Windows NT Server	$809	$1,129	$1,468	$2,447	$3,939	$9,037
SQL Server	1,399	1,999	3,999	7,599	13,179	31,779
Exchange Server	999	1,369	2,139	3,699	6,129	14,229
SMS	924	1,199	1,723	2,499	4,349	9,899
SNA Server	734	1,059	1,703	2,659	4,909	11,659
Total	4,865	6,755	11,032	18,903	32,505	76,603
Per Client	973	676	441	378	325	306

When this book was written, Microsoft hadn't published official pricing for BackOffice Server and Clients using Windows NT Server 4.0. Table 21.7 shows Microsoft's prices for "Common Customer Usage Requirements" for BackOffice 2.0 with Windows NT Server 3.51. Although Microsoft may increase the price of BackOffice Server and Client licenses to reflect the approximate $130 increase in the price of the 10-client version of Windows NT Server 4.0, such a surcharge isn't a major factor in comparing the savings between single-server versions of individual and bundled BackOffice purchases.

Table 21.7 Approximate Total Licensing Cost and Cost per Client for BackOffice 2.0 with Windows NT 3.51						
License	Number of Clients					
	5	10	25	50	100	250
Server	$2,199	$2,199	$2,199	$2,199	$2,199	$2,199
Clients	1,345	2,690	5,524	9,800	19,600	49,000
Total	3,544	4,889	7,723	11,999	21,799	51,199
Per Client	709	489	309	240	218	205

Microsoft also offers pricing models for 500 and 1,000 clients, which are wholly unrealistic for single-server BackOffice installations.

The Annuity Model for BackOffice Upgrades

Press reports from the July 31, 1996, Microsoft briefing for security analysts quote Bill Gates as saying that the BackOffice software market is "an annuity business." Much of Microsoft's income derives from license fees for the more-or-less yearly updates of the Microsoft Office and BackOffice full-package product. Updates to BackOffice occur at a more frequent rate because of the lack of synchronization among component upgrades, as discussed earlier in the "Aiming at a Moving BackOffice Target" section. The costs of updating servers and clients can be considerable. For example, updating from Windows NT Server 3.51 to 4.0 costs $539 for a 10-user license, and updating 20 clients carries a price tag of $339, both about 50 percent of the original license fees.

Microsoft defines the following types of server-side product upgrades:

■ *Major upgrades* are defined as an increment to the integer value of the product version. The upgrade from Windows NT 3.51 to 4.0 is an example of a major upgrade. Major upgrades require upgrading client and server software.

■ *Minor upgrades* are defined as an increment to the first decimal digit of the version number. The upgrade of SQL Server from version 6.0 to 6.5 and System Management Server from 1.1 to 1.2 are examples of minor upgrades. Minor upgrades also require upgrading client and server software, but Microsoft says that the price for a minor upgrade "will typically be half of the charge for a major upgrade."

■ *Step-ups* (sometimes called *updates*) are defined as an increment to the second decimal digit of the version number. The step-up from Windows NT Server 3.5 to 3.51 is an example. Step-ups replace the server but not the client software.

> **Note**
>
> Service packs, which ordinarily correct bugs or provide minor changes to client or server software, are free when downloaded from Microsoft's FTP site or Web server.

One of the problems facing network and system administrators at large firms is the ability to forecast the cost of upgrading clients and servers accurately. Not only is it difficult to predict when Microsoft will release a new upgrade or step-up, but pricing is likely to be unpredictable, too. Thus, Microsoft has gone into the "software insurance" business with a fixed-price annuity, called *maintenance*, for server-side upgrades.

Microsoft offers maintenance for its BackOffice family of server products under the Microsoft Select or Microsoft Open License programs. Maintenance is a fixed-fee, two-year agreement, which automatically updates all your BackOffice component and Client Access Licenses when Microsoft updates or steps up a product. According to Microsoft, the cost of the program is about 15 percent per year of the total ERPs for your existing license count. One of the more interesting features of the annuity is that you don't have to "be current" to enroll. In Microsoft's terms, you can "get current" and "remain current" for two years for an amount that might be less than the cost of a single major upgrade, depending on how many BackOffice components you license.

> **Tip**
>
> If you have a large Windows NT Server 3.51 installation that you plan to upgrade to version 4.0, make sure that you investigate a maintenance agreement before placing an order for the upgrade. A maintenance agreement that includes the current upgrade can reduce two-year upgrade costs substantially. If you're running System Management Server, you'll want to make the minor upgrade to version 1.2, and SNA Server had a major upgrade to version 3.0 in the works when this book was written.

Using Windows NT Server 4.0's License Manager

Most System Management Server users were disappointed to learn that version 1.2 still doesn't include a license metering feature. Microsoft includes a relatively simple License Manager application in Windows NT Server 4.0, which performs rudimentary license metering for applications that operate in per-server licensing mode. Control Panel's License tool also is involved in license management.

Control Panel's License Tool

Windows NT Server 4.0's License Management service introduces a new term, *enterprise server*, to define a master Primary Domain Controller (PDC) to which other PDCs in the domain and trusting domains replicate license information. An enterprise server can be a PDC or a plain server. In a single-domain environment, the PDC is the master server for license management purposes. You define the enterprise server or master server with Control Panel's License tool. The License tool also lets you specify the license mode for each service on the computer, the number of per-server licenses, and replication frequency and time. Only the License Manager can administer per-seat licenses.

To use Control Panel's License tool, follow these steps:

1. From Control Panel, double-click the License tool to open the Choose Licensing Mode dialog. Select the server component you want to manage from the Product list. Figure 21.1 shows Windows NT Server selected for the per-server licensing mode.

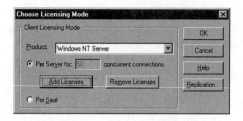

Fig. 21.1   Control Panel's Choose Licensing Mode dialog.

2. Click the Add Licenses button to add per-server licenses for the selected component in the New Client Access License dialog. Use the spin buttons or type a new number in the Quantity box (see fig. 21.2). The For License Mode option buttons and the Comment text box are disabled. Click OK to close the dialog.

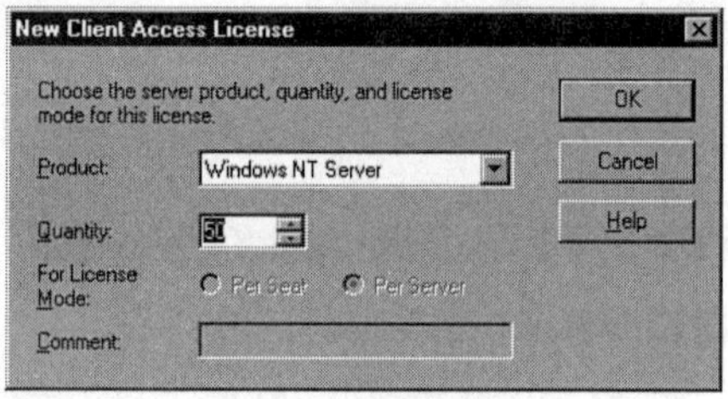

Fig. 21.2   Adding per-server licenses for Windows NT Server 4.0.

You can use the Remove Licenses button of the Choose Licensing Mode dialog to reduce the number of per-server licenses for a component, if necessary, to reflect actual license purchases.

3. If you add licenses, the Per Server Licensing dialog appears (see fig. 21.3). Mark the check box to indicate that you agree with the terms of the licensing agreement, and then click OK.

4. Click Replication in the Choose Licensing Mode dialog to open the Replication Configuration dialog to specify an enterprise server, if necessary, and to set the replication frequency or time for the local server. If you don't specify an enterprise server, the PDC for the server's domain is the master server for licensing purposes (see fig. 21.4). Click OK to close the dialog.

5. Click OK to close the Choose Licensing Mode dialog.

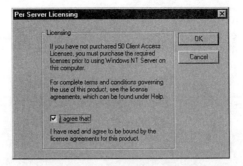

Fig. 21.3   Confirming agreement with the licensing terms for per-server mode.

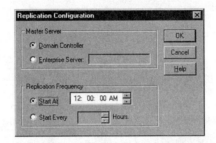

Fig. 21.4   Establishing the master server and a replication frequency in the Replication Configuration dialog.

Note

With the exception of specifying the replication options, you can use License Manager to perform all the functions of the License tool. Also, the License tool lets you set the number of per-seat licenses.

License Manager

License Manager is Microsoft's aid to keeping you honest in the licensing department. Unlike some other network operating system and server application suppliers, Microsoft trusts its customers to purchase the required number of server Client Access Licenses for their organizations. License Manager lets you set the number of Client Access Licenses for BackOffice components operating in per-seat, not per-server, mode. Also, you can monitor and administer per-seat and per-server licenses for any server in the domain or in a trusting domain.

To use License Manager, follow these steps:

1. From the Start menu choose Programs, Administrative Tools, and License Manager to open License Manager's window. If you haven't entered per-seat license information, the Purchase History page is empty.

2. Click the Products View tab to display a summary of product licensing. In figure 21.5, the Windows NT Server item displays the total number of per-server licenses for two servers (OAKLEAF0 and OAKLEAF3). The entry for System Management

Server displays a warning that three client seats have been allocated, but no per-client licenses have been purchased. The three allocated seats are the server on which SMS is installed (OAKLEAF0), a Windows 95 client (OAKLEAF1), and a Windows NT 4.0 BDC (OAKLEAF3).

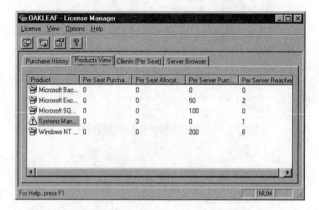

Fig. 21.5 The Products View page of License Manager for a system installed from the BackOffice Test Platform distribution CD-ROM but installed with per-server licensing.

3. To monitor clients with unlicensed usage of per-seat server applications, click the Clients (Per Seat) tab. Figure 21.6 displays the three PCs (two of which are servers) that show unlicensed usage of SMS.

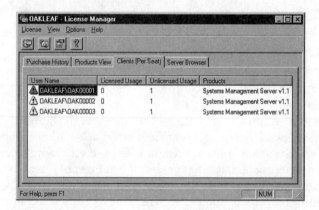

Fig. 21.6 The Clients (Per Seat) page, displaying unlicensed usage of SMS by two servers (OAK00001 and OAK00003) and a client (OAK00002).

4. To monitor or administer the number of per-seat licenses, or to change from per-server to per-seat licensing, click the Server Browser tab and expand the list to display each server and its services (see fig. 21.7).

5. To change a component from per-server to per-seat licensing, double-click the component to display the Choose Licensing Mode dialog (see fig. 21.8).

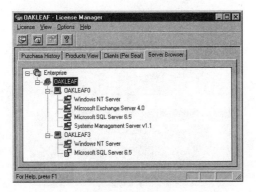

Fig. 21.7 Displaying BackOffice components in License Manager's Server Browser page.

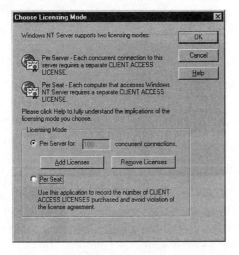

Fig. 21.8 The Choose Licensing Mode dialog.

6. Select Per Seat and click OK. A License Violation message box appears, offering you the opportunity to cancel your choice (see fig. 21.9, top). Click No to receive another confirmation message (see fig. 21.9, bottom); click Yes to change the licensing mode.

> **Note**
>
> The License Violation message that appears after selecting per-seat licensing doesn't conform to Microsoft's stated policy that you can change from per-server to per-seat licensing without violating your license.

7. Click OK in the Choose Licensing Mode dialog to continue with the mode change. Mark the I Agree That check box of the Per Seat Licensing dialog (see fig. 21.10), and then click OK to effect the mode change. All per-server license entries for the product are deleted.

V

Microsoft BackOffice

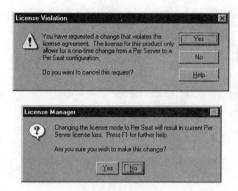

Fig. 21.9   Doubly confirming that you want to change licensing mode from per-server to per-seat.

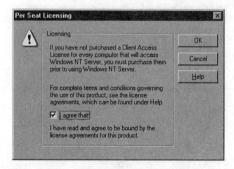

Fig. 21.10   The final dialog in the licensing mode change process.

8. From the License menu choose New License to display the New Client Access License dialog. Unlike the dialog displayed by Control Panel's License tool, the Per Seat option is set (but disabled), and the Comment text box is enabled.

9. Select the component to which to add Client Access Licenses in the Product drop-down list box, set the number of licenses in the Quantity box, and then type a description of the transaction in the Comment text box (see fig. 21.11). Click OK to add the new licenses, mark the I Agree That check box of the Per Seat Licensing dialog, and click OK to add the per-seat licenses.

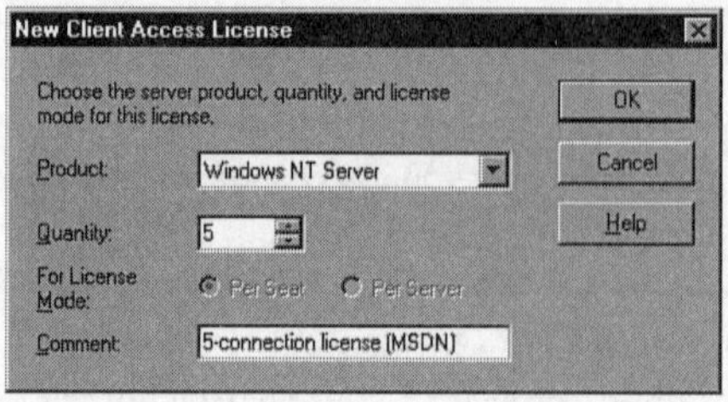

Fig. 21.11   Adding new per-seat licenses for a BackOffice component.

10. Repeat steps 5 through 9 for each component except SMS. For SMS, you need to add Client Access Licenses with only steps 8 and 9.

Note

You don't necessarily need to change the mode of all your BackOffice servers to per-seat mode unless you've purchased the BackOffice server bundle or are using the BackOffice Test Platform from MSDN. An alternative in these two cases is to specify the number of client licenses for the BackOffice product.

---

11. Click the Purchase History tab to verify your transactions (see fig. 21.12).

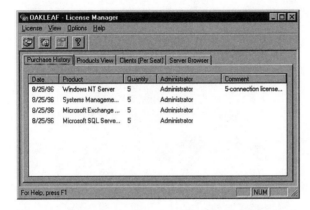

Fig. 21.12   The Purchase History page, displaying changes to per-seat licensing mode.

12. Click the Products View tab to verify that per-server licenses no longer appear (see fig. 21.13). Close License Manager.

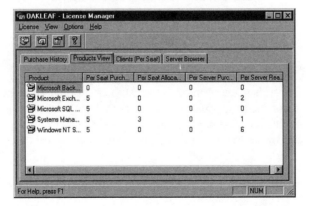

Fig. 21.13   The Products View, confirming that prior per-server licenses have been eliminated.

License violations appear as Stop events in Event Viewer's Application Log window (see fig. 21.14). Double-clicking the event item displays an Event Detail dialog (see fig. 21.15).

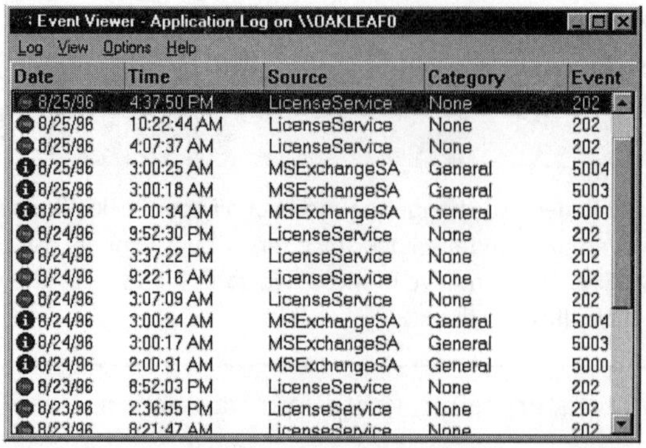

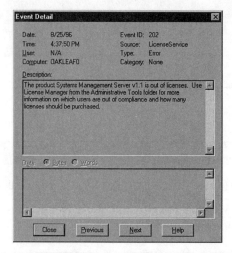

Fig. 21.14 Out-of-license events generated by License Manager.

Fig. 21.15 The Event Detail dialog, displaying an out-of-license event for System Management Server.

From Here...

This chapter provided an introduction to the BackOffice product, and the licensing requirements and costs of the individual components that make up Microsoft's BackOffice family. Using Control Panel's License tool and License Manager to assure compliance with Microsoft's licensing terms for server licenses and Client Access Licenses also was covered.

For additional information on the three most commonly used services of BackOffice, see the following chapters:

- Chapter 22, "Running Microsoft SQL Server 6.5," describes the basic features of Microsoft's most recent update to SQL Server, which includes new database replication features and a SQL Web Page Wizard.

- Chapter 23, "Messaging with Microsoft Exchange Server," introduces you to installation and management of Microsoft Exchange Server 4.0, Microsoft's new client/server replacement for file-oriented Microsoft Mail 3+.

- Chapter 24, "Administering Clients with System Management Server," covers the basics of planning, administration, and management for Microsoft SMS 1.1 and 1.2.

V

Microsoft BackOffice

Chapter 22

Running Microsoft SQL Server 6.5

Unlike the other members of the BackOffice suite, Microsoft SQL Server is a mature product with a long development history. Sybase Corp. released in 1987 the first version of SQL Server, a client/server relational database management system (RDBMS). In 1988, Sybase, Microsoft, and Ashton-Tate (the developer of dBASE) codeveloped a version of SQL Server for OS/2, the operating system of Microsoft's LAN Manager and IBM's LAN Server. Ashton-Tate, which later was acquired by Borland International, dropped out of the triumvirate, and Microsoft alone marketed the OS/2 version as Microsoft SQL Server. Sybase SQL Server for UNIX minicomputers and Microsoft SQL Server for PC-based systems remained almost indistinguishable through the last OS/2 version, 4.21.

Microsoft and Sybase went their separate ways in 1993, primarily as a result of Microsoft's port of SQL Server 4.21 to Windows NT as version 4.21a. In 1995, Microsoft introduced SQL Server 6.0 and, in April 1996, released the current 6.5 version. SQL Server 6.0 and 6.5 are optimized for Windows NT and include a comprehensive graphical management tool, SQL Enterprise Manager, for administering SQL Server databases. Like other members of the BackOffice family, SQL Server runs as a service and uses Windows NT's security system to control access to SQL Server objects, such as databases, tables, views, and stored procedures.

This chapter assumes basic familiarity with the terminology of client/server RDBMSs and their table objects, such as columns (fields), indexes, key fields, foreign keys, and constraints, as well as basic SQL syntax. The primary emphasis of the chapter is on installing SQL Server 6.5, installing and using SQL Enterprise Manager, and establishing basic database security.

Positioning SQL Server in the RDBMS Market

Microsoft's version of SQL Server traditionally has been relegated to the *departmental* database category, whereas UNIX RDBMSs (such as Oracle, Sybase,

This chapter shows you how to

- Install SQL Server 6.5

- Install SQL Server utilities on a client PC

- Use SQL Enterprise Manager to create database objects

- Use Access 95 and the Upsizing Wizard to import table structures and data

- Add indexes to tables on an immediate or scheduled basis

- Set up database security

and Informix) and mainframe products (primarily IBM's DB2) have *enterprise* status. The generally accepted definitions of these two categories is as follows:

- *Enterprise RDBMSs* support large-scale transaction processing applications, such as airline reservation systems running on mainframes and very large UNIX "boxes" (minicomputers). Enterprise RDBMSs often involve database sizes in the terabyte (1,000G) range. Licensing costs for enterprise RDBMSs start in the $100,000 range and often are in the million-dollar class. Users pay substantial amounts for yearly software maintenance.

- *Departmental RDBMSs* are dedicated to specific applications (such as inventory control or manufacturing requirements planning) or functions (such as finance or marketing). Departmental RDBMSs support database sizes between about 100G and a terabyte. Departmental RDBMSs can serve the needs of most smaller firms with sales of under $25 million or so.

Note

Microsoft's aggressive pricing of SQL Server has brought the average licensing costs for departmental RDBMSs into the $10,000 and less range. Smaller firms now can start with a single SQL Server 6.5 installation and 10 client PCs with an up-front cost of less than $2,000 for licenses.

Microsoft's goal is to reposition SQL Server from its current departmental niche to enterprise status while maintaining its rock-bottom price point. Microsoft is about halfway to its target with SQL Server 6.5. In the meantime, Microsoft is counting heavily on small- to mid-sized firms to increase SQL Server's market share. Integration of SQL Server 6.5 with Internet Information Server 2.0 through the Internet Database Connector, SQL Server's Web Assistant, and easy connectivity to SQL Server with the members of Microsoft Office and Visual Basic also contribute to SQL Server's acceptance for a broad range of database applications.

◀◀ See "Using the Internet Database Connector," p. 750

◀◀ See "Using SQL Server Web Assistant to Distribute Activity Reports," p. 742

Note

Microsoft RDBMS competitors also are jumping on the Windows NT bandwagon. Oracle announced in late August 1996 at the Windows NT Internet Solutions show that the firm is porting Oracle7, Oracle WebServer, application development tools, and other Oracle RDBMS applications to Windows NT. Oracle says it also plans to ship two-node and four-node cluster versions of its Parallel Server by early 1997. Most of the other major players in the client/server RDBMS market offer downsized Windows NT versions of their UNIX-based products, often called *workgroup servers*.

Data warehousing and *data marts* are two of today's hot database topics. Data warehousing involves extracting data stored in a variety of formats within enterprise RDBMSs, as well as legacy network and hierarchical databases (typified by IBM's VSAM), into separate databases that provide fast response to user queries. The objective is to separate ad hoc decision-support activities (queries) from transaction-processing operations and format the data into a consistent relational structure. *Rollups* of mainframe transaction databases are the traditional method of providing this separation. Rollups create a second database that summarizes daily, weekly, and/or monthly transactions. A data warehouse stores the rolled-up data for an entire corporation in a separate set of relational databases, usually on a UNIX box.

There are several suppliers of RDBMSs that are designed specifically for data warehousing; Red Brick Systems was one of the first firms to enter the data warehouse RDBMS business. Oracle offers its Oracle Express Server for data warehousing. The size of a data warehouse easily can grow into the terabyte range.

Data marts are smaller-scale versions of data warehouses devoted to a single department or function, such as sales, finance, or marketing. Properly designed data marts can be combined to create a distributed data warehouse. Microsoft is only beginning to stick its toe in the data mart water. SQL Server 6.5 has added ROLLUP and CUBE statements to Transact-SQL (SQL Server's flavor of SQL) for summarizing (aggregating) data. Microsoft recommends SQL Server for use with data marts less than 200G in size having fewer than 5,000 simultaneous users. These limits, although insufficient for major-scale data warehouses, are adequate for most of today's data marts.

Installing SQL Server 6.5

One of the primary advantages of SQL Server over its competitors is the ease of installation and startup. You can install SQL Server 6.5 in less than 30 minutes. Before you install SQL Server 6.5 for the first time or as an upgrade to an earlier version, be sure to do the following:

- Read the Readme.txt file on the distribution CD-ROM for your server's processor, typically in the \Sql65\I386 folder. The Readme.txt file contains late-breaking information on SQL Server 6.5 that isn't in the Books Online documentation. The Readme.txt file also contains details on disk space requirements for installation and actions you must take when upgrading from prior versions.

- Provide sufficient free disk space for the installation. Although a new installation requires about 80M of free space, you should have at least 110M free on the logical drive to which you install SQL Server, so you can install a master database device of 50M or larger. You can use other local logical drives to accommodate user databases and transaction logs.

> **Note**
>
> Less free space is required when upgrading SQL Server 4.21a or 6.0 to version 6.5. You must have free space available in your Master.dat device. Check the Readme.txt file for the exact disk and device free space requirements for upgrading.

■ Set up your local tape backup drive, if you haven't already done so. If you're using third-party network backup software, make sure that the tape drive is accessible from the Windows NT server on which you're installing SQL Server. (SQL Server's built-in tape backup function won't back up to a remote tape drive.)

◀◀ See "Using the Windows NT Server 4.0 Backup Application," p. 288

Installing Files from the Distribution CD-ROM

To install SQL Server 6.5 from the distribution CD-ROM, follow these steps:

1. Run Setup.exe from the SQL Server 6.5 folder for your processor type, usually \Sql65\I386, to start the Setup program.

2. When the Welcome dialog appears, click Continue to open the Enter Name and Organization dialog.

3. Complete the Name, Company, and, optionally, the Product ID text boxes (see fig. 22.1), and then click Continue to open the Verify Name and Company dialog.

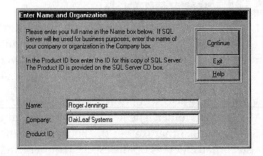

Fig. 22.1 Entering user and organization names.

4. Confirm your entries and click Continue to open the Microsoft SQL Server 6.5 – Options dialog. If this is a new installation, select Install SQL Server and Utilities (see fig. 22.2). Otherwise, select Upgrade SQL Server. Click Continue to open the Choose Licensing Mode dialog.

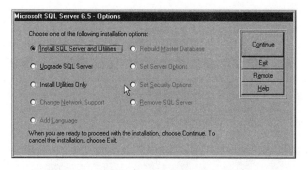

Fig. 22.2 Specifying a new installation of SQL Server 6.5 and its utility applications.

5. Select the Licensing Mode for your installation (see fig. 22.3). The default is Per Server, which you can change later to Per Seat. Click Add Licenses to open the New Client Access License dialog.

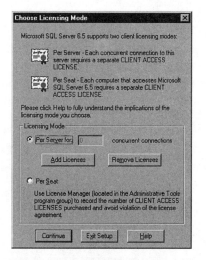

Fig. 22.3 Setting the licensing mode for SQL Server.

◀◀ See "Per-Seat vs. Per-Server Licensing," p. 780

6. Type the number of Client Access Licenses you own in the Quantity box, or use the spin buttons to set the number of licenses (see fig. 22.4). If you selected Per Seat in step 5, you can enter a note in the Comment text box that appears when you use Windows NT 4.0's License Manager application. Click OK to display the Per Server (or Per Seat) Licensing dialog.

V

Microsoft BackOffice

Fig. 22.4   Setting the initial number of Client Access Licenses.

 ◀◀ See "Using Windows NT Server 4.0's License Manager," p. 787

> **Note**
>
> If you're installing from the BackOffice Test Platform CD-ROM of the Microsoft Developer Network Enterprise Subscription, you're entitled to five simultaneous connections to SQL Server.

7. Mark the I Agree That check box (see fig. 22.5) and click OK to add the Client Access Licenses. Click Continue in the Choose Licensing Mode dialog to open the SQL Server Installation Path dialog. (You might need to reconfirm the number of Client Access Licenses at this point.)

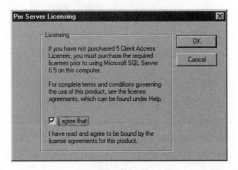

Fig. 22.5   Confirming that you've purchased the number of Client Access Licenses you added.

8. Select the local volume on which to install SQL Server and accept the default installation folder, unless you have a reason for doing otherwise (see fig. 22.6). Click Continue to open the MASTER Device Creation dialog.

Fig. 22.6 Specifying the local disk volume and the installation folder for SQL Server.

9. You can place the master device on a different volume and/or in a different folder, if you want. It's recommended that you specify a size of at least 50M for the master device (Master.dat file) of a production SQL Server installation (see fig. 22.7). Click Continue to open the SQL Server Books Online dialog.

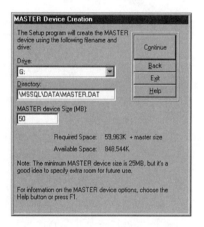

Fig. 22.7 Setting the volume and folder for the master device.

10. Microsoft provides SQL Server's documentation in a searchable Books Online format, similar to a help file. Unless you have another SQL Server installation with Books Online installed, select the Install on Hard Disk option (see fig. 22.8). Click Continue to display the Installation Options dialog.

11. Mark the Auto Start SQL Server at Boot Time and Auto Start SQL Executive at Boot Time check boxes (see fig. 22.9). Autostarting SQL Server is especially important if you use SQL Server for logging Internet Information Server 2.0 activity.

V

Microsoft BackOffice

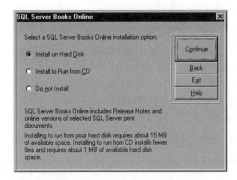

Fig. 22.8 Options for installing the SQL Server 6.5 online documentation.

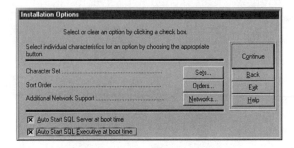

Fig. 22.9 Setting options to start SQL Server and SQL Executive during Windows NT's boot process.

 ◀◀ See "Logging to an ODBC Data Source," p. 729

12. The default character set (code page) for SQL Server 6.5 is the ISO character set. If you want to change the code page, click the Sets button in the Installation Options dialog to open the Select Character Set dialog (see fig. 22.10). Choose the code page to use from the Select Character Set list and click OK to close the dialog.

> ### Caution
>
> Make sure that you understand the ramifications of using a code page other than the default ISO character set. If you later must change the character set, you must re-create all your databases from backups. The ISO character set has been the standard for SQL Server since version 4.21a.

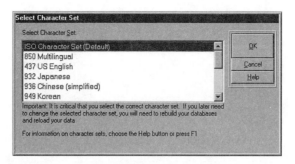

Fig. 22.10 Selecting a character set for your databases.

13. The default sort order for SQL Server 6.5 is dictionary order, case-insensitive. Early versions of SQL Server used case-sensitive sort order. If you must change the sort order, click the Sorts button in the Installation Options dialog to open the Select Sort Order dialog (see fig. 22.11). The same warning that applies to changing code pages also applies to sort order changes. Select the sort order you want and click OK to close the dialog.

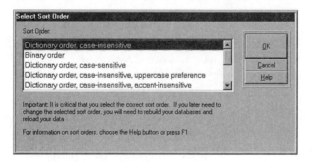

Fig. 22.11 Selecting a sort order.

14. The default network protocol for SQL Server is named pipes, which is sufficient for most Windows NT Server installations. To change or add network protocols, click the Networks button in the Installation Options dialog to open the Select Network Protocols dialog. You can add multiple protocols by marking the protocol name in the Install/Uninstall Networks list (see fig. 22.12). After making your selection, click OK to close the dialog.

15. Click Continue in the Installation Options dialog to open the SQL Executive Log On Account dialog.

16. SQL Executive, a service for automating execution of SQL Server processes, needs a login account to start during the boot process. The default is the domain Administrator account (see fig. 22.13), which must previously have been granted Log On as a Service rights. If you don't want to assign a user account for SQL Executive at this point, select the Install to Log On as a Local System Account option. Click Continue to begin copying files.

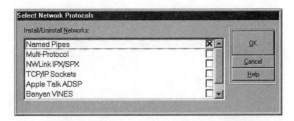

Fig. 22.12 Changing or specifying additional network protocols.

Fig. 22.13 Specifying the user account for the SQL Executive service.

17. Setup copies files to the destination folder you selected earlier in this process, and then creates the master database and other devices and objects. When Setup completes, you see the Microsoft Server SQL 6.5 – Completed dialog. Click Exit to Windows NT.

The Setup process adds a SQL Server 6.5 program group menu to the Programs menu with the choices shown in figure 22.14. At this point, SQL Server is installed, but neither SQL Server or SQL Executive is running.

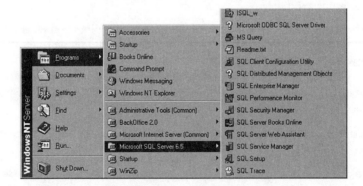

Fig. 22.14 Microsoft SQL Server 6.5's program group menu choices.

Starting SQL Server and SQL Executive

Before you can configure SQL Enterprise manager for your newly installed SQL Server system, you must start SQL Server 6.5. To start SQL Server and SQL Executive after installation without rebooting Windows NT, do the following:

1. From the Start menu choose Programs, Microsoft SQL Server 6.5, and SQL Service Manager to open the SQL Service Manager window.

2. The Server drop-down list box displays the name of the local SQL Server. Select MSSQLServer from the Services drop-down list and double-click Start/Continue to start SQL Server 6.5 (see fig. 22.15, left).

3. Select SQLExecutive from the Services list and double-click Start/Continue to start SQL Executive (see fig. 22.15, right).

Fig. 22.15 Starting SQL Server 6.5 and SQL Executive with the SQL Service Manager.

> **Note**
>
> You don't need to start SQL Executive to use SQL Enterprise Manager, but it's a good idea to start the service at this point to verify that the service is operable.

Using SQL Enterprise Manager

SQL Enterprise Manager, called *Starfighter* during its development, is a graphical management tool for SQL Server 6.x. SQL Enterprise Manager replaces the SQL Administrator and SQL Object Manager of SQL Server 4.21a. With very few exceptions, SQL Enterprise Manager lets you perform any administrative operation on SQL Server 6.5 that can be performed by a Transact-SQL script (query). You can run SQL Enterprise Manager locally on the server or from a Windows 95 or Windows NT client. Only ISQL/w, the graphical query manager, is available for 16-bit Windows clients. Most servers are located in restricted-access areas, so managing SQL Server 6.5 from a 32-bit client is the most common practice.

Installing SQL Enterprise Manager on a 32-Bit Client

To install SQL Enterprise Manager on a client running Windows 95 or Windows NT Workstation, follow these steps:

1. Run SQL Server 6.5's Setup.exe from the distribution CD-ROM, either from the client's CD-ROM drive or from a shared CD-ROM drive. The Setup program automatically recognizes that it's running on a client.

2. After Setup starts, click Continue to open the Install/Remove Client Utilities dialog (see fig. 22.16). With the Install Client Utilities option selected, click Continue to open the Install Client Utilities dialog.

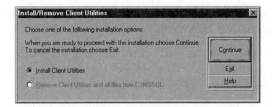

Fig. 22.16 Starting installation of the SQL Server utilities on a client PC.

3. Specify the local Drive and Directory in which to install the utilities, and then mark the Utilities to Be Installed check boxes to specify the applications you want (see fig. 22.17). In most cases, ISQL/w, SQL Enterprise Manager, and SQL Security Manager suffice for remote administration. Click Continue to install the client files.

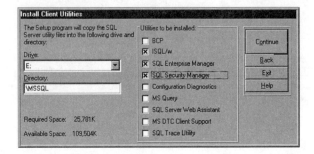

Fig. 22.17 Selecting the SQL Server client utilities to install.

4. After Setup copies the files to your local drive, the Microsoft SQL Server 6.5 – Completed dialog appears. Setup makes changes to the path, so you must reboot the client to make full use of all the utilities.

The examples in this chapter use SQL Enterprise Manager and SQL Security Manager running on a Windows 95 client.

Registering Servers

Before you can use SQL Enterprise Manager with your newly installed server and any other SQL Server 6.x server(s) previously installed, you must register the server(s) with SQL Enterprise Manager by following these steps:

1. From the Start menu choose Programs, Microsoft SQL Server 6.5 Utilities, and SQL Enterprise Manager. Click OK to close the Tip of the Day dialog, if it appears.

2. If you're running SQL Enterprise Manager for the first time, the Register Server dialog appears automatically. Otherwise, choose Register Server from the Server menu to open the Register Server dialog.

3. In the Server combo box, type the name of the Windows NT server on which the SQL Server you want to register resides. If you installed SQL Server for integrated or mixed security (Trusted Connection), accept the default Use Trusted Connection

option (see fig. 22.18). Otherwise, select Use Standard Security and type your administrator account (usually **sa**, the default account) in the Login ID text box and your password (empty if you haven't yet set a password for the sa account) in the Password text box.

Fig. 22.18 Registering a SQL 6.5 server with SQL Enterprise Manager.

4. If you want to create a server group for management purposes and add the new server to the group, click Groups to display the Manage Server Groups dialog. Type the group name in the Name text box, and then select whether you want a Top Level Group or a Sub-Group of the default SQL 6.5 group (see fig. 22.19). Click Add, and then click Close to return to the Register Server dialog.

Fig. 22.19 Creating a subgroup of the SQL 6.5 server group.

5. Click Register, and then click Close to return to the SQL Enterprise Manager with your new server added to the Server Manager window (see fig. 22.20).

6. Click the + icon next to the entry for your new server, to display the SQL Server objects and object collections installed during the SQL Server Setup process (see fig. 22.21). You can expand any entry that displays the + icon.

Microsoft BackOffice

V

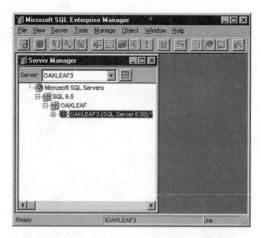

Fig. 22.20 SQL Enterprise Manager with the new server registered.

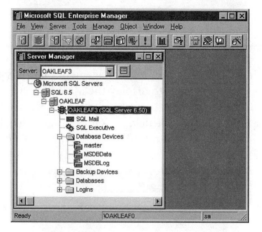

Fig. 22.21 Server Manager's window, with the server and Database Devices entries expanded.

7. Repeat steps 2, 3, and 5 to register any additional servers in your domain or trusting domain(s).

8. To view or change the configuration of a server, right-click the server entry and choose Configuration from the popup menu to open the default Server Options page of the Server Configuration/Options property sheet (see fig 22.22). You use the Configuration page to establish default values and to tune SQL Server parameters for optimum performance. If you plan to use SQL Server replication and this server will act as a publishing and/or distribution server, set the memory value to a minimum of 8,192 pages (see fig. 22.23). Click Cancel to close the property sheet.

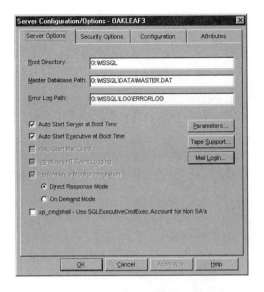

Fig. 22.22 The Server Options page of the Server Configuration/Options property sheet.

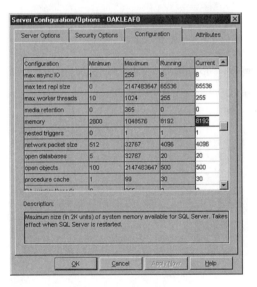

Fig. 22.23 The Configuration page, displaying default values and tuning parameters for SQL Server 6.5.

V

Microsoft BackOffice

Note

You can configure SQL Mail and SQL Executive by right-clicking the entries in the Server Manager window and choosing Configure to display a Configuration dialog or property sheet.

Specifying and Testing Backup Tape Devices

Only the diskdump backup device is installed by Setup. To enable and test your Windows NT Server backup tape drive for use with SQL Server 6.5's backup feature, follow these steps:

1. Right-click the Backup Devices item in the Server Manager window and choose New Backup Device from the popup menu to open the New Backup Device dialog.

2. Type a description of the drive in the Name text box and select Tape Backup Device. Accept the default \\.\TAPE0 entry in the Location text box; TAPE0 is the device name Windows NT assigns to the first tape drive of a server (see fig. 22.24). If you use a separate tape drive to back up SQL Server, type the device designator (such as \\.\TAPE1) in the Location text box. Mark the Skip Headers check box if you don't want to assign an ANSI header number to the backup tape. Click Create to add the new backup device.

Fig. 22.24 Adding a tape backup device to SQL Server 6.5.

3. Expand the Backup Devices entry in the Server Manager window to display the new tape backup device (see fig. 22.25).

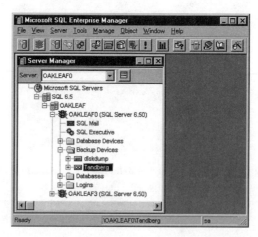

Fig. 22.25 The new tape backup device added to Server Manager's Backup Devices list.

4. Insert an inactive backup tape in your tape drive and use Windows NT's Backup tool to erase the tape. You must run the Backup tool from the server, unless you have third-party backup software.

5. Right-click your tape backup device entry in Server Manager's window and select Restore from the popup menu. In the Database Backup/Restore dialog, click the Backup tab, if necessary. Select the pubs demonstration database from the Database Backup drop-down list and your tape backup device from the Backup Devices list. Mark the Initialize Device check box and accept the No Expiration Date option (see fig. 22.26). Click Backup Now to open the Backup Volume Labels dialog.

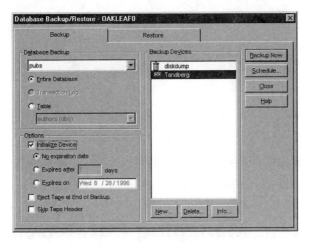

Fig. 22.26   Setting backup parameters for a test backup of the pubs sample database.

6. Accept the default volume label, or type a six-character Volume number in the Backup Volume Labels dialog (see fig. 22.27). Then click OK to back up the database.

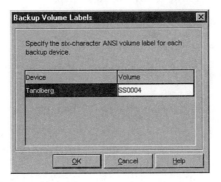

Fig. 22.27   Assigning an ANSI volume label to the backup tape.

7. A Backup Progress dialog confirms the backup operation, and then a message box indicates that backup is complete. Click OK to return to the Database Backup/ Restore dialog.

8. Click the Restore tab and select pubs from the Database list. After the drive searches the tape and finds the pubs database backup, the Restore page looks like figure 22.28. Click the Restore Now button to restore the database. A Restore Progress dialog and message box confirm success of the restore operation. Click OK twice to close the message box and the Database Backup/Restore dialog.

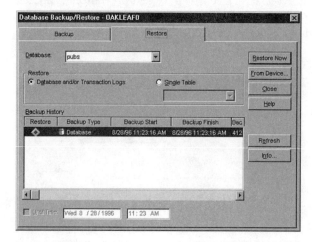

Fig. 22.28 The Restore page displaying the parameters for restoring the pubs database from the backup tape.

Creating and Managing Database Devices

Setup installs default database devices (master, MSDBData, and MSDBLog) and databases (msdb, pubs, and tempdb). As a general rule, you don't use existing database devices for user databases. A *database device* is a file with the .dat extension in which SQL Server stores databases and/or log data.

Adding user databases involves the following basic steps:

1. Create a new database device of the appropriate size for the database.

2. If the database is to be used for transaction processing, also create a log device.

3. Add the table(s) that comprise the database and, if applicable, import existing data to the tables.

4. Assign appropriate permissions to users of the database.

The following sections describe how to use SQL Enterprise Manager to create a new database device and database, and then use Access 95's Upsizing Wizard to create and populate the tables with existing data from a copy of Access 95's Northwind.mdb sample database. The advantage of using Access 95's Upsizing Wizard is that the wizard creates the tables, indexes, and triggers to maintain referential integrity automatically.

Creating a New Database Device

To create a new SQL Server 6.5 database device, follow these steps:

1. In SQL Enterprise Manager, select the server in the Manage Servers window, and then choose Database Devices from the Manage menu to open the Devices window. The default database devices created by the Setup program appear as shown in figure 22.29.

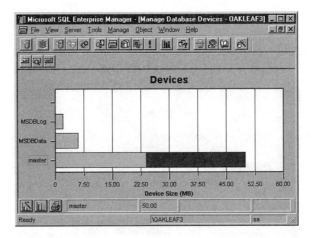

Fig. 22.29 The default database devices created by SQL Server 6.5's Setup program.

2. Click the New Device button (at the left on the second toolbar), or choose New Device from the File menu to open the New Database Device dialog.

3. Type the name of the device in the Name text box—in this example, **Northwind**. As you type the name, the default path and file name appear in the Location text box. Select the logical drive on which to create Northwind.dat from the Location drop-down list. This is an example database, so don't mark the Default Device check box.

4. Type the initial size of the device in the Size text box, or use the slider to set the size (see fig. 22.30). 8M is more than adequate for Northwind data and the temporary files created during the export process. Click Create Now to create the device file.

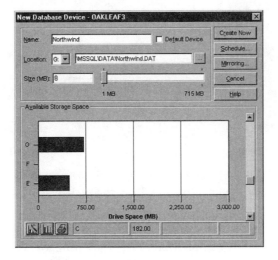

Fig. 22.30 Setting the location and size of a new database device.

V

Microsoft BackOffice

5. Click OK when a message box informs you that the device is created. Your new device appears in the Devices window. The brown bar (the darker area in fig. 22.31) indicates that the entire device is available to contain the database.

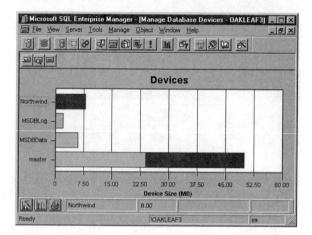

Fig. 22.31 The new database device added to the Devices window.

6. From the Manage menu choose Databases to open the Databases window, which displays the default databases installed by Setup (see fig. 22.32).

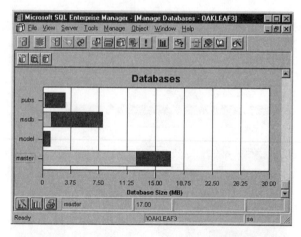

Fig. 22.32 Four of the databases installed by SQL Server 6.5's Setup program.

7. Click the New Database button (at the left on the second toolbar), or choose New Database from the File menu to open the New Database dialog.

8. Type the name of the database—**nwind** for this example—in the Name text box and select Northwind in the Data Device drop-down list. (Traditionally, SQL Server databases use lowercase names.) Don't mark the Create for Load check box, which is used when loading a database from a backup. For the moment, you also don't want to specify a log device. By default, the size of the database is equal to the size of the database device; set the database size to 5M (see fig. 22.33).

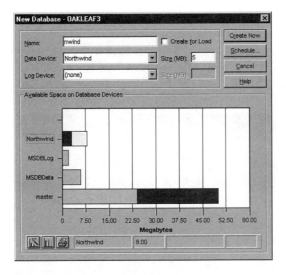

Fig. 22.33 Setting the properties of a new database.

9. Click the Create Now button to create the database. The new nwind database appears in the Databases window (see fig. 22.34).

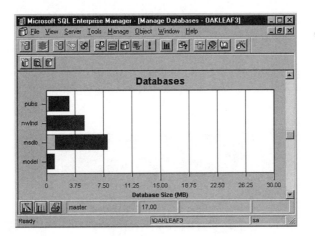

Fig. 22.34 A new database, nwind, added to the database device.

Importing Table Structures and Data

You must have Access 95 and the Access 95 Upsizing Wizard to import the data from a copy of Northwind.mdb into the SQL Server database. You can download a free copy of the Upsizing Wizard (2.4M, which expands to 7.8M) from **http://www.microsoft.com/accessdev/accinfo/accinfo.htm**. Use Access 95's Add-In

Manager to add the Upsizing Wizard to Access's Tools, Add-Ins menu. Compact Northwind.mdb into another database, such as Upsize Northwind.mdb, before starting the upsizing process.

To upsize the copy of Northwind.mdb to SQL Server, follow these steps:

1. Launch Access 95 (if necessary), open the Upsize Northwind database, and from the Tools menu choose Add-ins and Upsize to SQL Server to open the Upsizing Wizard (see fig. 22.35).

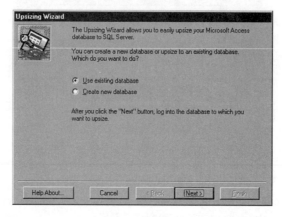

Fig. 22.35 Selecting use of the newly created database in the first dialog of the Access Upsizing Wizard.

2. With the Use Existing Database option selected, click Next to display the SQL Data Sources dialog, and then click the New button to open the Add Data Source dialog.

3. Select SQL Server from the Installed ODBC Drivers list (see fig. 22.36) and click OK to open the ODBC SQL Server Setup dialog. Click the Options button to expand the dialog.

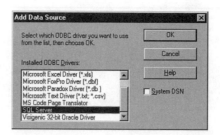

Fig. 22.36 Selecting the SQL Server ODBC 2.5 driver for a new ODBC data source.

4. Type the name of the ODBC data source in the Data Source Name text box, provide an option description of the data source, type the name of the SQL Server in the Server combo box, fill in the Database Name text box, and clear the Convert OEM to ANSI Characters check box (see fig. 22.37). Click OK to close the dialog and return to the SQL Data Sources dialog.

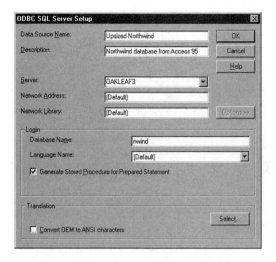

Fig. 22.37   Setting the property values of the new ODBC data source.

5. Select the new data source in Select Data Source list (see fig. 22.38) and click OK to open the SQL Server Login dialog.

Fig. 22.38   Selecting the new ODBC data source for the upsizing operation.

6. Type your SQL Server login ID—usually sa with no password, at this point. Click the Options button to expand the dialog (see fig. 22.39). Click OK to open the next Upsizing Wizard dialog.

Fig. 22.39   Entering the login ID and password for the data source.

7. Click the >> button to copy all the entries from the Available Tables list to the Export to SQL Server list (see fig. 22.40). Click Next to continue.

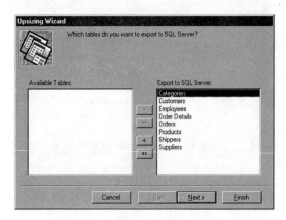

Fig. 22.40   Selecting all the tables in the Access database for export to SQL Server.

8. Mark the Indexes, Validation Rules, Defaults, and Table Relationships check boxes; then select the Use Triggers option to maintain referential integrity. If you choose the Use DRI (Declarative Referential Integrity) option, you lose cascading deletions.

9. Select Yes, Let Wizard Decide whether to add timestamp fields to tables, and mark the Attach Newly Created SQL Server Tables (to your Access database) and Save Password and User ID with Linked Tables check boxes (see fig. 22.41). Click Next if you want the option of having the Wizard prepare an Access upsizing report; otherwise click Finish (see fig. 22.42).

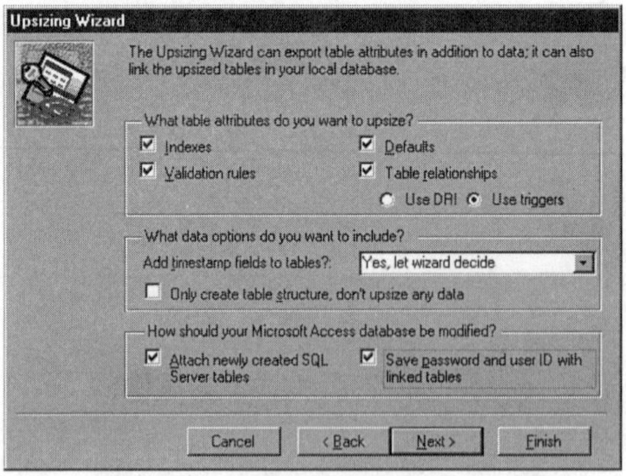

Fig. 22.41   Specifying parameters for the upsizing operation.

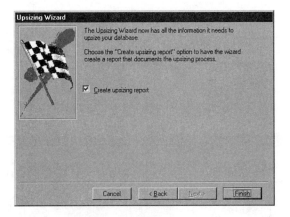

Fig. 22.42 Requesting the wizard to prepare an upsizing report.

10. The wizard provides a progress bar that reports the wizard's steps. When upsizing is complete, the attached tables appear as shown in figure 22.43. Tables attached by ODBC are identified by an arrow and a globe icon; the Access source tables are renamed to *TableName*_local. Click OK to terminate the wizard.

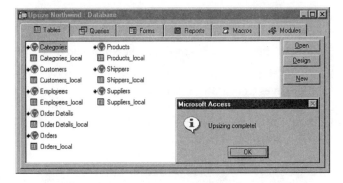

Fig. 22.43 New references to SQL Server tables attached by the Upsize Northwind ODBC data source.

You can test the performance of the attached tables by opening any of the Access forms in the database, such as the Customer Orders form.

> **Note**
>
> If you don't have Access 95 or the Upsizing Wizard, you can use the pubs demonstration database in the examples of the sections that follow. Choose one of the primary pubs tables, such as authors. The pubs database doesn't include demonstration triggers.

Working with SQL Tables, Indexes, Tasks, and Triggers

Importing table structures and data from an existing Access database provides tables that you can use to gain familiarity with the table-related features of SQL Enterprise Manager. To work with the tables you imported in the preceding section, follow these steps:

1. Select your new database, nwind, in the Server Manager window; then choose <u>T</u>ables from the <u>M</u>anage menu to open the Manage Tables window. The default <new> entry in the Table list lets you add a new table to the database and specify the properties of each column.

2. Select one of the imported tables, such as Orders, from the Table list. The properties of each column (field) of the table appears in the list (see fig. 22.44).

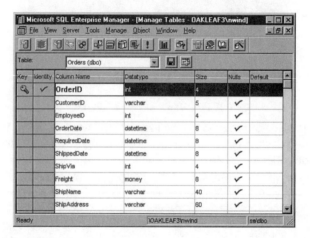

Fig. 22.44 Properties of the first 12 columns (fields) of the Northwind Orders table.

3. Click the Advanced Features button (with the + icon) of the second toolbar to open a set of properties pages that show Primary Key/Identity, Foreign Keys, Unique Constraints, and Check Constraints, if any. For the Orders table, only a Primary Key and Identity Column are defined (see fig. 22.45). Click the Advanced Features button again to return to the column list.

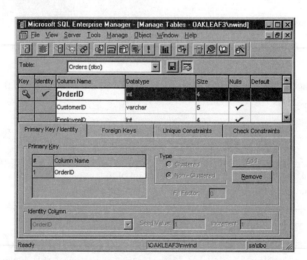

Fig. 22.45 Displaying Primary Key/Identity properties with the Advanced Features option of the Manage Tables window.

4. To add an index to a column, such as RequiredDate, choose Indexes from the Manage menu to open the Manage Indexes dialog.

5. Select (New Index) in the Index combo box, and then type an index name, such as **RequiredDate**, Index text box. Select the RequiredDate column in the Available Columns in Table list and click the Add button to add the column to the Columns in Index (Key) list (see fig. 22.46). Click the Build button to start the indexing process.

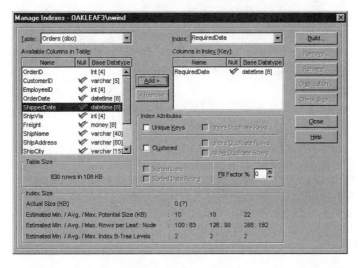

Fig. 22.46 Setting the properties of a new index on an existing table.

6. In the Index Build message box (see fig. 22.47), click the Schedule As Task button to open the Schedule Index Build dialog.

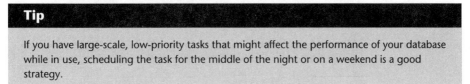

Tip

If you have large-scale, low-priority tasks that might affect the performance of your database while in use, scheduling the task for the middle of the night or on a weekend is a good strategy.

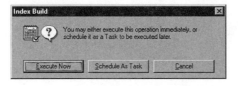

Fig. 22.47 Choosing whether to execute an indexing task immediately or at a later time.

7. You have the option of running the task Immediately, One Time, or as a Recurring task (see fig. 22.48). For this example, select Immediately and click OK. Click OK when the Run Task message box appears (see fig. 22.49).

Microsoft BackOffice

V

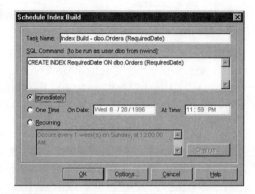

Fig. 22.48 Selecting scheduling options for the indexing task.

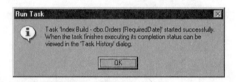

Fig. 22.49 Confirmation of the scheduling of your task.

8. To view the Task History dialog described in the Run Task message box, choose Scheduled Tasks from the Server menu to open the Task List page of the Manage Scheduled Tasks window (see fig. 22.50). This page displays all scheduled tasks, regardless of status.

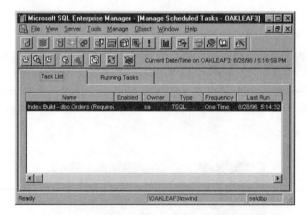

Fig. 22.50 Viewing scheduled tasks on the Task List page of the Manage Scheduled Tasks window.

9. Double-click the task to open the Edit Task dialog, which displays the task properties (see fig. 22.51). Click the History button to display the Task History dialog (see fig. 22.52). Click Close in the Task History dialog and then click Cancel in the Edit Task dialog to return to SQL Enterprise Manager.

Fig. 22.51   The Edit Task dialog, an intermediary on the way to viewing task history.

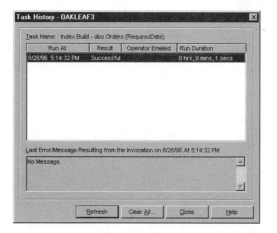

Fig. 22.52   Checking the execution of the task in the Task History dialog.

Viewing Triggers

The traditional method of enforcing referential integrity of SQL Server databases is by the use of triggers in transaction processing operations. *Triggers* are stored procedures that execute when a client application requests an INSERT, UPDATE, or DELETE operation on a table. The Transact-SQL code of the trigger performs one or more tests, usually on one or more related tables. If the test succeeds, the operation executes; otherwise, the trigger cancels the operation and posts an error message.

To view a typical pair of triggers that the Access Upsizing Wizard creates to maintain referential integrity, follow these steps:

1. With the nwind database selected in Server Manager's window, choose Triggers from the <u>M</u>anage menu to open the Manage Triggers window. You edit existing triggers or create new triggers in this window.

2. Select the Orders table from the Table list.

3. Click the icon to open the Trigger list and select Orders_ITrig (INSERT trigger on the Orders table). The Transact-SQL code for the trigger appears in the window (see fig. 22.53). The CREATE TRIGGER *name* ON *tablename* FOR INSERT AS statement specifies an INSERT trigger.

Fig. 22.53 Part of the Transact-SQL code for an INSERT trigger.

4. Open the Trigger list and select Order_UTrig (UPDATE trigger on the Orders table). The CREATE TRIGGER *name* ON *tablename* FOR UPDATE AS statement specifies an UPDATE trigger.

> **Note**
>
> A single table supports only three triggers, one each for INSERT, UPDATE, and DELETE operations. Triggers are self-contained stored procedures that don't accept or return parameter values. The only output from a trigger is an error message posted by a RAISERROR statement.

Viewing Standard Stored Procedures

Many of the functions performed by SQL Enterprise Manager use *stored procedures*, which are precompiled queries that accept and return parameter values. The master database holds stored procedures that can be executed against any database on the server. Stored procedures specific to a database are stored with the tables of the database. Traditionally, SQL Server names stored procedures with an sp_ prefix, as in sp_addserver.

To view example stored procedures in the master database, proceed as follows:

1. Select the master database in the Server Manager window, and then choose Stored Procedures from the Manage menu to open the Manage Stored Procedures window.

2. Select one of the stored procedures in the Procedures list, such as sp_addserver, to display the Transact-SQL code for the procedure (see fig. 22.54).

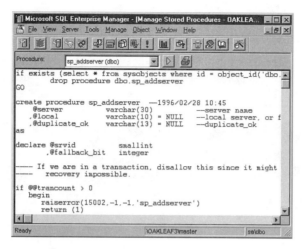

Fig. 22.54 Part of the Transact-SQL code for the sp_addserver stored procedure.

Parameters of stored procedures are identified by an ampersand (@) prefix, as in @server, followed by the SQL data type and size, if applicable, such as varchar(30). You also can create local variables with the declare @varname datatype statement.

Executing Queries

SQL Enterprise Manager includes the equivalent of the ISQL/w graphical query tool. You can write your own queries or execute Transact-SQL scripts (queries) stored as *.sql files. To execute a query, follow these steps:

1. Choose SQL Query Tool from the Tools menu to open the Query window.

2. Select the database from the DB list.

3. Type the query in the Queries page (see fig. 22.55).

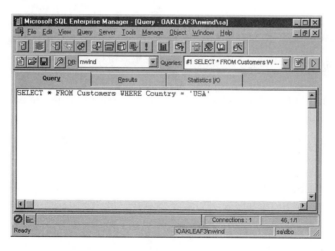

Fig. 22.55 A SELECT query against the nwind database.

Microsoft BackOffice

V

4. Choose Execute from the Query menu, or click the green arrow button at the right of the second toolbar.

5. Select the Results page to display the result of your query (see fig. 22.56). SELECT queries return the query result set; INSERT, UPDATE, and DELETE queries return the number of rows affected.

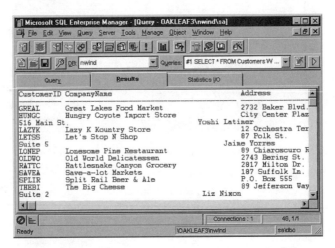

Fig. 22.56   The result set of the query shown in figure 22.55.

Setting Up Transaction Logging

Transaction logs provide a history of all changes made to the tables of the database by INSERT, UPDATE, and DELETE operations. The purpose of a transaction log is to provide the means to reconstruct a database to its state immediately before a catastrophic failure that requires restoring data from the last backup. The basic backup and restore sequence with a transaction log is as follows:

1. Immediately after making a full backup of the database, the transaction log is deleted (dumped).

2. In the event of a failure of the database file, the database is restored from the last backup.

3. The transaction log is executed against the database to bring the content of the database tables to their state immediately before the failure.

You establish transaction logging by specifying a log device for the database when you create the new database. Transaction logging is enabled by default, and the transaction log shares space with the data in the database. A transaction log in the same database or stored on the same physical device provides no protection against failure of the drive that stores the file for the database device. You can't change the log device after the database is created.

To determine the log device for a database, double-click the database entry in Server Manager to display the Database page of the Edit Database property sheet. The nwind database, created earlier in the "Importing Table Structures and Data" section, stores its log with the data (see fig. 22.57). In this case, there's no advantage to maintaining a transaction log, so you can click Truncate to recover the log space used. To prevent further log entries, display the Options page and mark the Truncate Log on Checkpoint check box (see fig. 22.58). Click OK to close the property sheet.

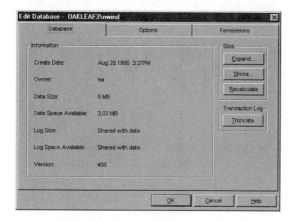

Fig. 22.57 The Database page of the Edit Database property sheet for the nwind database.

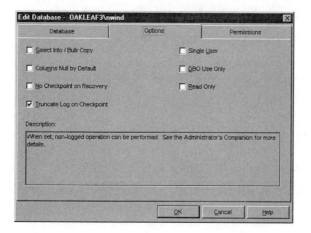

Fig. 22.58 Preventing transaction logging with the Truncate Log on Checkpoint option.

To create a database with a transaction log, follow these steps:

1. In the Manage Devices window, create a new database device of the appropriate size. (Refer to the earlier section "Creating and Managing Database Devices.")

2. Create another database device for the transaction log on a different local fixed-disk drive.

3. Create a new database, selecting the database device in the Data Device combo list and the database device for the transaction log in the Log Device combo list (see fig. 22.59).

4. Click Create Now to create the database and the transaction log.

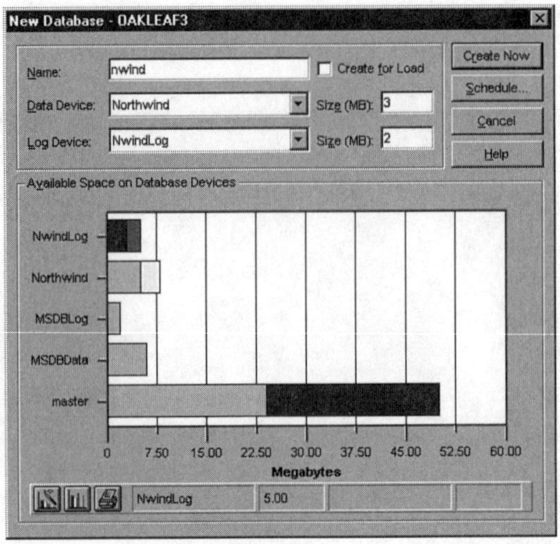

Fig. 22.59 Specifying a transaction log device for a new database.

Establishing Database Permissions

SQL Server offers the three following types of user login security:

- *Standard security* requires SQL Server users to specify a login ID and a password to gain access to the server. You set up individual SQL Server accounts for each server user in the Manage Logins window of SQL Enterprise Manager.

- *Integrated security* uses Windows NT security to authenticate SQL Server users with their Windows NT login IDs and passwords. Integrated security is limited to clients that connect with the default named pipes protocol. You use SQL Security Manager to assign group logins to the server.

- *Mixed security* lets SQL Server installations that are set up to accept multiple network protocols take advantage of integrated security for clients by using named pipes. Users of clients connecting by a protocol other than named pipes must supply a login ID and password.

Integrated security is the most common choice for SQL Server 6.5 with clients running Windows 95 or Windows NT Workstation. Regardless of the type of security you choose, the default system administrator account, sa, has all permissions for all databases and is the default owner (dbo, database owner) for all SQL Server objects.

Note

In the examples of this chapter, the sa account uses the default empty password. SQL Server's sa account and Microsoft Access's default Admin account have similar authority. Be sure to assign a password to the sa account before using SQL Server for production applications. To change the

(continues)

> (continued)
>
> sa password in SQL Enterprise Manager, choose <u>L</u>ogins from the <u>M</u>anage menu, select sa in the Login Name list, type a password in the Password text box, and click the Modify button.

Using SQL Security Manager to Assign Group Accounts

You can assign all users in a specified group access to one or more SQL Server databases with the SQL Security Manager. Ordinarily, you employ User Manager for Domains to create a specific Windows NT group for access to each database, and then add to the group the users who need database access. In the following example, the Domain Users group is used for simplicity.

◄◄ See "Using the Group Management Wizard," p. 450

To set up a SQL Server user group from Domain Users, follow these steps:

1. From the Start menu choose Programs, Microsoft SQL Server 6.5 Utilities, and SQL Security Manager to launch SQL Security Manager.

2. In the Connect Server dialog, type the name of the server, your login ID, and password, if necessary (see fig. 22.60). Click Connect to connect to the server.

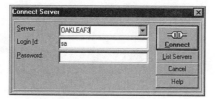

Fig. 22.60   Completing the Connect Server dialog to open SQL Security Manager.

3. To view administrators with sa (system administrator) status, choose <u>S</u>a Privilege from the <u>V</u>iew menu. Double-click the group names to expand the list and display login IDs with sa privileges (see fig. 22.61).

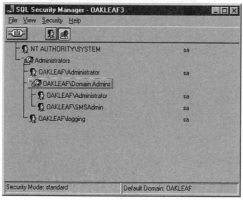

Fig. 22.61   Displaying users with system administrator (sa) privileges.

V

Microsoft BackOffice

4. From the <u>V</u>iew menu choose <u>U</u>ser Privilege. The No Accounts Have Been Granted User Authority message appears.

5. Choose <u>G</u>rant New from the <u>S</u>ecurity menu to open the Grant User Privilege dialog.

6. Select the Groups on Default Domain option and select the database user group in the Grant Privilege list.

7. Mark the Add Login IDs for Group Members and Add Users to Database check boxes. Select the database for the group from the drop-down list (see fig. 22.62). Click the Grant button to add the users.

Fig. 22.62 Adding Domain Users as the Domain$Users group of SQL Server.

> ### Note
>
> SQL Server doesn't permit spaces in names of objects, including names of groups. SQL Server automatically replaces spaces in group names with dollar signs ($).

8. As the users are added, the number of Login IDs, Users, and Groups appear in the Adding SQL Server Login IDs/Users dialog (see fig. 22.63).

Fig. 22.63 A summary of users and groups added to the Domain$Users group.

9. If errors occur during the login process, click Error Detail to expand the dialog and check the source of the errors (see fig. 22.64).

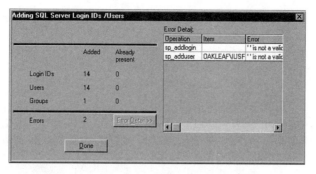

Fig. 22.64 Displaying errors during the addition of SQL Server users.

10. Click Done to close the dialog and display the added user accounts (see fig. 22.65).

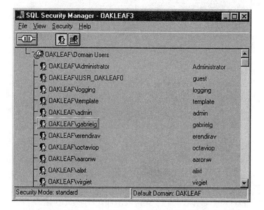

Fig. 22.65 The new user accounts displayed in the SQL Security Manager window.

11. Double-click one of the user accounts to display the Account Detail dialog. If you want to add another database for the user, select the database in the Available Databases list and click Add. Select the default database for the user in the Databases Currently Defined In list and click the Set Default database (see fig. 22.66).

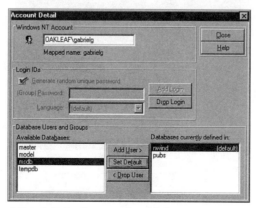

Fig. 22.66 The Account Detail dialog for a newly added user.

Viewing Logins and Setting Permissions in SQL Enterprise Manager

SQL Enterprise Manager includes complete facilities for managing SQL Server user accounts (logins) and database permissions for each account. To view the logins you added from the Windows NT Domain Users group in the preceding section and set specific user permissions for database objects, follow these steps:

1. Close and relaunch SQL Enterprise Manager, and then expand the Logins item of Server Manager's window for the server to which the users were added. Each user login, together with default users added by SQL Server, appears as shown in figure 22.67.

Fig. 22.67 Logins added to the OAKLEAF3 server from the Domain$Users group.

2. Double-click the user item to display the Manage Logins dialog for the user (see fig. 22.68). You can add or remove permissions for databases by clicking cells of the Permit column, and set one default database by clicking a cell in the Default column. Click Close to close the dialog.

Fig. 22.68 Displaying the details of the users account in the Manage Logins dialog.

3. Double-click the database in Server Manager to display the Edit Database dialog, and then display the Permissions page. By default, users in the Domain$Users group don't have permissions to modify the database. If you want to grant the Domain$Users group permission to create a view, click the Create View button (see fig. 22.69). When you click OK, the permission is granted to all members of the group.

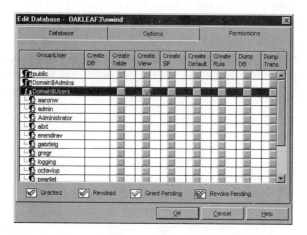

Fig. 22.69 Adding Create View permission for the Domain$Users group.

To drop a user group from a database, select the database item in Server Manager, and then choose Groups from the Manage menu to open the Manage Groups dialog. Select the group you want to drop in the Group drop-down list (see fig. 22.70), and then click the Drop button. Confirm in the message box that you want to drop the group.

Fig. 22.70 Selecting a user group to drop in the Manage Groups dialog.

From Here...

This chapter covered the basic operations involved in installing SQL Server 6.5 under Windows NT Server 4.0. Instructions for installing the SQL Server 6.5 Utilities on clients running Windows 95 and Windows NT Workstation 4.0 also were given. The chapter provided examples of creating new database devices, databases, and importing table structures and data to SQL Server databases. The chapter closed with a brief description of SQL Server's integrated security features.

V

Microsoft BackOffice

The following chapters contain material related to the content of this chapter:

■ Chapter 12, "Managing User and Group Accounts," describes how to use Windows NT Server 4.0's User Manager for Domains, take advantage of the new Add User Accounts and Group Management wizards, and utilize the built-in user groups of Windows NT.

■ Chapter 20, "Administering Intranet and World Wide Web Sites," describes how to use a SQL Server 6.5 database for logging the activity on your intranet or Internet site.

■ Chapter 24, "Administering Clients with System Management Server," covers the basics of planning, administration, and management for Microsoft SMS 1.x. SMS 1.x uses SQL Server 6.5 to store all of its client management information.

Chapter 23

Messaging with Microsoft Exchange Server

Microsoft Exchange Server 4.0 (called *Exchange* in this chapter) brings client/server messaging to the BackOffice suite of Windows NT Server-based applications. Microsoft's goal for Exchange was to create a scalable, enterprise-wide messaging system with a centralized administrative model. To support the need for forms and other custom enhancements, Microsoft added programmability to Exchange with a Forms Designer and support for the Visual Basic for Applications (VBA) programming language.

Exchange replaces or supplements current mail systems using the *shared file system* (SFS). SFS includes Microsoft Mail version 3.x and its support components, such as gateways and multi-postoffice interchange capabilities. By offering the option to replace *or* supplement an SFS, Microsoft provides a number of options for migrating your existing mail system(s) to Exchange.

This chapter describes the overall architecture of Exchange, how Exchange relates to current implementations of Microsoft Mail 3.x, and what you need to know about Exchange and its workings before installation. It's important to understand that Exchange is an especially intricate product that requires a great deal of forethought before you bring it online. The chapter takes you through a typical installation and also discusses selecting options from the custom installation. The chapter also explains what you can expect as you set up Exchange for use in messaging environments serving only a few users, or many thousands of users.

Comparing Microsoft Exchange and Microsoft Mail

Exchange is the first enterprise-wide electronic mail system to take full advantage of the client/server messaging model. Most Exchange users are likely to run Microsoft Mail, Lotus cc:Mail, or another SFS mail application. Before you install Exchange, it's important to understand how Exchange works and how Exchange's client/server architecture varies from the SFS approach.

In this chapter, you learn

- How Exchange messaging varies from Microsoft Mail

- How to install Exchange Server

- How to use Exchange's Server Optimizer, Client Load Simulator, and Server Migration utilities

- How to install the Exchange client

- How to use the Exchange Administrator utility

Microsoft Mail 3.x

When you create a Microsoft Mail postoffice on a mail server, the Setup program generates a large number of individual subdirectories with names ranging from ATT to XTN. These subdirectories are the holding locations for messages as well as postoffice management information. Each Microsoft Mail user connected to the postoffice has read/write access to these subdirectories. The user's MS Mail client application works with the subdirectories to post and retrieve mail. Microsoft Mail 3.x also supports Schedule+ 1.x's sharing of schedule information and its capability to send and receive meeting-related messages. The mail server also stores shared schedules and meeting-related messages.

> **Note**
>
> The terms *directory* and *subdirectory*, rather than *folder* and *subfolder*, are used in this book when discussing applications that predate the current version of Microsoft BackOffice, Windows NT 4.0, and Windows 95.

SFS has no active server-based processes to manipulate messages. The shared folders are limited to storing information for searching and retrieval by the client application. There is no concept of intelligent, server-side processing of messages and other requests of the mail system, other than transferring messages between postoffices.

Mail systems typically are divided into multiple postoffices, usually assigned to physical locations, departments, or other logical groupings of users of the system. Microsoft Mail's Message Transfer Agent (MTA), which usually resides on a dedicated machine, periodically polls each postoffice and transfers messages between the postoffices. Figure 23.1 illustrates how the MTA transfers messages between postoffices.

Postoffices not physically on the same network as the MTA call in to other postoffices to deliver and pick up mail. The MTA receives and processes the call, making available the messages that are pertinent to the calling postoffice. The MTA can be configured to receive calls and deliver any outgoing mail during the incoming call. The MTA also can be configured to place calls automatically, delivering mail to remote postoffices either on a scheduled basis or when the mail arrives at the MTA.

When a user calls in from the field with a laptop PC and a modem, the MTA is the process responsible for answering the call and delivering the mail to the calling user. The MTA handles mail headers, message content, and management of the remote user's mailbox. If you have remote postoffice traffic with many remote users calling in for their mail and a large number of active postoffices, the MTA is likely to become a significant bottleneck. Some ingenious workarounds for the MTA bottleneck range from dedicated systems that handle specific types of traffic, to elaborate circular transfers of mail between several different MTAs.

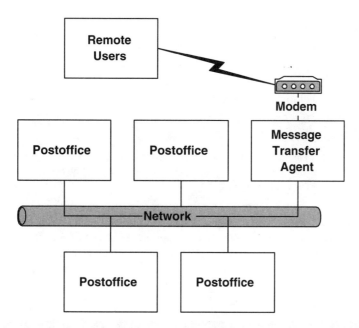

Fig. 23.1 Using the Message Transfer Agent (MTA) to link local and remote postoffices.

> **Note**
>
> Exchange supports multiple connectors, the software that connects external mail systems. Connectors serve the same purpose as the MTA of Microsoft Mail. Unlike Microsoft Mail 3.x's MTAs, you don't need a dedicated system to transfer mail through each Exchange connector you install.

An example of a challenge presented by the MTA approach to messaging is the number of phone lines required to support remote mail access and Remote Access Service (RAS) to connect to the LAN. With the MTA setup, you're required to have one line to support the remote mail and one line to support Remote Access Service. Microsoft Mail 3.x has a number of other encumbrances that are eliminated by the use of Exchange. Most of these encumbrances derive from the product's early development time frame and need for backward compatibility.

Microsoft Exchange Server

Exchange drastically changes the messaging process from Microsoft Mail's SFS and MTA implementation. It's very easy to underestimate the significance of these changes. The following list shows just a few of the changes and enhancements that Exchange introduces to the messaging model:

- Intelligent client/server messaging
- Security systems integrated with Windows NT
- Fully extensible client

- Fully extensible server

- Proxy address support

- Replication support

- Application development support

> **Note**
>
> It's likely that you'll implement your system in a stepped fashion, one piece at a time. The combination of features that best serve your messaging environment may not be readily apparent when you first start up your Exchange system.

Intelligent Client/Server Messaging. By introducing intelligent back-end (server) processes, Exchange greatly enhances users' experience with mail. When a message is submitted, the server works through the routing of the message and determines the recipients for the message. The server determines the connectors or gateways through which the message should be routed, and initiates the process of sending the message to the recipient or posting the message in a public folder.

> **Tip**
>
> Exchange lets you enable folders as valid recipients. You can post a message to a public folder, making it available to other people for their reference. You can include a folder in a distribution list. A typical application for public folders is managing phone messages. You can send a phone message to the intended recipient and have the system automatically post a copy of the message to a Phone Messages public folder for record-keeping.

If the mail message is to multiple recipients, Exchange parses each recipient's name and starts the correct routing process. If the message is to multiple recipients at a single physical site, only a single copy of the message is needed. Exchange, in essence, issues a pointer to the single message stored on the server. When the user opens the message, the pointer presents the original message.

If you issue a very large message to several people using SFS, you can take down an entire mail postoffice. SFS makes one copy of the message for each person on the distribution list. With Exchange, each user sees the same copy of the message.

> **Tip**
>
> Exchange lets you send messages using the BCC, or Blind Carbon Copy, field. By doing so, however, you prevent Exchange from issuing the same message to more than one person using the "pointer" approach outlined here. You effectively eliminate the single-copy-to-multiple-users feature of Exchange. If you're sending a message to many people, avoid using the BCC field when possible.

Client/server messaging introduces a very important feature to mail systems—the capability to have the server preprocess messages on behalf of the recipient. The Inbox

Assistant of the Exchange client lets you establish rules that govern the processing of your incoming messages. Figure 23.2 shows how to establish a rule that causes any message from Steve Wynkoop to be deleted on receipt.

Fig. 23.2 Setting up rules for incoming messages with the Exchange client's Inbox Assistant.

You can use the Inbox Assistant's rules even when you're not logged on to Exchange. The power of the Inbox Assistant is that your rules are server-based. The rules are implemented on and controlled by the server; when established, rules don't require further intervention by the client application. Figure 23.3 shows the Edit Rule dialog of the Exchange client in which you can specify one or more actions based on the message address, subject, or text in the body of the message.

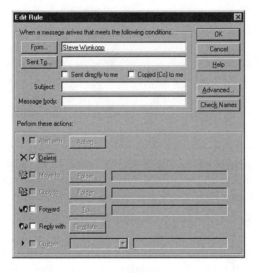

Fig. 23.3 Using the Exchange client's Edit Rule dialog to specify conditional message actions.

Integrated Security Systems. Traditional electronic mail systems require mail users to be defined separately and distinctly from network users. Exchange weaves the process of defining and working with users into the basic Windows NT 4.0 user administration process. You maintain all network and Exchange user information in one place. Integration with Windows NT Server 4.0's security system is the subject of the later section, "Working with User Manager and Exchange Mailboxes."

Fully Extensible Client. When you install the Exchange client, you can select from a number of *providers*, which are the source of information for the client software. Providers range from the Exchange system to proprietary network providers, such as The Microsoft Network (MSN) and CompuServe. Figure 23.4 shows the Add Service to Profile dialog's list of mail providers for the Exchange client running on Windows 95. Only the Internet Mail, Microsoft Mail, Personal Address Book, and Personal Folders appear when installing the Exchange client on machines running Windows NT 4.0. (Microsoft Mail appears only if you're using Microsoft Mail 3.x.)

Fig. 23.4 Adding providers to Exchange in the Add Service to Profile dialog.

The Exchange client fulfills the concept of Microsoft's *universal inbox*. You can add Microsoft or third-party providers to the client application so that you can direct all your electronic communication to a common location. Faxes, electronic mail from all sources, and various types of electronic documents can be managed by the server and organized through systems of Exchange folders.

> **Note**
>
> Exchange folders aren't the same as disk folders (directories and subdirectories). Exchange folders have many of the same characteristics as disk folders, such as hierarchical structures, but reside as individual records in Exchange's message store, a database similar in structure to Microsoft Access's .mdb files.

The interface to the provider layer in Exchange is open, so it's possible to create a provider that queries a SQL Server or Access database, or to provide an interface to other less structured sources of information, such as stock-quotation services.

Fully Extensible Server. Exchange answers the demand for a robust mail server by adding functionality to the mail-processing environment. This includes Proxy Address Support, Replication Support, and Native Application Development Support. When you combine these features with the client/server environment provided by Exchange, you begin to see the reason that Exchange's implementation is so powerful. The following sections explain how each feature is used in your messaging environment.

Proxy Address Support. Exchange lets you define multiple addresses per recipient. When users are initially set up in Exchange, they often are assigned a number of addresses, depending on where the users' accounts originated. You can establish addresses for each mail system in which the user previously had an account. By adding proxy addresses, Exchange automatically forwards mail for the prior account to the new Exchange mailbox.

Replication Support. One of the more important features of Exchange is the capability to replicate information across servers. Information is stored in folder structures on the server. When information is added, changed, or removed from these folders, Exchange automatically updates all servers that contain that folder. Exchange has a conflict-resolution plan that handles conflicting updates.

Exchange uses the messaging subsystem to update folder structures. When a change occurs in a replicated folder, only the changed information is mailed to all other servers with the same folder. When the updates are completed, the recipient server sends a confirmation back to the originating server. This store-and-forward process provides assurance that folder changes flow between servers, just as messages flow between the servers. If a server is down—perhaps due to a severed network connection—the Exchange messaging engine stores the messages until the server becomes available. At that time, the messages are transmitted and folder changes are applied, in the order in which they originated.

Exchange replication is a fully automatic background process. Replication is also a server-based process, so regardless of whether your client software is running, the server makes sure that all folders are synchronized by applying updates as soon as possible after a folder content change.

Application Development Support. Mail isn't just for sending meeting requests, short notes, or other text-based messages. Mail is an excellent medium for managing the information flow between servers. You can count on the mail system to send not only your text messages, but also application information, such as expense account entries in Excel worksheets, database updates, and requests to run queries on a database server.

For sending information to other applications or performing operations on databases, you create custom Exchange forms to organize and, in some cases, validate the information before submission to a public folder. When you design an Exchange form, you're developing an Exchange application. The form resides in a folder on the server; you open a blank copy of the form to create a structured Exchange message. Only the information you supply, plus a pointer to the form you used, is stored, making forms a very efficient method of communication.

Client/Server Messaging and Remote Procedure Calls

As mentioned earlier in this chapter, Exchange is a true client/server messaging environment, dividing the functionality of the mail system between server and client processes to optimize the combination of performance, functionality, and features. The client/server implementation makes possible automatic replication and rules that run even when you're not logged on.

Exchange servers communicate with Exchange clients using remote procedure calls (RPCs). An RPC opens a channel of network communication between the server and a client, allowing the two systems to converse. In this context, *conversing* means that the client or server can make and fulfill requests from the other. RPCs let a client run a process on the server as though the process were run on the client PC. Windows NT uses RPCs for various networking operations.

Exchange uses RPCs to maintain the updates between server-based information stores and the information stores on your local system. When you install the Exchange client, the following two new working files are created on the client PC:

- *Personal Address Book* (PAB). The client's PAB, which contains a list of mail, fax, and other types of addresses, can be installed for server or client-side storage. If you select to install and store the file on the client computer, you are prompted for the location in which to store it.

- *Personal Information Store* (PST). The client's PST file, installed to the location you specify during setup, contains personal folders to store the user's messages, attachments, and folder structures. Unless you regularly delete locally stored messages and their attachments, the .PST file becomes quite large.

Note

You can have more than one PST on a system and even in a given profile. This can be helpful if you have multiple mail addresses, as may be the case if you're the Exchange administrator or the administrator for a Web site.

Exchange clients use RPCs to converse with the server in order to make sure that local information stores are synchronized with the corresponding server store. By storing a local copy of e-forms that are used, users have ready access to the mail messages and attachments relating to those messages.

You may recall that the electronic forms are installed at the folder level. This has some real advantages over past implementations that were more server-based installations.

Installing Exchange Server

When you install Exchange, you find many new steps, terms, and approaches to the mail system that vary from Microsoft Mail's setup. It's important to understand how these terms affect your installation of the system. Exchange uses four terms to define the topology of the mail system, as listed in table 23.1, in order of increasing scope.

Table 23.1   Exchange Topology Terminology

Term	Definition
Client	Any machine running the Exchange 4.0 client software that isn't a Server.
Server	The system that's performing the task of managing the folders, messages, and tasks associated with the clients for which it's responsible. A Server runs the Exchange Server 4.0 software and participates in replication with other servers in your Exchange network.

Term	Definition
Site	Consists of one or more Servers.
Organization	Consists of one or more Sites.

Figure 23.5 illustrates the relationship between Servers, Sites, and Organizations.

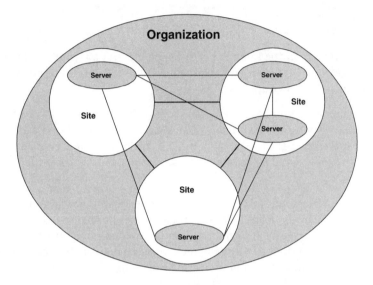

Fig. 23.5 The hierarchical organization of Servers, Sites, and Organizations.

The key to establishing a solid Exchange site is planning. You must take the time to plan for and name the servers, sites, and organizations that comprise your messaging system. You can relate sites and organizations in this context to domains in the Windows NT Server model. Sites can replicate folders and messages between themselves and, of course, can process electronic mail to and from other sites.

> **Note**
>
> Choose organization, site, and server names carefully before you install Exchange. After you install Exchange, changing fundamental implementation details, such as the site name or organization name, requires you to reinstall Exchange Server 4.0.

On the Exchange CD-ROM, you can find planning materials in the \Migrate folder, which contains tools and planning guides to aid your e-mail conversion effort. Microsoft's Web site provides white papers that cover Exchange planning, migration, and deployment at **http://www.microsoft.com/exchange/plan.htm**. Most of the white papers are session summaries from the Microsoft Exchange Planning Workshop held in September 1995, when Exchange was in the final beta-testing stage.

V

Microsoft BackOffice

Maximizing Exchange Server Performance

To ensure the best possible performance, install Exchange Server 4.0 on a dedicated Windows NT 4.0 server that's neither a Primary or a Backup Domain Controller. As a point of compromise, if this isn't feasible, you can use the Exchange server as a temporary Backup Domain Controller until the server's domain duties affect Exchange's performance.

◀◀ See "Understanding the Roles of Domain Controllers," p. 570

Running SQL Server 6.5 on the same server as Exchange isn't a recommended practice, because Exchange and SQL Server each require a substantial amount of memory resources and are disk-intensive applications.

As a point of reference, if you have users that employ the e-mail system in a typical manner, sending and receiving approximately 50 messages a day, count on needing as much as 50M of disk space per user on your system. To some extent, the server's disk space requirement can be alleviated by moving the users' mail databases (.pst files) to their local machines.

Additional requirements for good performance include an absolute minimum of 32M of RAM, disk drives that are as fast as possible, and as few additional server processes active as possible. Of course, in an ideal world, this would be a dedicated server with multiple processors and lots of RAM. Reality usually dictates that you scale the server as your mail system grows, starting small and later increasing the performance on the system.

The best indication of server performance is the length of time it takes from the time a message leaves a user's outbox to the time it arrives in the recipients' inbox within a common mailbox. If this time lag is excessive compared with the same timing when you initially install your system, consider the following options:

■ If at all possible, add RAM to the server. Adding RAM usually provides the greatest performance boost to your system. You can use the Windows NT Performance Monitor to check the percentage utilization for the paging file. If you see more than 60 percent utilization, add more RAM.

◀◀ See "Using Performance Monitor," p. 501

■ Check to make sure that you have enough disk space on your system to support mail transfers, the swap file, public folders, and the mail stores for the individuals on your system. High-performance, Fast and Wide SCSI drives provide a performance boost.

Planning for Exchange Accounts

One of the most important considerations in planning your Exchange installation is the creation of Exchange accounts. Following are three recommendations to reduce the time and effort needed to establish mail accounts for Exchange users:

- *Install Windows NT Server 4.0 and Exchange at the same time.* If you can install Exchange at the same time that you're setting up your domain, you save the need to create users twice. If you set up the users first or install Exchange into an existing system with users already defined, you must define the users manually in Exchange through the Exchange Administrator utility. If you create users after Exchange is installed, the process of creating users and their mailboxes is integrated into Windows NT User Manager.

- *Use an existing Microsoft Mail 3.x postoffice as a starting point.* If you already have an existing MS Mail 3.x postoffice, you can copy the users defined for Microsoft Mail installation as the starting point for your new Exchange server. This saves the time defining users on the system, as the migration utility either creates new user accounts as needed or assigns Exchange accounts to existing Windows NT accounts as they move from Microsoft Mail to Exchange.

- *Set up accounts so that they share user names.* When you set up Windows NT accounts, you should use the same user names in Windows NT that you'll use for Exchange. This allows Exchange to map mailbox names directly to user names, saving conversion time and effort.

Running the Exchange Setup Program

The process of installing Exchange comprises the following basic steps:

1. Designate the software components and mail connectors you want to install. The native Exchange connectors provide connectivity to MS Mail postoffices, SMTP mail connections, and X.400 networks. Other connectors are available from third-party vendors, including wireless services and connectivity to other information sources.

2. Select the licensing mode, Per Server or Per Seat, for Exchange. Per Server mode requires an Exchange client license for each simultaneous server connection; Per Seat requires a client license for each PC that uses Exchange server.

> **Note**
>
> The Exchange client included with Windows 95 and Windows NT 4.0, now called Windows Messaging, isn't the Exchange client for Exchange Server 4.0. This issue created considerable confusion during the early days of Windows 95. You must install the Exchange client from the CD-ROM on each PC that you want to connect to Exchange Server; the new, licensed client replaces the existing Windows 95 Exchange client.

3. Indicate the names for the site and organization for your server.

V

Microsoft BackOffice

4. Optionally run the migration/optimization wizards to expedite the e-mail conversion process and provide the maximum performance from your server hardware.

> **Caution**
>
> Before running the Exchange setup application, be sure to set the maximum size of your server's paging file to 100M plus the amount of RAM on your computer using the Performance page of Control Panel's System tool. Installation of Exchange 4.00a (released in August 1996) may fail if you don't have a sufficiently large Pagefile.sys.

To install Exchange from the Exchange Server distribution CD-ROM, follow these steps:

1. In Explorer, navigate to the *d*:\Setup\i386 folder and double-click Setup.exe to start the setup process. If your server uses a different processor, select the appropriate \Setup folder. (This step doesn't apply if you're installing from the BackOffice integrated setup application.) Click OK to bypass the initial copyright dialog and open the Microsoft Exchange Server Setup dialog (see fig. 23.6).

Fig. 23.6   Selecting Exchange installation options and the default installation folder.

2. If you want to change the default installation folder, click the Change Directory button, enter the drive and folder for the installation in the Change Directory dialog, and then click OK to return to the Microsoft Exchange Server Setup dialog.

3. Click the button for the type of installation—Typical, Complete/Custom, or Minimum. Click Complete/Custom to open the dialog that lets you specify the Exchange components to install (see fig. 23.7). Only the Microsoft Exchange Server item lets you specify additional installation options.

4. With the Microsoft Exchange Server option selected, click the Change Option button to display the list of Microsoft-supplied connectors to install (see fig. 23.8). The SMTP/Internet Mail Connector and X.400 Connector are extra-cost items not included with the basic Exchange Server license. If you have sufficient disk space, install the Sample Applications for later reference.

Fig. 23.7   Selecting the Exchange components to install.

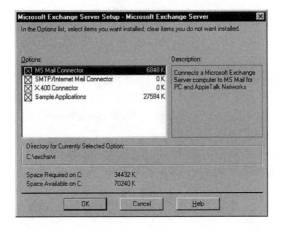

Fig. 23.8   Selecting the e-mail connector and specifying installation of the Sample Applications.

After choosing the options to install, click OK to close the dialog, and then click Continue to open the Choose Licensing Mode dialog.

5. Select the licensing mode for Exchange—Per Server or Per Seat (see fig. 23.9). Click the Add Licenses button to display the New Client Access License dialog (see fig. 23.10). Type the number of licenses purchased (or use the spin buttons). Click OK to open the Per Server or Per Seat dialog, mark the I Agree That… check box and click OK.

6. Click Continue in the Choose Licensing Mode dialog to open the Per Server or Per Seat Licensing dialog; again mark the I Agree That… check box, and click OK. (Microsoft wants to make sure that you doubly agree with its licensing terms.)

7. If this is your first or only Exchange server, or if it's a server that won't rely on another server, select the Create a New Site option in the Organization and Site

V

Microsoft BackOffice

dialog and type the site and organization names in the text boxes (see fig. 23.11). When you click OK, you're asked to confirm that you want to install a new site. Click Yes to open the Site Services Account dialog.

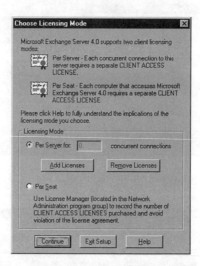

Fig. 23.9 Choosing between Per Server and Per Seat Exchange licensing.

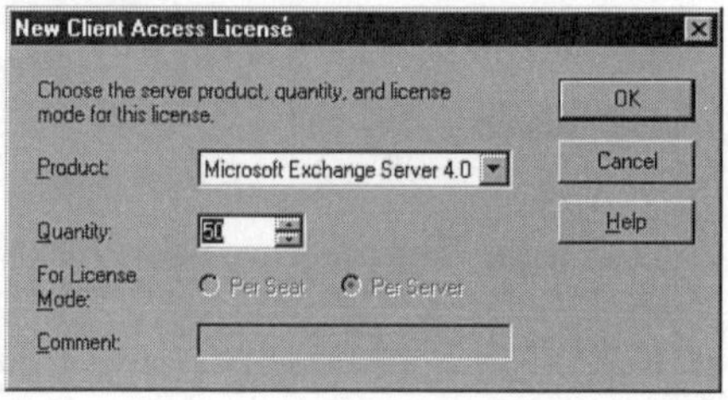

Fig. 23.10 Adding client licenses in accordance with your purchase.

8. The default Exchange Administrator account is the user ID with which you logged on to Windows NT before the setup process (see fig. 23.12). It's a good idea to create a new account in the Domain Admins group, such as ExchAdmin, so Exchange doesn't use your account to run services. The new account must have Log On as a Service and Restore Files and Directories rights, as well as full rights for file operations. To specify a different account name, click Browse to run User Manager for Domains. Type the password for the account and click OK. Click OK when the message box indicates that the necessary rights have been added to the account.

Exchange now has the information it needs to install the files onto your server. The actual process of moving the files to the server can be quite lengthy; the footprint for Exchange is more than 100M, and setting up Exchange objects takes a considerable period of time. Consider taking a coffee break while the installation process completes.

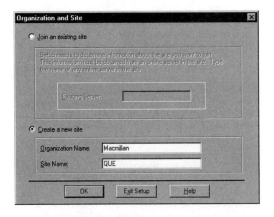

Fig. 23.11 Providing the organization and site names for a new Exchange installation.

Fig. 23.12 Specifying the Windows NT account (domain and user ID) and password for the Exchange Administrator account.

Using the Exchange Server Optimizer Utility

When completed, the installation process offers you the opportunity to run the Optimizer utility (see fig. 23.13). It's strongly recommended that you run this utility to optimize your hardware and software configuration for the number and types of users of Exchange. Run the Optimizer utility immediately after you set up the Exchange server. Although you can skip the optimization step during installation and run the utility later, starting with the optimum configuration assures that users will gain the maximum performance available from the messaging system.

The Optimizer performs the following basic operations:

- It determines the best locations for the Exchange-related files.

- It configures memory usage, taking into account other services running on the server.

- It sets parameters for the number of users and the load you expect on your server.

Fig. 23.13   The final Exchange Server Setup dialog that offers the option of running the Exchange Server Optimizer.

The Optimizer offers suggestions; you have the opportunity to override these suggestions as the Optimizer completes each step. Running the Optimizer is a non-destructive process; you can rerun the Optimizer whenever you change your system configuration or the number of users changes significantly.

To maximize your server's performance for Exchange, follow these steps:

1. Click the Run Optimizer button to open the initial dialog that provides an explanation of the optimizing process. The Optimizer must stop all Exchange services to proceed.

2. Click Next to stop Exchange services and display the user and server configuration dialog (see fig. 23.14). Select the number of users to be served by this installation—usually the number of client licenses you purchased for Exchange. For a conventional installation, the default server types—Private Store, Public Store, and Multi-server—are satisfactory. If this server connects to other servers, specify the total number of Exchange users in your organization.

3. If you have other services, such as SQL Server, running on the server, mark the Limit Memory Usage check box and specify the maximum amount of RAM you want to allocate to Exchange. The minimum value is 24M, but Microsoft recommends a minimum of 32M for Exchange. If you don't limit RAM usage, Exchange can consume all available RAM, which degrades the performance of other services. If your server is devoted to Exchange, don't limit RAM usage. Click Next to begin the Optimizer's analysis process, which takes a minute or two to complete.

4. Click Next after the disk test segment of the process completes to display the dialog that recommends relocation of Exchange files (see fig. 23.15). If you have more than one logical drive, the Optimizer usually recommends that at least one file be relocated. You can accept the recommendations or alter the Suggested Location values. Click Next to continue.

5. If any files are to be relocated, a dialog appears with a check box that you must mark before the relocation process occurs. The dialog recommends backing up the

existing files; this recommendation is applicable when you run Optimizer on a production Exchange server. Click Next to relocate the file(s) and display the final Optimizer dialog.

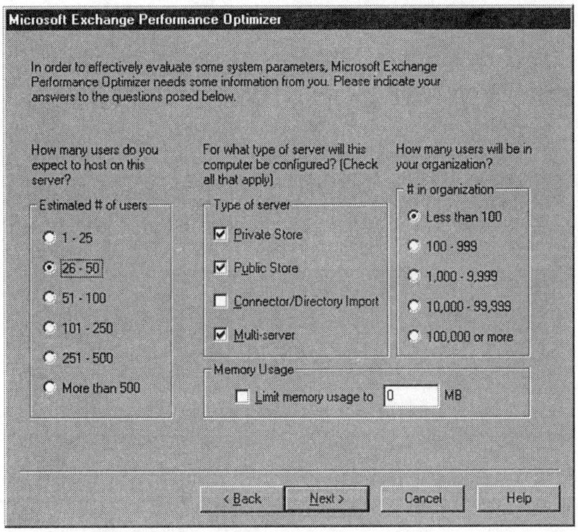

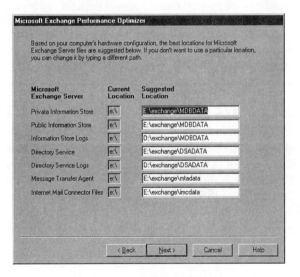

Fig. 23.14   Configuring the Optimizer.

Fig. 23.15   The Optimizer's suggestions for relocating Exchange files.

6. Click Finish to restart Exchange services (see fig. 23.16). If you want to start Exchange later, mark the Do Not Restart These Services check box, and then click Finish.

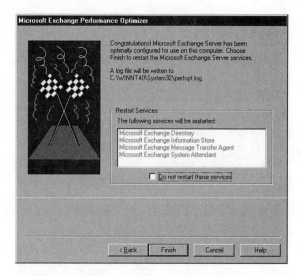

Fig. 23.16 The final dialog of the Exchange Optimizer, offering the option to restart Exchange services.

> **Note**
>
> You can run the Optimizer at any time from the Microsoft Exchange Optimizer choice that's installed in the Microsoft Exchange program menu. You have the same options as when running Optimizer during installation, and you can upsize your server configuration whenever necessary. It's a good idea to run the Optimizer whenever you have a significant change in the configuration of your server. Such changes include adding a large number of users to the system, adding memory, and adding services to or removing services from the server.

Using the Client Load Simulator Utility

The Client Load Simulator (LoadSim) is a complex, intricate tool that lets you load-test your Exchange configuration. Microsoft developed LoadSim to evaluate the performance of Exchange in a wide range of configurations. Using LoadSim effectively requires a thorough knowledge of Exchange features and topology. A complete description of the use of LoadSim is beyond the scope of this book; thus, only a brief description of how to install and start LoadSim is provided here. LoadSim places a controllable user load on the server to provide the following information:

■ The response of your configuration to a specified number of users

■ The effect of growth patterns on the performance of your Exchange system

By using the Load Simulator periodically after you implement Exchange, you can project how your system will respond as its workload increases. You can use this information to justify the acquisition of new equipment, memory, or other resources that may be required to optimize your system. LoadSim uses a significant percentage of your server's resources, so it's best to run LoadSim overnight or on weekends, if your Exchange server is in production.

> **Note**
>
> Running LoadSim creates an Exchange profile (*Servername-##*) for every simulated user. If you specify a load test with 100 users, LoadSim creates 100 exchange users and user profiles. The test profiles ordinarily don't present a problem, because it's uncommon to run a production Exchange client on the server. You can use the Exchange client to delete the test profiles, if necessary.

To install and run the Client Load Simulator, follow these steps:

1. Install the Exchange 4.0 Client on the computer on which you intend to run the Simulator (usually the Exchange server). The Exchange Server installation process doesn't install a local Exchange client on the server. You can run the Simulator from a client PC; however, networking bottlenecks are likely to interfere with accurate measurement.

2. Create a new folder and copy all the files from the \Support\LoadSim\i386 (or other processor) folder of the Exchange CD-ROM.

3. Copy Loadsim.doc from the \Support\LoadSim folder and review the instructions for use of the Simulator.

4. From Explorer, run Loadsim.exe to open LoadSim's main window.

5. Choose <u>T</u>est Topology from the <u>C</u>onfiguration menu, and then click the Add Server button of the Test Topology dialog to open the Server Properties sheet. Type the organization, site, and server names, plus the number of accounts for the server in the text boxes.

6. LoadSim lets you add multiple sites and servers to the test. Type the number of public folders and root folders to test (see fig. 23.17). Click OK twice to close the property sheet and the dialog.

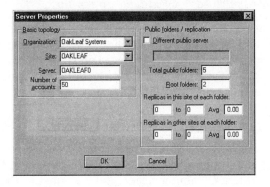

Fig. 23.17 Adding an Exchange server and basic test parameters for LoadSim.

Microsoft BackOffice

V

7. Choose Load Simulation Parameters from the Test menu to open the LoadSim User Profile Properties sheet. Click the New button to enter a new test description name, specify the test duration, and select task options (see fig. 23.18). For a trial run, specify 1 iteration. Click Medium Usage to specify the profile for a typical user. You can further customize the test user in the other property pages. When done, click OK to close the property sheet.

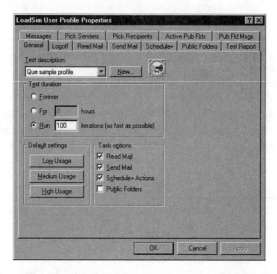

Fig. 23.18 Setting the basic test user parameters in the LoadSim User Profile Properties sheet.

8. Choose Generate Directory Import Files from the Configuration menu to create a .csv file from your server's directory data.

9. Choose Import Users from the Configuration menu to automatically create user accounts for the number of users you specified in step 5.

10. From the File menu, choose Save to save your configuration as a *Config*.sim file. LoadSim automatically loads your .sim file on startup.

11. From the Test menu, choose Run to start the simulation process. Each operation is logged in LoadSim's main window (see fig. 23.19). The progress bar below the menu bar displays the number of users logged on at any instant and the number of messages sent as the test runs. You can stop the test at any time by choosing Stop from the Test menu.

12. After you complete (or stop) the test, LoadSim creates a Loadsim.log file in the default folder. Use the Lslog.exe utility to display the result of the file with the command line `lslog answer loadsim.log`. Lslog.exe displays the weighted average response time in milliseconds. Figure 23.20 shows a Weighted Avg value of 2.143 seconds for a short test. Obtaining meaningful Weighted Avg values requires long (several-hour) tests with a variety of message types and sizes.

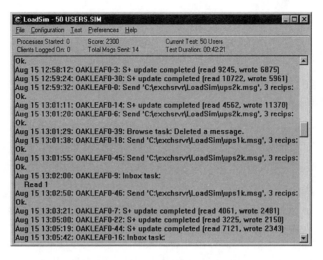

Fig. 23.19   LoadSim's progress report for a test simulation.

```
C:\exchsrvr\LoadSim>lslog answer loadsim.log
Sorting...
Category        Weight Hits    95th Percentile
SEND              1     11      2955
    Sub-weight   16      5      3905
    Sub-weight    5      1      5458
    Sub-weight   60      5      2494
READ             10     14      2363
REPLY             1      2      4707
REPLY ALL         1      1       341
FORWARD           1      0         0
MOVE              1      1       261
DELETE            2      5      1202
SUBMIT            0     14      2924
RESOLVE NAME      0     11      1112
LOAD IMSG         0     12      4106
DELIVER           0     14      5618
Weighted Avg     16     85      2143

C:\exchsrvr\LoadSim>
```

Fig. 23.20   Displaying the result from the Loadsim.log file with the Lslog.exe utility.

The Loadsim.doc file describes in more detail user parameters and how to analyze data to forecast Exchange performance with additional users. Users are divided into Light, Medium, and Heavy usage categories by the utility, and these categories are used to stress the server based on the profile of your users. Before running the utility, it's important to have a profile of your users' mail usage patterns so that the utility reports data from a realistic loading of your system.

Using the Migration Wizard

In an ideal situation, you install your Exchange server at the same time you install and configure your Windows NT domain and its associated users. The ideal is likely to be the exception rather than the rule when installing Exchange, because most Exchange installations are upgrades to existing mail systems.

If you're now using one or more popular mail systems supported by Exchange, you use the Migration Wizard to transfer user accounts, mailboxes, and shared folders. The Wizard supports migration of the following mail systems:

- Microsoft Mail, by using direct postoffice conversion

- Lotus cc:Mail system conversion

- AppleTalk mail, IBM Profs, IBM OfficeVision/VM, DEC ALL-IN-1, and MEMO MVS systems, all by using formatted migration files

In each case, the users' mailboxes are converted and placed into the Exchange system.

Migrating from Microsoft Mail 3.x

Most new Exchange installations now occur within organizations using Microsoft Mail 3.x; as a result, Microsoft Mail migration receives the most detailed explanation in this chapter. The process for migrating from Lotus cc:Mail is almost identical to that for Microsoft Mail. Using the Migration Wizard to convert an existing Microsoft Mail system involves these basic steps:

1. Specify the postoffice administrator's ID.

2. Locate and validate the MS Mail postoffice.

3. Import to Exchange some or all names from the postoffice.

4. Create the Windows NT user accounts, if necessary, for the new accounts.

Deciding on the Migration Procedure. The Migration Wizard offers the following two options for converting your MS Mail postoffice to Exchange:

- *Two-step migration* lets users run Exchange and Microsoft Mail side by side. You configure the Exchange client to use both the MS Mail postoffice and the Exchange server. The client delivers mail from both sources to users' inboxes. This process lets users become comfortable with the new mail system before converting entirely to Exchange. It also eases user anxiety that occurs when switching over to a new system in a single step. By moving to the Exchange server in steps, you help people become accustomed to the new interface and at the same time minimize your impact should any problems arise.

- *One-step migration* completes the conversion by transferring all your users to the Exchange server in one step. This method, which Microsoft recommends, is the easiest but can cause friction in some environments because of users' tendency to be wary of abrupt change. Users who rely on e-mail as their principal means of business communication are likely to resist an instantaneous conversion.

Consider the following approach for your transition from Microsoft Mail 3.x to Exchange:

1. Install the new Exchange client on your users' PCs. This lets users become accustomed to the new look and feel of the Exchange client and lets you set up the client to use the existing Microsoft Mail postoffice. The changes to the Exchange

client are the most visible to the users, and allowing them to see their existing mail messages in the new environment eases the transition process.

2. Convert the user list to Exchange in accordance with the method described later in the "Using the Two-Step Approach" section. The two-step process allows users to start using the Exchange server at their own pace, while remaining in touch with their previous mail system.

3. After you determine that the user accounts are set up correctly and that users are familiar with the new system, complete the final step and convert mail, folders, and other information to the Exchange server. After you fully convert, shut down the Microsoft Mail postoffice.

The following sections describe how to use the Migration Wizard with the recommended two-step scenario and the more drastic one-step method.

Preparing for Migration. Before proceeding with the two-step or one-step conversion, back up at least your MS Mail postoffice folder. Although migration doesn't remove user information or other files from the MS Mail postoffice, there's always the possibility of file corruption during the process.

If your prospective Exchange users don't have Windows NT user accounts, it's a good idea to create a template account for use in the installation process. Perhaps the easiest way to ensure the best security is to create a template account with the group memberships and other rights you desire, and with the Must Change Password option selected. By combining this with the ability to create accounts and use the account name as the password, you can ensure that the account is secured after the user signs on the first time.

> **Caution**
>
> Implementing the template option may require experimentation. If some of your clients are running network or operating system software that doesn't support changing of passwords during the sign-on process, the user may be locked out of the system. Be sure to test the template account on all operating system and network operating system combinations that are the target of your conversion efforts.

To preview the migration process, you can create a new MS Mail postoffice on the server, add a few test users and messages, and then run the Migration Wizard on the test postoffice. You can quickly create a workgroup postoffice from a Windows 95 client by using the Microsoft Mail Postoffice tool of Windows 95's Control Panel. Add a few users, and then use the Migration Wizard to create test Exchange mailboxes and user accounts.

> **Caution**
>
> Have all users log out of MS Mail until the production conversion process is complete. Operations on the MS Mail postoffice during conversion can cause unexpected events, such as loss of messages.

V

Microsoft BackOffice

Using the Two-Step Approach. The first step of two-step migration creates users on the Exchange server that match the mailboxes on the MS Mail system. This process creates the necessary user accounts on Exchange and Windows NT. The user names for the new Windows NT accounts are the same as the e-mail alias; new accounts aren't created for users whose Windows NT account uses their e-mail alias as the user name. The two-step process allows the users access to Exchange, but their existing mail, folders, and shared folders aren't converted from MS Mail.

After you complete your test phase, you use the second step of the two-step option to extract and import the message files, folders, and shared folders from the MS Mail system into the Exchange server's message store. Users have been created, as necessary, so you move only existing MS Mail messages to the Exchange message store.

> **Note**
>
> It's important to understand the enhanced benefits you have when you move to public folders from shared folders. With public folders, you can enable rules, filters, and smart, server-based processing on the posted objects. Public folders are similar to Usenet newsgroups or Lotus Notes databases, because public folders support conversation threading and can present views based on the conversation threads.

The two-step process is a simple variation of the one-step method described in the next section.

Using the One-Step Approach. If you select the one-step approach, the entire MS Mail postoffice is converted to the Exchange environment, carrying with it the address books, groups, folders, and mail for the users of the system. The conversion process involves the following basic steps:

- Selecting the information to convert

- Selecting the user accounts to convert

- Selecting the server on which the accounts are created, if more than one server exists at the site

When the conversion is completed, you shut down the MS Mail postoffice; users then connect only to the new Exchange server.

To run the Migration Wizard in the one-step process, follow this procedure:

1. From the Start menu, choose Microsoft Exchange and then Migration Wizard to open the first Wizard dialog (see fig. 23.21). Select Migrate from MS Mail for PC Networks and click Next.

2. The second dialog describes the requirements for permanent coexistence of MS Mail and Exchange, which doesn't apply to the one-step or two-step process. Click Next.

Fig. 23.21 Choosing the mail system to convert to Exchange in the Migration Wizard's opening dialog.

3. Type or browse for the path to your existing MS Mail postoffice, enter the Administrator account name and password for the postoffice (see fig. 23.22), and click Next.

Fig. 23.22 Specifying the MS Mail postoffice location and Administrator account name and password.

4. Select One Step Migration (see fig. 23.23) and click Next.

5. Specify the types of MS Mail information to import. By default, all MS Mail content is imported to Exchange (see fig. 23.24). If you haven't already created Exchange accounts by the two-step process, make sure that the Information to Create Mailboxes check box is marked. Click Next.

6. Click Select All to specify that all MS Mail users are migrated to Exchange (see fig. 23.25). Alternatively, you can migrate only a set of test users to Exchange, and then move the remaining users after the test period is over. Click Next.

7. Type the name of the Exchange server to store the mailbox accounts and messages (see fig. 23.26). Click Next.

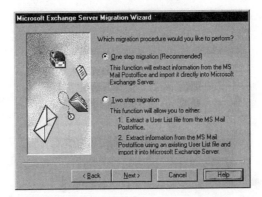

Fig. 23.23 Selecting one-step or two-step migration.

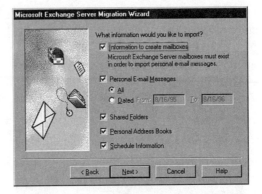

Fig. 23.24 Selecting the MS Mail information to migrate to Exchange.

Fig. 23.25 Specifying the user accounts to convert to Exchange.

Fig. 23.26   Providing the Exchange server name for MS Mail migration

8. Select the type of user access to shared MS Mail folders. The Migration Wizard applies the same permissions to all shared folders; you can change the permissions with the Exchange Administrator. The most common option is Author Access: Read, Create, Edit Items (see fig. 23.27). Click Next.

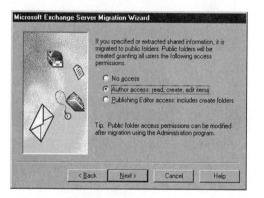

Fig. 23.27   Setting permissions for shared MS Mail folders converted to Exchange Public Folders.

9. Select the default recipient container to hold user accounts, as shown in figure 23.28. (If you ran LoadSim, described earlier in the section "Using the Client Load Simulator Utility," you also have a LoadSim container that holds the LoadSim test accounts.) If you created a template account for new Windows NT user accounts, click Browse and select the account from the Groups and Users list. Use of a template account is optional. Click Next.

10. Specify the type of password to create for new Windows NT accounts created from MS Mail mailboxes. The simplest method is Create Accounts and Use Alias as a Password. If you select this option, the template account should specify the User Must Change Password at Next Logon option. If your server is connected to more than one domain, select the domain for the new user accounts (see fig. 23.29). Click Next to begin the conversion process.

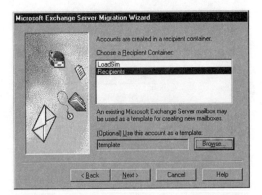

Fig. 23.28 Specifying the recipient container for Exchange accounts and a template file for creating Windows NT accounts.

Fig. 23.29 Selecting the type of password to create for new Windows NT accounts and specifying the domain for the accounts.

11. During conversion, a status dialog appears to indicate the progress of adding users and migrating messages (see fig. 23.30). When migration is complete, you receive the message shown in figure 23.31. Click OK to terminate the Migration Wizard.

When migration completes, your users sign on to the new Exchange server from the Exchange client and see all their existing mail.

Using Migration Files

When you convert a postoffice using migration files, you use a fixed-format file, created by an Exchange extractor application, as the source for the import process. The extractor programs included on the Exchange Server CD-ROM are located in the following folders:

- \Migrate\Tools\Macmail for the Microsoft Mail for AppleTalk Networks Source Extractor

- \Migrate\Tools\Host\All-in-1 for the Digital ALL-IN-1 Source Extractor

- \Migrate\Tools\Host\Memo for the Verimation Memo Source Extractor

- \Migrate\Tools\Host\Profs for the IBM PROFS/OV Source Extractor

Fig. 23.30 The status dialog during an early part of the conversion process.

Fig. 23.31 The message box indicating that migration is complete.

The Readme.txt file in the folder details the use of the extractor with the Migration Wizard. In general, you follow these steps to create and use the extractor files:

1. Use the extractor to create the migration source file.

2. Provide the path and file name to the migration source file to the Migration Wizard.

3. Follow the resulting prompts to select users, destination servers, and other parameters controlling the creation of user accounts.

The extractor options vary according to the features of your existing mail system. The extractor exports the messages stored in the system, private, and shared message storage locations (called *folders* in Exchange). After you create the migration source file, the Migration Wizard prompts you through the steps necessary to import the information into Exchange.

Installing the Exchange Client

Installing the client software for Exchange is a requirement for your users, even if they have the Exchange client shipped with Windows 95 or the newer Microsoft Windows Messaging client. The installation of the client software adds the messaging subsystem drivers necessary to connect to the server, use Exchange's advanced features, and provide access to the public folders on the server.

The following basic steps are required to install the client software for your users:

- Install the client software on the server and make it accessible to the users of your server

- Install the software from the server onto the client systems

- Set up profiles for the clients, specifying the messaging services to use

Installing the Client Software on the Server

The client software isn't included on the Exchange Server CD-ROM; instead, use the Exchange Clients CD-ROM, which also may include other BackOffice applications. Complete the following steps for each platform you want to support for a given server:

1. Copy the software for each type of Exchange client to be supported. Client software (English locale) is located in \DOS, \Win16, \Win95, and \Winnt subfolders of the \Exchange\Clients\Eng folder. The most recent release of Exchange also includes a Macintosh client. The simplest method is to copy the entire \Exchange\Clients\ Eng folder to your server, and then delete the subfolders for client types you don't need. The \Winnt subfolder contains clients for i386, Alpha, MIPS, and PowerPC platforms; delete the clients for the platforms you don't need.

2. Create share(s) on your system to provide client access to the software for installation.

3. Optionally, customize the client setup program to establish default profile values for the Exchange clients.

> **Note**
>
> Review the Readme.wri document in the \Exchange\Clients\Eng folder before having users install the client software. The Readme.wri file contains a substantial amount of information regarding potential installation problems and how to tune clients for optimum performance.

To set up the share to the different directories, you have the following options:

- Set up a high-level client share that gives users access to all the client software folders. This approach allows users to connect to a single share and select the client for their operating environment. The advantage of this is that your client installation instructions can be the same for all users on your network.

- Create individual shares to each operating environment folder. This approach lets users select the client software to install from a more readable share name, such as Exch_Win31 or Exch_Win94, with a full share description.

You can customize the client setup program from the Start menu by choosing Microsoft Exchange and then Microsoft Exchange Setup Editor. The Setup Editor lets you preset some user options, as well as specify the services to install. The Setup Editor doesn't let you automatically install the Internet Mail, Microsoft Fax, Microsoft Network, or CompuServe mail providers for Windows 95 clients, so Setup Editor is of limited use for Windows 95 clients. The client software files you copy from the CD-ROM have the read-only attribute set. You must remove the read-only attribute from the Exchng.stf setup file in the setup folder before saving a modified setup file.

Installing the Client Software

It's likely that most Exchange users run Windows 95 and already have the Windows 95 version of Exchange on their PCs. Follow these steps to install the full Exchange client software on a Windows 95 machine:

1. Close all programs running on the client. If necessary, log on to the Windows NT domain with the user name and password with the new account created from the client's MS Mail account.

2. Use Network Neighborhood to connect to the client server share of the Win95 client.

3. Double-click Setup.exe to start the client setup process. Click Continue when the first setup dialog appears.

4. Complete the Name and Organization entries, if they aren't filled in from default values on the client. Click OK twice to confirm the entries.

5. Setup detects the older version of Exchange, usually in the \Program Files\ Microsoft Exchange folder. Unless you must retain the older version, click OK to overwrite the Windows 95 version.

6. Click the Custom button to allow selection of installation options. (If you use the two-step installation process, you must use Custom setup to install the Microsoft Mail MAPI service provider.)

7. If the client needs to connect to Microsoft Mail, select Exchange, click the Change Option button, and then select Information Services (see fig. 23.32); then click Change Option again to open the Microsoft Exchange – Information Services dialog. Otherwise, skip to step 9.

8. Click the Select All button to mark all the check boxes (see fig. 23.33), and then click OK to close the dialog. Click OK to close the Microsoft Exchange – Exchange dialog.

9. The Exchange client includes an updated version of Schedule+ that works with Exchange Server. If you want to install or update Schedule+ (required if you're migrating now to Exchange), select Schedule+ and click Change Option to open the Microsoft Exchange Schedule+ dialog. You can save a substantial amount of disk space if you install only required options (see fig. 23.34). Click OK to return to the Microsoft Exchange – Custom dialog.

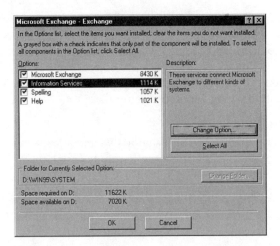

Fig. 23.32   Selecting Exchange components for installation.

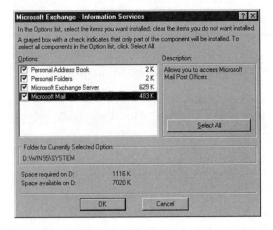

Fig. 23.33   Adding the Microsoft Mail MAPI service provider to the Information Services installed.

10. Click Continue to copy the required files to the client's fixed disk, which is a three- to five-minute process, depending on network traffic and the speed of the client PC.

> **Note**
>
> Steps 3 through 10 also apply to installing the client software on the server, which is required to run the LoadSim utility described earlier in the "Using the Client Load Simulator Utility" section. You need to install only the Exchange provider to run LoadSim.

11. If you added the Microsoft Mail provider in step 7, click Yes when the message box asks whether you want to use Microsoft Exchange to access Microsoft Mail postoffices.

12. At the final dialog, restart Windows 95 to complete the installation.

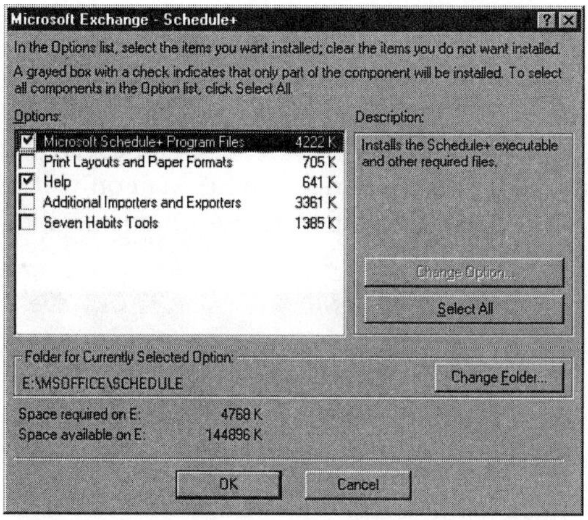

Fig. 23.34   Specifying required options for Schedule+.

Specifying Client Options

After the Exchange software is installed on the client system, you can establish multiple client profiles that each specify the set of information providers. To view client profiles, double-click Windows 95's Control Panel's Mail and Fax tool or Windows NT's Mail tool; then click Show Profiles in the Services page of the Microsoft Exchange Properties sheet to open the Mail and Fax property sheet. When you install the client software, the existing Exchange profile, if any, is saved and a new profile is created (see fig. 23.35). After you verify that the current MS Exchange Settings profile works, you can delete the MS Exchange Settings (old) profile.

Fig. 23.35   Exchange profiles created by the Exchange client during replacement of the Windows 95 Inbox.

You add new profiles by clicking the Add button to start the Windows 95 Inbox Setup Wizard or the Windows NT Microsoft Exchange Setup Wizard. The following steps describe how to set up a new profile using the Inbox Setup Wizard:

1. Mark the check boxes for the Information Services (MAPI providers) for the client's new profile (see fig. 23.36). Windows NT 4.0's wizard doesn't include Microsoft Fax, The Microsoft Network Online Service, or CompuServe Mail options. The following steps depict installing Exchange and MS Mail only; if you specify Microsoft Fax or an online service, you also must choose a modem. Click Next to continue.

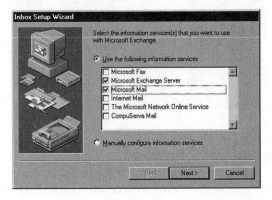

Fig. 23.36 Selecting the information services (MAPI service providers) for the client.

2. Type a description for the new profile in the Profile Name text box (see fig. 23.37). Click Next.

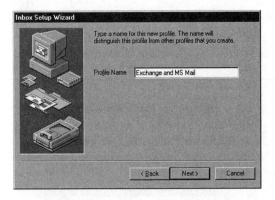

Fig. 23.37 Specifying a descriptive name for the new profile.

3. Type the name of your Exchange server and the full mailbox name for the user, not the e-mail alias (see fig. 23.38). Click Next.

Fig. 23.38   Entering the name of the Exchange server and the user's mailbox name.

4. If the client is a laptop PC, select Yes to allow off-network operation; otherwise, select No (see fig. 23.39). Click Next.

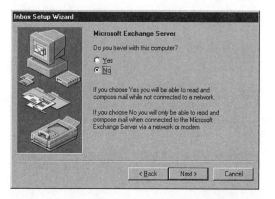

Fig. 23.39   Choosing between installation for a laptop or a desktop PC.

5. If you specified Microsoft Mail in step 1, type or browse for the MS Mail postoffice location (see fig. 23.40). If you pick the wrong location, you receive an error message. Click Next.

6. Type the password for the user's MS Mail account (see fig. 23.41). Click Next.

7. Type or browse for the location of an existing Personal Address Book (PAB). Existing PABs usually are located in the \Windows folder but may be located elsewhere (see fig. 23.42). If the Windows 95 user has no PAB, which is unlikely, leave the text box empty to let the Wizard create a .pab file. Click Next.

Fig. 23.40 Specifying the location of the existing Microsoft Mail postoffice.

Fig. 23.41 Verifying the user's MS Mail account and entering the mailbox password.

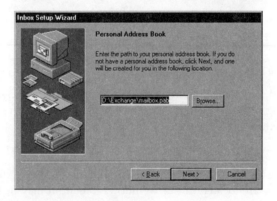

Fig. 23.42 Specifying the location of an existing Personal Address Book.

> **Note**
>
> Use the existing .pab file for each profile you create. If you specify a new .pab file, the user must re-create all of his PAB entries.

8. Select the Do Not Add Inbox to the StartUp Group option unless you want the user to check for mail on starting Windows 95 (see fig. 23.43). Click Next.

Fig. 23.43 Choosing whether to add the inbox to Windows 95's StartUp program group.

9. The last wizard dialog confirms the information services you specified in step 1 (see fig. 23.44). Click Finish to create the new profile and terminate the wizard.

Fig. 23.44 Confirming the information services to install before completing the new profile.

10. To make the new profile active, select the new profile name in the When Starting Microsoft Exchange, Use This Profile drop-down list (see fig. 23.45). Then click Close to close the Mail and Fax property sheet.

Fig. 23.45 Making the new profile the default when starting Microsoft Exchange.

After installing the new Exchange client, test the connection to the Exchange server. If you used the Migration Wizard for MS Mail and specified conversion of shared folders, a Microsoft Mail Shared Folders item appears in the Explorer-like left pane (see fig. 23.46).

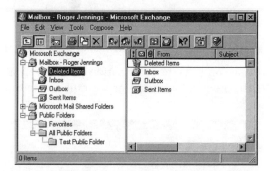

Fig. 23.46 The Windows 95 version of the Exchange client, providing access to MS Mail shared folders.

Working with User Manager and Exchange Mailboxes

Windows NT user accounts and Exchange mailboxes are closely integrated, so User Manager for Domains provides simultaneous addition of new Windows NT users and Exchange mailboxes. After you set up Exchange, a new menu choice, Exchange, appears in User Manager's window. The Exchange menu has Options and Properties choices for setting up users and their mailboxes. Choosing Options opens the General (only) page of the Options property sheet, in which you specify the name of the default Exchange server and recipients container for all new Exchange users (see fig. 23.47). Choosing Properties opens the property sheet for the selected user.

Fig. 23.47 Setting default options for adding new Exchange users.

When you create a new user, you follow the same steps as you did before the installation of Exchange. After you choose New User from the User menu and set up the account, however, you're presented with a new property sheet containing several pages. The General properties page lets you define the user's presence on the Exchange server (see fig. 23.48). Table 23.2 summarizes the information you enter on each page of the *Username* Properties sheet.

Fig. 23.48 Setting General properties for a new Exchange mailbox.

Table 23.2   Summary of Property Pages for the Exchange User Property Sheet

Page	Description
General	This page sets up the base account. You specify the alias, descriptive display name, and address information for the mailbox. This page also specifies the Windows NT user account that's associated with the mailbox.
Organization	This page lets you specify the user's manager and subordinates. This information is useful for applications to query in resolving a relative reference. For example, if an application needs to send an e-mail message to the user's supervisor, the destination is looked up here.
Phone/Notes	This page allows you to specify a number of phone numbers for this user. You can also enter a series of notes about the user.
Distribution Lists	This page allows you to select from existing lists those lists to which this user should belong.
E-mail Addresses	On this page, you establish proxy addresses (described earlier in the "Proxy Address Support" section) for accounts. More than one proxy address may be created, depending on the number of connectors installed on the server. A user may have one or more addresses associated with each connector that's running on the server and available to the user.
Delivery Restrictions	This page lets you specify the individuals from whom you will or won't accept e-mail. This can be a helpful junk mail filter. The message originator is notified of refused mail if it's declined at your mailbox.
Delivery Options	This page offers the option of setting up "Send on behalf of" privileges for users. This privilege allows users to, for example, send mail for a supervisor or co-worker. Another common use for this feature is to send mail on behalf of a shared mail account. For example, perhaps you have a technical support account, TechSupport, that's actually monitored by more than one individual. By using this feature, other users can originate mail from the TechSupport account.
Custom Attributes	Custom attributes are simply fields in which you can place information pertinent to your operation. These are free-form fields.
Advanced	Advanced options include several metering options that control system and disk space usage, mail display names, and others. This page may be helpful in managing users that tend to have a great deal of mail and require large amounts of disk space to store it. You can manage such users' disk space usage on this tab and help prevent storage outages.

Note

The property pages, connectors, and other objects in the Exchange environment are extensible by third parties. In some cases, when you install a product that works with Exchange, property sheets may be added to or changed from those of the default installation.

After you click OK to close the *Username* Properties sheet, you're returned to User Manager and are ready to add the next user to the system.

Using the Exchange Administrator Utility

The Exchange Administrator application provides global access to the server and all of its components. With Exchange's object-oriented approach to the messaging environment, the Administrator displays a hierarchy of containers and objects to ease the administrative process. You add new mailboxes for users with existing Windows NT accounts with the Administrator. The primary use of the Administrator, however, is to set the properties of other objects, such as connectors, through a multitude of property pages. Publishing limitations preclude a complete description of the Administrator's capabilities; only a brief overview of the Exchange Administrator is presented here.

You launch the Administrator from the Start menu by choosing Programs, Microsoft Exchange, and Microsoft Exchange Administrator. When Administrator's window opens, much of the object hierarchy is collapsed. Click the + icon of the item you want to expand; a – icon indicates that the item is fully expanded (see fig. 23.49).

Fig. 23.49   Exchange Administrator's window, with the first two object hierarchies expanded.

The Recipients container stores all mailbox accounts. Selecting the Recipients container, the default for new users, in the left pane displays all the container accounts in the right pane (refer to fig. 23.49). Double-clicking an individual recipient item displays the *Username* Properties sheet, as shown earlier in figure 23.48.

The Administrator is also where you install additional connectors for your system and other Exchange objects. You install new objects by choosing New Other from the File menu, which displays the submenu shown in figure 23.50. You manage existing objects by double-clicking the item at the lowest level (leaf node) of the hierarchy to display its property sheet. Figure 23.51 shows the Internet Mail Connector Properties sheet.

You can create Custom Recipients for third-party connectors added to your Exchange server. For example, if you want to create a recipient that's accessible only through a third-party wireless or paging connector, you create a John Smith–Pager recipient. This recipient is associated only with the wireless or paging gateway, and messages sent to this user automatically are sent through the wireless or pager connector.

Microsoft BackOffice

V

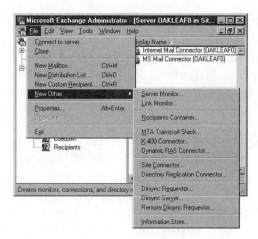

Fig. 23.50 New object choices presented by the File menu's New Other submenu.

Fig. 23.51 The Internet Mail Connector Properties sheet.

The Administrator is an effective tool for managing all Exchange objects. You can provide comprehensive distribution list management, user management, and connector support for your Exchange system. The specific options available depend on the services, transports, and connectors you install.

From Here...

This chapter provided only a brief overview of Exchange Server's client/server messaging capabilities. A full exposition of the features of Exchange requires a book in itself. Step-by-step procedures were provided for installing Exchange Server, using the

MS Mail Migration Wizard, and installing the Exchange client, along with the process of adding Exchange mailboxes for new user accounts with User Manager for Domains. The chapter closed with a short section on the Exchange Administrator application. For more information relating to topics covered in this chapter, refer to these chapters:

- Chapter 12, "Managing User and Group Accounts," describes how to use Windows NT Server 4.0's User Manager for Domains, take advantage of the new Add User Accounts and Group Management wizards, and utilize the built-in user groups of Windows NT.

- Chapter 16, "Distributing Network Services with Domains," covers Windows NT Server's trusted domains and other distributed networking features that allow a single-user logon for multiple network servers and server-based applications, such as Exchange, running on LANs and WANs.

- Chapter 18, "Managing Remote Access Service," explains how to configure Windows NT Server 4.0's RAS component to support dial-in access by mobile users to Exchange mail.

V

Microsoft BackOffice

Chapter 24

Administering Clients with System Management Server

This chapter introduces Microsoft System Management Server (SMS). The intent of this chapter isn't to provide a detailed system administration guide for SMS; such scope requires an entire book. Instead, this chapter describes the fundamentals of SMS, including its key components and how these components are integrated in LAN and WAN environments. This basic understanding is a necessity for IS staff planning to implement SMS, because SMS is a complex product and has extensive capabilities. When you achieve a basic understanding of SMS, you can plan the customization of SMS to suit your network environment. Detailed recommendations for installation and planning SMS are available from Microsoft's SMS home page at **http://www.microsoft.com/SMSmgmt/**.

The key factor in a successful SMS system design and rollout is an understanding of how SMS operates and a thorough knowledge of your LAN and WAN topology. Some of the functions performed by SMS are bandwidth critical, so where you place SMS servers and how you define their functions has a significant impact on the network performance. If you're planning on an enterprise-wide SMS rollout, you gain insight into how each component of SMS fits into your overall network strategy and how SMS affects your network as you read this chapter.

Introducing System Management Server

Organizations spend large amounts of money on upgrading, maintaining, and supporting the hardware and software for desktop computing. The PC support group typically is forced to revisit priorities in order to resolve end-user issues and, at the same time, design, deploy, and maintain new enterprise-wide applications and infrastructure. At the same time, PC support often must deal with budget restrictions and staff reductions as a result of downsizing, outsourcing, and/or re-engineering.

In this chapter, you learn

- The features and capabilities of SMS 1.2

- System requirements for SMS

- How to install SMS on a Windows NT Server

- How to design SMS queries

- How to install SMS software on client PCs

V

Microsoft BackOffice

Some of the major issues that PC support staff face are

- Quick end-user support and problem resolution

- Support of multiple offices in a LAN and WAN environment

- Support for multiple platforms and desktop operating systems

- Installing or upgrading many PCs with new or updated software in a very short period

- Support for multiple protocols in the enterprise

- Maintaining the hardware and software inventory for all desktop PCs

Microsoft System Management Server version 1.2 is the third major release of this application to address the preceding issues. Microsoft released version 1.2 on August 19, 1996. Following are the most important new features of SMS 1.2:

- Remote control of Windows NT Workstation and Server 3.51 or 4.0. You can log on to Windows NT machines remotely. (Version 1.1 added Windows 95 remote control capabilities.)

- Inventory runs as a service on Windows NT machines. A user doesn't need to be logged on to check software and hardware inventory.

- Improved performance loading Management Information Format (MIF) files on the central SMS database.

- Program Group Control (PGC) provided for Windows 95 and Office 95.

- Simple Network Management Protocol (SNMP) trap receiving and forwarding. This lets you specify events that are forwarded to network management applications, such as HP OpenView. You can receive traps from routers, hubs, and other active network components.

System Management Server provides centralized management of the networked PCs. Centralized management includes identification, control, maintenance, and software upgrade of all the PCs on the LAN and/or WAN. The following sections describe the primary features of SMS 1.1+, its server requirements, and its support for network operating systems and protocols.

Remote Control and Troubleshooting

Remote control and troubleshooting (also called *help* or *help desk*) lets you view a client PC's display and control the client's keyboard and mouse. The help feature allows you to run the PC without being physically present at the client's location. You also can conduct a text chat session with the user, remotely execute programs, read files, or even reboot the client operating system. End-user support requests are addressed from a central location, thereby saving valuable time and resources.

> **Note**
>
> SMS 1.1 is limited to remote control of MS-DOS, Windows 3.x, Windows for Workgroups 3.1+, and Windows 95 clients. SMS 1.2 lets you remotely control machines running Windows NT 3.51 and 4.0.

Hardware and Software Inventory

The capability to take an inventory of hardware and software installed on client PCs (also called *asset management*) is one of the features most requested by IS technical support staff. By using this SMS feature, you can automatically install the SMS client management agent on client machines without visiting each machine. The agent identifies the hardware and software on each desktop PC and reports the results back to the server. This feature also allows hardware and software audits. Asset management is used with SMS's software distribution and installation features, as well as its software metering capabilities.

Software Distribution and Installation

The software distribution and installation feature of SMS sets up applications on individual PCs and servers at local and remote sites. You can deliver a predefined software Package to targeted systems by using drag-and-drop methods. You also can define targeted Groups or Machines to create customized distribution and installation procedures.

A Package can be any type of file, including an executable file, so SMS can be used to run a program automatically without installing it on the targeted machine. For example, you can package an antivirus program to run every day at midnight. With the asset management feature of SMS, you can identify and deliver a Package only if a specified criterion is met by the destination client.

Network Protocol Analysis

System Management Server includes an extended version of Windows NT Server 4.0's Network Monitor tool. For example, if a user has difficulty logging on to the network, you can capture packets and then easily discover that the user's password is invalid. SMS's Network Monitor lets you remotely capture, filter, decode, analyze, edit, and replay network protocol packets, including TCP/IP, IPX/SPX, NetBIOS, AppleTalk, NCP, and SMB. You can set up dedicated network monitoring workstations when you run the remote capture agent in a session of a client running Windows NT Workstation. The primary difference between the SMS and Windows NT Server 4.0 versions of Network Monitor is that the SMS version can connect to remote Network Monitor agents across routed networks.

◀◀ See "Using Windows NT 4.0's Network Monitor," p. 545.

Remote Performance Monitoring

By using Performance Monitor, you can check the events generated by remote PCs running Windows NT Workstation and Server. The primary difference between SMS's and Windows NT Server 4.0's Performance Monitors is that you can run the SMS version remotely on a client running Windows NT Workstation.

V

Microsoft BackOffice

◄◄ See "Using Performance Monitor," p. 501

Customized Data Analysis, Transfer, and Reporting

System Management Server relies on a SQL Server database, named SMS, to store data gathered by SMS. The SMS database contains 84 user tables. The Identification_SPEC table contains one record for each PC for which you install the SMS client; other related tables store information on each PC's hardware and installed software.

You can design custom reports by using Microsoft Access, Visual Basic, or any other ODBC-compliant application development tool that can query the SMS database. For example, you can create an Access or Visual Basic front end to extract PC inventory data from the SMS database and to generate a new table compatible with the asset management features of an accounting application.

Differences Between SMS and Network Management Applications

Microsoft doesn't position SMS as an enterprise network management application. Network management software such as HP OpenView or Computer Associates CA-Unicenter TNG typically discover and then maintain the internetwork devices such as hubs and routers. A network management tool can turn on and off ports of hubs and routers using SNMP. SMS, on the other hand, discovers and maintains only the end-node devices, primarily PC clients. This is an important distinction between these two types of products because they complement one another, and both are necessary for large-scale network management.

◄◄ See "Considering Network Management Needs," p. 70

> **Note**
>
> Microsoft and Computer Associates announced on August 28, 1996, an agreement to collaborate on an enterprise network management system based on CA-Unicenter TNG and Microsoft's Internet technology, such as Internet Explorer, ActiveX controls, and the HyperMedia Management Schema (HMMS) and HyperMedia Management Protocol (HMMP) for network management. HMMS is designed to make network management information available via Web browsers. It's likely that future versions of SMS also will offer HMMS and HMMP for integration with CA-Unicenter TNG.

Server Requirements

Following are the minimum specifications for a server running SMS 1.2:

- Windows NT Server 3.5+ or 4.0

- SQL Server for Windows NT version 4.21+

- An Intel-based system with a 486/66 or faster processor, or a RISC system supported by Windows NT

- 32M of memory dedicated to SMS

- A fixed disk with at least 100M free and a NTFS partition for installing SMS (SMS won't install on a FAT partition)

- CD-ROM drive

- Network adapter card

- All requirements for running Windows NT Server 4.0

Note

System Management Server processes may be divided among multiple servers to reduce the requirements for a single server in large installations. The preceding minimum requirements are for a relatively small SMS installation.

Supported Networks

System Management Server is supported on the following local area networks:

- Windows NT Server

- Microsoft LAN Manager 2.1+

- Novell NetWare 3.1+ (requires installation of Gateway Service for NetWare)

- IBM LAN Server 3.x and 4.0

Wide Area Network Options

System Management Server supports the following WAN and remote access connection protocols:

- TCP/IP

- IPX/SPX

- ISDN

- X.25

- LU 6.2 (requires Microsoft SNA Server)

Clients Supported

SMS 1.2 supports the following clients:

- MS-DOS 5.0+

- Windows 3.1+

- Windows for Workgroups 3.11

- Windows 95

- Windows NT 3.x and 4.0 (remote control with SMS 1.2 requires Windows NT 3.51 or 4.0)

- Apple Macintosh System 7.x

- IBM OS/2 version 2.x, or OS/2 Warp

Planning for System Management Server

Planning is required to use SMS effectively. The planning requirement for SMS is similar in scope to that for Microsoft Exchange Server installations, described in Chapter 23, "Messaging with Microsoft Exchange Server." The following sections describe the topology of SMS sites and the SMS components you install at the sites.

> **Note**
>
> Microsoft publishes a series of white papers that deal with SMS planning and deployment. You can view or download these white papers from **http://www.microsoft.com/SMSmgmt/ plan.htm**.

Enterprise Site Topology

Figure 24.1 illustrates an enterprise-wide, multiple-server SMS configuration with a number of roles for the SMS servers installed at each location. In figure 24.1, the Chicago, New York City, and London servers are connected directly in a WAN environment. Each site has multiple clients connected via a LAN. The Milan site is supported by the London office.

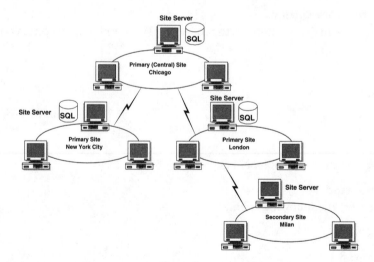

Fig. 24.1   A typical enterprise topology of SMS sites.

For the purposes of SMS, a *site* is a group of servers and clients in a LAN and/or WAN environment that are typically located in a single geographical area. In the example in figure 24.1, Chicago, New York City, London, and Milan are all sites.

A *Primary Site* is one with a SQL database. A Primary Site with a SQL Server installation is responsible for collecting all information from the nodes in that site. Chicago, New York City, and London are all Primary Sites.

A site without a SQL server, such as Milan, is called a *Secondary Site* and is supported by the Primary Site. All the information collected in a Secondary Site by SMS agents is reported to the Primary Site; therefore, bandwidth availability between primary and secondary sites is a major design consideration.

The SMS enterprise design also includes the concept of *parent* and *child* relationships. A parent site is one that has a Primary or Secondary Site as a child site. In figure 24.1, Chicago and London are parent sites, and New York City and Milan are child sites. A Primary Site can be a parent site if a Secondary Site is below it. A Primary Site can also be a child site. A Secondary Site, such as Milan, is always a child site.

The hierarchical design of SMS has major advantages over a simple collection of Primary Sites. One key advantage is that all the reports can be sent to a central administration office and, therefore, centralized enterprise management is achieved. This site is called a *Central Site* and must be a Primary Site with access to SQL Server. All the sites in the SMS hierarchical structure report to the Central Site. A second advantage of a hierarchical design is that adding sites to an existing environment becomes a simple task, because a site can easily be added as a child in the hierarchy tree of the SMS installation.

Component Terminology and Concepts

After you establish your enterprise design, you must define the role of the SMS servers in these sites. SMS can play many roles in the overall design strategy. The selection of roles depends on the complexity of the network, bandwidth availability of the LAN and WAN, the number of sites, and other factors. You must first understand the SMS role at each site. The terminology for SMS server roles is as follows:

- *Site Server*. This is the server that runs SMS. Each site must have at least one Site Server, which monitors and manages the site. It's also responsible for collecting the information from the clients and providing instructions for different tasks. The Site Server collects all the inventory information from clients.

- *Distribution Server*. A software distribution environment needs a server that's responsible for distributing new or updated software to all the desired nodes. This is the responsibility of the Distribution Server. This server can run NetWare, Windows NT Server, IBM LAN Server, or Microsoft LAN Manager. The Distribution Server sends a copy of the software to one client machine, to a group of client machines, or to all client machines to which it connects. The Distribution Server can be (and often is) the same server on which you install SMS.

- *Logon Server*. This server is responsible for validating user logons. Also during logon, the Logon Server collects client information such as inventory. If the Logon Server is the Primary Site server, this information is placed in the SQL server. If the Logon Server is a separate server, it will act as an agent and deliver all the information to the site server.

- *SQL Server*. As mentioned in previous sections, SMS requires SQL Server to provide the database component for system management. The overall system is more efficient if all the servers have access to their own SQL Server to minimize reporting activity and network bandwidth. If you can't justify a SQL Server in every site, you can use multiple secondary sites that report to the Primary Site. In such a case, you must carefully analyze bandwidth usage.

■ *Helper Server*. Helper Servers are used to offload some of the processing from the site server. If you have a large environment and many clients, you can transfer some functions from the site server to the Helper Server, such as the scheduler, despooler, inventory processor, and senders. The Helper Server lets you balance the load among machines running SMS to achieve better performance.

In smaller environments, a single server can be responsible for all the preceding roles. Installing a dedicated SQL Server on the same machine as SMS usually provides better performance by avoiding LAN traffic constraints. In larger environments, however, multiple servers play specific roles to provide efficient and timely transfer of information and files to and from clients.

Installing System Management Server

System Management Server must be installed on a Windows NT Primary or Backup Domain controller (PDC or BDC) and, if a Primary Site, must have access to SQL Server locally or over a network. The first SMS installation must be a Primary Site and usually is the Central Site; after you install the Primary Site, you can install other primary and secondary sites that report to the Central Site. Chapter 16, "Distributing Network Services with Domains," describes the relationships between Primary and Backup Domain Controllers.

Note

Microsoft provides a Reviewer's Guide for SMS 1.2 at **http://www.microsoft.com/ SMSmgmt/revgd/**. The Reviewer's Guide provides detailed installation instructions and user guidelines for evaluating SMS 1.2.

Creating a Service Account

Before you install SMS on any Windows NT server, you must create the user account for the SMS service. You create this account, typically called SMSAdmin, with User Manager for Domains as follows:

1. Open User Manager for Domains, and then choose New User from the User menu to open the New User dialog.

2. Type SMSAdmin as the Username, and then specify a Full Name, Description, and Password. (The password must not be the same as the value of Username.)

3. Clear the User Must Change Password at Next Logon check box, and mark the User Cannot Change Password and Password Never Expires check boxes (see fig. 24.2).

4. Click the Groups button to open the Group Memberships dialog, select Domain Admins in the Not Member Of list, and click Add. Select Domain Admins in the Member Of list, and then click Set to make Domain Admins the Primary Group (see fig. 24.3). Click OK to close the Group Memberships dialog, and then click OK again to close the New User dialog.

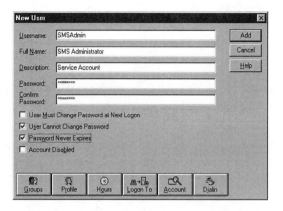

Fig. 24.2   Specifying the properties of the SMSAdmin account.

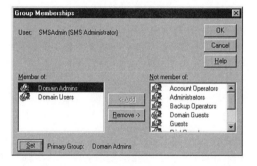

Fig. 24.3   Adding the SMSAdmin account to the Domain Admins group.

5. Select SMSAdmin in the Username list. From the Policies dialog choose User Rights to open the User Rights Policy dialog. Mark the Show Advanced User Rights check box and select SMSAdmin in the Grant To list. Select Log On as a Service from the Right drop-down list, and click Add (see fig. 24.4). Click OK to close the dialog.

6. Exit User Manager for Domains.

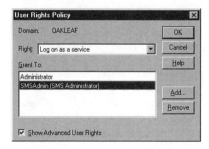

Fig. 24.4   Adding the Log On as a Service right to the SMSAdmin account.

Setting Up SQL Server

You must specify that SQL Server (MSSQLServer) and SQL Executive start as a service during Windows NT Server's boot process. Use Control Panel's Services tool to verify that the Startup property of these two services is set to Automatic, and both services are started before installation of SMS. Chapter 22, "Running Microsoft SQL Server 6.5," covers installing and using SQL Server 6.5.

If you intend to run SQL Server and SMS on the same Windows NT Server, SMS creates the SQL devices and databases automatically. If you run SQL Server on a separate Windows NT Server, you must manually create the SMSData and SMSLog devices with SQL Enterprise manager. The default sizes of the SMSData and SMSLog devices are 45M and 8M, respectively.

 ◀◀ See "Creating and Managing Devices," p. 814.

Installing System Management Server on the Primary Site Server

System Management Server installation takes 15 to 20 minutes. You must install SMS to an NTFS partition. To install SMS, follow these steps:

1. Run SETUP.BAT from the \Smssetup folder of the distribution CD-ROM. This batch file determines which platform (x86, Alpha, or MIPS) to install and starts the Setup program.

2. Click Continue in the first message box, complete the Registration dialog entries, and click Continue to display the Installation Options dialog. Click the Install Primary Site button.

   Figure 24.5 shows the Installation Options dialog for SMS 1.1. (SMS 1.2 offers a slightly different range of options, including installing Crystal Reports.)

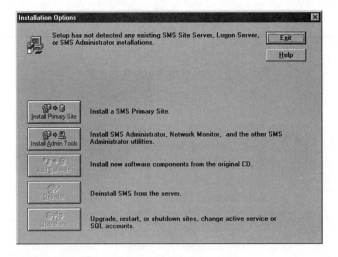

Fig. 24.5   The Installation Options dialog for SMS 1.1.

3. Mark the I Agree That check box of the Licensing dialog and click OK. SMS offers only per-seat, not per-server, client licensing.

4. Click Continue to bypass the dialog that describes the prerequisites for installing SMS.

5. In the Installation Directory dialog, accept the default or change the location of the folder to store the SMS files (see fig. 24.6). The drive must be formatted as NTFS. Click Continue.

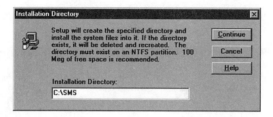

Fig. 24.6 Specifying the folder for installation of SMS's primary components.

6. In the Setup Install Options dialog, click Continue to install the default System Management Server components (see fig. 24.7). Alternatively, you can specify installation options for other platforms by clicking the Custom button.

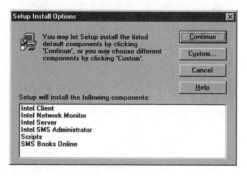

Fig. 24.7 The default installation options for SMS 1.1.

7. In the SQL Database Configuration dialog, type the password and confirmation password for the default sa (system administrator) account. The rest of the entries are completed for you with default values (see fig. 24.8). If you use a SQL Server installation on another machine, type the name of the server in the SQL Server Name text box. You can change the path, device file name, and size of the local SQL Server devices by clicking the Device Creation button to open the SQL Device Creation dialog (see fig. 24.9). Click Continue.

8. If you haven't set a sufficient number of SQL Server connections (minimum of 20), the SQL Connections dialog appears. Enter a reasonable number of connections to service your users and SMS (see fig. 24.10). Click Set to continue.

V

Microsoft BackOffice

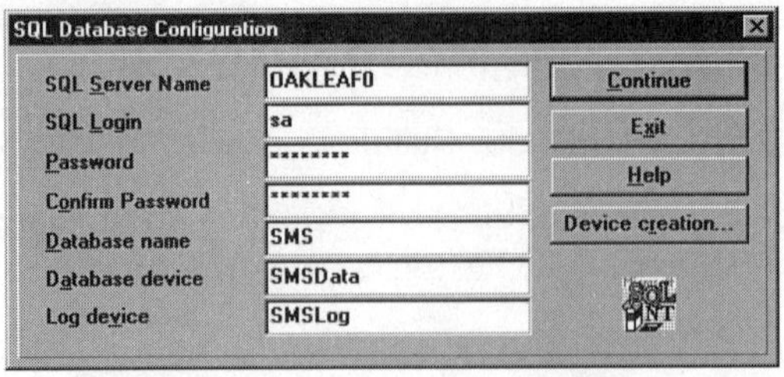

Fig. 24.8 Specifying the SQL Server name, logon account, password, database name, and devices.

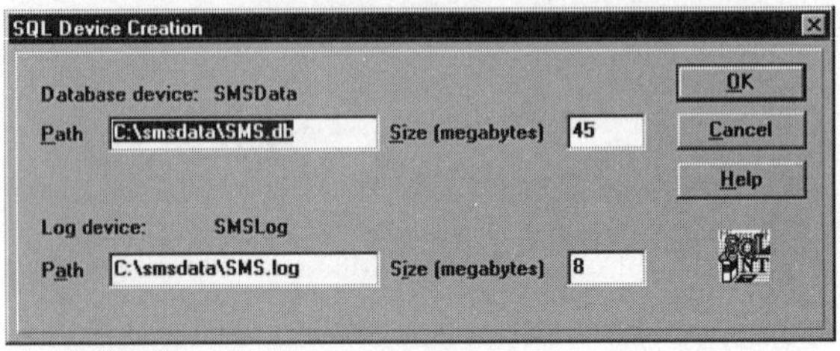

Fig. 24.9 Altering the location and/or size of the local SQL Server devices created for SMS.

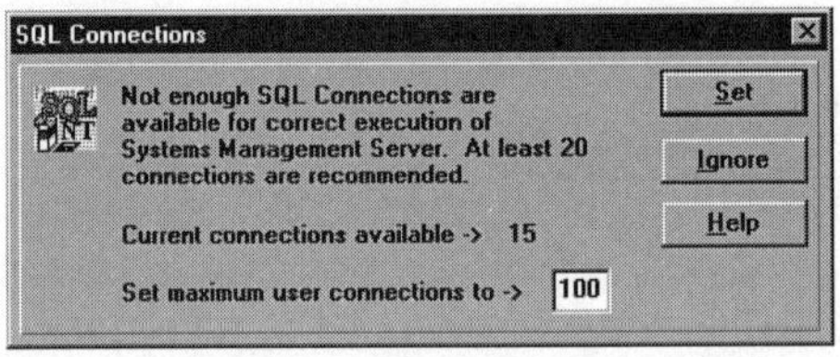

Fig. 24.10 The message box that appears if you have fewer than 20 connections specified for the SQL Server installation used with SMS.

9. In the Primary Site Information dialog, type a three-character Site Code and a descriptive Site Name. Accept the default values for Site Server and Site Server Domain. For a conventional installation using Windows Networking or TCP/IP, mark the Automatically Detect All Logon Servers check box. Type **SMSAdmin** in the Username text box and the password you assigned to SMSAdmin (see fig. 24.11). Click Continue.

The Setup program copies files, completes the database installation, and starts the SMS services. A Setup Progress dialog (see fig. 24.12) displays the status of the installation, which usually takes about 10 to 15 minutes. When the SMS Setup process is complete, click OK in the Setup Success message box to have the Setup program create a Start menu SMS program group. It isn't necessary to restart the server after installing SMS.

If you plan to install other Primary Sites, the process is basically the same as that described in preceding steps. You must assign a unique site code to each site. The steps that let you group SMS sites into a hierarchy are detailed near the end of this chapter in the section "Building Sites for Enterprise Networks."

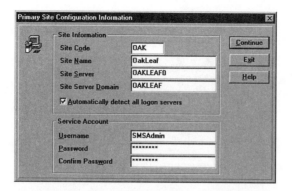

Fig. 24.11   Specifying the configuration information for the Primary Site.

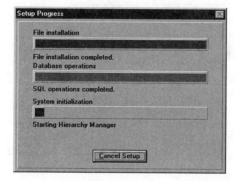

Fig. 24.12   The Setup Progress dialog's display near the end of the SMS installation process.

Using SMS Administrator

The Microsoft SMS Administrator application is SMS's primary management tool. To run SMS Administrator (SMS Admin), follow these steps:

1. From the Start menu choose Programs, System Management Server, and SMS Administrator to start SMS Admin.

2. The Microsoft SMS Administrator Login dialog displays the default SQL Server name, database, and logon ID (see fig. 24.13). Type the password for the SQL Server sa account and click OK.

3. The Open SMS Window dialog is intended for new users of SMS Admin. (You can prevent future appearances of this dialog by clearing the Show This Dialog at Startup check box.) As you select the various window types, a description of the window appears (see fig. 24.14). Spend a few minutes reading the description for each window. Select Sites, if necessary, and click OK to display SMS Admin with the Sites window active.

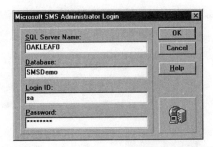

Fig. 24.13 Specifying the parameters required to start SQL Admin.

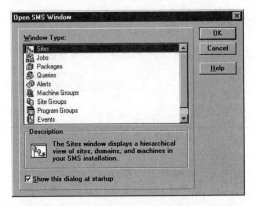

Fig. 24.14 Selecting the SMS window to display.

> **Note**
>
> The SQLDemo database shown in figure 24.13 is used in the SQL Admin examples that follow. The SQL Server query (Sms.sql) and database (SmsDemo.dat) is included on the SMS Server 1.2 distribution CD-ROM. If you don't have SMS Server 1.2, you can save Sms.sql as a text file and download Smsdemo.dat from **http://www.microsoft.com/SMSmgmt/demodata.htm**. Installation instructions for SMSDemo are located at **http://www.microsoft.com/SMSmgmt/revgd/sms02e.htm**.

The SMS Admin application, modeled on Windows Explorer, is deceptively simple. SMS Admin has 10 window styles that you use to perform administrative duties or monitor SMS operations. Table 24.1 lists the window name and the description (from the Open SMS Window dialog) of the window's function.

Table 24.1 SMS Administrator's Window Names and Descriptions

Window	Description
Sites	Displays a hierarchical view of sites, domains, and machines in your SMS installation
Jobs	Allows you to create and administer jobs at your SMS installation

Window	Description
Packages	Manages software packages that SMS can inventory or install on any workstation
Queries	Manages stored queries used to locate assets and workstations
Alerts	Manages alerts used to monitor and act on change in your SMS system
Machine Groups	Allows you to group servers and workstations together for administrative purposes
Site Groups	Allows you to group sites together for administrative purposes
Program Groups	Allows you to manage the contents of shared SMS program groups
Events	Allows you to monitor the status and actions of other components in your SMS system
SQL Server Messages	Displays messages from SQL Server caused by SMS Administrator

Use of the SMS Admin windows is described in the following sections.

Sites Window

The Sites window displays all the SMS sites in a hierarchical list. The right pane displays the next level of the hierarchy selected in the list. Figure 24.15 shows the site hierarchy from the SMSDemo database; the Canada and USA Primary Sites are expanded to show the first level of detail, their child sites, and the domains to which the sites belong.

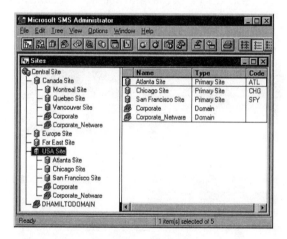

Fig. 24.15 The Sites window of SMS Admin displaying a partial expansion of the SMSDemo site hierarchy.

Double-clicking an entry in the Sites list expands the hierarchy for the site. For example, figure 24.16 shows in the right pane the client PCs of the Engineering group of the San Francisco site. The right pane displays the NetBIOS Name of the computer, SMSID (an SMS internal code), LogOn Name, SystemType (client platform), and SystemRole (Workstation or Server).

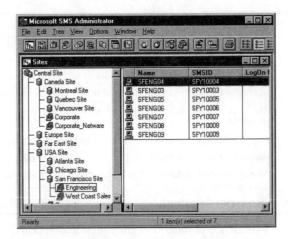

Fig. 24.16 The fully expanded hierarchy of the San Francisco site.

Double-clicking a client item in the right pane displays the Personal Computer Properties MDI child window for the client (see fig. 24.17). You select the properties to view or actions to take in the Properties list. Most of the information in the Attribute and Value list is derived from performing SMS's PC inventory function, which the SMSDemo database simulates. Table 24.2 lists the properties and actions available in the Personal Computer Properties window.

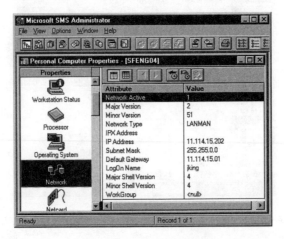

Fig. 24.17 Displaying network attributes and values in the Personal Computer Properties window.

Note

In the case of the demonstration system used in these examples, you can display only properties that are stored in the SQLDemo database. Actions such as obtaining Workstation Status or performing the Help Desk (remote control) function require the SMS client software to be installed on the client PC and an active network connection to the client.

Table 24.2 Properties and Actions Available in the Personal Computer Properties Window

Property/Action	Description
Identification	Displays the NetBIOS name, SMS Name, System Role and Type, and other identifying features of clients and server
Workstation Status	Displays the date and time of the Last Hardware Scan, Last Software Scan, Files Not Installed, and other status parameters
Processor	Displays the processor type and speed, and indicates whether the processor includes a floating-point coprocessor
Operating System	Displays the DOS version (if applicable) and the Windows version running on the client
Network	Displays various information on the current network connection maintained by the client
Netcard	Displays the code for the network interface card ($EPRO for Intel EtherExpress 16 Pro)
Disk	Displays the type and size of each removable disk drive and each partition of fixed disk drive(s)
PC Memory	Displays the amount of RAM and the paging file size, if applicable
Serial Port	Displays serial port parameters for COM1 through COM4
Parallel Port	Displays parallel port parameters for installed parallel port adapters
Video	Displays the type of graphics adapter installed, the name of the manufacturer, and the adapter's BIOS date
Mouse	Displays information about the installed mouse driver
PC BIOS	Displays the BIOS Manufacturer, Category, and Release Date
IRQ Table	Displays the address and use of interrupts 0 through 15
Environment	Displays the content of each environment variable in the DOS environment
Help Desk	Lets you start the Remote Control, Remote Boot, and Remote Chat features
Diagnostics	Opens the Diagnostics window, which lets you query the current status of the machine's CMOS ROM, hardware, and network connection
Network Monitor	Lets you start the remote Network Monitor for the machine
User Information	Provides the full user name and logon ID of the machine's current or last user

Packages Window

A *package* is the very basic element for software distribution and software installation. A package is used by a prescribed job, which delivers the package to a client. A package contains the information about the software, including the files in the software, configuration information, and identification information. When a package is prepared, you can install it on the client, install it on a server to be used as a shared application, or maintain inventory on the package. SMS has three defined package properties: Workstation, Sharing, and Inventory.

Workstation Packages. As the name suggests, this package is used to install software on a workstation (the targeted client machine). The installation is on the workstation, so you must specify the commands and files needed for the package. Therefore, the client uses a Package Command Manager (PCM).

V

Microsoft BackOffice

PCM is installed and set up automatically when SMS first inventories the client PC. PCM periodically checks with SMS to determine whether there are any packages to be installed. If so, PCM pulls the package from the distribution server and follows the installation instructions. PCM installs the software on the workstation in two ways:

- It lets the end user decide when to install the package. You also can specify a deadline so that the package is installed even if the user refuses to install the package during the prescribed period of time.

- It installs the package unattended overnight. This process requires that the end user leave the client PC turned on.

Sharing Packages. This method of software distribution is good for large sites with several servers. When using these sharing packages, the software is installed on the network file servers. There are several advantages to this method:

- *Fault tolerance* allows the application to be available to the end user, even if the file server that the end user utilizes isn't available.

- *Balanced loading* allows the servers with less traffic to perform as application servers, if necessary.

- *Metering* allows SMS to maintain the number of end users accessing the application.

- *Consistent end-user interface* provides the user with a program group tailored to his requirements, regardless of the computer used to log on.

The Program Control Group is responsible for checking the local server's applications database to see whether the user who logged on has access to any server applications. This process occurs when the user logs on from any computer on the network. When validated, the Program Control Group builds and displays program groups and application icons.

When the user launches an application, the Program Control Group checks with the local server application database to see which distribution servers have the application. It then connects the user to an available server.

The load-balancing and fault-tolerance features derive from the fact that the Program Control Group connects to any available application distribution server. Because of this capability, you can install applications on several servers to allow multiple servicing points (load balancing), and ensure that users always have access to their network application (fault tolerance).

Inventory Packages. The Inventory package defines the rules that SMS uses to identify, inventory, and collect applications and files on the local workstation. The packages you define are saved in the SMS database and appear in the Packages window of SMS Admin.

Package Definition File. A Package Definition File (PDF) is a text file that contains predefined Workstations, Sharing, and Inventory property settings for a package. To create a new package, you can use the Import command from the Package Properties dialog and use one of SMS's predefined PDFs to specify the properties for that package.

SMS includes PDFs for some of the more popular applications, such as Microsoft Excel and Microsoft Word; other software publishers also create PDFs. Figure 24.18 shows the creation of a new package for installation of Word 6.0c. Clicking the Sharing button lets you specify the location of the package and the share name (see fig. 24.19).

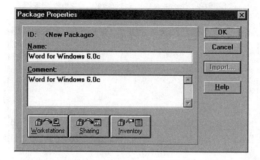

Fig. 24.18   Creating a new package from a PDF file included with SMS.

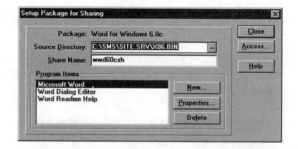

Fig. 24.19   Setting up the package source and specifying a server share name.

Jobs Window

After a package is created, it can be delivered to a targeted machine or set of machines with a job. These jobs are displayed in the Jobs window (see fig. 24.20).

There are four types of jobs in SMS. One job type is called *System Job* and is created automatically by SMS to deal with configuration issues. Following are the three types of jobs that you can create:

- *Run Command on Workstation* is used to deliver a package source directory with the package command to the targeted workstation. The user runs the commands by choosing a package in the Package Command Manager.

- *Shared Package on Server* is an automated installation of a network application. The job sends the package source directory to a network server. The directories that are needed are shared. This makes the package available to users with the specified permissions.

- *Remove Package from Server* deletes a package that has been installed on one or more servers.

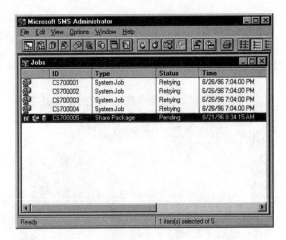

Fig. 24.20   Four System Jobs and one Share Package pending in SMS's Jobs window.

To create a new job, follow these steps:

1. From the File menu choose Open, and select Jobs from the Open SMS Window dialog.

2. From the File menu choose New to open the Job Properties dialog. Type a brief description of the job in the Comment text box, and choose the Job Type from the drop-down list (see fig. 24.21).

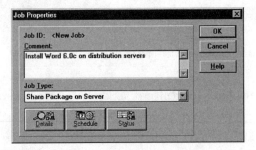

Fig. 24.21   Creating a new Share Package job.

3. Click the Details button to open the Job Details dialog. Select the Package for the job from the drop-down list and specify the Job Target, Send Phase, and Distribute Phase details (see fig. 24.22). Click OK twice to close the Job Details and Job Properties dialogs.

Queries Window

In a large network you need a flexible tool to let you easily search the database to find machines that match your requested criteria. For example, you might want to find machines that have the necessary disk space for a Windows 95 installation, Intel-based machines that run DOS, or machines that have been upgraded with a particular application.

Fig. 24.22   Specifying the details for the new Share Package job.

System Management Server's Queries window lets you run quick queries to inventory clients meeting specific criteria. The workstation information is collected by the inventory agent when SMS client software is installed. The inventory information is saved in a set of SQL Server tables. The Queries window executes SQL SELECT queries against these tables and automates the process of writing the SQL statements for these queries.

After the server and client software are installed, it's a good idea to run the query tool to get a report on the status of the machines in the network so you can plan your software distribution accordingly. You must first create and then execute a query. Follow these step to create and execute a query:

1. In SMS Admin, choose Open from the File menu, and then open the Queries window. SMS includes a variety of useful predefined queries (see fig. 24.23).

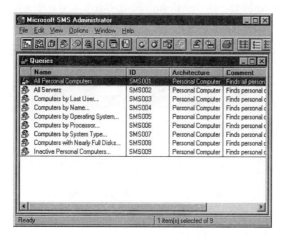

Fig. 24.23   The Queries window displaying the default queries included with SMS 1.1.

V

Microsoft BackOffice

2. From the File menu choose New to open the Query Properties dialog.

3. In the Query Name text box, type **Windows NT Computers** and click Add OR to open the Query Expression Properties dialog.

4. In the Operating Systems group, select the Operating System Name attribute, select Is in the Operator list, and select Microsoft Windows NT in the Value list. Click OK to close the dialog and return to the Query Properties dialog (see fig. 24.24).

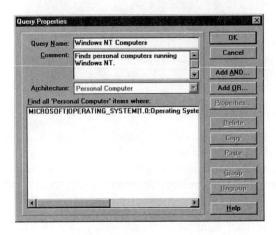

Fig. 24.24   A new query displayed in the Query Properties dialog.

5. Click OK to close the Query Properties dialog and add the query to the list in the Queries window.

6. From the File menu choose Execute Query to open the Execute Query dialog. Select the Windows NT Computers query from the Query drop-down list, accept the default Identification in the Query Result Format list, and optionally mark the Limit to Sites and Include Subsites check boxes (see fig. 24.25).

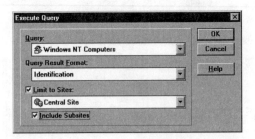

Fig. 24.25   Selecting the query, query format, and sites to inventory.

7. Click OK to execute the query. The query result set appears as shown in figure 24.26 for the SMSDemo database.

The preceding steps create and execute a simple query that has only one criterion. By using additional Add AND or the Add OR functions, however, you can add more operators to define more query details. For example, you can add an AND operator with the System Role of the machine and choose Server. Such a query detects only Windows NT servers.

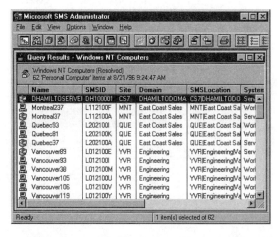

Fig. 24.26   The query result set for the Windows NT Computers query using the SMSDemo database.

Alerts Window

System Management Server lets you create alerts that are triggered based on criteria you define. For example, you can define a rule that specifies whether your server disk is 70 percent full. An alert is sent to one or more system administrators. Alerts may be sent by e-mail, or you can set up the system to page the system administrator.

Machine Groups Window

System Management Server lets you group machines together so that you can perform administrative tasks for a group systematically. Suppose that you want to upgrade all high-end workstations in the western region to Windows 95. First, you create a new group simply by using the File menu's New command. Then you can run a query for all the machines that are in the western region, have an Intel Pentium chip, and have 16M of RAM. When the result is delivered, you simply drag and drop all these machines in the group that you created. Now you can perform your upgrade to this group. Grouping machines can provide a simpler administrative system, particularly if you have a large network.

Site Groups Window

Similar to grouping the machines in your enterprise, SMS allows you to group different sites together for easier manageability. For example, if Los Angeles and San Francisco are two of the sites in the western region, you can put them together in one group.

Program Groups Window

This tool allows the administrator to customize programs in a program group that will be delivered to targeted workstations. As a result, you can control the desktop contents and provide desktop consistency.

Events Window

This tool lets you monitor Windows NT events generated by SMS. Figure 24.27 shows the Events window with events triggered by operations using the SMSDemo database. You double-click the event item to display the Event Detail dialog (see fig. 24.28).

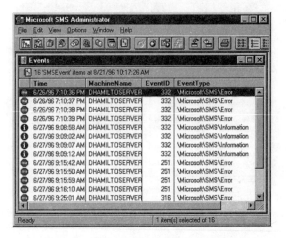

Fig. 24.27   The Events window displaying Windows NT events generated while using the SMSDemo database.

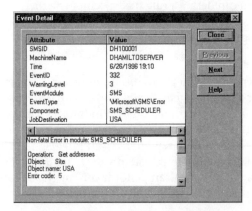

Fig. 24.28   Displaying detailed information about a selected event.

Installing and Configuring Client Software

One of the better features of SMS is its capability to automatically install the required client software on PCs. If you have only a small number of clients, you can install the software manually.

Manual Client Software Installation

When SMS is installed, the SMS_SHR share is created, which includes the RUNSMS.BAT batch file. This is the only file you need to run to install the SMS client software on

Windows 3.1x, Windows for Workgroups 3.1x, Windows 95, and Windows NT machines. Running this file from the workstation automatically installs the required components onto the client and then inventories the machine's hardware and software. The inventory of the client is performed during installation, which takes 30 to 60 seconds.

Automatic Installation

To automatically install the client software, the system logon script must be updated. To enable logon scripts from within SMS, follow these steps:

1. In SMS Admin, open the Sites window and select the site entry in the left pane.

2. From the File menu choose Properties to open the Site Properties dialog (see fig. 24.29).

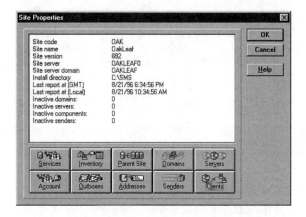

Fig. 24.29 Site characteristics displayed in the Site Properties dialog.

3. Click Clients to open the Clients dialog, which displays the default set of Current Properties for clients.

4. Click the Proposed Properties option button to enable the dialog's settings.

5. Click the Automatically Configure Workstation Logon Scripts check box; you can specify that the client execute the SMS commands at the start or the end of the script (see fig. 24.30).

6. Click OK to return to the Site Properties dialog box.

7. Click OK and click Yes when asked whether you want to update the site.

The preceding steps enable SMS to update the Windows NT server's logon scripts for each user and to amend the NetWare system logon scripts, if applicable, on all servers within the site being managed. The next time the client logs on, the script installs the SMS client software.

Client Inventory Management

As explained earlier in the "Hardware and Software Inventory" section, inventory management is one the primary functions of SMS. When the client software is installed, the Inventory Agent reads the CMOS (EEPROM) chip of the client and runs an abbreviated version of the Microsoft Diagnostics program to collect the hardware information. The client application then scans the hard disk to collect information about the software installed. After the initial collection, the Inventory Agent runs periodically, based on a schedule you determine.

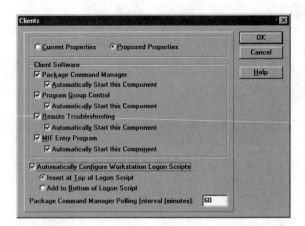

Fig. 24.30 Specifying the addition of the SMS client installation to client logon scripts.

Each time Inventory Agent runs, it collects the hardware and software information and reports it to the Logon Server. The Logon Server doesn't need to be a Windows NT Server; other servers, such as NetWare 3.1+, can be used to collect this information.

The Primary Site server then collects the information from the Logon Server(s). The site server determines whether there have been any updates on the workstation and updates its Microsoft SQL database with the new information. This information can also be sent up in the hierarchy of the SMS in a large environment as described earlier in this chapter.

The software information collected by the Inventory Agent can be either a Comprehensive Audit or a Detailed Identification. The differences between the two methods are as follows:

- *Comprehensive Audit* uses a set of simple rules in a rule file to compare the installed applications with the given parameter. Microsoft provides a number of these rules for Microsoft applications. You can edit this file to add or delete applications.

- *Detailed Identification* lets you define details such as name, size, date, and other parameters for a file. This information is saved in the database. Inventory Management uses this information to compare the file on the disk against the parameters you provide. When Inventory Agent finds a match, the information is included in the inventory report.

Figure 24.31 shows the client's Package Command Manager with a pending Audit Software package created from the Audit.pdf file included with SMS 1.1. When the user clicks the Execute button, the result of the audit is staged for transfer to the Primary Site.

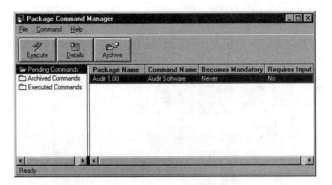

Fig. 24.31 A pending Comprehensive Audit job displayed in the client's Package Command Manager.

Remote Control

To perform Remote Control or Help Desk functions on a targeted machine, the Remote Control Agent must be running on the client. The command line for the Remote Control Agent is placed in the client's AUTOEXEC.BAT file during initial installation of the client software. For you or Help Desk personnel to support a machine, access rights must be granted to them by the machine's user. For security reasons, some machines might be made inaccessible to support personnel.

Note

You must restart the client PC after installing the SMS client software to enable the Remote Control Agent.

To enable Help Desk support, follow these steps for each client PC:

1. From the Start menu choose Programs, SMS Client, and Remote Control to start the Remote Control Agent.

2. From the Start menu choose Programs, SMS Client, and Help Desk Options to open the Help Desk Options dialog (shown with the default options in fig. 24.32).

3. Clear or mark the options you want for the client.

4. If you make changes to the options, click Save As Default and Save As Current, and then click Exit.

With these options shown enabled in figure 24.32, the user is notified when someone takes control of the machine remotely. If the machine is always to be supported remotely, it's good idea to add the Remote Control Program to the Startup program menu.

To remotely control a client PC from the SMS Admin application, follow these steps:

1. From the File menu choose Open, and select the Sites window. Expand the sites list as needed to display the entry for the client in the right pane.

2. Double-click the client item to open the Personal Computer Properties window.

V

Microsoft BackOffice

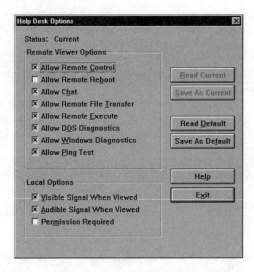

Fig. 24.32 The client's Help Desk Options for the Remote Control Agent.

3. Scroll to and click the Help Desk icon. SMS tries to connect to the client's Remote Control Agent with each supported protocol until a connection is established. When the connection is established, buttons are enabled for those services permitted by the client (see fig. 24.33).

Fig. 24.33 Making a connection from SMS to the client's Remote Control Agent.

4. Click Remote Control to open an image of the client's display (see fig. 24.34). Depending on the relative resolution of the server and client displays, you see all or part of the client screen, surrounded by a yellow and black border.

5. Click the button with the hand icon at the upper right of the display to open a small Area window that you can use to position the server viewport for the client display.

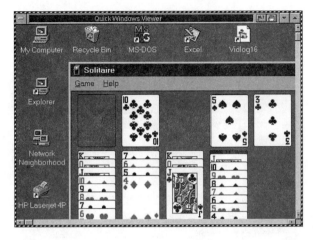

Fig. 24.34 Part of a remotely controlled client's 800×600 screen displayed on a server with 640×480 resolution.

6. Click the Alt button to enable server keystrokes to be sent to the client. Click the Alt button again to disable sending keystrokes.

In addition to Help Desk, a number of tools are available from the Diagnostics tool in the Properties pane. When you click one of the Diagnostics buttons, the server interrogates the client. Figure 25.35 illustrates the result of a Ping Test on a client.

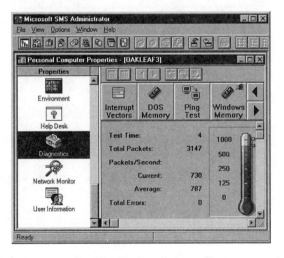

Fig. 24.35 Running a real-time Ping Test diagnostic on a client.

Network Monitor

The Network Monitor tool captures frames from a remote computer by running the Network Monitor Agent (see fig. 24.36). The capability to capture frames from a remote client is what distinguishes SMS's Network Monitor from that which comes with Windows NT 4.0. Clicking Start Network Monitor opens NetMon with the client selected (see fig. 24.37). After you capture the data, you can highlight certain data or filter the data based on your desired criteria.

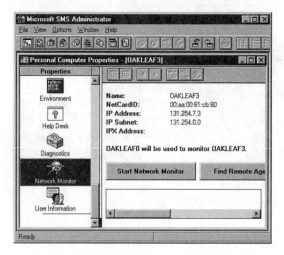

Fig. 24.36 Starting Network Monitor for a remote client.

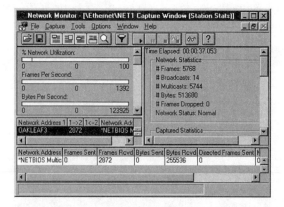

Fig. 24.37 Network Monitor displaying the result of a Ping Test of the client.

◀◀ See "Using Windows NT 4.0's Network Monitor," p. 545

Building Sites for Enterprise Networks

After you create your Central Site and set up the central server, you can begin creating child sites and add them to the SMS hierarchy. The hierarchical structure provides flexible system administration for the entire network. For example, you can provide decentralized Help Desk capabilities by designating some of the child sites as Primary Sites. The inventory data continues to be sent up the hierarchy to the Central Site server for overall administration and asset management. You can allow some of the Secondary Sites, which don't have local databases, to be managed by the Primary Sites.

Communication Between Sites with Senders

A *Sender* is a service in Microsoft Windows NT that SMS uses to transmit instructions and data from one site to another. The use of Senders is an important factor in the enterprise design, because the available bandwidth may vary depending on the connection, which in turn affects overall system performance.

Three types of Senders are available with SMS: LAN, RAS, and SNA. Other Senders, such as MAPI, may be created in the future. If your SMS is located in a LAN environment (typically Ethernet or Token Ring), a LAN Sender is used to connect the servers. This is usually the case for multiple servers in a server room, or a campus-wide network with a high-speed backbone. Remote Access Service (RAS) is another method of connecting the servers together; RAS is the subject of Chapter 18, "Managing Remote Access Service." RAS can use X.25, conventional modems, or ISDN connections. X.25 connections are common and particularly useful for international connections. The third connection method, Microsoft SNA, is used to connect to the IBM environment.

If you use a RAS connection, you must pay special attention to the primary and secondary sites. The Secondary Site doesn't have a database, so all the information is transmitted over the connection to the database of the Primary Site server in a raw format. In general, RAS isn't recommended for this configuration. If a RAS connection is used between two Primary Sites, performance is likely to be acceptable, at least over a 112kbps ISDN line, because the data from one database is compressed before it's delivered to the other primary server.

Remote control via connections other than LANs or T-1 lines is likely to be unsatisfactory. Remote control requires that the client's screen graphics be sent over the connection to your display. Sufficient bandwidth is required so that the normal network traffic isn't affected when Help Desk is operating.

When distributing packages such as Microsoft Office or Windows 95, there should be enough bandwidth to complete the installation in a reasonable period. Although SMS allows job scheduling so that the packages can be delivered during the time when the network is least utilized, it's unrealistic to assume that an efficient installation can be performed over a RAS connection.

Coexistence with NetWare Environments

If you're running Novell NetWare 3.x servers in your environment, you can add a Microsoft SMS to the network and use all of its features without any changes to the NetWare server or the client. The NetWare server can be used as a logon server and/or a distribution server. You need to add only a few lines to the user's logon script to run the installation program. You must install Gateway Services for NetWare to fully use SMS in a heterogeneous networking environment.

V

Microsoft BackOffice

The best way to manage NetWare servers and workstations is to group them together so that they're managed as one unit. NetWare 3.x doesn't support a domain concept and therefore doesn't offer a single logon account. Because most NetWare 3.x servers don't share the same user account database, an SMS account with supervisory rights must be created in each server that needs to participate in the SMS hierarchy. The account allows SMS to communicate with the NetWare server and to install a software package for distribution, or retrieve the inventory data from the NetWare server.

From Here...

This chapter demonstrated that System Management Server provides a number of capabilities that reduce the cost of ownership of PCs by providing an efficient method of supporting PC users. SMS is a much more feature-rich and complicated network application, that requires an understanding of a number of MIS-related issues such as LAN and WAN connections, network bandwidth, and organization structure. With proper planning, which includes setting up a pilot project before rollout, SMS enhances the system administrator and end-user environments.

The following chapters contain information related to the topics covered in this chapter:

- Chapter 16, "Distributing Network Services with Domains," covers Windows NT Server's trusted domains and other distributed networking features that allow a single-user logon for multiple network servers and server-based applications running on LANs and WANs.

- Chapter 17, "Integrating Windows NT with Heterogeneous Networks," shows you how to set up and administer Windows NT Server within a Novell NetWare or UNIX networking environment.

- Chapter 18, "Managing Remote Access Service," explains how to configure Windows NT Server 4.0's RAS component to support dial-in access to shared network resources by mobile users.

Glossary

10BaseT   The most common network cabling method for Ethernet, which handles traffic at a speed of 10mbps. 10BaseT uses a pair of unshielded twisted conductors to connect between a network interface card (NIC) and an Ethernet hub. 10Base2 (thin Ethernet, or *thinnet*) uses coaxial cable connections between computers and doesn't require a hub. 100BaseT is a newer medium that supports up to 100mbps. See *Ethernet*, *hub*, and *NIC*.

accelerator key   A key combination that provides access to a menu choice, macro, or other function of the application instead of selection with the mouse, usually combining Alt+*key*. Sometimes called a *shortcut key*, but shortcut keys usually consist of Ctrl+*key* combinations.

Access Control List (ACL)   Part of Windows NT's security description that controls access to a Windows NT object, such as a file. The owner of an object can change access control entries in the list to grant or revoke permissions (access rights) for the object.

access token   A Windows NT object that identifies a logged-on (authenticated) user. The access token contains the user's security ID (SID), the groups to which the user belongs, and other security information. See *SID*.

activation   An ActiveX and OLE term meaning to place an object in a running state, which includes binding the object, or to invoke a method of the object. See also *binding*.

active   In Windows, the currently running application or the window to which user input is directed; the window with the focus. See also *focus*.

ActiveX   A family of Microsoft object technologies, formerly called *OLE*, based on the Common Object Model (COM), serving as one of the foundation of Microsoft's Internet products. See *COM* and *DCOM*.

ActiveX control   An insertable COM object (component) that usually provides user interface components and can fire events. ActiveX controls are lightweight versions of OLE Controls (.OCXs)

address   The numerical value, usually in hexadecimal format, of a particular location in your computer's RAM.

address space   Memory allocated to an application by the operating system. See *virtual address space*.

aggregate object   An ActiveX and OLE term that refers to an object class that contains one or more member objects of another class.

alert   In Windows NT, a message sent between two simultaneously executing threads that results in an asynchronous procedure call (APC) executed by the receiving thread. Also means a message indicating abnormal operation of a Windows NT process.

ANSI   An abbreviation for the *American National Standards Institute*. In the Windows context, ANSI refers to the ANSI character set. Windows 95 and Windows NT include both ANSI (suffix A) and Unicode (suffix W) versions of Windows API functions. See *ASCII* and *Unicode*.

API   An abbreviation for *application program interface*. Generically, a method by which a program can obtain access to or modify the operating system. See also *DLL*.

applet   A Windows application that's supplied as a component of another Windows application, rather than as a retail product. The Notepad and Wordpad applications supplied with Windows NT are examples of applets.

application   The software product that results from the creation of a program, often used as a synonym for the programming (source) code that creates it. Applications are distinguished by the environment for which they're designed (for example, Windows, DOS, Macintosh, UNIX) and their purpose. Windows applications carry the executable file extension, .EXE.

application Close button   The small, square button with an × caption at the extreme right of the title bar of an application running in Windows NT and Windows 95. Clicking the application Close button closes the running application.

application Control-menu box   The small, square button with a miniature application icon at the extreme left of the title bar of an application window. Clicking the application Control-menu box displays the application Control menu. Double-clicking the application Control-menu box closes the application.

ASCII   Abbreviation for *American Standard Code for Information Interchange*. A set of standard numerical values for printable, control, and special characters used by PCs and most other computers. Other commonly used codes for character sets are ANSI (used by Windows 3.1+), Unicode (used by Windows 95 and Windows NT), and EBCDIC (Extended Binary-Coded Decimal Interchange Code, used by IBM for mainframe computers). See *Unicode*.

asymmetric multiprocessing   A multiprocessing technique in which individual processors are dedicated to particular tasks, such as running the operating system or performing user requests. See *SMP*.

asynchronous   A process that can occur at any time, regardless of the status of the operating system or applications that are running. An example is Windows NT's asynchronous procedure call (APC).

asynchronous I/O   Input/output operations in which an application issues an I/O request to a device, and then continues operation while the device transfers data. Asynchronous I/O greatly speeds fixed-disk file operations. See *synchronous I/O.*

auditing   Windows NT's capability to record and report security-related events, such as accessing, creating, or deleting files.

authentication   The process of verifying (validating) a user's logon ID and password, usually used to provide access to network resources.

Automation   An ActiveX (OLE) term that refers to a means of manipulating another application's objects by the use of a programming language, most commonly Visual Basic for Applications (VBA).

Automation controller   An ActiveX-compliant Windows application with an application programming (macro) language, such as VBA, that can reference and manipulate objects exposed by ActiveX components and Automation servers. *Automation controller* replaces the term *OLE Automation client.*

Automation server   Technically, any OLE 2-compliant Windows application that supports OLE Automation operations by exposing a set of objects for manipulation by OLE Automation client applications. In ActiveX terminology, ActiveX components are Automation servers.

autoplay   A feature of Windows 95's and Windows NT 4.0's CD-ROM file system (CDFS) that automatically executes a program on the CD-ROM when inserted into the CD-ROM drive.

back up   To create a file (backup file) that duplicates data stored in one or more files on a client or server computer.

background   In multitasking computer operations, a running application or process that isn't visible on-screen and isn't receiving user-generated input.

batch   A group of statements processed as an entity. Execution of DOS batch files (such as AUTOEXEC.BAT) and SQL statements are examples of a *batch process.*

BDC   An abbreviation for *Backup Domain Controller,* a Windows NT server that provides an alternative source of authentication for network users. Account and group information from a Primary Domain Controller (PDC) is replicated periodically to each BDC in the domain. See *PDC.*

binary file   A file whose content doesn't consist of lines of text. Executable (.EXE), dynamic link library (.DLL), and most database files are stored in binary format.

binding   In ActiveX and OLE, a term for the act of connecting a component (server object) to a controller (OLE client).

bit   The smallest piece of information processed by a computer. A bit, derived from the contraction of BInary digiT (or Binary digIT) has two states—on (1) or off (0). Eight bits make up a *byte;* 16 bits combined is called a *word.*

bitmap   The representation of a screen or printed image, usually graphic, as a series of bytes.

bitwise   A process that evaluates each bit of a combination, such as a byte or word, rather than process the combination as a single element. Logical operations and masks use bitwise procedures.

blitting   The process of using the BitBlt() function of Windows' Gdi32.exe to modify a bitmap using bit block transfer.

Boolean   A type of arithmetic in which all digits are bits—that is, the numbers may have only two states: on (true or 1) or off (false or 0). Widely used in set theory and computer programming, Boolean, named after mathematician George Boole, also is used to describe a data type that may have only two states: true or false.

break   To cause an interruption in program operation. Ctrl+C is the standard DOS break-key combination but seldom halts operation of a Windows application. Esc is more commonly used in Windows to cause an operation to terminate before completion.

BRI   An abbreviation for *Basic Rate Interface,* the standard ISDN service for business and residential Internet connections. BRI has two 56kbps B (bearer) channels and one 16kbps D (data) channel, providing a maximum bandwidth of 112kbps. See *ISDN* and *PRI.*

bridge   An active network device used to divide a network into mutually isolated segments while maintaining the whole as a single network. Bridges operate at the data-link layer of the OSI Reference Model. See *OSI.*

buffer   An area in memory of a designated size (number of bytes or characters) reserved, typically, to hold a portion of a file or the value of a variable.

business rules   A set of rules for entering data in a database that are specific to an enterprise's methods of conducting its operations. Business rules are in addition to rules for maintaining the domain and referential integrity of tables in a database. Business rules most commonly are implemented in a three-tier client/server database environment. See *three-tier.*

cache   A block of memory reserved for temporary storage. Caches usually store data from disk files in memory to make access to the data faster. By default, Windows NT caches all disk read and write operations.

cache manager   A component of Windows NT's I/O system that uses the virtual memory (VM) manager to create temporary storage in the paging file to speed disk I/O operations. See *VM.*

caret   The term used by Windows to indicate the cursor used when editing a text field, usually shaped as an I-beam. The caret, also called the *insertion point,* can be positioned independently of the mouse pointer.

CDFS   The 32-bit *CD-ROM file system* shared by Windows NT and Windows 95.

channel   A dedicated communication connection between a transmitting and receiving device. Channel is also used to identify an I/O port in mini- and mainframe computers.

CISC   *Complex instruction set computer*, a microprocessor whose internal instructions often involve many individual execution steps and thus many clock cycles. The Intel 80x86 processors are the most common CISC devices. See *RISC*.

class identifier   See *CLSID*.

client   The device or application that receives data from or manipulates a server device or application. The data may be in the form of a file received from a network file server, or an object created from an ActiveX component or OLE server. See *Automation controller*.

CLSID   An identification tag that's associated with an ActiveX or OLE 2.0 object created by a specific component or server. CLSID values appear in the Registry and must be unique for each type of object that the server can create. See *Registry*.

clustering   A server architecture that emulates multiprocessing by interconnecting two or more individual computers in order to share the application processing load. Microsoft's future clustering technology for Windows NT now carries the code name *Wolfpack*. A number of third parties offer proprietary clustering hardware and software for Windows NT Server 4.0.

collection   A group of objects of the same class that are contained within another object. Collections are named as the plural of their object class.

COM   An acronym for *Component Object Model*, the name of Microsoft's design strategy to implement OLE 2+ and ActiveX. Distributed COM (DCOM) allows networked and cross-platform implementation of ActiveX and OLE 2+ operations and Automation. See *Automation* and *DCOM*.

common dialogs   A standardized set of dialog boxes common to Windows 95 and Windows NT 4.0. Common dialogs include File Open, File Save, Print, and Printer Setup.

Component Object Model   See *COM*.

compound document   A document that contains OLE objects created by an application other than the application that originally created or is managing the document.

concurrency   The condition when more than one user has access to a specific set of records or files at the same time. Concurrency is also used to describe a database management system's capability to handle simultaneous queries against a single set of tables.

concurrent application   An application capable of simultaneous execution in multiple address spaces. Windows NT uses threads of execution to support concurrent applications.

console   A character-based interface to an operating system. Windows NT uses the Command Prompt tool as the console.

container   An object or application that can create or manipulate compound documents. For example, Internet Explorer is a container for ActiveX objects.

context switching   The process of saving an executing thread or process and transferring control to another thread or process. Windows NT 4.0's context switching, one of the major bottlenecks in COM operations, is substantially faster than in Window NT 3.x.

control   A synonym for a visible dialog or window object, such as include labels, text boxes, lists, combo lists, option buttons, and command buttons.

Control-menu box   See *application Control-menu box* and *document Control-menu box*.

control object   In Windows NT, objects that control system tasks, such as asynchronous and deferred procedure calls.

custom control   A control object not native to the application, such as an ActiveX control or a Visual Basic Extension control (VBX).

data definition   The process of describing databases and database objects such as tables, indexes, views, procedures, rules, default values, triggers, and other characteristics.

data dictionary   The result of the data definition process. Also used to describe a set of database system tables that contain the data definitions of database objects.

data integrity   The maintenance of rules that prevent inadvertent or intentional modifications to the content of a database that would be deleterious to its accuracy or reliability. See *domain integrity* and *referential integrity*.

database   A set of related data tables and other database objects, such as a data dictionary, which are organized as a group.

database administrator   The individual responsible for the administrative functions of client-server databases. The database administrator (DBA) has privileges (permissions) for all commands that may be executed by the RDBMS and is ordinarily responsible for maintaining system security, including access by users to the RDBMS itself and performing backup and restoration functions.

database device   A file in which databases and related information, such as transaction logs, are stored. Database devices usually have physical names, such as a file name (Master.dat), and a logical name, such as master.

database owner   The user who originally created a database. The database owner has control over all the objects in the database but may delegate control to other users. The database owner is identified by the prefix dbo in SQL Server.

DCOM   An acronym for *Distributed Common Object Model* that allows communication and manipulation of objects over a network connection. Windows NT 4.0 is the first Microsoft operating system to support DCOM (formerly called NetworkOLE). See *COM*.

DDE   An abbreviation for *dynamic data exchange*, an early Interprocess Communication (IPC) method used by Windows and OS/2 to transfer data between different applications. Automation (formerly OLE Automation) provides a more robust IPC method.

deadlock   A condition that occurs when two users with a lock on one data item attempt to lock the other's data item. Most RDBMSs detect this condition, prevent its occurrence, and advise both users of the deadlock situation.

default   A value assigned or an option chosen when no value is specified by the user or assigned by a program statement.

demand lock   Precludes more shared locks from being set on a data resource. Successive requests for shared locks must wait for the demand lock to be cleared.

device   A computer system component that can send or receive data, such as a keyboard, display, printer, disk drive, or modem. Windows NT uses device drivers to create device objects that connect applications to devices.

DHCP   Abbreviation for *Dynamic Host Configuration Protocol*, an Internet standard protocol that allows IP addresses to be pooled and assigned as needed to clients. Windows NT 4.0 includes DHCP Manager, a graphical DHCP configuration tool. See *IP* and *IP address*.

dialog   A popup modal child window, also called a *dialog box*, that requests information from the user. Dialogs include message boxes, input boxes, and user-defined dialogs for activities such as choosing files to open.

DIB   An acronym for *device-independent bitmap*, a Windows-specific bitmap format designed to display graphic information. DIB files take the extension .DIB and use a format similar to the .BMP format.

directory list   An element of a file-selection dialog that selectively lists the subfolders of the designated folder of a specified logical drive.

dispatcher   A Windows NT operating system component that schedules the execution of application threads.

distributed database   A database, usually of the client/server type, that's located on more than one database server, often at widely separated locations. Synchronization of data contained in distributed databases is most commonly accomplished by the two-phase commit or replication methods. See *replication* and *two-phase commit*.

disk mirroring   Creating on two or more physical disk drives exact duplicates of a disk volume to make files accessible in case of failure of one drive of the mirror set. See *RAID*.

disk striping   Distributing the data for a single logical disk volume across two or more physical disk drives. Simple disk striping (RAID 0) provides faster I/O operation.

Disk striping with parity (RAID 5) provides faster I/O and protection from failure of a physical disk in a stripe set. See *RAID*.

DLC   An abbreviation for *Data Link Control*, a Windows NT protocol used to communicate with mainframes and networked laser printers.

DLL   An abbreviation for *dynamic link library*, a file containing a collection of Windows functions designed to perform a specific class of operations. Most DLLs carry the .DLL extension, but some Windows DLLs, such as Gdi32.exe, use the .EXE extension. Functions within DLLs are called (invoked) by applications as necessary to perform the desired operation.

document   A programming object containing information that originates with the user of the application, rather than created by the application itself. The data for documents usually is stored in disk files.

document Control-menu box   The small, square button at the upper left of the menu bar of an application that uses the multiple document interface (MDI). Clicking the document Control-menu box displays the document Control menu. Double-clicking the document Control-menu box closes the document (but not the application).

domain   In Windows NT, a group of workstations and servers that share a common Security Accounts Manager (SAM) database and allow a user to log on to any resource in the domain with a single user ID and password.

domain integrity   The process of assuring that values added to fields of a table comply with a set of rules for reasonableness and other constraints. See *business rules* and *three-tier*.

dynamic data exchange   See *DDE*.

dynamic link library   See *DLL*.

environment   A combination of the computer hardware, operating system, and user interface. A complete statement of an environment follows: a Pentium PCI-bus computer with 64M of RAM, a Wide and Fast SCSI host adapter, SVGA display adapter, sound card, and two-button mouse, using the Windows NT Server 4.0 operating system.

environmental subsystem   In Windows NT, the four sets of APIs that support Win32, MS-DOS, POSIX, and OS/2 applications.

Ethernet   A networking medium that was developed at the Xerox Palo Alto Research Center (PARC) in the 1970s; was improved by Xerox, Intel, and Digital; and is now the most popular cabling method for LANs. The IEEE 802.3 specification for Ethernet is the most common implementation.

event   Most commonly, the occurrence of an action taken by the user, such as right-clicking the mouse, that's recognized by the operating system and passed to the foreground application. Windows NT and its server applications generate events, such as problem reports, without user intervention.

event-driven   The property of an operating system or environment, such as Windows, that implies the existence of an idle loop. When an event occurs, the idle loop is exited and event-handler code, specific to the event, is executed. After the event handler has completed its operation, execution returns to the idle loop, awaiting the next event.

exception   An error, such as division by zero, detected by hardware or by the operating system. Fatal exceptions halt execution of an application and, in a few circumstances, kill the operating system.

executable   Code, usually in the form of a disk file, that can be run by the operating system in use to perform a particular set of functions. Executable files in Windows carry the extension .EXE and can obtain assistance from dynamic link libraries (DLLs) in performing their tasks.

executive   In Windows NT, the components of the operating system that run in the kernel (ring 0) and handle interprocess communication, interrupt requests, and object security. Graphics operations have been moved from user mode to kernel mode in Windows NT 4.0 to speed performance. See *kernel mode* and *user mode*.

failover   A fault-tolerant clustering architecture in which two servers share a common set of fault-tolerant fixed disk drives. In the event of failure of one of the servers, the other transparently assumes all server processing operations. See *clustering* and *fault tolerance*.

FAT   An acronym for *file allocation table*, the disk file system used by MS-DOS, Windows 95, and (optionally) Windows NT. Windows NT is compatible with the 16-bit FAT system, but not the optional 32-bit FAT (FAT32) for Windows 95 that Microsoft announced in mid-1996. See *HPFS* and *NTFS*.

fault tolerance   A computer system's capability to maintain operability, despite failure of a major hardware component such as a power supply, microprocessor, or fixed-disk drive. Fault tolerance requires redundant hardware and modifications to the operating system. Windows NT Server includes fault tolerance for a failed disk drive by disk mirroring (RAID 1) or disk striping with parity (RAID 5). Clustering provides fault tolerance for individual computers. See *clustering* and *RAID*.

fiber   A lightweight thread, introduced in Windows NT 4.0, that makes it easier for developers to optimize scheduling within multithreaded applications. See *thread*.

focus   A Windows term indicating the currently selected application, or one of its windows, to which all user-generated input (keyboard and mouse operations) is directed. The title bar of a window with the focus is colored blue for the default Windows color scheme.

foreground   In multitasking operations, the application or procedure that's visible and to which user-generated input is directed. In Windows, the application that has the focus is in the foreground.

front end   When used with database management systems, an application, a window, or a set of windows by which the user may access and view database records, as well as add to or edit them.

function   A subprogram called from within an expression in which a value is computed and returned to the program that called it through its name. Functions are classified as internal to the application language when their names are keywords.

gateway   A hardware device or software program used to translate between incompatible protocols. A gateway can function at any one layer of the OSI Reference Model or at several layers simultaneously. For example, a gateway is used to translate between mail systems, such as SNMP and MHS. (Internet terminology uses the term *gateway* in place of *router*.)

global   Pertaining to an entire entity, such as a Windows NT domain or a collection of trusted/trusting domains. Windows NT distinguishes global groups from local groups; local groups have permissions only for objects on the server in which the local group exists.

group   A collection of network or database users with common permissions for particular objects, such as shared files or database tables. See also *permissions*.

HAL   An acronym for *hardware abstraction layer*, a Windows NT DLL that links specific computer hardware implementations with the Windows NT kernel. Windows NT 4.0 includes HALs for 80x86, Alpha, MIPS, and PowerPC hardware platforms.

handle   An unsigned long (32-bit) integer assigned by Windows NT or Windows 95 to uniquely identify an instance (occurrence) of an object, such as a file or a window.

host   Any computer on a network using the Internet Protocol (IP). See *IP* and *IP address*.

HPFS   An abbreviation for the *High-Performance File System* used by OS/2 and (optionally) Windows NT 3.x. Windows NT 4.0 doesn't support HPFS but can connect via a network to files on HPFS volumes of Windows NT 3.x PCs.

HTML   An abbreviation for *HyperText Markup Language*, a variant of SGML (Standardized General Markup Language), a page-description language for creating files that can be formatted and displayed by World Wide Web browsers.

hub   A concentrator that joins multiple clients by means of a single link to the rest of the LAN. A hub has several ports to which clients are connected directly, and one or more ports that can be used to connect the hub to the backbone or to other active network components. A hub functions as a multiport repeater; signals received on any port are immediately retransmitted to all other ports of the hub. Hubs function at the physical layer of the OSI Reference Model.

icon A 32-by-32-pixel graphic image used to identify the application in the Explorer window and in other locations in the application chosen by the programmer (such as the Help About dialog). Windows NT 4.0 and Windows 95 also use 16-by-16-pixel small icons to identify the application in the title bar and elsewhere where small icons are specified.

idle In Windows, the condition or state in which both Windows and the application have processed all pending messages in the queue from user- or hardware-initiated events and is waiting for the next event to occur. In Windows NT multiprocessing, one idle thread exists for each processor.

impersonation In Windows NT, the capability of a thread in one process to assume the security identity of another process. Impersonation is employed by a named pipe to acquire and use the security ID of the service requester.

index For arrays and collections, the position of the particular element with respect to others, usually beginning with 0 (arrays) or 1 (collections) as the first element. When used with database files or tables, *index* refers to a lookup table, usually in the form of a file or component of a file, that relates the value of a field in the indexed file to its record or page number and location in the page (if pages are used).

initialize In programming, setting all variables to their default values and resetting the point of execution to the first executable line of code.

in-place activation The capability to activate an object (launch another application) and have the container application take on the capabilities of the other application. The primary feature of in-place activation (also called *in-situ activation*) is that the other application's menu choices merge with or replace the container application's menu choices in the active window.

in-process A term applied to Automation servers, also called *Automation DLLs*, that operate within the same process space (memory allocation) of the Automation controller manipulating the server. In-process servers commonly are called *InProc servers*. See *out-of-process*.

installable file system In Windows NT, the capability to load a file system (such as NTFS, CDFS, FAT, or HPFS) dynamically, depending on the format of the file to be opened.

instance A term used by Windows to describe the temporal existence of a loaded application or one or more of its windows.

instantiate The process of creating an instance of an object in memory.

interface A noun describing a connection between two dissimilar devices or COM objects, such as Automation clients and servers. A common phrase is *user interface*, meaning the "connection" between the display-keyboard combination and the user. Use of *interface* as a verb is jargon.

interrupt An asynchronous message, usually issued by an I/O device, requesting the service of an operating system's or device driver's interrupt handler.

intranet A private network that uses Internet protocols and common Internet applications (such as Web browsers) to emulate the public Internet. Intranets on LANs and high-speed WANs provide increased privacy and improved performance compared with today's Internet.

invocation path The route through which an object or routine is invoked. If the routine is deeply nested, the path can be quite circuitous.

invoke To cause execution of a block of code, particularly a procedure or subprocedure. *Invoke* also is used to indicate application of a method to an object.

I/O manager A component of the Windows NT executive that handles all input/output (I/O) requests.

IP An abbreviation for *Internet Protocol*, the basic network transmission protocol of the Internet.

IP address The 32-bit hexadecimal address of a host, gateway, or router on an IP network. For convenience, IP addresses are specified as the decimal value of the four address bytes, separated by periods, as in 124.33.15.1. Addresses are classified as types A, B, and C, depending on the subnet mask applied. See *subnet mask.*

IPX/SPX Abbreviation for Internetwork Packet Exchange/Sequenced Packet Exchange, the transport protocol of Novell NetWare, supported by Windows NT's NWLink service. See *NWLink.*

ISDN An abbreviation for *Integrated Services Digital Network*, a switched telephone service that provides mid-band digital communication capabilities used for Internet connections and for remote access to LANs, as well as voice communication. Windows NT 4.0 has built-in support for ISDN modems, more properly called *network terminators.* See *BRI* and *PRI.*

item The name given to one of the elements contained in a list box or drop-down list, or the list component of a combo box.

kernel mode The mode in which the Windows NT system runs, providing the operating system with access to system memory and other hardware devices.

key A collection of one or more Registry values (properties) that relate to a single object.

key or key field In relational database tables, a field that identifies a record by its value. Tables are usually indexed on key fields. For a field to be a key field, each data item in the field must possess a unique value.

LAN An acronym for *local area network.* A LAN is a system comprising multiple computers that are physically interconnected through network adapter cards and cabling.

launch To start a Windows application.

library A collection of functions, compiled as a group and accessible to applications by calling the function name, together with any required arguments. DLLs are one type of library; those used by compilers to provide built-in functions are another type.

linked object   A source document in a compound document that's included by reference to a file that contains the object's data, rather than by embedding the source document in the compound document.

livelock   A request for an exclusive lock on a file or data item that's repeatedly denied because of shared locks imposed by other users.

local area network   See *LAN*.

locale   The environment for an operating system or application, usually based on a specific language or a dialect of a language. Windows NT uses the National Language Support (NLS) API to provide localization.

lock   In databases, a restriction of access to a table, portion of a table, or data item imposed to maintain data integrity of a database. Locks may be *shared* (more than one user can access the locked element or elements) or *exclusive* (the user with the exclusive lock prevents other users from creating simultaneous shared or exclusive locks on the element or elements).

logical   The manifestation of physical devices in software, including operating systems. For example, a logical disk drive may consist of a part of the space on a single disk drive or, using Windows NT's capability of spanning drives, space on multiple disk drives.

logon   The process by which Windows NT detects an attempt of a user to gain access to the operating system. Successful completion of the logon process authenticates the user.

LRPC   An abbreviation for *lightweight remote procedure call* used for communication between ActiveX controllers (OLE clients) and ActiveX components (OLE servers) residing on a single computer. See *remote procedure call (RPC)*.

MAC   An acronym for *Media Access Control*, the globally unique hardware address of an Ethernet network interface card.

machine language   Program code in the form of instructions that have meaning to and can be acted on by the computer hardware and operating system used. Object files compiled from source code are in machine language, as are executable files that consist of object files linked with library files. Windows NT is individually compiled for the machine language of each platform that uses a different processor.

map   To translate a physical memory address to a virtual memory (VM) address, or vice versa. See *VM*.

MAPI   Acronym for the Windows *Messaging API* originally created by Microsoft for use with Microsoft Mail, which implements Simple MAPI. Microsoft Exchange Client and Server implements MAPI 1.0 (also called Extended MAPI).

metafile   A type of graphics file, used by Windows and other applications, that stores the objects displayed in the form of mathematical descriptions of lines and surfaces. Windows NT 4.0 supports enhanced metafiles (EMF) for improved printing performance.

method   One of the characteristics of an object and a classification of keywords in VBA. Methods are the procedures that apply to an object. Methods that are applicable to a class of objects are inherited by other objects of the same class and may be modified to suit the requirements of the object.

MIB   An acronym for *Management Information Base*, a set of attributes for active network components, including servers, used by SNMP. Windows NT provides MIBs for server shares, sessions, and users, plus DHCP and WINS data. See *SNMP*.

mini-server   An applet with OLE server capabilities that you can't run as a stand-alone application. Microsoft Graph is an example of a mini-server (despite the size of its executable file).

mirroring   See *disk mirroring*.

MISF   An abbreviation for *Microsoft Internet Security Framework*, a set of high-level security services that rely on CryptoAPI 2.0 functions to provide certificate- and password-based authentication. MISF also incorporates secure channel communication using SSL (Secure Sockets Layer) 2.0 and 3.0, plus PCT (Personal Communications Technology), SET (Secure Electronic Transactions) for credit-card purchases, and the Microsoft Certificate Server for issuing authentication certificates.

modal   A dialog that must be closed before the user can take further action.

modeless   A window or dialog that the user may close or minimize without taking any other action—the opposite of *modal*.

multiprocessing   The capability of a computer with two or more CPUs to allocate tasks (threads) to a specific CPU. See *SMP*.

multitasking   The capability of a computer with a single CPU to simulate the processing of more than one task at a time. Multitasking is effective when one (or more) of the applications spends most of its time in an idle state, waiting for a user-initiated event such as a keystroke or mouse click.

multithreaded   An application that contains more than one thread of execution; a task or set of tasks that executes semi-independently of other task(s).

multiuser   Concurrent use of a single computer by more than one user, usually through the use of remote terminals. UNIX is inherently a multiuser operating system. *Multiuser* is often used as a term to describe an application that allows multiple users to view and update a single shared file, such as a Microsoft Access .MDB file.

named pipes   A method of interprocess communication, originally developed for OS/2, that provides a secure channel for network communication.

NBF An abbreviation for *NetBEUI Frame*, the transport packet structure used by NetBEUI.

NCBS An abbreviation for *Network Control Block Session*, a NetBIOS connection using the NetBEUI Frame protocol. Clients issue an NCB CALL and the destination server returns an NCB LISTEN to establish the session.

NDIS An acronym for Microsoft's *Network Driver Interface Specification* for writing device drivers for network interface cards (NICs) that work with Windows 3.x, Windows 95, and Windows NT.

NetBEUI An acronym for *NetBIOS Extended User Interface*, the transport protocol of Microsoft Networking. NetBEUI isn't a routable network, so its popularity is declining in comparison with TCP/IP.

NetBIOS An acronym for *Network Basic Input/Output System*, the original network API for MS-DOS and the foundation for NetBEUI.

NFS An abbreviation for *Network File System*, a file format and set of drivers created by Sun Microsystems Incorporated that allows DOS/Windows and UNIX applications to share files on disk drives running under UNIX. NFS relies on remote procedure calls (RPCs) for communication between clients and servers.

NIC An acronym for *network interface card*, a plug-in adapter card that provides the physical connection to the network. The most common NICs support 10BaseT network media; 100BaseT NICs, which are 10 times faster, are gaining acceptance in Windows NT networks.

NT An abbreviation for *New Technology* used by Windows NT. Windows NT is a registered trademark of Microsoft Corporation, so the full name of the operating system, *Windows NT*, is used in this book.

NTFS An abbreviation for *New Technology File System*, Windows NT's replacement for the DOS FAT (File Allocation Table) and OS/2's HPFS (High-Performance File System). NTFS offers many advantages over other file systems, including improved security and the ability to reconstruct files in the event of hardware failures. Windows 3.1+ and Windows 95 can access files stored on NTFS volumes via a network connection but can't open NTFS files directly.

NWLink Microsoft's implementation of the Novell NetWare IPX/SPX protocol for Windows NT Server and Workstation. See *IPX/SPX*.

object In programming, an element that combines data (properties) and behavior (methods) in a single container of code. Objects inherit their properties and methods from the classes above them in the hierarchy and can modify the properties and methods to suit their own purposes.

object code Code in machine-readable form that can be executed by your computer's CPU and operating system, usually linked with libraries to create an executable file.

object library   A file with the extension .OLB that contains information on the objects, properties, and methods exposed by an .EXE or .DLL file of the same file name that supports Automation.

object manager   A Windows NT executive component that manages operating system resources. In Windows NT, all system resources are objects.

object permissions   Permissions granted by the network administrator for users to access shared Windows NT objects. Object permissions also may be granted to users through group membership.

ODBC   An abbreviation for the Microsoft *Open Database Connectivity* API, a set of functions that provide access to client-server RDBMSs, desktop database files, text files, and Excel worksheet files through ODBC drivers. Windows NT 4.0 and Windows 95 use 32-bit ODBC 2.5. ODBC most commonly is used to connect to client/server databases, such as Microsoft SQL Server.

OLE Automation   See *Automation*.

OLE Control   See *ActiveX control*.

OLE DLL   A synonym for an in-process Automation server implemented as a Windows DLL. See *in-process*.

OpenDoc   A standard proposed by Apple Computer, Borland International, Lotus Development, Novell, and other Microsoft competitors to supplant or replace COM, DCOM, and OLE.

option button   A synonym for *radio button*, the original terminology in the CUA specification. Option buttons are circular control objects whose centers are filled when selected. If grouped, only one option button of a group may be selected.

OSI   Abbreviation for *Open System Interconnection*, the model for standard levels of networking functions and the services performed at each level. The seven-level OSI standard is defined by the International Standards Organization (ISO).

out-of-process   An (OLE) Automation server in the form of an executable (.EXE) file that operates in its own process space (memory allocation) and uses LRPCs (lightweight remote procedure calls) to communicate with the Automation client. The term *OutOfProc* often is used as shorthand for out-of-process.

page   A block of contiguous virtual memory (VM) addresses that Windows NT moves between physical RAM and a disk (paging) file as needed to support network operations and applications. Paging is used when physical RAM can't store the required data. See *VM*.

page fault   An event that occurs when a thread refers to an invalid (out-of-date) VM page. The VM manager must refresh the page from the page file. See *VM*.

paged pool   System memory that can be paged to Windows NT's Pagefile.sys paging file. The non-paged pool (approximately 4M for Windows NT 4.0) must reside in RAM and can't be paged to disk.

parameter   The equivalent of an argument but associated with the procedure that receives the value of an argument from the calling function. The terms *parameter* and *argument*, however, are often used interchangeably.

PDC   An abbreviation for *Primary Domain Controller*, the Windows NT server in a domain that's responsible for maintaining user and group accounts for a domain. Primary and Backup Domain Controllers authenticate domain users during the logon process. See *BDC* and *logon*.

permissions   Authority given by the system administrator, database administrator, or database owner to perform operations over a network or on data objects in a database.

persistent object   An object that's stored in the form of a file or an element of a file, rather than only in memory.

port   A connection to an external hardware device, such as a modem (serial port) or a printer (printer). In Windows NT, a communications channel object for local procedure calls.

PPP   An abbreviation for *Point-to-Point Protocol*, the most common Internet protocol for connection to TCP/IP networks via conventional and ISDN modems. See *SLIP*.

PPTP   An abbreviation for *Point-to-Point Tunneling Protocol*, a Microsoft-sponsored protocol, included with Windows NT 4.0, that uses encryption to assure privacy of communication over the Internet. See *VPN*.

preemptive multitasking   The multitasking process used by Windows NT and Windows 95 in which the operating system assures that all active threads have the opportunity to execute. Preemptive multitasking prevents a single thread from monopolizing a processor.

PRI   An abbreviation for *Primary Rate Interface*, an ISDN service for high-speed communication. PRI has 23 64kbps B (bearer) channels and one 64kbps D (data) channel, which may be used as independent channels or bonded to provide bandwidths higher than 64kbps. See *ISDN* and *BRI*.

primary key   The column or columns of a table whose individual or combined values (in the case of a composite primary key) uniquely identify a row in a table.

property   One of the two principal characteristics of objects (the other is methods). Properties define the manifestation of the object—for example, its appearance. Properties may be defined for an object or for the class of objects to which the particular object belongs, in which case they are said to be inherited.

property sheet   A dialog used to set the value(s) of properties of an object, such as an ActiveX control or an operating system component. As an example, Control Panel's Network tool is a property sheet. The tabbed elements of a property sheet are called *property pages*.

protected subsystem   A process that operates in a block of virtual memory that's not shared with other processes. Windows NT's protected subsystems prevent an errant process from killing the entire operating system.

protocol A description of the method by which networked computers communicate. Windows NT allows the simultaneous use of multiple network protocols, including TCP/IP, NetBEUI, and IPX/SPX.

protocol stack Network protocol software that implements a specific protocol, such as TCP/IP.

query A request to retrieve data from a database with the SQL SELECT instruction or to manipulate data stored in tables.

RAID An acronym for *redundant array of inexpensive disks*, a method of connecting multiple disk drives to a single controller card to achieve faster data throughput, data storage redundancy for fault tolerance, or both. See *disk mirroring, disk striping,* and *fault tolerance.*

raising exceptions A process by which the operating system transfers control to a block of software (exception handler) when an error or unexpected condition occurs. Windows NT's exception handler adds items to the event log.

RDBMS An abbreviation for *relational database management system.* An RDBMS is an application that can create, organize, and edit databases; display data through user-selected views; and, in some cases, print formatted reports.

record In database applications, a single element of a relational database table that contains each field defined for the table. A record is the logical equivalent of the row of a spreadsheet.

redirector Software that intercepts requests for remotely provided services, such as files in server shares, and sends the request to the appropriate computer on the network.

referential integrity Rules governing the relationships between primary keys and foreign keys of tables within a relational database that determine data consistency. Referential integrity requires that the value of every foreign key in every table be matched by the value of a primary key in another table.

Registry A database that contains information required for the operation of Windows NT and Windows 95, plus applications installed under Windows NT and Windows 95. The Windows Registry takes the place of Windows 3.1+'s REG.DAT, WIN.INI, and SYSTEM.INI files, plus *PROFILE*.INI files installed by Windows 3.1 applications. The Registry also includes user information, such as user IDs, encrypted passwords, and permissions. Windows NT and Windows 95 include RegEdit.exe for editing the Registry. The Windows NT and Windows 95 Registries differ in structure, and thus are incompatible.

relational database See *RDBMS.*

Remote Automation Object An out-of-process (OLE) Automation server, usually called an RAO, that resides on a server and is accessible to RAO-compliant applications that connect to the server. RAOs comprise the middle tier of three-tier client/server database applications. See *business rules* and *three-tier.*

remote procedure call (RPC)   An interprocess communication method that allows an application to run specific parts of the application on more than one computer in a distributed computing environment. Windows NT 4.0's DCOM uses RPCs for network communication between COM objects.

replication   The process of duplicating server shares and database objects (usually tables) in more than one location, including a method of periodically rationalizing (synchronizing) updates to the objects. Database replication is an alternative to the two-phase commit process. Microsoft SQL Server 6+ supports replication of databases across multiple Windows NT servers. Updating Windows NT Backup Domain Controllers (BDCs) from a Primary Domain Controller (PDC) occurs by replication of the Security Accounts Manger (SAM) database.

RISC   An acronym for *Reduced Instruction Set Computer*, a processor that uses a simplified set of internal operating instructions to speed execution. RISC processors supported by Windows NT 4.0 are Alpha, MIPS, and PowerPC. See *CISC*.

rollback   A term used in transaction processing that cancels a proposed transaction which modifies one or more tables and undoes changes, if any, made by the transaction before a COMMIT or COMMIT TRANSACTION SQL statement.

router   An active network component that connects one network to another network. Routers operate at the network layer of the OSI and work with packets that include logical addressing information.

routine   A synonym for *procedure*.

SAM   An acronym for *Security Accounts Manager*, a Windows NT subsystem that maintains a database of user account names and passwords for authentication.

scalable   The property of a multiprocessing computer that defines the extent to which addition of more processors increases aggregate computing capability. Windows NT Server 4.0 is generally considered to be scalable to eight Intel processors.

server   A computer on a LAN that provides services or resources to client computers by sharing its resources. Servers may be dedicated, in which case they share their resources but don't use them themselves, except in performing administrative tasks. Servers in client/server databases are ordinarily dedicated to making database resources available to client computers. Servers can also be used to run applications for users, in which case the server is called an *application server*. Peer-to-peer or workgroup servers, such as servers created by using PCs running Windows NT Workstation to share disk folders, are another class of server.

shared application memory   Memory that's allocated between processes involved in a lightweight remote procedure call (LCRP). See also *LRPC*.

shortcut key   A key combination that provides access to a menu choice, macro, or other function of the application in lieu of selection with the mouse.

SID   An acronym for *security ID*, a numeric value that identifies a logged-on user who has been authenticated by Windows NT or a user group.

SLIP An abbreviation for *Serial Line Interface Protocol*, the first common method of connecting via a modem to TCP/IP networks, now less widely used. See *PPP*.

SMB An abbreviation for *Server Message Block*, a networking protocol used by NetBEUI to implement Microsoft Networking.

SMP An abbreviation for *symmetric multiprocessing*, implemented in Windows NT, which distributes tasks among CPUs using a load-sharing methodology. Applications must be multithreaded to take advantage of SMP. See *asymmetric multiprocessing*.

SNMP An abbreviation for *Simple Network Management Protocol*, an Internet standard that defines methods for remotely managing active network components such as hubs, routers, and bridges.

source code The readable form of code that you create in a high-level programming language. Source code is converted to machine-language object code by a compiler or interpreter.

source document A term used by OLE 1.0 to refer to a compound object in a container document.

SQL An acronym, pronounced either as "sequel" or "seekel," for *Structured Query Language*, a language developed by IBM Corporation for processing data contained in mainframe computer databases. (*Sequel* is the name of a language, similar to SQL, developed by IBM but no longer in use.) SQL has now been institutionalized by the creation of an ANSI standard for the language.

stack See *protocol stack*.

stored procedure A set of SQL statements (and with those RDBMSs that support them, flow-control statements) that are stored under a procedure name so that the statements can be executed as a group by the database server. Some RDBMSs, such as Microsoft and Sybase SQL Server, precompile stored procedures so that they execute more rapidly. Jet 3.0's Remote Data Object is optimized for use with stored procedures.

stripe set See *disk striping* and *fault tolerance*.

Structured Query Language See *SQL*.

subnet mask A local bit mask (set of flags) that specifies which bits of the IP address specify a particular IP network or a host within a subnetwork. An IP address of 128.66.12.1 with a subnet mask of 255.255.255.0 specifies host 1 on subnet 128.66.12.0. The subnet mask determines the maximum number of hosts on a subnetwork.

synchronous I/O An input/output method in which the process that issues an I/O request waits for the requested process to complete before returning control to the application or operating system. See *asynchronous I/O*.

system administrator   The individual(s) responsible for the administrative functions for all applications on a LAN or users of a UNIX cluster or network, usually including supervision of all databases on servers attached to the LAN. If the system administrator's (SA's) responsibility is limited to databases, the term *database administrator* (DBA) is ordinarily assigned.

system databases   Databases that control access to databases on a server or across a LAN. Microsoft SQL Server has three system databases: the master database, which controls user databases; tempdb, which holds temporary tables; and model, which is used as the skeleton to create new user databases. Any database that's not a user database is a system database.

T-1   The most common moderate-speed telecommunications connection between LANs to create a WAN. Dedicated T-1 lines provide 1.544mbps of bandwidth. T-1 lines also are the most common method of connecting servers to the Internet.

table   A database object consisting of a collection of rows (records) divided into columns (fields) that contain data or null values. A table is treated as a database object.

TCP/IP   Abbreviation for *Transport Control Protocol/Internet Protocol*, the networking protocol of the Internet, UNIX networks, and the preferred protocol for Windows NT networks. TCP/IP is a routable network that supports subnetworks. See *IP*.

TDI   An abbreviation for *Transport Driver Interface*, used by Windows NT to implement multiple network protocols by using various network interface cards.

thread   A part of a process, such as an executing application, that can run as an object or an entity. Threads of execution are basis of Windows NT's symmetrical multiprocessing capability. See *multiprocessing* and *SMP*.

three-tier   The architecture of a database application, usually involving a client-server RDBMS, where the front-end application is separated from the back-end RDBMS by a middle tier application. The middle tier usually is implemented as a remote Automation server, which implements the database connection, enforces business rules, and handles transfer of data to and from databases of the RDBMS. See *business rules* and *Remote Automation Object*.

time stamp   The date and time data attributes applied to a disk file when created or edited. Time stamp is a database type for SQL Server and the ODBC API.

toggle   A property of an object, such as a check box, that alternates its state when repeatedly clicked with the mouse or activated by a shortcut key combination.

Token Ring   A network medium developed by IBM in which each computer in the ring passes a token, which carries network messages, to the adjacent computer. Token Ring provides each computer on the ring with guaranteed capability to transmit at regular intervals; Ethernet doesn't provide such a guarantee. Token Ring is specified by the IEEE-802.5 standard. See *Ethernet*.

transaction   A group of processing steps that are treated as a single activity to perform a desired result. A transaction might entail all the steps necessary to modify the values in or add records to each table involved when a new invoice is created. RDBMSs that are capable of transaction processing usually include the capability to cancel the transaction by a rollback instruction or to cause it to become a permanent part of the tables with the COMMIT or COMMIT TRANSACTION statement.

Transact-SQL   A superset of ANSI SQL used by Microsoft and Sybase SQL Server. Transact-SQL includes flow-control instructions, and the capability to define and use stored procedures that include conditional execution and looping.

trap   Windows NT's method of intercepting an event (such as an interrupt request or an unexpected result) that occurs during execution of a thread.

trigger   A stored procedure that occurs when a user executes an instruction that might affect the referential integrity of a database. Triggers usually occur before the execution of an INSERT, DELETE, or UPDATE statement so that the effect of the statement on referential integrity can be examined by a stored procedure before execution. See also *stored procedure*.

trust   In Windows NT domain terminology, a relationship between domain controllers in which users who are members of the trusted domain can access services on another trusting domain without the need to log on to the trusting domain.

two-phase commit   A process applicable to updates to multiple (distributed) databases that prevents a transaction from completing until all the distributed databases acknowledge that the transaction can be completed. The replication process has supplanted two-phase commit in most of today's distributed client/server RDBMSs. See *replication*.

UNC   An abbreviation for *Unified Naming Convention*, the method of identifying the location of files on a remote server. UNC names begin with \\. Windows NT and Windows 95 support UNC; 32-bit Windows applications must support UNC to qualify for application of Microsoft's "Designed for Windows NT" logo. All Microsoft Office 95 and later applications support UNC.

Unicode   A replacement for the 7-bit or 8-bit ASCII and ANSI representations of characters with a 16-bit model that allows a wider variety of characters to be used. Unicode is especially useful for representing the written characters of Asian languages. Windows NT and Windows 95 support Unicode.

uniform data transfer (UDT)   The interprocess communication (IPC) method used by OLE 2+. OLE 1.0 uses DDE for IPC.

unique index   An index in which no two key fields or combinations of key fields on which the index is created may have the same value.

UNIX   Registered trademark of a multiuser operating system, now administered by the Open Systems Foundation (OSF). Extensions and modifications of UNIX include DEC Ultrix, SCO UNIX, IBM AIX, and similar products.

UPS   An abbreviation for *uninterruptible power supply*, a device used to power a computer in the event of a primary power outage.

user mode   The processor mode used by Windows NT to run applications launched by users. Threads running in user mode are restricted to calling system services. See *kernel mode*.

UTP   An abbreviation for *unshielded twisted pair*, the type of cabling used to implement 10BaseT and 100BaseT network media.

VBA   An abbreviation for *Visual Basic for Applications*, the official name of which is "Visual Basic, Applications Edition." VBA is Microsoft's common application programming (macro) language for Access, Excel, Project, and the Visual Basic programming environment.

VDM   Abbreviation for *virtual DOS machine*, a Windows NT protected subsystem for running DOS applications in a console window.

virtual address space   The range of unique virtual memory addresses allocated to the threads of a single Windows NT process. See *VM*.

view   The method by which the data is presented for review by the user, usually on the computer display. Views can be created from subsets of columns from one or more tables by implementing the SQL CREATE VIEW instruction.

Visual Basic for Applications   See *VBA*.

VM   Abbreviation for *virtual memory*, a method of mapping a combination of RAM and images of RAM stored in a paging file to provide an address space larger than that available from the RAM installed in the computer.

VM manager   The Windows NT executive service that loads memory images stored in a paging file on demand, as well as saves memory images in the paging file when no longer needed by a thread.

VPN   An abbreviation for *Virtual Private Network*, a means of establishing secure communication channels on the Internet using various forms of encryption. See *PPTP*.

WAN   An acronym for *wide area network*. A WAN is a system for connecting multiple computers in different geographical locations by switched telephone network or leased data lines; by optical or other long-distance cabling; or by infrared, radio, or satellite links.

WDM   An abbreviation of *Windows Driver Model*, a 32-bit architecture for creating device drivers that run under both Windows NT and Windows 95. Microsoft hadn't issued the WDM specification when Windows NT 4.0 was released.

Win32   An API for running 32-bit Windows applications under Windows NT and Windows 95. The Win32 APIs of Windows NT and Windows 95 vary. To use Microsoft's "Designed for Windows NT" logo, applications must run under Windows NT 4.0 and Windows 95.

Win32S A subset of the Win32 API designed to add limited 32-bit capabilities to Windows 3.1+. Very few applications have been written to the Win32S API, which appears to have become obsolete.

WINS An acronym for *Windows Internet Naming Service*, a proprietary Microsoft application that maps easily remembered Windows machine names to the corresponding IP addresses.

Winsock An abbreviation for *Windows Sockets*, a networking API for implementing Windows applications that use TCP/IP, such as FTP and Telnet.

working set The set of active virtual memory pages for a process stored in RAM at a given instant.

workstation A client computer on a LAN or WAN that is used to run applications and is connected to a server from which it obtains data shared with other computers. *Workstation* is also used to describe a high-priced PC that uses a high-performance microprocessor and proprietary architecture to create what some call an "open" system.

WOSA Acronym for *Windows Open Services Architecture*, which is the foundation for such APIs as ODBC, MAPI, and TAPI. Microsoft also develops special vertical-market WOSA APIs for banking, financial, and other industries.

WOW An acronym for *Windows on Win32*, a subsystem of Windows NT that allows 16-bit Windows applications to run in protected memory spaces called *virtual DOS machines*. See *VDM*.

Index

Symbols

% Disk Time counter
(Performance
Monitor), 515
% Network Utilization
counter, 542
10-tape rotation
method, 276
100BaseT, Ethernet high-speed
variants, 134
100VG–AnyLAN, Ethernet
high-speed variants,
134-135
10BaseT cabling, 913
16-bit FAT file systems,
189-190
21-tape rotation
method, 277-278
32-bit FAT file systems,
189-190
32-bit protected mode, 333
32-bit TCP/IP, installing for
Windows for Workgroups
3.11 clients, 388-391
56kbps connection
DS0 circuit, 693-694
implementation
criteria, 693-694
Internet connection
types, 693-694
64-bit Windows NT
developing, 89-91
see also Microsoft Cairo,
89-91
8mm tape, helical scan
tapes, 286-287

A

About Registry Editor
command (Help
menu), 322
accelerator key, 913
Access 95, importing data to
SQL Server, 817-821
Access 95 Upsizing
Wizard, 817
access audits
Create Link, 326
Create Subkey, 326
Delete, 326
Enumerate Subkey, 326
Notify, 326
Query Value, 326
Read Control, 327
Set Value, 326
Write DAC, 327
Access Control List
(ACL), 913
Access Control Page
completing, 342-343
share level access control,
setting, 342-343
user level access control,
setting, 343
access links (frame relay
connectivity), 696
Access Through Share
Permissions dialog
box, 461, 611
access token, 913
accessing
FTP sites, 703-705
Macintosh clients
Windows NT file
resources, 404-412
Windows NT printer
resources, 404-412
Windows NT
Server, 403-404
Microsoft Networking clients
via NetWare, 601
off-site data storage, 281

Windows NT Registry by
administrators, 324-328
Windows NT Server
files from UNIX
host, 642-643
NetWare clients,
614-622
**Account command (Policies
menu),** 442
**Account Information
dialog,** 436
account lockout policy,
setting, 444
**Account Operators
group,** 446
Account Policy dialog, 442
activation, 913
active network components
bridges, selecting, 155-156
bridges versus routers, 157
collapsed backbones,
159-161
enterprise hubs, 159
Ethernet switches,
implementing, 159-161
gateways, 158
hubs, 153
NICs, selecting, 149-152
repeaters, 152-153
routers, selecting, 156-157
selecting, 149-163
summary
recommendations,
162-163
virtual LANs, 161-162
ActiveX controls, 913
Microsoft Internet client
platforms, 689
property sheets, 22
ActiveX scripting, Microsoft
Internet client
platforms, 689
ActiveX server scripting,
Microsoft Internet client
platforms, 689
activity reports
distributing via SQL Server
Web Assistant, 742-747
generating test copy,
746-747

**Adaptec AAA-130 host
adapter, RAID 5,** 240-241
**Adaptec AAC-330 host
adapter, RAID 5,** 240-241
**Add Computer to Domain
command (Server
menu),** 577
Add Data Source dialog, 736
**Add Key command (Edit
menu),** 321
**Add Network Adapter
dialog,** 388
**Add Network Protocol
dialog,** 389
Add Printer Wizard, 25
**Add Printer Wizard
dialog,** 483
Add RAS Device dialog, 677
**Add Static Mappings
dialog,** 559
**Add Through Share
Permissions dialog,** 461
**Add to Alert command
(Edit menu),** 509
Add to Alert dialog, 509
Add to Chart dialog, 504
**Add To Log command
(Edit menu),** 512
Add To Log dialog, 512
**Add Trusting Domain
dialog,** 587
**Add User Account Wizard,
creating user
accounts,** 437-442
**Add User Account Wizard
dialog,** 442
**Add User Accounts
Wizard,** 23
**Add Users and Groups
dialog,** 410, 455
**Add Value command
(Edit menu),** 321
**Add/Remove Programs
Wizard,** 25
adding
AppleTalk printers for
Macintosh clients,
407-412
backup domain
controller, 575

domains
global groups, 448
local groups, 446-448
Windows NT
clients, 575-577
logging table, 730-731
Microsoft Networking clients
in NetWare protocol
stack, 601-603
non-domain servers,
572-573
NTFS
file access
permissions, 471-472
folder access
permissions, 476-477
Performance Monitor
alerts, 509-510
RAID 5 dedicated controller
card, 240-241
remote clients to shared
folders, 374-376
share permissions, 461-464
SQL Server
backup tape device,
812-814
indexes to databases,
823-825
user databases, 814-830
user accounts, 423-426
Address Database dialog, 538
**Address Resolution
Protocol,** 545
address space, 914
**Addresses command (Capture
menu),** 538
administration privileges in
remote management,
370-371
administrative shares,
463-464
**Administrative Tools
command (Programs
menu),** 246-259
**Administrative Tools menu
commands**
Backup, 292
Disk Administrator, 246
Administrative Wizards
Add Printer, 23-26
Add User Accounts, 23-26

Add/Remove Programs, 23-26
  Group Management, 23-26
  Install New Modem, 23-26
  License, 23-26
  Managing File and Folder Access, 23-26
  Network Client Administrator, 23-26
Administrative Wizards command (Programs menu), 437
Administrator account
  executing multiple instances, 418-419
  group membership, assigning, 428-429
  managing built-in accounts, 422-423
  responsibilities, 422-423
  setting passwords, 202
Administrators group, 445
Advanced Installation Options dialog, 709
Advanced IP Addressing dialog, 555
Advanced page options, configuring World Wide Web server, 722-723
Advanced Settings for COM*x* dialog, 485
advanced user rights, 454
aggregate object, 914
Alert Options dialog, 510
alerts (Performance Monitor)
  adding, 509-510
  customizing, 510-511
  setting, 508-511
  viewing, 508-509
Alerts command (View menu), 509
Alerts window (System Management Server Administrator), 903
allocating
  networks, remaining funds, 82-83
  TCP/IP, IP addresses, 351-352
alternate 10-tape rotation method, 276-277
Always IN-2000, 188

Amdahl Corporation
  EnVista Availability Manager, 52
  scalable server systems, 52
  Web site, 52
American National Standards Institute (ANSI), 914
American Standard Code for Information Interchange, 914
Apple Macintosh networking protocols, 122
applet, 914
AppleTalk
  enabling Services for Macintosh, 401-403
  Migration Wizard, migration support, 858
  Multi-Protocol Router, 31
  printers
    adding for Macintosh clients, 407-412
    troubleshooting, 411-412
  Windows NT Server networking protocols, 117
  Windows NT Server Services for Macintosh, 117
application layer, OSI seven-layer model, 110-111
application programming interface (API), 914
application servers, 165-167
  configuring, 166-167
  CPU usage, monitoring, 521-522
  memory usage, monitoring, 522-526
  optimizing Windows NT Server, 521-526
  network throughput, maximizing, 523-526
  virtual memory, examining, 522-523
application-level encryption, 62-64
applications
  COM, developing, 39-40
  controlling with Task Manager, 23

Arcada Backup Exec, 296-297
Arcada Web site, 296
archive bits
  file backup types, 264
  setting, 264
ARCnet
  developed by DataPoint Corporation, 130
  media access methods, 130
arp command, 545
Arrange Icons command (Window menu), 322
arrays
  RAID, sizing, 233-234
  stacked RAID, 232-233
assigned cylinder scheduling, RAID 1 read performance, 225
assigning
  DHCP, IP addresses, 115-116
  folder share permissions, 467-468
  group membership, 428-429
  groups, access rights, 831-833
  user group rights, 454-455
asymmetric multiprocessing, 914
asymmetric processing, 169-170
asynchronous cache, 169
asynchronous I/O, 915
asynchronous SCSI, 173-174
Asynchronous Transfer Mode (ATM)
  features, 136-137
  media access methods, 136-137
attaching domain resources, 398-400
Audit Log, viewing, 327-328
audit options, setting for Internet Information Server (IIS), 713-727
auditing Windows NT Registry accesses, 326-327
Auditing command (Security menu), 322

authenticating
 Windows NT clients,
  580-582
 World Wide Web server,
  passwords, 713-716
authentication, 915
Auto Refresh command
 (Options menu), 322
autodial, Windows NT Server
 communication
 features, 654
automatic client setup,
 332-333
automatic client software
 installation (System
 Management Server), 905
automatic rebuild
 option, 233-234
  RAID product
   features, 236-238, 238
automatic server
 reconnection, 332-333
automatic synchronization of
 domains, 574-575
Automation controller, 915
autoplay, 915
Available AppleTalk Printing
 Devices dialog, 407

B

backing up
 files, NTBACKUP
  program, 291-297
 Windows NT Registry, 318
 Windows NT Server
  data, 192-193
BackOffice, *see* Microsoft
 BackOffice
Backup Browser, 555
Backup command
 (Administrative Tools
 menu), 292
backup domain controller
 configuring, 571
 domains, adding, 575
 installing in Windows NT
  Server, 192
 primary domain controller,
  promoting to, 571-572

Registry values,
 modifying, 574-575
 selecting in Setup
  program, 201-202
backup hardware
 selecting, 283-288
 tape drives, 284-287
 WORM drives, 288
 writable optical drives,
  287-288
backup information,
 displaying (NTBACKUP
 program), 299-300
Backup Information dialog
 box, 295
backup media capacities,
 purchasing, 273
Backup Operators group, 446
Backup Status dialog, 296
backup tape devices (SQL
 Server)
 adding, 812-814
 specifying, 812-814
 testing, 812-814
Backup Volume Labels
 dialog, 813
Banyan VINES, network client
 drivers, 339-341
Basic Rate Interface (BRI),
 694-696, 916
basic user rights, 454
BHS Software Web site, 553
Binary command (Edit
 menu), 321
binary files, 915
 transferring via FTP
  service, 703-705
binding, 915
 TCP/IP clients, 353
binding order,
 modifying, 519
bitmap, 916
bitwise, 916
blackouts, power protection
 issues, 178-179
blitting, 916
bonding, 694-696
Boolean data type, 916
bridges, 916
 data-link layer, 155-156
 network traffic, 528-529
 networks, 125-126

selecting active network
 components, 155-156
 Spanning Tree Algorithm
  (STA), 156
 versus routers, 157
broadcasting
 IPX/SPX protocol, 529
 NetBEUI protocol, 528-529
Browser Monitor, 550
Browser Status, 550
budget considerations,
 networks, 74-76
buffer, 916
building
 network business
  objectives, 56-57
 universal clients, 645-649
built-in accounts
 Administrator account,
  managing, 422-423
 Guest account, 423
built-in groups, 445-446
bursting capacity, 697
bus topology, 139-141
bus types
 selecting servers, 172-177
business organizations
 building networks, 56-57
 intranets, 46-47
buttons
 Edit Display Filter (Network
  Monitor), 35
 Start Capture (Network
  Monitor), 34
 Stop Capture and View
  (Network Monitor), 34
byte striping, RAID 3,
 226-228

C

cable types, 141-147
 coaxial, 141-142
 conductor size, 144
 fiber optic, 146-147
 shielded twisted pair,
  142-143
 unshielded twisted
  pair, 143-146

cables
  developing standards, 147
  ease of maintenence
    148-149
  Ethernet
    specifications, 132-133
  expandibility,
    designing, 148-149
  quality standards, 145-146
  system recommendations,
    147-148
cabling
  designing networks,
    138-139
  electrical topology,
    139-141
  logical topology, 139-141
  physical topology, 139-141
cache, 916
cache manager, 916
cache memory
  asynchronous, 169
  L1, 168-169
  L2, 168-169
  pipeline burst, 169
  sizing processors, 168-169
  synchronous, 169
caching data, RAID 5,
  230-231
Cairo, *see* Microsoft Cairo
University of California at
  Berkeley, RAID model
  development, 218-219
Capture Detail pane (Network
  Monitor), 34-36
capture filter, designing,
  35-36
Capture Hex pane (Network
  Monitor), 34-36
Capture menu commands
  Addresses, 538
  Networks, 536
  Stop and View, 537
Capture Summary pane
  (Network Monitor), 34-36
caret, 916
Carrier Sense Multiple
  Access with Collision
  Detection, 132-133
Cascade command (Window
  menu), 322

CD-recordable drives
  capacities, 287-288
  costs, 287-288
  disadvantages, 287-288
Certificate Request dialog box
  (Key Manager), 36
Change System Settings
  command (Options
  menu), 385
Change System Settings
  dialog, 385
Chart command (View
  menu), 506
Chart Options dialog, 507
charting system statistics
  (Performance
  Monitor), 505-508
charts (Performance Monitor)
  creating, 505-506
  customizing, 507-508
  deleting objects, 507
  displaying, 504-505
  editing, 507
checking Pentium floating-
  point division bug, 202
Choose Licensing Mode
  dialog, 788
circular queue, RAID 1 read
  performance, 224-226
CISC (Complex Instruction
  Computer Set), 917
CISC processors,
  selecting, 167-168
Class A IP addresses, 114-116
Class B IP addresses, 114-116
Class C IP addresses, 114-116
client access, granting
  (Remote Access
  Admin), 668-669
client access licenses,
  Microsoft BackOffice,
  781-782
Client for Microsoft Networks
  configuring network
    clients, 343-344
  file sharing
    installing, 356-357
    potential security
      problem alert, 357
  network client drivers,
    339-341

  printer sharing
    installing, 356-357
    potential security
      problem alert, 357
Client for NetWare, 30
  configuring network
    clients, 344-345
  file sharing
    installing, 357-358
    potential security
      problem alert, 357
  network client drivers,
    339-341
  printer sharing
    installing, 357-358
    potential security
      problem alert, 357
Client Load Simulator
  (Exchange Server)
  analyzing results, 856-857
  executing, 854-857
  installing, 855-857
client PCs
  network support,
    installing, 333-334
  NICs
    installing, 334-336
    modifying settings,
      336-338
  selection guidelines, 150
  supported protocols, 119
client-side features
  Event Viewer, 27-28
  Remote Program Load
    (RPL), 28
  Remote Server
    Administration, 27-28
  Server Manager, 27-28
  System Policy Editor, 26-28
  User Manager, 27-28
  User Profile Editor, 26-28
client software (Exchange
  Server)
  configuring 866-874
  installing, 866-874
client/server messaging
  Exchange Server
    features, 840-841
  incoming mail,
    processing, 840-841
  remote procedure calls
    (RPCs), 843-844

clients
authentication
services, 580-584
automatic software
installation, System
Management Server, 905
binding TCP/IP, 353
domains, moving, 577
manual software installation,
System Management
Server, 904-905
System Management Server,
supported, 885-886
**clone NICs versus name
brands, 151-153**
**Close command (Registry
menu), 320**
clustering, 917
servers, 177
coaxial cable
selection criteria, 142
types
Ethernet 10Base2
coax, 141-142
Ethernet coax, 141-142
RG-62, 141-142
**Collapse Branch command
(Tree menu), 319-321**
collapsed backbones
active network
components, 159-161
implementing, 159-161
**COM (Component Object
Model), 917**
business services, 39-40
data services, 39-40
user services, 39-40
command-line tools
arp command, 545
hostname command, 545
ipconfig command, 546
nbstat command, 546
nestat command, 547
ping command, 548
route command, 548
traceart command, 549
commands
Administrative Tools menu
Backup, 292
Disk Administrator, 246

Capture menu
Addresses, 538
Networks, 536
Stop and View, 537
Computer menu
Promote to Primary
Domain
Controller, 572
Send Message, 572
Synchronize Entire
Domain, 579
Configuration menu
Generate Directory
Import Files, 856
Import Users, 856
Test Topology, 855
Disk menu, Network
Connections, 386
Display menu, Filter, 539
Edit menu
Add Key, 321
Add to Alert, 509
Add To Log, 512
Add Value, 321
Binary, 321
Delete, 321
Delete From Chart, 507
DWord, 321
Edit Chart Line, 507
Multi String, 321
String, 321
Time Window, 514
Exchange menu
Options, 874
Properties, 874
Fault Tolerance menu
Create Stripe Set with
Parity, 257
Establish Mirror, 255
File menu
New Chart, 506
New Database, 734, 816
New Device, 815
New Log Settings, 512
Open Web, 770
Run Task, 747
Help menu
About Registry
Editor, 322
Contents, 322
How to Use Help, 322
Search for Help, 322

License menu, New
License, 792
Log menu, Security, 327
Manage menu
Database Devices, 814
Stored Procedures, 826
Tables, 732
Triggers, 825
Mapping menu
Show Database, 531
Static Mappings, 559
Operations menu, Hardware
Setup, 292
Options menu
Auto Refresh, 322
Change System
Settings, 385
Confirm on Delete, 322
Data From, 513
Font, 322
Read Only Mode, 322
Save Settings on
Exit, 322
Partition menu
Commit Changes
Now, 247
Create, 252
Create Stripe Set, 246
Restore, 250
Save, 250
Policies menu
Account, 442
Trust Relationships, 587
Printer menu, Connect
Network Printer, 394
Programs menu
Administrative
Tools, 246-259
Administrative
Wizards, 437
DHCP Manager, 637
Microsoft SQL
Server, 807
Remote Access
Admin, 668-669
SMS Administrator, 893
SQL Enterprise
Manager, 808
SQL Security
Manager, 831

Windows NT
Diagnostics, 317-318
WINS Manager, 641
Registry menu
Close, 320
Connect Network
Registry, 324, 372
Exit, 320
Load Hive, 320
Open, 320
Print Subtree, 320
Printer Setup, 320
Restore, 320
Restore Key, 318
Save Key, 318, 320
Save Subtree As, 320
Select Computer, 320
Unload Hive, 320
Security menu
Auditing, 322
Owner, 322
Permissions, 322
Server menu
Add Computer to
Domain, 577
New Backup
Device, 812
Register Server, 808
Scheduled
Tasks, 747, 824
Test menu, Load Simulation
Parameters, 856
Tools menu
Format, 248
Map Network
Drive, 399
SQL Query Tool, 827
Tree menu
Collapse Branch,
319-321
Expand All, 321
Expand Branch, 321
Expand One Level,
319-321
User menu
Copy, 426
New Global Group, 448
New Local Group, 447
New User, 423
Properties, 427
Select Domain, 420
Select Users, 427

View menu
Alerts, 509
Chart, 506
Data Only, 321
Display Binary
Data, 321
Find Key, 321
HTML, 771
Log, 511
Refresh, 321
Refresh All, 321
Select Columns, 23
Split, 321
Tree and Data, 321
Tree Only, 321
User Privilege, 832
Window menu
Arrange Icons, 322
Cascade, 322
Tile, 322
Windows menu,
Drives, 293
**commerce, securing on
Internet, 37-39**
**Commit Changes Now
command (Partition
menu), 247**
**committed information rate
(CIR), 697**
**communicating (System
Management Server)**
senders, 911
sites, 911
TAPI, 40-41
Compaq Computers
Netelligent, 52
scalable server systems, 52
Web site, 52
**Complete Trust model,
590-592**
implementing, 590-592
completing
Access Control Page,
342-343
Network property sheet,
identification page,
341-342
**Complex Instruction Set
Computer,** *see* CISC
Component Object Model,
see COM

compound document, 917
**comprehensive audit,
Inventory Agent
results, 906-907**
Computer menu commands
Promote to Primary Domain
Controller, 572
Send Message, 572
Synchronize Entire
Domain, 579
computer viruses
data communication
security, 60-64
McAfee VirusScan for
Windows NT, 61-64
concurrency, 917
concurrent application, 917
**CONFIG.SYS files, Windows
NT Registry, 328-329**
configuration files, viewing
Windows 3.1 clients,
384-385
Windows for Workgroups
3.11 client, 391-392
**Configuration menu
commands**
Generate Directory Import
Files, 856
Import Users, 856
Test Topology, 855
**Configure Gateway
dialog, 610**
**Configure LPT Port
dialog, 484**
**Configure Port Usage
dialog, 665**
configuring
application servers,
166-167
backup domain
controller, 571
database devices, 815-817
DHCP, 637-638
dial-up networking,
665-668
Directory Service Manager
for NetWare, 625-630
Exchange Server
client software, 866-874
mailboxes, 874-876
File and Print Services for
NetWare (FPSN), 620-622

file servers, 166-167
folder replication, 480-482
   export server, 480-482
   import computer,
    480-482
Gateway Service for
  NetWare, 605-606
   print gateway, 611-614
locally attached server
  printers, 483-488
Macintosh clients, printing
  services, 406-412
modem dial-up
  connections, 665-668
network clients, 343-346
   Client for Microsoft
    Networks, 343-344
   Client for NetWare
    Networks, 344-345
network printer
  servers, 488-498
network protocols
   NetBEUI, 347-348
   NWLink, 348-350
   TCP/IP, 351-356
NTBACKUP program,
  289-291
primary domain
  controller, 570-571
printers
   properties, 491-498
   shared resources,
    483-488
servers, memory, 171-172
Setup program
   fixed-disk drives,
    199-200
   network adapters, 203
SQL Security Manager, group
  accounts, 831-833
SQL Server, transaction
  logging, 828-830
TCP/IP, DNS configuration
  page, 354-355
user accounts, lockout
  options, 444
Windows 3.11 for
  Workgroups, universal
  clients, 646

Windows 95
  dial-up networking,
   670-676
  network protocols,
   347-355
  user.dat file, 364-366
Windows NT 4.0
  Workstation clients,
   TCP/IP, 395-398
Windows NT Server
  dial-up
   networking, 676-683
  RAS, 659-669
  video display, 210-211
  volume sets, 244-245
WINS, 640-642
World Wide Web server
  Advanced page
   options, 722-723
  Directories page
   options, 716-719
  Logging page
   options, 720-721
  Service page
   options, 713-716
**Confirm on Delete command
(Options menu), 322**
confirming Setup program
  network bindings, 208
  network settings, 205-208
  system information, 199
**Conflicting Device List,
network adapter
settings, 337-338**
**Connect Network Printer
command (Printer
menu), 394**
**Connect Network Printer
dialog, 394**
**Connect Network Registry
command (Registry
menu), 324, 372**
**Connect Network Registry
dialog, 372**
Connect Server dialog, 831
**Connect to Printer
dialog, 489**
connecting
  domains via low-speed
   connections, 420-421

IDC
  ODBC data
   sources, 750-752
  Web pages, 750-752
Internet methods, 692-698
LANs, cable types, 141-147
Macintosh clients to
  Windows NT Server,
  400-412
Net Watcher, remote
  clients, 373-376
RAS Multilink Channel
  Aggregation, servers,
  38-39
Windows 3.1 clients
  file resources, 386-387
  printer resources,
   386-387
Windows for Workgroups
  3.11 clients
  file resources, 394-395
  printer resources,
   394-395
Windows NT
  Workstation clients
  file resources, 398-400
  printer resources,
   398-400
connectivity
  default gateway problems,
   identifying, 554
  router problems,
   identifying, 554
  troubleshooting
   networks, 553-554
**constructing domain
names, 699-700**
consultants
  Microsoft Certified System
   Engineer, 81
  network management
   outside help, 80-81
  selecting, 81
containers, 918
**Contents command (Help
menu), 322**
context switching, 918
control object, 918

controlling
domains with Administrator account, 422-423
Task Manager applications, 23
converting FAT to NTFS, 190
Copper Distributed Data Interface (CDDI)
media access methods, 136
Twisted-Pair Physical Media Dependent (TPPMD), 136
copy backups
failed hard drive, re-creating, 265
file backup types, 265
Copy command (User menu), 426
Copy of Username dialog, 426
copying
domains, user group attributes, 448-449
Setup program files, 200-201
user accounts, 426
counters (Performance Monitor), 502-505
Internet Information Server (IIS), 747-749
CPU usage, monitoring, 521-522
Create command (Partition menu), 252
Create Default dialog, 361-364
Create Link (Access Audit), 326
Create Logical Drive dialog, 253
Create New Key dialog (Key Manager), 36
Create Stripe Set command (Partition menu), 246
Create Stripe Set dialog, 246
Create Stripe Set with Parity command (Fault Tolerance menu), 257
Create Stripe Set with Parity dialog, 257
Create Subkey (Access Audit), 326

creating
databases, logs, 829-830
driver disks, 188
emergency repair disks, 250-259
Exchange Server
mailboxes, 874-876
user profiles, 869-874
folder shares, 459-464
Gopher Server tag files, 725-727
Group Management Wizard, groups, 450-453
IDC files, ODBC data source, 752
Jobs window, system jobs, 899-900
logging database, 730
logging table
Jet 3.0, 734-735
SQL Server, 731-734
Microsoft dbWeb, Web pages, 758-764
New User dialog, user accounts, 424-426
ODBC data sources
Jet 3.0 databases, 738-740
SQL Server databases, 736
Performance Monitor, new charts, 505-506
PPTP, virtual private networks (VPNs), 37-39
RAID drive configurations, 250-259
RAID 0, stripe sets, 246-259
RAID 1, mirror sets, 252-259
RAID 5, stripe sets, 256-259
replication user, 478
SQL Server database devices, 814-817
SQL Server Web Assistant, Web pages, 742-747
standard volumes, 255-256
System Management Server, service accounts, 888-889
user accounts (Add User Account Wizard), 437-442

User Manager for Domains, multiple copies, 418-419
Windows 3.1 clients, installation disks, 378-379
Windows NT Server
emergency repair disk, 202, 211-212
ODBC system database, 735-740
setup boot disks, 194-195
custom control, 918
customizing (Performance Monitor)
alerts, 510-511
charts, 507-508
Cutler, David, head of Windows NT development team, 86-91

D

daily copy backups
file backup types, 268
file date stamps, utilizing, 268
data
backing up, 192-193
ensuring integrity of file backups, 271-272
importing to SQL Server from Access 95, 817-821
RAID 1 read performance, 224-226
RAID 1 write performance, 225
viewing in Performance Monitor, 513-514
data analysis (System Management Server), 884
data caching, RAID 5, 230-231
data channels, bonding, 694-696
data communication security
application-level encryption, 62-64
firewalls, 63-64

networks, 60-64
packet switching, 61-64
packet-level
  encryption, 63-64
router-based
  encryption, 63-64
data communication
  technology, 69-70
data compression, 97-99
data disaster plan,
  developing, 282-283
Data From command (Options
  menu), 513
Data From dialog box, 513
data integrity, 918
Data Link Control, *see* DLC
data-link layer, bridges,
  155-156
data marts, 799
Data Only command (View
  menu), 321
data packets, Routing Internet
  Protocol (RIP), 31
data redundancy
  RAID 0, 219-222
  RAID 1, 222-226
  RAID 2, 226
  RAID 3, 226-228
  RAID 4, 228
  RAID 5, 228-231
  RAID 6, 231-232
  RAID 7, 231-232
  RAID levels, 218-219
  stacked RAID, 232-233
  volume sets, 244-245
data restoration plan
  backup integrity, 282-283
  developing file
    backups, 282-283
  emergency repair kit,
    282-283
  minimal server
    downtime, 282-283
  spare tape drives, 282-283
  well-trained staff, 282-283
data table structures,
  importing, 817-821
Data Technology Corporation,
  187-188
data transfer
  SCSI methods, 173-174
    fast SCSI, 173-174
    SCSI-1, 173-174

SCSI-2, 173-174
  ultra SCSI, 173-174
  wide SCSI, 173-174
data warehousing, 799
  Oracle Express Server, 799
data-link layer
  logical link control
    (LLC), 109
  media access control
    (MAC), 109
  OSI seven-layer
    model, 108-109
Database Backup/Restore
  dialog, 813
database devices
  configuring, 815-817
  creating with SQL
    Server, 814-817
Database Devices command
  (Manage menu), 814
databases
  access, limiting, 831-833
  adding to SQL Server,
    814-830
  displaying, Microsoft
    dbWeb, 758-764
  dynamic access
    intranets, 750
    servers, 750
    Web sites, 750
  establishing permissions
    (SQL Server), 830-831
  logs, creating, 829-830
  modifying properties (SQL
    Server), 821-825
  procedures, viewing,
    826-827
  queries, executing, 827-828
  replicating, 478
  security
    considerations, 757-758
  tasks, scheduling, 824-825
  transaction logging,
    setting, 828-830
  triggers, viewing, 825-826
  viewing WINS, 531-533
Datamation Magazine, 43-44
Datamation Web site, 44
Dataphone Digital
  Service, 693

date/time, setting (Windows
  NT Server), 209-210
DC-2000 (QIC drives),
  284-285
DC-600 (QIC drives), 284-285
DCOM (Distributed Common
  Object Model)
  as known as
    NetworkOLE, 40
  OLE Automation
    server, 39-40
  three-tier architecture,
    39-40
DDE (dynamic data
  exchange), 919
deadlock, 919
decoupled disk drives,
  RAID 4, 228
dedicated controller cards,
  adding, 240-241
default gateways, 554
defining
  Internet domain
    names, 699-700
  user profiles, 429-433
Delete (Access Audit), 326
Delete command (Edit
  menu), 321
Delete From Chart command
  (Edit menu), 507
deleting
  domains, user groups
    from, 449
  Performance Monitor chart
    objects, 507
demand lock, 919
departmental RDBMS
  database, 798
departmental servers, 164
designing
  cables
    ease of maintenance,
      148-149
    expandibility, 148-149
  domains, 593-594
  Network Monitor, capture
    filter, 35-36
  network cabling, 138-139
detailed identification,
  Inventory Agent
  results, 906-907

determining
  networks
    fault-tolerance, 64-66
    user needs, 57-59
    workgroup needs, 57-59
  server memory
    requirements, 170-172
  user rights, 454
developing
  64-bit Windows NT, 89-91
  applications (COM), 39-40
  cable standards, 147
  data communication
    security for servers, 60-64
  file backups
    data restoration
      plan, 282-283
    strategies, 270-283
  Microsoft Cairo, 89-91
  networks, time
    schedule, 70
  physical security for
    servers, 59-64
  Web sites, 689-690
    Microsoft SiteBuilder
      Workshop, 690
  Windows NT, 86-87
  Windows NT 3.1, 87
  Windows NT 3.1 Advanced
    Server, 87
  Windows NT 3.5, 87-88
  Windows NT 3.51, 87-88
  Windows NT 4.0, 88-89
  Windows NT Server,
    network
    implementation, 55-77
device settings page
  (*Printername* **Properties**
  sheet), 498
device-independent
  bitmap, 919
DHCP (Dynamic Host
  Configuration
  Protocol) 919
  advantages, 634-635
  configuring, 637-638
  installing, 635-636
  IP addresses,
    assigning, 115-116
  managing, 637-638
  Windows NT Server, UNIX
    integration tools, 634-638

DHCP Manager command
  (Programs menu), 637
DHCP Relay Agent, 204
dial-in permissions,
  setting, 437
dial-up access method
  implementation
    criteria, 692-693
  Internet connection
    types, 692-693
dial-up networking, 333
  architecture, selecting,
    655-658
  configuring, 665-668
    Windows 95
      clients, 670-676
    Windows NT
      clients, 676-683
  testing
    Windows 95
      clients, 670-676
    Windows NT
      clients, 676-683
Dialin Information
  dialog, 437
dialogs
  Access Through Share
    Permissions, 461, 611
  Account Information, 436
  Account Policy, 442
  Add Data Source, 736
  Add Network Adapter, 388
  Add Network Protocol, 389
  Add Printer Wizard, 483
  Add RAS Device, 677
  Add Static Mappings, 559
  Add Through Share
    Permissions, 461
  Add to Alert, 509
  Add to Chart, 504
  Add To Log, 512
  Add Trusting Domain, 587
  Add User Account
    Wizard, 442
  Add Users and
    Groups, 410, 455
  Address Database, 538
  Advanced Installation
    Options, 709
  Advanced IP
    Addressing, 555
  Advanced Settings for
    COM*x*, 485

Alert Options, 510
Available AppleTalk Printing
  Devices, 407
Backup Information, 295
Backup Status, 296
Backup Volume Labels, 813
Certificate Request (Key
  Manager), 36
Change System
  Settings, 385
Chart Options, 507
Choose Licensing
  Mode, 788
Configure Gateway, 610
Configure LPT Port, 484
Configure Port Usage, 665
Connect Network
  Printer, 394
Connect Network
  Registry, 372
Connect Server, 831
Connect to Printer, 489
Copy of *Username*, 426
Create Default, 361-364
Create Logical Drive, 253
Create New Key (Key
  Manager), 36
Create Stripe Set, 246
Create Stripe Set with
  Parity, 257
Data From, 513
Database Backup/
  Restore, 813
Dialin Information, 437
Directory Permissions, 474
Display Filter, 539
Edit Chart Line, 507
Enter Name and
  Organization, 800
Enter Path, 374
File and Print Services
  for NetWare on
  Servername, 620
File and Print Sharing, 357
File New Database, 734
Files Needed, 290, 676
Files Opened by Users on
  Servername, 621
Format Drive *D:*, 248
Grant User Privilege, 832
Group Memberships, 428
Hardware Setup, 292
Have Disk, 368

Help Desk Options, 907
Identification
  Changes, 579
Input Log File
  Timeframe, 514
Insert Disk, 250, 536
Install Driver, 290
Install From Disk, 367
Install New Modem, 660
Install/Remove Client
  Utilities, 807
Logon Hours, 433
Logon Workstations, 435
Make New
  Connection, 670
Manage Exported
  Directories, 481
Manage Indexes, 823
Manage Logins, 733, 834
Map Network Drive, 399
Microsoft TCP/IP
  Configuration, 390
Network Client
  Administrator, 378
Network Connections, 386
Network Drivers, 388
Networks, 388
New Backup Device, 812
New Client Access
  License, 788, 792
New Database Device, 815
New Global Group, 448
New Local Group, 447
New Share, 610
New User, 423
ODBC SQL Server
  Setup, 737
Open SMS Window, 893
Open Web, 770
Owner, 498
Per Seat Licensing, 791
Per Server Licensing, 788
Per Server or Per Seat
  Licensing, 849
Permit Access On or Deny
  Access On, 723
Primary Site
  Information, 892
Printer Auditing, 497
Printer
  Permissions, 410, 496
Printer Ports, 407

Printers – Network
  Connections, 386
Propagate NetWare Accounts
  to Windows NT
  Domain, 628
Query, 743
Query Expression
  Properties, 902
Query Properties, 902
RAS Server TCP/IP
  Configuration, 667
Register Server, 808
Registry Key Auditing, 326
Registry Key
  Permissions, 325
Remote Access
  Permissions, 668
Remote Access Setup, 665
Repair Disk Utility, 211
Replication
  Configuration, 789
Restore Information, 298
Restore Progress, 813
Run, 417
Select Capture
  Network, 536
Select Components, 203
Select Computer, 505
Select Domain, 420
Select Network
  Adapters, 334
Select Network Component
  Type, 334
Select Network
  Protocol, 395
Select Network
  Service, 401, 536, 607
Select OEM Option, 615
Select Users, 427
Server Based
  Setup, 359, 362
Server Type, 201
Set Up Machine, 362
Settings for COM*x*, 484
Setup Complete, 766
Share Network Client
  Installation Files, 378
Shared Folders, 374
Site Services Account, 850
SMS Administrator
  Login, 893
Source Path, 359

Special Directory
  Access, 475
Special File Access, 475
Start Copying Files, 766
Start Up Settings, 393
System Data
  Sources, 736, 737
Task History, 824
TCP/IP Setup, 395
Test Topology, 855
Tip of the Day, 808
Trust Relationships, 587
User Environment
  Profile, 429, 433
User Rights Policy,
  455, 715
Users on *Servername*, 620
Verify Name and
  Company, 800
View HTML, 771
Virtual Memory, 524
Volumes Usage on
  Servername, 621
Windows NT Setup, 607
WINS Server
  Configuration, 641
differential backups
  failed hard drive,
    restoring, 267-268
  file backup types, 267-268
**digital audio tape, helical scan
  tapes, 286-287**
**Digital Clusters for
  Windows NT, 51**
Digital Data Service, 693
**Digital Equipment
  Corporation**
  Failover Manager, 51
  scalable server systems, 51
  Web site, 51
digital linear tape
  average lifetime, 286
  capacities, 286
**Directories page options,
  configuring (World Wide
  Web server), 716-719**
**Directory Permissions
  dialog, 474**
**Directory Replicator service,
  executing, 478-480**
**directory repository, Object
  File System (OFS), 89-91**

Directory Service Manager
for NetWare
configuring, 625-630
installing, 623-625
managing, 625-630
Synchronization Manager,
executing, 625-630
Windows NT Server
integration tools, 622-623
disabling Guest account, 423
disconnecting folder
shares, 463-464
Disk Administrator command
(Administrative Tools
menu), 246
disk bottlenecks
hardware solutions,
515-518
minimizing with
Performance
Monitor, 515-518
software solutions, 517-518
disk controllers
disk subsystems, 175-177
selecting servers, 175-177
disk drives
RAID, selecting, 236-238
RAID 1 usage, 222-226
Disk menu command,
Network Connections, 386
disk mirroring, 244-245, 919
Disk Queue Length counter
(Performance
Monitor), 515
disk storage
enterprise backup
solutions, 280
Hierarchical Storage
Management (HSM),
279-280
multiple volumes,
managing, 270-271
organizing file
backups, 270-271
disk striping, 244-245, 919
disk striping with
parity, 244-245
disk subsystems
disk controllers, 175-177
Enhanced Integrated Device
Electronics (EIDE)
drive, 172
SCSI drives, 172-174
selecting servers, 172-177

Diskeeper for Windows
NT, 520
diskless clients, Remote
Program Load (RPL), 28
diskless workstations, remote
boot clients, 151
dispatcher, 919
Display Binary Data
command (View
menu), 321
Display Filter dialog, 539
Display menu commands,
Filter, 539
displaying
folder shares, 463-464
Microsoft dbWeb
databases, 758-764
NTBACKUP program,
backup information,
299-300
Performance Monitor
charts, 504-505
query results, HTML
code, 756-757
Web pages (World Wide
Web server), 701-702
Distributed Component
Object Model, see DCOM
distributed computing,
remote procedure
calls, 102-105
distributed database, 919
distributing activity reports
(SQL Server Web
Assistant), 742-747
Distribution Server, 887-888
DLL, 920
DNS (Domain Name Services)
installing, 707
IP addresses,
translating, 30-31
mapping IP addresses,
698-700
name resolution, 698-700
troubleshooting,
560-562
network, Internet
connections, 67-69
versus WINS, 30-31
Windows NT Server, 30-31
DNS configuration
page, 354-355

domain accounts, setting
passwords, 443
Domain Admins group, 445
domain controllers
Backup Domain
Controller, 570-573
domains, moving, 578-579
flat network, 582-584
installing, 192
memory requirements, 584
placing, 582-584
Primary Domain
Controller, 570-573
remote offices, 582
server farms, 582-584
Domain Guests group, 446
domain integrity, 920
Domain Master Browser, 555
Domain Monitor, 550
Domain Name Services,
see DNS
domain names
constructing, 699-700
defining on Internet,
699-700
establishing, 707
networks, Internet
connections, 67-69
root domain, 699-700
service prefix, 699
Domain Planner (Windows
NT Resource Kit), 594
Domain Users group, 446
domains
account lockout policy,
setting, 444
adding Backup Domain
Controller, 575
Administrator account
controlling, 422-423
responsibilities, 422-423
architectural
overview, 567-580
authenticating Windows NT
clients, 580-582
authentication
services, 580-584
automatic synchronization,
modifying, 574-575
Complete Trust
model, 590-592
defined, 416
design criteria, 593-594

establishing trusts, 586-588
folder shares, Managing
Folder and File Access
Wizard, 464-468
global groups, adding, 448
Guest account, 423
hybrid domain model,
592-593
joining Windows NT
Server, 208
local groups, adding,
446-448
low-speed connection,
utilizing, 420-421
machine accounts, 576-577
moving
clients, 577
domain controllers,
578-579
Multiple Master
model, 589-590
renaming, 579-580
resources, attaching,
398-400
Security Account Manager,
manually synchronizing,
573-574
security identifiers, 569
security overview, 567-580
Single Domain model,
588-589
Single Master model, 589
synchronization process
overview, 573
trust relationships, 584-586
trusted, 585-586
trusting, 585-586
user group attributes,
copying, 448-449
user groups, deleting, 449
Windows NT clients,
adding, 575-577
downloading
Microsoft Internet
products, 689
Microsoft SiteBuilder
Workshop, 690
ODIPKT packet
drivers, 647-648
Requests For Comments
(RFCs), 632

Windows 95 Service Pack 1,
363-364
WINPKT packet
drivers, 648-652
drive configurations
creating RAID, 250-259
saving, 250-259
driver disks
creating, 188
hardware, SCSI host
adapters, 188
drives, selecting (NTBACKUP
program), 292-294
Drives command (Windows
menu), 293
drops, power protection
issues, 178-179
DS0 circuit, 693
Dual Inline Memory Modules
(DIMMs), 170-172
Dual Inline Package
(DIP), 170
dual loading power
supplies, 237-238
dual-attached stations, Fiber
Distributed Data Interface
(FDDI), 135-136
dumb external arrays,
241-243
dumb hubs, 154-155
duplexing, RAID 1, 222-226
DWord command (Edit
menu), 321
dynamic database
access, 750
HTML code,
examining, 756-757
Dynamic Host Configuration
Protocol, *see* DHCP
dynamic rebuild option,
RAID 238

E

Edit Chart Line command
(Edit menu), 507
Edit Chart Line dialog, 507
Edit Display Filter button
(Network Monitor), 35

Edit menu commands
Add Key, 321
Add to Alert, 509
Add To Log, 512
Add Value, 321
Binary, 321
Delete, 321
Delete From Chart, 507
DWord, 321
Edit Chart Line, 507
Multi String, 321
String, 321
Time Window, 514
editing
Performance Monitor
charts, 507
Windows NT Registry
remotely, 323-324
eight-processor servers, 29
electing Master
Browser, 555-556
electrical topology, 139-141
Electronic Industries
Association and Telephone
Industry
cable standards,
developing, 147
unshielded twisted pair
cables, quality
grades, 145-146
eliminating network
protocols, 518
emergency repair disk
creating 202, 211-212,
250-259
duplicates, creating,
211-212
enabling
Gateway Service for
NetWare, gateway, 609
Services for Macintosh,
AppleTalk protocol,
401-403
Windows 95 clients, remote
management, 370-375
encryption
application-level, 62-64
packet-level, 63-64
router-based, 63-64
Enhanced Integrated Device
Electronics (EIDE) drive, disk
subsystems, 172

Enter Name and Organization
dialog, 800
Enter Path dialog, 374
enterprise backup
solutions, 280
Intel Storage Express, 280
Legato's Network
Archivist, 280
Palindrome's Backup
Director, 280
enterprise hubs
active network
components, 159
prohibitive costs, 159
enterprise RDBMS
database, 798-799
enterprise servers, selection
criteria, 164
enterprise site topology
child sites, 886-887
parent sites, 886-887
primary sites, 886-887
secondary sites, 886-887
System Management
Server, 886-887
"enterprise-wide"
networking, 41-44
entry values, modifying
(Windows NT
Registry), 305-306
Enumerate Subkey (Access
Audit), 326
environmental subsystems
(Windows NT)
POSIX.1 subsystem, 97
Virtual DOS machines
(VDMs), 97
Windows NT, 95-97
Windows on Win32
(WOW), 97
EnVista Availability
Manager, 52
error checking and correcting
memory, 171-172
Establish Mirror command
(Fault Tolerance
menu), 255
establishing
domain names, 707
networks minimum
configuration, 82
security, 59-64

SQL Server, database
permissions, 830-831
trusts for domains, 586-588
Windows NT Server network
connections, 208
Ethernet, 920
bus topology, 139-141
cable specifications,
132-133
Carrier Sense Multiple Access
with Collision
Detection, 132-133
data transmission
process, 132-133
high-speed variants,
133-135
100BaseT, 134
100VG–AnyLAN,
134-135
Full Duplex
Ethernet, 134
media access
methods, 132-133
sample connections,
132-133
selection
recommendation,
137-138
Ethernet 10Base2 coax,
141-142
Ethernet coax, 141-142
Ethernet switches
cut-through
processing, 160-161
implementing, active
network
components, 159-161
overview, 159-161
store-and-forward
processing, 160-161
Event Viewer
audit logs, viewing,
327-328
functions, 27-28
Events window (System
Management Server
Administrator), 904
examining
application servers, virtual
memory, 522-523
dynamic database access,
HTML code, 756-757
IDC source file, 754-756

exchange accounts, planning
(Exchange Server), 847
Exchange Administrator
functions, 877-878
launching, 877-878
Exchange menu commands,
Options, 874
Exchange Server
Client Load Simulator,
executing, 854-857
client software
configuring, 866-874
installing, 866-874
distribution CD-ROM,
installing, 848-851
exchange accounts,
planning, 847
features
application development
support, 843
fully extensible
client, 842
fully extensible
server, 842
integrated security,
841-842
intelligent client/server
messaging, 840-841
proxy address
support, 842
replication support, 843
hardware
requirements, 846
installation planning,
844-851
installation options,
848-851
licensing fees, 783-784
mailboxes
configuring, 874-876
creating, 874-876
properties, 876
messaging overview, 837
messaging process, 839-843
Microsoft BackOffice,
bundled
components, 778-779
Migration Wizard,
implementing, 857-865
Optimizer, executing,
851-854
performance,
optimizing, 846

Personal Address Book (PAB), 844
Personal Information Store (PST), 844
reconfiguring installation with Optimizer, 852-854
remote procedure calls (RPCs), 843-844
replication support, store-and-forward process, 843
role of Exchange Administrator, 877-878
setup program, launching, 847-851
software requirements, 846
user profiles, creating, 869-874
versus Microsoft Mail, 837
executing
Directory Replicator service, 478-480
Directory Service Manager for NetWare, 625-630
Exchange Administrator, 877-878
Exchange Server
Client Load Simulator, 854-857
Optimizer, 851-854
Setup program, 847-851
Internet Service Manager, 710-711
License Manager, 789-794
Network Monitor, 536-541
NTBACKUP program, 294-297
Performance Monitor, 501-502
remote procedure calls, 102-105
servers, System Policy Editor, 368-369
Setup program, 196
SQL Enterprise Manager queries, 827-828
SQL Server, 806-807
database tasks, 823-825
System Management Server, data analysis, 884
System Management Server Administrator queries, 901-903

User Manager for Domains, 417-418
multiple instances, 418-419
Windows NT Diagnostics Utility, 317-318
Windows NT Server network installation, 203-208
Setup program, 194
Executive Software Web site, 520
existing infrastructure, incorporating, 66-69
existing operating systems, installing Windows NT Server, 196-197
Exit command (Registry menu), 320
Expand All command (Tree menu), 321
Expand Branch command (Tree menu), 321
Expand One Level (Tree menu), 319
Expand One Level command (Tree menu), 321
expanding servers in trusted domains, 29
export folders, 477-478
export servers, configuring, 480-482
external ISDN adapters, 656-658
external modems, installing, 660-665
external RAID enclosures, 241-243
extractor programs, launching (Migration Wizard), 864-865

F

failed hard drive
re-creating
copy backups, 265
normal backups, 264-265

restoring
differential backups, 267-268
incremental backups, 265-267
failover, 921
failover clustering, 51
Failover Manager, Digital Equipment Corporation, 51
Fast Ethernet, high-speed LANs, 28-29
FAT (File Allocation Tables), 458, 921
formatting, 199
NTFS, converting, 190
Windows NT Server, 189-190
fault tolerance, 921
cost versus performance, 65-66
networks
determining, 64-66
Microsoft Web site, 65-66
NTFS feature, 97-99
Fault Tolerance menu commands
Create Stripe Set with Parity, 257
Establish Mirror, 255
Fiber Distributed Data Interface (FDDI)
dual-attached stations, 135-136
fiber optic cable, 135-136
media access methods, 135-136
singly attached stations, 135-136
fiber optic cable
Fiber Distributed Data Interface (FDDI), 135-136
selection criteria, 146-147
file access permissions (NTFS)
adding, 471-472
modifying, 470-471
removing, 470-471
types, 469-470
viewing, 470-471
File Allocation Table, *see* FAT

File and Print Services for
NetWare,   31, 600-601
   configuring,   620-622
   features,   615-619
   installing,   615-619
   managing,   620-622
   versus Gateway Service for
      NetWare,   614-615
File and Print Services for
NetWare on
Servername,   620
File and Print Sharing
dialog,   357
file backups
   Arcada Backup Exec,
      296-297
   backup media capacities,
      purchasing,   273
   data restoration plan,
      developing,   282-283
   disk storage,
      organizing,   270-271
   enterprise backup
      solutions,   280
   future software and
      hardware options,   300
   grandfather-father-son
      method,   277-278
   Hierarchical Storage
      Management (HSM),
      279-280
   integrity, ensuring,
      271-272
   off-site data, storing,   281
   open files,   272-273
   rotation methods
      four-tape,   274-276
      10-tape,   276
      21-tape,   277-278
      alternate 10-tape,
         276-277
      organizing,   274-279
      Tower of Hanoi,
         278-279
   selection criteria for
      servers,   268-270
   strategies, developing,
      270-283
   tape drives, selecting,
      271-272

types
   archive bit,   264
   copy backups,   265
   daily copy backups,   268
   differential
      backups,   267-268
   incremental
      backups,   265-267
   normal backups,
      264-265
   selecting,   268-270
file date stamps,   268
file fragmentation
(NTFS),   520-521
File menu commands
   New Chart,   506
   New Database,   734, 816
   New Device,   815
   New Log Settings,   512
   Open Web,   770
   Run Task,   747
File New Database
dialog,   734
file servers,   165-167
   configuring,   166-167
   optimizing in Windows NT
      Server,   514-521
file sharing, installing
   Client for Microsoft
      Networks,   356-357
   Client for NetWare
      Networks,   357-358
   network clients,   356-358
   LANs,   28-29
file systems
   16-bit FAT,   189-190
   32-bit FAT,   189-190
   formatting,   199
   NTFS,   189-190
File Transfer Protocol, *see* FTP
files
   backing up (NTBACKUP
      program),   291-297
   copying (Setup
      program),   200-201
   handling NTFS,   97-99
   restoring (NTBACKUP
      program),   297-300
Files Needed dialog,   290, 676
Files Opened by Users on
   Servername dialog,   621

Filter command (Display
menu),   539
Find Key command (View
menu),   321
fine-tuning Windows NT
Server installation,   202-203
firewalls
   Microsoft Proxy Server,
      37-39
   network security,   63-64
fixed-disk drives
   configuring, Setup
      program,   199-200
   copying files, Setup
      program,   200-201
   partitioning,   199
      Windows NT
         Server,   188-190
flat networks,   582-584
folder access permissions
(NTFS)
   adding,   476-477
   modifying,   474-477
   removing,   474-477
   viewing,   474-477
folder replication
   configuring,   480-482
   export folders,   477-478
   export server,
      configuring,   480-482
   import computer,
      configuring,   480-482
   import folders,   477-478
   launching,   478-480
folder shares
   creating,   459-464
   disconnecting,   463-464
   displaying,   463-464
   Managing Folder and File
      Access Wizard,   464-468
   overview,   458-459
   permissions
      assigning,   467-468
      modifying,   466-468
      renaming,   467-468
   removing,   460-464
Foldername Properties
sheet,   22
folders
   replicating,   477-478
   selecting (NTBACKUP
      program),   292-294

Font command (Options menu), 322
Format command (Tools menu), 248
Format Drive *D*: dialog, 248
formatting
FAT, 199
file systems, 199
NTFS, 199
SQL Server Web Assistant, query results, 742-747
four-Pentium Pro motherboard, 29
four-processor servers, 29
four-tape rotation method, 274-276
frame relay connectivity
access links, 696
bursting capacity, 697
committed information rate (CIR), 697
connection speed, 696
implementation criteria, 696-697
Internet connection types, 696-697
FrontPage 1.1, 688-689
FrontPage Editor
viewing HTML code, 770-772
Web pages, modifying, 770-772
FrontPage Explorer, 770-772
FTP (File Transfer Protocol) Server
binary files, transferring, 703-705
Internet Information Server (IIS) component, 703-705
service options, setting, 723-725
FTP sites, accessing, 703-705
FTP Software NFS Client (InterDrive 95), 339-341
Full Duplex Ethernet, 134
fully extensible client
Exchange Server features, 842
universal inbox concept, 842

fully extensible server, 842
future growth
network considerations, 73-74
networks, planning, 72-74

G

Gates, Bill, role in feud with Novell, 598
gateways, 922
enabling (Gateway Service for NetWare), 609
Gateway (and Client) Services for NetWare, 204
Gateway Services for NetWare (GSNW), 30, 600-601
account management, 603-605
gateway, enabling, 609
implementing, 603-614
installing, 607-609
logon scripts, 603-605
NDS support, 603-605
NetWare, configuring, 605-606
preferred NetWare server, selecting, 609
print gateway
configuring, 611-614
installing, 611-614
shared rights, 603-605
shares, activating, 609-611
versus File and Print Services for NetWare, 614-615
gateways
active network components, 158
networks, 125-126
similarity to routers, 158
specifying TCP/IP, 352-353
general page (*Printername* Properties sheet), 491-498
Generate Directory Import Files command (Configuration menu), 856

generating test copy of activity reports, 746-747
geometric cylinder scheduling, RAID 1 read performance, 225-226
GetMac utility, 551
global groups
adding domains, 448
creation criteria, 449
defined, 416
GM Access Common Dealership Environment (CDE), 43-44
Gopher server
ANSI documents, 705
ASCII documents, 705
installing, 707
Internet Information Server (IIS) component, 705
service options, setting, 725-727
tag files, creating, 725-727
grandfather-father-son method, 277-278
see also 21-tape rotation method
Grant User Privilege dialog, 832
granting
client access, 668-669
remote management administration privileges, 370-371
group accounts
access rights, assigning, 831-833
configuring SQL Security Manager, 831-833
Group Management Wizard, 24
groups
creating, 450-453
naming, 451-453
local versus global, selecting, 452-453
overview, 450-453
group membership, assigning, 428-429
Group Memberships dialog, 428

groups
creating (Group Management Wizard), 450-453
naming (Group Management Wizard), 451-453
System Management Server, targeted software installation, 883
Guest account, disabling, 423
Guests group, 446

H

handling NTFS files, 97-99
hardware
Exchange Server requirements, 846
future file backup technology, 300
implementing RAID, 238-243
minimum configuration, establishing, 82
SCSI host adapters, 188
solutions for disk bottlenecks, 515-518
specifying servers, 163-182
SQL Server requirements, 799-800
System Management Server inventoring, 883
Inventory Agent, 905-907
hardware abstraction layer (HAL), 922
Windows NT Executive, 93-95
Hardware Compatibility List (HCL)
obtaining, 95
servers, conforming, 165
updates, obtaining, 187
hardware RAID
upgrading server, 239-240
versus software RAID, 243-245

Hardware Setup commmand (Operations menu), 292
Hardware Setup dialog, 292
Have Disk dialog, 368
helical scan tapes
8mm tape, 286-287
digital audio tape, 286-287
Help Desk, launching (System Management Server), 907-909
Help Desk Options dialog, 907
Help menu commands
About Registry Editor, 322
Contents, 322
How to Use Help, 322
Search for Help, 322
Helper Server, 888
Hierarchical Storage Management (HSM), 279-280
near-line storage, 279-280
offline storage, 279-280
online storage, 279-280
High Performance File System (HPFS), 458
high-speed variants, Ethernet, 134
high-end servers, selection criteria, 164-167
high-speed LANs, Fast Ethernet, 28-29
historical development
Windows NT 3.1, 87
Windows NT 3.1 Advanced Server, 87
Windows NT 3.5, 87-88
Windows NT 3.51, 87-88
Windows NT 4.0, 88-89
hives (Windows NT Registry), 309-310
HKEY_CLASSES_ROOT, 307, 315-316
HKEY_CURRENT_CONFIG, 307, 315
HKEY_CURRENT_USER, 309-310, 316
HKEY_LOCAL_MACHINE, 307
HARDWARE subkeys, 314
SAM (Security Account Manager), 310-311
SECURITY, 311

SOFTWARE, 311-312
subkeys, 310-314
SYSTEM, 312-314
HKEY_LOCAL_MACHINE\SAM (Windows NT Registry hive), 309-310
HKEY_LOCAL_MACHINE\ SECURITY (Windows NT Registry), 309-310
HKEY_LOCAL_MACHINE\ SOFTWARE (Windows NT Registry), 309-310
HKEY_LOCAL_MACHINE\ SYSTEM (Windows NT Registry hive), 309-310
HKEY_USERS, 307, 316
HKEY_USERS\DEFAULT (Windows NT Registry hive), 309
home folders, specifying, 431-433
host adapters, 175-177
hostname command, 545
hot pluggable power supplies, RAID, 237-238
hot spare disks, RAID, 236-238
hot swappable disks, RAID, 236-238
How to Use Help command (Help menu), 322
HTML (HyperText Markup Language), 922
displaying query results, 756-757
examining dynamic database access, 756-757
FrontPage Editor, viewing, 770-772
HTML command (View menu), 771
hubs, 922
active network components`, 153
dumb, 154-155
enterprise, 159
managing, 154-155
stackable, selecting, 154
stand-alone, selecting, 153-154
unmanaged, 154-155
hybrid domain model, 592-593

I

IBM, integrating SNA
  environments, 124-125,
  649-650
icons
  My Computer icon, 21
  Network Neighborhood, 21
IDC (Internet Database
  Connectors)
  Microsoft Internet client
    platforms, 689
  ODBC data source
    creating files, 752
    connecting, 750-752
  query parameters,
    specifying, 752
  source file,
    examining, 754-756
  Web pages,
    connecting, 750-752
**Identification Changes
  dialog, 579**
identification page,
  completing (Network
  property sheet), 341-342
identifying
  connectivity
    default gateway
      problems, 554
    router problems, 554
  Windows NT Server
    licensing terms, 201
    server computer
      name, 201
**IEEE 802 series, media access
  methods, 130**
**IEEE 802.5 series, Token
  Ring, 131-132**
IEEE networking model
  logical link control
    (LLC), 109
  media access control
    (MAC), 109
impersonation, 923
implementing
  active network components,
    Ethernet switches,
    159-161
  collapsed backbones,
    159-161

Complete Trust
  model, 590-592
Gateway Service for
  NetWare, 603-614
hybrid domain model,
  592-593
incremental backups,
  265-267
Migration Wizard, 857-865
  one-step approach,
    860-864
  two-step approach, 860
Multiple Master
  model, 589-590
Net Watcher, remote
  usage, 373-374
off-site data storage, 281
Performance Monitor
  remote machines,
    504-505
  TCP/IP networks, 545
Policy Editor, remote
  usage, 371-373
PPTP, 685-686
RAID hardware, 238-243
RAID 0, 219-222, 235
RAID 1, 235
RAID 2, 226
RAID 3, 226-228, 235
RAID 4, 228
RAID 5, 228-231, 235
RAID 6, 231-232
RAID 7, 231-232
RDBMS transaction
  recovery, 101-102
Registry Editor, remote
  usage, 372-373
Single Domain model,
  588-589
Single Master model, 589
stacked RAID,
  232-233, 235
System Monitor, remote
  usage, 373
TAPI communication
  services, 40-41
User Manager for
  Domains, 416-417
virtual LANs, 161-162
Web pages through
  Performance
  Monitor, 747-749

Windows 95 universal
  clients, 649
import folders, 477-478
**Import Users command
  (Configuration menu), 856**
importing
  Access 95 data to SQL
    Server, 817-821
  SQL Server table
    structures, 817-821
Inbox Setup Wizard, 869-874
incremental backups
  failed disk drives,
    restoring, 265-267
  file backup types, 265-267
  implementing, 265-267
**indexes, adding to databases
  (SQL Server), 823-825**
**.INI files (Windows NT
  Registry), 328-329**
initialization files, viewing
  Windows 3.1 clients,
    384-385
  Windows for Workgroups
    3.11 client, 391-392
**Input Log File Timeframe
  dialog box, 514**
Input/Output Manager (IOM)
  elements, 94-95
  Windows NT Executive
    component, 94-95
Insert Disk dialog, 250, 536
Install Driver dialog, 290
**install folder, specifying
  (Setup program), 199-200**
Install From Disk dialog, 367
**Install New Modem
  dialog, 660**
**Install New Modem
  Wizard, 25**
**Install/Remove Client Utilities
  dialog box, 807**
installation folders
  creating for Windows 3.1
    clients, 378-379
  executing, Setup
    program, 196
  preparing Windows NT
    Server, 195-197
  selecting, Setup
    program, 197-198

installing
Client for Microsoft
Networks
file sharing, 356-357
printer sharing, 356-357
Client for NetWare Networks
file sharing, 357-358
printer sharing, 357-358
Client Load Simulator,
855-857
DHCP, 636
Directory Service Manager
for NetWare, 623-625
DNS, 707
error checking and
correcting memory,
171-172
Exchange Server, 844-851
client software, 866-874
distribution CD-ROM,
848-851
File and Print Services for
NetWare (FPNW),
615-619
Gateway Service for
NetWare, 607-609
print gateway, 611-614
Gopher server, 707
Internet Information
Server, 203
Internet Information Server
(IIS), 203, 706-710
Microsoft dbWeb, 758-764
Microsoft FrontPage,
764-770
network clients, 339-341
file sharing, 356-358
printer sharing, 356-358
Network Monitor, 535-541
Performance Monitor, SMNP
service, 542-545
RAS
external modems,
660-665
internal modems,
660-665
Services for Macintosh
400-403
SQL Enterprise
Manager, 807-808

SQL Server, 799-807
distribution CD-ROM,
800-806
System Management Server,
primary site server,
890-893
System Policy Editor,
367-369
Windows 3.1 clients,
network drivers, 379-383
Windows 95
network support,
333-334
NICs, 334-336
Windows 95 clients
network, 359-364
PolEdit, 367-370
Windows for Workgroups
3.11
NetWare support,
646-647
packet driver
support, 647-652
TCP/IP support,
646-647
Windows for Workgroups
3.11 clients, 32-bit
TCP/IP, 388-391
Windows NT 4.0
Workstation 4.0 clients
TCP/IP, 395-398
Windows NT
domain, 397-398
Windows NT Server
decision overview,
185-192
domain controller, 192
existing operating
systems, 196-197
hardware
compatibility, 187
networks, 195-196
summary steps, 193-194
Windows 95 setup
copy, 359-364
WINS, 639
instantiate, 923
integrated security
Exchange Server
features, 841-842
SQL Server
databases, 830-831

**Integrated Services Digital
Network,** *see* ISDN
integrating
TCP/IP and NetBIOS,
529-533
Windows NT Server
IBM SNA
environments,
649-650
NetWare, 599-601
UNIX, 632-633
Intel processors
four-Pentium Pro
motherboard, 29
Pentium versions, 168
selecting, 168
Intel Storage Express, 280
interacting
Windows NT Registry
.INI files, 328-329
CONFIG.SYS files,
328-329
**Interconnected Windows NT
server, networking
protocols,** 122-123
internal ISDN adapters,
656-658
**internal modems,
installing,** 660-665
**International Data
Corporation,** 19
Internet
commerce, securing, 37-39
connection types, 692-698
56kbps
connection, 693-694
dial-up access, 692-693
frame relay
connectivity, 696-697
ISDN connection,
694-696
T-1 connections,
697-698
T-3 connections,
697-698
databases, security
considerations, 757-758
DNS
name resolution,
698-700
network
connections, 67-69

domain names
   defining, 699-700
   networks
     connections, 67-69
downloading Microsoft
   products, 689
Gopher server, 705
IP addresses, 67-69
ISP selection, 691
Microsoft BackOffice future
   components, 778-779
Netscape versus
   Microsoft, 44-45
networking protocols,
   123-124
strategies by Microsoft,
   44-45
WINS network
   connections, 67-69
**Internet Assistant for
Access, 688-689**
**Internet Assistant for
Excel, 688-689**
**Internet Assistant for
PowerPoint, 688-689**
**Internet Assistant for
Word, 688-689**
Internet Database Connectors,
see IDC
**Internet domain names versus
IP addresses, 116**
**Internet Engineering Task
Force (IETF), 632-633**
   PPTP submission, 685-686
   Requests For Comments
     (RFCs), 113-116, 632-633
   TCP/IP, regulating, 113-116
**Internet Explorer 3.0,
19, 687-689**
**Internet Information Server
(IIS)**
   audit options, setting,
     713-727
   components
     FTP service, 703-705
     Gopher Server, 705
     World Wide Web
       server, 700-702
   features, 36-39
   hardware
     requirements, 706

installation, testing,
   711-713
installing, 203-204,
   706-710
interaction with Windows
   NT domains, 705-706
Internet Database Connector
   (IDC), 37-39
Internet Service
   Manager, 710-711
launching, 48-50
logging options,
   setting, 713-727
logging table format,
   730-731
Microsoft BackOffice,
   bundled
     components, 778-779
Microsoft Index Server,
   37-39
Microsoft Proxy Server,
   37-39
Performance Monitor
   counters, 747-749
prior version,
   upgrading, 707-710
property sheets, 48-50
RAM requirements, 706
SSL certificates,
   obtaining, 36-39
Internet Server API, 689
**Internet Service Manager,
executing, 710-711**
**Internet service provider (ISP),
selecting, 691**
**Internet tools (Windows NT
Server), 36-39**
**intranet servers, networking
protocols, 123**
**intranet tools (Windows NT
Server), 36-39**
intranets, 924
   databases, security
     considerations, 757-758
   defined, 46-47
   dynamic database
     access, 750
   features, 47
   LANs, 19
   WANs, 19

**Inventory Agent (System
Management Server)**
   client hardware, 905-907
   client software, 905-907
   comprehensive audit,
     906-907
   detailed
     identification, 906-907
**inventory packages (Packages
window), 898-899**
invocation path, 924
IP (Internet Protocol)
   addresses, 924
   allocating TCP/IP, 351-352
   assigning DHCP, 115-116
   Class A, 114-116
   Class B, 114-116
   Class C, 114-116
   DNS mapping, 698-700
   mapping WINS, 530-533
   networks, Internet
     connections, 67-69
   resolving, 354-355
   routing process, 115-116
   subnet masks, 115-116
   TCP/IP, 114-116
   translating DNS, 30-31
   versus Internet domain
     names, 116
ipconfig command, 546
IPX/SPX, 598, 924
   as known as NWLink, 117
   broadcasting, 529
   routable protocol, 117
   Windows NT Server
     networking
     protocols, 117
**ISDN (Integrated Services
Digital Network), 924**
   adapters, 695-696
   availability, 696
   Basic Rate Interface
     service, 694-696
   bonding, 694-696
   cost, 696
   Ethernet adapters, 656-658
   implementation
     criteria, 694-696
   Internet connection
     types, 694-696

lines, 38-39
routers, 696
  RAS architecture,
    656-658

J-K

Java, Microsoft Internet client
  platforms, 689
Jet 3.0
  creating
    logging database, 730
    logging table, 734-735
    ODBC data
      sources, 738-740
Jobs window (System
  Management Server)
  job types, 899-900
  Site Groups Management
    Server Administrator, 903
  system jobs, creating,
    899-900
joining Windows NT Server
  domain, 208
jumper configurable
  NICs, 150-151

kernel mode services, 924
  versus user mode
    services, 96-97
  Windows NT
    Executive, 93-95
keys, 306-307
  Registry Editor,
    modifying, 318-320

L

L1 cache memory, 168-169
L2 cache memory, 168-169
labeling NTBACKUP program
  media, 291-292
LAN cabling
  bus topology, 139-141
  ring topology, 140-141
  star topology, 139-141

LANalyzer for Windows, 534
LANs (local area networks),
  924
  cable types, 141-147
  data communication
    security, 60-64
  file sharing, 28-29
  Multi-Protocol Routing
    (MPR) service, 630-631
  senders, 911
launching
  Directory Replicator
    service, 478-480
  Directory Service Manager
    for NetWare, 625-630
  Exchange
    Administrator, 877-878
  Exchange Server
    Client Load
      Simulator, 854-857
    Optimizer, 851-854
    Setup program, 847-851
  Gateway Service for NetWare
    shares, 609-611
  Internet Information Server
    2.0, 48-50
  Internet Service
    Manager, 710-711
  License Manager, 789-794
  Migration Wizard extractor
    programs, 864-865
  Network Monitor, 536-541
  Performance Monitor,
    501-502
  SQL Server, 806-807
  System Management Server
    Help Desk
      functions, 907-909
    Network Monitor,
      909-910
    Remote Control
      Agent, 907-909
  System Management Server
    Administrator, 893-895
  System Monitor, 373
  System Policy Editor,
    368-369
  Task Manager, 23
  User Manager for
    Domains, 417-418
  Windows NT Diagnostics
    Utility, 317-318

Legato's Network
  Archivist, 280
library function, 104-105
License Manager
  launching, 789-794
  per-seat licensing, 789-794
  per-server licensing,
    789-794
License menu commands,
  New License, 792
License Tool (Windows NT
  Server), 787-794
License Wizard, 25
licensing
  Exchange Server, 783-784
  Microsoft BackOffice,
    779-787
    components, total
      costs, 785-786
  SNA Server, 784-785
  SQL Server, 782-783
  System Management
    Server, 784
  Windows NT Server, 782
licensing terms
  identifying on Windows NT
    Server, 201
  Per Seat, 201
  Per Server, 201
lightweight remote procedure
  calls (LRPCs), 40-41
limiting database
  access, 831-833
linked object, 925
livelock, 925
load balancing, 518
Load Hive command (Registry
  menu), 320
Load Simulation Parameters
  command (Test menu), 856
local area networks, see LANs
local groups
  adding to domains,
    446-448
  creation criteria, 449
  defined, 416
Local Procedure Call (LPC)
  Facility, 94-95
local service servers, 165
localization with
  Unicode, 98-99

locally attached printers, configuring, 491-498

locally attached server printers, configuring, 483-488

lockout options, configuring, 444

Log command (View menu), 511

log files (Performance Monitor)
creating databases, 829-830
recording data, 511-514
viewing data, 513-514

Log menu command, Security, 327

logging
ODBC data source, 729-747
specifying ODBC data source, 740-741
transactions, 101-102

logging database
creating, 730
Jet 3.0, creating, 730
SQL Server, creating, 730

logging off users by logon hours, 435

logging options
Internet Information Server (IIS), 713-727
World Wide Web server, 713-723

Logging page options, configuring (World Wide Web server), 720-721

logging table
adding, 730-731
Internet Information Server (IIS) format, 730-731
Jet 3.0, creating, 734-735
SQL Server
creating, 731-734
querying, 732-734

logical link control (LLC), 109

logical topology for cabling, 139-141

logins, viewing (SQL Enterprise Manager), 834-835

logon hours
control methods, 433-435
expired, 435
logging off users, 435
managing networks, 433-435
setting multiple user accounts, 434-435

Logon Hours dialog, 433

logon privileges, restricting, 435-436

logon scripts
replicating, 478
setting for user accounts, 431-433

Logon Server, 887-888

Logon Workstations dialog, 435

long filename support, 333

Lotus cc:Mail, migration support to Exchange Server, 858

low-level TCP/IP parameters, 353-354

low-speed connections
modems, 420-421
partial T-1 line, 420-421
Switched-56, 420-421

low-speed domain connections, 420-421

M

MacFile Tools (Services for Macintosh)
attributes, 404-405
files, 404-405
users, 404-405
volumes, 404-405

machine accounts, 576-577

machine directory, performing setup for Windows 95 client, 362-364

Machine Groups window (System Management Server Administrator), 903

machine language, 925

Macintosh clients
Apple User Authentication Module (UAM), 403-404
printing services
configuring, 406-412
troubleshooting, 411-412
Windows NT Server
accessing, 403-404
connecting, 400-412
file resources, accessing, 404-412
printer resources, 404-412

magneto-optical drives
high media costs, 288
low capacities, 288

mail accounts, migrating from Microsoft Mail, 858-864

mailboxes (Exchange Server)
configuring, 874-876
creating, 874-876

mailslots, 527

mainframes, RAID 1 protection, 224-226

Make New Connection dialog, 670

Manage Exported Directories dialog, 481

Manage Indexes dialog, 823

Manage Logins dialog, 733, 834

Manage menu commands
Database Devices, 814
Stored Procedures, 826
Tables, 732
Triggers, 825

management needs
hardware, 71-72
networks, planning, 70-72
software, 71-72

managing
built-in accounts (Administrator account), 422-423
DHCP, 637-638
Directory Service Manager for NetWare, 625-630
disk storage, 270-271

File and Print Services for
NetWare (FPSN), 620-622
FrontPage Explorer, Web
pages, 770-772
hubs, 154-155
Internet Information Server
2.0, 48-50
Microsoft FrontPage, Web
site content, 764-772
multiple user
accounts, 432-433
networks
logon hours, 433-435
resources, 77-79
user account
information, 436
User Manager for Domains,
user groups, 416-417
user profiles, 429-433
Windows NT Server built-in
accounts, 421-423
WINS, 640-642
World Wide Web server
content, 718-719
**Managing File and Folder
Access Wizard, 24**
folder shares, 464-468
**mandatory user
profiles, 430-431**
**manual client software
installation (System
Management Server),
904-905**
**Map Network Drive command
(Tools menu), 399**
**Map Network Drive
dialog, 399**
**MAPI (Messaging Application
Programming
Interface), 925**
mapping
DNS, IP addresses, 698-700
WINS, IP addresses,
530-533
Mapping menu commands
Show Database, 531
Static Mappings, 559
**marketing strategies for
Windows NT Server,
41-44**

**marshaling layer (TAPI),
40-41**
mass storage drivers
detecting with Setup
program, 198
Windows NT End-User
License Agreement, 198
Master Browser, 555
election process, 555-556
master file table, *see* **MFT**
**maximizing network
throughput, 523-526**
**Maynard 16-bit SCSI
Adapter, 188**
**McAfee VirusScan for
Windows NT, 61-64**
media (NTBACKUP program)
labeling, 291-292
preparing, 291-292
**media access control
(MAC), 109**
media access methods
ARCnet, 130
Asynchronous Transfer
Mode (ATM), 136-137
Copper Distributed Data
Interface (CDDI), 136
Ethernet, 132-133
Fiber Distributed Data
Interface (FDDI), 135-136
IEEE 802 series, 130
recommendations, 137-138
selecting, 129-130
Token Ring, 130-132
**MediaVision Pro Audio
Spectrum-16, 188**
memory
configuring servers,
171-172
determining requirements
for servers, 170-172
domain controllers, 584
error checking and
correcting, 171-172
SIMM, 170-172
usage, monitoring 522-526
**Merchant Services, Microsoft
Internet products, 688-689**
**Message Transfer Agent
(MTA), 838-839**

**messages, store-and-forward
processing, 843**
metadata (MFT), 99-101
metafile, 926
MFT (Master File Table)
attributes
bitmap, 100-101
data, 100-101
extended, 101
filename, 100-101
index allocation,
100-101
index root, 100-101
security descriptor,
100-101
standard, 100-101
user-defined, 101-106
volume
information, 101
defined, 99-101
metadata, 99-101
Microsoft
Internet strategies, 44-45
Internet client platforms
ActiveX controls, 689
ActiveX scripting, 689
ActiveX server
scripting, 689
Internet Database
Connector, 689
Internet Server API, 689
Java support, 689
Internet products
downloading, 689
FrontPage 1.1, 688-689
Internet Assistant for
Access, 688-689
Internet Assistant for
Excel, 688-689
Internet Assistant for
PowerPoint, 688-689
Internet Assistant for
Word, 688-689
Internet Explorer
3.0, 687-689
Internet Information
Server 2.0, 688-689
Merchant Services,
688-689
Proxy Server, 688-689
Search Server, 688-689

SQL Server business
strategy, 798-799
versus Netscape
browser, 44-45
Microsoft BackOffice
annuity model, 786-787
bundled components
Exchange Server,
778-779
Internet Information
Server (IIS), 778-779
SNA Server, 778-779
SQL Server, 778-779
System Management
Server, 778-779
Windows NT
Server, 778-779
client access licenses,
781-782
future Internet
components, 778-779
licensing, 779-787
market penetration, 777
per-seat versus per-server
licensing, 780-781
sales, 777
server licenses, 781-782
total licensing costs,
785-786
upgrading, 786-787
Microsoft Cairo
64-bit Windows NT, 89-91
delays in development, 20
development, 89-91
Object File System
(OFS), 89-91
projected release
date, 20, 89-91
property sheets, 22
**Microsoft Certified System
Engineer, 81**
Microsoft dbWeb
databases, displaying,
758-764
installing, 758-764
Web pages, creating,
758-764
Microsoft DHCP Server, 205
Microsoft DNS Server, 205
Microsoft FrontPage
installing, 764-770
Web site content,
managing, 764-772

Microsoft Index Server
also known as Tivoli, 37-39
Internet Information Server
(IIS), 37-39
obtaining, 37-39
**Microsoft Knowledge
Base, 553**
**Microsoft LAN Manager for
UNIX, 643-644**
Microsoft Mail
mail accounts,
migrating, 858-864
Message Transfer Agent
(MTA), 838-839
messaging process, 838-839
shared file system, 838-839
subdirectories, 838-839
versus Exchange
Server, 837
Microsoft Networking clients
NetWare, accessing, 601
NetWare protocol stack,
adding, 601-603
**Microsoft Open Licensing
Pack (MOLP), 782**
**Microsoft Project, PERT
(Program Evaluation and
Review Technique), 77-79**
Microsoft Proxy Server
also known as
Catapult, 37-39
Internet Information Server
(IIS), 37-39
obtaining, 37-39
**Microsoft SiteBuilder
Workshop,
downloading, 690**
**Microsoft SQL Server
command (Programs
menu), 807**
**Microsoft TCP/IP
Configuration dialog, 390**
**Microsoft TCP/IP
Printing, 205**
Microsoft Technet CD, 553
Microsoft Web site, 689
fault-tolerance on
networks, 65-66
Windows NT Server
network
implementation, 59

migrating
Microsoft Mail mail
accounts, 858-864
Windows NT Server to
NetWare, 650-652
**Migration Tool for
NetWare, 651-652**
Migration Wizard
extractor programs,
launching, 864-865
implementing in Exchange
Server, 857-865
migrating mail
accounts, 858-864
migration
preparation, 859-860
migration support
AppleTalk, 858
Lotus cc:Mail, 858
Microsoft Mail, 858
one-step approach,
858-864
recommendation for transfer
of mail accounts, 859-864
two-step approach,
858-864
**minimal conventional DOS
memory usage, 333**
minimizing
NTFS file
fragmentation, 520-521
Performance Monitor, disk
bottlenecks, 515-518
**minimum configuration,
networks, 82**
mirror sets
creating, RAID 1, 252-259
creating standard
volumes, 255-256
system booting in Windows
NT Server, 245
mirroring
advantages/
disadvanatges, 222-226
RAID 1, 222-226
SCSI host adapter, 239-240
**mixed security (SQL
Server), 830-831**
modal, 926
modeless, 926

modems
dial-up access
method,   692-693
dial-up networking
configurations,   665-668
multiple external,   655-658
multiple internal,   655-658
RAS Multilink Channel
Aggregation,   38-39
single internal,   655-658
TAPI,   40-41
Windows NT Server support
list,   661-665
modifying
Backup Domain Controllers,
Registry values,   574-575
control sets
(HKEY_LOCAL_MACHINE\
SYSTEM),   312-314
domains, automatic
synchronization,   574-575
folder shares,
permissions,   466-468
FrontPage Editor, Web
pages,   770-772
monitors,   210-211
multiple user accounts,   427
network adapters,
settings,   336-338
network protocols, binding
order,   519
NTFS
file access
permissions,   470-471
folder access
permissions,   474-477
share permissions,   461-464
SQL Server, database
properties,   821-825
User Manager, user
accounts,   427-428
Windows 95, NIC
settings,   336-338
Windows for Workgroups
3.11 clients, network
protocols,   389-391
Windows NT Registry
values,   305-306
monitoring
application servers
CPU usage,   521-522
memory usage,   522-526
RAS connections,   683-685

monitors, modifying,
210-211
moving
clients in domains,   577
domain controllers,
578-579
**MS-DOS networking
protocols,**   121
**Multi String command (Edit
menu),**   321
**Multi-Link PPP protocol,
bonding,**   694-696
**Multi-Protocol Routing (MPR)
service,**   31
features,   630-631
Windows NT Server
integration tools,   630-631
multiple client support,
331-333
**multiple copies, creating (User
Manager for
Domains),**   418-419
**multiple data streams
(NTFS),**   98-99
**multiple external modem,
RAS architecture,**   655-658
**multiple instances, executing
(User Manager for
Domains),**   418-419
**multiple internal modem, RAS
architecture,**   655-658
Multiple Master model,
589-590
**multiple network protocols,
spanning,**   597
multiple protocols,   332-333
binding order,
modifying,   519
multiple user accounts
logon hours, setting,
434-435
modifying,   427
user profiles,
managing,   432-433
**multiple volumes, managing
disk storage,**   270-271
multiprocessing,   926
multitasking,   926
**multithreaded
operations,**   658-659, 926
symmetrical
multiprocessing,   29
My Computer icon,   21

N

**name brand NICs versus
clones,**   151-153
**name resolution
troubleshooting**
DNS,   560-562
WINS,   560-562
named pipes,   104-105, 926
**naming groups (Group
Management Wizard),**
451-453
**National Software Testing
Laboratories (NTSL),**   28
**native services (Windows NT
Executive),**   93-95
nbstat command,   546
nestat command,   547
Net Watcher
remote client,
connecting,   373-376
remote usage,
implementing,   373-374
**NetBEUI (NetBIOS Extended
User Interface),**   598
configuring network
protocols,   347-348
non-routable protocol,   113
Windows NT Server
networking
protocols,   112-113
NetBEUI Frame,   112-113
NetBEUI protocol
broadcasting,   528-529
named pipes,   104-105
non-routable,   528-529
**NetBIOS, IP addresses,
mapping,**   530-533
NetBIOS Datagram,   530
**NetBIOS Extended User
Interface,** *see* **NetBEUI**
NetBIOS Interface,   204
NetBIOS Name,   530
**NetBIOS protocol, network
messages (Performance
Monitor),**   511
NetBIOS Session,   530
NetBT protocol
RFC 1001,   529-533
RFC 1002,   529-533

Netelligent, 52
Netscape versus Microsoft, Internet battleground, 44-45
Netsetup.exe, installing, 359-364
NetWare
  accessing (Microsoft Networking clients), 601
  adding protocol stack (Microsoft Networking clients), 601-603
  configuring (Gateway Service for NetWare), 605-606
  installing support (Windows for Workgroups 3.11), 646-647
  integrating Windows NT Server, 599-601
    File and Print Services for NetWare (FPSN), 600-601
    Gateway Service for NetWare (GSNW), 600-601
  market share, 600-601
  migrating to Windows NT Server, 650-652
  Migration Tool for NetWare, 651-652
  selecting preferred server (Gateway Service for NetWare), 609
  universal clients, building, 645
NetWare Client 32, 340-341
NetWare clients, accessing Windows NT Server, 614-622
NetWare server
  interaction with System Management Server, 911-912
  networking protocols, 123
NetWatch, 551
network adapters
  compatibility list, 336
  configuring with Setup program, 203
  selecting (Windows NT Server), 190-191

settings
  Conflicting Device List, 337-338
  modifying, 336-338
  viewing, 336-338
network bindings, confirming (Setup program), 208
Network Client Administrator dialog, 378
Network Client Administrator Wizard, 25
network clients
  Banyan VINES, 339-341
  Client for Microsoft Networks, 339-341
    configuring, 343-344
  Client for NetWare Networks, 339-341
    configuring, 344-345
  file sharing, installing, 356-358
  FTP Software NFS Client (Interdrive 95), 339-341
  installing, 339-341
  NetWare Client 32, 340-341
  Novell 16-bit ODI NetWare, 339-341
  Primary Network Logon, setting, 345-346
  printer sharing, installing, 356-358
  removing, 341
  SunSoft PC-NFS, 339-341
Network Connections command (Disk menu), 386
Network Connections dialog, 386
Network Device Interface Specification (NDIS), 111
network drivers (Windows 3.1 clients)
  installing, 379-383
  setting, 385-386
Network Drivers dialog, 388
network drives, home folders, specifying, 431-433
Network File Systems, UNIX, 643

Network General Web site, 534
Network General's Expert Sniffer, 534
network installation, executing (Windows NT Server), 203-208
network interface card, see NIC
network layers
  OSI seven-layer model, 109
  routers, 156-157
network management
  Microsoft Certified System Engineer, 81
  outside help
    consultants, 80-81
    obtaining, 80-81
    resellers, 80-81
    vendors, 80-81
  selecting consultants, 81
  vendors, selecting, 83
Network Monitor
  Capture Detail pane, 34-36
  capture filter, designing, 35-36
  Capture Hex pane, 34-36
  Capture Summary pane, 34-36
  functions, 33-36
  installing, 535-541
  launching, 536-541
    System Management Server, 909-910
  network performance troubleshooting, 33-36
  overview, 535-541
  tools and agents, installing, 536-541
  window, viewing, 33-36
Network Monitor Agent, 205
Network Monitor Tools and Agent, 205
Network Neighborhood
  icon, 21
  renaming, 21
network operating system, see NOS
network printer servers, configuring, 488-498

Network property sheet, completing, 341-342
network protocols
analysis by System
Management Server, 883
and troubleshooting,
527-533
binding order,
modifying, 519
configuring in Windows
95, 347-355
eliminating, 518
IPX/SPX, 598
modifying Windows for
Workgroups 3.11
clients, 389-391
NetBEUI, 598
configuring, 347-348
NWLink, configuring,
348-350
protocol analyzers,
troubleshooting, 533-535
TCP/IP, 599
configuring, 351-356
network services
binding TCP/IP, 353
DHCP Relay Agent, 204
Gateway (and Client)
Services for NetWare, 204
Internet Information
Server, 204
Microsoft DHCP
Server, 205
Microsoft DNS Server, 205
Microsoft TCP/IP
Printing, 205
NetBIOS Interface, 204
Network Monitor
Agent, 205
Network Monitor Tools and
Agent, 205
Remote Access Service, 205
Remoteboot Service, 205
RIP for Internet
Protocol, 205
RIP for NWLink, 205
RPC Configuration, 204
RPC support for
Banyan, 205
SAP Agent, 205
selecting in Setup
program, 204-205

Services for Macintosh, 205
SNMP Service, 205
Windows Internet Name
Service, 205
**network settings, confirming
(Setup program), 205-208**
**networking processes
(Windows NT Server)**
servers, 105-106
workstations, 105-106
networking protocols
Apple Macintosh, 122
AppleTalk, 117
DLC 117
Interconnected Windows NT
server, 122-123
Internet, 123-124
intranet servers, 123
IPX/SPX, 117
MS-DOS, 121
NetBEUI, 112-113
NetBEUI Frame, 112-113
NetWare server, 123
NWLink, 117
OS/2, 122
RAS, 118
selection criteria, 126
streams, 118-119
TCP/IP, 113-116
UNIX server, 123
UNIX workstations, 122
Windows 3.1, 121
Windows 95, 120
Windows for Workgroups
3.1x, 120-121
Windows NT Server, 112
Windows NT Workstation
4.0, 119-120
NetworkOLE, *see* **DCOM**
networks
active components,
selecting, 149-163
bridges, 125-126
bridging traffic, 528-529
browsing,
troubleshooting, 554-556
budget considerations,
planning, 74-76
business objectives,
building, 56-57
cable design
guidelines, 148-149

cabling, designing, 138-139
cabling system
recommendations,
147-148
coaxial cable, 141-142
connectivity
troubleshooting, 553-554
data communication
technology, planning,
69-70
developing
implementation, 55-77
electrical topology,
cabling, 139-141
existing infrastructure
incorporating, 66-69
replacing, 68-69
fault-tolerance
cost versus
performance, 65-66
determining, 64-66
fiber optic cable, 146-147
folder shares
creating, 459-464
Managing Folder and File
Access Wizard,
464-468
overview, 458-464
removing, 460-464
future growth,
planning, 72-74
gateways, 125-126
global groups, adding, 448
installing over Windows NT
Server, 195-196
Internet connections
domain names, 67-69
IP addresses, 67-69
interoperability, 124-126
intranets, 46-47
IPX/SPX protocol,
broadcasting, 529
local groups, adding,
446-448
logical topology,
cabling, 139-141
logon hours,
managing, 433-435
management needs,
planning, 70-72
maximizing
throughput, 523-526

minimum configuration,
establishing, 82
NetBEUI protocol
broadcasting, 528-529
physical topology,
cabling, 139-141
placing domain
controllers, 582-584
PPTP, 37-39
printers, sharing, 482-498
project management
software, utilizing, 77-79
proxy servers, 125-126
remaining funds,
allocating, 82-83
resources
managing, 77-79
upgrading, 82-83
routers, 125-126
routing,
troubleshooting, 557
security
application-level
encryption, 62-64
data communication,
60-64
establishing, 59-64
firewalls, 63-64
packet switching, 61-64
packet-level
encryption, 63-64
physical, 59-64
router-based
encryption, 63-64
servers, selecting, 164-165
shielded twisted pair
cables, 142-143
specifying connection (Setup
program), 203
System Management Server,
supported, 885
time schedule,
developing, 70
topologies, 139-141
troubleshooting aids
Microsoft Knowledge
Base, 553
Microsoft Technet
CD, 553
Network Monitor, 33-36

Windows NT Resource
Center, 553
Windows NT Resource
Kit, 550-552
trust relationships,
troubleshooting, 557-560
unshielded twisted pair
cables, 143-146
user needs,
determining, 57-59
user training, planning,
76-77
viewing media speed
(Performance
Monitor), 519-520
workgroup needs,
determining, 57-59
**Networks command (Capture
menu), 536**
Networks dialog, 388
**New Backup Device command
(Server menu), 812**
**New Backup Device
dialog, 812**
**New Chart command (File
menu), 506**
**New Client Access License
dialog, 788, 792**
**New Database command (File
menu), 734, 816**
**New Database Device
dialog, 815**
**New Device command (File
menu), 815**
**New Global Group command
(User menu), 448**
**New Global Group
dialog, 448**
**New License command
(License menu), 792**
**New Local Group command
(User menu), 447**
New Local Group dialog, 447
**New Log Settings command
(File menu), 512**
New Share dialog, 610
**New User command (User
menu), 423**
New User dialog, 423
control options, 424-426
user accounts,
creating, 424-426

**NIC (network interface
card), 927**
client PCs, selection
guidelines, 150
diskless workstations, remote
boot clients, 151
features, 149-150
installing on Windows 95,
334-336
jumper configurable,
150-151
modifying settings in
Windows 95, 336-338
name brand versus
clone, 151-153
remote boot clients, 151
selecting active network
components, 149-152
servers, selecting, 151-152
software configurable,
150-151
non-domain servers
adding, 572-573
reasons for
installation, 572-573
**non-routable protocol,
NetBEUI, 113**
NonStop ServerWare, 51-52
**Noorda, Ray, role in feud with
Microsoft, 598**
normal backups
failed hard drive,
re-creating, 264-265
file backup types, 264-265
**Norton Utilities for Windows
NT, 520**
**NOS (network operating
system)**
integration feud between
Microsoft and Novell, 598
network protocol
differences, 598-599
Notify (Access Audit), 326
**Novell 16-bit ODI NetWare,
network client drivers,
339-341**
**Novell IPX, Multi-Protocol
Router, 31**
Novell NetWare 4.1, 19
**Novell NetWare
interoperability, 30-31**

NSLookup, 551
NT File System (NTFS), 458
NTBACKUP program
    Arcada Backup Exec,
        296-297
    backup information,
        displaying, 299-300
    configuring, 289-291
    drives, selecting, 292-294
    executing, 294-297
    files
        backing up, 291-297
        restoring, 297-300
    folders, selecting, 292-294
    media
        labeling, 291-292
        preparing, 291-292
    options, selecting, 294-297
NTBet
    NetBIOS Datagram, 530
    NetBIOS Name, 530
    NetBIOS Session, 530
NTFS (NT File System)
    converting FAT, 190
    features
        data compression,
            97-102
        fault-tolerance, 97-102
        localization with
            Unicode, 98-99
        multiple data
            streams, 98-99
        recoverability, 97-102
        security, 97-102
        support for fixed-disk
            drives, 97-102
    file access
      permissions, 468-469
        adding, 471-472
        modifying, 470-471
        removing, 470-471
        types, 469-470
        viewing, 470-471
    file fragmentation,
        minimizing, 520-521
    file permissions,
        overview, 468-469
    files, handling, 97-99
    folder access

permissions, 468-469
    adding, 476-477
    modifying, 474-477
    removing, 474-477
    types, 472-473
    viewing, 474-477
formatting, 199
MFT, 99-101
MFT attributes
    bitmap, 100-101
    data, 100-101
    extended, 101
    filename, 100-101
    index allocation,
        100-101
    index root, 100-101
    security descriptor,
        100-101
    standard, 100-101
    user-defined, 101-106
    volume
        information, 101
recoverable writing to
    file, 102
Windows NT Server,
    189-190
NWLink
    configuring, 348-350
    networking protocols, 117

O

Object File System (OFS),
    Microsoft Cairo, 89-91
Object Manager (OM)
    (Windows NT
    Executive), 94-95
object permissions, 928
obtaining
    Hardware Compatibility List
        (HCL), 95
        updates, 187
    Internet Information Server
        (IIS), SSL certificates,
        36-39
    Microsoft Index Server,
        37-39

Microsoft Proxy Server,
    37-39
network management,
    outside help, 80-81
SMNP service, TCP/IP
    statistics, 542-545
Windows Sockets, 646-647
ODBC data source
    connecting via IDC,
        750-752
    creating IDC files, 752
    Jet 3.0 databases,
        creating, 738-740
    logging, 729-747
    setting, 735-740
    specifying for logging,
        740-741
    SQL Server databases,
        creating, 736
ODBC SQL Server Setup
    dialog, 737
ODBC system database,
    creating, 735-740
ODIPKT
    packet driver support,
        647-648
    packet drivers,
        downloading, 647-648
off-site data storage
    accessibility, 281
    file backups, 281
    implementing, 281
OLE Automation server,
    39-40
one-step migration, 858-864
one-way trust
    relationships, 584-586
online UPS, 179-180
Open command (Registry
    menu), 320
open files
    backups strategy, 272-273
    file backups, 272-273
Open SMS Window
    dialog, 893
Open Systems
    Interconnection, see OSI
Open Web command (File
    menu), 770
Open Web dialog, 770

opening Remote
Registry, 324
operating systems (Windows
NT Server)
scalability, 28-29
summarizing features,
91-92
Operations menu command,
Hardware Setup, 292
Optimizer
analysis process, 852-854
Exchange Server installation,
reconfiguring, 852-854
executing in Exchange
Server, 851-854
optimizing
Exchange Server
performance, 846
Windows NT Server
application server,
521-526
file servers, 514-521
print servers, 514-521
Options command (Exchange
menu), 874
Options menu commands
Auto Refresh, 322
Change System
Settings, 385
Confirm on Delete, 322
Data From, 513
Font, 322
Read Only Mode, 322
Save Settings on Exit, 322
Oracle Express Server, 799
organizations and
intranets, 46-47
organizing file backups
disk storage, 270-271
rotation methods, 274-279
OS/2
networking protocols, 122
versus Windows
technology, 86-87
OSI (Open Systems
Interconnection)
seven-layer model
application layer,
110-111
data-link layer, 108-109
network layer, 109
physical layer, 108

presentation layer, 110
session layer, 110
transport layer, 109-110
versus Windows NT
layers, 111-112
outside help
consultants, 80-81
Microsoft Certified System
Engineer, 81
obtaining network
management, 80-81
resellers, 80-81
vendors, 80-81
Owner command (Security
menu), 322
Owner dialog, 498

P

package definition file
(Packages window),
898-899
Packages window
inventory packages,
898-899
package definition
file, 898-899
sharing packages, 898-899
System Management Server
Administrator, 897-899
workstation packages,
installing, 897-898
packet drivers, installing
(Windows for Workgroups
3.11), 647-652
packet switching, 61-64
packet-level encryption,
63-64
page fault, 928
page swapping, 525-526
paged pool, 928
pair count, unshielded twisted
pair cables, 144
Palindrome's Backup
Director, 280
Partition menu commands
Commit Changes
Now, 247
Create, 252
Create Stripe Set, 246

Restore, 250
Save, 250
partitioning fixed-disk
drives, 188-190, 199
passwords
authenticating (World Wide
Web server), 713-716
setting in domain
accounts, 443
paths, specifying, 430-431
PCI buses, 172-177
peer-to-peer
networking, 105-106, 333
Pentium floating-point
division bug, checking, 202
Pentium Pro servers, 168
per-seat licensing
advantages/
disadvantages, 780-781
License Manager, 789-794
versus per-server
licensing, 780-781
Per Seat Licensing dialog
box, 791
Per Seat licensing terms, 201
per-server licensing
advantages/
disadvantages, 780-781
License Manager, 789-794
versus per-seat
licensing 780-781
Per Server Licensing
dialog, 788
Per Server licensing
terms, 201
Per Server or Per Seat
Licensing dialog, 849
Performance Monitor
% Network Utilization
counter, 542
alerts
adding, 509-510
customizing, 510-511
setting, 508-511
viewing, 508-509
as network troubleshooting
tool, 541-545
chart objects, deleting, 507
charts
customizing, 507-508
displaying, 504-505
editing, 507

counters, 502-505
   Internet Information
     Server (IIS), 747-749
CPU usage,
  monitoring, 521-522
disk bottlenecks
   % Disk Time
     counter, 515
   Disk Queue Length
     counter, 515
   minimizing, 515-518
executing, 501-502
implementing in Web
  pages, 747-749
log files
   recording data, 511-514
   viewing, 513-514
memory usage,
  viewing, 522-526
network media speed,
  viewing, 519-520
network messages, 511
new chart, creating,
  505-506
object behavior, 502-505
remote machines,
  implementing, 504-505
scaling factors, 749
SMNP service,
  installing, 542-545
system statistics, 502-505
  charting, 505-508
TCP/IP networks,
  implementing, 545
virtual memory, 522-523
  viewing, 525-526
**Performance Monitor
command (Start
menu), 501**
**performance statistics,
viewing, 373**
permissions
  folder shares
   assigning, 467-468
   modifying, 466-468
   renaming, 467-468
  setting
   printers, 496-498
   SQL Enterprise
    Manager, 834-835
   Windows NT
    Registry, 325-327
  setting for dial-ins, 437

**Permissions command
(Security menu), 322**
**Permit Access On or Deny
Access On dialog, 723**
persistent object, 929
**Personal Address Book
(PAB), 844**
**Personal Information Store
(PST), 844**
**personal user profiles,
430-431**
**PERT (Program Evaluation
and Review Technique),
77-79**
physical layer (OSI), 108
**physical security on
networks, 59-64**
**physical topology,
cabling, 139-141**
ping command, 548
pipeline burst cache, 169
**placing domain
controllers, 582-584**
planning
  Exchange Server
   exchange accounts, 847
   installation, 844-851
  networks
   budget
    considerations, 74-76
   data communication
    technology, 69-70
   future growth, 72-74
   interoperability,
    124-126
   management needs,
    70-72
   user training, 76-77
  System Management Server
   installation, 886-888
  Web sites, 689-690
   Microsoft SiteBuilder
    Workshop, 690
plenum cabling, 145
**Point-to-Point Protocol
(PPP), 118**
**Point-to-Point Tunneling
Protocol,** *see* **PPTP**
Policies menu commands
  Account, 442
  Trust Relationships, 587

Policy Editor
  installing for Windows 95
   clients, 367-370
  remote usage,
   implementing, 371-373
POSIX.1 subsystem, 97
power protection issues
  blackouts, 178-179
  drops, 178-179
  servers, 178-179
  spikes, 178-179
  surges, 178-179
PPP Multilink, 654
**PPTP (Point-to-Point
Tunneling Protocol)**
  advantages over
   modems, 685-686
  IIS integration, 37-39
  implementing, 685-686
  Internet commerce, 37-39
  submission to Internet
   Engineering Task Force
   (IETF), 685-686
  virtual private network
   (VPN), creating, 37-39
  virtual private
   networks, 685-686
  Windows NT Server
   communication
   features, 654
**preemptive
multitasking, 658-659, 929**
preparing
  NTBACKUP program,
   media, 291-292
  Windows NT Server
   installation folder,
   195-197
presentation layer (OSI), 110
**pricing, Windows NT Server
strategies, 41-44**
Primary Domain Controller
  configuring, 570-571
  installing 192
  promoting Backup Domain
   Controller, 571-572
  role, 570-571
  Security Account Manager
   (SAM), 570-571
  selecting in Setup
   program, 201-202

primary key, 929
Primary Network Logon,
setting, 345-346
Primary Site Information
dialog, 892
primary site server, installing
(System Management
Server), 890-893
print gateway (Gateway
Service for NetWare)
configuring, 611-614
installing, 611-614
Print Operators group, 446
print servers,
optimizing, 514-521
Print Subtree command
(Registry menu), 320
Printer Auditing dialog, 497
Printer menu commands,
Connect Network
Printer, 394
Printer Permissions dialog,
410, 496
Printer Ports dialog, 407
Printer Setup command
(Registry menu), 320
printer sharing
Client for Microsoft
Networks, 356-357
Client for NetWare
Networks, 357-358
network clients, 356-358
Printername Properties sheet
Device Settings page, 498
General page, 491-498
Scheduling page, 492-498
Security page, 495-498
Sharing page, 494-498
printers
File and Print Services for
NetWare, 31
network servers versus
locally attached, 483-498
permissions, setting,
496-498
properties,
configuring, 491-498
selecting for Windows NT
Server, 190
shared resources,
configuring, 483-488
sharing on networks,
482-498

Printers-Network Connections
dialog box, 386
printing
server-based rendering, 29
Windows NT Server
features, 29
printing services (Macintosh
clients)
configuring, 406-412
troubleshooting, 411-412
procedures, viewing (SQL
Server), 826-827
Process Manager (PM)
(Windows NT
Executive), 94-95
processing client/server
messaging, 840-841
processors
asymmetric processing,
169-170
cache memory, sizing,
168-169
CISC, 167-168
Intel, 168
RISC, 167-168
selecting servers, 167-168
symmetric processing,
169-170
Program Groups window
(System Management Server
Administrator), 903
Programs menu commands
Administrative Tools,
246-259
Administrative
Wizards, 437
DHCP Manager, 637
Microsoft SQL Server, 807
Remote Access Admin,
668-669
SMS Administrator, 893
SQL Enterprise
Manager, 808
SQL Security Manager, 831
Windows NT
Diagnostics, 317-318
WINS Manager, 641
project management software,
utilizing, 77-79
Promote to Primary Domain
Controller command
(Computer menu), 572

promoting Backup Domain
Controller to Primary
Domain Controller,
571-572
Propagate NetWare Accounts
to Windows NT Domain,
628
Properties command
(Exchange menu), 874
Properties command (User
menu), 427
Properties menu command,
Options, 874
property sheets
ActiveX Controls, 22
Microsoft Cairo, 22
Windows NT Server, 22
protected subsystem, 929
protocol analyzers
LANalyzer for
Windows, 534
Network General's Expert
Sniffer, 534
troubleshooting network
protocols, 533-535
protocol stack, 930
protocols
binding order,
modifying, 519
client PCs, 119
networks, eliminating, 518
network
interoperability, 124-126
selecting in Setup
program, 204
selection criteria, 126
providing Windows NT Server
identification, 191
names, 191
proxy address support
(Exchange Server), 842
Proxy Server, 688-689
see also, Microsoft Proxy
Server
proxy servers on
networks, 125-126
Pulse, 574
PulseConcurrency, 574
purchasing
client access licenses,
781-782

Exchange Server
licenses,   783-784
file backups,   273
server licenses for Microsoft
BackOffice,   781-782
SNA Server licenses,
784-785
SQL Server licenses,
782-783
System Management Server
licenses,   784
Windows NT Server
licenses,   782

Q

QIC (quarter-inch cartridge)
drives
proposed drive
standards,   284-285
sizes
DC-600,   284-285
DC-2000,   284-285
QIC-3010,   284-285
QIC-3020,   284-285
TR-1,   285
TR-2,   285
TR-3,   285
TR-4,   285
QIC-3010 (QIC drives),
284-285
QIC-3020 (QIC drives),
284-285
quality grades (cabling)
cable selection
criteria,   145-146
Electronic Industry
Association/Telephone
Industry,   145-146
quantifying
RAID, lost data,   233-234
RAID 0,   220-222
Quarter-Inch Cartridge
Standards Committee
284-285
quarter-inch cartridges,
see QIC

queries
executing
SQL Enterprise
Manager,   827-828
System Management
Server Administrator,
901-903
parameters, specifying,   752
results
formatting with SQL
Server Web
Assistant,   742-747
HTML code,
displaying,   756-757
writing,   741-742
Queries window (System
Management Server
Administrator),   900-903
Query dialog,   743
Query Expression Properties
dialog,   902
Query Properties dialog,   902
Query Value (Access
Audit),   326
querying logging table
(SQL Server),   732-734
queuing theory,   222

R

RAID (Redundant Array of
Inexpensive Disks),   930
as server option,   238-239
automatic rebuilds,
233-234
defined by the University
of California at Berkeley,
218-219
drive configurations,
creating,   250-259
external enclosures,
241-243
dumb external
arrays,   241-243
smart external
arrays,   241-243

hardware,
implementing,   238-243
levels,   218-219
lost data, quantifying,
233-234
non-standard levels
RAID 6,   231-232
RAID 7,   231-232
options in Windows NT
Server,   244
overview,   217-218
product features
automatic rebuild,
236-238
disk drive
selection,   236-238
dual loading power
supplies,   237-238
hot pluggable power
supplies,   237-238
hot spare disks,   236-238
hot swappable
disks,   236-238
management
software,   238
role of RAID Advisory Board
(RAB),   219
SCSI host adapter,
mirroring,   239-240
sizing arrays,   233-234
software for Windows NT
Server,   243-245
stacked
implementation,   232-233
summary
recommendations,
259-260
upgrading server,   239-240
RAID 0
data chunk size,   220-222
implementation
criteria,   219-222, 235
primary applications,   222
queuing theory,   222
stripe set, creating,   246-259
striping,   220-222
Windows NT Server
option,   244
zero-redundancy array
option,   219-222

RAID 1
advantages/
   disadvantages, 222-226
common in
   mainframes, 224-226
defined, 222-226
disk drive usage, 222-226
duplexing, 222-226
implementation
   criteria, 235
mirror sets, creating,
   252-259
mirroring, 222-226
read performance, 224-226
   assigned cylinder
      scheduling, 225
   circular queue, 224-226
   geometric cylinder
      scheduling, 225-226
   regional cylinder
      scheduling, 225-226
   round-robin
      scheduling, 224-226
Windows NT Server
   option, 244
write performance, 225-226
RAID 2
defined, 226
implementation
   criteria, 226
RAID 3
byte striping with dedicated
   parity disks, 226-228
defined, 226-228
implementation
   criteria, 226-228, 235
long sequential disk
   accesses, 226-228
RAID 4
decoupled disk drives, 228
defined, 228
implementation
   criteria, 228
RAID 5
caching data, 230-231
dedicated controller card
   Adaptec AAA-130 host
      adapter, 240-241
   Adaptec AAC-330 host
      adapter, 240-241
   adding, 240-241

defined, 228-231
implementation
   criteria, 228-231, 235
read performance, 229-231
sector striping with
   distributed parity,
   228-231
stripe sets, creating,
   256-259
transaction
   processing, 230-231
Windows NT Server
   option, 244
write performance, 229-231
   two-phase commit
      process, 230-231
RAID 6
defined, 231-232
implementation
   criteria, 231-232
non-standard RAID
   levels, 231-232
RAID 7
defined, 231-232
implementation
   criteria, 231-232
non-standard RAID
   levels, 231-232
RAID Advisory Board (RAB)
committees, 219
development of RAID
   standards, 219
product certification, 219
**RAID Advisory Board Web
site, 219**
raising exceptions, 930
RAM (random access memory)
domain controllers, 584
minimum requirements for
   servers, 171-172
**RAS (Remote Access
Service), 205**
configuring for Windows NT
   Server, 659-669
external modems,
   installing, 660-665
internal modems,
   installing, 660-665
monitoring connections
   (Remote Access Admin
   application), 683-685

Point-to-Point Protocol
   (PPP), 118
PPTP, 685-686
senders, 911
Serial Line Internet Protocol
   (SLIP), 118-119
Windows NT Server
   modem configuration,
      662-665
   networking
      protocols, 118
RAS architecture
external ISDN
   adapters, 656-658
internal ISDN
   adapters, 656-658
ISDN Ethernet
   adapters, 656-658
ISDN routers, 656-658
multiple external
   modem, 655-658
multiple internal
   modems, 655-658
selecting, 655-658
single internal
   modems, 655-658
**RAS Multilink Channel
Aggregation, 38-39**
**RAS Server TCP/IP
Configuration dialog, 667**
**RDBMS (relational database
management systems)**
data mart, 799
data warehousing, 799
departmental, 797-799
enterprise, 797-799
scalability, 29
SQL Server market
   share, 797-799
transaction recovery,
   implementing, 101-102
**Read Control (Access
Audit), 327**
**Read Only Mode command
(Options menu), 322**
read performance
RAID 1, 224-226
RAID 5, 229-231
**recommending media access
methods, 137-138**

reconfiguring Optimizer
(Exchange Server), 852-854
recording data to log files
(Performance
Monitor), 511-514
re-creating
copy backups, 265
normal backups, 264-265
redirector, 930
Reduced Instruction Set
Computer, *see* RISC
processors
redundant array of
inexpensive disks, *see* RAID
referential integrity, 930
Refresh All command (View
menu), 321
Refresh command (View
menu), 321
REG_BINARY (Windows NT
Registry data type),
308-309
REG_DWORD (Windows NT
Registry data type),
308-309
REG_EXPAND_SZ (Windows
NT Registry data type),
308-309
REG_MULTI_SZ (Windows NT
Registry data type),
308-309
REG_SZ (Windows NT Registry
data type), 308-309
regional cylinder scheduling,
RAID 1 read
performance, 225-226
Register Server command
(Server menu), 808
Register Server dialog, 808
registering servers (SQL
Enterprise Manager),
808-811
Registry Editor
keys, 318-320
access, restricting,
325-327
menu commands, 320-322
remote usage,
implementing, 372-373
value entries, 318-320

Registry Key Auditing
dialog, 326
Registry Key Permissions
dialog, 325
Registry menu commands
Close, 320
Connect Network
Registry, 324, 372
Exit, 320
Load Hive, 320
Open, 320
Print Subtree, 320
Printer Setup, 320
Restore, 320
Restore Key, 318
Save Key, 318, 320
Save Subtree As, 320
Select Computer, 320
Unload Hive, 320
Registry values, modifying
in Backup Domain
Controllers, 574-575
regulating TCP/IP, 113-116
Relational Database
Management Systems, *see*
RDBMS
Remote Access Admin
application
client access, granting,
668-669
RAS connections,
monitoring, 683-685
Remote Access Admin
command (Programs
menu), 668-669
Remote Access Permissions
dialog, 668
Remote Access Services,
see RAS
Remote Access Setup dialog
box, 665
remote boot client NICs, 151
remote clients
connecting via Net
Watcher, 373-376
shared folders
adding, 374-376
removing, 374-376

Remote Control Agent,
launching (System
Management Server),
907-909
remote control capacity
(System Management
Server), 882-883
remote domains, 559-560
remote editing in Windows
NT Registry, 323-324
remote machines, 504-505
remote management
administration, 370-371
administration privileges,
granting, 370-371
enabling with Windows 95
clients, 370-375
user-level security, 370-371
remote offices, 582
remote procedure calls,
102-105, 843-844
distributed
computing, 102-105
executing, 102-105
library function, 104-105
named pipes, 104-105
RPC client runtime,
104-105
RPC server runtime,
104-105
server function, 104-105
Remote Program Load (RPL)
diskless clients, 28
functions, 28
Remote Registry,
opening, 324
Remote Server Administration
functions,
27-28
remote server shares,
virtualizing (World Wide
Web server), 719-720
remote usage
implementing
Net Watcher, 373-374
Policy Editor, 371-373
registry Editor, 372-373
System Monitor, 373
performance statistics,
viewing, 373

Remoteboot Service, 205
removing
folder shares, 460-464
network clients, 341
NTFS
file access
permissions, 470-471
folder access
permissions, 474-477
shared folders, 374-376
renaming
domains, 579-580
folder share
permissions, 467-468
My Computer icon, 21
Network Neighborhood, 21
Repair Disk Utility
dialog, 211
repair option, selecting (Setup
program), 197-198
repairing Windows NT Server
installation, 213-215
repeaters, selecting, 152-153
replacing networks, existing
infrastructure, 68-69
replicating
databases, 478
folders, 477-478
logon scripts, 478
Replication Configuration
dialog, 789
replication support (Exchange
Server), 843
replication user,
creating, 478
Replication Governor, 574
Replicator group, 446
Request For Comments (RFCs)
downloading, 632
Internet Engineering Task
Force (IETF), 113-116
supported in Windows NT
Server, 632-634
resellers, outside help, 80-81
resolving IP addresses,
354-355
restarting Windows NT
Server, 212
Restore command (Partition
menu), 250

Restore command (Registry
menu), 320
Restore Information
dialog, 298
Restore Key command
(Registry menu), 318
Restore Progress dialog, 813
restoring
differential backups,
267-268
incremental backups
failed disk drives,
265-267
failed hard drives,
265-267
NTBACKUP program
files, 297-300
restricting
Registry keys, access,
325-327
workstation logon
privileges, 435-436
retrieving documents (Gopher
server), 705
RFC 1001, NetBT
protocol, 529-533
RFC 1002, NetBT
protocol, 529-533
RG-62 coax cable, 141-142
ring topology, LAN
cabling, 140-141
RIP for Internet
Protocol, 205
RIP for NWLink, 205
RISC processors,
selecting, 167-168
rollback, 931
root domain, 699-700
rotation methods
four-tape, 274-276
10-tape, 276
21-tape, 277-278
alternate 10-tape, 276-277
grandfather-father-son
method, 277-278
organizing file
backups, 274-279
Tower of Hanoi, 278-279
round-robin scheduling,
RAID 1 read performance,
224-226

routable protocols
IPX/SPX, 117
TCP/IP, 114-116
route command, 548
router-based encryption,
63-64
routers
identifying problems with
connectivity, 554
network layers, 156-157
networks, 125-126
selecting active network
components, 156-157
versus bridges, 157
routing
IP addresses, 115-116
troubleshooting on
networks, 557
Routing Internet Protocol
(RIP), 31
RPC client runtime, 104-105
RPC Configuration, 204
RPC server runtime, 104-105
RPC support for Banyan, 205
Run command (Start
menu), 211
Run dialog, 417
Run Task command (File
menu), 747

S

SAM (Security Account
Manager), 310-311
SAMBA, 644
SAP Agent, 205
Save command (Partition
menu), 250
Save Key command (Registry
menu), 318-320
Save Settings on Exit
command (Options
menu), 322
Save Subtree As command
(Registry menu), 320
saving drive
configurations, 250-259

scalability
  relational database
    management systems
    (RDBMSs), 29
  symmetrical
    multiprocessing, 28-29
scalable server systems
  Amdahl Corporation, 52
  Compaq Computers, 52
  Digital Equipment
    Corporation, 51
  Tandem Computers, 51-52
  Windows NT Server, 50-52
Scheduled Tasks command
  (Server menu), 747, 824
scheduling database
  tasks, 824-825
Scheduling page (*Printername*
  Properties sheet), 492-498
SCSI bus termination,
  174-175
SCSI drives
  asynchronous, 173-174
  disk subsystems, 172-174
  selecting, 172-174
  synchronous, 173-174
  versus EIDE drives for
    servers, 174
SCSI host adapters
  Always IN-2000, 188
  Data Technology
    Corporation 3290, 188
  driver disks, hardware, 188
  Maynard 16-bit SCSI
    Adapter, 188
  MediaVision Pro Audio
    Spectrum-16, 188
  mirroring, 239-240
  Trantor T-128, T-130B, 188
  UltraStor 124f EISA Disk
    Array Controller, 188
Search for Help command
  (Help menu), 322
Search Server, 688-689
sector striping, RAID 5,
  228-231
securing Internet
  commerce, 37-39
security
  Apple User Authentication
    Module (UAM), 403-404
  application-level
    encryption, 62-64

database guidelines,
  757-758
domain overview, 567-580
establishing on
  networks, 59-64
firewalls on networks,
  63-64
NTFS feature, 97-99
packet switching on
  networks, 61-64
packet-level encryption
  on networks, 63-64
PPTP, 37-39
router-based encryption
  on networks, 63-64
Windows NT Registry,
  324-328
Security Account Manager,
  synchronizing domains
  manually, 573-574
Security Account Manager
  (SAM)
  primary domain
    controller, 570-571
Security command (Log
  menu), 327
security identifiers, Windows
  NT Server, 569
Security menu commands
  Auditing, 322
  Owner, 322
  Permissions, 322
Security page (*Printername*
  Properties sheet), 495-498
Security Reference Monitor
  (SRM) (Windows NT
  Executive), 93-95
Select Capture Network
  dialog, 536
Select Columns command
  (View menu), 23
Select Components
  dialog, 203
Select Computer command
  (Registry menu), 320
Select Computer dialog, 505
Select Domain command
  (User menu), 420
Select Domain dialog, 420
Select Network Adapters
  dialog, 334

Select Network Component
  Type dialog, 334
Select Network Protocol
  dialog, 395
Select Network Service
  dialog, 401, 536, 607
Select OEM Option
  dialog, 615
Select Users command (Users
  menu), 427
Select Users dialog box, 427
selecting
  active network
    components, 149-163
    bridges, 155-156
    NICs, 149-152
    routers, 156-157
  backup hardware, 283-288
  CISC processors, 167-168
  coaxial cable, 142
  consultants for network
    management, 81
  dial-up networking
    architecture, 655-658
  disk drives, RAID, 236-238
  file backups
    tape drives, 271-272
    types, 268-270
  Gateway Service for
    NetWare, preferred
    NetWare server, 609
  Group Management Wizard,
    local versus global
    groups, 452-453
  hubs
    stackable, 154
    stand-alone, 153-154
  Intel processors, 168
  ISP, 691
  media access method,
    129-130
  network management
    vendors, 83
  networking protocols, 126
  network servers, 164-165
  NICs
    client PCs, 150
    servers, 151-152
  NTBACKUP program
    drives, 292-294
    folders, 292-294
    options, 294-297

protocols, 126
RAID options, summary recommendations, 259-260
RAS architecture, 655-658
repeaters, 152-153
RISC processors, 167-168
SCSI drives, 172-174
servers
  bus types, 172-177
  components, 165-167
  disk controllers, 175-177
  disk subsystems, 172-177
  processors, 167-168
Setup program
  Backup Domain Controllers, 201-202
  installation option, 197-198
  network services, 204-205
  Primary Domain Controllers, 201-202
  protocols, 204
  repair option, 197-198
  stand-alone servers, 201-202
Token Ring, 137-138
UPS, 180-181
User Manager for Domains, new domain, 420
Windows NT Server
  CD-ROM drives, 190
  network adapters, 190-191
  printers, 190
Send Message command (Computer menu), 572
senders
communicating (System Management Server), 911
types
  LAN, 911
  RAS, 911
  SNA, 911
Serial Line Internet Protocol (SLIP), 118-119
Server Based Setup dialog, 359, 362

server farms, 582-584
server function, 104-105
server licenses, Microsoft BackOffice, 781-782
Server Manager functions, 27-28
Server menu commands
  Add Computer to Domain, 577
  New Backup Device, 812
  Register Server, 808
  Scheduled Tasks, 747, 824
Server Message Blocks (SMBs), 527
server NICs
  processor usage, 151-152
  selecting, 151-152
  speed requirements, 151-152
Server Operators group, 446
Server Optimizer, *see* **Optimizer**
Server Type dialog, 201
server usability, 20-26
  Administrative Wizards, 23-26
  Task Manager, 23
  Windows 95 user interface, 20-21
  Windows Explorer, 22
server-based setup program, installing, 359-364
ServerNet cluster, 51-52
servers
  10-tape rotation method, 276
  21-tape rotation method, 277-278
  30-pin SIMM packages, 170
  72-pin SIMM packages, 170
  alternate 10-tape rotation method, 276-277
  asymmetric processing, 169-170
  bus types, selecting, 172-177
  clustering, 177
  components, selecting, 165-167
  conforming, Hardware Compatibility List (HCL), 165

  connecting via RAS Multilink Channel Aggregation, 38-39
  data communication security, 60-64
  disk controllers, selecting, 175-177
  disk subsystems, selecting, 172-177
  dynamic database access, 750
  EIDE versus SCSI drives, 174
  eight-processor, 29
  enterprise site topology (System Management Server), 886-887
  file backups, selection criteria, 268-270
  four-processor, 29
  four-tape rotation method, 274-276
  GM Access Common Dealership Environment (CDE), 43-44
  hardware RAID, upgrading, 239-240
  hardware, specifying, 163-182
  Hardware Compatibility List (HCL), obtaining, 165
  host adapters, 175-177
  identifying computer name, 201
  load balancing, 518
  local service, 165
  memory, configuring, 171-172
  memory requirements, determining, 170-172
  Pentium Pro processor, 168
  Performance Monitor scaling factors, 749
  physical security, 59-64
  power protection issues, 178-179
  processors, selecting, 167-168
  protocol analyzers, troubleshooting, 533-535
  RAID option, 238-239

RAM minimum
    requirements,   171-172
registering with SQL
    Enterprise Manager,
    808-811
scalability,   28-29
scalability through
    clustering,   50-52
SCSI bus termination,
    174-175
SCSI drives,   172-174
selecting
    networks,   164-165
    NICs,   151-152
symmetric processing,
    169-170
System Management Server,
    minimum
    specifications,   884-885
system policies,
    setting,   366-369
System Policy Editor
    executing,   368-369
    installng,   367-369
Tower of Hanoi rotation
    method,   278-279
trusted domains,
    expanding,   29
types
    departmental,   164
    enterprise,   164
    high-end,   164-167
    workgroup,   164
UPS,   178-182
user profiles, setting,
    364-366
warranties,   165
Windows 95 clients,
    installing,   359-364
Windows NT networking
    processes,   105-106
service accounts, creating
(System Management
Server),   888-889
Service page options,
configuring (World Wide
Web server),   713-716
service prefix,   699

Services for Macintosh,   205
AppleTalk protocol,
    enabling,   401-403
MacFile Tools
    attributes,   404-405
    files,   404-405
    users,   404-405
    volumes,   404-405
Windows NT Server,
    installing,   400-403
Services Page (Windows
Diagnostics Tool),   31-33
session layer (OSI),   110
Set Up Machine dialog,   362
Set Value (Access Audit),   326
setting
Access Control Page
    share level access
        control,   342-343
    user level access
        control,   343
archive bits,   264
databases, transaction
    logging,   828-830
domain accounts,
    passwords,   443
domains, account lockout
    policy,   444
FTP Server service
    options,   723-725
Gopher server service
    options,   725-727
Internet Information Server
    (IIS)
    audit options,   713-727
    logging options,
        713-727
multiple user accounts,
    logon hours,   434-435
network clients,   345-346
ODBC data sources,
    735-740
Performance Monitor
    alerts,   508-511
printer permissions,
    496-498
servers
    system policies,   366-369
    user profiles,   364-366

SQL Enterprise Manager
    permissions,   834-835
TCP/IP
    low-level
        parameters,   353-354
    WINS configuration
        page,   352
user account logon
    scripts,   431-433
User Profile Editor
    profiles,   26-28
user dial-in
    permissions,   437
Windows 3.1 clients,
    network drivers,   385-386
Windows NT Registry
    permissions,   325-327
Windows NT Server
    administrator
        password,   202
    Macintosh
        printers,   406-412
    time/date,   209-210
World Wide Web server,
    logging options,   713-723
settings
modifying network
    adapters,   336-338
viewing network
    adapters,   336-338
Windows NT Registry,
    304-305
Settings for COMx
dialog,   484
setup boot disks
creating
    Windows NT
        Server,   194-195
Setup Complete dialog,   766
Setup program
Backup Domain Controllers,
    Selecting,   201-202
concluding,   209
executing in Windows NT
    Server,   194
files, copying,   200-201
fixed-disk drives,
    configuring,   199-200
install folder,
    specifying,   199-200

installation folder,
  executing, 196
installation option,
  selecting, 197-198
launching, 847-851
mass-storage driver,
  detecting, 198
network adapters,
  configuring, 203
network bindings,
  confirming, 208
network connection,
  specifying, 203
network installation,
  executing, 203-208
network services,
  selecting, 204-208
Pentium floating-point
  division bug,
  checking, 202
Primary Domain Controllers,
  selecting, 201-202
protocols, selecting, 204
repair option,
  selecting, 197-198
stand-alone servers,
  selecting, 201-202
system information,
  confirming, 199
seven-layer model (OSI)
  application layer, 110-111
  data-link layer, 108-109
  network layer, 109
  physical layer, 108
  presentation layer, 110
  session layer, 110
  transport layer, 109-110
share-level access control,
  setting (Access Control
  Page), 342-343
Share Network Client
  Installation Files
  dialog, 378
share permissions
  adding, 461-464
  modifying, 461-464
    folder shares, 466-468
  overview, 460-461
shared application
  memory, 931

shared files
  Microsoft Mail
    approach, 838-839
  Windows 95 Service Pack 1,
    updating, 363-364
shared folders
  adding remote clients,
    374-376
  removing remote
    clients, 374-376
Shared Folders dialog, 374
shared resources
  configuring
    locally attached server
      printers, 483-488
    network printer
      servers, 488-498
    printers, 483-488
shares, activating (Gateway
  Service for NetWare),
  609-611
sharing
  networks, printers on,
    482-498
  UNIX, Windows NT
    files, 642-644
sharing packages (Packages
  window), 898
sharing page (*Printername*
  Properties sheet), 494-498
sheath material (cables)
  plenum cabling, 145
  polyvinyl chloride, 145
  unshielded twisted pair
    cables, 145
shielded twisted pair
  cables, 142-143
Show Database command
  (Mapping menu), 531
SIMM (Single Inline Memory
  Module)
  memory type, 170-172
  sockets, 171-172
  30-pin packages, 170-172
  72-pin packages, 170-172
Simple Network Management
  Protocol, *see* SMNP
simultaneous network
  connections, 332-333
Single Domain model,
  588-589

Single Inline Memory Module,
  see SIMM
single internal modem,
  655-658
Single Master model, 589
single network logons,
  332-333
singly attached stations, Fiber
  Distributed Data Interface
  (FDDI), 135-136
site hieracrchy, displaying
  (Sites window), 895
Site Server, 887-888
Site Services Account
  dialog, 850
sites
  Amdahl Corporation, 52
  Arcada, 296
  BHS Software, 553
  communicating with System
    Management Server, 911
  Compaq Computers, 52
  Datamation, 44
  Digital Equipment
    Corporation, 51
  Executive Software, 520
  Microsoft, 689
  Network General, 534
  RAID Advisory Board, 219
  Softway, 92
  Tandem Computers, 52
  TechWeb, 44
  VeriSign, 36
Sites window
  properties, 895-897
  site hierarchy,
    displaying, 895
  System Management Server
    Administrator, 895-897
sizing
  arrays for RAID, 233-234
  processors, cache
    memory, 168-169
  UPS, 181-182
Small Computer System
  Interface, see SCSI
small-office/home-office
  (SOHO) markets, 21
smart external arrays,
  RAID, 241-243

SMBTrace, 551
SMS Administrator command (Programs menu), 893
SMS Administrator Login dialog, 893
SNA Server
  licensing fees, 784-785
  Microsoft BackOffice, bundled components, 778-779
  senders, 911
SNMP service (Simple Network Management Protocol), 205
  installing Performance Monitor, 542-545
  TCP/IP statistics, obtaining, 542-545
software
  automatic installation for clients (System Management Server), 905
  Exchange Server requirements, 846
  future file backup technology, 300
  manual installation for clients (System Management Server), 904-905
  minimum configuration, establishing, 82
  solutions for disk bottlenecks, 517-518
  SQL Server requirements, 799-800
  System Management Server inventoring, 883
    Inventory Agent, 905-907
  Windows NT Server, RAID, 243-245
software configurable NICs, 150-151
software RAID versus hardware RAID, 243-245
Softway Web site, 92
source code, 932
Source Path dialog, 359
spanning multiple network protocols, 597

Spanning Tree Algorithm (STA), 156
Special Directory Access dialog, 475
Special File Access dialog, 475
specifying
  IDC query parameters, 752
  ODBC data source for logging, 740-741
  server hardware, 163-182
  Setup program
    install folder, 199-200
    network connection, 203
  SQL Server, backup tape devices, 812-814
  TCP/IP gateway, 352-353
  user profiles
    home folders, 431-433
    paths, 430-431
  Windows NT Server
    company name, 201
    user name, 201
spikes, power protection issues, 178-179
Split command (View menu), 321
SQL Enterprise Manager
  functions, 807
  installing, 807-808
  logins, viewing, 834-835
  permissions, setting, 834-835
  queries, executing, 827-828
  servers, registering, 808-811
SQL Enterprise Manager command (Programs menu), 808
SQL Query Tool command (Tools menu), 827
SQL Security Manager, group account configurations, 831-833
SQL Security Manager command (Programs menu), 831
SQL Server
  backup tape device,
    adding, 812-814
    specifying, 812-814
    testing, 812-814

creating
  logging database, 730-736
  logging table, 731-734
database devices, creating, 814-817
database permissions, establishing, 830-831
database properties, modifying, 821-825
databases
  adding indexes, 823-825
  executing tasks, 823-825
  integrated security, 830-831
  mixed security, 830-831
  standard security, 830-831
distribution CD-ROM, installing, 800-806
hardware requirements, 799-800
installing, 799-807
launching, 806-807
licensing fees, 782-783, 798-799
Microsoft BackOffice, bundled components, 778-779
Microsoft business strategy, 798-799
querying logging table, 732-734
RDBMS market share, 797-799
scheduling tasks for databases, 824-825
software requirements, 799-800
standard stored procedure, viewing, 826-827
table structures, importing, 817-821
transaction logging, configuring, 828-830
triggers, viewing, 825-826
user databases, adding, 814-830
SQL Server Web Assistant
  activity reports, distributing, 742-747
  generating test copy of activity reports, 746-747

query results,
formatting, 742-747
Web pages, creating,
742-747
SSL (Secure Sockets Layer)
certificates, obtaining,
36-39
stackable hubs,
selecting, 154
stacked RAID
benefits, 232-233
defined, 232-233
implementation
criteria, 235
stand-alone hubs,
selecting, 153-154
stand-alone servers, selecting
(Setup program), 201-202
standard security (SQL
Server), 830-831
standard stored procedures,
viewing (SQL Server),
826-827
standard volumes, creating
mirrors, 255-256
standby UPS, 179-180
star topology, LAN
cabling, 139-141
Start Capture button (Network
Monitor), 34
Start Copying Files
dialog, 766
Start menu commands
Performance Monitor, 501
Run, 211
Start Up Settings dialog, 393
static mapping in remote
domains, 559-560
Static Mappings command
(Mappings menu), 559
static rebuild option,
RAID, 238
Stop and View command
(Capture menu), 537
Stop Capture and View button
(Network Monitor), 34
store-and-forward
processing, 160-161
Exchange Server replication
support, 843
stored procedure, 932

Stored Procedures command
(Manage menu), 826
storing file backups
off-site, 281
strategies
marketing Windows NT
Server, 41-44
pricing Windows NT
Server, 41-44
streams
lower layer, 118-119
upper layer, 118-119
Windows NT Server
networking
protocols, 118-119
String command (Edit
menu), 321
stripe sets, creating
RAID 0, 246-259
RAID 5, 256-259
striping
queuing theory, 222
RAID 0, 220-222
subkeys
(HKEY_LOCAL_MACHINE\
HARDWARE), 314
subkeys (Windows NT
Registry), 307
subnet masks, 932
IP addresses, 115-116
SunSoft PC-NFS, 339-341
surges, power protection
issues, 178-179
symmetric processing,
169-170
symmetrical multiprocessing,
658-659
four-Pentium Pro
motherboard, 29
multithreading, 29
scalability, 28-29
Synchronization Manager,
executing, 625-630
synchronization process,
domain overview, 573
Synchronize Entire Domain
command (Computer
menu), 579
synchronizing domains
manually (Security Account
Manager), 573-574
synchronous cache, 169

synchronous I/O, 932
synchronous SCSI, 173-174
system booting, 245
System Data Sources
dialog, 736-737
system failures, recoverable
writing to file, 102
system information,
confirming (Setup
program), 199
system jobs, creating (Jobs
window), 899-900
System Management Server
(SMS)
automatic client software
installation, 905
data analysis,
executing, 884
Distribution Server,
887-888
enterprise site
topology, 886-887
features, 882
hardware inventory, 883
Help Desk functions,
launching, 907-909
Helper Server, 888
installation planning,
886-888
installation
requirements, 888
interaction with
NetWare, 911-912
Inventory Agent, 905-907
licensing fees, 784
Logon Server, 887-888
manual client software
installation, 904-905
Microsoft BackOffice,
bundled
components, 778-779
minimum server
specifications, 884-885
Network Monitor,
launching, 909-910
network protocol
analysis, 883
primary site server,
installing, 890-893
Remote Control Agent,
launching, 907-909

remote control
  capacity, 882-883
senders,
  communicating, 911
service accounts,
  creating, 888-889
Site Server, 887-888
sites, communicating, 911
software inventory, 883
supported clients, 885-886
supported networks, 885
targeted software
  installation, 883
troubleshooting, 882-883
WAN protocols, 885
System Management Server
Administrator
  Alerts window, 903
  Events window, 904
  Jobs window, 899-900
  launching, 893-895
  Machine Groups
    window, 903
  Packages window, 897-899
  Program Groups
    window, 903
  queries, executing, 901-903
  Queries window, 900-903
  Site Groups window, 903
  Sites window, 895-897
  windows overview,
    894-895
System Monitor
  launching, 373
  remote usage,
    implementing, 373
System Network Architecture
(SNA), IBM AS/400, 124
system partitions,
converting, 190
System Policy Editor
  executing servers, 366-369
  functions, 26-28
  installing on servers,
    367-369
  Policy mode, 368-369
  Registry mode, 368-369
system statistics, charting
(Performance
Monitor), 505-508

T

T-1 connections
  connection speed, 697-698
  implementation
    criteria, 697-698
  Internet connection
    types, 697-698
T-3 connections
  connection speed, 697-698
  implementation
    criteria, 697-698
  Internet connection
    types, 697-698
table structures, importing
(SQL Server), 817-821
Tables command (Manage
menu), 732
tag files, creating (Gopher
server), 725-727
Tandem Computers
  NonStop ServerWare, 51-52
  scalable server systems,
    51-52
  ServerNet cluster, 51-52
  Web site, 52
tape drives
  backup hardware, 284-287
  backup media capacities to
    server size, 273
  digital linear tape, 286
  helical scan tapes, 286-287
  QIC drives, 284-285
  selecting file backups,
    271-272
TAPI (Telephony Application
Programming Interface)
  basic architecture, 658-659
  communication services,
    implementing, 40-41
  compatibility, 40-41
  components, 40-41
  marshaling layer, 40-41
  multithreaded
    operations, 658-659
  preemptive
    multitasking, 658-659
  symmetrical
    multiprocessing, 658-659

thunking layer, 40-41
  Windows NT Server
    communication
    features, 654
  Windows Open Services
    Architecture, 654
targeted software installation
(System Management Server)
  groups, 883
  users, 883
Task History dialog, 824
Task Manager
  applications,
    controlling, 23
  launching, 23
tasks (SQL Server)
  executing in
    databases, 823-825
  scheduling in
    databases, 824-825
TCP/IP (Transmission Control
Protocol/Internet
Protocol), 599
  32-bit protocol, installing for
    Windows for Workgroups
    3.11 clients, 388-391
  clients, binding, 353
  configuring network
    protocols, 351-356
  DNS configuration page,
    configuring, 354-355
  gateway, specifying,
    352-353
  implementing on
    Performance
    Monitor, 545
  installing to Windows NT
    Workstation 4.0 clients,
    395-398
  installing support for
    Windows for Workgroups
    3.11, 646-647
  intranets, 46-47
  IP addresses, 114-116
    allocating, 351-352
  low-level parameters,
    setting, 353-354
  Multi-Protocol Router, 31
  obtaining statistics via SNMP
    service, 542-545

regulating, Internet
Engineering Task Force
(IETF), 113-116
routable protocol, 114-116
single Internet
protocol, 123
standards, Internet
Engineering Task Force
(IETF), 632-633
troubleshooting, 529-533
Windows NT Server
networking
protocols, 113-116
Windows NT Server
diagnostic tools, 632-633
Windows NT Server
integration, 30-31
Windows NT Server
utilities, 632-633
WINS configuration page,
setting, 352
TCP/IP Setup dialog, 395
TechWeb Web site, 44
Telephony Application
Programming Interface,
see TAPI
Test menu commands, Load
Simulation Parameters, 856
Test Topology command
(Configuration menu), 855
Test Topology dialog, 855
testing
Internet Information Server
(IIS) installation, 711-713
SQL Server backup tape
devices, 812-814
Windows 95 clients, dial-up
networking, 670-676
Windows NT clients, dial-up
networking, 676-683
Thinking Machines Inc., 226
thunking layer, 40-41
Tile command (Window
menu), 322
Time Window command (Edit
menu), 514
time/date, setting (Windows
NT Server), 209-210
Tip of the Day dialog
box, 808

Token Ring, 933
data transmission
process, 130-132
features, 130-132
IEEE 802.5 series, 131-132
media access
methods, 130-132
selection criteria, 137-138
Tools menu commands
Format, 248
Map Network Drive, 399
SQL Query Tool, 827
topologies
bus, 139-141
electrical, 139-141
logical, 139-141
networks, 139-141
physical, 139-141
ring, 140-141
star, 139-141
Tower of Hanoi rotation
method, 278-279
TR-1 (QIC drives), 285
TR-2 (QIC drives), 285
TR-3 (QIC drives), 285
TR-4 (QIC drives), 285
tracert command, 549
transaction logging,
configuring (SQL
Server), 828-830
transaction processing,
RAID 5, 230-231
transaction recovery,
implementing
RDBMS, 101-102
transferring binary files (FTP
Server), 703-705
translating IP addresses
(DNS), 30-31
Transmission Control
Protocol/Internet Protocol,
see TCP/IP
Transport Driver Interface
(TDI), 111-112
transport layer (OSI),
109-110
Trantor T-128 & T-130B, 188
Tree and Data command
(View menu), 321

Tree menu commands
Collapse Branch, 319-321
Expand All, 321
Expand Branch, 321
Expand One
Level, 319, 321
Tree Only command (View
menu), 321
triggers, 934
viewing in SQL Server,
825-826
Triggers command (Manage
menu), 825
troubleshooting
and network
protocols, 527-533
DNS name resolution,
560-562
Macintosh clients printer
services, 411-412
Network Monitor, network
performance, 33-36,
541-545
network protocols, protocol
analyzers, 533-535
networks
browsing, 554-556
command-line
tools, 545-549
connectivity, 553-554
routing, 557
trust relationships,
557-560
System Management
Server, 882-883
TCP/IP, 529-533
Windows 3.1 clients, 387
Windows NT Resource
Kit, 550-552
Windows NT Server
tools, 31-36
WINS name
resolution, 560-562
with Network
Monitor, 535-541
trust relationships
one-way, 584-586
overview, 584-586
troubleshooting
networks, 557-560
two-way, 584-586

Trust Relationships command (Policies menu), 587
Trust Relationships dialog, 587
trusted domains, 585-586
    expanding servers, 29
    Windows NT Directory Service, 29
trusting domains, 585-586
trusts
    domains, establishing, 586-588
    limitations, 588
Twisted-Pair Physical Media Dependent (TPPMD)
    Copper Distributed Data Interface (CDDI), 136
two-step migration, 858-864
two-phase commit process, 934
    RAID 5 write performance, 230-231
two-way trust relationships, 584-586

U

UltraStor 124f EISA Disk Array Controller, 188
uniform data transfer (UDT), 934
Uniform Resource Locators, *see* URLs
uninterruptable power sources, *see* UPS
unique index, 934
universal clients
    building, 645
    configuring, Windows 3.11 for Workgroups, 646
    implementing, Windows 95, 649
universal inbox, 842
UNIX
    accessing files with Windows NT Server, 642-643
    integrating with Windows NT Server, 632-633
    Microsoft LAN Manager for UNIX, 643-644

    Network File Systems, 643
    SAMBA, 644
    universal clients, building, 645
    Windows NT files, sharing, 642-644
    Windows NT Server, integration tools, 633-642
UNIX integration tools
    DHCP, 634-638
    WINS, 638-639
UNIX servers, networking protocols, 123
UNIX workstations, networking protocols, 122
Unload Hive command (Registry menu), 320
unmanaged hubs, 154-155
unshielded twisted pair cables
    conductor size, 144
    pair count, 144
    quality grades, 145-147
    selection criteria, 143-146
    sheath material, 145
updating shared files, 363-364
upgrading
    Internet Information Server (IIS), 707-710
    Microsoft BackOffice, 786-787
    network resources, 82-83
    server hardware, RAID, 239-240
    Windows NT Server from previous Windows version, 186-187
UPS (uninterruptible power sources)
    manageability, 182
    selecting, 180-181
    servers, 178-182
    sizing, 181-182
    specifications, 180-181
    types
        online, 179-180
        standby, 179-180
URLs (Uniform Resource Locators)
    prefixes, 727
    Web browsers, 727

user accounts
    adding, 423-426
    copying with User Manager, 426
    creating
        Add User Account Wizard, 437-442
        New User dialog, 424-426
    defined, 415
    group membership, assigning, 428-429
    information, managing, 436
    limiting access to databases, 831-833
    lockout options, configuring, 444
    logon scripts, setting, 431-433
    modifying with User Manager, 427-428
    user rights, determining, 454
user content, managing (World Wide Web server), 718-719
user databases, adding (SQL Server), 814-830
User Environment Profile dialog, 429, 433
user groups
    copying attributes from domains, 448-449
    defined, 415
    deleting from domains, 449
    managing, 416-417
    printer permissions, setting, 496-498
    types, 445-446
    user rights, assigning, 454-455
user-level access control, setting (Access Control Page), 343
User Manager for Domains
    functions, 27-28
    implementing, 416-417
    launching, 417-418
    low-speed domain connection, 420-421

multiple copies,
  creating, 418-419
multiple instances,
  executing, 418-419
new domain, selecting, 420
user accounts
  copying, 426
  modifying, 427-428
user groups,
  managing, 416-417
User menu commands
  Copy, 426
  New Global Group, 448
  New Local Group, 447
  New User, 423
  Properties, 427
  Select Domain, 420
**user mode services versus
  kernel mode services,** 96-97
user names, specifying, 201
**User Privilege command
  (View menu),** 832
User Profile Editor
  functions, 26-28
  profiles, setting, 26-28
user profiles
  creating, 869-874
  defining, 429-433
  home folders,
    specifying, 431-433
  managing, 429-433
    multiple user
      accounts, 432-433
  paths, specifying, 430-431
  setting on servers, 364-366
  types, 430-431
user rights
  advanced, 454
  assigning, 454-455
  basic, 454
  determining, 454
**User Rights Policy dialog
  box,** 455, 715
**user.dat file,
  configuring,** 364-366
users
  dial-in permissions,
    setting, 437
  folder shares
    creating, 459-464
      Managing Folder and File
        Access Wizard,
        464-468

overview, 458-459
  removing, 460-464
logon hours, logging
  off, 435
System Management Server,
  targeted software
  installation, 883
training, 76-77
workstation logons,
  restricting, 435-436
**Users menu commands, Select
  Users,** 427
**Users on _Servername_
  dialog,** 620
utilizing
  daily copy backups, 268
  project management
    software, 77-79

V

value entries, modifying
  (Registry Editor), 318-320
**value entries (Windows NT
  Registry),** 308-309
vendors
  network management,
    outside help, 80-81
  selecting for network
    management, 83
**Verify Name and Company
  dialog,** 800
VeriSign Web site, 36
**video display,
  configuring,** 210-211
View HTML dialog, 771
View menu commands
  Alerts, 509
  Chart, 506
  Data Only, 321
  Display Binary Data, 321
  Find Key, 321
  HTML, 771
  Log, 511
  Refresh, 321
  Refresh All, 321
  Select Columns, 23
  Split, 321

Tree and Data, 321
Tree Only, 321
User Privilege, 832
viewing
  Audit Log, 327-328
  HTML code with FrontPage
    Editor, 770-772
  network adapter
    settings, 336-338
  Network Monitor
    window, 33-36
  NTFS
    file access
      permissions, 470-471
    folder access
      permissions, 474-477
  Performance Monitor
    alerts, 508-509
    log files, 513-514
    memory usage, 522-526
    network media
      speed, 519-520
    virtual memory,
      525-526
  remote usage performance
    statistics, 373
  SQL Enterprise Manager,
    logins, 834-835
  SQL Server
    standard stored
      procedures, 826-827
    triggers, 825-826
  Windows 3.1 clients
    configuration files,
      384-385
    initialization files,
      384-385
  Windows for Workgroups
    3.11 client
      configuration files,
        391-392
      initialization files,
        391-392
  WINS databases, 531-533
virtual address space, 935
**Virtual DOS machines
  (VDMs),** 97
virtual LANs
  active network
    components, 161-162
  implementing, 161-162

virtual memory
examining application
servers, 522-523
page swapping, 525-526
viewing with Performance
Monitor, 525-526
Virtual Memory dialog, 524
**Virtual Memory Manager
(VMM) (Windows NT
Executive), 94-95**
**virtual private networks
(VPNs)**
PPTP, 37-39, 685-686
**virtualizing remote server
shares, 719-720**
volume sets
advantages/
disadvantages, 244-245
configuring, 244-245
**Volumes Usage on *Servername*
dialog box, 621**

W

**WANs (wide area
networks), 935**
enterprise site
topology, 886-887
supported protocols (System
Management Server), 885
warranties for servers, 165
Web
managing site content
(Microsoft
FrontPage), 764-772
sites
Amdahl
Corporation, 52
Arcada, 296
BHS Software, 553
Compaq Computers, 52
Datamation, 44
Digital Equipment
Corporation, 51
Executive Software, 520
Microsoft, 689
Network General, 534

RAID Advisory
Board, 219
Softway, 92
Tandem Computers, 52
TechWeb, 44
VeriSign, 36
Web browsers
Netscape versus
Microsoft, 44-45
URL overview, 727
Web pages,
displaying, 701-702
Web pages
connecting via IDC,
750-752
creating
Microsoft dbWeb,
758-764
SQL Server Web
Assistant, 742-747
databases, security
considerations, 757-758
displaying with World Wide
Web server, 701-702
managing with FrontPage
Explorer, 770-772
modifying in FrontPage
Editor, 770-772
Performance Monitor,
implementing, 747-749
Web sites
dynamic database
access, 750
planning, 689-690
wide area networks, *see* WANs
Win32, 935
Win32S, 936
Window menu commands
Arrange Icons, 322
Cascade, 322
Tile, 322
Windows 3.1
networking protocols, 121
upgrading to Windows NT
Server, 186-187
Windows 3.1 clients
configuration files,
viewing, 384-385
connecting to Windows NT
Server, 378-387

initialization files,
viewing, 384-385
installation disks,
creating, 378-379
network drivers
installing, 379-383
setting, 385-386
Windows NT file resources,
connecting, 386-387
Windows NT printer
resources,
connecting, 386-387
Windows NT Server,
troubleshooting, 387
**Windows 3.11 for
Workgroups, universal
clients, 646**
Windows 95
compatibility with
applications in Windows
NT, 92
diskless clients, 28
installing setup copy,
359-364
NetBEUI
configurations, 347-348
network protocols,
configuring, 347-355
network support,
installing, 333-334
networking features
32-bit protected
mode, 333
automatic client
setup, 332-333
automatic server
reconnection, 332-333
dial-up networking, 333
long file-name
support, 333
minimal conventional
DOS memory
usage, 333
multiple client
support, 331-333
multiple protocol
support, 332-333
peer-to-peer
networking, 333

simultaneous network
connections, 332-333
single network
logons, 332-333
networking protocols, 120
NICs
installing, 334-336
modifying settings,
336-338
non-supported features on
Windows NT Server, 21
NWLink
configurations, 348-350
small-office/home-office
(SOHO) markets, 21
TCP/IP
configurations, 351-356
universal clients,
implementing, 649
upgrading to Windows NT
Server, 186-187
user interface in Windows
NT Server, 20-26
user.dat file,
configuring, 364-366
Windows 95 clients
dial-up networking
configuring, 670-676
testing, 670-676
machine directory setup,
performing, 362-364
network, installing,
359-364
PolEdit, installing, 367-370
remote management,
enabling, 370-375
**Windows 95 Disk
Defragmenter, 520**
**Windows 95 Registry versus
Windows NT Registry, 306**
Windows 95 Service Pack 1
downloading, 363-364
features, 363-364
updating shared files,
363-364
**Windows Diagnostics Tool,
Services Page, 31-33**
Windows for Workgroups 3.11
NetWare support,
installing, 646-647
packet driver support,
installing, 647-652

TCP/IP support,
installing, 646-647
upgrading to Windows NT
Server, 186-187
Windows Sockets,
obtaining, 646-647
Winsock
implementation, 646-647
**Windows for Workgroups 3.11
client**
configuration files,
viewing, 391-392
initialization files,
viewing, 391-392
**Windows for Workgroups 3.11
clients**
32-bit TCP/IP,
installing, 388-391
network protocols,
modifying, 389-391
Windows NT file resources,
connecting, 394-395
Windows NT printer
resources,
connecting, 394-395
Windows NT Server,
connecting, 387-395
**Windows for Workgroups
3.1x, networking
protocols, 120-121**
**Windows Hardware
Engineering Conference
(WinHEC), 65, 87**
**Windows Internet Name
Service, 205**
**Windows menu command,
Drives, 293**
Windows NT
David Cutler, head of
development, 86-91
elements in Windows NT
Executive, 93-95
environmental
subsystems, 95-97
POSIX.1 subsystem, 97
Virtual DOS machines
(VDMs), 97
Windows on Win32
(WOW), 97
Hardware Compatibility List
(HCL), 95

historical development,
86-87
Windows technology
versus OS/2
technology, 86-87
IBM SNA environments,
integrating, 649-650
networking
architecture, 111-112
networking processes
servers, 105-106
workstations, 105-106
new layers
Network Device Interface
Specification
(NDIS), 111
Transport Driver Interface
(TDI), 111-112
operating system features,
summarizing, 91-92
peer-to-peer
networking, 105-106
remote procedure
calls, 102-105
user mode services versus
kernel mode services,
96-97
versus OSI network
layers, 111-112
Windows 95 applications,
compatibility, 92
**Windows NT 3.1, historical
development, 87**
**Windows NT 3.1 Advanced
Server, historical
development, 87**
**Windows NT 3.5, historical
development, 87-88**
Windows NT 3.51
historical development,
87-88
Shell Update Release
(SUR), 88-89
**Windows NT Workstation 4.0
clients**
domain resources,
attaching, 398-400
TCP/IP, installing, 395-398
Windows NT domain,
installing, 397-398

Windows NT file resources,
connecting, 398-400
Windows NT printer
resources,
connecting, 398-400
Windows NT clients
adding domains, 575-577
authenticating, 580-582
dial-up networking
configuring, 676-683
testing, 676-683
**Windows NT Diagnostics
command (Programs
menu), 317-318**
**Windows NT Diagnostics
Tool, 31-33**
**Windows NT Diagnostics
Utility, executing, 317-318**
**Windows NT Directory
Service, trusted
domains, 29**
**Windows NT End-User License
Agreement, 198**
Windows NT Executive
components
Input/Output Manager
(IOM), 94-95
Local Procedure Call
(LPC) Facility, 94-95
Object Manager
(OM), 94-95
Process Manager
(PM), 94-95
Security Reference
Monitor (SRM), 93-95
Virtual Memory Manager
(VMM), 94-95
hardware abstraction layer
(HAL), 93-95
Input/Output Manager,
elements, 94-95
kernel mode services, 93-95
native services, 93-95
Windows NT file resources
accessing, Macintosh
clients, 404-412
connecting
Windows 3.1
client, 386-387
Windows for Workgroups
3.11 clients, 394-395

Windows NT
Workstation 4.0
clients, 398-400
sharing UNIX, 642-644
Windows NT printer resources
accessing Macintosh
clients, 404-412
connecting
Windows 3.1
clients, 386-387
Windows for Workgroups
3.11 clients, 394-395
Windows NT
Workstation 4.0
clients, 398-400
Windows NT Registry
.INI files, interacting,
328-329
accesses, auditing, 326-327
administrator access,
324-328
backing up, 318
caution concerning
changing values, 305-306
CONFIG.SYS files,
interacting, 328-329
data types
REG_DWORD, 308-309
REG_EXPAND_SZ,
308-309
REG_MULTI_SZ,
308-309
REG_SZ, 308-309
hives, 309-310
HKEY_CURRENT_USER,
309-310
HKEY_LOCAL_MACHINE\
SAM,
309-310
HKEY_LOCAL_MACHINE\
SECURITY, 309-310
HKEY_LOCAL_MACHINE\
SOFTWARE, 309-310
HKEY_LOCAL_MACHINE\
SYSTEM, 309-310
HKEY_USERS\DEFAULT,
309
HKEY_CLASSES_ROOT,
315-316
HKEY_CURRENT_CONFIG,
315

HKEY_CURRENT_USER,
316
HKEY_USERS, 316
importance of
settings, 304-305
keys, 306-307
HKEY_CLASSES_ROOT,
307
HKEY_CURRENT_
CONFIG, 307
HKEY_CURRENT_USER,
307
HKEY_LOCAL_MACHINE,
307
HKEY_USERS, 307
permissions, setting,
325-327
remote editing, 323-324
security, 324-328
storage information,
303-304
subkeys, 307
value entries
components, 308-309
data types, 308-309
names, 308-309
values, modifying, 305-306
versus Windows 95
Registry, 306
**Windows NT Resource
Center, 553**
Windows NT Resource Kit
Browser Monitor, 550
Browser Status, 550
Domain Monitor, 550
Domain Planner, 594
GetMac, 551
NetWatch, 551
networks,
troubleshooting, 550-552
NSLookup, 551
SMBTrace, 551
WNTIPcfg, 552
Windows NT Server 4.0
accessing Macintosh
clients, 403-404
administrative shares,
463-464
Administrative
Wizards, 23-26

administrator password,
  setting, 202
AppleTalk printers,
  troubleshooting, 411-412
application server,
  optimizing, 521-526
application server APIs, 29
archive bits, 264
authentication
  services, 580-584
built-in accounts
  Administrator
    account, 422-423
  Guest account, 423
  managing, 421-423
built-in groups, 445-446
CD-ROM drives,
  selecting, 190
client-side features
  Event Viewer, 27-28
  Remote Program Load
    (RPL), 28
  Remote Server
    Administration, 27-28
  Server Manager, 27-28
  System Policy
    Editor, 26-28
  User Manager, 27-28
  User Profile Editor,
    26-28
command-line tools
  arp command, 545
  hostname
    command, 545
  ipconfig command, 546
  nbstat command, 546
  nestat command, 547
  ping command, 548
  route command, 548
  tracert command, 549
communication features
  autodial, 654
  PPP Multilink, 654
  PPTP, 654
  TAPI, 654
company name,
  specifying, 201
connecting
  Macintosh clients,
    400-412
  Windows for Workgroups
    3.11 clients, 387-395

Windows NT
  Workstation 4.0
  clients, 395-400
data, backing up, 192-193
Datamation Magazine,
  43-44
desktop appearance, 22
DHCP configurations,
  637-638
DHCP installation, 636
disk mirroring, 244-245
disk striping, 244-245
disk striping with
  parity, 244-245
DNS tool, 30-31
domain controllers
  installing, 192
  selecting, 201-202
domains
  interaction with Internet
    Information Server
    (IIS), 705-706
  joining, 208
emergency repair disk,
  creating, 202, 211-212
"enterprise-wide"
  network, 41-44
existing operating systems,
  installing, 196-197
FAT, 189-190
File and Print Services for
  NetWare (FPSN), 600-601
file servers,
  optimizing, 514-521
file systems, 458
  File Allocation
    Table, 458
  High Performance File
    System (HPFS), 458
  NT File System, 458
fixed-disk drives,
  partitioning, 188-190
Foldername Properties
  sheet, 22
Gateway Service for NetWare
  (GSNW), 600-601
GM Access Common
  Dealership Environment
  (CDE), 43-44
hardware compatibility,
  installing, 187
identification,

providing, 191
installation
  fine-tuning, 202-203
  finishing, 209
  repairing, 213-215
installation decisions,
  185-192
installation folder,
  preparing, 195-197
installation summary
  steps, 193-194
installing Services for
  Macintosh, 400-403
integration tools
  Directory Service
    Manager for
    NetWare, 622-623
  Multi-Protocol Routing
    (MPR) Service,
    630-631
Internet tools, 36-39
interoperability,
  planning, 124-126
intranet tools, 36-39
License tool, 787-794
licensing fees, 782
licensing terms,
  identifying, 201
list of supported
  modems, 661-665
Macintosh printers,
  setting, 406-412
market share, 600-601
marketing strategies, 41-44
Microsoft BackOffice,
  bundled
  components, 778-779
Microsoft Cairo, delays in
  development, 20
Migration Tool for NetWare,
  implementing, 651-652
modem configuration,
  662-665
multiple network protocols,
  spanning, 597
names, providing, 191
NetWare
  integrating, 599-601
  migrating, 650-652
NetWare clients,
  accessing, 614-622

network adapters,
  selecting, 190-191
network connection,
  establishing, 208
network features, 28-29
network implementation
  budget
    considerations, 74-76
  business objectives,
    56-57
  data communications
    technology, 69-70
  developing, 55-77
  existing
    infrastructure, 66-69
  fault-tolerance, 64-66
  future growth, 72-74
  management needs,
    70-72
  Microsoft Web site, 59
  security, 59-64
  time schedule, 70
  user needs, 57-59
  user training, 76-77
  workgroup needs, 57-59
network installation,
  executing, 203-208
networking protocols, 112,
  598-599
  AppleTalk, 117
  DLC, 117
  IPX/SPX, 117
  NetBEUI, 112-113
  NetBEUI Frame,
    112-113
  NWLink, 117
  RAS, 118
  streams, 118-119
  TCP/IP, 113-116
networks, installing,
  195-196
non-support of Windows 95
  functions, 21
Novell NetWare
  interoperability, 30-31
NTBACKUP program,
  289-291
NTFS, 189-190
ODBC system database,
  creating, 735-740

overview of new
  features, 20
previous Windows version,
  upgrading, 186-187
print servers,
  optimizing, 514-521
printer emulation via File
  and Print Services for
  NetWare, 31
printers, selecting, 190
printing enhancements, 29
projected corporate
  sales, 43-44
property sheets, 22
RAID 0, 244
RAID 1, 244
RAID 5, 244
RAID options, 244
RAS, configuring, 659-669
restarting, 212
sales information, 19
scalability features, 28-29
scalable server systems,
  50-52
security identifiers, 569
server computer name,
  identifying, 201
server usability, 20-26
setup boot disks,
  creating, 194-195
Setup program,
  executing, 194
software RAID, 243-245
strategies, pricing, 41-44
supported InterNIC
  RFCs, 632-634
system booting, 245
Task Manager, 23
TCP/IP diagonstic
  tools, 632-633
TCP/IP integration, 30-31
TCP/IP utilities, 632-633
time/date, setting, 209-210
troubleshooting, Windows
  3.1 clients, 387
troubleshooting tools,
  31-36, 533-553
universal clients,
  building, 645
UNIX, integrating, 632-633

UNIX host, accessing
  files, 642-643
UNIX integration
  tools, 633-642
    DHCP, 634-638
    WINS, 638-639
user name, specifying, 201
versus Novell NetWare 4.1
  sales, 19
video display,
  configuring, 210-211
volume sets,
  configuring, 244-245
Windows 3.1 clients,
  connecting, 378-387
Windows 95 setup copy,
  installing, 359-364
Windows 95 user
  interface, 20-26
Windows Explorer, 22
Windows NT Diagnostics
  Tool, 31-33
WINS configuration,
  640-642
WINS installation, 639
**Windows NT Server Services
for Macintosh**, 117
**Windows NT Setup
dialog**, 607
**Windows NT Workstation 4.0,
networking protocols,**
119-120
**Windows on Win32
(WOW)**, 97
**Windows Open Services
Architecture (WOSA)**, 654
**Windows Sockets, obtaining
(Windows for Workgroups
3.11)**, 646-647
**Windows technology versus
OS/2 technology**, 86-87
WINPKT
  packet driver support,
    648-652
  packet drivers,
    downloading, 648-652
**WINS (Windows Internet
Naming Service)**
  advantages, 638-639
  configuration
    parameters, 640-642

configuring, 640-642
databases, viewing,
  531-533
installing, 639
IP addresses, mapping,
  530-533
managing, 640-642
name resolution,
  troubleshooting, 560-562
network, Internet
  connections, 67-69
versus DNS, 30-31
Windows NT Server, UNIX
  integration tools, 638-639
**WINS configuration page,
setting, 352**
**WINS Manager command
(Programs menu), 641**
**WINS Server Configuration
dialog, 641**
wizards
  Add Printer, 25
  Add User Accounts, 23
  Add/Remove Programs, 25
  Group Management, 24
  Install New Modem, 25
  License, 25
  Managing File and Folder
    Access, 24, 466
  Network Client
    Administrator, 25
WNTIPcfg, 552
**workgroup servers, selection
criteria, 164**
**workstation packages
(Packages window),
897-898**
workstations
  logon privileges,
    restricting, 435-436
  Windows NT networking
    processes, 105-106
World Wide Web server
  Advanced page options,
    configuring, 722-723
  content, managing,
    718-719
  Directories page options,
    configuring, 716-719
  HTML formatting, 700-702
  Internet Information Server
    (IIS) components,
    700-702

logging options,
  setting, 713-723
Logging page options,
  configuring, 720-721
password
  authentication, 713-716
remote server shares,
  virtualizing, 719-720
Service page options,
  configuring, 713-716
SGML formatting, 700-702
Web pages,
  displaying, 701-702
**WORM (Write Once, Read
Many) drives**
  capacities, 288
  cost, 288
writable optical drives
  backup hardware, 287-288
  CD-recordable drives,
    287-288
  magneto-optical
    drives, 288
**Write DAC (Access
Audit), 327**
write once, read many,
  see **WORM**
write performance
  RAID 1, 225-226
  RAID 5, 229-231
**writing queries for logs,
741-742**

X - Y - Z

**zero-redundancy array option,
RAID 0, 219-222**

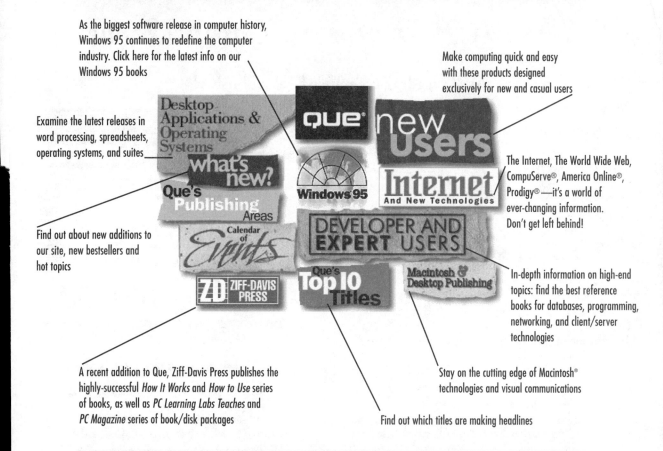

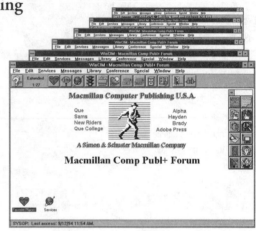